Psychology:
A New Introduction

for A2

Richard Gross
Rob McIlveen
Hugh Coolican
Alan Clamp
Julia Russell

London: Hodder & Stoughton,   0340800224

Hodder & Stoughton

A MEMBER OF THE HODDER HEADLINE GROUP

British Library Cataloguing in Publication Data

A catalogue record for this title is available from the British Library

ISBN 0 340 800 224

First published 2000

Impression number 10 9 8 7 6 5 4 3 2 1
Year   2005 2004 2003 2002 2001

Typeset by GreenGate Publishing Services, Tonbridge, Kent.

Printed and bound in Spain for Hodder and Stoughton Educational, a division of Hodder Headline plc, 338 Euston Road, London NW1 3BH, by Graphycems.

Contents

Preface

Our aim in this book is to provide a comprehensive and detailed, yet readable and accessible, introduction to the diverse and constantly changing discipline of psychology. This second edition has been completely re-written and re-structured in line with the new A2 (A level) specifications. The book is divided into two main sections, Unit 4 and Unit 5.

Unit 4 consists of *Social Psychology* (Chapters 1–9), *Physiological Psychology* (Chapters 10–18), *Cognitive Psychology* (Chapters 19–27), *Developmental Psychology* (Chapters 28–36), and *Comparative Psychology* (Chapters 37–45).

Unit 5 comprises *Individual Differences* (Chapters 46–54) and *Perspectives* (Chapters 55–59).

In addition, there are two Appendices, dealing with Data Analysis (tests of statistical significance) and Report Writing. Appendix 3 comprises Statistical Tables.

Whilst the sequence of chapters and much of the content is based on the new AQA (A) specification, we believe that the book will also be invaluable to those studying the AQA (B), OCR, and EDEXCEL specifications.

All the important features of the first edition have been retained, including an introduction and overview, conclusions and a detailed summary for every chapter. The Perspectives chapters include several exercises, aimed at helping students to draw on (and revise) their knowledge of the subject as a whole. Also for revision purposes, the index contains page numbers in bold which refer to definitions and main explanations of particular concepts for easy reference. Each chapter also has several website addresses for those who wish to research material further via the Internet.

There are also self-assessment questions for each chapter, based on the question format used in the examinations (i.e. essay-style questions). The overall approach is designed to be interactive and user-friendly.

We won't pretend that psychology is easy, and there is no substitute for hard work. We hope – and believe – that this book will make the task of studying psychology both less arduous and even a little more enjoyable than it would otherwise be. Good luck!

Richard Gross
Rob McIlveen
Hugh Coolican
Alan Clamp
Julia Russell

Acknowledgements

We would like to thank Dave Mackin, Anna Churchman, Celia Robertson and Denise Stewart at GreenGate Publishing for the excellent job they have made of preparing the text. Also, thanks to Greig Aitken for his co-ordination of the project and his helpful, often imaginative, artwork suggestions. Finally, thanks to Tim Gregson-Williams.

PICTURE CREDITS

The publishers would like to thank the following for permission to reproduce photographs and other illustrations in this book:

Page 4, (Fig 1.1), BFI Stills, Posters and Designs; p.7 (Fig 1.3), BFI Stills, Posters and Designs; p.8 (Fig 1.4) Copyright House of Viz/John Brown Publishing Ltd; p.13 (Fig 2.1), Corbis; (Fig 2.2), Copyright House of Viz/John Brown Publishing Ltd; p.16 (Fig 2.3), Margaret Bourke-White, *Life Magazine* © 1937 Time Inc.; p.21 (Fig 3.1), Grimsby & Scunthorpe Newspapers Ltd; p. 24 (Fig 3.2), PA News; (Fig 3.3) Associated Press; p.26 (Fig 3.4), Tony Stone Images. Chip Henderson; p.27 (Fig 3.6), Private Eye; p.28 (Fig 3.7) Action Images; p.30 (Fig 3.8), Concord Video and Film Council; p.32 (Fig 3.9), Action Plus; p.34 (Fig 4.1), *Illustrated London News*; p.35 (Fig. 4.2), from Festinger, L. *et al.* (1950), *Social Pressures in Informal Groups: A Study of Human Factors in Housing.* Stanford University Press; (Box 48.2) from Nicholson, J. (1977) Habits. London: Macmillan; p.37 (Fig 4.5), Private Eye; p.38 (Fig 4.6), The Hutchison Picture Library; (Fig 4.7), The British Psychological Society from *The Psychologist*, 1995, 8, 77; p.40 (Fig 4.8), Rex Features, London by Mike Daines; p. 44 (Fig 5.2), Ken Pyne, from *The Relationship – A Cartoon Novel of Romance in the 80s*, (1981) Little, Brown & Co (UK), © Ken Pyne, 1981; p.58 (Fig 6.1), Corbis-Bettman; p.59 (Fig 6.2), Zefa © R.Halin-Zefa; p.63 (Fig 6.3), from *The Sunday Times* © Times Newspapers Limited; p.66 (Fig 7.1), All Sport; p.70 (Fig 7.3), Camera Press Ltd; p.71 (Fig 7.4), Corbis-Bettman; p.72 (Fig 7.5), Prentice-Dunn, S. & Rogers, R.W. (1983) *Journal of Personality and Social Psychology*, 43, 503–513. Copyright © 1983 by the American Psychological Association. Reprinted with permission; p.79 (Fig 8.1), *The Mirror* 1999; p.81 (Fig 8.3), from Darley J.M. & Latané B. (1968) Bystander intervention in emergencies: Diffusion of responsibility. *Journal of Personality and Social Psychology*, 8, 377–383. Copyright © 1968 by the American Psychological Association. Reprinted with permission; p.83 (Fig 8.4), from Piliavin J.A. *et al.* (1981) *Emergency Intervention.* Academic Press, Inc.; p.84 (Fig 8.5), Associated Press; p.89 (Fig 9.1), BFI Stills, Posters and Designs; p.93 (Fig 9.3), BFI Stills, Posters and Designs; p.95 (Fig 9.4), © BBC; (Fig 9.5), Telegraph Colour Library. Photograph: Elke Hesser; p.100 (Fig 10.3) from Penfield, W. & Boldrey, E. (1937) 'Somatic, motor and sensory representation in the cerebral cortex as studies by electrical stimulation'. Brain, 60, 389–442. By permission of Oxford University Press; p.103 (Fig 10.4), *The Guardian*, 1996; p.110 (Fig 11.4), Jim Torrance; p.126, (Fig 12.9) The Far Side © Creators Syndicate International; p.131 (Fig 13.1), www.CartoonStock.com; p.141, (Fig 14.1), AKG London; p.143 (Fig 14.3), www.CartoonStock.com; p.149 (Fig 15.1), AKG London; p.151 (Table 15.1), from *Psychology*, Fourth Edition by Spencer A. Rathus, copyright © 1990 Holt, Rinehart & Winston, reproduced by permission of the publisher; p.152 (Fig 15.2), The Telegraph Group Limited, London, 1996; p.161 (Fig 16.2), from *Psychology: Science,*

Behaviour and Life, Second Edition, by Robert L. Crooks, copyright © 1991 Holt, Rinehart & Winston, reproduced by permission of the publisher; p.162 (Fig 16.3), BFI Stills, Posters and Designs; p. 166 (Fig 17.1), The Far Side © Creators Syndicate International; p.168 (Fig 17.2), V&A Picture Library; p.194 (Fig 19.4), from Neisser, U. & Becklen, R. *Cognitive Psychology*, 1975, 7, 480–494. Academic Press, Inc p.199 (Fig 20.1), BFI Stills, Posters and Designs; p.203 (Fig 20.3), Life File © Emma Lee; p.205 (Fig 20.4), *Private Eye*; p.210 (Fig 21.2) from Biederman, I. *Computer Vision, Graphics and Image Processing*, 1985, 32, 29–73. Academic Press Inc; p.211 (Fig 21.5), from Yarbus, A.L. *Eye Movements and Vision*, 1967, Plenum; p.213 (Fig 21.7), from Bradshaw J.L. & Wallace, G. *Perception & Psychonomics*, 1971, 443-448. Psychonomic Society Publications; p.214 (Fig 21.8), from Thompson. P. *Perception*, 1980, 483-484. Pion Ltd; p.215 (Fig 21.9), from Young, A.W. *et al. British Journal of Psychology*, 1985, 76, 495-523. British Psychological Society; p.216 (Fig 21.10), from Bruce, V. & Young, A.W. *British Journal of Psychology*, 1986, 77, 305-327. British Psychological Society; p.223 (Fig 22.5), Isia Leviant; p.230 (Fig 23.2) Weidenfeld & Nicolson Ltd; (Fig. 23.4a) Kaiser Porcelain Ltd; p.231 (Fig. 23.4b), Cordon Art, M.C. Escher's Circle Limit IV © 1997 Cordon Art – Baarn-Holland; (Box 14.1, shell) Worth Publishers Inc from David G. Myers *Exploring Psychology* (1993) Second Edition, New York: Worth Publishers; p. 235 (Fig. 23.6f), *The British Journal of Psychology*; p.236 (Fig 23.8d), Cordon Art, M.C. Escher's *Relativity* © 1997 Cordon Art – Baarn-Holland;. p.239 Professor Richard L. Gregory; p.243 (Fig 23.15), Eastern Counties Newspapers Ltd; p.249 (Figs 24.1, 24.2), Alex Semenoick; p.250 (Fig 24.3) Alex Semenoick; p.255 (Fig 24.8), from *The Journal of Social Psychology*, 52, 183–208 (1960). Reprinted with permission of the Helen Dwight Reid Educational Foundation, published by Heldref Publications 1319, 18th St., N.W., Washington D.C. 20036–1802. Copyright © 1960; p.256 (Fig 24.9), *Scientific American*; p.260 (Fig 25.1), David Gaskill; p.264 (Fig 25.3), PA News; p.269 (Fig 26.1), Reproduced by permission of The Agency (London) Ltd © Graham Rawle 1999; p.277 (Fig 26.6), Times Newspapers Limited © Peter Brookes/The Times; p. 285 (Fig 27.1) from Köhler, W. (1925), *The Mentality of Apes*, Kegan Paul, Trench, Trubner & Co., Ltd.; p.286, Prentice-Hall; p.290 (Fig 27.3), Hulton Getty; (Fig 27.4), Corbis-Bettman; p.303 (Fig 28.6), Paul Chapman Publishing Ltd, from Sutherland, P. (1992) *Cognitive Development Today: Piaget and His Critics*, copyright © Paul Chapman Publishing Ltd, London; p.312 (Fig 29.1), Rex Features Ltd; p.315 (Fig 29.3) BFI Stills, Posters and Designs; p.322 (Fig 30.1), ZEFA; p.323 (Fig 30.2), Alpha Press Agency Ltd; p.327 (Fig 30.3), Associated Press/Topham; (Fig 30.4) Topham Picture Point; p.334 (Fig 31.2) Ronald Grant Archive; p.338 (Fig 31.3) Edward Arnold / © Antony McEvoy; p.343 (Fig 32.1), Popperfoto; p.345 (Fig 32.2), The Johns Hopkins University Press, from Money J. and Ehrhardt A. (1972) Man and Woman, Boy and Girl © 1972, The Johns Hopkins University Press; p.348 (Fig 32.3 top), Life File © Nicola Sutton; (bottom) Sally and Richard Greenhill, © Sally Greenhill; p.350 (Fig 32.4), PA News; p.353 (Fig 33.1), The Kobal Collection; p.356 (Fig 33.3), Super Stock; p.361 (Fig 33.4), Ronald Grant Archive; p.361 (Fig 33.5), Routledge, from Coleman J.C. and Hendry L. *The Nature of Adolescence*, Second Edition, published 1990 by Routledge; p.366 (Fig 34.1), BBC Worldwide Ltd; p.367 (Fig 34.3), BFI Stills, Posters and Designs; p.369 (Fig 34.4), The Ronald Grant Archive; p.370 (Fig 34.5), The Mc-Graw–Hill Companies from *Psychology*, Fifth Edition by Santrock, J. *et al.*, copyright © 1997 The McGraw–Hill Companies, reproduced by permission of the publishers; p.376 (Fig 35.1), Sally and Richard Greenhill © Kate Mayers; p.378 (Fig 35.2), PA News; p.379 (Fig 35.3), Ronald Grant Archive; p.380 (Fig 35.5), *Scientifc American*; p.385, (Fig 36.2) © BBC; p.387 (Fig 36.3), Times Newspapers Limited © Peter Brookes/ The Times, 1996; p.389 (top), Topham Picture Point; (bottom) Sally and Richard Greenhill; p.391 (Fig 36.6), © BBC; p.395 (Fig 36.7), PA News; p.400 (Fig 37.1), Illustrated London News; p.401 (Fig 37.2), www.CartoonStock.com; p.405 (Fig 37.4), Frank Lane Picture Agency © Mark Newman; p.407 (Fig 37.5), Frank Lane Picture Agency © R Wilmshurst; p.416 (Fig 38.10), PA News; p.419 (Fig 38.11), The Far Side © Creators Syndicate International; p.424 (Fig 39.1), Courtesy Masao Kawai, Primate Research Institute, Kyoto University; p.428 (Fig 39.6), from Köhler, W. (1925), *The Mentality of Apes*, Kegan Paul, Trench, Trubner & Co., Ltd.; p.430 (Fig 39.8), photograph by Donna T. Bierschwale, courtesy of the University of Southwestern Louisiana New Iberia Research Center, Laboratory of Comparative Behavioural Biology; p.432 (Fig 39.9), photograph by Donna T. Bierschwale, courtesy of the University of Southwestern Louisiana New Iberia Research Center, Laboratory of Comparative Behavioural Biology; p.442 (Fig 40.7), from *The Cambridge Encyclopaedia of Ornithology*: 1991, Cambridge University Press; (Fig 40.8), BBC Natural History; p.443 (Fig 40.9), BBC Natural History; (Fig 40.10), Frank Lane Picture Agency © Eichorn/Zingel; p.449 (Fig 41.1), Ardea London Ltd © David and Katie Urry; p.451 (Fig 41.3), BBC Publications. Reproduced from *Animal Language* by Michael Bright with the permission of BBC Worldwide Limited; p.452 (Fig 41.4), Frank Lane Picture Agency © Silvestris; p.459 (Fig 41.7), Georgia State University; p.464 (Fig 42.1), Time Life International; p.465 (Fig 42.2), from *Animal Behaviour* (5th edition) by John Alcock © 1993 Sinauer; (Fig 42.3), from Animal Behaviour 57 © 1999, Academic Press, London; p.466 (Fig 42.4), BBC Natural History; p.473 (Fig 43.2), Science Photo Library © D Phillips; (Fig 43.3), Frank

Lane Picture Agency © M. Walker; p.475 (Fig 43.4), Super Stock; p.483 (Fig 44.2), Ronald Grant Archive; p.484 (Fig 44.3), AKG London; p.504 (Fig 44.1), The Kobal Collection; p.513 (Fig 47.1), BFI Stills, Posters and Designs; p.529 (Fig 49.1), Private Eye; p.530 (Fig 49.2) The Bridgeman Art Library, *The Garden of Earthly Delights: Hell*, right wing of triptych, detail of 'Tree Man', c1500, (panel) by Hieronymous Bosch (c1450–1516); p.540 (Fig 50.1), Illustrated London News; p.545 (Fig 50.3), Steve Goldberg/Monkmeyer Press Photo Service; p.552 (Fig 51.1), Rex Features, London © SIPA-PRESS; p.559 (Fig 52.1), www.CartoonStock.com; p.561 (Fig 52.2), Science Photo Library, Will and Deni Mcintyre; p.567 (Fig 53.1), Colorific/ Mark Richards/ Dot Pictures; p.576 (Fig 54.1), The Telegraph Photo Library; p.595 (Fig 55.1), from Hofstede G. (1980) *Culture Consequences*, copyright © 1980 Sage Publications Inc., reprinted by permission of Sage Publications.; p.604 (Fig 56.4), PA News; p.613 (Fig 57.1), AKG London; p.620 (Fig 57.2), Corbis; p.625 (Fig 58.1), Corbis; p.626 (Fig 58.2), Wide World Photo, Inc.; p.627 (Figs 58.3, 65.4), The Bettman Archive; p.645 (Fig 59.6), from Horowitz, F.D. Exploring Developmental Theories (1987) Erlbaum.

The publisher would also like to thank the following for permission to reproduce text extracts:

p.18 (Box 2.9), from Durkin, K. *Developmental Social Psychology, From Infancy to Old Age* (1995) Blackwell Publishers; p.89 (Box 9.3), © Times Newspapers Limited, 1997; p.94 (Box 9.9), from Gunter B. and McAleer J.L. (1990) *Children and Television – The One-Eyed Monster?* Reprinted by permission of Routledge; p.95 (Box 9.11), Mark Griffiths from *The Psychologist*, 9, 410–407.

Every effort has been made to obtain necessary permission with reference to copyright material. The publishers apologise if inadvertently any sources remain unacknowledged and will be glad to make the necessary arrangements at the earliest opportunity.
Index compiled by Frank Merrett, Cheltenham, Gloucester.

UNIT 4

Social, Physiological, Cognitive, Developmental and Comparative Psychology

Social Psychology

1 *Attribution of Causality*

INTRODUCTION AND OVERVIEW

How do we explain our own and other people's behaviour? *Attribution theory* deals with the general principles governing how we select and use information to arrive at *causal explanations* for behaviour. *Theories of attribution* draw on attribution theory's principles, and predict how people will respond in particular situations (or *life domains:* Fiske & Taylor, 1991).

Rather than being a single body of ideas and research, attribution theory is a collection of diverse theoretical and empirical contributions sharing several common concerns. Six different traditions form attribution theory's 'backbone' (Fiske & Taylor, 1991). These are: Heider's (1958) *'commonsense' psychology*, Jones & Davis's (1965) *correspondent inference theory*, Kelley's (1967, 1972, 1983) *covariation and configuration models*, Schachter's (1964) *cognitive labelling theory*, Bem's (1967, 1972) *self-perception theory*, and Weiner's (1986, 1995) *motivational theory of attribution*.

This chapter critically considers the contributions made by Heider, Jones and Davis, and Kelley, and research studies relating to these contributions. The models and theories view people as being logical and systematic in their explanations of behaviour. In practice, however, people tend to make attributions quickly, use much less information than the theories and models suggest, and show clear tendencies to offer certain types of explanations for particular behaviours (Hewstone & Fincham, 1996). This chapter also examines some of the *biases* in the attribution process and why these biases occur.

HEIDER'S 'COMMONSENSE' PSYCHOLOGY

Heider (1958) argued that the starting point for studying how we understand the social world is the 'ordinary' person. Heider posed questions like 'How do people usually think about and infer meaning from what goes on around them?' and 'How do they make sense of their own and other people's behaviours?' These questions relate to what he called *'commonsense' psychology*. In Heider's view, the 'ordinary' person is a *naïve scientist* who links observable behaviour to unobservable *causes*, and these causes (rather than the behaviour itself) provide the meaning of what people do.

What interested Heider was the fact that members of a culture share certain basic assumptions about behaviour. These assumptions belong to the belief system that forms part of the culture as a whole, and distinguishes one culture from another. As Bennett (1993) has observed:

'It is important that we *do* subscribe to a common psychology, since doing this provides an orienting context in which we can understand, and be understood by, others. Imagine a world in which your version of everyday psychology was fundamentally at odds with that of your friends – without a shared 'code' for making sense of behaviour, social life would hardly be possible'.

Box 1.1   Dispositional and situational attributions

Heider pointed out that in our culture at least, we explain people's behaviour in terms of *dispositional* (or personal/internal) factors, such as ability or effort, and *situational* (or environmental/external) factors, such as circumstances or luck. When we observe somebody's behaviour, we are inclined to attribute its cause to *one or other* of these two general sources.

Although Heider did not formulate his own theory of attribution, he inspired other psychologists to pursue his original ideas. As well as his insight relating to personal and situational factors as causes of behaviour, three other ideas have been particularly influential (Ross & Fletcher, 1985):

- When we observe others we tend to search for enduring, unchanging, and dispositional characteristics;

- We distinguish between intentional and unintentional behaviours;

- We are inclined to attribute behaviours to events (causes) that are present when the outcome is present and absent when the outcome is absent.

JONES AND DAVIS'S CORRESPONDENT INFERENCE THEORY

Suppose you are on a bus and see someone give up his or her seat to an elderly person. If, from this behaviour, you think 'what a kind and unselfish person', you are making what Jones & Davis (1965) call a *correspondent inference*. This is because the disposition you attributed to the person ('kind and unselfish') corresponds to the behaviour itself (giving up a seat for another person is 'kind and unselfish'). However, we do not always attribute behaviour to people's dispositions, and sometimes explain their behaviour by reference to the circumstances or situation in which it occurred. So why do we make correspondent inferences about dispositions in some cases but not others?

Box 1.2   Intentionality

Jones and Davis argue that a precondition for a correspondent inference is the attribution of *intentionality*: the behaviour is deliberate rather than accidental. Two conditions are seen as being necessary for this. First, we have to be confident that the person *knew* the behaviour would have the effects it did, and second that the person had the *ability* to perform that behaviour. Only if we are confident that a behaviour was not accidental can we proceed to try to explain its occurrence in dispositional terms.

Once a behaviour has been judged to be intentional, we then look for a disposition that could have caused it. One way we do this is through the *analysis of non-common effects*. Suppose there are several places you could visit for your holiday. All are hot and have bars and discos, and all *except one* has hotels offering full board. If you were to choose the place that offers self-catering, it could be inferred that you had a strong preference for being independent and did not wish to be tied to regular meal times.

According to Jones and Davis, the smaller the number of differences between the chosen course of action and those that are not, the more confidently a dispositional attribution can be made. We can be even more confident about the importance of a behaviour's distinctive consequence the more *negative* elements there are involved in the chosen action. For example, if self-catering means having to walk to restaurants, and meals are more expensive than at a hotel, your desire for independence would assume even greater importance to someone explaining your behaviour.

Box 1.3   Other factors influencing the likelihood of a dispositional attribution

Free choice: If we know that a person freely chose to behave in a particular way, we usually assume that the behaviour reflects an underlying disposition. However, if we know that a person was pressed to act in that way, behaviour is more likely to be attributed to external causes.

Expectedness and social desirability: Some behaviours are so expected and socially acceptable that they tell us little about a person's dispositions (such as when a politician shakes hands with people and kisses babies). However, unexpected and socially undesirable behaviour is much more informative (Jones *et al.*, 1961). This is largely because when we behave unexpectedly or in a socially undesirable way (such as making jokes and laughing at a funeral), we are more likely to be shunned, ostracised or disapproved of.

Prior expectations: The better we know people, the better placed we are to decide whether their behaviour on a particular occasion is 'typical'. If it is 'atypical' ('she doesn't normally react like that'), we are more likely to dismiss it, play down its significance, or explain it in terms of situational factors.

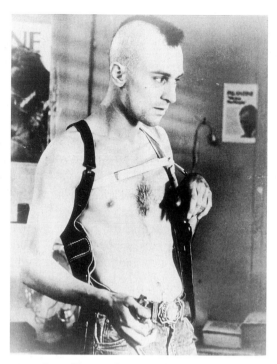

Figure 1.1 *According to Jones and Davis, any anti-social behaviour displayed by this person (Travis Bickle in* Taxi Driver*) is likely to be attributed to his anti-social disposition*

Whilst there are data consistent with Jones and Davis's theory, several weaknesses in it have been identified. Eiser (1983) has argued that intentions are *not* a precondition for correspondent inferences (see Box 1.2, page 2). For example, when someone is called 'clumsy', that dispositional attribution does not imply that the behaviour was intentional. In Eiser's view, behaviours which are unintended or accidental are beyond the scope of Jones and Davis's theory. Also, whilst behaviour which disconfirms expectations is informative, so sometimes is behaviour which confirms expectations, a good example being behaviour that confirms a *stereotype* (Hewstone & Fincham, 1996: see Chapter 2, pages 13–15).

KELLEY'S COVARIATION AND CONFIGURATION MODELS

Jones and Davis's theory continues to attract interest. However, most of the studies supporting it did not measure *causal* attributions (Gilbert, 1995). Inferring a disposition is not the same as inferring a cause, and each appears to reflect different underlying processes (Hewstone & Fincham, 1996). Both of Kelley's (1967, 1972, 1983) models are concerned with the processes that determine whether an *internal* or *external* attribution is made for a behaviour's cause.

The covariation model

This tries to account for the attributions made when we have some degree of knowledge about how a person whose behaviour we want to explain (the 'actor') usually behaves in various situations, and how other people behave in the same situation. According to the *principle of covariation*:

> 'An effect is attributed to one of its possible causes with which, over time, it covaries'.

This means that if two events repeatedly co-occur, we are more likely to infer that they are causally related than if they rarely co-occur. According to Kelley, an attribution about some effect (or behaviour) depends on the extent to which it covaries with *consensus, consistency,* and *distinctiveness* information.

Box 1.4   Consensus, consistency and distinctiveness information

Consensus refers to the extent to which other people behave in the same way towards the same stimulus. For example, if one person is laughing at a particular comedian and other people are as well, consensus is *high*. However, if nobody else is laughing, consensus is *low*.

Consistency refers to the stability of behaviour, that is, the extent to which a person has reacted in the same way to the same stimulus on other occasions. If, for example, a person is laughing at a comedian now, and has laughed at this comedian on previous occasions, consistency is *high*. However, if the person has not laughed at this comedian on previous occasions, consistency is *low*.

Distinctiveness refers to the extent to which a person reacts in the same way towards other similar stimuli or entities. For example, if a person is laughing at a comedian and has laughed at other comedians, distinctiveness is *low* (there is nothing about the behaviour that makes it distinctive). However, if the person does not find other comedians funny, distinctiveness is *high* (laughing at this comedian *is* a distinctive behaviour).

Kelley proposed that how these three types of information *covary* determines the type of attribution made. Consider, for example, explaining the behaviour of Peter, who is late for a psychology tutorial. As can be seen in Figure 1.2 (see page 5), Kelley's model predicts that Peter's behaviour will be explained differently when the information about him and other students covaries in certain ways.

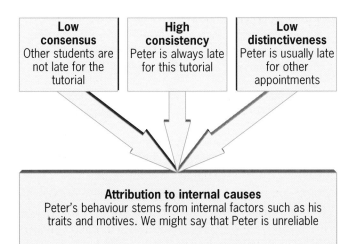

Attribution to internal causes
Peter's behaviour stems from internal factors such as his traits and motives. We might say that Peter is unreliable

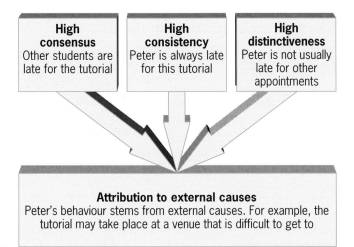

Attribution to external causes
Peter's behaviour stems from external causes. For example, the tutorial may take place at a venue that is difficult to get to

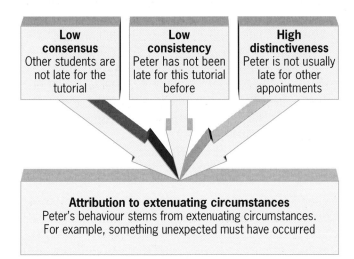

Attribution to extenuating circumstances
Peter's behaviour stems from extenuating circumstances. For example, something unexpected must have occurred

Figure 1.2 *Predictions made by Kelley's covariation model given different types of consensus, consistency and distinctiveness information*

Several studies have shown that when people are asked to explain a behaviour (such as Peter being late for his tutorial), and are given information which covaries in certain ways, attributions tend to be made in accordance with Kelley's predictions (McArthur, 1972; Harvey & Weary, 1984). However, just because people make attributions as if they are using covariation 'rules', does not *necessarily* mean that they are (Hewstone & Fincham, 1996). Several researchers have attempted to look at exactly how people make causal attributions, the most promising of these being Hilton & Slugoski's (1986) *abnormal conditions focus model*.

Box 1.5   The abnormal conditions focus model

According to Hilton and Slugoski, Kelley's three types of information are useful to the extent that the behaviour requiring explanation contrasts with the information given. Thus, with low consensus information, the *person* is abnormal, whereas with low consistency information the *circumstances* are abnormal. With high distinctiveness information, the *stimulus* is abnormal. The model proposes that we attribute as a cause the necessary condition that is abnormal when compared with the background of the target event (Slugoski & Hilton, 2000). This model may explain certain findings that Kelley's model has difficulty with, one of these being that the three types of information do not appear to be used to the same extent (Major, 1980).

The configuration model

Kelley recognised that in many situations (most notably when we do not know the actor), we might not have access to any or all of the covariation model's three types of information. Yet we can still offer explanations for behaviour. The configuration model was Kelley's attempt to account for attributions about behaviour given a single occurrence of it by a particular individual.

When we make 'single event attributions' we do so using *causal schemata* (Kelley, 1972). These are general ideas (or ready-made beliefs, preconceptions, and even theories: Hewstone & Fincham, 1996) about how certain kinds of causes interact to produce a specific kind of effect.

Causal schemata are a 'causal shorthand' (Fiske & Taylor, 1991) for explaining behaviour quickly and easily. We develop causal schemata through experience, and the two most extensively researched are *multiple sufficient causes* and *multiple necessary causes*.

Box 1.6   Multiple sufficient causes and multiple necessary causes

Multiple sufficient causes: With some behaviours, any number of causes are *sufficient* to explain their occurrence. For example, a footballer who advertises aftershave may do so because he genuinely believes it is a good product, or because he is being paid a large sum of money to advertise it – either of these is a sufficient cause. In such circumstances, we follow the *discounting principle* (Kelley, 1983), according to which:

'Given that different causes can produce the same effect, the role of a given cause is discounted if other plausible causes are present'.

With the footballer advertising aftershave, it is more reasonable to assume that money explains the behaviour, and so we discount the other possible cause.

Multiple sufficient causes are also associated with the *augmenting principle* (Kelley, 1983). According to this:

'The role of a given cause is augmented or increased if the effect occurs in the presence of an inhibitory factor'.

So, we are more likely to make an internal attribution (to effort and ability) when a student passes an exam after (say) suffering the death of a relative than would be the case for a student who had passed without having suffered such a loss.

Multiple necessary causes: Experience tells us that to stand any chance of winning a marathon, for example, a person must be fit, highly motivated, have trained hard for several months, wear the right sort of running shoes, and so on. Even if all these conditions are met, success is not guaranteed. However, the *absence* of any one of them is likely to produce failure. Thus, there are many causes needed to produce certain behaviours (typically those which are unusual or extreme).

BIASES IN THE ATTRIBUTION PROCESS

Kelley's is a *normative model* of the attribution process (it tells us how people *should* make causal attributions). As has been seen, however, people are far less logical and systematic (less 'scientific') than the model requires (Pennington *et al.*, 1999). A more accurate account of how causal attributions are made may come from an analysis of the systematic errors and biases that occur in the attribution process. A bias is:

'... the tendency to favour one cause over another when explaining some effect. Such favouritism may result in causal attributions that deviate from predictions derived from rational attributional principles like covariation' (Zebrowitz, 1990).

Although almost all behaviour is the product of *both* the person and the situation, we tend to emphasise one or other of these when making attributions. Perhaps this is because we want to be seen as competent interpreters of behaviour, and so we naïvely assume that simple explanations are better than complex ones (Jones & Nisbett, 1971). Our tendency to act as *'cognitive misers'* means that we do not analyse the interactions between personal and situational factors even if a lot of information is available. Three important attributional biases are the *fundamental attribution error*, the *actor–observer effect*, and the *self-serving bias*.

The fundamental attribution error

The *fundamental attribution error* (FAE) – also known as the *correspondence bias* (Gilbert, 1995) – is the tendency to overestimate the importance of personal or dispositional factors and underestimate the importance of external or situational factors as explanations for other people's behaviours (Ross, 1977). The FAE, then, is a failure to use the discounting principle (see Box 1.6) and has been demonstrated in numerous studies.

Key **STUDY**

Box 1.7   An experimental demonstration of the FAE

Napolitan & Goethals (1979) had students talk, one at a time, with a young woman who acted in either an aloof and critical, or warm and friendly manner. Before the experiment began, half the students were told that the woman's behaviour would be spontaneous. The other half were told that, for the purposes of the experiment, she had been *instructed* to act in an unfriendly (or friendly) way.

Even though the students had been told the woman was behaving in a particular way for the purposes of the experiment, they disregarded that information. So, if she acted in a friendly (or unfriendly) way towards them, they inferred that she really was a warm (or cold) person. Only if the students interacted with the woman twice, and saw her act in a friendly way on one occasion and an unfriendly way on the other, did they consider the situational reasons for her behaviour.

Figure 1.3 *Even if we are told this person is pretending to look frightened (in a scene from* The Blair Witch Project*), we are highly likely to believe that she really is frightened*

Jones & Nisbett (1971) have proposed two explanations for the FAE. First, we have a different *focus of attention* when we view ourselves and others. When we behave, we see the world around us more clearly than we see our own behaviour. However, when we observe somebody else behaving, we focus attention on what seems most salient and relevant, namely their behaviour, and not on the person's situation. Second, *different types of information* are available to us about our own and other people's behaviour. We, for example, have more consistency information available because we are likely to be able to remember how we acted on previous occasions in the same circumstances, and also have a better idea of the stimuli to which we are attending.

By explaining behaviour in personal or dispositional ways, other people seem more predictable, enhancing our sense of control over the environment (Ross, 1977). Gilbert (1995) sees the FAE as an efficient and automatic process of inferring dispositions from behaviour which, on average, produces accurate perceptions by perceivers who are too 'cognitively busy' to make conscious corrections based on situational causes.

In some circumstances, however, we *overestimate* the importance of situational factors as causes for other people's behaviour. For example, Quattrone (1982) showed that when people are alerted to the possibility that behaviour may be influenced by environmental constraints, there is a tendency to perceive those constraints as causes. This occurs even though such behaviour can be explained in terms of the actor's dispositions. For this reason, Zebrowitz (1990) prefers the term 'bias' to 'error' in this respect (see page 6). In Zebrowitz's view:

'This bias may be limited to adults in Western societies and it is most pronounced when they are constrained to attribute behaviour to a single cause'.

Certainly, the FAE is by no means universal (Fletcher & Ward, 1988). In our society, we tend to believe that people are responsible for their own actions. In India, however, people are more embedded in their family and caste networks, and are more likely to recognise situational constraints on behaviour. As a result, situational attributions are more likely for other people's behaviour (Miller, 1984).

Key S T U D Y

Box 1.8   The FAE and the importance of consequences

In Western culture, the likelihood of the FAE being made depends on the importance of the consequences. The more serious a behaviour's consequences, the more likely the actor is to be judged responsible for it. Walster (1966) gave participants an account of a car accident in which a young man's car had been left at the top of a hill and rolled down backwards.

Participants told that the car had crashed into a shop, injuring the shopkeeper and a small child, rated the young man as being more 'guilty' than those told that the car had crashed into and damaged another vehicle. Participants told that very little damage was done to the car, and that no other vehicle was involved, rated him least 'guilty' of all. Similarly, Chaikin & Darley (1973) found that the FAE was more likely when a person was described as having spilt ink over a large and expensive book than over a newspaper.

Two other factors influencing the likelihood of the FAE occurring are *intentionality* and *personal relevance*. Darley & Huff (1990) found that participants' judgements of the damage caused by an action depended on intentionality. Three groups of participants read the same description of some damage that had been done. However, one was told that the damage had been done intentionally, one that it was a result of negligence, and one that it had occurred naturally. Estimations of the damage done were inflated by those told that it had been done intentionally.

The greater the personal (or *hedonic*) relevance an action has (the more it affects us personally), the more likely the FAE is. So, if the large and expensive book used as stimulus material in Chaikin and Darley's study (see Box 1.8) had been described as belonging to us, the FAE would be more likely than if it was described as belonging to someone else.

The actor–observer effect

The *actor–observer effect* (AOE) refers to the tendency to make different attributions about behaviour depending on whether we are performing ('acting') it or observing it. Actors usually see behaviour as a response to the situation, whereas observers typically attribute the same behaviour to the actor's intentions and dispositions (that is, observers make the FAE).

There are several explanations for the AOE. One of these proposes that because we do not like to be 'pigeon-holed', we tend not to explain our own behaviour in terms of trait labels. However, we have no such reservations about pigeon-holing others. Because we like to see ourselves as being flexible and adaptive, and others as understandable and predictable, we explain the same behaviour differently depending on who is performing it (Gross, 1999).

A second explanation is based on the amount of information actors and observers have at their disposal. Actors know they have behaved differently in other situations, and would behave differently in this one if conditions were changed. Unless they know the actor well, observers have no such information and so assume that actors have behaved similarly in the past (and consequently make a dispositional attribution).

A third possible explanation suggests that people do not usually look at or perceive themselves (unless in a mirror). When explaining their own behaviour, they attend to things they can see or are most conspicuous, namely the external situation or environment. As observers, though, other people are attended to because they are the most interesting thing in the environment, and a dispositional attribution becomes more likely. Storms (1973), for example, found that when people are induced to view *themselves* as observers (by means of a videotape of themselves from the perspective of an observer) they do make internal attributions (see Figure 1.4). Additionally, when people are induced to view others from the same perspective they view themselves (by, for example, empathising with them), external attributions for their behaviours tend to be made (Regan & Totten, 1975).

Figure 1.4 *An illustration of the actor–observer effect: Actors look for situational causes of their behaviour whilst observers look for dispositional causes*

(Copyright House of Viz/John Brown Publishing Ltd)

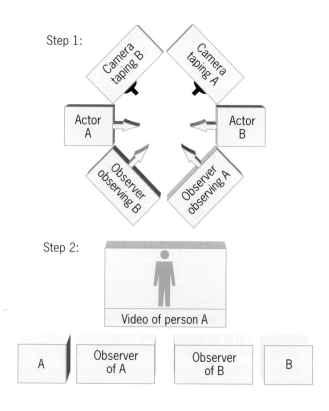

Figure 1.5 *Diagram depicting the arrangement in Storms' (1973) experiment*

The self-serving bias

From what has just been said about the AOE, it might be thought that actors *always* explain their own behaviour in external terms. Everyday experience, though, indicates that this is not so. Certainly, people who fail an examination often explain this in terms of poor teaching or very difficult questions, and not in terms of a lack of intelligence. When people pass an examination, however, they don't usually explain their success in terms of 'easy questions' or 'soft marking'. Most people explain success in terms of dispositional factors like 'effort', 'ability', 'high intelligence' and so on. The tendency for us to 'take credit' when things go right and 'deny responsibility' when they go wrong is called the *self-serving bias* (SSB) (Miller & Ross, 1975). It has been demonstrated in a variety of settings.

Box 1.9 Some illustrations of the self-serving bias

- Lau & Russell (1980) found that American football players and coaches tended to credit their wins to internal causes (such as determination), but blamed their defeats on external causes (such as bad luck or injuries).

- Gilovich (1983) showed that gamblers at sports events attribute winning bets to the greater ability of the winning team. Losing bets are explained in terms of 'flukes', such as refereeing errors or unforeseen factors.

- Students who taught boys whose performance in maths was rigged to 'improve', explained the improvement in terms of their teaching skills. Those who taught boys whose performance did not 'improve' explained performance in terms of the boys' poor motivation or intelligence (Johnson *et al.*, 1964).

- Students tend to regard exams in which they do well as good indicators of their abilities, and exams in which they do badly as poor indicators. When students do well, teachers are more likely to assume responsibility for their performance than when they do badly (Arkin *et al.*, 1980).

- When politicians are victorious in elections, they tend to attribute their success to internal factors such as their personal service to constituents. When they are defeated, this is usually attributed to external factors such as national trends (Kingdon, 1967).

Two broad types of explanation for the SSB have been advanced. One proposes that it can best be explained in *motivational* or *'need-serving'* terms, such as the need to enhance or protect self-esteem (Greenberg *et al.*, 1982). If a person explains success in terms of dispositional factors, self-esteem is enhanced (a *self-enhancing bias*). If failure is explained in terms of external factors, self-esteem is protected (a *self-protecting bias*). Alternatively, the SSB could reflect a motivation to appear in a favourable light to other people (Weary & Arkin, 1981).

The second position explains the SSB in *cognitive* or *information-processing* terms. Miller & Ross (1975) and Feather & Simon (1971) argue that we typically intend and expect to succeed at a task, although there are, of course, occasions on which we expect to be unsuccessful. Intended and expected successful outcomes tend to be attributed internally to factors, such as 'trying hard'. Unintended and unexpected outcomes tend to be attributed to external factors, such as 'bad luck'. Disentangling the role played by motivational and cognitive factors in the SSB is difficult, but evidence suggests that both are involved (Pennington *et al.*, 1999).

An interesting exception to the SSB comes from observations of the attributions made by clinically depressed people. They tend to explain failures in terms of their own inadequacies, and successes in terms of external factors such as luck or chance (Abramson *et al.*, 1978). This attributional style has also been observed in non-depressed women. According to Davison & Neale (1994), women are more likely to cope with stress by blaming themselves for their plight, and to attribute their achievements to external factors (see Chapter 50). Although these differences in attributional style can help to explain why married people differ in their degree of happiness (see Chapter 5), the exact reasons for different attributional styles remain to be discovered.

Attributional therapy (Abramson & Martin, 1981) is a relatively recent cognitive approach to the treatment of depression, which derives from research described in Chapter 50 into the revised theory of *learned helplessness* (see page 541). Attributional therapists hold that, in some cases, depressed people make unrealistic or faulty attributions concerning their own behaviours, and that these can cause considerable distress (Weiner, 1995). Therapists attempt to break the vicious circle experienced by people low in self-esteem. This involves training them to perceive successes as resulting from internal factors, and at least some failures from external factors beyond their control.

Key STUDY

Box 1.10 Attributional therapy and depression

Rabin *et al.*, (1986) gave 235 depressed adults a ten-session programme that initially explained the advantages of interpreting events in the way that non-depressed people do. After this, they were trained to reform their habitually negative patterns of thinking and labelling by, for example, being given 'homework assignments' in which they recorded each day's positive events and the contributions they had made to them. Compared with a group of depressed people given no programme, the group receiving the ten-session programme reported experiencing significantly less depression.

CONCLUSIONS

This chapter has looked at some theories of attribution and biases in the attribution process. Theories of attribution are helpful in understanding how we arrive at explanations for people's behaviours but, because of various biases, they cannot tell the whole story. As normative theories of the attribution process, theories of attribution tell us how we *should* make causal attributions for behaviour, rather than how we actually *do* make them.

Summary

■ **Attribution theory** deals with the general principles governing causal explanations in a variety of situations. **Theories of attribution** draw on these principles to predict how people will respond in particular situations/life domains. Attribution theory is a collection of diverse theoretical and empirical contributions.

■ Heider's 'commonsense' psychology sees people as **naïve scientists**, inferring unobservable causes (or meaning) from observable behaviour. In western culture, behaviour is explained in terms of both **personal** (dispositional/internal) and **situational** (environmental/external) factors.

■ Jones and Davis were concerned with explaining why we make **correspondent inferences** about people's dispositions. One way of looking for dispositions that could have caused behaviour is through the **analysis of non-common effects**. The likelihood of dispositional attributions is influenced by **free choice**, **expectedness** and **social desirability**, and **prior expectations**.

■ Kelley was concerned with the processes by which internal and external attributions are made for the causes of behaviour. In his **covariation model**, the principle of covariation says that we are more likely to infer that two events are causally related if they repeatedly co-occur.

■ Attributions about some effect/behaviour depend on the extent of its covariation with information regarding **consensus**, **consistency** and **distinctiveness**. How these types of information covary determine the attribution made.

■ Although Kelley's model is supported by evidence, this does not necessarily mean that people do use covariation 'rules'. The **abnormal conditions focus model** sees the three types of information as being useful to the extent that they contrast with the behaviour being explained.

■ Kelley's **configuration model** tries to account for 'single event attributions' in terms of multiple sufficient and multiple necessary **causal schemata**. The former are associated with the **augmenting principle**, and we choose between two or more possible causes by using the **discounting principle**.

- People are less rational and scientific than Kelley's **normative** model requires. A more accurate account of the attribution process involves looking at **systematic biases** in the attribution of cause.

- The **fundamental attribution error** (FAE) is the tendency to exaggerate the importance of internal/dispositional factors relative to external/situational factors. Its likelihood depends on the importance of a behaviour's **consequences** and **personal/hedonic relevance**.

- In the **actor–observer effect** (AOE), actors see their behaviours as responses to situational factors, whereas observers explain the same behaviours in dispositional terms. The effect may occur because actors have more information than observers about their own behaviours, or because of perceptual differences.

- People do not, as the AOE implies, always explain their own behaviour in terms of situational factors. Whilst failures are often explained in this way, successes tend to be explained in dispositional ways. This is the **self-serving bias** (SSB).

- The SSB may occur because of a need to enhance or protect self-esteem. Alternatively, a cognitive/information processing explanation proposes that we attribute intended/expected outcomes internally and unintended/unexpected outcomes externally.

- The SSB is reversed in clinically depressed people. The reasons for this **attributional style**, also displayed by some non-depressed women, are not known. **Attributional therapy** attempts to treat depression by changing attributional style.

Essay Questions

1 Discuss **two** theories relating to the attribution of causality. *(24 marks)*

2 Describe and evaluate research studies into any **two** errors or biases in the attribution process (e.g. self-serving bias; fundamental attribution error). *(24 marks)*

WEB ADDRESSES

http://www.as.wvu.edu/~sbb/comm221/chapters/attrib.htm
explorer.scrtec.org/explorer/explorer-db/html/783751634-447DED81.htm
http://www.midcoast.com.au/~lars/Attribution_Bias
http://www.vcu.edu/hasweb/psy/faculty/fors/ratt1.html
http://www.psych.purdue.edu/~esmith/search.html

2 *Social Perception*

INTRODUCTION AND OVERVIEW

The concept of a '*stereotype*' was introduced to psychology by Lippmann (1922). The word derives from its use in printing, where it refers to a printing mould or plate which, when cast, is difficult to change (Reber, 1985). Research into stereotyping has a long history. The first part of this chapter examines research relating to the origins and maintenance of social and cultural stereotyping.

Related to stereotypes are *social representations*. These are shared beliefs and expectations held by the society in which we live or the group to which we belong (Moscovici, 1961, 1976). The second part of this chapter reviews research relating to social representations, and considers its contribution to our knowledge of how we share, transmit, and reflect upon our understanding of the social world.

IMPLICIT PERSONALITY THEORY AND ILLUSORY CORRELATIONS

In his study of the processes involved in interpersonal perception, Asch (1946) showed that when people are presented with characteristics describing a person, they often go beyond the information given and assume that the person also possesses certain other characteristics. For example, when people were presented with a list containing the words 'intelligent', 'skilful', 'industrious', 'warm', 'determined', 'practical' and 'cautious', they also inferred that the person was 'serious' rather than 'frivolous' and 'persistent' rather than 'unstable'. Asch also found that certain words (*central traits*) had more impact on the inferences made than others (*peripheral traits*). Thus, 'warm' and 'cold' had a greater effect than 'polite' and 'blunt'.

Box 2.1 The halo effect

Asch's finding that including 'warm' in a list of traits produces a more positive impression of a person compared with the same list including 'cold', demonstrates the *halo effect*. If told that a person has a particularly *favourable* characteristic (such as being 'warm'), we tend to attribute other favourable characteristics to him/her (a *positive* halo). If told that a person has a particularly *unfavourable* characteristic (such as being 'cold'), we attribute other unfavourable characteristics to him/her (a *negative* halo).

According to Bruner & Tagiuri (1954), our perception of others is not based on what they are 'really' like, but on our own general 'theory' or expectations about them. Everyone has ideas about which personality traits go with, or are consistent with, others, and use these to 'fill in the gaps' in their representations of other people. Bruner and Tagiuri coined the term *implicit personality theory* (IPT) to describe the unconscious inference processes that enable us to form impressions of others based on very little evidence.

Bruner and Tagiuri propose that IPTs are shared by everyone and are consistent within a culture. This explains why, for example, many people think that intellectuals have larger than average skulls, and thick lips mean gluttony (Leyens & Codol, 1988). Indeed, so entrenched are such beliefs, despite evidence to the contrary, that the term *illusory correlation* (see also page 14) has been used to describe them (Chapman & Chapman, 1969).

Although IPT is at least partly derived from our background culture, individual experiences of interacting with, and making judgements about, people also provide us with a set of assumptions and inferences. These may *not* be shared with others. For example, one student in a class who hears that a new member is 'vivacious' might feel differently from another, depending on their personal experiences (Abrahams & Shanley, 1992).

Moreover, since certain languages, such as Eskimo and Maori, embody very different theories about people from those embodied in English (Harré, 1983), the resulting perception of others is likely to be very different: they begin with a very different set of basic categorisations. As Abrahams & Shanley (1992) note, we share a basic theory of others through our language, but we develop personal variations through particular social experience.

Figure 2.2 *Millie Tant is the embodiment of the stereotype of feminists as held by non-feminists*

(Copyright House of Viz/John Brown Publishing Ltd)

Figure 2.1 *This Inuit Eskimo's perception of other people is shared with other Eskimo-speakers, but differs from that of members of other, non-Eskimo-speaking cultures*

STEREOTYPES AND STEREOTYPING

IPT has been demonstrated using different experimental techniques, and manifests itself in several ways (Gahagan, 1980). One of these is the phenomenon of *stereotyping*. In IPT, a single item of information about a person generates inferences about other aspects of that person's character. In stereotyping, information is limited to some highly visible aspect of a person such as sex, race, nationality, and so on. This information generates judgements about what any person belonging to a given group is like (an *individual stereotype*), and that all people belonging to a given group possess the same characteristics (a *group stereotype*). Social stereotypes, then, can be defined as grossly oversimplified and generalised abstractions that people share about their own or another group (Levy *et al.*, 1998).

Key STUDY

Box 2.2 Ethnic stereotyping

Early research examined how different ethnic groups were stereotyped, and whether people actually hold traditional social stereotypes as portrayed in the media. Katz & Braly (1933) asked Princeton University students to indicate which five or six of a list of 84 words describing personality were most closely associated with each of ten ethnic groups (including Germans, Negroes, Jews and Turks). Katz and Braly used agreement across students as the criterion for a stereotype's existence. Thus, if 75 per cent or more of students assigned the trait of, say, 'obedience' to a given ethnic group, that was taken as evidence of the existence of a stereotype.

There was substantial agreement amongst the students with the traditional social stereotypes, especially derogatory traits. For example, Negroes were stereotyped as 'lazy' and 'ignorant', whilst Jews were stereotyped as 'shrewd', 'mercenary' and 'grasping'. Disturbingly, these stereotypes were held despite the fact that the majority of students had not actually had any personal contact with members of most of the ethnic groups. Presumably, the students had absorbed the images of these groups as portrayed by the media. The results were also used to compare the favourability of different ethnic groups. In 1933, Americans had the 'best' stereotype, and Turks the 'worst'.

Using Katz and Braly's methodology, other researchers examined how stereotypes change over time. For example, Gilbert's (1951) study of Princeton students showed that the stereotypes reported by Katz and Braly had become significantly weaker. Thus, only 41 per cent thought Negroes were 'superstitious' (compared with 84 per cent reported by Katz and Braly), 47 per cent thought Jews were 'shrewd' (70 per cent), and 62 per cent thought Germans were 'scientifically minded' (78 per cent).

Karlins *et al.* (1969) found that whilst Americans were seen as 'industrious', 'intelligent', but not particularly 'materialistic' in 1933, they were seen as 'materialistic' but not particularly 'industrious' or 'intelligent' in 1967. This research also revealed changes in the favourability of ethnic groups. By 1969, for example, Turks had improved markedly, whilst Americans had lost their position slightly. Interestingly, in both Gilbert's and Karlins *et al.*'s studies, the student participants expressed great irritation at being asked to make generalisations (Baron & Byrne, 1997).

One criticism of research in this area is that it forces judgements and is subject to the artefacts of *social desirability responding* (Gahagan, 1991). As noted above, in studies that followed Katz and Braly's, students were markedly less willing to engage in the exercise. Since negative stereotypes have become less acceptable, people would be less likely to offer them even if they were held.

Key S T U D Y

Box 2.3   Overcoming social desirability responding

One way of overcoming social desirability responding was devised by Razran (1950). Participants were led to believe they would be rating pictures of girls according to various psychological qualities. Later, they were shown the same pictures but each girl was identified with an Irish, Italian or Jewish-sounding name. Razran used changes in the ratings previously given as evidence of ethnic stereotyping. Girls with Jewish-sounding names were rated higher in terms of 'intelligence' and 'ambition', but lower on 'niceness'. Razran argued that since the participants did not know they were involved in a study on stereotyping, their responses were free from social desirability responding.

Explaining stereotyping: the 'grain of truth' hypothesis

According to Campbell (1967), stereotypes originate from two major sources – a person's experience with another person or group of people, and the communication of those experiences to others. For example, if the stereotypical view of the Scots is that they are extremely thrifty, someone at some time *must* have encountered a thrifty Scot. Equally, if Germans are stereotyped as 'getting up at dawn to reserve a sunbed', somebody must have observed this on at least one occasion.

At some time, then, the stereotypical characteristic attributed to a given group must have been an attribute of at least one member of that group. Later on, the process of communication would establish the stereotype as a truism in people's minds. Stereotypes therefore originate in someone's experience, and consequently must contain at least a 'grain of truth' (Allport, 1954). The fact that people do make inferences corresponding with their experiences was shown by Wegner *et al.* (1976).

Key S T U D Y

Box 2.4   Inferences and experience

Wegner *et al.* (1976) gave one group of participants a series of personality traits designed to cultivate the inference that the traits of 'persuasiveness' and 'realism' were *positively correlated*. A second group was read similar descriptions, but these were designed to cultivate the inference that the two traits were *negatively correlated*.

Afterwards, both groups were asked to read other descriptions that made no reference to 'persuasiveness' or 'realism'. However, each participant was asked to rate how 'persuasive' and 'realistic' the individual described appeared to be. Participants given positive correlation descriptions between the traits perceived a more positive correlation than those given descriptions suggesting a negative correlation. Thus, experiences can change expectations about behaviour.

The 'grain of truth' hypothesis assumes that a person, who was at one time in a particular situation, made a perfectly logical inference (the person's expectancies and inferences matched his or her experiences *exactly*). However, people sometimes see two variables as being related when in fact they are not (*illusory correlation*: see page 12).

In connection with stereotypes, people perceive differences between two or more social groups in terms of the strength of correlation between membership in one group and certain characteristics, even when such differences do not exist (Pennington, et al, 1999). For example, Sanbonmatsu *et al.* (1987) found that their participants saw people of Cuban descent as being more violent than people of European descent, even though being Cuban or European is equally unrelated to this characteristic.

Explaining illusory correlations

Illusory correlations may occur because expectations about certain events distort the ways in which we process information.

Key STUDY

Box 2.5 The distorting effects of expectations on information

Hamilton & Gifford (1976) asked participants to read two short statements about various people. Two-thirds of those they read about were identified as members of 'Group A'. The other one-third were identified as members of 'Group B'. Statements about the people were either 'desirable' ('John, a member of Group A [Group B] visited a sick friend in hospital') or 'undesirable' ('Roy, a member of Group B [Group A] always talks about himself and his problems').

Within each group, the majority (two-thirds) were described by 'desirable' qualities. However, even though there were twice as many Group A members as Group B members, neither group had a higher *proportion* of 'desirable' or 'undesirable' members. Although there was no relationship between membership of either group and 'desirability', participants thought that there was, since when they read about all the people and then reported their impressions of the 'typical' member of each group, the Group B member was rated as less desirable than the Group A member.

Wegner & Vallacher (1976) have argued that illusory correlation is similar to the fundamental attribution error (see Chapter 1, page 6). Just as other people's behaviours tend to be explained in terms of personal rather than situational factors, 'odd' behaviour can be explained by attributing it to a person's membership in an unusual group of people. When two distinctive events co-occur one or more times, we tend to conclude that they are causally related (Mullen & Johnson, 1990). According to Wegner and Vallacher, although people's inference systems are built from their transactions with reality, our perceptions sometimes go awry, and we make inferences about relationships that were never there at all.

Moreover, once an illusory correlation is made, we tend to seek out, notice, and remember information that supports the belief. This is called the *confirmation bias* (see Box 27.3, pages 287–288). As a result, the belief in non-existent correlations grows stronger. Such illusory correlations can give rise to serious inferential errors (Gahagan, 1991). For example, an employer who believes that being blonde and having fun are causally linked, may conclude that blondes are a poor choice for responsible jobs since they are too busy having fun (Baron & Byrne, 1997).

Stereotyping: a normal or abnormal cognitive process?

Many North American psychologists (e.g. Katz & Braly, 1933) have condemned stereotypes for being both false and illogical, and users of stereotypes have been seen as prejudiced and even pathological. According to Taylor & Porter (1994), there are compelling reasons why Americans should condemn stereotyping and wish to rid society of this evil. One is political ideology, according to which everyone who lives in America is first and foremost 'American', regardless of their country of origin or their ethnic/cultural background. This has been called the 'melting pot', in which differences between people are 'boiled away', leaving just one culture.

Some European social psychologists, however, were brought up in contexts in which it is normal to categorise people into groups, where society is expected to be culturally diverse, and where people are proud of their identity. A good example is Tajfel (1969). Drawing on his own experiences, Tajfel challenged the American view of stereotyping. For Tajfel, stereotyping can be reconceptualised as the product of quite normal cognitive processes common to all (non-prejudiced) people.

Box 2.6 Stereotyping and categorisation

Tajfel sees stereotyping as a special case of *categorisation* (see Chapter 3, page 27), which involves an exaggeration of similarities within groups and of differences between groups (the *accentuation principle*). According to Oakes *et al.* (1994), Tajfel's contribution is widely seen as having been revolutionary, one effect of his ideas being to move researchers away from studying the *content* of stereotypes and towards the study of the *process* of stereotyping in its own right.

Brislin (1993) has argued that stereotypes should not be viewed as a sign of abnormality. In his view:

'They reflect people's need to organise, remember, and retrieve information that might be useful to them as they attempt to achieve their goals and to meet life's demands'.

Like Allport (1954), Brislin sees stereotypes as 'categories about people', and categories (in general) and stereotypes (in particular) are shortcuts to thinking. From a cognitive perspective, there is nothing unique about stereotypes: they are universal and inevitable and 'an intrinsic, essential and primitive aspect of cognition' (Brown, 1986).

As noted earlier, though, stereotypes have been defined as oversimplified and generalised abstractions (or *exceptionless generalisations*), so that, for example, *every* skinhead is assumed to be aggressive, and *every* American materialistic. However, it is doubtful that stereotypes are factually true, because no group is completely homogeneous and individual differences are the norm. Yet in Katz & Braly's (1933) study (see Box 2.2, page 13), the instruction to list traits typical of each ethnic/national group was thought to have been understood by the participants as an instruction to list the traits *true of all members* of each group (Brown, 1986).

However, early studies like Katz and Braly's never actually found out exactly what was understood by the word 'typical'. As noted previously (see page 14), some students in follow-up studies objected to doing what was asked of them. In fact, a substantial number actually refused to take part in the study, sensing that characterising ethnic groups at all would be interpreted as ignorant or even morally wrong.

Figure 2.3 *Whilst Americans as a group may enjoy the highest standard of living in the world, there are many exceptions to this stereotyped belief*

The view of stereotyping as a normal cognitive process has led to interesting developments in research, particularly with respect to prejudice and discrimination (Taylor & Porter, 1994). Some of the findings that have emerged are considered in Chapter 3 (see Box 3.5, page 24). What can be said here is that relying on stereotypes to form impressions of strangers (*category-driven processing*) is:

'... the least effortful cognitive route we can take, whereas relying on the unique characteristics of the target person [*attribute-driven processing*] is the most effortful route' (Fiske & Neuberg, 1990).

Perhaps stereotypes are resistant to change because they represent a way of simplifying our complex social world (Shih *et al.*, 1999).

SOCIAL REPRESENTATIONS

Whilst stereotypes illustrate the shared nature of cognition, we do not all share the same knowledge constructs or form precisely the same opinions about other people. However:

'It is apparent ... that a great deal of information, and hence meaning, is collectively shared by sets of individuals, groups or societies. This is a natural consequence of the social life we lead, which involves a plethora of communication and sources of information ... Our perception is determined by the ecological context in which we

---

Key STUDY

Box 2.7   What does 'typical' mean?

That 'typical' does *not* appear to mean an exceptionless generalisation was shown by McCauley & Stitt (1978). They had students answer questions requiring them to estimate things like the percentage of American cars that are Chevrolets. Interspersed with these questions were 'critical' questions about the percentage of Germans that are efficient, extremely nationalistic, scientifically minded, pleasure-loving, and superstitious. There were also questions about the percentage of people in the world who possessed these characteristics.

McCauley and Stitt found that none of the estimates given about Germans was close to 100 per cent, so clearly 'typical' is not an exceptionless generalisation, and does not seem to mean 'true of all'. What 'typical' apparently means is 'true of a higher percentage of the group in question than people in general', or *characteristic* (Brown, 1986).

exist. Our religious beliefs, political and social ideologies, ideas about right and wrong, and even scientific theories are for the most part defined by the social contexts in which they occur' (Leyens & Dardenne, 1996).

As mentioned at the beginning of this chapter, Moscovici (1961, 1976) coined the term *social representations* (SRs) to refer to the shared beliefs and explanations held by the society in which we live or the group to which we belong. Specifically, Moscovici (1981) defines SRs as:

> '... a set of concepts, statements and explanations originating in daily life in the course of inter-individual communications'.

In his view, SRs in our society are equivalent to the myths and belief systems that exist in traditional societies, and are 'the contemporary version of common sense'. Such representations explain how 'the strange and the unfamiliar become, in time, the familiar' (Farr & Moscovici, 1984).

A group or society's SRs provide the framework within which its members can share, transmit, and reflect upon their understanding of the world. To that extent, SRs are 'the essence of *social* cognition' (Moscovici, 1998) because they help us master and make sense of the world, and enhance our communication about it with others. Two main processes used to realise the functions of SRs are *anchoring* and *objectifying*. *Anchors* are established concepts within a pre-existing system to which new experiences can be related (Hayes, 1998). *Objectifying* involves making abstract things concrete in a way that most people can understand, so that they become generally accepted as 'knowledge'.

Objectification can be achieved by means of *personification* and *figuration*. For example, Moscovici (1961) showed that people have simplified (and often mistaken) ideas about psychoanalytic theory, but know the name Sigmund Freud. Similarly, there are few of us who have much understanding about the origins of the universe or evolutionary theory, but most of us have heard the names Stephen Hawking and Charles Darwin. These are all examples of the *personification* of complex ideas, that is, linking an idea with a particular person's name that represents those ideas.

Complex ideas can also be converted into images and metaphors that represent the concept in question. This is *figuration*. For example, when British general elections occur, the concept of a 'swing' to one political party as a result of people's voting behaviours is depicted in the form of a pendulum. This shows the effect a change in voting behaviour would produce on the national balance of power. In Freud's psychodynamic model, the impulsive (or *id*) aspect of a person's personality is often portrayed as a devil, whilst the moralistic (or *superego*) aspect is portrayed as an angel. Both of these images

stand on the shoulders of the person him or herself (the *ego*: see, for example, Gross *et al.*, 2000).

Perhaps the best example of figuration is the formula $E = mc^2$, where E = energy, m = mass, and c^2 = the speed of light squared, a formula derived from the theory of relativity personified by Albert Einstein. As Leyens & Dardenne (1996) have observed:

> 'Even this trivial amount of knowledge is sufficient to maintain conversation at a party, which is good evidence that cognitions can be socially shared'.

Box 2.8 Social representations of 'split–brain' research

In the 'split-brain operation', the nerve fibres connecting the two cerebral hemispheres are severed (see Chapter 12, page 121). The purpose of this is to control the severity of epileptic seizures by confining abnormally amplified brain activity to one cerebral hemisphere. As a result of studying patients who had undergone this operation, Sperry and his colleagues discovered that, as a *broad generalisation*, the two cerebral hemispheres are specialised for different kinds of mental activity, with the left showing superior linguistic and mathematical skills, and the right superior skills on spatial tasks.

Moscovici & Hewstone (1983) have argued that Sperry and his colleagues' findings have been transformed in the public mind to the belief that people are 'logically left-brained' or 'intuitively right-brained', depending on how they behave. What was a tentative description of how the brain is organised has become a general statement about the social and economic differences between people and societies.

Social representations in childhood

Durkin (1995) has reviewed evidence relating to SRs in childhood and of development itself. Drawing on Emler *et al.*'s (1990) and Corsaro's (1993) research, Durkin argues that children attempt to transform the puzzling and ambiguous features of the adult world (such as the rules that adults impose on them) by incorporating them into their own collective practices, so making 'the unfamiliar familiar'.

Box 2.9 SRs in childhood

Teachers in an Italian nursery prohibited the children from bringing personal objects to school. From a four-year-old's perspective, this presumptuous constraint makes little sense (the whole point of having personal objects is that they are fun to play with), but the children know that grown-ups set the rules. So, the sensible thing to do is smuggle small playthings in, concealed in one's pockets. Of course, having got around the system it is essential to share the achievement with one's peers, who can appreciate the risks undertaken and the delights of the illicit goods. This calls for discretion, and all disclosures have to be made out of sight of the agents of repression. But through these defiant arrangements, the rules themselves are given meaning and transformed into a basis for social organisation.

According to Corsaro (1993), the children are trying to make sense of the adult rule by anchoring it in the collective security of their own culture. As they begin to incorporate the rule, and find ways of working around it, so they themselves lend it a form of objectivity: it influences how they organise their shared activities. By avoiding someone's authority and persuading your peers to avoid it, the authority is confirmed. In this way, through working jointly within the rules that adults impose, children begin to reconstruct jointly a SR of how the world (or their fragment of it) is regulated.

(From Durkin, 1995)

Durkin argues that development itself is something about which any society has SRs. As he says:

'A society has a belief system, a set of expectations and explanations, concerning what children should be like and what should be done with them. These social representations influence the context in which the young are raised'.

One such SR is *intelligence*, a construct which eludes a definition that everyone agrees with, but is widely believed in our society to be a useful 'thing' to have. Our beliefs about what determines intelligence influence how we behave towards others. For example, teachers who believe that intelligence is a genetically determined and inherited 'thing' are likely to teach children differently from teachers who see intelligence as something acquired through experience (Hayes, 1998).

Other research into social representations

Although SRs have been discussed as shared beliefs, different groups within a single society may have different SRs, and this can lead to differences between them. Di Giacomo (1980) studied Belgian university students staging a protest movement about changes to student grants. The representations held by the student leaders and those of the main student body were different. Principally, the concept of 'student–worker solidarity' was held by the student leaders, but not by the main student body. As a result, when the leaders called for action there was very little student support for it.

Box 2.10 The central figurative nucleus

The stability of SRs has also attracted research interest. Whilst particular SRs may be held by individuals and societies, they are not completely unchanging and may be altered by a variety of sources, one being the mass media. Moscovici (1984) explains the durable but open-to-change nature of SRs in terms of a *central figurative nucleus*, the part of the SR that virtually everyone in a group or culture shares (Hayes, 1998). This is linked to a number of *peripheral elements* that provide additional detail about something. Changes in SRs occur when major changes in the peripheral elements break the link between them and the central core (Farr, 1998).

SR theory's major weakness concerns its abstract or 'fuzzy' nature (Jahoda, 1988). As a result, critics argue that it does not suggest many hypotheses that can be experimentally investigated and that it is *non-falsifiable*: any data obtained can be interpreted in a way consistent with the theory. The first criticism is refuted by the various studies described in this section. However, the second criticism is more difficult to defend, and a major task of SR theorists is to address the theory's 'fuzziness'.

CONCLUSIONS

This chapter has reviewed some of the theory and research relating to social and cultural stereotyping and SRs. Stereotypes are not exceptionless generalisations, and may even be a normal rather than abnormal cogni-tive process. Research into social representations reveals information about how we share, transmit, and reflect upon our understanding of the world. However, its crit-ics have challenged the theory's 'fuzzy' nature and non-falsifiability.

Summary

- When forming impressions of people, we tend to go beyond the information given about them and assume they also possess other characteristics. People's **central traits** (e.g. 'warm' and 'cold') have more impact on inferences than **peripheral traits** (e.g. 'polite' and 'blunt').

- Inferring other favourable (unfavourable) character-istics on the basis of a positive (negative) characteristic is called a **positive (negative) halo effect**.

- **Implicit personality theories** (IPTs) are beliefs about which personality traits belong together. We use IPTs to 'fill in the gaps' when we have little information about people. IPTs are shared by everyone and con-sistent within a culture.

- Some IPTs are so entrenched they illustrate **illusory correlation**, the tendency to see variables as being related when they are not. Social experiences and language also contribute to impression formation.

- IPT manifests itself in **stereotyping**, in which impres-sions about someone are built around something highly visible, such as sex or race. There are both individual and group stereotypes.

- The existence of stereotypes can be explained by the **'grain of truth' hypothesis**, which says that at some time the stereotypical characteristic attributed to a given group must have been displayed by at least one member of that group.

- Illusory correlations contradict the 'grain of truth' hypothesis. They may occur because expectations about certain events distort how we process informa-tion. When an illusory correlation is made, belief in it grows stronger through the **confirmation bias**.

- Stereotyping may be the product of normal cognitive processes, specifically as a special case of categorisa-tion involving the **accentuation principle**.

- Stereotypes are not exceptionless generalisations. Research indicates that 'typical' does not mean 'true of all members'. Rather, it seems to mean character-istic of the group in question.

- Relying on stereotypes to form impressions of strangers (**category-driven processing**) is less cognitively demanding than relying on the unique characteristics of a person (**attribute-driven processing**). Stereotypes may be resistant to change because they are a way of simplifying our complex social world.

- **Social representations** (SRs) are shared beliefs and explanations held by the societies in which we live, or the groups to which we belong. SRs explain how the strange and familiar become, in time, the familiar.

- Two major processes involved in SRs are **anchoring** and **objectifying**. The latter can be achieved through **personification** (linking complex ideas with a particu-lar person's name) and **figuration** (converting complex ideas into images and metaphors).

- Children attempt to transform the puzzling and ambiguous features of the adult world by incorporat-ing them into their own collective practices, thereby making the unfamiliar familiar.

- All societies have SRs about development itself, a set of expectations concerning what children should be like and how they should be treated. Different groups within a particular society may have different SRs.

- SRs are subject to change, one major source being the mass media. The **central figurative nucleus** is linked to several peripheral elements. When this link is bro-ken, the SR changes.

- SR theory's major weakness is its abstract or 'fuzzy' nature, making it difficult to test experimentally. It may also be non-falsifiable.

Essay Questions

1 Discuss research into the nature of social representations. *(24 marks)*

2 Describe and evaluate psychological insights into social **and/or** cultural stereotyping. *(24 marks)*

WEB ADDRESSES

http:www.csbs.utsa.edu/users/jreynolds/popcul.txt
http://www.psc-cfp.gc.ca/prcb/mono3-e.htm
http:www.msu.edu/user/amcconne/research/html
http://socpsych.jk.uni-linz.ac.at/SocReps/SRNet.html
http://lito.lse.ac.uk/socpsy/depthome.html

3 *Prejudice and Discrimination*

INTRODUCTION AND OVERVIEW

Social psychologists have long been interested in prejudice and discrimination. *Age* (see Chapter 36), *sex* (see Chapter 55), *sexuality* (see Chapter 55), and *race* have all been investigated in this respect. That prejudice and discrimination exist in our own society is undeniable. For example, in July 1999, the UK Transplant Support Agency accepted racist conditions for a kidney donation (Norton & Herbert, 1999). Just two weeks later *The Times* newspaper carried an article describing how the Ku Klux Klan, a white supremist organisation, has established branches across rural England and Wales (Barrowclough, 1999). This chapter looks at theories of the origins and maintenance of *racial prejudice and discrimination*, and at explanations and research studies relating to their reduction.

DEFINING PREJUDICE AND DISCRIMINATION

Literally, 'prejudice' means to pre-judge, and we are all prejudiced towards and against certain things. In everyday language, 'prejudice' and 'discrimination' are typically used synonymously. For social psychologists, however, the two words have subtly different meanings. Prejudice is a special type of *attitude* (a psychological tendency that is expressed by evaluation of a particular entity: Hewstone *et al.*, 1996). As an example of an extreme type of attitude, prejudice comprises three components (the *cognitive*, *affective* and *behavioural)* common to all attitudes.

The cognitive component is the *beliefs* and *preconceived expectations* (or *stereotypes*: see Chapter 2) a person has about a particular group or its individual members. These may be positive, but are generally negative. The affective component of prejudice is the *feelings* or *emotions* (which may be positive, but are mostly negative) that a particular group or its members incite in us. The behavioural component is the way a person *acts* towards a group or its members. This component constitutes *discrimination*, and ranges from anti-locution (such as the telling of racist jokes) to the genocide (or extermination) of an entire group (Allport, 1954; Hirsch, 1995). Discrimination, then, is *not* the same thing as prejudice. Rather, it is the behavioural component of prejudice.

Figure 3.1 *Racist slogans and graffiti are an all-too-familiar form of discrimination*

THE PREJUDICED PERSONALITY

The most famous attempt to establish a link between *personality* and prejudice is that of Adorno *et al.* (1950). They reported the results of a research programme aimed at understanding the *anti-semitism* (opposition to, or intolerance of, Jews) and *ethnocentrism* (or 'general prejudice') that had emerged in Nazi Germany in the 1930s. Adorno *et al.* hypothesised that a person's political and social attitudes formed a coherent pattern that was 'an expression of deep-lying trends in personality'.

Box 3.1 Prejudice and early experience

Adopting a Freudian perspective (see Chapter 31), Adorno *et al.* argued that personality development was shaped by a child's parents. In normal development, parents strike a balance between disciplining a child and the child's self-expression. If, however, parents adopted an excessively harsh disciplinary regime which did not allow self-expression, the child would *displace* aggression against the parents on to some alternative target (because the consequences of displacing aggression towards the parents would elicit too much fear).

Adorno *et al.* reasoned that likely targets for displaced aggression would be those perceived as being weaker or inferior, such as members of ethnic or deviant groups who could not fight back, and who possessed the hostility towards authority repressed in the child itself. Adorno *et al.* devised several personality inventories which measured anti-semitism (*AS scale*), ethnocentrism (*E scale*), political–economic conservatism (*PEC scale*), and potentiality for fascism (*F scale*).

The AS scale measured 'stereotyped negative opinions' describing the Jews as threatening, immoral, and categorically different from non-Jews, and hostile attitudes urging various forms of restriction, exclusion, and suppression as a means of solving the 'Jewish problem' (Brown, 1965). The E scale measured:

> '... a view of things in which one's own group is the centre of everything, and all others are scaled and rated with reference to it ... Each group ... boasts itself superior ... and looks with contempt on outsiders [and each] thinks its own folkways the only right one.' (Sumner, 1906).

The PEC scale measured attachment to things as they are and a resistance to social change. The F scale measured implicit authoritarian and anti-democratic trends in personality, which make someone with such a personality susceptible to explicit fascist propaganda.

Box 3.2 Some items appearing on the F scale

For each statement, respondents are asked to decide whether they strongly agree, moderately agree, slightly agree, slightly disagree, moderately disagree or strongly disagree. The scale is arranged so that high scorers strongly agree with the statements and low scorers strongly disagree with them.

1 Obedience and respect for authority are the most important virtues children should learn.

2 Young people sometimes get rebellious ideas, but as they grow up they ought to get over them and settle down.

3 Sex crimes, such as rapes and attacks on children, deserve more than mere imprisonment. Such criminals ought to be publicly whipped or worse.

4 When a person has a problem or worry, it is best for him not to think about it, but to keep busy with more cheerful things.

5 Some day it will probably be shown that astrology can explain a lot of things.

6 People can be divided into two distinct classes: the weak and the strong.

7 Human nature being what it is, there will always be war and conflict.

8 Nowadays, when so many different kinds of people move around and mix together so much, a person has to protect himself especially carefully against catching an infection or disease from them.

9 The wild sex life of the old Greeks and Romans was tame compared to some of the goings-on in this country, even in places where people might least expect it.

Adorno *et al.* found that high scorers on the F scale (*authoritarian personalities*) also tended to score highly on the other scales, and were more likely to have had the sort of childhood described in Box 3.1. However, although it is tempting to conclude that childhood experiences lead to the formation of a prejudiced personality, many criticisms have been made of Adorno *et al.*'s research.

The F scale (and, indeed, the other scales) can be criticised on methodological grounds. It was constructed so that agreement with a statement *always* indicated authoritarianism (see Box 3.2). Constructing a scale like this often leads to *acquiescent response sets*, that is, the tendency to agree with the remainder of a questionnaire's items (irrespective of their content) when the first few have been agreed with. Other methodological criticisms include:

- the biased nature of the original sample (white, middle class, non-Jewish, Americans);

- the use of retrospective questions (about childhood);

- experimenter effects (the interviewers *knew* the interviewee's scores on the F scale).

Box 3.3 Dogmatism and toughmindedness

Adorno *et al.* also only identified people on the political *right*. According to Rokeach (1948, 1960), *dogmatism* (a rigid outlook on life and intolerance of those with opposing beliefs regardless of one's own social and political position) is a major characteristic of prejudice. Similarly, prejudice may arise from a personality dimension Eysenck (1954) called *toughmindedness*. The toughminded individual is attracted to extreme left-wing *or* right-wing political ideologies.

Empirically, predictions derived from Adorno *et al.*'s theory have not always been supported. For example, Pettigrew (1958) found that F scale scores were no higher among Southerners in the USA than among Northerners, even though anti-black attitudes were more common in the south than the north of the USA when Pettigrew conducted his research.

An approach based on personality is *reductionist* (see Chapter 57), simplistic and ignores sociocultural and demographic factors. Indeed, personality factors are *weaker* predictors of prejudice than age, education, socioeconomic status, and the region of a country in which a person lives (Maykovich, 1975). The *social* nature of prejudice and discrimination requires a social explanation.

Box 3.4 Prejudice in society and conformity to social norms

If prejudice is due to personality *differences*, then it is hard to see how an entire society or subgroup within a society (with many differences between people) would be prejudiced. Such an approach also has difficulty in explaining why prejudice rises and declines in a society. The change from positive to negative attitudes towards the Japanese by Americans following the bombing of Pearl Harbour in 1940 cannot possibly be explained by reference to the factors proposed by Adorno *et al.*

A much better explanation here is in terms of *conformity to social norms*. For example, Minard (1952) showed that whilst 80 per cent of a sample of white coalminers in the USA were friendly towards blacks *underground*, only 20 per cent of the sample were friendly *above ground*. This finding suggests that a different set of norms operated above and below ground. However, this approach fails to explain why prejudice continues even if a social norm *changes* (as has been the case in South Africa). Perhaps more importantly, it also fails to explain where the social norm to be prejudiced towards a particular group originated from (Reich & Adcock, 1976).

Evidence suggests that the authoritarian personality is *self-perpetuating*. Authoritarian parents tend to produce authoritarian children, and there is a strong correlation between parents' and their offspring's F scale scores (Cherry & Byrne, 1976). However, level of education is also negatively correlated with authoritarianism. Presumably, the provision of, and access to, education would go some way to reducing prejudice (Pennington *et al.*, 1999: see page 30). Additionally, changing patterns of child rearing (which Adorno *et al.* saw as being crucially important) might reduce prejudice. By allowing children to express hostility, the need to displace it on to ethnic and other groups would not arise.

THE FRUSTRATION–AGGRESSION APPROACH

According to Dollard *et al.*'s (1939) *frustration–aggression hypothesis*, frustration always gives rise to aggression, and aggression is always caused by frustration (see also Chapter 7). Frustration (being blocked from achieving a desirable goal) has many sources. Sometimes, *direct aggression* against the source of the frustration may be possible, and sometimes not. Drawing on Freudian theory, Dollard *et al.* proposed that when we are prevented from being aggressive towards the source of frustration, we *displace* it on to a substitute, or 'scapegoat' (see Box 3.1, page 22).

The choice of a scapegoat is not usually random. In England during the 1930s and 1940s, the scapegoat was predominantly the Jews. In the 1950s and 1960s, it was West Indians, and since the 1970s it has mainly been Asians from Pakistan. In one retrospective correlational study, Hovland & Sears (1940) found that the number of lynchings of blacks in America from 1880 to 1930 was correlated with the price of cotton: as cotton's price dropped, the number of lynchings increased. Presumably, the economic situation created frustration in the white cotton farmers who, unable to confront those responsible for it (the government), displaced their aggression on to blacks.

Although Hovland and Sears' interpretation of their data has been challenged (Hepworth & West, 1988), other research (e.g. Doty *et al.*, 1991) has confirmed that prejudice rises significantly in times of social and economic threat (a point explored further below). Whilst these findings are consistent with the concept of displaced aggression, the fact that some rather than other minority groups are chosen as scapegoats suggests that there are usually socially approved (or legitimised) groups that serve as targets for frustration-induced aggression. As the prominent Nazi Hermann Rausching observed: 'If the Jew did not exist, we should have to invent him' (cited in Koltz, 1983).

Figure 3.2 *According to the frustration–aggression approach, discrimination against outsiders (in this case eastern-European asylum seekers) is a form of displaced aggression*

Box 3.5   Scapegoating in the laboratory

Scapegoating has been demonstrated in the laboratory in several ways. Weatherley (1961) had an experimenter insult students, who were either low- or high-scorers on a measure of anti-semitism, as they completed another questionnaire. After this, the students were asked to write short stories about pictures of men, two of whom had Jewish-sounding names. Low and high scorers did not differ in the amount of aggression displayed in their stories about the pictures of men with non-Jewish sounding names. However, high scorers displayed more aggression than low scorers towards the pictures of men with Jewish-sounding names. Similar effects have been found when frustration is induced in other ways, such as making people feel like failures (Crocker *et al.*, 1987).

CONFLICT APPROACHES

Relative deprivation theory

According to *relative deprivation theory*, the discrepancy between our *expectations* (the things we feel entitled to) and *actual attainments* produces frustration (Davis,

1959; Davies, 1969). When attainments fall short of rising expectations, relative deprivation is particularly acute and results in collective unrest. For example, the immediate cause of the 1992 Los Angeles riots was an all-white jury's acquittal of four police officers accused of beating a black motorist, Rodney King. Against a background of rising unemployment and deepening disadvantage, this was seen by blacks as symbolic of their low value in the eyes of the white majority (Hogg & Vaughan, 1998). The great sense of injustice at the acquittal seemed to demonstrate acutely the injustice which is an inherent feature of both discrimination and relative deprivation.

Figure 3.3 *The 1992 Los Angeles riots were triggered by an all-white jury's aquittal of four Los Angeles police officers accused of beating a black motorist, Rodney King*

The Los Angeles riots are an example of *fraternalistic relative deprivation*, based on a comparison either with dissimilar others or with other groups (Runciman, 1966). This is contrasted with *egoistic relative deprivation*, based on comparison with other similar individuals. For example, Vanneman & Pettigrew (1972) found that whites who expressed the greatest anti-black attitudes were those who felt most strongly that whites *as a group* are badly off relative to blacks. Since, in objective terms, whites are actually better off, this shows the subjective nature of relative deprivation.

According to Vivian & Brown (1995), the most militant blacks appear to be those with higher socioeconomic and educational status. They probably have higher expectations, both for themselves and for their group, than non-militant blacks. Consequently, they experience relative deprivation more acutely.

The frustration–aggression and relative deprivation theories would argue that preventing frustration, lowering people's expectations, and providing them with less anti-social ways of venting their frustration should result in a reduction of prejudice and discrimination. However, the practical problems of putting back the 'historical clock', or changing social conditions in quite fundamental ways, are immense.

Realistic conflict theory

Data obtained from many nations and historical periods show that the greater the competition for scarce resources, the greater the hostility between various ethnic groups. For example, the Ku Klux Klan was founded in 1866, just after the American civil war. Established in Tennessee, in the defeated South, it attracted mainly poor whites who believed that their livelihood was threatened by the newly freed black slaves. Shortly afterwards, it became a para-military organisation attacking and often murdering blacks (Barrowclough, 1999).

Sherif's (1966) *realistic conflict theory* proposes that intergroup conflict arises when interests conflict. When two distinct groups want to achieve the same goal but only one can, hostility is produced between them. Indeed, for Sherif, conflict of interest (or *competition*) is a *sufficient* condition for the occurrence of hostility or conflict. This claim is based on a field study conducted by Sherif *et al.* (1961).

Key **STUDY**

Box 3.6   The 'Robber's Cave' field experiment

Sherif *et al.*'s (1961) experiment involved 22 eleven- and twelve-year-old white, middle class, well-adjusted American boys who were attending a summer camp at Robber's Cave State Park in Oklahoma. The boys were divided in advance into two groups of 11 and housed separately, out of each other's sight.

As a result of their co-operative activities, such as pitching tents and making meals, the two groups quickly developed strong feelings of attachment for their own members. Indeed, a distinct set of norms for each group emerged, defining their identity. One group called themselves the 'Rattlers' and the other the 'Eagles'. A week later, the groups were brought together, and a series of competitive events (for which trophies, medals and prizes would be awarded) was organised.

The two groups quickly came to view one another in highly negative ways, manifesting itself in behaviours such as fighting, raids on dormitories, and refusing to eat together. The competition threatened an unfair distribution of rewards (the trophy, medals, and prizes), and the losing group saw the winners as undeserving.

The view that competition is sufficient for intergroup conflict has, however, been challenged. For example, Tyerman & Spencer (1983) studied boy scouts at their annual camp. The boys already knew each other well, and much of what they did was similar to what Sherif's boys had done. The scouts were divided into four 'patrols' which competed in situations familiar to them from previous camps, but the friendship ties which existed between them prior to their arrival at the camp were maintained across the patrols. Under these conditions, competition remained friendly and there was no increase in ingroup solidarity.

In Tyerman and Spencer's view, the four groups continued to see themselves as part of the whole group (a view deliberately encouraged by the scout leader), and therefore Sherif *et al.*'s results reflect the *transitory* nature of the experimental groups. The fact that the scouts knew each other beforehand, had established friendships, were familiar with camp life, and had a leader who encouraged co-operation, were all important contextual and situational influences on their behaviour. So, whilst conflict *can* lead to hostility, it is not sufficient for it and this weakens the explanatory power of Sherif's theory.

Reducing prejudice by pursuing common goals

Sherif *et al.* (1961) initially attempted to resolve the conflict they created between the two groups of children by having them watch movies, attend a party, and eat meals together. However, this was unsuccessful and none of the situations, either individually or collectively, did anything to reduce friction. Indeed, the situations actually resulted in increased hostility between the groups.

Box 3.7   Co-operation and superordinate goals

Another approach used by Sherif *et al.* was more successful. This involved creating situations in which the problems both groups faced could only be solved through *co-operation* between them. For example, the researchers arranged for the camp's drinking water supply to be cut off, with the only way of restoring it requiring both groups to work together. Similarly, on a trip to an overnight camp, one of the trucks carrying the boys got 'stuck', and the only way in which it could resume the journey was if all the boys pulled together on a large rope.

Sherif *et al.* found that by creating these *superordinate goals* (goals that can only be achieved through co-operation), the group divisions gradually disappeared. Indeed, at the end of the experimental period, the boys actually suggested travelling home together on one bus. Sixty-five per cent of friendship choices were made from members of the *other* group, and the stereotypes previously held became much more favourable.

Sherif *et al.*'s findings have subsequently been replicated in other similar studies (e.g. Clore *et al.*, 1978) in a variety of contexts (such as inter-racial sports teams: Slavin & Madden, 1979). However, imposing superordinate goals is not always effective, and may sometimes *increase* antagonism towards the outgroup if the co-operation fails to achieve its aims (Brown, 1996). It may also be important for groups engaged in co-operative ventures to have distinctive and complementary roles to play, so that each group's contributions are clearly defined. When this does not happen, liking for the other group may actually decrease, perhaps because group members are concerned with the ingroup's integrity (Brown, 1996).

The pursuit of common goals has also been investigated in studies of co-operative learning in the classroom. Aronson (1992) was originally approached by the superintendent of schools in Austin, Texas, to give advice about how inter-racial prejudice could be reduced. Aronson *et al.* (1978) devised an approach to learning that involved mutual interdependence among the members of a class.

Box 3.8   The jigsaw classroom technique

In Aronson *et al.*'s *jigsaw classroom technique*, students (regardless of their race) are placed in a situation in which they are given material that represents one piece of a lesson to be learned. Each child must learn his or her part and then communicate it to the rest of the group. At the end of the lesson, all children are tested on the whole lesson and given an individual score. Thus, the children must learn the full lesson, and there is complete *mutual interdependence* because each is dependent on the others for parts of the lesson that can only be learned from them.

Aronson originally studied white, black and hispanic students, who met for three days a week for a total of six weeks. At the end of this period, the students showed increased self-esteem, academic performance, liking for their classmates, and some inter-racial perceptions, compared with a control group given six weeks of traditional teaching. Aronson's method has been used in many classrooms, with thousands of students, and the results consistently show a reduction in prejudice (Singh, 1991).

Importantly, though, whilst the children who had actually worked together came to like each other better as individuals, this research has not been longitudinal and so the consequences of cooperative learning have only shown *short-term* benefits. Whether the changes last, and whether they *generalise* to other social situations, is unclear. However, at least in the short term, the pursuit of common goals can be effective, especially with young children in whom prejudiced attitudes have not yet become deeply ingrained.

Figure 3.4 *Pursuit of common goals: multi-racial children working in harmony*

SOCIAL CATEGORISATION AND SOCIAL IDENTITY APPROACHES

Whether conflict is a *necessary* condition for prejudice and discrimination (whether hostility can arise in the absence of conflicting interests), has been addressed by several researchers. According to Tajfel *et al.* (1971), merely being in a group and being aware of the existence of another group are sufficient for prejudice and discrimination to develop.

Evidence for this comes from Tajfel *et al.*'s study of 14- and 15-year-old Bristol schoolboys. Each boy was told that he would be assigned to one of two groups, which would be decided according to some purely arbitrary criterion (such as the toss of a coin). They were also told that other boys would be assigned in the same way to either their group or the other group. However, none of the boys knew who these others were, and did not interact with them during the study.

Box 3.9 The task used in Tajfel *et al.*'s (1971) minimal group experiment

Each boy worked alone in a cubicle on a task that required various matrices to be studied (see Figure 3.5) and a decision to be made about how to allocate points to a member of the boy's own group (but not himself) and a member of the other group. The boys were also told that the points could be converted to money after the study. The top line in the figure represents the points that can be allocated to the boy's own group, and the bottom line the points to the other group. For example, if 18 points are allocated to the boy's own group, then 5 are allocated to the other group. If 12 are allocated to the boy's own group, 11 are allocated to the other group.

MATRIX 4	18	17	16	15	14	13	12	11	10	9	8	7	6	5
	5	6	7	8	9	10	11	12	13	14	15	16	17	18

Figure 3.5 *One of the matrices used by Tajfel* et al. *(1971)*

At the end of the study, Tajfel *et al.* scored the boys' allocations to see if they chose for fairness, maximum gain to their own group, or maximum difference in favour of their own group. Although the matrices were arranged so that both groups would benefit from a co-operative strategy, the boys allocated points to the advantage of their own group and to the disadvantage of the other group.

Social categorisation theory

Several other studies using Tajfel *et al.*'s method (called the *minimal group paradigm*) have found that people favour their own group over others (Tajfel & Billig, 1974; Brewer & Kramer, 1985). According to *social categorisation theory* (Hewstone & Jaspars, 1982), this is because people tend to divide the social world into two categories, 'us' (the *ingroup*) and 'them' (the *outgroup*). In Tajfel's view, discrimination cannot occur until this division has been made (categorisation being a *necessary* condition for discrimination), but when it is made it produces conflict and discrimination (categorisation is a *sufficient* condition as well). Amongst the criteria used for categorisation are race, nationality, religion and sex.

Research into ingroups and outgroups shows that ingroup members see themselves in highly favourable terms, as possessing desirable characteristics, and being strongly liked. Linville *et al.* (1989) call the ingroup's tendency to see all kinds of differences among themselves

the *ingroup differentiation hypothesis*. The opposite perceptions apply to outgroup members. Additionally, outgroup members are evaluated less favourably and the ingroup sees them as being more alike in attitudes, behaviour and even facial appearance. The view that 'they all look the same to me' is called the *illusion of outgroup homogeneity* (Quattrone, 1986), and may be a natural cognitive process. The illusion of outgroup homogeneity effect has clear social implications, especially as far as the legal justice system is concerned.

Box 3.10 The illusion of outgroup homogeneity

JUDGE DENIES 'ASIAN' REMARK WAS RACIST

A judge who told an all-white jury that Asians 'all look the same' to him has refused to apologise. The judge made the comments during the trial of a young Asian man accused of robbery. After viewing photographs of a dozen Asians, he told the jury: 'I have in front of me photographs of 12 Asian men, all of whom look exactly the same, which I'm sure you'll appreciate.'

He insisted his remark had been misinterpreted. 'I want to make it clear that (my) observation, far from being an accidental affront to any section of the community, was merely intended to indicate that on examination of the photographs, the appearance of those people depicted was similar. The comment – which perhaps should not have been made – was, if anything, directed by implication to warn the jury that there was nothing singularly striking about any of the persons depicted in the photographs, in so far as identification is an issue in this case. That comment has been taken as carrying with it some sort of insult. I'm appalled that anybody could suppose that such an inference was fairly to be drawn.'

(Adapted from *The Daily Telegraph*, 22 February, 1995)

Figure 3.6 *The 'us' and 'them' mentality*

There has, however, been disagreement with the view that intergroup conflict is an *inevitable* consequence of ingroup and outgroup formation. For example, Wetherell (1982) studied white and Polynesian children in New Zealand and found the latter to be much more generous towards the outgroup, reflecting cultural norms which emphasised co-operation. Also, the minimal group paradigm itself has been criticised on several grounds, most notably its *artificiality* (Schiffman & Wicklund, 1992; Gross, 1999).

Figure 3.7 *How the 'ingroup' and 'outgroup' are defined can change depending on the circumstances. Here, the ingroup (England supporters) incorporates a large number of what are usually outgroups (supporters of other clubs)*

Social identity theory

Exactly why people tend to divide the social world into 'us' and 'them' is not completely clear. However, Tajfel (1978) and Tajfel & Turner (1986) propose that group membership provides people with a *positive self-image* and a sense of 'belonging' in the social world. According to *social identity theory* (SIT), people strive to achieve or maintain a positive self-image. There are two components of a positive self-image: *personal identity* (our personal characteristics and attributes which make us unique) and *social identity* (a sense of what we are like, derived from the groups to which we belong).

Box 3.11   Social identities, comparison and competition

Each of us actually has several social identities, which correspond to the number of different groups we identify with. In relation to each one, the more positive the group's image, the more positive social identity and hence self-image will be. To enhance self-esteem, group members make *social comparisons* with other groups. To the extent that the group sees

itself in favourable terms as compared with others, self-esteem is increased. However, since every group is similarly trying to enhance self-esteem, a clash of perceptions occurs, and prejudice and discrimination arise through what Tajfel calls *social competition*.

SIT has been applied beyond the laboratory (see Brown, 1988, for a review of applications to wage differentials, ethnolinguistic groups, and occupational groups). The theory also helps us understand how prejudice is maintained. Phenomena like the *confirmatory bias* (the tendency to prefer evidence which confirms our beliefs: see Chapter 27), *self-fulfilling prophecies* (in which our expectations about certain groups determine their behaviour) and the promotion of our own group's identity, can all be understood when viewed in terms of SIT.

Whilst there is empirical support for SIT, much of it comes from the minimal group paradigm which, as noted, has been criticised. More importantly, the available evidence shows only a positive ingroup bias and not derogatory attitudes or behaviour towards the outgroup, which is what we normally understand by 'prejudice'. So, although there is abundant evidence of intergroup discrimination, this apparently stems from raising the evaluation of the ingroup rather than denigrating the outgroup (Vivian & Brown, 1995).

The 'contact hypothesis' of prejudice reduction

People who are separated, segregated, and unaware of one another have no way of checking whether an interpretation of another group's behaviour is accurate. Because any interpretation is likely to be consistent with a (negative) stereotype held about that group, the stereotype will be strengthened. Equally, if we do not know why members of a particular group behave the way they do, we are likely to see them as being more dissimilar from ourselves than is actually the case.

Related to this so-called *autistic hostility* is what Bronfenbrenner (1960) terms the *mirror-image phenomenon*. In this, enemies come to see themselves as being in the right (each has 'God on its side') and the other in the wrong. In the same way, each attributes to the other the same negative characteristics (the 'assumed dissimilarity of beliefs').

Box 3.12 Why does enhanced contact reduce prejudice and discrimination?

By enhancing or increasing contact between separated and segregated groups, prejudice and discrimination may be reduced for at least four reasons:

- Increased contact might be effective because it leads people to realise that their attitudes are actually more similar than they assumed. The recognition of *similarity* between people leads to increased liking and attraction (see Chapter 4, pages 36–37).

- Increased contact may have benefits through the *mere exposure effect* (according to which, the more we come into contact with certain stimuli, the more familiar and liked they become: Zajonc, 1968).

- Favourable contact between two groups may lead to an opportunity to *disconfirm the negative stereotypes* held about them.

- Increased contact may lead to a *reduction in outgroup homogeneity* (see page 27), because the outgroup members lose their strangeness and become more differentiated. As a result, they are seen as a collection of unique individuals rather than interchangeable 'units'.

It is generally agreed, however, that increased contact by itself is not sufficient to reduce prejudice, and may even have the opposite effect. Despite evidence that we prefer people who are familiar, if contact is between people of consistently *unequal* status, then 'familiarity may breed contempt'. Many whites in the United States have always had a great deal of contact with blacks, but with blacks in the role of dishwashers, toilet attendants, domestic servants, and so on. Contacts under these conditions may simply reinforce the stereotypes held by whites of blacks as inferior (Aronson, 1980).

Similarly, Amir (1994) has argued that the central issues to address are those concerning the important conditions under which increased intergroup contact has an effect, who is affected by it, and with respect to what particular outcomes. Some of these issues were addressed by Allport (1954). According to his *contact hypothesis*:

'Prejudice (unless deeply rooted in the character structure of the individual) may be reduced by equal status contact between majority and minority groups in the pursuit of common goals. The effect is greatly enhanced if this contact is sanctioned by institutional supports (i.e. by law, custom or local atmosphere) and provided it is of a sort that leads to the perception of common interests and common humanity between members of the two groups'.

Most programmes aimed at promoting harmonious relations between groups that were previously in conflict have adopted Allport's view, and stressed the importance of *equal status contact* (see below) and the *pursuit of common* (or *superordinate*) *goals* (see pages 25–26).

Equal status contact

One early study of equal status contact was conducted by Deutsch & Collins (1951). They compared two kinds of housing project, one of which was thoroughly integrated (blacks and whites were assigned houses regardless of their race) and the other segregated. Residents of both were intensively interviewed, and it was found that both casual and neighbourly contacts were greater in the integrated housing and that there was a corresponding decrease in prejudice among whites towards blacks. Wilner *et al.* (1955) showed that prejudice is particularly reduced in the case of next-door neighbours, illustrating the effect of *proximity* (see Chapter 4, pages 35–36).

Related to these studies are the findings reported by Minard (1952), Stouffer *et al.* (1949), and Amir (1969). As noted previously (see Box 3.4, page 23), Minard studied white coalminers in the USA and found that whilst 80 per cent of his sample were friendly towards blacks *underground*, only 20 per cent were friendly *above ground*. This suggests that prejudice was reduced by the equal status contact between the two groups when they were working together, but that the *social norms* which operated above ground at that time did not permit equality of status. Similarly, Stouffer *et al.* (1949) and Amir (1969) found that inter-racial attitudes improved markedly when blacks and whites served together as soldiers in battle and on ships, but that their relationships were less good when they were at base camp.

From the evidence considered, it would seem that if intergroup contact does reduce prejudice, it is not because it encourages interpersonal friendship (as Deutsch and Collins would claim), but rather because of changes in the nature and structure of *intergroup relationships*. Brown & Turner (1981) and Hewstone & Brown (1986) argue that if the contact between individual groups is *interpersonal* (people are seen as individuals and group memberships are largely insignificant), any change of attitude may not generalise to other members of the respective group. So, and at the very least, people must be seen as typical members of their group if generalisation is to occur (Vivian *et al.*, 1994). The problem here is that if, in practice, 'typical' means 'stereotypical' and the stereotype is negative, reinforcement of it is likely to occur. Thus, any encounter with a 'typical' group member should be a pleasant experience (Wilder, 1984).

SOCIAL LEARNING THEORY

According to *social learning theory* (SLT: see also Chapter 38), children acquire negative attitudes towards various social groups as a result of 'significant others' (such as parents, peers and teachers) exposing them to such views or rewarding them for expressing such attitudes.

For example, Ashmore & Del Boca (1976) found that children's racial attitudes are often closely aligned with those of their parents, and children might internalise the prejudices they observe in them.

Another 'significant other' is the mass media. If some groups are portrayed by the mass media in demeaning or comic roles, then it is hardly surprising that children acquire the belief that these groups are inferior to others (Coolican, 1997). The mass media which have the greatest, and most immediate impact, and to which children are most exposed, are television and films. However, others include newspapers, magazines, textbooks and the internet (see Chapter 9).

SLT approaches to prejudice reduction

If children's attitudes are shaped by their observations of 'significant others', then, presumably, discouraging those others from expressing prejudiced views and discriminatory behaviour should help to prevent prejudice and discrimination from developing. Whilst psychologists cannot interfere in parent–child relationships, they can alert parents to the prejudiced views they are expressing and the important costs attached to them (Baron & Byrne, 1997).

Parents could also encourage *self-examination* in their children (Rathus, 1990). For example, some of the things we say or do reflect our prejudices without us being aware of this. Rathus gives the example of a Catholic referring to an individual as 'that damned Jew'. It is extremely unlikely that a Catholic would say 'that damned Catholic'. Parents could, therefore, stress to their children the importance of remembering to attribute behaviour to people as *individuals* rather than *group representatives* (Hogg & Vaughan, 1998).

Several researchers have looked at the extent to which directly experiencing prejudice and discrimination may help children to understand them and, as a result, reduce their occurrence. McGuire (1969) showed that providing children with counter-arguments to attitudes and behaviours they might experience as adults lessens prejudice and discrimination. A well-documented example of this approach was taken by Jane Elliott, an American schoolteacher (Elliott, 1977).

As a way of helping her nine-year-old students understand the effects that prejudice and discrimination can have, she divided them into two groups on the basis of their eye colours. Elliott told her students that brown-eyed people are more intelligent and 'better' than blue eyed people. Brown-eyed students, though in the minority, would therefore be the 'ruling class' over the inferior blue-eyed students and would be given extra privileges. The blue-eyed students were told that they would be 'kept in their place' by restrictions such as being last in line, seated at the back of the class, and

given less break time. They were also told that they would have to wear special collars as a sign of their low status.

Figure 3.8 *Stills from the film of Elliott's classroom experiment, in which wearing collars as an overt sign of low status was part of the discrimination sanctioned by the teacher*

Within a short time, the blue-eyed students began to do more poorly in their schoolwork, became depressed and angry, and described themselves in negative ways. The brown-eyed students became mean, oppressed the others, and made derogatory statements about them. The next day, Elliott told her students that she had made a mistake and that it was really blue-eyed people who were superior. With the situation reversed, the pattern of prejudice and discrimination quickly switched from the blue-eyed students to the brown-eyed students as victims.

At the end of her demonstration, Elliott debriefed her students. She told them that its purpose was to provide them with an opportunity to experience the evils of prejudice and discrimination in a protected environment. Interestingly, the consequences of the demonstration were not short-lived. In a follow-up study of the students when they were 18, Elliott (1990) found that they reported themselves as being more tolerant of differences between groups and actively opposed to prejudice.

Key STUDY

Box 3.13   The greens and oranges

The implications of Elliott's informal demonstration were investigated by Weiner & Wright (1973). They randomly assigned white nine-year-olds to either a 'green' or an 'orange' group, group membership being indicated by an appropriately coloured armband. First, the 'green' pupils were labelled inferior and denied social privileges. After a few days, the labelling was reversed. Children in a second class were not treated in this way and served as a control group.

Once the children had experienced being in the 'green' and 'orange' conditions, they and the control group children were asked if they wanted to go on a picnic with black children from another school. Ninety-six per cent of children from the 'green–orange' group expressed a desire to go compared with only 62 per cent of the control group. The experience of prejudice and discrimination evidently led the 'green–orange' children to think that discrimination on the basis of colour is wrong. This suggests that experience of being discriminated against can make children more aware of the sensitivities and feelings of outgroup members.

Racism and childhood identity

According to Milner (1996, 1997), the development of children's racial attitudes has been seen as an essentially *passive* process, in which parents and others provide behaviours which children then absorb and reproduce. Racial attitude development is seen as being the result of irresistible social and cultural factors which impinge on the child from a variety of sources, with the child's only active participation being an attempt to make 'cognitive sense' of the messages s/he receives.

Whilst Milner accepts that a variety of sources provide the *content* of children's racist attitudes, he argues that:

> 'There has been a tendency to make a rather facile equation between, on the one hand, children's racial attitudes, and culturally mediated racism on the other. It is as though we have said a) "children have rather hostile racial attitudes", and b) "our cultural products contain many instances of implicit or explicit racism", and therefore a) must be caused by b)'.

Milner does not see sources such as children's books as containing enough 'raw material' in themselves to account for the development of their racial attitudes. In his view, children play an *active* role in the development of their racial awareness and rudimentary attitudes. Rather than solely absorbing adults' attitudes in 'junior form' or seeking to construct a cognitively well-ordered world, they are motivated by *needs* to locate themselves and their groups within that social world 'in ways which establish and sustain positive self- and social-regard or identity'. This is consistent with social identity theory (see page 28).

The principal need in a society with a competitive ethos (such as our own) is to understand the complexity of the social world and locate oneself at an acceptable station within it. Aligning oneself with a particular category might lead to social acceptance or to marginality or ostracism. Identification with a particular childhood category membership, then, has a positive aspect whose value is much sought after, and negative racial attitudes *may* fulfil this function for the majority-group child in a multi-racial society. As Milner points out, though, negative racial attitudes cannot (by definition) fulfil the same function for the minority group. This can be seen in the phenomenon of *misidentification*.

Box 3.14 Misidentification

Clark & Clark (1947) asked black and white children aged between three and seven to choose a black or white doll to play with. Regardless of their own colour, the children consistently chose the white dolls, saying that they were prettier and nicer. These findings were replicated by other researchers, and it was also shown that the 'doll tests' are a valid measure of self-concept related to ethnic identification (Ward & Braun, 1972). However, their status has subsequently been challenged (Owuso-Bempah & Howitt, 1999).

Morland (1970) found that when the level of actual discrimination increases, so self-contempt increases. Thus, more black children from Southern states in America chose a white child as a preferred playmate than was the case for black children from the Northern states. As Rowan (1978) has remarked:

'What this means is that when whites are taught to hate blacks, blacks themselves come to hate blacks – that is, themselves. When whites are taught that blacks are inferior, blacks come to see themselves as inferior. In order to cease to be inferior, they have (it sometimes seems to them) to cease to be black'.

The *self-denigration* by minority groups was addressed by civil rights and black politico-cultural movements that encouraged a positive connotation about blackness with slogans like 'Black is Beautiful'. As a result of these movements, the misidentification phenomenon all but disappeared, even among young children who might not be expected to be attuned to the relevant cultural and political messages (Milner, 1997). But what about the majority group? As Milner notes:

'If it is true that majority-group children may actively seek, or be drawn to, a set of racial attitudes partly because the superior/inferior group relations they portray satisfies the developing need for a positive social identity, then this might seem to underscore both the inevitability and ineradicability of racism, among the majority group'.

However, Milner argues that many other things can serve the purpose of satisfying the need for a positive social identity (supporting a winning soccer team, for example), and far from embedding racism deeper in the child's 'psychological economy', this notion actually undercuts the significance of childhood racism. For Milner, racist ideas may have more to do with the developing identity needs of children than with the objects of those attitudes, and may be rapidly superseded by other sources of status and self-esteem.

This would account for Pushkin & Veness's (1973) finding that racial attitudes peak in hostility around the age of six to seven and decline subsequently. Moreover, if racial attitudes were central in a child's identity, they would endure into adulthood, but (with a few exceptions) this does not seem to happen. That hostile racial attitudes may be transient phenomena 'would be encouraging for multiracial education and for the wider society' (Milner, 1997).

Figure 3.9 *France's multi-ethnic 1998 World Cup winning soccer team. Supporting soccer teams is one way of satisfying the need for a positive social identity*

CONCLUSIONS

Several theories of prejudice and discrimination have been advanced. Some see prejudice as stemming from individual factors, some concentrate on the role of external factors, and some emphasise the impact of group membership. Whilst all have some support, none is yet accepted as a definitive theory. Since prejudice and discrimination cannot be explained in a simple way, it is hardly surprising that proposals for their reduction have not always met with success.

Summary

- Prejudice is an extreme **attitude**, comprising the three components common to all attitudes. These are **cognitive**, **affective** and **behavioural**. The behavioural component constitutes **discrimination**.

- Adorno *et al.* argued for the existence of a prejudiced personality (the **authoritarian personality**). However, their research is methodologically suspect and has little experimental support. It fails, for example, to explain prejudice in entire societies or sub-groups, or the decline of prejudice in societies.

- **Conformity to social norms** is a better explanation for the above, although this does not explain prejudice's origins or its continuation following changes in social norms.

- The **frustration–aggression hypothesis** proposes that when aggression cannot be expressed directly against a frustration's source, it is displaced onto a substitute or **scapegoat**. Minority groups are often used as scapegoats.

- **Relative deprivation theory** proposes that the discrepancy between expectations and attainments produces frustration, which leads to prejudice and discrimination. **Fraternalistic relative deprivation** is based on comparisons with either dissimilar others or other groups. **Egoistic relative deprivation** is based on comparisons with similar individuals.

- According to **realistic conflict theory**, intergroup conflict arises when interests conflict. According to Sherif *et al.*, competition between groups is a sufficient condition for hostility, although some evidence disputes this.

- One way to resolve conflict is through the **pursuit of common goals**. However, this is only effective when **superordinate goals**, which can be achieved through **cooperation**, are created.

■ Co-operative learning in the classroom has been studied using the **jigsaw technique**, which creates mutual **interdependence** between students. Although effective in the short term, little is known about the technique's long-term benefits, and whether they generalise to other situations.

■ Based on studies using the **minimal group paradigm**, Tajfel *et al.* argue that conflict is not necessary for prejudice and discrimination. Merely belonging to a group and being aware of another group's existence is sufficient. **Social categorisation theory** explains this in terms of the division of the world into 'us' (the **ingroup**) and 'them' (the **outgroup**).

■ According to **social identity theory** (SIT), people strive to achieve or maintain a positive self-image. The more positive a group perceive its image to be, the more positive each individual member's social identity is.

■ Social comparison with other groups enhances self-esteem, but since every group is trying to enhance self-esteem, a clash of perceptions occurs, and prejudice and discrimination arise through **social competition**.

■ There is considerable experimental support for SIT, but much of it comes from the minimal group paradigm, which has been criticised for its **artificiality**. Additionally, the evidence tends to show a **positive ingroup bias**, rather than negative attitudes/behaviour towards the outgroup, which is what prejudice and discrimination normally imply.

■ The **contact hypothesis** of prejudice reduction proposes that there must be **equal status contact** if prejudice is to be reduced. Any reduction in prejudice that occurs probably does so because of changes in the nature and structure of **intergroup relationships**.

■ **Social learning theory** (SLT) proposes that children acquire negative attitudes towards particular social groups as a result of significant others exposing them to such views, or reinforcing them for expressing such attitudes.

■ Providing children with the opportunity to experience prejudice and discrimination directly in a protected environment may help in their reduction, by increasing children's understanding. This was demonstrated in Elliot's 'brown-eyes–blue-eyes' study and Weiner and Wright's 'green–orange' experiment.

■ Children do not passively absorb and reproduce parents' and others' behaviour. The content of racial attitudes may be provided by social/cultural sources, but children are actively involved in the development of their racial awareness and attitudes.

■ Adopting negative racial attitudes may help majority-group children achieve acceptance in a multi-racial, competitive society. However, these attitudes cannot fulfil this function for minority group children, as seen in **misidentification**.

■ Racist attitudes may be more to do with children's developing identity needs than with the objects of those attitudes. This would account for racial hostility peaking at ages six to seven.

Essay Questions

1 Describe and evaluate **two** theories of the origins of prejudice. *(24 marks)*

2 Discuss explanations **and** research studies relating to the reduction of prejudice and/or discrimination. *(24 marks)*

WEB ADDRESSES

http:www.socialpsychology.org/social.html#prejudice
http://www.noctrl.edu/~ajomuel/crow/topicprejudice.htm
http://www.colorado.edu/conflict/peace/problem/prejudisc.htm

4 Attraction and the Formation of Relationships

INTRODUCTION AND OVERVIEW

According to Duck (1995), the study of interpersonal relationships is one of the most fertile and all-embracing aspects of social scientific research. This chapter examines explanations and research studies relating to *interpersonal attraction*, and theories and research studies relating to the *formation of relationships*. It begins, however, by briefly considering *affiliation* as a precondition for relationship formation.

AFFILIATION

Affiliation is a basic need for the company of others. According to Duck (1988), we are more affiliative and inclined to seek other people's company in some circumstances than others. These include moving to a new neighbourhood, and terminating a close relationship. One of the most powerful factors influencing affiliation, however, is *anxiety*.

Key STUDY

Box 4.1 The effects of anxiety on affiliation

In one of Schachter's (1959) experiments, female students were led to believe that they would receive electric shocks. Half were told that the shocks would be extremely painful (*high anxiety condition*) and half that they would not be at all painful (*low anxiety condition*). The students were then told that there would be a delay whilst the equipment was being set up, and that they could wait on their own or with another participant. Two-thirds of those in the high anxiety condition chose to wait with another participant, whilst only one-third in the low anxiety condition chose this option.

In another experiment, Schachter told *all* participants that the shocks would be extremely painful. This time, though, the members of one group were given the option of waiting alone or with another participant who would also be receiving the shocks. Members of a second group were given the option of waiting alone or with a student waiting to see her teacher. Those in the first group preferred to sit with another participant, whilst those in the second group preferred to be alone. This suggests that if we have something to worry about, we prefer to be with others in the same situation as us.

Figure 4.1 *Greta Garbo famously wanted to be alone. The need to be affiliative differs according to the circumstances*

Anxiety's role in affiliation has also been demonstrated in other studies. For example, Kulik & Mahler (1989) found that most patients awaiting coronary bypass surgery preferred to share a room with someone who had already undergone such surgery, rather than with someone who was waiting to undergo it. The main motive for this preference seemed to be the need for *information* in order to reduce the stress caused by the forthcoming operation (Buunk, 1996).

FORMING RELATIONSHIPS: INTERPERSONAL ATTRACTION

According to Clore & Byrne (1974), we are attracted to people whose presence is *rewarding* for us. These rewards may be direct (and provided by the other person) or indirect (the other person takes on the emotional tone of the surrounding situation). The more rewards someone provides for us, the more we should be attracted to them. Although rewards are not the same for everyone, several factors are important in influencing the initial attraction between people through their reward value. These include *proximity, exposure, familiarity, similarity, physical attractiveness, reciprocal liking, complementarity* and *competence*.

Proximity

Proximity means geographical closeness. It is a minimum requirement for attraction because the further apart two people live, the less likely it is that they will have the chance to meet, become friends or marry each other. Festinger *et al.* (1950) found that students living in campus accommodation were most friendly with their next-door neighbours and least friendly with those at the end of the corridor. Students separated by four flats hardly ever became friends and, in two-storey flats, residents tended to interact mainly with people who lived on the same floor. On any one floor, people who lived near stairways had more friends than those living at the end of the corridor (see Figure 4.2).

Festinger *et al.*'s findings have been replicated in numerous studies. For example, home owners are more likely to become friendly with their next-door neighbours, especially when they share a drive (Whyte, 1956), and apartment dwellers tend to form relationships with those on the same floor (Nahemow & Lawton, 1975). At school, students are more likely to develop relationships with those they sit next to (Segal, 1974).

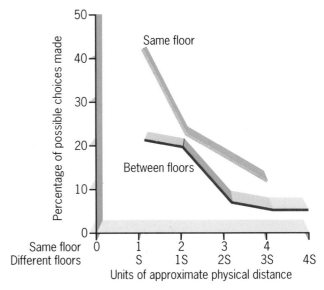

Figure 4.2 *Data from Festinger* et al.'*s (1950) investigation. The 'units of approximate physical distance' refer to how many doors apart people lived. For example, 3S means 3 doors and a stairway apart*

Box 4.2 Physical proximity and personal space

There are, however, 'rules' governing physical proximity. Sommer (1969) and Felipe & Sommer (1966) showed that when a stranger sits next to or close to someone, that person experiences an unpleasant increase in arousal. This is because his or her *personal space* (Hall, 1959: a sort of 'invisible bubble' around a person in which it is unpleasant for others to be) has been invaded.

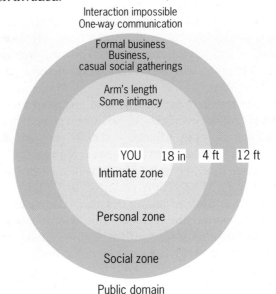

Figure 4.3 *Hall's four zones of personal space (From Nicholson, 1977)*

In Hall's view, we learn *proxemic rules*. These prescribe the physical distance that is appropriate between people in daily situations, and the kinds of situation in which closeness or distance is proper. These rules are not the same in all cultures, and there are individual differences with regard to them, even within the same culture (violent criminals, for example, are more sensitive to physical closeness than non-violent criminals). Successful relationships may require an initial establishment of 'boundary understandings', that is, strangers must be *invited* into our personal space rather than 'invade' it.

Exposure and familiarity

Proximity provides increased opportunity for interaction (*exposure*) which, in turn, increases how familiar others become to us (*familiarity*). Far from breeding *contempt*, familiarity apparently breeds *contentment* (unless we initially dislike something, in which case we tend to dislike it even more: Grush, 1976). This is what Zajonc (1968) calls the *mere exposure effect,* and several studies have found a positive correlation between frequency of exposure to stimuli and liking for them (e.g. Brooks & Watkins, 1989). Argyle (1983) has argued that increased exposure to, and familiarity with, others causes an increased *polarisation* of attitudes towards each other. Usually, this is in the direction of greater liking, but only if the interaction is as equals.

The impact of familiarity on attraction was demonstrated by Newcomb (1961). He found that whilst similarity of beliefs, attitudes and values (see below) was important in determining liking, the key factor was familiarity. So, even when students were paired according to the similarity or dissimilarity of their beliefs, attitudes and values, room-mates became friends far more often than would be expected on the basis of their characteristics.

Other research has shown that our preference for what is familiar even extends to our own facial appearance. For example, Mita *et al.* (1977) showed people pictures of themselves as they appear to others and mirror-images (how we appear to ourselves when we look in a mirror). Most people preferred the latter – this is how we are used to seeing ourselves. However, their friends preferred the former – this is how others are used to seeing us. It seems, then, that in general we like what we know and what we are familiar with.

Similarity

Evidence suggests that 'birds of a feather flock together', and that the critical similarities are those concerning *beliefs*, *attitudes*, and *values* (Cramer, 1998). For example,

Newcomb (1943) studied students at an American college with a liberal tradition among teaching staff and senior students. Many students coming from conservative backgrounds adopted liberal attitudes in order to gain the liking and acceptance of their classmates.

Box 4.3   Some other research findings relating to similarity and attraction

- We are more strongly attracted to people who share our attitudes. Moreover, the greater the proportion of shared attitudes, the greater the attraction.

- The more dogmatic we are, the more likely we are to reject people who disagree with us.

- When we believe that politicians share our attitudes, we may fail to remember statements they made that *conflict* with our attitudes.

- Some attitudinal factors are more important than others. One of the most important is religion.

(Based on Howard *et al.*, 1987)

Rubin (1973) suggests that similarity is rewarding for at least five reasons:

- Agreement may provide a basis for engaging in joint activities.

- A person who agrees with us helps to increase confidence in our own opinions which enhances self-esteem. In Duck's (1992) view, the validation that friends give us is experienced as evidence of the accuracy of our personal construction of the world.

- Most of us are vain enough to believe that anyone who shares our views must be a sensitive and praiseworthy person.

- People who agree about things that matter to them generally find it easier to communicate.

- We may assume that people with similar attitudes to ourselves will like us, and so we like them in turn (*reciprocal liking*: see pages 39–40).

According to *balance theory* (Heider, 1946; Newcomb, 1953), people like to have a clear, ordered and consistent view of the world so that all the parts 'fit together'. If we agree with our friends and disagree with our enemies, then we are in a state of balance (Jellison & Oliver, 1983). As Figure 4.4 shows (see page 37), the theory predicts that two people (A and B) will like each other if their opinions about something (X) are the same. If A and B's opinions about X are different, however, they will not like each other. This imbalance can be resolved either by A or B changing his or her opinion, or by A and B disliking each other.

A slightly different approach to understanding similarity's importance is provided by Rosenbaum's (1986) *repulsion hypothesis*. Rosenbaum argues that whilst other people's agreement with our attitudes provides balance, this psychological state is not especially arousing. However, when people disagree with our attitudes, we experience arousal and discomfort as a result of the imbalance. So, disagreement has more effect than agreement. Whilst similarity is important, then, the role of dissimilarity in attraction should not be ignored.

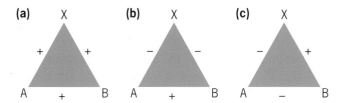

Figure 4.4 *Balance theory predicts that two people, A and B, will like each other (+) if their opinions about something (X) are both favourable, as shown in (a), or unfavourable, as shown in (b). A and B will dislike each other if their opinions about X are different, as shown in (c). (After Heider, 1946, and Newcomb, 1953)*

Physical attractiveness

A large body of evidence supports the general view that *physical attractiveness* influences the impression we form of the people we meet. For example, attractive-looking people are believed to have attractive personalities, such as being sexually warm and responsive, kind, strong, outgoing, nurturant, interesting, and so on (Dion *et al.*, 1972).

Box 4.4 Some research findings relating to attractiveness

Compared with unattractive people, attractive people are:

- more popular and sought after;
- assumed to be higher in positive traits such as intelligence;
- more likely to be employed even when their physical attractiveness is not a prerequisite for a job;
- perceived as happier, more sensitive, more successful, and more socially skilled.

(Based on Feingold, 1992)

Given the importance of *stereotypes* in influencing first impressions (see Chapter 2), it seems that attractive people have a 'head start' in this early phase of relationship

development (Eagly *et al.*, 1991). Interestingly, though, it is not always in our best interests to be seen as being highly attractive. For example, Dermer & Thiel (1975) found that female participants judged extremely attractive women to be egoistic, vain, materialistic, snobbish, and less likely to be successfully married.

Furthermore, although mock jury experiments and observational studies have shown that attractive people are more likely to be found *innocent* of crimes (Michelini & Snodgrass, 1980), there are exceptions to this. For example, if a woman is standing on trial for fraud, accused of having charmed a man into giving her money for some non-existent cause, she is *more* likely to be found guilty if she is very attractive. In terms of attribution theory, her good looks may result in the jury being more likely to make a *correspondent inference* (see Chapter 1, pages 3–4).

Figure 4.5 *Beauty is in the eye of the beholder!*

Albeit unconsciously, adults may treat children differently according to their physical appeal, and may expect attractive children to be better behaved than less attractive ones (Stephan & Langlois, 1984). When the former behave badly, their behaviour is more likely to be explained by adults in *situational* ('it wasn't really their fault') rather than *dispositional* (something about them made them behave that way) terms. According to Dion & Dion (1995), stereotyping based on facial attractiveness appears at least as early as six.

Interestingly, some studies indicate that even infants as young as two months have a marked preference for attractive faces over unattractive ones. For example, Langlois *et al.* (1990) showed that when infants are presented with pairs of colour slides of adult faces rated by adults as being unattractive and attractive, they spend longer looking at the attractive face. According to Langlois *et al.*, such a finding:

> '... challenges the commonly held assumption that standards of attractiveness are learned through gradual exposure to the cultural standard of beauty and are merely "in the eye of the beholder"'.

Box 4.5 Who is attractive? The role of culture and gender

Different cultures have different criteria concerning physical beauty. For example, chipped teeth, body scars, artificially elongated heads and bound feet have all been regarded as attractive (Ford & Beach, 1951). In Western culture, definitions of beauty change over time, a particularly good instance of this being the 'ideal' figure for women (Tovee *et al.*, 1998). Traditionally, facial beauty has been generally regarded as more important in women than men. For men, stature (particularly height), a muscular body, and (at least at present) firm, rounded buttocks, influence how attractive they are judged to be (Jensen-Campbell *et al.*, 1995).

The above examples apparently show that 'attractive' cannot be defined objectively. However, 'average' (not too big or too small) may be one way of moving away from a purely subjective definition. For example, Langlois & Roggman (1994) digitised the faces of a number of college students and used a computer to average them. Students judged the composite faces as more appealing than 96 per cent of the individual faces.

Brehm (1992) has argued that in the context of personal advertisements and commercial dating services, the primary 'resource' (or reward) offered by females seeking a male partner is still physical attractiveness, which matches what men actually seek from a female partner. However, Buss (1989) has argued that this is a universal phenomenon rather than one confined to Western culture (see Box 4.8, page 40).

Figure 4.6 *Facial scarring (left) and artificially elongated necks (right) are considered to be attractive in many non-Western cultures*

What makes a pretty face?

Bruce *et al.* (1994) examined the relationship between facial distinctiveness and attractiveness. They found that the variables were not correlated, and that 'distinctiveness' can be accounted for in terms of a physical deviation from the norm. Exactly what the 'norm' is was addressed by Perret *et al.* (1994). They asked white male and female undergraduates to rate each of 60 young adult white female faces for attractiveness.

After this, an 'average' composite was constructed from the photographs using Langlois and Roggman's computer averaging method (see Box 4.5). An attractive composite was made from the 15 faces rated as being most attractive, and a highly attractive composite by exaggerating the shape of the attractive composite by 50 per cent. The composites were then rated by female and male students. Both sexes preferred the attractive composite to the average one, and the highly attractive composite to the attractive one.

Figure 4.7 *Computers can be used in a variety of ways to study facial attractiveness. (From Perret* et al., *1994)*

Perret *et al.* then attempted to replicate their findings cross-culturally. Young female Japanese adult faces were rated by Japanese and white raters. The results did not differ from those in the original study. The most attractive face generally had higher cheek bones, a thinner jaw and larger eyes relative to facial size. There was also a shorter distance between the mouth and chin and the nose and mouth. These findings suggest there is a systematic difference between an 'average' and 'attractive' face, but cast doubt on the view that attractiveness is averageness (see also Young & Bruce, 1998, and Chapter 21). What also seems to be important, at least in men, is *symmetry*. Men with more symmetrical bodies are perceived as more attractive and desirable than non-symmetrical men, and apparently have physical and personal attributes 'necessary to be successful in direct competition tactics in heterosexual encounters' (Simpson *et al.*, 1999: see also Chapter 43, pages 474–476).

Interestingly, evidence indicates that certain factors associated with physical attractiveness can cause psychological distress in those who do not possess them. Research into impression formation indicates that bald and balding men are generally rated less favourably in terms of physical and social attractiveness, self-assertiveness, personal likeability and life success.

Wells *et al.* (1995) wanted to know if men with hair loss suffer the kinds of psychological distress that might accompany such unfavourable impressions. They studied 182 men of various ages and whose hair loss ranged from none to severe.

The participants were asked to complete a personality questionnaire which revealed that, irrespective of their age, the greater their hair loss, the more likely they were to report low self-esteem, feelings of depression and unattractiveness, and signs of neuroticism and psychoticism. These effects tended to be largest amongst the younger men.

The matching hypothesis

According to *social exchange theory* (Thibaut & Kelley, 1959; Blau, 1964; Homans, 1974; Berscheid & Walster, 1978 see Chapter 5, pages 44–45), people are more likely to become romantically involved if they are fairly closely matched in their ability to reward one another. Ideally, we would all like to have the 'perfect partner' because, the theory says, we are all selfish. However, since this is impossible we try to find a compromise solution. The best general bargain that can be struck is a *value-match* (a subjective belief that our partner is the most rewarding we could realistically hope to find).

Several studies have tested the matching hypothesis (Walster *et al.*, 1966; Dion & Berscheid, 1974; Berscheid *et al.*, 1971; Silverman, 1971; Murstein, 1972; Berscheid & Walster, 1974). These studies generally show that people rated as being of high, low or average attractiveness tend to choose partners of a corresponding level of attractiveness. Indeed, according to Price & Vandenberg (1979):

'The matching phenomenon [of physical attraction between marriage partners] is stable within and across generations'.

The findings from the various matching hypothesis studies imply that the kind of partner we would be satisfied with is one we feel will not reject us, rather than one we positively desire. Brown (1986), however, maintains that the matching phenomenon results from a well-learned sense of what is 'fitting', rather than a fear

of being rebuffed. For Brown, then, we learn to adjust our expectations of rewards in line with what we believe we have to offer others.

The term *'mate selection'* refers to choosing someone we hope will be our lifetime partner. Because identical twins share the same genes and, typically, the same environment (see Chapters 29 and 59), their choice of a mate might be expected to be similar. However, using 738 sets of identical twins, Lykken & Tellegren (1993) found that this was not the case, and the spouses of an identical twin-pair were hardly more likely to be similar than were spouses of random pairs of same-sex adults. When the researchers asked the twins how they felt about their co-twin's choice of mate, less than half (of both sexes) reported that they were attracted to their co-twin's choice. Indeed, just as many reported negative attitudes.

Lykken and Tellegren argue that if people adopt reasonably discriminating criteria to guide mate selection, then those of identical co-twins should be more similar (even though these criteria will differ from person to person). The evidence, though, suggests that whilst we do tend to choose from among people like ourselves, identical twins are not likely to be drawn to the same choice. According to Lowe (1994), this suggests that:

'Although most human choice behaviour is fairly rational, the most important choice of all – that of a mate – seems to be an exception'.

Reciprocal liking

In *How to Win Friends and Influence People*, Carnegie (1937) advised people to greet others with enthusiasm and 'praise' if we wanted them to like us. It is certainly a very pleasant experience when someone compliments and generally seems to like us. Indeed, we often respond by saying 'flattery will get you everywhere'. When we are the recipients of compliments and liking, we tend to respond in kind, or *reciprocate*. This often influences those to whom we respond to like us even more (Pennington *et al.*, 1999).

According to Aronson's (1980) *reward–cost principle*, we are most attracted to a person who makes entirely positive comments about us over a number of occasions, and least attracted to one who makes entirely negative comments. This is not, however, particularly surprising or interesting. More interesting is Aronson & Linder's (1965) *gain–loss theory*. According to this, someone who starts off by disliking us and then comes to like us will be more liked than someone who likes us from the start. Equally, someone who begins by liking us and then adopts a negative attitude towards us, will be disliked more than someone who dislikes us from the start.

Complementarity

As noted earlier , 'birds of a feather flock together'. But do 'opposites attract'? *Complementarity* refers to the reinforcement of opposing traits to the benefit of both people in a relationship, and there is a little evidence to support the view that some relationships are based on complementarity rather than similarity (Dryer & Horowitz, 1997). For example, Winch (1958) found that 'happy' marriages are often based on each partner's ability to fulfil the needs of the other (*complementarity of emotional needs*). In Winch's study, women who displayed a need to be nurturant were often married to men who needed to be nurtured.

If complementarity does occur in relationship formation, it is probably because opposing traits *reinforce* each other and benefit both individuals. However, apart from Winch's research, the evidence for complementarity is weak, and it is more likely that complementarity develops during a relationship. There is, though, stronger evidence for *complementarity in resources*. Whilst attractiveness is important for both men and women, men give a higher priority to 'good looks' in their female partners than women do in their male partners. In the case of being a 'good financial prospect' and having a 'good earning capacity', however, the situation is reversed (Brehm, 1992: see Chapter 43).

Key S T U D Y

Box 4.8   Sex differences in complementarity in resources

According to Buss (1988, 1989), sex differences in complementarity of resources 'appear to be deeply rooted in the evolutionary history of our species'. Buss bases this claim on a study of 37 cultures involving 5114 women and 4360 men. In Buss's view, the chances of reproductive success should be increased for men who mate with younger, 'healthy' adult females as opposed to older, 'unhealthy' ones. Fertility is a function of a female's age and health, which affects pregnancy and her ability to care for her child.

Since reproductive success is crucial to the survival of a species, natural selection should favour those mating patterns that promote the offspring's survival. Men often have to rely on a woman's physical appearance to estimate her age and health, with younger, healthier women being perceived as more

attractive (Singh, 1993). For women, mate selection depends on their need for a provider to take care of them during pregnancy and nursing (Highfield, 2000). Men who are seen as powerful and as controlling resources that contribute to the mother and child's welfare will be seen as especially attractive (women display a '*resource acquisition preference*').

Figure 4.8 *Sociobiologists argue that men's desire for attractive female partners, and women's desire for good providers, represents a universal sex difference rooted in human evolutionary history*

There are, however, several issues concerning Buss's findings and the *sociobiological* approach on which his claims are based. For example, sociobiological theory seems to take male–female relationships out of any cultural or historical context (captured by the use of the term 'mate selection': see Box 4.7, page 39). It is equally plausible to argue that women have been forced to obtain desirable resources through men because they have been denied direct access to political and economic power. Sigall & Landy (1973) argue that a woman has been traditionally regarded as a man's property, wherein her beauty increases his status and respect in the eyes of others.

Importantly, Buss ignores the fact that in his cross-cultural study, 'kind' and 'intelligent' were universally ranked above 'physically attractive' and 'good earning power' by both men and women. Buss's argument also fails to account for homosexual relationships (see Chapter 6, pages 60–62). Such relationships clearly do not contribute to the species' survival, despite being subject to some of the same sociopsychological influences as heterosexual relationships. Finally, Eagly & Wood (1999) have reanalysed Buss's data in terms of gender equality in societies. In societies with greater gender equality, the sex differences reported by Buss are weaker. Moreover, the female preference for selecting 'resource acquisition' characteristics is more important in cultures with low 'reproductive freedom' (e.g. contraception) and educational inequality (Kasser & Sharma, 1999).

Competence

Whilst we are generally more attracted to competent than incompetent people, there are exceptions to this. For example, when a highly talented male makes an embarrassing error, we come to like him *more* (Aronson *et al.*, 1966). Presumably, this is because the error indicates that, like the rest of us, he is 'only human'. Additionally, Aronson *et al.* found that when a person of average ability makes an error, he is liked less, and his error is seen as being just another example of his incompetence. These findings seem to be confined to men, possibly because men are more competitive and like other competent people better when they show a weakness (Deaux, 1972).

Box 4.9　Beyond attraction

There has been criticism of the quality and validity of data in interpersonal attraction and relationship formation research. One of the strongest critics has been Duck (1995), who argues that much research is:

'... typically based on scrutiny of the point of interaction at which the partners were, at best, strangers to each other. The studies [use] college students, for the most part, and [focus] only on immediate judgements of attractiveness or expressions of desire to see the other person again [and are] rarely followed up or checked for correspondence to later realities of actual interaction or second meetings'.

Duck has called for appropriate caution to be taken about such data, and for the scope of research to be broadened beyond studies of 'initial attraction'. He cites commuter marriages, 'electronic' relationships (such as those formed on the Internet, see Chapter 6, pages 62–64), and relationships among the elderly as areas attracting interest.

Duck's review of the ever-growing literature in this area indicates that the study of social relationships has recovered from what he describes as:

'... the [biased] discussions ... that used to make up the bulk of ... our social psychology textbooks'.

Whilst a general text such as this cannot possibly even briefly review *all* of the areas currently under investigation, Chapters 5 and 6 at least begin to look at the wider concerns of social relationships research.

CONCLUSIONS

This chapter has looked at explanations and research studies relating to interpersonal attraction, and theories and research studies relating to the formation of relationships. Many factors have been shown to influence initial attraction between people, although criticisms can be made of research in this area.

Summary

■ **Affiliation** is a precondition for relationship formation and is the basic need for other people's company. When anxious, people prefer the company of others in the same situation. One motive for this is the need for stress-reducing information.

■ We are attracted to people who **reward** us, either directly or indirectly. The greater the rewards, the greater the attraction. Several factors influence initial attraction through their reward values.

■ **Proximity** is a minimum requirement for attraction. Studies show that proximity increases the likelihood of relationship formation. However, there are 'rules' governing physical proximity which differ between and within cultures.

■ Proximity increases opportunity for **exposure** to others. This increases **familiarity** through the **mere exposure effect** and/or increased **polarisation of attitudes**. Familiarity appears to breed contentment rather than contempt. The preference for what is familiar even extends to our own facial appearance.

■ **Similarity** is rewarding for various reasons. For example, we are likely to see people who agree with us as sensitive and praiseworthy, as well as easier to communicate with. Through reciprocal liking, we like people who share our attitudes because we assume they will like us.

■ **Balance theory** proposes that we like to have an ordered and consistent world view. However, the **repulsion hypothesis** says that the imbalance produced by disagreement is more arousing.

■ **Physical attractiveness** also influences impression formation. Compared with unattractive people, attractive people are (in general) perceived more favourably.

■ Standards of attractiveness are evidently culturally determined, and different cultures have different criteria concerning physical beauty. In Western cultures at least, these change over time.

■ According to **social exchange theory**, people are more likely to become romantically involved the more closely they are matched in their abilities to reward each other. In the absence of a perfect partner, we settle for a **value-match** (the **matching hypothesis**).

■ **Reciprocal liking** tends to occur when others pay us compliments and show they like us. **Gain–loss theory** claims that someone who begins by disliking us and then comes to like us will be more liked than someone who likes us from the start. The reverse is true for someone who likes us initially, but then comes to dislike us.

■ Relationships can be based on **complementarity of emotional needs** rather than similarity. However, complementarity develops during a relationship and, rather than personality traits, it involves resources, such as physical beauty and money.

■ The evidence for complementarity of emotional needs is weak, and is much stronger for **complementarity in resources**. Sociobiologists claim that there is a universal preference in men for physical beauty in women, whereas women universally prefer men who are good financial prospects. However, this claim has been challenged.

■ Duck argues that most research into relationship formation focuses on first meetings and judgements of initial attraction, and fails to follow up relationship development. More interesting research goes beyond 'initial attraction'.

Essay Questions

1 Critically consider research relating to interpersonal attraction. *(24 marks)*

2 Discuss psychological insights into the formation of relationships *(24 marks)*

WEB ADDRESSES

http://www.octrl.edu/~ajomuel/crow/topicattraction.htm
http://www.socialpsychology.org/social.htm#romance
miavx1.muohio.edu/~psybersite/attraction/
http://faculty.edu.umuc.edu/~motsowit/psyc334.htm/

5 *Maintenance and Dissolution of Relationships*

INTRODUCTION AND OVERVIEW

Chapter 11 looked at some of the factors that influence initial attraction to others and hence the likelihood that we will try to form relationships with them. This chapter examines theories and research studies relating to the *maintenance* and *dissolution* of relationships. It also considers some psychological explanations of love.

STAGE THEORIES OF RELATIONSHIPS

As we all know and expect, relationships develop and change over time. Indeed, relationships which stagnate, especially if sexual/romantic in nature, may well be doomed to failure (Duck, 1988: see pages 46–48). Several theories charting the course of relationships have been proposed. These typically cover both sexual and non-sexual relationships, although they sometimes make specific mention of marriage/marriage partners.

Kerckhoff and Davis's 'filter' theory

According to Kerckhoff & Davis (1962), relationships pass through a series of 'filters'. They base this claim on a comparison between 'short-term couples' (less than 18 months) and 'long-term couples' (more than 18 months). Initially, similarity of *sociological* (or *demographic*) variables (such as ethnic, racial, religious, and social class backgrounds) determines the likelihood of people meeting in the first place. To some extent, our choice of friends and partners is made *for us*. To use Kerckhoff's (1974) term, 'the field of availables' (the range of people who are realistically, as opposed to theoretically, available for us to meet) is reduced by social circumstances.

The next 'filter' involves people's *psychological* characteristics and, specifically, agreement on basic values. Kerckhoff and Davis found this was the best predictor of a relationship becoming more stable and permanent. Thus, those who had been together for less than 18 months tended to have stronger relationships when the partners' values coincided. With couples of longer standing, though, similarity was not the most important factor. In fact, *complementarity of emotional needs* (see page 40)

was the best predictor of a longer term commitment, and this constitutes the third 'filter'.

Murstein's stimulus–value–role (SVR) theory

Murstein (1976, 1987) sees intimate relationships proceeding from a *stimulus* stage, in which attraction is based on external attributes (such as physical appearance), to a *value* stage, in which similarity of values and beliefs becomes more important. Then comes a *role* stage, which involves a commitment based on successful performance of relationship roles, such as husband and wife. Although all these factors have some influence throughout a relationship, each one assumes its greatest significance during one particular stage.

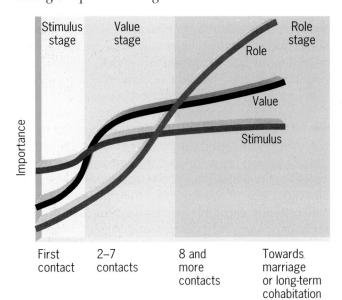

Figure 5.1 *States of courtship in Murstein's SVR theory (From Gross, 1996)*

Levinger's theory

For Levinger (1980), relationships pass through five stages rather than the three proposed by Murstein. These are: acquaintance or initial attraction, building up the relationship, consolidation or continuation, deterioration and decline, and ending. At each stage, there are positive factors that promote the relationship's development, and corresponding negative factors that prevent its development or cause its failure.

For example, and as seen in Chapter 4, repeated interaction with someone makes initial attraction more likely, whilst infrequent contact makes it less likely. Similarity of attitudes and other characteristics helps a relationship to build, whilst dissimilarity makes building difficult (Levinger's second stage), and so on. However, the major limitation of Levinger's theory and, indeed, other stage theories, is that there is only weak evidence for a fixed sequence of stages in interpersonal relationships (Brehm, 1992). As a result, Brehm suggests that it is better to talk about 'phases' that take place at different times for different couples.

WHAT KEEPS PEOPLE TOGETHER?

If we consider what our important relationships have in common, we would find that all are rewarding for us and yet all can at times be complex, demanding, and even painful. If relationships involve both positive and negative aspects, then what determines our continued involvement in them?

Social exchange theory

Social exchange theory was mentioned briefly in Chapter 4 (see page 39). It provides a general framework for analysing all kinds of relationship, both intimate and non-intimate, and is really an extension of *reward theory* (also discussed briefly in Chapter 4: see page 35).

According to Homans (1974), we view our feelings for others in terms of *profits* (the amount of *reward* obtained from a relationship minus the *cost*). The greater the reward and lower the cost, the greater the profit and hence the attraction. Blau (1964) argues that interactions are 'expensive' in the sense that they take time, energy and commitment, and may involve unpleasant emotions and experiences. Because of this, what we get out of a relationship must be more than what we put in.

Similarly, Berscheid & Walster (1978) have argued that in any social interaction there is an exchange of rewards (such as affection, information and status), and that the degree of attraction or liking will reflect how people evaluate the rewards they receive relative to those they give. However, whether or not it is appropriate to think of relationships in this economic, and even capitalistic, way has been hotly debated.

Figure 5.2 *According to social exchange theory, we stay in relationships which are 'profitable' for us. Different individuals will define the costs and rewards involved in different ways*

Box 5.1   Should relationships really be seen in economic terms?

Social exchange theory sees people as fundamentally selfish, and views human relationships as based primarily on self-interest. Like many theories in psychology, social exchange theory offers us a *metaphor* for human relationships and should not be taken too literally. However, although we like to believe that the joy of giving is as important as the desire to receive, it is true that our attitudes towards other people are determined to a large extent by our assessments of the rewards they hold for us (Rubin, 1973).

Equally, though, Rubin does not believe that social exchange theory provides a complete, or even adequate, account of human relationships. In his view:

'Human beings are sometimes altruistic in the fullest sense of the word. They make sacrifices for the sake of others without any consideration of the rewards they will obtain from them in return'.

Altruism is most often and most clearly seen in close interpersonal relationships (and is discussed further in Chapter 8).

Consistent with Rubin's view, Brown (1986) distinguishes between 'true' love and friendship (which are altruistic) and less admirable forms which are based on considerations of exchange. For example, Fromm (1962) defines true love as giving, as opposed to the false love of the 'marketing character' which depends upon expecting to have favours returned.

Support for this distinction comes from Mills & Clark (1980), who identify two kinds of intimate relationship. In the *communal couple*, each partner gives out of concern for the other. In the *exchange couple*, by contrast, each keeps mental records of who is 'ahead' in the relationship and who is 'behind'.

Equity theory

Social exchange theory is really a special case of a more general account of human relationships called *equity theory*. The extra component in equity theory that is added to reward, cost and profit is *investment*. For Brown (1986):

> 'A person's investments are not just financial; they are anything at all that is believed to entitle him [or her] to his [or her] rewards, costs, and profits. An investment is any factor to be weighed in determining fair profits or losses'.

Equity means a constant ratio of rewards to costs, or profit to investment. So, it is concerned with *fairness* rather than equality. Equity theory does not see the initial ratio as being important. Rather, it is *changes* in the ratio of what is put into a relationship and what is got out of it that cause us to feel differently about the relationship. For example, we might feel that it is fair and just that we should give more than we get, but if we start giving very much more than we did and receiving very much less, we are likely to become dissatisfied with the relationship (Katzev *et al.*, 1994).

Some versions of social exchange theory do actually take account of factors other than the simple and crude profit motives of social interactors. One of these was introduced by Thibaut & Kelley (1959).

Box 5.2 **The concepts of comparison level and comparison level for alternatives (Thibaut & Kelley (1959)**

Comparison level (CL) is essentially the average level of rewards and costs a person is used to in relationships, and is the basic level expected in any future relationship. So, if a person's reward:cost ratio falls below his or her CL, the relationship will be unsatisfying. If it is above the CL, the relationship will be satisfying.

Comparison level for alternatives (CL alt.) is essentially a person's expectation about the reward:cost ratio which could be obtained in other relationships. If the ratio in a relationship exceeds the CL alt., then a person is doing better in it than he or she could do elsewhere. As a result, the relationship should be satisfying and likely to continue. If the CL alt. exceeds the reward:cost ratio, then a person is doing worse than he or she could do elsewhere. As a result, the relationship should be unsatisfying and unlikely to continue.

The concept of CL alt. implies that the endurance of a relationship (as far as one partner is concerned) could be due to the qualities of the other partner and the relationship, *or* to the negative and unattractive features of the perceived alternatives, *or* to the perceived costs of leaving. This, however, still portrays people as being fundamentally selfish, and many researchers (e.g. Duck, 1988) prefer to see relationships as being maintained by an equitable distribution of rewards and costs for both partners. In this approach, people are seen as being concerned with the equity of outcomes both for themselves and their partners.

Murstein *et al.* (1977) argue that concern with either exchange or equity is negatively correlated with marital adjustment. According to Argyle (1988), people in close relationships do not think in terms of rewards and costs at all until they start to feel dissatisfied. Murstein & MacDonald (1983) have argued that the principles of exchange and equity do play a significant role in intimate relationships. However, they believe that a conscious concern with 'getting a fair deal', especially in the short term, makes *compatibility* (see below) very hard to achieve, and that this is true for friendship and, especially, marriage (see Box 5.1 and Mills and Clark's *exchange couple*).

The role of similarity in maintaining relationships

As seen in Chapter 4 (page 36), evidence suggests that similarity is an important factor in relationship formation. It also plays a major role in the maintenance of relationships.

Key **S T U D Y**

Box 5.3 **Similarity in relationship maintenance**

Hill *et al.* (1976) studied 231 steadily dating couples over a two-year period. At the end of this period, 103 (45 per cent) had broken up, and when interviewed often mentioned differences in interests, background, sexual attitudes, and ideas about marriage as being responsible. By contrast, those who were still together tended to be more alike in terms of age, intelligence, educational and career plans, as well as physical attractiveness.

Hill *et al.* found that the maintenance or dissolution of the relationship in the couples they studied could be predicted from initial questionnaire data collected about them. For example, about 80 per cent of those who stayed together described themselves as being 'in love', compared with 56 per cent of those who did not stay together.

Of couples in which both members initially reported being equally involved in the relationship, only 23 per cent broke up. However, where one member was much more involved than the other, 54 per cent broke up. The latter type of couple is a highly unstable one in which the person who is more involved (putting more in but getting less out) may feel dependent and exploited. The one who is less involved (putting less in but getting more in return) may feel restless and guilty (implying some sense of fairness).

Other research has confirmed the general rule that the more similar two people in a relationship see themselves as being, the more likely it is that the relationship will be maintained. Thus, individuals who have similar needs (Meyer & Pepper, 1977), attitudes, likes and dislikes (Newcomb, 1978), and are similar in attractiveness (White, 1980), are more likely to remain in a relationship than dissimilar individuals.

Another way of looking at compatibility is *marital satisfaction*. In a review of studies looking at marital satisfaction and communication, Duck (1992) found that happy couples give more positive and consistent non-verbal cues than unhappy couples, express more agreement and approval for the other's ideas and suggestions, talk more about their relationship, and are more willing to compromise on difficult decisions.

The importance of positive interactions was shown by Spanier & Lewis (1980). They propose that there are three main components in relationships that last. These are 'rewards from spousal interaction', 'satisfaction with lifestyle', and 'sufficient social and personal resources'. These rewards include regard for one's partner, and emotional gratification. When these elements are positive, spouses or partners are more likely to report satisfaction with their relationship, and it is more likely to endure (Buss & Shackelford, 1997).

MARITAL UNHAPPINESS AND DIVORCE

Duck (1988, 1992) has identified several factors which make it more likely that a marriage will either be unhappy or end in divorce.

Key STUDY

Box 5.4 Factors contributing to marital unhappiness and divorce

- Marriages in which the partners are *younger than average* tend to be more unstable. This can be related to Erikson's concept of intimacy (see Chapter 34), whereby teenage marriages, for example, involve individuals who have not yet fully established their sense of identity and so are not ready for a commitment to one particular person. Additionally, there seems to be a connection between the rising divorce rate and *early parenthood*, which gives young couples little time to adjust to their new relationships and marital responsibilities. The arrival of a baby brings added financial and housing problems.

- Marriages between couples from *lower socioeconomic groups and educational levels* tend to be more unstable. These are also the couples who tend to have children very early on in their marriage.

- Marriages between partners from *different demographic backgrounds* (race, religion, and so on) also tend to be more unstable. This finding can be related to Kerckhoff and Davis's 'filter' theory (see page 43).

- Marriages also tend to be more unstable between people who have experienced *parental divorce* as children or who have had a *greater number of sexual partners* than average before marriage.

Relationships are, of course, highly complex, and the factors identified in Box 5.4 cannot on their own adequately explain why marriage break-ups occur (Duck, 1995). For example, only a proportion of marriages involving the young, those from lower socioeconomic groups, or different demographic backgrounds, actually end in divorce. Equally, many divorces occur between couples who do *not* fit these descriptions.

There is a link between *communication strategies* employed early on in married life and subsequent marital unhappiness, with manipulative and coercive styles being good predictors of the dissatisfaction experienced by wives but *not* by husbands (McGhee, 1996). *Rejection sensitivity* (which is associated with misinterpreting ambiguous events negatively, and expecting the worst to happen in a romantic relationship) is also associated with the disintegration of a relationship (De La Ronde & Swann, 1998)

Brehm (1992) identifies two broad types of cause for marital unhappiness and divorce, these being *structural* (including gender, duration of the relationship, the presence of children, and role-strain created by competing demands of work and family) and *conflict resolution*.

Gender differences

Men and women appear to differ in their perceptions of their relationship problems. In general, women report more problems, and evidence suggests that the degree of female dissatisfaction is a better predictor than male unhappiness of whether the relationship will end (Brehm & Kassin, 1996). This could mean that women are more sensitive to relationship problems than men. Alternatively, it could be that men and women enter into relationships with different expectations and hopes, with men's generally being fulfilled to a greater extent than women's.

Consistent with this possibility is evidence of gender differences in the specific *types* of relationship problems that are reported. For example, whilst men and women who are divorcing are equally likely to cite communication problems as a cause for the dissolution of their relationships, women stress basic unhappiness and incompatibility more than men do. Again, men seem to be particularly upset if there is 'sexual withholding' by female partners, whilst women are distressed by their male partners' aggression.

Duration of relationships and the passage of time

The longer partners have known each other before they marry, the more likely they are to be satisfied in their marriage and the less likely they are to divorce. However, couples who have cohabited before marriage report fewer barriers to ending the marriage, and the longer a relationship lasts the more likely it is that people will blame their partners for negative events.

Two major views of changes in marital satisfaction are Pineo's (1961) *linear model* and Burr's (1970) *curvilinear model*. According to the linear model, there is an inevitable fading of the romantic 'high' of courtship before marriage. The model also proposes that people marry because they have achieved a 'good fit' with their partners, and that any changes occurring in either partner will reduce their compatibility. For example, if one partner becomes more self-confident (which, ironically, may occur through the support gained from the relationship), there may be increased conflict between two

equals who now compete for 'superiority' in the relationship. The linear model is supported by at least some evidence (Blood & Wolfe, 1969).

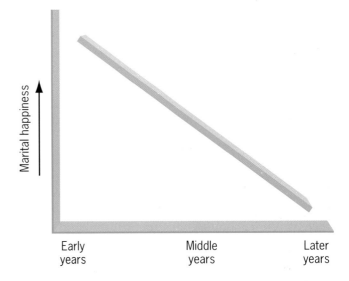

Figure 5.3 *The linear model of marital satisfaction (From Gross, 1996)*

The curvilinear model of martial satisfaction proposes that marital happiness is greatest in the earliest years of marriage, reaches a low in the middle years, and then begins to rise again in the later years. The middle years of marriage are often associated with the arrival and departure of children. The model proposes that marital happiness declines when children are born and during their growing up, but increases as they mature and leave home. However, whilst it is generally agreed that a decline in marital happiness begins in the early years, whether happiness ever does increase or merely 'levels off' is debatable.

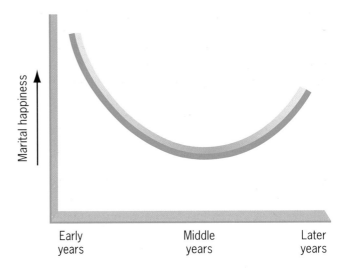

Figure 5.4 *The curvilinear model of marital satisfaction (From Gross, 1996)*

Gilford & Bengston (1979) argue that it is an oversimplification to talk about marital 'satisfaction' or 'happiness'. In their view, it is much more productive to look at the *pattern of positive rewards* and the *pattern of negative costs* that occur in a marriage. The early years of marriage are associated with very high rewards and very high costs. In the middle years, there is a decline in both, whilst in the later years there is a continuing decline in costs and an increase in rewards.

Conflict resolution

According to Duck (1988), some kind and degree of conflict is inevitable in all kinds of relationship. However, the process of resolving conflicts can often be a positive one that promotes the relationship's growth (Wood & Duck, 1995). The important question is not whether there is conflict, but *how* this conflict can best be dealt with. Unfortunately, the recurrence of conflicts, indicating a lack of agreement and an inability to resolve the conflict's underlying source, may lead the partners to doubt each other as 'reasonable persons'. This might produce a 'digging in of the heels', a disaffection with each other, and, ultimately, a 'strong falling out' (Berry & Willingham, 1997).

Key **STUDY**

Box 5.5 **Attributional patterns and conflict resolution**

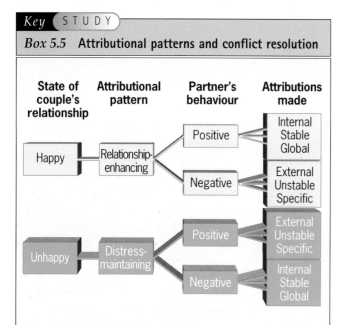

Figure 5.5 *Attributions made by happy and unhappy couples according to Bradbury & Fincham (1990) (From Brehm, 1992)*

Bradbury & Fincham (1990) have argued that happy and unhappy couples resolve their conflicts in typically different ways, and that these can be understood as different *attributional patterns* (see Chapter 1). Happy couples use a *relationship-enhancing*

---

attributional pattern, in which a partner's negative behaviour is explained in terms of situational and other variable causes. By contrast, unhappy couples use a *distress-maintaining* attributional pattern, in which a partner's negative behaviour is explained in terms of underlying and unchanging personality dispositions (Fincham, 1997).

Rule-breaking, deception and jealousy

Argyle & Henderson (1984) have conducted many studies looking at the *rules* people use in different types of relationship. By rules, they mean shared opinions or beliefs about what should and should not be done. According to Argyle and Henderson, the two major functions of rules are to regulate behaviour in order to minimise potential sources of conflict, and to check on the exchange of rewards which motivate people to stay in relationships. Their research has uncovered rules which are thought to apply to all or most types of relationship, such as 'respecting other people's privacy', 'not discussing what has been said in confidence' and 'being emotionally supportive'.

Additional rules apply in particular types of relationship. Argyle and Henderson's findings indicate that relationships fall into clusters, with similar rules applying within a particular cluster. One such cluster includes spouse, sibling and close friends, whilst another includes doctor, teacher and boss. *Deception* is probably the most important rule that should not be broken. However, what counts as deception will depend on the nature of the relationship: if we cannot trust a friend or a partner, then the relationship is almost certainly doomed.

Jealousy can be defined as 'a concern about losing, or having to share, something one has' (De Silva, 1997), and is one of the more destructive factors in a relationship. Amongst the characteristics which define a jealous person are:

- the belief that a partner has been sexually unfaithful;

- an obsession with a partner's previous relationships;

- the need to maintain the exclusive attention of a partner.

According to De Silva, a jealous disposition is strongly correlated with low self-esteem, neuroticism and feelings of inadequacy (see also Chapter 6, pages 59–60).

SOME EFFECTS OF RELATIONSHIP DISSOLUTION

In his review of relevant studies, Duck (1992) found that people in disrupted relationships are more susceptible than others of the same sex and age group to coronary heart disease, alcoholism, drug dependency, and sleep disturbances. The relationship between marital status and vulnerability to mental disorders has been extensively investigated by Cochrane (1983, 1996), who has found that marital status is one of the strongest correlates of risk of mental health hospital admissions.

Key S T U D Y

Box 5.6 Marital status and mental health

Allowing for age differences, Cochrane found that the divorced are five-and-a-half times more likely than the married to be admitted to a mental hospital in any one year. Stress could account for this, since the relationship between stress and illness is strongly supported by evidence (see Gross *et al.*, 2000). Additionally, a loss of 'protective' factors that marriage might provide (such as home-building, sexual satisfaction, intimacy, security and so on) could also be important. Even the *'selection for marriage' hypothesis* might have something to contribute given that, with about 40 per cent of British marriages ending in divorce, divorce is becoming 'normal'. According to the hypothesis, a predisposition to illness *reduces* the likelihood of a person marrying, either because an unwell person is not motivated to marry and/or because s/he is an unattractive proposition to potential spouses.

There may, however, be an important gender difference regarding the effects of divorce, depending on the point of the dissolution process being considered. Whilst much has been made of the detrimental effects of divorce on men, as opposed to women, these usually occur *after* the relationship has ended. Men discover that they miss the emotional support that marriage can provide, and that on their own they have very little opportunity to express feelings to friends around them. With women, it is the stage *before* divorce, during marital stress, when they are far more likely than men to become depressed. This is the point when marriage is probably worse for female mental stability than divorce itself.

In a survey involving over a 100 couples, Fincham (1997) compared levels of marital discord and symptoms of depression in men and women. According to Fincham:

'Our result suggests something pretty clear and robust and raises all sorts of interesting questions. It is widely believed that marriage protects men from mental health problems but if you look at women you find the opposite' (cited in Cook, 1997).

The situation for men (depression predicted marital stress) is the mirror-image of what happens for women, for whom marital stress predicted depressive symptoms. Women seem to value relationships more than men, and when the marital relationship is not working, this can cause depression. According to Fincham, women may feel greater responsibility for making the relationship work, so that when it does not, they blame themselves and this makes them more susceptible to depression (see Chapter 1, page 9).

There is, however, much evidence to suggest that the social support given to people following the dissolution of a relationship can *reduce* the probability of psychological distress and ill-health (McGhee, 1996). For example, Buehler & Legge (1993) found that companionship and other reassurance to self-esteem improved the level of psychological well-being in a sample of 144 women with children. If women are better at confiding in others (especially other women: see page 226), they are more likely to receive social and emotional support following divorce, whereas men are more likely to be socially and emotionally isolated.

THE PROCESS OF RELATIONSHIP DISSOLUTION

As noted above, relationships are highly complex, and this is as true of relationship dissolution as it is of relationship formation and maintenance. The complexity of relationship dissolution is evident not just in the case of marriage, but in all sorts of relationships, such as friendships and sexual relationships. The complexity is even greater if the relationship is a long-term one that has embraced many parts of a person's emotional, communicative, leisure and everyday life (Duck, 1988).

One way of looking at the break-up of a relationship is to regard it as a *process*, rather than an event, which takes place over a period of time. For Duck (1988):

'Breaking up is not only hard to do, but also involves a lot of separate elements that make up the whole rotten process'.

Several models of the stages through which relationships pass as they dissolve have been proposed. If there are aspects that characterise many, if not all, dissolving relationships, it might be possible to identify the kinds of counselling or other 'repair work' that may work best for dissatisfied couples who want to avoid dissolving their relationships. Such models are, therefore, of more than theoretical importance (McGhee, 1996).

Lee's model

Lee (1984) has proposed that there are five stages in *pre-marital* romantic break-ups. First of all, *dissatisfaction* (D) is discovered. This dissatisfaction is then *exposed* (E). Some sort of *negotiation* (N) about the dissatisfaction occurs, and attempts are made to *resolve* (R) the problem. Finally, the relationship is *terminated* (T).

Key S T U D Y

Box 5.7   Pre-marital break-ups

Lee surveyed 112 premarital break-ups and found that (E) and (N) tended to be experienced as the most intense, dramatic, exhausting and negative aspects of the whole experience. Those who skipped these stages (by just walking out of the relationship) reported feeling less intimate with their ex-partners, even when the relationship had been progressing smoothly. Lee also found that in those cases where the passage from (D) to (T) was particularly prolonged, people reported feeling more attracted to their ex-partners and experienced the greatest loneliness and fear during the break-up.

Duck's model

Duck's (1982, 1988) model of relationship dissolution consists of four phases, each of which is initiated when a threshold is broken. The first, *intrapsychic phase*, begins when one partner sees him- or herself as being unable to stand the relationship any more. This initiates a focus on the other's behaviour, and an assessment of how adequate the partner's role performance is. Also, the individual begins to assess the negative aspects of being in the relationship, considers the costs of withdrawal, and assesses the positive aspects of being in an alternative relationship. Duck uses the term 'intrapsychic' because the processes are occurring only in the individual's mind, and have not yet shown themselves in actual behaviour.

The next threshold is when the individual considers him- or herself as being justified in withdrawing from the relationship. This leads to the *dyadic phase*, and involves the other partner. Here, the dissatisfied individual must decide whether to confront or avoid the partner. When this decision is made, negotiations occur about, for example, whether the relationship can be repaired and the joint costs of withdrawal or reduced intimacy.

If the negotiations in this phase are unsuccessful, the next threshold is when the dissatisfied partner determines that he or she means the relationship to end. This leads to the *social phase*, so-called because it involves consideration of the social implications of the relationship's dissolution. This state of the relationship is made public, at least within the individual's own social network, and publicly negotiable face-saving/blame-placing stories and accounts of the relationship's breakdown may be given. 'Intervention teams', such as family or very close friends, may be called in to try to bring about a reconciliation.

Unless the 'intervention teams' are successful, the next threshold is when the relationship's dissolution becomes inevitable. This leads to the final *grave-dressing phase*. In this, the partners attempt to 'get over' the relationship's dissolution and engage in their own 'post-mortem' about why the relationship dissolved, a version of events which is then given to friends and family. Each partner needs to emerge from the relationship with an intact reputation for relationship reliability. 'Dressing the grave' involves 'erecting a tablet' which provides a credible and socially acceptable account of the relationship's life and death. Whilst helping to save face, it also serves to keep alive some memories and to 'justify' the original commitment to the ex-partner. For Duck (1988):

> 'Such stories are an integral and important part of the psychology of ending relationships ... By helping the person get over the break-up, they are immensely significant in preparing the person for future relationships as well as helping them out of old ones'.

Table 5.1   *A summary of the phases involved in Duck's (1982, 1988) model of relationship disolution*

Breakdown–dissatisfaction with relationship

Threshold: *'I can't stand this any more'*

INTRAPSYCHIC PHASE

- Personal focus on partner's behaviour
- Assess adequacy of partner's role performance
- Depict and evaluate negative aspects of being in the relationship
- Consider costs of withdrawal
- Assess positive aspects of alternative relationships
- Face 'express/repress dilemma'

Threshold: *'I'd be justified in withdrawing'*

DYADIC PHASE

- Face 'confrontation/avoidance dilemma'
- Confront partner
- Negotiate in 'Our Relationship Talks'
- Attempt repair and reconciliation?
- Assess joint costs of withdrawal or reduced intimacy

Table 5.1 continued

Threshold: *'I mean it'*

SOCIAL PHASE

- Negotiate post-dissolution state with partner
- Initiate gossip/discussion in social network
- Create publicly negotiable face-saving/blame-placing stories and accounts
- Consider and face up to implied social network effect, if any
- Call in intervention team

Threshold: *'It's now inevitable'*

GRAVE-DRESSING PHASE

- 'Getting over' activity
- Retrospective; reformative post-mortem attribution
- Public distribution of own version of break-up story

(From Gross, 1996)

As well as Lee and Duck's models, several others have been advanced to explain the process of relationship dissolution (Furnham & Heaven, 1999). These include Rusbult's (1987) *exit–voice–loyalty– neglect model*, which proposes four basic responses to relationship dissatisfaction. These are *exit* (leaving the relationship), *neglect* (ignoring the relationship), *voice* (articulating concerns), and *loyalty* (staying in the relationship and accepting the situation and the other's behaviour).

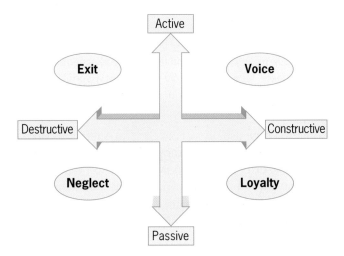

Figure 5.6 *Rusbult's exit–voice–loyalty–neglect model*

The two *'active'* strategies in the face of dissatisfaction are exit and voice, whilst the two *'passive'* strategies are neglect and loyalty. Exit and neglect are *'destructive'*, whereas voice and loyalty are *'constructive'*. According to McGhee (1996), the usefulness of this model, and the accuracy of its predictions about which type of couple will engage in which type of strategy, have been sup-

ported by studies conducted in both Britain (Goodwin, 1991) and America (Rusbult, 1987).

Felmlee (1995) has proposed the *fatal attraction model of relationship breakdown*. Felmlee argues that the perceived characteristics in a person that initially attract someone to him or her are the very characteristics that lead to the breakdown of a relationship. So, a characteristic that initially makes a person appear 'exciting', say, to another, later on makes that person 'unpredictable', and the relationship breaks down because of this perceived unpredictability.

Marital reconciliation

We have looked in detail at the process of relationship breakdown. Other research has attempted to identify the factors which might predict successful marital reconciliation.

Key STUDY

Box 5.8 **Wineberg's (1994) study of marital reconciliation**

Wineberg studied 506 white women who had attempted reconciliations in their first marriages. Women who had made 'successful' reconciliations, and were still married a year later, were compared with those who had made 'unsuccessful' reconciliations and were separated/divorced within a year of the attempted reconciliation. Wineberg found that, overall, 30 per cent of reconciliations were successful, and that important factors linked with the reconciliation included:

- both partners being of the same religion (especially if one partner had changed religion in connection with the marriage);
- cohabitation with a partner before marriage;
- marriage with a partner of the same age.

Different factors were associated with marital dissolution, including age at separation, duration of marriage, and education. Wineberg argues that although these factors may be reflected in the decision to separate, there are other factors that may have a bearing on whether an attempted reconciliation is successful. Amongst these are social and religious ties, advice from family and friends, and life after separation.

LOVE

Liking and loving

According to Rubin (1973), liking and loving are not the same. Liking is the positive evaluation of another and consists of *respect* and *affection*. Rubin sees loving as being more than an intense liking. In his view, loving is qualitatively different and composed of *attachment, caring* and *intimacy*. Attachment is the need for the physical presence and support of the loved one. Caring is a feeling of concern and responsibility for the loved one. Intimacy is the desire for close and confidential contact, and wanting to share certain thoughts and feelings with the loved one more fully than with anyone else. Rubin's idea of caring corresponds to Fromm's (1962) definition of love as 'the active concern for the life and growth of that which we love'.

Much of the support for Rubin's distinction between liking and loving comes from people's responses on scales devised by him to measure them. Amongst other things, Rubin found that lovers tend to give similar but not identical positive responses to items on both scales. So, we tend to like the people we love, but the relationship is not perfect. Also, high-scorers on the love scale are more likely to say that they expect to marry their partners. This means that love is correlated with an anticipated permanent relationship.

The love scale can also be applied to same-sex friends. Here, Rubin found that females reported loving their friends more than men did. Other research has shown that women's friendships tend to be more intimate than men's, and that spontaneous joint activities and exchange of confidences occur more in women. For men, loving may be channelled into single, sexual relationships whilst women may be better able to experience attachment, caring and intimacy in a wider range and variety of relationships (Rubin & McNeil, 1983).

Table 5.2   *Some items from Rubin's (1973) liking scale and love scale*

Respondents are asked to indicate if a particular statement reflects accurately their perception about another person.

Liking scale

1   I think that _____ is unusually well adjusted.

2   I have great confidence in _____'s good judgement.

3   _____ is the sort of person whom I myself would like to be.

Love scale

1   If _____ were feeling bad, my first duty would be to cheer him/her up.

2   I feel that I can confide in _____ about virtually everything.

3   If I could never be with _____ I would feel miserable.

It has been argued that a concept like love cannot be measured at all, let alone by using pencil-and-paper devices. Rubin, though, has shown that partners high on the love scale engage in more eye contact than dating couples who are lower on it. For Rubin (1973), this is good evidence that the love scale has at least *some* validity (see Cramer, 1998, for a review of attempts to conceptualise and measure love).

Types of love

For some researchers, love is a label that we learn to attach to our own state of physiological arousal. However, for most of the time love does not involve intense physical 'symptoms', and it is perhaps better to view it as a sort of attitude that one person has towards another (Rubin & McNeil, 1983). It seems likely that the sort of love a couple married for 50 years experiences is different from that of a couple 'going steady' at college.

Berscheid & Walster (1978) distinguish between *romantic* love and *companionate* love. Romantic love (or *passionate* love) is characterised by intense feelings of tenderness, elation, anxiety, and sexual desire. It is also associated with increased activity in the sympathetic branch of the autonomic nervous system. According to Hatfield & Rapson (1987):

'Passionate love is like any other form of excitement. By its very nature, excitement involves a continuous interplay between elation and despair, thrills and terror ... Sometimes men and women become entangled in love affairs where the delight is brief, and pain, uncertainty, jealousy, misery, anxiety, and despair are abundant. Often, passionate love seems to be fuelled by a sprinkling of hope and a large dollop of loneliness, mourning, jealousy, and terror'.

Romantic love usually occurs early in a relationship but does not last very long. Companionate love (sometimes called *true* or *conjugal* love) is the affection that remains after the passion of romantic love has subsided, and is essential if a relationship is to be maintained. Companionate love is less intense than romantic love and involves thoughtful appreciation of one's partner. It is also characterised by a tolerance for weaknesses and a desire to solve conflicts and difficulties in a relationship (Grote & Frieze, 1994).

Several taxonomies of love have been proposed (Furnham & Heaven, 1999). According to Sternberg (1986, 1988), love has three basic components, *intimacy, passion* and *decision/commitment*. The presence or absence of these produces different types of love.

Box 5.9 Sternberg's triangular theory of love

Intimacy is the emotionally based part of love, and refers to feelings of closeness, connectedness and bondedness in loving relationships.

Passion is the motivational component of love. It refers to the drives that lead to romance, physical attraction and sexual consummation.

Decision/commitment is the cognitive 'controller' in a loving relationship. The short-term decision involves acceptance of such a relationship. The long-term aspect involves the commitment to maintain the relationship.

Table 5.3 *Types of love and their components*

Kind of love	Component		
	Intimacy	Passion	Decision/commitment
Non–love	Absent	Absent	Absent
Liking	Present	Absent	Absent
Infatuated love	Absent	Present	Absent
Empty love	Absent	Absent	Present
Romantic love	Present	Present	Absent
Companionate love	Present	Absent	Present
Fatuous love	Absent	Present	Present
Consummate love	Present	Present	Present

Consider, for example, *infatuated love*. This includes those relationships which we describe as being 'love at first sight'. The love is aroused by passion, but there is no intimacy or decision/commitment. Such relationships can arise almost instantaneously and end just as quickly.

Sternberg's three dimensions help us to understand various relationships. However, most loving relationships fit between the categories because the various components of love are expressed along dimensions, not discretely (Houston *et al.*, 1991). Also, alternatives to Sternberg's theory exist, most notably the six basic love styles identified by Hendrick *et al.* (1986), which recognises that 'love' means different things to different people, even the partners themselves (Bellur, 1995).

Box 5.10 The formula for love?

According to Byrne (cited in Harlow, 1999a), love is a mix of five factors: *sexual attraction, psychological arousal, a desire for intimacy, an intense need to be wanted and agreed with*, and *a recurring fear of losing the loved one*. Based on experiments and interviews carried out in North America, Britain and Holland, each of these five factors can be given a different weighting to produce the following formula:

$$\textbf{LOVE} = (1.7 \times \textbf{A}) + (1.5 \times \textbf{B}) + (1.5 \times \textbf{C}) + (1.5 \times \textbf{D}) + (1.3 \times \textbf{E})$$

where:

- **A** is the feeling for an average friend;
- **B** is the emotional arousal felt for an average friend;
- **C** is the desire to be physically close to an average friend;
- **D** is how much you want that person to want you;
- **E** is the increased fear that the relationship will break up.

Each of A to E can be rated on a ten-point scale, and a total score derived using the formula. If the score for a friend is greater than that for a lover, a person is *not* in love.

Love across cultures

According to Moghaddam *et al.* (1993), much of the theory and research relating to social relationships is a reflection of the dominant values of North America, from where many theories and an even larger number of studies originate (see also Chapters 6 and 55).

Box 5.11 The importance of cross-cultural analyses

Goodwin (1995) has argued that cross-cultural analyses of relationships are important for at least three reasons.

- They allow competing theories to be compared and assessed according to whether they are universal or the products of particular cultural or historical conditions.
- Contact between people from different cultural backgrounds is increasing in both frequency and intensity. As people acculturate to a new society, their relationships with those around them are

important in determining their psychological well-being.

- Increasing business and leisure contacts raise important issues about cross-cultural communications, and understanding the rules of commerce in different cultures is an important part of a business person's armoury.

One of the main dimensions on which cultures differ is *individualism–collectivism* (see Chapters 6 and 55). Individualism places greatest emphasis on personal achievement and self-reliance. Collectivism, by contrast, places priority on the welfare and unity of the group. Although this division is somewhat simplified (because some cultures seem to be highly individualist in some settings and more collectivist in others), it is useful in helping to summarise some of the cross-cultural variations in personal relationships.

Goodwin (1995) argues that love, 'at least in its passionate stomach churning Hollywood manifestation', is largely a Western and individualistic phenomenon, and that in Western cultures marriage is seen as the

culmination of a 'loving' relationship. In cultures where 'arranged marriages' occur, the relationship between love and marriage is the other way around, and marriage is seen as the basis on which to explore a loving relationship (Bellur, 1995). As Bellur notes, the cultural background in which people have learned about love is important in shaping their concept of it.

The fact that love is seen as something that will develop in the arranged marriage does not necessarily mean that such a marriage will be unhappy. Indeed, evidence suggests that these marriages may produce *more* happiness than 'love' marriages. For example, Gupta & Singh (1992) found that couples in India who married out of love reported diminished feelings of love if they had been married for more than five years. By contrast, those who had undertaken arranged marriages reported more love if they were not newly-weds.

These findings reveal that passionate love 'cools' over time, and that there is scope for love to flourish within an arranged marriage. In the case of those cultures in which arranged marriages occur, then, courtship is accepted to a certain degree, but love is left to be defined and discovered after marriage (Bellur, 1995). Cultural differences in relationships are considered further in the following chapter.

CONCLUSIONS

This chapter has examined theories and research studies relating to the maintenance and dissolution of relationships, and considered some psychological explanations of love. Several theories of relationship maintenance have been advanced, all of which can claim some degree of experimental support. Relationship dissolution has also been the subject of

extensive research and theorising. There are many factors and effects associated with the dissolution of relationships, and several explanations of the processes that occur during relationship dissolution. Although love may be a difficult phenomenon to conceptualise and measure, several different types of love have been identified, and differences between cultures with respect to this complex phenomenon studied.

Summary

- Relationships change and develop over time. Several stage theories have attempted to chart the courses of both sexual and non-sexual relationships. These include Kerckhoff and Davis's **filter theory**, Murstein's **stimulus–value–role theory**, and Levinger's five stage theory.

- Stage theories suffer from the limitation of there being weak evidence for a fixed sequence of stages. It may be better to talk about 'phases', which occur at different times for different people.

- **Social exchange theory** provides a framework for analysing all kinds of relationship. Variations on the theory see people as being fundamentally selfish. However, it has been argued that humans are capable of genuine altruism, and this is most clearly seen in close interpersonal relationships.

- Social exchange theory is really a special case of **equity theory**, which adds the concept of investment to those of reward, cost and profit. Changes in the reward:cost/profit:investment ratio determine how we feel about a relationship.

- **Similarity** plays an important role in compatability and the maintenance of relationships. People who have similar needs, attitudes, likes and dislikes, and are similar in attractiveness, are more likely to remain in a relationship than dissimilar people.

- Although factors such as age, socio-economic status and parental divorce are associated with relationship **dissolution**, they cannot on their own completely explain it.

- **Communicative strategies** employed early on in married life are linked with subsequent marital happiness. **Structural causes** and **conflict resolution** are also linked to marital unhappiness and divorce.

- Two models of changes in marital satisfaction are Pineo's **linear model** and Burr's **curvilinear model**. The former proposes a gradual decline in marital happiness, whereas the latter suggests that happiness increases after declining in the middle years.

- Happy and unhappy couples display different attributional patterns when resolving their conflicts. The pattern is **relationship-enhancing** in happy couples, and **distress-maintaining** in unhappy couples.

- Relationship dissolution is associated with several harmful consequences. In men, most of these effects occur after a relationship has dissolved. In women, they are more likely before relationship dissolution (during marital stress).

- Dissolution is best thought of as a process rather than an event. Several models have attempted to identify the stages or phases relationships pass through as they dissolve. These include Lee's **five stage model**, Duck's **four phase model**, Rusbult's **exit–voice–loyalty–neglect model** and Felmlee's **fatal attraction model**.

- Successful **marital reconciliation** is linked to several factors, including the partners being of the same age and religion, and cohabitation with the partner before marriage. Unsuccessful reconciliation is associated with age at separation, duration of marriage, and education.

- According to Rubin, **love** is qualitatively different from liking. Rubin's **love scales** are one way of measuring love, although the validity of pencil-and-paper devices has been questioned.

- Berscheid and Walster distinguish between **romantic (passionate) love** and **companionate (true** or **conjugal) love**. According to Sternberg, the three basic components of love are **intimacy**, **passion** and **decision/commitment**. The presence or absence of these produces different types of love.

- **Cross-cultural studies** of love suggest that passionate love is largely a Western and individualistic phenomenon, and marriage is a culmination of a loving relationship. In cultures which favour **arranged marriages**, the reverse is true, and marriage is seen as the basis for love to develop.

Essay Questions

1 Describe and evaluate research relating to the maintenance **or** dissolution of relationships. *(24 marks)*

2 Discuss psychological insights into 'love'. *(24 marks)*

WEB ADDRESSES

http://www.socialpsychology.org/social.htm#cultural
http://www.socialpsychology.org/social.htm#family
http://www.socialpsychology.org/social.htm#divorce
http://www.erlbaum.com/html/500.htm

6 Cultural and Sub-cultural Differences in Relationships

INTRODUCTION AND OVERVIEW

Chapters 4 and 5 looked at how relationships are formed, maintained, and sometimes dissolved. Much of the research in these areas has been concerned only with relationships in Western cultures. The first part of this chapter examines explanations and research studies relating to *differences* in relationships between Western and non-Western cultures.

Research into relationships has also tended to concentrate on how relationships are formed, maintained and dissolved in *heterosexual* people. The second part of this chapter considers 'understudied' relationships, and investigates research findings concerning gay and lesbian relationships. It also looks at 'electronic' friendships (that is, relationships formed on the Internet).

CULTURAL DIFFERENCES IN RELATIONSHIPS: AN OVERVIEW

Although different types of relationships are found in many cultures, their importance varies considerably between them. For example, whilst Western cultures place great emphasis on the desirability of *romantic love* in dyads (two-person groupings), most non-Western cultures attach greater importance to family ties and responsibilities (Segall *et al.*, 1990). A related, more general, difference is that interpersonal relationships in Western cultures tend to be *individualistic*, *voluntary* and *temporary*, whereas those in non-Western cultures are more *collectivist*, *involuntary* and *permanent* (Moghaddam *et al.*, 1993: see Chapter 5, page 54 and Box 55.6, page 594). According to Moghaddam *et al.* (1993):

> 'The cultural values and environmental conditions in North America have led North American social psychologists to be primarily concerned with first-time acquaintances, friendships and intimate relationships, primarily because these appear to be the relationships most relevant to the North American urban cultural experience'.

In other words, there is a tendency for Western psychologists to equate 'relationships' with 'Western relationships', which is a form of *ethnocentrism* (specifically, *Anglo-* or *Eurocentrism*: see Chapter 55, page 594). However, wide and important cultural variations are found even when the 'same' relationship (such as marriage) is being considered.

CULTURE AND MARRIAGE

Westerners think of *monogamy* (marriage to one spouse at any one time) as the normal, even moral, form of marriage (Price & Crapo, 1999: see Chapter 35). Indeed, this belief is enshrined in the law (*bigamy* is a criminal offence), and reflects basic Judeo-Christian doctrine. However, cultures differ in their marital arrangements. In addition to the monogamous pattern, there are several other patterns. *Polygamy* (having two or more spouses at once) can take the form of *polygyny* (one man having two or more wives) or, less commonly, *polyandry* (one woman with two or more husbands). Another arrangement is *mandatory marriage to specific relatives*, as when a son marries the daughter of his father's brother (his first cousin: Triandis, 1994).

Monogamy is 'natural' from a Western perspective, and probably fewer than 0.5 per cent of human societies have practised *polyandry* as a common or preferred form of marriage (Price & Crapo, 1999). However, throughout Tibet and the neighbouring Himalayan areas of India, Nepal and Bhutan, polyandry has been common for generations. In this region, it usually takes the form of a woman marrying two or more brothers (*fraternal polyandry*), which minimises population growth in order to cope with scarce resources (Tibet is a land of scarce resources and relatively little productive land). It keeps brothers together and slows the growth of the family, since several brothers will produce only the number of children their one wife can bear. In this way, land does not need to be divided up (as would happen if each brother married monogamously), and a single family is preserved as an economic unit (Westermarck, 1894; Goldstein, 1979).

Key STUDY

Box 6.1 Polyandry amongst the Nyinba

Levine (1988) studied polyandry among the Nyinba, a group of ethnic Tibetans who live in the rugged Himalayan region of North-western Nepal. Polyandry has profound effects on social life, especially domestic relations. From a Western viewpoint, polyandry might be expected to contrast sharply with the male dominance that is common in polygynous marriages. However, Levine observed that polyandry creates a family whose central core is a group of men, usually brothers, who emphasise their solidarity and control over society's economic life. Thus, polyandrous families are dominated by men, who are favoured over women in 'special systems of property inheritance and succession to positions of household authority' (Levine, 1988).

Nyinba notions of kinship strongly emphasise the relationship between fathers and children. Each brother in the family thinks of himself as the 'real' father of specific children. This provides the basis for organising the community into larger groups of paternally related kin.

The large numbers of unmarried adult women are vital to the economy of Tibet, where large numbers of agricultural workers are needed. According to Schuler, families in Chumik typically prefer a daughter as a first-born child, because a daughter can help her mother with work. Families prefer to keep daughters in the household as long as they can, because their daughters' labour is economically important. They adopt various strategies to keep their daughters unmarried, so they can keep working in the family for as long as possible. They may even demand that the in-laws allow a married daughter to return home to work during the day for an extended period during each harvest season for several years after she marries. Chumikwa society frowns on remarriage after divorce or widowhood.

Although remaining single offers women the opportunity for somewhat greater freedom than is enjoyed by married women, the lot of unmarried women is a difficult one, and most would *prefer* to be married. Since a family's land is inherited by its sons but worked by women, daughters who do not marry become part of the lower social class of landless workers, a class Chumikwans describe as descendants of earlier slaves. The harsh life of unmarried women helps to maintain the more comfortable lifestyle and higher social status of landowning men and their wives. Unmarried women pass on their low social status to any children they may have, since these children are defined as illegitimate.

The status of women in polyandrous societies

Whilst the focus of Levine's (1988) study of the Nyinba was on men's status, Schuler (1987) was concerned with the status of women in polyandrous societies. Schuler studied polyandry in Chumik (a Tibetan society similar to the Nyinba), in which about 22 per cent of women aged 35 and over, and 29 per cent of those over 45, have never been married. Although these figures correspond closely to rates of non-marriage reported for other polyandrous societies, exactly what happens to these women has been largely ignored.

Unlike Islamic countries and India, polyandrous Tibetan men and women mix freely in public. There is no seclusion of women, and women seem to be vocal and influential. Their status, therefore, appears to be high, and the fact that they could have several husbands seems to reinforce this impression. However, this view represents a false romanticisation of the position of women, and ignores the implications that widespread non-marriage has for the status of women in such societies.

IS ROMANTIC LOVE UNIQUE TO WESTERN CULTURE?

As noted in Chapter 5 (see page 54), passionate, romantic love has been interpreted as a largely Western and individualistic phenomenon. The popular ('Hollywood') view is that people fall in love and then commit themselves to each other through marriage. However, this concept of romantic love may be more universal, and more complex, than has sometimes been claimed.

When Kephart (1967) asked Americans 'If someone had all the other qualities you desired in a marriage partner, would you marry this person if you were not in love?', well over twice as many men replied 'no' as did women. When Simpson *et al.* (1986) repeated the study, more than 80 per cent of *both* men and women said 'no'. This can be explained at least partly by the fact that, twenty years later, financial independence has allowed women to choose marriage partners for reasons other than material necessity. However, this does *not* explain why romantic love has become so central for both American men *and* women (Moghaddam, 1998).

Box 6.2   Exporting love from Hollywood to the rest of the world

According to Moghaddam (1998), romantic love is not exclusive to Western societies. The notion of people falling in love is found in one form or another in most human societies, even where marriages are traditionally arranged by families or friends. For example, an analysis of songs and folklore in 166 societies indicates that 'Western' romantic love is recognised in more than 85 per cent of them (Jankowaik & Fischer, 1992). However, Moghaddam (1998) believes that:

'What is unique about romantic love in late twentieth-century Western societies is its pervasiveness: the idea that everyone should marry only when they are in love. Such an idea is fairly new historically and is still limited to Western societies'.

Perhaps no other feature of Western culture is being exported or internationalised more than romantic love 'Hollywood style'. Over the last century, there has been an increasing acceptance in Western societies of the idea that one should marry for love, and that it is right to end the relationship when love dies (see Chapter 5). As societies become industrialised and more individualistic, the percentage of people who believe that love must precede marriage increases.

Figure 6.1 *Love 'Hollywood style', here portrayed by Elizabeth Taylor and (ironically) Rock Hudson*

Cultural differences still exist. For example, Levine *et al.* (1995) studied young people in Australia, Brazil, England, Hong Kong, India, Japan, Mexico, Pakistan, the Philippines, Thailand, and the USA. When given the question previously asked by Kephart (1967) and Simpson *et al.* (1986: see page 57), participants from India, Thailand and Pakistan gave the highest proportion of 'yes' replies, whilst those from England and the USA gave the lowest. These are collectivist and individualist cultures, respectively.

If romantic love is an integral part of freely *choosing* our partners, then we might expect it to be endorsed most strongly in individualist cultures. Sprecher *et al.* (1994) asked students in the USA, Japan and Russia, 'Are you in love right now?' The majority in all countries said 'yes', with the highest scores in Russia (a collectivist culture). However, the use of such simple questions risks concealing cultural differences in what people actually mean by 'being in love' (Smith & Bond, 1998). Rothbaum and Tsang (cited in Smith & Bond, 1998) analysed the content of American and Chinese love songs. They found that Chinese songs made more references to sadness, the future, and the context in which the love occurred, whilst American songs focused more directly on the loved one. However, there were no overall differences in the intensity of emotion expressed.

Based on studies conducted in Canada, the Caribbean, Senegal, Uganda, the USA, and South Africa, Smith & Bond (1998) conclude that:

'There are relatively universal ways in which people speak about their attachment to others. However, the more detail we add to the measures, explicating exactly what attitudes and behaviours are entailed within the generalised notion of love or romance, the more differences we start to find'.

There are also important differences *within* culturally diverse societies, such as Britain, America and Canada. For example, first generation Indian immigrants to Canada (those born abroad who subsequently emigrated to Canada) tend to endorse the idea that *marriage precedes love* more than second generation Indian Canadians (whose parents came from abroad but who were themselves born in Canada: Vaidyanathan & Naidoo, 1991). Similarly, Dion & Dion (1993) found that Asian Canadians tend to interpret love as more friendship- and caring-based than something 'mysterious', compared with European Canadians. Both these findings are consistent with the distinction between collectivist and individualist cultural beliefs and practices, such as arranged marriages.

ARRANGED MARRIAGES: GOOD OR BAD?

Gupta & Singh (1992) found that love is more likely to develop and grow during the course of an arranged marriage compared with 'love' matches (see Chapter 5, page 54). Arranged marriages are far more common in collectivist cultures, where the whole extended family 'marries' the other extended family. This is distinct from individualist cultures, in which the *individuals* marry one another (Triandis, 1994). In one modern collectivist culture, Japan, almost a quarter of marriages are arranged (Iwao, 1993).

In general, divorce rates among those who marry according to parents' wishes are much *lower* than among those who marry for love. This is one argument in favour of arranged marriages. As Triandis (1994) argues:

> 'Marriage, when seen as a fifty-year relationship, is more likely to be a good one if people enter it after careful, rational analysis, which is more likely to be provided by older adults than by sexually aroused young people ...'.

However, divorce rates among couples who entered arranged marriages are *rising*, an indication that personal freedom is gaining importance and that traditional structures which define set roles for family members are no longer viable (Bellur, 1995). Among the more liberal-minded Asians living in the West, arranged marriages operate more like a dating facility ('arranged meetings' rather than 'arranged marriages'). The transition from meeting to marrying occurs when both parties formally agree to the commitment, with love being left to be defined and discovered after marriage (Bellur, 1995).

Figure 6.2 *Marriage represents a very different type of major transition, depending, among other things, upon cultural background. The wedding ceremony shown here is the culmination of detailed and prolonged planning by the bride and groom's families, with the couple themselves having little choice or control*

SEXUAL JEALOUSY

According to Ford & Beach (1951), only 53 per cent of societies studied by anthropologists *forbid* extramarital sex by both husbands and wives. Indeed, there are several societies that permit or even encourage sexual relationships to which Americans (and most other Westerners) would probably respond with jealousy. For example, Rivers (1906) found that the Toda of the southern Deccan Plateau of India considered it inappropriate for a man to refuse his wife's request to have an affair with another man. He was expected to show no jealousy over such a relationship.

According to Reiss (1986), all human societies are aware of sexual jealousy in marriage and have cultural rules for dealing with it. Hupka (1981) studied jealousy in 92 societies and found that the more important the marriage was thought to be, the more jealousy people showed. Reiss believes that jealousy is universal, but is expressed more readily in some societies than others. Within a society, the expression of jealousy by men and women is influenced by their respective social power: the greater the power, the greater the expression of jealousy (Reiss, 1986).

Cultures also seem to differ in terms of the behaviours that *trigger* sexual jealousy. In many cultures, marriages and sexual relationships are strictly regulated by concepts of kinship that are not applicable to relationships in Western cultures. For example, orthodox Jews require a man to marry his deceased brother's widow. Among the Nayar of India, a husband and wife did not always live together, and the husband would visit his wife at her home. She would conceive most of her children by various men with whom she had short-term relationships, but this was no basis for jealousy by the primary husband. However, he would express jealousy if she showed a lack of interest in him – either sexually or non-sexually (Price & Crapo, 1999). Probably the most common triggers of jealousy are sexual behaviours, but the specific type of behaviour that elicits sexual jealousy varies from culture to culture.

Key **STUDY**

Box 6.3 What triggers sexual jealousy?

Buunk & Hupka (1987) studied over 2000 students, in Hungary, Ireland, Mexico, the Netherlands, (former) Soviet Union, the USA and (former) Yugoslavia. They were asked to rate a series of items regarding 'sexual' behaviours, such as one's partner dancing or flirting with someone else, in terms of how much it bothered them and how uneasy it made them feel (measures of jealousy).

Men and women differed only in their reactions to their partners' kissing and to sexual fantasies. In all countries, women reported a greater degree of jealousy than men about kissing, but men were more negative about their partners expressing sexual fantasies concerning someone else. Men and women indicated similar levels of jealousy about flirting, and neither men nor women seemed bothered about their partners dancing with or hugging someone else of the opposite sex.

Overall, the similarities between the seven countries studied were greater than the differences. No single country was consistently more positive or negative than the others in response to the various items, although flirting and sexual relationships were the most likely causes of jealousy across all the countries. In all societies there are certain behaviours that will evoke sexual jealousy, even if it is not considered appropriate to express that jealousy (Price & Crapo, 1999).

UNDERSTUDIED RELATIONSHIPS

Homosexual relationships

Sexual orientation (or *preference*) refers to an individual's enduring sexual attraction towards members of a particular gender. *Heterosexuals* display a sexual preference for people of the *opposite* sex, whereas *homosexuals* display a sexual preference for people of the *same* sex. Around three to four per cent of men are exclusively homosexual, compared with around one per cent of women. Under one per cent report being *bisexual*, that is, displaying a sexual attraction to both same and different sex people (although there may be a stronger preference for one or the other). According to Hass (1979), 14 per cent of American boys and 11 per cent of girls report some kind of homosexual experience before the age of 15, although much of this is experimental and does not lead to a lasting homosexual orientation.

For many years, homosexual relationships were dismissed as destructive, exploitative and inauthentic (Kitzinger & Coyle, 1995), and homosexuality was identified as a *sexual deviation* in DSM-II, the American Psychiatric Association's (APA) classification of mental disorders (see Chapter 46). In 1973, however, under pressure from many professionals and gay activist groups, the APA recommended that the term sexual deviation be replaced by *sexual orientation disturbance*. This was to be applied to male ('gay') and female ('lesbian') homosexuals who are 'disturbed by, in conflict with, or wish to change their sexual orientation'.

When DSM-III was published in 1980, another new term, *ego-dystonic homosexuality*, (EDH) was introduced. This referred to someone who is homosexually aroused, finds this arousal to be a persistent source of distress, and wishes to become heterosexual. Since homosexuality was no longer deemed a mental disorder, there was no inclusion in DSM-III of predisposing factors (as there was for all disorders) but they were included for EDH, namely, the individual homosexual's internalisation of society's negative attitudes (*homophobia* – the fear of homosexuals – and *heterosexism* – anti-homosexual prejudice and discrimination).

DSM-III's revision in 1987 (DSM-III-R) did not include EDH. However, one of several 'catch-all' categories, *sexual disorder not otherwise specified*, includes 'persistent and marked distress about one's sexual orientation'. This is retained in DSM-IV, which was published in 1994 (see page 501). The latest edition of the World Health Organisation's classificatory system (ICD-10, 1992: see page 502) also includes ego-dystonic sexual orientation in the category *disorders of adult personality and behaviour*. Until the 1960s, homosexuality among consenting adults was illegal. In 1995, the age of consent was lowered to 18. Nothing has happened to homosexuality itself during the last 30 years, but attitudes towards it have changed (Joyce & Schrader, 1999).

Yet despite an apparent acceptance of homosexuality, homosexual relationships are still discriminated against and not officially sanctioned (Yip, 1999). The lack of social support afforded homosexual couples is manifested in many ways, such as a family's refusal to accept a homosexual relationship and their failure to acknowledge key aspects of a couple's joint life (such as anniversaries). Homosexual couples are also discriminated against in material terms, such as pension schemes or relocation allowances that exclude a same-sex partner. These factors may make the maintenance of a homosexual relationship more difficult, and the absence of support may deprive homosexual couples of the help they need to overcome difficulties and crises in their relationships (Kitzinger & Coyle, 1995).

Box 6.4   The isolation of gays and lesbians

Gays and lesbians are isolated from mainstream society as a result of the current social climate. There are not many public places where it is considered safe to meet, let alone to establish a relationship. At present, there is still no, or very little, legal protection, religious affirmation or widespread social acceptance for same-sex couples. This is illustrated by the *Lisa Grant versus South West Trains* case, in which Lisa Grant took her company to the European Court of Justice for refusing to issue her lesbian partner with a travel pass. If she had been in a heterosexual partnership, married or not, the travel pass would have been a simple matter of entitlement. The Court, however, eventually ruled in favour of South West Trains on the grounds that discrimination based on sexual orientation in this case fell outside the remit of current legislation. Such limits of social structure result in the lack of a solid support base, which makes the maintenance of a same-sex partnership difficult.

(From Yip, 1999)

According to Kitzinger & Coyle (1995), since the mid-1970s psychological research on homosexuality has moved away from a 'pathology' model towards a framework characterised by four themes. These are:

- a belief in the basic underlying similarity of homosexual and heterosexual people;
- a rejection of the concept of homosexuality as a central organising principle of the personality in favour of recognising the diversity and variety of lesbians and gay men as individuals;
- an assertion that homosexuality is as natural, normal and healthy as heterosexuality;
- denial of the notion that lesbians or male homosexuals pose any threat to children, to the nuclear family, or the future of society as we know it.

Bee (1994) argues that homosexual partnerships are far more like heterosexual relationships than they are different from them. Thus, following an extensive study of both homosexual and heterosexual relationships and individuals, Peplau (1981) concluded that:

'We have learned, among other things, that the values and experiences of homosexual couples are similar to those of heterosexuals in many ways. Whatever their sexual preferences, most people strongly desire a close and loving relationship with one special person. For both homosexuals and heterosexuals, intimate relationships can – and often do – provide love and satisfaction. But neither group is immune to the perils of relationships - conflict and possible break-up. Whatever their sexual preferences, people in intimate relationships today struggle to reconcile a longing for closeness with a desire for independence and self-realisation'.

Subsequent research has supported Peplau's conclusions. For example:

- homosexual and heterosexual relationships are more likely to endure if the partners are similar in terms of their backgrounds and level of commitment (Peplau, 1991);
- homosexual and heterosexual partners are more satisfied with a relationship when there are more rewards and fewer personal costs associated with it (Kurdeck, 1994).

However, Kitzinger & Coyle (1995) argue that certain factors are found to be omitted or distorted when homosexual relationships are assessed in terms derived from heterosexual relationships. These include *cohabitation, sexual exclusivity*, and *sex role*. Cohabitation is much less common for homosexuals than heterosexuals. The reasons for this are unclear, but probably include:

- concern amongst 'closet' homosexuals about the increased visibility entailed in openly living with a person of the same sex;
- concerns, where children are involved, from the homosexual parent, the other spouse and/or the courts about the effects of cohabitation;
- alleviating the burden of disentangling joint property should the relationship end;
- a concern *not* to duplicate the conditions of heterosexual marriage; and
- a desire for the autonomy and flexibility possible with separate living arrangements.

Compared with married heterosexuals, sexual exclusivity (only having one sexual partner) is less common in lesbian relationships and *much less* common in gay relationships (Peplau, 1982). However, the ideal of sexual exclusivity is based on an assumed heterosexual norm or 'blueprint' (Yip, 1999), which many gays and lesbians reject. Sexual non-exclusivity may lead to relationship breakdown in heterosexuals, largely because it is likely to be 'secretive'. In homosexual couples, those who have sex outside their relationships:

'... tend to do so after negotiation of relationship rules and sexual activity guidelines, in the context of an open relationship ... and are consequently less likely to experience their own, or their partners' sexual affairs as signalling the end of the couple relationship' (Kitzinger & Coyle, 1995).

In terms of sex roles, most gays and lesbians actively reject traditional husband–wife or masculine–feminine roles (as clearly exist in heterosexual relationships) as a model for enduring relationships (Peplau, 1991). Equality in status and power is the preferred approach, and relationships which are not equal are less likely to be maintained.

Box 6.5   Role sharing in homosexual relationships

Despite the existence of some gay and lesbian couples that replicate the so-called 'heterosexual model', most of these couples demonstrate a high degree of role-sharing rather than 'role complementarity'. In the area of domestic division of labour, for example, gender appears to be the most significant factor in task allocations for heterosexual couples, with the wife performing most of the household tasks. In lesbian couples, however, all tasks are *shared* (performed together), whilst gay male couples are likely to specialise in tasks, depending on each partner's own preferences and skills.

On the whole, gay and lesbian couples seem to embrace 'the ethic of equality and reciprocity', deliberately rejecting the 'heterosexist model' which is characterised by power inequality. This is particularly true for lesbians who have previously been in 'unequal' heterosexual relationships.

(Adapted from Yip, 1999)

As Yip (1999) notes, gays and lesbians constitute a largely *hidden* population, which raises important methodological issues about research on same-sex couples. Respondents recruited for studies:

- are typically opportunistic and *not* drawn from a wider sample;
- tend to offer themselves for analysis;
- are white, young, urban-based and well educated;
- are drawn from friendship networks or gay and lesbian organisations and groups.

Whilst much detailed research is needed to document a more complete and inclusive picture of same-sex relationships, it is, as Kitzinger & Coyle (1995) note, time for psychology to:

'... move beyond the mere acceptance of homosexual lifestyles to a better understanding of the differences between homosexual and heterosexual relationships'.

'Electronic' friendships

According to an Anglo-American study in which over 1000 students were interviewed, one in ten 'surfs' the *Internet* for up to four hours a day, as well as using a computer for things like coursework or essay writing. Even the typical student uses the Internet an hour a day for 'fun' (Harlow, 1999b). As Wallace (1999) has noted:

'From almost total obscurity, the Internet swiftly leapt into our lives. Once an arcane communication medium for academics and researchers, it now sustains almost any human activity you can imagine, from shopping to sex, from research to rebellion'.

Box 6.6   Who uses the Internet?

Computer and Internet users are stereotypically portrayed as socially unskilled male teenagers, with little or no social life or self-confidence. They have been labelled 'nerds', 'geeks' and 'anoraks'. Up until recently, this stereotype was partly true. However, the spread of cheaper and easier-to-use home computers has meant that women and retired people have also become regular 'users'. 'Net obsession', defined as surfing the Internet for more than four hours a day, may be evident in as many as 400,000 Britons, that is, ten per cent of computer owners.

(Based on Griffiths, 1999, and Harlow, 1999b)

Computer users can communicate with others in several ways. These include electronic mail (*email*), *asynchronous discussion forums* (in which contributors start or join discussions to which others contribute at a later time), *newsgroups* (a variation on asynchronous discussion forums) and *synchronous chats*. In these, people who are 'online' can enter a 'chat-room' and discuss issues in real-time. A message is typed, and others contribute, with each message scrolling up the screen.

The factors influencing initial attraction between people that were discussed in Chapter 4 are relevant to the study of 'electronic friendships', and much of what happens in adult relationship-formation can evidently be found in the formation of electronic relationships. According to Wallace (1999), *proximity, exposure* and *familiarity* (see pages 35–37) translate into *intersection frequency*, that is, how often a person who participates in a 'chat-room' is encountered. The more one person anticipates encountering and communicating with another (and this can be facilitated through a 'buddy list' indicating who is on line at a particular time), the more likely a personal relationship is to be established.

As noted in Chapter 4, evidence suggests that 'birds of a feather flock together' (see page 36), and that the critical *similarities* are those concerning *beliefs, attitudes* and *values*. This might also apply in electronic relationships. A chat-room user or message board poster may be initially attracted to another because of their agreement about some topic. As more information is shared, though, it might become apparent that the correspondents are really more dissimilar than they initially believed. In such circumstances, the frequency and length of correspondence between two people would be expected to decrease, and eventually cease. This is exactly what happens.

Box 6.7 Physical attractiveness and electronic relationships

Physical attractiveness influences the impressions we form of the people we meet (see pages 37–39). However:

'In some interactions, the Internet pulls the rug out from under our tendency to rely on good looks in interpersonal attraction, at least initially. This gives people an opportunity to get to know one another without the weight of all the physical attractiveness stereotypes. If interactive video and voice become more accessible and widely used, the equation will change again. But for the time being ... beauty's power is restrained'. (Wallace, 1999)

Wallace describes a student who rarely contributed in face-to-face discussions, and described himself as being 'not very attractive'. When he did contribute, he was usually ignored by others. Online, however, he could not be dismissed because of his looks, and this gave him the confidence to contribute. What Wallace calls 'the Internet's level playing field' with respect to physical attributes, may bring out the best in this student, even in 'real life'.

As well as birds of a feather flocking together, opposites can attract, and some adult relationships are based on *complementarity* rather than similarity (see pages 40–41). Little research has been conducted into the role of complementarity in electronic relationship-formation. What has been shown, though, is that people who like to display their technical expertise like those who ask for and appreciate their help.

Box 6.8 DotComGuy

From January 1, 2000, Mitch Maddox has been confined to a small and initially otherwise empty house in Dallas, Texas, for a period of 12 months. Maddox aims to show that it is possible to exist with just a laptop computer, a high speed Internet connection and a credit card. He is allowed to receive visitors, but he must buy all his needs over the Internet, and may leave the house only in the event of serious illness or injury or a death in his immediate family.

Maddox, who has legally changed his name to DotComGuy, is convinced that the first months of the new millennium could bring romance. He is confident of finding a 'cyber soulmate' in what he hopes could turn into a real-life version of the on-line romance played out between Tom Hanks and Meg Ryan in the film *You've Got Mail*. DotComGuy says:

'I'm sure I'm going to meet someone out there. I have already called her DotComGirl in my mind ... I want to show people how they can create more time for themselves by using their computers'.

He can be reached at me@DotComGuy.com.

(Adapted from Rhodes, 1999)

Figure 6.3 *'DotComGuy' is confident that the Internet will provide him with a romantic partner*

Electronic friendships and romantic attachments are apparently just as common and 'deep' as relationships formed in other ways, at least to those who are involved in them (Wallace, 1999). According to Parks & Floyd (1996) and Scherer & Bost (1997):

- two-thirds of people who responded to a survey reported that they had formed a personal relationship with somebody in a newsgroup;

- more women than men reported forming online relationships;

- like other relationships, electronic relationships vary in their intensity and duration;

- opposite-sex relationships are more common than same-sex relationships;

- self-disclosure is an important part of online relationships;

- under ten per cent of online relationships are 'romantic';

- people who are 'Internet dependent' are more likely than non-dependent users to form online relationships.

However:

'The relationships that form [on the Internet] are vulnerable because of the way humans are, and the way the Internet is. People may disclose too much, too soon, and they may idealise and fantasise in unrealistic ways. The role-playing, deceptions and gender-swapping [that people often engage in] make the Internet a bit hazardous for developing relationships, and it is not at all uncommon for a person you are growing to like on the net – as a friend or romantic partner – to just vanish into thin air'. (Wallace, 1999)

CONCLUSIONS

There has been a tendency for Western psychologists to equate 'relationships' with 'Western relationships'. However, research reviewed in the first part of this chapter suggests that there are important differences between Western and non-Western cultures in this regard. There has also been a tendency for research to concentrate on heterosexual relationships. However, research reviewed in the second part of this chapter indicates that 'understudied' relationships, such as gay and lesbian and those formed on the Internet, are also important to understand.

Summary

- Interpersonal relationships in Western cultures tend to be **individualistic**, **voluntary** and **temporary**, whereas those in non-Western cultures tend to be more **collectivist**, **involuntary** and **permanent**.

- There has been a tendency for Western psychologists to equate 'relationships' with 'Western relationships'. This is a form of **ethnocentrism**, specifically, **Anglo-** or **Eurocentrism**.

- Westerners think of **monogamy** as the norm, even moral form of marriage. However, cultures differ in their marital arrangements. **Polygamy** can take the form of **polygyny** or **polyandry**. Another arrangement is **mandatory marriage to specific relatives**.

- **Fraternal polyandry** has been common for generations in Tibet and its neighbouring Himalayan areas. It keeps brothers together, and slows the growth of the family since several brothers will produce only the number of children their one wife can bear. Land does not need to be divided up, and a single family is preserved as an economic unit.

- Women who do not marry in polyandrous societies have low social status. Unmarried women pass on their low social status to any children they may have, since these children are defined as illegitimate.

- The concept of **romantic love** may be more universal, and more complex, than has sometimes been claimed. The notion of people falling in love is found in one form or another in most human societies, even where marriages are traditionally arranged by families or friends.

- There are also important differences within culturally diverse societies. These differences are consistent with the distinction between collectivist and individualist cultural beliefs and practices.

- All human societies recognise **sexual jealousy** in marriage, and have cultural rules for dealing with it. However, jealousy is expressed more readily in some societies than others. Cultures also seem to differ in terms of the behaviours that trigger sexual jealousy.

- For many years, **homosexual relationships** were dismissed as destructive, exploitative and inauthentic, and homosexuality was identified as a sexual deviation. However, although there is now an apparent acceptance of homosexuality, such relationships are still discriminated against and not officially sanctioned.

- Research suggests that homosexual partnerships are far more like heterosexual relationships than they are different from them. For example, in both types of relationship, partners are more satisfied when there are more rewards and fewer personal costs involved.

- Certain factors are found to be omitted or distorted when homosexual relationships are assessed in terms derived from heterosexual relationships. These include **cohabitation**, **sexual exclusivity**, and **sex role**.

- Gays and lesbians constitute a largely hidden population, which raises important methodological issues about research on same-sex couples. For example, they are typically opportunistic and not drawn from a wider sample, and tend to be white, young, urban-based and well educated.

- The factors influencing initial attraction between people are also relevant to the study of '**electronic friendships**'. Much of what happens in adult relationship-formation can evidently be found in the formation of electronic relationships.

- Electronic friendships and romantic attachments are apparently just as common and 'deep' as relationships formed in other ways, at least for those who are involved in them.

- Electronic relationships are, however, vulnerable because of the way humans are, and the way the Internet is. People may disclose too much, too soon, and they may idealise and fantasise in unrealistic ways.

Essay Questions

1 Discuss psychological insights into differences in relationships between Western and non-Western cultures. *(24 marks)*

2 Describe and evaluate research into **one** type of 'understudied' relationship (e.g. gay and lesbian or 'electronic' friendships). *(24 marks)*

WEB ADDRESSES

http://www.socialpsychology.org/social.htm#cultural
http://www.socialpsychology.org/social.htm#sexuality
http://www.socialpsychology.org/social.htm#lesbigay

PART 3: PRO- AND ANTI-SOCIAL BEHAVIOUR

7 The Nature and Causes of Aggression

INTRODUCTION AND OVERVIEW

Philosophers and psychologists have long been interested in human aggression. According to Hobbes (1651), people are naturally competitive and hostile, interested only in their own power and gaining advantage over others. Hobbes argued that to prevent conflict and mutual destruction, people needed government. This pessimistic view about people's nature was shared by Freud and Lorenz, who offered theories of aggression in psychoanalytic and ethological terms respectively. This chapter, however, examines several *social psychological theories of aggression*, including research studies relating to them. It also considers research into the effects of *environmental stressors* on aggressive behaviour. The chapter begins by considering the nature of aggression.

THE NATURE OF AGGRESSION

Baron & Richardson (1994) define anti-social behaviours as those 'which show a lack of feeling and concern for the welfare of others'. One anti-social behaviour is *aggression*. Used as a noun, 'aggression' usually refers to some behaviour intended to harm or destroy another person who is motivated to avoid such treatment. Penrod (1983) calls this *anti-social aggression*, to distinguish it from those instances when, for example, a person defends him- or herself from attack (*sanctioned aggression*) or when, for example, an aircraft hijacker is shot and killed by security agents (*pro-social aggression*). When used as an adjective, 'aggressive' sometimes conveys an action carried out with energy and persistence, and may even be regarded as socially desirable (Lloyd *et al.*, 1984).

Moyer (1976) and Berkowitz (1993) see aggression as always involving behaviour, either physical or symbolic, performed with the intention of harming someone. They reserve the word *violence* to describe an extreme form of aggression in which a deliberate attempt is made to inflict serious physical injury on another person or damage property.

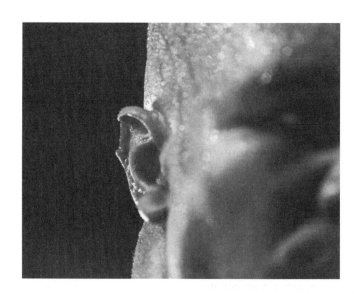

Figure 7.1 *Evander Holyfield: a victim of Mike Tyson's violence*

THE FRUSTRATION–AGGRESSION HYPOTHESIS

According to Freud (1920, 1923), the purpose of all *instincts* is to reduce tension or excitement to a minimum and ultimately eliminate them. Freud's early writings emphasised what he called *Eros*, the human drive for pleasure. This later came to include self-preservation (the ego instincts). After the great loss of lives in World War 1, however, he proposed the existence of *Thanatos*, a drive directed towards self-destruction and death.

Freud thought that because Eros and Thanatos conflicted, the self-directed aggression of the latter was satisfied by being turned *outward*, and that some other thing or person must be destroyed if we are not to destroy ourselves. So, unless a more acceptable way of expressing Thanatos could be achieved (through a *cathartic activity* such as sport), people would act aggressively from time to time to discharge built-up aggressive energy. In Freud's view, just as we need to eat, drink and express our sexual needs periodically, so we also need to express our hostile and destructive impulses.

Freud's ideas on aggression had little impact until the publication of *Frustration and Aggression* by Dollard *et al.* (1939). Intended partly to 'translate' Freudian psychoanalytic concepts into learning theory terms, the frustration–aggression hypothesis proposed that:

> 'Aggression is always a consequence of frustration and, contrariwise ... the existence of frustration always leads to some form of aggression'.

In everyday language, 'frustration' refers to an unpleasant feeling produced by an unfulfilled desire. Dollard *et al.*, however, defined frustration as:

> 'An interference with the occurrence of an instigated goal-response at its proper time in the behaviour sequence'.

Put differently, frustration prevents an *expected reinforcer's* occurrence.

Whilst Dollard *et al.* shared Freud's view that aggression was an innate response, they argued that it would only be elicited in specific situations. Thus, whenever an important need was thwarted, the resulting frustration would produce an aggressive response. This does not mean that aggression is always directed towards the object of the frustration. Aggression may be delayed, disguised or displaced from its most obvious source to a more accessible target. An example of such displacement behaviour is *scapegoating* which, as was seen in Chapter 3 (see pages 23–24), is one theory of prejudice and discrimination.

Evidence consistent with Dollard *et al.*'s hypothesis was reported by Barker *et al.* (1941). Young children were shown an attractive set of toys, but prevented from playing with them. When the children were eventually allowed access to the toys, they threw them, stomped on them, and smashed them. These behaviours did not occur in a comparison group of children who were not frustrated. Despite this support, however, the original version of the frustration–aggression hypothesis has attracted much criticism.

Box 7.1   Some criticisms of the original frustration–aggression hypothesis

According to Miller (1941), frustration is an instigator of aggression, but situational factors (such as *learned inhibition* or the *fear of retaliation*) may prevent actual aggression from occurring. So, whilst frustration may make aggression more likely, it is far from being a *sufficient* cause of aggressive behaviour. Miller also suggested that frustration can produce several possible responses, of which aggression is only one. These include withdrawal, apathy, hopelessness, depression, and sometimes an increased effort to achieve the goal.

Frustration can produce different responses in different people in different situations. Berkowitz (1993) has suggested that aggression is most likely when a person is close to achieving a goal, or the frustrator is perceived as being arbitrary or illegitimate. So, we are not usually bothered by a failure to reach a goal unless we believe that the frustrator intentionally or improperly interfered with our efforts.

This *attribution of intention* perspective (Kulik & Brown, 1979) is consistent with the definition of aggression as the (perceived) intention to harm another person. If there are mitigating circumstances, the attribution made by the victim may change. Interestingly, research indicates that children who display chronic aggression have a strong *attributional bias* (see Chapter 1) towards seeing others as acting against them with hostile intent, especially in ambiguous situations. These biased attributions often lead to retaliatory aggression (Taylor *et al.*, 1994).

BERKOWITZ'S CUE–AROUSAL (OR AGGRESSIVE CUE) THEORY

Whilst frustration and aggression are related, frustration does *not* always lead to aggression (see Box 7.1). Berkowitz (1966, 1978, 1989) was the first to point out that aggression, like any other behaviour, can be *reinforced*. For example, a hired assassin kills for *money*, and frustration does not play a causal role in an assassin's behaviour. Moreover, things other than frustration can produce aggressive behaviour. For example, if two non-humans are placed in a cage and receive electric shocks to their feet, they are likely to fight (Carlson, 1987).

Berkowitz proposed that frustration produces *anger* rather than aggression. However, frustration is psychologically painful, and anything that is psychologically (or, indeed, physically) painful can produce aggression. According to Berkowitz, two conditions act together to produce aggression when frustration occurs. The first is a *readiness* to act aggressively. The second is the presence of *environmental cues* associated either with aggressive behaviour or with the frustrating person or object. For Berkowitz, then, whilst we might become angry as a response to frustration, aggressive behaviour will be elicited only when certain environmental cues are present (see also pages 73–75).

Box 7.2   Three tests of Berkowitz's cue–arousal theory

- Geen & Berkowitz (1966) had a stooge, who was introduced as either Kirk Anderson or Bob Anderson, insult and berate participants for failing to solve a jigsaw puzzle. Participants then watched a film in which the actor Kirk Douglas was brutally beaten. Afterwards, participants were given the opportunity to administer supposed electric shocks to the stooge. Participants gave higher intensity 'shocks' to the stooge called Kirk. Geen and Berkowitz argued that because of its association with brutality in the film, 'Kirk' served as a cue to aggressive behaviour.

- Berkowitz & Geen (1966) introduced the stooge as Bob Kelly, Bob Dunne or Bob Riley. Dunne was the name of the victorious character in the film in which Kirk Douglas was brutally beaten. Douglas's character was called Kelly. The stooge received 'shocks' of greater intensity when he was called Kelly. Presumably, the character called Kelly was associated with an instance of successful aggression, and this made it more likely that anger would be converted into aggression (Berkowitz, 1993).

- Berkowitz & LePage (1967) had participants perform a task which was then evaluated by a stooge. The evaluation involved the stooge delivering electric shocks to the participant. The number of shocks produced different levels of anger in participants. Later, participants were required to evaluate the stooge, also by delivering electric shocks. Participants were taken to a 'control room' and shown the shock apparatus. For some, a shotgun and revolver had been placed on a nearby table. Sometimes, participants were told that these belonged to the stooge, and sometimes they were given no explanation for their presence. In two other conditions, there were either badminton rackets and shuttlecocks on the table or no objects at all.

Angry participants delivered most shocks when the weapons were associated with the stooge, and only slightly fewer shocks when they were present but not associated with the stooge. The no objects and badminton rackets conditions led to significantly fewer shocks being delivered. Berkowitz (1968) called this *the weapons effect*. In his view:

'Guns not only permit violence, they can stimulate it as well. The finger pulls the trigger, but the trigger may also be pulling the finger'.

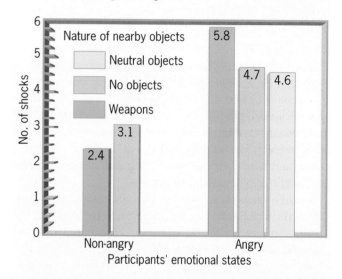

Figure 7.2 *Mean number of shocks given as a function of presence of weapons (From Gross, 1996, and based on Berkowitz & Le Page, 1967)*

Whilst several researchers have failed to replicate the weapons effect (Mummendey, 1996), Berkowitz (1995) cites several examples of successful replications in a number of countries. Indeed, in Sweden, Frodi (1975) reported the weapons effect among high-school boys even when they had not been angered by means of receiving electric shocks.

The results of Berkowitz's own experiments and those of other researchers suggest that frustration and pain are *aversive stimuli*. Other aversive stimuli occurring in the physical environment include *noise*, *crowding* and *temperature* (see pages 73–75).

ZILLMAN'S EXCITATION-TRANSFER THEORY

According to Zillman (1982), arousal from one source can be transferred to, and energise, some other response. This is because arousal takes time to dissipate. When we are aroused, aggression may be heightened provided that the aroused person has some disposition to react aggressively, and provided that the arousal is incorrectly attributed to the aggression-provoking event rather than to the correct source.

In one test of this, Zillman & Bryant (1974) created a state of arousal in participants by requiring them to ride bicycles. For some, a high level of arousal was induced, whilst for others a low level was induced. Then, participants played a game during which they were verbally insulted by a stooge. When participants were later given the opportunity to deliver a harsh noise in headphones worn by the stooge, significantly more noise was delivered by highly aroused participants.

Box 7.3   Excitation transfer and sexual arousal

Excitation-transfer theorists have been particularly interested in the relationship between *sexual arousal* and aggression (Zillman & Bryant, 1984). Unfortunately, the data have been inconsistent. 'Soft' pornography apparently either decreases or has no effect on aggression, whereas 'hard core' pornography can lead to an increase in aggressive behaviour (Donnerstein *et al.*, 1987). Also, sexual excitement, combined with aggressive behaviour in the sexually arousing material, has been shown to produce an increase in aggression (Donnerstein & Berkowitz, 1981). The effects of observing aggressive behaviour are considered briefly in the following section, and in greater detail in Chapter 9.

Excitation-transfer theory sees the relationship between arousal and aggression as a *sequence*, in which arousal is generated and then, depending on its perceived causes, labelled, producing a specific emotion such as anger (Mummendey, 1996). Berkowitz (1990), however, disputes the existence of 'unspecific' or 'neutral' arousal. According to his *cognitive–neoassociationistic approach*, anger and aggression are *parallel* rather than sequential processes, because aversive events automatically lead to the instigation of aggression, depending on what situational cues are present (Mummendey, 1996).

SOCIAL LEARNING THEORY

According to social learning theory (SLT), aggressive behaviours are learned through *reinforcement* and the *imitation* of aggressive 'models' (Bandura, 1965, 1973, 1994: see Chapter 31). Reinforcement of aggressive behaviour can occur in a number of ways. For example, a child who behaves aggressively in order to play with attractive toys will quickly learn to repeat the behaviour in the future. Non-tangible reinforcement, such as praise for 'being tough', can also increase the tendency to behave aggressively.

Imitation is the reproduction of learning through observation (*observational learning*), and involves observing other people who serve as models for behaviour. Bandura *et al.* (1961, 1963) demonstrated how a child's aggressive tendencies can be strengthened through *vicarious reinforcement* (seeing others being rewarded for behaving aggressively).

Key STUDY

Box 7.4   Bandura *et al.*'s research into the effects of observing aggressive behaviour

Bandura's procedure involved three-, four- and five-year-old children observing an adult model behaving aggressively towards an inflated plastic 'Bobo' doll. Later, the children were allowed to play with the doll themselves. Those who saw the adult model being reinforced for displaying aggressive behaviour performed significantly more imitative aggressive acts than those who saw the model's behaviour being neither reinforced nor punished. Those who saw the model being punished for behaving aggressively made fewest imitative responses of all.

However, Bandura *et al.* pointed out the important distinction between *learning* and *performance*. The fact that a child does not perform an imitative behaviour does not necessarily mean that it has not been learned. In other experiments, Bandura (1965) showed that when children who had seen the model being punished for his behaviour were themselves offered rewards for behaving aggressively, they showed they had learned (or acquired) the model's behaviours just as well as those who saw the behaviours being reinforced (see also Box 31.4, pages 338–339).

Whilst there are methodological concerns with Bandura *et al.*'s research which make it difficult to generalise their findings to the 'real world', SLT has received support from a number of quarters (Hollin & Howells, 1997). For example, children who are raised by aggressive and physically abusive parents often behave in the same way. Indeed, for Straus *et al.* (1980), 'each generation learns to be violent by being a participant in a violent family'. SLT has also contributed to our understanding of the role played by the media in both pro- and anti-social behaviour. This contribution is considered in Chapter 9.

DEINDIVIDUATION THEORY

In an early study of the aggressive behaviour sometimes associated with *crowds*, Le Bon (1879) noted that:

> 'Isolated, a man may be a cultured individual; in a crowd he is a barbarian. [Crowd behaviour is] an irrational and uncritical response to the psychological temptations of the crowd situation'.

In Le Bon's view, the question that needed answering was why crowds act in ways that are uncharacteristic of the individuals comprising them, and in ways contrary to their everyday norms. Le Bon identified several situational determinants of behaviour which come into operation when a crowd is assembled, these being *suggestibility*, *social contagion*, *impersonality* and *anonymity* (see Gross & McIlveen, 1998). The last of these has been the subject of most research.

Figure 7.3 *According to Le Bon, crowd behaviour is an irrational and uncritical response to the psychological temptations of the crowd situation*

Anonymity and deindividuation

Le Bon believed that the more *anonymous* the crowd, the greater was its potential for extreme action, because anonymity removes the sense of *individuality* from members. When a person does not feel that he or she is being singled out as an individual, and when attention is not paid to others as individuals, restraints on behaviour are removed and a person is 'free' to indulge in behaviour that would ordinarily be controlled. The reason for this is that moral responsibility for behaviour has been shifted from the individual person to the *group* of which he or she is a member.

Whilst Le Bon wanted to know why people in crowds act in uncharacteristic ways and contrary to their everyday norms, Fromm (1941) was more concerned with the *motives* that lead some people to hide their individuality in crowds. Le Bon and Fromm's concerns were combined by Festinger *et al.* (1952), who proposed the concept of *deindividuation*, defining it as:

> '... a state of affairs in a group where members do not pay attention to other individuals *qua* individuals and, correspondingly, the members do not feel they are being singled out by others'.

According to Festinger *et al.*, membership of a group not only provides us with a sense of identity and *belongingness* (see Chapter 3, page 28), but allows us to merge with the group, forego our individualities, and become anonymous. This may lead to a reduction of inner constraints and inhibitions. A field experiment demonstrating the effects of anonymity was reported by Zimbardo (1969). Zimbardo reasoned that a big city is a more anonymous place than a small town, because people are more likely to know one another in a small town. For the big city, the Bronx area of New York was chosen. The little town was the Stanford area of Palo Alto, California.

In each location, a similar car was parked in a street adjoining a university campus. The car's number plates were removed and its bonnet raised in order to make it appear that it had been abandoned. Research assistants photographed the car and filmed people's behaviour from hidden locations. In New York, the car's battery and radiator were removed within ten minutes of it being parked. Within a day, just about everything else that could be removed was. Within three days, there was little left of the car, a result of 23 incidents of 'destructive contact'. These were nearly always observed by a passerby, who occasionally stopped to chat with the perpetrator. Moreover, the incidents were carried out in daylight by well-dressed, clean-cut whites who, argued Zimbardo, were the very people who would protest against such behaviour and demand a greater police presence! By contrast, the car left in Palo Alto was left alone for seven days. Indeed, on the day it rained, a passer-by lowered the car's bonnet in order to protect its engine!

Box 7.5 Some research showing the effects of deindividuation

- Defining deindividuation as 'a subjective state in which people lose their sense of self-consciousness', Singer *et al.* (1965) found that reduced individuality within a group was associated with a greater liking for the group and a larger number of obscene comments being made in a discussion of pornography. In a follow-up study, Singer *et al.* found that although deindividuated participants liked their group more, they conformed to it less.

- In one of several studies conducted by Zimbardo (1969), female undergraduates were required to deliver electric shocks to another student as 'an aid to learning'. Half the participants wore bulky laboratory coats and hoods that hid their faces. These participants were spoken to in groups of four and never referred to by name. The other half wore their normal clothes, were given large name tags to wear, and introduced to each other by name. They could also see each other dimly whilst giving the shocks.

   Both sets of participants could see the student supposedly receiving the shocks, who pretended to be in extreme discomfort. The hooded participants gave twice as much shock as the other group. Moreover, the amount of shock given by the hooded participants, unlike that given by the other group, did not depend on whether they were told that the student receiving the shocks was 'honest, sincere and warm' or 'conceited and critical'.

- Watson (1973) investigated 23 different cultures. Those warriors who depersonalised themselves with face paints or masks were significantly more likely than those with exposed faces to kill, torture or mutilate captured enemies.

- Diener *et al.* (1976) observed 1300 'trick-or-treating' American children one Halloween night. When the children were anonymous, as a result of wearing costumes which prevented them from being recognised, and went from house to house in large groups, they were more likely to steal money and candy.

Diener's theory of deindividuation

According to Diener (1980):

'A deindividuated person is prevented by situational factors in a group from becoming *self-aware*. Deindividuated persons are blocked from an awareness of themselves as separate individuals and from monitoring their own behaviour'.

Diener argues that in everyday life we are frequently unaware of our individual identities or of ourselves as separate persons. Indeed, when we perform well-learned behaviours, express well-thought-out cognitions, or enact culturally scripted behaviour, we are not consciously aware. In some circumstances, such as when we are evaluated by others or when a behaviour does not produce an expected outcome, self-awareness and behavioural self-regulation are initiated. In other circumstances, such as when we are immersed in a group, self-awareness and individual self-conception are blocked, and it is this which Diener believes leads to deindividuation. When deindividuation occurs, certain self-regulatory capacities are lost. These include a weakening of normal restraints against impulsive behaviour, a lack of concern about what others will think of our behaviour, and a reduced capability to engage in rational thinking.

Figure 7.4 *The Ku Klux Klan: deindividuated individuals but an easily identifiable group*

Prentice–Dunn and Rogers' theory of deindividuation

Prentice-Dunn & Rogers (1983) argue that it is possible to distinguish between two types of self-awareness. *Public self-awareness* refers to a concern about the impression we are giving others who will hold us accountable for our behaviour. *Private self-awareness* refers to the attention we pay our own thoughts and feelings.

Public self-awareness can be reduced by three factors. For example, we would be difficult to identify in a crowd and this would make us feel *anonymous*. If other members were behaving anti-socially, a *diffusion of responsibility* (see Chapter 8, page 81) would also occur because one person alone could not be blamed for the group's actions. Finally, other group members' behaviours would set some sort of standard or *norm* for behaviour and supply models to *imitate*.

Private self-awareness can also be reduced by several factors. For example, in a crowd attending a rock concert, our attention would be directed outward, and we might become so engrossed in what was going on (singing, dancing, and/or drinking alcohol, for example) that we would 'forget' who we are. Prentice-Dunn and Rogers argue that deviant behaviour can occur through a loss of either of these forms of self-awareness, although this occurs through different routes.

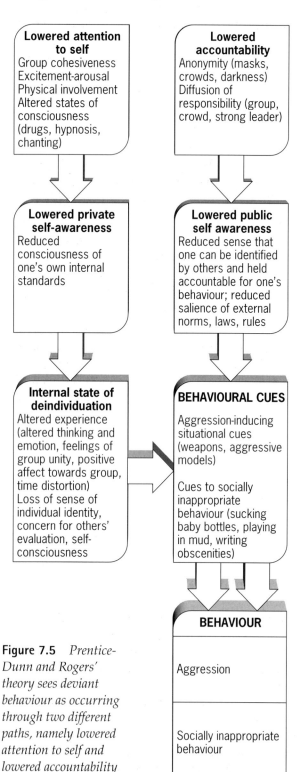

Figure 7.5 *Prentice-Dunn and Rogers' theory sees deviant behaviour as occurring through two different paths, namely lowered attention to self and lowered accountability (From Prentice-Dunn & Rogers, 1983)*

When we are publicly self-aware, we engage in rational calculations about the likelihood of being punished for deviant behaviour. A deindividuated state, however, is an *irrational state of altered consciousness*. As Figure 7.5 illustrates, Prentice-Dunn and Rogers' theory does not see reductions in public or private self-awareness by themselves as causing deviant behaviour. Rather, both factors make us susceptible to *behavioural cues*, one being other people's behaviour in a crowd.

The data presented in Box 7.5 (pages 70–71) are consistent with both theories described above. These theories may also explain other phenomena such as the 'baiting crowd' in cases of threatened suicide. For example, in an analysis of 21 incidents of potential suicides threatening to jump from buildings, Mann (1981) found that in ten cases, people were more likely to shout 'Jump!' when they were part of a large crowd, when it was dark, and when the victim and crowd were distant from one another (as is the case when the victim threatens to jump from a tall building). Baiting was also linked to other behavioural cues (see above), such as high temperatures and how long the episode lasted.

An evaluation of deindividuation research

Although there is much experimental support for the concept of deindividuation, several cautions should be exercised. First, participants in Zimbardo's (1969) study outlined in Box 7.5 wore clothing resembling that worn by the Ku Klux Klan, an American racist group (see Figure 7.4, page 71). This uniform may have acted as a *demand characteristic*, in that it might have led American participants to believe that more extreme behaviour was expected of them (Johnson & Downing, 1979). In support of this, Johnson and Downing found that when participants wore surgical masks and gowns, they delivered significantly *less* electric shock than those participants whose names and identities were emphasised. This suggests that the participants' clothing and related *behavioural expectations*, rather than deindividuation, may have led to differences in behaviour.

Similarly, Brown (1985) has pointed out that in another of Zimbardo's (1969) studies, the participants were Belgian soldiers rather than the female undergraduates investigated in the study described in Box 7.5. When these soldiers wore the hoods, they did *not* behave more aggressively. Instead, they became self-conscious, suspicious and anxious. Their apparently *individuated* counterparts, who wore army-issue uniform, retained their 'normal' level of deindividuation resulting from their status as *uniformed soldiers*. One of the functions of uniforms in the 'real world' is to *reduce* individuality and hence, at least indirectly, to increase deindividuation (Brown, 1985). Indeed, dispossessing someone of the clothes they normally wear is a major technique of depersonalising them in 'total institutions' such as prisons and psychiatric hospitals (Goffman, 1968, 1971).

Also, whilst the anonymity produced by wearing, say, police or military uniform may increase the likelihood of deindividuated behaviour, such anonymity may make the wearers of these uniforms appear less human and affect the perceptions and attitudes of others (Brown, 1985).

Box 7.6   Do crowds resent the anonymity of their opponents?

In a disturbance in the Notting Hill area of London in 1982, 100 police officers were sent to the scene wearing special flameproof suits. According to *The Times* newspaper:

'(The) uniform, combined with a hard helmet and visor, does not include a police serial number, making it difficult for anyone who wishes to identify and complain against an individual officer to pursue a grievance. A middle-aged West Indian, who was in a restaurant when it was raided, said yesterday:

'When they came through the door they looked like zombies, dressed in full black with headgear. All they had was one white stripe saying 'police' on it. We could not know in the world who they were, their faces were covered and they had helmets.''

(Taken from Brown, 1985)

Finally, deindividuation does not necessarily produce anti-social behaviour. Gergen *et al.* (1973) showed that in some circumstances when people cannot be identified, more *affiliative* behaviours can occur. In their study, groups of six men and six women were placed in either a normally lit room (control group) or a completely dark room (experimental group). The participants, who had never met one another, were told that there was nothing special the experimenters wanted them to do. The experimenters left the participants for one hour, tape recorded what they said and, when the experiment was over, asked them what had happened.

During the first 15 minutes, the experimental group participants mainly explored the room and chatted idly to one another. In the following 30 minutes, the conversation turned to more serious matters. In the final 15 minutes, the participants began to get physical in that half of them hugged one another. Some of them became quite intimate, and 80 per cent reported feeling sexually aroused! It seems that we can become uninhibited in the dark where the norms of intimacy no longer prevail. We feel less accountable for our behaviour in such situations, but this state of deindividuation can be to the mutual benefit of all (Gergen & Gergen, 1981).

Box 7.7   The social constructionist approach

The most recent theoretical approach to understanding aggression comes from *social constructionists*. Mummendey (1996) has proposed that whether or not a behaviour is aggressive or non-aggressive depends on whether the behaviour (or, in the case of failing to help someone, the non-behaviour) is *judged* to be aggressive either by an observer or by the performer. In Mummendey's view, the appraisal of a behaviour as aggressive involves going beyond a description to an *evaluation* of it.

For Mummendey:

'When asking about the causes of aggression, more is of interest than simply the conditions for the occurrence of that behaviour. Of even greater importance are the conditions for judging the individual behaviour as "aggressive".'

Mummendey's own research (Mummendey & Otten, 1989) and that of others (e.g. Mikula, 1994) suggests that the intention to harm, actual harm, and norm violation are the main criteria people use to label behaviour as aggressive. In looking for the cause of aggressive behaviour, then:

'We should not concentrate on the conditions that energise individual drives or reduce the rational control of behaviour. Rather, we should look for the conditions (at least from the actor's point of view) which make intentionally harming another person seem both situationally appropriate and justified' (Mummendey, 1996).

THE EFFECTS OF ENVIRONMENTAL STRESSORS ON AGGRESSION

Contrary to popular belief, aggression is not always provoked by the words or deeds of other people (Baron, 1977). Often, aggression is elicited or encouraged by a wide range of factors that are not closely related to ongoing social interaction. Regardless of its specific causes, however, aggression remains a form of social behaviour directed towards other people (see page 66). Baron identifies three major causes that relate to the *physical environment*, namely, *noise*, *crowding* and *temperature*, and others which involve *situational conditions*, including *aggressive cues* (see pages 67–68), *heightened arousal* (see pages 68–69), and *drugs* (including alcohol).

Causes relating to the physical environment

Noise

Geen & O'Neal (1969) found that high-intensity noise increased aggression only in participants who had previously witnessed a violent film. Those who had watched a non-violent film were no more aggressive in a high-intensity noise condition than those in a low-intensity noise condition.

Key **STUDY**

Box 7.8   The effects of noise on aggression

Donnerstein & Wilson (1976) asked male participants to each write an essay which a confederate then evaluated either favourably (*non-angered condition*) or quite critically (*angered condition*). After this, participants were given the opportunity to 'turn the tables' on the confederate by assuming the teacher role and evaluating *his* essay through administering electric shocks (a measure of aggression). Whilst serving as the teacher, participants wore headphones and were exposed to one-second bursts of either low-intensity (65 db) or high-intensity (95 db) noise. Participants in the 'angered' condition were much more likely to administer more and longer shocks if they heard high–intensity noise, whilst those in the non-angered condition were largely unaffected by noise intensity.

In a second, related experiment, Donnerstein and Wilson added a no-noise control condition, and exposed participants to noise *before* they could deliver shocks to the confederate. In a further condition, participants were led to believe they could terminate the aversive noise simply by asking. The findings from the first study were confirmed and the last (new) condition made no difference (that is, noise intensity had *no effect* on aggression). Donnerstein and Wilson suggested that when participants believed they could terminate the noise at will, it was less arousing and unpleasant for them (see Gross *et al.*, 2000).

In Bandura's (1973) terms, the heightened physiological arousal produced by loud noise (or any other environmental condition) will only result in overt aggression if such behaviour represents a strong or *dominant* response. Given the frequency with which we are all exposed to provocation and annoyance from others, the experimental findings suggest that high noise levels present in many urban areas may contribute to – if not actually initiate – interpersonal aggression (Baron, 1977).

Crowding

Common sense suggests that the greater the number of people present in a given space, the greater the likelihood that two or more of them will become involved in aggressive encounters (see pages 70–73). However, research findings suggest a much more complex picture.

Box 7.9   Some research findings relating to the effects of crowding

- There is little evidence of a correlation between urban density and crime, or between crowding and the incidence of violent crimes (murder, rape, and aggravated assault: Baron, 1977). However, there is a high correlation between density and violence in prisons (Cave, 1998). For example, Cox *et al.* (1984) reported that a 30 per cent reduction in the prison population produced a 60 per cent reduction in assaults on other inmates, particularly in male prisons.

- Laboratory studies have also produced mixed results. For example, Freedman *et al.* (1972) found that crowding increased aggression (defined as the severity of sentences recommended for people found guilty in tape-recorded trials) in all-male groups. However, the *opposite* effect was found for all-female groups, and there was no significant effect of crowding in mixed groups. In a study of four- and five-year-olds, crowding appeared to *reduce* aggressive behaviour (Loo, 1972).

- According to Freedman (1975), crowding by itself has neither good nor bad effects. Rather, it serves to *intensify the individual's typical reactions to the situation, either positive or negative*.

Temperature

Riots in the USA and elsewhere during the 1960s and early 1970s were attributed by the media of the time to (amongst other factors) the *ambient temperature*. Prolonged exposure to temperatures in the high 80s and low 90s Fahrenheit was seen as shortening tempers, increasing irritability, and generally setting the stage for the outbreak of collective violence (Baron, 1977). These large 'common-sense' and informal observations are supported by more systematic obseration, which has shown that a large proportion of the serious violence in the late 1960s in major American cities occurred during hot summer months in heat-wave or near heat-wave conditions (Goranson & King, 1970; US Riots Commission, 1968). Increases in ambient temperature are also linked with increases in domestic violence (Cohn, 1993) and violent suicides (Maes *et al.*, 1994). However, there is no correlation between rape and temperature (Rotton, 1993).

Griffitt (1970) and Griffit & Veitch (1971) also found evidence for the temperature–aggression link. Under uncomfortably hot conditions, people become more irritable, more prone to outbursts of temper, and more negative in their reactions to others, compared with people in comfortably cool conditions. However, Baron (1972) found that higher temperatures (91–95 Fahrenheit) actually *reduced* aggression amongst both angered and non-angered participants. It seemed that participants were motivated more by trying to end the experiment as quickly as possible (so they could escape) than aggressing against the confederate who had angered them. These, and other findings, suggest that the relationship between temperature and aggression is not a straightforward, linear one.

Key STUDY

Box 7.10 The curvilinear relationship between temperature and aggression

Baron & Bell (1975) reasoned that two factors might strongly affect the dominance of participants' tendancy to aggress: (a) the degree of provocation by the confederate (see Box 7.8, page 74); and (b) exposure to an aggressive model. The combination of these two factors would increase the probability of aggression to quite high levels. Under conditions of high provocation *and* exposure to an aggressive model, high ambient temperature would be most likely to cause aggression.

However, this prediction was *not* supported. Regardless of exposure to the model, high temperatures increased later aggression by non-angered participants, but actually *inhibited* aggression in those who had been provoked. In post-experimental questionnaires and debriefing sessions, participants exposed to prior provocation and high temperatures said that their predominant wish was for the experiment to end (as in Baron's, 1972, experiment: see text above).

Perhaps, then, the crucial psychological process underlying the impact of temperature on aggression is *not* increased arousal (as previously thought), but the degree of *induced negative affect* (level of unpleasant feelings). In this case, trying to *minimise the discomfort* becomes the dominant response, rather than aggression. This would account for the observed reduction in aggression. In the absence of provocation, the negative effect induced by high temperatures may have produced annoyance and irritation, making aggression more dominant. This suggests a *curvilinear*

relationship between temperature and aggressing, as shown in Figure 7.6.

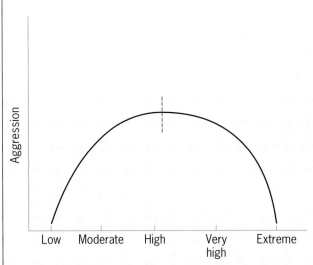

Level of negative affect experienced by potential aggressors

Figure 7.6 *Hypothetical relationship between negative affect (unpleasant feelings) and aggression. At first, aggression increases as negative affect arises. Beyond some determinable point, however, further increments in negative affect lead to decreasing aggression (From Baron, 1977)*

Several experimental studies have tested the proposed curvilinear relationship (e.g. Baron & Bell, 1976), and the results are generally consistent with it (Halpern, 1995). As predicted, unpleasantly *low* temperatures have similar effects to uncomfortable heat (e.g. Bell & Baron, 1977, cited in Baron, 1997).

Causes relating to situational conditions

Alcohol and other drugs

It is popularly believed that 'the conscience is soluble in alcohol', that is, learned inhibitions against expressing aggression seem to be among the more common aspects of conscience that are ignored when under the influence of alcohol (Taylor *et al*, 1994). It is often assumed that underlying this *disinhibition* is a physiological process, in which alcohol reduces the normal control exercised by the brain's cortex over the more primitive brain areas. Another form of disinhibition is *deindividuation* (see pages 70–73). According to Hogg & Vaughan (1998), the link between alcohol and aggression seems well established, and experimental studies suggest that a *causal* relationship operates.

Box 7.11   The effects of alcohol and social pressure on aggression

Taylor & Sears (1988) assigned male students to either an alcohol or a placebo (a ginger-ale drink disguised with the taste of vodka) condition. They were then put into a competitive situation with another participant, in which their response times were measured. In each pair, the slower responder on a given trial received an electric shock from the opponent. The shock intensity could vary, and was selected by each person *before* each trial began. In fact, the opponent's shock setting, and the win/loss frequency (50 per cent), were determined by the experimenter. In four sequential blocks of trials (see Figure 7.7), social pressure was exerted: participants were encouraged to give high intensity shocks by a watching confederate.

As Figure 7.7 illustrates, there was an *interaction* between alcohol and social pressure. Participants who had consumed alcohol were more susceptible to social pressure, and continued to give high-intensity shocks even after the pressure was later withdrawn.

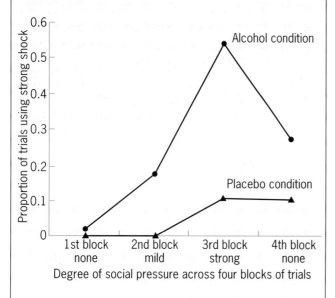

Figure 7.7 *The effects of alcohol and social pressure on men's willingness to deliver electric shocks to a passive opponent (From Taylor* et al., *1994)*

In Taylor and Sears' study, the opponent always behaved non-aggressively, posing no threat or attack. The results showed, therefore, that alcohol can *increase* aggression even in response to instigators that do not involve threat, attack or frustration. Statistics for real-life situations are suggestive, but not clear-cut, in this regard. Alcohol consumption *is* disproportionately associated with physical violence. For example, intoxicated offenders commit 60 per cent of murders in the USA, as well as comparably high proportions of other violent crimes, such as rape (including date rape), robbery, assault, domestic violence, and child abuse (Lisak & Roth, 1988; Steele & Southwick, 1985).

However, the causal pathways are complex (Hogg & Vaughan, 1998). For example, stress and lifestyle factors appear to contribute to high levels of *both* alcohol consumption and aggression. In other words, alcohol does not cause aggression – they are merely *correlated*. Also, violent people tend to drink a lot of alcohol, and at least as much as that which actually promotes violence (Bradbury, 1984).

Although *marijuana* is a disinhibiting drug (like alcohol), experimental studies have shown that it tends to *reduce* aggression (Taylor *et al.*, 1994). Neither chronic nor occasional use of marijuana increases aggressive behaviour (Abel, 1977). Both PCP ('angel dust') and crack cocaine *do* seem to trigger violent reactions, but systematic behavioural research into their effects is still in its infancy (Taylor *et al.*, 1994).

CONCLUSIONS

This chapter has examined the nature of aggression and several social psychological theories of its causes. Research studies suggest that all of the theories can claim some degree of experimental support, although this is stronger for some of them than others. Research into the effects of environmental stressors was also considered. Although these stressors are associated with aggression, the precise mechanisms by which they exert their effects are, for at least some of them, more complex than might be imagined.

Summary

- Different types of aggression include **anti-social**, **sanctioned** and **pro-social**. Aggression always involves some behaviour intended to harm another person. **Violence** is an extreme form of aggression.

- The **frustration–aggression hypothesis** proposes that aggression is always a consequence of frustration, and frustration always leads to some form of aggression. However, neither of these proposals is true.

- According to **cue-arousal theory**, frustration produces **anger**. However, this results in aggression only if there are a **readiness** to act aggressively and **environmental cues** associated with aggressive behaviour or a frustrator.

- Experimental tests of cue–arousal theory measure aggression when participants are frustrated in the presence/absence of aggressive cues, such as guns (the **weapons effect**).

- **Excitation-transfer theory** sees the arousal–aggression relationship as a sequence. However, the existence of 'unspecific' 'neutral' arousal has been questioned. The **cognitive approach** sees anger and aggression as parallel processes.

- **Social learning theory** sees aggressive behaviours as being learned through **reinforcement** and **imitation** (closely related to **observational learning**). Aggressive tendencies can be strengthened by **vicarious reinforcement**.

- **Deindividuation** is a state of affairs in a group where members do not pay attention to other individuals as individuals and, correspondingly, the members do not feel that they are being singled out by others.

- According to Diener, deindividuated people are prevented from forming an awareness of themselves as separate individuals, and from monitoring their own behaviours. This occurs when immersed in a group, resulting in certain self-regulatory capacities being lost.

- It is possible to distinguish between **public** and **private self-awareness**, and aggressiveness can increase through a loss of either type of self-awareness. However, this happens indirectly, either through inducing deindividuation or being made more susceptible to behavioural cues.

- Whilst the concept of deindividuation is supported by evidence, some findings are open to alternative explanations. Also, under certain circumstances, deindividuation can increase **affiliation**.

- According to the **social constructionist** approach, behaviour is aggressive or non-aggressive as judged to be so, either by an observer or actor. Calling a behaviour 'aggressive' involves an **evaluation** of it.

- Causes of aggression relating to the physical environment include **noise**, **crowding** and **temperature**. However, the relationship between all of these environmental stressors and aggression is not straightforward.

- Causes of aggression relating to situational conditions include **aggressive cues**, **heightened arousal**, and **alcohol** and other **drugs**. The relationship between alcohol and aggression seems well established, and may even be causal. With other drugs, the relationship is less clear-cut.

Essay Questions

1 Describe and evaluate research relating to any **two** social psychological theories of aggression. *(24 marks)*

2 Discuss research into the effects of environmental stressors on aggressive behaviour. *(24 marks)*

WEB ADDRESSES

http://www.socialpsychology.org/social.htm#violence
http://www.socialpsychology.org/social.htm#generalviolence
http://www.noctrl.edu/~ajomuel/crow/topic.aggression.htm

8 Altruism and Bystander Behaviour

INTRODUCTION AND OVERVIEW

In August 1999, under the heading 'A crime to shame the nation', *The Mirror* newspaper published the photograph shown in Figure 8.1 (see below). The journalist wrote:

> 'A choirgirl of 13 was gang raped by four youths on a sunny afternoon – and no one did a thing to help. The innocent child was attacked on a path overlooked on three sides by a housing estate. People heard her screaming, but not one made a move to step in or call police. Yesterday, detectives described the outrage in south London as a "new low". The girl's mother said: "I can't understand it. How can these people live with themselves?"' (Edwards, 1999)

Contrast the above with a newspaper report in which a book-dealer on a business trip from Bristol to London, was taken 194 miles to York after he helped to carry a woman's luggage on to her train. He was trapped when the doors locked automatically. As the passenger remarked:

> 'Nobody was helping this poor woman, so I gave her a hand. I couldn't believe my eyes when the automatic doors closed and a few seconds later the train started moving ... I only stopped at the station for a cup of coffee and I ended up at the other end of the country' (reported in O'Neill, 1996).

These two accounts are probably the tip of an iceberg of incidents that actually find their way into our national newspapers. We may be appalled at the behaviour of people in the first incident, and admire the individual's behaviour in the second. This chapter examines explanations and research studies relating to human altruism and bystander behaviour. The issue of *cultural differences* in pro-social behaviour is discussed in Chapter 30, in the context of moral reasoning.

Box 8.1 The tragic case of Kitty Genovese

At 3.20 a.m., 23 March 1964, 28-year-old Kitty Genovese was fatally wounded by a knife-wielding stalker close to her apartment in the Queens district of New York. Miss Genovese's screams of 'Oh my God, he stabbed me!' and 'Please help me!' woke up 38 of her neighbours in the apartment block. Their lights went on, and they opened their windows to see what was happening. One neighbour even turned *out* his light and pulled a chair to the window to get a better view of the disturbance. As Miss Genovese lay dying, her attacker fled, only to return to sexually assault her and stab her again. Despite her shouts for help, it was not until 3.50 a.m., half an hour after the attack had begun, that the police were made aware as a result of a neighbour's telephone call. When police later questioned the witnesses, they were unable to explain their inaction.

Figure 8.1 *One of the consequences of bystander apathy*

EXPLAINING 'BYSTANDER APATHY': THE DECISION MODEL OF BYSTANDER INTERVENTION

According to Milgram (cited in Dowd, 1984), Kitty Genovese's murder:

> '... touched on a fundamental issue of the human social condition. If we need help, will those around us stand around and let us be destroyed, or will they come to our aid?'.

The first researchers to investigate systematically the circumstances in which bystanders are and are not likely to intervene to help others were Latané & Darley (1968). At the time of Miss Genovese's murder, America's commentators attributed her neighbours' indifference to a cold and apathetic (urban) society:

> 'It can be assumed ... that their apathy was indeed one of the big-city variety. It is almost a matter of psychological survival, if one is surrounded and pressed by millions of people, to prevent them from constantly impinging on you, and the only way to do this is to ignore them as often as possible. Indifference to one's neighbour and his troubles is a conditioned reflex in New York as it is in other big cities' (Rosenthal, 1964).

However, Latané and Darley showed that the reasons for Miss Genovese's neighbours' apathy were *not* quite as straightforward as this. As a result of their research, they proposed a five-step decision model of bystander intervention.

The model suggests that before a person helps a stranger, five decisions must be made. First, a situation requiring help must be *noticed*. If a situation has not been noticed, then intervention cannot occur. Second, the event that has been noticed must be *defined* as a situation in which help is needed. If the decision that help is needed is made, then, in the third step, the potential helper must *assume personal responsibility* for helping. If this occurs, the potential helper must then *select a way to help*. If a way is selected, the potential helper must decide whether to *implement it*.

The decision model represents a logical sequence of steps, such that a 'no' answer at any step results in the bystander not intervening, with help only being given when a 'yes' answer has been given in all five steps.

Defining the situation as one where help is needed

Latané and Darley have shown that we are less likely to define a situation as being dangerous if other people are present, a phenomenon they called *pluralistic ignorance*.

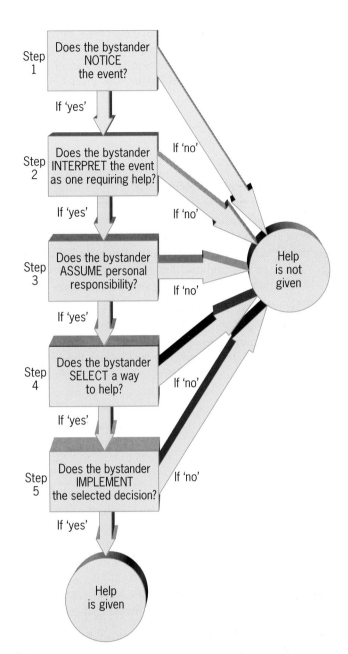

Figure 8.2 *Latané and Darley's five-step decision model of bystander intervention and non-intervention (Based on Schroeder et al., 1995)*

Box 8.2   Some experimental demonstrations of pluralistic ignorance

- **Latané & Darley (1968):** Participants were taken to a room to fill out a questionnaire either alone or with others. After a while, steam, which resembled smoke, began to pour out through a wall vent. Participants reacted most quickly when they were alone. With others present, they often failed to react, even though the steam was so thick it was difficult to see the questionnaire! In Latané and Darley's words, the participants:

'... continued doggedly working on the questionnaire and waving the fumes away from their faces. They coughed, rubbed their eyes, and opened the window – but they did not report the smoke'.

- **Latané & Rodin (1969):** Participants sitting in a room waiting to be called for an experiment heard a voice from an adjoining room (actually the voice of a female experimenter) cry out and moan for nearly a minute. Participants were significantly slower to respond and offer help when they were with other people than when they were alone.

- **Clark & Word (1974):** In a similar experiment to Latané and Rodin's, a 'workman' carried a ladder and venetian blinds past a room in which participants were sitting. Shortly afterwards, a loud crash was heard. Again, the more people there were in the room, the less likely help was to be given, *unless* the workman made it clear what had happened.

Interviews conducted with participants after the experiments described in Box 8.2 indicated that one reason for people's failure to help was *social influence*. Many participants indicated that they had looked at, and tended to follow, the reactions of others. Since these others were trying (and evidently succeeding) to appear calm, participants defined the situation as 'safe'. Thus, each participant influenced others into thinking there was no cause for alarm.

Another reason for failing to help is the potential *embarrassment* of incorrectly defining a situation. One person snatching money from another *might* be a potential 'mugging', but it may also be the result of a harmless bet between two friends. The fear of making a social blunder, and being subject to ridicule if a situation is ambiguous, also deters people from helping (Pennington *et al.*, 1999).

Interestingly, Latané & Rodin (1969) found that when two friends were placed in an ambiguous situation, their response to a potential emergency was just as quick as when either was alone, and much quicker than when two *strangers* were together or when a naïve participant was with a 'stooge' instructed *not* to respond. Presumably, with people we do not expect to see again, we are deterred from acting because we will not have the opportunity to explain ourselves if our

interpretations are incorrect (Shotland & Heinold, 1985).

There is, however, evidence indicating that when an emergency *clearly* requires bystander intervention, help is much more likely to be given, even when a large number of people witness the emergency (see below). For example, Clark & Word (1974) staged a realistic 'accident' (in which a 'technician' supposedly received a severe electric shock) in a room next to one in which individual participants or participants in groups of two or five were completing a questionnaire. All participants responded and went to the 'technician's' assistance.

Assuming personal responsibility or diffusing responsibility?

Whilst some witnesses to Kitty Genovese's murder claimed they believed the attack to be a 'lover's tiff', it is doubtful if pluralistic ignorance was operating, since her screams when the attacker returned would have made the situation unambiguous (if, after the first attack, it was not already).

Key **STUDY**

Box 8.3   An emergency in the laboratory

In a laboratory simulation of an emergency, Darley & Latané (1968) led students, who were in separate cubicles, to believe they were participating in a group discussion of the problems of living in a high-pressure urban environment. To avoid any embarrassment and preserve anonymity, the students were told that the discussion would take place over an intercom system, and that only the person whose microphone was switched on could be heard. The students were also told that each would talk for two minutes and then comment on what the others had said.

Some students were told that there were five others in the discussion group, some that there were two others, and some that there was only one other. In actual fact, the other 'participants' were pre-recorded tapes played through the intercom system. Early on in the 'discussion', one of the 'participants' hesitantly admitted that he had epilepsy, and that the anxiety and stress of urban living made him prone to seizures. Later on, the 'participant' had a 'seizure', began to speak incoherently, and stammered out a request for help before lapsing into silence.

As Figure 8.3 shows, almost all (85 per cent) participants left the room to offer help when they believed themselves to be the only other person. However, when they believed there were witnesses other than themselves, they were much less likely to leave the room, and the likelihood of helping lessened the more witnesses there were. Also, participants responded more quickly when they believed themselves to be the only other person present.

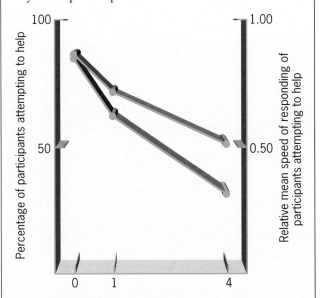

Figure 8.3 *Percentage of participants attempting to help (by leaving their room to look for the 'victim' within five minutes) as a function of the number of others believed to be present, and the relative mean speed of responding of participants attempting to help (Adapted from Darley & Latané, 1968)*

Darley and Latané called the phenomenon they observed in their experiment *diffusion of responsibility*, suggesting that, as probably happened in the Kitty Genovese murder, people reason that somebody else should, and probably will, offer assistance. The consequence of no one feeling responsible is that the victim is not helped, and the more people present, the less likely it is that any one of them will give assistance (the *inverse law of helping behaviour*).

When participants in Darley & Latané's (1968) experiment were interviewed about their behaviour, they were actually *not* indifferent, callous or apathetic to the student's plight. Indeed, Darley and Latané reported that:

'If anything they seemed more emotionally aroused than the [participants] who reported the emergency',

and they typically asked the experimenter who entered the room whether the victim was being taken care of. Darley and Latané's explanation for the participants' behaviour was that they were caught in a conflict

between a fear of making fools of themselves and ruining the experiment by over-reacting (the anonymous nature of the experiment had previously been stressed as important by the experimenter), and their own guilt and shame at doing nothing.

Piliavin *et al.* (1981) have pointed out that Darley and Latané's experiment actually shows a *dissolution* rather than a diffusion of responsibility. In Darley and Latané's experiment, participants could not observe other people's behaviours and 'reasoned' that someone must have intervened. In other situations, responsibility is accepted by the participant but shared by all witnesses. The term diffusion best applies in these circumstances, whilst dissolution is a better descriptor for what happened in Darley and Latané's experiment.

Whether this distinction is important or not is debatable. What is important is the reliability with which the inhibitory effects of the presence of others on helping behaviour occurs. Latané *et al.* (1981) reviewed over 50 studies, conducted in both the laboratory and the natural environment, in which a variety of 'emergencies' were staged. In almost all of them (but see page 82), the *bystander effect* was observed.

Choosing a way to help: the role of competence

Related to diffusion of responsibility, and something which may interact with it, is a bystander's *competence* to intervene and offer help. When bystanders have the *necessary skills* (such as a knowledge of first aid: 'Let me through, I'm a doctor'), helping is more likely. However, in the presence of others, one or more of whom we believe to be better equipped to help, diffusion of responsibility is *increased*. Thus, the inhibitory effects of other people may not necessarily indicate bystander apathy – non-helpers may sincerely believe that someone else is more likely, or better qualified in some way, to help (Schroeder *et al.*, 1995).

Key STUDY

Box 8.4 Proximity and competence

Bickman (1971) replicated Darley & Latané's (1968) 'seizure' experiment (see Box 8.3), but manipulated the participants' beliefs about the victim's proximity. Those who believed that another person was as close to the victim as they were (in the same building), and equally capable of helping, showed diffusion of responsibility and were less likely to help than those who believed they were alone. However, when participants believed that the other person was in another building, and therefore less able to help, they helped as much as those who believed they were alone.

An evaluation of the decision model

Schroeder *et al.* (1995) argue that Latané and Darley's model provides a valuable framework for understanding why bystander non-intervention occurs. Moreover, whilst the model was originally designed to explain intervention in emergency situations, it has been successfully applied in other situations ranging from preventing someone from drinking and driving to deciding whether to donate a kidney to a relative. However, the model does not tell us *why* 'no' decisions are taken at any of the five steps, particularly once the situation has been defined as an emergency. Additionally, it focuses on why people *don't* help, and pays much less attention to why they *do*.

Also, whilst the presence of others is a powerful and well-established factor influencing bystander behaviour, other factors have been shown to increase or decrease helping behaviour. In Piliavin *et al.*'s (1969) study, a stooge pretended to collapse in a subway carriage. Sometimes the stooge carried a cane, and sometimes a bottle in a brown paper bag (and wore a jacket which smelled strongly of alcohol). Help was much more likely to be given to the 'victim' with the cane (helped 90 per cent of the time within 70 seconds, compared with 20 per cent for the other victim).

In one of Piliavin & Piliavin's (1972) experiments, the 'victim' who 'collapsed' bit off a capsule of red dye resembling blood, and let it run down his chin. This reduced the helping rate to 60 per cent, with those who witnessed the event being likely to enlist the help of others whom they believed to be more competent. In another experiment, Piliavin and Piliavin studied the effect of the victim having an ugly facial birthmark. They found that helping dropped from 86 per cent when the victim was not disfigured to 61 per cent when he was.

Box 8.5   Some situational and individual differences in bystander behaviour

- According to Amato (1983), help is less likely to be given in *urban* than *rural* environments. This is because the conditions that discourage bystander intervention (such as the situation's ambiguity) are more likely to be met in cities than rural areas. Amato studied 55 cities and towns in Australia selected on the basis of size and geographical isolation. Using a variety of measures of helping behaviour, Amato found that city size was negatively correlated with all but one measure of helping. A population of about 20,000 was the point at which helping behaviour was inhibited. If the findings from these Australian cities and towns

generalise to Britain, then helping behaviour would be expected to be an infrequently occurring phenomenon even in some smaller towns.

- People are more likely to help when put in a *good mood* than when mood is neutral or negative (Brown & Smart, 1991).

- In Europe and America, *husband and wife disputes* are considered to be private affairs. In Mediterranean and Latin cultures, however, anyone can intervene in a dispute between *any* two people (Wade & Tavris, 1993).

- People who feel a *moral obligation* to a victim, have deeply held *moral values* or personal feelings for the victim, and/or *empathy* with the victim, are more likely to act as helpers (Dovidio *et al.*, 1990).

- People with a *high need for approval* from others are more likely to help than people low on this need (Deutsch & Lamberti, 1986).

- People who score high on measures of *fear of being embarrassed* in social situations are less likely to offer help (McGovern, 1976).

- *Women* are more likely than men to *receive* help (Eagly & Crowley, 1986), and victims who are similar in appearance to the potential helper are more likely to receive help than victims dissimilar in appearance (Hensley, 1981). Interestingly, most victims themselves do not actually like to ask for help and feel they will be viewed as being less competent if they accept it (De Paulo & Fisher, 1981). In a *reverse bystander effect*, victims are generally less likely to *seek* help as the number of potential helpers increases (Williams & Williams, 1983).

Piliavin *et al.*'s research is also interesting in terms of the operation of a diffusion of responsibility. Earlier (see page 81) it was noted that in *almost* all studies looking at the effects of the presence of others on helping behaviour, an inhibitory effect has been found. However, Piliavin *et al.* (1969) found that help was just as likely to be given on a crowded subway as on a relatively empty one. To explain this, Piliavin offered an alternative model of the conditions under which help is and is not likely to be given.

AROUSAL: COST–REWARD MODEL

Although originally proposed as an explanation for the results obtained in their 'subway studies' (see earlier text), Piliavin *et al.* (1981) and Dovidio *et al.* (1991) subsequently revised and expanded this model to cover both emergency *and* non-emergency helping behaviour.

The model emphasises the interaction between two sets of factors. The first are *situational*, *bystander* and *victim characteristics*, along with what Piliavin and his colleagues call *'we-ness'*. The second are *cognitive* and *affective* reactions. Situational characteristics include things like a victim asking for help rather than not asking for help. Bystander characteristics include both *trait* factors (such as the potential helper being an empathic person) and *state* factors (such as the potential helper being in a positive or negative mood). Victim characteristics include things like the victim's appearance and other factors identified in Box 8.5 (see page 82). 'We-ness' refers to what Piliavin *et al.* call:

'... a sense of connectedness or the categorisation of another person as a member of one's own group'.

The various characteristics produce certain *levels of arousal*. Whether or not helping behaviour occurs depends on *how* the arousal is interpreted or *attributed*. For example, if it can be attributed to the victim's distress rather than to other factors, helping is more likely to occur because the arousal is unpleasant and the bystander is motivated to reduce it. However, the exact way in which arousal is reduced depends upon the *rewards and costs* involved in helping and not helping. Piliavin *et al.* suggest that bystanders weigh the costs and benefits of intervening, and the result of this *hedonic calculus* determines whether or not they help.

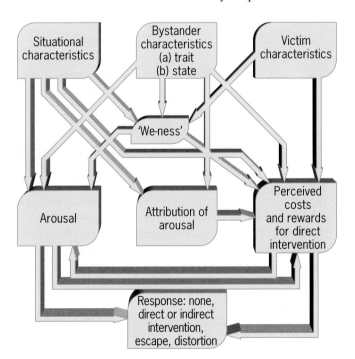

Figure 8.4 *Piliavin* et al.*'s alternative to the decision model proposed by Latané and Darley. The model emphasises the interaction between the potential helper, the situation and the victim, and the cognitive and affective reactions of the potential helper (From Piliavin* et al., *1981)*

In the case of helping, rewards include enhanced self-esteem, praise from others, and even financial reward. In the case of not helping, rewards include time and the freedom to go about our normal business (Bierhoff & Klein, 1988). Costs of helping include lost time, effort, physical danger, embarrassment, the disruption of ongoing activities, and psychological aversion (as in the case of a victim who is bleeding or drunk). The costs of not helping include guilt, others' disapproval, and cognitive and/or emotional discomfort associated with knowing that a person is suffering.

When the costs of helping are low and the costs of not helping are low, the likelihood of intervention will be fairly high, although bystanders' behaviours will vary according to individual differences and the norms operating in a particular situation.

> **Box 8.6 The application of Piliavin** *et al.***'s model to some of the data reported by Piliavin** *et al.* **(1969) and Piliavin & Piliavin (1972)**
>
> 1 **Circumstances:** The costs of helping are low (e.g. there is little danger to the self) and the costs of not helping are high (e.g. one may receive criticism for not helping).
>
> **Prediction:** Direct intervention and helping are very likely.
>
> **Finding:** A person carrying a cane who collapses is helped 90 per cent of the time within 70 seconds.
>
> 2 **Circumstances:** The costs of helping are high (e.g. the situation is dangerous or the person seems very strange) and the costs of not helping are high (something needs to be done).
>
> **Prediction:** Indirect helping, such as calling for an ambulance, will be fairly likely to occur.
>
> **Finding:** People are more likely to get somebody else to help when they see a person who collapses with 'blood' running down his chin.
>
> 3 **Circumstances:** The costs of helping are high (e.g. the person could be violent) and the costs of not helping are low ('who would blame me if I didn't help?').
>
> **Prediction:** The likelihood of helping is very low.
>
> **Finding:** People are less likely to help a 'victim' who collapses smelling of alcohol and carrying a bottle in a brown paper bag.

Whilst arousal and helping are often only *correlated*, the model clearly sees the former as *causing* the latter. According to Dovidio *et al.* (1991), evidence indicates that emotional reactions to other people's distress play an important role in motivating helping. The model proposes that bystanders will choose the response that most rapidly and completely reduces the arousal, incurring as few costs as possible. So, the emotional component provides the motivation to do *something*, whilst the cognitive component determines what the most effective response will be. As far as costs are concerned, what is high cost for one person might be low cost for another, and costs may even differ for the same person from one situation to another or from one occasion to another.

Piliavin *et al.*'s original model was subsequently elaborated to take account of the role played by other factors, such as bystander personality and mood, the clarity of the situation, characteristics of the victim, the relationships between the victim and potential helpers, and attributions made by potential helpers of the victim's deservingness. Not surprisingly, many of these variables interact, and contribute to how aroused the bystander is and the perceived costs and rewards for direct intervention.

'Personal costs' versus 'empathy costs'

Two costs associated with not helping are *personal costs* (such as self-blame and public disapproval) and *empathy costs* (such as knowing that the victim is continuing to suffer). According to Dovidio *et al.* (1991):

'In general ... costs for *not* helping affect intervention primarily when the costs for helping are low'.

Although *indirect helping* becomes more likely as the costs for helping increase (as in serious emergencies), indirect helping is relatively infrequent, possibly because it is difficult for bystanders to 'pull away' from such situations in order to seek other people to assist (Schroeder *et al.*, 1995).

Box 8.7   Cognitive reinterpretation and bystander behaviour

The most common (and positively effective) way of resolving the high-cost-for-helping/high-cost-for-not-helping dilemma (as shown in (2) in Box 8.6) is *cognitive reinterpretation*. This can take one of three forms, namely:

- redefining the situation as one *not* requiring help;
- diffusing responsibility;
- denigrating (blaming) the victim.

Each of these has the effect of reducing the perceived costs of not helping. However, cognitive reinterpretation does not mean that bystanders are uncaring. Rather, it is the fact that they do care that creates the dilemma in the first place.

Impulsive helping

Piliavin *et al.*'s model suggests that help is least likely to be given in high-cost (life-threatening) situations. In some situations, however, people act in almost reflexive ways, irrespective of the personal consequences and the number of others present (Anderson, 1974). Such examples of *impulsive helping* appear to occur in (but are not limited to) situations which are clear and realistic, and in which the potential helper has some sort of prior involvement with the victim.

As Piliavin *et al.* (1981) have noted:

'Not coincidentally, [these] factors ... have also been demonstrated to be related to greater levels of bystander arousal'.

Piliavin *et al.* argue that when people encounter emergency situations they cannot avoid, they become 'flooded' with intense arousal and this produces a narrowing of attention which is directed towards the victim's plight. In their view, cost considerations become peripheral and not attended to and, more speculatively:

'There may be an evolutionary basis for ... impulsive helping'.

Figure 8.5 *When Hurricane Hortense hit Puerto Rico in 1996, at least eight people were killed in flash floods and mudslides. Here, José Louis de Leon and Miguel Rodriguez brave the flood to attach a rope to the home of the Gomez family, and bring one-year-old Cassandra, her three brothers and sister and father, to the safety of dry land*

BYSTANDER BEHAVIOUR: UNIVERSAL EGOISM OR EMPATHY–ALTRUISM?

One conclusion that might be drawn from studies on bystander behaviour is that we are an essentially selfish species, motivated to minimise costs and behave in ways that cause us least displeasure. An *altruistic act* is one performed to benefit others and which has no expectation of benefit or gain for the benefactor (and may even involve some degree of cost). So, is a responsive bystander's behaviour ever motivated by a *genuine* wish to benefit others?

Universal egoism

Universal egoism is the view that people are fundamentally selfish, a dominant view in the social sciences which sees altruism as an impossibility (Dovidio, 1995). There are many examples of apparently altruistic behaviour in non-humans. For example, in certain songbirds an individual which detects a predator signals this by making a vocal 'alarm call', which causes those in the immediate vicinity to form a flock (for other examples of such apparent altruism, see Chapter 37).

Box 8.8 The paradox of altruism

From a Darwinian perspective, altruistic behaviour is *not adaptive*, because it reduces the likelihood of an individual who raises an alarm surviving (the predator is likely to be attracted to the signal's source). According to sociobiologists, this *'paradox of altruism'* can be resolved if apparently altruistic behaviour is viewed as *selfish* behaviour 'in disguise'.

Sociobiologists argue that an individual animal should be seen as a *set of genes* rather than a separate 'bounded organism', and that these *'selfish genes'* (Dawkins, 1976) aim to secure their own survival. For a detailed account of how this can be achieved – notable examples include Hamilton's, 1964, *kin selection theory* and Trivers', 1971, *delayed reciprocal altruism theory* – see Chapter 37.

Theories that explain the apparently altruistic behaviour of non-humans can, at least for sociobiologists, be applied to humans (Wilson, 1978). Piliavin *et al.*'s model is clearly one form of universal egoism, in that it sees the decision making relating to probable rewards and costs as ultimately being concerned with arriving at a course of action that is really directed towards *self-benefit*.

Empathy–altruism

The *empathy–altruism hypothesis* accepts that much of what we do is egoistic, including much that we do for others. However, this hypothesis argues that in some circumstances we feel *empathic concern* when people are in difficulty, and we help in order to relieve the distress of *others* rather than our own emotional distress (Roker *et al.*, 1998). The emotions associated with empathic concern

include sympathy, compassion, and tenderness, and can be distinguished from the more self-oriented emotions of discomfort, anxiety and upset (which corresponds to the distinction between personal and empathic costs for not helping: see page 84). Whilst personal distress produces an egoistic desire to reduce our own distress, empathic concern produces an altruistic desire to reduce others' distress, and these are *qualitatively* different.

According to Darley (1991), who is clearly a universal (or at least a Western capitalist) egoist:

'In the United States and perhaps in all advanced capitalistic societies, it is generally accepted that the true and basic motive for human action is self-interest. It is the primary motivation, and is the one from which other motives derive. Thus it is the only 'real' motivation, a fact that some bemoan but most accept ... To suggest that human actions could arise for other purposes is to court accusations of naïvety or insufficiently deep or realistic analysis.'

BIOLOGICAL AND PSYCHOLOGICAL ALTRUISM

Whilst there is some plausibility in sociobiological accounts of altruism, sociobiologists have failed to make the distinction between *biological* (or *evolutionary*) *altruism* and *psychological* (or *vernacular*) *altruism*. Biological altruism is the kind displayed by, for example, birds and rabbits when they give alarm signals. We would not normally attribute their behaviours to altruistic 'motives' or 'intentions' (it would be *anthropomorphic* to do so). Rather, such behaviour is better seen as part of the animal's biologically determined behavioural repertoire (Sober, 1992).

Psychological altruism is displayed by the higher mammals, in particular primates and especially humans. Whether humans are capable of biological altruism has been the subject of much debate. For Brown (1988):

'Human altruism goes beyond the confines of Darwinism because human evolution is not only biological in nature but also cultural and, indeed, in recent times primarily cultural.'

However, biological altruism *may* be triggered under very specific conditions. With impulsive helping (see page 84), people react in a rapid and almost reflexive way in certain conditions (an example being a natural disaster such as an earthquake or a flood: see Figure 8.5, page 84).

Impulsive helping is generally unaffected by social context or the potential costs of intervention (Piliavin *et al.*, 1981). In clear and realistic situations, especially those involving friends, relatives or acquaintances, the bystander is (as noted previously) most concerned with the costs for the victim of not receiving help. This is very close to Sober's definition of evolutionary altruism. Our ability to carry out sophisticated reasoning (as in psychological altruism), along with more primitive, non-cognitive, biological mechanisms, may permit us to perform a range of altruistic behaviours well beyond those of other species (Schroeder *et al.*, 1995).

CONCLUSIONS

Research into human altruism and bystander behaviour has told us much about the conditions under which we are likely to behave (or not behave) pro-socially towards others. Nearly forty years after the brutal murder of Kitty Genovese, we seem to be closer to understanding bystander intervention and apathy.

Summary

- Latané and Darley were the first to systematically investigate the circumstances under which bystanders are/are not likely to intervene to help others. Their interest was stimulated by the murder of Kitty Genovese in front of 38 witnesses, none of whom did anything to help her.

- Latané and Darley proposed a five-step **decision model** of bystander intervention. According to this, a situation must first be **noticed** before it can be **defined** as one requiring help. The potential helper must then **assume personal responsibility** and **select a way to help** before **implementing it**. This is a logical sequence of steps, such that a negative decision at any time leads to non-intervention.

- In other people's presence, we are less likely to define a situation as dangerous, and hence less likely to act (**pluralistic ignorance**). Potential **embarrassment** and fear of **ridicule** for making a social blunder in an ambiguous situation also deter people from helping. However, when an emergency **clearly** requires bystander intervention, help is much more likely to be given even when many witnesses are present.

- In the presence of others, however, people often believe that another person will act. As a result of this **diffusion of responsibility**, help is not given. The more people that are present, the less likely any one of them is to offer assistance (the **inverse law of helping behaviour**). Helping also depends on **competence**. When bystanders have the necessary skills, they are likely to respond.

- The decision model has also been successfully applied to non-emergency situations. However, it fails to say why 'no' decisions are taken, and concen-

trates on why people **don't** help rather than why they do.

- Factors other than the presence of others also influence helping behaviour. **Situational factors** include type of environment (urban versus rural), whilst **individual factors** include mood.

- Piliavin *et al.*'s **arousal: cost–reward model** emphasises the interaction between (a) situational, bystander and victim characteristics, plus 'we-ness', and (b) cognitive and affective reactions. These characteristics produce **arousal**. How this arousal is attributed determines whether or not helping occurs. Exactly how arousal is reduced depends on the **hedonic calculus** of the rewards and costs for helping or not helping.

- **Rewards for helping** include enhanced self-esteem and praise from others. **Not helping** brings rewards such as being free to carry on with one's normal behaviour. **Costs of helping** include lost time and physical danger. **Costs of not helping** include guilt, others' disapproval and the discomfort of knowing someone is suffering.

- Two costs associated with not helping are **personal** and **empathy costs**. These become relevant when the costs of helping are low. As the costs increase, so **indirect helping** becomes more likely but remains relatively infrequent.

- The high-cost-for-helping/high-cost-for-not-helping dilemma can be resolved through **cognitive reinterpretation**. This can take the form of **redefining the situation** as one not requiring help, **diffusing responsibility**, or **blaming the victim**. All of these reduce the costs of not helping.

- The model predicts that helping is least likely in high cost (life-threatening) situations. However, **impulsive helping** sometimes occurs regardless of personal consequences and the presence of others.

- **Universal egoism** sees people as being fundamentally selfish and unable to perform truly **altruistic acts**. According to **sociobiologists**, all apparently altruistic behaviour is really **selfish** behaviour in disguise.

- Piliavin *et al.*'s model is a form of universal egoism, since the cost/reward analysis is ultimately concerned with **self-benefit**. By contrast, the empathy–altruism hypothesis acknowledges that we sometimes feel **empathic concern** for others' distress.

- Sociobiology fails to distinguish between **biological/evolutionary altruism** and **psychological/vernacular altruism**. The former is seen in various non-humans, and is part of their biologically determined behavioural repertoires. The latter is displayed by higher mammals, in particular primates and especially humans.

Essay Questions

1 Discuss psychological research studies into the behaviour of bystanders. *(24 marks)*

2 Describe and evaluate **one or more** explanations relating to human altruism or bystander behaviour. *(24 marks)*

WEB ADDRESSES

http:www.//ios.org/pubs/Article16.asp
http://www.socialpsychology.org/social.htm#prosocial
http://www.noctrl.edu/~ajomuel/crow/topic.altruism.htm
http://fccjvm.fccj.cc.h.vs/~jwisner/social.html/

9 Media Influences on Pro- and Anti-social Behaviour

INTRODUCTION AND OVERVIEW

Chapters 7 and 8 looked at theory and research relating to pro- and anti-social behaviour. This chapter examines the influence of the *media* on these two types of social behaviour. The media are:

'... the methods and organisations used by specialist groups to convey messages to large, socially mixed and widely dispersed audiences' (Trowler, 1988).

Most research has looked at the media's (in particular television's) influence on anti-social behaviour. However, there has been a growing interest in the relationship between the media and pro-social behaviour. This chapter examines explanations and research studies relating to media influences on pro- and anti-social behaviour.

HOW MUCH AGGRESSIVE BEHAVIOUR IS SHOWN ON TELEVISION?

The average American child sees 32,000 murders, 40,000 attempted murders, and 250,000 acts of violence on television before the age of 18 (Ahmed, 1998). The basic method of quantifying the amount of violence shown on television involves simple counting techniques. Researchers define violence objectively, and then code samples of television programmes for incidents which match those definitions.

Box 9.1 Gerbner's studies of violence on American television (Gerbner, 1972; Gerbner & Gross, 1976; Gerbner *et al.*, 1980, 1986)

Defining violence as:

'... the overt expression of physical force against others or self, or the compelling of an action against one's will on pain of being hurt or killed',

Gerbner's team have found that since 1967 the percentage of television shows containing violent episodes has remained about the same, but the number of violent episodes per show has gradually increased. In 1986, there was an average of around five violent acts per hour on prime-time television. On children's weekend shows, mostly consisting of cartoons, about 20 violent acts per hour occurred.

Gerbner's analysis provided the framework for British research initiated by Halloran & Croll (1972) and the BBC's Audience Research Department. Both studies found that violence was a common feature of programming, although it was not as prevalent on British as on American television. Cumberbatch (1987), commissioned by the BBC, analysed all programmes broadcast on the (then) four terrestrial channels in four separate weeks between May and September 1986.

Key STUDY

Box 9.2 The main findings from Cumberbatch's (1987) study

Cumberbatch found that 30 per cent of programmes contained some violence, the overall frequency being 1.14 violent acts per programme and 1.68 violent acts per hour. Each act lasted around 25 seconds, so violence occupied just over 1 per cent of total television time. These figures were lower if boxing and wrestling were excluded, but higher (at 1.96 violent acts per hour) if verbal threats were included.

Death resulted from violent acts in 26 per cent of cases, but in 61 per cent of acts no injuries were shown, and the victim was portrayed as being in pain or stunned. In 83 per cent of cases, no blood was shown as a result of a violent act, and considerable blood and gore occurred in only 0.2 per cent of cases. Perpetrators of violent acts were much more likely to be portrayed as 'baddies' than 'goodies', and violence occurred twice as frequently in law-breaking than in law-upholding contexts.

Cumberbatch argued that whilst violence, and concerns about it, had increased in society in the decade up to 1987, this was *not* reflected by a proportional increase on television, even in news broadcasts. He concluded that:

> 'While broadcasters may take some comfort from our data on trends in television violence, they must expect to be continually reminded of their responsibilities in this area and be obliged to acknowledge that a significant minority of people will remain concerned about what's on the box'.

More recently, the BBC and ITV commissioned Gunter & Harrison (1998) to look at the frequency of violence on terrestrial and satellite channels.

Key S T U D Y

Box 9.3   Some findings from Gunter & Harrison's (1998) analysis of violence on British television

The researchers monitored 2084 programmes on eight channels over four weeks in October 1994 and January/February 1995. The findings include:

- On BBC 1 and 2, ITV and Channel 4, 28 per cent of programmes contained violent acts, compared with 52 per cent on Sky One, UK Gold, Sky Movies and the Movie Channel.

- Violence occupied 0.61 per cent of time on the terrestrial channels and 1.53 per cent on the satellite stations.

- The greatest proportion of violent acts (70 per cent) occurred in dramas and films; 19 per cent occurred in children's programmes.

- Most violent acts occurred in contemporary settings in inner-city locations. The majority of perpetrators were young, white males.

- One per cent of programmes contained 19 per cent of all violent acts. *Double Impact*, shown on the Movie Channel, for example, contained 105 violent acts, as against an average of 9.7.

- The United States was the most common location for violence (47 per cent), followed by the United Kingdom (12 per cent). The third most likely location was a cartoon setting (7 per cent), and then science fiction locations (4 per cent).

On the basis of the finding that violent acts account for one per cent of programme content on terrestrial channels and less than two per cent on some satellite stations, and the fact that one per cent of programmes contained 19 per cent of all violent acts, Gunter and Harrison concluded that:

'The picture that emerges is not one of a television system permeated by violence, but rather one in which violence represents only a tiny part of the output and where it tends to be concentrated principally in a relatively small number of programmes' (cited in Frean, 1995).

An almost identical conclusion was reached by the American Academy of Paediatrics (Murray & Whitworth, 1999).

As well as television, violent behaviour can also be seen at the *cinema* or on *video* (and what is shown may or may not be subsequently screened on television). Evidence indicates that a large percentage of 9–11-year-olds have watched 18-rated videos, including the particularly violent *Nightmare on Elm Street*, *The Silence of the Lambs*, and *Pulp Fiction* (Ball & Nuki, 1996; Wark & Ball, 1996).

Figure 9.1 *Jean-Claude van Damme performs another aggressive act in* Double Impact

THE EFFECTS OF TELEVISION ON CHILDREN'S BEHAVIOUR

Research into the effects of television on children's behaviour began in America in the 1960s, following the publication of the results of Bandura *et al.*'s 'Bobo doll experiments' (see Chapter 7, page 69). These 'first generation' (or 'phase one': Baron, 1977) studies involved filmed (or symbolic) models. Essentially, Bandura *et al.* showed that children can acquire new aggressive responses not previously in their behavioural repertoire merely through exposure to a filmed or televised model.

If children could learn new ways of harming others through such experiences, then the implication was that media portrayals of violence might be contributing to increased levels of violence in society (Baron, 1977). However, Bandura (1965) warned against such an interpretation in the light of his finding that the learning of aggressive responses does not necessarily mean that they will be displayed in a child's behaviour (see Chapter 7, page 69). Nevertheless, the *possibility* that such effects could occur was sufficient to focus considerable public attention on Bandura *et al.*'s research.

How much television do people watch?

American research conducted since 1965 suggests that the time people in a typical household spend in front of the television has, in general, been steadily increasing (Burger, 1982; Liebert & Sprafkin, 1988). However, these data are typically derived from paper-and-pen surveys concerning viewing habits and may not be reliable.

Anderson *et al.* (1986) installed automated time-lapse video recording equipment in the homes of 99 families consisting of 462 people aged between one and 62. The recordings began when the television was switched on and stopped when it was switched off. One camera used a wide-angled lens to record people's behaviour in the room where the television was, whilst a second focused on the television screen itself.

Key STUDY

Box 9.4   The main findings from Anderson *et al.*'s (1986) study

- No one actually watches the television for more than 75 per cent of the time it is on.

- Children spend an average of 12.8 hours per week with the television on, and 9.14 hours looking at it. Adults spend an average of 11.5 hours per week with the television on, and 7.56 hours looking at it.

- Adult females pay significantly less attention to television than do children. Adult males look at the television more than females do, but watch it less than school-aged children.

- The number of hours spent looking at television increases up to the age of ten, after which it decreases, levels off at about age 17, and continues around the same level (ten hours per week) into adulthood.

Exactly why people have the television on but do not watch it is an interesting question in its own right! However, Anderson *et al.*'s findings suggest that data about how much television people *watch* should be treated with caution.

Figure 9.2 *The fact that the television is on does not necessarily mean anyone is looking at it*

How do viewers perceive violence?

Much of the concern over television's effects has centred on children. Cumberbatch (1987) found that whilst violence was more likely after 9 p.m., and whilst violence in children's programmes was rare, a notable exception was *cartoons*. Whether children perceive cartoons as representing 'reality' is debatable.

According to Gunter & McAleer (1997), viewers can be highly discriminating when it comes to portrayals of violence, and do not invariably read into television content the same meanings researchers do. Thus, merely knowing how often certain pre-defined incidents occur in programmes does not tell us how significant these features are for viewers.

Viewers' perceptions of how violent television content is, then, may not agree with objective counts of violence in programmes. However, *realism* appears to be an important element in viewers' perceptions of violence, since real-life incidents in news and documentary programmes are generally rated as being more violent than those in fictional settings. Children are very similar to adults as far as their judgements of the *amounts* of violence are concerned. However, their *ratings* of violence differ and, with cartoons, an objectively high number of violent acts may be subjectively perceived as hardly containing any. Subjective assessment of violence should, therefore, be incorporated into assessments of the amount of violence shown on television (Gunter & McAleer, 1997).

Methods used to study television violence

What Baron (1977) calls 'phase two' research (research into the effects of media violence) has been conducted using various methodological approaches. *Correlational studies* typically involve asking people which programmes they like best and which they watch most often. These data are then correlated with measures of aggression given by parents, teachers, self-reports, peers, and so on. Evidence from such studies has generally been inconsistent, but one finding is that the overall amount of viewing is related to self-reports of aggressive behaviour. Of course, it is possible that those who watch violent television are *different* in some way from those who do not, and the inability to infer cause and effect in correlational studies weakens this methodology.

Laboratory studies are designed to enable the causal link between watching violent television and behaving aggressively to be established (if it exists). Liebert & Baron (1972) randomly assigned children to two groups. One watched *The Untouchables*, a violent television programme, whilst the other watched an equally engaging and arousing, but non-violent, sports competition. Afterwards, the children were allowed to play. Those who had watched the violent programme behaved more aggressively than the others.

The problem with laboratory studies is that most use small and unrepresentative samples who are exposed to the independent variable under highly contrived and unnatural viewing conditions. The measures of television viewing and aggression tend to be so far removed from normal everyday behaviour that it is doubtful whether such studies have any relevance to the real world (Gunter & McAleer, 1997). Much more ecologically valid are *field experiments*. In these, children or teenagers are assigned to view violent or non-violent programmes for a period of a few days or weeks.

Measures of aggressive behaviour, fantasy, attitude and so on are taken before, during and after the period of controlled viewing. To ensure control over actual viewing, children in group or institutional settings are studied, mostly from nursery schools, residential schools, or institutions for adolescent boys. In general, the results show that children who watch violent television are more aggressive than those who do not (Parke *et al.*, 1977).

The weakness of the field experiment, however, is that the setting cannot be as well controlled as that of the laboratory experiment. As a result, we cannot be certain that the *only* difference between the children is who watches violent and non-violent television, especially when participants are not assigned randomly to conditions. In Parke *et al.*'s study, for example, 'cottages' (or pre-existing *groups*), rather than individuals, were assigned to the viewing conditions. Also, and by definition, such participants (juvenile delinquent males in Parke *et al.*'s study) are not representative of children or adolescents in general.

Box 9.5   Longitudinal panel studies

Like experiments, but unlike correlational studies, *longitudinal panel studies* can say something about cause and effect, *and* normally use representative samples. Their aim is to discover relationships that may exist or develop *over time* between television viewing and behaviour. These studies, then, look at television's *cumulative* influence and whether or not attitudes and behaviour are linked with watching it.

American (e.g. Lefkowitz *et al.*, 1972; Eron & Huesmann, 1985; Phillips, 1986) and British research (e.g. Sims & Gray, 1993; Bailey, 1993) shows that such a link exists. Sims and Gray, for example, reviewed an extensive body of literature linking heavy exposure to media violence and subsequent aggressive behaviour. Similarly, Bailey's study of 40 adolescent murderers and 200 young sex offenders showed repeated viewing of violent and pornographic videos to be 'a significant causal factor'. This was particularly important in adolescents who abused while they were babysitting, where videos provided 'a potential source of immediate arousal for the subsequent act', including imitating violent images.

However, at least some studies have failed to find such a link. Milavsky *et al.* (1982) found only small associations between exposure to violent programmes and verbal and physical aggression amongst 3200 elementary school children and adolescents. Variables such as family background, social environment, and school performance were actually much better predictors of aggressiveness, if not crime (Ford, 1998).

One of the most useful kinds of study is the *natural experiment*, in which the researcher does not manipulate an independent variable, but takes advantage of a fortuitous and naturally occurring division. Williams (1986) studied a community ('Notel') where television had only been recently introduced. This community was compared with one in which there was a single television channel and another with several channels. Verbal and physical aggression in both male and female 6–11-year-olds increased over a two-year period following the introduction of television to 'Notel', but no such increase occurred in the communities that already had television.

Key STUDY

Box 9.6 A natural experiment on the island of St Helena

In July 1994, a study began to look at the effects of the introduction of television to St Helena. This remote island in the south-east Atlantic has fewer than 6000 inhabitants, none of whom had ever seen live television. Of its 9–12-year-olds, only 3.4 per cent have behavioural problems, compared with 14 per cent of children in London. Of the three– to four-year-olds, less than seven per cent have behavioural problems, compared with 12 per cent in London. The figure of 3.4 per cent for the 9–12-year-olds is the lowest ever recorded for any age range anywhere in the world.

Prior to several 24-hour channels (including BBC World Television, MNET [a South African commercial service] and the American satellite channel, CNN) being introduced, the only access the islanders had to news was on short-wave radio from the BBC World Service. Whilst the island has three video libraries, it does not have a cinema.

The study's leader, Tony Charlton, is looking at the effects of the introduction of television on 59 pre-school children, who will be monitored until they are 13, and all 800 children on the island who are of first and middle-school age. According to Charlton:

'The children on the island represent a unique control group – it is extraordinarily difficult to find a group that doesn't have television'.

Prior to the study beginning, Charlton noted that:

'It could be that excessive viewing interferes with the development of social skills and mental capacities which children need to acquire. But there could be enormous educational benefits'.

In the fourth year of the seven-year study, *pro-social behaviour* (defined as helping others and playing amicably) has not only been maintained since television's introduction, but has actually *improved* slightly.

(Based on Cooper, 1994, McIlroy, 1994, Frean, 1994, Lee, 1996, and Midgley, 1998)

Despite the findings described above, on the basis of the studies that have been carried out, involving at least 100,000 participants (Hearold, 1986), many researchers believe that there *is* a link between television and aggressive behaviour in children and adolescents (Singer, 1989). Indeed, the American National Institute of Mental Health's (1982) review of 2500 studies led it to conclude that:

'The consensus amongst most of the research community is that violence on television does lead to aggressive behaviour by children and teenagers who watch the programmes. This conclusion is based on laboratory experiments and field studies. Not all children become aggressive, of course, but the correlations between violence and aggression are positive. In magnitude, television violence is as strongly correlated with aggressive behaviour as any other behavioural variable that has been measured'.

How does television exert its effects?

Four specific effects of television violence have been investigated. These are *arousal, disinhibition, imitation* and *desensitisation*.

Box 9.7 Television's effects

Arousal: Arousal is a non-specific, physiological response, whose 'meaning' will be defined by the viewer in terms of the type of programme being watched (Zillman, 1978). It has been claimed that watching violence on television increases a viewer's overall level of emotional arousal and excitement (Berkowitz, 1993). However, there does not seem to be any strong overall relationship between perceiving a programme as violent and verbal or physiological reports of emotional arousal (Gadow & Sprafkin, 1993; Bryant & Zillman, 1994). Interestingly, the more *realistic* the violence is perceived as being, the greater the reported arousal and involvement are likely to be.

Disinhibition: Disinhibition is the reduction of inhibitions about behaving aggressively oneself, or coming to believe that aggression is a permitted or legitimate way of solving problems or attaining goals. Berkowitz's *cue–arousal* (*aggressive cue*) *theory*, discussed in Chapter 7, is relevant here.

Imitation: Perhaps the most *direct* link between watching television and the viewer's own behaviour is imitation. This, of course, is directly related to Bandura *et al.*'s studies of imitative aggression (see pages 89–90). However, social learning theorists acknowledge the role of cognitive factors as mediating between stimulus and response (Bandura, 1994).

How television violence is perceived and interpreted, and the issue of realism, are clearly important *intervening* variables for both children and adults.

Desensitisation: Desensitisation is the reduction in emotional response to television violence (and an increased acceptance of violence in real life) as a result of repeatedly viewing it. As with drug tolerance, increasingly violent programmes may be required to produce an emotional response (Gadow & Sprafkin, 1989). In one study implicating desensitisation, Drabman & Thomas (1974) showed eight-year-olds a violent or non-violent programme before witnessing a 'real' (but actually staged) fight between two other children. Those who saw the violent programme were much less likely than those who saw the non-violent programme to tell an adult that a fight was occurring.

Reconsidering media violence

The debate about media violence and aggression's relationship is far from being resolved (Harrower, 1998). In Britain, the link between the two was brought back into the spotlight following two-year-old James Bulger's murder by two teenage boys in February, 1993. At their trial, Mr Justice Moreland said:

> 'It is not for me to pass judgement on their upbringing, but I suspect that exposure to violent video films may, in part, be an explanation' (cited in Cumberbatch, 1997).

The call for legislation controlling the supply of videos to children was supported by many psychologists, including Newson (1994), whose report (*Video Violence and the Protection of Children*) was also endorsed by many psychiatrists and paediatricians.

Figure 9.3 *The claim that there is a direct causal link between watching media violence (such as* A Clockwork Orange) *and violent behaviour is, at the least, an oversimplification*

Cumberbatch (1997), however, has questioned the validity of the evidence on which Newson's report was based. He notes that whilst it might be true that the father of one of the murderers of James Bulger had rented the video *Child's Play 3* some weeks before the murder occurred (as one British tabloid claimed), his son was not living with him at that time, disliked horror films, and was upset by violence in videos. Similarly, it was claimed that the massacre of 16 people in Hungerford in 1987 was inspired by the murderer seeing the character 'Rambo' in the film *First Blood*. In fact, there is no evidence to support this claim (Cumberbatch, 1997).

More recently, two fourteen-year-old British schoolboys were convicted of attempted murder, apparently as a result of watching the film *Scream*. In the film, college students became victims of fatal knife attacks by two of their classmates. At their trial, though, the schoolboys denied that the film had influenced their behaviour (Stokes, 1999).

Cumberbatch has also criticised Comstock & Paik's (1991) conclusion that, based on Huesmann & Eron's (1986) cross-national survey in six countries (Holland, Australia, USA, Israel, Poland and Finland), viewing television violence at an early age is a predictor of later aggression.

Box 9.8 Cumberbatch's criticisms of the claim that viewing television violence at an early age is a predictor of later aggression

- The Dutch researchers concluded that their results showed no effects of television, and refused to allow their findings to be included in Huesmann and Eron's edited book of the research study.

- The Australian research showed no significant correlations between early television violence viewing and later aggression.

- The American study found that when initial aggression was controlled for, the correlation between early television viewing and later aggression was significant only in *girls*.

- Israeli researchers found significant effects in their city samples but not in their Kibbutz samples.

- In Poland, the researchers agreed that a greater preference for violent viewing was predictive of later aggression, but that 'the effects are not large and must be treated cautiously'.

- The Finnish researchers appeared to misunderstand their own data. Rather than there being a *positive* correlation between viewing violent television and aggressive behaviour, the correlation is actually *negative*, indicating that the more television is watched, the *less* aggressive children were later.

(Adapted from Cumberbatch, 1997)

Cumberbatch (1997) cites several other studies (e.g. Hagell & Newburn, 1994) which also cast doubt on claims about the connection between media violence and aggression in children. In his view:

'It is all too easy to scaremonger. However, we should remember that Britain is still a safe, highly regulated country. UK television has roughly half the amount of violence as most countries studied. It is ironic that the media seem largely to blame for the particularly British moral panic about our behaviour'.

THE MEDIA AND PROSOCIAL BEHAVIOUR

According to Gunter & McAleer (1997):

'Concern about the possible anti-social influences of television far outweighs the consideration given to any other area of children's involvement with television ... Television programmes contain many examples of good behaviour, of people acting kindly and with generosity. It is equally logical to assume that these portrayals provide models for children to copy'.

Television violence and catharsis

One positive effect of television might be that witnessing others behaving aggressively helps viewers to get their aggressive feelings 'out of their systems', and hence be less likely to behave aggressively. The claim that television can act as a form of *vicarious catharsis* is based partly on the theories of aggression advanced by Freud and Lorenz (see Gross & McIlveen, 1998).

The evidence does not, however, support the view that television is cathartic for everybody. If a discharge of hostile feelings can occur at all, it is probably restricted to people of a particular *personality type* or those who score high on cognitive measures of *fantasy*, *daydreaming* and *imagination* (Singer, 1989). For only some people, then, does television violence have positive effects and provide a means of reducing aggressive feelings (Gunter & McAleer, 1997).

Television and pro-social behaviour

If television can have harmful effects as a result of watching anti-social behaviour then, presumably, it can have beneficial effects by promoting pro-social behaviour.

According to Gunter (1998), the evidence for the pro-social effects of television can be grouped into four types.

Box 9.9 The evidence for the pro-social effects of television

- **Laboratory studies with specially produced instructional film or video materials:** Specially prepared materials have been shown to influence courage, the delay of gratification, adherence to rules, charitable behaviour, friendliness, and affectionate behaviour.

- **Laboratory studies with educational broadcasts specially produced for social skills teaching purposes:** Television productions designed to enhance the social maturity and responsibility of young viewers include *Sesame Street* and *Mister Rogers' Neighborhood*. Children who watch these programmes are able to identify and remember the cooperative and helping behaviours emphasised in certain segments of them. Some programmes are better at encouraging pro-social behaviour in children than others, but the reasons for this are unclear.

- **Laboratory studies with episodes from popular TV series:** Specially manufactured television programmes or film clips influence children's pro-social tendencies, at least when the pro-social behaviour portrayed is very similar to that requested of the child. However, only some evidence indicates that ordinary broadcast material can enhance a wide range of helping behaviours.

- **Field studies relating amount of viewing of pro-social television content to strength of pro-social behaviour tendencies:** Children who watch little television, but watch a lot of programmes with high levels of pro-social content, are more likely than others to behave pro-socially. However, the correlations between viewing habits and pro-social behaviour are lower than those between viewing habits and anti-social behaviour.

In part, this may be because pro-social behaviours are verbally mediated and often subtle, whereas anti-social behaviours are blatant and physical. Children learn better from simple, direct and active presentation, and so aggressive behaviours may be more readily learned. Also, the characters who display pro-social behaviour (typically female and non-white) and anti-social behaviour (typically male and white) may confound the relative influence of pro-social and anti-social behaviours with the types of character that portray them.

(From Gunter & McAleer, 1997, and Gunter, 1998)

On the basis of their review of the literature, Gunter & McAleer (1997) concluded that:

'Televised examples of good behaviour can encourage children to behave in friendlier and more thoughtful ways to others'.

An alternative approach to what Greenfield (1984) has called *television literacy* involves teaching children to be 'informed consumers' of television. This includes distinguishing between social reality and the (at least sometimes) make-believe world of television, understanding the nature and purpose of advertisements, and interpreting and assessing sex-role and minority-group stereotyping.

Figure 9.4 *Teletubbies: models of pro-social behaviour, or as some critics have claimed, models of undesirable linguistic habits?*

Key S T U D Y

Box 9.10 **Teaching children to be 'informed consumers' of television**

Huesmann *et al.* (1983) allocated young children known to be 'heavy' watchers of television to a control or experimental group. The experimental group received three training sessions designed to reduce the modelling of aggressive behaviour seen on television. They were taught that television does not portray the world as it really is, that camera techniques and special effects give the illusion that characters are performing their highly aggressive and unrealistic feats, and that most people use other methods to solve the problems encountered by characters in television programmes. Compared with the control group, the experimental group showed less overall aggressive behaviour and lowered identification with televised characters. These effects had persisted when the participants were followed up two years later.

Computer games and pro-social behaviour

According to Griffiths (1998), little is known about the long-term effects of playing violent computer games. However, great concern has been voiced that such games may have a more adverse effect on children than television because of the child's *active involvement* (Keegan, 1999). Griffiths's review of research indicates that the effects of long-term exposure to computer games on subsequent aggressive behaviour 'are at best speculative'. As regards pro-social behaviour, computer games have received support from a number of researchers (e.g. Loftus & Loftus, 1983; Silvern, 1986).

Box 9.11 The positive effects of computer games

- Computer games have become an integral part of modern language teaching in America because they are seen:

  ' ... as a motivating device, a means for providing comprehensible input and a catalyst for communicative practice and the negotiation of meaning' (Hubbard, 1991).

However, whether a game is perceived as educational depends on factors such as the player's age, gender, proficiency level and educational background.

- Computer games give children access to 'state of the art' technology, a sense of confidence, and equip them with computer-related skills for the future (Surrey, 1982).

- Computer games may also promote social interaction. In a study on the impact of computers on family life, Mitchell (1983, cited in Griffiths, 1993) found that families generally viewed computer games as promoting interaction in a beneficial way through co-operation and competition.

- The aggressive content of some computer games may be cathartic (see page 94) in that it allows players to release their stress and aggression in a non-destructive way, and has the effect of relaxing the players (Kestenbaum & Weinstein, 1985). Other benefits include enhancing cognitive skills, a sense of mastery, control and accomplishment, and a reduction in other youth problems due to 'addictive interest'(!) in video games (Anderson & Ford, 1986).

(Adapted from Griffiths, 1993)

According to Griffiths (1997a), there appear to be some genuine applied aspects of computer game playing, although he notes that many of the assertions made in Box 9.11 were subjectively formulated and not based on empirical research findings.

AND FINALLY ...

In a lecture given in 1994, the BBC newsreader Martyn Lewis claimed that television producers were failing to reflect the true state of the world through their tendencies to ignore positive news (Lewis & Rowe, 1994). BBC managers attacked Lewis's views, charging that he was calling for news to be trivialised in order to make it more palatable, a charge Lewis vigorously denied.

Johnson and Davey (cited in Matthews, 1997a) conducted a study in which three groups of participants were shown news bulletins with positive, negative or neutral blends of stories. After the bulletins, those shown the negative blend of stories were considerably more worried and depressed about their own lives (rather than the issues they had seen in the bulletin).

According to Davey:

'Television producers need to think very carefully about the emotional impact news might have on their viewers'.

Davey sees slots like 'And finally ... ' on ITN's late night news as being beneficial:

'Having a light piece at the end is no bad thing. The trouble is [the broadcast] then gives a quick summary of all the news at the end, so it's not as effective as it could be'.

Reporting on solutions as well as problems, then, may be beneficial for all of us.

CONCLUSIONS

There has been much research into media influences on pro- and anti-social behaviour. The evidence reviewed in this chapter suggests that the media can exert an influence on the expression of both pro- and anti-social behaviour, although it is dangerous to talk about this in simple cause-and-effect terms.

Summary

- American research has shown an increase in the amount of violence depicted on television since 1967. In Britain, television violence is not as prevalent, and represents only a very small proportion of the total output. Interestingly, whilst the television might be switched on for longer in households than was the case in the 1960s, people are not always attentive to it.

- Bandura *et al.* exposed children to filmed (symbolic) models. They found that children can acquire new aggressive responses merely through exposure to a filmed or televised model. These findings implied that media portrayals of violence might contribute to violence in society.

- Cartoons contain a great deal of violence, and yet are aimed mainly at children. However, viewers' **perceptions** of violent television content may not correspond with **objective counts** of violent incidents. Real-life incidents in news and documentaries are generally rated as more violent than those in fictional settings.

- **Correlational studies** indicate that the overall amount of television watched is related to self-reports of aggressive behaviour. However, cause and effect cannot be inferred from such studies, and those who watch violent programmes may **differ** in some way from those who do not.

■ **Laboratory experiments** are designed to detect causal links between watching television and behaviour. However, most use small, unrepresentative samples, and their measures are far removed from everyday behaviour.

■ **Field experiments** are more ecologically valid. They involve controlled viewing over an extended time period. Data consistently indicate that children who watch violent television are more aggressive than those who do not. However, field experiments lack control, and often use unrepresentative samples.

■ **Longitudinal panel studies** say something about cause and effect, **and** use representative samples. They look at the **cumulative influence** of television. Some studies have shown a link between heavy exposure to media violence and aggression, but others have not.

■ **Natural experiments** look at communities/societies before and after the introduction of television. Some studies have shown increases in aggressive behaviour following the introduction of television, whilst others have not.

■ The four specific effects of television that have been investigated are **arousal**, **disinhibition**, **imitation** and **desensitisation**. All of these have been shown to increase following exposure to media violence.

■ Some researchers suggest that the link between media violence and aggressive behaviour is overstated. They believe that it is difficult to justify the overall conclusion that viewing television at an early age predicts later aggression.

■ As well as being a potential influence on anti-social behaviour, television may influence **pro-social behaviour**. The evidence that television may exert a pro-social effect comes from **laboratory studies** using **prepared television/filmed material**, broadcast material specially produced for **teaching social skills**, programme materials from **popular TV series**.

■ **Field studies** also indicate that the amount of pro-social content viewed is related to the strength of pro-social behaviour. However, this relationship is weaker than that between viewing habits and anti-social behaviour. This may be because anti-social behaviours (which are blatant and physical) are learnt more easily than verbal and subtle pro-social behaviours.

■ Little is known about the long-term effects of playing **violent computer games**, but the child's **active involvement** makes them potentially more harmful than television. There is some evidence for the pro-social effects of such games, but much of this has not been gathered in carefully controlled ways.

■ The **benefits** of computer games include providing motivation, a sense of confidence, mastery and control, and computer-related skills for the future. They also provide an opportunity for releasing stress and aggression in a non-destructive way.

■ News bulletins can induce anxiety and depression in viewers. Producers of news programmes should think carefully about the emotional impact news might have on their audiences.

Essay Questions

1 Discuss research studies relating to media influences on pro-social behaviour. *(24 marks)*

2 Critically consider explanations relating to media influences on anti-social behaviour. *(24 marks)*

WEB ADDRESSES

http://www.apa.org/pubinfo/violence.html
http://www.cdc.gov/od/oc/media/fact/violence.htm
http://www.dukeedu/~cars/vmedia.html
http://www.medialit.org/Violence/indexviol.htm

Physiological Psychology

PART 1: BRAIN AND BEHAVIOUR

10 Methods of Investigating the Brain

INTRODUCTION AND OVERVIEW

Although psychologists are far from completely understanding the relationship between brain structures and behaviour, knowledge about the brain grows almost daily. But how do we know what we know? This chapter looks at the nature of the methods used to investigate the brain, and some of their strengths and limitations.

The various methods can be discussed under separate headings. *Clinical/anatomical methods* involve 'accidental interventions', such as injury to, and disease of, the brain. *Invasive methods* involve 'deliberate intervention', such as stimulating the brain either electrically or chemically, or causing deliberate injury to it. Finally, *non-invasive methods* involve recording the brain's activity without making deliberate interventions.

CLINICAL/ANATOMICAL METHODS

Perhaps the most obvious way of studying the brain is to look at the behavioural consequences of *accidental* damage to it. This approach assumes that if damage to a particular part of the brain part causes a behavioural change, then it is reasonable to propose that the damaged part ordinarily plays a role in the behaviour affected.

Box 10.1 Some studies of accidental brain damage

In the late nineteenth century, Broca and Wernické studied patients who had suffered a stroke (or *cerebrovascular accident*). A stroke occurs when a blood vessel in the brain is damaged or blocked. This causes brain tissue to be deprived of the oxygen and nutrients carried by the blood, and the tissue dies. Broca's patients had difficulty producing speech, but

no difficulty understanding it. Wernické's patients, however, could produce speech (although it was often unintelligible), but could not understand it. *Postmortems* revealed that Broca's patients had suffered damage in one brain area, whilst Wernické's had suffered damage in a different area. The role played by these areas is discussed in detail in Chapter 12.

Clinical and anatomical studies compare what people could do *before* their brain damage with what they can do *afterwards*. Unfortunately, there are rarely precise enough records of people's behaviour before the damage was sustained. As a result, this approach is useful for very obvious behavioural changes (such as the inability to produce language), but less helpful where more subtle effects are involved (such as changes in personality).

Also, it is sometimes difficult to determine the precise location and amount of damage that has been caused by a particular injury. More practically, researchers must wait for the 'right kind' of injury to occur so that a particular brain part can be investigated. In post-mortem studies, of course, researchers must wait until the individual has died (Stirling, 2000).

INVASIVE METHODS

Ablation and lesion production

Ablation involves surgically removing or destroying brain tissue, and observing the behavioural consequences. Flourens pioneered the technique in the 1820s, and showed that removal of thin tissue slices from the cerebellum of rabbits, birds and dogs resulted in them displaying a lack of muscular coordination and a poor sense of balance, but no other obvious behavioural difficulties. Flourens concluded that the cerebellum, two convoluted hemispheres which extend outward to the back of the skull, plays a vital role in muscular coordination and balance, a conclusion which was essentially correct.

Surgical removal can be achieved by *cutting* the tissue with a knife, *burning* it out with electrodes, or *sucking* it away through a hollow tube attached to a vacuum pump. Although ablation studies are still conducted on non-humans, they are limited in what they can tell us about the *human* brain. Another problem is the issue of *control* versus *involvement* in behaviour. Behaviour may change when part of the brain is removed, but we cannot be certain that the removed part controlled the behaviour or was merely involved in it. Since many parts of the brain work together to produce a particular behaviour, we cannot be sure what behaviour changes mean when a part is removed.

Lesion production involves deliberately injuring part of the brain and then observing the consequences of the injury (*lesion*) on behaviour. Whilst an animal is under anaesthetic, a hole is drilled in its skull and an electrode inserted into a particular brain site. Then, an electrical impulse of a voltage larger than those occurring naturally in the brain is delivered to the site. This 'burns out' a small area surrounding the electrode. Because the sites involved are usually located deep within the brain, a *stereotaxic apparatus* (see Figure 10.1) is used to precisely locate the area to be lesioned.

Once the animal has recovered, its behaviour is observed to see whether the lesion has produced immediate, delayed, or no apparent changes in behaviour, and whether any changes are permanent or disappear with time, re-training or therapy. Lesion studies have produced some important findings. For example, lesions in one area of the *hypothalamus* cause extreme overeating in rats, and they become grossly overweight. A lesion in a different area, however, produces the opposite effect and, at least initially, they refuse to eat any sort

of food (see Chapter 16). Whilst lesion production is not used on humans *purely* for research purposes, lesions have been used therapeutically (Stirling, 2000). In the *split-brain* operation, certain nerve fibres are severed to try to reduce the severity of epileptic seizures (see Chapter 12).

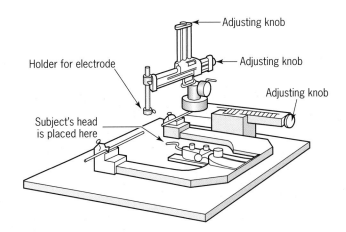

Figure 10.1 *A stereotaxic apparatus (stereotax). When used in conjunction with a stereotactic atlas, which provides three-dimensional co-ordinates for any brain structure, a lesion can be made precisely in a particular part of the brain.*

Lesion production studies tell us something about how different parts of the brain are *normally* connected. As with ablation studies, however, we must be extremely cautious in interpreting data from them. Again, since the subjects of research are *always* non-humans, findings may not generalise to humans. Additionally, whilst a lesion is produced in a specific area, the possibility that behaviour changes occur as a result of other damage caused by the procedure cannot be ruled out. The problem of 'control versus involvement' in the production of behaviour changes is also a concern with lesion studies.

Electrical stimulation of the brain (ESB)

ESB involves inserting one or more electrodes into a living animal's brain, and applying an electric current which does not cause any damage. Careful adjustment of the current produces a 'false' nerve impulse, which the brain treats as a real impulse from a sensory receptor.

ESB has produced some dramatic findings. For example, Delgado (1969) walked into a bullring equipped with a bull fighter's cape and a radio transmitter. Delgado had implanted a radio-controlled electrode into the *limbic system* of a 'brave bull', a variety bred to respond with a raging charge to the sight of a human being. When the bull charged, Delgado sent an impulse to the electrode in the bull's brain. Fortunately for

Delgado, the bull stopped its charge. The implications of this finding, and the role played by the limbic system, are discussed in Chapter 18.

Key STUDY

Box 10.2 'Pain' and 'pleasure' centres in the brain?

Olds & Milner (1954) found that electrical stimulation of the *hypothalamus* caused rats to increase the frequency of whatever behaviour they were engaged in. In one experiment, they connected the implanted electrode to a control mechanism that the rat could operate. Stimulation of one part of the hypothalamus appeared to be extremely pleasurable for the rat, since it would forego food, water and sex to carry on stimulating its brain at a rate of 100 times a minute and over 1900 times an hour. As well as discovering an apparent 'pleasure centre' in the brain, Olds and Milner also found that placing the electrode in a different location led to an animal that had operated the control mechanism once never operating it again, suggesting the existence of a 'pain centre'.

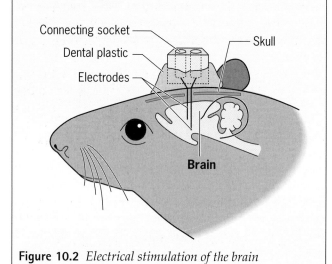

Figure 10.2 *Electrical stimulation of the brain*

Delgado's and Olds and Milner's studies illustrate some of the findings from stimulating structures *deep* within the brain. However, in other studies the *cerebral cortex* (see Chapter 11) has been electrically stimulated. The classic research in this area was conducted by Penfield in the 1940s and 1950s (e.g. Penfield, 1947). Penfield routinely performed surgery on epileptics, and to minimise the disruption of normal functions as a result of this surgery, he would stimulate the cortex and observe what happened. Because there are no pain receptors in the brain, the person awaiting surgery could be kept conscious whilst the stimulation was given, and could report on the experiences produced by the stimulation (see also Chapter 11, page 110).

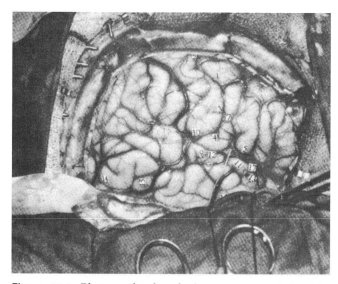

Figure 10.3 *Photograph taken during surgery carried out by Penfield. The barely visible numbers refer to the parts of the cortex stimulated*

(Oxford University Press)

ESB has provided much information about the brain's workings, and has also been used *therapeutically*. Perhaps its most useful application has been in the reduction of pain. For example, ESB can be used to 'block' pain messages in the spine before they reach the brain, and this relieves the severe pain experienced by people with illnesses such as cancer.

Clearly, ESB is a useful way of 'mapping' the connections between areas or structures of the brain. If stimulation of one area produces increased activity at another, it is reasonable to assume that the two are connected. Equally, if stimulation of a specific brain site produces a behaviour, that site must at least be involved in that behaviour. However, caution must be exercised before drawing too many conclusions from research findings.

Box 10.3 Some limitations of ESB

Valenstein (1977) offers three cautions:

- No single brain area is likely to be the *sole* source of any given behaviour or emotion;

- ESB-provoked behaviour does not perfectly mimic natural behaviour. Rather, it produces compulsive and stereotypical behaviour. For example, an animal whose eating behaviour is initiated by ESB might only eat one type of food;

- ESB's effects may depend on many other factors, since people exhibit very different behavioural responses to identical stimulation administered at different times.

For Valenstein:

'The impression that brain stimulation in humans can repeatedly evoke the same emotional state, the same memory, or the same behaviour is simply a myth. The brain is not organised into neat compartments that correspond to the labels we assign to behaviour'.

Micro-electrode recording

Instead of electrical stimulation, some researchers insert tiny electrodes (*micro-electrodes*) to *record* a single *neuron's* (or nerve cell's) activity in a living animal's brain. Micro-electrodes are about one ten-thousandth of a millimetre in diameter, and enable the 'sound' of a neuron to be recorded without the 'noise' emanating from neighbouring neurons.

Using a stereotaxic apparatus (see Figure 10.1, page 99), the electrode is inserted into the brain. It is then attached to an electrical connector cemented to the brain. Finally, the scalp is sewn together. The electrical connector is attached to a wire leading to apparatus that records the cell's electrical activity as various tasks are performed. Micro-electrodes are sophisticated enough to detect an electrical charge of one-millionth of a volt.

Recordings of the activity of single neurons have produced interesting findings, particularly into the workings of the visual system. Chapters 22 and 27 look at the research conducted by Hubel and Wiesel into the visual system. These researchers have been able to build up a detailed picture of some of the ways in which the monkey's brain deals with visual information. However, since the brain has billions of neurons, each of which connects with many others, building up a picture of how the brain works using this method is very slow indeed. Moreover, since micro-electrodes can destroy brain tissue, their use has been confined to non-humans, making the generalisation of findings to humans difficult.

Chemical stimulation of the brain

This technique is also used with non-humans, and involves introducing a chemical into the brain to determine its behavioural and physiological effects. Typically, a thin tube (or micro-pipette) is inserted into the brain, with the open end touching the area being studied. A smaller tube is filled with a few crystals of a chemical substance and inserted into the implanted tube. The chemical is then released at the site being stimulated.

Box 10.4 Chemical stimulation and anatomic pathways

Chemical stimulation has been used to trace anatomic pathways in the brain using radioactive 2-deoxyglucose, a form of sugar. Following the injection, an animal is made to perform a certain task. Those cells involved in the task use more sugar, and so radioactivity builds up in them. After the task, the animal is 'sacrificed'. The brain is then frozen and thin slices of it are pressed against photographic film (which is sensitive to radioactivity). This indicates which brain cells were particularly active during the task's performance.

The chemical used depends on the nature of the study. Perhaps the most commonly used chemicals are those believed to affect synaptic transmission. These produce longer-lasting effects than those induced by electrical stimulation, and allow researchers to make their observations over longer periods of time. However, the data are often difficult to interpret, with different non-humans responding differently to the *same* chemical. Since non-humans respond differently to one another, we should be cautious in generalising any results to humans.

As well as the practical problems involved in the various methods described above there are, of course, serious ethical issues (see Chapter 56). Both practical problems and ethical issues have led researchers to look for alternative ways of studying the brain which do not involve direct intervention.

NON-INVASIVE METHODS

Recording the brain's electrical activity

Neurons in the brain communicate with one another by releasing chemical messengers called *neurotransmitters*. In 1875, it was discovered that these chemical changes also produce recordable electrical discharges. Half a century later, Berger, a German neurologist, devised a technique which allowed the electrical activity to be continuously recorded.

Key STUDY

Box 10.5 Electrical activity in the brain

Working on the assumption that the part of the brain which is electrically active during some behaviour is involved in that behaviour, Berger (1929) attached two flat silver plates (which acted as electrodes) to his son's scalp. The electrodes were connected to a *galvanometer*, which measures small electric currents. After much effort, Berger successfully recorded regular electrical activity from the electrodes, and suggested that the activity was affected by *conscious experience*.

Berger's work was largely ignored until 1934, when Adrian and Matthews confirmed his findings using a newly invented device, the *electroencephalogram* (or EEG). An EEG machine measures changes in the electrical activity of different brain parts. There are characteristic patterns of electrical activity which are common to everyone at a particular age or stage of development. However, everyone's individual brain activity is as unique and distinctive as their fingerprints.

Using special jelly, small disc-like electrodes are attached to the scalp. Via wires, these pass electrical information to an amplifier capable of detecting impulses of less than a ten-thousandth of a volt, and then magnifying them one million times. With older machines, the amplifier passes its information to pens which trace the impulses on paper revolving on a drum. This produces a permanent record of the oscillating waves produced by the electrical activity.

Box 10.6 The measurement of 'brain waves'

EEG activity can be described in terms of *frequency* (the number of complete oscillations of a wave that occur in one second, which is measured in cycles per second or Hertz (Hz)) and *amplitude* (half the height from the peak to the trough of a single oscillation). Whilst amplitude is important, frequency is more commonly used to describe the brain's electrical activity. The four main types of 'brain wave' are:

- **Delta** (1–3 Hz) – mainly found in infants, adults in 'deep' sleep, or adults with brain tumours;

- **Theta** (4–7 Hz) – commonly seen in children aged between two and five. In adults, it has been observed in *dissocial personality disorder*;

- **Alpha** (8–13 Hz) – this wave is seen in adults who are awake, relaxed, and whose eyes are closed;

- **Beta** (13 Hz and over) – this is found in adults who are awake, alert, have their eyes open, and are concentrating on a task.

The EEG allows researchers to examine the brain's activity in response to specific experiences as they occur. Whilst we are awake, the brain's electrical activity changes in response to sights, sounds and other sensory

information. The EEG is also extensively used in clinical diagnosis to detect abnormal brain activity, since EEG patterns from tumours and damaged brain tissue, for example, are very distinctive. Indeed, the EEG has been invaluable in the diagnosis of *epilepsy*, a condition characterised by abnormal bursts of electrical activity (which may be 20 times that of normal) occurring in rapidly firing individual neurons.

In addition to recording electrical activity in the brain, electrodes can also be attached to the skin beneath the chin and near the outer corners of the eyes. The activity recorded from the chin muscles is called an *electromyogram* (EMG), and provides information about muscle tension or relaxation. The activity recorded from near the outer corner of the eyes is called an *electrooculogram* (EOG), and shows the electrical activity that occurs when the eyes move. A machine that measures more variables than just the electrical activity of the brain is called a *polygraph*.

As well as being used for diagnostic purposes, the EEG is the indispensable tool of those interested in understanding the nature and functions of *sleep* and *dreaming*. Chapters 14 and 15 discuss sleep and dreaming research, and refer extensively to EEG, EMG and EOG measures. As those chapters illustrate, muscle, eye and brain activity is *not* constant over the course of a night's sleep.

The brain contains billions of neurons. Recordings from the scalp therefore reflect the *gross* and simultaneous activity of millions of neurons. For some researchers, the EEG is analogous to standing outside Wembley Stadium on Cup Final day and hearing the crowd roar. A goal could have been scored, but by which side? It could be a penalty, but to whom? It might even be the crowd's response to a streaker running across the pitch! Whilst the EEG reveals that *something* is happening it does not indicate exactly what.

Key STUDY

Box 10.7 Computerised electroencephalography

One way of partially overcoming EEG's limitations involves repeatedly presenting a stimulus and having a computer filter out the activity unrelated to it. This is called *computerised electroencephalography*. The filtering out leaves an *evoked potential*, which can be useful in identifying activity patterns associated with particular behaviours.

For example, Donchin (1975) recorded the EEG activity of participants who were exposed to various familiar or predictable stimuli, occasionally interspersed with unfamiliar or unpredictable stimuli. Donchin found that the perception of an unexpected event was consistently associated with the production of an evoked potential called P300. Donchin's research suggests that evoked potentials can be helpful in understanding the relationship between brain activity and mental processes.

More recently, researchers have taken advantage of the fact that the brain's electrical activity creates magnetic fields that can be detected outside the skull. *Magnetoencephalograms* (or MEGs) detect these very weak fields (which are of the order of one billionth of the earth's magnetic field). The brain's electrical signals are distorted when they pass through the skull, making it difficult to identify their point of origin. Magnetic fields are unaffected by bone, and the MEG measures the magnetic field's strength and its source. The biggest weakness of MEG is that the magnetic fields are easily disrupted, and this makes measurement extremely difficult (Charlton, 1996). Despite this, MEG has been used successfully to detect disorders like epilepsy, multiple sclerosis and Alzheimer's disease.

EEG *imaging* is also useful in studying the brain. This allows researchers to measure the functioning of the brain 'on a millisecond by millisecond basis' (Fischman, 1985). The activity is recorded by 32 electrodes placed on the scalp. The information is fed to a computer, which translates it into colour-coded moving images on a television monitor, different colours indicating different activity levels. The technique was originally developed for research into convulsive seizures. However, it has also been used to predict learning disabilities in children and for mapping the brain activity of people suffering from mental disorders. A similar method, which uses 64 or 128 electrodes and is called a *geodesic sensor net*, has been developed for similar purposes (Highfield, 1996a).

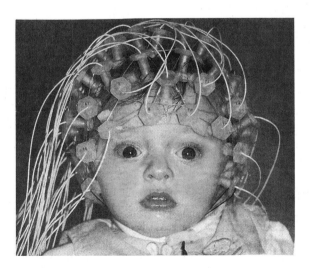

Figure 10.4 *A geodesic sensor net being used to study brain activity in an infant*

Scanning and imaging devices

Psychologists know the location of lesions in the brains of laboratory animals because they put them there (Carlson, 1988). Prior to the 1970s, the location of lesions in the human brain could only be identified when the individual died and if the family gave their permission for an autopsy. Since the 1970s, however, a new approach to studying the brain has allowed researchers to identify the location of lesions in *living* individuals, as well as providing other information about the brain's workings.

Computerised axial tomography

For many years, neurologists took X-rays of the head to study brain damage, usually using dyes injected into the circulatory system to make the blood vessels in the brain more visible. However, the flat picture produced by a standard X-ray was not always informative. In the early 1970s, *computerised axial tomography* (CAT) was introduced and made the use of X-rays much more informative.

In CAT, the brain is examined by taking a large number of X-ray photographs of it. A person's head is placed in a large doughnut-shaped apparatus, which has an X-ray source located on one side and an X-ray detector on the other. As the apparatus is rotated through many different orientations (or axes), the amount by which the X-rays penetrate the brain is recorded by the detector. This information is fed to a computer which creates detailed images – the CAT scan – which are displayed as a three-dimensional representation of the brain's structures.

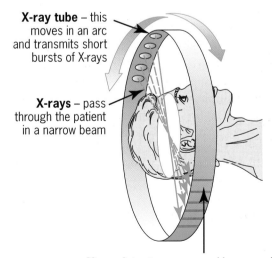

X-ray tube – this moves in an arc and transmits short bursts of X-rays

X-rays – pass through the patient in a narrow beam

X-ray detector – arranged in an arc. Each detector comprises an X-ray sensitive crystal plus a light detector called a photodiode. Information about the number and position of these light flashes is relayed to the computer

Figure 10.5 *Diagrammatic representation of CAT*

CAT is helpful to surgeons because it aids decision-making about the procedures that will be followed in an operation on the brain. For psychologists, CAT can help to determine whether a particular behavioural problem has an identifiable physical basis.

Magnetic resonance imaging

A more sophisticated approach than CAT is *magnetic resonance imaging* (MRI). Like CAT, MRI provides a three-dimensional image of brain structures. Although MRI uses similar equipment to CAT, a strong magnetic field rather than X-rays is used to form images of the brain. The person undergoing MRI is placed in a doughnut-shaped tunnel that generates a magnetic field several thousand times stronger than the earth's magnetic field. Then, harmless radio waves are introduced which excite hydrogen atoms in the brain. This causes changes in the magnetic field, which are recorded by a computer and then transformed into a colour-coded image on a television monitor.

MRI is used to identify structural disorders and to study the normal brain. One advantage over CAT is its sensitivity and the clarity of the images produced. MRI can, for example, identify the smallest tumour with pinpoint accuracy, and locate the slightest reduction in blood flow in an artery or vein. Unfortunately, both CAT and MRI can only provide a still image of a cross-section of the brain. Whilst this provides useful information about the brain's structure, it tells us very little about its function. However, *functional magnetic resonance imaging* (fMRI) overcomes MRI's limitations.

In fMRI, blood flow in the brain is monitored continuously over time. Haemoglobin in the blood contains iron, and has magnetic properties that can be detected. When there are changes in blood flow, the magnetic 'profile' changes. This is probably because oxygenated blood flow changes when neurons in a brain area become more active (Dobson, 1999a). One advantage of fMRI is that it is very fast. Small changes in blood flow can be observed that correlate with physiological activity in the cerebral cortex, occurring in tens to hundreds of milliseconds (David *et al.*, 1994). Another advantage is that there is no concern over exposure to radioactive substances used with some methods (see below), and therefore no limit to the number of scans a person may undergo.

Box 10.8 Transcranial magnetic stimulation (TMS)

TMS involves generating an intense magnetic field over part of the skull's surface, which creates an electrical field that temporarily interferes with the activity of the cerebral cortex. Stimulation at different frequencies increases or decreases the rate of learning of a task. By choosing the right frequency, it might be possible to use TMS to stimulate the formation of new connections in the brain, such as in those areas identified through fMRI as important in recovery after a stroke. TMS may also be a more benign alternative to *electroconvulsive therapy* (ECT: see Chapter 52), which is used with depressed people who do not respond to drug treatment.

(Adapted from Ferry, 1999)

Positron emission tomography

Positron emission tomography (PET) allows researchers to examine the relationship between brain activity and mental processes. PET works by measuring metabolic activity within the brain. A person undergoing PET is first injected with a small amount of harmless radioactive material 'bonded' to a substance, such as glucose, that the body metabolises. Since the brain's primary form of energy is glucose, the areas which are most active absorb more of it.

The glucose is broken down by the brain, but the radioactive material is not. As it decays, and it has completely decayed within three hours, it emits positively charged particles (*positrons*). These are detected by sensors arranged around the head. This information is then fed to a computer, which produces colour-coded images of the activity occurring throughout the brain. Like CAT and MRI, PET is of great help in diagnosing abnormalities. For example, it is used to locate tumours and growths, which gives surgeons vital information about the likelihood of essential brain structures being damaged by surgery.

As noted, PET takes advantage of the fact that at any given time some areas of the brain will be more active than others. PET's biggest advantage over CAT and MRI is that it can be used to provide images of what is going on in the brain *during* various behaviours. For example, when a person shuffles a pack of cards, there is increased activity in the part of the brain concerned with the regulation of skilled performance. When a person looks at a picture, the area of the brain concerned with the processing of visual information becomes active. PET can also be used to identify areas of the brain that are active when we are *thinking*.

Key STUDY

Box 10.9 The hippocampus and the 'knowledge'

Maguire *et al.* (1997) used PET to show that the part of the brain called the *right hippocampus* is involved in memories for routes between two places. When 11

London taxi drivers were asked to recall a complex route, the right hippocampus became active. When asked to recall information about landmarks in London and other cities, however, different brain parts were activated. This suggests that the right hippocampus plays an important role in 'route recall'. Indeed, the hippocampus is actually *larger* in the taxi drivers compared with a matched group who do not drive taxis (Maguire *et al.*, 2000).

PET is also useful in revealing differences between the brains of people with and without certain mental disorders. For example, the pattern of neural activity in the schizophrenic brain is different from that in the non-schizophrenic brain, suggesting that this disorder may have a physical cause (see Chapter 49).

Spets and squids

New imaging and scanning devices are presently being developed and tested. These include the *superconducting quantum interference photon device* (SQUID) and *single photon emission tomography* (SPET). Like PET, SPET and SQUID are able to map the different brain areas that are either functioning or not functioning during a task's performance. Although very expensive (costing around £350,000), their advantage is that they can focus on very small areas of the brain, occupying less than a fiftieth of a cubic inch in volume.

SPET measures the blood that flows into different brain areas. When mental activity takes place, a great deal of blood is needed. In areas where there is little activity, less blood is required. With SPET, a person is first injected with a small amount of radioactive iodine, which makes the blood vessels, including those in the brain, mildly radioactive. The person is then placed so that the head lies in a ring of detectors, each of which turns the radiation emitted by the iodine into a pulse of light which itself is transformed into a minute electronic

signal. By carefully analysing the signals, a computer builds up cross-sections of the brain at various depths depending on the part of the brain being studied.

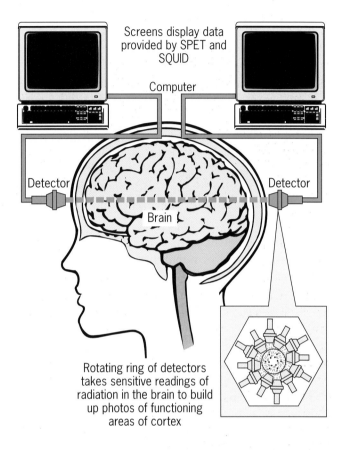

Figure 10.6 *Diagrammatic representation of SPET*

SPET has already produced some spectacular results. For example, prolonged and heavy use of alcohol causes *Korsakoff's psychosis*, a severe impairment in memory. Using SPET, it has been shown that there is a significant loss of functioning in the front part of the brain. SPET is also useful in detecting the brain areas affected in people with learning difficulties.

CONCLUSIONS

This chapter has discussed some of the methods by which the brain can be investigated. Although they all tell us something about the brain's structure and function, each has weaknesses which limit the power of the conclusions that can be drawn from them.

Essay Questions

1 Discuss any **two** methods used to investigate the brain. *(24 marks)*

2 Describe and evaluate the strengths and limitations of **one** non-invasive method used to investigate the brain. *(24 marks)*

Summary

- Three major ways of investigating the brain are **clinical/anatomical methods**, **invasive methods** and **non-invasive methods**.

- Studies of the behavioural consequences of **accidental brain damage** assume that if damage to part of the brain causes a particular behavioural change, the damaged part ordinarily plays a role in that behaviour.

- With many cases of accidental damage, however, not enough is known about the individuals before the damage occurred. Also, it can be difficult to determine the precise location and amount of damage, and research requires the 'right kind' of injury to have occurred.

- **Ablation** involves surgically removing/destroying the brain tissue of non-humans and observing the behavioural effects. However, such research tells us nothing about humans, and because parts of the brain may work together in a particular behaviour, we do not know whether a part controls, or is merely involved in, behaviour.

- The problems with ablation also occur in **lesion production**, in which part of the brain is deliberately injured and the effects observed. Lesion production has been used therapeutically in humans to treat **epilepsy**. These **split-brain** operations have interesting psychological consequences.

- **Electrical stimulation of the brain** (ESB) involves inserting electrodes into the brain and passing a non-damaging current which the brain treats as a real impulse. Alternatively, the cerebral cortex is stimulated. ESB has been used therapeutically, and is a useful way of mapping the connections between various brain structures.

- The activity of single neurons can be studied using **micro-electrode recording**. This has contributed to our understanding of the visual system, but the vast number of neurons in the visual system alone makes it a painstaking method.

- **Chemical stimulation of the brain** involves the introduction of a chemical to the brain by means of a micro-pipette. The effects produced last longer than in electrical stimulation, but since different non-humans respond differently to the same chemical, interpreting findings is difficult.

- To overcome the practical problems and ethical issues of methods using direct intervention, researchers also use non-invasive methods. These involve recording the brain's electrical activity, and scanning and imaging it.

- The **electroencephalogram** (EEG) measures the simultaneous electrical activity of millions of neurons. However, whilst it has been used extensively in research into sleep and dreaming, and as a diagnostic tool, it provides only general information about the brain. **Computerised electroencephalography,** the **magnetoencephalogram** (MEG) and **EEG imaging** provide much more specific information, although they too have limitations.

- Various imaging techniques are used to investigate the brain. These include **computerised axial tomography** (CAT) and **magnetic resonance imaging** (MRI). However, both are limited to still images of the brain's structure. Newer techniques, such as **functional magnetic resonance imaging** (fMRI) and **transcranial magnetic stimulation** (TMS) may be even better than CAT and MRI.

- **Positron emission tomography** (PET) is an imaging technique that measures the brain's metabolic activity. The advantage of PET over CAT and MRI is that it can measure brain activity during a task's performance.

- The **superconducting quantum interference device** (SQUID) and **single photon emission tomography** (SPET) are among the most recent imaging and scanning techniques. Both can examine tiny areas of the brain, and have already yielded important information.

WEB ADDRESSES

http://www.hhmi.org/sense/e/e110.htm
http://www.brain.com/
http://www.maclester.edu/~psych/whathap/UBNRP/Imaging/pet/html
http://www-hbp.scripps.edu/
http://www.mni.mcgill.ca/

11 Localisation of Function in the Cerebral Cortex

INTRODUCTION AND OVERVIEW

The cerebral cortex is the surface layer of the brain and, as noted in Chapter 4 (see page 69), it developed about two million years ago, but only in some mammals. The cortex is typically ½–3 mm thick, but at its deepest it extends to about 10 mm. As well as being the last brain part to stop growing and differentiating, it undergoes greater structural change and transformation after birth than any other structure.

This chapter examines the functional organisation of the cerebral cortex, and looks at specific processes and behaviours which are *localised*, that is, have relatively precise and circumscribed cortical locations. It also considers those cortical areas which are apparently involved in certain higher cognitive processes such as learning, thinking and memory. Finally, the chapter examines the debate between those who believe that functions are localised in the cortex (*'localisation' theorists*) and those who believe that psychological functions are controlled by neurons throughout the brain (*'distributed functions' theorists*).

AN INTRODUCTION TO THE CEREBRAL CORTEX

The *cerebral cortex* is folded into a pattern of 'hills' and 'valleys' called *convolutions*. These give the brain its cauliflower-like appearance. The convolutions are produced during the brain's development, when the cortex folds back on itself. Its total surface area is around 2400 cm², and the convolutions are nature's way of confining it to a skull that has to be narrow enough to pass through the birth canal. The convolutions also facilitate the interconnections between different parts of the cortex needed to control complex behaviours.

Although some non-human species possess a cortex, it is much smaller in surface area, shallower, and less convoluted than that of humans. Generally, the greater proportion of brain devoted to the cortex, the more complex and flexible an animal's possible range of behaviours is. The cortex, then, accounts for our fantastic information-processing capabilities. If it ceases to function, a person vegetates without sensory experiences, voluntary movement or consciousness.

The larger 'hills' (or 'bulges') are called *gyri* (the singular being *gyrus*). The deeper 'valleys' are called *fissures* or *sulci* (the singular being *sulcus*). One of these, the *longitudinal fissure* runs down the middle of the brain, and divides it into two halves (the right and left *cerebral hemispheres*). Two other naturally occurring fissures in each hemisphere are the *lateral fissure* (or *fissure*

of Sylvius) and the central fissure (or *fissure of Rolando*: see Figure 11.1 below).

Box 11.1 The four lobes of the brain

Using the lateral and central fissures, each hemisphere can be divided into four distinct areas or *lobes*, which are named after the bones beneath which they lie. These are the *frontal*, *parietal*, *occipital* and *temporal* lobes.

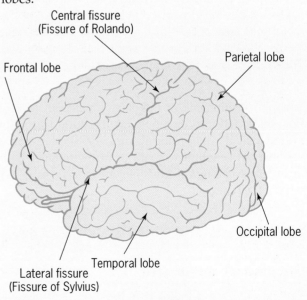

Figure 11.1 *The four lobes of the brain*

This division is a convenient 'geographical' one but, as will be seen, each lobe carries out many functions, some of which involve interactions with the others. A much better way of 'mapping' the cortex is in terms of areas of it that, during the course of evolution, have become specialised to perform certain tasks. Three cortical areas can be identified in terms of the general functions they perform. These are the *motor*, *sensory* and *association areas*, and all are considered in this and the following chapter.

LOCALISATION THEORY

According to *localisation theory*, different areas of the brain and cortex are specialised for different psychological functions. This theory can be traced back to the work of Gall, an Austrian physician. He noticed that some of his friends with particularly good memories also had large protruding eyes. His explanation for this was that the front of their brains (which he believed to be the location of memories) was so well developed that it had pushed out the eyes. On the basis of this and other observations, Gall developed *phrenology*.

Box 11.2 Phrenology

Phrenologists see the brain as composed of a number of separate organs, each of which is responsible for a different psychological trait. The unusual growth of any of these organs would create a bump on the skull, and people's characters could be determined by the pattern of bumps on their skulls. For example, a bump on the back of the head indicated that a person was 'cautious', whilst a bump on the side of the head indicated a 'secretive' individual. A bump just above the ears apparently meant that a person was 'destructive' and, potentially, a 'criminal'.

Although fashionable in the early nineteenth century, phrenology fell into disrepute on the quite reasonable ground that it was wrong (Carter, 1998). However, it was 'just right enough' to continue further interest in the idea that psychological functions are *localised* in certain parts of the brain.

PRIMARY CORTICAL AREAS

The primary motor area

Penfield (1947) and Penfield & Roberts (1959) showed that stimulation of part of the frontal lobe near to the central fissure in one cerebral hemisphere caused twitching of specific muscles in the *opposite* side of the body. Delgado (1969) dramatically illustrated this when he stimulated a part of the primary motor area in a patient's *left* hemisphere. This caused the patient to form a clenched fist with his *right* hand. When asked to try to keep his fingers still during the next stimulation, the patient could not achieve this and commented, 'I guess, Doctor, that your electricity is stronger than my will'.

Box 11.3 Contralateral and ipsilateral conections

The first structure that emerges from the spinal cord as it widens on entering the skull is called the *medulla oblongata*. This regulates vital functions such as heart rate, blood pressure, respiration and body temperature, and contains all the nerve fibres connecting the spinal cord to the brain. Most of these cross the medulla oblongata so that, generally, the one half of the body is connected to the *opposite* side of the brain. This is called a *contralateral connection*. It is contrasted with an *ipsilateral connection*, in which nerve fibres from one half of the body go to the *same* half of the brain.

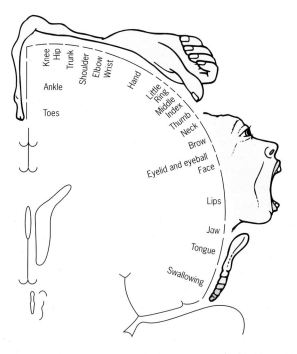

Figure 11.2 *A cross-section through the cortex showing the primary motor area and how the parts of the body are represented*

Penfield discovered that when he stimulated the *top* of the primary motor area (or *motor strip*), a twitching in the *lower* part of the body (such as the leg) occurred.

However, stimulation of the *bottom* part of the motor strip produced movement in the *upper* part of the body (such as the tongue). Penfield concluded that the body must be represented in an approximately upside-down fashion in the primary motor area. He also found that those body areas which require precise control, such as the fingers and mouth, have more cortical area devoted to them than those requiring less precise control.

Key **S T U D Y**

Box 11.4 The primary motor area and movement

The primary motor area itself is not responsible for 'commanding' the 600 muscles in the body involved in voluntary movement. These commands are initiated in other cortical locations. However, once a command has been given, neurons in the primary motor area are activated, and send their information to the muscles that perform movements. What Penfield's (1947) research identified was exactly where the response messages from the brain start their return trip to the muscles and glands of the body. Damage to the primary motor area does not produce complete paralysis. However, it often results in a loss of control over 'fine' movements (especially of the fingers).

The primary sensory areas

Whilst some cortical parts are specialised for motor functions, others govern sensory functions and receive their information in a precise, orderly way from the thalami, subcortical structures that act as a 'sensory relay station', and send sensory information to cortical areas for interpretation.

The primary somatosensory area

As has just been seen, the primary motor area *transmits* information out to the body. Certain types of incoming information are *received* by the *primary somatosensory area*, located in the parietal lobe, just across the central fissure. It is a thin 'strip' along which information from the skin senses (such as touch, temperature, pressure and so on) is represented. It also receives information concerning *taste*.

Micro-electrode stimulation of the primary somatosensory area might produce the sensation that the arm, for example, is being touched or pinched or that the leg 'feels hot'. Like the primary motor area, the body is represented in an approximately upside-down fashion, and those body parts which are more sensitive (such as the face and genitals) have more cortex devoted to them. Relatively insensitive parts of the body, such as the trunk, have considerably less area devoted to them.

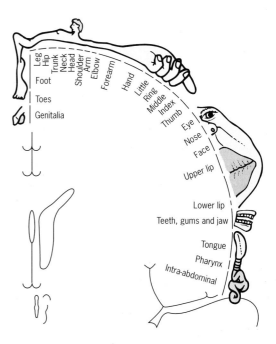

Figure 11.3 *A cross-section through the cortex showing the primary somatosensory area and how the parts of the body are represented*

Box 11.5 Sensitivity and the primary somatosensory area

There is a clear relationship between the *importance* of a body part and the amount of cortex devoted to it. In animals that use their forepaws to explore the environment (such as the racoon), there is a large amount of forepaw cortical representation. In rats, the amount of primary somatosensory area devoted to the whiskers is very large. If a human is unfortunate enough to lose a finger, the somatosensory part responsible for receiving input from that finger becomes available to receive input from other fingers. As a result, the other fingers become *more sensitive* (Fox, 1984). Similarly, in Braille readers the cortical area devoted to the tip of the right forefinger is considerably enlarged as compared with the left, and is larger than that in non-Braille readers (Robertson, 1995).

As with the primary motor area, the primary somatosensory area in the *left* hemisphere registers information about the *right* side of the body. If the primary somatosensory area is damaged, deficits or disturbances in the sense of touch result. The extent of these depends on the amount of damage. With very mild damage, a person might not be able to make fine distinctions between the temperature of objects, but could tell the difference between 'hot' and 'cold'. With more severe damage, this might not be possible.

Figure 11.4 *If the area of each body part were proportionate to its sensitivity, a human would appear like this. This is called a* homunculus

The primary auditory area

The primary auditory area lies in the temporal lobe of each hemisphere, along the lateral fissure. When auditory information is detected by the ear, it is transmitted via the thalami to the primary auditory area, and causes neurons there to be activated. Penfield discovered that stimulation of these neurons caused his

patients to report hearing sounds such as 'the ringing of a door bell' or 'the engine of a car'. The neurons in this area are highly specialised, with some responding only to low-pitched sounds and others only to high-pitched sounds.

Most auditory information from one ear travels to the primary auditory area in the opposite hemisphere. However, some information is processed on the same side. In hearing, then, there are both contralateral and ipsilateral connections. Slight damage to the primary auditory area produces 'partial hearing loss'. The more extensive the damage, the greater is the loss.

The primary visual area

One of Penfield's first findings was that parts of the cortex are specialised to receive visual sensory information. For example, when a stimulating electrode was applied to the occipital lobe, his patients reported 'seeing' different kinds of visual displays. Penfield (1947) reported the descriptions given by his patients as follows:

> 'Flickering lights, dancing lights, colours, bright lights, star wheels, blue-, green- and red-coloured discs, fawn and blue lights, radiating grey spots becoming pink and blue, a long white mark, and so on'.

Although his patients never reported a complete picture of the visual displays they experienced, Penfield's findings convinced him that the brain's primary visual area is located in the occipital lobe. When this area is damaged, blindness (or a 'hole') occurs in part of the visual field. The rest of the visual sense is, however, intact. Indeed, by moving the eyes, those parts of the visual world which cannot be seen can be brought into view, although the person will still be blind in some part of the visual field.

Chapter 22 looks in detail at the structures and processes involved in visual perception. However, it is worth briefly describing here how visual information reaches the primary visual area of the cortex. When light strikes the *retina* of the eyes, it is converted into electrical information which then passes along each eye's *optic nerve*. At the *optic chiasma*, the nerve fibres from each eye meet and divide up.

The fibres from the half of each eye's retina closest to the nose cross over, and continue their journey in the hemisphere on the opposite side. The fibres from each eye's retina closest to the temples do not cross over, and continue their journey in the hemisphere on the same side. The visual world can be divided into a *left visual field* and a *right visual field*. As Figure 11.6 illustrates (see page 111), information from the *left* visual field is processed by the *right* cerebral hemisphere, whilst information from the *right* visual field is processed by the *left* cerebral hemisphere.

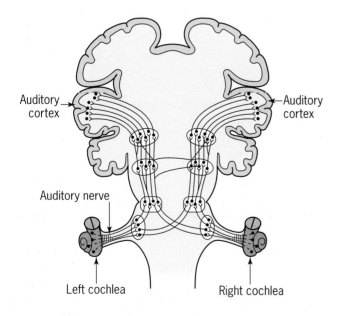

Figure 11.5 *The major pathways of the auditory nerve fibres*

Auditory cortex

Auditory cortex

Auditory nerve

Left cochlea

Right cochlea

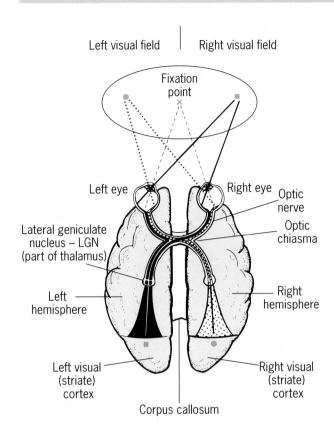

Figure 11.6 *The major pathways of the visual nerve fibres*

This occurs because of the crossing over of the fibres at the optic chiasma, and means that each hemisphere receives information from both eyes. Although it might be simpler if each eye transmitted information to the hemisphere on the same side, damage to one eye would mean that a hemisphere would not receive any visual input. By having the more complex arrangement, damage to one eye does *not* result in a hemisphere 'missing out' on visual information. Information travels along the optic nerve and to the *lateral geniculate nuclei*, part of the thalami. From there, it is sent to the primary visual area.

ASSOCIATION AREAS IN THE CORTEX

The primary motor and sensory areas account for a relatively small proportion of the cortex's surface area. The primary motor area sends information to adjacent areas of the cortex called the *motor association areas*. Each of the primary sensory areas sends information to adjacent *sensory association areas*.

Motor association areas

These are involved in the planning and execution of movements. Information about which movements are to

be executed are sent to the primary motor area. The motor association areas receive their information from several areas and integrate this into plans and actions. One region of the cortex is necessary for the production of spoken *language*, and is described in detail in Chapter 12.

Left parietal lobe damage makes hand movements difficult. Figure 11.7 shows the attempt of a person with such damage to draw a bicycle. Although the proportions of the elements making up the bicycle are quite good, the drawing looks clumsy and might have been done by a child. The motor association area's ability to integrate information into plans and actions is probably disrupted following left parietal lobe damage.

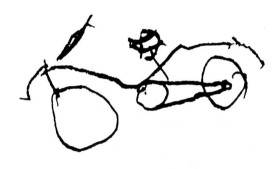

Figure 11.7 *Drawing of a bicycle by a person with left parietal lobe damage*

The motor association areas in the left parietal lobe, then, play an important role in the ability to keep track of the location of the body's moving parts (Carlson, 1988). This view is strengthened by the finding that people with left parietal lobe damage often have difficulty with tasks requiring them to point to a part of the body. They may, for example, point to the shoulder when asked to point to the elbow. Left parietal lobe damage results in 'faulty data' being sent to the primary motor area, which leads to poor execution of movement.

Sensory association areas

Each of the primary sensory areas sends information to adjacent sensory association areas. As was seen earlier, the primary somatosensory area mediates our awareness of what is happening in the body and on its surface. Severe damage to this area produces *sensory neglect*.

Box 11.6 Sensory neglect

In sensory neglect, the affected person loses all awareness of the opposite side of the body. For example, a person having a shave will shave only one side of the face, eat food on only one side of the plate, and draw only one half of an object (Halligan, 1995).

Figure 11.8 *Drawing of a parrot by a person with left-side neglect*

Associations in the parietal lobe play a role in *integrating* complex sensory functions as shown in *cross-modal matching*. If an object is placed in your hand but kept out of sight, you would, when *shown* an array of objects in which it was included, be able to pick it out. This is because ordinarily we can integrate visual and tactile information. When the parietal lobe association areas are damaged, however, this task is extremely difficult.

The *auditory association area* is located towards the back of the occipital lobes on the side of the temporal lobes. If the left hemisphere's auditory association area is damaged, severe language disturbances occur. For example, speech comprehension is lost, presumably because the neurons involved in decoding speech sounds have been destroyed. Additionally, the ability to read is lost, and whilst the person may still be capable of producing language, its quality is very poor indeed and just a meaningless jumble of words (see Chapter 12). Right hemisphere damage, by contrast, does not affect the production or comprehension of speech to any great degree. It does, however, affect the ability to perceive the *location* of sounds, and to recognise non-speech sounds, such as rhythms and tones.

In contrast to the effects produced by damage to the primary visual area, damage to the *visual association area* (which includes parts of the temporal and parietal lobes, as well as the occipital lobes) does not produce blindness. However, whilst the primary sensory function of vision is not impaired, the ability to *recognise* objects by sight is, a condition called *visual agnosia*.

Key **STUDY**

Box 11.7 The man who mistook his wife for a hat

Sacks (1985) described a man who could not even recognise his own wife. At the end of one testing session, the man started to look for his hat. He reached over to his wife and began to lift her head, seemingly believing it to be his hat. Evidently, he had mistaken his wife's head for his own hat. Damage to some parts of the visual association area, then, produces deficits in the visual recognition of familiar objects.

Damage to the occipital lobes results in the inability to recognise the elements of a visual scene, such as curves and angles. Damage to the right parietal lobe results in great difficulty integrating an object's parts into a consistent whole. In contrast to the drawing of the bicycle produced by a person with left parietal lobe damage (see Figure 11.7, page 111), a person with a damaged right parietal lobe produces a drawing which is smoothly executed and well-detailed, but does not have all of the parts placed appropriately.

Figure 11.9 *Drawing of a bicycle by a person with right parital lobe damage*

Box 11.8 Higher order analyses of sensory information

As has been seen, sensory association areas are located near to their primary sensory area counterparts, and receive information only about one sense modality. However, other sensory association areas receive information from more than one sense modality. These perform higher-order analyses of sensory information and represent abstract information in ways that are independent of individual sense modalities.

When we think about the word 'dog', for example, we can picture a visual image of a particular dog, the sound of its bark, and (perhaps) the pain we felt when it once bit us. We can also think about the visual representation of the word 'd-o-g' and the sound of the word 'dog'. Our thoughts can be stimulated when we see a dog, hear the word being said, or read a book in which the word is printed. The centres of higher-order analysis include areas on the borders between the temporal, parietal and occipital lobes.

Association areas not involved in motor or sensory functions

Even given what has been described, there are still large cortical areas that do not seem to be involved in either motor or sensory aspects of behaviour. Although knowledge is limited, it is known that these other areas are involved in the more complex psychological processes of learning, thinking, memory, and so on. Indeed, the term 'association areas' was originally used to describe them, because it was believed that they were used in higher cognitive processes such as forming associations between things.

Box 11.9 Einstein's parietal lobes

Although Albert Einstein's brain was no heavier than most people's, his parietal lobes were larger. Additionally, Einstein's lateral fissure (see Figure 11.1, page 107) was smooth and almost missing. The lack of this fissure might have allowed nerve cells in Einstein's brain to make connections more easily and be more highly integrated. The parietal lobe plays a role in working out mathematical concepts as well as understanding movement and processing visual information. The temporal lobe is involved in hearing and speech development (see Chapter 12). The lack of a clear dividing line between the temporal and parietal lobe might also explain Einstein's own description of his scientific thinking:

'Words do not seem to play a role, [but there is] an associative play of more or less clear images of a visual and muscular type.'

(Adapted from Murray, 1999)

The frontal lobes are larger in humans than in any other species. For that reason, they were once thought to be 'the seat of intelligence'. However, frontal lobe damage does not cause significant impairments in intellectual functioning. Rather, it seems to affect the ability to set goals, plan actions and make decisions. Put differently, frontal lobe damage affects *intentions*.

Box 11.10 Perseveration and the frontal lobes

Damage to the frontal lobes results in the inability to change a behaviour in response to change in a situation. For example, Cotman & McGaugh (1980) described a man who worked in a carpenter's shop. Although he could sand a piece of wood, the man did not know to stop when the sanding was complete. As a result, he sanded completely through the wood and continued sanding the work bench below. Similarly, Luria (1980) reported the case of a man who kept trying to light a match that was already lit. The term *perseveration* has been used to describe these behaviours.

Card-sorting tasks also illustrate perseveration. In these, a person is given a series of cards each of which has one or more patterns on it in one of several colours. People with frontal lobe damage have few difficulties sorting the cards according to colour, but when asked to sort them according to shape, they have great difficulty and continue sorting according to colour. Frontal lobe damage in non-humans results in the inability to remember the solution to a simple problem for more than a few seconds (Rosenkilde & Divac, 1976). Similarly, humans have difficulties in remembering the solutions to problems, especially those which require switching back and forth from one solution to another.

Frontal lobe damage is also associated with changes in personality. For example, a person may react with indifference to emotionally-provoking events, and being informed of the death of a close relative may produce no over-emotional reaction even though the individual understands what has happened. Other consequences of frontal lobe damage include a lack of insight, uncritical acceptance of the failure to solve a task and the inability to perceive sarcasm in written and conversational speech (McDonald & Pearce, 1996). Excessive damage produces *behavioural inertia*, in which a person lacks spontaneity, remains motionless and stares vacantly into space.

Surgically damaging the frontal lobes became a 'popular' way of treating some mental disorders in the 1930s and 1940s. *Psychosurgery* is still used to treat some mental disorders, and its applications and limitations are discussed further in Chapter 52.

One final consequence of frontal lobe damage is the production of *reflexive behaviour* normally seen only in babies, such as sucking an object placed near the mouth.

Possibly, one role of the frontal lobes is to suppress such activities (which are presumably the result of activity in the more 'primitive' parts of the brain) when they are no longer needed.

Box 11.11 The association areas and memory

The association areas in the temporal lobes play an important role in memory. Penfield (1947) claimed that stimulating these areas caused a person to recall a 'dream-like' reliving of a past event. For example, when he stimulated an area of a young woman's temporal lobe, she said:

'I think I heard a mother calling her little boy somewhere. It seemed to be something that happened years ago ... in the neighbourhood where I live'.

When the same part was stimulated moments later, she said:

'Yes. I hear the same familiar sounds. It seems to be a woman calling; the same lady'.

When Penfield moved the electrode slightly and stimulated the woman's cortex she said:

'I hear voices. It is late at night, around the carnival somewhere – some sort of travelling circus. I just saw lots of big wagons that they use to haul animals in'.

Association areas in the temporal lobe also play a role in both social behaviour and certain emotional responses. In some types of temporal lobe damage, a person becomes a compulsive talker who harangues anyone who is (or potentially could be) listening, even if listeners have not the slightest interest in what is being said. This finding suggests that the association areas of the temporal lobe (especially, it seems, of the right hemisphere) play a role in evaluating the appropriateness of thoughts and speech. If the temporal lobes are damaged, the ability to carry out such evaluations is impaired (Carlson, 1988).

Key STUDY
Box 11.12 Loser's lobes?

Damasio *et al.* (cited in Matthews, 1997b) gave brain damaged and non-brain damaged people packs of cards. Some individual cards in each pack were worth money, whilst some cards in two of the packs carried large financial penalties. Non-brain damaged people quickly learnt to choose cards from packs that did not carry the penalties. Whilst brain-damaged

individuals eventually realised the packs were different, they still chose cards from them. Non-brain damaged individuals attributed their decisions to a 'hunch' and Damasio *et al.* suggest that the ventromedial frontal cortices, the parts affected in the damaged individuals, were responsible for these poor decisions. These regions are believed to store information about past rewards and punishment. In the absence of reliable 'hunches', poor decisions invariably occur (see Chapter 27).

HOLISM AND DISTRIBUTED FUNCTIONS AS ALTERNATIVES TO LOCALISATION

The findings relating to cortical areas lend strong support to localisation theory. However, localisation has not been universally accepted. According to *holistic theory*, psychological functions are controlled by neurons throughout the brain. Lashley (1926) studied the effects of destroying various parts of rats' brains on their abilities to remember the way through a complex maze. Although the rats displayed some difficulties, Lashley found that destruction of one particular area did not lead to greater difficulties than destruction of any other area.

Box 11.13 Learning just is not possible!

In a follow-up experiment, Lashley varied the *amount* of cortex destroyed in rats who had learned their way through the maze. He found that the greater the amount of cortex destroyed, the greater the effects, and called this the *law of mass action*. However, he also found that even rats with considerable damage could still find their way through the maze. In 1950, Lashley gave up his search for the part of the brain where memories were stored and remarked that, on the basis of his studies, the only conclusion he could reach after 25 years of research was that 'learning just is not possible!'

A compromise between localisation and holism is the idea of *distributed functions* (or *distributed control*). According to this perspective, psychological functions depend on the activity of, and connections between, several different but specific locations (Stirling, 2000). A particularly good example of this is the cortical areas involved in *language*, and these are considered in detail in the following chapter.

CONCLUSIONS

The cerebral cortex plays a vital role in behaviours and mental processes. As well as dealing with motor and sensory aspects of behaviour, it is also responsible for higher cognitive processes. When the cortex is damaged, various behavioural deficits occur. With the introduction of the non-invasive methods of studying the brain described in Chapter 10, we can confidently expect knowledge of the cortex and its functions to increase dramatically.

Summary

- According to **localisation theory,** a scientific successor to **phrenology**, different cortical areas are specialised for different psychological functions.

- The **primary motor area** is involved in movement, although it is not responsible for 'commanding' the muscles involved in voluntary movement. However, when a command has been given, primary motor area neurons send their information to muscles that perform movements.

- The body is represented in an approximately **upside-down** fashion in the primary motor area, and since the area in the left hemisphere sends information to the right side of the body (and vice versa), it is **contralaterally connected**. Parts of the body requiring precise control have more cortical area devoted to them.

- The **primary somatosensory area** receives information about the skin senses and taste via the thalami. It is contralaterally connected, and the body is represented in an approximately upside-down fashion. Sensitive and important body parts have more cortex devoted to them.

- The **primary auditory area** is both **ipsilaterally** and contralaterally connected. It receives auditory information via the thalami. Stimulation produces the experience of hearing sounds.

- Light striking the retina is converted to electrical information. This passes along the **optic nerve**. At the **optic chiasma**, the fibres from the half of each retina closest to the nose cross over to the opposite hemisphere. The fibres from the half of each retina closest to the temples continue in the hemisphere on the same side.

- Stimulation of the **primary visual area** results in the experience that something has been seen. If the area is damaged, blindness (or a 'hole') occurs in part of the visual field. However, moving the eyes can bring the 'missing' part of the visual world into view.

- The primary motor and sensory areas send information to adjacent **motor** and **sensory association** areas. Motor association areas are involved in the planning and execution of movements. Damage to these areas produces deficits in the ability to integrate information into plans and actions, and an inability to keep track of the location of the body's moving parts.

- Damage to the somatosensory association areas produces **sensory neglect**, a loss of awareness of one side of the body. Deficits in **cross-modal matching** can also occur.

- Damage to the **auditory association area** in the left hemisphere results in severe language disturbances. Right hemisphere damage affects the ability to perceive a sound's location and the recognition of non-speech sounds.

- When the **visual association areas** are damaged, **visual agnosia** occurs. The type of agnosia depends on the area damaged.

- Some association areas receive information from more than one sense modality, and perform higher-order analyses of sensory information, as well as representing information in abstract ways.

- Large areas of the cortex are not obviously involved in either sensory or motor aspects of behaviour. Rather, they are involved in complex psychological processes such as learning, thinking and memory.

- The **frontal lobes** are involved in setting goals, planning actions and making decisions. Damage to them results in the inability to change behaviour in response to situational change (as in **perseveration**). Damage is also associated with personality changes and a lack of insight.

- **Temporal lobe** association areas play an important role in memory, social behaviour and certain emotional responses. Damage impairs the ability to evaluate the appropriateness of thoughts and speech.

- In contrast to localisation theory, **holism** maintains that psychological functions are controlled by neurons throughout the brain. The idea of **distributed functions** is a compromise between these two positions.

Essay Questions

1 Discuss psychological research into the functional organisation of the cerebral cortex. *(24 marks)*

2 Critically consider the view that psychological functions are localised in the cerebral cortex. *(24 marks)*

WEB ADDRESSES

http://www.Isadc.org/web2/lang_brain.html
http://www.ability.org.uk/index.html
http://www.core.binghampton.edu/~flobe
http://neuro.med.cornell.edu/VL/

12 Lateralisation of Function in the Cerebral Cortex

INTRODUCTION AND OVERVIEW

Chapter 18 described the role played by certain cortical areas in mental processes and behaviour. These areas are found in *both* cerebral hemispheres. However, for the overwhelming majority of people, some functions and processes are associated with *one or other* cerebral hemisphere rather than both. When this is the case, the functions and processes are said to be *lateralised*.

The first part of this chapter examines the cortical areas involved in *language* which, for most people, are lateralised in the *left* cerebral hemisphere. The second part looks at other hemisphere asymmetries of function, and at the intriguing question of whether the two cerebral hemispheres represent two kinds of 'mind'.

THE DISTRIBUTED CONTROL OF LANGUAGE

As noted in Chapter 11 (see Box 11.2, page 108), Gall's phrenology fell into disrepute because it was wrong. However, Gall did make some suggestions which were more or less correct. One of these concerned *speech*. Gall proposed that the frontal lobes of the brain were specialised for speech. An admirer who was particularly impressed with phrenology offered the sum of 500 French francs to anyone who could find a person with frontal lobe damage who did *not* have a speech disorder.

Key STUDY

Box 12.1 'Tan'

The admirer's offer led Broca (see Box 10.1, page 98), a French physician, to examine patients who had difficulty producing speech. His first case, 'Tan', was so named because this was the only word he could say. 'Tan' was originally admitted to hospital because he had a serious leg infection, but it was his difficulty in producing speech that most interested Broca.

Shortly after being admitted, 'Tan' died as a result of his infection and Broca conducted a post-mortem on him. This indicated that 'Tan' had suffered strokes which caused multiple *lesions* in a cortical area in the frontal lobe of the *left* hemisphere. In the next three years, Broca reported eight other cases, all with the same problem as 'Tan', and all with lesions in a specific part of the left frontal lobe.

Around the same time that Broca was reporting his findings, Wernické (see Box 10.1, page 98) described patients who had difficulty in understanding language, but were able to produce it, even though what was produced was usually meaningless. Wernické identified a region in the temporal lobe of the *left* cerebral hemisphere as being responsible for the deficit. The cortical areas identified by Wernické and Broca are now called *Wernické's area* and *Broca's area* respectively.

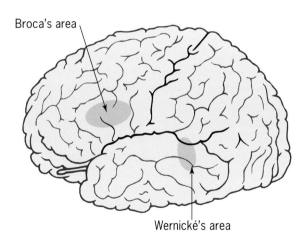

Figure 12.1 *The location of Broca's and Wernické's areas in the left cerebral hemisphere*

Language disorders arising from brain damage are called *aphasias*. However, Milner (1971) argues that the term should only be used to describe complete language loss, *dysphasia* being a more accurate term to describe a partial loss of language (the word aphasia comes from the Greek word 'aphitos' which means 'speechless'). The type of aphasia a person suffers tells us interesting things about the cortical area whose damage produced it.

Broca's aphasia

A person with damage to Broca's area experiences *Broca's aphasia* (sometimes called *ataxic, expressive, non-fluent* or *motor aphasia*). Usually, a Broca's aphasic can comprehend spoken or written language either normally or nearly normally. However, the person has great difficulty in producing speech (as Broca observed over 100 years ago). Typically, speech production is slow, laboured, non-fluent and difficult for the listener to understand.

For example, Geschwind (1979) reported the case of a Broca's aphasic who was asked about his dental appointment. He replied, 'Yes ... Monday ... Dad and Dick ... Wednesday nine o'clock ... ten o'clock ... doctors ... teeth'. As this example shows, Broca's aphasics find it difficult to produce 'function words', (words with grammatical meaning such as 'a', 'the' and 'about'). Their language consists almost entirely of 'content words' (words which convey meaning such as nouns, verbs, adjectives and adverbs). Consequently, Broca's aphasia has a *telegraphic* quality to it (see Chapter 26, page 273). In milder cases, the person might be aware that speech is not correct, and may become irritated by being unable to produce the intended words.

Box 12.2 Phonemic paraphrasias and agraphia in Broca's aphasia

Another characteristic of Broca's aphasia is the production of *phonemic paraphrasias*. In these, certain words are mispronounced. For example, instead of saying 'lipstick' the person might say 'likstip'. Sometimes, Broca's aphasia is accompanied by difficulty in writing (*agraphia*). Broca's area stores the 'motor plans' for the formulation of words. Normally, these plans are passed to the *primary motor area* (see Chapter 11, pages 108–109) which initiates the processes that will convert them to spoken language. When Broca's area is damaged, 'faulty data' are sent to the primary motor area, and this results in the characteristic deficits in speech production.

Wernické's aphasia

Damage to Wernické's area produces *Wernické's aphasia* (sometimes called *receptive, sensory,* or *fluent aphasia*). Its major characteristic is a difficulty in understanding spoken and written language. Luria (1973), for example, described a person who was puzzled by the question: 'Is an elephant bigger than a fly?' He told Luria that he 'just didn't understand the words smaller or bigger' and that he:

'... somehow thinks the expression "a fly is smaller than an elephant" means that they're talking about a very small elephant and a big fly'.

In another case, Kertesz (1979) reported the response given by a person who was asked, 'What kind of work did you do before you came into the hospital?' The person replied:

'Never, now mista oyge I wanna tell you this happened when he rent. His – his kell come down here and is – he got ren something. It happened. In these ropiers were with him for hi – is friend – like was. And it just happened so I don't know, he did not bring around anything. And he did not pay for it. And he roden all o these arranjen from the pedis on from his pescid. In these floors now and so. He hadn't had em round here'.

Similarly, Rochford (1974) reports the case of a man who was asked why he had been admitted to hospital. The man replied:

'Boy I'm sweating, I'm awful nervous, you know, once in a while I get caught up, I can't mention the tarripoi, a month ago, quite a little I've done a lot well. I'm pose a lot, while, on the other hand, you know what I mean'.

These examples show that Wernické's aphasics have difficulty in understanding language and the language they produce is, at least in some cases, virtually unintelligible and lacking coherence. Thus, when asked to describe a picture of two boys stealing biscuits behind a woman's back, a patient of Geschwind's replied:

'Mother is away here working her work to get better, but when she's looking the two boys looking in the other part. She's working another time' (Geschwind, 1979).

The verbal outpourings of Wernické's aphasics have been described as 'a peculiar and outwardly meaningless language form'. Freud (1891) described such utterances as 'an impoverishment of words with an abundance of speech impulse'. Freud might have viewed such verbal behaviour as an indication of a serious mental disorder. However, as Williams (1981) has noted:

'The aphasic patient nearly always tries hard to communicate, whereas in [the seriously mentally disturbed individual] communication seems to be irrelevant'.

One characteristic of Wernické's aphasia which is evident in some of the examples given above is the production of *jargon*, that is, nonsense words or *neologisms* (see also Chapter 49). For example, when Rochford (1974) asked a Wernické's aphasic to name a picture of an anchor, the aphasic called it a 'martha argeneth'. Similarly, when Kertesz (1979) asked a Wernické's aphasic to name a toothbrush and a pen, the aphasic responded with 'stok-tery' and 'minkt'.

Box 12.3 Wernické's aphasia: semantic paraphrasias and comprehension

Merely because a Wernické's aphasic does not answer a question correctly, it cannot be inferred that the question has not been understood. Wernické's aphasia is also characterised by *semantic paraphrasias*, in which the word that is produced does not have the intended meaning, although it may be related to the intended word. For example, instead of producing the word 'table', the word 'chair' may be produced. To assess comprehension, *non-verbal* responses must be elicited. One test asks the person to point to various objects on a table. If the person is asked to 'point to the one you unlock a door with' and responds by pointing to an object which is not a key, the request has not been understood.

Wernické's aphasics are capable of using some language including function words, complex verb tenses and subordinate clauses. However, there are few content words, and the words that are produced often do not make sense. Since people with damage to Wernické's area have difficulty in understanding language (and may themselves be unaware that they have a speech deficit), it is possible that they are unable to monitor their own language and this accounts for its incoherence.

It is reasonable to propose that Wernické's area stores memories of the sequences of sounds contained in words. This allows us to recognise individual words when we hear them, and produce words ourselves. If Wernické's area is damaged, sounds cannot be recognised as speech and so the individual cannot comprehend what has been said.

Anomic aphasia

In terms of producing and understanding language, *anomic* (sometimes called *amnesic* or *nominal*) *aphasics* have few problems. However, they are unable to find correct nouns to name objects. The anomic aphasic will, for example, hesitate whilst nouns are being sought and sometimes produce an inaccurate noun. Alternatively, things may be expressed clumsily as the person tries to get around the difficulty.

Most of us experience this to a degree. In severe cases of anomic aphasia, however, the person has difficulty in naming common objects such as a pen or a pair of scissors. In some cases, the anomic aphasic will *circumlocute*,

or speak in a roundabout way. A shoe, for instance, might be described as 'something to put one's foot in'.

Key **STUDY**

Box 12.4 The angular gyrus

Penfield & Roberts (1959) encountered an anomic aphasic who could not *name* a comb, but could *describe* it as 'something I comb my hair with'. Thus, 'comb' could be used as a verb but not as a noun. According to Beaumont (1988), this suggests that:

'There is obviously a part of the language system which, given a particular meaning, retrieves the appropriate word from some store and it is this which is disordered in anomic aphasia'.

Anomic aphasia is the result of damage to the *angular gyrus*, which is located in the posterior part of the parietal lobe, and therefore it is this which plays the role described by Beaumont.

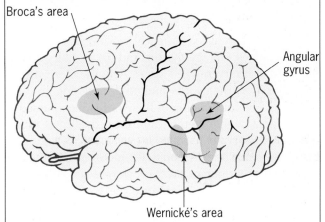

Figure 12.2 *The location of the angular gyrus in relation to Broca's and Wernické's areas*

Conduction aphasia

The typical symptom of *conduction* (or *central*) *aphasia* is difficulty in repeating a sentence that has just been heard. Although conduction aphasics can understand and produce speech relatively well, and give an account of a presented sentence in their own words, *exact* reproduction is not possible. For example, an American conduction aphasic tested in the 1960s was simply asked to repeat the word 'president'. He replied, 'I know who that is – Kennedy' (Geshwind, 1972). Another aphasic, asked to repeat the sentence, 'The auto's leaking gas tank soiled the roadway', responded with, 'The car tank's leaked and made a mess on the street'. Conduction aphasia occurs as a result of lesions interrupting the nerve fibres (the *arcuate fasciculus* or 'arch-shaped bundle') which connect Broca's area with Wernické's area. So, because Broca's and Wernické's areas are undamaged, speech production and comprehension are preserved, but the ability to repeat words is lost (Stirling, 2000).

Transcortical aphasia

A final type of aphasia is *transcortical aphasia*. Transcortical aphasics have few comprehension skills (*transcortical sensory aphasia* or *TSA*), cannot produce normal speech (*transcortical motor aphasia* or *TMA*) or, more usually, both (*mixed transcortical aphasia* or *MTA*). They are, however, able to repeat back what somebody has said to them. Although TSA is similar to Wernické's aphasia, and TMA to Broca's aphasia, the essential difference is that the damage has occurred *beyond* Wernické's and Broca's areas.

The relationship between cortical areas and language

Over 100 years ago, Wernické formulated a model of how the brain produces language. This was refined by Geschwind (1979). The *Wernické–Geschwind model* proposes that when asked to repeat a word just *heard*, the word is passed (via the thalami and the auditory area of the cortex) to Wernické's area. Activity there allows recognition of the words and understanding of their meaning. The formulation of the word is then passed to Broca's area, where memories of the sequence of movements necessary to produce it are stored. Broca's area then passes this information to the motor area of the cortex which programmes the various muscles in the face, tongue and larynx to reproduce the word (see Figure 12.3). This model explains why damage to Wernické's area leaves speech intact but disrupts language comprehension and the formation of meaningful sentences. It also explains why damage to Broca's area affects language production.

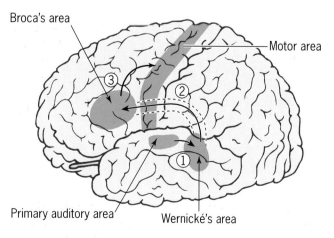

Figure 12.3 *The processes involved in speaking a heard word (see text)*

When asked to repeat a word we have *read*, a slightly different process occurs. First, the words are registered in the visual area of the cortex. Then, they are sent to the angular gyrus. This cortical area transforms a word's visual appearance into a code which is recognised and understood in Wernické's area (see Box 12.4, page 119). Once this area has received the code and understood the word's meaning, the formulation is then sent to Broca's area and the sequence of events for producing the word is initiated.

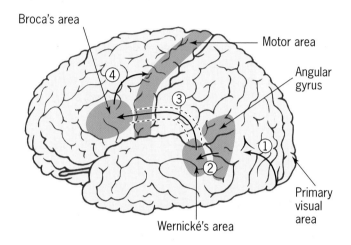

Figure 12.4 *The processes involved in speaking a written word (see text)*

The last two decades have seen significant progress in understanding the brain structures responsible for language (Banich, 1997). Research using PET (see Chapter 10) has been especially revealing. Findings indicate that when people are asked to say a particular word, Broca's area becomes highly active. However, when asked to generate a verb that would be appropriate for a particular noun (such as 'cook' for 'oven'), other cortical areas are activated (Raichle, 1994).

Language: localisation, lateralisation and holism

Chapter 11 introduced the term *localisation* to describe the fact that some specific functions and processes have relatively precise and circumscribed locations. From what has been said, language can be considered a localised function along with those described in Chapter 11. At the beginning of this chapter, it was noted that the cortical areas associated with language are *lateralised*. So, language is both localised and lateralised.

Box 12.5 Language and handedness

For most of us, language is lateralised in the *left* hemisphere. However, there are some exceptions to this general rule as Satz's (1979) review of research discovered. All but around 5 per cent of us are right-handed, and in around 95 per cent of right-handers language is localised in the left hemisphere. In the remaining 5 per cent of right-handers, language is localised in the *right* hemisphere. In left-handers, Satz found things to be more complex. In about 75 per cent of left-handers, language is localised in the left hemisphere. Although none of the studies reviewed by Satz indicated that left-handers had language localised in the right hemisphere, the remaining 25 per cent showed *bilateral representation*, that is, the language structures were more or less equally represented in *both* hemispheres.

To add to this complex picture, Kimura (1993) has reported that some left-handers show a localisation of language which is exactly the opposite of that observed in the vast majority of right-handers. In other words, some left-handers do have language localised in the right hemisphere.

There also seems to be sex differences in terms of how the brain is organised for speech production. Kimura (1993) has argued that women are less likely to incur aphasia than men, and that men show a greater degree of lateralisation than women for linguistic tasks (although some research disputes this: Frost *et al.*, 1999). Kimura does not believe that *bilateral representation* of language in women explains this effect. Her research shows that women are more likely to suffer aphasia when the front part of the brain is damaged, whilst in men aphasia is more likely following damage to the back part of the brain. Since restricted damage within a hemisphere more frequently affects the back part of the brain in both men and women, speech functions would be less likely to be disrupted in the latter because the relevant cortical area is less often affected.

There is no generally accepted explanation of why language is represented in the left and/or right hemispheres. However, the brain appears to have remarkable *plasticity*, especially during childhood (see Box 12.6). When an area is damaged, other areas are apparently able to reorganise themselves and take over the damaged part's functions. This appears to be particularly the case with language. Lashley (1926) called this phenomenon the *law of equipotentiality,* and Luria (1973) argued that the process occurs through *functional reorganisation*. In this, surviving brain circuits reorganise themselves to achieve the same behavioural goal in a different way (Robertson, 1995). This would explain why some victims of a minor stroke recover at least some abilities that were seemingly lost as a result of the stroke.

Box 12.6 Sturge–Weber syndrome and brain plasticity

In Sturge–Weber syndrome, the blood vessels of the left side of the brain become constricted during foetal development. As a result, the left side becomes shrunken with many calcium deposits. Following removal of the left half of his brain, a ten-year-old boy who was previously mute learnt to speak at an age considered by some researchers to be too late to acquire language (see Chapter 26). Several explanations for this phenomenon have been proposed, one of the most plausible being that the damaged left side was inhibiting the right from 'taking over' (Connor, 1997).

Holistic theories (which were outlined in Chapter 11 as an alternative to the theory of localisation) are capable of explaining the brain's plasticity. Localisation, holism and distributed control are probably all true to some degree.

HEMISPHERE ASYMMETRIES AND THE 'SPLIT-BRAIN'

Fechner, one of experimental psychology's pioneers, knew that the brain is *bilaterally symmetrical*, consisting of two hemispheres which are very similar (though not identical) to each other. In 1860, he asked what would happen if a living person's brain were split in half. His own answer was that each half would have a different conscious experience, that is, he believed that two 'minds' existed inside the one brain.

Fechner thought that the experiment which would answer his question could not be conducted. In the 1960s, however, studying the effects of dividing the brain in two became possible as a by-product of surgery to control epileptic seizures. Up until the 1960s, attempts to control epilepsy involved removing the presumed disordered parts of the brain. However, this approach was limited in its success, and researchers sought other treatment methods.

Box 12.7 The corpus callosum and the commissurotomy

The *corpus callosum* is a dense mass of commissural (or 'joining') fibres which connect the two cerebral hemispheres, and convey information back and forth from them. Provided that the hemispheres are connected, each receives information about the other's activities almost simultaneously.

In the early 1960s, Vogel and Bogen (see Bogen, 1969) proposed that epileptic seizures were caused by an amplification of brain activity that 'bounced' back and forth between the hemispheres. As a therapy of last resort, they suggested severing the corpus callosum, an operation called a *commissurotomy*. Their rationale was that severing the corpus callosum's 250 million axons would prevent the reverberation of brain activity, and cause it to be confined to one hemisphere. Since the operation involved splitting the hemispheres apart, people who underwent it became known as *split-brain patients*.

Research with cats and monkeys revealed that commissurotomy did not seem to cause any ill-effects. When the operation was carried out on epileptic patients, the results also suggested that there were no ill-effects apart from, as one patient joked, producing a 'splitting headache'! (Gazzaniga, 1967). As Sperry (1964) remarked:

> 'In casual conversation over a cup of coffee and a cigarette, one would hardly suspect that there was anything unusual about [the patient]'.

From a therapeutic perspective, the operation was a great success because the severity of the epileptic seizures was dramatically reduced, if not eliminated. From a psychological perspective, the operation provided the opportunity to investigate whether the hemispheres were specialised for particular functions, and allowed Fechner's question to be addressed. As will be seen, the results of many investigations also laid to rest the view that the corpus callosum served no function other than 'to keep the hemispheres from sagging'.

In their research with cats, Sperry *et al.* also severed part of the nerve fibres connecting the eyes and the brain (see Figure 11.6, page 111). This operation meant that a cat's left and right eyes sent information exclusively to its left and right hemispheres respectively. In one experiment, they placed an eye patch over a cat's left eye and then taught it to perform a particular task. When the task had been learned, the eye patch was switched to the other eye and the cat tested on the task it had just learned. It behaved as though it had *never* learned the task at all.

On the basis of this, the researchers concluded that one half of the brain did not (literally) know what the other half was doing, and that the corpus callosum functions as a means by which information can be transmitted back and forth, so that each hemisphere is aware of the sensations and perceptions of the other. Sperry *et al.* wondered if the corpus callosum served the same function in humans. Of course, it would be unethical to sever some of

the optic nerve fibres in humans if it could not be justified on therapeutic grounds (and even then, some would still consider it to be unethical).

Ordinarily, we constantly move our eyes, and hence both hemispheres receive information about the visual world whether we have experienced a commissurotomy or not. Sperry (1964) devised a way of sending visual information to one hemisphere at a time. Before looking at this methodology, two findings described in Chapter 11 should be recapped.

Box 12.8 The visual system: a recap

Each cerebral hemisphere is primarily connected to the opposite side of the body. So, an object placed in the left hand is sensed by neurons in the right hemisphere. The nerve fibres from the half of each retina closest to the temples send information to the hemisphere on the same side. However, the nerve fibres from each half of the retina closest to the nose send information to the opposite hemisphere. It is possible to divide up the visual world into a left and right visual field. As Figure 11.6 illustrates (see page 111), each hemisphere only receives information about the visual field on its opposite side. Thus, visual sensations in the left visual field are processed only by the right hemisphere, whereas the left hemisphere processes information only from the right visual field (see also Chapters 21 and 22).

Normally, each hemisphere more or less immediately shares its information with the other. In 'split-brain' patients, however, the severing of the corpus callosum means that information cannot be conveyed from hemisphere to hemisphere. As noted, we constantly move our eyes, and this allows both hemispheres to receive visual information whether the corpus callosum has been severed or not. Sperry's method of delivering information to only one cerebral hemisphere involved presenting a stimulus to one visual field at a speed that was too quick for eye movements to allow it to enter the other, and hence be perceived by both hemispheres. He discovered that a visual stimulus presented for about one tenth of a second allowed it to be perceived only by one hemisphere.

Key STUDY

Box 12.9 Presenting stimuli to each visual field individually

In Sperry's basic procedure, a patient is seated in front of a projector screen with the hands free to handle objects behind the screen, but obscured from sight by it. The patient is asked to gaze at a 'fixation point' in the centre of the screen. Visual stimuli are then 'back-projected' to the left of the fixation point (the left visual field) or to the right of it (the right visual field) for one tenth of a second or less. As noted, this allows the stimulus to be perceived, but is too quick for eye movements to allow it to enter both visual fields.

When a picture of an object is shown to the *right* visual field, and the patient is asked to report verbally what was shown, the task is done easily. However, when a picture is shown to the *left* visual field, the task cannot be done and the patient typically reports that 'there is nothing there'. Such a finding appears bizarre, but can be easily explained by applying what is known about the organisation of the visual system and what was said on pages 117–121 about the location of the structures responsible for language production and comprehension.

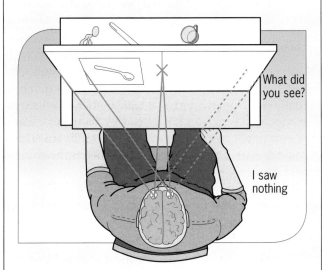

Figure 12.5 *Responses given by a split-brain patient when material is presented to the right (above) and left (below) visual fields*

All of Sperry *et al.*'s split-brain patients had their language structures in the left hemisphere (to which right visual field information goes). So, when an object was shown in the right visual field, the left hemisphere responded verbally and correctly. However, since the right hemisphere does not possess Broca's area, it cannot respond verbally. Thus, when an object is shown in the left visual field, the *verbal response* to the question 'What did you see?' comes from the left hemisphere. Since nothing was presented in the right visual field, the left hemisphere truthfully responds by saying that it saw nothing!

The apparent difference in the left and right hemispheres' abilities to produce spoken language led some researchers to use the terms *major* or *dominant* and *minor* or *subordinate* to describe the left and right respectively, as though the right hemisphere were some sort of 'second-class citizen' (Nebes, 1974). However, whilst the right hemisphere might not be able to respond verbally, it is far from linguistically incompetent.

Key STUDY

Box 12.10 Assessing the right hemisphere's linguistic abilities

A picture of an object was shown in the left visual field and hence perceived by the right hemisphere. When the patient was asked what had been presented, the response 'nothing' was given, a response which emanated from the left hemisphere (which had indeed seen nothing in the right visual field). However, when the patient was asked to use the left hand (which was placed beneath the screen so that it could not be seen) to select the object from a variety of objects, it was correctly selected. The left hand is controlled by the right hemisphere, and since it was able to select the object, the right hemisphere must have at least some understanding of language (Sperry *et al.*, 1969).

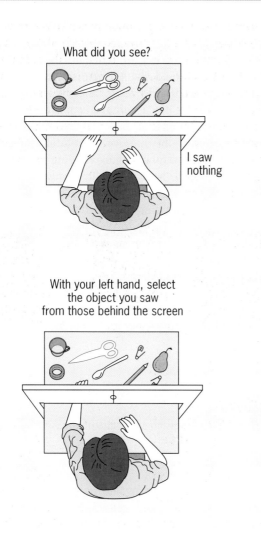

What did you see?

I saw nothing

With your left hand, select the object you saw from those behind the screen

Figure 12.6 *Although the right hemishere cannot verbalise a response, the left hand can correctly select an object the patient denies seeing*

In a variation of the study just described, a picture of a cigarette was presented to the right hemisphere. The patient was asked to use the left hand (again placed beneath the screen so that it could not be seen) to pick out an object *most closely related* to the picture presented. Of all the objects that could have been selected, an ashtray was the one consistently selected by the patients. However, when asked to verbally identify the picture that had been shown or the object selected by the left hand, the patient was unsuccessful, the right hemisphere being unable to verbalise a response and the left being in complete ignorance of the picture presented.

As well as showing that the right hemisphere has some verbal abilities, even if they cannot be articulated, these findings also suggest that the left hemisphere seemingly has no idea of, or access to, the perceptions and memories of the right hemisphere. This was also shown in studies using the *divided field technique*.

Box 12.11 The divided field technique

In the divided field technique, a word or picture is presented to the left visual field (right hemisphere) and a different word or picture *simultaneously* presented to the right visual field (left hemisphere).

In one study using this technique, the word 'case' was presented to the right visual field, and the word 'key' simultaneously presented to the left visual field. When asked to report what had been seen, the patient replied 'case'. However, when asked to use the left hand to write the word that had been presented, the patient wrote 'key'. When asked what particular kind of 'case', the patient's left hemisphere would respond with 'in case of fire' or 'the case of the missing corpse' and so on. Any reference to 'key case' was purely fortuitous. The creative, narrative talent of the left hemisphere has been called the '*interpreter mechanism*', and has been implicated in *false memory syndrome* (Gazzaniga, 1998).

Another study required the patient to find the objects that corresponded to the words shown to the left and right visual fields, using the left and right hands (both of which were behind the projector screen and could not be seen). When the right-hemisphere-controlled left hand came across the object that had been shown to the left hemisphere it ignored it completely, as did the left-hemisphere-controlled right hand when it came across the object that the left hand was looking for!

Gazzaniga (1983) claimed that on the basis of 20 years of empirical research:

> 'The cognitive skills of a normal disconnected right hemisphere without language are vastly inferior to the cognitive skills of a chimpanzee'.

However, the results of many studies have shown that whilst the right hemisphere might not be able to report verbally on its experiences, it has linguistic and cognitive capabilities which far exceed Gazzaniga's claims. As Levy (1983) has remarked, this is hardly surprising because it is unlikely that the 'eons of human evolution' would have left 'half the brain witless'.

An immediate critical response to Gazzaniga's claims came from Zaidel (1983). He developed a technique of presenting stimuli to the left or right visual field using a special contact lens that moves with the eye. This allows a stimulus to be presented for a much longer period than is the case using the original method of studying split-brain patients.

In one study, Zaidel gave vocabulary questions that required the right hemisphere to choose a picture that corresponded to a particular word. Although it did not perform as well as the left hemisphere, its performance was roughly equivalent to that of a ten-year-old child. This, and other findings, led Zaidel to conclude that:

> 'The precise limits of right hemisphere language capacity are not yet known [and] there is increasing evidence for right hemisphere involvement in normal language'.

Indeed, the right hemisphere has been shown to be better than the left at understanding familiar idioms and metaphors, such as 'turning over a new leaf'. The right hemisphere may, therefore, play an important (if underrated) role in language, a point acknowledged by Gazzaniga (1998).

The right hemisphere is also superior to the left at *copying drawings* (see Figure 12.7). Although the left hand is not as dextrous as the right (the right being the preferred hand in the patients that were studied), it is better able to reproduce the spatial arrangement of the example shown. The more coordinated right hand seems to be incapable of duplicating three-dimensional forms.

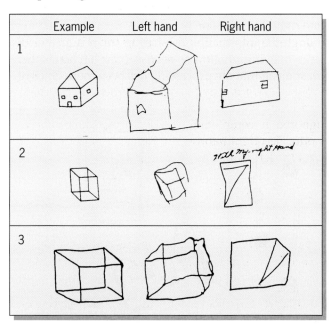

Figure 12.7 *The abilities of the right and left hemispheres to reproduce a visual stimulus using the left and right hands respectively*

A further right hemisphere superiority is in *recognising faces*. Using the divided field technique, pictures of different faces are presented to the left and right visual fields. When asked to select which face had been presented from an array of several other faces, the picture shown to the right hemisphere is consistently chosen whereas the one shown to the left hemisphere is consistently ignored. A slightly different approach to studying face recognition was taken by Levy *et al.* (1972). They showed patients

chimerics (composite pictures of two different faces), one half of the face being projected to each of the hemispheres (see Figure 12.8). When asked to describe verbally the picture that had been seen, the left hemisphere dominated but was not particularly accurate in its description. When asked to select a picture that had been seen, the right hemisphere dominated and was more accurate in its selection. This indicates that the left hemisphere processes information in linguistic terms whereas the right responds to the face as a total picture.

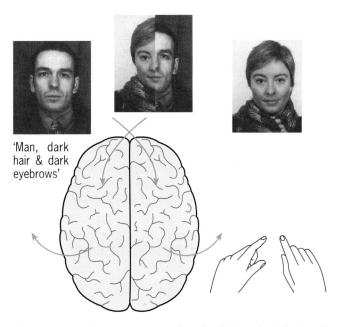

Figure 12.8 *Responses given by the left and right hemispheres to a chimeric*

Box 12.12 Analytic and synthetic hemispheres?

The terms *analyser* and *synthesiser* have been used to describe the left and right hemispheres respectively. The left hemisphere is evidently skilled at handling discrete information that can be stated verbally in the form of mathematical propositions. Faces, for example, are analysed in terms of their components ('deep-set eyes', 'blonde hair' and so on). The right hemisphere is superior when information cannot be adequately described in words or symbols. With a face, the right hemisphere synthesises all the information and recognises it as a whole. The perceptual superiority of the right hemisphere was also demonstrated by Sperry (1974). When the right hemisphere is instructed to arrange some blocks to match a picture, the left hand is highly competent. When the left hemisphere performs the same task using the right hand, its performance is so bad that, via the left hand, the right hemisphere 'interrupts' and takes over!

Outside the laboratory, the left and right hemispheres occasionally do battle (termed *'hemispheric competition'*). A female split-brain patient's left hand might pick out a particular dress to wear, only for the right hand to push the dress away and select another. This finding alone supports the view that the left and right hemispheres may be simultaneously conscious in different ways, and partly answers Fechner's question (see pages 121 and 127).

Evidence also suggests that split-brain patients can sometimes perform *better* in some situations than people who have not had a commissurotomy. Ellenberg & Sperry (1980) sent one simple decision task to the right hemisphere and another simultaneously to the left. The split-brain patients were much better able to perform both tasks than were people with an intact corpus callosum. Under normal circumstances, then, the two hemispheres work together at solving tasks whereas in split-brain patients they are able to work independently.

As interesting as these data are, it has been suggested that they be treated with caution on the grounds that those who have been studied might not be representative of people in general. It was mentioned earlier that split-brain patients have all had a history of epileptic seizures, and it could be that the differences between the hemispheres occur as a result of changes in brain organisation brought about by the epilepsy (Stirling, 2000). To talk about 'cerebral asymmetries' and 'hemispheric specialisation' requires that the same phenomena occur in people who have not had a history of epilepsy and/or undergone a commissurotomy.

HEMISPHERE ASYMMETRIES AND THE INTACT BRAIN

There are several ways in which asymmetries in the intact brain can be studied. One of these is the *Wada test* (Wada & Rasmussen, 1966).

Box 12.13 The Wada test

This involves injecting sodium amytal (a fast-acting barbiturate) into the left or right carotid artery. Because this artery sends blood primarily to the cerebral hemisphere on the same side, it is possible to temporarily anaesthetise a hemisphere and observe what happens. Just before the injection, the person is instructed to put his/her arms in the air and begin counting backwards from one hundred. The arm on the opposite side of the artery injected will suddenly fall limp. If the person can continue counting backwards, then the language structures must be in the non-injected hemisphere since the injected hemisphere has been anaesthetised.

The Wada test is only used prior to brain surgery to assess whether language structures might be affected. Other ways of assessing asymmetries include EEG, measurements of blood flow and glucose consumption (see Chapter 10), and studying people who have suffered strokes. It is also possible to use variations of the techniques originally employed to study 'split-brain' patients.

In one of these, different stimuli are simultaneously presented to the left and right visual fields for one-tenth of a second. In some cases, the stimulus to the right visual field will be reported by the person, whereas in others the stimulus presented to the left visual field will be reported. Reporting of the right visual field stimulus implies that the left hemisphere is better at processing the type of information presented. If the left visual field stimulus is reported, this implies that the right hemisphere is better.

This finding is *not* inconsistent with the claim that the right hemisphere cannot verbalise its responses. In the normal brain, the two hemispheres communicate with one another. Information about a stimulus presented to the right hemisphere must cross into the left hemisphere to be verbalised. The fact that the stimulus presented to the right hemisphere is verbally reported first, even though the information has had to travel a greater distance than information presented to the left hemisphere, must mean that the processing has been more efficient.

Innocent and carefree, Stuart's left hand didn't know what the right was doing.

Figure 12.9 *It looks like 'hemispheric competition' is developing in Stuart!*

Similarly, auditory information can be simultaneously presented to the left and right ears. The results of studies using *dichotic listening tasks* (see Chapter 19) indicate a right ear advantage for words, suggesting a left hemisphere superiority for processing verbal material. However, non-verbal auditory material (such as music) tends to produce a left ear advantage, suggesting a right hemisphere superiority in processing this information.

On the basis of many studies using people with intact brains, Ornstein (1986) concluded that the left hemisphere is specialised for *analytical* and *logical thinking*, especially in verbal and mathematical functions. It also processes information *sequentially* (one item at a time) and its mode of operation is *linear*. By contrast, the right hemisphere is specialised for *synthetic thinking*, in which it is necessary to bring different things together in order to form a whole. This is particularly true for spatial tasks, artistic activities, body image and face recognition. The right hemisphere also processes information more *diffusely* (several items at once) and its mode of operation is more *holistic* than linear.

Box 12.14 Left and right brains?

The conclusions drawn by Ornstein, coupled with the results of many studies not described in this chapter, suggest that the hemispheres perform somewhat different functions. This has led to the idea of people being 'logically left-brained' or 'intuitively right-brained' depending on the ways they behave (Gazzaniga, 1998). Indeed, (best-selling) books have been published which claim to show us how to 'unlock the door to the neglected right side of the brain'.

Although hemispheric differences seem to be well-established, psychologists generally believe the claims made in popular books to be both exaggerated and grossly oversimplified. Whilst the terms 'verbal' and 'non-verbal' hemispheres are reasonable first approximations, the data are actually much more complicated. Under normal circumstances, the two hemispheres work together, communicating by means of the corpus callosum, and their functions overlap to at least some degree. Moreover, some of the tasks which are ordinarily dealt with by one hemisphere can be performed by the other. As Sperry (1982) has observed, 'the left-right dichotomy is an idea with which it is very easy to run wild'.

AN ANSWER TO FECHNER'S QUESTION?

The results from the many studies on split-brain patients seem to agree with Fechner's own answer to the question he posed over 100 years ago. What we see when the brain is bisected is, according to Sperry, essentially a divided organism with two mental units each possessing its own private sensations, perceptions, thoughts, feelings and memories. These units compete for control over the organism.

Ornstein (1986) has asked whether a commissurotomy produces a 'splitting' (or 'doubling') of mind, or whether it helps to manifest a duality that is actually present all the time. As has been seen, Sperry, and at least some of his colleagues, clearly believe the former. Others, however, take the latter view. For example, Pucetti (1977) has argued that split-brain patients are not special in having two minds, because even when the hemispheres are connected, we *are* two minds. Normally, Pucetti argues, we appear to be unified and synchronised beings, because the separate existence of the two selves is undetectable. All the commissurotomy does is to make apparent the duality that is there all the time. According to this *double brain theory*, the mind, 'self', or personality can be essentially 'reduced' to a hemisphere of the brain (see also Chapter 47).

Parfit (1987) accepts the idea that the split-brain patient has two streams of consciousness, but does not believe that we should regard them as constituting two persons because in a sense, there is *none*. Parfit distinguishes *ego theory* (a theory of what people are) from *bundle theory* (which explains the unity of consciousness by claiming that ordinary people are, at any time, aware of having several different experiences). At any time, split-brain patients do not have one state of awareness of several different experiences. Rather, they have two such states (and *not* two separately existing egos). As Parfit has observed, split-brain patients have great theoretical importance, because they 'challenge some of our deepest assumptions about ourselves'.

CONCLUSIONS

The ability to produce and understand language is one of many remarkable human abilities. The first part of this chapter examined the cortical areas involved in language, and described the behavioural consequences of damage to them. The cortical areas involved in language are lateralised in the left hemisphere for most people. However, for a small number they are later-alised in the right hemisphere, and for an even smaller number language is bilaterally represented. The second part of the chapter looked at other hemisphere asymmetries of function. Research with split-brain patients, and those with intact corpus callosa, suggests that the left and right hemispheres play different roles in mental processes and behaviour. The question of whether dividing the brain results in a doubling of consciousness has yet to be satisfactorily resolved.

Summary

- Based on post-mortems, Broca concluded that lesions in a small cortical area in the left frontal lobe (**Broca's area**) were responsible for deficits in **language production.**

- Wernické identified damage to an area in the temporal lobe (**Wernické's area**) as being responsible for **language comprehension**.

- **Aphasias** are language disorders arising from brain damage. **Broca's aphasia** results in difficulty producing language, and listeners find it difficult to understand. Speech is **telegraphic** and characterised by **phonemic paraphrasias**. Difficulty in writing (**agraphia**) may also occur. Broca's aphasia is a result of Broca's area sending 'faulty data' to the primary motor area.

- **Wernické's aphasia** is characterised by difficulties in understanding spoken and written language. Speech may be unintelligible and lack coherence. It is characterised by **neologisms**, **semantic paraphrasias**, and the **absence of content words**.

- Wernické's area stores memories of the sequences of sounds contained in words, which allows us to recognise spoken individual words. Damage to it means that sounds cannot be recognised as speech, and so comprehension is absent.

- **Anomic aphasia** involves the inability to retrieve appropriate words to name things, and **circumlocution** sometimes occurs. The aphasia is the result of damage to the **angular gyrus** which, given a particular meaning, retrieves the appropriate word from some store.

- In **conduction aphasia**, the person has difficulty in repeating a sentence that has just been heard. The aphasic can, however, put the sentence into his/her own words. Lesions interrupting the **arcuate fasciculus**, which connects Broca's and Wernické's areas, cause conduction aphasia.

- **Transcortical motor aphasia** is similar to Broca's aphasia, and **transcortical sensory aphasia** to Wernické's aphasia. In **mixed transcortical aphasia**, both the production and comprehension of language are affected.

- The **Wernické–Geschwind model** implicates the auditory area, Wernické's area, Broca's area and the motor area in speaking a word that has been heard. When a word that has been read is spoken, the primary visual area, angular gyrus, Wernické's area, Broca's area and the motor area are involved.

- As well as being **localised**, language is, in most people, **lateralised** as well. For most people it is lateralised in the **left** hemisphere. For a small number it is localised in the **right** hemisphere. For an even smaller number, language is **bilaterally represented**.

- Speech may be more bilaterally organised in women than men, and women are less likely to incur aphasia. However, it is unlikely that bilateral organisation in women explains this.

- The brain's **plasticity** is particularly marked in the case of language. This flexibility is at its maximum during childhood, and even removal of a complete hemisphere does not prevent normal language development. Such a finding is consistent with **holism**.

- Whether the cerebral hemispheres play the same or different roles in mental processes and behaviour has long interested psychologists, and can be traced back to a question posed by Fechner in 1860.

- As a treatment for severe forms of epilepsy, the fibres of the corpus callosum are severed in an operation called a **commissurotomy**. This allows the roles played by the hemispheres to be investigated in **'split-brain' patients.**

- Stimuli presented to the left visual field are perceived by the right hemisphere. Right visual field stimuli are perceived by the left hemisphere. Split-brain patients verbally report what is presented to the right visual field, but verbally deny perceiving anything in the left visual field. This is because the language structures are in the left hemisphere.

- The left and right hemispheres have been called the **major/dominant hemisphere** and the **minor/subordinate hemisphere** respectively. However, the right hemisphere has some understanding of language, even if it cannot verbalise this.

- The right hemisphere is superior at copying drawings and recognising faces. The left hemisphere processes pictures of faces linguistically, whilst the right responds to the face as a total picture.

- The left hemisphere has been described as an **analyser**, because it is skilled at handling discrete information that can be stated verbally. The right hemisphere has been described as a **synthesiser**, since it is superior when information cannot be adequately described in words or symbols (as in recognising a face).

- Generalising data from split-brain patients is difficult, since their epilepsy may have caused changes in brain organisation. However, studies of asymmetries in the intact brain have yielded similar findings.

- The left hemisphere is apparently specialised for **analytical** and **logical** thinking. The right hemisphere is apparently specialised for **synthetic** thinking. This is a useful first approximation, but the hemispheres normally work together and their abilities tend to overlap.

- According to Sperry, the bisected brain is two mental units competing for control of the organism. Pucetti believes people have two minds even when the hemispheres are connected, and the commissurotomy simply makes obvious the duality that is there all the time. This is called **double brain theory**.

- According to **bundle theory**, we are normally aware of having several different experiences, and this accounts for the unity of consciousness. Split-brain patients have two states of awareness of several different experiences, as opposed to being two distinct egos (**ego theory**).

Essay Questions

1 Discuss research into the lateralisation of function in the cerebral cortex. *(24 marks)*

2 Describe and evaluate research into the organisation of language in the brain. *(24 marks)*

WEB ADDRESSES

http://ezinfo.indiana.edu/~pietsch/cv.html
http://neuro.med.cornell.edu/VL
http://hcs.harvard.edu/~husn/BRAIN/index.html
http://www.med.harvard.edu/AANLIB/home.html

PART 2: BIOLOGICAL RHYTHMS, SLEEP AND DREAMING

13 *Biological Rhythms*

INTRODUCTION AND OVERVIEW

According to Marks & Folkard (1985):

'Rhythmicity is a ubiquitous characteristic of living cells. In the human it is evident within the single cell, in individual behaviour, and at the population level'.

A bodily rhythm is *a cyclical variation over some period of time in physiological or psychological processes*. This chapter looks at research studies into *circadian*, *infradian* and *ultradian* biological rhythms, and the roles played by *endogenous pacemakers* and *external Zeitgebers*. It also examines some of the consequences of disrupting biological rhythms.

CIRCADIAN RHYTHMS

Circadian rhythms are consistent cyclical variations over a period of about 24 hours (the word circadian comes from the Latin 'circa' meaning 'about' and 'diem' meaning 'a day'), and are a feature of human and non-human physiology and behaviour. As Aschoff & Wever (1981) have noted, 'there is hardly a tissue or function that has not been shown to have some 24-hour variation'. These include heart rate, metabolic rate, breathing rate and body temperature, all of which reach maximum values in the late afternoon/early evening, and minimum values in the early hours of the morning. It might seem obvious that such rhythms would occur since we are active during the day and inactive at night. However, the rhythms persist if we suddenly reverse our activity patterns (see pages 137–139).

The concentration of the body's *hormones* also varies over the day. However, the time at which a hormone is concentrated varies from one hormone to another. In women, *prolactin* (which stimulates the production of milk) peaks in the middle of the night, and this explains why women are more likely to go into labour then.

Box 13.1 Chronotherapeutics

The symptoms of many illnesses fluctuate over the 24-hour cycle. For example, the symptoms of hay fever are worst around dawn, and there is a tendency for heart attacks to occur in the morning when the blood is more prone to clotting. Awareness of these '*sickness cycles*' has now been incorporated into treatment called *chronotherapeutics* ('chronos' means 'time'). For example, anticoagulant drugs are more effective at night, when the blood is a little thinner in density. Anti-cholesterol drugs (called *statins*) function better in the evening, because they target a cholesterol-affecting enzyme that is active at night.

(Based on Dobson, 1999b)

Ordinarily, we are surrounded by *external cues* about the time of day. These are called *Zeitgebers*, which comes from the German, meaning 'time-giver'. The process of resetting a rhythm to some periodically recurring environmental variable is called *entrainment*. Siffre (1975) spent six months underground in a cave where no natural sounds or light could reach him. Although he had adequate food, drink, exercise and so on, and whilst he was in contact with the outside world via a permanently staffed telephone, he had no means of telling the time of day. Siffre's physiology and behaviour remained cyclical, but his day lengthened to 25 hours.

Figure 13.1 *Eventually, this budding blues singer will develop a sleep–waking pattern that will not disrupt his mum and dad's*

Similarly, Folkard *et al.* (cited in Huggett & Oldcroft, 1996) had six students spend a month isolated from any external cues. Temperature and activity levels were recorded constantly, and mood levels were measured every two hours using computer tasks. One student was asked to play her bagpipes regularly to see if the body's sense of rhythm was affected by the absence of external cues. Folkard *et al.*'s findings confirmed the existence of several *internal* (or *body*) *clocks* (called *oscillators*).

One of these lies in the *suprachiasmatic nuclei* (SN), paired aggregations of neurons located in the *hypothalamus*. The SN receives information from the retina (via a direct neural pathway called the *retinohypothalamic tract*). This information about light and dark synchronises our biological rhythms with the 24-hour cycle of the outside world. If the SN is damaged, or the connection between it and retina severed, circadian rhythms disappear completely, and rhythmic behaviours become random over the day. Indeed, people born without eyes cannot regulate their internal clocks, nor can non-humans whose eyes have been bred out.

The cycle length of rhythms is dependent on genetic factors (Green, 1998). If hamsters are given brain transplants of SN from a mutant strain whose biological rhythms have a shorter cycle than those of the recipients, the recipients adopt the same activity cycles as the mutant strain (Morgan, 1995). Interestingly, the location of the transplant does not appear to be important, suggesting that the SN might rely on chemical signals rather than nerve connections.

Box 13.2 The evolution of internal clocks

According to Loros *et al.* (cited in Highfield, 1996b), primitive bacteria developed an internal clock from molecular machinery that responds to light, so they could anticipate the coming of the sun's rays and change their metabolism accordingly. Two proteins, White Collar 1 and 2, regulate light responses, are essential to the circadian rhythm, and work in the dark without light stimulation. The proteins were first discovered in a fungus and then in the fruit fly, and it is likely that all biological clocks share common molecular components. The Atlantic salmon, for example, possesses a light-sensitive substance (*VA opsin*), which is *not* involved in vision. It is, however, an ancient signalling substance that developed before substances involved with vision. So, the ability to regulate body clocks came *before* the ability to see (Ahuhja, 1998).

The finding that animals transplanted with the SN of others adopt the same activity patterns as their donors (see above), coupled with the fact that the circadian rhythm cannot be experimentally manipulated beyond certain limits (Folkard *et al.*, 1985), strongly suggests that bodily rhythms are *primarily* an internal (or *endogenous*) property that does not depend on external (or *exogenous*) cues.

One of the most interesting circadian rhythms is the sleep–waking cycle. Although some people have as little as 45 minutes of sleep each night, the average person has around seven-and-a-half hours per 24-hour day. However, this is about 90 minutes a night less than a century ago (Brooks, 1999). People in all cultures sleep, and even those who take a midday 'siesta' have an extended period of five to eight hours sleep each day.

The need for sleep does not seem to be *determined* by the cycle of light and darkness. For example, Luce & Segal (1966) found that people who live near the Arctic circle, where the sun does not set during the summer months, sleep about seven hours during each 24-hour period. *External* cues, then, would not seem to be of primary importance as far as sleep and waking are concerned. Of more importance is the *group two oscillator*, an internal clock which sends us to sleep and wakes us up.

Although external cues are not of primary importance in the sleep–waking cycle, they do play a role. When night falls, the eyes inform the SN and, via the *paraventricular nucleus (PNV)*, the *pineal gland*. This gland is so called because it resembles a pine cone. It is believed to have evolved by the convergence and fusion of a second pair of *photoreceptors* (Morgan, 1995). This resultant 'third eye' secretes the hormone *melatonin* (see also page 138). Melatonin influences neurons that produce the neurotransmitter *serotonin*, which is concentrated in a brain structure called the *raphe nuclei*. When a certain level of melatonin is reached, serotonin is released, and acts on the brain's *reticular activating system* (RAS).

Box 13.3 The monoamine hypothesis of sleep

It has long been known that the RAS is involved in *consciousness*. For example, stimulation of the RAS causes a slumbering cat to awaken, whereas destruction of the RAS causes a permanent coma (Moruzzi & Magoun, 1949). Jouvet (1967) showed that destruction of the raphe nuclei produces sleeplessness and, on the basis of his finding that serotonin is concentrated in this brain structure, Jouvet concluded that serotonin must play a role in the induction of sleep. Since serotonin is a *monoamine* neurotransmitter, Jouvet called his theory the *monoamine hypothesis of sleep*.

Jouvet discovered that *parachlorophenylalanine* (PCPA), a substance which inhibits serotonin synthesis, prevents sleep. However, if its effects are reversed (by means of *5-hydroxytryptophan*), then sleep is reinstated. This suggests that whilst serotonin may not play *the* role in sleep induction, it certainly plays *a* role (see Chapter 14).

INFRADIAN RHYTHMS

Infradian rhythms last for *longer* than one day, and have been known about for centuries. The infradian rhythm that has attracted most research interest is *menstruation*. Menstruation is an endocrine cycle, and several such cycles are experienced by everybody. However, none is as well marked as menstruation, and others are much more difficult to study.

Every 28 days or so, female bodies undergo a sequence of changes with two possible outcomes: conception or menstruation. Conventionally, we portray menstruation as the *beginning* of a cycle. In fact, the menstrual period is the end of a four-week cycle of activity during which the womb has prepared for the job of housing and nourishing a fertilised egg.

The onset of the 28-day cycle is often irregular at first, but becomes well established in a matter of months. The cycle can change to fit in with events in the environment. For example, women who spend a lot of time together often find that their menstrual periods become synchronised (Sabbagh & Barnard, 1984). Why this happens is

not known, but one hypothesis attributes it to the unconscious detection of chemical scents called *pheromones* secreted at certain times during the menstrual cycle (Russell *et al.*, 1980).

Hormonal changes at the time of menstruation can cause women painful physical problems. For example, *prostaglandin* production causes uterine contractions. Many of these go unnoticed, but when they are strong and unrelieved, they can be particularly uncomfortable. Fortunately, prostaglandin-inhibiting drugs (such as *Ibuprofen*) can relieve the pain. Much more controversial is the claim that the menstrual cycle can cause psychological problems.

The term *pre-menstrual syndrome* (PMS) has been used to describe a variety of behavioural and emotional effects occurring at several phases of the menstrual cycle, which affect around 10–40 per cent of women of reproductive age (Choi, 1999). Typically, these occur around four to five days before the onset of menstruation, and include mild irritation, depression, headaches and a decline in alertness or visual acuity. One commonly reported experience is a day or so of great energy, followed by lethargy that disappears with the onset of menstrual bleeding (Luce, 1971). PMS has also been associated with a change in appetite. Some women develop a craving for certain types of food, whereas others lose their appetite completely.

Key STUDY
Box 13.4 PMS and behaviour change

The most pervasive social impacts of PMS are the psychological and behavioural changes which occur. Dalton (1964) reported that a large proportion of crimes were clustered in the pre-menstrual interval along with suicides, accidents, and a decline in the quality of schoolwork and intelligence test scores. A small percentage of women do experience effects that are strong enough to interfere with normal functioning, (an exteme which DSM-IV (see Chapter 46) classifies as *premenstrual dysmorphic disorder*. However, these women are not, contrary to Dalton's claim, more likely to commit crimes or end up on psychiatric wards. Any effects that do occur are a result of increased stress levels and other health fluctuations (Hardie, 1997).

Choi (1999) has called for a change in the prevalent negative attitude towards PMS. Her research indicates that some women have *positive* premenstrual experiences, such as heightened creativity and increased energy (Choi & McKeown, 1997).

For a long time, PMS was attributed to a denial of femininity or a resistance to sexual roles. However, the effects of PMS occur in all cultures, indicating a *physiological cycle* rather than a pattern of behaviour imposed by culture. Support for this comes from the finding that similar effects to those experienced by women occur in primates.

The *pituitary gland* governs the phases of the menstrual cycle by influencing changes in the *endometrium* (the walls of the uterus) and the preparation of the ovum. Timonen *et al.* (1964) showed that during the lighter months of the year conceptions increased, whilst in the darker months they decreased. The light levels might have had some direct or indirect influence on the pituitary gland, which then influenced the menstrual cycle.

Key STUDY

Box 13.5 Menstruation in the absence of Zeitgebers

Reinberg (1967) studied a young woman who spent three months in a cave relying on only the dim light of a miner's lamp. Her day lengthened to 24.6 hours, and her menstrual cycle shortened to 25.7 days. Even though she was in the mine for only three months, it was a year before her menstrual cycle returned to its normal frequency. Reinberg speculated that it was the level of light in the cave which had influenced the menstrual cycle.

Consistent with this was his finding that among 600 girls from northern Germany, *menarche* (the onset of menstruation, which occurs at puberty) was much more likely to occur in winter. Interestingly, menarche is reached earlier by blind girls than sighted girls. It is likely that the pineal gland is somehow affected by melatonin's secretion, and this affects both the menstrual cycle and, given that there are increased conceptions during the lighter months of the year, the reproductive system in general.

ULTRADIAN RHYTHMS

Ultradian rhythms are *shorter* than a day, and have been demonstrated in many physiological and behavioural processes including oral activity (such as smoking cigarettes), renal excretion and heart rate. The most well-researched ultradian rhythms are those occurring during *sleep*. Sleep is not a single state, and within a night's sleep several shorter rhythms occur.

Before the EEG's invention (see Chapter 10), sleep could not be studied scientifically because there was no way of accessing what was going on inside the sleeper's

head. Loomis *et al.* (1937) used the EEG to record the electrical activity in a sleeping person's brain. They discovered that the brain was electrically active during sleep, and that certain types of activity seemed to be related to changes in type of sleep. It seemed that the waves tended to get 'bigger' as sleep got 'deeper'.

Box 13.6 REM sleep

In 1952, eight-year-old Armond Aserinsky's father Eugene connected him to an EEG machine to see if repairs carried out on it had been successful. Electrodes were also placed near Armond's eyes to try to record the rolling eye movements believed to occur during sleep. After a while, the EOG started to trace wildly oscillating waves. Aserinsky senior thought that the machine was still broken, but after several minutes the EOG fell silent. Periodically, however, the wildly oscillating waves returned. When Armond was woken by his father during one such period, Armond reported that he had been dreaming.

Aserinsky senior eventually realised that the EOG was indicating fast, jerky eye movements beneath Armond's closed eyelids. He further observed that whilst the EOG was active, Armond's EEG indicated that his brain was highly active as well, even though the boy was sound asleep. Aserinsky & Kleitman (1953) reported that the same phenomenon occurred when EOG and EEG measurements in adults were recorded. They used the term *rapid eye movement sleep* (or REM sleep) to describe the period of intense EOG activity.

Dement & Kleitman (1957) showed that when people were woken up during REM sleep and asked if they were *dreaming*, they usually replied that they were. When woken at other times during the night, in non-rapid eye movement sleep (or NREM sleep), they occasionally reported dream-like experiences, but their descriptions usually lacked the vivid visual images and fantastic themes that were described during REM sleep awakenings.

The EEG allows researchers to measure the electrical activity occurring in the brain over the course of a night's sleep. Rechtschaffen & Kales (1968) devised criteria to describe changes in the brain's electrical activity. These divide NREM sleep into four stages, each of which is characterised by distinct patterns of electrical activity.

When we are awake and alert, the EEG shows the low amplitude and high frequency *beta waves* (see Box 10.6, page 102 for a description of beta waves and the waves that follow). Once we are in bed and relaxed, beta waves are replaced by *alpha waves* of higher amplitude but slower frequency. Gradually, we begin to fall asleep. Breathing and heart rate slow down, body temperature drops and muscles relax. The onset of sleep is marked by the appearance of irregular and slower *theta waves*, and we have entered *Stage 1* of sleep.

The transition from relaxation to Stage 1 is sometimes accompanied by a *hypnagogic state*, in which we experience dream-like and hallucinatory images resembling vivid photographs. Such images have been linked to creativity. We may also experience the sensation of falling, and our bodies might suddenly jerk. Although the EMG indicates that the muscles are still active, the EOG indicates slow, gentle, rolling eye movements. Because Stage 1 sleep is the lightest stage of sleep, we are easily awakened from it. If this occurs, we might feel that we have not been sleeping at all.

After about a minute, the EEG shows another change which marks the onset of *Stage 2* sleep. Although the waves are of medium amplitude with a frequency of around 4–7 cycles per second (cps), Stage 2 sleep is characterised by brief bursts of activity with a frequency of 12–14 cps. These are called *sleep spindles*, but why they appear is not precisely understood.

Box 13.7 K-complexes

Another characteristic of Stage 2 sleep is the presence of *K-complexes*. These are the brain's response to external stimuli, such as a sound in the room in which we are sleeping, or internal stimuli such as a muscle tightening in the leg. Whilst it is possible to be woken fairly easily from Stage 2 sleep, the EOG registers minimal eye movements and the EMG shows little activity in the muscles.

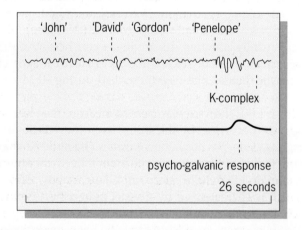

Figure 13.2 *EEG response of a person in Stage 2 sleep to the presentation of several names, one of which is his wife's*

After around 20 minutes in Stage 2, electrical activity increases in amplitude and becomes even slower, dropping to around 1–3 cps. When these slow *delta waves* account for 20–50 per cent of the EEG, we have entered *Stage 3* sleep. After a brief period of time, delta waves will account for more than 50 per cent of the EEG, and will slow to around ½–2 cps which marks the onset of *Stage 4* sleep. In both Stages 3 and 4 of sleep, we are extremely unresponsive to the environment and it is very difficult for us to be woken up. The EOG shows virtually no eye movements and our muscles are completely relaxed. Noises and lights do not disturb us as they would have done in the earlier stages of sleep.

In Stage 4, heart rate, blood pressure and body temperature are at their lowest. We have descended the '*sleep staircase*' and have moved from a very light to a very deep sleep. Our first episode of Stage 4 sleep lasts for around 40 minutes. After this, we begin to 'climb' the sleep staircase, passing briefly through Stage 3, before entering Stage 2 in which we spend around ten minutes.

Instead of re-entering Stage 1, however, something very different registers on the EEG machine, and we start showing the irregular eye movements and brain activity first observed by Aserinsky (see Box 13.6, page 133). We are now experiencing our first episode of REM sleep. REM sleep occurs in all mammals except the dolphin and spiny anteater, but does not occur in fish, reptiles and amphibians, and occurs only briefly in a few birds of prey. It is therefore likely that REM sleep is related to the development of brain structures found in mammals.

Interestingly, the EMG in REM sleep indicates that the body's muscles are in a state of *virtual paralysis*, which occurs as a result of inhibitory processes (the occasional twitches of our hands and feet are presumably a result of these processes weakening briefly). The probable function of this paralysis is discussed in Chapter 15. Although our muscles may be paralysed, heart rate and blood pressure begin to fluctuate rapidly, and respiration alters between shallow breaths and sudden gasps. Males may experience erections, and females corresponding changes in their sexual organs.

The fact that the eyes and brain of a person in REM sleep are very *active* whilst the muscles are virtually *paralysed*, coupled with the observation that a person in REM sleep is very difficult to wake up, has led to it also being called *paradoxical sleep*. Our first period of REM sleep lasts for about 10 minutes. The end of it marks the completion of the first ultradian sleep *cycle*.

When REM sleep ends, we enter Stage 2 sleep again and spend around 25 minutes in that stage. After passing briefly through Stage 3, we enter Stage 4 and spend about 30 minutes in a very deep sleep. After ascending the sleep staircase once more, another episode of REM sleep occurs, which also lasts for around ten minutes. We have now completed the second sleep cycle.

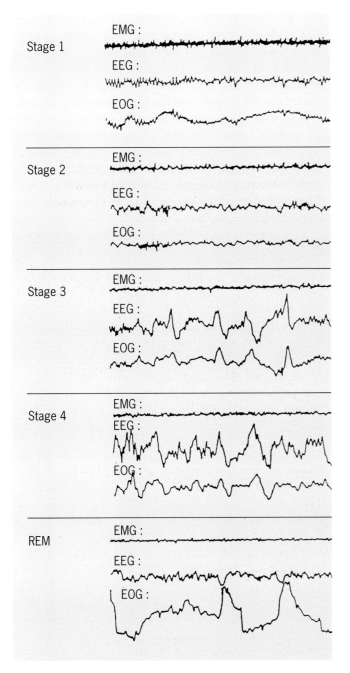

Figure 13.3 *EMG, EEG and EOG recordings associated with the various stages of sleep*

The entry into Stage 2 sleep marks the beginning of the third cycle. However, instead of descending the sleep staircase (after about an hour in Stage 2), we enter REM sleep and might spend as long as 40 minutes in that stage. Again, the end of REM sleep marks the end of another cycle. Unlike the first two cycles, then, the third cycle does not involve any Stage 3 or 4 sleep. This is also true of the fourth cycle. It begins with around 70 minutes of Stage 2 sleep, which is immediately fol-lowed by a fourth episode of REM sleep. This might last as long as an hour. By the end of the fourth cycle, we

will have been asleep for around seven hours. The fifth cycle will probably end with us waking up, and for that reason it is known as the *emergent cycle*. We may awake directly from REM sleep, or from Stage 2, and might experience *hypnopompic images* (vivid visual images that occur as we are waking up: cf. the hypnagogic images mentioned earlier). As was true in the third and fourth cycles, the emergent cycle does not consist of any Stage 3 or 4 sleep.

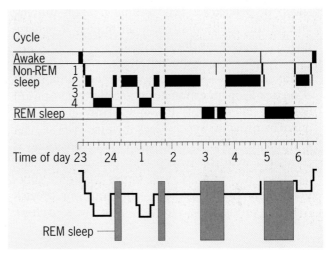

Figure 13.4 *A characteristic profile of a night's sleep. (From Borbely, 1986)*

Typically, then, we have five or so cycles of sleep, each of which lasts, on average, for around 90 minutes. The exact pattern of sleep varies from person to person, and what has been described is very much an 'average', since the time between REM and NREM sleep varies both between and within people. So, as well as people differing in terms of their sleep cycles, the pattern can vary within the same person from night to night. What does seem to be true for everyone, though, is that Stages 3 and 4 of sleep occur only in the first two cycles of sleep, and whilst REM sleep occurs in every cycle, episodes of it increase in length over the course of the night.

Our pattern of sleeping also changes as we get older. Newborn infants sleep for around 16 hours a day, and spend approximately half this time in REM sleep. One-year-olds sleep for around 12 hours a day, and REM sleep occupies about one-third of this time. In adulthood, we spend only around a quarter of an eight-hour period of sleep in REM sleep, and in very old age the amount of REM sleep time decreases even further. Stage 4 sleep also changes as we get older. At age 60, Stage 4 sleep has all but disappeared. As a result, we tend to be more easily awakened when we are older even though we may have been very sound sleepers when younger.

Key STUDY

Box 13.8 The physiology of REM sleep

Destruction of the *locus coeruleus* (a small patch of dark cells located in a brain structure called the *pons*) causes REM sleep to disappear completely. This suggests that the pons plays a role in regulating REM sleep. Moreover, if neurons in a different part of the pons are destroyed, REM sleep remains, but muscle tension (which is ordinarily absent during REM sleep) is *maintained*. This results in a cat moving around during REM sleep, even though it is completely unconscious (Jouvet, 1983).

For reasons that are not well understood, the inhibitory processes normally operating during REM sleep do not operate in some people. Sufferers of *REM behaviour disorder* may 'thrash violently about, leap out of bed, and may even attack their partners' (Chase & Morales, 1990). As noted previously, dreaming is correlated with REM sleep and, presumably, being paralysed during REM sleep serves the useful function of preventing us from acting out our dreams (which, presumably, Jouvet's cat was doing).

'*Sleepwalking*', then, cannot ordinarily occur during REM sleep (see Box 15.1, page 150).

The locus coeruleus produces the neurotransmitters *noradrenaline* and *acetylcholine*. Jouvet proposed that these are responsible for REM sleep's onset and the associated loss of muscle tone. *Carbachol*, a chemical which imitates acetylcholine but has a more prolonged action, leads to longer periods of REM sleep. *Scopolamine*, a chemical which inhibits acetylcholine's action, leads to a delay in REM sleep's onset. Both of these findings support Jouvet's proposal.

Sleep cycles themselves may occur as a result of the relationship between the raphe nuclei and locus coeruleus (Jouvet, 1983). The raphe nuclei are believed to initiate sleep by acting on the RAS. Thereafter, interactions between the raphe nuclei and the locus coeruleus generate the NREM–REM sleep cycle. When one structure overcomes the other, wakefulness occurs. However, the picture is probably much more complicated than has been painted here, and almost certainly the result of complex interactions between various brain structures.

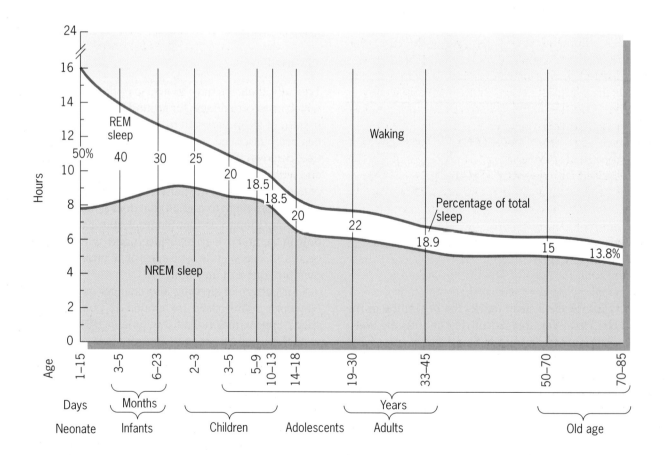

Figure 13.5 *Changes in sleep patterns with age*

DISRUPTING BIOLOGICAL RHYTHMS

Shift work

Humans can adjust their bodily rhythms if necessary, at least to a degree. In many societies, what Moore-Ede (1993) calls 'twenty-four hour societies', some people are required to do *shift work*. Monk & Folkard (1992) define shift work as 'any regularly taken employment outside the day working window, defined arbitrarily as the hours between 07:00 and 18:00'. Occupations that satisfy this definition include postal and milk-delivery workers and bakers.

Although night workers report sleeping less than day workers, research suggests that various performance deficits occur when work is carried out at night which are *additional* to any effects that can be attributed to a lack of sleep (Reilly *et al.*, 1997). These include:

- decreased attention;
- a slowing down of reasoning skills;
- impaired reaction time;
- disturbed perceptual–motor skills.

It is therefore not surprising that there is a tendency for accidents due to 'human error' to happen at night. For example, the human errors which caused the *Three Mile Island* (04:00) and *Chernobyl* (01:23) nuclear reactor accidents occurred during the night shift, and at the peak times for the 'sleep impulse' (Green 1998). However, it should be noted that increased errors may not be solely attributable to working at night. Increased errors or accidents may also be a consequence of poor lighting and/or the use of a 'skeleton staff' at night, who may be less supervised than day-workers (Reilly *et al.*, 1997).

There is a sense, though, in which occupations such as milk delivery do not constitute 'shift work', because the work does not 'shift' to different times of the day. However, some organisations require their employees to work according to a *rotating shift system*. Typically, these are either *rapidly rotating shifts* (two to three days per shift) or *weekly rotating shifts* (five to seven days per shift). One common pattern is to divide the day into three eight-hour shifts, such as 22:00–06:00 (the 'night' shift), 06:00–14:00 (the 'early' shift) and 14:00–22:00 (the 'late' shift), and then apply a rapidly or weekly rotating shift cycle, with employees moving *back* one shift every time, that is, from an early shift, to a night shift, to a late shift.

Unfortunately, people differ in how quickly they can reverse their rhythms. For example, some people can apparently achieve a reversal in five to seven days, whereas it may take 14 days for others. Some people may not ever achieve a complete reversal (Monk *et al.*, cited in Irwin, 1997). Additionally, not all physiological functions reverse at the same time. For most people, heart rate and blood pressure 'entrain' quickly (Baumgart *et al.*, 1989). However, *adrenocorticotrophic hormone* production takes longer than a week to reverse.

During a shift changeover period, all the body's functions are in a state of *internal desynchronisation* (Aschoff & Wever, 1981), which is very stressful and accounts for much of the exhaustion, malaise and lassitude associated with changing work shifts. In shift work, the Zeitgebers stay the same, but workers are forced to adjust their natural sleep–waking cycles in order to meet the changing demands of changing work schedules.

Key S T U D Y

Box 13.9 Shifting shifts to improve performance

As noted above, one of the most common shift patterns requires workers to move *back* one shift every time, once a week. However, workers who rotate shifts in this way report experiencing insomnia, digestive problems, irritability, fatigue and depression. They also have more accidents at work and are less productive. When laboratory animals are subjected to this kind of rotating schedule of light and dark, they suffer from increased heart disease and a shorter lifespan.

Czeisler *et al.* (1982) studied a group of shift-workers following the shift pattern described above. Czeisler *et al.* discovered that it generally takes people around 16 days to adjust to a new shift pattern, and so recommended that the shift rotation period changed from seven to 21 days. They also recommended that the shifts rotated *forwards* in time (taking advantage of the body's natural preference for a slightly longer than 24-hour cycle).

The results of these two changes were dramatic, rapid and remarkable. The workers themselves reported liking the new schedules, enjoying better health, and making more productive use of their leisure time. From the employer's perspective, the change was also successful, because there was an increase in productivity and a decrease in the number of errors leading to accidents.

Transferring shift-workers from a current schedule to one that begins later is an example of *phase delay*, whereas transferring from a current schedule to one that begins earlier is a *phase advance*. What Czeisler *et al.*'s findings show is that companies operating phase-delay schedules are more likely to benefit from their employees.

Jet lag

The world is divided into 24 time zones, centred around Greenwich, London. These time zones determine the relationship between Greenwich Mean Time (GMT) and the time somewhere else. Places to the east of Britain are 'ahead', whilst those to the West are 'behind'. So, at the same moment it may be noon in Britain, but 07:00 in New York and 21:00 in Japan. When we fly to the west, we 'gain' time (we can 'relive' some hours), but when we fly to the east, we 'lose' time (part of the day is 'lost').

The biological implications of crossing time zones are not very important to people on a cruise liner, because the rate of travel is slow enough to be accommodated by the body (Reilly *et al.*, 1997). However, a cluster of symptoms, collectively known as '*jet lag*', are suffered by the majority of people when several time zones are crossed in a short space of time (as happens when we travel by jet). Although the symptoms of jet lag differ from person to person, amongst the more common are:

- tiredness during the 'new' daytime and an inability to sleep at night;
- decreased mental performance, especially on vigilance tasks;
- decreased physical performance, especially where precise movement is required;
- a loss of appetite, indigestion and even nausea;
- increased irritability, headaches and mental confusion.

In general, then, jet lag is experienced as a general malaise or feeling of disorientation (Reilly *et al.*, 1997).

Box 13.10 East-to-west versus west-to-east jet lag

Most people suffer much less jet lag when travelling in an east–west direction than a west–east direction. When travelling west, we are 'chasing the sun', and the day is temporarily *lengthened* (which corresponds to a *phase delay* change in shift work). Travelling in an easterly direction '*shortens*' the day (and corresponds to a *phase advance* in shift work). As noted previously (see pages 130–131), Siffre's (1975) experiences indicate that the natural (or free-running) circadian rhythm of the biological clock is around 25 hours. Travelling east, then, shortens what is for the body an already shortened day. Travelling west lengthens the day, which is what the body 'prefers'. The idea way to travel would be always going east–west, in short hops of one time zone per day. This would make each day of the journey more-or-less equal to the body's preferred rhythm.

Melatonin (see page 131) plays a crucial role in the experience of jet lag. Because it is produced mainly at night, melatonin is known as 'the hormone of darkness'. After a long flight, the cyclical release of melatonin remains on

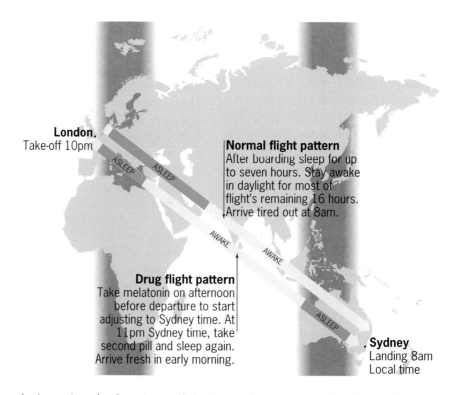

London.
Take-off 10pm

ASLEEP   ASLEEP

Normal flight pattern
After boarding sleep for up to seven hours. Stay awake in daylight for most of flight's remaining 16 hours. Arrive tired out at 8am.

AWAKE   AWAKE

Drug flight pattern
Take melatonin on afternoon before departure to start adjusting to Sydney time. At 11pm Sydney time, take second pill and sleep again. Arrive fresh in early morning.

ASLEEP

. Sydney
Landing 8am
Local time

Figure 13.6 *Taking a synthetic version of melatonin may help air travellers overcome the effects of jet lag*

the day/night pattern of the home country for several days. This could account for the fatigue felt during the day and insomnia at night. In 1995, a synthetic version of melatonin was produced and marketed in America as a way of overcoming insomnia and jet lag. Although currently banned in the UK, because not enough is known

about its effects, it has been shown that if jet-lagged volunteers are given melatonin during the evening, far fewer report feeling jet-lagged than volunteers who receive only a placebo (Blakemore, 1988: see Figure 13.6, page 138). Melatonin's effects are probably mediated by the melatonin receptors in the SN (Minors, 1997).

CONCLUSIONS

This chapter has looked at circadian, infradian and ultradian bodily rhythms. Although bodily rhythms are affected by exogenous Zeitgebers, they are primarily an internal (or endogenous) property. Disruption of these rhythms, through shift work or crossing time zones, can have serious effects on a number of measures of performance.

Summary

- **Circadian rhythms** are consistent cyclical variations over a period of about 24 hours. Examples include heart rate, metabolic rate, breathing rate and body temperature. These rhythms persist even if activity patterns are reversed or external cues about the time of day removed.

- One **internal clock** (or **oscillator**) lies in the **suprachiasmatic nuclei** (SN). This receives information directly from the retina, and synchronises biological rhythms with the 24 hour cycle of the outside world. If the SN is damaged, circadian rhythms disappear.

- The cycle length of rhythms depends on genetic factors, and internal clocks evolved so that organisms could anticipate the coming of the sun's rays and change their metabolism accordingly. It is likely that all biological clocks share common molecular components.

- The sleep–waking cycle is largely independent of culture and the cycle of light and dark. It is determined by internal events governed by the **group two oscillator.**

- Brain structures implicated in the sleep–waking cycle include the **raphe nuclei** and **reticular activating system** (RAS). **Melatonin** and **serotonin** are important chemicals involved in the induction of sleep.

- **Infradian rhythms** last longer than one day. The most extensively researched of these is menstruation. **Pre-menstrual syndrome** (PMS) refers to a variety of physical and psychological effects occurring at several phases of the menstrual cycle.

- PMS does not predispose women to criminal behaviour or mental disorders. Any behaviour changes found are better explained in terms of increased stress levels and other health fluctuations. PMS is evidently a universal physiological cycle, independent of culture.

- The phases of the menstrual cycle are controlled by the **pituitary gland.** This gland may be influenced by (seasonal) light levels, since **menarche** has been found to be most likely to occur in winter and is reached earlier by blind than sighted girls.

- **Ultradian rhythms** are shorter than one day. The most well-researched are those that occur during sleep. Sleep consists of a number of cycles lasting around 90 minutes. NREM sleep consists of four stages, each characterised by a distinct pattern of electrical activity.

- REM sleep seems to be related to the development of brain structures found only in mammals. In REM sleep, the musculature is virtually paralysed. The brain is highly active during REM sleep and a person woken from it typically reports experiencing a dream.

- There are important developmental changes in sleep patterns. Newborns spend about half of their 16 hours of sleep per day in REM sleep. In adulthood, about a quarter of total sleep time is spent in REM sleep. This decreases further in late adulthood, which is also accompanied by the virtual disappearance of Stage 4 sleep.

- One brain structure implicated in REM sleep is the **locus coeruleus**, which is part of the **pons**. Sleep cycles themselves may be a result of the relationship between the locus coeruleus and the **raphe nuclei**.

- Bodily rhythms are disrupted by **shift work**, especially during a shift changeover, when the body's functions are in a state of **internal desynchronisation**. By rotating shifts forwards instead of backwards, many of the problems associated with shift work can be reduced.

- Crossing time zones in a short space of time leads to **jet lag**. This tends to be more severe when travelling west to east than east to west. This is because easterly travel causes a disruptive **phase advance**, whereas westerly travel causes a less disruptive **phase delay**.

Essay Questions

1 Discuss the role played by endogenous pacemakers **and** exogenous Zeitgebers in any **one** biological rhythm. (*24 marks*)

2 Describe and assess the consequences of disrupting biological rhythms. (*24 marks*)

WEB ADDRESSES

http://www.circadian.com
http://www.cbt.virginia.edu/cbtindex.html
http://bioclox.bot.biologie.uni-tuebingen.de/Html_we/english/Books/ren96/ren96/node57.html

14 *Sleep*

INTRODUCTION AND OVERVIEW

As was seen in Chapter 13, everyone ordinarily sleeps at least once a day. Spending approximately seven hours in this altered state of consciousness means that just under one-third of our lifetimes are spent fast asleep! Indeed, seven hours sleep per day is probably not enough, and we may need to spend as long as ten hours asleep in order to function optimally (Thomas, 1999).

This chapter examines theories and research studies relating to the evolution and functions of sleep. It also considers the implications that findings from studies of total and partial sleep deprivation have for theories of sleep.

STUDIES OF TOTAL SLEEP DEPRIVATION

It has long been known that depriving people of sleep can have detrimental effects. For example, sleep deprivation has served dubious military purposes over the ages. The ancient Romans used *tormentum vigilae* (or the *waking torture*) to extract information from captured enemies, and in the 1950s the Koreans used sleep deprivation as a way of 'brainwashing' captured American airforce pilots (Borbely, 1986).

The first experimental study of sleep deprivation was conducted by Patrick & Gilbert (1898). They deprived three 'healthy young men' of sleep for 90 hours. The men reported a gradually increasing desire to sleep, and from the second night onwards two of them experienced perceptual disorders. When they were allowed to sleep normally, all three slept for longer than they usually did, and the psychological disturbances they experienced disappeared.

Box 14.1 The record breakers

In 1959 Peter Tripp, a New York disc-jockey, staged a charity 'wakeathon' in which he did not sleep for eight days. Towards the end of his wakeathon, Tripp showed some disturbing symptoms, including hallucinations and delusions. The delusions were so intense that it was impossible to give him any tests to assess his psychological functioning. In 1965, Randy Gardner, a 17-year-old student, stayed awake for 264 hours and 12 minutes, aiming to get himself into the *Guinness Book of Records*. For the last 90 hours of his record attempt, he was studied by sleep researcher William

Dement. Although Gardner had difficulty in performing some tasks, his lack of sleep did not produce anything like the disturbances experienced by Peter Tripp.

Afterwards, Gardner spent 14 hours and 40 minutes asleep, and when he awoke he appeared to have recovered completely. On subsequent nights, Gardner returned to his usual pattern of sleeping for eight hours per day, and did not seem to suffer any permanent physiological or psychological effects from his long period without sleep.

Figure 14.1 *Goya's* The Sleep of Reason Produces Monsters

Going without sleep for over 200 hours has subsequently been achieved by a number of people, none of whom appears to have experienced any long-term detrimental effects (Lavie, 1998). This *might* suggest that the major consequence of going without sleep is to make us want to go to sleep!

As interesting as the cases of Tripp, Gardner and others are, they tell us little about the effects of *total sleep deprivation,* because they did not take place under carefully controlled conditions. However, many controlled studies have been conducted. The effects of sleep deprivation over time have been summarised by Hüber-Weidman (1976).

Key **STUDY**

Box 14.2 The effects of sleep deprivation over time

Night 1: Most people are capable of going without sleep for a night. The experience may be uncomfortable, but it is tolerable.

Night 2: The urge to sleep becomes much greater. The period between 3–5 a.m., when body temperature is at its lowest in most of us, is crucial. It is during this period that sleep is most likely to occur.

Night 3: Tasks requiring sustained attention and complex forms of information processing are seriously impaired. This is particularly true if the task is repetitive and boring. If the task is interesting, or the experimenter offers encouragement, performance is less impaired. Again, the early hours of the morning are most crucial.

Night 4: From this night onwards, periods of *micro-sleep* occur. We stop what we are doing and stare into space for a few seconds. The end of micro-sleep is accompanied by a return to full awareness. Confusion, irritability, misperception and the *'hat phenomenon'* occur. In this, a tightening around the head is felt as though a hat that was too small was being worn.

Night 5: As well as the effects described above, *delusions* may be experienced. However, intellectual and problem-solving abilities are largely unimpaired.

Night 6: Symptoms of *depersonalisation* occur, and a clear sense of identity is lost. This is called *sleep deprivation psychosis.*

(From Hüber-Weidman, 1976)

The effects described above are psychological rather than physiological, and little physical harm follows sleep deprivation. Reflexes are unimpaired, and heart rate, respiration, blood pressure and body temperature show little change from normal. Hand tremors, droopy eyelids, problems in focusing the eyes, and heightened sensitivity to pain seem to be the major bodily consequences.

Additionally, the effects of sleep deprivation do not accumulate over time. If we normally sleep for eight hours a day and are deprived of sleep for three days, we do not sleep for 24 hours afterwards. Thus, we do not need to make up for *all* the sleep that has been missed, although we do make up for some (see Box 14.1, page 141).

The experiences of Peter Tripp (see Box 14.1) are unusual. Whilst some temporary psychological disturbances occur following sleep deprivation, sleep deprivation has no significant long-term consequences on normal psychological functioning. Tripp's experiences are, therefore, unlikely to be *solely* attributable to a lack of sleep. It is more likely that *stress*, which sleep deprivation can also cause, produces abnormal behaviour in susceptible individuals.

Key **STUDY**

Box 14.3 Sleep deprivation in non-humans

Whilst it might be tempting to conclude that sleep has little value, and a lack of it few harmful effects, such a conclusion is not justified. For example, Rechtschaffen *et al.* (1983) placed a rat on a disc protruding from a small bucket of water, with an EEG monitoring its brain activity. Every time brain activity indicated sleep, the disc rotated. This forced the rat to walk if it wanted to avoid falling in the water.

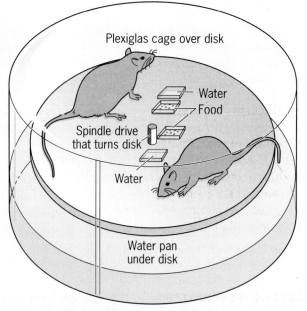

Figure 14.2 *Apparatus used in the experiment conducted by Rechtschaffen et al.*

A second rat, also connected to an EEG, was on the disc. However, whenever its brain activity indicated sleep the disc did *not* rotate. Thus, one rat was allowed to sleep normally whereas the other was not. After 33 days, all sleep-deprived rats had died, whereas those that slept normally appeared not to have suffered. The cause of death could not be precisely determined, but given a progressive physical deterioration in the rats, the ability to regulate their own heat may have been fatally impaired.

Unfortunately, the results of sleep deprivation studies on rats tells us little about the effects of sleep deprivation on humans, and there are clearly serious ethical objections to subjecting humans to the length of time the rats were deprived of sleep. However, Lugaressi *et al.* (1986) reported the case of a man who abruptly began to lose sleep at age 52. He became increasingly exhausted, and eventually developed a lung infection from which death resulted. A post-mortem revealed that neurons in areas of the brain linked to sleep and hormonal circadian rhythms were almost completely destroyed.

Irrespective of the effects of sleep deprivation, unless we are constantly encouraged to remain awake, we fall asleep, and we do so in virtually any position anywhere. People do not like to be kept awake, and there seems to be a need to sleep even though sleeplessness itself does not, at least as far as we know, appear to be particularly harmful. Perhaps, then, people sleep just to avoid feeling sleepy. However, such a suggestion isn't particularly helpful, and researchers have tried to understand sleep's exact functions.

EVOLUTIONARY THEORIES OF SLEEP FUNCTION

Meddis (1975, 1979) has pointed to evidence indicating that different species characteristically sleep for different periods of time, and that the amount of time spent asleep is related to an animal's need and method of obtaining food, and its exposure to predators. Animals that cannot find a safe place to sleep, have high metabolic rates that require a lot of food gathering, or are at risk from predators, sleep very little.

Box 14.4 The sleeping habits of some non–humans

The short-tailed shrew has a safe burrow, but sleeps very little since its high metabolic rate means that it must eat around the clock or die. Animals that are preyed upon, such as cattle, sheep and deer, sleep only about two hours a day, and even then take only 'brief naps'. By contrast, predator species (such as lions and tigers) or those that have safe sleeping places or can satisfy their needs for food and water fairly quickly, sleep for much longer. Like the short-tailed shrew, the ground squirrel has a safe burrow but, being a larger animal, it has a lower metabolic rate and does not need to eat so often. It sleeps for 14 hours a day. The gorilla, which does not need to sleep in a burrow to protect itself, also sleeps for 14 hours a day.

In a variation of Meddis's theory, Webb (1982) has suggested that sleep enables us to conserve energy when there is no need to expend it, or when expending energy would probably do more harm than good. Webb argues that sleep is an instinctual behavioural response which does not satisfy a physiological need in the way that food does. Rather, natural selection would favour an organism that kept itself out of danger when danger was most likely to occur. Sleep can therefore be seen as a response which is useful for a species' survival.

"I've set the alarm for half past April. That'll give us a bit of a lie in."

Figure 14.3 *Some researchers believe that sleep serves a function similar to hibernation*

Since we usually do not walk or roam about when we are asleep and (usually) sleep at night, sleep can be seen as an adaptive behaviour that keeps us quiet and out of harm's way. This is the *hibernation theory of sleep function*. In our evolutionary past, the enforced inactivity of sleeping allowed us to survive for a least two reasons:

• Sleeping at night would reduce the risk of predation or accidents;

- Since the likelihood of finding food at night would be much reduced, more energy would have been spent hunting than would have been gained by the results of hunting (Hobson, 1995).

However, even though we may be quiet and out of harm's way whilst asleep, we are *potentially* vulnerable. As Evans (1984) has remarked:

'The behaviour patterns involved in sleep are glaringly, almost insanely, at odds with common sense'.

Some evolutionary theorists argue that preyed upon species sleep for short periods because of the constant threat of predation. Others argue that preyed upon species sleep for longer periods in order to keep out of the way of predators. The sleep pattern of any species can thus be explained in one of these two ways by evolutionary theories, which makes them *non-falsifiable* in this respect.

Box 14.5 Sleep in the dolphin

Dolphins are aquatic mammals, but cannot sleep under water given that they have to come up for air periodically. The bottle-nosed dolphin's solution to this problem is for one cerebral hemisphere to sleep whilst the other stays awake. After a 30–60 minute period, the two hemispheres reverse their roles. Indus dolphins adopt a different strategy, sleeping for seconds at a time over the whole day (Mukhametov, 1984). This might be because the Indus river in which they live is full of large debris, and so they need to be constantly vigilant to avoid serious injury (Bentley, 2000).

RESTORATION THEORIES OF SLEEP FUNCTION

Safety and energy conservation could be two functions of sleep. However, whilst the neural mechanisms for sleep might have evolved to satisfy such needs, they may well have taken on additional or alternative functions. Most of us spend around 16 hours a day using up energy. According to Oswald (1966, 1980), the purpose of sleep is to restore depleted energy reserves, eliminate waste products from the muscles, repair cells and recover physical abilities that have been lost during the day.

Key STUDY

Box 14.6 Sleep and energy expenditure

The length of time we remain awake is related to how sleepy we feel, and at the end of a busy day we are all 'ready for bed'. Shapiro *et al.* (1981) found that people who had competed in an 'ultra-marathon', a running race of 57 miles, slept an hour and a half longer than they normally did for two nights following the race. Shapiro *et al.* also found that Stage 4 sleep occupied a much greater proportion of total sleep time (about 45 per cent) than normal (about 25 per cent), whilst the proportion of time spent in REM sleep decreased.

The restorative processes that occur during sleep are not precisely known (Green, 1998). Some studies have shown that a lack of exercise does *not* substantially reduce sleep, which it might be expected to do if sleep served an exclusively restorative function. Ryback & Lewis (1971) found that healthy individuals who spent six weeks resting in bed showed no changes in their sleep patterns. Adam & Oswald (1977, 1983) have suggested that certain kinds of tissue restoration, such as cell repair, occur during sleep, whilst Webb & Campbell (1983) believe that neurotransmitter levels are restored during sleep.

The *pituitary gland* releases a growth hormone during Stage 4 sleep which is important for tissue growth, protein and RNA synthesis, and the formation of red blood cells. This suggests that Stage 4 sleep plays a role in the growth process. As noted in Chapter 13 (see page 135), the total time spent in Stage 4 sleep decreases with increasing age, and this might be related to a relative lack of need for growth hormone. Disruption of Stage 4 sleep in healthy people produces symptoms similar to those experienced by fibrositis sufferers, who are known to experience a chronic lack of Stage 4 sleep (Empson, 1989). Since fibrositis is a disorder which causes acute inflammation of the back muscles and their sheaths, which is experienced as pain and stiffness, it is tempting to accept the suggestion that sleep serves a restorative function.

Box 14.7 Sleep and psychological restoration

A different approach to restoration theory suggests that sleep may serve a *psychological* as well as (or instead of) a physiological restorative function. For example, Kales *et al.* (1974) have shown that insomniacs suffer from far more psychological problems than healthy people, whilst Hartmann (1973) has reported that we generally need to sleep more during periods of stress, such as occurs when we change a job or move house. Berry & Webb (1983) found a strong correlation between self-reported levels of anxiety and 'sleep efficiency', and also discovered that the better the sleep attained by the participants in their study, the more positive were their moods on the following day.

Although the evidence is not conclusive, it is possible that sleep helps us recover from the psychological as well as the physiological exertions of our waking hours (see also Chapter 15).

STUDIES OF REM SLEEP DEPRIVATION

REM sleep has been of particular interest to researchers, largely because of its paradoxical nature (see Chapter 13, page 134). REM sleep might serve particular functions, and much research has investigated this. As with sleep in general, the easiest way to address the role of REM sleep has been to deprive people of it and observe the consequences of the deprivation.

Key STUDY

Box 14.8 REM starvation

Dement (1960) had volunteers spend several nights at his sleep laboratory. They were allowed to sleep normally, but whenever they entered REM sleep they were woken up. A control group of volunteers was woken up the same number of times but only during NREM sleep. Compared with the control group, the REM sleep-deprived group became increasingly irritable, aggressive and unable to concentrate on performing various tasks. As the experiment progressed, the REM sleep-deprived group started to show *REM starvation*. After several nights, they attempted to go into REM sleep as soon as they went to sleep, and it became increasingly difficult to wake them when they did manage to enter REM sleep.

On the first night, Dement had to wake the REM-deprived sleepers an average of 12 times each, but by the seventh night they had to be woken an average of 26 times, suggesting that the need for REM sleep was steadily increasing. Similarly, Borbely (1986) found that a REM sleep-deprived individual made 31 attempts to enter REM sleep on the first night, 51 attempts on the second, and over 60 on the third!

When people are allowed to sleep normally after REM sleep deprivation most, but not all, show a REM sleep *rebound effect* (they spend longer in REM sleep than is usually the case). This suggests that we try to make up for 'lost' REM sleep time, although firm conclusions cannot be drawn since the rebound effect is *not* observed in everyone. In general, the evidence suggests that we can adjust to REM sleep deprivation in much the same way that we can adjust to not eating for several days if necessary (Webb, 1975). REM sleep seems to be necessary, then, though depriving people of it does not appear to be psychologically harmful.

Key STUDY

Box 14.9 REM sleep, anxiety and alcohol

Some researchers have looked at the effects of REM sleep deprivation on the reduction of anxiety. Greenberg *et al.* (1972) had participants watch a film of a circumcision rite performed without anaesthetic. On first viewing, the film elicits a high level of anxiety which gradually subsides on repeated viewing. However, Greenberg *et al.* found that people deprived of REM sleep did *not* show a reduction in their anxiety when they viewed the film on subsequent occasions. This suggests that REM sleep may, at least partly, act to reduce the anxiety of events that have occurred during the waking day.

Alcohol suppresses REM sleep without affecting NREM sleep. When heavy alcohol users abstain, a REM rebound effect occurs. The effect can be very disturbing, and the sharp increase in dreaming often leads to a resumption of heavy drinking. With severe alcohol abuse, a kind of REM rebound effect may occur during the waking hours. This manifests itself as the disturbing hallucinations experienced during alcohol withdrawal (Greenberg & Pearlman, 1967).

As noted earlier, the evidence generally suggests that there are few harmful effects following REM sleep deprivation. Indeed, according to Dement (1974):

'Research has failed to prove substantial ill-effects result from even prolonged selective REM deprivation'.

Whilst this may be true, the occurrence of the REM rebound effect, and the fact that REM-deprived sleepers try to enter REM more and more over the course of time, suggests that REM sleep may serve important functions (see Chapter 15).

RESTORATION THEORIES OF REM SLEEP FUNCTION

According to Oswald (1966, 1980), REM sleep is related to brain 'restoration' and growth. Studies have shown a greater rate of *protein synthesis* during REM sleep than in NREM sleep, and protein synthesis may serve as 'an organic basis for new developments in the personality' (Rossi, 1973). However, whether REM sleep *causes* increased protein synthesis, or increased protein synthesis is the *result* of the increased activity of nerve cells that occurs during REM sleep, is less clear.

REM sleep does, however, differ over the lifespan, and accounts for around 50 per cent of the total sleep time (TST) of a newborn baby compared with only 20 per cent of the TST of an adult (see Figure 13.5, page 136). Indeed, in almost every mammalian species, adults sleep less than infants and spend less time in REM sleep as they get older. REM sleep may, therefore, promote the protein synthesis necessary for cell manufacture and growth, which is essential to the developing nervous system's maturation. The decline observed in adulthood may reflect a decrease in the rate of development of the brain's information processing capabilities.

Box 14.10 REM, learning and brain 'insults'

REM sleep deprivation has the effect, in non-humans at least, of impairing *learning*. Bloch (1976) has shown that REM sleep increases when non-humans are given training on a new task, and that this increase is greatest during the steepest part of the learning curve. Perhaps, then, the protein synthesis that occurs during REM sleep is a contributory factor in the formation of long-term memories (see below). In humans, the consequence of a massive 'insult' to the brain by, for example, a drug overdose or electroconvulsive therapy (ECT: see Chapter 52), is in an increase in the amount of time spent in REM sleep, as though some attempt was being made to repair the damage done.

Even those who support the restoration theory of REM sleep function accept that REM sleep uses a substantial amount of energy (such as increased blood flow to the brain). Such activity would actually *prevent* high levels of protein synthesis. In view of this, Oswald (1974) suggests that both Stage 4 *and* REM sleep are involved in the restoration of *body tissue*.

SOME OTHER THEORIES OF REM SLEEP FUNCTION

Memory consolidation theory

REM sleep may stimulate neural tissue and consolidate information in memory. Empson & Clarke's (1970) participants heard unusual phrases before bedtime and were given a memory test about them the next morning. Those deprived of REM sleep remembered less than those woken the same number of times during the night but from other stages of sleep. This finding has been replicated on several occasions using various material (e.g. Tilley & Empson, 1978), although we should note that there is no evidence to suggest that *hypnopaedia* – learning whilst we are asleep – takes place (Rubin, 1968).

As noted in Chapter 13 (see page 134), REM sleep occurs in all mammals except the spiny anteater and dolphin, but not in non-humans such as fish, whose behaviour is less influenced by learning. It was also noted that the proportion of time spent in REM sleep declines with increasing age when, possibly, the need to consolidate memories is of less importance. The evidence concerning memory consolidation during REM sleep is mounting, and it is probable that memory consolidation is an important function of REM sleep (Kudrimoto *et al.*, 1996).

The sentinel theory

The observation that EEG activity resembles activity patterns observed during waking, and that short periods of wakefulness sometimes occur at the *end* of REM sleep, led Snyder (1970) to suggest that REM sleep serves the function of allowing animals to check their surroundings periodically for signs of danger. Snyder sees the end of REM acting as a *sentinel* (or look-out) to ensure that animals are free from danger. Whilst this is an interesting suggestion, its main weakness lies in the fact that it sees only the *end* of REM sleep as serving any function. The time spent in REM sleep presumably serves no function at all. It is unlikely that many sleep researchers would agree with this.

The oculomotor system maintenance theory

Some researchers who might agree with Snyder are those who subscribe to the oculomotor system maintenance theory of REM sleep function. According to this, REM sleep's function is to keep the eye muscles toned up. About once every 90 minutes during sleep, the eye muscles are given some *exercise* to keep them in trim.

Box 14.11 REM: Stirring up the fluid

In a variation of the oculomotor system maintenance theory, Maurice (1998) suggests that REMs are designed to stir up the fluid in the eye. This fluid needs to circulate to carry oxygen from blood vessels in the iris to the cornea, which has relatively few blood vessels. When the eyes are closed and motionless, the fluid hardly moves. When it is open, motion or convection currents stimulated by the cooler air around the eyeball keep the fluid stirred. However, people deprived of REM do not suffer eye problems, and the *REM rebound effect* that sometimes follows REM sleep deprivation is also hard for Maurice's account to explain (Bentley, 2000).

CONCLUSIONS

This chapter has examined theories and research studies relating to the evolution and functions of sleep. Many theories have been advanced, and typically tested by means of partial or total sleep deprivation. Presently, no theory is firmly supported by experimental evidence. For some researchers, however, the question of why we sleep has a very simple answer. We sleep because we need to *dream*. If this is the case, another interesting question arises, concerning the functions of dreaming. This question is addressed in Chapter 15.

Summary

- **Sleep deprivation** is used as a way of studying the functions of sleep. Controlled studies suggest a pattern of psychological reactions whose severity increases with increasing deprivation. After six nights without sleep, **sleep deprivation psychosis** occurs, although this disappears after a period of 'recovery sleep'. There is little evidence that physical harm follows sleep deprivation.

- Long-term sleep deprivation in rats fatally impairs the ability to regulate their own heat. Case studies of humans who lose sleep as a result of brain damage, also indicate that long-term deprivation is fatal.

- Meddis's **evolutionary theory** of sleep function proposes that sleep time is related to an animal's metabolic rate, method of obtaining food and exposure to predators. Animals which have a high metabolic rate, gather food in the open, and are preyed upon, have little sleep.

- Webb's **hibernation theory** proposes that because natural selection would favour an animal that kept itself out of danger, sleep has survival value. In the evolutionary past of humans, sleeping at night would have reduced the risk of predation/accidents and conserved energy.

- Some evolutionary theorists argue that preyed-upon species sleep for short periods because of the constant threat of predation. Others argue that such species sleep longer to avoid predation. This account of different sleep times is non-falsifiable.

- **Restoration theories** propose that sleep restores depleted energy levels, eliminates waste products from the muscles, repairs cells and recovers lost physical abilities. Stage 4 sleep, strongly suspected of being involved in the growth process, increases after excessive physical exertion. Reduced Stage 4 sleep in the elderly may reflect a reduction in the need for growth hormone.

- Sleep, especially REM sleep, may also serve a psychological restorative function. People deprived of REM sleep show **REM starvation**, and try to enter REM as soon as they return to sleep. Most people also show a 'rebound effect' following deprivation of REM sleep.

- REM sleep may be involved in brain restoration and growth, since more protein synthesis occurs in it than in NREM sleep. Because REM sleep decreases with age, it may promote maturation of the developing nervous system and increase the brain's information-processing capabilities.

- REM sleep in non-humans increases during learning, especially in the steepest part of the learning curve, and so may be involved in long-term memory formation and consolidation. Studies using humans also point to a role in memory consolidation.

- Snyder's **sentinel theory** proposes that the brief awakenings which sometimes occur at the end of a period of REM sleep allow an animal periodically to monitor its environment for signs of danger. However, this function only concerns the end of REM sleep, not REM sleep itself.

- One **oculomotor system maintenance theory** proposes that REM sleep's function is to keep the eye muscles toned up. Another suggests that eye movements provide the cornea with oxygen from blood vessels.

Essay Questions

1 Discuss **two** theories relating to the functions of sleep. (*24 marks*)

2 Critically consider the implications of findings from studies of total and/or partial sleep deprivation for any **one** theory of sleep function. (*24 marks*)

WEB ADDRESSES

http://bisleep.medsch.ucla.edu/
http://faculty.Washington.edu/chudler/sleep.htm
http://www.lboro.ac.uk/departments/hu/groups/sleep/karger.htm

15 *Dreaming*

INTRODUCTION AND OVERVIEW

Dreams have long been of interest to both laypeople and psychologists. Some cultures, for example, believe dreams to be the experiences of a world that is not available during the waking hours. Others see dreams as messages from the gods. Attempts to discover the meaning of dreams can be found in Babylonian records dating back to 5000 BC. The Bible, Talmud, and Homer's *Iliad* and *Odyssey* all give accounts of the meaning of dreams. In the Bible, for example, dreams provided revelations. It was during a dream that Joseph learned there was to be a famine in Egypt. This chapter describes research findings relating to the nature of dreams, and examines *psychological* and *neurobiological* theories of the functions of dreaming.

THE NATURE OF DREAMS

The pioneering research of Dement, Aserinsky and Kleitman, which was described in Chapter 13, revealed much about dreaming. As noted, REM sleep is correlated with dreaming, and so instead of relying on the sometimes hazy recall of a dreamer waking at the end of an eight-hour period of sleep, the waking of a dreamer during a REM sleep episode enabled a vivid account of a dream to be obtained.

Everyone shows the pattern of four to five REM sleep episodes per night. When woken from REM sleep, people report dreaming about 80 per cent of the time. Thus, those who claim that they don't dream really mean that they don't *remember* their dreams. Although there are wide individual differences, those dreams that are remembered tend to be the ones occurring closest to waking up. People blind from birth also dream, and have auditory dreams which are just as vivid and complex as the visual dreams of sighted people.

Dreams may be realistic and well organised, disorganised and uninformed, in black and white or colour, and emotional or unemotional. Although dreaming is most likely to occur in REM sleep, some occurs in NREM sleep (Strauch & Meier, 1996). REM sleep dreams tend to be clear, highly detailed, full of vivid images and often reported as fantastic adventures with a clear plot. The eye movements that occur during REM sleep are *sometimes* correlated with a dream's content, but there is no one-to-one correspondence (Dement & Kleitman, 1957). NREM sleep dreams typically consist of fleeting images, lack detail, have vague plots and involve commonplace things.

Figure 15.1 The Nightmare *by Johann Heinrich Füssli*

Most dreams last as long as the events would last in real life (Burne, 1998). Although time seems to expand and contract during a dream, 15 minutes of events occupies about 15 minutes of dream time. The actual content of a dream can be affected by pre-sleep events. For example, people deprived of water often dream of drinking (Bokert, 1970). Also, whilst the brain is relatively insensitive to outside sensory input, some external stimuli can either wake us up (see Box 13.7, page 134) or be incorporated into a dream. For example, Dement & Wolpert (1958) lightly sprayed cold water onto dreamers' faces. Compared with sleepers who were not sprayed, they were much more likely to dream about water, incorporating waterfalls, leaky roofs and, occasionally, being sprayed with water, into their dreams.

Sex differences in dreaming have also been reported, with females typically dreaming about indoor settings and males about outdoor settings (Hall, 1984). Male dreams also tend to be more aggressive than female dreams. Contrary to popular belief, only a small proportion (one in ten in men and one in 30 in women) of dreams are clearly sexual in content (Hall & Van de Castle, 1966).

Box 15.1 Lucid dreaming and sleepwalking

Lucid dreamers report having dreams in which they knew they were dreaming and felt as if they were conscious during the dream. They can test their state of consciousness by attempting to perform impossible acts, such as floating in the air. If the act can be performed, a lucid dream is occurring. Some lucid dreamers can control the course of events in a dream, and skilled dreamers can signal the onset of a lucid dream by moving their eyes in a way pre-arranged with the sleep researcher. Evidently, the technology now exists for all of us to become lucid dreamers (Martin, 1999).

Contrary to popular belief, sleepwalking does not occur during REM sleep. It cannot, since the musculature is in a state of virtual paralysis during REM sleep (see Box 13.8, page 136). As noted, the paralysis presumably prevents us from *acting out* a dream. Sleepwalking occurs during the *deeper stages* of sleep when the musculature is *not* paralysed.

A great deal is known about the process of dreaming, but what functions does it serve? Some researchers believe that dreaming has no functions. Kleitman (1963), for example, has suggested that:

'The low-grade cerebral activity that is dreaming may serve no significant function whatsoever'.

Others believe that dreams have important psychological functions.

PSYCHOLOGICAL THEORIES OF THE FUNCTIONS OF DREAMING

Freud and 'the interpretation of dreams'

The first person to seriously consider the psychology of dreaming was Freud (1900) in *The Interpretation of Dreams*. Freud argued that a dream was a sort of 'psychic safety valve', which allowed a person to harmlessly discharge otherwise unacceptable and unconscious wishes and urges.

During the waking hours, these wishes and impulses are excluded from consciousness because of their unacceptable nature. During sleep, they are allowed to be expressed through the medium of dreams. As noted above, Freud saw them as relieving psychic tensions created during the day and gratifying unconscious desires. He also saw them as 'protecting sleep', by providing imagery that would keep disturbing and repressed thoughts out of consciousness.

Box 15.2 Manifest and latent content

Freud argued that unconscious desires are not gratified directly in a dream. What he called the *manifest content* of a dream (the dream as reported by the dreamer) is a censored and symbolic version of its deeper *latent content* (its actual meaning). According to Freud, a dream's meaning has to be 'disguised' because it consists of drives and wishes (*wish fulfilment*) that would be threatening to us if they were expressed directly. Freud believed that the process of 'censorship' and 'symbolic transformation' accounted for the sometimes bizarre and highly illogical nature of dreams.

For Freud, dreams provide the most valuable insight into the motives that direct a person's behaviour, and he described a dream as 'the royal road to the unconscious'. The task of a dream analyst is to decode the manifest content of a dream into its latent content. Analysts call the objects that occur in a dream, and which camouflage its meaning, *symbols*. A gun, for example, might actually be a disguised representation of the penis. A person who dreamt of being *robbed* at gunpoint might be unconsciously expressing a wish to be sexually dominated. A person who dreamt of *robbing* someone at gunpoint might be unconsciously expressing a wish to be sexually dominant.

Table 15.1 *Sexual symbols in Freudian dream interpretation*

Symbols for the male genital organs

aeroplanes	fish	neckties	tools	weapons
bullets	hands	poles	trains	
feet	hoses	snakes	trees	
fire	knives	sticks	umbrellas	

Symbols for the female genital organs

bottles	caves	doors	ovens	ships
boxes	chests	hats	pockets	tunnels
cases	closets	jars	pots	

Symbols for sexual intercourse

climbing a ladder	entering a room
climbing a staircase	flying in an aeroplane
crossing a bridge	riding a horse
driving a car	riding a roller coaster
riding a lift	walking into a tunnel or down a hall

Symbols for the breasts

apples	peaches

Freud believed that no matter how absurd a dream appeared to be to the dreamer, it always possessed meaning and logic. However, he did accept that there was a danger in translating the symbols, and warned that dreams had to be analysed in the context of a person's waking life as well as his/her associations with the dream's content: a broken candlestick may well represent a theme of impotence, but as Freud himself (a lover of cigars) famously remarked, 'sometimes a cigar is only a cigar'.

It is, of course, possible that dreams have meaning and might reveal important issues and conflicts in a person's life. However, Freud's view that these issues and conflicts are always disguised has been criticised (Griffin, 1998). For example, a person who is concerned with impotence is just as likely to dream about impotence as about a broken candlestick. As Fisher & Greenberg (1977) have noted:

'There is no *rationale* for approaching a dream as if it were a container for a secret wish buried under layers of concealment'.

Freud's claim that part of the function of dreaming is to 'protect sleep' has also been challenged. Evidence suggests that disturbing events during the day tend to be followed by related disturbing dreams, rather than 'protective imagery' (Foulkes, 1971; Cohen, 1973). Hall (1966),

amongst others, has noted that the content of most dreams is consistent with a person's waking behaviour. Thus, there is little evidence to support the view that the primary function of dreaming is to act as a release for the expression of unacceptable impulses.

The major problem for Freud's theory of dream function is that the *interpretation* of a dream is not something that can be *objectively* achieved, even if the interpreter is a trained psychoanalyst. According to Collee (1993):

'Metaphor is a notoriously ambiguous form of communication. You can suggest to me the meaning of having luminous feet, but the image will almost always mean something entirely different to you from what it means to me. So dreams end up in much the same category as tarot cards or tea leaves: just a system of images which the dream expert can manipulate to tell you exactly what they think you need to hear'.

Box 15.3 Dreams and illness

Another theory of dreams developed by Freud derives from practices in ancient Greece. At the Temple of Aesculapius, the physician Epidaurus administered drugs to people who, having slept and dreamt, then told him about their dreams. On the basis of the descriptions provided, Epidaurus was able to tell them the nature of their illness. Like the ancient Greeks, Freud believed that dreams were the body's way of telling us about physical illness. Psychoanalytic interest lies in the finding that dreams may precipitate illness or contribute to the distress of illness (Le Fanu, 1994).

A 'problem-solving' theory

Webb & Cartwright (1978) see dreams as a way of dealing with problems relating to work, sex, health, relationships and so on that occur during the waking hours. Cartwright *et al.* (1984) argue that whatever is symbolised in a dream *is* the dream's true meaning and, unlike Freud, they see no reason to distinguish between a dream's manifest and latent content. Like Freud, however, Cartwright *et al.* make much use of the role of metaphor in dreaming.

They suggest that a person dreaming of, say, being buried beneath an avalanche whilst carrying several books might be worried about being 'snowed under' with work. Dreaming of a colleague trying to stab you in the neck might indicate that the colleague is a 'pain in the neck'. Webb & Cartwright (1978) have claimed support for their theory from several studies. In one, participants were presented with common problems which needed solving. Those allowed to sleep uninterrupted generated far more realistic solutions than those deprived of REM sleep.

Additionally, Hartmann (1973) found that people experiencing interpersonal or occupational problems entered REM sleep earlier, and spent longer in it, than people without such problems. For Webb & Cartwright (1978), then, dreams are a way of identifying and dealing with many of life's problems. As they have noted, people going through crises need the support of friends and family, a little bit of luck and 'a good dream system'.

NEUROBIOLOGICAL THEORIES OF THE FUNCTIONS OF DREAMING

'Reprogramming' theories

According to Evans (1984), the brain needs to periodically shut itself off from sensory input in order to process and assimilate new information and update information already stored. This shutting off is REM sleep, during which the brain 'mentally reprograms' its memory systems. The dreams we experience are the brain's attempts at interpreting this updating.

Support for this theory has been claimed from studies which show that REM sleep increases following activities requiring intense or unusual mental activity (such as performing complex and frustrating tasks). For example, Herman & Roffwarg (1983) had participants spend the waking day wearing distorting lenses that made the visual world appear upside down. After this experience, which demands considerable mental effort, participants spent longer than usual in REM sleep. Evans' theory would explain this in terms of the brain needing to spend a longer period of time 'off-line', processing and assimilating the experience. The finding that older people spend shorter periods of time dreaming is also consistent with Evans' theory: presumably, the older we get, the less need there is to reprogram our memory systems.

Key (STUDY)

Box 15.4 To sleep, perchance to experience amygdalocortical activation and prefrontal deactivation?

Maquet *et al.* (1996) persuaded participants connected to an EEG machine to sleep in a PET scanner, their heads pinned in place by a special face mask. The PET scans confirmed the existence of activity in the pons during REM sleep (see Box 13.8, page 136), and also indicated activity in the left thalamus, which receives signals from the brainstem. Of most interest, though,

was the activity in the left and right amygdalas. Since one role of these structures is the formation and consolidation of memories of emotional experience, it seems likely that REM sleep is, as theorists like Evans (1984) have proposed, involved in memory processing.

Maquet *et al.* also found *reduced* activity in the prefrontal cortex, which is involved in self-awareness and the planning of behaviour. They argue that the 'dampening down' of this area may prevent us from realising that a dream is actually unreal, and may be why dreams appear real. The prefrontal cortex's reduced activity may also explain the distortions in time that occur in a dream and the forgetting of a dream after waking.

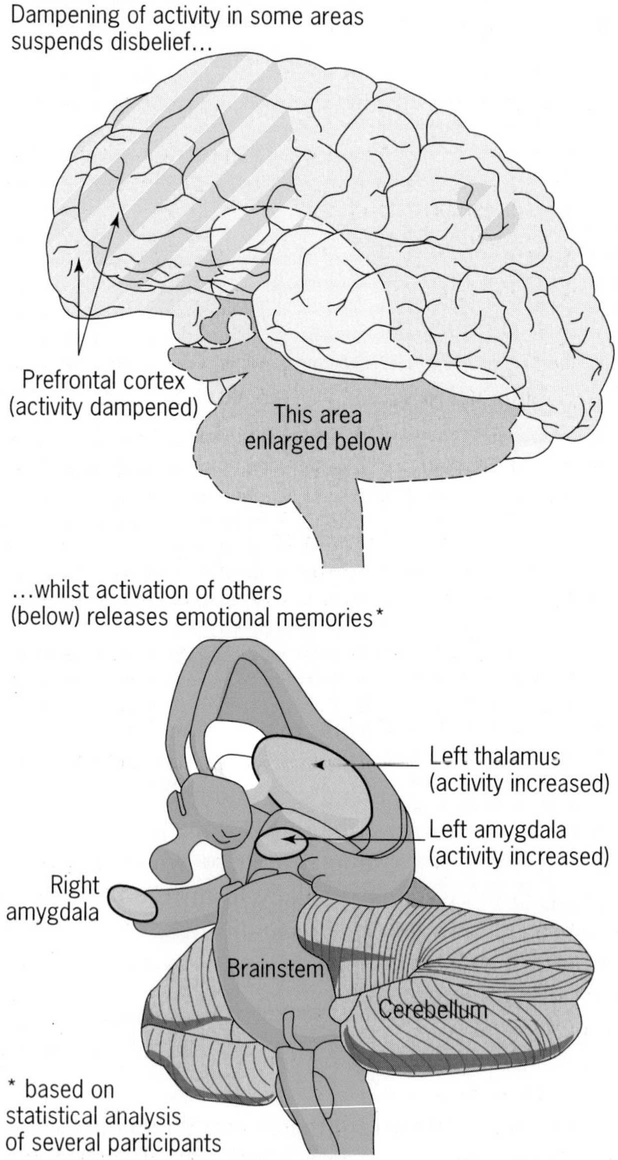

Dampening of activity in some areas suspends disbelief...

Prefrontal cortex (activity dampened)

This area enlarged below

...whilst activation of others (below) releases emotional memories*

Left thalamus (activity increased)

Left amygdala (activity increased)

Right amygdala

Brainstem

Cerebellum

* based on statistical analysis of several participants

Figure 15.2 *Maquet* et al.'s *findings (The Telegraph Group Limited, London, 1996)*

An alternative 'reprogramming' theory has been offered by Foulkes (1985). Like some other sleep researchers, Foulkes argues that dreams occur as a result of spontaneous activity in the nervous system. Foulkes argues that this activity can be related to our cognitive processes. The activation that occurs in the brain may well be spontaneous and random, but our cognitive systems are definitely *not* random. According to Foulkes *et al.* (1988), these systems, which we use in interpreting new experiences, themselves try to interpret the brain activity that occurs during REM sleep. Because of the structure imposed on the activation by our cognitive systems, dreams consist of events that generally occur in a way that makes at least some sense.

Box 15.5 Foulkes' functions of dreams

For Foulkes, dreams have at least four functions.

- First, most dreams usually refer to and reflect the dreamer's memories and knowledge. One function might therefore be to relate *newly* acquired knowledge to one's own self-consciousness.

- Second, a dream might help integrate and combine specific knowledge and experiences acquired through the various senses with more general knowledge acquired in the past.

- Third, dreams often contain events that could, or might, have happened to us, but did not. By dreaming about something that has not yet occurred, but which might, a dream may serve the function of programming us to be prepared for dealing with new, unexpected events.

- Fourth, since dreams are shaped by basic cognitive systems, they may reveal important information about the nature of our cognitive processes.

A third 'reprogramming' theory, which is a variation of the second function of dreams proposed by Foulkes, has been advanced by Koukkou & Lehman (1983). They argue that during a dream we combine ideas and strategies of thinking which originated in childhood with recently acquired relevant information. A dream is therefore a restructuring and reinterpretation of data already stored in memory.

Like some other theorists, Koukkou and Lehman clearly see dreams as being *meaningful*. However, some researchers have challenged this view, arguing that dreams are a meaningless consequence of brain activity during sleep.

Hobson and McCarley's 'activation-synthesis' theory

Hobson (1989) showed that in cats, certain neurons deep within the brain fire in a seemingly random manner during REM sleep. The firing of these neurons *activates* adjacent neurons which are involved in the control of eye movements, gaze, balance, posture and activities such as running and walking.

As noted in Chapter 14, most body movements are inhibited during REM sleep. However, signals are still sent to the parts of the cerebral cortex responsible for visual information processing and voluntary actions when we are awake. Thus, although the body is not moving, the brain receives signals which suggest that it is. In an attempt to make sense of this contradiction, the brain, drawing on memory and other stored information, attempts to *synthesise* the random bursts of neural activity. The result of its efforts is the dream we experience, and hence the term *'activation-synthesis'* (Hobson, 1995).

The process of synthesis results in the brain imposing some order on the chaotic events caused by the firing of neurons, but it cannot do this in a particularly sophisticated way. This would explain why dreams often comprise shifting and fragmentary images. As Hobson & McCarley (1977) have noted, the dream itself is the brain's effort 'to make the best out of a bad job'. For Hobson and McCarley, then, dream content is the by-product of the random stimulation of nerve cells rather than the unconscious wishes suggested by Freud. Whereas Freud saw dreams as 'the royal road to the unconscious', Hobson and McCarley see them as inherently random and meaningless.

Box 15.6 Giant cells and 'synaptic ammunition'

Hobson (1988) has also offered an explanation of why the brain is *periodically* activated during the sleep cycle. He argues that *giant cells*, which are found in the reticular activating system and the pons, are responsible for the onset of REM sleep and are sensitive to the neurotransmitter *acetylcholine*. When acetylcholine is available, the giant cells fire in an unrestrained way, but when no more is available they stop.

Hobson uses the analogy of a machine gun which can fire bullets very quickly when the cartridge is full, but can do nothing once it has emptied. The end of REM sleep occurs because there is no more 'synaptic ammunition'. When synaptic ammunition, in the form of acetylcholine, becomes available again, the giant cells start firing and another period of REM sleep begins.

Hobson and McCarley's theory has attracted considerable support because of its apparent explanatory power. For example, our strong tendency to dream about events that have occurred during the day presumably occurs because the most current neural activity of the cortex is that which represents the concerns or events of the day. Commonly experienced dreams about falling are, presumably, the brain attempting to interpret activity in the neurons involved in balance, whilst dreams about floating are the brain's attempt to interpret neural activity in the inner ear.

Activation-synthesis theory is also capable of explaining why we do not experience smells and tastes during a dream. This is because the neurons responsible are not stimulated during REM sleep. Our inability to remember dreams occurs because the neurons in the cortex that control the storage of new memories are turned 'off'. Finally, evidence concerning the role of acetylcholine in REM sleep is also consistent with Hobson and McCarley's theory (see Box 13.8, page 136).

Yet whilst Hobson believes that activation synthesis theory has 'opened the door to the molecular biology of sleep' (and closed it on the Freudian approach to dreaming: Bianchi, 1992), it has not escaped criticism. According to Foulkes (1985), the content of dreams is influenced by our waking experiences and, therefore, dreams cannot be as random and psychologically meaningless as Hobson and McCarley suggest.

In response to this, Hobson (1988) has accepted that:

> 'The brain is so inexorably bent upon the quest for meaning that it attributes and even creates meaning when there is little or none in the data it is asked to process'.

However, although dreams might contain 'unique stylistic psychological features and concerns' which provide us with insights into our 'life strategies' and, perhaps, ways of coping, the activation synthesis theory most definitely sees dreams as the result of brain stem activities rather than unconscious wishes.

Crick and Mitchison's 'reverse learning' theory

According to Crick & Mitchison (1983), the function of dreaming is to enable the brain to get rid of information it doesn't need by weakening undesirable synaptic connections, and erasing 'inappropriate modes of brain activity' which have been produced either by the physical growth of brain cells or experience. Crick and Mitchison propose that during REM sleep, random firing of neurons in the brain sets off undesirable connections, such as hallucinations and fantasies, that have overloaded the cortex. By 'flushing out' the excessive accumulation of 'parasitic information', more space is made available in memory for useful information. 'We

dream in order to forget', they write, and call this process *reverse learning* or *unlearning*.

Box 15.7 Why don't dolphins and spiny anteaters have REM sleep?

Crick and Mitchison argue that their theory is supported by the finding that all mammals except the spiny anteater and dolphin have REM sleep (when dreaming is most likely to occur). Both of these mammals have an abnormally large cortex for their size, which Crick and Mitchison believe is because they do not dream. Consequently, they need an especially large cortex to accommodate all the useless information they have accumulated, which cannot be disposed of.

For Crick and Mitchison, then, dreams serve a biologically useful process in that they keep the nervous system functioning effectively. However, a dream's content is an accidental result that does not lend itself to meaningful interpretation. Indeed, remembering dreams is *bad* for us because we are storing again the very information we were trying to dispose of!

Box 15.8 Dreams and creativity

One problem for theories which see dreams as meaningless events is that history is littered with stories of discoveries or creations that came to people during a dream. The chemist August Kekulé von Stradonitz once dreamed of six snakes chasing each other in such a way that the snake in front was biting the snake behind. From this, he deduced the structure of the benzene ring. James Watt, puzzled about how to make engine parts run more smoothly, dreamt of molten metal fragments falling from the sky. As they fell, they formed into globes. This 'drop-cooling' is how ball-bearings were first manufactured (Martin, 1999).

One observation that most theories of dreaming have difficulty in accounting for is that something very much like REM sleep occurs in the developing foetus. What unconscious wishes could a developing foetus have? What 'parasitic information' could a foetus be getting rid of? According to Jouvet (1983), the only possible explanation is that REM sleep serves to program processes in the brain necessary for the development and maintenance of genetically determined functions, such as *instincts*. This theory suggests that REM sleep generates a sensory activity pattern in the brain – the dream – that is independent of the external world (Borbely, 1986). Jouvet sees the activity of nerve cells that occurs in REM sleep as representing a code which is capable of activating information stored in the genes. This inborn instinctive behaviour is 'practiced' during REM sleep. After birth, it is combined with acquired or learned information. Alternatively, though, REM sleep might just serve the function of stirring up fluid in the eye (see Box 14.11, page 147).

CONCLUSIONS

This chapter has reviewed psychological and neurobiological theories of the function of dreaming. These see dreams as being either meaningful *or* meaningless. Because they are difficult to test, none can be rejected or accepted. An answer to the question of what functions dreaming serve cannot be given without reservation. As Collee (1993) has observed:

'There is a danger in thinking about the body in teleological terms – imagining that everything has a function, whereas we know that a lot of what happens is accidental. Yawning is one example of such accidents of nature, seeming to be just the useless by-product of various important respiratory reflexes. Dreams might have no function at all or they might have a heap of different functions all jumbled together so that one obscures the other. They might just be the films your brain plays to entertain itself while it is sleeping.'

Summary

- The correlation between REM sleep and dreaming enables dreams to be studied scientifically. Everyone experiences four to five episodes of REM sleep per night, and when woken from it report dreaming 80 per cent of the time.

- Some dreams occur in NREM sleep, but there are important differences in quality and content between them and REM sleep dreams.

- Events in dreams tend to last as long as they would in real life, and a dream's content can be affected by pre-sleep events and events occurring during REM sleep.

- There are differences in men and women's dreams, although we have fewer dreams about sex than is commonly believed.

- **Lucid dreamers** are aware that they are dreaming, and can sometimes control the events that are occurring. Sleepwalking cannot occur in REM sleep since the musculature is virtually paralysed. Sleepwalking must occur in stages of sleep other than REM sleep.

- According to Freud, a dream is a 'safety valve' which allows us to harmlessly discharge otherwise unacceptable and unconscious urges and wishes. The dream reported by the dreamer (its **manifest content**) is a censored and symbolic version of its actual meaning (**latent content**).

- Freud's theory has been widely criticised, and there is little evidence to support it. The non-falsifiability of dream interpretation is the theory's major weakness.

- Dreams have also been proposed as ways of solving problems. People experiencing interpersonal/occupational problems enter REM sleep earlier, and spend longer in it, than those without such problems.

- Evans' **reprogramming theory** suggests that dreams are the brain's attempt at interpreting the processing and assimilation of new information, and updating information already stored. Support for this comes from the finding that REM sleep time increases following activities requiring intense/unusual mental activity.

- Foulkes' **reprogramming theory** claims that a dream is an attempt to interpret the random and spontaneous brain activity that occurs in REM sleep. A dream usually makes some sense because our cognitive system imposes its structure on this otherwise meaningless activity.

■ **Activation-synthesis theory** suggests that dreams are essentially meaningless, and reflect the brain's unsophisticated attempt to make sense of the electrical activity that occurs in REM sleep. A dream occurs when giant cells in the reticular activating system and the pons are activated by **acetylcholine**.

■ Activation-synthesis theory has much apparent explanatory power. However, if dreams are influenced by our waking experiences, then dreaming cannot be completely random and meaningless.

■ Crick and Mitchison's **reverse learning theory** proposes that dreams enable the brain to erase information that is no longer needed, by weakening certain synaptic connections. The 'flushing out' of 'parasitic information' creates more space in memory for useful information.

■ Crick and Mitchison see the absence of REM sleep in the spiny anteater and dolphin as consistent with their theory, since both of these have abnormally large cortexes for their size. An abnormally large cortex would be needed if there were no way of removing useless information.

Essay Questions

1 **a** Outline the nature of dreams. (*6 marks*)

   b Outline and evaluate **one** psychological theory of the functions of dreaming. (*18 marks*)

2 Discuss the view that the functions of dreaming are better explained by neurobiological rather than psychological accounts. (*24 marks*)

WEB ADDRESSES

http://www.iag.net/~hutchib/.dream/
http://www.spiritonline.com/dreams/why.html
http://dreamemporium.com/

16 Brain Mechanisms of Motivation

INTRODUCTION AND OVERVIEW

The word 'motive' comes from the Latin 'movere' which means 'move'. Motives are inner directing forces that arouse an organism and direct its behaviour towards some goal. Geen (1995) describes motivation as 'the processes involved in the initiation, direction, and energisation of individual behaviour'. For Miller (1962), the study of motivation involves:

'... all those pushes and prods – biological, social, and psychological – that defeat our laziness and move us, either eagerly or reluctantly, to action'.

The study of motivation, then, is the study of the *why* of behaviour which, in a sense is what psychology is all about! This chapter examines theories and research studies relating to the role of brain structures in the motivational states of hunger and thirst. It also examines the impact that external factors can have on these states.

HUNGER

To survive, the body must have appropriate amounts of food, water, air, sleep and heat. Our bodies contain complex mechanisms that maintain proper levels of these essentials. The body's tendency to maintain a steady state is called *homeostasis*.

Box 16.1 Homeostasis

Homeostasis comes from the Greek 'homos' meaning 'same' and 'stasis' meaning 'stand-still'. Homeostasis is the maintenance of a proper balance of physiological variables such as body temperature, fluid concentration and the amount of nutrients stored in the body. The *hypothalamus* receives information from sensory receptors inside the body, and is therefore well informed about changes in physiological status. It also contains specialised receptors that monitor the various characteristics of blood flowing through the brain, such as its temperature, nutrient levels and the concentrations of dissolved salts. Hypothalamic functions can involve either non-behavioural physiological changes, such as regulating temperature by sweating or increasing metabolic rate, or stimulating actual behaviours, such as taking off or putting on a coat.

(From Gross & McIlveen, 1998)

Homeostasis has been likened to a *thermostat*: when room temperature rises above the *set-point*, the heating system switches off and remains this way until the temperature falls to the set-point. This analogy has dominated much biopsychological thinking, and underlies some of the proposals concerning hunger and thirst.

If hunger and eating are at least partially, if not wholly, controlled by some internal homeostatic mechanism, what are the means by which the body's need for food is conveyed to the brain, and what part of the brain receives these messages and sends signals to the body to initiate eating?

When we are hungry, the walls of the stomach contract producing 'hunger pangs'. When the stomach is full we 'feel bloated' or *satiated*. An early theory of eating proposed that the *stomach*, via the *vagus nerve* (the connection between the stomach/gastrointestinal tract and the brain), sent information to the brain informing it about hunger and satiety.

Box 16.2 Cannon & Washburn's (1912) experiment

Washburn swallowed a balloon which was inflated by air introduced through an attached tube. His stomach contractions forced air out of the balloon and activated a recording device. Whenever Washburn felt a hunger pang, he pressed a key which activated another recording device. Each time he reported a hunger pang, a large stomach contraction occurred, suggesting that hunger is controlled by the stomach.

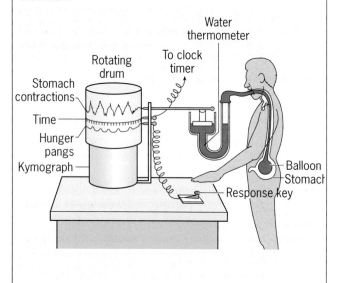

Figure 16.1 *Cannon and Washburn's set-up*

As appealingly simplistic as this common sense approach to hunger is, the picture is actually much more complicated than Cannon and Washburn's findings suggest. For example, people whose stomachs have been surgically removed because of cancer still report feeling hungry, and cutting the vagus nerve has little effect on food intake in both humans and non-humans (Pinel, 1993).

Although Cannon exaggerated the importance of stomach contractions in causing hunger, the stomach/gastrointestinal tract does play an influential role. Even if the vagus nerve is cut, signals arising from the gut can be communicated to the brain via the circulatory system. Additionally, the presence of food in the stomach (*stomach loading*) is important in the regulation of feeding, since if the exit from the stomach to the small intestine is blocked, rats will still eat normal-sized meals. Information about the stretching of the stomach wall must therefore be passed to the brain (via the vagus nerve), and the brain is somehow able to control food intake. As well as the stomach, other internal stimuli involved in eating have been identified.

Box 16.3 Some internal stimuli involved in eating

The mouth: Clearly, chewing and swallowing must provide some sensations of satiety. If they didn't, we might eat for a long time after we had eaten enough, since it takes the digestive tract time to metabolise food and send signals to the brain about food levels. Janowitz & Grossman (1949) found that when a tube was implanted into a dog's throat so that food did not reach the stomach, it stopped eating (although it resumed eating sooner than a normal dog). The *secondary taste cortex* appears to be responsible for telling us what a pleasant experience tasting food is (Irwin, 1996).

The liver: Injections of glucose to the liver cause a decrease in eating, and specialised cells in the liver convey information to the brain via a nerve connection (Russek, 1971).

Hormones: Eating behaviour may be influenced by hormones. One hormone, *cholecystokinin-8* (CCK-8), is produced by the intestinal walls. Injections of this can cause satiety (Dockray *et al.*, 1978). CCK-8 may, therefore, inform the brain about food levels in the intestines, although exactly how it does this is not yet known (see also Box 16.6, pages 159–160).

The depletion of fats, carbohydrates, glucose, vitamins/mineral salts, and proteins/amino acids may all play some role in initiating action in the stimuli identified in Box 16.3. The effects of changes in *blood-glucose* levels and the amounts of *body fat* have received most attention, and several theories have been proposed to explain how such changes relay information about hunger and satiety.

Glucostatic and lipostatic theories

According to *glucostatic theory*, the primary stimulus for hunger is a decrease in blood-glucose level *below* a certain *set-point*. Satiety occurs when levels rise above the set-point. Since glucose is the body's (and especially the brain's) primary fuel, this theory is intuitively appealing. It is also supported by evidence. Thus, when glucose is injected into the system, eating is usually inhibited. When insulin injections (which lower blood-glucose levels) are given, eating is stimulated.

Key S T U D Y

Box 16.4 Glucostats

Glucostatic theory proposes the existence of a *glucostat*, an analogue of the thermostat. Mayer & Marshall (1956) injected mice with *gold thioglucose*, reasoning that the glucose would bind to hypothesised *glucoreceptors* (wherever they happened to be) and, because gold is a *neurotoxin*, the tissue would be destroyed. When post-mortems were conducted, damage was found in the *ventromedial hypothalamus* (VMH). Since the injected mice ate large quantities of food following the injection, and since the injection damaged the VMH, Mayer and Marshall concluded that the VMH must be a *satiety centre* which 'tells' mice to stop feeding (and might serve the same function in humans). The role of the VMH in eating is discussed further on pages 160–161.

Glucostatic theory is also supported by the finding that a fall in blood-glucose level before a spontaneous meal is not just related to the onset of eating, but actually *causes* it. For example, Campfield *et al.* (1985) found that if very small amounts of glucose were injected into the veins of rats as a decline in their blood-glucose levels occurred, the predicted meal they would take was 'postponed' as though the injection had removed the hunger signal.

Mayer and Marshall saw the *rate* of glucose *utilisation*, rather than its *absolute level*, as being the most important factor in eating. However, there is little evidence for this and at least some to contradict it (Geiselman, 1983). Furthermore, although blood-glucose levels might be important, they cannot be the only signal to stop and start eating. An animal that eats a meal low in carbohydrates, but high in fats or protein, still eats a relatively constant amount of calories even though its blood-glucose level is reduced slightly. If eating was exclusively controlled by blood-glucose levels, it would overeat and become fat (Carlson, 1988).

Box 16.5 Lipostatic theory

Another explanation of the homeostatic mechanism regulating eating concentrates on the role of fats (or *lipids*) in *adipocytes*. Clumps of adipocytes form the

fatty (or *adipose*) body tissues, and body fat is normally maintained at a relatively constant level. According to Nisbett's (1972) version of *lipostatic theory*, everyone has a body-weight set-point around which body weight fluctuates within quite narrow limits, and this is determined by fat levels in the adipocytes. Evidence supporting lipostatic theory comes from the observation that short-term dieting programs do *not* produce long-term weight loss. As soon as dieting stops, the lost weight is regained.

Also, when a rat's *lateral hypothalamus* (LH) is damaged, it stops eating, even when food is freely available, to the point of starvation. This condition is called *hypophagia*. Originally, hypophagia was taken to indicate that the LH normally functions to *stimulate* feeding. Keesey & Powley (1975), however, showed that this is not the case. They deprived rats of food so that their body weight was significantly lowered. The LH was then lesioned. Instead of eating less, which should have occurred if the LH does normally stimulate feeding, the rats ate *more*.

The most plausible interpretation of this finding is that the LH affects feeding *indirectly* (rather than directly) by altering the body-weight set-point: when a rat's weight is reduced before the lesion is made, its feeding increases after the lesion in order to reach the new and higher set-point. The role of the LH is discussed further on pages 161–162.

Glucostatic theory was intended to explain the relatively short-term processes of initiating and terminating eating, whereas lipostatic theory was a way of explaining long-term feeding habits and body weight regulation. Both, however, share the belief that pre-determined set-points exist. Some researchers disagree, and prefer to see body weight as drifting around a *settling-point*, or a level at which the various factors that influence it try to achieve equilibrium. Rather than seeing the processes involved in eating as analogous to a thermostat, Pinel (1993) prefers the analogy of a 'leaky barrel', in which the level of fat in the body is regulated around a natural settling-point just as water is in a leaky barrel.

Box 16.6 Glucagon-like peptide and cholecystokinin-8

According to Bloom *et al.* (cited in Nuttall 1996), people prone to gluttony may be underproducing *glucagon-like peptide 1* (GLP-1), a substance produced in the brain and intestine after a filling meal. Bloom *et al.* believe that GLP-1 is produced in response to an extension of the intestine and/or an increase in blood-sugar level. It is also involved in the release of insulin to help digest food.

A synthetic version of GLP-1 may improve treatment for overeating, as may substances which affect *cholecystokinin-8* (CCK-8). CCK-8 carries messages between nerves in the digestive system and acts within the brain. It dampens appetite, and is normally destroyed by a natural enzyme. However, *butabindide*, a synthetic compound, prevents the enzyme from working and allows CCK-8's influence to continue.

External stimuli for hunger

As if the picture concerning the internal stimuli for eating were not complex enough, it is also clearly the case that eating can be affected by *external* factors.

Box 16.7 Some external factors influencing eating

Habit: If we miss a meal, our hunger does not continue to grow indefinitely. Rather, it subsides some time after the meal would normally be taken and then grows just before the scheduled time of the next one. Hunger, then, increases and decreases according to a learned schedule of eating.

Environment: We are much more likely to eat and feel hungry in the presence of others who are eating. Even when we have just eaten, we may join friends for some company only to find ourselves joining in their meal!

Culture: What is accepted as food is shaped by culture (and, indeed, by habits acquired early in life). Ducks' feet and frogs' legs, for example, are enjoyed by members of some cultures but are rarely eaten in our own culture.

Palatability: The sight, smell and taste of food can all influence our eating. For example, children who have just eaten, and do not feel at all hungry, will still eat M & Ms (Rodin & Slochower, 1976). Whilst we have an innate preference for sweet tastes, we can also learn the relationship between taste and the post-ingestion consequences of eating food (Pinel, 1993). *Taste aversion studies* show that animals learn to avoid novel tastes which are followed by illness (see Chapter 38). By contrast, a sick rat that tastes a novel food and then recovers will display an acquired preference for that flavour, a phenomenon termed the *medicine preference effect*.

As Box 16.7 indicates, eating is far from a straightforward behaviour to explain. The many internal and external factors interact, often in complex ways. For example, however palatable a food is, several small but different foods are more interesting than one large and specific food. Given access to only one type of food, we demonstrate *sensory-specific satiety*, that is, we become tired of it. Rather than eat four yoghurts of the same flavour, then, we prefer to eat four different flavoured yoghurts. Sensory-specific satiety encourages the consumption of a varied diet, and we are also capable of learning which diets best meet our biological needs. Mexicans, for example, increased the calcium in their bodies by mixing small amounts of mineral lime in their tortillas.

The fact that we sometimes eat when we are not hungry, and some people (such as hunger strikers) do not eat when they are hungry, indicates that hunger is neither necessary nor sufficient for eating, even though there is usually a close relationship between them (Blundell & Hill, 1995).

The hypothalamus and eating

In 1902, Frolich, a Viennese physician, observed that tumours near the hypothalamus caused overeating (hyperphagia) and *obesity*. In the late 1930s, the introduction of stereotaxic apparatus (see Figure 10.1, page 99) enabled researchers to assess the effects of experimentally induced damage to areas of the hypothalamus on the eating behaviour of non-humans.

Earlier, it was noted that Mayer & Marshall's (1956) findings suggested that 'glucoreceptors' might be located in the VMH, and that the VMH might act as a satiety centre. In fact, the VMH's role as a *satiety centre* had been proposed some years previously by Hetherington & Ranson (1942). They showed that a VMH lesioned rat will overeat and become grotesquely fat, doubling or even trebling its normal body weight.

Box 16.8 VMH hyperphagia syndrome

The *VMH hyperphagia syndrome* has two distinct phases. The *dynamic phase* begins as soon as the rat regains consciousness following surgery. This phase is characterised by several weeks of overeating and rapid weight gain. As the rat approaches its maximum weight, eating gradually declines to a level just sufficient to maintain a stable level of obesity. The *static phase* is a period of stability in which it 'defends' its new body weight. If deprived of food until it loses a substantial amount of weight, the rat will temporarily increase its intake until the lost weight is gained. If, however, it is force-fed, it will temporarily reduce its intake until the excess is lost. Research also revealed that if the VMH is electrically or chemically stimulated (or 'turned on'), rats will terminate eating until the stimulation is stopped.

Figure 16.2 *A hyperphagic rat*

The role of the LH in eating behaviour was referred to earlier on when considering Keesey & Powley's (1975) findings. The *hypophagic* effects of LH damage were first reported by Anand & Brobeck (1951) who found that if the damage was extensive enough, rats would actually starve to death. Additionally, electrically stimulating the LH caused a rat to start eating. These findings led to the conclusion that the LH was the 'start feeding' centre, in contrast to the VMH's role as the 'stop feeding' centre.

The findings concerning the VMH and the LH led to the *dual hypothalamic control theory of eating*. According to this, the VMH and LH receive information about nutrient levels in the body and operate together to maintain a relatively constant level of satiety. Thus, the LH 'turns' hunger on and the VMH 'turns' it off. It is likely that the hypothalamus can initiate and terminate eating but needs information from peripheral regulatory factors, such as those proposed by glucostatic and lipostatic theories, to do this (Green, 1994). However, the precise interaction between the VMH and LH is still unclear.

Box 16.9 Lipogenesis and lipolysis

Traditionally, biopsychologists have assumed that obesity is a consequence of overeating in VMH lesioned animals. However, obesity may be a *cause* of overeating. VMH lesions might increase *lipogenesis* (the body's tendency to produce fat) and decrease *lipolysis* (its tendency to release fats into the bloodstream). Because this would result in calories being converted to fat at a much higher than normal rate, an animal would be forced to keep eating in order to ensure that it had enough calories in its blood for immediate energy needs. One finding which supports this possibility is that rats with VMH lesions accumulate more fat than controls, even when they eat the same amount of food (Friedman & Stricker, 1976).

The VMH's role is further complicated by the observation that VMH lesioned rats show an increased 'fussiness' about the *taste* of food. Ordinarily, hungry rats will eat food even if it has an unpleasant taste (as, for example, occurs when bitter-tasting quinine is added to it). Such food will not be eaten by VMH lesioned rats even if they become *underweight* (Teitelbaum, 1955). This suggests that such rats become more sensitive to *external cues* (such as the taste of food) than to *internal cues* (such as blood-sugar level), and so the VMH may also play a role in this aspect of eating.

It has also been found that whilst VMH-damaged rats eat more food than normal, they do so only if it is freely available. If they have to work for food by, for example, having to press a lever or lift a heavy lid, they actually eat less than non-damaged rats. Some obese humans behave in a parallel way and also respond to the availability of food (Miller, 1995). They are, for example, less willing to find food or prepare it in some way. Although human obesity is almost certain to have physiological correlates, eating is influenced by many other factors, and an account of obesity based only on physiological factors is probably too simplistic.

Findings concerning the LH are also more complex than dual hypothalamic theory proposes. For example, whilst rats with LH lesions initially do not eat, they can be coaxed into eating by first being fed through a tube. After several weeks of this, they begin to eat by themselves provided they are given palatable food (Teitelbaum & Epstein, 1962). These findings challenge the idea that the LH is a discrete 'eating centre', as does the finding that LH damage causes behaviour changes that are *not* related to eating. Rats with LH damage fail to groom themselves, have difficulty with balance and show little interest in almost *any* stimuli. The additional finding that eating can be elicited by stimulation of other hypothalamic areas and by the amygdala, hippocampus, thalami and frontal cortex, also challenges the simple idea that the LH is a discrete 'hunger centre'.

As noted earlier, LH damage affects weight indirectly by altering the body-weight set-point. This might also be the case with the VMH. Such findings seem to indicate that the VMH and LH are not *absolutely* essential for regulating hunger and eating. So, whilst the immediate effect of VMH and LH lesions might be to destroy the capacity to regulate eating and body weight, this is not necessarily the case over the long term. However, the fact that lesions in these structures apparently affect the set-point strongly implicates them in long-term weight control.

The belief that the hypothalamus is the neurological basis of hunger has not, then, always produced data which can be explained simply. The anatomical complexity of the hypothalamus makes it even more difficult to assess its role. For example, VMH lesions also damage the axons connecting the *paraventricular nucleus* (PVN) with certain parts of the brain stem. If CCK (see Box 16.6, pages 159–160) is injected into the PVN, food intake is inhibited (Pinel, 1993).

Additionally, neurotransmitters in the *medial hypothalamus* appear to play an important role in eating behaviour. We tend to eat sweet or starchy carbohydrate-laden foods when we are tense or depressed (Carlson, 1987). Carbohydrates help increase *serotonin* levels, and depression is associated with lower than normal levels of it (see Chapter 50). *Noradrenaline*, by contrast, stimulates carbohydrate intake. One potential application of this is the use of food substitutes that mimic the biochemical effects of carbohydrates to treat stress-related food cravings.

With advances in methodology, new information about the processes involved in eating and its regulation by the brain continues to be gained. Current biopsychological thinking views the hypothalamus as just *one part* of a brain system that regulates eating. Other areas (such as the *limbic system*) may also play important roles.

Box 16.10 Obesity and genetics

O'Rahilly *et al.* (cited in Radford, 1997) studied two severely obese cousins, one male and one female, each having more than 50 per cent body fat. They found very low levels of *leptin*, a protein produced in the body by fat cells. They also found that in each cousin there was a small change in the same place in the DNA code in the gene that controls leptin's supply.

Leptin's role is apparently to keep the brain informed about fat stores, and regulate appetite and the rate at which calories are consumed, so helping to keep body weight stable. Whether low levels of leptin, or limits to the rate at which leptin can travel to the brain, is the most important factor, continues to be researched.

THIRST

The dry mouth theory of thirst

As with eating, several theories have been proposed to explain the onset and termination of drinking. According to the *dry mouth theory of thirst*, receptors in the mouth and throat play a major role in determining thirst and satiety. However, 'sham drinking' studies, in which liquid swallowed down the throat does not pass into the stomach, indicate that whilst animals drink a normal amount and then stop, they return to drinking quickly afterwards unless water is placed in the stomach. Thus, internal signals, rather than the amount that has been swallowed, appear to govern how much is drunk.

Figure 16.3 *In this still from* Ice Cold in Alex, *John Mills' brain is calculating how much he needs to drink in order to slake his thirst (see Box 16.11)*

Box 16.11 The satiation of thirst

Denton *et al.* (cited in Highfield, 1999a) made ten volunteer participants thirsty by injecting them with a saline solution. MRI scanning (see Chapter 10, page 104) indicated a complex pattern of activation and dampening in the cingulate area of the cortex, the hippocampus, thalami, amygdala and cerebellum. When the participants were allowed to wash out their mouths with water, but not swallow, there was little change in brain activity and no reduction in thirst. Participants were then allowed to drink until they were no longer thirsty. The brain activation elicited by thirst disappeared within three minutes, consistent with the participants saying they had drunk enough.

Denton *et al.*'s study shows that although the body's biochemistry remains disturbed by a lack of water for some time, drinking stops because the brain can calculate how much is needed to quench the thirst. It bases this calculation on sensations from the mouth, impulses from the throat that suggest how much water has been swallowed, and how much the stomach has swollen (see below). Each of these individually is not enough to satisfy a thirst. Rapid satiation of thirst is adaptive, since it allows an animal to drink quickly from a water hole and leave with minimum exposure to predators.

(Adapted from Highfield, 1999a)

The hypothalamus and drinking

One important internal signal in drinking is *cellular dehydration*. Certain cells in the *lateral preoptic* area of the hypothalamus are apparently sensitive to cellular dehydration, and their activation causes us to drink until enough has been consumed to restore the balance. The fluid levels inside the cells are affected by salt levels in the blood. When these are high, water leaves the cells by *osmosis* (and hence this type of thirst is often referred to as *osmotic thirst*). It is this that causes the cells to become dehydrated.

The *osmoreceptors*, the name given to the cells, seem to shrink themselves when the brain is fluid-depleted, and as a result of this two hypothalamic effects occur. The first is the production of *antidiuretic hormone* (ADH) by the pituitary gland. This causes the kidneys to reabsorb water which would otherwise be excreted as urine. The second is the generation of thirst.

In addition to cellular dehydration, a lowered water level reduces the volume of blood in the body which lowers blood pressure. This *volumetric thirst* stimulates *baroreceptors* located in the heart, kidneys and veins. *Volumetric thirst* is caused by bleeding, vomiting, diarrhoea and sweating. The baroreceptors then trigger the secretion of ADH, which causes the kidneys to retain water. The kidneys release the hormone *angiotensin*, which circulates to the hypothalamus, resulting in the initiation of drinking behaviour.

Box 16.12 Primary and secondary drinking

Like hunger, thirst is influenced by external as well as internal factors. *Primary drinking* occurs when there is a physiological need. However, we sometimes engage in *secondary drinking*, or, drinking not caused by a physiological need. An example of secondary drinking would be the consumption of many pints of beer during the course of an evening. Secondary drinking probably occurs as a result of learning and reinforcement. Drinking beer, for example, makes us feel good, and drinking tea when offered a cup in the afternoon is a sociable thing to do. We may even drink because we wish to be like someone portrayed in a media 'message'. Moreover, what we drink can be influenced by many external factors. Ice-cold lemonade in February, for example, is as popular a drink as a cup of piping hot cocoa on a sunny August afternoon.

CONCLUSIONS

Although the relationship between the body and brain is complex, in the motivated behaviours of eating and drinking it has been at least partially explained by biopsychological research. One important brain structure in eating and drinking is the hypothalamus, which receives information from various parts of the body concerning tissue needs. Yet whilst the hypothalamus is important, so are other brain structures. Moreover, external factors play an influential role in eating and drinking. Exclusively physiological accounts of these behaviours are, therefore, unlikely to be true.

Summary

- **Motives** are inner directing forces that arouse an organism and direct its behaviour towards a goal. To survive, the body needs food, water, air, sleep and heat. **Homeostasis** provides a balance of these physiological variables.

- The stomach plays a role in hunger and satiety as do the mouth, liver and various hormones such as cholecystokinin-8 (CCK-8). The depletion of fats, carbohydrates, glucose, vitamins/mineral salts and proteins/amino acids may all initiate action in internal stimuli involved in eating.

- Theories of hunger and eating have concentrated on changes in blood-glucose levels and the amount of body fat. **Glucostatic theory** proposes that hunger occurs when blood-glucose levels fall below a certain **set-point**; satiety occurs when they rise above the set-point.

- **Glucostats** (an analogue of a thermostat) may exist in the **ventromedial hypothalamus** (VMH). However, whilst glucostatic theory is supported by evidence, the view that glucose utilisation is the only factor in eating is unlikely to be true.

- **Lipostatic theory** proposes that everyone has a body-weight set-point around which body weight fluctuates within quite narrow limits, and that this is determined by fat levels in **adipocytes.**

- Glucostatic and lipostatic theories share the belief that pre-determined set-points exist. However, an alternative view is of a **settling point,** a level at which the various factors that influence body weight try to reach equilibrium.

- Eating is influenced by external factors including habit, the social environment, culture and a food's palatability. We have an innate preference for sweet tastes, but can learn the relationship between taste and the consequences of ingesting certain foods.

- Internal and external factors interact in a complex way. For example, access to only one type of (palatable) food produces **sensory-specific satiety**, which encourages the consumption of a varied diet. Hunger is neither necessary nor sufficient for eating, although they are usually correlated.

- Lesions to the VMH produce **hyperphagia**, which has a **dynamic phase** (in which maximum weight is attained) and a **static phase** (in which the new weight is defended). Extensive **lateral hypothalamus** (LH) damage causes rats to starve to death, whilst stimulating the LH causes eating to begin.

- **Dual hypothalamic control theory** sees the LH as a 'start feeding' centre and the VMH as a 'stop feeding' centre. The VMH and LH operate to maintain a relatively constant level of satiety.

- VMH lesions may increase **lipogenesis** and decrease **lipolysis**. Because this would cause calories to be converted to fat at a higher than normal rate, an animal would need to keep eating to ensure it had enough calories for immediate energy needs. This would suggest that obesity is a cause, not a consequence, of overeating.

- VMH-lesioned rats show increased fussiness about food's taste, suggesting they are more sensitive to external than internal cues. Such rats will only consume more food if they do not have to work for it, which parallels what is seen in obese humans.

- LH-lesioned rats will eventually eat by themselves, which suggests the LH is not a discrete feeding centre. Eating can occur when other areas of the hypothalamus and structures in the limbic system are stimulated.

- According to the **dry mouth theory of thirst,** receptors in the mouth and throat play a role in thirst and satiety. However, sham drinking studies suggest that internal signals determine how much is drunk.

- **Osmoreceptors** in the hypothalamus are sensitive to cellular dehydration, which is caused by high salt levels in the blood. This results in water leaving cells by osmosis (**osmotic thirst**). To counter this, ADH is produced and thirst generated.

- Reduced water levels reduce blood volume, which lowers blood pressure. This **volumetric thirst** stimulates **baroreceptors**. These trigger the secretion of ADH, which causes water retention by the kidneys. The kidneys release **angiotensin** to the hypothalamus, leading to drinking. Stopping drinking may be the result of cells in the small intestine sending messages to the hypothalamus.

- **Primary drinking** is caused by internal needs, whereas **secondary drinking** is caused by external needs. These needs also determine what is drunk.

Essay Questions

1 Describe and evaluate **two** theories relating to the role of brain structures in any **one** motivational state (e.g. hunger). (*24 marks*)

2 Discuss research studies into brain mechanisms involved in a motivational state such as hunger. (*24 marks*)

WEB ADDRESSES

http://www.dana.org/dana/bwn_html/bwn_0698.htm/
http://www.medserv.dk/comp/1999/04/14/story04.htm
http://www.cc.emory.edu/WHSC/YERKES/NEWSROOM/kuharrls.htm
http://www.ndif.org/Translation/jstran_160.html

17 Theories of Motivation

INTRODUCTION AND OVERVIEW

One major aim of psychological research is to explain what motivates us to act in certain ways. Several theories of motivation have been proposed. As might be expected given the findings described in Chapter 16, some of these adopt a distinctly *physiological* approach. Others, however, are primarily *psychological*. Yet others are a *combination* of the physiological and psychological. This chapter examines some theories of motivation and explores the contrast between them. It begins, however, by looking at different types of motive.

TYPES OF MOTIVE

The range of motivation is very broad. As will be seen, some behaviours, such as drinking a glass of water, can be explained in terms of reducing a 'need'. Others, such as smoking cigarettes when we know they cause disease, must have more complex explanations. To assess theories of motivation requires *types* of motive to be identified. Three main categories of human behaviour are *biologically-based motives*, *sensation-seeking motives* and *complex psychosocial motives*.

Figure 17.1 *Even a chicken may need no greater motivation to cross the road than to get to the other side!*

Biologically-based motives

Biologically-based motives are rooted primarily in body tissue needs (or *drives*) such as those for food, water, air, sleep, temperature regulation and pain avoidance. Although these needs are in-built, their expression is often learned. For example, hunger is caused by food deprivation, and we learn to search the environment effectively for food to satisfy this basic need.

Sensation-seeking motives

Sensation-seeking motives are apparently largely unlearned needs for certain levels of stimulation. They depend more on external stimuli than do biologically-based motives, and their main function is to affect the environment. These motives aim to *increase* rather than decrease the amount of stimulation, and are most evident in the way we attempt to create our own sensations when placed in *sensory isolation*. Other sensation seeking motives include *activity*, *curiosity*, *exploration* and *manipulation*.

The need to be *active* affects all animals. When an animal is deprived of activity, it is much more active than normal when subsequently released. Whether activity is a separate motive or a combination of motives, unlearned or learned, is unclear. Sensory deprivation studies, in which virtually all sensory input is cut off, indicate that sensory deprivation appears to be intolerable. As well as hallucinations, people have difficulty in thinking clearly. They also experience boredom, anger and frustration. However, voluntary sensory restriction has also been associated with increased ability to gain control over negative habits such as smoking, but this is much milder than studies in which virtually all stimulation is cut off.

Curiosity and *exploration* are activated by the new and unknown, and appear to be directed to no more a specific goal than 'finding out'. For example, children will play with toys even though there is no extrinsic reward for doing so. *Unfamiliarity* and *complexity* are sometimes preferred because they may be more appealing. Thus, a non-human that has just copulated will show an interest in sexual behaviour when presented with a 'novel' partner. Non-humans will also learn discrimination problems when the reward is nothing more than a brief look around the laboratory in which they are housed.

Manipulation is directed towards a specific object that must be touched, handled, or played with before we are satisfied. 'Do Not Touch' signs in museums, for example, are there because curators know that the urge to touch things is irresistible. This motive is limited to primates who have agile fingers and toes, and seems to be related to the need to have *tactile experience* and a need to be *soothed*. The 'worry beads' manipulated by Greeks would be an example of the latter. Three other sensation-seeking motives are *play*, *contact* and *control*.

Box 17.1 Play, contact and control

Play: Many species have this innate motive, and the young enjoy *practice play*, that is, behaviour which will later be used for 'serious' purposes. Such activity might not appear to have any immediate consequences for the fulfilment of biological needs (Bolles, 1967). Much of the behaviour normally associated with play can be thought of in terms of the drives for curiosity, exploration and manipulation.

Contact: This refers to the *need* to touch other people, and is broader and more universal than the need for manipulation. It is not limited to touching with the fingers and toes, and can involve the whole body. Unlike manipulation, which is active, contact can be passive.

Control: The need for control is linked to the need to be free from restrictions from others, and to determine our own actions and not be dictated to. When our freedom is threatened, we tend to react by reasserting it, a phenomenon which Brehm (1966) calls *psychological reactance* (see Chapter 57). *Learned helplessness* (Seligman, 1975: see Chapter 50) is important here. Whilst initial negative experiences produce psychological reactance, further negative experiences produce a state in which we perceive ourselves as being unable to do anything else. All of us have a belief about the things that control events in our everyday lives (Rotter, 1966). Rotter's *locus of control* questionnaire attempts to distinguish between *inter-nals*, who see themselves as being responsible for events in their lives, and *externals*, who see events in the outside world as being particularly influential.

It is generally believed that the motivation to seek stimulation evolved because of its survival value. Organisms motivated to explore their environment, and acquire information about it, would be more likely to survive because of an increased awareness of resources and potential dangers. Such behaviour would allow them to change their environment in beneficial ways.

Complex psychosocial motives

These share little, if any, relationship with biological needs. They are acquired by learning and aroused by psychological events rather than body tissue needs. Unlike the latter, which must be satisfied, there is no biological requirement for complex psychosocial motives to be met (although much of our happiness and misery is associated with them). Murray (1938) identified 20 motives, although some have been more extensively researched than others (Baumeister & Leary, 1995).

Need for achievement (nAch) is the need to meet or exceed some standard of excellence. nAch is measured using the *thematic apperception test*, which consists of ambiguous pictures about which a story must be told (McClelland, 1958). The story content is scored for achievement and other important motives held to reflect 'hidden forces' motivating behaviour. Differences between individuals have been correlated with child rearing practices such as an emphasis on competition, praise-giving, encouragement to take credit for success, and *modelling*, where parents serve as models to their children by being high in nAch themselves.

Need for affiliation (nAff) is the desire to maintain close, friendly relations with others. Schachter (1959) found that people high in nAff find it painful to make their own decisions or be by themselves over extended periods of time. In anxiety-provoking situations, people high in nAff prefer to be with others provided they are also experiencing anxiety. According to *social comparison theory* (Festinger, 1954), this is because we prefer to affiliate with people with whom we can compare our feelings and behaviours (see Chapter 4).

Need for power (nPower) is a concern with being in charge, having status and prestige, and bending others to our will. This has both positive and negative features. For example, leaders high in nPower can impede group decision-making by failing to allow full discussion, and by not encouraging full consideration of others' proposals. nPower is also linked to *child rearing*. Children allowed to be aggressive to siblings tend to produce children high in nPower, possibly because allowing children to exercise power at an early age encourages them to continue this later on.

Need for approval (nApp) is the desire to gain approval or some kind of sign that others like us and think we are good. The characteristics of people with a high need for approval have been studied using Crowne & Marlowe's (1964) *social desirability scale*. This measures the extent to which people try to gain others' approval by behaving in socially desirable ways. Whilst there are wide individual differences, people high in nApp are conformist and tend to change their behaviour when they know they are being observed.

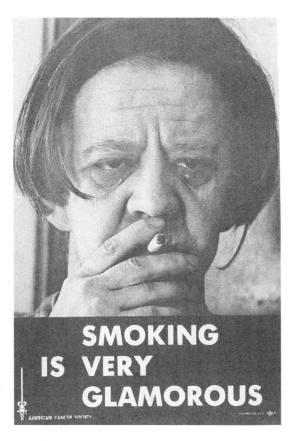

Figure 17.2 *Whilst some behaviours can be explained in terms of reducing a 'need', others, such as smoking cigarettes when we know they cause disease, must have more complex explanations*

INSTINCT THEORIES

According to these, we possess *innate* or genetically predetermined dispositions to act in a particular way towards a certain stimulus. Instinct theories were popu-

lar in the early twentieth century, largely due to Darwin's (1859) emphasis on the similarity between humans and other animals. Indeed, James (1890) argued that humans were *more* influenced by instincts because we are motivated by *psychosocial instincts* such as 'jealousy' and 'sympathy', as well as biological instincts. James did not provide any evidence for such instincts, and compiled a list of them from arguments about their evolutionary advantages, and observations of his own children's behaviour.

Box 17.2 How many instincts are there?

Several attempts were made to identify instincts fostering self-survival. McDougall (1908) proposed 12 'basic' instincts, including 'hunger' and 'sex'. However, lists of instincts grew larger until there were as many instincts as psychologists studying them. Indeed, since around 15,000 instincts were identified, there were probably more (Tolman, 1923). Some instincts (such as 'cleanliness' and 'modesty') had little to do with basic survival, and instinct gradually lost its meaning, becoming a way of *labelling* rather than explaining behaviour. Moreover, an instinct's existence was inferred from the behaviour it was trying to explain. A 'cleanliness' instinct, for example, was inferred from the observation that most people keep themselves clean, and the fact that people keep themselves clean was taken as evidence of this 'cleanliness' instinct. This *circular reasoning* did not enhance instinct theory's reputation.

In the 1930s, instinct theory was revised by *ethologists*. They coined the term *fixed action pattern* (FAP) to describe an unlearned behaviour, universal to a particular species and occurring (or *released*) in the presence of a naturally occurring stimulus (or *sign stimulus*). Tinbergen (1951, 1966), for example, demonstrated that the sign stimulus of a red belly elicited the FAP of aggressiveness in the three-spined stickleback.

Today's ethologists believe that whilst behaviour is innate or pre-programmed, it can be modified by environmental requirements. The greylag goose, for example, has an innate tendency to retrieve an egg that has rolled from its nest. However, if the egg has rolled to a dangerous place, this behaviour may change.

Whether instincts really are innate is, however, debatable. Some behaviours that ethologists identify as innate are influenced by experiences *before birth*. For example, the duckling's ability to discriminate maternal calls is linked to its behaviour within the egg. At some point, the duckling's bill penetrates the egg's interior membrane and it begins to 'talk to itself'. This self-vocalisation is critical to the duckling's ability at birth to identify the maternal call of its species (Gottleib, 1975).

Box 17.3 Sociobiology

Sociobiologists argue that innate tendencies play an important role in complex forms of *human* behaviour. Sociobiologists see the primary motivation of all organisms as ensuring the future survival of their *genes*. Our behaviour is basically *selfish*, because it is designed to ensure our genes survive. Far from caring for others and behaving empathically, altruistic acts are actually examples of 'genetic selfishness' designed for gene survival. Although influential, some researchers regard sociobiology as oversimplifying human behaviour. They argue that whilst altruism may have a genetic component, the role of situational and personal variables cannot be ignored (see Chapters 8 and 37).

DRIVE THEORIES

During the 1920s, 'instinct' was replaced by *drive*, a term originated by Woodworth (1918) who likened human behaviour to the operation of a machine. Woodworth saw machines (and hence humans) as being relatively passive, and drive was the power that made them (and humans) 'go'. Two major drive theories have been particularly influential. These are *homeostatic drive theory*, which is a physiological theory, and *drive reduction theory*, which is primarily a learning theory.

Homeostatic drive theory

Cannon (1929) viewed homeostasis (see Box 16.1, page 157) as an optimum level of physiological functioning that maintains an organism in a constant internal state. When imbalance occurs, something must happen to correct it. For example, if body temperature deviates from the normal 98.4°F, sweating occurs to bring it down or shivering occurs to raise it.

When body temperature rises, we do not always need to 'do' anything, since sweating is autonomic and physiological. However, with an imbalance caused by a *tissue need* (a physiological need for food or drink), the animal must behave in a way which will procure these. It is here that the concept of a *homeostatic drive* becomes important: a tissue need leads to an internal imbalance, which causes a homeostatic drive. The drive leads to an appropriate behaviour which restores the balance and reduces the tissue need which produced the drive.

The internal environment requires a relatively regular supply of raw materials from the external world. Some of these, such as oxygen intake, are involuntary and continuous. Others, such as eating and drinking, are voluntary and discontinuous. Although we talk about a hunger and thirst drive, we do not talk about an oxygen drive (Green, 1980). Because of eating and drinking's voluntary nature, hunger and thirst have been the most researched homeostatic mechanisms and, as was seen in Chapter 16, they are also the drives most researched in terms of the brain mechanisms involved.

Drive reduction theory

An animal deprived of food is in a state of *need* and experiencing some sort of tissue deficit. Drive reduction theory proposes that this need state leads to an *unpleasant* state of bodily arousal (a *drive state*). Drive states activate behaviour to *reduce* the tension associated with them. Behaviours that achieve this are strengthened, whilst those that do not are weakened. According to drive reduction theory, then, organisms are *pushed* into behaviours arising in connection with tissue needs. A thirsty animal is motivated to reduce the unpleasant drive state by drinking. Once achieved, the behaviour ceases and arousal recedes.

Box 17.4 Are drives and needs always parallel?

Whilst drives and needs are mostly parallel, sometimes they are not. A person who is hungry, for example, might have an overwhelming need for food but may be so weak that the drive to search for nutrition is absent. Originally, drive reduction theory focused on biological needs or *primary drives* such as hunger and thirst. However, through association we also learn *secondary* or *acquired drives* which help reduce primary drives. A drive for money is a secondary drive that enables us to buy food and drink to reduce the primary drives of hunger and thirst, and eliminate the tension they produce (see Chapter 37).

Drive reduction theory is still popular with some researchers, not least because biologically-based motives fit in with it. However, at least four reasons exist for doubting its usefulness as a comprehensive theory of motivation. First, whilst a hunger and thirst drive make sense because they reduce tension or arousal, we would need to invent a drive for all motivated behaviour which reduced a drive. This is as absurd as it is impossible. For example, rats will eat saccharin for hours even though it has no nutritional value and so cannot reduce hunger or thirst (Sheffield & Roby, 1955).

To talk of a 'saccharin eating drive' (or, for another behaviour, a 'stamp collecting drive') does not make sense. So, some behaviours are *not* obviously motivated by drives associated with physiological need states, and these are difficult for drive reduction theory to explain.

Second, at least some behaviour *increases* rather than reduces various drives. Some hungry people, for example, will refuse a biscuit with a mid-morning cup of coffee in order to increase their enjoyment of a lunch-time meal. Others make lengthy efforts to prepare a meal instead of having a snack, even though a snack would quickly reduce the hunger.

Third, the theory proposes that when tension is reduced the behaviour that led to it will itself be reduced. This does not always happen. For example, if given the opportunity to explore our surroundings, we engage in *more* exploration rather than less. All of the sensation motives in Box 17.1, seem to go against drive reduction theory unless there is a 'manipulation drive', 'curiosity drive', and so on, which simply labels rather than explains behaviour (one of the criticisms made of instinct theories).

The fourth, and most compelling evidence against drive reduction theory, comes from research into the effects of *electrical self-stimulation of the brain*.

Key STUDY

Box 17.5 Electrical self-stimulation of the brain (ES-SB)

Olds & Milner (1954) discovered that placing an electrode in a rat's *hypothalamus* and allowing it to stimulate its brain resulted in it doing so thousands of times an hour. This behaviour *never* satiated, and was done in preference to anything else. Thus, although exhausted, a rat would continue pressing the lever, cross an electrified grid to gain access to it, and ignore sexually receptive females (see also Box 10.2, page 101).

Similar findings were obtained in other species including goldfish, dolphins, monkeys and humans. Olds and Milner proposed the existence of a *pleasure centre* in the brain. Later research suggested that the main reward site for (ES-SB) is the *median forebrain bundle* (MFB), a nerve tract running from the brain stem up to the forebrain and through the lateral hypothalamus.

Olds and Milner also found that placing the electrodes elsewhere in the brain produced the opposite effects. Thus, rats would do everything they could to *avoid* brain stimulation, suggesting the existence of a *pain centre*. This research indicates that reinforcement does *not* consist of drive reduction, but appears to *increase* drive levels.

Stimulation of parts of the hypothalamus activates neurons which release dopamine to the *nucleus accumbens*. It is likely that dopamine and the nucleus accumbens are part of some sort of 'reward pathway', and that ES-SB is a 'short cut' to pleasure which eliminates the need for drives and reinforcers. However, although ES-SB has been demonstrated in all species that have been studied:

'It remains rather mysterious ... [and] acts as a reminder that however much we may uncover about motivated behaviours ... there are still many aspects of motivation, even in the rat, to be uncovered' (Green, 1994).

OPTIMUM LEVEL OF AROUSAL THEORY

Sometimes we are motivated to reduce tension. As noted, however, on other occasions we behave as though we want to *increase* tension or excitement without satisfying any biological need (Myers, 1998). Driving a Formula one car at 180 miles per hour, or parachuting from an aeroplane, are yet other observations which are difficult for drive reduction theory to explain.

The fact that we sometimes want to decrease and sometimes increase *arousal* suggests we have a preference for an *optimum level* of stimulation that is neither too low nor too high (Renner, 1992). Like drive reduction theory, *optimum level of arousal* (OLA) *theory* proposes that when arousal is too high we try to lower it by decreasing stimulation. Unlike drive reduction theory, OLA theory proposes that when arousal level falls below a certain level we are motivated to raise it by increasing stimulation.

Although most of us fall between the extremes, there are wide individual differences in the OLA we seek. People with low levels may prefer to lead sedentary lives, whereas those with high levels may prefer to engage in activities like driving a Formula one car or parachuting from an aeroplane. Zuckerman (1979) calls such people *sensation-seekers*.

OLA theory's major problem is one that also applies to drive reduction theory. Because we cannot measure an organism's drive or arousal level, we cannot say what its OLA should be. Thus, the theory identifies an organism's optimum level by its behaviour. If it seeks out stimulation it must be functioning below its optimum level, and if it avoids stimulation it must be functioning above it. This is an unsatisfactory and circular way of measuring OLA.

EXPECTANCY (OR INCENTIVE) THEORY

The theories considered so far address an animal's internal or biologically-based state, and propose that some level of tension or arousal motivates (or *pushes*) it to perform certain behaviours. A different idea is that *external stimuli* motivate (or *pull*) us in certain directions in the absence of known physiological states.

These stimuli are called *incentives*, and according to the *expectancy* (or *incentive*) *theory* of motivation, the expectation of a desirable goal motivates us to perform a behaviour. The expectation of an undesirable goal motivates us not to perform a behaviour. Expectancy theorists, then, address what induces us to act and what inhibits our actions.

Numerous studies have shown that incentives can act as powerful motivators. As mentioned earlier (see page 169), rats will work hard for a sip of saccharin even though saccharin has no nutritional value and therefore cannot reduce a tissue need. Rats simply like the taste of saccharin and are motivated to experience it! People who are no longer hungry, and whose tissue needs have been satisfied, will sometimes eat chocolate after a meal.

Box 17.6 Work motivation

Expectancy theory's most important application is in *work motivation,* our tendency to expend effort and energy on a job. Mitchell & Larson (1987) have shown that we will demonstrate a high level of work motivation if we believe that:

- hard work will improve performance;

- good performance will yield rewards (such as a pay increase); and

- such rewards are valued.

Rotter (1966) has proposed that expectations *and* values affect whether a behaviour is performed or not. For example, whether you ask someone out for the evening is determined to some degree by past experiences. If you have been unsuccessful in the past, your expectations are low and you would be less likely to try again. However, if you assign great value to the goal of taking someone out for the evening, expectations of failure might be overcome.

Box 17.7 Intrinsic and extrinsic rewards and motivation

The relationship between *intrinsic* and *extrinsic reward* is also important. Intrinsic refers to the pleasure and satisfaction a task brings. Some tasks themselves are rewarding to us. Extrinsic refers to the rewards that are given beyond a task's intrinsic pleasures. The relationship between these rewards is not straightforward, since being given rewards for behaviours we intrinsically enjoy *lessens* our enjoyment of them.

Sometimes, then, extrinsic reward can undermine intrinsic motivation. On other occasions, extrinsic rewards can be given without reducing intrinsic motivation. For example, a reward given as a recognition of competence can maintain rather than reduce intrinsic motivation. However, giving rewards for something quite happily done for pleasure can 'rob' a person of that pleasure and reduce intrinsic motivation (see Chapter 57).

OPPONENT-PROCESS THEORY

Some motives are clearly *acquired* and become powerful and driving forces in our lives. According to Solomon & Corbit (1974), some acquired motives (such as taking drugs) initially bring about a basic pleasure, but each pleasurable experience eventually triggers some kind of 'pain'. In the case of taking drugs, the pain would be the unpleasant symptoms of withdrawal. Equally, other acquired motives, like parachuting from an aeroplane for the first time, bring about an initial suffering (in the form of terror) but eventually trigger a pleasurable experience (the elation of having completed a parachute jump).

Solomon and Corbit's *opponent-process theory* could also be considered a theory of *emotion* since, in essence, they are suggesting that every emotional experience elicits a more intense opposite emotional experience persisting long after the primary emotion has passed. Solomon and Corbit argue that the opposite emotion lasts longer than the primary emotion it developed from, and acts to diminish the primary emotion's intensity. In the case of parachuting from an aeroplane, for example, each successful jump lessens the associated fear whilst the elation of the experience remains. Opponent process theory is considered here, rather than in Chapter 18, because it is similar to theories of motivation that propose the maintenance of 'steady states'.

Box 17.8 Opponent–process theory and drug addiction

Opponent-process theory has been particularly useful in explaining *drug addiction*, although Solomon and Corbit see it as being equally useful in explaining acquired motives such as social attachments and love. With drug addiction, the theory argues that the initial pleasure produced by a drug is followed by a gradual decline and then a minor craving for it. When addiction occurs, the drug is taken to avoid the pain of withdrawal rather than the experience of pleasure, and this provides the motivational forces for continued drug-taking.

Opponent-process theory sees behaviour as being influenced by what happens in the long rather than the short term. Repeated pleasurable (or unpleasurable) experiences eventually lose their pleasantness (or unpleasantness) and shift the driving force from pleasure to pain or pain to pleasure.

MASLOW'S THEORY

According to Maslow (1954, 1968), many theories of motivation are 'defensive', and see human behaviour as occurring in a mechanical fashion and aimed at nothing more than survival and tension reduction. In Maslow's view, and that of other *humanistic psychologists*, behaviour is also motivated by the conscious desire for *personal growth*. Maslow argued that our needs could be organised into a *hierarchy*.

At the lowest level of the hierarchy are basic *physiological needs* (such as food and drink) deriving from bodily states that *must* be satisfied. Maslow argues that we all start life at this lowest level (where drive reduction theory operates). As we move up the hierarchy, so the needs become more *complex* and *psychological*. The hierarchy culminates in *self-actualisation*, our self-initiated striving to become whatever we believe we are capable of being.

Maslow labelled behaviours related to survival or deficiency needs *'deficiency'* (*D-motives*), because they satisfy such needs and represent a means to an end. Behaviours relating to self-actualisation are 'growth' or *'being'* needs (*B-motives*). Maslow saw them as being performed for their own sake, since they are intrinsically satisfying.

Maslow argued that the needs at one level must be 'relatively satisfied' before those at the next level could direct and control behaviour. Before enjoying reading a book, for example, the 'stomach pangs' of hunger should ideally be attended to first. Maslow believed that

few people achieve self-actualisation, because most are stalled along the way by insurmountable social or environmental barriers. However, he also believed that all of us could reach the final level in the hierarchy for brief periods, which he called *peak experiences*.

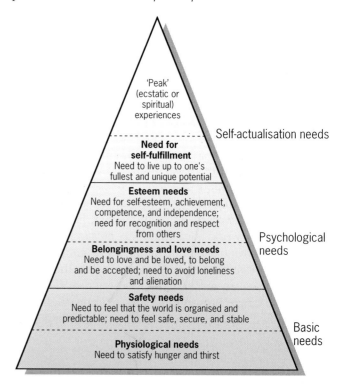

Figure 17.3 *One version of Maslow's hierarchy of needs*

Maslow's critics have argued that towards the highest level of the hierarchy the ordering is wrong. In a sense, such criticism is trivial because it is the idea of a *needs* hierarchy that is useful, rather than its exact nature and order. Also, the term 'relatively satisfied' with respect to moving from one level to another was used, rather than 'completely satisfied'. Maslow would accept that basic physiological needs do not need to be completely satisfied for higher needs to be addressed, and might use the example of the hungry artist working on a 'masterpiece' to illustrate this.

Despite its intuitive appeal, Maslow's theory may be criticised on other grounds. For example, it is difficult to operationally define concepts like self-actualisation, and without such definitions it is impossible to test the theory experimentally. Also, some people don't seem to show any interest in going beyond physiological, safety, and love needs. Thus, it has been proposed that there is too much individual variation for the hierarchy to apply to everyone.

Maslow's conclusions about 'self-actualisation' have also been criticised. These were based on his observations of people he considered to be 'self-actualised', and included historical figures, famous living individuals, and even some of his friends whom he admired greatly. Such an approach does not follow the traditions of the scientific process (Wahba & Bridwell, 1976).

FREUD'S THEORY

The theories considered so far assume that motives are *conscious*. Freud, however, argued that behaviour is controlled by *unconscious* motives. Indeed, these could be called 'instincts', and Freud's theory could be discussed as an instinct theory of motivation. Originally, Freud saw all human behaviour as being rooted in *Eros*, the drive for 'bodily pleasure'. After the carnage of World War 1, he argued that behaviour was also directed by a drive for self-destruction (which has been called *Thanatos:* see Chapter 7, page 67).

The view that behaviour is controlled by unconscious motives has attracted much controversy and stimulated considerable theoretical and research interest. However, whether any (let alone all) behaviour is controlled by unconscious motives is difficult to assess, because we cannot measure 'unconscious motivation' directly. So, whilst such motives might exist, there is no direct evidence for them, and for this reason alone Freud's theory is not a plausible explanation of human motivation (see also Chapters 3, 32, 54 and 57).

CONCLUSIONS

This chapter has looked at several theories of motivation. Some are primarily physiological, some are primarily psychological, and some are combined approaches. Several different types of motive exist, and different theories apply better to some motives than others. However, in any given behaviour (such as hunger), at least some supporting evidence can be found for one or other of the theories that have been considered.

Summary

- Several different types of motive exist. **Biologically-based motives** are in-built body tissue needs (or 'drives') such as those for food, water, air, sleep, temperature regulation and pain avoidance.

- **Sensation-seeking motives** are largely unlearned needs for increasing stimulation. They are most evident in conditions of sensory isolation or deprivation, and include activity, curiosity and exploration, manipulation, play, contact and control.

- Complex **psychosocial motives** are learned and unrelated to body needs. They include the needs for achievement, affiliation, power and approval.

- **Instinct theories** explain motivation in terms of innate dispositions. Attempts to identify instincts stopped being useful when they merely acted as descriptive labels for the behaviours they were inferred from.

- **Ethologists** replaced 'instinct' with **fixed action pattern**, and recognised the role played by environmental stimuli. **Sociobiologists** argue that innate patterns play a crucial role in complex human behaviours, and all animal behaviour is motivated by 'the selfish gene'.

- Psychologists replaced 'instinct' with 'drive'. Two major approaches are **homeostatic drive theory** and **drive reduction theory**.

- Some homeostatic needs (e.g oxygen intake) are involuntary and continuous, and satisfied automatically. Tissue needs, however, are involuntary and discontinous, and cause a homeostatic drive which leads to an appropriate behaviour.

- Drive reduction theory maintains that behaviour successful in reducing unpleasant drive states will be strengthened. However, whilst some behaviours are motivated by drives associated with tissue needs, the majority are not.

- Like drive theory, **optimum level of arousal** (OLA) **theory** proposes that arousal is sometimes reduced by decreasing stimulation. Unlike drive theory, however, OLA theory proposes that we sometimes try to **increase** stimulation.

■ **Expectancy** (or **incentive**) **theory** sees the expectation of a desirable environmental goal as 'pulling' us towards it. The expectation of an undesirable goal has the opposite effect. The value placed on a goal is also important. A distinction can be made between **intrinsic** and **extrinsic rewards**.

■ **Opponent-process theory** proposes that every emotional experience triggers an opposite emotional experience which persists longer, is more intense, and reduces the primary emotion's intensity.

■ Maslow's **hierarchy of needs** places **physiological needs** at the bottom and **self-actualisation** at the top.

Maslow distinguishes between behaviours related to survival or deficiency needs (**D-motives**) and those relating to self-actualisation, 'growth' or 'being' needs (**B-motives**).

■ D-motives are a means to an end, whereas B-motives are intrinsically satisfying. Most people do not achieve self-actualisation, but reach the hierarchy's top for brief periods called **peak experiences**.

■ Freud's belief that behaviour is controlled by **unconscious motivation** has attracted much interest. However, it is difficult to assess since unconscious motivation cannot be directly measured.

Essay Questions

1 Discuss **one** physiological and **one** psychological approach to explaining motivation. *(24 marks)*

2 Distinguish between physiological and psychological approaches to explaining motivation. *(24 marks)*

WEB ADDRESSES

http://www.csun.edu/~vcpsyOOh/students/explore.htm
http://www.tecfa.unige.ch/themes/sa2/act-app-dos2-fic-drive.htm
http://www.cho.fis.utoronto.ca/FIS/Courses/LIS1230/LIS1230sharma/motive6.htm
http://www.exxnet.com:2000/resources/motivate.htm
http://sol.brunel.ac.uk/~jarvis/bola/motivation/masmodel.htm

18 *Emotion*

INTRODUCTION AND OVERVIEW

The study of emotion has always occupied a prominent position in psychology. Much research has been devoted to identifying the brain structures involved in emotional behaviour and experience. The first part of this chapter examines the role played by the cerebral cortex, hypothalamus, limbic system and cerebral hemispheres in this regard. The second part of the chapter considers some theories of emotional experience. The first two (the James–Lange and Cannon–Bard theories) emphasise the role of *physiological* factors. The second two (Schachter's and Lazarus's theories) emphasise the role of *non-physiological* factors, in the form of cognitive processes.

EMOTION AND THE BRAIN

The role of the cortex and hypothalamus in emotion

Bard (1928) found that destroying parts of the *cerebral cortex* in cats and dogs resulted in a much lowered threshold of emotional excitation. For example, following *decortication* (removal of part or all of the cerebral cortex), a cat would present a typical picture of 'full-blown rage'. It hissed, growled, screamed and spat, arched its back, and displayed elevated heart rate and blood pressure. However, this aggression occurred in response to the slightest provocation and was poorly directed. For example, the responses occurred if the cat had its tail pinched, *but* were directed at the ground in front of it rather than the source of the pinching.

Bard concluded that the cortex normally acts as an *inhibitor* of sub-cortical structures, and that these structures were responsible for the production of emotional behaviour. The responses elicited by decorticated non-humans were called *sham rage* because they seemed to be the integrated expression of rage, but without the awareness and persistence characteristic of normal emotion.

Bard discovered that the rage produced by removal of the cortex largely disappeared if the *hypothalamus* was also removed. The involvement of the hypothalamus in the full expression of emotional behaviour has been shown in many studies of non-humans. For example, destruction of the lateral hypothalamus produces a *quiet*

biting attack (which does not appear to be accompanied by strong emotion, and which ends when the prey ceases to move). However, *affective attack* (the behaviours exhibited by a decorticated cat and described above) is produced by stimulation in the region of the ventromedial nucleus of the hypothalamus. If the *dorsal* part of the hypothalamus is stimulated, a non-human makes frantic attempts to escape the cage in which it is housed, and displays physiological responses indicative of increased activity in the sympathetic branch of the autonomic nervous system (ANS). If it is restrained, it will frequently attack in an attempt to escape.

As well as cats, such findings have also been obtained in rats, monkeys and several other non-humans. In humans, however, the picture is less clear. Sem-Jacobsen (1968) found that hypothalamic stimulation had little effect on emotional experiences, and studies of people with hypothalamic damage caused by disease have also shown little change in subjective emotional reactions. The hypothalamus, then, cannot be responsible for emotional experience, and it has also been found that it is not uniquely involved in organising emotional behaviour.

Key **STUDY**

Box 18.1 Separating the hypothalamus from the rest of the brain

Because large hypothalamic lesions will kill an animal by causing severe disruption to the *endocrine system*, special apparatus is needed to cut around the hypothalamus to sever all the connections between it and the rest of the brain, whilst leaving connections to the pituitary gland intact. Ellison & Flynn's (1968) technique involved two knives that could be rotated around the hypothalamus, leaving it as an 'island' in the brain. However, even when the hypothalamus was separated from the rest of the brain, some kinds of aggressive behaviour could still be elicited in cats. These occurred in response to 'natural stimulation' (such as the sight of a mouse) and artificial electrical stimulation of other parts of the brain, although slightly higher levels of electrical current were necessary as compared with those before the isolation.

The role of the limbic system in emotion

Klüver & Bucy (1937) conducted several studies investigating the effects of damage to the temporal lobes in monkeys. Essentially, they found five main consequences which together are known as the *Klüver–Bucy syndrome*. First, the monkeys ate any sort of food that was presented to them, including that which they had rejected prior to the operation, and displayed a tendency to put anything movable into their mouths (*hyperorality*). Second, they suffered *visual agnosia* (the inability to recognise objects by sight: see Chapter 11, page 112). Third, increased, and often inappropriate, sexual activity (*hypersexuality*) was displayed. A fourth consequence was that the monkeys became tamer and safer to handle. Finally, they displayed an apparent absence of fear. For example, they would repeatedly put their fingers into the flame of a burning match.

Klüver and Bucy also investigated the effects of *limbic system* damage. Much of the early research into the limbic system was concerned with its role in olfaction. However, Klüver and Bucy showed that damage to the limbic system had effects on monkey's emotional behaviour. For example, as well as displaying increased sexuality, they also displayed decreased fearfulness and increased aggression towards one another. Researchers thus began to explore the possibility that limbic system structures may be responsible for emotional expression. Klüver and Bucy noted that destruction of the *amygdala* made wild and ferocious monkeys tame and placid. Removing the amygdala of a monkey dominant in a social group, for example, caused it to lose its place in the dominance hierarchy when it returned to the colony. When the amygdala was lesioned, stimuli that would normally elicit an aggressive response failed to do so. Such effects were not confined to monkeys, and subsequent research showed that lesions to the amygdala in

species such as the rat, wolverine and lynx also resulted in timidity and placidity.

In cats, the effects of electrical stimulation of the amygdala depend on the part stimulated. In one part, stimulation results in the cat arching its back, hissing and showing all the signs of preparing to attack. However, stimulation in another part results in the cat cowering in terror when caged with a small mouse. Of course, there is always a danger in generalising the results obtained with non-humans to human beings. However, some evidence suggests that the amygdala plays a similar role in humans.

Box 18.2 The case of Charles Whitman

Several years ago, Charles Whitman killed his wife and mother before making his way to the University of Texas. Once there, he killed 15 people he did not know and wounded another 24 before being killed himself by the police. It seems that Whitman was aware of his aggressiveness since, just before he embarked on the killings, he wrote of the agony he was experiencing:

'I don't quite understand what compels me to type this letter … I am supposed to be an average, reasonable and intelligent young man … However, lately I have been a victim of many unusual and irrational thoughts … I talked with a doctor once for about two hours and tried to convey to him my fears that I felt overcome (sick) by overwhelming violent impulses. After one session I never saw the doctor again and since then I have been fighting my mental turmoil alone, and seemingly to no avail. After my death I wish that an autopsy would be performed on me to see if there is any visible physical disorder.' (cited in Johnson, 1972)

An autopsy revealed a small tumour in Whitman's brain. Although the wounds caused by the police gunfire made it difficult to establish the tumour's precise location, it appeared to be in (or at least close to) the amygdala (Sweet *et al.*, 1969).

Klüver, Bucy and others' findings concerning the amygdala were instrumental in the development of *psychosurgery* (see Chapters 12 and 52). Mark & Ervin (1970) studied a young woman called Julia, who was admitted to hospital after committing, seemingly without any reason, twelve separate attacks on people. Tests suggested that Julia's amygdala was damaged, and her family agreed to surgeons conducting psychosurgery (in the form of a small lesion in the amygdala) to try and reduce her aggressive behaviour. In follow-up studies, Mark and Ervin reported that Julia's aggressive behaviour had been greatly reduced (see also Chapter 52).

Key STUDY

Box 18.3 The surgical treatment of emotional disturbances

'Case 34 was admitted and kept in (hospital) ... He was a young man of 25 years ... admitted because he was always violent. He was constantly aggressive and destructive. He could not be kept in general wards and had to be nursed in an isolated cell. It was difficult to establish any sort of communication with him. *Bilateral stereotaxic amygdalectomy* was performed. Following the operation he was very quiet and could be safely left in the general wards. He started answering questions in slow syllables.' (Balasubramamiam *et al.*, 1970)

Balasubramamiam *et al.*'s method of assessing the effectiveness of psychosurgery on the hyperactive or violent behaviour of their patients is presented below (after Carlson, 1977):

Grade	Criteria
A	There is no need of any drug. Patient is able to mingle with others.
B	Very much docile and given to occasional outbursts only.
C	Manageable when given drugs although not leading a useful life.
D	Transient improvement.
E	No change.
F	Died.

According to these criteria, 'Case 34' would be graded as an 'A'. Do you think the patient was cured as a result of psychosurgery, or does 'manageability' seem to be the important criterion? Should there be a category for patients whose condition is made *worse* by psychosurgery? (See Chapters 52 and 56.)

Calder *et al.* (cited in Spinney, 1997) report the case of D.R., a woman in her early 50s who has suffered from severe epilepsy since the age of 28. D.R. had an operation to treat her epilepsy, which resulted in total destruction of the left amygdala and partial destruction of the right. She seems unable to differentiate whether people are happy, angry or sad from the tone of their voice, and incapable of detecting facial expressions of emotion. Such findings are consistent with the view that the amygdala interprets emotional signals regardless of their source.

D.R. evidently cannot appraise dangerous situations, and consequently shows no sense of fear. For example, she finds it difficult to understand television programmes where the plot involves fear or danger, and on one occasion came close to putting her hand into a pot of boiling water before being stopped by her husband. Her response was to shrug the incident off and laugh. D.R. is not unique, and in other cases where the amygdala has been damaged (through, for example, encephalitis), similar effects have been observed (Young, 1997).

Another part of the limbic system, the *septum*, has also been implicated in emotional behaviour. Brady & Nauta (1953) found that septal lesions resulted in the lowering of a rat's 'rage threshold'. For example, if a person approached the cage in which a septally lesioned rat was housed, it showed signs of extreme emotional arousal, such as screaming and jumping wildly. If a person placed a hand into the cage, the rat would launch a vicious attack on it. However, in mice, a septal lesion produces an increase in 'flight' behaviour rather than 'affective rage'. In rats, increased emotionality gradually subsides, until within a few weeks it is all but absent. In mice, hyperemotionality remains indefinitely (Carlson, 1977).

As well as these differences, it has been shown that most other non-humans do *not* display emotionality as a result of a septal lesion. Thus, making *general* statements about the septum's role in emotional behaviour is not possible, since the effects of lesions apparently depend on the species studied.

On the basis of data obtained from non-human studies and his own investigations of brain-damaged people, Papez (1937) proposed that a complex set of interconnected pathways and centres in the limbic system underlies emotional experience. The *Papez circuit* (see Figure 18.1, page 178) forms a closed loop running from the *hippocampus* to the *hypothalamus* and from there to the *anterior thalamus*. The circuit continues via the *cingulate gyrus* and the *entorhinal cortex* back to the hippocampus.

Unfortunately, Papez's proposals have not stood the test of careful anatomical study. MacLean (1949) modified the circuit, and suggested that the amygdala and hippocampus play a central role in the mediation of aggression but the cingulate gyrus does not. Whilst the *Papez–MacLean limbic model* has been influential, researchers have cautioned against the idea that there are specific 'emotion centres' (especially 'aggression centres') in the brain, since the brain is not neatly organised into structures that correspond to categories of behaviour.

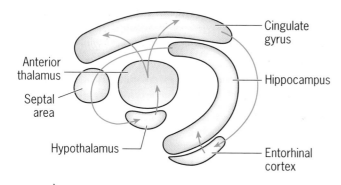

Figure 18.1 *The Papez circuit*

Box 18.4 The 'brave bull' reassessed

One who has claimed evidence for an 'aggression centre' is Delgado (1969), whose research was briefly described in Chapter 10 (see pages 99–100). In a much-publicised demonstration, Delgado showed that stimulating a charging bull's limbic system resulted in the 'brave bull' stopping in its tracks. However, Valenstein (1973) challenged Delgado's interpretation of his results. After watching film of Delgado's demonstration, Valenstein noted that the bull always circled to the right when Delgado stimulated its brain. Rather than being pacified as a result of the stimulation, Valenstein argues that the bull was simply 'confused' and 'frustrated' and just gave up!

Research has begun to clarify the role that limbic system structures play in emotional behaviour. Much of this has concentrated on the amygdala, and it has been found that the amygdala has direct connections with sensory channels (Connor, 1998). According to LeDoux (1996), when the amygdala receives sensory information, an emotional response, can be elicited *independently* of the cortex. This has been called a *pre-cognitive emotional response*, since it occurs without the cortex having made any appraisal of the appropriateness of a particular emotional response.

Perhaps you have had the experience of someone creeping up on you. On turning round, your initial response is to jump (and perhaps scream), but when the cortex appraises the situation and recognises the person as someone you know, your initial emotional response disappears (sometimes to be replaced by another response – anger!). LeDoux suggests that we can view the initial emotional response as being mediated by the amygdala, which acts as a sort of 'early warning system'

and allows us to experience emotion without cognition. The cortex then assesses the situation and determines whether the 'system' is responding appropriately or inappropriately.

The cerebral hemispheres and emotion

Since the development of PET and other non-invasive methods of investigating the brain, it has been possible to investigate the activity occurring in the brain during a task's performance (see Chapter 10). As noted in Chapter 12, evidence suggests that the two *cerebral hemispheres* are not functionally symmetrical but are specialised for the performance of different tasks.

In a case study reported in 1908, a mentally disturbed woman repeatedly tried to choke herself with her left hand. As she did this, her right hand would try to pull the left away from her throat. As well as this self-destructive behaviour, the woman engaged in other destructive behaviours such as ripping her bed pillows and tearing her sheets. However, she only did this with her left hand. After the woman died, a post-mortem was conducted. This revealed that her *corpus callosum* was badly damaged.

As was seen in Chapter 12, the corpus callosum connects the two cerebral hemispheres and allows them to exchange information, so that each is aware of the other's activities. When the corpus callosum is surgically divided, the channel of communication is disrupted and the hemispheres are no longer in contact. In a sense, the woman described above was like a split-brain patient and, on the basis of her behaviour, it has been suggested that the two hemispheres might differ in terms of their comprehension and communication of emotion.

Box 18.5 Indifference and catastrophic reactions

Studies of brain damaged people have told us something about the role of the hemispheres in emotion. In Chapter 11, it was noted that damage to the motor area of the right hemisphere leads to paralysis of the body's left side. However, people with right hemisphere damage seem to be completely unmoved by this and continue to make plans as though they could walk normally. This is termed an *indifference reaction*. Damage to the motor area of the left hemisphere causes paralysis of the body's right side. Far from being unmoved by this, people with left hemisphere damage display a *catastrophic reaction*, that is, an episode of severe anxiety and depression which is probably a result of their awareness of the major damage the brain has suffered.

The findings described above suggest that the left and right hemispheres differ in terms of their reactions to emotion-provoking stimuli. Because of the undamaged right hemisphere's catastrophic response to the consequences of damage to the left hemisphere, it seems reasonable to propose that the right hemisphere is specialised for recognising emotion-provoking stimuli and for organising the appropriate pattern of emotional responses.

Equally, because of the left hemisphere's indifference reaction to the consequences of damage to the right, it seems reasonable to propose that the left hemisphere cannot recognise the emotional significance of this damage, and so continues to make plans without taking it into consideration. Whilst the left hemisphere is *aware* of the damage, then, it does not seem to be 'bothered' by it.

Key STUDY

Box 18.6 The right hemisphere and the recognition of emotional expression

Studies of people with normally functioning left and right hemispheres have *generally* confirmed that the hemispheres differ in terms of their reactivity to emotion-provoking stimuli. Ley & Bryden (1979) showed participants drawings of faces displaying different emotional expressions. The drawings were presented one at a time to either the left or right hemisphere, using a modified version of the method employed with split-brain patients which enables information to be presented to one hemisphere only (see pages 122–123). After a drawing had been displayed, it was replaced by another which was shown in the centre of the visual field. This meant that it was perceived by both hemispheres. The participants had to decide whether the emotion displayed in the second picture was the same as, or different from, the emotion displayed in the first.

When the drawings displayed *clear* emotional states (such as a big smile), fewer recognition errors were made by the right hemisphere. When the drawing displayed no emotion or a 'mild' emotional state, there was no difference in recognition between the hemispheres. These findings suggest that the right hemisphere has a definite advantage in the recognition of clear or strong facial expressions of emotion. This also appears to be the case when emotions are expressed *paralinguistically*, that is, utterances which convey their meaning in terms of voice tone, emphasis, pausing, and so on.

It was noted earlier that right hemisphere damage results in an indifference reaction from the left and, as Box 18.6 illustrates, the right hemisphere seems to be better than the left at recognising facial and paralinguistic expressions of emotion. To suggest that the left hemisphere is completely non-emotional would, however, be incorrect (Davidson, 1992).

Box 18.7 The left and right hemispheres and positive and negative emotions

Several studies indicate that the left hemisphere is more active during the experience of *positive* emotions. For example, research using PET (see Chapter 10, page 104) indicates that when people are given 'good' news, asked to think about 'positive' events, or required to discriminate happy faces from neutral ones, the left hemisphere is more active than the right (Tomarken & Davidson, 1994; Gur *et al.*, 1994). By contrast, the right hemisphere is more active when people are given 'bad' news or asked to think about 'negative' events (and recall from page 178 that the woman who engaged in destructive behaviour did so only with her right-hemisphere-controlled left hand).

Support for the left/right, positive/negative distinction comes from studies of clinically depressed people, which also show a tendency for the frontal lobes of the right hemisphere to be more active (Miller, 1987).

The different areas of the cortex *within* the right hemisphere may also play slightly different roles. Ross (1981) describes several examples of people with damage to the frontal lobe of the right hemisphere who had difficulty in *producing* facial gestures and tone of voice to express emotion. However, their ability to *recognise* other people's emotional expression appeared to be unaffected. By contrast, people with damage to the right parietal/temporal lobe seemed to be able to produce emotional expressions but were unable to recognise those expressed by other people. Damage to both the right frontal and parietal/temporal lobes resulted in the inability to both produce and recognise emotional expression.

There is an interesting similarity between Ross's (1981) findings and those described in Chapter 12 on the localisation and lateralisation of language. Whether there are discrete areas in the right hemisphere for the production and understanding of emotional expression, which are analogous to Broca's and Wernicke's areas in the left hemisphere, is an interesting possibility. However, the findings reported by Ross need to be replicated by other researchers before we can begin to talk about the 'localisation and lateralisation of emotion'.

The apparently differential responses of the right and left hemispheres to positive and negative emotions has also led to much speculation. According to Sackheim (1982), the two hemispheres operate in a *reciprocal* manner with activity in one (caused by either a positive or negative emotion-provoking stimulus) producing reciprocal activity in the other. Such activity might function to ensure that an emotion was not experienced in an inappropriately intense way. Extremely excited reactions might, therefore, be due to the right hemisphere failing to reciprocate the activity in the left hemisphere, whilst extremely sad or angry reactions might result from the left hemisphere failing to reciprocate the activity in the right hemisphere.

Box 18.8 Antisocial (dissocial) personality disorder and the hemispheres

Amongst other things, people with dissocial personality disorder are emotionally cold, superficially charming, and less responsive to facial cues of distress than non-dissocial people (Blair *et al.*, 1997). Day & Wong (1996) measured the time taken by dissocial and non-dissocial individuals to respond to negative emotional words presented to the left and right visual fields (and hence the right and left hemispheres respectively: see Chapter 12, page 122).

Whilst non-dissocial people showed a right ('emotional') hemisphere advantage, dissocials exhibited no significant hemisphere advantage. The researchers had predicted the dissocials would show a left ('analytical') hemisphere advantage, so the findings did not completely support their hypotheses. However, the absence of a right hemisphere advantage does suggest differences between dissocials and non-dissocials in the processing of negative information.

THEORIES OF EMOTION

Some theories of emotion attempt to explain how emotion-provoking events produce subjective emotional experiences. Others attempt to explain how emotions develop. Here, theories of *emotional experience* will be considered. In everyday language, we use the words 'emotions' and 'feelings' interchangeably. However, 'feelings' are but one element of an emotion (Briner, 1999), and it is possible to identify four integral components of human emotions. These are *subjective feelings*, *cognitive processes*, *physiological arousal* and *behavioural reactions*. The relationship between these components, and the relative emphasis given to one or more of them, distinguishes the various theories.

The James–Lange theory

Common sense tells us that bodily changes (such as crying) occur because an emotion-arousing stimulus (receiving bad news) produces an emotion (feeling sorry). However, James (1884) and, independently, Lange (1885) offered a theory running counter to common sense. According to the *James–Lange theory* of emotion, emotional experience is the *result* rather than the cause of bodily and/or behavioural changes to some emotion-provoking stimulus.

Box 18.9 James on emotion

According to James (1884):

'The bodily changes follow directly the perception of the exciting fact, and ... our feelings of the same changes as they occur is the emotion. Common sense says that we ... are sorry, and weep. The hypothesis to be defended here says that this order of sequence is incorrect, that the one mental state is not immediately induced by the other and that the bodily manifestations must first be interposed between. The more rational statement is that we feel sorry because we cry'.

When we experience some stimulus, then, physiological reactions and behavioural responses occur, and trigger the emotional experience. For the James–Lange theory, emotions are a *by-product* (or *cognitive representation*) of automatic physiological and behavioural responses.

James and Lange argued that the brain receives *sensory feedback* from the body's internal organs *and* parts that respond to emotion-provoking stimuli. The feedback the brain receives is recognised and then labelled appropriately. Although running counter to common sense, you might be able to think of a situation in which you reacted in a fairly automatic way. An example would be slipping down the stairs and grabbing the bannisters. Only when you had stopped yourself would you become aware of feeling frightened, as though the sudden change in your behaviour *caused* the fear, quite apart from *why* you grabbed the bannisters.

Because it was counter-intuitive, the theory received much attention. Cannon (1927) identified three major problems. The first concerned the pattern of physiological activity fed back to the brain. Cannon argued that each emotion would need its own distinct pattern of activity otherwise the cortex would not be able to 'determine' which emotion should be experienced. Many studies have found distinct patterns of physiological activity associated with different emotional states (Dalgleish, 1998). However, many other studies have reported the absence of such differences.

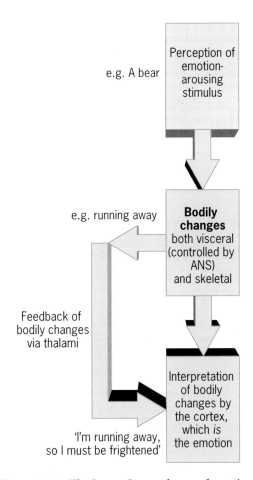

Figure 18.2 *The James–Lange theory of emotion*

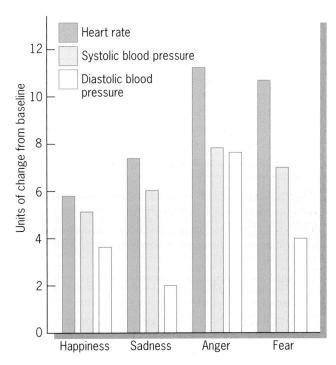

Figure 18.3 *Data reported by Schwartz* et al. *(1981) concerning physiological changes when participants recall particular emotion-provoking events*

Ax (1953) and Schwartz *et al.* (1981: see Figure 18.3) are amongst those who reported data supportive of the James–Lange theory. They showed that emotions like fear, anger, happiness, and sadness are different in terms of heart rate and body temperature, muscular activity in the face, blood pressure, and neural activity in the frontal lobes.

Wolf & Wolff (1947) and Mandler (1962) have supported Cannon's criticisms by showing that different people may display different patterns of physiological activity when experiencing the same emotion, and that the same person may respond differently when experiencing the same emotion on several occasions.

Cannon also argued that James and Lange were wrong to propose that physiological changes themselves produce changes in emotional states. This criticism was based on Marañon's (1924) study in which participants were injected with *adrenaline*, which increases ANS activity. Following the injection, participants were asked to describe their emotional state. Most reported a physical change with *no* emotional overtones, and those who did report a change described it as an 'as if' change in emotional state rather than an actual change.

Cannon's third criticism was that total separation of the viscera from the CNS did *not* result in the absence of emotional experience (the James–Lange theory predicts that emotional experience *would* be absent in such conditions). Cannon based this criticism on his own and other researchers' findings indicating that when visceral feedback was abolished in dogs and cats, emotional experience was not affected. However, apart from the fact that we do not know about the emotional experiences of non-humans, Cannon seems to have ignored James's views about the body, and in particular the *muscles*, as well as the viscera. Even if visceral feedback were abolished, an animal would still receive feedback from the muscles, and this might contribute to some sort of emotional experience.

Key STUDY

Box 18.10 **Emotional experience following spinal cord damage**

If feedback from the internal organs through the ANS were important, then humans with spinal cord damage would not be capable of experiencing emotion of the same intensity they experienced before the damage (if, indeed, they experienced *any* sort of emotion). Hohmann (1966) studied several patients with spinal cord injuries. Some had damaged relatively low portions of the spinal cord, which meant that feedback from the internal organs still reached the brain through the higher undamaged portions. Others had spinal cord damage much further up and received little or no information from the internal organs.

Hohmann asked his patients to recall an event that had aroused fear, anger, grief, or sexual excitement before their injury, and a comparable event that had occurred after it. As measured by self-reports of emotional intensity, there was a diminishing of emotional experience for events after the injury. Also, the higher up the spinal cord the injury was, the less intense were the emotional experiences reported in terms of their *feelings*, but not necessarily their *behaviours*. As one patient put it:

> 'I was at home alone in bed and dropped a cigarette where I couldn't reach it. I finally managed to scrounge around and put it out. I could have burnt up right there, but the funny thing is, I didn't get all shook up about it. I just didn't feel afraid at all, like you would suppose. Now I don't get a feeling of physical animation, it's a sort of cold anger. Sometimes I cry when I see some injustice. I yell and cuss and raise hell, because if you don't do it sometimes I've learned people will take advantage of you, but it doesn't have the heat that it used to. It's a mental kind of anger'.

Hohmann's data cast doubt on Cannon's criticism. However, Hohmann's and other studies finding similar effects (e.g. Jasnos & Hakmiller, 1975) have been criticised on the grounds that they are liable to experimenter and social desirability effects, and the possibility that patients might suppress their feelings as a way of coping with their extreme circumstances (Trieschmann, 1980). Generously, the findings concerning the lack of emotional response in the absence of visceral feedback can be seen as supporting the James–Lange theory, but the potential methodological shortcomings in supportive studies should be acknowledged.

Despite the criticisms levelled at it, the James–Lange theory has stood the test of time remarkably well. In discussing its relevance, James (1890) suggested that it had practical importance as well. Since emotions are no more than the perception of physiological and behavioural responses, we could:

> '... conquer undesirable emotional tendencies ... by assiduously, and in the first instance cold-bloodedly, going through ... the *outward movements* of those contrary dispositions which we prefer to cultivate'.

For James, then, by smiling at someone who makes us angry our anger would eventually disappear. It is generally agreed that emotional states are *reflected* by our facial expressions, but some researchers believe that the reverse may be true as well. Tomkins (1962) has argued that specific facial displays are *universally* associated with neural programmes linked to various emotions.

Certainly, some facial expressions of emotion seem to be recognised by people in all cultures irrespective of their experiences (Myers, 1998), and studies which induce people to express facially a particular emotion (smiling, for example) are associated with self-reported changes in emotional state and distinct patterns of physiological activity (as Schwartz *et al.*'s study showed – see page 181) comparable to those that occur during actual emotional experiences.

Box 18.11 Facial feedback theory

Facial feedback theory argues that facial expressions can produce changes in emotional state as well as mirror them. As James suggested, we do seem to feel happier when we smile, sadder when we frown, and so on. In several studies, people have been asked to imagine a pleasurable event such as winning a large sum of money, or an unpleasurable event such as being placed in a fear-provoking situation. Then, they are asked to enhance or suppress tension in certain facial muscles. Consistent with facial feedback theory, subjective reports of emotional experience have been shown to change (McCanne & Anderson, 1987).

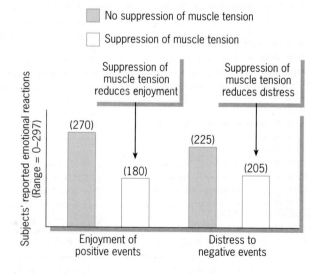

Figure 18.4 *Data reported by McCanne & Anderson (1987) supporting the facial feedback hypothesis*

Contraction of the facial muscles apparently heightens physiological arousal, and this possibly leads us to report changes in perceived emotional state (Myers, 1998). It has been proposed that contraction of the facial muscles affects blood flow to the brain and this influences the release of serotonin and noradrenaline, which are believed to play a role in emotion (see Chapter 50). However, irrespective of the mechanisms involved, it is not hard to see how facial feedback theory could have applications as a potential treatment for certain emotional disorders.

There is, of course, a danger in exaggerating the claims from any area of research. Critics of facial feedback theory have identified several methodological problems with some studies (such as the possibility that the participants' expectations and distracting elements in the experimental setting may affect their emotional states), and whilst research may show statistically significant effects, these could be *behaviourally* insignificant. Nonetheless, the possibility that the British 'stiff upper lip' may influence our emotional experiences cannot be entirely ruled out!

The Cannon–Bard theory

As shown in the previous section, Cannon did not believe that different emotions are associated with different patterns of physiological and bodily activity. He saw all emotions as producing the *same* pattern of responses which correspond to the *fight-or-flight* response, which prepares us to deal with an emergency. According to Cannon (1927) and Bard (1928), external stimuli activate the *thalami* which send sensory information to the cortex for interpretation, and simultaneously send *activation messages* through the PNS to the viscera and skeletal muscles.

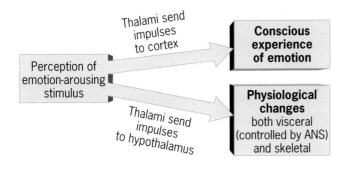

Figure 18.5 *The Cannon–Bard thalamic theory of emotion*

The Cannon–Bard theory claims that information sent to the cortex produces the sensations of emotion *at the same time* as physiological and behavioural responses are produced. However, these are *independent* of one another. Thus, the experience of emotion neither causes, nor is a result of, physiological and behavioural responses. Heightened physiological and behavioural activity occurs in response to the emotion-provoking stimulus, rather than the experience of emotion it produces.

The claim that physiological and bodily activity is a 'side-effect' of emotion and plays no role in it is, as was seen earlier, not supported by evidence. Also, Cannon was almost certainly wrong to ascribe a central role to the thalami. As has been shown, other brain structures, principally the hypothalamus and limbic system, appear to be much more directly involved in emotional experience. However, despite the theory's limitations, it does at least highlight the important role played by the brain in emotional responses.

Schachter's theory

According to Schachter (1964), Cannon was wrong in believing that bodily changes and emotional experiences are independent. Schachter also saw the James–Lange theory as being mistaken in its claim that changes in physiological activity cause emotional experience. Schachter's theory proposes that emotional experience depends on two factors. The first is *physiological arousal* in the ANS. The second is the *cognitive appraisal* (or interpretation) of the physiological arousal.

Thus, like James and Lange, Schachter sees arousal as preceding emotional experience and being necessary for it. However, physiological arousal itself is not sufficient. If an emotion is to be experienced, the arousal must be appraised in an emotional way. In Marañon's study (see page 181), the participants had a clear explanation for their physiological arousal, namely the injections they were given. For Schachter, it is hardly surprising they did not report emotional experiences, because their cognitive appraisals of the heightened physiological activity could be explained in a non-emotional way.

Schachter argues that the degree of arousal determines an emotion's intensity, provided that arousal is interpreted in an emotional way. The interpretation itself determines the emotion that is experienced. Notice how different this is from the James–Lange theory. That theory sees each emotional state as being determined by a *different* pattern of physiological activity. Schachter's theory assumes that the same physiological changes underlie all emotions, and that it is the *meaning* attributed to them that generates different emotions. Because the theory proposes arousal *and* cognition as the central elements in emotional experience, it is sometimes referred to as the *two-factor theory of emotion*.

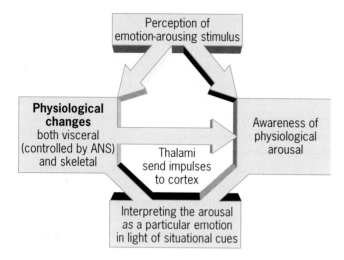

Figure 18.6 *Schachter's theory of emotion*

Key S T U D Y

Box 18.12 **Hypothesised effects of the various manipulations in Schachter & Singer's (1962) experiment**

Epinephrine-informed condition: These participants have been told of the *real* effects the 'vitamin' injection will have. Whilst they will show increases in physiological arousal, they will interpret this in a non-emotional way, because the effects they are experiencing are the effects they have been told to expect. Factor 1 (arousal) is present, but Factor 2 (cognitive appraisal in an emotional way) is not. Therefore, participants should not experience any change in their emotional states.

Epinephrine-misinformed condition: These participants have been given *false* information about the effects the 'vitamin' injection will have. An increase in physiological arousal will occur, but the participants will not be able to explain it in terms of the injection's effects, since the effects they are experiencing are not those they have been told to expect. Factor 1 (arousal) is present as is Factor 2 (cognitive appraisal potentially explaining the arousal in an emotional way). In the absence of a suitable non-emotional explanation for their arousal, participants would be expected to cognitively appraise their environment for a logical explanation and a suitable label for the arousal they are experiencing. In a room with somebody behaving 'angrily' or 'euphorically', the participant might conclude that he too was feeling angry or euphoric. Participants in this condition should experience change in their emotional states.

Epinephrine-ignorant condition: These participants have been given *no information* about the effects the 'vitamin' injection will have. Like participants in the epinephrine-misinformed condition, they will experience arousal and will have no obvious explanation for it, since they have not been told that the injection will produce any change in their physiological activity. Since both Factor 1 (arousal) and Factor 2 (cognitive appraisal potentially explaining the arousal in an emotional way) are present, these participants too should experience changes in their emotional states.

Control condition: Participants in this condition have received 'vitamin' injections, but the substance they have been injected with produces no change in physiological activity (it is merely a saline solution). Therefore Factor 1 (arousal) is not present. Since arousal is necessary for the experience of emotion, participants should not show any change in their emotional states.

Schachter tested his theory in an ingenious experiment (Schachter & Singer, 1962). Male college students were informed that they would be participating in an experiment looking at the effects of the vitamin compound 'Suproxin' on vision, and that this would necessitate them receiving vitamin injections. In fact, they were given injections of *epinephrine* (or *adrenaline*), a hormone that causes an increase in heart rate, respiration rate, blood pressure, and produces muscle tremors.

Participants in the *epinephrine-informed condition* were told of these effects, whilst participants in the *epinephrine-misinformed condition* were given *false* information about epinephrine's effects. These participants were told that the injection would cause 'itching', 'facial numbness' and a 'headache'. In a third (*epinephrine-ignorant*) condition, participants were given no information at all about the injection's effects. Participants in a *control condition* were injected with a saline solution, which did not cause changes in physiological activity, and were told nothing about this injection's effects.

After receiving his injection, the participant was taken to a 'waiting room' before supposedly having his vision tested. Once there, he was introduced to another 'participant' (actually a 'stooge'), who was part of the experimental set-up. With some participants, the stooge pretended to fill out a questionnaire, a copy of which was also given to the genuine participant to complete. As he completed the questionnaire, the stooge began to act '*angrily*' and complain loudly about the personal nature of the questions it contained. After a while, he ripped up the questionnaire and stormed out of the room. With other participants, the stooge pretended to behave '*euphorically*', according to a pre-determined script of behaviours, including making paper aeroplanes, throwing crumpled up paper into a basket, and generally 'messing around'.

The participant's emotional responses were assessed by observers, who watched through a one-way mirror and coded the responses according to a pre-determined schedule. This included the extent to which the stooge's behaviours were copied. At the end of the stooge's 'routine', the genuine participant was given a questionnaire to fill in that included questions about his emotional state. The results provided *some* support for Schachter's theory, with participants showing emotional changes generally in line with the experimental predictions.

Thus, in the 'epinephrine-misinformed' and 'epinephrine-ignorant' conditions, participants appeared to use the stooge's behaviour as a cue for identifying and labelling their own emotional states, at least as regards the observers' measurements. Participants in the 'epinephrine-informed' condition had a ready explanation for their arousal, and showed little change in their emotional states. The finding that participants' emotional states seemed to change irrespective of whether they were in the 'angry' or 'euphoric' condition is also important, because it supports the view that the same type of physiological arousal can be associated with different emotions (recall James and Lange's view concerning different patterns of physiological activity being associated with different emotions).

Other research also supports Schachter's theory. In Dutton & Aron's (1974) experiment, participants were unsuspecting males aged between 18 and 35 who happened to be visiting the Capilano Canyon in British Columbia, Canada. Whilst they were on the extremely unstable suspension bridge 230 feet above the canyon, participants were interviewed by an attractive female who asked them questions as part of a survey she was allegedly conducting on reactions to scenic attractions. In a comparison condition, different participants were interviewed by the same female, but on a solid wooden bridge upstream of the canyon.

In both conditions, participants were asked to invent a short story about an ambiguous picture of a woman. This was later scored for amount of sexual content, taken to reflect a participant's sexual attraction towards the interviewer. Those interviewed on the suspension bridge (the '*high arousal*' condition) invented stories with significantly more sexual imagery than those interviewed on the solid wooden bridge (the '*low arousal*' condition). This study seems to confirm the view that the physiological arousal accompanying all emotions is similar, and that it is the interpretation of the arousal which is important, even though we may occasionally *misidentify* an emotional state. In this case, the participants seemed to mislabel their fear as sexual attraction towards the interviewer.

Box 18.13 Misattribution therapy

Findings such as those reported by Dutton and Aron have led to Schachter's theory being applied as a form of therapy. Although Schachter did not explicitly say so, his theory really identifies *two* cognitive components that must be present for emotion to be experienced (Reisenzein, 1983). First, cognitive appraisal must interpret the situation in an emotional way. Second, this appraisal must 'connect up' (Gordon, 1978) with the arousal and be attributed to the emotional source.

In *misattribution therapy*, people are taught to attribute their arousal to some other source. For example, a therapist dealing with a person who is afraid of spiders might give that person a pill and tell him/her that the pill causes heightened physiological activity. When the person is in the presence of a spider, the heightened physiological activity occurring as a result of fear is attributed to the effects of the pill (even though the pill actually produces no effects). By misattributing increased physiological activity to the pill rather than the spider, it would not be labelled as 'fear'. After a programme of exposure to spiders under these conditions, spiders would become much less frightening to the person (see also Chapter 1, page 9).

Schachter's influential theory has been described as a 'juke box' theory of emotion, in which arousal is the coin we put into the juke box and cognition is the button we press to select an 'emotional tune' (Mandler, 1984). However, although the theory highlights the important role played by cognition in the experience of emotion, we should be cautious about accepting it uncritically (Gross, 1999).

One important problem concerns the *replication* of the original findings reported by Schachter & Singer (1962). Some studies (e.g. Marshall & Zimbardo, 1979) have failed to report *any* effects of the arousal and cognition manipulations. Others (e.g. Maslach, 1978) have found different effects to those reported by Schachter and Singer. In her experiment, Maslach discovered that participants were less likely to imitate the stooge's behaviour, and more likely to apply negative emotional labels to their arousal, irrespective of the social situation in which they were placed.

Hilgard *et al.* (1979) have documented several specific criticisms concerning Schachter and Singer's original experiment:

- Epinephrine does not affect everyone in exactly the same way. Indeed, Schachter and Singer actually eliminated from their analysis the data provided by five participants who later reported they experienced no physiological effects. When the data from these discarded participants are included in the analysis, the difference between conditions disappears!

- Schachter and Singer omitted to assess the mood of the participants *before* they were given the injection. It is possible that a participant in a good mood to begin with might have responded more positively to the stooge irrespective of any injection.

- Some people are extremely afraid of injections. Schachter and Singer appear to have mistakenly assumed that receiving an injection is affectively neutral.

It should also be noted that everyday experience suggests that many of our emotions are triggered spontaneously, and do not result from interpreting and labelling unexplained arousal. Some sorts of stimuli might produce the emotion of fear long before we have any opportunity to assess cognitively the reason for, say, an increased heart rate. A more complete theory of emotion, then, needs to take this into account.

Lazarus's theory

Of several theories that use *cognitive appraisal* as a central component, the most well-known is that proposed by Lazarus (1982, 1999), who argues that some cognitive processing is an essential pre-requisite for the experience of emotion.

Box 18.14 Lazarus on emotion

According to Lazarus (1982):

'Emotion reflects a constantly changing person–environment relationship. When central life agendas (e.g. biological survival, personal and social values and goals) are engaged, this relationship becomes a source of emotion ... Cognitive activity is a necessary pre-condition of emotion because to experience an emotion, people must comprehend – whether in the form of a primitive evaluative perception or a highly differentiated symbolic process – that their well-being is implicated in a transaction, for better or worse'.

With some emotions, in some situations, cognitive appraisal occurs in a conscious, rational and deliberate way, and up to a point we are able to exercise conscious control over our emotions. However, the view that cognition has primacy over emotion has been disputed. Zajonc (1984), for example, has argued that cognition and emotion operate as *independent* systems. He believes that in certain circumstances an emotional response may *precede* the onset of cognition and, in other circumstances, an emotional response may occur in the *absence* of any type of cognitive appraisal. For example, when we meet a person for the first time, we often form a positive or negative impression even though we have processed very little information about that person. In Zajonc's view, we have evolved the capacity to detect affective qualities *without* cognitive mediation (see LeDoux, 1996, page 178).

Lazarus, however, disagrees and argues that primitive emotional responses (such as fear) might not involve any conscious processing, but certainly do involve rapid and unconscious appraisal (and as illustrated in the quote above, Lazarus uses the term *primitive evaluative perception* to describe this). Zajonc has also been criticised on the grounds that some of the things he identifies as emotional states are not emotional states at all. One of these, 'startle', is essentially a *reflex* response, and Lazarus would not disagree with the view that it occurs in the absence of any cognitive appraisal!

In support of Lazarus, Ekman *et al.* (1985) have noted that whilst 'startle' is a response to a sudden loud noise which is produced automatically in *all people*, there is no known stimulus which reliably produces the same *emotion* in everybody. As Eysenck & Keane (1995) have noted:

'There is no doubt that Lazarus's studies have far more direct relevance to everyday emotional experiences than do those of Zajonc. This provides grounds for assuming (albeit tentatively) that emotional experience is generally preceded by cognitive processes, even if that is not invariably the case'.

CONCLUSIONS

The first part of this chapter examined the role played by several brain structures in the experience of emotion. Although the structures examined are involved in emotion, the existence of 'emotional centres' (especially 'aggression centres') has yet to be supported completely by experimental evidence. Theories of emotional experience have also been considered. Whilst some of these are supported by evidence, there is presently no single comprehensive theory of emotional experience.

Perhaps a single comprehensive theory will never be found. Ethical considerations preclude inducing strong emotions as part of psychological research. Whilst participants can be asked to make facial expressions corresponding to a particular emotion, they cannot be expected to actually experience strong emotions. Only those situations which are motivationally relevant for people can reliably produce strong emotions, and it would be unethical to create these in laboratory settings.

Summary

- Decortication in cats and dogs produces a lower threshold of poorly directed emotional excitation (**sham rage**). This suggests that the cortex normally inhibits sub-cortical structures which are actually responsible for emotional behaviour.

- Sham rage largely disappears if the hypothalamus is removed. Destruction of the lateral hypothalamus produces a **quiet biting attack**. Stimulation near the ventromedial nucleus causes sham rage (or **affective attack**). Stimulation of the dorsal hypothalamus produces aggressive escape behaviours and increased activity in the sympathetic branch of the ANS.

- When the hypothalamus is separated from the rest of the brain, some kinds of aggressive behaviour are still elicited in cats. In humans, the role of the hypothalamus in emotion is less clear.

- The **Klüver–Bucy syndrome** was first observed in monkeys, and is the result of temporal lobe damage. The syndrome is characterised by hyperorality, visual agnosia, hypersexuality, placidity when handled, and a total lack of fear.

- Damage to the limbic system in monkeys causes increased sexuality, decreased fear and increased aggression. Destruction of the amygdala changes wild and ferocious monkeys into tame and placid ones. Similar effects occur in other species.

- Damage to the amygdala in humans is also associated with increased aggressiveness. The amygdala evidently functions to interpret emotional signals regardless of their source.

- The amygdala has direct connections with sensory channels, allowing emotional responses to be elicited independently of the cortex (**pre-cognitive emotional response**). This acts as an 'early warning system', after which the cortex appraises the appropriateness of an emotional response.

- Lesions in the rat septum lowers the 'rage threshold' for a brief period. In mice, lesions produce an increase in 'flight' behaviour which remains indefinitely. In other species, however, emotionality does not follow septal lesions.

- The **Papez circuit** is a closed loop in the limbic system which may underlie emotional experience. However, anatomical study has failed to confirm the circuit's existence. The **Papez–MacLean limbic model** sees the amygdala and hippocampus as being of major importance.

- Damage to the motor area of the right hemisphere produces left-side paralysis, but an affected person often displays an **indifference reaction** to this. Damage to the left hemisphere produces a **catastrophic reaction** to the paralysis and brain damage.

- When facial or paralinguistic expressions of emotion are presented to the left and right hemispheres of people with intact brains, the right hemisphere is better able to recognise these. However, the **left hemisphere** is more active when people experience **positive** emotions, and the **right** more active when **negative emotions** are experienced.

- Dissocial personalities do not show the right hemisphere advantage for the processing of negative emotional words that non-dissocials exhibit. This absence suggests that dissocials process information differently from non-dissocials.

■ The **James–Lange theory** proposes that emotional experience is the result, rather than cause, of bodily/behavioural responses to an emotion-arousing stimulus. Emotions are therefore a by-product (or **cognitive representation**) of automatic physiological and behavioural responses.

■ Some studies have found that different patterns of physiological activity are associated with different emotions. However, others have failed in this respect. In other ways, the James–Lange theory has also sometimes been supported and sometimes not.

■ One implication of the theory is that changes in facial expression may induce changes in emotional state and physiological activity. This **facial feedback theory** is supported by experimental evidence.

■ The **Cannon–Bard theory** of emotion proposes that external stimuli activate the thalami, which send sensory information to the cortex for interpretation and simultaneously, but independently, send activation messages to the viscera and skeletal muscles.

■ **Schachter's two-process theory** of emotion sees physiological arousal in the ANS as being a necessary, but not sufficient condition for emotional experience. For an emotion to be experienced, the arousal must be interpreted in an emotional way. The same physiological changes underlie all emotions, but the meaning attributed to them determines the emotion experienced.

■ Schachter and Singer tested this theory in an experiment in which participants' arousal levels and their likely explanations for the arousal were manipulated. The results provided some support for the theory, as have studies conducted by other researchers.

■ Despite its influence, Schachter's theory has been criticised. Importantly, researchers have been unable to replicate the findings from the original experiment. A further criticism is that many emotions are triggered spontaneously, and do not arise from interpreting and labelling unexplained arousal.

■ The possibility that some stimuli elicit emotions before there is opportunity to cognitively assess physiological change has been addressed in **Lazarus's theory** of emotion. However, the view that cognition has primacy over emotion has been disputed by Zajonc.

Essay Questions

1 Discuss the role that brain structures play in the experience of emotion. (*24 marks*)

2 Describe and evaluate any **two** theories of emotion.
(*24 marks*)

WEB ADDRESSES

http://www.emotion.ccs.brandeis.edu/emotion.html
http://www.erin.utoronto.ca/~w3psy398/answerkey2.html
http://serendip.brynmawr.edu/bb/
http://vassun.vassar.edu/~psych/FacultyPages/SPnotes2.html
http://www.britannica.com/bcomm/eb/article16/0,5716,33116+1,00.html

Cognitive Psychology

19 *Focused Attention*

INTRODUCTION AND OVERVIEW

According to Titchener (1903), a student of Wundt:

'The doctrine of attention is the nerve of the whole psychological system'.

However, because of their belief that a stimulus array's properties were sufficient to predict the perceptual response to it, Gestalt psychologists (see Chapter 23) believed the concept of attention was unnecessary, whilst behaviourists argued that since 'attention' was unobservable, it was not worthy of experimental study (see Chapter 58).

Interest in the study of attention re-emerged following the publication of Broadbent's (1958) *Perception and Communication*. Broadbent argued that the world is composed of many more sensations than can be handled by the perceptual and cognitive capabilities of the human observer. To cope with the flood of available information, humans must *selectively attend* to only some information and somehow 'tune out' the rest. To understand our ability to selectively attend to things, researchers study *focused attention*. This chapter considers some theories and research studies concerned with focused *auditory* and *visual* attention.

FOCUSED AUDITORY ATTENTION

Cherry's dichotic listening and shadowing research

Broadbent's (1958) book was partly an attempt to account for the *cocktail-party phenomenon* (Cherry, 1953), that is, the ability to focus attention on one conversation whilst ignoring other conversations going on around us. In his initial experiments, Cherry's participants wore headphones through which pairs of spoken prose 'messages' were presented to both ears simultaneously (*binaural listening*). Cherry found that various physical differences affected the ability to select one of the messages to attend to, in particular voice intensity, the speaker's location and the speaker's sex. He also found that when these differences were controlled for in the two messages (so that each message was, say, spoken in an equally intense female voice), their meaning was extremely difficult to separate.

In later experiments, participants were presented with one message to the right ear and, simultaneously, a *different* message to the left ear (*dichotic listening*) instead of two messages through both ears. Participants were required to repeat out loud *one* of the messages, a procedure known as *shadowing*. Its purpose is to ensure that one of the messages is being attended to. Whilst participants were able to carry out the shadowing requirement, little of the non-shadowed message was remembered.

Box 19.1 Other research findings using shadowing

Little of the non-shadowed message was remembered, even when the same word was presented 35 times to the non-shadowed ear (Moray, 1959). Also, if the message was spoken in a foreign language or changed from English to a different language, participants did not notice this. Whilst speech played backwards was reported as having 'something queer about it', most participants believed it to be normal speech. However, a pure tone of 400 cycles per second was nearly always noticed, as was a change of voice from male to female or female to male (Cherry & Taylor, 1954). These data suggested that whilst the physical properties of the message in the non-shadowed ear were 'heard', semantic content (its meaning) was completely lost. People quickly gave up Cherry's original question about how we can attend to one conversation, and began asking why so little seemed to be remembered about the other conversations (Hampson & Morris, 1996).

Broadbent's split-span studies

Broadbent (1954) reported the results of a series of studies using the *split-span procedure*. In this, three digits (such as 8, 2 and 1) are presented via headphones to one ear at the rate of one every half a second. Simultaneously, three different digits (such as 7, 3 and 4) are presented to the other ear. The task is to listen to the two sets of numbers and then write down as much as can be remembered.

The digits can be recalled either (a) according to the ear of presentation (*ear-by-ear recall*: the numbers above could be recalled as either 8,2,1,7,3,4 or 7,3,4,8,2,1), or (b) according to their chronological order of presentation (*pair-by-pair recall*). Since the digits have been presented in pairs, this would involve recalling the first pair (8,7 or 7,8), followed by the second pair (2,3 or 3,2) and finally the third pair (1,4 or 4,1).

When people are simply given a list of six digits at a rate of one every half a second, serial recall is typically 95 per cent accurate. However, Broadbent found that the split-span procedure produced accurate recall only 65 per cent of the time. Moreover, pair-by-pair recall was considerably poorer than ear-by-ear recall. If given a choice, people preferred ear-by-ear recall.

SINGLE-CHANNEL THEORIES OF FOCUSED AUDITORY ATTENTION

Single-channel theories propose that somewhere in information processing there is a 'bottleneck' or *filter* which allows some information to be passed on for further analysis, either discarding the other information or processing it only to a limited degree. The three theories that have been proposed essentially differ over whether the filtering takes place *early* or *late* in information processing, and hence they differ in terms of the nature of, and extent to which, processing of the non-attended material occurs.

Broadbent's early selection filter theory

Broadbent's (1958) theory was the first systematic attempt to explain both Cherry's findings and those of split-span experiments. Broadbent assumes that our ability to process information is *capacity limited*. Information from the senses passes 'in parallel' to a *short-term store*, a temporary 'buffer system' which holds information until it can be processed further and, effectively, extends the duration of a stimulus. The various types of information (such as two or more voices) are then passed, preserved in their original form, to a *selective filter*. This operates on the basis of the information's *physical characteristics*, selecting one source for further analysis and rejecting all others.

Information allowed through the filter reaches a *limited capacity channel* (and the filter is necessary precisely because the channel is capacity limited). This corresponds to the 'span of consciousness' (James, 1890) or what we experience as happening *now*. The information allowed through the filter is analysed in that it is recognised, possibly rehearsed, and then transferred to the motor effectors (muscles) and an appropriate response initiated.

Because Broadbent considered the short-term store to be capable of holding information for a period of time before it decayed away, two simultaneous stimuli *can* be processed provided that the processor can get back to the store before the information in it has decayed away. So, attending to one thing does not necessarily mean that everything else is lost. However, Broadbent believed that switching attention between channels took a substantial period of time, and so processing information from two channels would always take longer, and be less efficient, than processing the same information from one channel.

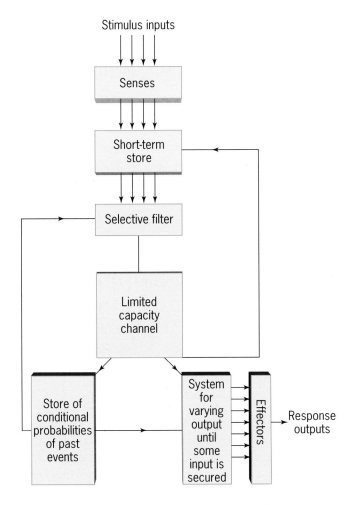

Figure 19.1 *Broadbent's theory of the flow of information between stimulus and response*

Tests of Broadbent's theory

Broadbent's theory could explain Cherry's findings concerning the fate of the non-shadowed message, because the non-shadowed message is not permitted to pass through the filter. It also explained the data from split-span experiments by proposing that the input to the relevant ear is the physical property on which the information is selected. However, the theory assumes that because the non-shadowed message is filtered out according to its physical characteristics, its *meaning* should not be subject to any sort of higher-level analysis.

However, when we are at a party, our attention sometimes switches from the person we are conversing with to another part of the room if we hear our *name* mentioned. This was demonstrated experimentally by Moray (1959), who found that when the participant's name was presented to the non-attended ear, attention switched to that ear about one-third of the time.

Box 19.2 Some experimental studies producing data inconsistent with Broadbent's theory

- Gray & Wedderburn (1960) showed that if participants were presented with 'Dear 2 Jane' in one ear and '3 Aunt 8' in the other, they were able to process the information alternately according to the ears, since they typically reported 'Dear Aunt Jane'. This indicates that the ears do not always function as different information channels, and that switching between channels is fairly easy to do.

- Treisman (1960) found that if meaningful material presented to the attended ear was switched in mid-sentence to the non-attended ear, participants would occasionally change the focus of their attention to the non-attended ear and shadow the material presented to it before changing back to the attended ear.

- Treisman (1964) discovered that if a French translation of the shadowed material was presented as non-shadowed material, some *bilingual* participants realised that the shadowed and non-shadowed material had the same meaning.

- Corteen & Wood (1972) conditioned participants to produce a *galvanic skin response* (or GSR, a minute increase in the electrical conductivity of the skin) whenever they heard a particular target word. A small electric shock was delivered immediately after the target word was heard. The target word produced a GSR when presented to the non-attended ear, and *synonyms* of it did as well. These findings were replicated by von Wright *et al.* (1975) using Finnish participants. However, in both experiments, GSRs did *not* occur on all the trials on which the conditioned words were presented.

- Mackay (1973) found that after the word 'bank' had been presented in a sentence and participants subsequently had to recognise the sentence they had heard, recognition was influenced by whether the word 'river' or 'money' had been presented to the non-attended ear.

The studies summarised in Box 19.2 suggest that the meaning of the input to the non-attended ear is processed at least sometimes. Further, Underwood's (1974) finding that participants *trained* at shadowing can detect two-thirds of the material presented to the non-attended ear casts doubt on Broadbent's claim that the non-shadowed message is always rejected at an *early* stage of processing. Additionally, when material used is sufficiently different, such as one being auditory and the other visual, memory for the non-shadowed message is good, indicating that it must have been processed at a higher level than proposed by Broadbent (Allport *et al.*, 1972).

Treisman's attenuation or stimulus-analysis system theory

According to Treisman (1960, 1964), competing information is analysed for things other than its physical properties, including sounds, syllable patterns, grammatical structure and the information's meaning (Hampson & Morris, 1996). Treisman suggested that the non-shadowed message was not filtered out early on, but that the selective filter *attenuated* it. Thus, a message not selected on the basis of its physical properties would not be rejected completely, but would be diminished in intensity (or 'turned down').

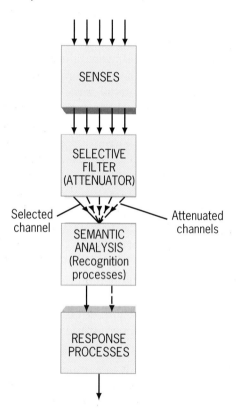

Figure 19.2 *Treisman's theory of the processes by which information is selectively attended to*

Both non-attenuated and attenuated information undergo the further analyses mentioned above. These may result in an attenuated message being attended to, depending on its features. Treisman suggested biologically relevant and emotionally important stimuli may be 'pre-sets' to which attention is switched, irrespective of the attenuated message's content. This accounts for our ability to switch attention to a different conversation when our name is mentioned. Since Treisman argues that it is the *features* of a stimulus which determine whether or not it is attended to, the concept of *probabilistic filtering* is perhaps a better

way of appreciating Treisman's theory than that of attenuation (Massaro, 1989).

The Deutsch–Norman late selection filter theory

Deutsch & Deutsch (1963) and Norman (1968, 1976) completely rejected Broadbent's claim that information is filtered out early on. According to the Deutsch–Norman theory, filtering or selection only occurs after *all inputs* have been analysed at a high level, for example, after each word has been recognised by the memory system and *analysed for meaning*.

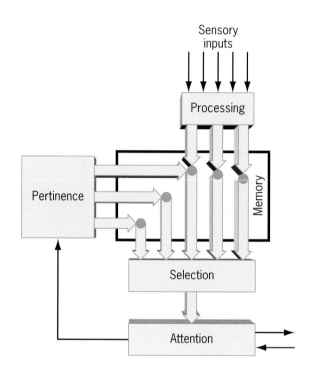

Figure 19.3 *The Deutsch–Norman theory of focused attention. All sensory inputs receive perceptual processing and are recognised in the sense that they excite their representations (the blue circles) in memory. The information selected is that which has the greatest pertinence (Norman, 1968)*

The filter is placed nearer the *response* end of the processing system, and hence it is a 'late' selection filter. Because processing will have already been undertaken on the information that has been presented before, some information will have been established as *pertinent* (most relevant) and have activated particular memory representations (hence the theory is sometimes called *pertinence theory*). When one memory representation is selected for further processing, attention becomes selective. The theory implies that we perceive everything we encounter, but are only consciously aware of some of it (Hampson & Morris, 1996).

Tests of Treisman's and the Deutsch–Norman theories

Both Treisman's and the Deutsch–Norman theories can account for the evident processing of non-shadowed material (which cannot be explained by Broadbent's theory). If the Deutsch–Norman theory is correct, then participants should be able to identify as many target words in the non-shadowed message as in the shadowed message, since the theory claims that both are completely analysed for meaning. Treisman & Geffen (1967), however, found that target words were much better detected in the shadowed message (87 per cent) than the non-shadowed message (eight per cent), an outcome consistent with Treisman's view that the non-shadowed message is attenuated.

Treisman and Geffen's findings assume that the shadowed and non-shadowed messages are *equally important*. Deutsch & Deutsch (1967) argued that this assumption was not met, because the requirement to shadow one message made the target words in that message more important. Treisman & Riley (1969) overcame this problem by requiring participants to *stop* shadowing whenever a target word was heard in *either* the attended *or* non-attended ear. Under such circumstances, performance was still better for the shadowed message (76 per cent) than for the non-shadowed message (33 per cent).

This finding is consistent with Treisman's theory, but inconsistent with the Deutsch–Norman claim that performance should not differ given that the targets were equally pertinent irrespective of the ear they were presented to. However, the detection rate for the non-attended ear in Treisman and Riley's study (33 per cent) was much higher than that in the Treisman and Geffen study (eight per cent), a finding which provides some support for the Deutsch–Norman theory.

Box 19.3 Experimental tests of the Deutsch–Norman theory

The theory predicts that participants asked immediately afterwards should be able to repeat back the words presented to the non-shadowed ear. However, the non-shadowed message gets into short-term memory for only a brief period and is then forgotten very quickly.

Norman (1969) found that participants *could* remember the last couple of words presented to the non-attended ear only if tested *immediately* rather than after a short continuation of the shadowing task, a finding replicated by Glucksberg & Cowan (1970). This relates to Neisser's (1967) *echoic memory* (see Gross *et al.* 2000). The Deutsch–Norman theory is also supported by the studies summarised in Box 19.2.

The Deutsch–Norman theory's major problem is its claim that *every* input's meaning is subjected to higher-level analysis, because this makes information processing rigid and inflexible. The data indicate that whilst not as much is known about information presented in the non-attended ear as predicted by the Deutsch–Norman model, more is known about such information than predicted by either Broadbent's or Treisman's theories! (Wilding, 1982).

Alternatives to single-channel theories of focused auditory attention

The major criticism of single-channel theories is their lack of *flexibility*, and several more 'flexible' theories have been advanced. According to Johnston & Heinz (1978), attentional selectivity can occur at several different stages of processing, depending upon the demands made by the experimental task. To minimise demands on capacity, selection is made as early as possible.

Johnston & Heinz (1979) and Johnston & Wilson (1980) have presented findings consistent with their view that processing is more flexible than predicted by single-channel theories. For example, Johnston and Wilson showed that participants processed words presented to *both* ears when they did not know to which ear particular target words would be presented, but did not do this when they did know. These data suggest that non-target words are processed only to the extent necessary to perform a task. Similarly, other alternative theories (such as Kahneman, 1973, and Norman & Bobrow, 1975) can also be applied to the phenomenon of *divided attention* (see Chapter 20).

FOCUSED VISUAL ATTENTION

According to Driver (1996):

> 'The cluttered scenes of everyday life present more objects than we can respond towards simultaneously, and often more than we can perceive fully at any one time. Accordingly, mechanisms of attention are required to select objects of interest for further processing. In the case of vision, one such mechanism is provided by eye movements, which allow us to fixate particular regions so that they benefit from the greater acuity of the fovea'.

The fovea (a very small area of the retina containing very sensitive *cone* cells: see Chapter 22, page 221) provides maximum acuity for visual stimuli. So, when we fixate on an object, maximum visual processing is given to the object that projects its image onto the fovea, whilst the resources given to the other part of the visual field are 'attenuated' (Anderson, 1995a).

Posner *et al.* (1978, 1980) found that when people are told to fixate on one part of the visual field, it is still possible to attend to stimuli seven or so degrees either side of the fixation point, and that attention can be shifted more quickly when a stimulus is presented in an 'expected' rather than an 'unexpected' location. Thus, visual attention is *not* identical to the part of the visual field which is processed by the fovea, but can be shifted without corresponding changes in eye movements. Indeed, such shifts in attention frequently *precede* the corresponding eye movement (Anderson, 1995a). Posner (1980) calls this phenomenon *covert attention*.

The internal mental spotlight and the zoom lens

Posner likened covert attention to an *internal mental spotlight* that 'illuminates' any stimulus in the attended region so that it is perceived in greater detail. It essentially duplicates the functions of eye movements internally, by allowing a particular region of space to be perceptually enhanced (Driver, 1996).

LaBerge (1983) required participants to judge whether the middle letter of five letters (such as LACIE) came from the beginning or end of the alphabet (*directed attention condition*). On some occasions, however, a stimulus such as +7+++ was presented, and the task was to determine whether the 7 was one of two letters (T or Z). LaBerge found that the speed of judgement was a function of the distance from the centre of attention. Thus, reaction times were fastest for items at the centre of the stimulus and slower at its periphery, even though all items were within the fovea's region.

LaBerge concluded that visual attention is most concentrated at the centre of the internal spotlight and least at its periphery. When material beyond its centre needs to be processed, the spotlight must be shifted to ensure maximal processing. Because this takes time, participants in Posner *et al.*'s experiments took longer to judge a stimulus when it appeared in an 'unexpected' location (Eriksen & Yeh, 1987).

LaBerge also found that when participants were required to attend to the whole five-letter word string (*global attention condition*), the 'width' of the spotlight's 'beam' increased as indicated by the lack of difference in reaction times for items at the centre and periphery. These findings led Eriksen (1990) to propose the *zoom-lens model* of visual attention which accepts the existence of an internal mental spotlight, but suggests that it has a beam which may be very narrow (in the case of LaBerge's letter task) or broad (in the case of LaBerge's word task). It is simply a *variable beam spotlight* (Groome *et al.*, 1999).

Whilst there is evidence that, consistent with the spotlight model, little or no processing occurs beyond

the spotlight (Johnston & Dark, 1986), both the spotlight and zoom-lens models have been contradicted in several studies.

> *Key* (STUDY)
>
> ### Box 19.4 Neisser & Becklen's (1975) study of selective visual attention
>
> Visual selective attention was studied by superimposing a film of three people playing a ball game on a film which showed two people's hands clapping (see Figure 19.4).
>
>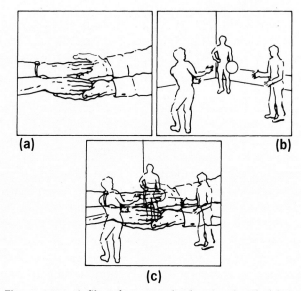
>
> **Figure 19.4** *A film of two people clapping hands (a), and three people playing a ball game (b), which have been superimposed (c)*
>
> The task was to follow one of the films and press a key to indicate that a 'critical event', such as the ball being thrown, had occurred. Whilst adults found it difficult to follow both events simultaneously, they were able to attend selectively to one or other of the films easily. This is difficult for the zoom-lens model to explain, since it proposes that the focus of attention is a given *area* in visual space rather than objects within that area (Eysenck & Keane, 1995). Using Neisser and Becklen's methodology, it has been shown that infants as young as four months can selectively follow one of the two episodes and, as a result, that selective visual attention is *innate* rather than learned (Bahrick *et al.*, 1981: see Chapter 24).

The fate of unattended visual stimuli

For Johnston & Dark (1986), stimuli beyond the focus of visual attention are subject to no or virtually no semantic processing. Any such processing is limited to mainly simple physical features. However, Driver (1996) disagrees. For example, when a picture is shown as the unattended stimulus on one trial, it slows the processing of an attended word with an identical or similar meaning on the next trial, a phenomenon called *negative priming*. The fact that processing of the attended stimulus is lessened suggests that the meaning of the unattended stimulus must have been subject to some sort of processing (Tipper & Driver, 1988).

Treisman's feature-integration theory

Treisman's (1988) theory was developed on the basis of findings using the *visual search procedure*. In this, participants are presented with an array of visual material in which a target item is embedded on some trials but absent on others, and the 'distractor' items can be varied so that they are similar to the target letter or different. The participant's task is to decide if the target is present or absent.

```
X  P  T  L  A  B  N  T

A  R  H  N  J  I  F  R

E  W  R  N  P  A  Z  X

A  H  Y  5  Y  T  E  S

A  N  H  C  E  S  T  I

G  D  T  K  D  Y  U  I
```

Figure 19.5 *A visual search array. The task is to find the number five in amongst the letters*

Neisser (1967) argued that when people perform a visual search task, they process many items simultaneously without being fully 'aware' of the exact nature of the distractor items. However, visual information processing might occur *pre-attentively* as a result of the nature of the stimuli presented (such as whether they have angular or curved features when the task is to detect a particular letter).

According to Treisman, attention must be focused on a stimulus *before* its features can be synthesised into a pattern. In one of Treisman & Gelade's (1980) experiments, participants were required to detect the presence of the letter T in amongst an array of I's and Y's. Because the horizontal bar at the top of a T, distinguishes it from an I and a Y, this could be done fairly easily just by looking for the horizontal bar. Participants took around 800 milliseconds to detect the T, and the detection time was not affected by the *size* of the array (that is, the number of I's and Y's).

In another experiment, the T was embedded in an array of I's and Z's. Here, looking for a horizontal bar on its own does not aid detection since the letter Z also has a horizontal bar on top of it. To detect a T, participants need to look for the *conjunction* of a horizontal and vertical line. They took around 1200 milliseconds to detect the T, that is, they took *longer* to recognise the conjunction of features compared with just a single feature. Moreover, detection time was *longer* when the size of the array was increased. On the basis of these (and other) findings, Treisman proposed her *feature-integration theory*.

Box 19.5 Treisman's feature–integration theory

According to Treisman, it is possible to distinguish between *objects* (such as a strawberry) and the *features* of those objects (such as being red, possessing curves, and being of a particular size). In the *first stage of visual processing*, we process the features of stimuli in the visual environment and do so rapidly and in *parallel*, without attention being required.

Next, the features of a stimulus are combined to form objects (such as a small, red strawberry). This *second stage of processing* is a slow and *serial* process (features are combined one after another). Processing is slower in this stage, because several stimuli must be processed.

Focusing attention on an object's location provides the 'glue' which allows meaningless features to be formed into objects, although features can also be combined on the basis of knowledge stored in memory (such as the knowledge that strawberries are typically red). When relevant stored knowledge is not available or focused attention absent, feature combination occurs in a random way. This can produce *illusory conjunctions* (for example, a blue banana) or odd combinations of features.

(Based on Anderson, 1995a, and Eysenck & Keane, 1995)

Criticisms of Treisman's theory and alternatives to it

Duncan & Humphreys (1992) have argued that the time taken to detect a target depends on the target's *similarity* to the distractors and the distractors' *similarity to one another*. According to their *attentional-engagement theory*, all the visual items in a display are initially segmented and analysed in parallel. After this, selective attention occurs in which items that are well matched to the description of the target item enter short-term visual memory.

Distractors which are similar to the target will *slow* the search process (because they are likely to be selected for short-term visual memory), as will non-targets that are dissimilar to each other but similar to the target (because items which are perceptually grouped will either be selected or rejected together for short-term visual memory). Since dissimilar distractors cannot be rejected together, the search process is slowed (Eysenck & Keane, 1995).

Treisman has claimed evidence for the occurrence of *illusory conjunctions* (see Box 19.5, page 195) in her visual search experiments. Treisman & Schmidt (1982), for example, required participants to identify two black digits flashed in one part of the visual field. In another part, letters in various colours were presented (such as a blue T or a red S). After reporting the digits, participants were asked what letters they had seen and their colour. Most reported seeing illusory conjunctions (such as a blue S) almost as frequently as correct conjunctions. This supports the view that accurate perception only occurs when attention is focused on an object. When it is not, the features of objects are processed but not always combined accurately.

Treisman & Sato (1990) have acknowledged that the degree of similarity between the target and the distractors is important, and the distance between Treisman's theory and Duncan and Humphreys' is narrowing, although the role of conjoining features and the importance of the similarity between non-targets remain important points of difference (Eysenck & Keane, 1995). Also, results from experiments in which moving items are intermingled with static items challenge Treisman's theory.

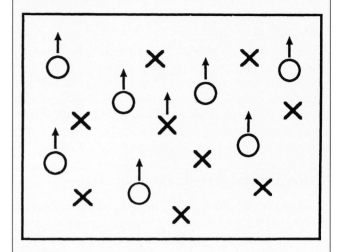

Figure 19.6 *A schematic representation of the display used by McLeod* et al. *(1991). The arrows indicate motion, and the task is to search for a single moving X amongst moving O's and intermingled static X's*

Visual attention and brain damage

Many researchers are interested in the brain regions involved in attention (e.g. Muller & Maxwell, 1994; Halligan, 1995; Driver, 1996). People who have suffered a right-hemisphere stroke involving the parietal cortex may completely ignore stimuli occurring on the opposite side to the affected hemisphere. For example, in right-hemisphere damage, they may fail to eat food from the left side of their plate and be unaware of their body on that side. The fascinating thing about this *unilateral visual neglect* is that these effects occur even though the pathways from the receptors to the central nervous system for the neglected information remain intact (see Box 11.6, pages 111–112).

According to Posner & Petersen (1990), the *parietal lobe* is responsible for disengaging attention from its present focus, and patients with damage to the pulvinar nucleus (part of the thalami) have difficulty in shifting attention to a new target (Rafal & Posner, 1987).

Interestingly, among four- to ten-year-old children, those who took *less* time to switch attention in a specially devised computer game were *more* likely to show awareness of traffic as they approached a busy road (Dunbar *et al.*, 1999).

Key STUDY

Box 19.6 McLeod *et al*.'s (1991) moving target experiment

Participants were asked to search for the presence or absence of a single moving X amongst static X's and moving O's (see Figure 19.6). The target is defined only by its specific conjunction of form and movement, since its shape is shared with the static X's and its movement with the O's. Treisman's theory would predict that serial attention was necessary for each item when searching the target, and hence that decision times would increase with an increasing number of distractors.

In fact, the target was found easily regardless of the display's size. This implies a *parallel process*, and in other experiments McLeod *et al.* showed that the parallel search arose because attention could be restricted to just the group of items with common motion to the exclusion of the static items. Because the target has a unique shape, it can be detected in parallel.

CONCLUSIONS

Research into focused auditory and visual attention indicates that we can attend selectively to certain information, and several theories have been advanced to explain how this is done. Some degree of processing of unattended material takes place in both the auditory and visual modalities, although the exact mechanisms by which this occurs have yet to be determined. However, certain parts of the brain are implicated in the ability to shift attention from one target to another.

Summary

- Whilst Titchener saw attention as of central importance to psychology, **Gestalt psychologists** thought it an unnecessary concept, and **behaviourists** rejected it as unworthy of experimental study.

- According to Broadbent, who was trying to account for Cherry's **cocktail-party phenomenon**, humans must **selectively attend** to some information and 'tune out' the rest.

- Using **binaural listening**, Cherry identified several physical differences affecting selective attention to one of two messages. When these differences were controlled for, it was very difficult to separate the meaning of the two messages.

- Cherry also used **dichotic listening**, in which participants had to **shadow** one of the messages. Although they could do this, they remembered little, if anything, of the non-shadowed message. Also, whilst the physical properties of the non-attended message were 'heard', its meaning was completely lost.

- In Broadbent's **split-span studies**, each ear was presented with different information. **Pair by pair** recall was considerably **poorer** than **ear-by-ear recall**.

- Three **single-channel theories** share the belief in a 'bottleneck' or **filter** which allows some information to be passed on for further processing, either discarding the rest or processing it only to a limited degree. They differ mainly in terms of how early or late the filtering take place.

- According to Broadbent's **early selection filter theory**, sensory information passes 'in parallel' to a **short-term store**, then onto a **selective filter**. This operates on the **physical characteristics** of the selected source, rejecting all the others.

- Broadbent's theory accounts for Cherry's findings and the split-span data. It also assumes that the **meaning** of the non-shadowed message will not be subjected to any higher-level analysis.

- People's ability to switch attention to the non-attended ear when their name is spoken, together with other research findings, are **inconsistent** with Broadbent's theory.

- According to Treisman's **stimulus-analysis system theory**, competing information is analysed for its physical properties, **and** for sounds, syllable patterns, grammatical structures and meaning. The selective filter **attenuates** the non-shadowed message. If this includes biologically and emotionally relevant stimuli ('pre-sets'), our attention will switch to the non-shadowed message.

- The **Deutsch–Norman late selection filter theory/pertinence theory** completely rejects Broadbent's claim that information is filtered out early on. Instead, selection only occurs after **all inputs** have been analysed at a high level. The filter is nearer the **response** end of the processing system (a late-selection filter).

- The Deutsch–Norman theory predicts that as many target words will be identified in the non-shadowed as the shadowed message. Also, participants should be able to repeat back the words presented to the non-attended ear if asked to do so **immediately**, otherwise they will be lost rapidly from short-term memory.

- Despite some experimental support, the Deutsch–Norman theory is inflexible. Although more processing of the non-shadowed message takes place than is claimed by either Broadbent or Treisman, it falls short of what is predicted by Deutsch and Norman.

- Alternatives to single-channel models include Johnston and Heinz's proposal that attentional selectivity can occur at several different processing stages depending on the experimental task's demands.

- Mechanisms involved in **focused visual attention** include eye movements that allow us to fixate specific regions of the visual field which can be projected on to the **fovea**.

- Visual attention is **not** identical to the part of the visual field processed by the fovea, as demonstrated by **covert attention**. This is like an **internal mental spotlight**, duplicating the functions of eye movements internally.

- When we must process material beyond the spotlight's centre, it is shifted to ensure maximal processing. According to Eriksen's **zoom-lens model of visual attention**, the internal spotlight has a beam which may be very narrow or very broad.

- According to Treisman's **feature-integration theory**, we can distinguish between **objects** and their **features**. The first stage processes the features of environmental stimuli, rapidly and in parallel, without attention being required. We then combine the features to form objects, which is done slowly and serially.

- Focusing attention on their location allows unitary features to be formed into their various objects, although these can also be combined on the basis of stored knowledge. **Illusory conjunctions** can arise in the absence of relevant stored knowledge or focused attention.

- According to Duncan and Humphreys' **attentional-engagement theory**, detection time depends on the similarity between the target and distractors and on their **similarity to one another**.

- Despite signs of convergence between Treisman and Duncan and Humphreys' theories, they still disagree over the role of combining features and of similarity between distractors. Evidence from studies of attention to moving displays is also inconsistent with Treisman's theory.

- In **unilateral visual neglect**, stroke victims ignore stimuli occurring on the opposite side to the affected hemisphere, even though the pathways from the receptors to the central nervous system remain intact. The parietal lobe seems to play an important role in switching attention.

Essay Questions

1   Describe and evaluate the contribution of psychological research to our understanding of focused (selective) attention. *(24 marks)*

2   Discuss **one** early-selection and **one** late-selection model of focused (selective) attention. *(24 marks)*

WEB ADDRESSES

http://www.bioscience.org/2000/v5/d/alain/fulltext.htm
http://www.diku.dk/~panic/eyegaze/node15.html
http://www.princeton.edu/~psych/psychsite/fac_treisman.html
http://www.multimedia.calpoly.edu
http://www.mb.jhu.edu

Divided Attention

Chapter 19 looked at studies requiring people to process the information from one of two stimulus inputs. Researchers interested in *divided attention* also typically present people with two stimulus inputs, but require responses to be made to *both* of them. Sometimes, we are able to do two things at once easily. Indeed, even though simultaneously attending to two conversations is difficult, it is not impossible (Underwood, 1974). Sometimes, though, it is extremely difficult to perform two tasks simultaneously (see Chapter 19).

The first part of this chapter looks at research findings into divided attention, including factors affecting *dual-task performance*. It then looks at theories explaining how our attention can be divided between two tasks. Some theorists have argued that, with sufficient practice, many processes become *automatic* and make no demands on attention. The second part of the chapter reviews the evidence concerning automatic (as distinct from *controlled*) processing, and considers how this can help us understand *slips associated with automatic processing* (performing behaviours that were not intended).

SOME DEMONSTRATIONS OF DUAL-TASK PERFORMANCE

Allport *et al.* (1972) showed that skilled pianists were able to successfully read music whilst shadowing speech. Later, Shaffer (1975) reported the case of an expert typist who could accurately type from sight whilst shadowing speech. However, perhaps the most striking example of dual-task performance comes from Spelke *et al.* (1976), who had two students spend five hours a week training at performing two tasks simultaneously. Initially, the students were required to read short stories whilst writing down dictated words.

At first, they found this difficult, and both their comprehension and writing suffered. After six weeks of training, however, they could read as quickly, and comprehend as much of what they read, as when reading without dictation. Interestingly, though, they could remember very little of what they had written down, even though thousands of words had been dictated to them over the course of the experiment.

At this point, the task was altered and the students had to write down the category a word belonged to, a task which required more processing of the words, whilst simultaneously reading the short stories. Again, the task was initially difficult, but the students eventually performed it without any loss in their story comprehension.

Figure 20.1 *Tasks that require us to perform more than one operation at the same time can be bewildering*

FACTORS AFFECTING DUAL-TASK PERFORMANCE

According to Hampson (1989), factors which make one task easier also tend to make the other easier because:

'Anything which minimises interference between processes or keeps them "further apart" will allow them to be dealt with more readily either selectively or together'.

Eysenck & Keane (1995) identify three factors which affect our ability to perform two tasks at once. These are *difficulty*, *practice* and *similarity*.

Box 20.1 The effects of difficulty, practice and similarity on dual-task performance

Difficulty: Generally, the more difficult tasks are, the less successful dual-task performance is. However, it is hard to define task difficulty objectively, since a task that is difficult for one person might not be for another (and this relates to practice: see below). Also, the demands made by two tasks individually are not necessarily the same when they are performed concurrently. Thus, performing two tasks together may introduce fresh demands and require interference to be avoided.

Practice: As has been seen, practice improves dual-task performance. This could be because people develop new strategies for performing each task, minimising interference between them. Another possibility is that practice reduces a task's attentional demands. Finally, practice may produce a more economical way of functioning using fewer resources (see pages 202–204).

Similarity: As was seen in both this and Chapter 19, Allport *et al.* (1972) showed that when people are required to shadow one message and learn pictorial information, both tasks can be performed successfully, presumably because they do not involve the same stimulus modality. Two tasks also disrupt performance when both rely on related memory codes (such as visual memory), make use of the same stages of processing (such as the input stage) or require similar responses to be made.

(Based on Eysenck & Keane, 1995)

A BRIEF INTRODUCTION TO THEORIES OF DIVIDED ATTENTION

The theories of selective attention described in Chapter 19 assume the existence of a limited capacity filter which is capable of dealing with one channel of information at a time. As Hampson & Morris (1996) have observed, these theories:

'... imply a series of stages of processing, starting with superficial, physical analysis, and working "upwards" towards the "higher" cognitive analyses for meaning'.

In Hampson and Morris's view, these processes are better thought of as an integrated mechanism, with the high and low levels interacting and combining in the recognition of stimuli, and that as a result it is better to look at the system's *overall processing*.

LIMITED CAPACITY THEORIES

Kahneman's theory

According to Kahneman (1973), humans have a limited amount of processing capacity, and whether tasks can be performed successfully depends on how much demand they make on the limited capacity processor. Some tasks require little processing capacity and leave plenty available for performing another task simultaneously. Others require much more and leave little 'spare' processing capacity.

Kahneman calls the process of determining how much capacity is available 'effort', and effort is involved in the allocation of that capacity. How much capacity a task requires depends on things like its difficulty and a person's experience of it. How capacity is allocated depends on *enduring dispositions*, *momentary intentions* and the *evaluation of the attentional demands* (see Figure 20.2, page 201). The central processor is responsible for the allocation policy and constantly evaluates the level of demand. When demand is too high, the central processor must decide how available attention should be allocated.

Kahneman sees *arousal* as playing an important part in determining how much capacity is available. Generally, more attentional resources are available when we are aroused and alert than when we are tired and lethargic. Attention can be divided between tasks as long as the total available capacity is not exceeded. This explains the findings from the dichotic listening tasks discussed in Chapter 19 by assuming that shadowing is a task which requires almost all of the capacity available, leaving the non-shadowed message insufficient capacity. Kahneman's theory also predicts that as skill on a task increases, so less capacity is needed for it and more becomes available for other tasks. Thus, in Underwood's (1974) study (see page 191), when people are *trained* at shadowing they become able to shadow *and* attend to the non-shadowed message.

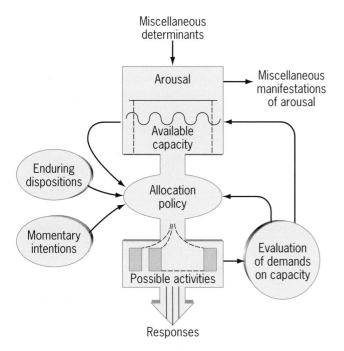

Figure 20.2 *Kahneman's theory of attention.* **Enduring dispositions** *are the rules for allocating capacity which are outside voluntary control. These include allocating capacity to novel stimuli and hearing one's own name used in a different conversation.* **Momentary intentions** *are voluntary shifts in attention such as listening to a message in a dichotic listening task.* **Evaluation of demands on capacity** *include rules for overload on the system, such as deciding to complete one task rather than failing to complete two*

Kahneman's theory suggests that attention is a much more flexible and dynamic system than suggested by the theories of focused attention described in Chapter 19. However, it does not address the issue of *how* decisions are made to channel attention, and the difficulty in defining the general limits of capacity has led some researchers to suggest that the concept of a limited capacity should be abandoned (Hampson & Morris, 1996).

Norman and Bobrow's theory

Following on from Kahneman, Norman & Bobrow (1975) have offered a *central capacity interference* account of attentional phenomena.

This theory's central feature is its distinction between *resource-limited* and *data-limited* processes. On a complex task, performance is related to the amount of resources devoted to it. As more resources are allocated, so task performance improves up to some point. Performance is thus *resource-limited*. On some tasks, though, applying more resources does not lead to improved performance because of external influences (as when participants are required to identify a quiet tone amongst loud, masking 'white' noise). This sort of task is *data-limited*, because performance can only be improved by altering the stimuli (such as by making the tone louder and/or the masking noise quieter).

This distinction between resource- and data-limited processes can explain findings from both focused and divided attention research. For example, Treisman & Geffen (1967: see page 193) found that participants shadowing words in one ear had difficulty recognising target words presented simultaneously to the other ear. Lawson (1966), however, found that under similar conditions, participants were able to detect target tones presented in the non-attended ear. This finding can be explained by proposing that the tone-detection process becomes data-limited much sooner than the word-recognition process.

Norman and Bobrow's theory can explain the results of various attention studies simply by talking about tasks in terms of their being data-limited or resource-limited. However, its biggest weakness is its inability to predict beforehand the results an experiment is likely to produce. Additionally, because the theory allows for differential allocation of resources to tasks, an experimenter can never know the level of resources allocated to a particular task. Any results can therefore be interpreted in a way consistent with the theory, and no results can ever be taken as negative evidence.

MULTI-CHANNEL THEORIES

Supporters of limited-capacity models defend their approach by pointing out that the attentional system breaks down as more and more is demanded from it, and that if data from divided-attention studies are considered carefully it is *not* true that two tasks can be performed together with no disruption at all (Broadbent, 1982). Nevertheless, several researchers have rejected the concept of a general purpose, limited-capacity processor completely. For Allport (1980, 1989, 1993), the concept of attention is often used synonymously with 'consciousness', with no specification of how it operates, and this has done little to increase our understanding of the very problems it is meant to explain.

Modules and multiple resources

According to Allport, it is difficult to see how the neurology of the brain could produce a system of processing capacity that was completely open to any of the tasks that might be presented (Hampson & Morris, 1996). It is much more profitable to view the data in terms of tasks competing for the same specialised processing mechanisms or *modules*, each of which has a limited capacity but none of which is uniquely 'central'.

When two tasks are highly similar, they compete for the same modules, and this leads to performance impairments. However, because dissimilar tasks use different modules, both can be performed simultaneously. A virtually identical theoretical account has been proposed by Navon & Gopher (1979) and Wickens (1992) in their *multiple-resource theory*. Certainly, the findings of dual-task studies (e.g. Allport *et al.*, 1972) are consistent with the idea of different processing mechanisms handling the requirements of different tasks.

Given the variation in the amount of interference that two tasks can produce for each other, it is plausible to propose that modules or multiple resources exist. However, this approach is also non-falsifiable, since any pattern of data can be explained by proposing the existence of a particular pattern of modules (Navon, 1984). Additionally, the *number* of modules has yet to be specified, and no attempt has been made to explain how people evaluate and integrate multiple sources of information. Lastly, if multiple resources operate in parallel, they must do so in a highly integrated way, given that our behaviour is typically coherent (Eysenck & Keane, 1995).

ATTEMPTS AT SYNTHESISING CAPACITY AND MODULE ACCOUNTS

According to Eysenck (1982, 1984, 1997a) and Baddeley (1986), a much better way of accommodating the data from divided-attention studies is to see capacity and module accounts as being complementary rather than competitive. *Synthesis models* propose the existence of a modality-free central capacity processor, which is involved in the coordination and control of behaviour, and specific processing systems. In Baddeley's (1986) model, for example, two independently operating and specific systems, an *articulatory/phenological loop* and a *visuo-spatial scratchpad* are proposed. These systems can explain why overt repetition of an overlearned sequence of digits does not interfere with verbal reasoning, since the former uses an *articulatory loop* and the latter a *central processor* (see Gross *et al.*, 2000).

AUTOMATIC PROCESSING

As has been seen, both laboratory evidence and everyday experience indicate that we can learn to perform two tasks simultaneously and highly efficiently. For some researchers, this is because many processes become *automatic* (in the sense that they make no attentional demands) if they are used (or practised) frequently enough. Two important theoretical contributions are those of Schneider & Shiffrin (1977) and Norman & Shallice (1986).

Schneider and Shiffrin's automaticity model

According to Schneider & Shiffrin (1977; Shiffrin & Schneider, 1977), it is possible to distinguish between *controlled* and *automatic* attentional processing. Controlled processing makes heavy demands on attentional resources, is slow, capacity limited, and involves consciously directing attention towards a task. Automatic processing, by contrast, makes no demands on attentional resources, is fast, unaffected by capacity limitations, unavoidable and difficult to modify (in the sense that it always occurs in the presence of an appropriate stimulus), and is not subject to conscious awareness.

The results of several studies (e.g. Gleitman & Jonides, 1978; Schneider & Fisk, 1982) are consistent with Schneider and Shiffrin's view, showing that if people are given practice at a task, they are able to perform it quickly and accurately, but their performance is resistant to change. An example of apparent automaticity in real life occurs when we learn to drive a car. At first, focused attention is required for each component of driving, and any distraction can disrupt performance. Once we have learned to drive, and as we become more experienced, our ability to simultaneously attend to other things increases.

Logan (1988) suggests that automaticity develops through practice, because automatic responses involve an almost effortless retrieval of an appropriate and well-learned response from memory. This does not involve conscious memory, because no thought processes intervene between the presentation of a stimulus and the production of an appropriate response. In Logan's view, then, automaticity occurs when stored information about the sequence of responses necessary to perform a task can be accessed and retrieved rapidly.

Figure 20.3 *A learner driver exhibits controlled processing to begin with; this will become automatic processing as his/her competence as a driver increases*

Despite its intuitive appeal, serious criticisms have been made of Schneider and Shiffrin's model (Eysenck & Keane, 1995). For example, it is unclear whether automaticity results from a speeding up of the processes involved in a task or a *change* in the nature of the processes themselves. Also, the view that automatic processing makes *no* demands on attention has been challenged by findings indicating that allegedly automatic tasks *do* influence the performance of simultaneously performed tasks (e.g. Hampson, 1989). Additional problems occur with the *Stroop effect*.

Key STUDY

Box 20.3 The Stroop effect

Stroop (1935) showed that if a colour word (such as 'blue') is presented in a colour with which the word conflicts (such as 'blue' being presented in red), participants find it difficult to name the *colour* the word has been presented in. Presumably, because reading is such a well learned, unavoidable and automatic activity, the word interferes with the requirement to name the colour.

An analogue of the Stroop effect can be tried here. The task is to say as quickly as you can the *number* of characters in each of the rows at the end of this box. Flowers *et al.* (1979) found that people have difficulty resisting saying the numbers that make up each row rather than counting the numbers, because number recognition is much more automated relative to number counting. Kahneman & Henik (1979) found that the Stroop effect is greater when the conflicting colour word is in the same location as the colour that has to be named than when it is in an adjacent location within the central fixation area.

This suggests that automatic responses are *not* always unavoidable (Eysenck, 1993).

```
        5   5   5
      1   1   1   1
            2
    3   3   3   3   3
          4   4
        5   5   5
    4   4   4   4   4
      5   5   5   5
            3
        4   4   4
      2   2   2   2
          3   3
        4   4   4
      1   1   1   1
            3
        2   2   2
```

The application of Schneider and Shiffrin's theory beyond the cognitive psychological domain has also met with limited success. One example is in social facilitation and impairment research. For over 100 years, social psychologists have tried to explain why people perform some tasks better (a *facilitation effect*) and others more poorly (an *impairment effect*) when other people watch their performance (Guerin, 1993).

According to Manstead & Semin (1980), 'simple' tasks are under what Adams (1976) calls *open-loop control* (equivalent to automatic processing). With such tasks, sequences of responses are run off without being monitored continuously. Abrams & Manstead (1981) propose that when we perform simple tasks, performance is suboptimal because not enough attention is paid to relevant feedback. When someone watches us perform a simple task, our attention is focused sharply on the performance, which causes feedback to be monitored more closely and performance to be improved (facilitated). According to this account, social facilitation effects only occur when a task is so well learned that continuous monitoring is not ordinarily required.

Manstead and Semin propose that 'complex' tasks are under what Adams calls *closed-loop control* (equivalent to controlled processing). Here, the performer is continuously monitoring feedback and modifying performance in the light of it. The set-backs which inevitably occur during the learning of complex tasks distract the performer's attention away from the immediate requirement of monitoring a subsequent stage of the task. This interrupts the steady progression of learning, leading to increased errors. When performance is observed, the observer acts as an additional source of distraction (especially when set-backs occur), presumably because of the performer's concern about being evaluated by those observers. This places further demands on an already-stretched attentional system, and results in an increase in errors.

Thus, the effects of being watched will only occur at or near the extremes of what Abrams & Manstead (1981) call a *task mastery continuum*. For them:

'The presence of a critical audience should improve the driving of a highly experienced driver, but impair that of a novice driver, since the latter would suffer from attentional overload whereas the former has spare attentional capacity which can be devoted to considering the audience's reaction to the task performance'.

Unfortunately, data exist which indicate that 'simple' task performance can be impaired by the presence of others whilst 'complex' task performance can be improved in their presence. Defining task difficulty objectively is not easy (see Box 20.1, page 200). However, unless it is assumed that the 'simple' tasks in such experiments were actually 'complex' and vice versa, the application of automatic and controlled processing to social facilitation and impairment is not strongly supported by evidence.

Norman and Shallice's SAS model

To overcome what Eysenck (1993) calls the 'unavoidability criterion', Norman & Shallice (1986) have proposed that processing involves *two* separate control systems, which they call *contention scheduling* and the *supervisory attentional system* (SAS). They accept that some behaviours involve *fully automatic processing,* and that this occurs with little conscious awareness of the processes involved, since it is controlled by schemas (or organised plans for behaviour: see page 205).

However, such processes are capable of disrupting behaviour, and so contention scheduling occurs as a way of resolving conflicts among schemas. This produces *partially automatic processing* which generally involves more conscious awareness than fully automatic processing, but occurs without deliberate direction or conscious control. *Deliberate control* involves the SAS and is involved in decision-making and trouble-shooting, allowing flexible responding to occur in novel situations. Baddeley (1997) claims that SAS is like the operation of free will, whilst contention scheduling leaves no place for free will (see Chapter 57).

According to Eysenck & Keane (1995), Norman and Shallice's model is superior to Schneider and Shiffrin's because it:

'... provides a more natural explanation for the fact that some processes are fully automatic whereas others are only partially automatic'.

Although not worked out in the same degree of detail, or empirically tested as extensively as Schneider and Shiffrin's automaticity model, Norman and Shallice's SAS model provides a very useful basis for conceptualising the central executive of Baddeley & Hitch's (1974) working-memory model (Baddeley, 1997: see Gross *et al.*, 2000).

ACTION SLIPS

These have been defined as the performance of unintended actions, or actions which deviate from the actor's intentions, and have been extensively researched by Reason (1979, 1992). Reason originally asked 36 participants to keep a diary record of the action slips they made over a four-week period. The participants recorded 433 action slips between them. Reason was able to place 94 per cent of these into one of five categories.

Box 20.4 Reason's five categories of action slips

1 **Storage failures:** These were the most common and accounted for 40 per cent of those recorded. They involve performing again an action that has already been completed. An example would be pouring a second kettle of boiling water into a tea pot of freshly made tea without any recognition of having made the tea already.

2 **Test failures:** These involve forgetting the goal of a particular sequence of actions and switching to a different goal. An example would be intending to turn on the radio but walking past it and picking up the telephone instead. These accounted for 20 per cent of those recorded, and presumably occur because a planned sequence of actions is not monitored sufficiently at some crucial point in the sequence.

3 **Sub-routine failures:** Accounting for 18 per cent of the action slips recorded, these involve either omitting or re-ordering the stages in a sequence of behaviour. An example would be making a pot of tea but failing to put any tea bags in it.

4 **Discrimination failures:** These involve failing to discriminate between two objects involved in different actions. An example would be mistaking toothpaste for shaving cream. These accounted for 11 per cent of the total recorded.

5 **Programme assembly failures:** This was the smallest category, accounting for five per cent of the total recorded. They involve incorrectly combining actions as in unwrapping a sweet, putting

the paper in your mouth, and throwing the sweet in the waste-paper bin.

(Based on Reason, 1992, and Eysenck, 1997b)

Paradoxically, action slips seem to occur with highly practised and over-learned actions (which should, therefore, be least subject to errors). Reason (1992) proposes that when we first learn to perform a behaviour, our actions are subject to *closed-loop control* (see page 203). In this, a central processor or attentional system guides and controls behaviour from start to finish. When we are skilled at a behaviour, it is under *open-loop control* (see page 203) and controlled by motor programs or other automatic processes.

Closed-loop control is slow and effortful, whereas open-loop control is fast and allows attentional resources to be given over to other activities. However, closed-loop control is less prone to error and responds more flexibly to environmental demands than open-loop control. As a result, action slips occur because of an over-reliance on open-loop control when closed-loop control (selectively attending to the task) should be occurring.

As seen in studies of focused attention (see Chapter 19), material not attended to is typically poorly remembered because it does not get stored in long-term memory. The most common type of action slip, storage failures, can thus be explained in terms of open-loop induced attentional failures leading to a failure to store (and hence recall) previous actions. As a result, an action may be repeated. Other slips also seem amenable to explanation in terms of open-loop control (Eysenck, 1997b).

"Damn! I keep forgetting it's AD not BC now..."

Figure 20.4 *What kind of action slip do you think this is?*

An alternative theoretical account has been advanced by Norman (1981) and elaborated by Sellen & Norman (1992). Their theory is based on the concept of the schema, first proposed by Bartlett (1932). Briefly, a schema is an organised mental representation of everything we understand by a given object, concept or event, based on past experience (see page 204).

Box 20.5 Sellen & Norman's (1992) schema theory of action slips

This distinguishes between *parent* and *child* schemas. Parent schemas are the highest-level schemas and correspond to an overall intention or goal (such as going to a football match). At a lower level are child schemas, which correspond to the actions involved in accomplishing the overall intention or goal (such as driving the car to the football ground, buying a ticket and so on). Each schema has a particular activation level, and a behaviour occurs when the activation level is reached (which depends on the current situation and current intentions) and appropriate 'triggering' conditions exist.

If (a) there is an error in the formation of an intention, (b) an incorrect schema is activated, (c) activation of the correct schema is lost, or (d) there is faulty triggering of an active schema, then an action slip occurs. Thus, a regular beer drinker may decide, because he or she is driving, not to drink alcohol on a visit to the pub with friends. However, without realising it, the drinker finds he or she has ordered a pint of beer in the pub as a result of faulty triggering.

Reason & Mycielska (1982) believe that a thorough understanding of the nature of action slips is necessary to avoid potential disaster occurring in the real world (see, for example, Box 27.6, page 290). Eysenck (1994) maintains that action slips would be eliminated if we were to use closed-loop control for all behaviours. However, this would be a waste of valuable attentional resources! The frequency of action slips reported by Reason's (1979) participants (an average of about one per day) suggests that people alternate between closed-loop and open-loop control as the circumstances dictate. For Eysenck (1994):

'The very occasional action slip is a price which is generally worth paying in order to free the attentional system from the task of constant monitoring of our habitual actions'.

Action slips represent the minor errors of an action system that typically functions very well indeed (Eysenck, 1997b). Similarly:

'Absent-minded errors demonstrate misapplied competence rather than incompetence'. (Reason, 1984)

Each type of action slip might require its own explanation, because whilst the mechanisms underlying them may appear similar, they might actually be very different (Eysenck & Keane, 1995). Additionally, any theoretical account depends on the validity of the data it attempts to explain. The diary method employed by Reason may supply weak data, because participants might not have detected some of their action slips or remembered to record them when they did (Eysenck, 1997b). As a result, the percentages reported by Reason may be inaccurate.

Box 20.6 Reason's (1992) 'oak–yolk effect' experiment

Participants are instructed to answer the following series of questions as quickly as possible.

Q What do we call the tree that grows from acorns?

A Oak

Q What do we call a funny story?

A Joke

Q What sound does a frog make?

A Croak

Q What is Pepsi's major competitor?

A Coke

Q What's another word for cape?

A Cloak

Q What do you call the white of an egg?

A Yolk

'Yolk' is, in fact, the wrong answer (correct answer = albumen). Reason found that 85 per cent of his participants made this error, compared with only five per cent of a control group given just the final question. However, are such trick-induced action slips comparable to those that occur spontaneously in everyday life? According to Sellen & Norman (1992), the laboratory environment is the least likely place to see truly spontaneous absent-minded errors.

Finally, in Eysenck & Keane's (1995) words:

'The number of occurrences of any particular kind of action slip is meaningful only when we know the number of occasions on which the slip might have occurred but did not. Thus, the small number of discrimination failures [reported by Reason] may reflect either good discrimination or a relative lack of situations requiring anything approaching a fine discrimination'.

CONCLUSIONS

It is sometimes possible to divide attention between two different tasks, although how this is achieved has not yet been satisfactorily explained. Two broad types of explanation are those which propose a general purpose limited-capacity processor, and those which identify modules, each with a limited capacity but none of which is central. The idea that many processes become automatic and make no demands on attention has some support, and helps explain why we sometimes perform behaviours we did not intend. Action slips involve behaviours that are highly practised and are the price we pay for not having to continuously monitor our actions.

Summary

■ Researchers interested in divided attention typically present people with two stimulus inputs, and require them to respond to both (**dual-task performance**). Three factors affecting dual-task performance are **task difficulty**, **practice** and **similarity**.

■ Two tasks disrupt performance when they both involve the same stimulus modality, rely on related memory codes, make use of the same processing stages, or require similar responses to be made.

■ Theories of selective attention assume the existence of a limited capacity filter, capable of dealing with only one information channel at a time. Instead of a series of processing stages, we should consider the system's **overall processing**.

■ According to Kahneman, humans have only a limited processing capacity. Different tasks require different amounts of processing capacity, leaving more or less available for performing other tasks.

■ The **central processor** controls the allocation policy and constantly evaluates demand level. **Arousal** is important for determining the amount of available capacity, and the more skilled we are at a particular task, the less capacity is needed.

■ Norman and Bobrow's **central capacity interference** theory distinguishes between **resource-limited** and **data-limited** performance. This can explain findings from both focused and divided-attention studies but cannot predict **beforehand** whether an experiment is likely to produce data-limited or resource-limited data.

■ Several researchers have rejected the concept of a general purpose, limited-capacity processor. They argue that the most useful way of interpreting the data is in terms of tasks competing for the same **modules**, each of which has a limited capacity but none of which is uniquely 'central'.

■ Two highly similar tasks compete for the same modules, leading to performance deficits, whilst dissimilar tasks use different modules and thus do not compete. This view is also taken by **multiple-resource theory**.

■ Eysenck and Baddeley believe that capacity and module accounts are complementary. **Synthesis models** propose the existence of a modality-free central capacity processor, which coordinates and controls behaviour, plus specific independent processing systems, such as Baddeley's **articulatory/phonological loop** and **visuo-spatial scratchpad**.

■ Schneider and Shiffrin distinguish between **controlled** and **automatic processing**. Practice makes performance fast and accurate, but resistant to change. According to Logan, practice leads to automaticity through effortless retrieval from memory of an appropriate and well-learned response, with no intervening conscious thought processes.

■ The '**Stroop effect**' shows that well-learned, unavoidable and automatic skills (such as reading) can interfere with other tasks (such as naming the colour of a written word).

■ **Contention scheduling** is used to resolve conflicts among **schemas** which control **fully automatic processing** and produces **partially automatic processing**. The **supervisory attentional system** (SAS) is involved in **deliberate control**, which allows flexible responses in novel situations.

■ The most common type of **action slips** are **storage failures**. Other categories include **test**, **sub-routine**, **discrimination** and **programme assembly failures**.

■ Paradoxically, action slips seem to involve actions that are highly practised or over-learned. Performance of new behaviours is subject to **closed-loop control**, whilst skilled performance is under **open-loop control**. Action slips reflect an over-reliance on open-loop control when focused attention is needed. Different types of action slip may require their own explanations.

Essay Questions

1   **a**   Describe research into controlled and automatic processing. *(12 marks)*

    b   Assess the extent to which such research helps us to identify the limits of divided attention.
(12 marks)

2   Discuss research into slips associated with automatic processing. *(24 marks)*

WEB ADDRESSES

http://www.cc.gatetech.edu/~jimmyd/summaries/index.html
http://ear.berkeley.edu/auditory_lab/
http://www.wws.princeton.edu/faculty/kahneman.htm

21 *Pattern Recognition*

INTRODUCTION AND OVERVIEW

Pattern recognition is the process by which we assign meaning to visual input by identifying the objects in the visual field (Eysenck, 1993). Although our ability to recognise, identify and categorise objects seems effortless, it actually comprises several remarkably complex achievements. Whilst we are usually aware only of structured, coherent objects:

> 'Our visual systems have to "decide" which edges, surfaces, corners and so on go together to form units or wholes'. (Roth, 1995)

A major contribution to our understanding of this process comes in the form of the Gestalt laws of perception, which are discussed in Chapter 23. Pattern (or object) recognition can be regarded as the central problem of perception and, indeed, the terms are almost synonymous. To this extent, all the theories of perception discussed in Chapter 23 can be thought of as trying to account for pattern recognition (PR).

However, this chapter begins by considering some additional theories, which are usually referred to as theories of PR (rather than perceptual theories), including the *template-matching hypothesis*, *Biederman's geon theory*, *prototype theories* and *feature detection theories*. The second part of the chapter discusses research into *face recognition* as a special case of PR.

THE CHALLENGE OF PR

As Roth (1995) says (see above), what theories of PR must do is explain the complexity of a process which 'is so ingrained in our experience that we rarely even notice that we do it' (Houston *et al.*, 1991). A way of illustrating this challenge is to consider the ease with which we are able to recognise the letter 'T', whether it is printed on paper, handwritten or spoken. As Figure 21.1 shows, the letter 'T' can be presented in many different ways.

T T *T* **T***T* **T T** *T* **T T** *T* **T** *T* / *T* **T** **T** *T* **T** *T* **T** *T* *T* **T T**

Figure 21.1 *Anyone for T?*

TEMPLATE-MATCHING HYPOTHESIS

According to the *template-matching hypothesis* (TMH), incoming sensory information is matched against miniature copies (or templates) of previously presented patterns or objects which are stored in long-term memory. Template-matching is used by computerised cash regis-ters, which identify a product and its cost by matching a bar code with some stored representation of that code.

Given the complexity of the environment, we would need to possess an incredibly large number of templates, each corresponding to a specific visual input. Even if we were able to use a wheelbarrow to carry around the cere-brum needed for this, the time needed to search for a specific template would be inordinately long, and we would never recognise unfamiliar patterns (Solso, 1995).

BIEDERMAN'S GEON THEORY

Biederman's (1987) *geon theory of PR* ('geon' stands for 'geometrical icon') or *recognition-by-components* model, is intended to overcome TMH's limitations. Biederman's starting point is the everyday observation that if we are asked to describe an object, familiar or unfamiliar, we tend to use the same basic strategy. We almost certainly divide it into parts or components (*parsing/segmentation*), comprising various 3-D shape concepts (*volumetric con-cepts* or *geons*), such as 'block', 'cylinder', 'funnel' and 'wedge'. The regions of the object used to divide it up are probably the regions of greatest *concavity* (where one part makes a sharp angle with another part). According to geon theory, a very large range of different objects can be described by combining geons in various ways. Geons (simple geometric 'primitives') can be combined to produce more complex ones.

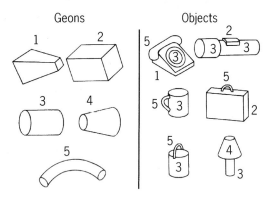

Figure 21.2 *Biederman's geons (left) and some of the objects they can combine to make (right)*

Component- or geon-based information extracted from the visual object is matched in parallel against stored representations of 36 geons that make up the basic set. The identification of any visual object is determined by whichever stored representation provides the best fit. However, for a *complete* object to be recognised, there must also be a store of complete object descriptions, in which both the characteristic geon set and *relationships* amongst it are specified (Roth, 1995).

An evaluation of geon theory

According to Roth (1995), Biederman's theory was designed to provide an intuitively plausible account of how we recognise objects in terms of their obvious components, and to explain the fact that this recognition is both rapid and accurate, despite variations in angle of viewing and the 'degraded' information available (such as poor lighting, one object obscuring another and so on).

Key STUDY

Box 21.1 Experimental tests of Biederman's theory

One general prediction is that since an appropriate arrangement of geons provides a very powerful cue for object recognition, this recognition will occur even when an object's full complement of geons is absent. To test this, Biederman (1987) produced line drawings of 36 common objects, differing in complexity (the number of basic geon components needed to draw them ranged from two to nine). For each drawing, there were 'partial' versions (one or more geons were missing), and each stimulus was presented for 100 ms via a tachistoscope. Participants had to name the object aloud as quickly as possible.

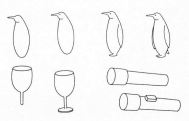

Figure 21.3 *Complete and partial versions of objects used in Biederman's experiment*

Error rates for 'partial' objects were extremely low, with 90 per cent accuracy even for complex objects with two-thirds of their components missing. So, even the simplest line drawings can be readily and correctly identified, provided the relevant geons are present. These findings are consistent with the model. Also, response times were almost as fast for partial as for complete objects, although complex complete objects were slightly more quickly identified than simple complete objects. This too is consistent with the model: if an object's geons are simultaneously matched with stored geon descriptions, then the more such geons are available, the faster the critical level needed for a 'match' will be reached.

A more stringent test is participants' ability to identify degraded versions of objects, in which the normal contours are disrupted. In a second experiment (using the same basic procedure as the first), stimulus objects like those in Figure 21.4 were presented.

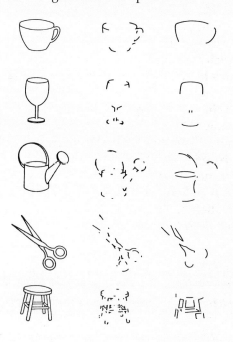

Figure 21.4 *The middle column shows degraded but 'recognisable' versions; the right-hand column shows 'non-recognisable' versions*

The middle column shows degraded versions which are still recognisable, whilst those in the right-hand column are non-recognisable. In the latter, the contours have been deleted at regions of concavity (at sharp angles which are important for dividing objects into geons). These stimuli were presented for 100, 200 or 750 ms, with 25, 45 or 65 per cent of their contours removed. Once again, results supported the model.

Roth (1995) believes that geons are intuitively appealing and also offer a relatively flexible and comprehensive system for describing objects. Geons include a range of different shapes that can be applied not only to artifacts such as chairs, tables and houses, but also mammals and other animals. Although the model makes clear predictions which can be experimentally tested (see Box 21.1), identification of the 36 geons and structural relationships is based more on 'hunch' than empirical evidence. There have been no tests of the model to determine whether it is *these* geons which are used in object recognition rather than other components.

PROTOTYPE THEORIES OF PR

Prototype theories propose that instead of storing templates, we store a smaller number of *prototypes* ('abstract forms representing the basic elements of a set of stimuli': Eysenck, 1993). Whereas TMH treats each stimulus as a separate entity, prototype theories maintain that similarities between related stimuli play an important part in PR. So, each stimulus is a member of a *category* of stimuli and shares basic properties with other members of the category.

The main weakness of this approach is its inability to explain how PR is affected by the *context* as well as by the stimulus itself (Eysenck, 1993). Knowing just what properties are shared by a category of stimuli is important, but not specified by the theories. What, for example, is an 'idealised' letter 'T' and what is the 'best representation of the pattern? This question has been addressed by *feature-detection theories*.

FEATURE-DETECTION THEORIES

Feature-detection theories form the most influential approach to PR, maintaining that every stimulus can be thought of as a configuration of elementary features. Gibson *et al.* (1968) argue that the letters of the alphabet, for example, are composed of combinations of 12 basic features (such as vertical lines, horizontal lines and closed curves).

Box 21.2 Some experimental findings supporting feature–detection theories

In *visual scanning* tasks, participants search lists of letters as quickly as possible to find a randomly placed target letter. Since finding a target letter entails detecting its elementary features, the task should be more difficult when the target and non-target letters have more features in common. This is exactly what researchers have found (e.g. Rabbitt, 1967). Additional support comes from *studies of eye movements and fixation*. Presumably, the more a feature in a pattern is looked at, the more information is being extracted from it. The perception of features within complex patterns depends on higher cognitive processes (such as attention and purpose), as well as the nature of the physical stimuli being looked at.

For example, Yarbus (1967) found that when participants were shown the scene in Figure 21.5, different patterns of eye movements were recorded depending on whether they were asked to: (1) examine the picture at will; (2) estimate the economic status of the people shown; (3) judge their ages; (4) query what they had been doing prior to the arrival of the visitor; (5) remember their clothing; (6) remember their positions (and objects in the room); or (7) estimate how long since the visitor had last seen the family.

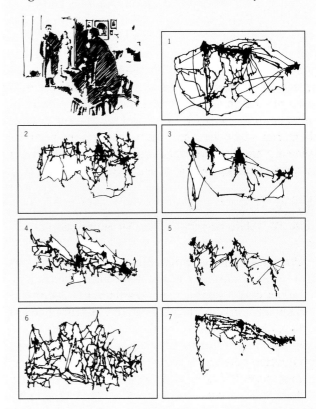

Figure 21.5 *Different patterns of eye movements corresponding to different instructions*

It is also well established that the visual systems of some vertebrates contain both peripheral (retinal) and central (cortical) cells that respond only to particular features of visual stimuli. In their pioneering research, Hubel & Wiesel (1968) identified three kinds of cortical cell (which they called 'simple', 'complex' and 'hypercomplex' to refer to the types of stimuli the cells respond to: see Chapter 22, pages 222–223). More recently, it has been claimed that there are face-specific cells in the infero–temporal cortex of the monkey (Ono *et al.*, 1993: see below, pages 216–217).

In humans, Perrett (cited in Messer, 1995) has identified cells that respond to specific aspects of a face or to a set of features. There may also be cells which respond to many different views of a face, 'summing' inputs from a variety of sources.

An evaluation of feature-detection theories

Whether such cells constitute the feature detectors proposed by feature-detection theories is unclear. These neurological detectors may be a necessary pre-condition for higher-level (or cognitive) pattern task analysis. However, feature-detection theories typically assume a *serial* form of processing, with feature extraction being followed by feature combination, which itself is then followed by PR (Eysenck, 1993). For example, Hubel and Wiesel saw the sequence of simple, complex and hyper-complex cells representing a serial flow of information, whereby only particular information is processed at any one time before being passed on to the next level upwards, and so on. The alternative and widely held view is that considerable *parallel* (non-serial) processing takes place in the visual cortex, and that the relationship between different kinds of cortical cell is more complex than originally believed. An early example of a non-serial processing computer program is Selfridge's (1959) *Pandemonium model*.

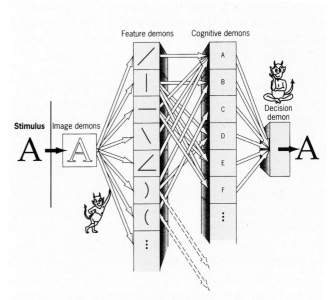

Figure 21.6 *A representation of Selfridge's Pandemonium model of pattern recognition (based on Ruch, 1984)*

Although *Pandemonium* was never intended as a model of human perception, Groome *et al.* (1999) ask what *assumptions* about human perception would need to be made if it were modelled in such terms. These could then be tested against human data. One such assumption is that context would have minimal effect on PR. This relates to a criticism that has been made of feature-detection theories in general, namely, failure to take sufficient account of the role played by *context* and *perceiver characteristics* (such as expectations: see Box 23.6, page 241). An ambiguous feature can produce *different* patterns, and different features can produce the *same* pattern, depending on the context.

Context can tell us what patterns are likely to be present and hence what to expect. Sometimes, we may fail to notice the *absence* of something (such as typing or printing errors) because of its high predictability. The influence of context and expectation illustrates *top-down/conceptually-driven processing*, whilst most feature-detection theories are *bottom-up/data-driven* (see theories of perception in Chapter 23). PR involves *selectively attending* to some aspects of the presented stimuli but not to others, aided by context. PR and *selective attention* are therefore closely related (Solso, 1995: see Chapters 19 and 20).

Box 21.3 Selfridge's (1959) Pandemonium model

Selfridge's computer program was designed to recognise Morse code and a small set of handwritten letters. The components of the model are known as *demons*, of which there are four kinds. *Image demons* simply copy the pattern presented (and these are analogous to the retina). *Feature demons* analyse the information from the image demons in terms of combinations of features. *Cognitive demons* are specialised for particular letters and 'scream' according to how much the input from the feature demons matches their special letter. Finally, a *decision demon* chooses the 'loudest scream' and identifies the letter as shown in Figure 21.6.

FACE RECOGNITION

Just as we can identify different categories of dogs or chairs, so we can identify 'baby's face', 'man's face' or

'Japanese face'. We also have some ability to identify individual dogs or chairs, but in the case of human faces this ability to identify *individuals* is of paramount importance (Bruce, 1995). Recognising faces is probably one of the most demanding tasks that we set our visual systems. Unlike most other cases of object identification, the task is to identify one specific instance of the class of objects known as faces (Groome *et al.*, 1999).

Strictly, *face recognition* (using the face to identify an individual) is part of the broader process of *face perception* (the whole range of activities where information is derived from the face, such as inferring emotional states from facial expressions). According to Eysenck & Keane (1995), substantial recent research has provided greater knowledge about the processes involved in face recognition than about those involved in most other forms of PR.

Are faces more than the sum of their parts?

Based on theories of basic level PR (such as Biederman's geon theory: see pages 209–211), faces could be described as a set of parts (the features) and their spatial arrangement. However, it seems more valid to describe faces in a more configural way (Bruce, 1995).

Box 21.4 The meanings of 'configural'

According to Bruce (1995), although psychologists tend to agree that a face is greater than the sum of its parts, studies of face perception have not always made explicit which sense of 'configural' is being investigated. She identifies three meanings:

- The *spatial relationships* between features are as important as the features themselves;
- Facial features *interact* with one another (for example, perception of mouth shape is affected by the shape of the nose);
- Faces are processed *holistically* (they are not analysed into separable features at all).

However, early research into face recognition implicitly assumed that a part-based description might be appropriate, comprising a list of features each with different specific values. Many psychologists during the 1970s used *artificially constructed faces*, such as Bradshaw & Wallace's (1971) use of Identikit. This refers to a set of varying line-drawn features used by the police to construct a criminal/suspect's face, based on a witness's description.

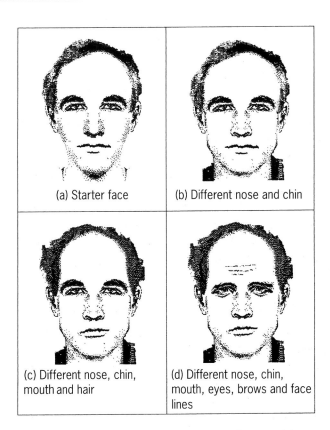

Figure 21.7 *Examples of Identikit faces used in Bradshaw & Wallace's (1971) experiment*

Bradshaw and Wallace presented pairs of faces and explored how quickly participants decided that two faces in a pair were different as a function of the number of features that differed. They found that the *more* differences between the two faces, the *faster* participants responded, and they concluded that facial features are processed independently and in sequence. Sergent (1984) reviewed several other studies which reached similar conclusions.

However, Sergent also noted that faces which differed in several features also differed more in terms of overall configuration than those differing only in a few. If features really are processed independently, the number of feature differences should not affect how quickly a 'difference' judgement is made (the judgement can be made as soon as any *one* feature difference is spotted). Accordingly, Sergent constructed eight slightly different faces from the same 'kit' of face features, but each had one of two different *chins*, *eye colours* and arrangements of internal features (*internal space*). 'Different' pairs (one, two or three feature differences) were intermixed with pairs of identical faces, and participants were asked to decide whether the 'different' pairs were the same or different.

Sergent confirmed Bradshaw and Wallace's finding that the more features that differed, the faster a 'difference' decision was made. However, when only a single feature differed, 'difference' decisions were faster when this involved *chins* (and this was true for all participants), and when something in addition to chins differed, the decisions were even faster. This latter finding suggests that there is *interactive processing* of different dimensions of facial appearance: a configuration emerges from a set of features that is more than the sum of its parts (see Box 21.4, page 213).

Are upright and inverted faces processed differently?

An interesting additional finding from Sergent's study was that when she repeated the experiment using *inverted* face images, the results supported the view that the face is processed as a set of *independent* features. Several other studies have confirmed this finding.

Box 21.5 Evidence relating to differential processing of upright and inverted faces

- Tanaka & Farah (1993) found that facial features learned in the context of an *upright* normal face were more likely to be identified correctly in the context of that face (as opposed to being tested in isolation). However, this advantage was not found for *inverted* faces. They concluded that the representation of whole faces is based on a *holistic* description, whilst inverted faces (as well as houses and scrambled faces: see Chapter 24) are represented as a set of *independent components*.

- According to Yin (1969), whilst upright faces are recognised more accurately than physical objects, the reverse is true for inverted faces. Somehow, the different features in inverted faces cannot be integrated to give a coherent impression. This is one of the best established findings in the field of face recognition (Bruce, 1995).

- Young *et al.* (1987) took pictures of well-known faces and sliced them horizontally to form separate upper and lower face halves. They then paired the upper half with a 'wrong' lower half. Participants were asked to name the top halves of faces presented either in isolation or when paired with the 'wrong' lower halves. The top halves were much harder to name when combined with the wrong lower halves than when shown alone, or when the two correct halves were misaligned. Young *et al.*'s explanation was that combining the two halves produced a 'new' configuration. Significantly, when composite faces were inverted, participants named them *more* accurately than when they were presented upright.

- In Thompson's (1980) *Thatcher illusion*, the eyes and mouth are cut out and inverted within the face. When viewed upright, this produces a grotesque appearance, but when inverted, it looks quite similar to the 'normal' version.

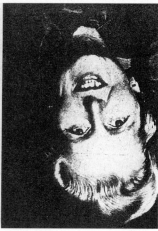

Figure 21.8 *The Thatcher illusion*

According to Bartlett & Searcy (1993), the most likely explanation of the Thatcher illusion is what they call the *configural processing hypothesis*. The relationship between the features is more difficult to perceive when the face is inverted (so the features are processed *independently*), and the strangeness of the grotesque face cannot be seen (since it arises from the *relationship between* the features).

If Bartlett and Searcy are correct, does this necessarily mean that there is something special about face recognition? A study by Diamond & Carey (1986) of dog breeders and judges suggests that *expertise* may be the crucial variable. These dog experts were just as affected by the inversion of dog pictures as non-experts were by the inversion of human faces. So, perhaps it is configural processing that enables experts to make fine discriminations within a particular category in which all the members share the same overall structure. When it comes to human face recognition, we all appear to be experts.

Disorders of face processing

Whilst we might all be experts at face recognition, there are rare but dramatic cases of people who are unable to recognise familiar faces, including those of their spouses, other relatives and friends. The most common such disorder is *prosopagnosia*.

Box 21.6 A case of prosopagnosia

McNeil & Warrington (1993) report the case of W.J., a 51-year-old man who suffered a series of strokes, causing lesions in his left occipital, frontal and temporal lobes. When shown a set of three photographs (one famous and two unfamiliar faces), he could not select the famous one. However, if he was asked 'Which one is ...?', his performance improved significantly (*covert recognition*). Following the onset of his prosopagnosia, he acquired a flock of sheep which he photographed. He knew them by number and could recognise at least eight of the 16 pictures. This represents remarkable evidence of an ability to learn to recognise individual sheep, whilst still being profoundly prosopagnosic for human faces (Groome *et al.*, 1999).

As the case of W.J. demonstrates, prosopagnosia appears to be a face-specific deficit. Several other case studies show that patients can still identify personal possessions (including non-human animals) and can recognise faces if tested indirectly (unconscious or covert recognition: Groome *et al.*, 1999). Covert recognition suggests that prosopagnosia is *not* a memory deficiency.

Some of these patients can derive particular kinds of meaning from faces (including emotional expression), despite being unable to recognise them. Conversely, some patients with a form of dementia find it difficult to recognise emotional expressions, whilst still able to classify famous faces according to occupation (which requires knowledge of personal identity: Kurucz & Feldmar, 1979). The task of recognising individual identity from a face, therefore, seems to be quite separate from that of recognising an emotional expression. Whilst the former requires recognition of an individual regardless of the expression, the latter requires recognising emotion irrespective of other aspects of facial appearance. Experiments with normal adults have shown that identity seems to be ignored when identifying emotional expressions, and expressions are identified no more quickly from familiar than from unfamiliar faces.

Models of face recognition

According to Bruce (1995), the complete identification of a known face requires not just that we recognise the pattern of the face as a familiar one, but that we know the context in which we have encountered the person and can retrieve his/her name. Studies of both normal and brain-damaged people suggest that there is a sequence of distinct *stages* involved in retrieving someone's identity, with failures at each stage characterised by different problems of identification.

Hay & Young (1982) were the first to outline a stage model, which was supported by the pattern of errors reported by Young *et al.* (1985) in their diary study of everyday failures in person identification. On the basis of their data, Young *et al.* proposed a model of the functional components involved in person identification, as shown in Figure 21.9.

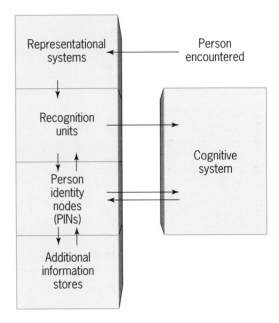

Figure 21.9 *Young* et al.*'s (1985) model of the functional components involved in person identification*

After representational processing, information about the face of the person encountered is processed by *recognition units*. These contain stored representations of known faces. If the currently viewed face matches one of these representations, information about the resemblance is signalled to *person identity nodes* (PINs), where basic information about personal identity is stored, and via which names and other details are accessed (from the *additional information stores*). Decisions as to whether or not a particular face is familiar, or about the person's identity, are made as a result of communication between these levels and the *cognitive system*.

This model was revised by Bruce & Young (1986). In their revised model, the stages of person identification (as shown in Figure 21.9) are put into the broader context of their relationship with the other uses made of facial information. The model comprises several different processing 'modules' linked in sequence or in parallel (see Figure 21.10, page 216).

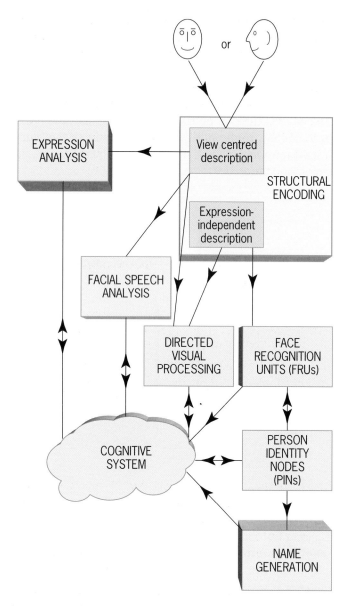

Figure 21.10 *Bruce & Young's (1986) functional model for face recognition*

An evaluation of the Bruce & Young (1986) model

According to Groome *et al.* (1999), the dissociation between processing of emotional expression and person identification makes good sense. We need to be able to recognise a face irrespective of which expression it is displaying and vice versa. Despite being broad, Bruce (1995) believes the model has the strength of being falsifiable.

Some relevant experimental evidence comes in the form of the *tip-of-the-tongue* (TOT) *phenomenon* for people's names (see Gross *et al.*, 2000). Brennen *et al.* (1990) wanted to know if participants in a TOT state, after being asked to identify someone from a description, could be helped to retrieve the name by viewing a picture of the person or by being given the initals of the missing name. Providing the initials allowed about half the missing names to be retrieved, but pictures produced just as little success as simply repeating the questions. These results are consistent with Bruce and Young's model. In a TOT state, participants must be at the stage of PINs, but are unable to reach the next stage of name retrieval. Seeing the face should not help, since there is no direct link between faces and names, but the initials provide partial cues to help name retrieval.

However, evidence of *covert recognition* in prosopagnosic patients (see Box 21.6, page 215) are difficult for the model to explain. Familiarity judgements are supposedly made on the basis of activation levels at FRUs, forming an early stage in the sequence of establishing the person's full identity. If patients consistently fail to make familiarity judgements at better than chance levels, they should be unable to access information from later ('deeper') levels (stages) in the system. Yet this is exactly what covert recognition entails. Partly as an attempt to overcome these difficulties, the model was revised and extended by Burton *et al.* (1990) and Bruce (1992: see Bruce, 1995).

Face recognition and the brain

Given that face perception is such a demanding perceptual task, it is not surprising that brain damage can result in deficits in face processing, such as prosopagnosia (Groome *et al.*,1999). According to Young & Bruce (1998):

'Because faces are of such fundamental social importance to a creature that lives in a complex society, extensive areas of the brain are involved in their perception.'

The functions of these areas are being revealed in studies of the effects of different types of brain injury and using modern neuro-imaging techniques to study face processing in the normal brain (see Chapter 10). The brain seems to 'farm out' different aspects of the task to different specialised areas. For example, some regions are more

Independent routes are drawn for the processing of emotional expressions, lip-reading ('facial speech') and identification, thus allowing the processing of information from both familiar and unfamiliar faces. *Directed visual processing* allows for certain kinds of operation to be performed on faces without accessing their identities (such as looking out for white-haired people when meeting your grandmother at the station). The route by which familiar faces are identified involves separate stages of representation of the face image (*structural encodings*), access of stored structural descriptions of known faces (*face recognition units*/FRUs), access of information about personal identity (via PINs), and finally, retrieval of proper names.

closely involved in determining an individual's identity from their facial appearance, and others in interpretation of facial expressions of emotion (Young *et al.*, 1993).

According to Ellis & Young (1990), when we look at the faces of people we know, we recognise who they are and parts of our brains set up preparatory emotional responses for the types of interaction that are likely to follow (the *'orienting response'*). Recognising who it is and the orienting response involve separate neurological pathways. If the pathway responsible for the orienting response is damaged, and the orienting response is impaired, faces that can still be recognised (and so look familiar) can somehow seem strange, (because they do not elicit the usual reactions).

This is what probably underlies Capgras' delusion (see Box 49.2, page 529), one of the most extensively studied forms of *delusional misidentification*. It involves the belief that one or more close relatives have been replaced by near-identical imposters, and it has been explained as a rationalisation of this highly disturbing sense of strangeness (Young & Bruce, 1998).

CONCLUSIONS

As noted at the beginning of this chapter, pattern recognition (PR) is closely related to perception. They both entail the identification and categorisation of objects, processes which seem effortless and automatic. In fact, however, they are extremely complex, and theories are needed to explain them. Several theories of PR have been proposed, some of which have been much more influential than others. Biederman's geon theory, for example, is generally considered to be a significant improvement on TMH, but it is feature-detection theories that have proved the most influential.

The chapter has also considered research into face recognition, which is really one aspect of face perception. Studies of brain-damaged patients whose face recognition abilities are impaired have figured prominently in this research area. Two models of face recognition have been discussed, showing the complexity of this fascinating aspect of PR.

Summary

- **Pattern recognition** (PR) is the process of assigning meaning to visual input by identifying the objects in the visual field. Like perception, with which it is almost synonymous, PR is a deceptively simple process.

- According to the **template matching hypothesis** (TMH), incoming sensory information is matched against miniature copies (or templates) of patterns/objects stored in long-term memory. However, TMH fails to account for our ability to recognise unfamiliar patterns.

- Biederman's **geon theory** (or **recognition-by-components** model) tries to overcome TMH's limitations. Descriptions of objects usually divide them into **volumetric concepts** or **geons**, and the regions used to divide them up are probably those of greatest **concavity**.

- A very large range of objects can be described by combinations from a basic set of 36 geons. Object identification is determined by whichever stored representations of geons provides the best fit, but the **relationships** between geons must also be specified for complete objects to be recognised.

- Geon theory has been supported by experiments using drawings of common objects with one or more geons missing ('partial' objects). A more stringent test involves the use of 'degraded' versions of objects, in which the normal contours are missing. Again, the results tend to support the theory.

- Geons are intuitively appealing and can be used to describe both physical objects and mammals/other animals. However, there is little empirical support for the specific geons which Biederman identifies.

- **Prototype theories** claim that what is stored is a small number of prototypes. Instead of treating every stimulus as a separate entity, prototype theories regard each stimulus as belonging to a **category** of stimuli. This approach fails to take account of **context** and to specify the properties which characterise different categories.

- **Feature-detection theories** are the most influential approach to PR. They maintain that every stimulus can be regarded as a configuration of elementary features. **Visual scanning tasks** and studies of **eye movements** and **fixations** lend empirical support to feature-detection theories. The latter also show that the perception of features within complex patterns depends on attention and purpose.

- Hubel and Wiesel identified three kinds of cortical cell which respond to particular types of stimulus, and there may be face-specific cells in the monkey cortex. There also appear to be cells in the human cortex that respond to specific aspects of faces.

- These cortical cells may or may not be the feature detectors proposed by feature-detection theories, but they are likely to be a necessary pre-condition for cognitive pattern task analysis. Whilst feature-detection theories typically assume a **serial** form of processing, it is widely believed that the visual cortex involves considerable **parallel** (non-serial) processing.

- Selfridge's **Pandemonium** computer program used parallel processing. Although not intended as a model of human perception, Pandemonium shares with other feature-detection theories the neglect of **context** and **perceiver characteristics** as influences on PR.

- Most feature-detection theories are **bottom-up/data-driven**, whilst the influence of context and expectations illustrates **top-down/conceptually-driven processing**.

- **Face recognition** involves the identification of **individual** faces. It is part of **face perception**, which includes inferring emotional states and other information from the face. Probably more is understood about face recognition than about any other aspect of PR.

- Although faces could be described in terms of basic components, it seems more valid to describe them in a more **configural** way. However, this can refer to different things, including the **interaction** between features and the **holistic** processing of the whole face.

- Early research often used **artificially constructed faces**, such as Identikit faces, and indicated that facial features are processed independently and in sequence. However, some features (such as chins) seemed to influence facial judgements more than others and there was evidence of **interactive processing**.

- According to the **configural processing hypothesis**, the relationship between the features is more difficult to perceive when the face is **inverted** (they are processed **independently**). In a normal upright face, the configuration of the features is crucial.

- Patients with **prosopagnosia** are unable to recognise familiar faces, despite an otherwise normal capacity for recognising individual objects or animals. However, they often display **covert** (unconscious) **recognition**.

- Studies involving prosopagnosics, patients with other face perception disorders, and normal adults also suggest that recognising individual identity is quite separate from recognising emotional expression.

- Studies of both normal and brain-damaged people indicate that there is a sequence of **stages** involved in retrieving someone's identity. These stages have been incorporated into various **models of face recognition**. In Bruce and Young's model, several different processing 'modules' are linked in sequence or in parallel, including **face recognition units** (FRUs) and **person identity nodes** (PINs).

- Whilst there is experimental support for this model (such as the TOT phenomenon for people's faces), it has difficulty explaining covert recognition in prosopagnosic patients.

- Studies of brain damage, and neuro-imaging studies of the normal brain, suggest that different areas of the brain are specialised for different aspects of face recognition. In **Capgras' delusion**, the normal integration of face recognition and orienting response appears to be impaired.

Essay Questions

1 Discuss **two** theories of pattern recognition in relation to visual perception. *(24 marks)*

2 Describe and evaluate research into face recognition. *(24 marks)*

WEB ADDRESSES

http://psych.st-and.ac.uk:8080/research/perception_lab/
http://www.dbv.informatik.uni-bonn.de/
http://www.csrug.nl/~peterkr/FACE/face.html
http://www.stir.ac.uk/departments/humansciences/psychology/staff/vb1/
http://www.white.media.mit.edu/vismod/demos/facerec/

22 The Visual System

INTRODUCTION AND OVERVIEW

Vision is the dominant sense in humans, and much of what we do depends on possessing an adequately functioning visual system. The visual system's importance is reflected by the fact that a greater proportion of the brain is devoted to vision than any other sense. Indeed, such is vision's importance that if we wear lenses that distort a square object into a rectangle, we perceive it as a rectangle even though it can be felt as a square, a phenomenon known as *visual capture*.

This chapter discusses the *structure and functions of the visual system,* and the nature of *visual information processing*. It begins by looking briefly at light, the 'messenger' that tells us about the colour, size, shape, location and texture of objects and surfaces. It then discusses the structure of the eye and the visual pathways from eye to brain. The final part of the chapter considers theories of *colour vision* and *colour constancy*.

LIGHT

Light consists of energy particles called *photons*. These have both electrical and magnetic properties, and so light is an example of *electromagnetic radiation*. Photons travel in waves that move forward and oscillate up and down. There are two important *characteristics* of light. The number of photons in a pulsating stream determines the *intensity* of a light wave. The distance between successive peaks of a light wave determines its *wavelength*. Wavelength is measured in *nanometres* (nm). One nanometre is one thousand millionth of a metre.

Light has three important *properties*. These are *brightness, hue* and *saturation*. The intensity of a light wave determines our experience of *brightness*. The more photons a light source emits, the brighter it appears. *Hue* is the colour we perceive something to be, and is partly determined by wavelength. Visible light is a very narrow section of the electromagnetic spectrum that includes radio waves, radar, microwaves and X-rays. Light visible to humans has a wavelength ranging from about 380 nm

to 760 nm. Longer wavelengths look red, whereas shorter wavelengths are perceived as violet. In between these extremes, the other colours of the rainbow can be found (see Figure 22.1, page 220).

Some colours, such as brown and white, are not in the spectrum of light. Colour, then, cannot be just a matter of wavelength. As will be seen, colours like brown are produced by a complex process in which various wavelengths are mixed by the visual system. White light is, in fact, radiation that includes *all* wavelengths within the visible range. *Saturation* determines how colourful light appears. White is a completely colourless state, and the more white that is present in a colour the less saturated it is. For example, when mint and vanilla chocolate are mixed, the green colour gradually diminishes to a very light green shade. Saturation, then, is the proportion of coloured (or *chromatic*) light to non-coloured (or *achromatic*) light.

Sir Isaac Newton demonstrated that white light is a mixture of wavelengths corresponding to all colours in the visible spectrum. He showed that when light is passed through a prism, the longer wavelengths are refracted least by the prism whilst the shorter wavelengths experience most refraction. By casting this light on to a screen, Newton revealed the full spectrum of colours (see page 224).

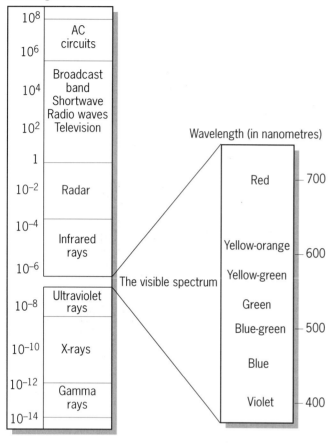

Figure 22.1 *The electromagnetic spectrum showing the visible portion to the right*

THE EYE

According to Ornstein (1986), the eye 'is the most important avenue of personal consciousness'. About 90 per cent of the information about the external world reaches us through the eye. The eyeball is enclosed by the *sclera*, a tough outer coat. The sclera is opaque, except at the front of the eye where it bulges out to form a transparent membrane (the *cornea*) through which light enters the eye. Via the cornea, light waves pass through a clear, watery fluid, (*aqueous humour*) which supplies oxygen and nutrients needed by the cornea and lens (see below). Through *refraction*, light waves are bent as they pass from one substance to another. This allows light from a large area to focus sharply on a small region of the *retina* (see Box 22.1).

The *iris* controls the amount of light entering the eye, and contracts or expands to vary the size of the *pupil* (a black aperture in the eye) through which light waves pass. Pupil size adjusts automatically to the amount of light, and is under the control of the autonomic nervous system (ANS). In dim lighting, the pupil dilates to allow more light to enter. In bright light, it contracts to limit the amount that enters.

Light must be focused to form a coherent image on the retina. This is achieved by the curvature of the cornea and of the *lens*, a crystalline structure held in place by *ciliary muscles* that control its shape. The curvature of the lens can be altered, so that different focal lengths can be accommodated, hence the term *accommodation* (Bowie, 1991). Looking into the distance causes the lens to be made thinner. Looking at objects close to us causes it to be made thicker. Abnormalities in eye shape often make it impossible for the lens to accommodate correctly. This causes *short-sightedness* (in which objects can be seen distinctly only over a short distance) or *long-sightedness* (in which distant objects can be seen clearly but near objects cannot).

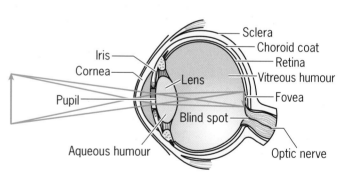

Figure 22.2 *Cross-section of the human eye*

After being refracted by the lens, light waves pass through a jelly-like substance (*vitreous humour*) before striking the retina, a delicate membrane which lines the back of the eye.

Box 22.1 The retina

The main parts of the retina are *cones*, *rods*, *bipolar cells* and *ganglion cells*, all of which are neurons. Rods and cones form one layer of the retina and are *photosensitive cells* (or *photoreceptors*), whose job it is to convert light energy into electrical nerve impulses. Bipolar and ganglion cells form the other two layers of the retina. The bipolar cells are connected to the ganglion cells and to rods and cones. The axons of the ganglion cells form the beginning of the *optic nerve*, the pathway by which information is sent to the brain.

We might expect the photoreceptors to be at the *front* of the retina, where they would be in the best position to intercept light waves. However, because of how it develops the retina is functionally inside out, with the rods and cones at the *back* (see Figure 22.3). This means that light waves must pass through the other two layers and the blood vessels that serve them. The work done by the photoreceptors requires amounts of energy that cannot be supplied by the fluid of the eye. Thus, the photoreceptors are next to the *choroid coat* of the retina, which is rich in blood vessels. Oxygen and other nutrients carried by the blood provide the photoreceptors with the necessary energy.

Each retina has about 120 million rods and 7 million cones. Rods help us to see *achromatic colour* (black, white and intermediate grey), and are specialised for vision in dim light (*scotopic vision*). They are sensitive only to light intensity, and therefore contribute to our perception of brightness but not colour. The photosensitive chemical contained in rods, *rhodopsin*, changes its structure in response to low levels of illumination. Different cones respond to different wavelengths and this helps us see *chromatic colour* (red, green, blue, and so on) and provides us with *photopic vision*. The cones are specialised for bright light vision and contain a chemical called *iodopsin*.

the cone-rich fovea. In dim light, however, the sharpest image will be obtained if we look slightly to one side of the object in order to stimulate the rods in the retina's periphery.

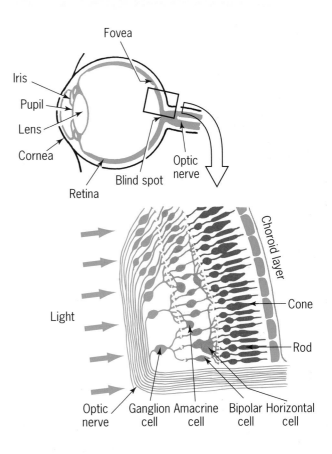

Figure 22.3 *The layers of cells in the retina. Note how light must travel through several layers before reaching the photoreceptors*

Box 22.2 The distribution of rods and cones

Rods and cones are distributed differently in the retina. Cones are much more numerous towards its centre. The *fovea*, a pit-like depression, is part of a cone-rich area called the *macula lutea* in which around 50,000 cones are concentrated. This dense packing explains visual *acuity* (or sharpness). The more densely packed the receptors are, the finer are the details of a pattern of light intensity which can be transformed into electrical energy.

Rods are distributed fairly evenly around the retina's periphery and are absent in the fovea. When we want to focus on an object in bright light, the most sharply defined image will be obtained by looking directly at the object, so that light is projected on to

When a photon strikes a receptor, a *photochemical reaction* occurs. This *transduces* light energy into neural signals. These are passed to bipolar cells, which in turn pass them to ganglion cells. These travel across the retina's inner surface and converge to form the optic nerve, which carries signals to the brain. The *optic disc* is the part of the retina where the optic nerve leaves the eye. There are no visual receptors at this point, and the optic disc is thus the eye's *blind spot*. Normally, we do not notice the blind spot, one reason being that our eyes are constantly moving. This allows us to receive the image that would fall on the blind spot in another part of the retina.

There are many more rods and cones than there are bipolar cells, and more bipolar cells than ganglion cells. This means that many rods (and cones) send their information to the same bipolar cell, and ganglion cells receive their information from many bipolar cells. Two other kinds of neuron in the retina, *horizontal cells* and *amacrine cells*, transmit information across the retina and allow interactions between adjacent rods, cones, bipolar cells and ganglion cells.

The number of photoreceptors sending information to the same bipolar cell varies. Around the retina's periphery, several hundred rods may send information to one bipolar cell. At the fovea, however, individual bipolar and ganglion cells may serve only one cone. This one-to-one relationship accounts for the better acuity of cone vision as compared with rod vision. However, because many rods send information to one bipolar cell, the cell is more likely to 'fire', and hence rods are better at detecting faint light.

Box 22.3 Receptive fields

Hubel & Wiesel (1962) identified the type of visual stimulus to which individual retinal cells are most sensitive. They inserted micro-electrodes (see Chapter 10) into the optic nerve of an anaesthetised cat. Some cells responded maximally when a spot of light fell on one particular, and usually circular, part of the retina. If the spot was moved to the surrounding part of the retina, the ganglion cells gradually stopped responding. Hubel and Wiesel called the sensitive areas the cell's *receptive field*, and concluded that a ganglion cell is connected to all or most of the rods and cones within a receptive field.

The receptive field of a ganglion cell is divided into two concentric, antagonistic parts, the *centre* and *surround* regions. Both may be either *on-regions* (in which an increase in light produces an increase in the cell's response, and a decrease in light produces a decrease in the cell's response) or *off-regions* (an increase in light produces a *decrease* in the cell's response, and a decrease in light produces an *increase* in the cell's response: Harris, 1998). At least three types of ganglion cell exist, each of which has a different kind of receptive field. One has an *on-centre* and an *off-surround*. This cell is more active when light falls in the centre of the receptive field and less active when it falls on the edge. A second has an *off-centre* and *on-surround*. A third has a larger receptive field and seems to respond to movements, especially sudden ones. This is called a *transient cell*. The combined activity of on- and off-centre cells provides a clear definition of contours where there is a sudden change in brightness. Such contours are essential in defining the shape of objects to be perceived (Beaumont, 1988).

FROM THE EYE TO THE BRAIN

As was seen in Chapter 11 (pages 110–111), visual sensory information travels to the thalami and from there to the *primary visual area* of the cortex. Optic nerve fibres terminate at synapses with cells of a part of the thalami called the *lateral geniculate nucleus* (LGN). The LGN in each of the thalami combines the information from both eyes before sending it to the cortex along the *geniculostriate path*. This and the visual area must be intact for the conscious experience of vision. However, in *blindsight*, the visual area may be extensively damaged but a person can identify objects without being consciously aware of them. Weiskrantz (1986), for example, reported a case in which a person was able to detect whether a visual stimulus had been presented even though he was subjectively blind! This suggests the existence of another pathway, which carries enough information to guide some actions in an unconscious way.

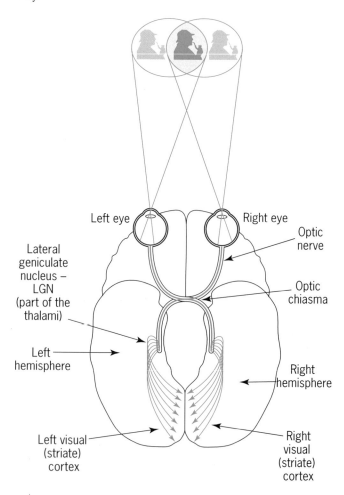

Figure 22.4 *The major pathways of the visual system, showing connections between the eyes and the visual (striate) cortex*

Hubel & Wiesel (1965) found that LGN cells had circular receptive fields just like ganglion cells. However, when they investigated cells in the cortex, a slightly different picture emerged. Using micro-electrodes to record the activity of single cells in the primary visual area of monkeys and cats, Hubel and Wiesel suggested the existence of three types of cortical cell that play a role in decoding light information.

Box 22.4 Simple, complex and hypercomplex cells

Simple cells respond only to particular features of a stimulus in a particular orientation and location in the visual field. For example, a vertical straight line in a specific location in the visual field might cause a particular neuron to 'fire'. However, if a horizontal line was in the same part of the visual field, the neuron would not respond.

Complex cells respond to a particular feature of a stimulus in a particular orientation *no matter where* it appears in the visual field. A complex cell, then, might respond to a vertical line wherever it was in the visual field. However, if the line's features or orientation changed, the cell would stop responding. Presumably, complex cells receive inputs from many simple cells which show the same features and orientation, and this accounts for their ability to respond to stimuli no matter where they appear in the visual field.

Hypercomplex cells respond to corners, angles, or bars of a particular length moving in a certain direction. Such cells presumably receive inputs from large numbers of complex cells. Although the existence of hypercomplex cells has been questioned (Bruce & Green, 1990), Hubel and Wiesel's research demonstrated that the visual area of the cortex is not a homogeneous mass of tissues with randomly scattered cells. Rather, it shows precise and regular arrangement of different cells, which Hubel and Wiesel termed the visual area's *functional architecture*.

Hubel & Wiesel (1977) showed that six main layers of the visual area of the cortex could be identified beneath the microscope. The visual area is apparently divided into roughly 1 mm square blocks of tissue that extend from the surface of the cortex down to the white matter below. These are called *hypercolumns*. Within the hypercolumns, cells have different receptive fields. Although there is a good deal of overlap of these receptive fields, all fall within some single retinal area (or what Hubel and Wiesel term an *aggregate field*).

Two further patterns of organisation are worth a mention. First, cells fall into two groups according to which eye is most effective in eliciting a response. Although cells in some layers have *binocular fields*, and respond to their optimal stimulus whichever eye it is presented to, they always respond more strongly to the stimulus to one eye or the other (*ocular dominance*). Cells sharing the same ocular dominance are grouped together into bands running across the visual area.

The second pattern of organisation is that cells are arranged in columns about 0.5 mm across according to their 'orientation preference'. If an electrode penetrates the cortex at right angles to the surface, then all the cells it encounters will have the same orientation preference regardless of whether they are simple or complex.

As well as the primary visual area, there are other visual association areas in the occipital, temporal and parietal lobes. Maunsell & Newsome (1987) have suggested the existence of at least 19 visual areas, each of which sends output to several others, and most (if not all) of which are matched by reciprocal connections running in the opposite direction. According to van Essen (1985), there are as many as 92 pathways linking the visual areas!

Each area appears to have its own specialised function. V5, for example, deals with motion (see Box 22.5, page 224). *Visual illusions* (see Chapter 23) might be caused by the breakdown of the rules used by the brain to process signals from the eye. One illusion, 'Enigma', is a painting in blue, black and white by the artist Isia Leviant. Although static, there seems to be a rotating movement within the solid rings of the picture.

Figure 22.5 *A black and white version of 'Enigma'. There appears to be a rotating movement in the solid rings of the picture*

Using PET (see Chapter 10), Zeki (cited in Highfield, 1997a) showed that the black and white version of the illusion stimulated V5 and surrounding areas. For some reason, the static picture causes activity in V5 and this accounts for the sensation of the circular movement even though there is no objective motion (see Chapter 23, pages 237–238).

Key S T U D Y

Box 22.5 Motion detection in the blind

It used to be thought that retinal signals pass to V1 (the primary visual processing area) which forms an image of a stimulus, and that after this other areas sort out attributes like form (V3), colour (V4) and motion (V5). Zeki (1992, 1993) has shown that this is not the case. He studied G.Y., a man blinded in an accident when he was seven. G.Y. could detect fast moving objects, such as cars, and the direction in which they were travelling. Scans confirmed that G.Y.'s V5 was active when he was 'seeing' fast motion, but his V1 was not. This suggests that fast movements are first processed by V5, whilst signals from slow movements arrive in V1 first. In Zeki's view, signals must go through V1 to see clearly, but even the blind can sometimes see through other areas in a rudimentary way.

Other examples of very specific visual impairments arising from brain damage support Zeki's claim that different aspects of visual processing occur in different parts of the brain. For example, damage to V5 produces *akinetopsia*, in which moving objects appear invisible even though the same objects can be seen quite clearly when stationary. Patients with *chromatopsia* (caused by widespread brain damage due to carbon monoxide poisoning) have intact colour vision, but almost all other visual abilities are impaired. Similarly, P.B. awoke from a four-month coma to find he was blind, except for the ability to make out colours (Zeki, cited in Highfield, 1999b), The converse of this is *achromatopia*. Following a stroke, E.H. reported that everything looked grey, although all other visual abilities were normal. A MRI scan revealed damage to V4 (Shuren *et al.*, 1996).

COLOUR VISION

As noted earlier, Newton demonstrated that white light is a mixture of all the colours of the spectrum. In further experiments, Newton investigated the effects of mixing various components of the spectrum. He found that mixing only two of the colours (such as yellow and

violet-blue or red and blue-green) produced white. However, this only occurred with colours far apart in the spectrum. If the light of two colours close together was mixed, light of an intermediate colour was produced. Newton devised a *colour circle*, in which colours that produced either white or neutral grey were placed at opposite ends of the circle's diameter (see Figure 22.6).

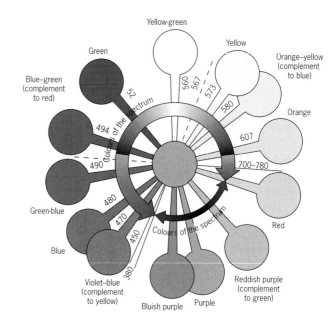

Figure 22.6 *The colour circle. When lights of complementary colours such as yellow and violet-blue are mixed, neutral grey is produced*

The pure colours arranged around the circle are *hues* and those opposite one another are called *complementary colours*. Those of us who have mixed coloured paints may be confused at this point. Surely, blue and yellow produce green, not grey or white. To overcome this confusion, we need to distinguish between *subtractive* and *additive colour mixing*.

Box 22.6 Subtractive and additive colour mixing

Hue is determined by the wavelength of light that is *reflected* rather than the wavelengths that are absorbed. Blue paint appears blue because the light it reflects is predominantly of short-medium wavelength (the blue-green part of the spectrum). The light it absorbs (or 'subtracts') is of a long wavelength. Yellow paint mostly reflects light of long-medium wavelength (the yellow-green part of the spectrum) and absorbs (or 'subtracts') the short wavelength light. When blue and yellow are mixed, *both* short and long wavelength light are absorbed (or 'subtracted') leaving only medium wavelength (or green) light to be reflected. This is *subtractive colour mixing*.

When *lights* with different wavelengths simultaneously stimulate the retina, the combining (or 'adding') of these wavelengths occurs. This is *additive colour mixing*. Thus, subtractive colour mixing takes place in the object we are viewing, whereas additive colour mixing takes place in the visual system. If you were to look closely at a colour television set, for example, you would see that a yellow object was actually composed of red and green.

Wavelength mixing experiments show that the human visual system is equipped to distinguish between different wavelengths and make comparisons between them. These experiments show that *any* colour can be produced by varying the proportions of just three (*primary*) wavelengths. Whilst there is no unique set of primaries, in practice there must be one *long* wavelength (e.g. red), one *medium* (e.g. green) and one *short* (e.g. blue) (Harris, 1998). For an artist, these are red, blue and yellow, since all the hues can be produced by a mixture of them. For psychologists, however, the primary colours are red, green and blue *light* since all the various hues can be obtained by mixing these.

Humans with normal vision can distinguish up to 150 colours formed from the combination of four basic hues (red, green, blue and yellow) and two hueless colours (black and white). Importantly, whilst wavelengths can be varied in a *continuous* manner from shorter to longer, changes in colour appear to be *discontinuous*. Thus, our perception of colour may seem to suddenly 'shift' from, say, blue to green, even though the change in wavelength was smaller than that between two 'blues'.

THEORIES OF COLOUR VISION

Two major theories of colour vision have been advanced. These are the *Young–Helmholtz theory* and the *opponent-process theory*.

The Young–Helmholtz theory

In 1802, Young demonstrated that the various combinations of red, green and blue light produce all the colours of the spectrum. About 50 years later, von Helmholtz suggested that the eye contains three types of receptor corresponding to red, blue and green, and that the perception of colour is somehow created by combining the information from them. Yellow, for example, would

result from the simultaneous stimulation of red and green receptors. According to the *Young–Helmholtz theory*, then, the *ratio* of the blue:green:red receptors which are activated determines the colour that is perceived.

Because the theory proposes that three types of receptor exist, it is also called the *trichromatic theory of colour vision* ('tri' means 'three' and 'chroma' means 'colour'). Over 100 years after it was proposed, research confirmed the existence of three distinct types of cone in the retina, each of which contains a slightly different *photopigment*. These cones are maximally sensitive to light at 435, 540 and 565 nm, wavelengths corresponding to blue, green and yellow-green (note that to be consistent with earlier convention, the yellow-green receptor is termed 'red'). Nathans (1989) has shown that there are specific genes which direct the three kinds of cones to produce photopigment sensitive to light in the three regions identified above. However, although each type of cone responds maximally to light in the three regions, light of a particular wavelength has been shown to stimulate *more* than one type of receptor (Ohtsuka, 1985).

Whilst the Young–Helmholtz theory can explain the effects of mixing colours of different wavelengths, it has difficulty in explaining *colour blindness* and the phenomenon of *negative after-images* (see Box 22.7). Both of these can be explained more easily by opponent-process theory.

Opponent-process theory

In 1870, Hering proposed that we see six primary colours rather than the three identified in the Young–Helmholtz theory. The additional three colours are yellow, black and white. Like Young and Helmholtz, Hering believed that there were three types of receptor. However, he suggested that each was responsive to *pairs* of colours. Two of these, the red-green and yellow-blue pairs are responsible for the perception of colour. The third, black-white, contributes to the perception of brightness and saturation (see page 219). As its name suggests, *opponent-process theory* proposes that each member of a pair is opposed to the other, so that when one (such as red) is excited, the other (green) is inhibited. This explains why we never experience a colour as being 'reddish-green' but do experience colours as 'reddish-yellow'.

Box 22.7 Colour blindness and negative after-images

As noted, Hering's theory can explain colour-blindness. People are *never* colour-blind to red and yellow but able to see green and blue. The most common type of colour-blindness is red-green (one of Hering's pairs). Whilst red and green (and the colours derived from them) cannot be seen, blue and yellow (and the colours derived from them) can. Yellow-blue (another of Hering's pairs) colour-blindness is much rarer but does occur. People who are either red-green or yellow-blue colour-blind are said to be *dichromatic* (whereas normal colour vision is *trichromatic*). People who are totally colour-blind are *monochromatic*, and see only black, white and shades of grey.

Opponent-process theory can also explain *negative after-images*. If you stare at a red surface for about 30 seconds and then look at a sheet of white paper, the sheet will appear green. Thus, the persistent sensation of a colour results in the perception of the complementary colour when the colour is removed. According to opponent-process theory, staring at red (say) forces the red-green receptors into 'red phase'. After a while, the red component tires. When our gaze is directed to a neutral surface, the light it reflects stimulates the red and green components equally, but only the green components are 'fresh' enough to fire.

According to Harris (1998), both theories are compatible, and neurophysiological evidence exists for both. The first stage of colour vision seems to be at the receptor level (cones) and is trichromatic. Studies of bipolar, ganglion and some cells in the LGN, however, suggest that the messages from the cones (stage two) are relayed to parts of the brain in opponent-process fashion (DeValois & Jacobs, 1984).

For example, some neurons transmitting information to the brain are excited by red light but inhibited by green light. Others work in the opposite way. A red-sensitive neuron excited by red light for half a minute might switch briefly to 'inhibitory mode' when the light is removed. This would result in us perceiving green as an after-image even if no light was present (Haber & Hershenson, 1980). Opponent-process theory does not seem to operate at the level of the cones, but along the neural path from the cones to the visual area. It may even be that the trichromatic system itself interacts in an opponent-process way.

COLOUR CONSTANCY

The colours we perceive are not *solely* determined by the wavelength of light reflected from an object. If they were, we might more often misjudge colours. This is because many artificial lights (unlike natural sunlight) do not contain a roughly equal mixture of all wavelenths, and light in many natural settings (such as forests) is predominantly one particular wavelength

(Harris, 1998). Amongst other factors affecting perception are *familiarity* with, and *knowledge* of, an object's colour. This is part of the phenomenon of *colour constancy*. The visual system is built to tell us about the permanent colours of objects, as opposed to the spectral composition of light falling on a local area of the retina (McCann, 1987).

Land (1977) provided a powerful demonstration of colour constancy. He used a *colour Mondrian*, consisting of a patchwork of randomly arranged and differently coloured matt papers. The display was illuminated by mixed light from projectors with red, green and blue filters. An independent brightness control was also available for each projector.

Observers then selected one of the colours, and Land measured the amounts of red, green and blue light coming from it. A second colour was then selected and the same measurements taken. The illumination was then changed so that the amount of red, green and blue light coming from the second colour was the *same* as that from the first colour. When all three projectors were turned on, observers were asked to report what colour they saw. All reported seeing the second colour, even though the physical properties of the light coming from it were the same as the first colour!

Box 22.8 Retinex theory

If perceived colour were determined solely by the spectral composition of the reflected light, the first and second colours would have been seen as the same. However, they were not, and the observers displayed colour constancy. To explain this, Land proposed the *retinex theory of colour constancy* ('retinex' is a combination of 'retina' and 'cortex'). According to this, there are three separate visual systems or retinexes, responsive primarily to long-wavelength light, medium-wavelength light and short-wavelength light. Each produces a separate lightness image and a comparison of these images is carried out.

The comparison determines the colour perceived. The three lightnesses provide the coordinates of a three-dimensional space and, whereas a colour space based on the *absolute* absorptions in the three classes of receptor predicts only whether two stimuli will *match*, a space based on the three lightnesses predicts how colours actually *look*. This is because between them they give the reflectance of the object in different parts of the spectrum (that is, a measure of their *relative absorptions*). Land's theory implies that the formation of lightnesses could occur in the retina *or* cortex, and that the retina-cortical structure acts as a whole.

Cells with suitable properties for retinex theory exist in the LGN, and Zeki (1980) found that the responses of individual cells in area V4 of macaque monkeys mirrored his own perception of surface colour as opposed to the physical composition of the light. These V4 cells seem to be genuinely colour- (rather than wavelength-) selective (Harris, 1998).

CONCLUSIONS

This chapter has examined the nature of light and the structure of the eye. Light information is transduced into electrical energy in the retina of the eye, and then passed on to the brain where it is decoded. Neurons specialised for various functions play an important role in this decoding process, and research has begun to identify areas of the cerebral cortex which are specialised for particular aspects of visual perception. Theories of colour vision and colour constancy have also been presented.

Summary

- Light consists of energy particles called **photons**. Two important characteristics of light are **intensity** and **wavelength**. Three important properties of light are **brightness, hue** and **saturation**. White light is a mixture of wavelengths corresponding to all colours in the visible spectrum.

- The eye is the organ of vision, and 90 per cent of information about the external world reaches us via the eye. Light ends its journey through the eye at the **retina**, which contains **cones, rods, bipolar cells** and **ganglion cells**.

- Rods and cones are **photoreceptors** which convert light energy into electrical energy. Each retina contains about 120 million rods. These are distributed around the retina's periphery and help us see **achromatic colour**, and are specialised for **scotopic vision**. Seven million cones help us see **chromatic colour**, and are specialised for **photopic vision**. Cones are concentrated towards the retina's centre.

- Bipolar cells are connected to ganglion cells and to rods and cones. **Horizontal** and **amacrine** cells transmit information across the retina allowing bipolar and ganglion cells and rods and cones to interact.

- Some ganglion cells have an **on-centre/off-surround** receptive field. Others have an **off-centre/on-surround** receptive field. **Transient cells** have a larger receptive field and are most responsive to sudden movements.

- Information from the eyes travels along the optic nerve to the thalami, and from there to the primary visual area of the cortex via the **geniculostriate path**. This pathway must be intact for conscious visual experience, but **blindsight** suggests the existence of another pathway allowing 'unconscious vision'.

- **Simple cells** respond only to particular orientations of a stimulus in a certain part of the visual field. **Complex cells** respond to a particular orientation wherever it appears. **Hypercomplex** cells respond to corners, angles or bars of a particular length moving in a certain direction.

- The visual area of the cortex consists of six layers, divided into **hypercolumns**. Cells within these have different receptive fields, all falling within an **aggregate field**. The primary visual field is also organised in terms of **binocular fields, ocular dominance** and **orientation preference**.

- There are many areas within the visual cortex, each of which appears to have its own specialised function. V3, V4 and V5, for example, are concerned with form, colour and motion respectively. This view of visual processing is supported by case studies of people with specific visual impairments (such as **akinetopsia, chromatopsia** and **achromatopsia**).

- In Newton's colour circle, pure colours correspond to hues, and those opposite one another are called **complementary colours. Subtractive** and **additive colour mixing** explain why mixing coloured paints (for example) results in a different colour from that when light of different wavelengths is mixed.

- People with normal vision can distinguish up to 150 colours formed from four basic hues and two hueless colours. Changes in wavelength can be varied **continuously**, but changes in colour are **discontinuous**.

- The **Young–Helmholtz theory** of colour vision proposes the existence of three types of receptor (cones) corresponding to red, blue and green hues. Colour perception is determined by the **ratio** of the receptors activated. However, the theory is unable to explain colour blindness and negative after-images.

- Hering's **opponent-process theory** proposes that three types of receptor are responsive to **pairs** of colours: red-green, yellow-blue and black-white. When one member of a pair is excited, the other is inhibited. This theory can account for colour blindness and negative after-images.

- Both theories have some validity and work in a complementary way at different levels or stages. Different cones are sensitive to different wavelengths, although messages from them are relayed to the visual area of the brain in opponent-process fashion.

- **Perceived colour** is only partly determined by the wavelength of reflected light from an object. **Familiarity** with, and **knowledge** of, an object's colour are also involved, and play a part in **colour constancy**.

- According to **Land's retinex theory**, there are three separate visual systems or retinexes, responsive to long-, medium- and short-wavelength light. Each produces a separate lightness image, and the **comparison** of these determines the colour perceived.

Essay Questions

1 Describe and evaluate research into the nature of visual information processing (e.g. the processing of colour). (*24 marks*)

2 **a** Outline the structure and functions of the visual system. (*12 marks*)

 b Assess the extent to which knowledge of the visual system's structure and functions helps us to understand visual information processing.
(*12 marks*)

WEB ADDRESSES

http://vision.arc.nasa.gov/VisionScience/
http://www.socsci.uci.edu/cogsci/vision.html
http://minerva.acc.virginia.edu/~mklab/
http://www.med.uni-muenchen.de/medpsy/vis/nvi/infpro.html

23 *Perceptual Organisation*

INTRODUCTION AND OVERVIEW

When we compare our experience of the world (one in which objects remain stable and constant) with what our sense organs receive in the form of physical stimulation (a state of near continuous flux), it is almost as if there are two entirely different 'worlds'. Psychologists call these *sensation* and *perception* respectively. Sensations are the experiences that physical stimuli elicit in the sense organs. Perception is the organisation and interpretation of incoming sensory information to form inner representations of the external world.

This chapter begins by looking at some basic visual perceptual phenomena, namely, *form* and *depth perception, perceptual constancy* and *visual illusions.* Many of the principles that govern human visual perception were first uncovered by the German 'school' of *Gestalt psychology,* and their contribution will be examined. The chapter then considers some major *theories* of visual perception. As Dodwell (1995) has observed:

'To perceive seems effortless. To understand perception is nevertheless a great challenge'.

One response to this challenge claims that our perception of the world is the end result of a process which also involves making *inferences* about what things are like. Those who subscribe to this 'end result' view, such as Bruner (1957), Neisser (1967) and Gregory (1972, 1980), are called *top-down* (or *conceptually-driven) perceptual processing theorists.* Making inferences about what things are like means that we perceive them *indirectly*, drawing on our knowledge and expectations of the world. Others argue that our perception of the world is essentially determined by the information presented to the sensory receptors, so that things are perceived in a fairly *direct* way. The most influential of these *bottom-up* (or *data-driven) perceptual processing theorists* is Gibson (1966, 1979).

GESTALT PSYCHOLOGY AND VISUAL PERCEPTION

Ehrenfels (1890) claimed that many groups of stimuli acquire a pattern quality which is greater than the sum of their parts. A square, for example, is more than a simple assembly of lines – it has 'squareness'. Ehrenfels called this 'emergent property' *Gestalt qualität* (or form quality). In the early 1900s, Gestalt psychologists (notably Wertheimer, Koffka and Köhler) attempted to discover the principles through which sensory information is interpreted. They argued that as well as creating a coherent perceptual experience that is more than the sum of its parts, the brain does this in regular and predictable ways, and that these organisational principles are largely innately determined. The claim about innateness is discussed in Chapter 24.

FORM PERCEPTION

In order to structure incoming sensory information, we must perceive objects as being separate from other stimuli and as having a meaningful form.

Figure and ground

The first perceptual task when confronted with an object (or *figure*) is to recognise it. To do this, we must perceive the figure as being distinct from its surroundings (or *ground*). A figure's *familiarity* can help determine whether it is perceived as figure or ground. However, unfamiliar and even meaningless forms are also seen as figures.

Figure 23.1 (see page 230) illustrates that familiarity is *not* necessary for form perception. If it were, we would have difficulty perceiving objects we had never seen before (Carlson, 1987). One of the strongest determinants of figure and ground is *surroundedness*. Areas enclosed by a *contour* are generally seen as figures, whereas the surrounding area is generally seen as ground. *Size*, *orientation* and *symmetry* also play a role in figure–ground separation.

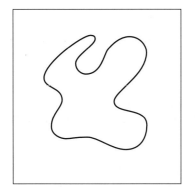

Figure 23.1 *Even unfamiliar objects are immediately perceived when the outline is closed*

Sometimes, though, there may not be enough information in a pattern to allow us to easily distinguish between figure and ground. A good example of this is shown in Figure 23.2 which illustrates the principle underlying *camouflage*.

Figure 23.2 *The dalmation dog (the figure) is difficult to distinguish from the ground because it has few visible contours of its own*

In *figure–ground reversal*, a figure may have clear contours, but is capable of being perceived in two very different ways because it is not clear which part of it is the figure and which the ground. A famous example is Rubin's vase (Rubin, 1915).

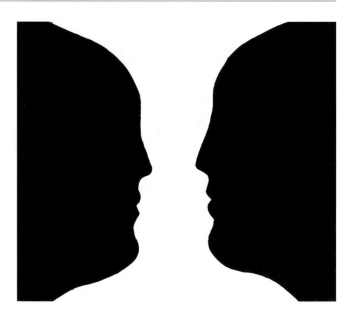

Figure 23.3 *A white vase on a black background or two faces in silhouette?*

In Rubin's vase, the figure–ground relationship continually reverses, so that it is perceived as either a white vase with a black background or two black profiles on a white background. However, the stimulus is *always* organised into a figure seen against a ground, and the reversal indicates that the same stimulus can trigger more than one perception (see page 236).

Figures 23.4 (a) and (b) show two examples of the ways in which figure–ground reversal has been used by artists.

Figure 23.4 (a) *The use of reversible ground by a potter. The vase, a commemoration of the Queen's Silver Jubilee (1977), can also be perceived as the profiles of the Duke of Edinburgh (left) and the Queen (right)*

Figure 23.4 (b) *A woodcut by the artist M.C. Escher. Either black devils or white angels can be seen in the ring*

Grouping

Once we have discriminated figure from ground, the figure can be organised into a meaningful form. Gestalt psychologists believed that objects are perceived as *gestalten* ('organised wholes', 'configurations' or 'patterns') rather than combinations of isolated sensations. They identified several 'laws' of perceptual organisation or grouping which illustrate their view that the perceived whole of an object is more than the sum of its parts.

These laws can be summarised under one heading, *the law of prägnanz*, according to which:

> 'Psychological organisation will always be as good as the prevailing conditions allow. In this definition, "good" is undefined' (Koffka, 1935).

'Good' can be defined as possessing a high degree of internal redundancy, that is, the structure of an unseen part is highly predictable from the visible parts (Attneave, 1954). Similarly, according to Hochberg's (1978) *minimum principle*, if there is more than one way of organising a given visual stimulus, we are most likely to perceive the one requiring the least amount of information to perceive it.

In practice, the 'best' way of perceiving is to see things as symmetrical, uniform and stable, and this is achieved by following the laws of prägnanz.

Box 23.1 Gestalt laws of perception

Proximity: Elements appearing close together – in space or time – tend to be perceived together, so that different spacings of dots produce four vertical lines or four horizontal lines:

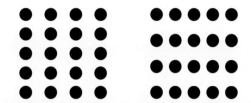

An auditory example would be the perception of a series of musical notes as a melody because they occur soon after one another in time.

Similarity: Similar figures tend to be grouped together. So, the triangles and circles below are seen as columns of similar shapes rather than rows of dissimilar shapes.

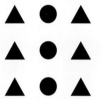

When we hear all the separate voices in a choir as an entity, the principle of similarity is operating.

Good continuation: We tend to perceive smooth, continuous patterns rather than discontinuous ones. The pattern below could be seen as a series of alternating semi-circles, but tends to be perceived as a wavy line and a straight line.

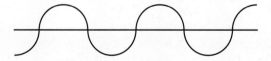

Music and speech are perceived as continuous rather than a series of separate sounds.

Closure: The law of closure says that we often supply missing information to close a figure and separate it from its background. By filling in the gaps, the illustrations are seen as a triangle and a seashell.

Part–whole relationship: As well as illustrating continuity and proximity, the three figures below illustrate the principle that 'the whole is greater than the sum of its parts'. Each pattern is composed of 12 crosses, but the gestalten are different, despite the similarity of the parts.

The same melody can be recognised when hummed, whistled or played with different instruments and in different keys.

Simplicity: According to this law, a stimulus pattern will be organised into its simplest components. The figure below is usually perceived as a rectangle with an overlapping triangle rather than as a complex and nameless geometric shape.

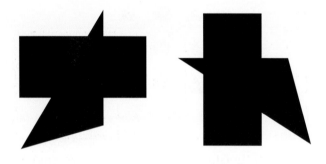

Common fate: Elements seen moving together are perceived as belonging together. This is why a group of people running in the same direction appear to be unified in their purpose.

An evaluation of the Gestalt contribution

A major philosophical influence on Gestalt psychology was *phenomenology*. This sees the world as we ordinarily experience it as being of central concern. Koffka, for example, believed that the most important question for perceptual psychologists was 'Why do things look as they do?', and for Köhler:

> 'There seems to be a single starting point for psychology, exactly as for all the other sciences: the world as we find it, naïvely and uncritically'.

The most comprehensive account of perceptual grouping is still that provided by the Gestaltists (Roth, 1986), and in Gordon's (1989) view, Gestalt psychology's dis-

coveries 'are now part of our permanent knowledge of perception'.

Many contemporary researchers, (e.g. Greene, 1990) however, have argued that, as originally expressed, the various Gestalt 'laws' are at best only descriptive and at worst extremely imprecise and difficult to measure (what, for example, makes a circle or square a 'good' figure?). Several studies (e.g. Navon, 1977) have attempted to address the various criticisms made of the Gestalt laws.

Key (S T U D Y)

Box 23.2 Navon's (1977) experimental test of Gestalt laws

Navon tested the idea that the whole is perceived before the parts that make it up by presenting participants with various stimuli as shown below.

```
H           H              H H H H
H           H           H H       H
H           H          H           H
H           H          H
HHHHHHHHHH  H           H H H H
H           H               H H H H
H           H                      H
H           H           H           H
H           H            H H       H
H           H              H H H H H
```

Navon distinguished between the *global* (or 'whole-like' features of a stimulus) and the *local* (or more specific and 'part-like' features). Each stimulus consisted of a large (global) letter made up of many small (local) letters. In some cases, the global and local letters matched (as shown in the stimulus on the left), and in some cases they did not (as shown on the right).

Participants had to identify either the large or the small letter as quickly as possible. Navon found that the time taken to identify the large letter was unaffected by whether the small letters matched or not. However, the time taken to identify the small letters *was* affected by whether the large letter matched or not, such that when the large letter was different, response times were longer. This suggests that it is difficult to avoid processing the whole and that global processing necessarily occurs before any more detailed perceptual analysis.

(Adapted from Eysenck & Keane, 1995)

Navon's data support claims made by Gestaltists. However, Gestalt laws are difficult to apply to the perception of solid (three-dimensional/3-D) objects (as opposed to two-dimensional/2-D drawings). Our eyes evolved to see 3-D objects, and when 3-D arrays have been studied, Gestalt laws have not been consistently upheld (Eysenck, 1993). The world around us comprises 'whole' scenes in which single objects are but 'parts' (Humphreys & Riddoch, 1987). As a result, many of the Gestalt displays, which involve *single* objects, have very low *ecological validity* in that they are not representative of 'the objects and events which organisms must deal with in order to survive' (Gordon, 1989).

DEPTH PERCEPTION

From the 2-D images that fall on our retinas, we manage to organise 3-D perceptions. This ability is called *depth perception*, and it allows us to estimate an object's distance from us. Some of the cues used to transform 2-D retinal images into 3-D perceptions involve both eyes and rely on their working together. These are called *binocular cues. Monocular cues* are available to each eye separately.

Binocular cues

Most preyed upon non-humans (such as rabbits) have their eyes on the side of the head, allowing them to see danger approaching over a wide area. Most predators (such as lions) have their eyes set close together on the front of the head, equipping them with binocular vision, which helps in hunting prey. Like non-human predators, humans have predatory vision, which influences the way we perceive the world. Four important binocular cues are *retinal disparity, stereopsis, accommodation* and *convergence*.

Because our eyes are nearly three inches apart, each retina receives a slightly different image of the world. The amount of *retinal disparity* (the difference between the two images) detected by the brain provides an important cue to distance. For example, if you hold your finger directly in front of your nose, the difference between the two retinal images is large (and this can be shown by looking at your finger first with the left eye closed and then with the right eye closed). When the finger is held at arm's length, retinal disparity is much smaller.

Ordinarily, we do not see double images, because the brain combines the two images in a process called *stereopsis* (literally, 'solid vision': Harris, 1998). This allows us to experience one 3-D sensation rather than two different images. In *accommodation*, which is a muscular cue, the lenses of the eyes change shape when we focus on an object, thickening for nearby objects and flattening for distant objects (see Chapter 22, page 220). *Convergence*, another muscular cue to distance, is the process by which the eyes point more and more inward as an object gets closer. By noting the angle of convergence, the brain provides us with depth information over distances from about six to 20 feet (Hochberg, 1971).

Monocular cues

Except with relatively near objects, each eye receives a very similar retinal image whilst looking ahead. At greater distances, we depend on monocular cues.

Box 23.3 Some monocular cues to depth

Relative size: The larger an object's image is on the retina, the larger it is judged to be. Larger objects are also judged to be closer.

Overlap (or Superimposition): If one object is partially covered by another, it is perceived as being further away. When a smaller object partially obscures a larger one, they seem closer together than if their position is reversed (a combination of overlap and relative size).

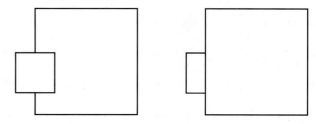

Relative height: Objects *below* the horizon and *lower down* in our field of vision are perceived as being closer. Objects *above* the horizon and *higher up* in our field of vision are perceived as being further away.

Texture gradient: This refers to the fact that textured surfaces nearby appear rougher than distant surfaces. Thus, at increasing distances the details of the surface blend together and the texture appears increasingly smooth.

Linear perspective: The apparent convergence of parallel lines is interpreted as a distance cue. The greater the convergence, the greater the perceived distance.

Shadowing: Opaque objects block light and produce shadows. Shadows and highlights give us information about an object's 3-D shape. In the illustration on the next page, the object on the left is perceived as a 2-D circle. The object on the right is perceived as a 3-D sphere because of the highlight on the surface and the shadow underneath.

Relative brightness: Objects that are close to us reflect more light to the eyes. The dimmer of two identical objects appears to be further away.

Aerial haze: Objects that are hazy are perceived to be further away than objects more in focus.

Aerial perspective: Objects at a greater distance appear to have a different colour (such as the bluish tint of a distant mountain).

Motion parallax: If we move, objects near to us appear to move more than objects far away from us. When we move past objects located at different distances from us, they appear to move across the visual field at different speeds, with those nearest to us moving most rapidly. Such differences in speed help us to judge both distance and depth.

PERCEPTUAL CONSTANCY

Having perceived an object as a coherent form and located it in space, we must next recognise the object without being 'fooled' by changes in its size, shape, location, brightness and colour. The ability to perceive an object as unchanging, despite changes in the sensory information that reaches our eyes, is called *perceptual constancy*.

Size constancy

As people move further away from us, the size of image they project on the retina decreases. However, rather than seeing people as 'growing smaller', we perceive them as being of a fixed height moving away from us. *Size constancy* occurs because the perceptual system takes into account an object's distance from the perceiver. So, perceived size is equal to retinal image size taking distance into account.

The perception of an *after-image* demonstrates how distance can be varied *without* changing the retinal image's size. If you stare at a bright light for a few seconds and then look away, you will experience an after-image. This has a fixed size, shape and position on the retina. However, if you quickly look at a nearby object and then an object further away, the after-image appears to shrink and swell, appearing to be largest

when you look at a more distant object. Real objects cast a smaller image the further away they are, and to maintain perceptual constancy the brain 'scales-up' the image (*constancy scaling*). The same constancy scaling is applied to an after-image, producing changes in its apparent size.

Shape constancy

We often view objects from angles at which their 'true' shapes are not reflected in the retinal image they project. For example, rectangular doors often project trapezoid shapes and round cups often project elliptical-shaped images. Just as with size constancy, the perceptual system maintains constancy in terms of shape.

Figure 23.5 *No matter what angle a door is viewed from, it remains a door*

However, shape and size constancy do not always work. When we look down at people from the top of a very tall building, they do *look* more like ants to us, even though we know they are people.

Location constancy

Moving our heads around produces a constantly changing pattern of retinal images. However, we do not perceive the world as spinning around. This is because *kinaesthetic feedback* from the muscles and balance organs in the ear are integrated with the changing retinal stimulation in the brain to inhibit perception of movement. To keep the world from moving crazily every time we move our eyes, the brain subtracts the eye-movement commands from the resulting changes on the retina, which helps to keep objects in a constant location.

Brightness constancy

We see objects as having a more or less constant brightness even though the amount of light they reflect changes according to the level of illumination. For example, white paper reflects 90 per cent of light falling on it, whereas black paper reflects only ten per cent. In bright sunlight, however, black paper still looks black even though it may reflect 100 times more light than does white paper indoors (McBurney & Collins, 1984). Perceived brightness depends on how much light an object reflects relative to its surroundings (*relative luminance*). If sunlit black paper is viewed through a narrow tube such that nothing else is visible, it will appear greyish because in bright sunlight it reflects a fair amount of light. When viewed without the tube it is again black, because it reflects much less light than the colourful objects around it.

Colour constancy

Familiar objects retain their colour (or, more correctly, their *hue*) under a variety of lighting conditions (including night light), provided there is sufficient contrast and shadow (see Chapter 22, page 226). However, when we do not already know an object's colour, colour constancy is less effective (Delk & Fillenbaum, 1965). If you have purchased new clothes under fluorescent light without viewing them in ordinary lighting conditions, you will no doubt agree.

ILLUSIONS

Although perception is usually reliable, our perceptions sometimes misrepresent the world. When our perception of an object does not match its true physical characteristics, we have experienced an *illusion*. Some illusions are due to the *physical distortion* of stimuli, whereas others are due to our *misperception* of stimuli (Coren & Girgus, 1978). An example of a *physical illusion* is the bent appearance of a stick when placed in water.

Gregory (1983) identifies four types of *perceptual illusion*. These are *distortions* (or *geometric illusions*), *ambiguous* (or *reversible) figures*, *paradoxical figures* (or *improbable and impossible objects*) and *fictions*.

Distortions

Figure 23.6 shows several examples of distortions. The Poggendorf illusion (Figure 23.6 (b)) is accentuated when the diagonal line is more steeply slanted and when the parallel bars are more separated. As the line is

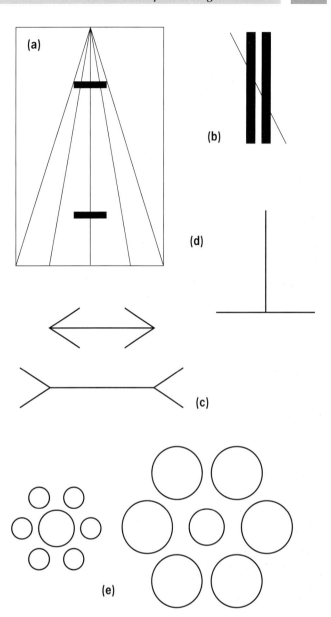

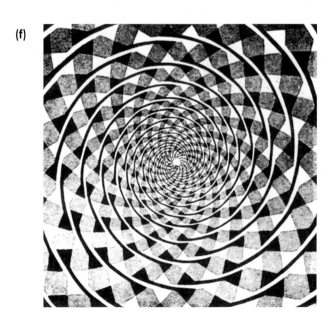

Figure 23.6 *Distortions (or geometric illusions). In the Ponzo illusion (a), the horizontal bar at the top is seen as being longer than the horizontal line at the bottom, even though they are both the same length. The Poggendorf illusion (b) suggests that the segments of the diagonal line are offset, even though they are not. The line with the outgoing fins in the Müller–Lyer illusion (c) appears to be longer than the line with the ingoing fins, but in fact they are the same length. In the horizontal–vertical illusion (d), the vertical line is seen as being longer, although it is the same as the horizontal line. In Titchener's circles (e), the central circle in the left-hand group is seen as being larger than the central circle of the right-hand group, but they are both the same size. Finally, in the twisted card illusion (f), the twisted cards appear to be a spiral pattern, but the circles are, in fact, concentric*

brought closer to the horizontal, the illusion disappears (MacKay & Newbigging, 1977). The horizontal–vertical illusion (Figure 23.6 (d)) illustrates our tendency to overestimate the size of vertical objects. This helps to explain why a small tree we have chopped down looks shorter than it did when it was standing (Coren & Girgus, 1978).

Ambiguous figures

In addition to Rubin's vase (see page 230), three other well-known reversible figures are shown in Figure 23.7 (a–c). In the Necker cube (Figure 23.7 (a)), the figure undergoes a *depth reversal*. The cube can be perceived with the crosses being drawn either on the back side of the cube or on the top side looking down. Although our perceptual system interprets this 2-D line drawing as a 3-D object, it seems undecided as to which of the two orientations should be perceived, and hence the cube spontaneously reverses in depth orientation if looked at for about 30 seconds.

Figure 23.7 (b) shows Boring's 'Old/Young woman'. This and Figure 23.7(c) are examples of reversible figures in which the change in perception illustrates *object reversal*. The figure can be perceived as the profile of a young woman's face with the tip of her nose just visible, or the young woman's chin can be perceived as the nose of the face of a much older woman. In Jastrow's reversible duck/rabbit head (Figure 23.7(c)), the object can be perceived either as the head of a duck with its beak pointing to the left or as a rabbit (the duck's beak becomes the rabbit's ears).

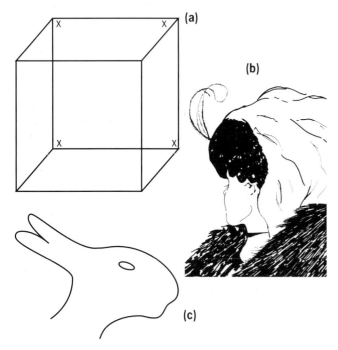

Figure 23.7 *Three ambiguous/reversible figures: (a) the Necker cube; (b) Boring's 'Old/Young Woman'; and (c) Jastrow's duck/rabbit head*

Paradoxical (impossible) figures

Whilst paradoxical figures look ordinary enough at first, on closer inspection we realise that they cannot exist in reality (hence 'paradoxical'). Figure 23.8 (a–d) illustrates four such paradoxical figures.

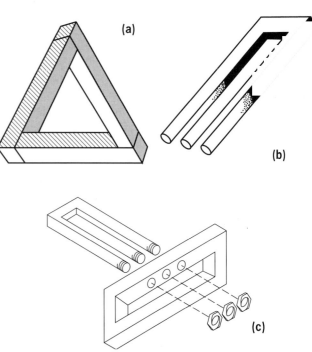

Figure 23.8 *Four paradoxical objects. (a) is the Penrose impossible triangle and (b) is variously known as 'Trident' and 'The devil's pitchfork'. In (c), Trident has been combined with another impossible object. (d) is M.C. Escher's* Relativity. *Although working in two dimensions, Escher has used perceptual cues in such a way as to encourage the viewer to perceive a three-dimensional figure*

According to Hochberg (1970), it takes us a few seconds to realise that a figure is impossible because we need time to fully examine or scan it and organise its parts into a meaningful whole. When we look at a figure, our eyes move from place to place at the rate of about three changes per second (Yarbus, 1967: see Box 21.2, page 211). So when we look at an impossible figure, it takes time to scan it and perceive its form, and only after this scanning can we appreciate its impossible nature.

Fictions

Fictions help explain how we perceive that objects possess a specific shape. The idea that shape is determined by the *physical contours* of an object (which cause edge-detectors in the cells of the visual system to fire) has been challenged by the existence of *subjective contours*, which are the boundaries of a shape perceived in the absence of physical contours (Kanizsa, 1976).

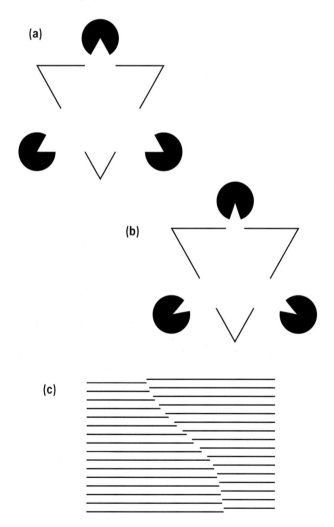

In Figure 23.9 (a), although no white triangular contour is physically present, we perceive the shape of a white triangle which appears to be opaque and lighter than the background. There are *some* contours that are physically present (the overlap of the triangle and the disc), and these *might* cause enough edge-detector cells to fire. However, this explanation cannot account for the fact that in Figure 23.9 (b), the partial and straight physical contours give rise to a *curved* triangle. Nor can it explain the subjective contour in Figure 23.9 (c), which is marked by lines in a totally different orientation (Krebs & Blackman, 1988).

It is the *relationship between its parts* that is the defining characteristic of a shape, rather than its physical contours (Rock, 1984). Physical contours are, of course, usually indicative of the location of an object's parts. However, the location of the parts can also be determined by subjective contours. As a result, the perception of shape must involve more than simply detecting the elements of a pattern (Krebs & Blackman, 1988).

We are surrounded by illusions in our everyday life. The use of perspective cues by artists leads us to infer depth and distance, that is, we add something to a picture which is not physically present, just as we do to the images projected on our television screens. Television pictures also use the *illusion of movement*.

THE PERCEPTION OF MOVEMENT

As we turn our heads and look around a room, the light from various objects stimulates successive and different parts of the retina. Despite this, we perceive the objects to be stationary. At a soccer match, we move our heads so that the light reflected by the players and ball is directed at the same area of the retina, but we know that the players and ball are moving. Cues used to perceive movement include the movement of the head and eyes, and knowledge about certain objects. Unfortunately, there is no single (and simple) way in which movement is perceived, and our conclusions about movement using environmental cues depend on how such cues are interpreted (Poggio & Koch, 1987).

Just as it is possible for changes in patterns of retinal stimulation not to be accompanied by the perception of movement, so it is possible to perceive movement without a successive pattern of retinal stimulation (Ramachandron & Anstis, 1986). This is called *apparent movement*.

Figure 23.9 *Three fictions. In (a), the 'white triangle' is banded by a subjective contour, rather than a continuous physical one. In (b), the subjective contours are curved. In (c), lines of different orientation produce a subjective contour*

Box 23.4 Some examples of apparent movement

The autokinetic effect: If you look at a stationary spot of light in an otherwise completely dark room, the light will appear to move. According to Gregory (1973), this illusion of apparent movement is produced by small and uncontrollable eye movements. Another explanation suggests that it is caused by the absence of a stimulating background to provide a frame of reference for measuring movement. This is supported by the fact that the autokinetic effect disappears if other lights are introduced (see also Gross *et al.*, 2000).

Stroboscopic motion: The illusion of movement is created by the rapid succession of slightly different stationary images. If these are presented sufficiently quickly (around 16 to 22 frames per second), an illusory impression of continuous movement is produced, and this is the mechanism by which moving pictures operate. With fewer than 16 frames per second, the moving picture looks jumpy and unnatural. Smooth *slow motion* is achieved by filming at a rate of 100 or more frames per second, and then playing back at about 20 frames per second.

The phi phenomenon: This is a simpler form of stroboscopic motion in which a number of separate lights are turned on and off in quick succession. This gives the impression of a single light moving from one position to another. Both stroboscopic motion and the phi phenomenon can be explained by the *law of good continuation* (see page 231).

Induced movement: This occurs when we perceive an object to be moving, although in reality it is stationary and its surroundings are moving. Movie stars, for example, are often filmed in a stationary car with a projection of a moving background behind them. Similarly, when the moon is seen through a thin cover of moving clouds, we sometimes perceive it to be moving very quickly. Another example is the experience of sitting in a car at traffic lights and noticing that we are 'moving backwards', when in fact the car at our side is moving forwards.

Motion after-effects: People who work on inspection belts in factories experience movement after-effects when the belt suddenly stops but is perceived as now moving backwards. Similarly, if you stare at a waterfall and then switch your gaze to the ground surrounding it, the ground appears to be moving in the opposite direction.

Such after-effects are generally accepted as being due to the overstimulation of particular movement-detector cells in the visual system. Because cells sensitive to, say, downward movement have been overstimulated, they are momentarily insensitive when the stimulation ceases. However, the cells sensitive to, say, upward movement are relatively more active, resulting in a motion after-effect.

At least some examples of apparent movement can be termed *intelligent errors*, because they result from perceptual strategies that work most of the time (Rock, 1983). Motion after-effects, however, can be more easily explained in physiological terms.

According to Braddick (1974), the human visual system seems to have two separate systems for measuring the speed and direction of individual features moving in the retinal image:

- a long-range, *feature-tracking* system seems to infer motion from one instant to the next, and this underpins our conscious impression of motion in films and television;

- a short-range, *motion-sensing* system seems to measure motion more directly by signalling changes in the image content over time.

Although neither system is fully understood, the basic requirements are in place even at the retina. *P-type* ganglion cells (see Chapter 22, pages 220–221) respond to abrupt *spatial* changes in the image, whilst *M-type* ganglion cells may respond to abrupt *temporal* changes. Additionally, the temporal cortex contains many cells selective for different types of motion, and most visual cortical cells prefer moving to stationary stimuli (Harris, 1998).

SOME THEORIES OF VISUAL PERCEPTION

Gregory's 'constructivist' theory

According to Gregory (1966):

> 'Perception is not determined simply by stimulus patterns. Rather, it is a dynamic searching for the best interpretation of the available data ... [which] involves going beyond the immediately given evidence of the senses'.

To avoid *sensory overload*, we need to select from all the sensory stimulation which surrounds us. Often, we also need to *supplement* sensory information because the total information that we need might not be directly available to the senses. This is what Gregory means by 'going beyond the immediately given evidence of the senses' and it is why his theory is known as *constructivist*. For

Gregory, we make *inferences* about the information the senses receive (based on Helmholtz's nineteenth-century view of perception as *unconscious inferences*).

Gregory's theory and perceptual constancies

Perceptual constancies (see pages 234–235) tell us that visual information from the retinal image is sketchy and incomplete, and that the visual system has to 'go beyond' the retinal image in order to test hypotheses which fill in the 'gaps' (Greene, 1990). To make sense of the various sensory inputs to the retina (*low-level information*), the visual system must draw on all kinds of evidence, including distance cues, information from other senses, and expectations based on past experience (*high-level knowledge*). For all these reasons, Gregory argues that perception must be an *indirect process* involving a construction based on physical sources of energy.

Gregory's theory and illusions

Gregory argues that when we experience a visual illusion (see pages 235–237), what we perceive may not be physically present in the stimulus (and hence not present in the retinal image). Essentially, an illusion can be explained in terms of a *perceptual hypothesis* which is not confirmed by the data, so that our attempt to interpret the stimulus figure turns out to be inappropriate. An illusion, then, occurs when we attempt to construe the stimulus in keeping with how we normally construe the world and are misled by this.

Box 23.5 Explaining the Ponzo illusion

In the Ponzo illusion, for example (see Figure 23.6 (a), page 235), our system can accept the equal lengths of the two central bars as drawn on a flat 2-D surface (which would involve assuming that the bars are equidistant from us), or it can 'read' the whole figure as a railway track converging into the distance (so that the two horizontal bars represent sleepers, the top one of which would be further away from an observer but appears longer since it 'must' be longer in order to produce the same length image on the retina).

The second interpretation is clearly inappropriate, since the figure is drawn on a flat piece of paper and there are no actual distance differences. As a result, an illusion is experienced.

All illusions illustrate how the perceptual system normally operates by forming a 'best guess' which is then tested against sensory inputs. For Gregory, illusions show that perception is an *active* process of using information to suggest and test hypotheses. What we perceive are not the data, but the interpretation of them, so that:

'A perceived object is a hypothesis, suggested and tested by sensory data' (Gregory, 1966).

As Gregory (1996) has noted, '... this makes the basis of knowledge indirect and inherently doubtful'.

Gregory argues that when we view a 3-D scene with many distance cues, the perceptual system can quickly select the hypothesis that best interprets the sensory data. However, reversible figures supply few distance cues to guide the system. For example, the spontaneous reversal of the Necker cube (see page 236) occurs because the perceptual system continually tests two *equally* plausible hypotheses about the nature of the object represented in the drawing.

One striking illusion is the *rotating hollow mask* (Gregory, 1970: see Figure 23.10). There is sufficient information for us to see the mask as hollow, but it is impossible *not* to see it as a normal face. The perceptual system dismisses the hypothesis that the mask is an inside-out face because it is so improbable, and note that in this case, the hypothesis we select is strongly influenced by our *past experiences of faces* (Gregory, 1970). With the impossible triangle (see Figure 23.8 (a), page 236), our perceptual system makes reasonable, but actually incorrect, judgements about the distance of different parts of the triangle.

Figure 23.10 *The rotating hollow mask. (a) shows the normal face which is rotated to (d), which is a hollow face. However, (d) appears like a normal face rotating in the opposite direction*

According to Gregory's *misapplied size constancy theory*, the Müller–Lyer illusion (see Figure 23.6 (c), page 235) can be explained in terms of the arrow with the ingoing fins providing linear perspective cues suggesting that it could be the *outside corner* of a building, and the ingoing fins the walls receding from us. This would make the arrow appear to be 'close'. In the arrow with the outgoing fins, the cues suggest that it could be the *inside corner* of a room, and the outgoing fins as walls approaching us. This would make the shaft appear 'distant' (see Figure 23.11).

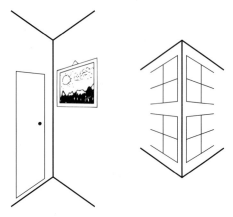

Figure 23.11 *A representation of the Müller–Lyer illusion as suggested by Gregory's misapplied size constancy theory*

However, the retinal images produced by the arrows are equal and, according to size constancy, if equally sized images are produced by two lines, one of which is further away from us than the other, then the line which is furthest from us must be longer! Because this interpretation is taking place unconsciously and quickly, we immediately perceive the illusion. Evidence suggests, though, that if the perspective cues are removed, the illusion remains, suggesting that the misapplied size constancy theory is itself misapplied (see Figure 23.12). Alternatively, the apparent distance of the arrow could be caused by the apparent size of the arrows rather than, as Gregory claims, the other way around (Robinson, 1972).

In a variation of the original Müller–Lyer illusion, Morgan (1969) placed a dot mid-way along the arrow (see Figure 23.13). The dot appears to be nearer the left-hand end, and the only way this can be explained by Gregory is to claim that the fins make the arrow appear to slope away from us, providing a rather odd perspective interpretation of the figure. According to Gregory (1972), such a slope can be demonstrated, although this claim has been disputed (Eysenck & Keane, 1995).

In the Müller–Lyer illusion, we *know* the arrows are the same length, yet we still experience the illusion. Our knowledge *should* enable us to modify our hypotheses in an adaptive way. Whilst some illusions can be explained

in terms of the same unconscious processes occurring (an example being size constancy), not all illusions are amenable to explanation in the way Gregory proposes (Robinson, 1972).

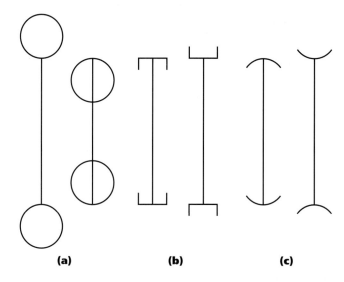

Figure 23.12 *The Müller–Lyer illusion with the depth cues removed (after Delboeuf, 1892)*

Figure 23.13 *Morgan's (1969) modified Müller–Lyer illusion*

Gregory's theory and 'perceptual set'

Perceptual set is also directly relevant to Gregory's view that perception is an active process involving selection, inference and interpretation. Allport (1955) describes perceptual set as:

> '... a perceptual bias or predisposition or readiness to perceive particular features of a stimulus'.

It refers to the tendency to perceive or notice some aspects of available sense data and ignore others. According to Vernon (1955), set acts as a *selector* (the perceiver has certain expectations which help focus attention on particular aspects of the incoming sensory information), and as an *interpreter* (the perceiver knows how to deal with the selected data, how to classify, understand and name them, and what inferences to draw from them).

Several factors can influence or induce set, most of them being *perceiver* (or *organismic*) *variables*, but some relate to the nature of the stimulus or the conditions under which it is perceived *(stimulus* or *situational variables)*. Both types of variable influence perception *indirectly*, through directly influencing set which, as such, is a perceiver variable or characteristic.

Box 23.6 Some findings relating to perceptual set

Motivation: People with some particular need (such as hunger) are more likely to perceive vague or ambiguous pictures as relating to that need (Sanford, 1937; McClelland & Atkinson, 1948).

Values: Lambert *et al.* (1949) found that when children were taught to value something more highly than they had previously done, they perceived the valued thing as being larger (*perceptual accentuation*).

Beliefs: The beliefs we hold about the world can affect our interpretation of ambiguous sensory signals. A person who believes in UFOs is likely to perceive an ambiguous object in the sky differently from a person who does not share that belief (Wade & Tavris, 1993).

Cognitive style: The way we deal with our environment appears to affect our perception of it. Some people perceive the environment as a whole and do not clearly differentiate the shape, colour and so on, of individual items. Others perceive the elements of the environment as separate and distinct (Witkin *et al.*, 1962).

Cultural background: The BaMbuti pygmies of Zaire, who seldom leave their forest environment and rarely encounter objects more than a few feet away, use perceptual cues differently from people with different cultural backgrounds (Turnbull, 1961: see also Chapter 24, pages 253–257).

Context and expectations: The interaction between context and expectations was demonstrated by Bruner & Postman (1949) and Bruner *et al.* (1952). When participants are asked to copy a briefly presented stimulus such as:

PARIS IN THE

THE SPRING

it is typically copied as PARIS IN THE SPRING (Lachman, 1984). One reason why *eyewitness testimony* is so unreliable is that our general expectation of people is that they will be of 'average height and weight', and this is what almost all eyewitness accounts describe people as being (Loftus, 1980: see Gross *et al.*, 2000).

An evaluation of Gregory's theory of perception

According to Gregory (1996), even a minimal amount of 'bottom-up' data (sensory signals) can produce detailed hypotheses. He cites Johansson's (1975) demonstration of *biological motion*, in which a few lights attached to a moving person seen in darkness evoke clear perceptions of a person walking or dancing. Gregory has also drawn on research indicating that vision 'works' by many physiologically distinct 'channels' which are produced by their own 'modules'. A rotating spiral, for example, does not actually change size but appears to expand or contract. Because size and motion are signalled by different 'channels', disagreement between them leads to a *physiological paradox* being experienced (see Chapter 22, page 223).

Gregory's theory raises many important questions which have yet to be answered satisfactorily (Gordon, 1989). For example, if perception is essentially constructive, then we need to know how it gets started and why there is such common experience among different people, all of whom have had to construct their own idiosyncratic perceptual worlds. Also, given that perception is typically accurate (and our hypotheses are usually correct), it seems unlikely that our retinal images are really as ambiguous and lacking in detail as Gregory suggests.

Gregory has been much more successful in explaining at least some types of illusion than in explaining perception as a whole (Eysenck & Keane, 1995). His theory may be most relevant when stimuli are ambiguous or incomplete, presented very briefly, or their processing interrupted (Groome *et al.*, 1999). In Gordon's (1989) view, constructivist theories have underestimated the richness of sensory evidence in the real world. For Gordon:

> 'It is possible that we perceive constructively only at certain times and in certain situations. Whenever we move under our own power on the surface of the natural world and in good light, the necessary perceptions of size, texture, distance, continuity, motion and so on, may all occur directly and reflexively'.

Gibson's theory of 'direct perception'

Constructivists use the retinal image as their starting point for explaining perception. According to Gibson (1966), this approach mistakenly describes the input for a perceiver in the same terms as that for a single *photoreceptor*, namely a stream of photons. For Gibson, it is better to begin by considering the input as a pattern of light extended over time and space (an *optic array* containing all the visual information from the environment striking the eye of a stationary perceiver). The optic array provides unambiguous, *invariant* information about the layout and relevant properties of objects in space, and this information takes three main forms: *optic flow patterns*, *texture gradient* and *affordances*. Perception essentially involves 'picking up' the rich information provided by the optic array in a direct way, which involves little or no (unconscious) information processing, computations or internal representations (Harris, 1998).

Optic flow patterns

During World War II, Gibson prepared training films describing the problems pilots experience when taking off and landing. He called the information available to pilots *optic flow patterns* (OFPs). As shown in Figure 23.14, the point to which a pilot moves appears motionless, with the rest of the visual environment apparently moving away from that point. Thus, all around the point there is an apparent radial expansion of textures flowing around the pilot's head.

The lack of apparent movement of the point towards which the pilot moves is an invariant, unchanging feature of the optic array. Such OFPs provide unambiguous information about direction, speed and altitude. OFPs in general refer to changes in the optic array as the perceiver moves about.

Figure 23.14 *The optic flow patterns as a pilot approaches the landing strip (From Gibson, 1950)*

Texture gradients

Textures expand as we approach them and contract as they pass beyond our head. This happens whenever we move toward something, so that over and above the behaviour of each texture element there is a 'higher-order' pattern or structure available as a source of information about the environment (and so the flow of the texture is *invariant*). *Texture gradients* (or *gradients of texture density*) are an important depth cue perceived directly without the need for any inferences. The depth cues identified in Box 23.3 (see pages 233–234) are all examples of directly perceived, invariant, higher-order features of the optic array. For Gibson, then, the third dimension (depth) is available to the senses as directly as

the other two dimensions, automatically processed by the sense receptors, and automatically producing the perceptual experience of depth.

Affordances

Affordances are directly perceivable, potential uses of objects (a ladder, for example, 'affords' climbing), and are closely linked with *ecological optics*. To understand an animal's perceptual system, we need to consider the environment in which it has evolved, particularly the patterns of light (the optic array) which reaches the eye (ecological optics). When an object moves further away from the eye, its image gets smaller (relative size), and most objects are bounded by texture surfaces and texture gradient gets finer as an object recedes. In other words, objects are not judged in complete isolation, and the optic array commonly contains far more information than that associated with a single stimulus array (often overlooked by the use of classical optics and laboratory experiments: Gordon, 1989).

An evaluation of Gibson's theory

According to Marr (1982), Gibson's concern with the problem of how we obtain constant perception in everyday life, on the basis of continually changing sensations, indicated that he correctly regarded the problem of perception as that of recovering from sensory information 'valid properties of the external world'. However, as Marr (1982) points out, Gibson failed to recognise two equally critical things:

> 'First, the detection of physical invariants, like image surfaces, is exactly and precisely an information-processing problem ... Second, he vastly underrated the sheer difficulty of such detection'.

Gibson's concept of affordances is part of his attempt to show that all the information needed to make sense of the visual environment is directly available in the visual input (a purely 'bottom-up' approach to perception). Bruce & Green (1990) argue that this concept is most powerful and useful in the context of *visually guided behaviour*, as in insects. Here, it makes sense to speak of an organism detecting information available in the light needed to organise its activities, and the idea of it needing to have a conceptual representation of its environment seems redundant.

However, humans act in a *cultural* as well as physical environment. It seems unlikely that no *knowledge* of writing or the postal system is needed in order to detect that a pen affords writing or a postbox affords posting a letter, and that these are directly perceived invariants. People see objects and events as what they are in terms of a culturally given conceptual representation of the world, and Gibson's theory says much more about '*seeing*' than about '*seeing as*'.

'Seeing' and 'seeing as'

Fodor & Pylyshyn (1981) distinguish between 'seeing' and 'seeing as'. For them:

> 'What you see when you see a thing depends upon what the thing you see is. But what you see the thing as depends upon what you know about what you are seeing'.

This view of perception as 'seeing as' is the fundamental principle of *transactionalism*. Transactionalists (such as Ames, cited in Ittelson, 1952) argue that because sensory input is always ambiguous, the interpretation selected is the one most likely to be true given what has been perceived in the past.

In the Ames *distorted room* (see Figure 23.15), the perceiver has to choose between two different beliefs about the world built up through past experience. The first is that rooms are rectangular, consist of right angles, and so

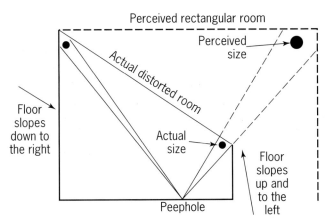

Figure 23.15 *The Ames room and a schematic representation of its 'secret'. The room is constructed in such a way that, when viewed with one eye through a peephole, a person at one end may appear very small and the person at the other end very tall, When they cross the room, they appear to change size. The room itself appears perfectly normal and regular to an observer*

on. The second is that people are usually of 'average' height. Most observers choose the first and so judge the people to be an odd size (although a woman who saw her husband in the room and judged the *room* to be odd shows that particularly salient past experiences can override more generalised beliefs about the world).

The Ames room is another example of a visual illusion, and the inability of Gibson's theory to explain mistaken perception is perhaps its greatest single weakness. Gibson argues that most 'mistaken perceptions' occur in situations very different from those which prevail in the natural environment. However, to suggest that illusions are nothing but laboratory tricks designed to baffle ordinary people is mistaken, since at least some produce effects that are similar to those found in normal perception. A striking example is the 'hollow mask' illusion described on page 239 (Bruce & Green, 1990).

A possible synthesis of Gregory's and Gibson's theories

Despite the important differences between Gibson's and Gregory's theories, they also agree on certain points.

Box 23.7 The main similarities and differences between Gibson and Gregory

Similarities

- Visual perception is mediated by light reflected from surfaces and objects.

- Some kind of physiological system is needed to perceive.

- Perception is an active process. (In Gibson's, 1966, view, 'a perceiving organism is more like a map-reader than a camera'.)

- Perceptual experience can be influenced by learning.

Differences

- Gregory believes that meaningless sensory cues must be supplemented by memory, habit, experience and so on in order to construct a meaningful world. Gibson argues that the environment (initially the optic array) provides us with *all* the information we need for living in the world. Perceptual learning consists not in 'gluing' together sensory 'atoms', but in coming to differentiate and discriminate between the features of the environment as presented in the optic array.

- To the extent that Gibson acknowledges the role of learning (albeit a different kind of learning from Gregory), he may be considered an *empirist* (see

Chapter 24), together with his emphasis on what is provided by the physical world. In other respects, though, Gibson can be considered a *nativist* (see Chapter 24). He was very much influenced by the Gestalt psychologists (see pages 229–233), stressing the organised quality of perception. However, whilst for Gibson the organised quality of perception is part of the physical structure of the light impinging on the observer's eye, for Gestaltists it is a function of how the brain is organised.

Eysenck & Keane (1995) argue that the relative importance of bottom-up and top-down processes is affected by several factors. When viewing conditions are good, bottom-up processing may be crucial. However, with brief and/or ambiguous stimuli, top-down processing becomes increasingly important. Gibson seems to have been more concerned with *optimal* viewing conditions, whilst Gregory and other constructivists have tended to concentrate on *sub-optimal* conditions (Eysenck, 1993). In most circumstances, both bottom-up and top-down processes are probably needed, as claimed by Neisser (1976).

Box 23.8 Neisser's (1976) analysis–by–synthesis model

Neisser assumes the existence of a *perceptual cycle* involving *schemata*, *perceptual exploration* and *stimulus environment*. Schemata contain collections of knowledge based on past experience, and these direct perceptual exploration towards relevant environmental stimulation. Such exploration often involves moving around the environment, leading the per-

ceiver to actively sample the available stimulus information. If this fails to match the information in the relevant schema, then the hypothesis is modified accordingly.

An initial *analysis* of the sensory cues/features (a bottom-up process) might suggest the hypothesis that the object being viewed is, say, a chair. This initiates a search for the expected features (such as four legs and a back), which is based on our schema of a chair (and this *synthesis* is a top-down process). However, if the environmental features disconfirm the original hypothesis (the 'chair' has only three legs and no back), then a new hypothesis must be generated and tested (it might be a stool), and the appropriate schema activated.

Neisser argues that perception never occurs in a vacuum, since our sampling of sensory features of the environment is always guided by our knowledge and past experience. Perception is an *interactive process*, involving both bottom-up feature analysis and top-down expectations.

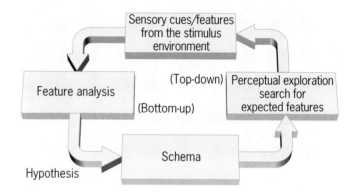

Figure 23.16 *Neisser's analysis-by-synthesis model of perception*

CONCLUSIONS

This chapter looked at some basic visual phenomena, namely form and depth perception, perceptual constancy and visual illusions. These are all concerned with perceptual organisation, and many of the principles governing perceptual organisation are commonly referred to as Gestalt laws.

The chapter also considered various theories of visual perception, two major examples being Gregory's constructivist ('top-down') and Gibson's direct ('bottom-up') approaches.

Whilst they may appear to contradict each other, it is possible to see them as complementary. According to Harris (1998):

'Perception is not just a single task but ... contributes in many different ways to everyday life ... Some of these ... are obviously more difficult than others and it seems likely that some can be accomplished directly, as Gibson maintained, whilst others may require sophisticated internal knowledge and are thus better described by the indirect approach.'

Summary

■ **Sensation** involves physical stimulation of the sense organs, whilst **perception** is the **organisation** and **interpretation** of incoming sensory information. Vision is the dominant sense modality in humans.

■ **Gestalt psychologists** identified innately determined **principles** through which sensory information is interpreted and organised, the most basic being **form perception** which organises incoming sensory information into **figure and ground**.

■ Laws for **grouping** stimuli together all rest on the belief that 'the whole is greater than the sum of its parts'. These laws can be summarised under Koffka's law of **prägnanz**. Major Gestalt laws of perception include **proximity**, **similarity**, **good continuation**, **closure**, **part–whole relationship**, **simplicity** and **common fate**.

■ The various 'laws' are merely descriptive and often imprecise and difficult to measure. Despite empirical support, Gestalt laws are difficult to apply to 3-D perception and to whole scenes (they lack **ecological validity**).

■ **Depth perception** allows us to estimate the distance of objects from us. **Monocular cues** are important for judging objects at greater distances. They include **relative size**, **overlap/superimposition**, **relative height**, **texture gradient**, **linear perspective**, **shadowing**, **relative brightness**, **aerial haze**, **aerial perspective** and **motion parallax**.

■ **Perceptual constancy** refers to the ability to recognise an object as unchanging despite changes in its **size**, **shape**, **location**, **brightness** and **colour**.

■ **Perceptual illusions** occur when a stimulus contains misleading perceptual cues. **Fictions** suggest that **subjective contours** are at least as important as **physical contours** in determining an object's perceived shape. Shape perception is defined by the **relationship** between the elements of a pattern, not simply by detection of the elements.

■ Four main kinds of perceptual illusion are **distortions/geometric illusions**, **ambiguous/reversible figures**, **paradoxical figures**, and **fictions**.

■ Other illusions include **perception of depth** in paintings/drawings and the **perception of movement** in television pictures. Examples of **apparent movement** include the **autokinetic effect**, **stroboscopic motion**, the **phi phenomenon**, **induced movement** and **motion after-effects**.

■ According to **top-down (conceptually-driven) perceptual processing theorists**, perception is the end result of an indirect process that involves making **inferences** about the world, based on knowledge and expectations.

■ **Bottom-up (data-driven) perceptual processing theorists** argue that perception is a **direct** process, basically determined by the information presented to the sensory receptors.

■ According to Gregory's **constructivist theory**, perception sometimes involves selecting from all the available sensory stimulation, but often we supplement it with **unconscious inferences**. The experience of illusions involves making a **perceptual hypothesis** which is not confirmed by the data.

■ According to Gregory's **misapplied size constancy theory**, we interpret the ingoing and outgoing fins of the arrows in the Müller–Lyer illusion as providing perspective cues to distance. However, removal of the perspective cues does not remove the illusion.

■ **Perceptual set** acts as a **selector** and **interpreter**, and can be induced by **perceiver/organismic** and **stimulus/situational variables**. Perceiver variables include **expectations** which often interact with context.

■ According to Gibson, the correct starting point for explaining perception is the **optic array**, which provides unambiguous/invariant information about the layout and properties of objects in space. Little or no (unconscious) information processing, computations or internal representations are needed.

■ **Optic flow patterns, texture gradients/gradients of texture density** and **affordances** are all **invariant**, unchanging and 'higher-order' features of the optic array. Texture gradients are an important cue to depth, which is directly available to the senses and automatically processed by the sense receptors.

■ **Affordances** are closely linked with **ecological optics**. Objects are not judged in isolation, and the optic array usually contains far more information than is provided by any single stimulus.

■ Humans act in a **cultural** as well as a physical environment, and Gibson seems to have overlooked the role of **knowledge** in perception. He also failed to distinguish between seeing and seeing as, the latter forming the basic principle of **transactionalism** as demonstrated by the Ames **distorted room** illusion.

■ Both Gibson and Gregory agree that perception is an active process, influenced by learning (making them **empirists**), although they propose different kinds of learning. Gibson is also a **nativist** in certain respects and was influenced by the Gestalt psychologists.

■ Bottom-up processing (Gibson) may be crucial under **optimal** viewing conditions, but under **sub-optimal** conditions, top-down processing (Gregory) becomes increasingly important.

■ According to Neisser's **analysis-by-synthesis model**, perception is an **interactive process,** involving both bottom-up feature analysis and top-down expectations (appearing at different stages of a perceptual cycle).

Essay Questions

1 Discuss research into any **two** examples of perceptual organisation (e.g. constancies; illusions). *(24 marks)*

2 Describe and evaluate **one** constructivist and **one** direct theory of visual perception. *(24 marks)*

WEB ADDRESSES

http://www.illusionworks.com/
http://www.yorku.ca/research/vision/eye
http://aspen.uml.edu/~landigrad/ILLUSION.HTML
http://pantheon.yale.edu/~chunlab/chunlab_projects.html

24 *Perceptual Development*

Chapters 22 and 23 showed that visual perception is a complex set of interconnected and overlapping abilities. Whether these are present at birth or develop through experience has been one of psychology's most enduring debates. This chapter examines the evidence concerning the development of visual perception. Whilst there are several approaches to studying the development of visual perception, this chapter concentrates on (a) studies involving human neonates (new-born babies) and infants, and (b) cross-cultural studies.

Theoretically, the study of neonates is the most direct way of assessing which perceptual abilities are present at birth and which develop through experience. Unfortunately, neonates cannot *tell* us about their visual experiences, and so researchers have had to devise ingenious ways to allow them to *infer* what the new-born baby can perceive (but we can never be certain that such inferences are correct!). As well as the findings, some of the methods used in this area will also be considered.

If consistent differences are found to exist between cultural groups, then, unless we have good independent reasons for believing that these are biologically based, they must be attributable to environmental factors.

THE 'NATURE' AND 'NURTURE' OF VISUAL PERCEPTION

According to Mehler & Dupoux (1994):

'In certain cultures different from our own, the baby was thought of as a repository of a soul that had already lived before, and therefore possessed of all faculties utilised by adults. Closer to us, generations of parents believed, on the contrary, that their children were born deaf and blind and that they remained in this condition for weeks, even months. The notion that the new-born was about as competent as a potted plant and that it had to learn to see, hear, memorise and categorise, was extremely influential in Western thought'.

Indeed, until 25–30 years ago, many medical textbooks stated that newborns are *blind* (Bee, 2000).

Philosophers and psychologists have long debated whether visual perceptual (and other) abilities are *innate* (or *inborn*) or the product of *experience* and *learning*. *Nativists* (or *innate theorists*) argue that we are born with certain capacities and abilities to perceive the world in particular ways. Whilst such abilities might be immature or incomplete at birth, they develop gradually thereafter, proceeding through a genetically determined

process of *maturation*, in which experience plays only a minor (if any) role. The Gestalt psychologists (see Chapter 23) illustrate this perspective.

Those who believe that our capacities and abilities develop through experience are called *empirists* (and can be distinguished from *empiricists*, who follow a methodological prescription which says that we should rely on observation, experience and measurement to obtain reliable knowledge: Wertheimer, 1970). For Locke (1690), the mind at birth is a *blank slate* (or *tabula rasa*) on which experience 'writes' and, in the case of visual perception, the world can only be understood through learning and experience (see Chapter 58). Locke's belief was supported by James (1890), according to whom:

'The baby, assailed by eyes, ears, nose, skin and entrails at once, feels it all as one great booming, buzzing confusion'.

STUDYING NEONATE AND INFANT VISUAL PERCEPTION

If visual perception is innate, then it should be possible to demonstrate perceptual abilities in human neonates.

If visual perception is dependent on experience, such attempts should be doomed to failure. Before looking at the perceptual world of the human neonate, we need to be familiar with some of the methods that have been used in this area.

Box 24.1 Some methods used to study neonate and infant perception

Spontaneous visual preference technique (or preferential looking): Two stimuli are presented simultaneously to the neonate. If more time is spent looking at one, it can reasonably be assumed that (a) the difference between the stimuli can be perceived, and (b) the stimulus which is looked at longer is preferred.

Sucking rate: In this, a dummy (or pacifier) is used and the sucking rate in response to different stimuli is measured. First, a *baseline sucking rate* is established and then a stimulus introduced. The stimulus may produce an increase or decrease in sucking rate but, eventually, *habituation* will occur, and the baby will stop responding. If the stimulus is changed and another increase or decrease in sucking rate occurs, it can be inferred that the baby has responded to the change as a novel stimulus and hence can tell the difference between the two stimuli.

Habituation: As well as being used as described above, habituation has been used as a method in its own right. If an external stimulus and a baby's representation of it match, then the baby presumably knows the stimulus. This will be reflected by the baby ignoring it. Mismatches will maintain the baby's attention, so that a novel (and discriminable) stimulus presented after habituation to a familiar stimulus re-excites attention.

Conditioned head rotation: In this, the infant is operantly conditioned (see Chapter 38) to turn its head in response to a stimulus. The stimulus can then be presented in, for example, a different orientation, and the presence or absence of the conditioned response noted. This method has been used to test for shape constancy (see pages 234 and 253) and in auditory perception to study basic abilities such as frequency, localisation and complexity (Bornstein, 1988).

Physiological measures: Two of the most important physiological measures are heart rate and breathing rate. If a physiological change occurs when a new stimulus is presented, it can be inferred that the infant can discriminate between the old and new stimuli.

Measures of electrical activity in the brain: By using electrodes attached to the scalp, researchers can look for *visually evoked potentials* (VEPs) occurring in response to particular stimuli. If different stimuli produce different VEPs, the infant can presumably distinguish between those stimuli (see Chapter 10).

THE PERCEPTUAL EQUIPMENT OF BABIES

At birth, the whole nervous system is immature. The optic nerve is thinner and shorter than in adults, and myelin sheath will not be fully developed until about four months. As a result, visual information is transmitted less effectively to the immature cortex. Also, at birth a baby's eye is about half the size and weight of an adult's, and the eyeball is shorter. This reduces the distance between the retina and lens which makes vision less efficient. So, although the new-born's eyeball is anatomically identical to an adult's, the relationship between the parts is different, and they do not develop at the same rate (see Chapter 22, page 220).

Box 24.2 What can babies see?

Colour perception: The retina, rods and cones are reasonably well developed at birth. Using habituation, Bornstein (1976) found that in the absence of brightness cues, three-month-olds could discriminate blue-green from white, and yellow from green (tests which are typically failed by those who are red-green colour blind). Most babies possess largely normal colour vision at two months, and some as early as one month (Bornstein, 1988).

Brightness: The fovea is also reasonably well developed at birth. The developing foetus reacts to bright light, and the *pupillary reflex* is present even in premature babies, with the *blink reflex* present at birth. These findings suggest that a baby's sensitivity to brightness is reasonably similar to an adult's. The ability to discriminate between lights of varying intensities improves with time and reaches adult levels within one year (Adams & Maurer, 1984).

Movement: The *optokinetic reflex* (or *optic nystagmus*), which enables us to follow a moving object, is present within two days of birth. Whilst it is less efficient than an adult's, it improves rapidly in the first three months. Horizontal movement is better tracked than vertical movement, but is still 'jerky'. This may be because *convergence* (essential for fixation and depth perception) is absent at birth, although fully developed by two to three months. *Accommodation* to the distance of objects is equivalent to that of an adult by about four months, and, like at least some of the above, is probably due to maturation (see Chapter 23, page 233).

Visual acuity: Gwiazda *et al.* (1980) used the preference method to show that the *threshold of visual acuity* (the ability to discriminate fine detail) is about 30 times poorer than in adults and, at birth, everything beyond 20 centimetres is seen as a blur. However, babies aged one to three months will learn to suck on a nipple connected to the focus on a projector to bring a blurred picture into focus (Kalnins & Bruner, 1973). Also, when electrodes are attached to a baby's scalp above its visual cortex, VEPs occur in response to visual stimuli, suggesting some degree of acuity at birth. Between six and 12 months, visual acuity comes within adult range (20/20 vision: Haith, 1990; Slater, 1994).

THE PERCEPTUAL ABILITIES OF BABIES

Pattern (or form) perception

Using the preferential looking technique, Fantz (1961) presented one- to 15-week-old babies with pairs of stimuli (see Figure 24.1). The stimuli were presented at weekly intervals, and Fantz measured how long the babies spent looking at each. There was a distinct preference for more *complex stimuli*, that is, stimuli which contain more information and in which there is more 'going on'. According to Fantz:

> 'The relative attractiveness of the two members of a pair depended on the presence of a pattern difference. There were strong preferences between stripes and bull's-eyes and between checkerboard and square. Neither the cross and circle nor the two triangles aroused a significant differential interest. The differential response to pattern was shown at all ages tested, indicating that it was not the result of a learning process'.

Fantz also found that preference for complexity is apparently a function of age (reflecting the fact that the eye, the visual nerve pathways and the visual cortex are poorly developed at birth). The babies tested at weekly intervals could discriminate between stimuli with progressively narrower stripes (cf. visual acuity in Box 24.2). Later, Fantz showed that two- to four-month-old babies prefer patterns to colour or brightness. In that experiment, six test objects were used (see Figure 24.2).

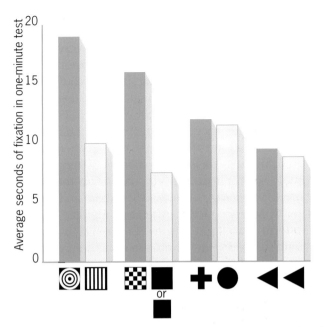

Figure 24.1 *Average time spent looking at various pairs of stimulus patterns in babies aged one to 15 weeks (from Fantz, 1961)*

These were flat discs six inches in diameter. Three were patterned (a face, a bull's-eye and a patch of printed matter), and three were plain (a red disc, a fluorescent yellow disc and a white disc). The discs were presented one at a time against a blue background, and the time spent looking at each was recorded. The face was preferred over both the printed matter and the bull's-eye, and all of these were preferred to the plain discs.

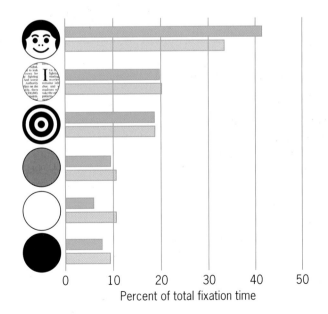

Figure 24.2 *Preference for complex stimuli over simple stimuli. The dark blue bars show the percentage of fixation time for two-to three-month-olds. The light blue bars show the percentage of fixation time for four-month-olds (From Fantz, 1961)*

The preference for increasing complexity suggests that the baby's capacity for differentiation steadily improves. Possibly, this is because its ability to *scan* becomes more efficient and thorough. Support for this comes from studies showing that very young infants confine their scanning to one corner of a triangle, suggesting a preference for areas of greatest contrast (Salapatek, 1975). Only later does the baby begin to explore all around the stimulus and inside it, and attend to the whole pattern and not just specific parts. Before two months of age, neonates probably discriminate between shapes on the basis of *lower-order variables* such as orientation and contrast (Slater & Morison, 1985). After two months, however, 'true form perception' begins (Slater, 1989), and they respond to *higher-order variables* (such as configurational invariance and form categories).

The perception of human faces

The most interesting and attractive stimulus experienced by a baby is the human face. It is three-dimensional, contains high contrast information (especially the eyes, mouth and hairline), constantly moves (the eyes, mouth and head), is a source of auditory information (the voice) and regulates its behaviour according to the baby's own activities. Thus, the human face combines complexity, pattern and movement (it is a *supernormal stimulus*: Rheingold, 1961), all of which babies appear innately to prefer. Whether this preference occurs because of this combination of factors, or whether there is an innate perceptual knowledge of a face *as a face*, was also addressed by Fantz (1961).

Fantz presented babies aged between four days and six months with all possible pairs of the three stimuli shown in Figure 24.3. The stimuli were coloured black, presented against a pink background, and of the approximate shape and size of an adult's head.

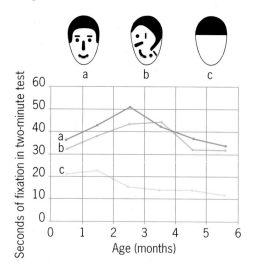

Figure 24.3 *Looking times for each of the stimuli used in Fantz's study of the perception of faces (From Fantz, 1961)*

Irrespective of age, the babies preferred to look at the schematic representation of a face (a) more than the 'scrambled' face (b). The control stimulus (c) was largely ignored. Even though the difference between (a) and (b) was small, Fantz concluded that 'there is an unlearned, primitive meaning in the form perception of infants', and that babies have an innate preference for 'facedness'.

Hershenson *et al.* (1965) pointed out that (a) and (b) were more *complex* than (c) and this might account for Fantz's findings, rather than a preference for looking at human faces. They controlled for complexity, and neonates were presented with all possible pairs of three equally complex stimuli. These were: (1) a real female face, (2) a distorted picture which retained the outline of head and hair but altered the position of the other features, and (3) a scrambled face (stimulus (b) in Fantz's experiment). They found *no* preference for any of the three stimuli, and concluded that a preference for real faces is *not* innate. In their view, such a preference does not appear until about four months of age.

Box 24.3 The perception of 'facedness'

Some researchers (e.g. Melhuish, 1982; Kleiner, 1987) have obtained findings which are inconsistent with Fantz's claims, whilst others (e.g. Walton *et al.*, 1992)) have shown that babies as young as 12–36 hours old display a clear preference for their mother's face over the face of a female stranger, when variables such as the overall brightness of the face and hair colour are controlled for. So far, there is no evidence of a preference for their father's face over a male stranger's, even when he has spent more time with the baby than the mother has. There is no obvious explanation for this (Bee, 2000).

Given the human face's complexity, it is hardly surprising that babies fail to make subtle distinctions about faces (such as distinguishing male from female) until mid- to late-infancy (Slater, 1994). Meltzoff & Moore (1992) have found that babies will, only minutes after birth, imitate a range of facial expressions they see an adult produce. For Slater (1994), this indicates that neonates can match what they see to some inbuilt knowledge of their own face, and can use this to produce a facial gesture which, in the case of sticking out their tongue, for example, they cannot see. The evidence indicates that:

'Some knowledge about faces is present at birth, suggesting that babies come into the world with some innate, genetically determined knowledge about faces' (Slater, 1994).

Depth perception in babies

Perhaps the most famous way of investigating infants' depth perception is Gibson & Walk's (1960) *visual cliff apparatus* (see Figure 24.4). This consists of a central platform on the *shallow* side of which is a sheet of plexiglass. Immediately below this is a black and white checkerboard pattern. On the other *deep* side is another sheet of plexiglass, this time with the checkerboard pattern placed on the floor, at a distance of about four feet. This gives the appearance of a 'drop' or 'cliff'. The baby is placed on the central platform and its mother calls and beckons to it, first from one side and then the other.

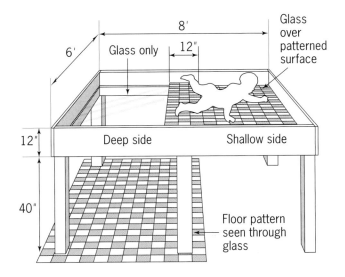

Figure 24.4 *Gibson and Walk's 'visual cliff' apparatus*

Gibson and Walk found that most babies aged between six and 14 months would not crawl onto the 'deep' side when beckoned by their mothers. This was interpreted as indicating that neonates have the innate ability to perceive depth. Those babies who did venture onto the deep side did so 'accidentally', either by backing onto it or resting on it. It is likely that their poor motor control was responsible for this, rather than their inability to perceive depth.

The very nature of the visual cliff apparatus, however, required the researchers to use babies who could *crawl*, the youngest being six months old. An alternative explanation of Gibson and Walk's findings would be that the babies had *learned* to perceive depth during their first six months. Gibson and Walk subsequently tested a number of members of *precocial species* (capable of moving about independently at or shortly after birth), namely, chicks, goat kids, lambs, and rats with their sensitive whiskers removed. None would venture onto the deep side. If forcibly placed on the deep side, the various non-humans would 'freeze'.

Key STUDY

Box 24.4 Testing much younger babies on the visual cliff

In an ingenious way of assessing babies younger than six months, Campos *et al.* (1970) used heart rate as an index of depth perception. Babies of various ages had their heart rates monitored whilst they were on the visual cliff. Older babies (nine months) showed an increased heart rate, a response presumably indicating fear. The youngest (two months) showed a *decreased* heart rate when placed on the 'deep' side. They were less likely to cry, more attentive to what was underneath them, and clearly not frightened by what they saw. No such changes were observed when the infants were placed on the 'shallow' side. It seems that even two-month-olds can perceive depth and that avoidance behaviour is probably learnt (perhaps after having a few experiences of falling).

Depth perception has also been studied by looking at how neonates react when an object approaches their face from a distance. For example, if a large box is moved towards a 20-day-old neonate's face, it shows an *integrated avoidance response*, that is, it throws back its head, shields its face with its hands, and even cries (Bower *et al.*, 1970). This suggests that the baby understands that the box is getting closer and, because it is potentially harmful, some sort of protective reaction is needed. Interestingly, the integrated avoidance response occurs even with one eye closed, but does not occur when equivalent pictures are shown on a screen. This indicates that *motion parallax* (see Chapter 23, page 234) is the critical cue for distance.

Bornstein (1988) has proposed that the roles of innate and experiential factors are both important and inseparable. For him:

'No matter how early in life depth perception can be demonstrated, no matter how late its emergence, it can never be proved that only experience has mattered'.

The perception of 3-D objects

Bower *et al.*'s (1970) discovery of the integrated avoidance response suggests that as well as perceiving depth, neonates see boxes as solid, 3-D objects. To explore this, Bower (1979) devised a piece of apparatus that creates illusions of 3-D objects. Babies aged 16 to 24 weeks were put in front of a screen. A plastic, translucent object was suspended between lights and the screen so that it cast a double shadow on the back. When the screen is viewed from the front and the baby wears polarising goggles, the double shadows merge to form the image of a solid 3-D object.

Bower found that none of the babies showed any surprise when they grasped a real and solid object, but when they reached for the apparent object, and discovered there was nothing solid to get hold of, they all expressed surprise and some were even distressed. This indicates that they expected to be able to touch what they could 'see', an ability Bower believes to be innate.

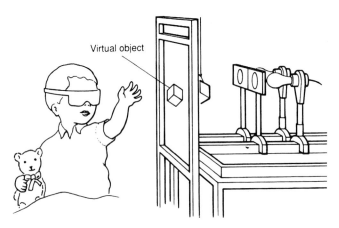

Figure 24.5 *Trying to grasp a 'virtual object' produces surprise in a 4–6-month-old baby*

Perceptual organisation: constancies and gestalt principles

Size constancy

Perceptual constancy is a major form of perceptual organisation, and seems to be a prerequisite for many other types of organisation (see Chapter 23). Despite a newborn's vision being much poorer than an adult's, its visual world is highly organised (Slater, 1994). According to empirists, constancy is learned, and so neonates are likely to be 'tricked' by the appearance of things. For example, if something looks smaller (it projects a smaller retinal image), then it *is* smaller. Nativists, however, would argue that neonates are innately able to judge the size of an object regardless of retinal image.

Key S T U D Y

Box 24.5 Bower's (1966) study of size constancy

To assess nativist and empirist claims, Bower (1966) initially conditioned two-month-olds to turn their heads whenever they saw a 30-centimetre cube at a distance of one metre (an adult popping up in front of the baby whenever it performed the desired behaviour served as a powerful reinforcer). Once the response was conditioned, the cube was replaced by one of three different cubes. The first was a 30-centimetre cube presented at a distance of three metres

(producing a retinal image one-third the size of the original). The second was a 90-centimetre cube presented at a distance of one metre (producing a retinal image three times the size of the original). The third was a 90-centimetre cube presented at a distance of three metres (producing exactly the same-sized retinal image as the conditioned stimulus).

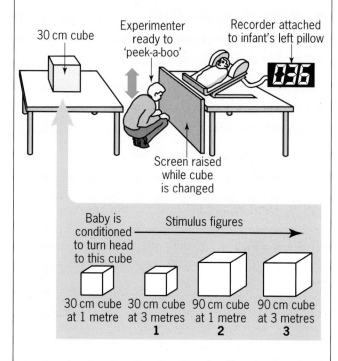

Figure 24.6 *The experimental set-up in Bower's study of size constancy*

Bower recorded the number of times each stimulus produced the conditioned response (CR), and used this as a measure of how similar the neonate considered the stimulus to be to the original. The original stimulus produced a total of 98 CRs, whilst the first produced 58, the second 54, and the third 22. The finding that most CRs occurred in response to the first stimulus indicates that the baby was responding to the actual size of the cube irrespective of its distance. This suggests the presence of size constancy, and supports the nativist view that this constancy is inbuilt.

The nativist position is further strengthened by the finding that fewest CRs occurred in response to the third stimulus. If size constancy was absent, as predicted by empirists, neonates would 'compare' retinal images and base their perception of similarity on these regardless of distance. Empirists, then, would have expected the third stimulus to produce the most CRs. Bower's findings have been replicated with two-day-olds by Slater *et al.*

(1990: cited in Slater, 1994). Although these findings demonstrate that size constancy is an organising feature of perception present at birth, learning still plays some part (Slater, 1994). For example, in the Slater *et al.* study, the procedure depends on infants learning the characteristics of the cubes in the early 'familiarisation trials'.

Shape constancy

According to Slater (1989), new-borns are able to extract the constant real shape of an object that is rotated in the third dimension, that is, they are capable of recognising an object's form independently of (transformations in) its spatial orientation. For example, Bower (1966) found that if a two-month-old infant was conditioned to turn its head to look at a rectangle, it would continue to make the CR when the rectangle was turned slightly to produce a trapezoid retinal image. For Bornstein (1988), the evidence concerning shape constancy indicates that 'babies still only in their first year of life can perceive form *qua* form'.

Feature, identity and existence constancy

Feature constancy is the ability to recognise the invariant features of a stimulus despite some detectable but irrelevant transformation. If a new-born has been *habituated* to a moving stimulus, it will display a *novelty preference* when shown the same stimulus paired with a novel shape, both of which are stationary. This indicates that the new-born perceives the familiar stationary stimulus as the same stimulus when it was moving, and that feature constancy is present at birth.

Feature constancy is a prerequisite for *identity constancy* (the ability to recognise a particular object as being exactly the same object despite some transformation made to it). Distinguishing between feature and identity constancy is extremely difficult. In Bower's (1971) study, babies younger or older than 20 weeks were seated in front of mirrors which could produce several images of the mother. Babies younger than 20 weeks smiled, cooed and waved their arms to *each* of the 'multiple mothers', whereas older babies became upset at seeing more than one mother. What this suggests is that only the older babies, who are aware that they have just one mother, possess identity constancy (see Gross *et al.*, 2000).

Existence constancy refers to the belief that objects continue to exist even when they are no longer available to the senses (which Piaget calls *object permanence*: see Chapter 28). Together, existence and identity constancy comprise the *object concept*, which typically appears around six months of age. Both existence and identity constancy are more sophisticated than shape, size and feature constancies, and it is possible that the object concept arises from the less sophisticated constancies.

Gestalt principles

Bower has also looked at how neonate perception is organised in terms of certain Gestalt principles (see Chapter 23). Bower wanted to discover if *closure* (or *occlusion*) is, as Gestalt psychologists claim, an inborn characteristic.

Key STUDY

Box 24.6 Bower's study of closure

Two-month-olds were conditioned to respond to a black wire triangle with a black iron bar across it (Figure 24.7 top). Then, various stimuli (Figure 24.7 bottom), were presented. Bower found that the CR was generalised to the complete triangle (A), suggesting that the babies perceived an unbroken triangle to lie behind the black iron bar. Given that they were unlikely to have encountered many triangles, Bower concluded that closure is almost certainly an inborn feature of neonate perceptual ability.

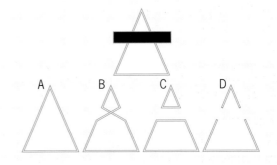

Figure 24.7 *The stimulus figures used in Bower's study of closure*

CROSS-CULTURAL STUDIES

Cross-cultural studies involve a comparison of how people from very different cultures perceive the same things. If we find consistent differences between different cultural groups, then unless there are good independent reasons for believing that those differences are biologically based, we must attribute them to environmental factors (such as social, ecological, linguistic, or some combination of these). Theoretically, then, cross-cultural studies enable us to discover the extent to which perception is structured by the nervous system (and so common to all humans) and by experience.

Studies using visual illusions

There is a long history of cross-cultural research into perceptual development using visual illusions.

- Rivers (1901) compared English adults and children with adult and child Murray Islanders (people from a group of islands between New Guinea and Australia) using the Müller–Lyer illusion and the horizontal–vertical illusion. The Murray Islanders were *less* susceptible to the Müller–Lyer illusion than their English counterparts, but *more* susceptible to the horizontal–vertical illusion.

- Allport & Pettigrew (1957) used the *rotating trapezoid* illusion. This is a trapezoid which has horizontal and vertical bars attached to it.

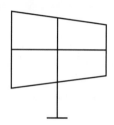

When attached to a motor and revolved in a circle, the trapezoid gives those from Western cultures the impression of being a window, and when rotated through 360°, most Western observers report seeing a rectangle that oscillates to and fro rather than a trapezoid rotating through 360° (which it actually is). Allport and Pettigrew reasoned that for people unfamiliar with windows (at least as people from Western cultures know them), expectations of rectangularity would be absent and the illusion not perceived. When the trapezoid was viewed with both eyes and from a short distance, Zulus (who live in a rather 'circular environment') were less likely than either urban Zulus or Europeans to perceive an oscillating rectangle and more likely to perceive a rotating trapezoid.

- Segall *et al.* (1963) used the Müller–Lyer illusion with members of African and Filipino cultures. As compared with white South Africans and Americans, the Africans and Filipinos were much *less* susceptible to the illusion. However, on the horizontal–vertical illusion, members of two African cultures (the Batoro and the Bayankole) were *most* susceptible. People of these cultures live in high, open country where vertical objects are important focal points and are used to estimate distances. For example, when a tree or pole falls away from you, it seems to grow shorter (*foreshortening*), but when it falls to the left or right across your field of vision its length does not appear to change (Price & Crapo, 1999). The Bete, who live in

a dense jungle environment, were least likely of all groups tested to see the illusion. The white South Africans and Americans fell between the extremes of the three African cultures.

- Stewart (1973) used the Ames distorted room (see page 243) with rural and urban Tongan children. The rural children were less likely to see the illusion than those living in urban environments and European children. This was also true for other illusions, including the Müller–Lyer.

Accounting for differential susceptibility to visual illusions

According to Segall *et al.*'s (1963) carpentered world hypothesis, people in Western cultures:

'... live in a culture in which straight lines abound and in which perhaps 90 per cent of the acute and obtuse angles formed on [the] retina by the straight lines of [the] visual field are realistically interpretable as right angles extended in space'.

Segall *et al.*, therefore, believe that we tend to interpret illusions, which are 2-D drawings, in terms of our past experiences. In the 'carpentered world' of Western societies, we add a third dimension (depth) which is not actually present in the drawing, and this leads to the illusion experience (cf. Gregory's account of visual illusions: see Chapter 23, pages 239–240).

Annis & Frost (1973) looked at the perceptual acuity of Canadian Cree Indians, who live in a non-carpentered environment consisting of summer tents and winter lodges with lines in all orientations. The task involved judging whether two lines were parallel or not, and pairs of lines in different orientations were used. The Crees had no difficulty in judging the lines no matter what angle they were presented at. However, whilst a comparison group of Crees who had moved away from their original environment were good at judging lines that were horizontal or vertical, they were less good with lines at an angle.

Whilst Annis and Frost's data are consistent with Segall *et al.*'s hypothesis, other studies are inconsistent with it. For example, Mundy-Castle & Nelson (1962) studied the Knysna forest dwellers, a group of isolated, white, illiterate South Africans. Despite the rectangularity of their environment, they were unable to give 3-D responses to 2-D symbols on a standard test and, on the Müller–Lyer illusion, their responses were not significantly different from black South Africans, although they were significantly different from literate white adults.

Studies using other perceptual phenomena

In various African cultures, children and adults find it difficult to perceive depth in both pictorial material *and* the real world. Turnbull (1961), for example, studied the BaMbuti pygmies who live in the dense rainforests of the Congo, a closed-in world without open spaces. When a BaMbuti archer was taken to a vast plain and shown a herd of buffalo grazing in the distance, he claimed he had never seen such *insects* before. When informed that the 'insects' were buffalo, the archer was offended. They then rode in a jeep towards the buffalo. The sight of the buffalo in the distance was so far removed from the archer's experience, that he was convinced Turnbull was using magic to deceive him. The archer lacked experience with *distance cues*, preventing him from relating distance to size (Price & Crapo, 1999).

Distance cues are also important in 'reading' pictures. In Hudson's (1960) study, people from various African cultures were shown a series of pictures depicting hunting scenes (see Figure 24.8). The participants saw each picture on its own and were asked to name all the objects in the scene to determine whether or not the elements were correctly recognised. Then they were asked about the *relationship* between the objects, such as 'Which is closer to the man?' If the 'correct' interpretation was made, and depth cues were taken into account, respondents were classified as having 3-D vision. If such cues were ignored, they were classified as having 2-D vision. Hudson reported that both children and adults found it difficult to perceive depth in the pictorial material, and whilst this difficulty varied in extent, it appeared to persist through most educational and social levels (Deregowski, 1972).

Deregowski refers to a description given of an African woman slowly discovering that a picture she was looking at portrayed a human head in profile:

> 'She discovered in turn the nose, the mouth, the eye, but where was the other eye? I tried turning my profile to explain why she could see only one eye, but she hopped round to my other side to point out that I possessed a second eye which the other lacked'.

The woman treated the picture as an object rather than a 2-D representation of an object, that is, she did not 'infer' depth in the picture. What she believed to be an 'object' turned out to have only two dimensions, and this is what the woman found bewildering. However, when familiar pictorial stimulus material is used, recognition tends to be better (Serpell, 1976). Thus, some (but not all) of the Me'en of Ethiopia found it much easier to recognise material when it was presented in the form of pictures painted on cloth (which is both familiar to them and free of distracting cues such as a border) than line drawings on paper (Deregowski, 1972).

Figure 24.8 *Hudson (1960) found that when shown the top picture and asked which animal the hunter is trying to spear, members of some cultures reply 'the elephant'. This shows that some cultures do not use cues to depth (such as overlap and known size of objects). The second picture shows the hunter, elephant and antelope in true size ratios when all are the same distance from the observer*

Evidence also indicates that the drawings in some of the studies emphasise certain depth cues whilst ignoring others, putting non-Western observers at a 'double disadvantage'. For example, in Hudson's (1960) pictures (see Figure 24.8), two depth cues were used (namely *relative size* and *overlap/superimposition*). However, cues like *texture gradient*, *binocular disparity* and *motion parallax* were absent from all of Hudson's pictures. When they were redrawn so as to show texture gradients (by, for example, adding grass to open terrain), more Zambian children gave 3-D answers than in Hudson's original study (Kingsley *et al.*, cited in Serpell, 1976). Research summarised by Berry *et al.* (1992) indicates that the absence of certain depth cues in pictorial material makes the perception of depth difficult for non-Western peoples.

Finally, much research in this area implies that the Western style of pictorial art represents the real world in an *objectively* correct way. 'Artistic excellence' is not identical with 'photographic accuracy' (Gombrich, 1960), and so it might be that people of non-Western cultures 'reject' Western art forms simply on *aesthetic grounds*. As a result, research may have mistakenly described *stylistic preference* as a difference in perception (Serpell, 1976).

Certainly, unfolded 'split', 'developed' or 'chain-type' drawings as shown in Figure 24.9 (left) were originally preferred by African children and adults to the 'orthogonal' or perspective drawings as shown in Figure 24.9 (right). This was often because the drawing lacked important features (legs in the case of Figure 24.9).

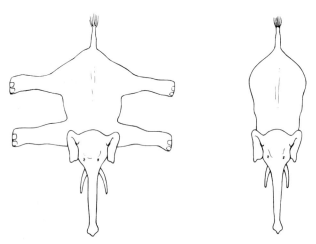

Figure 24.9 *Members of certain African cultures generally prefer the 'split elephant' drawing shown on the left to the top-view perspective drawing shown on the right*

(From Deregowski (1972), 'Pictorial perception and culture'. Copyright © (1972) by Scientific American, Inc. All rights reserved.)

Also, the small lines used by cartoonists to imply motion were the least understood of all the pictorial conventions shown to rural African children (Duncan *et al.*, 1973). When shown a picture in which the artist had drawn a head in three different positions above the same trunk to indicate that the head was turning round, half the children thought the character depicted was deformed (see Figure 24.10 (a)). Likewise, Western observers require guidance from an anthropologist to understand the art forms of American Indians (see Figure 24.10 (b)).

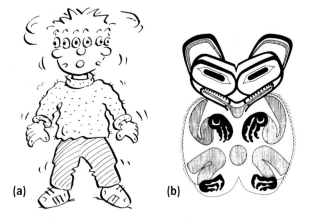

(a)   **(b)**

Figure 24.10 *Is the work of an artist from one particular culture (a) always understandable to a viewer from a different culture (b)?*

Whilst some psychologists believe that the physical environment (or ecology) is closely linked with perceptual experiences, others believe that ecology actually *determines* perceptual experience. However, they cannot agree about the key features of such cultural experiences, and so neither of the beliefs can be strongly supported.

Nature, nurture or an interaction of both?

According to Bee (2000), as researchers have become increasingly ingenious in devising ways of testing infants' perceptual skills, they have found more and more skills already present in new-borns and very young infants. There is growing evidence to support Kagan's (1971) claim that:

> 'Nature has apparently equipped the newborn with an initial bias in the processing of experience. He does not ... have to learn what he should examine'.

Slater (1994) is a little more cautious. *Auditory* perception and learning about the auditory world (not dealt with in this chapter) are well advanced even in very young babies, and a nativist view is closest to the truth. However, in the case of vision, the truth lies somewhere in between a nativist and empirist view. Evidence suggests that the new-born infant:

> '... comes into the world with a remarkable range of visual abilities ... Some rudimentary knowledge and understanding of important stimuli such as objects and faces is present at birth, and experience builds on this genetically or evolutionarily provided range of abilities'. (Slater, 1994)

Some of the strongest evidence in support of the role of nurture comes from cross-cultural studies like those discussed above. Additional support comes from deprivation studies using non-humans, and studies of human cataract patients (see Gross, 1996). Based on his analysis of adults who have had their sight restored following cataract-removal surgery, Hebb (1949) distinguished between *figural unity* (the ability to detect the presence of a stimulus, including scanning objects and distinguishing figure from ground) and *figural identity* (naming or in some other way identifying a familiar object through vision alone). Hebb concluded that the simpler figural unity is innate, whilst the more complex figural identity depends on learning.

Although generalising from adult cataract patients to neonates is far more problematical than Hebb believed, it is difficult to dispute the claim that some visual abilities are probably largely genetically determined whilst others are much more dependent on learning and experience. However, nature and nurture are *never* entirely separable. For example, the neonate's ability to discriminate between the mother's face and that of a similar-looking female *must* be the result of experience, but the *capacity* to make the distinction must be built in. As Bee (2000) says, whenever there is a dispute between nativists and empirists:

> 'Both sides are correct. Both nature and nurture are involved'.

CONCLUSIONS

As this chapter has shown, evidence from studies of human neonates and very young infants suggests that some visual perceptual abilities are probably innate. However, evidence from cross-cultural studies suggests that experience plays a vital role. Rather than seeing themselves as nativists or empirists, most psychologists see a *transactional perspective* as being the most profitable one to adopt as far as visual perception is concerned. Whilst we may be born with capacities to perceive the world in certain ways, stimulation and environmental influences in general are crucial in determining how, and even whether, these capacities actually develop.

Summary

- Studying neonates is the most direct way of assessing which perceptual abilities are **innate/inborn** and which develop through **experience** and **learning**, although researchers must make **inferences** about neonates' experiences.

- Methods used to study neonate perception include **spontaneous visual preference/preferential looking, sucking rate, habituation, conditioned head rotation, physiological measures** and **measures of electrical brain activity**, such as **visually evoked potentials** (VEPs).

- **Nativists/innate theorists** argue that we are born with capacities and abilities to perceive the world in particular ways. If absent at birth, these abilities develop through **maturation** involving little or no learning.

- **Empirists** (as distinct from **empiricists**) see the mind at birth as a **blank slate** (or **tabula rasa**), and argue that our perceptual abilities develop through learning and experience.

- **Colour vision** appears by about two months. The **pupillary** and **blink reflexes** are both present at birth, suggesting that a baby's sensitivity to **brightness** is quite similar to an adult's. The **optokinetic reflex/optic nystagmus** appears soon after birth and quickly improves. **Convergence** and **accommodation** only reach adult levels by three to four months.

- The new-born's **threshold of visual acuity** is much poorer than an adult's, but improves during the first six to 12 months. One- to three-month-olds will learn to suck on a nipple in order to bring a blurred picture into focus, and VEPs can be produced in new-borns.

- Fantz found a preference for more **complex stimuli** among one- to 15-week-old babies. However, this preference is a function of age and reflects the maturation of the visual system. The preference for increasing complexity may be related to the increasingly efficient ability to **scan** the whole stimulus. Before two months, babies discriminate between shapes on the basis of **lower-order variables**, after which they respond to **higher-order variables**.

- The **human face** combines complexity, pattern and movement, all of which babies innately prefer, in an attractive and stimulating form (it is a **supernormal stimulus**). Fantz claimed that babies innately know a face **as a face**. However, he failed to control adequately for **complexity**.

- Although babies fail to make subtle distinctions about faces until mid- to late infancy, they can imitate a range of facial expressions minutes after birth and they also show a very early preference for the mother's face.

- Using the **visual cliff apparatus**, Gibson and Walk concluded that neonates can innately perceive **depth**. However, the youngest babies studied were old enough to have **learned** depth perception, although members of **precocial species** avoid the cliff's deep side shortly after birth/hatching. Measuring changes in heart-rate on the visual cliff suggests that depth perception is probably innate, whilst avoidance behaviour is probably learnt.

- Twenty-day-old babies display an **integrated avoidance response** to an approaching object, with **motion parallax** as the critical cue for distance. This, and babies' expectations that they can touch what they can see, suggests that neonates possess **3-D perception**.

■ Bower's experiment using cubes of different sizes presented from various distances provides support for the nativist view, at least as regards **size constancy**. Bower also found evidence of **shape constancy** in two-month-olds.

■ New-borns are apparently capable of recognising an object's form independently of (transformations in) its orientation in space. **Feature constancy** also seems to be innate, and is a prerequisite for **identity constancy**, which is displayed by babies over 20 weeks old. Identity constancy together with **existence constancy** comprise the **object concept**, which normally appears at about six months.

■ Bower has shown that two-month-olds display the Gestalt principle of **closure**, strongly suggesting that this is an inborn ability.

■ **Cross-cultural studies** compare the perceptions of members of very different cultural groups, often using **visual illusions**. Consistent differences between different groups must be attributed to social, ecological or linguistic factors, unless there is good independent reason to attribute them to biological factors.

■ According to Segall *et al.*'s **carpentered world hypothesis**, members of Western cultures tend to interpret illusion figures by adding depth that is not actually in them. Whilst Annis and Frosts's study of Canadian Cree Indians supports the carpentered world hypothesis, several other studies are inconsistent with it.

■ Turnbull's study of the BaMbuti pygmies demonstrated lack of experience with **distance cues**, which is important in interpreting pictures. Hudson's studies using pictures depicting hunting scenes found that both children and adults from a variety of African cultures, regardless of their educational or social levels, had difficulty perceiving depth.

■ Hudson's drawings only used **relative size** and **overlap/superimposition**, omitting other depth cues (such as **texture gradient**) and making the task more difficult for non-Western peoples. When they were redrawn so as to include other depth cues, the number of 3-D responses increased.

■ People from non-Western cultures might be 'rejecting' Western art forms, expressing a **stylistic preference**, rather than showing an inability to perceive depth in pictures. Just as rural African children are unfamiliar with artistic conventions as used in Western cartoons, so Western observers need guidance to understand the art forms of American Indians.

■ Increasingly ingenious research has revealed more and more inborn abilities. However, a nativist view might apply more to auditory than to visual abilities, in which the truth lies in between a nativist and empirist view.

■ Hebb's distinction between **figural unity** and **figural identity** was based on his analysis of adult cataract patients, and so it is difficult to generalise the findings to neonates. However, not only does the influence of nature and nurture vary between different abilities, but they are always both involved.

■ Most psychologists adopt a **transactional perspective**, according to which stimulation and environmental influences are crucial in determining how and whether inborn perceptual capacities actually develop.

Essay Questions

1 Critically consider research into the development of perception. *(24 marks)*

2 a Describe how neonates have been used in the study of perceptual development. *(6 marks)*

  b Critically consider the contribution of such studies to our understanding of perceptual development.
(18 marks)

WEB ADDRESSES

http://www.tue.nl/ipo/oldhome/html
http://mambo.ucsc.edu/
http://www.long.su.se/staff/hartmut/imito.htm
http://www.ecdgroup.com/archive/ecd06.html
http://www.uia.org/uiademo/h0665.htm

25 | *Language and Culture*

INTRODUCTION AND OVERVIEW

Knowing what we want to say but being unable to 'put it into words', is one of several examples of thought taking place without language (Weiskrantz, 1988). However, the exact relationship between language and thought has been the subject of much debate amongst philosophers and psychologists. For some, thought is dependent on, or caused by, language, which represents a major aspect of culture. Others believe that language is dependent on, and reflects, thought or an individual's level of cognitive development. Yet others maintain that thought and language are initially quite separate activities, which come together and interact at a certain point in development.

This chapter reviews the evidence relating to each of these major theoretical perspectives concerning language and thought's relationship. It begins by briefly examining the view that language and thought are the same.

LANGUAGE AND THOUGHT ARE THE SAME

Watson's 'peripheralist' approach

The earliest psychological theory of language and thought's relationship was advanced by the behaviourist Watson (1913). In his view, thought processes are really no more than the sensations produced by tiny movements of the speech organs too small to produce audible sounds. Essentially, then, thought is talking to oneself very quietly. Part of Watson's rejection of 'mind' was his denial of mentalistic concepts such as 'thought', and hence his reduction of it to 'silent speech' (see Box 58.2, pages 627–628).

Watson's theory is called *peripheralism* because it sees 'thinking' occurring peripherally in the *larynx*, rather than centrally in the brain. Movements of the larynx *do* occur when 'thought' is taking place. However, this only indicates that such movements may *accompany* thinking, not that the movements *are* thoughts or that they are *necessary* for thinking to occur.

Smith *et al.* (1947) attempted to test Watson's theory by injecting Smith himself with *curare*, a drug that causes total paralysis of the skeletal muscles without affecting consciousness. The muscles of the speech organs and the respiratory system are paralysed, and so Smith had to be kept breathing artificially. When the drug's effects had worn off, Smith was able to report on his thoughts and perceptions during the paralysis.

Additionally, Furth (1966) has shown that people born deaf and mute, and who do not learn sign language, can also think in much the same way as hearing and speaking people. For Watson, deaf and mute individuals should be incapable of thought because of the absence of movement in the speech organs.

THOUGHT IS DEPENDENT ON, OR CAUSED BY, LANGUAGE

Several theorists believe that thought is dependent on, and reflects, language. Bruner (1983), for example, has argued that language is essential if thought and knowledge are not to be limited to what can be learned through our actions (the *enactive mode of representation*) or images (the *iconic mode*). If the *symbolic mode* (going beyond the immediate context) is to develop, then language is crucial.

Social constructionists (e.g. Gergen, 1973) have argued that our ways of understanding the world derive from other people (past and present) rather than from objective reality. We are born into a world where the conceptual frameworks and categories used by people in our culture already exist. Indeed, these frameworks and categories are an essential part of our culture, since they provide meaning, a way of structuring experience of both ourselves and the world of other people. This view has much in common with the 'strong' version of the *linguistic relativity hypothesis*, the most extensively researched of the theories arguing that thought is dependent on, or caused by, language.

The linguistic relativity hypothesis

According to Wittgenstein (1921), 'The limits of my language mean the limits of my world'. By this, he meant that people can only think about and understand the world through language, and that if a particular language does not possess certain ideas or concepts, these could not exist for its native speakers. The view that language determines *how* we think about objects and events, or even determines *what* we think (our ideas, thoughts and perceptions), can be traced to the writings of Sapir (1929), a linguist and anthropologist, and Whorf (1956), a linguist and student of Sapir. Their perspective is often called the *Sapir–Whorf linguistic relativity hypothesis*, and is sometimes referred to as the *Whorfian hypothesis* in acknowledgement of the greater contribution made by Whorf. For Whorf (1956):

> 'We dissect nature along the lines laid down by our native languages. The categories and types that we isolate from the world of phenomena we do not find there because they stare every observer in the face; on the contrary, the world is presented in a kaleidoscopic flux of impressions that has to be organised by our minds – and this means largely by the linguistic systems in our minds. We cut nature up, organise it into concepts and ascribe significance as we do, largely because we are parties to an agreement to organise it this way – an agreement that holds throughout our speech community and is codified in patterns of our language'.

According to Whorf's *linguistic determinism*, language determines our concepts, and we can only think through the use of concepts. So, acquiring a language involves acquiring a 'world view' (or *Weltanschauung*). People who speak different languages have different world views (hence linguistic '*relativity*').

Whorf claimed that the Inuit Eskimos have over 20 words for snow (including 'fluffy snow', 'drifting snow' and 'packed snow'), whereas Standard Average European languages (such as English) have only one. Similarly, the Hanuxoo people of the Philippines use 92 words for 'rice', depending on whether it is husked or unhusked and its mode of preparation. The Shona people (Zimbabwe) have only three words for colour, and the Dani (New Guinea) just two. 'Mola' is used for bright, warm hues, whereas 'mili' is used for dark, cold hues. The Hopi Indians (whose language Whorf studied for several years) have two words for flying objects. One applies to birds, and the other to anything else that travels through the air (Rathus, 1990).

Whorf also saw a language's *grammar* as determining an individual's thought and perception. In the Hopi language, for example, no distinction is made between past, present and future which, compared with English, makes it a 'timeless language'. In European languages, 'time' is treated as an *objective* entity, with a clear demarcation between past, present and future. Although the Hopi language recognises duration, Hopis talk about time only as it appears *subjectively* to the observer. For example, rather than saying 'I stayed for ten days', Hopis say 'I stayed until the tenth day' or 'I left on the tenth day'.

Figure 25.1 *At least as far as British politicians are concerned, the relationship between language and thought is (in the eyes of the media) a clear-cut one!*

In English, nouns denote objects and events, and verbs denote actions. In the Hopi language, 'lightning', for example, is a verb, since events of necessarily brief duration must be verbs. As a result, a Hopi would say 'it lightninged'.

Testing the linguistic relativity hypothesis (LRH)

Miller & McNeill (1969) distinguish between *three* different versions of the LRH, all of which are consistent with it but vary in the *strength* of claim they make. The *strong* version claims that *language determines thought*. The *weak* version claims that *language affects perception*, and the *weakest* version claims that *language influences memory*, such that information which is more easily described in a particular language will be better remembered than information more difficult to describe.

Key **STUDY**

Box 25.2 Carroll & Casagrande's (1958) test of the 'strong' version of the LRH

Carroll and Casagrande compared Navaho Indian children who either spoke only Navaho (Navaho–Navaho) or English and Navaho (English–Navaho) with American children of European descent who spoke only English. The children were tested on the development of *form* or *shape recognition*. The Navaho language stresses the importance of form, such that 'handling' verbs involve different words depending on what is being handled. For example, long and flexible objects (such as string) have one word form, whereas long and rigid objects (such as sticks) have another.

American children of European descent develop object recognition in the order: size, colour, and form or shape. If, as the strong version of the LRH claims, language influences cognitive development, then the developmental sequence of the Navaho children should differ from the English-only American children, and their form or shape recognition abilities should be superior. This is what Carroll and Casagrande found, thus supporting the strong version of the LRH. However, they also found that the English–Navaho group showed form recognition *later* than the English-only American children, which does *not* support the LRH strong version.

Carroll and Casagrande attributed the poor performance of the English–Navaho children to their experience of shape classification at nursery school, which made them an atypical sample.

Attempts at testing the 'weak' and 'weakest' versions of the LRH have typically involved the perception and memory of *colour*. Since language users such as the Jalé

(New Guinea) only have terms for black and white, whilst those of the Ibibio culture (Nigeria) have terms for black, white, red and green, tests of colour perception and memory should be more difficult for the Jalé than the Ibibio. Since the Ibibio word for green encompasses the English green, blue and yellow, the Ibibio should find colour perception and memory tasks more difficult than English speakers.

Early tests appeared to support the two weaker versions of the LRH. For example, Brown & Lenneberg (1954) found that Zuni Indians, who have a single word to describe yellows and oranges, did make more mistakes than English speakers in recognising these colours. However, the results (and those of other researchers using a similar methodology) were challenged by Berlin & Kay (1969). They found that whilst cultures may differ in the number of basic colour terms they use, all cultures draw their basic (or *focal*) terms from only 11 colours. These are black, white, red, green, yellow, blue, brown, purple, pink, orange and grey. Moreover, the colour terms emerge in a particular sequence in the history of languages.

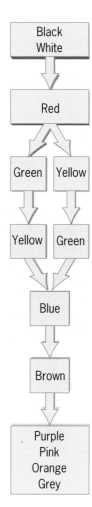

Figure 25.2 *The sequence in which focal colours emerge (Berlin & Kay, 1969)*

So, for cultures with only two colours, these will always be black and white, whereas in cultures with three colours, these will always be black, white and red (Newstead, 1995). As Newstead has observed:

'This, then, gives a rather different perspective on the use of colour terms. It had been assumed that verbal labels were chosen more or less arbitrarily, and that those chosen influenced the way in which colour was perceived. Berlin and Kay's findings suggest that there are certain focal colours which will always be labelled if colour terms are used at all. This suggests an alternative explanation for Brown and Lenneberg's findings: that the colours which participants in their study had found easier to learn were the focal colours and these were easy to remember not because they had verbal labels but because they were the most basic colours'.

A study which supports Berlin and Kay's findings, and the alternative explanation for Brown and Lenneberg's, is that conducted by Heider & Oliver (1972).

Heider (1972) concluded that:

'Far from being a domain well suited to the study of the effects of language on thought, the colour-space would seem a prime example of the influence of underlying perceptual-cognitive factors on the formation and reference of linguistic categories'.

By this, Heider means that her data are better explained in terms of *physiological factors* underlying colour vision, rather than linguistic factors. Thus, people are sensitive to focal colours because the human visual system processes reality in a certain way (Lakoff, 1987). Indeed, evidence suggests that focal colours can be discriminated *before* any verbal labels for them have been learned. Bornstein (1988), for example, has argued that pre-verbal infants categorise the visible spectrum in a similar way to adults, in that categorisation occurs on the basis of the relatively discrete hues of blue, green, yellow and red (see Chapter 24, page 248). However, a study of another New Guinea people, the Berinmo, casts doubt on Heider's interpretation and seems to support the weakest and weak versions of the LRH.

Key **STUDY**

Box 25.3 Heider & Oliver's (1972) study of colour naming

As noted, the Dani have only two words for colours, whereas native English speakers have words for 11 basic colours. Heider and Oliver gave both Dani and English-speaking participants a coloured chip which they were allowed to look at for five seconds. After a 30-second delay, participants were asked to pick out a chip of the same colour among a set of 40 different coloured chips. On the weakest version of the LRH, the Dani's colour vocabulary should have influenced their memory for colours, and on the weak version they should have had difficulty in discriminating similar colours of a slightly different hue that they had labelled with the same name.

The results showed that whilst the Dani-speaking and English-speaking participants made many mistakes, there were no significant differences between them in their rate of confusion of similar colours, despite the differences in their colour vocabularies. In other research, Heider showed that both Dani and English speakers were better at recognising focal colours than non-focal colours, and that the Dani found it much easier to learn labels for focal than non-focal colours.

Key **STUDY**

Box 25.4 Colour naming among the Berinmo

Robertson *et al.* (cited in Hanlon, 1999) studied the Berinmo people of New Guinea, who live a simple hunter–gatherer lifestyle in remote forests. They have five colour names: one for green, blue and purple, another for yellow, orange and brown, a third for all dark colours, a fourth for white and all light colours; and a fifth for all shades of red and pink. Using a procedure similar to Heider & Oliver's (1972), Robertson *et al.* found that the Berinmo could only remember those colours which matched their colour names, and that they were unable to discriminate between colours which their language did not discriminate (for example, green and blue).

Although all the focal colours were 'represented' by the Berinmos' five colour names, the fact that green, blue and purple were lumped together, as were yellow, orange and brown, and red and pink, seems inconsistent with the claim that colour terms emerge in a particular order in the history of languages (see Figure 25.2):

'While it has been assumed that a lot of low-level things like colour perception have taken place at a low, almost a genetic level, we found that even something as simple as colour is affected by culture'. (Robertson, cited in Hanlon, 1999)

An evaluation of the LRH

According to Sapir and Whorf, the differences between language speakers determine differences in how the world is perceived, thought about and remembered. The world *is* different depending on what language we speak (or 'think in'). However, Berry *et al.* (1992) and Jackendoff (1993) have argued that Whorf's evidence was anecdotal rather than empirical, and that he exaggerated the differences between Hopi and other languages. Moreover, far from having 'over 20' words for 'snow', the Inuit Eskimos have relatively few such words (Newstead, 1995), and no more than do English speakers (Pinker, 1997). According to Pagel (1995), Whorf simply got his facts wrong.

There is an important difference between a language's grammar and our perceptual experience. The fact that Hopi can be translated into English (and vice versa) implies that there is a universally shared knowledge of the world that is independent of the particular language in which it is expressed (Pagel, 1995).

Whorf also appears to have overlooked *why* Inuit Eskimos have more than one word for snow. One possibility is that the more significant an experience or environmental feature is for us, the larger the number of ways in which it can be expressed. So, instead of language determining our perceptions, our perceptions (which reflect what is important for us) might influence our language. As Solso (1995) says:

> 'The development of specific language codes ... is dependent on cultural needs; the learning of these codes by members of a language group also involves the learning of significant values of the culture, some of which must be related to survival'.

Solso's view is supported by the fact that English-speaking skiers *do* learn to discriminate between varied snow conditions and *invent* a vocabulary to describe these differences. Such terms include 'sticky snow', 'powder', 'corn' and 'boilerplate' (or ice: Crooks & Stein, 1991). Similarly, the Hanunoo people of the Philippines have modified their language in response to environmental conditions. For example, women have developed a more complex vocabulary for shades of blue to distinguish the colours of dyed textiles that have been introduced into their society (Price & Crapo, 1999).

It is now widely accepted that Whorf overestimated the importance of language differences. As Berry *et al.* (1992) have observed:

> 'Language as an instrument for thinking has many cross-culturally variant properties. As humans, we may not all be sharing the same thoughts, but our respective languages do not seem to predestine us to different kinds of thinking'.

What language may do, though, is to affect the ease of information processing. Newstead (1995), for example, describes research conducted by Hunt & Agnoli (1991) which supports this view. The English word 'seven' has two syllables, whereas the equivalent French word ('sept') has only one. The English word 'eleven' has three syllables whereas the French word 'onze' has one. Hunt and Agnoli argue that when a name is shorter, information is processed more quickly, and so French speakers would have an advantage over English speakers when performing mental arithmetic involving these numbers, at least in processing terms.

According to Price & Crapo (1999), the study of semantic domains (such as colour naming) helps us to discover what is important in the daily lives of different cultural groups, as well as the changing cultural history of a society.

The LRH, social class and race

Social-class differences in language and thought

Bernstein (1961) was interested in language's role as a social (rather than individual) phenomenon, especially its relation to cultural deprivation. He showed that whilst there were generally no differences between the verbal and non-verbal intelligence test performance of boys from public schools, boys from lower working class homes often showed considerable differences, with non-verbal performance sometimes being as much as 26 points better than verbal performance. Bernstein argued that working and middle class children speak two different kinds (or codes) of language, which he called *restricted code* and *elaborated code* respectively.

Because Bernstein saw the relationship between potential and actual intelligence as being mediated through language, he argued that the lack of an elaborated code would prevent working class children from developing their full intellectual potential. The different language codes underlie the whole pattern of relationships (to objects and people) experienced by members of different classes, as well as the patterns of learning which their children bring with them to school (see Table 25.1, page 264).

Supportive of Bernstein's views is Hess & Shipman's (1965) finding that social-class differences influence children's intellectual development. In particular, there was a lack of *meaning* in the mother–child communication system for low-status families. Language was used much less to convey meaning (to describe, explain, express and so on) and much more to give orders and commands to the child.

However, instead of seeing 'restricted' and 'elaborated' as distinct types of language code, they are better thought of as two ends of a continuum. Also, the terms 'restricted' and 'elaborated' imply a value judgement of middle class speech as being superior to working class speech (closer to 'standard' or 'the Queen's' English). The lack of objectivity makes this judgement difficult to defend.

Table 25.1 *Characteristics of restricted and elaborated codes (Bernstein, 1961)*

Restricted code

1 Grammatically crude, repetitive and rigid, limited use of adjectives and adverbs, greater use of pronouns than nouns. Sentences are often short, grammatically simple and incomplete.

2 Context-bound: the meaning is not made explicit but assumes the listener's familiarity with the situation being described, e.g. 'He gave me it'; listener cannot be expected to know what 'he' or 'it' refers to.

3 'I' is rarely used, and much of the meaning is conveyed non-verbally.

4 Frequent use of uninformative but emotionally reinforcing phrases, such as 'you know', 'don't I'.

5 Tends to stress the present, the here-and-now.

6 Doesn't allow expression or abstract or hypothetical thought.

Elaborated code

1 Grammatically more complex and flexible. Uses a range of subordinate clauses, conjunctions, prepositions, adjectives and adverbs. Uses more nouns than pronouns. Sentences are longer and more complex.

2 Context-independent: the meaning is made explicit, e.g. 'John gave me this book'.

3 'I' is often used, making clear the speaker's intentions, as well as emphasising the precise description of experiences and feelings.

4 Relatively little use of emotionally reinforcing phrases.

5 Tends to stress the past and future, rather than the present.

6 Allows expression of abstract or hypothetical thought.

(From Gross, 1996)

Black English

A version of English spoken by segments of the African-American community is called 'Black English'. For example, when asked to repeat the sentence 'I asked him if he did it, and he said he didn't do it', one five-year-old girl repeated the sentence like this: 'I asks him if he did it, and he says he didn't did it, but I knows he did' (Labov, 1973). Bernstein argued that Black English is a restricted code, and that this makes the thinking of Black English speakers less logical than that of their white elaborated-code counterparts.

One major difference between Black and Standard English relates to the use of verbs (Rebok, 1987). In particular, Black English speakers often omit the present tense copula (the verb 'to be'). So, 'he be gone' indicates Standard English 'he has been gone for a long time' and 'he gone' signifies that 'he has gone right now'. Black English is often termed *sub-standard* and regarded as illogical rather than *non-standard* (Bereiter & Engelman, 1966). According to Labov (1970), Black English is just one dialect of English, and speakers of both dialects are expressing the same ideas equally well.

Whilst the grammatical rules of Black English differ from those of Standard English, Black English possesses consistent rules which allow the expression of thoughts as complex as those permitted by Standard English (Labov, 1973). Several other languages, such as Russian and Arabic, also omit the present-tense verb 'to be', and yet we do not call them 'illogical'. This suggests that black dialects are considered sub-standard as a matter of convention or prejudice, and *not* because they are poorer vehicles for expressing meaning and thinking logically. However, because the structure of Black English does differ in important ways from Standard English, and since intelligence tests are written in Standard English, Black English speakers are at a linguistic disadvantage (as, indeed, are white working class children: see Chapter 55).

Figure 25.3 *With his tongue-in-cheek celebrity interviews, Ali G. has demonstrated that non-standard English does* not *equal sub-standard English*

Labov also showed that the social situation can be a powerful determinant of verbal behaviour. A young boy called Leon was shown a toy by a white interviewer and asked to tell him everything he could about it. Leon said very little and was silent for much of the time, even when a black interviewer took over. However, when Leon sat on the floor and shared a packet of crisps with his best friend and with the same black interviewer introducing topics in a local black dialect, Leon became a lively conversationalist. Had he been assessed with the white or black interviewers on their own, Leon would have been labelled 'non-verbal' or 'linguistically retarded'.

Black children may actually be *bilingual*. In their home environment, the school playground and their neighbourhoods, they speak the accepted vernacular. In the classroom, however, and when talking to any one in authority, they must adopt Standard English with which they are unfamiliar. This results in short sentences, simple grammar and strange intonation. Out of school, however, their natural language is easy, fluent, creative and often gifted. So, whilst Black English is certainly *non-standard*, it is another language with its own grammar which is certainly not sub-standard.

Box 25.5 'Ebonics': an ongoing debate

Ebonics is a fusion of the words 'ebony' and 'phonics' and was coined in 1975 as an alternative to the term 'Black English'. In 1996, Ebonics (or African–American Vernacular English/AAVE) was officially recognised by the Oakland public school board in California, and schools were ordered to teach 28,000 black children in their own 'tongue'. The board claimed that Ebonics was a separate language, genetically rooted in the West-African and Niger–Congo language system, rather than a dialect of standard American English (Hiscock, 1996; Whittell, 1996).

In early 1997, the school board edited its statement so that the word 'genetically' referred to linguists' use of the word for the roots of a language rather than to a gene pool. They also indicated that it was not the intent to teach in Ebonics, but rather to have teachers use the vernacular to understand their children (Zinberg, 1997). Both conservatives and liberals in America claim that the decision to require Ebonics to be taught would be 'political correctness run amok' (Cornwell, 1997). Educationalists such as Zinberg disagree. In her view, many students are:

'... bewildered, then angered and finally alienated from the schools where their language and self-esteem are belittled by a seemingly insensitive system'.

Although regional dialects in the USA are diverging, there is no evidence of convergence between black and white vernaculars (Rickford, cited in Hawkes, 1998). By contrast, British blacks and whites still speak the same language, partly because there is no segregation in housing in Britain as there is in the USA (Labov, cited in Hawkes, 1998).

LANGUAGE IS DEPENDENT ON, AND REFLECTS, THOUGHT

According to Piaget (1950), children begin life with some understanding of the world and try to find linguistic ways of expressing their knowledge. As language develops, it 'maps' onto previously acquired cognitive structures, and so language is dependent upon thought (Piaget & Inhelder, 1969). For example, according to Piaget's concept of *object permanence* (the realisation that objects continue to exist even when they cannot be seen: see Chapter 28, pages 296–297), a child should begin talking about objects that are not present in its immediate surroundings only after object permanence had developed.

Corrigan (1978) showed that children were able to talk about absent objects only after they had demonstrated an advanced level on an object permanence test. Similarly, children who had the ability to conserve liquid quantity (to recognise that different-shaped containers can hold the same amount of liquid: see Chapter 28) understood the meaning of phrases and words such as 'as much as', 'bigger' and 'more'. However, children who could not conserve did not improve their performance of the correct use of these words after having been given linguistic training (Sinclair-de-Zwart, 1969).

In Piaget's view, children can be taught words, but they will not *understand* them until they have mastered certain intellectual skills during the process of cognitive growth. So, language can exist without thought, but only in the sense that a parrot can 'speak'. Thought, then, is a necessary forerunner to language if language is to be used properly.

Contrary to Piaget's view that thought structures language, Luria & Yudovich (1971) suggest that language plays a central role in cognitive development. However, it is probably much more reasonable to conclude that language reflects, to an extent, our understanding of the world.

Box 25.6 Luria & Yudovich's (1971) study

Luria and Yudovich studied five-year-old twin boys whose home environment was unstimulating. They played almost exclusively together and had only a very primitive level of speech. The boys received little adult encouragement to speak, and made little progress towards the symbolic use of words. Essentially, their speech was *synpraxic*, a primitive form in which words cannot be detached from the action or object they denote.

The twins hardly ever used speech to describe objects or events or to help them plan their actions. They could not understand other people's speech, and their own constituted a kind of signalling rather than symbolic system. Although they never played with other children, and played with each other in a primitive and monotonous way, they were otherwise normal.

After being separated, one twin was given special remedial treatment for his language deficiency, but the other was not. The former made rapid progress and, ten months later, was ahead of his brother. However, both made progress, and their synpraxic speech died away. For Luria and Yudovich:

'The whole structure of the mental life of both twins was simultaneously and sharply changed. Once they acquired an objective language system, [they] were able to formulate the aims of their activity verbally, and after only three months we observed the beginnings of meaningful play'.

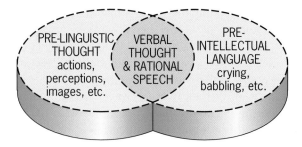

Figure 25.4 *A diagrammatic representation of Vygotsky's views on the relationship between language and thought*

Vygotsky believed that between ages two and seven, language performs two functions. The first is an *internal* function, which enables internal thought to be monitored and directed. The second is an *external* function, which enables the results of thinking to be communicated to others. However, children cannot yet distinguish between the two functions and, as a result, their speech is *egocentric*. Thus, they talk out loud about their plans and actions, and can neither think privately nor communicate publicly to others. Instead, they are caught somewhere between the two and cannot distinguish between 'speech for self' (what Piaget calls *autistic speech*) and 'speech for others' (*socialised speech*).

Vygotsky believed that around age seven (when children typically enter Piaget's *concrete operational* stage of intellectual development: see Chapter 28, pages 299–300), overt language begins to be restricted to communication, whilst the thought function of language becomes internalised as internal speech or verbal thought. Piaget saw egocentric speech as a kind of 'running commentary' on the child's behaviour, and believed that around age seven it was replaced by socialised (or communicative) speech.

Box 25.7 The function of egocentric speech

Vygotsky (1962) showed that when six- or seven-year-olds are trying to solve a problem and a mishap occurs (such as a pencil breaking) which requires them to revise their thinking, they often *revert* to overt verbalisation. Adults sometimes do the same in similar situations, especially when they believe that no one can hear them. For example, we will often re-trace our steps out loud (such as 'Now, I know I didn't have it when I went in the room, so what did I do before that?'). Vygotsky concluded that the function of egocentric speech was similar to that of inner speech. It does not merely accompany the child's activity but:

'... serves mental orientation, conscious understanding; it helps in overcoming difficulties, it is speech for oneself, intimately and usefully connected with the child's thinking. In the end it becomes inner speech' [see Figure 25.4].

THOUGHT AND LANGUAGE ARE INITIALLY SEPARATE ACTIVITIES WHICH INTERACT AT A CERTAIN POINT OF DEVELOPMENT

According to Vygotsky (1962), language and thought begin as separate and independent activities (see Chapter 28). Early on, thinking occurs without language (consisting primarily of images) and language occurs without thought (as when babies cry or make other sounds to express feelings, attract attention or fulfil some other social aim). Around age two, however, *pre-linguistic thought* and *pre-intellectual language*:

'... meet and join to initiate a new kind of behaviour [in which] thought becomes verbal and speech rational' (Vygotsky, 1962).

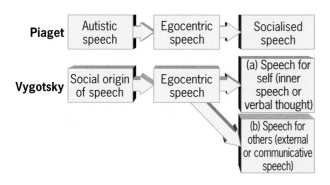

Figure 25.5 *The difference between Piaget and Vygotsky with respect to egocentric speech*

Eventually, Piaget accepted Vygotsky's view concerning the function and fate of inner speech. Both inner speech and egocentric speech differ from speech for others in that they do not have to satisfy grammatical conventions. Thus, both are abbreviated, incomplete and concerned more with the essential meaning rather than how it is expressed. For Vygotsky, inner speech is a 'dynamic, shifting and unstable thing which "flutters" between word and thought' (see Figure 25.4 page 266).

Overt speech can sometimes resemble inner speech in its abbreviated nature long after egocentric speech has been replaced. For example, people who know each other well may talk in an abbreviated form that would not be used with strangers. Understanding occurs because the more familiar we are with others, and the more experiences we have in common, the less explicit our speech has to be. 'Beer?', for example, asked with a rising inflection and in a particular context, would be interpreted as 'Would you like another beer?' in a similar way to how adults interpret the holophrastic speech of young children (see Chapter 26, page 272). In Bernstein's terms, we use restricted code when talking in familiar surroundings to familiar others, whose view of the world we assume to be similar to ours.

CONCLUSIONS

Whilst there are many examples indicating that thought can occur without language, the exact relationship between thought and language remains unclear. What is certain, however, is that no one account of this relationship is true and all others false; several theoretical perspectives can claim some support from the experimental literature. However, since language represents such a central feature of culture, both shaping it and being shaped by it, any theory which fails to take account of cultural factors is likely to be inadequate.

Summary

- According to Watson's **peripheralism**, thought is no more than sensations produced by tiny movements of the larynx which are too small to produce audible sounds. Whilst these movements accompany thought, they are not necessary for thinking to occur. Thinking can occur despite complete paralysis, and people born deaf and mute are also capable of thinking.

- Bruner argues that language is essential for thought and knowledge to progress beyond the **enactive** and **iconic modes of representation** to the **symbolic mode**. **Social constructionists** claim that conceptual frameworks and categories provide meaning within a culture, a way of structuring our experience of ourselves and the world.

- According to the **Sapir–Whorf linguistic relativity hypothesis** (LRH), language determines **how** we think about objects and events, and even **what** we think. This is related to **linguistic determinism**. Both the vocabulary and grammar of a language help to determine a world view.

- Miller and McNeill distinguish between the **'strong'**, **'weak'** and **'weakest'** versions of the LRH. The 'weak' and 'weakest' versions have typically been tested through perception and memory of **colour**. The fewer colour words there are in a language, the more difficult native speakers should find tests of colour perception and memory.

- Early studies seemed to support these two versions. However, according to Berlin and Kay, whilst cultures may differ in the number of basic colour terms they use, all cultures draw their colour terms from only 11 **focal** colours, which emerge in a particular sequence in the history of languages.

- Berlin and Kay's findings are supported by Heider and Oliver's comparison of Dani-speaking and English-speaking participants' rate of confusion of similar colours. Heider also found that the Dani learnt labels for focal colours much more easily than for non-focal colours. She argues that her data are better explained in terms of **physiological factors** underlying colour vision than linguistic factors.

- Whorf's evidence was anecdotal rather than empirical, and he exaggerated the differences between Hopi and other languages. Also, he mistakenly equated language's grammar with perceptual experience. Translation between languages implies a universally shared knowledge of the world independent of any particular language.

- Bernstein claimed that working class children speak a **restricted code** and middle class children an **elaborated code**. The relationship between actual and potential intelligence is mediated through language, so working class children are prevented from developing their full intellectual potential.

- Language codes underlie the patterns of learning children bring with them to school. However, identifying two basic types of code is an oversimplification, and the terms 'restricted' and 'elaborated' imply a value judgement.

- Differences between Standard and **Black English**, which Bernstein sees as a restricted code, have resulted in the latter being called **sub-standard**, rather than **non-standard**. According to Labov, this is an expression of prejudice, and the fact that intelligence tests are written in Standard English puts Black English speakers at a real disadvantage.

- Black children may be **bilingual**, using the accepted register fluently at home and with their peers, but adopting unfamiliar standard English in the classroom.

- According to Piaget, language 'maps' onto previously acquired cognitive structures, so that language is dependent on thought. One example is **object permanence**. Similarly, children who cannot yet **conserve** will not benefit from linguistic training on the use of conservation-related terms. Words can only be understood if certain intellectual skills have already been mastered. So, thought **structures** language.

- According to Vygotsky, language and thought are initially separate and independent activities. At around age two, **pre-linguistic thought** and **pre-intellectual language** begin to interact to form verbal thought and rational speech.

- Between the ages of two and seven, language performs both an **internal** and **external** function. The child's failure to distinguish between them results in **egocentric speech**, which largely disappears around age seven. For Vygotsky, this indicates the separation of the two functions. The function of egocentric speech is similar to that of inner speech, which is what it eventually becomes.

Essay Questions

1 Critically consider research into the relationship between language and thought. *(24 marks)*

2 'The limits of my language mean the limits of my world.' (Wittgenstein, 1921)

   Discuss ways in which social **and/or** cultural aspects of language use may influence thought. *(24 marks)*

WEB ADDRESSES

http://www.cdipage.com/phonics.htm
http://www.june29.com/HLP
http://www.arts.uwa.edu.au/lingwww/LIN102-99/notes/whorf.html
http://www.lclarke.edu/~soan/context/htm

26 *Language Acquisition*

INTRODUCTION AND OVERVIEW

Until quite recently, the study of language was largely the domain of *linguistics*, which is concerned primarily with language's *structure* (its *grammar*). However, psychologists have become interested in language from the perspective of how it develops, whether it is unique to humans, and its relationship to cognitive processes. The 'marriage' between psychology and linguistics is called *psycholinguistics*, which studies the perception, understanding and production of language, together with the development of these activities. This chapter begins by looking at what language is and its major components, and then describes the course of language development in humans (the major milestones).

According to learning theory, associated with Skinner and Bandura, language development can be attributed primarily to environmental input and learning. Another position argues that whilst the environment may supply the *content* of language, grammar is an inherent, biologically determined capacity of human beings. According to Chomsky, Lenneberg and McNeill, the process of language development is essentially one of *acquistion* (as distinct from *learning*).

The final part of the chapter considers the evidence for and against the learning theory and biological approaches, as well as some alternative approaches. Significant amongst these are approaches which stress the relationship between language and children's cognitive development, and children's interactions with other language users.

WHAT IS LANGUAGE?

According to Brown (1965), language is an arbitrary set of symbols:

> '... which, taken together, make it possible for a creature with limited powers of discrimination and a limited memory to transmit and understand an infinite variety of messages and to do this in spite of noise and distraction'.

Whilst other species are able to *communicate* with each other (see Chapter 41), they can do so only in limited ways, and it is perhaps the 'infinite variety of messages' part of Brown's definition that sets humans apart from non-humans. For example, wild chimpanzees use over 30 different vocalisations to convey a large number of meanings, and repeat sounds in order to intensify their meaning. However, they do not string these sounds together to make new 'words' (Calvin, 1994). The claim that chimpanzees are capable of using language is based largely, and until recently, on *deliberate training* (see Chapter 41). Human language is mastered spontaneously and quite easily within the first five years of life.

Brown (1973) pointed out that humans do not simply learn a repertoire of sentences but:

> '... acquire a rule system that makes it possible to generate a literally infinite variety of sentences, most of them never heard from anyone else'.

Figure 26.1 *A single missing letter can totally change a word's meaning – and with it, the meaning of the entire sentence*

This rule system is called *grammar* (or *mental grammar*). However, for psycholinguists, grammar is much more than the parts of speech we learn about in school. It is concerned with the description of language, the rules which determine how a language 'works', and what governs patterns of speech (Jackendoff, 1993).

THE MAJOR COMPONENTS OF GRAMMAR

Grammar consists of *phonology*, *semantics* and *syntax* (see Figure 26.3, page 271).

Phonology

Phonologists are concerned with a language's sound system, what counts as a sound and what constitutes an acceptable sequence of sounds. Basic speech sounds are called *phones* or *phonetic segments* and are represented by enclosing symbols inside square brackets. For example, [p] is the initial phone in the word 'pin'. Some languages have as few as 15 distinguishable sounds and others as many as 85. The English language has some 46 phones (Solso, 1995).

Only those phones which affect the meaning of what is being said matter. For example, the difference between [p] and [d] matters because it can lead to two words with different meanings (such as 'pin' and 'din'). Because [p] and [d] cannot be interchanged without altering a word's meaning, they belong to different functional classes of phones called *phonemes* (*phonological segments*).

Languages differ in their numbers of phonemes. *Phonological rules* constrain the permitted sequence of phonemes, which are just sounds and correspond roughly to the vowels and consonants of a language's alphabet. However, languages (including English) can have more phonemes than letters in the alphabet (see above). This is because some letters, such as 'o', can be pronounced differently (as in 'hop' and 'hope'). The development of speech sounds continues for several years after birth (see page 272) and most children *recognise* sounds in adult speech before they can *produce* them. So, in response to the instruction: 'I am going to say a word two times and you tell me which time I say it right and which time I say it wrong: *rabbit, wabbit*', a child might reply: '*Wabbit* is wight and *wabbit* is wong', indicating that the 'r' sound can be recognised but not yet produced (Dale, 1976).

Semantics

Semantics is the study of the *meaning* of language, and can be analysed at the level of *morphemes* and *sentences*. Morphemes are a language's basic units of meaning and consist mainly of *words*. Other morphemes are *prefixes*

(letters attached to the beginning of a word, such as 'pre' and 're') and *suffixes* (word-endings, such as 's' to make a plural). Some morphemes, such as the plural 's', are 'bound' (they only take on meaning when attached to other morphemes), but most morphemes are 'free' (they have meaning when they stand alone, as most words have). Single words, however, have only a limited meaning and are usually combined into longer strings of phrases and sentences, the other level of semantic analysis.

Syntax

Syntax refers to the rules for combining words into phrases and sentences. One example of a *syntactic rule* is word order. This is crucial for understanding language development. Clearly, the sentences 'The dog bit the postman' and 'The postman bit the dog' have very different meanings!

Figure 26.2 *"Then you should say what you mean," the March Hare went on.*

"I do," Alice hastily replied; "at least – at least I mean what I say – that's the same thing, you know."

"Not the same thing a bit!" said the Hatter. "Why, you might just as well say that 'I see what I eat' is the same thing as 'I eat what I see'!"

Another example of a syntactic rule occurs in the sentence 'The dog chased the ...'. In English, only a *noun* can complete this sentence. Some sentences may be syntactically correct but have no semanticity. For example, 'The player scored a goal' and 'The goal post scored a banana' are both syntactically correct, but one has much more meaning than the other. Whilst sentences have sounds and meanings, syntax refers to the *structures* which relate the two.

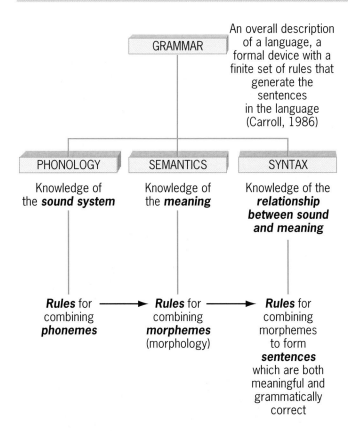

Figure 26.3 *The major components of grammar (Adapted from Gross, 1996)*

For many psychologists, language development follows a universal timetable, that is, regardless of their language or culture, all children pass through the same sequence of stages at approximately the same ages (although children may vary with respect to their rate of development). Whilst this belief implies the role of *maturation*, environmental factors are also necessary in that children can only come to speak a language if they are exposed to it. The claim that children are *programmed* to develop language if exposed to it is one of the competing theoretical views examined below (pages 277–279).

It is generally agreed that there are three major stages in language development. These are the *pre-linguistic stage* (0–12 months), the *one-word stage* (12–18 months), and the *stage of two-word sentences*. This third stage is divided into two sub-stages: *Stage 1 grammar* (18–30 months) and *Stage 2 grammar* (30 months and beyond).

The pre-linguistic stage (0–12 months)

In their first year, babies are essentially pre-linguistic. They make various sounds with their vocal organs (including crying) long before they can talk. Crying tends to dominate in the first month, with parents grad-

ually learning to discriminate between the various cries (Gustafson & Harris, 1990). By one month, babies are able to distinguish between phonemes (such as 'ba' and 'pa') and other sounds, even though these may be physically and acoustically almost identical (Aslin *et al.*, 1983). Quite possibly, this perceptual ability (*categorical speech perception*) is innate (see page 278).

At about six weeks, *cooing* begins. This is associated with pleasurable states and does not occur when babies are hungry, tired or in pain. Although vowel sounds may be produced at this age, they are different from those that will be made later and from which the first words will be formed. This is because the baby's oral cavity and nervous system are not sufficiently mature to enable it to produce the sounds necessary for speech.

Box 26.1 The development of babbling

This is the major development in the first year of life, and usually begins between six and nine months. Phonemes are produced and take the form of combinations of consonants and vowels (such as *ma* and *da*). These may be repeated to produce *reduplicated monosyllables* (such as *mama* and *dada*). Although these are very different from the earlier cooing sounds, they have no meaning.

Babbling and pre-babbling vocalisations differ in two main ways. First, babies spend more time making noises, especially when alone in their cots (*spontaneous babbling*), and they seem to enjoy exercising their voices for the sake of it. Second, babbling has intonational patterns, just like speech, with rising inflections and speech-like rhythms. By one year, syllables are often produced over and over again (as in *dadadada*), a phenomenon called *echolalia*.

Babbling occurs at around the same age in all babies regardless of culture, and even deaf babies of deaf–mute parents show a kind of 'sign-babbling' (Petitto, 1988). These findings suggest that the onset of babbling is based on maturation. However, smiling, soft sounds and pats on the abdomen can all increase the frequency of babbling (Rheingold *et al.*, 1959).

Babies initially produce only a few phonemes, but within a short period almost every available phoneme is produced, whether or not it belongs in what will become the baby's native language. The onset of this *phonemic expansion* is probably maturational. At around nine or ten months, *phonemic contraction* begins, and phoneme production is restricted to those used in the baby's native language. Thus, babies whose native languages will be different can be distinguished by the sounds they produce. Additionally, deaf babies usually *stop* babbling at around nine or ten months, presumably because of the lack of feedback from their own voice.

Phonemic contraction does not mean that all phonemes have been mastered. By two and a half years of age, only about 60 per cent of the phonemes used in English are mastered, and complete mastery will not be achieved until around age seven.

One-word stage

Typically, children produce their first word at around one year, although there is considerable variability in this (Rice, 1989). Babies do not, of course, suddenly switch from babbling to the production of words, and non-words (*jargon*) continue to be produced for up to another six months. The baby's first words (or articulate sounds) are often invented, and not like 'adult words' at all. Scollon (1976) has defined a word as 'a systematic matching of form and meaning'. On this definition, 'da' is a word if it is consistently used to refer to a doll, since the same sound is being used to label the same thing or kind of thing, and there is a clear intention to communicate.

However, an infant's earliest words are usually *context-bound*, produced only in very limited and specific situations or contexts in which particular actions or events occur (Barrett, 1989). For example, one infant, at least initially, only produced the word 'duck' whilst hitting a toy duck off the edge of a bath. The word was never used in any other context (Barrett, 1989).

Barrett has argued that an infant's first words often do not serve a communicative purpose as such. Rather, because they typically occur as accompaniments to particular actions or events (as in the case above), they function as 'performatives'. Some words may be more like the performance of a ritualised action than the expression of a lexical meaning to another person. However, words seem to have either an *expressive function*, in that they communicate internal states (such as pleasure and surprise) to others, or a *directive function*, in which the behaviour of others is directed (by, for example, requesting or obtaining and directing attention).

Box 26.2 Holophrases: making a sentence out of a word

The one-word stage is also characterised by the use of *holophrases*. In holophrastic speech, a single word (such as 'milk') is used to convey a much more complex message (such as 'I want some more milk' or 'I have spilt my milk'). Because holophrases are accompanied by gestures and tone of voice to add full meaning to an individual word, they may be seen as precursors of later, more complex sentences (Greenfield & Smith, 1976). They represent 'two-word meanings' (word

plus gesture) before two words are actually used together in speech (Bates *et al.*, 1987). They are, however, dependent upon the recipient of the holophrase making the 'correct' interpretation.

Nelson (1973) identified six categories of words and calculated the percentage of children's first 50 words (typically acquired by 19 to 20 months) that fell into each category.

Table 26.1 *Nelson's six categories and the percentage of children's first 50 words falling into each of them*

1 *Specific nominals.* Names for unique objects, people or animals (14 per cent).
2 *General nominals.* Names for classes of objects, people or animals, e.g. 'ball', 'car', 'milk', 'doggie', 'girl', 'he', 'that' (51 per cent).
3 *Action words.* Describe or accompany actions or express or demand attention, e.g. 'bye-bye', 'up', 'look', 'hi' (13 per cent).
4 *Modifiers.* Refer to properties or qualities of things, e.g. 'big', 'red', 'pretty', 'hot', 'all gone', 'there', 'mine' (9 per cent).
5 *Personal-social words.* Say something about a child's feelings or social relationships, e.g. 'ouch', 'please', 'no', 'yes', 'want' (8 per cent).
6 *Function words.* Have only grammatical function, e.g. 'what', 'is', 'to', 'for' (4 per cent).

(Taken from Gross, 1996)

Nelson argued that it is not just the amount of exposure to objects and words that is important in word acquisition. Rather, given that specific and general nominals and action words make up the vast majority of those produced (78 per cent), it is the child's *active involvement* with its environment that determines many of its first words.

Children *understand* more words than they can produce. For example, a child who uses 'bow-wow' to refer to all small animals will nonetheless pick a picture of a dog, rather than any other animal, when asked to select a 'bow-wow' (Gruendel, 1977). The child's *receptive vocabulary* (the words it can understand) is therefore much bigger than its *expressive vocabulary* (the words it uses in speech).

Even before age two, children begin acquiring words at the rate of about 20 per day (Miller, 1978). Whilst some of these are context-bound, they gradually become *decontextualised* as the one-word stage progresses. Other words are used from the start in a decontextualised way (Barrett, 1989). As the one-word stage progresses, so the child becomes able to ask and answer questions and provide comments on people and objects in the immediate environment. These abilities enable the child to participate in very simple conversations with other people.

Stage of two-word sentences

Like the one-word stage, this stage is universal (although individual differences become more marked) and, like the transition from babbling to the one-word stage, the transition to the two-word stage is also gradual (Slobin, 1979). As well as continued vocabulary development, the understanding of grammar grows, and Brown (1965) divides this stage into *Stage 1 grammar* (18 to 30 months) and *Stage 2 grammar* (after 30 months).

Stage 1 grammar (18–30 months)

Here, the child's speech is essentially *telegraphic* (Brown, 1965), that is, only those words which convey the most information (*contentives*) are used. Purely grammatical terms (*functors*), such as the verb 'to be', plurals and possessives, are left out. For example, children will say 'There cow' to convey the underlying message 'There is a cow'. It seems that irrespective of their culture, children express basic facts about their environment (Brown, 1973). However, this may *not* be a universal feature of telegraphic speech. Where contentives (or inflections) are stressed more than in English, as in Turkish, for example, children seem to use them much earlier (Gleitman & Wanner, 1988).

Telegraphic speech has a *rigid word order*, which seems to preserve a sentence's meaning. For example, if asked 'Does John want some milk?', the child might reply 'John milk' (or, later on, 'John want milk'). Adult speech, by contrast, does not rely exclusively on word order to preserve meaning, as in the passive form of a sentence. So, 'John drank the milk' and 'The milk was drunk by John' both convey the same meaning, even though the two sentences' word order is different.

Children's imitations of adult sentences are also simple and retain the original sentence's word order. For example, 'John is playing with the dog' is imitated as 'Play dog' (*imitation by reduction*: Brown, 1965). Complementary to this is *imitation with expansion*, in which the adult imitates the child's utterances by inserting the 'missing' functors. The rigid order of the child's utterances makes it easier to interpret their meaning, but gestures and context still provide important clues (as with the one-word stage).

Compared with talking to one another, adults talking to children tend to use much shorter sentences and simpler syntax, raise the pitch of their voice for emphasis, and repeat or paraphrase much of what the child says. This *motherese (or infant-directed speech)* helps to achieve a mutual understanding with children who have not yet mastered the full complexity of language. Sensitivity to the child's vocabulary and its intellectual and social knowledge is an example of a *pragmatic rule* for ensuring a degree of shared understanding (Greene, 1990) and also supports a social interaction approach to language acquisition (see pages 279–281).

Children's two-word utterances are not just random word combinations, but systematic expressions of specific semantic relations (see Table 26.2). Brown (1970) has distinguished between two main types of semantic relations: those expressed by combining a single constant term or pivot word (such as 'more') with another word which refers to an object, action or attribute (such as 'milk'), and those that do not involve the use of constant or pivot words. The appearance of two-word utterances can therefore be attributed to the child's acquisition of two different types of combinatorial rule, namely *pivotal* and *categorical rules*. There is considerable individual variation in the type of two-word utterances which different children produce. Some rely largely on pivotal rules, whereas others rely primarily on categorical rules (Barrett, 1989).

Table 26.2 *The eight most common semantic relationships produced by children in the two-word stage*

Semantic relationships	Examples
agent + action	mommy give, daddy sit
action + object	give money, open door
agent + object	mommy car, Angel bone
action + location	sit there, fall floor
entity + location	plane rug, phone table
possessor + possession	my mommy, baby bed
entity + attribute	truck red, house pretty
demonstrative + entity	dat tree, dis mop

(From Brown, 1973)

Box 26.3 Cromer's cognition hypothesis

Word order in two-word utterances seems to reflect the child's pre-linguistic knowledge. According to Cromer's (1974) *cognition hypothesis*, language structures can only be used correctly when permitted by our cognitive structures. Children form schemata to understand the world and then talk about it. A good example is *object permanence*, which is a prerequisite for understanding that words can represent things. If a child did not already understand the relationships between objects, people and events in the real world, its first words would be like random unconnected lists. These are important concepts in Piaget's developmental theory (see Chapter 28), and are consistent with his view of language development reflecting the child's stage of cognitive development (see page 281).

Stage 2 grammar (from about 30 months)

This lasts until around age four or five, and whilst it may be different for different languages, the rule-governed nature of language development is universal. The child's vocabulary grows rapidly and sentences become longer and more complex. *Mean length of utterance* (MLU) is the number of words in a sentence divided by the total number of sentences produced. So, a child who produced 100 sentences with 300 words would have a MLU of 3.00.

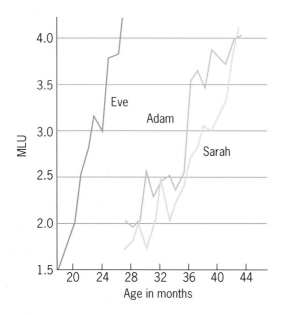

Figure 26.4 *Mean length of utterance (MLU) plotted against age in months for three children (Based on Brown, 1973)*

The increase in MLU shown above is due largely to the inclusion of the functors that are omitted from the telegraphic speech of Stage 1 grammar. For example, 'Daddy hat' may become 'Daddy wear hat' and finally 'Daddy is wearing a hat'. Sentences also become longer because conjunctions (such as 'and' and 'so') are used to form compound sentences like 'You play with the doll and I play with the ball'. Stage 2 grammar, then, really begins with the first use of purely grammatical words. Whilst most children up to 20 months still use one- or two-word sentences, by 24 months the longest sentences include four to five words. By 30 months, this has risen to between eight and ten. This is strongly linked to vocabulary development (Fenson *et al.*, 1994).

Brown (1973) has found a distinct regularity among English-speaking children in terms of the order in the addition of grammatical complexities. Similarly, de Villiers & de Villiers (1979) have found that, irrespective of culture, children acquire functional words in the same general order but at different rates. Each function word corresponds to a syntactic rule. Several studies show that when children begin to apply these rules (such as the rule for forming plurals), they are not just imitating others.

Box 26.4 Berko's (1958) study of rule formation in children

Berko showed children a picture of a fictitious creature called a wug and told them 'This is a wug'.

They were then shown a second picture in which there were two of the creatures and told 'Now there is another one. There are two of them.'

The children were asked to complete the sentence 'There are two ...'. Three- and four-year-olds answered 'wugs' despite never having seen a 'wug' before. Although the children could not have been imitating anybody else's speech, and had not been told about the rule for forming plurals, they were able to apply this rule. Significantly, they were not consciously aware of having acquired the rule for forming a plural, and could not say what the rule was.

The rule-governed nature of language is also shown in children's grammatical *mistakes*. For example, whilst the rule 'add an "s" to a word to form a plural' usually works, there are exceptions to it (such as 'sheep' rather than 'sheeps' and 'geese' rather than 'gooses'). Similarly, the rule 'add "ed" to form the past tense' usually works, but not in the case of 'cost' and 'go'. The observation that children use words like 'costed' and 'goed', without ever having heard others use them, suggests that they are applying a rule rather than using imitation. In these cases, however, the rule is being *overgeneralised* or the language *over-regularised*.

Box 26.5 An example of how the misapplication of a rule is greater than any desire to imitate (Gleason, 1967)

The following is a transcript of an interaction between a mother and her child:

CHILD: My teacher holded the baby rabbits and we patted them.

MOTHER: Did you say your teacher held the baby rabbits?

CHILD: Yes.

MOTHER: What did you say she did?

CHILD: She holded the baby rabbits and we patted them.

MOTHER: Did you say she held them tightly?

CHILD: No, she holded them loosely.

By age four or five, basic grammatical rules have been acquired, and by five or six, children have acquired most of what they need to know about phoneme construction. However, a typical five-year-old will have difficulty understanding *passive* sentences. There are also many irregular words still to be learned, and this aspect of grammatical development will take several more years.

By age 13, most English-speaking children have a vocabulary of 20,000 words, and by age 20, this will have risen to 50,000 or more (Aitchison, 1996), a vocabulary which is acquired at an *average rate* of ten words *per day* (Pinker, 1994).

THEORIES OF LANGUAGE DEVELOPMENT

Learning theory

Classical conditioning

The earliest theory implicating learning principles suggested that much of language is developed through *classical conditioning* (Houston *et al.*, 1991: see Chapter 38). Consider, for example, the development of the sound 'mama'. If this initially neutral sound (which will eventually become a *conditioned stimulus*) is repeatedly paired with the *unconditioned stimulus* of the mother, then the baby's responses to her become classically conditioned to 'mama'. Equally, words like 'hot' may acquire their meaning through repeated pairings with a certain class of unconditioned stimuli such as fires, radiators and so on.

Operant conditioning

According to Skinner (1985):

'Verbal behaviour evidently came into existence when, through a critical step in the evolution of the human species, the vocal musculature became susceptible to operant conditioning'.

Skinner (1957) first applied operant conditioning principles to explain language development when he argued that:

'A child acquires verbal behaviour when relatively unplanned vocalisations, selectively reinforced, assume forms which produce appropriate consequences in a given verbal community'.

Whilst Skinner accepted that pre-linguistic vocalisations, such as cooing and babbling were probably inborn (see page 271), he argued that adults *shape* the baby's sounds into words by *reinforcing* those which approximate the form of real words. Through selective reinforcement, words are shaped into sentences with correct grammar being reinforced and incorrect grammar ignored.

One form of positive reinforcement is the child getting what it asks for (*mands*). For example, 'May I have some water?' produces a drink that reinforces that form of words. Reinforcement may also be given by parents becoming excited and poking, touching, patting and feeding children when they vocalise. The mother's delight on hearing her child's first real word is exciting for the child, and so acquiring language becomes reinforcing in itself.

Skinner also believed that *imitation* plays an important role. When children imitate, or produce *echoic responses* of verbal labels (*tacts*), they receive immediate reinforcement in the form of parental approval to the extent that the imitations resemble correct words. As children continue to learn new words and phrases through imitation, so their language becomes progressively more like that of adults (Moerk & Moerk, 1979).

An evaluation of Skinner's theory

Brodbeck & Irwin (1946) found that, compared with institutionalised children who received less attention, children whose parents reinforced their early attempts at meaningful sounds tended to vocalise more. Parents often reinforce children when they imitate adult language, and using *behaviour modification* Lovaas (1987) has shown that selective reinforcement can be used successfully to teach language to emotionally disturbed or developmentally delayed children (see Chapter 53). However, Skinner's views have been challenged by a number of researchers.

Box 26.6 Does selective reinforcement have any influence on children's grammar?

- Mothers respond to the 'truth value', or presumed meaning of their children's language, rather than to its grammatical correctness or complexity. Mothers extract meaning from, and interpret, their children's incomplete and sometimes primitive sentences (Brown *et al.*, 1969).

- Tizard *et al.* (1972) argue that attempts to correct grammatical mistakes or teach grammar have very little effect (see also pages 274–275). Indeed, vocabulary develops more slowly in children of mothers who systematically correct poor word pronunciation and reward good pronunciation (Nelson, 1973).

- Slobin (1975) found that children learn grammatical rules *despite* their parents, who usually pay little attention to the grammatical structure of their children's speech and often reinforce *incorrect* grammar. According to Slobin:

  'A mother is too engaged in interacting with her child to pay attention to the linguistic form of [its] utterances'.

These findings suggest that whilst parents usually respond to (or reinforce) true statements and criticise or correct false ones, they pay little regard to grammatical correctness. Even if they do, this has little effect on language development.

Whilst imitation must be involved in the learning of accent and vocabulary, its role in complex aspects of language (syntax and semantics) is less obvious. As was seen above, when children do imitate adult sentences, they tend to convert them to their own currently operating grammar. So, between 18 and 30 months, the child's imitations are as telegraphic as its own spontaneous speech. However, a child is more likely to imitate a correct grammatical form after an adult has *recast* the child's own sentences than when the adult uses the same grammatical form spontaneously in normal conversation (Farrar, 1992; Nelson, 1977). Recasting, though, is relatively rare (or sometimes non-existent) in normal toddler–parent conversations, yet children still acquire a complex grammar (Bee, 2000). Furthermore, since at least some adult language is ungrammatical, imitation alone cannot explain how children ever learn 'correct language'. Even if we do not always speak grammatically ourselves, we still know the difference between good and bad grammar.

In response to these criticisms, Bandura (1977a) has broadened the concept of imitation. He accepts that the

exact imitation of particular sentences plays a relatively minor role in language development, but argues that children may imitate the *general* form of sentences, and fill in these general forms with various words. *Deferred imitations* are those word sequences and language structures stored in a child's memory for long periods before being used (often in the same situation in which they were first heard). *Expanded imitations* are repetitions of sentences or phrases not present in the original form (Snow, 1983). Children's language production sometimes exceeds their competence in that they imitate forms of language they do not understand. By storing examples of adult language in memory, children have a sort of 'delayed replay' facility that enables them to produce language forms after they have been acquired (see Chapter 31, pages 339–340).

Box 26.7 Some reasons for disputing learning theory's explanation of language development

- If language is established through reinforcement, we would expect that all children living under widely varying social conditions would acquire language in different ways. The existence of a culturally universal and invariant sequence in the stages of language development, which occurs under highly variable conditions, contradicts this. Indeed, even children born to, and raised by, deaf parents apparently acquire language in the same sequence as other children (Slobin, 1986).

- Learning theory cannot explain the *creativity of language*, that is, native speakers' ability to produce and understand an infinitely large number of sentences never heard or produced before by anyone. As Chomsky (1968) states:

  'The normal use of language is innovative, in the sense that much of what we say in the course of normal language use is entirely new [and] not a repetition of anything that we have heard before'.

- Learning theory has difficulty explaining children's spontaneous use of grammatical rules which they have never heard or been taught. These rules are often overgeneralised and incorrectly used, and (as noted in Box 26.6) children are largely impervious to parental attempts to correct grammatical errors.

- Learning theory cannot account for children's ability to understand sentence as opposed to word meaning. A sentence's meaning is not simply the sum of the meanings of the individual words. The structure of language is comparable to the structure of perception as described by the Gestalt psychologists (Neisser, 1967: see Chapter 23). Learning theory might account for how children learn the meaning of individual nouns and verbs, which have an obvious reference, but it cannot explain acquisition of the meaning of grammatical terms.

Chomsky's LAD and the biological approach

Although language cannot develop without some form of environmental input, Chomsky (1957, 1965, 1968), Lenneberg (1967) and McNeill (1970) believe that environmental factors could never explain language development adequately. Chomsky proposed the existence of an innate *language acquisition device* (LAD), whereby children are born already programmed to formulate and understand all types of sentences even though they have never heard them before.

Chomsky (1957) argued that language is much more complex and much less predictable than Skinner believed. Central to his theory of *transformational gram-*

Rule (1) An S (sentence) consists of (or can be broken down into) NP (noun phrase) and VP (verb phrase)

Rule (2) NP ⟶ Article + (Adjective) + Noun

(The brackets denote 'optional')

Rule (3) VP ⟶ Verb + NP

Rule (4) Article ⟶ a(n), the

Rule (5) Adjective ⟶ big, small, red, etc.

Rule (6) Noun ⟶ boy, girl, stone, etc.

Rule (7) Verb ⟶ hit, threw, helped, etc.

These are *Lexical Rewrite Rules.*

The commas imply that only *one* word should be selected from the list

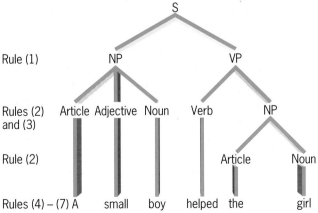

Figure 26.5 *Some of Chomsky's phrase-structure rules and an example of a sentence produced by using them*

mar (TG) are *phrase-structure rules*, which specify what are and are not acceptable utterances in a speaker's native language. When applied systematically, these rules generate sentences in English (or any other language: see Figure 26.5). Whilst phrase-structure rules specify *some* important aspects of language, they do not specify them all (Chomsky, 1957: see Box 26.8).

Box 26.8 Deep structure and surface structure, and transformational grammar

Chomsky distinguished between a sentence's *deep structure* and its *surface structure*. Surface structure refers to *syntactical* structure (the actual words or phrases used in the sentence). Its deep structure more or less corresponds to the sentence's *meaning*. Chomsky argued that when we hear a spoken sentence, we do not 'process' or retain its surface structure, but transform it into its deep structure. The understanding or knowledge of how to transform a sentence's meaning into the words that make it up (and vice versa) is called *transformational grammar* (TG). This understanding or knowledge is an innate LAD, and is what enables us to produce an infinite number of meaningful sentences.

A single surface structure may have more than one deep structure, as in the sentence 'The missionary was ready to eat'. In one representation it is the missionary who is ready to consume a meal, whilst in another the missionary has been made ready for consumption by others. Conversely, different surface structures can have the same deep structure (as in the sentences 'A small boy helped the girl' and 'The girl was helped by a small boy').

Figure 26.6 *As 'New Labour' took over from 'Old Labour', two veteran socialists (Arthur Scargill and Tony Benn) contemplated the party's future. Scargill's question has two deep structures and, given all the 'Old Labour' policies that have, along with Scargill and Benn, been put in the dustbin, we might expect Benn's reply simply to be 'No'. Benn's reply to the alternative deep structure is out of context, and hence the cartoon is funny*

For Chomsky, children are equipped with the ability to learn the rules for transforming deep structure into various surface structures, and they do this by looking for certain kinds of linguistic features common to all languages, such as the use of consonants and vowels, syllables, modifiers and so on. Collectively, these linguistic features (*linguistic universals*) provide the deep structure. They must be universal because all children can learn with equal ease any language to which they are exposed. So, a child born in England of English parents who went to live in China soon after its birth would learn Chinese, if brought up by a Chinese-speaking family, just as easily as a native-born Chinese child. Chomsky argues that only some kind of LAD can account for children's learning and knowledge of grammatical rules in view of the often ungrammatical and incomplete samples of speech they hear.

Chomsky did not suggest that we go through the procedures of phrase structure and TG each time we prepare to speak a sentence (Hampson & Morris, 1996). For Chomsky, a language's grammar is an idealised description of the *linguistic competence* of its native speakers. Any model of how this competence is applied in actual *performance* must acknowledge certain psychologically relevant factors such as memory, attention, the workings of the nervous system and so on (Lyons, 1970).

Box 26.9 Some evidence supporting Chomsky's theory

- The human vocal organs, breathing apparatus, auditory system and brain are all specialised for spoken communication.

- Babies as young as two days old can discriminate between 'ba' and 'pa' sounds (Eimas, 1975). According to Chomsky, these phonetic discriminations can be thought of as the first linguistic universals the baby discovers.

- All adult languages appear to have certain linguistic universals, and TG is acquired in some form by all people (unless brain damaged or reared in isolation) irrespective of their culture and despite enormous variations in the ability to learn other skills (Lenneberg, 1967). The fact that a person with an IQ of 50 may have difficulty in learning simple tasks but still learns to talk, indicates that language develops independently of factors that affect the learning of those tasks. For Lenneberg, this shows that language acquisition must be controlled by genetic factors that are (at least partially) independent of those controlling general intelligence.

- Some twin studies have revealed the existence of a 'private language', intelligible only to the twins (Malmstrom & Silva, 1986). Likewise, studies of some deaf children in Nicaragua have revealed a parallel phenomenon with sign language (Gerrard, 1997). These languages are apparently not a variation of ordinary language, but have the characteristics of ordinary languages (such as verbs, nouns and syntax). This supports the view that knowledge of syntax is innate.

- Studies of congenitally deaf children have shown the emergence of 'gestural language', even though the children received no encouragement or training from their parents (Goldin-Meadow & Feldman, 1977). This suggests that language is very difficult to suppress even in adverse environmental circumstances:

> 'The baby is somehow primed to learn "language" in some form, be it spoken or gestural'. (Bee, 2000)

Lenneberg has argued that the years leading to puberty constitute a *critical period* for language development, based on the still-developing brain's relative lack of specialisation. Children born brain damaged and who lose their language abilities can relearn at least some of them because other, non-damaged, parts of the brain seem to take over. However, adolescents or adults who experience an equivalent amount of damage are unable to regain abilities corresponding to the site of the injury, because the brain is now specialised (or 'committed') and no longer 'plastic' (see Chapter 12, page 121). Evidence exists, however, which suggests that the first ten years or so may not necessarily be the critical period Lenneberg has argued for.

Key STUDY
Box 26.10 The case of Genie (Curtiss, 1977)

Genie was an American child raised in conditions of extreme (de)privation until her discovery at the age of 13 years and seven months. Amongst other appalling treatment, Genie was beaten if she made any noise, and had learned to suppress almost all vocalisations except for a whimper. According to Curtiss, 'Genie was unsocialised, primitive, hardly human'.

Genie could understand a handful of words (including 'rattle', 'bunny' and 'red'), but always responded to them in the same way. Essentially, then, she had to learn language at the age of nearly 14. She never developed normal language skills, and by age 18 could produce only short sentences which lacked important aspects of grammar (such as the use of pronouns).

Her vocabulary expanded and she could hold a conversation, but her use of intonation was poor and only those who knew her well could understand much of what she said. Genie herself had great difficulty in understanding complex syntax. Nonetheless, the fact that she was capable of learning any language at all weakens Lenneberg's claim for a critical period. However, her obvious linguistic retardation is consistent with the existence of a *sensitive period* for language development.

An evaluation of Chomsky's theory

If phrase structure and TG do describe language, it is not unreasonable to ask whether the actual processes involved in preparing to speak actually follow the same steps. In general, investigations have failed to find strong evidence for the application of Chomsky's rules when people speak and listen (Hampson & Morris, 1996).

Aitchison (1983) agrees with Chomsky's claim that children are 'wired' with the knowledge that language is rule-governed, and that they make a succession of hypotheses about the rules underlying speech. However, she disputes the claim that the LAD also consists of TG (what she calls 'Content Cuthbert'). Aitchison prefers a *process* approach, in which children are seen as having inbuilt puzzle-solving equipment that enables them to process linguistic data along with other sorts of data ('Process Peggy').

By contrast, Chomsky (1979) argues that an innate language ability exists *independently* of other innate abilities, because the mind is constructed of 'mental organs' which are:

'... just as specialised and differentiated as those of the body ... and ... language is a system easy to isolate among the various mental faculties'.

Some alternatives to learning theory and biological approaches

Recently, there has been a growing acceptance that neither learning theory nor nativist approaches offers a complete account of language development. Instead, an *integrated* view maintains that children cannot acquire language until an appropriate maturational level has been reached, but that language development is more closely related to environmental input and cognitive development than Chomsky proposes. Maratsos (1983) has identified several assumptions made by *integrative theorists*.

Box 26.11 Some assumptions made by integrative theorists

* Children are highly motivated to communicate and therefore are *active* rather than *passive* language learners.

* Children can learn the major aspects of grammar because they have already acquired important concepts on which grammar is based (namely that events involve agents, actions, objects of actions and so on). For this reason, learning a grammar does not require much information processing.

* Other aspects of language can be explained by the language parents use to talk to children.

* Those grammatical rules that do not fit in with children's natural cognitive processes, and are not conveyed adequately through parental input, are unnatural and difficult for the child. They are also acquired very late (such as the passive voice in English).

The language and social–interaction approach

One alternative explanation of the rule-bound nature of children's speech, which represents a departure from the grammatical competence approach inspired by Chomsky, is that it arises from the child's *pre-linguistic knowledge*. During the 1970s, psychologists began to look at language development in the first 12 to 18 months of life, because the basic skills acquired then contribute substantially to the syntactic skills characteristic of adult language.

A purely syntactic analysis of language cannot explain how children 'discover' their language, that is, how they learn that there is such a thing as language which can be used for communicating, categorising, problem-solving and so on. However, Smith *et al.*'s (1998) *language and social-interaction approach* sees language as being used to communicate needs and intentions, and as an enjoyable means of entering into a community.

Several studies have indicated how babies initially master a social world onto which they later 'map' language. Snow (1977), for example, notes that adults tend to attach meaning to a baby's sounds and utterances. As a result, burps, grunts, giggles and so on are interpreted as expressions of intent and feeling, as are non-verbal communications (such as smiling and eye contact). Snow sees this as a kind of primitive conversation (or *proto-conversation*), which has a rather one-sided quality in that it requires a 'generous' adult attributing some kind of intended meaning to the baby's sounds and non-verbal behaviours. From this perspective, the infant is an inadequate conversational partner.

Box 26.12 Visual co-orientation and formats: two-way interaction

Much more two-way exchanges are *visual co-orientation* (or joint attention) and *formats* (Collis & Schaffer, 1975). Visual co-orientation involves two individuals coming to focus on some common object. This puts an infant's environmental explorations into a social context, so that an infant-object situation is converted into an infant-object-mother situation (Schaffer, 1989). The joint attention this entails provides opportunities for learning how to do things. So, as parents and children develop their mutual patterns of interaction and share attention to objects, some activities recur, as happens in joint picture-book reading.

Bruner (1975, 1978) uses Collis and Schaffer's term 'formats' to refer to rule-bound activity routines in which the infant has many opportunities to relate language to familiar play (as when the mother inserts name labels into a game or activity), initially in *indicating* formats and later in *requesting* them. These ritualised exchanges stress the need for *turn-taking*, and so help the baby to discover the social function of communication. As a result, the infant can learn about the structures and demands of social interaction, and prepare and rehearse the skills that will eventually become essential to successful interchanges such as conversation.

LASS: the active adult

According to Bruner (1983), formats comprise the *language acquisition support system* (LASS). He is concerned with the pragmatics and functions of language (what language is used for). In Bruner's view:

> 'Entry into language is entry into discourse that requires both members of a dialogue pair to interpret a communication and its intent. Learning a language ... consists of learning not only the grammar of a particular language, but also learning how to realise one's intentions by the appropriate use of that grammar'.

The emphasis on intent requires a far more active role on the adult's part in helping a child's language acquisition than just being a 'model', or providing the input for the child's LAD. According to Moerk (1989), 'the LAD was a lady', that is, the lady who does most of the talking to the child (namely its mother). Mothers simplify linguistic input and break it down into helpful, illustrative segments for the child to practise and build on. This view sees language development as a very sophisticated extension of the processes of meaningful interaction that the caregiver and child have constructed over several months (Durkin, 1995).

The active child

Another way of looking at the 'partnership' between adults and infants is to see the infant (rather than the adult) as being the more 'active' partner in their relationship. The view of language as a *cause–effect analytic device* has been summarised by Gauker (1990), for whom:

> 'The fundamental function of words is to bring about changes in the speaker's environment ... Linguistic understanding consists of a grasp of these causal relations'.

Box 26.13 The emergence of communicative intentionality

According to Gauker (1990), language comprises a set of symbols whose use results in a change of behaviour in the listener. The use of words as communicative tools is shown in the *emergence of communicative intentionality*. During the pre-linguistic stage, children have no awareness that they can gain a desired effect indirectly by changing somebody else's behaviour. So, they may cry and reach for something, but not direct the cry towards the caregiver or look back at the caregiver. The cry merely expresses frustration and is not a communicative signal designed to affect the other's behaviour. This 'analysis' of means–ends relationships (what causes what) solely as a product of one's own actions, is called *first-order causality*.

The emergence of communicative intentionality involves *second-order causality*, the awareness that it *is* possible to bring about a desired goal by using another person as a tool. Pointing gestures and glances now rapidly proliferate as a means of asking others to look at or act upon an object. According to Savage-Rumbaugh (1990), the child is beginning to understand in a general sense:

> '... that it is possible to "cause" others to engage in desired actions through the mechanism of communication about those actions'.

(Based on Gauker, 1990)

This use of animate tools (other people) parallels the use of inanimate tools (physical objects), and this is an important feature of what Piaget (1952) calls *sensorimotor intelligence* (see Chapter 28). Some kind of *instrumental understanding* (what leads to what) seems to underlie both activities.

It is, however, more difficult to analyse language *comprehension* in terms of a cause–effect analysis than it is to analyse *language production*, since what do we cause to happen when we understand things that have been said to us? Based on her work with chimpanzees, Savage-Rumbaugh (1990) concludes that language comprehension is clearly the driving force underlying the language acquisition process, and that under normal circumstances, language production is just one outcome of the development of language comprehension (see Chapter 41).

Piaget and language development

According to Piaget (1952), the growth of language can be predicted from an understanding of children's cognitive skills. He believed that children must first understand concepts before they can use words that describe them. Piaget's views are an important contribution to the debate concerning the language and thought relationship (see Chapter 25, pages 265–266).

CONCLUSIONS

This chapter has described the course of language development. Many psychologists believe that there is a biologically determined 'timetable' for language development, whilst others emphasise the role of conditioning. Although the evidence suggests that biologically based accounts are probably closer to the truth, it is unlikely that they offer a complete account of language development. According to Bee (2000):

'The fact that children learn complex and varied use of their native tongue within a few years remains both miraculous and largely mysterious.'

Summary

- **Psycholinguistics** is the study of the perception, understanding and production of language and their development.

- Language involves the acquisition of a rule system (**grammar/mental grammar**), which consists of **phonology**, **semantics** and **syntax**.

- During the **pre-linguistic stage** (0–12 months), babies make various non-speech sounds including crying and **cooing**. **Babbling** (starting at six to nine months), however, involves the production of phonemes.

- **Phonemic expansion** is replaced at around nine or ten months by **phonemic contraction**. This reflects the baby's sampling of phonemes used in its 'linguistic environment'.

- There is a gradual transition from babbling to the **one-word stage**. The child's first words are often invented and **context-bound**, denoting specific actions, events or objects. They perform less of a communicative function and more of a performative function.

- The one-word stage is also characterised by **holophrases**, whose full meaning is provided by accompanying gestures and tones of voice. They can be thought of as precursors of later, more complex sentences.

- The **two-word stage** is universal, and can be divided into **Stage 1 grammar** (18–30 months) and **Stage 2 grammar** (30 months and beyond).

- Language in Stage 1 grammar is **telegraphic**, consisting of **contentives** but no **functors,** and involving a **rigid word order**. The child's **imitation by reduction** is complemented by the adult's **imitation with expansion**.

- **Two-word utterances** represent systematic expressions of specific semantic relations, such as **pivotal rules** and **categorical rules**. These are **combinatorial** rules, and children show considerable individual variation in which type they use for forming two-word utterances.

- Word order seems to reflect the child's pre-linguistic knowledge, as claimed by Cromer's **cognition hypothesis**. Similarly, Piaget believes that language development reflects the child's stage of cognitive development.

- The rule-governed nature of **Stage 2 grammar** is universal. Sentences become longer and more complex, as measured by the **mean length of utterance** (MLU). MLU increase is due largely to the inclusion of functors missing from Stage 1 telegraphic speech.

- There appears to be a universal developmental sequence of grammatical complexities/functional words. Each functor corresponds to a **syntactic rule**. The rule-governed nature of language is also illustrated in children's grammatical mistakes, which often involve the **overgeneralised/over-regularised** application of a rule.

- According to Skinner, verbal behaviour is acquired through **operant conditioning**. Whilst cooing and babbling are probably inborn, adults **shape** these into words by **reinforcing** sounds which approximate real words. Selective reinforcement shapes words into grammatically correct sentences.

- Children whose parents reinforce their early attempts at meaningful sounds tend to vocalise more, compared with institutionalised children. However, mothers respond to the 'truth value' of their children's language rather than to its grammatical correctness or complexity.

- Whilst **imitation** is necessary for the learning of accent and vocabulary, it cannot explain the development of syntax and semantics, and imitation of adult speech reflects the child's currently operating grammar. However, children may imitate the **general** forms of sentences and then fill these in with various words.

- Learning theory cannot explain the culturally universal and invariant sequence in the stages of language development. It also fails to explain the **creativity of language**.

- According to Chomsky, children are innately equipped with a **language acquisition device** (LAD) which consists essentially of **transformational grammar** (TG). Central to TG are **phrase-structure rules**. TG enables us to transform **surface** into **deep structure** and vice versa.

- LAD is used to look for **linguistic universals**, which collectively provide the deep structure. Children can learn any language to which they are exposed with equal ease.

- Lenneberg's proposed **critical period** is based on the finding that only in adolescents and adults does brain damage cause permanent loss of the corresponding abilities, since the brain is now specialised, unlike the child's 'plastic' brain.

- According to **integrative theorists**, children are **active** learners of language whose learning of grammar is based on important concepts already acquired. The **language and social-interaction approach** emphasises children's **pre-linguistic knowledge**. Language is used to communicate needs and intentions.

- Babies initially master a social world onto which they later 'map' language, as demonstrated by **proto-conversations**. More two-way exchanges include **visual co-orientation** and **formats**, the latter comprising the **language acquisition support system** (LASS).

- Seeing language as a **cause–effect analytic device** depicts the child as a more 'active' partner, using words as a tool for bringing about a change in the listener's behaviour. The **emergence of communicative intentionality** parallels the use of physical objects, an important feature of Piaget's **sensorimotor intelligence**.

Essay Questions

1 Discuss **one** environmental and **one** nativist theory of language acquisition. *(24 marks)*

2 Critically consider psychological research into the process of language acquisition. *(24 marks)*

WEB ADDRESSES

http://www.cogsci.ac.uk/~harnad/Papers/Psy104/pinker.langacq.html
http://carla.acad.umn.edu
http://williamcalvin.com/1990s/1994SciAmer.htm
http://ww2.med.jhu.edu/peds/neonatology/poi3.html

27 Problem-solving and Decision-making

INTRODUCTION AND OVERVIEW

The basic cognitive processes considered in the previous chapters are all aspects of 'thought'. However, there is more to thinking than perception, attention and language. Two closely related aspects of thinking of interest to cognitive psychologists are *problem-solving* and *decision-making*. This chapter considers research into the processes involved in solving problems and making decisions, including practical issues relating to risk-taking behaviour in everyday life.

THE NATURE OF PROBLEMS

Stages in problem-solving (PS)

A problem is a situation in which there is a discrepancy between a present state and some goal state, with no obvious way of reducing it. PS is an attempt to reduce the discrepancy and achieve the goal state, and progresses through a series of logical stages (Bourne *et al.*, 1979). These are *defining or representing the problem, generating possible solutions* and *evaluating possible solutions*. Some researchers have claimed that there is an *incubation stage* (in which no attempt is made to solve the problem) occurring between the generating and evaluating stages.

Representing and defining problems

How problems are represented (such as in verbal, visual or mathematical form), their form of presentation and our ability to 'weed out' unimportant information can all influence the understanding of a problem (Duncker, 1945; Simon & Hayes, 1976). Ill-defined and complex problems are more difficult to solve than well-defined and simple ones (Matlin, 1989).

Once we understand a problem, we can *generate possible solutions*. Sometimes, finding a solution is straightforward, and simply involves retrieving information from long-term memory (LTM). On other occasions, certain tendencies and biases operate which lead us to overlook potential solutions and so we 'get stuck'. This is why generating lots of possible solutions can be useful in some contexts.

Once possible solutions have been generated, they can be *evaluated*. As with generating solutions, the evaluation of solutions is sometimes straightforward, especially when the problem is clearly defined or represented. With unclear or poorly defined problems, though, the generated solutions are typically difficult to evaluate. Also, the various stages in PS do not necessarily occur in a fixed order, and we may move between stages or go back to the defining or representing stage.

Types of problems

Garnham (1988) distinguishes between two broad classes of problem, *adversary* and *non-adversary*. Adversary problems are those in which two or more people compete for success, as in chess. In non-adversary problems, other people are involved only as problem setters for the problem solver.

PS: FROM BEHAVIOURISM TO INFORMATION-PROCESSING

According to behaviourists, PS is essentially a matter of *trial-and-error* and *accidental success* (Thorndike, 1911: see Chapter 38). Behaviourists argued that as acquired habits are learned, so PS (essentially a chain of stimulus–response associations) improves. Whilst trial-and-error can be effective in solving some problems, the behaviourist approach was challenged by *Gestalt psychologists*. They maintained that our perceptions are organised according to the laws of proximity, closure, similarity and so on (see Chapter 23).

The Gestalt approach to PS looked at how we impose *structure* on a problem by understanding how its elements are related to one another. Thus, rather than being 'senseless drill and arbitrary associations' (as Katona, 1940, argued was the case with the behaviourist approach), PS occurs through *meaningful apprehension of relations*.

Gestalt psychologists distinguished between *reproductive thinking* and *productive thinking* (Maier, 1931). In reproductive thinking, past solutions are applied to new problems. Whilst past experience can lead to success, it can also hinder PS (see below). In productive thinking, problems are solved by the principle of *reorganisation*, or solving a problem by perceiving new relationships among its elements.

Consider, for example, trying to arrange six matchsticks into four equilateral triangles with each side equal to one stick. If you try to arrange the matchsticks by pushing them around on a table, the problem cannot be solved. Through reorganisation, though, and realisation that the matchsticks do not *have* to be arranged in two dimensions, the problem can be solved (as shown in Figure 27.5 on page 294). The principle of reorganisation is similar to what Köhler (1925) called *insight* in his studies of PS in chimpanzees.

Key STUDY

Box 27.1 Köhler's studies of PS in chimpanzees

Köhler suspended an out-of-reach bunch of bananas from the ceiling of the cage of a chimpanzee called Sultan. In the cage were several items that could be used to reach the bananas (such as different length sticks), although none on its own was sufficient. Eventually, Sultan solved the problem by placing empty boxes beneath the bananas and climbing on the boxes.

Figure 27.1

Later, Köhler allowed Sultan to see a box being placed in the corridor leading to his cage. Sultan was then taken to his cage where, again, bananas were suspended from the ceiling. Sultan's first strategy was to remove a long bolt from the open cage's door. Quite suddenly, though, he stopped, ran down the corridor, and returned with the box which was again used to retrieve the bananas.

For Köhler, Sultan's behaviour was a result of sudden perceptual reorganisation or *insight*, which was different from trial-and-error learning. Other experiments showed that Sultan's perceptual reorganisation was maintained as a plan of action. So, when the bananas were placed *outside* the cage, Sultan still built several boxes. Experience can sometimes be an obstacle to PS! (For further discussion of Köhler's experiments, see Chapter 39, pages 428–429.)

Whilst Gestalt psychologists made a significant contribution to our understanding of the processes involved in solving certain types of problem, they did not develop a theory that applies to all aspects of PS. Although the concepts of 'insight' and 'restructuring' are attractive because they are easily understood (especially when accompanied by perceptual demonstrations), they are radically understated as theoretical constructs (Eysenck & Keane, 1995). Thus, it is very unclear under what conditions they will occur and exactly what insight involves.

Information-processing approaches analyse cognitive processes in terms of a series of separate stages. In the case of PS, the stages are those mentioned earlier, that is, representing the problem, generating possible solutions and evaluating those solutions.

GENERATING POSSIBLE SOLUTIONS: ALGORITHMS AND HEURISTICS

Algorithms

An *algorithm* is a systematic exploration of every possible solution until the correct one is found. For example, to solve the anagram YABB, we could list *all* the possible combinations of letters, checking each time to see if the result is a word. Thus, we might generate BBAY (non-word), BYAB (non-word) and so on, until we eventually arrive at BABY. Algorithms *guarantee* a solution to a problem, and are effective when the number of possible solutions is small (as in the above example). However, when the number of possible solutions is large, algorithms are *time consuming* (unless we are fortunate enough to find the solution early).

Heuristics

Heuristics are 'rules of thumb' which, whilst not guaranteeing a solution to a problem, can result in solutions being reached more quickly (Newell *et al.*, 1958). These 'fuzzy' procedures are based on intuition, past experience and any other relevant information. With solving anagrams, for example, a heuristic approach would involve looking for letter combinations that are and are not permitted in the English language. BB is not a permitted combination of letters at the beginning of a word, and so this would immediately exclude BBAY as a solution to the example above. Although unlikely with four-letter anagrams, heuristic devices applied to longer anagrams might not be successful, and we might miss a solution based on a lack of intuition, past experience and other relevant factors.

Heuristic devices include *analogies* and *means–end analysis* (Newell & Simon, 1972). Analogies involve recognising that a particular problem is similar to one encountered before. In means–end analysis (or *working backwards*), the search for a solution begins at the goal (or end) and works backwards to the original state (the means being the steps that must be taken to get from the present state – the problem – to the goal of solving the problem).

Box 27.2 An illustration of means–end analysis

In one version of the game of 'Nim', 15 matchsticks are placed in front of two players. Each player is allowed to remove at least one matchstick but not more than five on each turn. Players take turns in removing matchsticks until one takes the last matchstick and so wins the game. In order to win, then, a player must reach his or her turn with one to five matchsticks left. By working backwards, we can see that if an opponent is left with six or 12 matchsticks, then it doesn't matter what he or she does because we will always win. The optimum strategy is therefore to remove enough matchsticks so as to leave the opponent with six or 12 of them.

Because it is often not possible to achieve the main goal in one step, working backwards can involve breaking down the main goal into a series of *sub-goals* or *sub-problems*, each of which must be solved before the main goal can be reached (*problem-reduction representation*). As each of the sub-problems is solved, so the distance between the original state and the goal state lessens (Newell & Simon, 1972). A good example is the 'hobbit and orcs' problem (Thomas, 1974). In this, the goal is to get three

hobbits and three orcs across a river in a boat that can carry a maximum of two creatures at a time. To take the boat back across the river, at least one hobbit or one orc must be on it. Moreover, the orcs must never outnumber the hobbits on either side of the river (because the orcs will eat the hobbits).

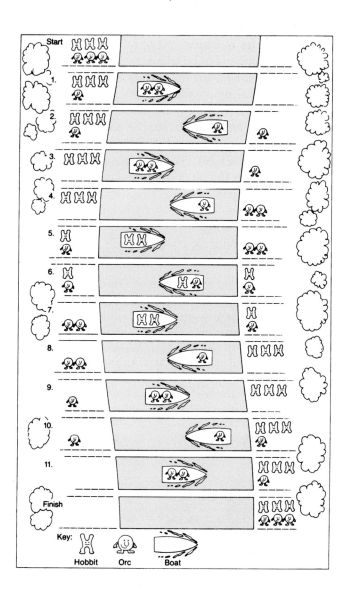

Figure 27.2 *The 'hobbits and orcs' problem*

(*From* Psychology: An Introduction 6/E. by Morris, © 1988. Reprinted by permission of Prentice-Hall, Inc., Upper Saddle River, NJ.)

Leaving aside the main goal of getting everybody across the river, we might begin, as shown in Figure 27.2, by sending two orcs across. Since there is no constraint on the same orc going back to the other side, we might have one make a return trip, pick up another orc, send one orc back, and then allow two hobbits to cross the river (see

Steps 1–5). By working on this particular sub-goal, we can eventually get all the hobbits and orcs across to the other side in 11 moves.

Unfortunately, measuring progress in this problem is difficult. Computers can be programmed to work out a sequence of all possible moves and then plot the quickest path to a solution (using a *check-every-move algorithm*). People, however, cannot hold this amount of information in a limited-capacity working memory. Also, in working backwards we sometimes have to move *further away* from the goal to achieve it. One reason why the 'hobbits and orcs' problem is so difficult is that at one point (Step 6), it becomes necessary to take a hobbit *and* an orc *back* to the side they started from, which apparently *increases* the distance from the final goal (Greene, 1987).

Evaluating potential solutions to a problem is the final PS stage. Where the problem and goal have been stated precisely, as in the 'hobbits and orcs' problem, evaluation is relatively simple. With poorly defined problems, it is much more difficult.

PROBLEMS IN SOLVING PROBLEMS

Earlier on, it was mentioned that certain tendencies and biases can hinder the ability to solve particular problems. Two circumstances in which past experience hinders rather than helps were identified by Gestalt psychologists. These are *mental set* (or *rigidity*) and *functional fixedness*. A third obstacle to PS is the *confirmation bias*.

Mental set

This is the tendency to continue using a previously successful strategy to solve new problems, even when more efficient strategies exist. Luchins (1942) and Luchins & Luchins (1959) asked people to imagine they had three different containers each of a different size. The task was to use the containers to obtain a specific amount of liquid. Once this problem had been solved, the task was repeated, but participants had to imagine a different set of three containers.

The first five problems can be solved using the formula B–2C–A (that is, fill container B, pour its contents into container C twice, and then pour what remains in container B into container A to leave the desired amount in container B). Whilst the sixth problem can also be solved using this formula, there is a more direct solution, namely A–C. The seventh problem *cannot* be solved using the formula B–2C–A, but can be solved using the formula A–C.

Table 27.1 *The water container problems used by Luchins & Luchins (1959)*

Problem No.	Containers with capacity in fluid ounces			Obtain exactly these amounts of water
	Container A	Container B	Container C	
1	21	127	3	100
2	14	163	25	99
3	18	43	10	5
4	9	42	6	21
5	20	59	4	31
6	23	49	3	20
7	10	36	7	3

Once people discovered a solution to the first problem, they continued to use it even when (in the case of the sixth problem) it was less efficient or (in the case of the seventh problem) did not apply. In Gestalt terms, mental set produces reproductive thinking when a problem calls for productive thinking (Scheerer, 1963).

Functional fixedness

Functional fixedness (or '*fixity*') is a type of mental set in which we fail to see that an object may have functions (or uses) other than its normal ones. Duncker (1945) gave participants a box of drawing pins and a candle, and instructed them to attach the candle to a wall so it would stay upright and burn properly. Whilst participants devised several inelegant solutions to the problem, they failed to empty the box, pin it to the wall and place the candle in it. However, when people are shown an *empty* box and the drawing pins are scattered on a table, the box is much more likely to be used as a candle holder (Glucksberg & Weisberg, 1966).

Box 27.3 Confirmation bias

This is the tendency to search for information that confirms our ideas and simultaneously overlook contradictory information. Wason (1960) gave participants the three-number sequence 2–4–6 and asked them to discover the rule that he had in his head which applied to the sequence. Participants were allowed to generate their own three-number sequences and ask if it conformed to the rule that applied to 2–4–6.

Wason's rule was actually very simple, namely 'any three ascending numbers'. However, 80 per cent of participants failed to discover it, despite being extremely confident that they had. Most formed a wrong idea about the rule (such as 'counting in twos') and then searched only for confirming evidence (such as 1–3–5 or 42–44–46) which also conformed to Wason's rule. What participants did not do was look for evidence that would disconfirm their hypotheses. Thus, 4–6–9 would *disconfirm* the counting-in-twos rule, but since it conforms to Wason's rule, it would have allowed thinking to shift.

DECISION-MAKING

Decision-making (DM) is a special case of PS in which we already know the possible solutions (or choices). Some decisions we have to make are relatively trivial. Others are more important, such as a married couple deciding whether or not to have children, or a student deciding which university to study at. In DM, then, we are faced with various alternative choices from which one must be selected and the others rejected.

Compensatory and non-compensatory models of DM

Compensatory models

If we were completely logical in our DM, we would evaluate how *all* of the desirable potential outcomes of a particular decision might *compensate* for the undesirable potential outcomes. According to the *additive compensatory model*, we start the DM process by listing common features of various alternatives and assigning arbitrary weights that reflect their value to us. The weights are then added up to arrive at a separate score for each alternative. Provided that the criteria have been properly weighted and each criterion has been correctly rated, the alternative with the highest score is the most rational choice given the available information.

Another compensatory model is the *utility-probability model*, which proposes that important decisions are made by weighting the desirability of each potential outcome according to its *utility* and *probability*. Utility is the value placed on potential positive or negative outcomes. Probability is the likelihood that the choice will actually produce the potential outcome.

Non-compensatory models

Evidence suggests that we actually use various, and less precise, *non-compensatory models*. In these, not all features of each alternative may be considered and features do not compensate for each other. There are at least four such models.

Box 27.4 Some non-compensatory DM models

Elimination by aspects: When faced with complex decisions, we eliminate various options if they do not meet particular criteria, irrespective of their quality on other criteria (Tversky, 1972). This assumes that we begin with a maximum criterion and use it to test the various options. If, after applying this criterion, more than one alternative remains, the second most important criterion is used. The procedure continues until just one option remains. This is the chosen option.

Maximax strategy: After comparing the various options according to their best features, we then select the one with the strongest best feature.

Minimax strategy: After considering the weakest feature of each option, we select the option whose weakest feature is most highly rated.

Conjunctive strategy: This involves setting a 'minimum' acceptable value on each option. Any option which does not meet, or exceed, this value as the criteria are considered from most to least important is discarded. The chosen option is that which does meet or exceed the minimum acceptable value on each criterion.

Heuristics in DM

Clearly, important decisions should be approached rationally and systematically. However, it is not always easy to make rational decisions, even in important matters, because of the absence of information about the various alternatives. Moreover, with all the decisions we have to make daily, there is not time to engage in the rational processes described above. We also have only a limited capacity for reasoning according to formal logic and probability theory (Evans & Over, 1996). As a result, we often rely on heuristics. Two of these are the *availability heuristic* (or *bias*) and the *representativeness heuristic* (or *bias*: Tversky & Kahneman, 1973).

Availability heuristic (or bias)

Sometimes, decisions must be made on the basis of whatever information is most readily available in LTM. The availability heuristic is based on the assumption that an event's probability is directly related to the frequency with which it has occurred in the past, and that more frequent events are usually easier to remember than less frequent events.

For example, if asked whether the letter 'K' appears more often as the first letter of words or as the third letter, you would probably say the former. In fact, 'K' is three times more likely to appear as the third letter, but because words beginning with 'K' come to mind more easily, we presume that they are more commonplace (Hastie & Park, 1986).

The availability heuristic also plays a role in our tendency to overestimate the chances of being the victim of a violent crime or a plane crash (Tyler & Cook, 1984). This is because the extensive media coverage of these statistically very rare events brings vivid examples of them to mind very readily.

Representativeness heuristic (or bias)

Tversky & Kahneman (1973) gave participants the following information about a person called 'Steve':

> 'Steve is very shy and withdrawn, invariably helpful, but with little interest in people, or in the world of reality. A meek and tidy soul, he has a need for order and structure, and a passion for detail'.

The participants were asked to decide how likely it was that Steve was involved in one of a number of occupations, including musician, pilot, physician, salesman and librarian. Most guessed he was a librarian, presumably because his personality characteristics matched certain stereotypes about librarians (see Chapter 2, pages 13–14). Whenever we judge the likelihood of something by intuitively comparing it with our preconceived ideas of a few characteristics that we believe represent a category, we are using the representative heuristic. The representativeness heuristic can also explain the *gambler's fallacy* (see Box 27.5) and the *base rate fallacy*.

Box 27.5 The gambler's fallacy

Consider the following possible outcomes of tossing a coin six times:

HHHHHH, TTTHHH and HTTHTH.

Most people believe the first outcome to be the *least* likely of the three and the third to be the *most* likely. In fact, the probability of the three sequences is *identical*. Our assumption that coin tossing produces a random sequence of heads and tails leads us to decide that the third is the most likely. Indeed, if people observe five consecutive heads and are asked to estimate the probability of the next toss being a head, they tend to suggest that a tail is the more likely outcome, even though the probability of either is actually 0.5. This tendency is called the *gambler's fallacy*.

In the *base rate fallacy*, we ignore important information about *base rates* (the relative frequency of different objects/events in the world). For example, Tversky & Kahneman (1973) asked participants to decide whether a student who could be described as 'neat and tidy', 'dull and mechanical' and 'a poor writer' was a computer-science student or a humanities student. Over 95 per cent decided the student studied computing. Even after they were told that over 80 per cent of students at their school were studying humanities, their estimates remained virtually unchanged. So, even when we know the relative frequency of two things, we tend to ignore this information and base a decision on how well something matches our stereotype, that is, how representative it is.

However, if prior odds are the *only* relevant information (base rates without the description of the student), then participants will estimate correctly. People may also be more inclined to take account of base rate information when it seems to be *causally* relevant (Tversky & Kahneman, 1980).

Box 27.6 Some other influences on DM

Belief perseverance: This is the tendency to cling to a belief even in the face of contrary evidence (Lord *et al.*, 1979). It can be overcome by *considering the opposite*. However, some false beliefs, such as stereotypes, are difficult to remove even when information exists which clearly discredits them.

Entrapment: When we make costly investments in something (such as a relationship) that goes wrong, we may come to feel that we have no choice but to continue, because withdrawal cannot justify the costs already incurred (Brockner & Rubin, 1985). For example, industrial disputes often continue beyond the stage where either side can hope to achieve any gains (Baron, 1989).

Over-confidence: This is the tendency to overestimate the accuracy of our current knowledge. This can occur because it is generally easier for us to remember successful decisions or judgements than unsuccessful ones. So, using the availability heuristic, we overestimate our success at particular tasks. Over-confidence can be overcome by providing feedback about the accuracy of decisions and judgements.

Loss aversion and costs against losses: Typically, we tend to reject riskier, though potentially more rewarding, decisions in favour of a certain gain *unless* taking a risk is a way to avoid loss (Tversky & Kahneman, 1986). We also tend to see losses as being more acceptable if we label them as 'costs' rather than 'losses' (although the evaluation of a cost depends on the context: Kahneman & Tversky, 1984).

Expectations: Expectations can affect both our perception of the world (see Chapter 23, page 241) and what is done with the perceived information. For example, the shooting down of an ascending Iranian airliner by an American warship occurred as a result of initial, but later corrected, computer information that the plane was a descending F14 fighter jet. The expectation of an attack led the ship's captain to pay more attention to his crew's reports of an emergency than to the new computer information (Wade & Tavris, 1993).

Hindsight: *Hindsight bias* refers to our tendency to overestimate the probability that something would have happened after it has happened, as if we knew this all along (Hawkins & Hastie, 1990).

Framing: When the same issue is presented (or *framed*) in two different but equivalent ways, we tend to make different judgements about it. For example, people respond more positively to ground beef if it is described as '75 per cent lean' rather than '25 per cent fat'. Also, medical treatments are seen as being more successful if framed as having a '50 per cent success rate' rather than a '50 per cent failure rate' (Levin & Gaeth, 1988).

COMPUTERS, PS AND DM

At the heart of the information-processing approach lies the *computer analogy*, the view that human cognition can be understood by comparing it with the functioning of digital computers (see Chapter 58). Newell *et al.*'s (1958) *general problem solver* (GPS) attempted to simulate the entire range of human PS. It was based on *verbal protocols* given by people as they attempted to solve particular problems, and employed the working-backwards heuristic (see page 286).

Tests of the GPS (e.g. Atwood & Polson, 1976) involved giving it and a person the same problem, and comparing the performance of both in terms of the number and types of steps taken and the solution arrived at. Results indicated that the GPS and people use similar strategies for solving particular problems, although measuring the 'goodness of fit' between verbal protocols (which are themselves suspect) and the 'traces' of a computer program is difficult (Garnham, 1988; Hampson & Morris, 1996).

Research has also looked at computer simulations of adversary problems (especially chess), where substantial *domain-specific knowledge* is required. Studies of experts and novices have revealed many important differences between them. These do not necessarily occur because experts are faster thinkers, have better memories or are cleverer than non-experts (Hampson & Morris, 1996). The gain from being an expert would seem to be that it places less strain on working memory. Since PS strategies depend on knowledge which is already available, 'the more you know, the less you have to think' (Greene, 1987).

Figure 27.3 *Neville Chamberlain, the British Prime Minister, returned home in September 1938 from seeing Hitler in Munich with a pledge of non-aggression. He over-confidently declared 'I believe it is peace in our time'.*

Figure 27.4 *Chess experts are only better at remembering the position of chess pieces when they are positioned as they might be during a game. If the pieces are placed randomly, the experts are no better than non-experts at memorising their positions (de Groot, 1966)*

Box 27.7 Expert systems

Expert systems (ESs or *intelligent knowledge-based systems*) are computer programs that apply knowledge in a specific area, enabling a computer to function as effectively as a human expert. ESs include MYCIN (Shortliffe, 1976), which helps doctors diagnose and treat infectious diseases, and PROSPECTOR (Feigenbaum & McCorduck, 1983) which helps geologists explore for minerals. ESs obtain their 'knowledge' from human experts. However, experts cannot always formulate explicitly the knowledge they use in solving particular problems, nor can they say how they combine different items of information to reach a decision about a particular case. As a result, ES production is both difficult and time consuming.

Whilst ESs have been shown to be useful, they are much less flexible than their human counterparts. In Boden's (1987) view:

'In almost every case, their 'explanations' are merely recapitulations of the previous firing of if-then rules ... for they still have no higher-level representations of the knowledge domain, their own problem-solving activity or the knowledge of their human user'.

Whether ESs can be provided with causal reasoning, so that they can reach a conclusion *and* explain the reason for it, is currently the focus of much research interest.

DM IN EVERYDAY LIFE

Gambling and risk-taking

Many laboratory studies have used gambling as a model of risk-taking behaviour, despite the fact that it is *not* typical of the risks we take in everyday life (Jones, 1998). However, the heuristics discussed above (which are based largely on laboratory studies) can help explain an increasingly common case of real-life gambling, namely, playing the National Lottery. Although the odds against winning the jackpot are 14 million to one (far greater than any other form of average gambling return), 90 per cent of the population are estimated to have bought at least one ticket, and 65 per cent claim to play regularly (Hill & Williamson, 1998). Given these odds, it is likely that the ordinary 'social gambler' does not think about the actual probability of winning, but relies on heuristic strategies for handling the available information (Griffiths, 1997b). (See Table 27.2, page 292.)

The fact that there are so many heuristics and biases, and that several can be applied to any one particular situation, gives them little predictive value (Griffiths, 1997b; Wagenaar, 1988). However, the availability bias, illusory correlations and illusion of control can help explain the persistence of gambling (Griffiths, 1997b; Hill & Williamson, 1998). Uncovering the false beliefs underlying people's mistakes when becoming involved in a risk situation can help to reduce the irrational thinking of a potential gambler (Griffiths, 1990; Walker, 1992).

Naturalistic DM

Unlike traditional research into DM, which typically studies decisions made by naïve participants in laboratory experiments, *naturalistic decision-making* (NDM) has emerged as a paradigm shift in applied DM research (Skriver, 1996). NDM researchers argue that only by studying experienced people can they gain insight into the way decision-makers utilise both their domain knowledge and contextual information, and how the contextual factors affect DM processes.

Areas of NDM research interest include military command and control, firefighting incident command, offshore installation emergency response, and medical DM (Heller *et al.*, 1992). How real decision-makers arrive at difficult, dynamic decisions in often ill-structured and changing environments is NDM's major concern.

Table 27.2 *Heuristic strategies and biases that might be used by lottery players*

Heuristic	Application to lottery participation
Availability bias (see pages 288–289)	Wide publicity concerning winners, and pleasant memories of an occasional small prize, make winning more salient than losing.
Randomness bias: not expecting a random sequence to have any apparent biases and regularities (Teigen, 1994).	Despite the mechanical and random nature of the draw, many people seem to be trying to *predict* which numbers will be drawn (Haigh, 1995). So, there is difficulty in choosing six random numbers from 49.
Representativeness bias: equating a 'random' sample with a 'representative' sample (Tversky & Kahneman, 1971: see also page 289).	A tendency to choose numbers that appear 'random' (irregular, no pattern), and avoid those which appear less random (adjacent numbers and repeating digits).
Gambler's fallacy: the belief that subsequent events will cancel out previous events to produce a representative sequence (Holtgraves & Skeel, 1992), and that the probability of winning will increase with the length of an ongoing run of losses (Wagenaar, 1988: see also Box 27.5, page 289).	Choosing numbers which have been least drawn (they are therefore 'due'), and overestimate the chances of winning.
Illusory correlations: the use of superstitious behaviour when it is believed variables correlate when they do not (Wagenaar, 1988: see Chapter 2, page 12).	Choosing 'lucky numbers' – birthdays, house numbers etc. – which causes players to discard statistical probabilities.
Flexible attribution: tendency to attribute success to personal skill and failures to some external influence (Wagenaar, 1988: see Chapter 1, page 8).	Preference for choosing own numbers rather than buying 'lucky dips', so that any win is due to player's own skill (*game of luck*), whereas losses are due to features of the game (*game of chance*).
Illusion of control: an expectancy of success which is greater than the objective probability warrants (Langer, 1975).	Being able to choose own numbers induces skill orientations, which cause players to feel inappropriately confident.
Sunk cost bias: continuing an endeavour once an investment has been made (Arkes & Blumer, 1985).	Continuing to buy lottery tickets whilst experiencing losses. The more money that is spent, the more likely people are to continue 'investing', and to inflate their estimations of winning.

(Based on Griffiths, 1997b, and Hill & Williamson, 1998)

CONCLUSIONS

Psychological research has revealed much about the cognitive processes underlying successful and unsuccessful PS and DM. Whilst we might think that our approaches to PS and DM are always rational and unbiased, the evidence indicates that this is not so, and that various factors influence the solutions we arrive at and the decisions we make. These include various biases and heuristics, which can help to explain 'social' gambling, such as playing the National Lottery.

Summary

- According to an **information-processing approach**, problem-solving progresses through a series of logical stages: **defining/representing the problem, generating possible solutions** and **evaluating possible solutions**. However, they may not always occur in this sequence.

- Ill-defined and complex problems are more difficult to solve than well-defined, simple ones. Generating possible solutions might simply involve retrieving information from LTM.

- The **behaviourist** view of PS as **trial-and-error** and **accidental success** was challenged by the **Gestalt** psychologists, who looked at how we impose **structure** on a problem through **meaningful apprehension of relations**. Maier distinguished between reproductive and productive thinking, the latter involving reorganisation (similar to insight). Whilst these concepts are easy to understand, they are more difficult to define.

■ Algorithms and heuristics are two ways of generating possible solutions to a problem. Algorithms guarantee a solution, but are time-consuming when the number of possible solutions is large. Heuristics do not guarantee a solution, but can help produce solutions more quickly. Examples include analogies and means–end analysis.

■ Means–end analysis involves working backwards from the goal or end (the solution) to the original state (the problem). The means are the steps required to get from one to the other. The main goal may have to be broken down into sub-goals/sub-problems through a process of problem-reduction representation.

■ Computers can be programmed with a check-every-move algorithm, but human working memory (WM) is unable to hold this amount of information. Also, we sometimes have to move further away from the goal in order to achieve it.

■ Mental set/rigidity, functional fixedness/fixity and the confirmation bias are ways in which past experience can hinder PS. In mental set, people continue to use a solution to past problems (reproductive thinking) even when the current problem requires productive thinking. Functional fixedness is a type of mental set in which we fail to see that an object may have functions/uses other than its normal ones.

■ Decision-making (DM) is a special case of PS in which we already know the possible solutions or choices. According to a compensatory model, we evaluate how all desirable potential outcomes might compensate for undesirable ones. Two examples are the additive compensatory model and the utility-probability model.

■ Non-compensatory models are less precise but more commonly used approaches, in which not all features of each alternative are considered, and features do not compensate for each other. Examples include elimination by aspects, maximax, minimax and conjunctive strategies.

■ Rational decisions cannot always be made because of the absence of information and time. So, we often resort to the availability and representativeness heuristics.

■ The availability heuristic assumes that an event's probability is directly related to its past frequency: more frequent events are easier to retrieve from LTM. The representativeness heuristic involves judging the likelihood of something by intuitively comparing it with preconceived ideas of a few characteristics believed to represent a category.

■ Central to the information-processing approach is the computer analogy. Newell *et al.*'s general problem solver (GPS) attempted to simulate the entire range of human PS. The GPS was based on verbal protocols using means–end analysis. When the GPS and a person are given the same problem to solve, they tend to use similar strategies.

■ Chess experts are only better at remembering board positions that could appear in an actual game, as opposed to random positions. Expertise reduces the strain on WM by enabling the expert to draw on already available knowledge.

■ Expert systems (ESs) are computer programs that apply knowledge in a specific area (such as medical diagnosis), enabling a computer to function as effectively as a human expert. However, human experts cannot always say explicitly how they solve particular problems or make particular decisions. This makes writing ESs difficult and time consuming.

■ ESs are much less flexible than human experts, lacking higher-level representations of the knowledge domain or their own PS activity. This prevents them from explaining how they reach a decision.

■ Gambling is a form of risk-taking behaviour. Playing the National Lottery can be explained in terms of several heuristic strategies and biases. These include the representativeness bias (which can explain the gambler's fallacy) and availability bias, randomness bias, illusory correlation, flexible attribution, illusion of control, and sunk cost bias. Identifying these biases may help potential gamblers to avoid gambling behaviour.

■ Naturalistic decision-making (NDM) is a new paradigm in applied DM research. NDM's major concern is how real decision-makers reach difficult, dynamic decisions in often ill-structured and changing environments, such as military command and control, firefighting incident command and medical DM. Such research may help prevent 'disastrous decisions'.

Essay Questions

1 Critically consider psychological research into problem-solving. (*24 marks*)

2 Discuss psychological research into risk-taking behaviour **and/or** errors in thinking about probability in relation to decision-making. (*24 marks*)

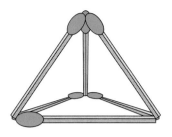

Figure 27.5 *Solution to the problem presented on page 285*

WEB ADDRESSES

http://mellers1.psyc.berkeley-edu:80/sjdm/
http://www.sjdm.org
http://www.eadm.org/
http://act.psy.cmu/ACT/papers/Lessons_Learned.html

Developmental Psychology

28 — *The Development of Thinking*

INTRODUCTION AND OVERVIEW

According to Meadows (1993, 1995), cognitive development is concerned with the study of 'the child as thinker'. *Information-processing theorists* see children as symbol manipulators. Vygotsky, by contrast, saw children as participants in an interactive process by which socially and culturally determined knowledge becomes individualised. However, the theory of cognitive development which has received most attention is that of Jean Piaget, for whom children's behaviour represents *adaptation to the environment*.

This chapter examines all three of these attempts to explain cognitive development, and considers their application to education.

PIAGET'S THEORY

Rather than trying to explain individual differences (why some children are more intelligent than others: see Chapter 29), Piaget was interested in how intelligence itself changes as children grow. He called this *genetic epistemology*.

According to Piaget, cognitive development occurs through the interaction of innate capacities with environmental events, and progresses through a series of *hierarchical, qualitatively different, stages*. All children pass through the stages in the same sequence without skipping any or, except in the case of brain damage, regressing to earlier ones (they are *invariant*). The stages are also the same for everyone irrespective of culture (they are *universal*). Underlying the changes are certain *functional invariants*, fundamental aspects of the developmental process which remain the same and work in the same way through the various stages. The most important of these are *assimilation*, *accommodation* and *equilibration*. The principal *cognitive structure* subject to change is the schema (plural *schemas* or *schemata*).

Schemas (or schemata)

A *schema* (or *scheme*) is the basic building block or unit of intelligent behaviour. Piaget saw schemas as mental structures which organise past experiences and provide a way of understanding future experiences. For Bee (2000), they are not so much categories as the *action of categorising* in some particular way. Life begins with simple schemas which are largely confined to inbuilt reflexes (such as sucking and grasping). These operate independently of other reflexes, and are activated only when certain objects are present. As we grow, so our schemas become increasingly complex.

Assimilation, accommodation and equilibration

Assimilation is the process by which we incorporate new information into existing schemas. For example, babies will reflexively suck a nipple and other objects such as a finger. To suck from a bottle or drink from a cup, the initial sucking reflex must be *modified* through *accommodation*. When a child can deal with most, if not all, new experiences by assimilating them, it is in a state of *equilibrium*. This is brought about by *equilibration*, the process of seeking 'mental balance'. However, if existing schemas are inadequate to cope with new situations, *cognitive disequilibrium* occurs. To restore equilibrium, the existing schema must be 'stretched' in order to take in (or 'accommodate') new information. The necessary and complementary processes of assimilation and accommodation constitute the fundamental process of *adaptation*.

Piaget's four stages of cognitive development

Each represents a stage in the development of intelligence (hence *sensorimotor intelligence*, *pre-operational intelligence* and so on), and is a way of summarising the various schemas a child has at a particular time. The ages shown in Table 28.1 are approximate, because children move through the stages at different rates due to differences in both the environment and their biological maturation. Children also pass through *transitional periods*, in which their thinking is a mixture of two stages.

Table 28.1 *Piaget's four stages of cognitive development*

Stage	Approximate age
Sensorimotor	Birth to two years
Pre-operational	Two to seven years
Concrete operational	Seven to 11 years
Formal operational	11 years onwards

The concept of developmental 'stages' is often taken to mean that development is *discontinuous*. However, for Piaget, development is a gradual and *continuous* process of change, although later stages build on earlier ones (which is why the sequence is invariant). The passage from one stage to the next occurs through cognitive disequilibrium. To achieve equilibrium, the child is 'forced' to higher levels of intellectual understanding (Krebs & Blackman, 1988).

The sensorimotor stage

This lasts for approximately the first two years of life. Infants learn about the world primarily through their senses ('sensori-') and by doing ('motor'). Based on observations of his own children, Piaget (1952) divided the sensorimotor stage into six sub-stages.

Box 28.1 The six sub–stages of the sensorimotor stage

Sub-stage 1 (Exercising reflexes; birth to one month): Reflexes are practised until they function smoothly. Infants have no intentionality and no understanding of an object.

Sub-stage 2 (Primary circular reactions; one to four months): Reflexes are extended to new objects, and infants coordinate simple schemas (such as grasping and looking). Behaviours causing specific events are repeated. Infants look briefly at where a disappearing object was last seen.

Sub-stage 3 (Secondary circular reactions; four to ten months): All the senses become co-ordinated, and the infant can anticipate events and results of actions. A *partially* hidden object can be found.

Sub-stage 4 (The coordination of secondary circular reactions; ten to 12 months): Infants represent objects in their minds, and demonstrate the beginning of symbolic behaviour and memory. A goal can be decided and then acted on. A *completely* hidden object can be found.

Sub-stage 5 (Tertiary circular reactions; 12 to 18 months): Infants search for environmental novelty and use several interchangeable schemas to achieve goals. Experiments are conducted to see what will happen. An object hidden under one of several covers can be found.

Sub-stage 6 (Invention of new means through mental combinations; 18 to 24 months): Infants think about a problem before acting, and thoughts begin to dominate actions. Objects can be mentally manipulated to reach goals. An object placed in a container and then hidden can be found.

(Based on Tomlinson-Keasey, 1985)

Object permanence

Frequent interaction with objects ultimately leads to the development of *object permanence*. As Box 28.1 shows, in sub-stage 2, an infant will look where an object disappears for a few moments, but will not search for it. If the object does not reappear the infant apparently loses interest. Piaget called this *passive exploration*, because the infant expects the object to reappear but does not actively search for it ('out of sight' is 'out of mind').

Figure 28.1 *If an object is made to disappear from an infant's sight, the infant seems to lose interest in it and does not actively search for it*

In sub-stage 3, an infant will reach for a partially hidden object, suggesting that it realises that the rest of it is attached to the visible part. However, if the object is *completely hidden*, infants make no attempt to retrieve it. In sub-stage 4, a hidden object will be searched for ('out of sight' is no longer 'out of mind'). Although the infant will retrieve a hidden object, it will persist in looking for it where it was *last* hidden, even when it is hidden somewhere else.

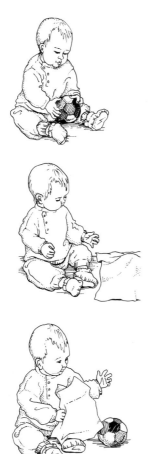

Figure 28.2 *Whilst a six-month-old child will not search for an object that has been removed from its sight, an eight-month-old child will, because it has developed some degree of object permanence*

Whilst this no longer occurs in sub-stage 5, object permanence is not yet fully developed. For example, suppose an infant sees an object placed in a matchbox, which is then put under a pillow. When the infant isn't looking, the object is removed from the matchbox and left under the pillow. If the matchbox is given to the infant, it will open it expecting to find the object. On not finding it, the infant will *not* look under the pillow. This is because it cannot take into account the possibility that something it has not actually seen might have happened (*failure to infer invisible displacements*). Once the infant can infer invisible displacements (in sub-stage 6), the development of object permanence is complete.

Object permanence's emergence occurs simultaneously with the emergence of a *fear of strangers* (see Gross *et al.*, 2000). By eight months, the infant probably has schemas for familiar faces, and faces that cannot be assimilated into these schemas cause distress (Kagan, 1984).

Box 28.2 The general symbolic function

Other cognitive structures that have developed by the end of the sensorimotor stage include *self-recognition* (the ability to name the self correctly in a mirror: Bertenthal & Fischer, 1978), and *symbolic thought*, such as *language*.

Two other manifestations of the *general symbolic function* are *deferred imitation* and *representational* (or *make-believe*) *play*. Deferred imitation is the ability to imitate or reproduce something that has been perceived but is no longer present (Meltzoff & Moore, 1983). Representational play involves using one object as though it were another. Like deferred imitation, this ability depends on the infant's growing ability to form mental images of things and people in their absence (to *remember*).

The pre-operational stage

Probably the main difference between this and the sensorimotor stage is the continued development and use of internal images (or 'interiorised' schemas), symbols and language, especially important for the child's developing sense of self-awareness. However, the child tends to be influenced by how things *look* rather than by logical principles or operations (hence the term 'pre-operational'). Piaget subdivided the stage into the *pre-conceptual sub-stage* (age two to four) and the *intuitive sub-stage* (age four to seven). The absolute nature of the pre-conceptual child's thinking makes relative terms such as 'bigger' or 'stronger' difficult to understand (things tend to be 'biggest' or just 'big'). The intuitive child can use relative terms, but its ability to think logically is still limited.

Seriation and artificialism

In *seriation*, the pre-conceptual child has difficulty arranging objects on the basis of a particular dimension, such as increasing height (Piaget & Szeminska, 1952). *Artificialism* is the belief that natural features have been designed and constructed by people. For example, the question 'Why is the sky blue?' might produce the answer 'Somebody painted it'.

Transductive reasoning and animism

Transductive reasoning involves drawing an inference about the relationship between two things based on a single shared attribute. If both cats and dogs have four legs, then cats must be dogs. This sort of reasoning can lead to *animism*, the belief that inanimate objects are alive. So, because the sun appears to follow us when we walk, it must be alive, just like people (Piaget, 1973).

Centration

This involves focusing on only a single perceptual quality at a time. A pre-conceptual child asked to divide apples into those that are 'big and red' and those that are 'small and green' will either put all the red (or green) apples together irrespective of their size, or all the big (or small) apples together irrespective of their colour. Until the child can *decentre*, it will be unable to classify things logically or systematically. Centration is also illustrated by *syncretic thought*, the tendency to link neighbouring objects or events on the basis of what *individual instances* have in common. By age five, however, most children can select a number of things and say what they have in common. Centration is also associated with the inability to conserve (see page 299).

Egocentrism

According to Piaget, pre-operational children are *egocentric*, that is, they see the world from their own standpoint and cannot appreciate that other people might see things differently. They cannot put themselves 'in other people's shoes' to realise that other people do not know or perceive everything they themselves do. Consider the following example (Phillips, 1969) of a conversation between the experimenter and a four-year-old boy:

Experimenter: 'Do you have a brother?'

Child: 'Yes.'

Experimenter: 'What's his name?'

Child: 'Jim.'

Experimenter: 'Does Jim have a brother?'

Child: 'No.'

Box 28.3 The 'Swiss mountain scene' test of egocentrism (Piaget & Inhelder, 1956)

The three papier-mâché model mountains (see Figure 28.3 below) are of different colours. One has snow on the top, one a house, and one a red cross. The child walks round and explores the model and then sits on one side whilst a doll is placed at some *different* location. The child is shown ten pictures of different views of the model and asked to choose the one that represents how the doll sees it.

Four-year-olds were completely unaware of perspectives different from their own and always chose a picture which matched their view of the model. Six-year-olds showed some awareness, but often chose the wrong picture. Only seven- and eight-year-olds consistently chose the picture that represented the doll's view. According to Piaget, children below the age of seven are bound by the *egocentric illusion*. They fail to understand that what they see is relative to their own position, and instead take it to represent 'the world as it really is'.

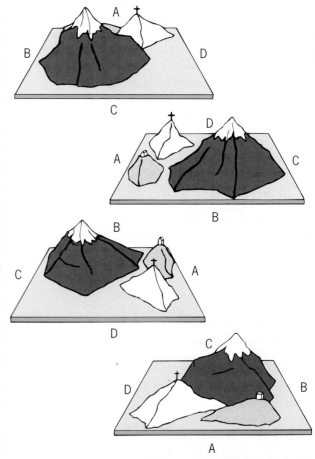

Figure 28.3 *Piaget and Inhelder's three-mountain scene, seen from four different sides (From Gross, 1996, and based on Smith & Cowie, 1991)*

Conservation

Conservation is the understanding that any quantity (such as number, liquid quantity, length and substance) remains the same despite physical changes in the arrangement of objects. Piaget believed that pre-operational children could not conserve because their thinking is dominated by objects' *perceptual appearance*.

The inability to conserve is another example of *centration*. With liquid quantity, for example, the child centres on just one dimension of the beaker, usually its height, and fails to take width into account. Only in the concrete operational stage do children understand that 'getting taller' and 'getting narrower' tend to cancel each other out (*compensation*). If the contents of the taller beaker are poured back into the shorter one, the child will again say that the two shorter beakers contain the same amount. However, it cannot perform this operation mentally and so lacks *reversibility* (understanding that what can be done can be undone *without any gain or loss*).

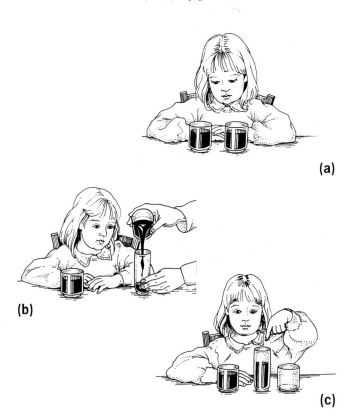

Figure 28.4 *Piaget's test for the conservation of liquid quantity. The child is shown two identical beakers and agrees that they contain the same amount of liquid (a). The contents of one of the beakers is then poured into another beaker which is taller but narrower (b). Although the child has seen the liquid being poured and agrees that none has been added or spilled in the process (Piaget calls this 'identity'), when asked if one beaker contains more or if the two have identical quantities, the pre-operational child typically says that the taller beaker contains more (c)*

Box 28.4 Tests for the conservation of number, length and substance or quantity

Conservation of number: Two rows of counters are placed in one-to-one correspondence. The child agrees that the two rows contain an equal number.

One row is then extended (or contracted). The child is asked whether each row still has the same number of counters.

Conservation of length: Two sticks are aligned and the child agrees that they are both the same length.

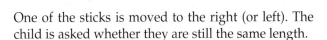

One of the sticks is moved to the right (or left). The child is asked whether they are still the same length.

Conservation of substance or quantity: Two identical Plasticine balls are presented. The child agrees that there is the same amount in each.

The shape of one ball is changed, and the child is asked whether there is still the same amount in each.

(Based on LeFrancois, 1986)

The concrete operational stage

The child is now capable of performing logical operations, but only in the presence of actual objects. S/he can conserve and shows reversibility and more logical classification.

Further examples of the child's ability to *decentre* include its appreciation that objects can belong to more than one class (as in the case of Andrew being Bob's brother *and* Charlie's best friend). There is also a significant decline in egocentrism (and the growing *relativism* of the child's viewpoint), and the onset of seriation and reciprocity of relationships (such as knowing that adding one to three produces the same amount as taking one from five).

One remaining problem for the concrete operational child is *transitivity* tasks. For example, if told that 'Alan is taller than Bob, and Bob is taller than Charlie' and asked whether Alan or Charlie is taller, children under 11 cannot solve this problem entirely in their heads. They can usually only solve it using real (or concrete) objects (such as dolls). Nevertheless, concrete operational children enjoy jokes that enable them to utilise abilities such as conservation, as in the following: Mr Jones went into a restaurant and ordered a whole pizza for his dinner. When the waiter asked if he wanted it cut into six or eight pieces, Mr Jones said 'Oh, you'd better make it six, I could never eat eight pieces!' (McGhee, 1976).

Box 28.5 Horizontal and vertical décalage

Some types of conservation are mastered before others, and their order tends to be invariant. *Liquid quantity* is mastered by age six to seven, *substance/quantity* and *length* by seven to eight, *weight* by eight to ten, and *volume* by 11 to 12. This step-by-step acquisition of new operations is called *décalage* (displacement or 'slips in level of performance'). In conservation, décalage is *horizontal* because there are inconsistencies *within* the same kind of ability or operation (a seven-year-old child can conserve number but not weight, for example). *Vertical* décalage refers to inconsistencies *between* different abilities or operations (a child may have mastered all kinds of classification, but not all kinds of conservation).

The formal operational stage

Whilst the concrete operational child is still concerned with manipulating *things* (even if this is done mentally), the formal operational thinker can manipulate *ideas or propositions* and can reason solely on the basis of verbal statements ('first order' and 'second order' operations respectively). 'Formal' refers to the ability to follow the form of an argument without reference to its particular content. In *transitivity problems*, for example, 'If A is taller than B, and B is taller than C, then A is taller than C' is a form of argument whose conclusion is logically true, regardless of what A, B and C might refer to.

Formal operational thinkers can also think *hypothetically*, that is, they can think about what *could* be as well as what actually *is*. For example, asked what it would be like if people had tails, they might say 'Dogs would know when you were happy' or 'Lovers could hold their tails in secret under the table'. Concrete operational thinkers might tell you 'not to be so silly', or say where on the body the tail might be, showing their dependence on what has actually been seen (Dworetzky, 1981). The ability to imagine and discuss things that have never been encountered is evidence of the continued decentration

that occurs beyond concrete operations: formal operational thinkers display *hypothetico-deductive reasoning*.

Key STUDY

Box 28.6 A demonstration of formal operational thinking

Inhelder & Piaget (1958) gave adolescents five containers filled with clear liquid. Four were 'test chemicals' and one an 'indicator'. When the proper combination of one or more test chemicals was added to the indicator, it turned yellow. The problem was to find this proper combination. Pre-operational children simply mixed the chemicals randomly, and concrete operational children, although more systematic, generally failed to test all possible combinations. Only formal operational thinkers considered all alternatives and systematically varied one factor at a time. Also, they often wrote down all the results and tried to draw general conclusions about each chemical.

An evaluation of Piaget's theory

Piaget's theory has had an enormous impact on our understanding of cognitive development. However, as Flavell (1982) has remarked:

'Like all theories of great reach and significance ... it has problems that gradually come to light as years and years of thinking and research get done on it. Thus, some of us now think that the theory may in varying degrees be unclear, incorrect and incomplete'.

Object permanence

Piaget's claims about the sensorimotor stage have been criticised in both general and specific terms. Bower & Wishart (1972), for example, found that *how* an object is made to disappear influences the infant's response. If the infant is looking at an object and reaching for it and the lights are turned off, it will continue to search for up to one and a half minutes (as filmed with special cameras). This suggests that it *does* remember the object is there (so, 'out of sight' is *not* 'out of mind': see page 299). Baillargeon (1987) has shown that object permanence can occur as early as three and a half months, and that it is *not* necessary for a baby younger than six months to see the whole object in order to respond to it.

Centration

One way to study centration (and classification) is through *class inclusion tasks*. If a pre-operational child is presented with several wooden beads, mostly brown but a few white, and asked 'Are they all wooden?', the child will respond correctly. If asked 'Are there more brown or more white beads?', the child will again respond correctly. However, if asked 'Are there more brown beads or more beads?', the child will say there are more brown beads. According to Piaget, the child fails to understand the relationship between the whole (the class of wooden beads) and the parts (the classes of brown and white beads). These are the *superordinate* and *subordinate* classes respectively. The brown beads are more numerous than the white and can be perceived in a more immediate and direct way than the wooden beads as a whole (despite the first question being answered correctly).

Piaget argued that this was another example of the inability to decentre. However, Donaldson (1978) has asked if the difficulty the child experiences is to do with what is expected of it and how the task is presented.

Box 28.7 Alternatives to Piaget's class-inclusion task

Donaldson describes a study with six-year-olds using four toy cows, three black and one white. The cows were laid on their sides and the children told they were 'sleeping'. Of those asked 'Are there more black cows or more cows?', 25 per cent answered correctly. However, of those asked 'Are there more black cows or more *sleeping* cows?', 48 per cent answered correctly.

Similarly, the word 'more' has a different meaning for children and adults (Gelman, 1978). Adults use 'more' to mean 'containing a greater number'. For children, however, 'more' refers to the general concept of larger, longer, occupying more space and so on.

Hodkin (1981) showed children two rows of sweets. When asked if there were more Smarties or more sweets, the children replied 'more Smarties'. However, when asked if there were 'more Smarties or more *of all of the sweets*, children replied that there were more of all of the sweets, showing that they could understand class inclusion.

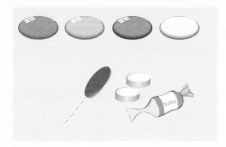

Top row = Smarties
Bottom row = Other kinds of sweets

Figure 28.5 *Stimuli used in Hodkin's (1981) experiment*

Egocentrism

Gelman (1979) has shown that four-year-olds adjust their explanations of things to make them clearer to a blindfold listener. If the children were entirely egocentric, such a finding would be unlikely. Nor would we expect four-year-olds to use simpler forms of speech when talking to two-year-olds, yet this is what they do (Gelman, 1979). We would, however, expect egocentric children to choose toys *they* liked for their mothers' birthday. However, at least some four-year-olds choose presents appropriate for their mothers (Marvin, 1975).

Critics of the 'Swiss mountain scene' test (see Box 28.3, page 298) see it as an unusually difficult way of presenting a problem to a young child. Borke (1975) and Hughes (cited in Donaldson, 1978) have shown that when the task is presented in a meaningful context (making what Donaldson calls 'human sense'), even three and a half-year-olds can appreciate the world as another person sees it. These are all examples of *perspective-taking*.

Key **STUDY**

Box 28.8 Perspective-taking, false beliefs and theory of mind

According to Flavell *et al.* (1990), there are two levels of *perspective-taking* ability:

- Level 1 (two-to three-year-olds): the child knows *that* some other person experiences something differently;

- Level 2 (four-to five-year-olds): the child develops a whole series of complex rules for figuring out precisely *what* the other person sees or experiences.

In a study of children's ability to distinguish between appearance and reality, Flavell (1986) showed children a sponge painted to look like a rock. They were asked what it looked like and what it 'really' was. Three-year-olds said either that it looked like a sponge and *was* a sponge, or that it looked like a rock and *was* a rock. However, four- and five-year-olds could say that it *looked* like a rock but was in fact a sponge.

Gopnik & Astington (1988) allowed children to feel the sponge before asking them the questions used in Flavell's study. They were then told: 'Your friend John hasn't touched this, he hasn't squeezed it. If John just sees it over here like this, what will he think it is? Will he think it's a rock or a sponge?'. Typically, three-year-olds said that John would think it was a sponge (which it is), whilst four- and five-year-olds said that he would think it was a rock (because he had not had the opportunity of touching/squeezing it). In other words, the older children were attributing John with a *false belief*, which they could only do by taking John's perspective.

Evidence like this has led several theorists (e.g. Gopnik & Wellman, 1994) to propose that four-to-five-year-olds have developed a quite sophisticated *theory of mind* (Premack & Woodruff, 1978). This refers to the understanding that people (and not objects) have desires, beliefs and other mental states, some of which (such as beliefs) can be false. The older children in Gopnick and Astington's study understood that John would not know something which they did.

Conservation

The ability to conserve also seems to occur earlier than Piaget believed. Rose & Blank (1974) showed that when the *pre-transformation* question (the question asked before one row of counters, say, is rearranged) was dropped, six-year-olds often succeeded on the conservation of number task. Importantly, they made fewer errors on the standard version of the task when tested a week later.

These findings were replicated by Samuel & Bryant (1984) using conservation of number, liquid quantity and substance. The standard version of the task unwittingly 'forces' children to produce the wrong answer against their better judgement by the mere fact that the same question is asked twice, before *and* after the transformation (Donaldson, 1978). Hence, children believe they are expected to give a *different* answer on the second question. On this explanation, contextual cues may override purely linguistic ones.

According to Piaget, it should not matter *who*, in the case of number conservation, rearranges the counters/Smarties or *how* this happens. Yet when 'Naughty Teddy', a glove puppet, causes the transformation 'accidentally', pre-operational children can conserve number and length (McGarrigle & Donaldson, 1974; Light *et al.*, 1979). This also applies when the transformation is made by a *person* other than the experimenter (Hargreaves *et al.*, 1982; Light, 1986).

Whilst Piaget's original procedure might convey the implicit message 'take note of the transformation because it is relevant', studies using accidental transformations might convey the message 'ignore the transformation, it makes no difference'. It follows that if some change actually takes place, the implicit message to ignore the transformation would make children give an incorrect answer. The standard Piagetian task involves an *irrelevant perceptual change* (nothing is added or taken away), but where some *actual change* occurs, children tested under the accidental/incidental transformation condition should do *worse* than those tested in the standard way. This out-

come has been obtained in several studies (Light & Gilmour, 1983; Moore & Frye, 1986).

Piaget believed that the attainment of a new stage arises from a major reorganisation of mental operations rather than the acquisition of new skills. Hence, attempts to teach children to conserve should be unsuccessful. In general, special training techniques may speed children's understanding of conservation, but only if they have reached the necessary stage of development. Such training appears at best:

> '... to move children through a period of formation and into the period of attainment more quickly than they would otherwise progress' (Krebs & Blackman, 1988).

Methodological criticisms

Piaget's observation of individual children, often his own, falls short of the controlled methodology characteristic of experimental psychology (see Gross *et al.*, 2000). His use of particular observations to demonstrate general points is also unscientific (Brainerd, 1978). However, both Ginsberg (1981) and Dasen (1994) see Piaget's methods as a superior way of exploring the subtleties of a child's abilities, since they are tailored to an individual child's requirements.

The universality of the stages

Although some researchers have accepted the validity of the stages, they have suggested that there are cultural differences in the rates of development in the various cognitive domains. For Dasen (1994):

> 'The *deep* structures, the basic cognitive processes, are indeed universal, while at the *surface* level, the way these basic processes are brought to bear on specific contents, in specific contexts, is influenced by culture. Universality and cultural diversity are not opposites, but are complementary aspects of all human behaviour and development'.

Dasen has argued that only one-third of adolescents and adults actually attains formal operations, and that in some cultures it is not the typical mode of thought. Conversely, others (e.g. Riegel, 1976; Labouvie-Vief, 1980) have argued that some people reach stages *beyond* the formal operational stage.

The role of social factors in cognitive development

According to Meadows (1995), Piaget implicitly saw children as largely independent and isolated in their construction of knowledge and understanding of the physical world (children as *scientists*). This excluded the contribution of other people to children's cognitive development. The *social* nature of knowledge and thought is a basic proposton of Vygotsky's theory (see pages 304–305).

According to Bee (2000):

'Despite the fact that many aspects of his [Piaget's] theory have been called into question by later research, his theory sets the agenda for most research in this area for the past thirty years and still serves as a kind of scaffolding for much of our thinking about thinking'.

Applying Piaget's theory to education

Piaget did not actually advocate a 'theory of instruction' (Ginsberg, 1981). However, his theory has three main implications for education (Brainerd, 1983). These are the concept of *readiness*, the *curriculum* (what should be taught), and *teaching methods* (how the curriculum should be taught).

What was said above about limits set on learning by children's current stage of development relates to the concept of readiness (see Box 28.9). Regarding the curriculum, appropriate content would include logic (such as transitive inference), maths (numbers), science (conservation) and space (Euclidean geometry). Teaching materials should consist of concrete objects that children can easily manipulate.

However, Ginsberg (1981) has argued that attempting to base a curriculum on the teaching of Piagetian stages is a misapplication of his theory. It would be more useful to *modify* the curriculum in line with what is known about the various Piagetian stages, without allowing them to limit teaching methods. Piaget's theory seems to suggest that there are definite sequences in which concepts should be taught. For example, different types of conservation appear at different times (see Box 28.5, page 300). However, many traditional schools do *not* base their teaching on this or other developmental sequences (Elkind, 1976).

Central to a Piagetian perspective is the view that childen learn from actions rather than from passive observation (*active self-discovery/discovery learning*). Regarding *teaching methods*, teachers must recognise that each child needs to construct knowledge for itself, and that deeper understanding is the product of active learning (Smith *et al.*, 1998).

Box 28.9 The role of the teacher in the Piagetian classroom

- It is essential for teachers to assess very carefully each individual child's current stage of cognitive development (this relates to the concept of readiness). The child can then be set tasks tailored to its needs which become *intrinsically motivating*.

- Teachers must provide children with learning opportunities that enable them to advance to the next developmental step. This is achieved by creating *disequilibrium* (see page 296). Rather than providing the appropriate materials and allowing children to 'get on with it', teachers should create a proper balance between actively guiding and directing children's thinking patterns and providing opportunities for them to explore by themselves (Thomas, 1985).

- Teachers should be concerned with the learning *process* rather than its end product. This involves encouraging children to ask questions, experiment and explore. Teachers should look for the reasoning behind children's answers, particularly when they make mistakes.

- Teachers should encourage children to learn from each other. Hearing other (and often conflicting) views can help to break down egocentrism (see page 298). Peer interaction has both a *cognitive* and a *social value*. As a result, small-group activity is as important as individual work.

- Teachers are the guides in children's process of discovery, and the curriculum should be adapted to each child's individual needs and intellectual level (Smith *et al.*, 1998).

Figure 28.6 *In the traditional classroom (top), the teacher is at the centre of the learning process, imparting ready-made ('academic/school') knowledge. By contrast, in the Piagetian classroom the child actively discovers knowledge for itself, often through interaction with other children in small groups (bottom)*

VYGOTSKY'S THEORY

Vygotsky outlined a major alternative to Piaget's theory, which was published in the former Soviet Union in the 1920s and 30s, but not translated into English until the early 1960s (Vygotsky, 1962).

Internalisation and the social nature of thinking

As noted in the *Introduction and overview*, Vygotsky believed that a child's cognitive development does not occur in a social vacuum. The ability to think and reason by and for ourselves (*inner speech* or *verbal thought*) is the result of a fundamentally *social* process. At birth, we are social beings capable of interacting with others, but able to do little either practically or intellectually by or for ourselves. Gradually, however, we move towards self-sufficiency and independence, and by participating in social activities, our abilities become transformed. For Vygotsky, cognitive development involves an active *internalisation* of problem-solving processes that takes place as a result of *mutual interaction* between children and those with whom they have regular social contact (initially the parents, but later friends and classmates).

This is the reverse of how Piaget (at least initially) saw things. Piaget's idea of 'the child as a *scientist*' is replaced by the idea of 'the child as an *apprentice*', who acquires the culture's knowledge and skills through graded collaboration with those who already possess them (Rogoff, 1990). According to Vygotsky (1981):

'Any function in the child's cultural development appears twice, or on two planes. First it appears on the social plane, and then on the psychological plane.'

Box 28.10 Pointing: an example of cultural development from the social to the psychological

Initially, a baby's pointing is simply an unsuccessful attempt to grasp something beyond its reach. When the mother sees her baby pointing, she takes it as an 'indicatory gesture' that the baby wants something, and so helps it, probably making the gesture herself. Gradually, the baby comes to use the gesture deliberately. The 'reaching' becomes reduced to movements which could not themselves achieve the desired object even if it were in reach, and is accompanied by cries, looks at the mother and eventually words. The gesture is now directed towards the mother (it has become a gesture 'for others') rather than toward the object (it is no longer a gesture 'in itself': Meadows, 1995).

Scaffolding and the zone of proximal development

Scaffolding refers to the role played by parents, teachers and others by which children acquire their knowledge and skills (Wood *et al.*, 1976). As a task becomes more familiar to the child and more within its competence, so those who provide the scaffold leave more and more for the child to do until it can perform the task successfully. In this way, the developing thinker does not have to create cognition 'from scratch' because there are others available who have already 'served' their own apprenticeship.

The internalised cognitive skills remain social in two senses. First, as mature learners we can 'scaffold' ourselves through difficult tasks (self-instruction), as others once scaffolded our earlier attempts. Second, the only skills practised to a high level of competence for most people are those offered by their culture: cognitive potential may be universal, but cognitive expertise is culturally determined (Meadows, 1995).

Since the 1980s, research has stressed the role of social interaction in language development, especially the facilitating effects of the use of child-contingent language by adults talking with children (Meadows, 1995: see Chapter 26, page 280). This 'fit' between adult and child language closely resembles the concept of 'scaffolding'.

Key STUDY

Box 28.11 Scaffolding

Wood *et al.* (1976) found that on a construction task with four- and five-year-olds, different mothers used instructional strategies of varying levels of specificity. These ranged from general verbal encouragement to direct demonstration of a relevant action. No single strategy guaranteed learning, but the most efficient maternal instructors were those who combined general and specific interventions according to the child's progress.

The most useful help is that which adapts itself to the learner's successes and failures (Bruner, 1983). An example would be initially using a general instruction until the child runs into difficulties. At this point, a more specific instruction or demonstration is given. This style allows the child considerable autonomy, but also provides carefully planned guidance at the boundaries of its abilities (Vygotsky's *zone of proximal development*).

The *zone of proximal development* (or ZPD) defines those functions that have not yet matured but are in the process of maturing (Vygotsky, 1978). These could be called the 'buds' or 'flowers' rather than the 'fruits' of development. The actual developmental level characterises mental development *retrospectively*, whilst the ZPD characterises mental development *prospectively*.

Applying Vygotsky's theory to education

Vygotsky defines intelligence as the capacity to learn from instruction. Rather than teachers playing an enabling role, Vygotsky believes that teachers should *guide* pupils in paying attention, concentrating and learning effectively (a *didactic* role: Sutherland, 1992). By doing this, teachers *scaffold* children to competence.

The introduction of the National Curriculum and national testing at various ages has returned Britain to the 'teacher-centred' or 'traditional' approach to young children's education. Whilst this approach was dominant up to the 1960s, it was 'revolutionised' by the Piagetian-influenced 'child-centred' or 'progressive' approach (see page 303). However, Vygotsky did not:

'... advocate mechanical formal teaching where children go through the motions of sitting at desks and passing exams that are meaningless to them ... On the contrary, Vygotsky stressed intellectual development rather than procedural learning' (Sutherland, 1992).

Vygotsky rejected any approach advocating that teachers have rigid control over children's learning. Rather, as with Piaget, teachers' control over children's activities is what counts. Teachers extend and challenge children to go beyond where they would otherwise have been.

Box 28.12 Applying the concept of the ZPD to education

Suppose a child is currently functioning at level 'x' in terms of attainment. Through innate/environmental means, the child has the potential to reach level 'x + 1'.

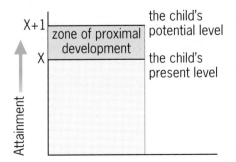

Figure 28.7 *Vygotsky's zone of proximal development*

The area between 'x' and 'x + 1' is the child's ZPD. The ZPD may be different for individual children, and children with large ZPDs will have a greater capacity to be helped than those with small ZPDs. Irrespective of the ZPD's size, Vygotsky saw the teacher as being responsible for giving children the cues they need or taking them through a series of steps towards the solution of a problem.

(Based on Sutherland, 1992)

Vygotsky also believed in *collaborative learning*. As well as being helped by teachers, more advanced children are important in helping less advanced children. Educators now believe that group learning and peer tutoring can offer an effective environment for guiding a child through its ZPD. This may be because these settings encourage children to use language, provide explanations, and work co-operatively or competitively, all of which help produce cognitive change (Pine, 1999).

Using the peer group for teaching was for a long time the basis of Marxist education in the former Soviet Union. According to Sutherland (1992):

'The socialist rationale was one of all children working for the general good rather than the capitalist one of each child trying to get out of school as much benefit as [s/he] can without putting anything back into it. The brighter child is helping society by helping the less able one since the latter ... will be more of an asset to society as a literate than as an illiterate adult'.

Whilst much of the research into collaborative learning has been undertaken with young children, there is evidence that group work and collaborative learning can also be effective in adult and higher education (Foot, 1994).

For Vygotsky, then, there is much educational value in direct teaching, but with the child as an active learner. Using tchniques derived from Vygotsky's work, Shayer (cited in Sylva, 1996) has shown that specially designed material for science teaching can increase 'learning ability' (gains on tests of psychological functioning) as well as educational test scores and standardised attainment tests (SATs). Moreover, such improvement also appears to generalise to performance in English and mathematics.

INFORMATION-PROCESSING THEORIES

According to Bee (2000), it is more accurate to talk of the information-processing (IP) *approach* than a distinct IP theory of cognitive development. This approach grew out of, and in some ways represents a reaction to,

Piaget's theory (Pine, 1999). Like Piaget, IP theorists believe that there are psychological structures in people's minds that explain their behaviour, and which are essentially independent of the individual's social relationships, social practices and cultural environment (Meadows, 1995).

Underlying the IP approach is the *computer analogy* (see Chapter 55). This examines more closely than Piaget's theory the way that major cognitive processes, such as memory and attention, come into play when children deal with particular tasks and problems (Pine, 1999). To understand cognitive *development*, we need to discover whether the basic capacity of the system, or the programs, change in any systematic way with age (Bee, 2000). One key assumption is that as children grow, they develop better strategies for remembering and organising knowledge and for encoding more aspects of a problem. To study the claim that children become better information processors as they develop, IP theorists use *task analysis*.

Box 28.13 Task analysis

To understand why children cannot solve problems that adults can, we need to understand a particular task's component steps (Oakhill, 1984). For example, five elements are necessary to solve the following problem: 'If Ann is not as bad as Betty, and Betty is not as bad as Carole, who is the best?'.

1 The child must perceive and encode the important statements (premises) contained in the question, which involves attending to it (see Chapter 19).

2 The premises must be stored in working memory (WM: see Gross *et al.*, 2000).

3 They must be combined in memory to form an integrated representation.

4 The question must be encoded.

5 The representation of the premises must be scanned to answer the question or formulate a conclusion about it.

IP theorists argue that children fail to solve such problems correctly because of errors in encoding the problem, being unable to hold information in memory for long enough, or because holding it in memory may interfere with other task performance (Trabasso, 1977).

Keeney *et al.* (1967) gave children of different ages a series of pictures to remember. Before being tested on recall, most eight- to ten-year-olds could be seen mouthing the picture series (rehearsal), whilst the five-year-olds did not do this. Although the younger children recalled far fewer items than the older children, they could be taught the rehearsal strategy and performed as well as the older children. So, their memory was just as good, but they did not use it as efficiently as the older children.

A large amount of research has found that as children grow they acquire more and more powerful strategies for remembering, use them more efficiently and flexibly, and apply them to an increasing variety of problems. Also, school-age children are capable of applying a wider range of different strategies to the *same* problem, so that if the first attempt fails, a back-up or alternative strategy can be used (Bee, 2000; Pine, 1999).

Box 28.14 How different is the IP approach from Piaget's?

IP theorists can explain cognitive development (the child makes better and more efficient use of basic cognitive processes) without having to assume any global reorganisation of the cognitive system (qualitatively different stages) as proposed by Piaget. For example, based on research using Piagetian-type tasks, Siegler (1976) claims that what changes as children develop is their acquisition of increasingly complex rules for problem-solving.

Consistent with Piaget's theory, Siegler's research suggests that there is a sequence in children's acquisition of new strategies, but this is still very different from identifying developmental stages. Nevertheless, it is mistaken to assume that a child either has or does not have a particular strategy in its repertoire at any time. When learning a new strategy in maths, for example, a child may forget to use it all the time or fail to see that it can be applied to new problems. One important developmental change is knowing where and when to use new strategies (Siegler, 1989). This is related to metacognition: see text below.

According to Bee (2000), some of the changes Piaget attributed to new mental structures can be more simply explained in terms of increased experience with tasks and problems, and faster and more efficient processing of information (all *quantitative* changes). At the same time:

> 'There also seems to be a real qualitative change in the complexity, generalisability, and flexibility of strategies used by the child'.

One form of new strategy (new 'software') is the child's increasing awareness of its own mental processes (*metacognition*). This is part of a larger category of *executive processes* (planning what to do and considering alternative strategies). It may be precisely such metacognitive/executive skills that gradually emerge with age. Performance on a whole range of tasks will be better if the child can monitor its own performance and recognise when a particular strategy is required or not. This self-monitoring improves fairly rapidly, beginning at school age (Bee, 2000).

According to Pascual-Leone (1980) and Case (1985), children do not use just one cognitive strategy in solving Piagetian tasks (as Piaget believed), but several, the number required being correlated with a problem's difficulty. Like Oakhill (1984), Pascual-Leone and Case also see WM as storing the information necessary to solve problems. The amount of memory space necessary is also correlated with the problem's complexity and, as the child develops, so available memory space increases. Pascual-Leone and Case also believe that certain strategies become *automatic* with practice, and so require less space in memory (see Chapter 20). An adult, for example, would instantly 'see' that $(10 + 6) - (10 + 6)$ equals zero. A child, however, would require time to solve this problem, since each component must be stored in memory before a solution can be reached.

Applying IP theories to education

One strength of the IP approach is its emphasis on memory and young children's limited capacity to process information. As well as memory's importance in the child's ability to operate effectively, knowledge also has a considerable influence on learning, and the more children know about a situation, the more successful they will be at dealing with it. As Sutherland (1992) has noted:

'Since knowledge is generally contained within language, the skill of storing knowledge in some valid linguistic form (whether this be oral memory or written) is a vital prerequisite of successful IP performance. One of the teacher's main roles is to help children find strategies for reducing their memory load – for instance to write down a list of the facts they need to solve a maths problem'.

Whilst young children can add numbers together when two digits are involved (e.g. 22 + 56), they make errors when three digits are used (Van Lehn, 1983). For example, faced with the problem:

231 +
 42

young children tend to either ignore the third column and arrive at 73 as the answer, or muddle up the hundreds and tens columns to produce 673. Van Lehn uses the term *repair* to refer to the process by which addition involving three digits can be successfully achieved. This process implies a teacher-led approach to teaching mathematics. However, IP theories also see *metacognition* (see above) as playing a vital role. In the case of learning to read, the child needs to be aware of which words it knows and does not know, which sentences it understands and does not understand, and how to get the information it needs. A variety of research shows that younger and poorer readers are less skilled at all these metacognitive tasks compared with older and better readers (Flavell *et al.*, 1993).

CONCLUSIONS

This chapter has discussed Piaget's theory, which revolutionised the way that cognitive development was investigated and understood. Some of the influences of Piaget's theory on the education of young children have also been described.

Two major alternatives to Piaget's theory have also been examined. Both Vygotsky's theory and the information-processing approach disagree with some of Piaget's basic assumptions, but each takes a very different view of what cognitive development involves. Whilst Vygotsky emphasises the social nature of cognitive change, both Piaget and the information-processing approach see development as occurring quite independently of social interaction. Both theories have contributed to our understanding of the education of young children.

Summary

■ Piaget sees behaviour as **adaptation to the environment**. His theory focuses on the organisation of intelligence and how it changes as children grow (**genetic epistemology**). Younger children's intelligence is **qualitatively** different from that of older children.

■ Cognitive development occurs through the interaction between innate capacities and environmental events, and progresses through a series of **hierarchical stages** which are **invariant** and **universal**.

■ Underlying the changes are **functional invariants**, the most important being **assimilation, accommodation** (which together constitute **adaptation**) and **equilibration**. The major cognitive structures that change are schemas/schemata.

■ A **schema/scheme** is the basic building-block of intelligent behaviour. Our first schemas are mainly inborn reflexes which operate independently of each other and become increasingly complex.

■ Piaget's four stages of cognitive development are the **sensorimotor, pre-operational, concrete operational** and **formal operational.**

■ During the **sensorimotor stage**, frequent interaction with objects ultimately leads to **object permanence**, which is fully developed when the child can **infer invisible displacements**.

■ By the end of the sensorimotor stage, **self-recognition** and **symbolic thought** have emerged. Schemas are now 'interiorised'. **Representational/make-believe play**, like **deferred imitation**, reflects the **general symbolic function.**

■ **Pre-operational** children have difficulty in **seriation** tasks and also display **artificialism, transductive reasoning** and **animism. Centration** involves focusing on a single perceptual quality to the exclusion of others, and is illustrated by the **inability to conserve**. To be able to classify things logically or systematically, the child must be able to **decentre**.

■ Pre-operational children are also **egocentric** and cannot understand that others may not know or perceive everything they themselves know or perceive (the **egocentric illusion**).

■ During the **concrete operational stage**, logical operations can only be performed in the presence of actual or observable objects. Some types of conservation appear before others **(horizontal décalage)**. A child who has mastered all kinds of classification but not all kinds of conservation displays **vertical décalage**.

■ **Formal operational** thinkers can manipulate ideas and propositions, can reason solely on the basis of verbal statements ('second order' operations) and think **hypothetically**.

■ Four- and five-year-olds are capable of **perspective-taking**, enabling them to attribute **false beliefs** to other people. This is a crucial feature of the child's **theory of mind**.

■ When the **pre-transformation** question is dropped in **conservation** tasks, children under seven often succeed. The standard version may unwittingly make children give the wrong answer against their better judgement.

■ Whilst **deep** structures (the basic cognitive processes) may be universal, how these are brought to bear on specific contents (at the **surface** level) is influenced by culture, and so is **culturally diverse**.

■ Although Piaget did not actually advocate a 'theory of instruction', his theory of cognitive development has three main implications for education: the **concept of readiness**, the **curriculum** and **teaching methods**.

■ Central to Piagetian views of the educational process is **active self-discovery/discovery learning**. Teachers assess each individual child's current stage of cognitive development to set **intrinsically motivating** tasks and provide learning opportunities that create **disequilibrium**.

■ Vygotsky sees the ability to think and reason by and for ourselves as the result of a fundamentally **social** process. The initially helpless baby actively **internalises** problem-solving processes through interaction with parents.

■ Vygotsky's child **apprentice** acquires cultural knowledge and skills through graded collaboration with those who already possess them (**scaffolding**).

■ The most useful assistance mothers can give their child's task performance is to initially use general instruction until the child experiences difficulties, then give more specific instruction. This relates to Vygotsky's **zone of proximal development** (ZPD).

■ For Vygotsky, intelligence is the capacity to learn from instruction. Teachers occupy a **didactic role**, guiding pupils in paying attention, concentrating and learning effectively. In this way, children are **scaffolded**. Vygotsky also believed in **collaborative learning**, whereby more advanced children ('substitute teachers') help other, less advanced ones.

■ **Information-processing** (IP) **theories** are based on the **computer analogy** and focus on cognitive processes. **Task analysis** is used to study how children's 'mental programs' and strategies for processing information develop.

■ Whilst children appear to acquire new strategies in a particular sequence, this is not equivalent to a Piagetian stage. Nevertheless, children can be inconsistent when using new strategies. Improvement with age is related to improved **monitoring** of performance, which is part of **metacognition**. This is part of a larger category of **executive processes**.

■ Emphasis on memory and young children's limited IP capacity can explain why they are poorer at tasks involving memorising and reading. Storing knowledge linguistically is a vital prerequisite of successful IP performance. Teachers have a crucial role to play in helping children to find strategies for reducing memory load.

Essay Questions

1 a Describe Piaget's theory of cognitive development (*12 marks*)

 b Assess the extent to which this theory is supported by research evidence. (*12 marks*)

2 Critically consider practical applications of **two** theories of cognitive development. (*24 marks*)

WEB ADDRESSES

http://129.7160.115/inst5931/piagetl.html
http://www.funderstanding.com/learningtheoryhow3.html
http://gwu.edu/~yip/piaget.html
http://www.uiademo/hum/h0146.htm
http://nces.ed.gov

29 The Development of Measured Intelligence

INTRODUCTION AND OVERVIEW

According to Sternberg & Grigorenko (1997), virtually all researchers accept that:

- both heredity *and* environment contribute to intelligence;
- heredity and environment *interact* in various ways;
- extremely poor, as well as highly enriched, environments can interfere with the realisation of a person's intelligence, regardless of his or her heredity.

This chapter considers claims about the influence of genetic and environmental factors on the development of measured intelligence. It begins by looking at evidence for the view that differences between people in intelligence test performance are largely determined by genetic factors. Then, it looks at evidence concerning the influence of both *pre-natal* and *post-natal* environmental factors, including the role of cultural differences. Finally, it examines the *interaction* between genetic and environmental factors.

GENETIC INFLUENCES

Studies of IQ stability

Since people's genetic inheritance is a constant, then if measured intelligence (an IQ test score) is largely determined by genetic factors, there should be a high degree of continuity in IQ throughout a person's life-span (McGurk, 1975). IQ is not normally used as a measure of intelligence below age two. Instead, a *developmental quotient* (DQ) is used. This assesses a child's developmental rate compared with the 'average' child of the same age (Bayley, 1969). The younger a child is when given a developmental test, the lower the correlation between its DQ and later IQ. Once IQ is measurable, it becomes a better predictor of adult IQ.

Whilst many studies have shown little fluctuation in IQ over time, there are many short-term fluctuations which are often related to disturbing factors in an individual's life. Although the stability coefficients reported by some researchers (e.g. Honzik *et al.*, 1948) are impressive, they are based on large numbers of people and tend to obscure individual differences.

Others have reported unimpressive stability coefficients. For example, McCall *et al.* (1973) found that in 140 middle class children, the average IQ change between the ages of two-and-a-half and 17 was 28 points. The most 'stable' children changed an average of ten points, whilst 15 per cent shifted 50 points or more in either direction. One child's IQ increased by 74 points!

Even in studies where the correlation between IQ at different ages is *statistically significant* (see Appendix 1), the stability coefficients are low and suggest greater fluctuation in scores than a simple genetic theory predicts. There is, therefore, a large amount of convincing evidence that a person's intelligence level can alter, sometimes substantially (Howe, 1997).

Family resemblance studies

These examine the correlation in intelligence test scores among people who vary in genetic similarity. If genetic factors influence IQ, then the closer the genetic relationship between two people, the greater should be the correspondence (or *concordance*) between their IQs.

Monozygotic (MZ) or identical twins are unique in having exactly the same genetic inheritance, since they develop from the same single fertilised egg. *Dizygotic* (DZ) or non-identical twins, by contrast, develop from two eggs, and are no more alike than ordinary siblings (they share about 50 per cent of their genes). If genes have any influence on the development of measured intelligence, then MZs should show the *greatest* correspondence in terms of their intelligence test performance (see also Gross *et al.*, 2000). Any difference between them would

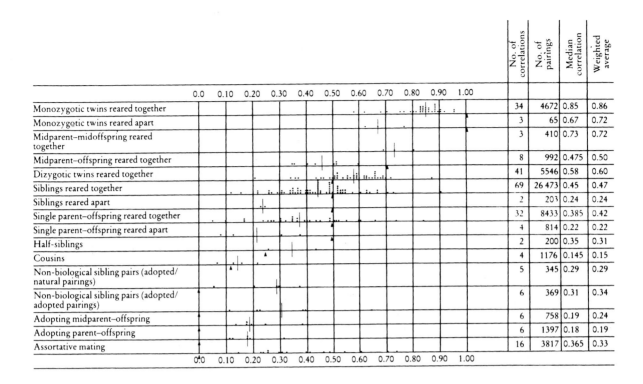

	0.0	0.10	0.20	0.30	0.40	0.50	0.60	0.70	0.80	0.90	1.00	No. of correlations	No. of pairings	Median correlation	Weighted average
Monozygotic twins reared together												34	4672	0.85	0.86
Monozygotic twins reared apart												3	65	0.67	0.72
Midparent–midoffspring reared together												3	410	0.73	0.72
Midparent–offspring reared together												8	992	0.475	0.50
Dizygotic twins reared together												41	5546	0.58	0.60
Siblings reared together												69	26 473	0.45	0.47
Siblings reared apart												2	203	0.24	0.24
Single parent–offspring reared together												32	8433	0.385	0.42
Single parent–offspring reared apart												4	814	0.22	0.22
Half-siblings												2	200	0.35	0.31
Cousins												4	1176	0.145	0.15
Non-biological sibling pairs (adopted/natural pairings)												5	345	0.29	0.29
Non-biological sibling pairs (adopted/adopted pairings)												6	369	0.31	0.34
Adopting midparent–offspring												6	758	0.19	0.24
Adopting parent–offspring												6	1397	0.18	0.19
Assortative mating												16	3817	0.365	0.33

Table 29.1 *Familial correlations for IQ. The vertical bar on each distribution indicates the median correlation. The arrow indicates the correlation predicted by a simple polygenic model (that is, the view that many pairs of genes are involved in the inheritance of intelligence) (From Gross, 1996, and based on Bouchard & McGue, 1981)*

have to be attributed to environmental or experiential influences. Many studies (e.g. Erlenmeyer-Kimling & Jarvik, 1963; Bouchard & McGue, 1981; Wilson, 1983) have shown that the closer people's genetic similarity, the more strongly correlated are their IQs. Table 29.1 presents a summary of Bouchard and McGue's world-wide review of 111 studies reporting IQ correlations between people of varying genetic similarity.

As Table 29.1 shows, the closer the genetic relationship between two individuals, the stronger the correlation between their IQ scores. So, the correlation between cousins (who share roughly 12.5 per cent of their genes) is weaker than that for parents and their offspring (who share roughly 50 per cent). The strongest correlation of all, however, is for MZs. At first sight, these data suggest that heredity is a major influence on IQ test performance. However, as the genetic similarity between people increases, so does the similarity of their environments: parents and offspring usually live in the same household, whereas unrelated people do not.

Studies of separated twins

One way of overcoming this problem is to compare the IQs of MZs *reared together* in the same environment with those raised *separately* in different environments. As

Table 29.1 shows, MZs reared together show a greater similarity in IQ scores than those reared separately. However, the fact that MZs reared separately are still more similar than same-sex DZs reared together suggests a strong genetic influence (Bouchard *et al.*, 1990). The data obtained from studies of separated MZs have, however, been criticised.

Box 29.1 Criticisms of twin studies

- 'Separated' twins often turn out not to have been reared separately at all. In Shields' (1962) and Juel-Nielsen's (1965) studies, some of the twins were raised in related branches of the parents' families, attended the same school and/or played together (Farber, 1981; Horgan, 1993). When these are excluded from analysis in Shields' study, for example, the correlation decreases from 0.77 to 0.51. Moreover, even if the twins are separated at birth, they have shared the same environment of the mother's womb for nine months. Their identical *pre-natal* experiences may account for the observed similarities in IQ (Howe, 1997).

- When twins have to be separated, the agencies responsible for placing them will try to match the respective families as closely as possible. When the environments are substantially different, there are marked IQ differences between the twins (Newman *et al.*, 1937).

- Experimenter and participant bias may also play an important role. In Newman *et al.*'s and Shields' studies, the experimenters *knew* which twins were identical and which had been separated. Participants in Bouchard *et al.*'s (1990) study were recruited by means of media appeals and 'self-referrals'. Kaprio (cited in Horgan, 1993) claims that Bouchard *et al.*'s study has tended to attract people who enjoy publicity, and therefore constitute an atypical sample.

- Different studies have used different IQ tests, making comparisons between them difficult. Moreover, some of the tests used were inappropriate and/or not standardised on certain groups.

- The most widely cited and best-known studies of MZs are those reported by Burt (e.g. 1966), who found high correlations between the IQs of 53 pairs of twins supposedly reared in very different environments. After noticing several peculiarities in Burt's procedures and data, Kamin (1974) and Gillie (1976) questioned the genuineness of Burt's research. Even Burt's most loyal supporters have conceded that at least some of his data were fabricated (e.g. Hearnshaw, 1979).

The various problems with twin studies undoubtedly led to an *overestimation* of genetic influences. However, methodological improvements have produced correlations that are still impressive and which, for Plomin & DeFries (1980):

> '... implicate genes as the major systematic force influencing the development of individual differences in IQ'.

A major ongoing study is that directed by Bouchard at the University of Minnesota. Separated and non-separated twins are given comprehensive psychological and medical tests, and answer some 15,000 questions! For some abilities (such as verbal ability), the correlations between MZs reared apart are very high, suggesting a strong genetic influence. However, for others (such as memory), the correlations are low or, as with spatial ability, inconsistent (Thompson *et al.*, 1991).

Figure 29.1 *Barbara Herbert and Daphne Goodship, one of the pairs of (English) separated identical twins reunited through their participation in the Minnesota twin study*

Adoption studies

Adopted children share half their genes but none of their environment with their biological parents, and they share at least some of their environment but none of their genes with their adoptive parents. One research methodology involves comparing the IQs of children adopted in infancy with those of their adoptive and biological parents. Support for the influence of genetic factors would be obtained if the correlation between the adopted children's IQ scores and their biological parents was stronger than that between the adopted children and their adoptive parents.

This is exactly what some studies have shown. Munsinger (1975) found that the average correlation between adopted children and their biological parents was 0.48, compared with 0.19 for adopted children and their adoptive parents. Also, by the end of adolescence, adopted children's IQs are correlated only weakly with their adoptive siblings who share the same environment but are biologically unrelated (Plomin, 1988).

One problem with adoption studies is the difficulty in assessing the amount of similarity between the biological and adoptive parents' environments. When the environments are very different (as when the children of poor, under-educated parents are adopted into families of high socio-economic status), substantial increases in IQ scores are observed.

Box 29.2 Adoption studies involving very different natural and adoptive parental environments

Scarr & Weinberg (1976) carried out a 'transracial' study of 101 white families, above average in intelligence, income and social class, who adopted black children. If genetics were the only factor influencing the development of measured intelligence, then the average IQ of the adopted children should have been more or less what it was before they were adopted. In fact, their average IQ was 106 following adoption, compared with an average of 90 before adoption.

This finding has been replicated in other studies. For example, Schiff *et al.* (1978) studied a group of economically deprived French mothers who had given up one baby for adoption whilst retaining at least one other child. The average IQ of the children adopted into middle class homes was 110, whilst that of the siblings who remained with the biological mother was 95. Similarly, French adoptees raised by parents of high socio-economic status were around 12 IQ points higher than adoptees raised by parents of low socio-economic status, irrespective of the socio-economic status of their biological parents (Capron & Duyme, 1989).

Scarr & Weinberg's (1976) data also indicated that children adopted early in life (within their first year) have higher IQs than those adopted later. So, when adoptive homes provide a superior intellectual climate, they can have a substantial effect on the development of measured intelligence. However, when the economic status of the biological and adoptive parents is roughly equal, the IQs of adopted children tend to be much more similar to those of the biological parents than the adoptive parents (Scarr & Weinberg, 1978).

Plomin & DeFries's Colorado Adoption Project (begun in 1975) is an ongoing study involving over 200 adopted children. By middle childhood, natural (birth) mothers and their children who were adopted were just as similar as control parents and *their* children on measures of both verbal and spatial ability. In contrast, the adoptees' scores do not resemble their adoptive parents' at all.

According to Plomin & DeFries (1998), these results are consistent with a growing body of evidence suggesting that the shared family environment does *not* contribute to similarities between family members:

'Rather, family resemblance on such measures [verbal and spatial ability] seems to be controlled almost entirely by genetics, and environmental factors often end up making family members different, not the same'.

(See Chapter 59 for a more detailed discussion of shared and non-shared environments.)

ENVIRONMENTAL INFLUENCES

Those who believe that the environment influences the development of measured intelligence do not deny that genetic factors play a role. However, they believe that measured intelligence can be strongly influenced by a whole range of (pre- and post-natal) environmental factors.

Pre-natal environmental influences

Pre-natal non-genetic factors account for the largest proportion of biologically caused learning difficulties and lowered IQ. Known pre-natal *teratogens* include certain infections (e.g. maternal *rubella*), toxic chemicals in the mother's body (e.g.drugs like heroin, cocaine and alcohol: see Box 29.3), radiation and pollutants. Other toxins are produced by the mother's own faulty metabolism, or as a result of incompatibility between the rhesus factors in the mother's body and that of her developing foetus (Frude, 1998).

Anxiety has also been found to lead to low birth-weight babies (due to impaired blood flow to the uterus: Teixeira, 1999). In turn, low birth-weight is associated with neurological impairment, lower IQ and greater problems in school (e.g. Hack *et al.*, 1994).

Box 29.3 Foetal alcohol syndrome

Foetal alcohol syndrome (FAS) is a consequence of the mother's excessive alcohol use during pregnancy. Children with FAS are typically smaller than average and suffer from *microcephaly* (an unusually small head and brain). They often have heart defects and a distinctive facial appearance (see Figure 29.2). FAS children are generally mildly retarded (IQ scores 50–55 to 70), although some may be moderately retarded (IQ 35–40 to 50–55) and others of average intelligence (anything above IQ 70–75). However, in those of average intelligence, there are significant academic and attentional difficulties (Sue *et al.*, 1994).

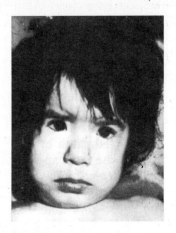

Figure 29.2 *A child with FAS (From Bee, 1992)*

Post-natal environmental influences

Rutter *et al.* (1998) studied a large sample of 111 institutionalised Romanian children adopted into English families within 24 months of birth. The children had experienced extreme privation, both physically and psychologically, and were all severely malnourished. Compared with 42 English adoptees, the Romanian children showed developmental deficiencies in weight, height and head circumference, as well as deficits in reaching developmental milestones.

However, by age four, they showed considerable physical and developmental catch-up, and 'spectacular' cognitive catch-up. Those who were adopted before six months had a clear advantage over the later-adopted children. Although their data do not allow a clear differentiation to be made, Rutter *et al.* conclude that the effects of malnutrition do not appear to be independent of the effects of the psychological privation.

Other studies, however, suggest that periodic or chronic subnutrition *can* adversely affect cognitive development in its own right. For example, when children in developing countries are given high-quality nutritional supplements in infancy and early childhood, their later IQ and vocabulary scores are higher than those of non-supplemented children (Pollitt & Gorman, 1994).

Box 29.4 Some post-natal environmental influences on the development of measured intelligence

Environmental 'insults', illness and disease: Exposure to lead is just one environmental factor associated with reduced IQ, and the effects may be irreversible (Tong, 1998). Anoxia (lack of oxygen) at birth, head trauma and various childhood illnesses (such as encephalitis) can cause brain damage and lower potential intelligence. In later life, brain damage from strokes, metabolic disturbances, brain infections, and diseases (e.g. Alzheimer's: see Chapter 36) can all adversely affect measured intelligence.

Family size and birth order: According to Zajonc & Markus (1975):

'Intelligence declines with family size; the fewer children in your family, the smarter you are likely to be. Intelligence also declines with birth order; the fewer older brothers or sisters you have, the brighter you are likely to be'.

A study of 200,000 children from large Israeli families (Davis *et al.*, 1977) supports Zajonc and Markus's claim, at least up to the seventh child. At this point, the trend reverses itself, so that the tenth-born child has a higher IQ than the ninth-born, who in turn has a higher IQ than the eighth-born. One possible explanation is that each new-born that enters a family lowers the 'intellectual environment', because the parents' intellectual capacity needs to be spread among a larger number of children. Alternatively, the mother's uterus might be less conducive to optimal pre-natal growth for later than earlier pregnancies, and this affects IQ (Crooks & Stein, 1991). However, neither explanation can account for the trend reported by Davis *et al.* after the seventh child.

Stressful family circumstances: Sameroff & Seifer's (1989) *Rochester longitudinal study* indicates that intellectual competence and general adjustment are correlated with a variety of 'family risk factors' including low parental work skills and a father who does not live with the family. Children with no risk factors score more than 30 IQ points higher than children with seven or eight risk factors.

(Based on Morris, 1988; Wade & Tavris, 1993; Zimbardo & Weber, 1994)

Environmental enrichment studies

Skeels (1966) followed up a group of children removed from orphanages into more stimulating environments 20 years earlier (Skeels & Dye, 1939). Most of those raised by foster mothers showed significant improvements in their measured intelligence, whereas those raised in the orphanage had dropped out of high school, or were still institutionalised or not self-supporting. Other studies of children raised in orphanages have also shown that environmental enrichment can have beneficial effects. The Rutter *et al.* (1998) study of Romanian orphans is a striking example.

Hunt (1961) and Bloom (1964) argued that intelligence was not a fixed attribute but depended on, and could be increased by, experience. This led to the United States government initiating a number of *intervention programmes*, based on the assumption that intelligence could be increased through special training.

Box 29.5 Operation Headstart

In 1965, *Operation Headstart* began. It was an ambitious compensatory programme designed to give culturally disadvantaged pre-school children enriched opportunities in early life. Operation Headstart started as an eight-week summer programme, and shortly afterwards became a full year's pre-school project. In 1967, two additional *Follow Through* programmes were initiated, in an attempt to involve parents and members of the wider community. Early findings indicated that there were significant short-term gains for the children, and this generated much optimism. However, when IQ gains did occur, they disappeared within a couple of years, and the children's educational improvement was minimal.

Similar to Operation Headstart was the *Milwaukee Project*. Heber & Garber (1975) worked with 40 poor, mostly black families, whose average IQ score was 75. Twenty of the women were given job training and sent to school (the 'experimental group'). The other twenty (the 'control group') received no job training or special education. The findings initially showed that the children of the 'experimental group' parents had an average IQ score of 126, 51 points higher than the average obtained by their mothers. The average score of the 'control group' children was 94, also higher than their mothers' average score.

Figure 29.3 *Eddie Murphy and Dan Ackroyd in* Trading Places, *which illustrates the crucial importance of social class background and opportunity as influences on individual achievement. The fact that they are also from different racial backgrounds highlights even more the role of environmental influence*

As with Headstart, however, the IQ gains diminished over time. Moreover, the children's academic gains were very modest, in that whilst the experimental group did have better reading scores than the controls, there was little difference between them in mathematics, in which both groups performed poorly. Like Headstart, the Milwaukee project showed that vigorous and relatively prolonged intervention can make a difference to severely disadvantaged children's cognitive performances. However, much of the gain is lost in the years following the end of the programme, at the time of starting school (Rutter & Rutter, 1992). Figure 29.4 illustrates this.

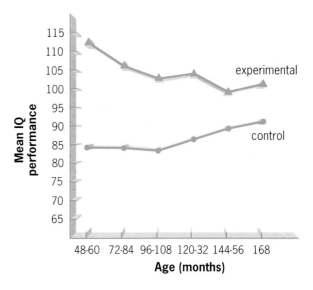

Figure 29.4 *IQ performance with increasing age of severely disadvantaged children participating in a broad-ranging intensive intervention programme in the pre-school years. (Data from Garber, 1988 and taken from Rutter & Rutter, 1992)*

Headstart in particular has been subject to several criticisms. Hunt (1969), for example, has claimed that it was inappropriate to the children's needs and did not provide them with the skills they had failed to develop at home during their first four years, and which are developed by most middle class children. Also, it emphasised IQ changes as an outcome measure in evaluating its effectiveness. Critics have argued that measures which reflect social competence, adaptability and emotional health are much better criteria of success (Weinberg, 1989). According to Bee (2000), because children are not randomly allocated to Headstart or non-Headstart, interpreting the differences becomes very difficult.

However, the criticisms were apparently premature, and several reviews looking at Headstart's long-term effects have concluded that the programme has brought about lasting changes in children's cognitive abilities (Brown & Grotberg, 1981), with the greatest gains being shown by children with the lowest initial IQ. Additionally, there is a *sleeper effect* at work, in that the impact of intervention programmes is cumulative (Collins, 1983).

Box 29.6 The longer-term effects of Headstart and other intervention programmes

Compared with non-participants, children enrolled in intervention programmes:

- will usually show gains of about ten IQ points. These gains occur whilst the programme is running, but then fade and disappear within the early years of elementary (primary) school (Zigler & Styfco, 1993);

- are *less* likely to be placed in special education/remedial classes, are *slightly less* likely to repeat a grade and *slightly more* likely to graduate from high school (Darlington, 1991; Haskins, 1989);

- tend to score higher on tests of reading, language and maths, with this 'achievement gap' widening between the ages of six and 14 (Collins, 1983);

- show better school adjustment than their peers (Zigler & Styfco, 1993);

- are more likely to want to succeed academically (Collins, 1983).

According to Bee (2000), although enrolled children do not necessarily *test* much higher than non-enrolled children, they *function* better in school. When some kind of supportive intervention continues into the early years of elementary school, and when the school is of a reasonable quality, the beneficial effects on school peformance are even more evident.

However, Howe (1998) believes that it would be inconceivable if the improvements in IQ produced by intervention programmes *did not* fade. In the case of Headstart schemes, for example, the urban environments where they have been set up have often involved squalor, addiction, violence, unemployment, poor housing and inadequate parenting. Together, these negative influences work to restrict a child's opportunities to practise and maintain recently acquired mental skills. This makes it highly likely that they will fade.

For Howe, evidence of fading simply confirms that intelligence is changeable. Similarly, even if the vast majority of intervention studies had failed to raise children's IQs at all, this would not be conclusive evidence that intelligence was fixed. Before 1972, the total amount of time a child would have spent in a Headstart programme was 180 hours. This rose to 720 hours after 1972. However, when compared with real-life exposure to language of children from different social class backgrounds, 720 hours represents a rather modest intervention:

'Regarded in that light, the finding that educational intervention programmes ... have nevertheless yielded large ... IQ gains would appear to provide rather conclusive evidence that IQ scores are highly changeable'. (Howe, 1998)

Hothousing

According to Scarr (1984):

'Parents who are very concerned about providing special educational lessons for their babies are wasting their time'.

Whether it is possible and, indeed, desirable to accelerate children's development is currently the subject of much debate. For some psychologists (including Scarr), development is largely a matter of *maturation*. Others believe that whilst accelerated progress can occur in some areas, other skills (such as language) are essentially pre-programmed and not much affected by early experience (Howe, 1995; see Chapter 26).

Howe (1990) and Howe & Griffey (1994) have reviewed the evidence concerning early acceleration. In their view, efforts to help babies gain basic skills (such as running and jumping) earlier than usual can be beneficial. Even language development can be accelerated such that at 24 months of age, children given special graduated language programmes were as linguistically capable as typical 32-month-olds. Specific benefits have been found in pronoun and plural use and, in general, children given special programmes are well ahead of those not given them (Howe, 1995).

However, researchers have cautioned against generalising about the effects of providing children with enriched environments. White (1971), for example, showed that infants in enriched visual surroundings (a highly colourful mobile suspended over their cribs) were advanced in some respects, but *delayed* in others. Similarly, studies of perceptual and motor development indicate that acceleration in one area of development can have a 'blunting' effect on development in other areas (Cratty, 1970).

Parents determined to make their child into a genius or prodigy can pressurise it with their high expectations, and by sending it to an organisation established to serve 'gifted children'. However, there is no convincing evidence that such organisations are actually effective (Llewellyn-Smith, 1996). Also, children who experience intensive *hothousing regimes* may miss other experiences which, whilst not necessarily 'educational', are important for healthy development (Howe, 1995). A child who successfully completes a mathematics degree before the age of 14 has clearly developed a useful skill. But s/he might not have developed important social skills (such as the ability to make friends), because of an inability to join in 'normal' children's conversations.

Box 29.7 Dimensions of family interaction affecting cognitive development

According to Bee (2000), how infants and young children are treated can make a real difference to their cognitive development, regardless of whether they come from poor working-class or middle-class families. These differences in early experience have been the focus of most of the research into environmental effects on IQ.

Bee identifies several dimensions of family interaction or stimulation which seem to make a difference. Parents of higher-IQ children, or whose IQs show an increase over time, tend to:

- provide *interesting* and *complex physical environments*, including play materials that are appropriate for the children's ages and developmental levels;

- be *emotionally responsive* and *involved with* the children: smiling when the children smile, answering their questions, and generally responding to the their cues;

- *talk to the children* often, using language that is diverse, descriptively rich and accurate;

- operate within the children's *zone of proximal development* (ZPD: see Chapter 28, page 305) during play and interaction;

- *avoid excessive restrictiveness*, punitiveness or control, providing opportunities for the children to ask questions, as opposed to giving commands;

- *expect* their children to do well and develop rapidly, especially academically.

A study which is relevant to Bee's second dimension was conducted by Crandell & Hobson (1999), involving 36 middle-class mothers and their three-year-olds. Children of *securely attached* mothers (based on a version of Main *et al.*'s (1985) *adult attachment interview*) scored 19 points higher on the Stanford–Binet intelligence scale compared with children of *insecure* mothers. In turn, the mother's attachment type was related to how well *synchronised* her behaviour was with the child's: the higher-IQ children tended to enjoy more synchronised interactions with their mothers.

THE INTERACTION BETWEEN GENETIC AND ENVIRONMENTAL FACTORS

Clearly, both genetic *and* environmental factors can influence the development of measured intelligence.

This relates to the first of the points made by Sternberg & Grigorenko (1997) in the *Introduction and overview*. The second point acknowledges that measured intelligence can be attributed to an *interaction* between genetic and environmental factors. As Weinberg (1989) has noted:

'Genes do not fix behaviour. Rather, they establish a range of possible reactions to the range of possible experiences that environments can provide. Environments can also affect whether the full range of gene reactivity is expressed. Thus, how people behave, or what their measured IQs turn out to be or how quickly they learn, depends on the nature of their environments and on their genetic endowments bestowed at conception'.

How much does each contribute?

To acknowledge that both genetic and environmental factors influence intelligence raises the question: *how much* does each contribute? Researchers have attempted to determine the *relative* contributions made by genetic and environmental factors. The term *heritability* is used by behaviour geneticists to refer to the mathematical estimate of how much variability in a particular trait is a result of genetic variability (Carlson, 1988). Eye colour, for example, is affected almost entirely by heredity and little, if at all, by environmental factors. As a result, the heritability of eye colour is close to 100 per cent.

Early heritability estimates for IQ of 80 per cent (Jensen, 1969) have been revised down more recently to around 50 to 60 per cent (Bouchard & Segal, 1988). However, to say that the heritability of measured intelligence is 50 to 60 per cent does *not* mean that 50 to 60 per cent of measured intelligence is determined by genetic factors. This is because heritability estimates apply only to a particular *population* or group of people at a particular time, and not to a single individual. So, of the variation in intelligence test scores *within a group of people*, about 50 to 60 per cent (if Bouchard and Segal's estimate is correct) can be attributed to genetic factors.

However, heritability describes *what is* rather than *what could be* (Pike & Plomin, 1999). If environmental factors within a population change (e.g. educational opportunities), then the relative impact of genes and environment will change. Even for a highly heritable trait such as height, environmental changes *could* make a large difference. Indeed, the huge increase in height during the twentieth century is almost certainly the result of improved diet (Pike & Plomin, 1999). As far as intelligence is concerned, heritability of 50 per cent means that environmental factors account for *as much* variance as genes do (Plomin & DeFries, 1998: see Chapter 59).

Box 29.8 Why between-group differences cannot be inferred from within-group differences

Lewontin (1976) asks us to consider ten tomato plants grown in poor soil. Their different heights are the result of genetic factors. If the same ten plants were grown in fertile soil, differences in height would again be due to genetic factors. However, the difference in the average height of the plants grown in poor and fertile soil is due to the environmental differences of the soils. So, even when the heritability of a trait is high *within* a particular group, differences in that trait *between* groups may have environmental causes (Myers, 1990).

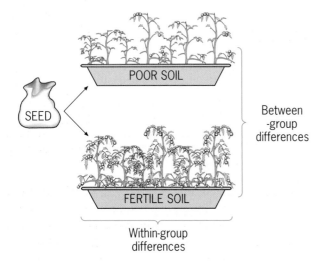

Figure 29.5 *Although we can account for within-group differences in terms of genetic factors, between-group differences may be caused by environmental factors (i.e. poor/fertile soil)*

If we apply the argument in Box 29.8 to Jensen's (1969) claim that 80 per cent of the differences between blacks and whites on IQ tests are due to blacks' *'genetic inferiority'*, then his claim must be rejected. *Environmental factors* which could account for such differences include *bias* in the tests used to measure intelligence. According to Segall *et al.* (1990), IQ tests are biased against those (such as blacks and other minorities) whose cultural background differs from that of the test's *normative sample* (whites). Segall *et al.* (1990) argue that all attempts at constructing 'culture-fair' or 'culture-free' tests have failed, and they conclude that:

> 'Clearly, culturally mediated experience always interacts with test content to influence test performance'.

This relates to the *emic–etic* distinction, and to the very concept of intelligence (see Chapter 55, pages 593–596, and Gross, 1999).

How do heredity and environment contribute?

If we accept that genetic and environmental factors *interact*, then the focus shifts from *how much* they contribute to *how* they exert their influence. An example of how this might occur is *cumulative deficit*. Dozens of studies show that children from poor families, or families where the parents are relatively uneducated, have lower IQ scores than those from middle-class families (Bee, 2000). This could reflect either genetic or environmental factors, or both.

However, these social class differences are *not* found before the age of two-and-a-half to three, after which they widen steadily. This suggests that the longer a child lives in poverty, the more negative the effects on IQ test scores and other measures of cognitive functioning become (Duncan, 1993; Smith *et al.*, 1997). Hence, the effects of any genetic differences that *may* be involved to begin with are *accentuated* by environmental factors, especially poverty. Poverty has a significant effect on children's IQ scores *over and above* what the parents' own genes may have contributed (Bee, 2000). Other examples of gene–environment interaction are discussed in Chapter 59.

CONCLUSIONS

This chapter has examined evidence which appears to support the claim that genetic factors are the major influence on the development of measured intelligence. It has also considered evidence which shows that both pre- and post-natal factors can influence individuals' performance on IQ tests. Clearly, both genetic *and* environmental factors can influence the development of measured intelligence. These factors are intertwined, not separate, which makes it essential to understand how they interact. For measured intelligence to develop to its full potential, people should be provided with an optimal environment, whatever their heredity may be.

Summary

- One way of investigating heredity's influence on measured intelligence is to study the **stability of IQ**. If IQ is largely determined by genetic factors, then it should remain stable throughout the life-span. Although several studies show high **stability coefficients**, these obscure sometimes very large individual differences, and there are many short-term fluctuations.

- **Family resemblance studies** involve examining the correlations in IQ among people who vary in genetic similarity. If genetic factors influence IQ test performance, then the closer the genetic relationship between two people, the greater the correspondence (**concordance**) between their IQ scores. **MZs** should show the **greatest** correspondence: any difference between them is attributable to environmental influences.

- Although there is evidence supporting this prediction, as people's genetic similarities increase so do the similarities of their environments. This can be overcome by comparing the IQs of MZs **reared together** with those raised **separately**. MZs reared separately are still more similar than same-sex DZs reared together, suggesting a strong genetic influence.

- Studies of separated MZs have been criticised on several important grounds. However, the Minnesota twin study indicates that for verbal ability the correlations among separated MZs are very high, although for memory they are low and for spatial ability inconsistent.

- Further support for the influence of genetic factors comes from **adoption studies**. When the economic status of the biological and adoptive parents is roughly equal, biological factors seem to be more influential. However, when children from disadvantaged parents are adopted into high socio-economic families, substantial gains in IQ can occur, as in 'transracial' studies. Also, children adopted within their first year have higher IQs than those adopted later.

- Whilst not denying the role of genetic factors, environmentalists argue that the development of measured intelligence can be strongly influenced by **environmental factors**.

- **Pre-natal** environmental influences (**teratogens**) which can produce lowered IQ scores include infections, drugs, radiation and pollutants. Anxiety can lead to low birth-weight babies, and excessive alcohol consumption can result in **foetal alcohol syndrome**.

- Human infants suffering **extreme malnutrition** and **psychological privation** have much lower IQs than similar children with adequate diets. **Environmental 'insults'**, **illness** and **disease** can all cause brain damage and lower potential intelligence. **Family size** and **birth order** are also related to intelligence, as are **stressful family circumstances** .

- **Intervention programmes** started with **Operation Headstart**. Early findings indicated significant short-term IQ gains, but these were short-lived and the educational improvement was minimal. Similar results were reported for the **Milwaukee Project**.

- Headstart was criticised for not providing the skills the disadvantaged children had failed to develop at home. It also overemphasised IQ as a measure of effectiveness, at the expense of social competence, adaptability and emotional health.

- Studies of the longer-term effects have concluded that Headstart has lasting cognitive benefits, especially for those whose IQ scores are initially the lowest. There is also a **sleeper effect**. Other intervention studies have also shown that cognitive abilities can be enhanced, as well as helping children to **function** better in school.

- Whether **hothousing** accelerates development is debatable. Acceleration in one area of development can have a 'blunting' or **delaying** effect on others. Children exposed to **hothousing regimes** may miss out on other experiences important for healthy development.

- The parents of higher-IQ children tend to provide **interesting** and **complex physical environments**, are **emotionally responsive**, **talk** to their children in a stimulating way, operate within the child's ZPD, **avoid excessive restrictiveness**, and **expect** their children to achieve.

- **Heritability** refers to **how much** of the variability in a particular trait is due to genetic variability **within a particular population or group of people** (not within a single individual). Even when a trait's heritability is high **within** a particular group, differences in that trait **between** groups may have environmental causes.

- Whilst heritability is concerned with the **relative** contributions of genes and environment, an equally important issue is **how** they **interact** to influence the development of measured intelligence. One example of this is **cumulative deficit**.

Essay Questions

1 Critically consider the role of genetic **and/or** cultural differences in the development of measured intelligence. (*24 marks*)

2 Describe and evaluate research into factors associated with the development of intelligence test performance. (*24 marks*)

WEB ADDRESSES

http://www.cycad.com/cgi-bin/Upstream/Issues/psychology/IQ/index.html
http://www.netlink.co.uk/users/vess/mensal.html
http://www.apa.org/monitor/may97/twinstud.html
http://www.abacon.com/bee/links/html
http://www.queendom.com.tests.html

30 *Development of Moral Understanding*

INTRODUCTION AND OVERVIEW

At birth, humans are *amoral* and do not possess any system of personal values and judgements about what is right or wrong. By adulthood, though, most of us possess *morality*. Psychologists, however, are not interested in morality as such, but in the *process* by which it is acquired. The nature of that process is seen very differently by different psychological theories, which attempt to answer quite different questions.

According to Haste *et al.* (1998), historically four main questions have been asked about moral development:

- How do conscience and guilt develop, acting as sanctions on our misdeeds? (This relates to Freud's psychoanalytic theory: see Chapter 31.)
- How do we come to understand the basis of rules and moral principles, so that we can make judgements about our own and others' behaviour? (The major theories here are those of Piaget, Kohlberg, and Eisenberg.)
- How do we learn the appropriate patterns of behaviour required by our culture? (This relates to learning theories, including Bandura's social learning theory: see Chapter 31.)
- How do we develop the moral emotions that motivate our concern for others? (Eisenberg's theory is also relevant here.)

This chapter is primarily concerned with the second question, and critically considers the theories of Piaget (1932), Kohlberg (1963) and Eisenberg (1982), including the influence of *gender* and *cultural variations*.

COGNITIVE–DEVELOPMENTAL THEORIES

According to Haste *et al.* (1998), the second question above has dominated research on moral development for 30 years, through work within the cognitive–developmental theoretical framework. Whilst it is Kohlberg's theory which has been the focus of research during this time, Piaget (1932) pioneered this approach to moral development. Cognitive–developmental theories maintain that it is the reasons *underlying* behaviour, rather than the behaviour itself, which make it right or wrong.

Piaget's theory

Piaget argued that morality develops gradually during childhood and adolescence. Whilst these changes are usually referred to as qualitatively different *stages* of moral development, Piaget explicitly did not use the concept of developmental stages in relation to moral development. Rather, he differentiated two *types* of moral orientation, namely *heteronomous* and *autonomous* (see Box 30.2, page 323). Instead of seeing morality as a form of cognition, Piaget discussed morality in the context of *affects* and *feelings* (Eckensberger, 1999).

Understanding rules

To discover how moral knowledge and understanding change with age, Piaget began by looking at children's ideas about the rules of the game of marbles. He believed that the essence of morality lies in rules, and that marbles is a game in which children create and enforce their own rules free from adult influence. Piaget felt that in this way he could discover how children's moral knowledge in general develops. As he noted:

> 'Children's games constitute the most admirable social institutions. The game of marbles, for instance, as played by boys, contains an extremely complex system of rules, that is to say, a code of laws, a jurisprudence of its own ... All morality consists in a system of rules'

Pretending he did not know the rules, Piaget asked children to explain them to him and, during the course of a game, to tell him who made the rules, where they came from, and whether they could be changed. He found that children aged between five and nine or ten tended to believe that the rules had always existed in their present form, and that they had been created by older children, adults or even God. The rules were sacred, and could not be changed in any way (an *external law*). Nevertheless, children unashamedly broke them to suit themselves, and saw nothing contradictory in the idea of both players winning the game.

Children aged ten and above understood that the rules were invented by children themselves and could be changed, but only if all players agreed. The function of rules was to prevent quarrelling and ensure fair play. They adhered rigidly to the rules, and discussed the finer points and implications of any changes. Piaget called this moral orientation towards co-operation with peers *mutual respect*, which he distinguished from the *unilateral respect* shown by younger children towards adult authority.

Figure 30.1 *According to Piaget, the rules of marbles could be used to study morality, since all morality consists of a system of rules*

Moral judgement and punishment

Piaget also told children pairs of stories about (hypothetical) children who had told lies, stolen or broken something.

Box 30.1 Examples of pairs of stories used by Piaget

Example 1a: A little boy called John was in his room. He was called to dinner and went into the dining room. Behind the door there was a chair and on the chair there was a tray with 15 cups on it. John couldn't have known that the chair was behind the door, and as he entered the dining room, the door knocked against the tray and the tray fell on the floor, breaking all of the cups.

Example 1b: One day, a little boy called Henry tried to get some jam out of a cupboard when his mother was out. He climbed onto a chair and stretched out his arm. The jam was too high up, and he couldn't reach it. But while he was trying to get it, he knocked over a cup. The cup fell down and broke.

Example 2a: A little girl called Marie wanted to give her mother a nice surprise and so she cut out a piece of sewing for her. But she didn't know how to use the scissors properly and she cut a big hole in her dress.

Example 2b: A little girl called Margaret went and took her mother's scissors one day when her mother was out. She played with them for a bit and then, as she didn't know how to use them properly, she made a hole in her dress.

Piaget asked children who they believed was the naughtier and should be punished more. He was more interested in the *reasons* the children gave for their answers than the answers themselves. Whilst five- to nine- or ten-year-olds could distinguish an intentional act from an unintentional one, they tended to base their judgements on the *severity* of the outcome or the sheer amount of damage done. So, John and Marie (see Box 30.1) were typically judged to be naughtier (*objective* or *external responsibility*).

By contrast, children aged ten or above judged Henry and Margaret to be naughtier, because they were both doing something they should not have been. Although the damage they caused was accidental, older children saw the motive or intention behind the act as being important in determining naughtiness (*internal responsibility*).

Regarding punishment, younger children believed that naughty people should pay for their crimes. In general, the greater the suffering the better, even though the form of punishment might be quite arbitrary. Such *expiatory* ('paying the penalty for') *punishment* is seen as decreed by authority and accepted as just because of its source (*moral realism*). Thus, when a child in a class does not admit to a misdeed and the rest of the class does not identify the offender, young children see *collective punishment* (i.e. the whole class is punished) as being acceptable.

Younger children often construed a misfortune which happens to someone who has behaved naughtily and 'got away with it' as a punishment for the misdeed (*immanent justice*). For example, a child who lied but was not found out and later fell and broke his arm was being punished for the lie. God (or an equivalent force) is in league with those in authority to ensure that 'the guilty will always be caught in the end'.

By contrast, older children saw punishment as bringing home to the offender the nature of the offence and as a deterrent to behaving wrongly in the future. They also believed that collective punishment was wrong, and that 'the punishment should fit the crime'. So, if one child stole another's sweets, the offender must give his or her own sweets to the victim (based on the *principle of reciprocity*) or be punished in some other appropriate way (see Figure 30.2). Older children no longer saw justice as being tied to authority (*moral relativism*), and there was less belief in immanent justice.

Figure 30.2 *Eric Cantona, the ex-Manchester United footballer, whose infamous attack on a Crystal Palace supporter in 1995 resulted in punishment by both the football authorities and the police. His community service, based on the principle of reciprocity, involved working with young footballers in and around Manchester.*

> **Box 30.2 Heteronomous and autonomous morality**
>
> Piaget called the morality of young children *heteronomous* ('subject to another's laws or rules'). Older children have *autonomous morality* ('subject to one's own laws or rules'), and see rules as the product of social agreements rather than sacred and unchangeable laws (the *morality of co-operation*).
>
> Piaget believed that the change from heteronomous to autonomous morality occurred because of the shift at about seven from egocentric to operational thought (see Chapter 28). This suggests that cognitive development is necessary for moral development, but since the latter lags at least two years behind the former, it cannot be sufficient. Another important factor is the change from *unilateral respect* (the child's unconditional obedience of parents and other adults) to *mutual respect* within the peer group (where disagreements between equals have to be negotiated and resolved).

An evaluation of Piaget's theory

Piaget believed that popular girls' games (such as hopscotch) were too simple compared with boys' most popular game (marbles) to be worthy of investigation. Whilst girls *eventually* achieve similar moral levels to boys, they are less concerned with *legal elaborations*. This apparent gender bias is also evident in Kohlberg's theory (see pages 324–329).

Children's understanding of *intention* is much more complex than Piaget believed, and children are able to bring this understanding to bear on moral decision-making. The pre-school child is *not* amoral (Durkin, 1995).

> **Box 30.3 Some experimental challenges to Piaget's claims regarding intention**
>
> - Piaget's stories make the *consequences* of behaviour explicit rather than the intentions behind it (Nelson, 1980). When three-year-olds see people bringing about negative consequences, they assume that their intentions are also negative. However, when information about intentions is made explicit, even three-year-olds can make judgements about them, *regardless* of the consequences. This suggests that three-year-olds are only *less proficient* than older children at discriminating intentions from consequences and in using these separate pieces of information to make moral judgements.

- Armsby (1971) found that 60 per cent of six-year-olds (compared with 90 per cent of ten-year-olds) judged the deliberate breaking of a cup as more deserving of punishment than accidental damage to a television set. This suggests that at least some six-year-olds are capable of understanding intention in the sense of 'deliberate naughtiness', and that a small amount of deliberate damage is naughtier than a large amount of accidental damage.

- According to some *information-processing theorists* (e.g. Gelman & Baillargeon, 1983: see Chapter 28), aspects of development which Piaget attributed to the increasing complexity and quality of thought, are actually the result of an increasing capacity for the storage and retrieval of information. Most five-year-olds say that John is naughtier because he broke more cups than Henry (see Box 30.1, page 322). This is because they can remember who broke more cups, but they *cannot remember all the other details of the stories*. When efforts are made to rectify this, five-year-olds often take intention into account, as well as the amount of damage.

Although evidence regarding the *process* of moral development is mixed, many of the age *trends* (not necessarily the ages) Piaget described are supported by later research. This includes cross-cultural data, mainly from Africa (Eckensberger & Zimba, 1997).

However, based on his idea of a balance between the individual and society, he did *not* assume that the developmental changes he observed in his Swiss sample would necessarily be found in other cultures. On the contrary, he claimed that the essential issue was whether the cultural context would allow certain developmental changes to occur. This general orientation towards *contextualisation* is evident in current cross-cultural research (Eckensberger, 1999), and an interesting example is a study of lying and truth-telling by Lee *et al.* (1997).

Box 30.4 Lying and truth-telling

Key **STUDY**

Lee *et al.* (1997) tested the claim that the understanding of lying is greatly influenced by the cultural norms and values in which individuals are socialised. One-hundred-and-twenty children from the People's Republic of China and 108 Canadian children (aged seven, nine and 11) were compared. They were presented with four brief stories, two involving a child who intentionally carried out a good deed (valued by adults in both cultures) and two involving a child who carried out a bad deed (viewed negatively by adults in both cultures). When the story characters were questioned by a teacher as to who committed the act, they either lied or told the truth. The children were asked to evaluate the story characters' deeds and their verbal statement as 'naughty' or 'good'.

Overall, the Chinese children rated truth-telling *less* positively and lie-telling *more* positively in *prosocial settings* compared with the Canadian children. This indicates that the emphasis on self-effacement and modesty in Chinese culture overrides Chinese children's evaluations of lying in some situations. Both groups rated truth-telling positively and lie-telling negatively in *antisocial situations*, reflecting the emphasis in *both* cultures on distinguishing between misdeed and truth/lie-telling.

Lee *et al.*'s results suggest a close link between sociocultural practices and moral judgement in relation to lying and truth-telling. China is a communist–collectivist society, which values the community over the individual and promotes personal sacrifice for the social good (see Chapter 55). Admitting a good deed is viewed as a violation of both traditional Chinese cultural norms *and* communist–collectivist doctrine.

By contrast, in Western culture 'white lies' and deceptions to avoid embarrassment are tolerated, and concealing positive behaviour is not explicitly encouraged (especially in the early school years). Taking credit for good deeds is an accepted part of individualistic self-promotion in the West, whilst in China it is seen as a character flaw. Whilst cognitive development plays an undeniable role (as argued by Kohlberg: see below), cultural and social factors are also key determinants in children's moral development (Lee *et al.*, 1997).

Kohlberg's theory

As noted earlier, Kohlberg's theory has dominated research in the field of moral reasoning for 30 years. Like Piaget, by whom he was greatly influenced, Kohlberg believed that morality develops gradually during childhood and adolescence. Also like Piaget, he was more interested in the *reasons* people give for their moral judgements, than the judgements themselves. For example, our reasons for upholding the law, as well as our views about whether there are circumstances in which breaking the law can be justified, might change as we develop.

Kohlberg assessed people's moral reasoning through the use of *moral dilemmas*. Typically, these involved a choice between two alternatives, both of which would be considered socially unacceptable. One of the most famous of these dilemmas concerns 'Heinz'.

Box 30.5 An example of a moral dilemma

In Europe, a woman was near death from a special kind of cancer. There was one drug that the doctors thought might save her. It was a form of radium that a druggist in the same town had recently discovered. The drug was expensive to make, but the druggist was charging ten times what the drug cost him to make. He paid $400 for the radium and charged $4000 for a small dose of the drug. The sick woman's husband, Heinz, went to everyone he knew to borrow the money, but he could only get together about $2000, which is half of what the drug cost. He told the druggist that his wife was dying and asked him to sell it cheaper or let him pay later. But the druggist said, 'No, I discovered the drug and I'm going to make money from it'. So Heinz got desperate and considered breaking into the man's store to steal the drug for his wife.

1 Should Heinz steal the drug?

  a Why or why not?

2 If Heinz doesn't love his wife, should he steal the drug for her?

  a Why or why not?

3 Suppose the person dying is not his wife but a stranger. Should Heinz steal the drug for the stranger?

  a Why or why not?

4 (If you favour stealing the drug for a stranger.) Suppose it's a pet animal he loves. Should Heinz steal to save the pet animal?

  a Why or why not?

5 Is it important for people to do everything they can to save another's life?

  a Why or why not?

6 Is it against the law for Heinz to steal? Does that make it morally wrong?

  a Why or why not?

7 Should people try to do everything they can to obey the law?

  a Why or why not?

  b How does this apply to what Heinz should do?

(From Kohlberg, 1984)

The original study (beginning in 1956) involved 72 Chicago boys (10–16 years), 58 of whom were followed up at three-yearly intervals for 20 years (Kohlberg, 1984; Colby *et al.*, 1983; Colby & Kohlberg, 1987). Based on the answers given by this sample to the Heinz and other dilemmas, Kohlberg identified six qualitatively different *stages* of moral development, differing in complexity, with more complex types being used by older individuals. The six stages span three *levels* of moral reasoning.

At the *pre-conventional level*, we do not have a personal code of morality. Instead, it is shaped by the standards of adults and the consequences of following or breaking their rules. At the *conventional level*, we begin to internalise the moral standards of valued adult role models. At the *post-conventional level*, society's values (such as individual rights), the need for democratically determined rules, and *reciprocity* (or *mutual action*) are affirmed (stage 5). In stage 6, individuals are guided by *universal ethical principles*, in which they do what their conscience dictates, even if this conflicts with society's rules.

Box 30.6 Kohlberg's three levels and six stages of moral development and their application to the Heinz dilemma

Level 1: Pre-Conventional Morality

Stage 1 (punishment and obedience orientation): What is right and wrong is determined by what is punishable and what is not. If stealing is wrong, it is because authority figures say so and will punish such behaviour. Moral behaviour is essentially the avoidance of punishment.

• Heinz *should* steal the drug because if he lets his wife die, he would get into trouble.

• Heinz *should not* steal the drug because he would get caught and sent to prison.

Stage 2 (instrumental relativist orientation): What is right and wrong is determined by what brings rewards and what people want. Other people's needs and wants are important, but only in a reciprocal sense ('If you scratch my back, I'll scratch yours').

• Heinz *should* steal the drug because his wife needs it to live and he needs her companionship.

• Heinz *should not* steal the drug because he might get caught and his wife would probably die before he got out of prison, so it wouldn't do much good.

Level 2: Conventional Morality

Stage 3 (interpersonal concordance or 'good boy–nice girl' orientation): Moral behaviour is whatever pleases and helps others and doing what they approve of. Being moral is 'being a good person in your own eyes and the eyes of others'. What the majority thinks is right by definition.

- Heinz *should* steal the drug because society expects a loving husband to help his wife regardless of the consequences.
- Heinz *should not* steal the drug because he will bring dishonour on his family and they will be ashamed of him.

Stage 4 (maintaining the social order orientation): Being good means doing one's duty – showing respect for authority and maintaining the social order for its own sake. Concern for the common good goes beyond the stage 3 concern for one's family: society protects the rights of individuals, so society must be protected by the individual. Laws are unquestionably accepted and obeyed.

- Heinz *should* steal the drug because if people like the druggist are allowed to get away with being greedy and selfish, society would eventually break down.
- Heinz *should not* steal the drug because if people are allowed to take the law into their own hands, regardless of how justified an act might be, the social order would soon break down.

Level 3: Post-Conventional Morality

Stage 5 (social contract–legalistic orientation): Since laws are established by mutual agreement, they can be changed by the same democratic process. Although laws and rules should be respected, since they protect individual rights as well as those of society as a whole, individual rights can sometimes supersede these laws if they become destructive or restrictive. Life is more 'sacred' than any legal principle, and so the law should not be obeyed at all costs.

- Heinz *should* steal the drug because the law is not set up to deal with circumstances in which obeying it would cost a human life.
- Heinz *should not* steal the drug because although he couldn't be blamed if he did steal it, even such extreme circumstances do not justify a person taking the law into his own hands. The ends do not always justify the means.

Stage 6 (universal ethical principles orientation): The ultimate judge of what is moral is a person's own conscience operating in accordance with certain universal principles. Society's rules are arbitrary and may be broken when they conflict with universal moral principles.

- Heinz *should* steal the drug because when a choice must be made between disobeying a law and saving a life, one must act in accordance with the higher principle of preserving and respecting life.
- Heinz *should not* steal the drug because he must consider other people who need it just as much as his wife. By stealing the drug he would be acting in accordance with his own particular feelings with utter disregard for the values of all the lives involved.

(Based on Rest, 1983; Crooks & Stein, 1991; Gross, 1996)

Both Piaget and Kohlberg saw cognitive development as necessary for, and setting a limit on, the maturity of moral reasoning, with the latter usually lagging behind the former. So, for example, formal operational thought (see Chapter 28) is needed to achieve stages 5 and 6, but it cannot *guarantee* it. Because formal operational thought is achieved by a relatively small proportion of people, it is hardly surprising that the percentage of those attaining stages 5 and 6 is only about 15 per cent (Colby *et al.*, 1983).

Table 30.1 *The relationship between Kohlberg's stages and Piaget's types of moral development, and Piaget's stages of cognitive development*

Kohlberg's levels of moral development	Age group included within Kohlberg's developmental levels	Corresponding type of morality (Piaget)	Corresponding stage of cognitive development (Piaget)
1 Pre-conventional (stages 1 and 2)	Most nine-year-olds and below. Some over nine	Heteronomous (five to nine or ten)	Pre-operational (two to seven)
2 Conventional (stages 3 and 4)	Most adolescents and adults	Heteronomous (e.g. respect for the law and authority figures) *plus* autonomous (e.g. taking intentions into account)	Concrete operational (seven to 11)
3 Post-conventional (stages 5 and 6)	10–15 per cent of adults, not before mid-thirties	Autonomous (ten and above)	Formal operational (11 and above)

Figure 30.3 *Mahatma Gandhi was a moral leader who defied his country's traditional moral and legal standards, in pursuit of humanistic causes. He seems to have been guided by universal ethical principles*

Figure 30.4 *Mother Theresa of Calcutta: another moral leader who, like Gandhi, pursued humanistic causes and was guided by universal ethical principles*

An evaluation of Kohlberg's theory

Findings from his longitudinal study showed that those who were initially at low stages had advanced to higher stages, suggesting 'moral progression' (Colby *et al.*, 1983). Based on these findings, Kohlberg argued that the first five stages are *universal* and that they occur in an *invariant sequence*. Similarly, Rest's (1983) 20-year longitudinal study of men from adolescence to their

mid-thirties showed that the developmental stages seem to occur in the order described by Kohlberg.

According to Snarey's (1987) review of 45 studies conducted in 27 different cultures, the data 'provide striking support for the universality of Kohlberg's first four stages'. However, Kohlberg & Nisan (1987) studied Turkish youngsters, both from a rural village and a city, over a 12-year period. Their scores overall were *lower* than Americans', and rural youngsters scored lower than the urban dwellers. Snarey *et al.* (1985) reported that Israeli youngsters (aged 12–24) educated in kibbutzim scored *higher* than Americans at all ages.

These findings suggest that cultural factors play a significant part in moral reasoning. According to the *socio-cultural approach*, what 'develops' is the individual's skill in managing the moral expectations of one's culture, expressed through linguistic and symbolic practices. This contrasts sharply with Kohlberg's cognitive–developmental model, which concentrates on individual processes 'inside the head' (Haste *et al.*, 1998).

Box 30.7 Cultural bias in Kohlberg's theory

As noted, stage 6 reasoning is based on supposedly 'universal' ethical principles, such as justice (which is central to Kohlberg's theory), equality, integrity and reverence for life. However, these are *not* universally held (Shweder, 1991; Eckensberger, 1994).

For example, South East Asian culture places family loyalty at the centre of their ethical system. Shweder *et al.* (1987) gave the Heinz dilemma to people living in Indian Hindu villages. One very morally sophisticated reasoner reached very different conclusions supported by very different arguments, from that expected in Western culture. He was clearly using a high stage of reasoning, but it was impossible to score him on the Kohlberg measure, because his arguments were too far removed from the Western position (Shweder, 1990).

Iwasa (1992) compared Americans and Japanese using the Heinz dilemma. There was no difference in the overall level of moral development, but there were qualitative differences in why human life was valued, reflecting cultural norms. Whilst Americans were concerned to prolong length of life, the Japanese were concerned to make it purer and cleaner. Hence, most Americans thought Heinz should steal, whilst most Japanese thought he should not.

Eckensberger (1999) maintains that Kohlberg's theory is not as 'Western based' as some critics have claimed. For example, the highest stages can be found in India,

Taiwan and Israel. It appears to be the degree of 'complexity' (industrialisation) – and not 'Westernisation' – that assists the development to higher stages.

Nevertheless, cultural psychologists believe that instead of looking for universal moral stages, we should be trying to understand moral *diversity*. A focus on justice may be very far from some cultures' primary ethical concerns:

> 'If the researchers try to measure justice reasoning, rather than eliciting people's usual moral framework, stage scores may be misleading, but more importantly, the results would fail to give a true picture of people's moral lives'. (Haste *et al.*, 1998)

This criticism of Kohlberg's theory as being biased towards Western cultural ideals (*Eurocentrism*) mirrors a second major criticism, namely that it is biased in favour of males (*androcentrism*: see Chapter 55). Gilligan (1982, 1993) has argued that because Kohlberg's theory was based on an all-male sample, the stages reflect a male definition of morality.

Whilst men's morality is based on abstract principles of law and justice, women's is based on principles of compassion and care. In turn, the different 'moral orientations' of men and women rest on a deeper issue, namely how we think about selfhood. An ethic of justice (male) is a natural outcome of thinking of people as *separate* beings, in continual conflict with each other, who make rules and contracts as a way of handling it. An ethic of caring/responsibility (female) follows from regarding selves as being *in connection* with one another.

However, the claim that women 'think differently' about moral issues has been challenged. According to Johnston (1988), each sex is competent in each mode, but there are gender-linked preferences. Whilst boys tended to use a justice orientation, if pressed they would also use the care orientation. Similarly, girls preferred a care orientation, but also switched easily. According to Haste *et al.* (1998), these findings support Gilligan's argument that there is more than one moral 'voice', but not her claim that the 'caring' voice was more apparent amongst women. Several studies show that sex differences in moral orientations are less important than the *kind of dilemmas* being considered.

Key STUDY

Box 30.8 Are males and females morally different?

Walker (1989) studied a large sample of males and females, aged five to 63. Participants were scored for both moral stage and orientation on both hypothetical and personally generated, real-life dilemmas. The only evidence of sex differences was for adults on real-life dilemmas.

When asked to produce real-life dilemmas, females reported more *relational/personal* ones and males reported more *non-relational/impersonal* dilemmas (Walker *et al.*, 1987). A *relational/personal* conflict involves someone with whom the participant had a significant and continuing relationship (e.g. whether or not to tell a friend her husband was having an affair). A *non-relational/impersonal* conflict involves acquaintances or strangers (e.g. whether or not to correct a shop assistant's error in giving too much change). *Regardless* of sex, *personal/relational* dilemmas produced a *higher* level of response than *impersonal/non-relational* dilemmas. This is the *opposite* of what Gilligan claimed, namely that Kohlberg's stages are biased against an ethic of care (Walker, 1996).

Both males and females tended to use the ethic of care mostly in personal dilemmas, and most people used *both* orientations to a significant degree, with no clear focus or preference. According to Walker (1996), the nature of the dilemma is a better predictor of moral orientation than is sex.

Walker (1984, 1995) also refuted Gilligan's claim that Kohlberg's scoring system was biased against females, making them more likely to be rated at the conventional level, and men at the post-conventional level. He reviewed all the available research evidence relating to sex differences (80 studies, 152 distinct samples, and over 10,000 participants) and found that, regardless of age category, the typical pattern was one of *non-significant differences*. Once any educational or occupational differences favouring men were controlled for, there was no evidence of a systematic sex difference in moral stage scores.

Kohlberg has also been criticised for his emphasis on moral *thinking* based on quite unusual hypothetical dilemmas. Moral reasoning and *behaviour* are not necessarily correlated (Gibbs & Schnell, 1985). Whilst moral reasoning may determine moral talk, 'talk is cheap' (Blasi, 1980), and what we say and what we do when faced with a moral dilemma often differ, particularly under strong social pressure (see Gross *et al.*, 2000). Moral development research should really look at what people *do*, rather than what they *say* they would do (Mischel & Mischel, 1976).

The higher stages in Kohlberg's theory are associated with education and verbal ability (Shweder *et al.*, 1987). Whilst 'college-educated' people give higher-level and more mature explanations of moral decisions, this does not make them more moral than the non-college-educated. The former might simply be more verbally sophisticated. Nor is post-conventional morality necessarily superior to conventional morality (Shweder, 1991), and even Kohlberg (1978) acknowledges that there may not be a separate sixth stage.

Eisenberg's theory of prosocial moral reasoning

Kohlberg's concept of moral reasoning is *prohibition-oriented*. In the case of Heinz, for example, one prohibition (stealing) is pitted against another (allowing his wife to die). However, not all 'moral conflicts' are like this. Eisenberg (1982, 1986; Eisenberg *et al.*, 1991) argues that if we want to understand developmental changes in helping or altruism (see Chapter 8), we need to examine children's reasoning when faced with a conflict between their own needs and those of others, in a context where the role of laws, rules, and the dictates of authority are minimal. This describes *prosocial moral reasoning*.

In a series of studies during the 1980s, Eisenberg presented children of different ages (sometimes followed up to early adulthood) with illustrated hypothetical stories, in which the character can help another person, but at a personal cost.

> **Box 30.9 A hypothetical story used by Eisenberg to assess prosocial reasoning**
>
> A girl named Mary was going to a friend's birthday party. On her way, she saw a girl who had fallen down and hurt her leg. The girl asked Mary to go to her home and get her parents so the parents could take her to the doctor. But if Mary did run and get the child's parents, she would be late for the birthday party and miss the ice cream, cake and all the games.
>   What should Mary do? Why?

Based on children's responses to this and other similar dilemmas, Eisenberg identified six stages of prosocial moral reasoning.

Table 30.2 *Stages of prosocial moral reasoning (based on Eisenberg, 1982, 1986)*

Level 1 (hedonistic, self-focused orientation): The individual is concerned with selfish, pragmatic, consequences, rather than moral considerations. For example, 'She shouldn't help, because she might miss the party'. What is 'right' is whatever is instrumental in achieving the actor's own ends/desires. Reasons for helping/not helping include direct gain to the self, future reciprocity, and concern for others whom the individual needs and/or likes.

[This is the predominant mode for pre-schoolers and younger primary-schoolers.]

Table 30.2 *continued*

Level 2 (needs of others orientation): The individual expresses concern for the physical, material and psychological needs of others, even though these conflict with his/her own needs. For example, 'She should help, because the girl's leg is bleeding and she needs to go to the doctor'. This concern is expressed in the simplest terms, without clear evidence of self-reflective role-taking, verbal expressions of sympathy, or reference to internalised affect, such as guilt.

[This is the predominant mode for many pre-schoolers and primary-schoolers.]

Level 3 (approval and interpersonal orientation and/or stereotyped orientation): Stereotyped images of good and bad persons and behaviours and/or considerations of others' approval/acceptance are used in justifying prosocial or non-helping behaviours. For example, 'It's nice to help' or 'Her family would think she did the right thing'.

[This is the predominant mode for some primary-schoolers and secondary-school students.]

Level 4a (self–reflective empathic orientation): The individual's judgements include evidence of self-reflective sympathetic responding, role taking, concern with others' humanness, and/or guilt or positive affect related to the consequences of one's actions. For example, 'She cares about people', and 'She'd feel bad if she didn't help because she'd be in pain'.

[This is the predominant mode for a few older primary schoolers and many secondary school students].

Level 4b (transitional level): The individual's justifications for helping/not helping involve internalised values, norms, duties or responsibilities, or refer to the need to protect the rights and dignity of others. But these are not clearly or strongly stated. For example, 'It's just something she's learnt and feels'.

[This is the predominant mode for a minority of people of secondary school age and older.]

Level 5 (strongly internalised stage): As for 4b, but internalised values, norms etc., are much more strongly stated. Additional justifications for helping include the desire to honour individual and societal contractual obligations, improve the conditions of society, and belief in the dignity, rights and equality of all human beings. It is also characterised by the wish to maintain self-respect for living up to one's own values and accepted norms. For example, 'She'd feel a responsibility to help others in need' or 'She'd feel bad if she didn't help because she'd know she didn't live up to her values'.

[This is the predominant mode for a very small minority of secondary-school students and no primary-schoolers.]

An evaluation of Eisenberg's theory

In a review of her research, Eisenberg (1996) points out that, as predicted, children almost never said they would help in order to avoid punishment or because of blind obedience to authority, such as adults. This would be expected, given that children are seldom punished for *not* acting in a prosocial way (but are often punished *for* wrongdoing). This differs greatly from what has been found for prohibition-oriented moral reasoning.

Whilst for Kohlberg other-oriented reasoning emerges relatively late, Eisenberg expected to find it by the pre-school years. Even four- to five-year-olds appeared to frequently orient to others' needs and show what seemed to be primitive empathy. Also, references to empathy-related processes (such as taking the other's perspective and sympathising) are particularly common in prosocial moral reasoning.

Contrary to Kohlberg's claims, even individuals who typically used higher-level reasoning occasionally reverted to lower-level reasoning (such as egotistic, hedonistic reasoning). This was especially likely when they chose *not* to help, suggesting the influence of *situational variables*. These are also implicated by some cross-cultural studies. For example, children raised on Israeli kibbutzim are especially likely to emphasise reciprocity between people, whereas city children (Israeli and from the USA) are more likely to be concerned with personal costs for helping others. If individuals' moral reasoning can vary across situations, then there is likely to be only a modest relationship between their typical level of moral reasoning and their actual prosocial behaviour. This is supported by Eisenberg's research.

One additional factor that has been implicated is emotion, in particular, *empathy*. Whether or not children help others depends on the *type* of emotional response that others' distress induces in them (rather than *whether or not* they respond emotionally). People who respond sympathetically/empathically (associated with, for instance, *lowered* heart rate) are more likely to help than those who experience personal distress (associated with *accelerated* heart-rate). This is consistent with Batson's work with adults (e.g. Batson & Oleson, 1991: see Chapter 8).

According to Eckensberger (1999), emotions (especially *positive emotions*) are increasingly being seen as the basis for moral development. This represents a move away from Kohlberg's theory and a return to Piaget's, in which feelings of mutual respect and empathy were seen as central.

CONCLUSIONS

This chapter has considered three major theories of morality, all belonging to the cognitive–developmental approach. Whilst Piaget, Kohlberg and Eisenberg all emphasise moral judgement and reasoning, and despite Piaget's influence on Kohlberg, all three theories see moral development differently. Piaget identified two major types of morality that change during childhood and adolescence, whilst Kohlberg identified six stages that develop through into adulthood. Eisenberg was concerned with stages of prosocial reasoning.

Summary

- **Cognitive–developmental theories** of moral development try to explain how we come to understand moral rules and principles as the basis for our moral judgements. It is the reasons **underlying** behaviour, rather than the behaviour itself, which makes it right or wrong.

- Piaget called five- to nine-year-olds' morality **heteronomous**. It is associated with **unilateral respect**, **objective/external responsibility**, **moral realism**, and belief in **expiatory punishment** and **immanent justice**. The morality of children over ten is **autonomous**, which is associated with **mutual respect**, **internal responsibility**, the **principle of reciprocity** and **moral relativism**.

- The change from heteronomous to autonomous occurs due to the shift from egocentric to operational thought, and freedom from unilateral respect and adult constraint to mutual respect within the peer group.

- Although children's understanding of **intention** is much more complex than Piaget believed, many of the **age trends** he described have been supported by later research. This includes cross-cultural studies, mainly from Africa.

- Piaget did not expect that children from different cultures would necessarily all develop in the same way. Much current cross-cultural research, such as Lee *et al.*'s study of lying and truth-telling, indicates that moral development is a highly **contextualised** process.

- Like Piaget, **Kohlberg** was interested in how moral thinking changes with age. He identified six qualitatively different **stages** in moral development, spanning three basic **levels** of moral reasoning: **pre-conventional**, **conventional** and **post-conventional morality**.

- Despite extensive empirical support for the sequence and universality of the (first four) stages, the **socio-cultural approach** maintains that **cultural factors** play a significant part in moral reasoning. For Kohlberg, the focus is what takes place within the individual's head.

- Kohlberg's theory has been criticised for its bias towards **Western** cultures. Ethical principles such as justice, equality, integrity and reverence for life are **not** universally held. Conversely, some societies have developed moral principles not covered by Kohlberg's theory.

- Gilligan regards Kohlberg's stages as based on a **male** definition of morality (an ethic of justice), with women's ethic of care/responsibility being largely ignored. Consequently, women are rated as being at the conventional level, whilst men are at the post-conventional level.

- However, both males and females are capable of using **both** types of moral orientation, and several studies show that sex differences are less important than the **kind of dilemmas** being considered. Nor is there any convincing evidence of a systematic sex difference in moral stage scores.

- Kohlberg has also been criticised for overemphasising moral **thinking**, which may not be a very accurate predictor of moral **behaviour**. Also, those who attain the highest stages may simply be more verbally sophisticated, rather than more moral, and a separate stage 6 may not even exist.

- Whilst Kohlberg's theory is **prohibition-oriented**, Eisenberg concentrates on the development of **prosocial moral reasoning**. Based on her use of hypothetical stories, she identified six stages: **hedonistic/self-focused orientation**, **needs of others orientation**, **approval and interpersonal orientation and/or stereotyped orientation**, **self-reflective empathic orientation**, **transitional level**, and **strongly internalised stage**.

- Many of the predictions derived from Eisenberg's theory have been supported, such as the finding that children rarely say they would help someone in order to avoid punishment. Her research has also indicated that **situational variables** influence moral reasoning which, in turn, suggests only a modest relationship between moral reasoning and actual prosocial behaviour.

- Emotion, especially **empathy**, is also thought to influence whether or not children help others. This and other **positive emotions** are becoming increasingly important in explanations of moral development.

Essay Questions

1 a Describe **one** theory of the development of moral understanding. (*12 marks*)

   b Evaluate this theory using alternative theories **and/or** research studies. (*12 marks*)

2 Critically consider the influence of gender **and/or** cultural variations in the development of moral understanding. (*24 marks*)

WEB ADDRESSES

http://www.awa.com/w2/erotic_computing/Kohlberg.stages.html
http://www.uk.eduInucci/MoralEd/overview.html
http://www.cortland.edu/www/c4n5rs/home.htm
http://www.unikonstanz.de/SIG-MDE/
http://www.nd-edu/~rbarger/Kohlberg.html

31 *Personality Development*

INTRODUCTION AND OVERVIEW

When psychologists use the term 'personality', they are usually trying to describe ways in which people are different. According to Bee (2000), 'personality' describes those *enduring individual differences* in how children and adults go about relating to the people and objects in the world around them. However, she believes that we also need to understand the *common developmental patterns* which children experience.

If 'development' implies systematic changes associated with age, then some of the theories that are commonly discussed as theories of personality development are not, strictly, developmental theories at all (e.g. social learning theory). Others (such as psychodynamic theories) stress these common patterns (or stages), with the result that individual differences become overshadowed.

This chapter considers two major psychodynamic theories of personality development, namely Freud's *psychoanalytic theory* and Erikson's *psychosocial theory*. After discussing the similarities and differences between them, it then examines Bandura's *social learning theory*. The chapter begins, however, by looking at the concept of *temperament* and its relationship to personality

TEMPERAMENT AND PERSONALITY

According to Bee (2000), the great bulk of research into individual differences in infants' and children's styles of interacting with the world has been couched in terms of temperament, *not* personality. A number of different classifications of temperament have been proposed. The best known are *easy*, *difficult* and *slow-to-warm-up* (Thomas & Chess, 1977), *emotionality*, *activity* and *sociability* (Buss & Plomin, 1984), and *behavioural inhibition* (Kagan *et al.*, 1990).

Whichever classification is favoured, it is generally agreed that temperament is genetically determined. However, what we inherit is *not*, say, a high level of emotionality, but rather a nervous system with a low threshold of arousal. Temperamental differences tend to persist through childhood and into adulthood, but the individual's *personality* is the product of an *interaction* between inborn temperament and the environment the child encounters or creates. Temperamental differences between infants and children can influence other people's responses to them, but temperament can also influence what an infant or child *chooses* to experience and how it *interprets* any particular experience (see Chapter 59).

So, whilst a child is born with certain behavioural and emotional tendencies, its eventual personality depends on the transaction between these and its environment. However, theories of temperament fail to tell us how these inborn individual differences may interact with *common developmental patterns*. These are the focus of psychodynamic theories.

PSYCHODYNAMIC THEORIES OF PERSONALITY

Gross *et al.* (2000) define 'psychodynamic' theories as those which focus on the active forces within the personality that motivate behaviour, and the inner causes of behaviour, in particular the unconscious conflict between the various personality structures. Whilst Freud's was the original psychodynamic theory, all those theories based on his ideas are also psychodynamic. Although all psychodynamic theories are concerned with personality development, this is dealt with most directly and explicitly by Freud (*psychosexual stages*) and Erikson (*psychosocial stages*).

Freud's psychoanalytic theory

Freud's account of personality development (e.g. 1923) is closely related to other aspects of his psychoanalytic theory, in particular the structure of the personality and motivation (see Gross *et al.,* 2000).

The psychic apparatus

Freud believed that the personality (or *psychic apparatus*) comprises three parts, the id, ego and superego. The id:

> '... contains everything that is inherited, that is present at birth, that is laid down in the constitution – above all, therefore, the instincts' (Freud, 1923)

The wishes and impulses arising from the body's needs build up a pressure or tension (*excitation*), which demands immediate release or satisfaction. Since the id's sole aim is to reduce excitation to a minimum, it is said to be governed by the *pleasure principle*. It is – and remains – the infantile, pre-socialised part of the personality. The two major id instincts are sexuality and aggression.

The ego is:

> '... that part of the id which has been modified by the direct influence of the external world.' (Freud, 1923)

It can be thought of as the 'executive' of the personality, the planning, decision-making, rational and logical part of us. It enables us to distinguish between a wish and reality (which the id cannot do), and is governed by the *reality principle*. Whilst the id demands immediate gratification of our needs and impulses, the ego will postpone satisfaction until the appropriate time and place (*deferred gratification*):

> 'The ego seeks to bring the influence of the external world to bear upon the id and its tendencies ... For the ego, perception plays the part which in the id falls to instinct. The ego represents ... reason and common sense, in contrast to the id, which contains the passions'. (Freud, 1923)

Not until the *superego* has developed can we be described as moral beings. It represents the *internalisation* of parental and social moral values:

> 'It observes the ego, gives it orders, judges it and threatens it with punishment, exactly like the parents whose place it has taken'. (Freud, 1933)

It is in fact the *conscience* which threatens the ego with punishment (in the form of guilt) for bad behaviour, whilst the *ego-ideal* promises the ego rewards (in the form of pride and high self-esteem) for good behaviour. These correspond to the *punishing* and *rewarding parent* respectively.

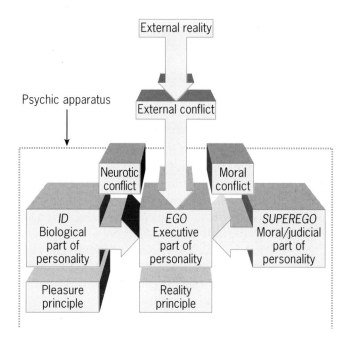

Figure 31.1 *The relationship between the id, ego and superego*

Psychosexual development

Although the id, ego and superego develop within the individual in that order, this is not strictly part of Freud's developmental theory. According to his theory of *infantile sexuality*, sexuality is not confined to physically mature adults, but is evident from the moment of birth. So, babies and young children have sexual experiences and are capable of sexual pleasure, which is derived from the rhythmical stroking or stimulation of any part of the body. However, *different* parts of the body (the *erogenous zones*) are particularly sensitive at different times during infancy and childhood, and become the focus of sexual pleasure (and frustration).

Whilst the sequence of these *psychosexual stages* is determined by *maturation* (biologically programmed), what is crucial is how a child is treated by others, especially the parents. Both excessive gratification *and* extreme frustration can result in an individual getting emotionally 'stuck' (*fixated*) at the particular stage at which this occurs, producing associated *adult personality traits*. For example, an *anal expulsive* trait is orderliness (a preoccupation with punctuality, routine, and everything being in its proper place), whilst *anal retentive* traits include parsimony (miserliness) and obstinacy. In this way, Freud was able to explain how individual differences arise from common developmental patterns (see the *Introduction and overview*).

Box 31.1 Freud's stages of psychosexual development

- **Oral stage (0–1 year):** The nerve-endings in the mouth and lips are highly sensitive, and the baby derives pleasure from sucking for its own sake (*nonnutritive sucking*). In the earlier *incorporative sub-stage*, the major oral activities are sucking, swallowing and mouthing. In the later *biting/aggressive sub-stage*, hardening gums and erupting teeth make biting and chewing sources of pleasure.

- **Anal stage (1–3 years):** The anal cavity and sphincter muscles of the bowel are now the main source of pleasure. In the earlier *expulsion sub-stage*, the child has its first encounter with external restrictions on its wish to defecate where and when it pleases, in the form of parents trying to potty-train it. Parental love is no longer unconditional, but now depends on what the child does. In the later *retention sub-stage*, parents come to be seen for the first time as authority figures:

  'By producing them [the contents of the bowels] ... [the infant] can express his active compliance with his environment, and by withholding them, his disobedience'. (Freud, 1905)

- **Phallic stage (3–5/6 years):** Sensitivity is now concentrated in the genitals, and masturbation (in both sexes) becomes a new source of pleasure. The child becomes aware of anatomical sex differences ('*phallic*' comes from the Greek word 'phallus' meaning penis), which marks the beginning of the *Oedipus complex*. The name derives from the classical Greek tragedy *Oedipus Rex*, in which Oedipus kills his father and marries his mother. Both boys and girls experience conflicting emotions in relation to their same- and opposite-sex parents, and how successfully these are resolved is crucial for future personality development. It is through the resolution of the Oedipus complex that a child's superego and sex role are acquired.

- **Latency period (5/6–puberty):** The sexual preoccupations of the earlier years are repressed, which allows the child's energies to be channelled into developing new skills and acquiring new knowledge. In relative terms, the balance between the id, ego and superego is greater than at any other time in the child's life.

- **Genital stage (puberty–maturity):** Latency represents the calm before the storm of puberty, which marks the beginning of adolescence. The relative harmony within the child's personality is disrupted by the id's powerful new demands in the form of heterosexual desires (see Chapter 33).

The Oedipus complex, identification and the superego

Boys, like girls, take their mothers as their first love-object (see Gross *et al.*, 2000). Starting at about three, a boy's love for his mother becomes increasingly passionate, and he does not wish to share her with anyone. The boy is also jealous of his father who already 'possesses' her and wants him out of the way ('dead'), so that he can have the mother all to himself. However, his father is bigger and more powerful than he is, and he eventually becomes afraid that his father will punish him by cutting off his penis (*fear of castration/castration anxiety*). He reaches this conclusion partly as a result of previous punishments for masturbation, and partly based on his observation that females do not have a penis.

To resolve the dilemma, the boy *represses* (makes unconscious) his desire for his mother and his hostile feelings for his father, and *identifies* with his father (he comes to act, think and feel as if he were his father). Through this *identification with the aggressor*, boys acquire the superego and the male sex role (see Chapter 32).

Figure 31.2 *Norman Bates (Anthony Perkins), the main character in Hitchcock's* Psycho, *identified very strongly with his dead mother. He attempted, unconsciously, to 'keep her alive' by, for example, dressing up in her clothes*

As for the girl, her Oedipus complex (sometimes referred to as the *Electra complex*) *begins* with the belief that she has already been castrated. She blames her mother for her lack of a penis, and experiences *penis envy* (she wants what males have). However, she eventually realises that this is unrealistic and substitutes the wish for a penis with the wish for a baby. This causes her to turn to her father as a love-object, in the hope that he will provide her with a (preferably male) baby.

In order to identify with the mother, the girl must give up her father as a love-object and move *back* to her mother (whilst boys only have to make one 'move', from the mother to the father). However, Freud was much less sure about *why* the girl identifies with the mother than he was about the boy's motive for identifying with the father. The stronger the motive, the stronger (or more complete) the identification, which in turn makes for a stronger superego. So, boys' fear of castration is associated with a strong identification with the father (the 'aggressor') and a strong superego. As Freud (1924) says:

> 'The fear of castration being thus excluded in a little girl, a powerful motive also drops out for the setting up of a superego'.

One suggestion Freud made was that the girl may fear loss of the mother's love. To keep the mother 'alive' inside her, she internalises her, becoming the 'good' child that her mother would want her to be (*anaclitic identification*). What he was quite sure about, however, was that identification with the mother is *less* complete. The girl's love for her father does not have to be as thoroughly abandoned as the boy's for his mother, and her Oedipus complex does not have to be so completely shattered (Mitchell, 1974). Consequently, females have weaker superegos *and* their identities as separate, independent persons are also less well developed.

Box 31.2 Are females morally and sexually inferior to men?

Because her identification with the mother is less complete, the girl relies more on external authority figures throughout her childhood, and has to be more compliant, and less 'naughty' (there is no equivalent of 'boys will be boys'). It is through his strong identification with the father that the boy achieves independence, which the girl will have to try to achieve in adolescence. According to Mitchell (1974):

> 'Many women, though nominally they leave home, understandably, never make it'.

However, there is little evidence to support this view. For example, Hoffman (1975) reviewed several studies in which children were left alone and tempted to violate a prohibition (such as look round to see a toy placed on a table behind them). There were usually no overall gender differences, but, if anything, girls were *better* able to resist temptation than boys were.

As noted, Freud saw women as having to make do with babies as penis-substitutes, a view that has aroused fierce criticism, particularly from feminist psychologists (see Chapter 55). For example, Horney (1924) and Thompson (1943), both eminent psychoanalysts, argued that what girls (and women) envy is *not* the penis as such, but males' superior social status (the penis is a *symbol* for male privilege). Moreover, it is *men*, not women, who equate lack of a penis with inferiority!

An evaluation of the Oedipus complex

Box 31.2 has considered some of the criticisms of Freud's account of sex differences in morality which follows from his theory of the Oedipus complex ('the central phenomenon of the sexual period of early childhood': Freud, 1924). Another criticism concerns its potential *cultural bias*. Freud assumed that the Oedipus complex was a *universal* phenomenon, but even if true for Western cultures, the Oedipus complex may not apply to every culture or to all historical periods (Segall *et al.*, 1990).

Key STUDY

Box 31.3 Malinowski's (1929) study of the Trobriand Islanders

Among the Trobriand Islanders of Papua, New Guinea, boys, traditionally, were disciplined by their maternal uncles (their mother's brother), rather than by their own biological fathers. It was an uncle's role to guide his nephew through to adulthood, and such societies are described as *avuncular*. However, the father remained the mother's lover. Hence, the two roles (disciplinarian and mother's lover) were adopted by *different* men, whereas in Viennese society at the time that Freud was proposing his theories, the boy's father played *both* roles.

As Segall *et al.* (1990) point out, by explaining the boy's hostility towards the father wholly in terms of sexual jealousy, Freud overlooked the possibility that he resented his father's power over him. What Malinowski found was that a Trobriand Island boy's relationship with his father was very good, free of the love–hate ambivalence which is central to Freud's Oedipus theory. By comparison, the relationship with the uncle was not usually so good.

However, this does not necessarily mean that Malinowski was right and Freud was wrong (Price & Crapo, 1999). Segall *et al.* (1990) suggest that more societies need to be examined, including both Western and avuncular.

Freud (1909) cited his case study of 'Little Hans' as supporting his Oedipal theory. This five-year-old developed a phobia of being bitten by a horse, which Freud interpreted as a fear of castration (see Chapter 51). A common criticism made of Freud's developmental theory as a whole is that it was based largely on the study of his *adult* patients. This makes the case of Little Hans especially important, because he was Freud's only *child* patient.

However, Freud saw Hans as a 'little Oedipus', having formulated his theory four years earlier (in *Three Essays on the Theory of Sexuality*, 1905). Hence, the case study is biased and provides no *independent* evidence to support Freud. In addition, Hans's therapy was conducted mainly by his own father, a supporter of Freud's ideas! Even more seriously, perhaps, other psychoanalytic theorists have provided alternative explanations of Hans's fear of horses, including Bowlby's (1973) reinterpretation in terms of attachment theory (see Gross, 1999).

According to Bee (2000), attachment research provides a good deal of support for the basic psychoanalytic hypothesis that the quality of the child's earliest relationships affects the whole course of later development. Both Bowlby (1973) and Erikson (1963: see below) regard early relationships as *prototypes* of later relationships. Despite the considerable evidence showing that all types of early privation are reversible (see Gross *et al.*, 2000), and accepting all the criticisms of the Oedipal theory, belief in the impact of early experience is a lasting legacy of Freud's developmental theory.

Erikson's psychosocial theory

Similarities and differences between Erikson and Freud

Erikson trained as a psychoanalyst under the supervision of Anna Freud, Sigmund Freud's daughter. She was much more interested in child analysis than her father had been, and this in turn influenced Erikson. He accepted Freud's *tripartite* theory of the structure of personality (id, ego, superego), and regarded the psychosexual stages of development as basically valid – as far as they went. However, for Erikson they did not go far enough. Because Freud saw personality development as inseparable from the development of the sexual instinct, once physical/sexual maturation is complete so

is personality development. Hence, there are five stages of psychosexual development (see Box 31.1, page 334), the last (genital) beginning with puberty and ending with sexual maturity.

Erikson, together with many other *neo-Freudians* argued that Freud *overemphasised* the role of sexuality, and largely neglected the influence of social and cultural factors in development. Since the latter continue to influence development throughout a person's life, what happens to us during the first five or six years is far less crucial (*deterministic*) in Erikson's theory than it is in Freud's. Erikson identifies eight *psychosocial stages* (the 'Eight Ages of Man' were originally proposed in 1950), the first five of which correspond to Freud's psychosexual stages. These are shown in Table 31.1.

Table 31.1 *Comparison between Erikson's and Freud's stages of development (based on Thomas, 1985; Erikson, 1950)*

No. of stage	Name of stage (psycho-social crisis)	Psycho-social modalities (dominant modes of being and acting)	Radius of significant relation-ships	Human virtues (qualities of strength)	Freud's psycho-sexual stages	Approx. ages
1	Basic trust versus basic mistrust	To get. To give in return	Mother or mother-figure	Hope	Oral	0–1
2	Autonomy versus shame and doubt	To hold on. To let go	Parents	Willpower	Anal	1–3
3	Initiative versus guilt	To make (going after). To 'make like' (playing)	Basic family	Purpose	Phallic	3–6
4	Industry versus inferiority	To make things. (completing) To make things together	Neighbour-hood and school	Competence	Latency	6–12
5	Identity versus role confusion	To be oneself (or not to be). To share being oneself	Peer groups and outgroups. Models of leadership	Fidelity	Genital	12–18
6	Intimacy versus isolation	To lose and find oneself in another	Partners in friendship, sex, competition, co-operation	Love		20s
7	Generativity versus stagnation	To make be. To take care of	Divided labour and shared household	Care		Late 20s –50s
8	Ego integrity versus despair	To be, through having been. To face not being	'Human-kind', 'my kind'	Wisdom		50s and beyond

According to Erikson's *epigenetic principle* (based on embryology), it is human nature to pass through a fixed, genetically predetermined sequence of stages. However, the sociocultural environment has a significant influence on the psychosocial modalities, the radius of significant relationships and institutions with which the individual interacts, and the nature of the psychosocial crisis at each stage.

As shown in Table 31.1 (see page 336), each stage centres around a developmental crisis involving a struggle between two opposing or conflicting personality characteristics. The first refers to the positive or functional (*adaptive*) outcome (e.g. trust), and the second to the negative or dysfunctional (*maladaptive*) outcome (e.g. mistrust). However, these are *not* either/or alternatives: every personality represents some mixture of trust and mistrust (and similarly for the other seven stages). Healthy development involves the adaptive quality outweighing the maladaptive (e.g. *more* trust than mistrust), so what matters is achieving the right balance.

Although the optimum time for developing a sense of trust, say, is during infancy, Erikson argued that it is possible to make up for unsatisfactory early experience at a later stage. However, this becomes increasingly difficult, since the individual will be facing *that* stage's conflict as well as the one being carried over. Conversely, a sense of trust acquired during infancy could be shattered, or at least shaken, if the child subsequently suffers deprivation (e.g. parental divorce: see Gross *et al.*, 2000). Either way, Erikson presents a much less deterministic view of development than Freud.

Basic trust versus basic mistrust (0–1)

The quality of care the baby receives determines how it comes to view its mother in particular and the world (including other people) in general: is it a safe, predictable, comfortable place to be, or is it full of danger and uncertainty? This is linked to the baby's ability to influence what happens to it, and hence to its trust in itself. If the baby's needs are met promptly and its discomforts quickly removed, if it is cuddled, played with and talked to, it develops a sense of the world as safe and of people as helpful and dependable (*trust*).

However, if its care is inconsistent and unpredictable it develops a sense of *mistrust*, fear and suspicion. These may take the form of apathy or withdrawn behaviour, reflecting a sense of being controlled and unable to influence what happens to it. A healthy balance of trust/mistrust allows the baby to accept fear of the unknown as part and parcel of having new experiences.

Autonomy versus shame and doubt (1–3)

The child's cognitive and muscle systems are maturing, making it more mobile and expanding its range of experiences and choices. The child is also beginning to think of itself as a person in its own right, separate from its parents and with a new sense of power. This is the basis for the child's growing sense of *autonomy* or independence. The child wants to do everything for itself, and parents have to allow it to exercise these new abilities. At the same time, they must ensure that the child does not 'bite off more than it can chew', since repeated failures and ridicule from others can induce a sense of *shame* and *doubt*.

The child must be allowed to do things at its own pace. Parents should not impatiently do things for it 'to save time', or criticise the child for its failures and the inevitable accidents. These accidents – and the stage as a whole – may become focused on toilet training. If this is too strict or starts too early, the child may feel powerless to control either its bowels or its parents' actions. This may result in a regression to oral activities (e.g. thumb-sucking), attention-seeking, or a pretence at autonomy by rejecting others' help and becoming very strong-willed.

Initiative versus guilt (3–6)

Physical, cognitive and social development are all happening very fast and the child is keen to try out its new abilities and skills. Its sense of *initiative* will be reinforced by being encouraged to ask questions and in other ways express its natural curiosity, being allowed to engage in physical activity, and indulge in fantasy and other kinds of play.

However, if parents find the child's questions embarrassing, intellectually difficult or a nuisance, its motor activity dangerous and its fantasy-play silly, then the child may come to feel *guilty* about intruding into other people's lives. This may inhibit the child's initiative and curiosity. Erikson believed that this guilt can be exaggerated by the Oedipus complex, but this merely represents one feature of a much wider picture. For Freud, as noted earlier, it was the core feature of this stage.

Industry versus inferiority (6–12)

Industry refers to the child's concern with how things work and how they are made, as well as its own efforts to make things. This is reinforced when the child is encouraged by parents and other adults, such as teachers, who begin to assume a very real significance in the child's life.

The peer group also assumes increasing importance. Children compare themselves with each other as a way of assessing their own achievements, and unfavourable comparisons can threaten the child's self-esteem. Unsuccessful completion of realistic tasks, not being allowed to make things, and not receiving the necessary guidance and encouragement from adults can all contribute to a sense of *inferiority*.

Identity versus role confusion (12–18) is discussed in Chapter 33 in relation to adolescence. *Intimacy versus isolation* (the twenties) and *generativity versus stagnation* (late twenties to fifties) relate to early and middle adulthood respectively, and are considered in Chapter 34. Finally, *ego integrity* (fifties and beyond) is looked at in relation to late adulthood in Chapter 36. Although in many ways an advance on Freud's developmental theory, Erikson's theory has itself come in for much criticism, including its gender bias (see Chapter 34, page 365, and Chapter 55).

SOCIAL LEARNING THEORY

Social learning theories (SLTs), such as those of Bandura (1977a) and Mischel (1973), originated in the USA in the 1940s and 1950s. They were an attempt to reinterpret certain aspects of Freud's psychoanalytic theory in terms of *conditioning theory* (classical and operant conditioning: see Chapter 38). In the 1960s and 1970s, Bandura and his colleagues tried to make Freud's concept of identification (see pages 334–335) more objective by studying it experimentally in the form of *imitation*. More specifically, many of these experiments were concerned with *aggression* (see Box 31.4 and Chapter 7), but SLT has been applied to many aspects of development, such as gender (see Chapter 32) and morality. This focus on *human social behaviour* is one feature that sets SLT apart from conditioning (or orthodox learning) theory.

Figure 31.3 *This father is modelling behaviour which his daughters are learning spontaneously, i.e. observing his behaviour is the crucial factor, rather than being directly reinforced for 'doing the dishes'*

Some important similarities and differences between SLT and orthodox learning theory

- Whilst SL theorists agree that all behaviour is learned according to the same learning principles, they are interested specifically in *human learning*.

- Although SL theorists agree that we should observe what is observable, they also believe that there are important cognitive or *mediating variables* which intervene between stimulus and response, and without which we cannot adequately explain human behaviour (see Box 31.5, pages 339–340).

- SL theorists emphasise *observational learning* or *modelling* (learning through watching the behaviour of others, called *models*). This occurs spontaneously, with no deliberate effort by the learner, or any intention by the model to teach anything.

Observational learning takes place without any reinforcement – mere exposure to the model is sufficient for learning to occur (Bandura, 1965). However, whether the model's behaviour is imitated depends partly on the *consequences* of the behaviour, both for the model and the learner. Reinforcement is important only in so far as it affects *performance* (not the learning itself: see Box 31.4).

Key STUDY

Box 31.4 Bandura's (1965) demonstration of learning versus performance

Bandura (1965) showed three groups of children a film of an adult behaving aggressively towards a bobo doll (a large, inflatable bounce-back toy, as shown in Figure 31.4).

Figure 31.4
- **Group A (control)** saw the adult kicking, pummelling and punching the bobo doll.

- **Group B (model-rewarded)** saw what group A saw, but a second adult appeared near the end of the film and commended the model's aggressive behaviour. Sweets and lemonade were offered to the model.

- **Group C (model-punished)** also saw the same filmed aggression, but this time a second adult scolded the model and warned against further aggression.

So, the only difference between the three groups was the *consequences for the model* of his/her aggression.

After the film, all the children (one by one) went into a playroom, which contained a large number of toys, including a bobo doll and a mallet. They were observed for ten minutes and the number of acts of *imitative aggression* was recorded for each child. Whilst group C children showed *significantly fewer* aggressive acts than groups A and B, there was no difference between these two groups. This suggests that *vicarious punishment* is more powerful than *vicarious reinforcement*.

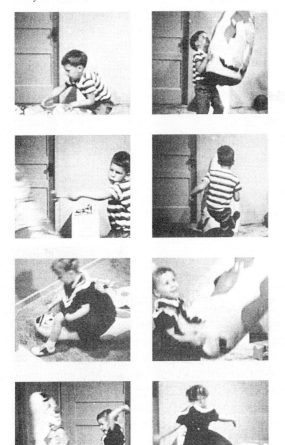

Figure 31.5 *After watching a film of an aggressive model who punched, kicked and hurled a bobo doll, these children spontaneously imitated the model's aggression*

More importantly, all the children were later asked to reproduce as much of the model's behaviour as they could, and were directly rewarded for each act of imitative aggression. Under these conditions, all three groups showed the *same* high levels of imitative aggression. This shows that group C children must have attended to and remembered the model's behaviour (i.e. *learned* from the model) to the same extent as those in groups A and B. However, this learning had not been apparent in their *performance* when they were originally observed, but only after receiving direct reinforcement. Hence, reinforcement (either vicarious or direct) was not needed for learning (acquisition), but it was for imitation (performance).

Reinforcement as information about the future

Bandura (1977a) challenged Skinner's claim that reinforcements and punishments *automatically* strengthen and weaken behaviour (see Chapter 38). For Bandura:

> 'Reinforcement serves principally as an informative and motivational operation rather than as a mechanical response strengthener'.

Reinforcement provides the learner with *information* about the likely consequences of certain behaviour under certain conditions, that is, it improves our prediction of whether a given action will lead to pleasant (reinforcement) or unpleasant (punishment) outcomes in the *future*. It also *motivates* us by causing us to anticipate future outcomes. Our present behaviours are largely governed by the outcomes we *expect* them to have, and we are more likely to try to learn the modelled behaviour if we value its consequences.

The role of cognitive factors in observational learning

The learning process is much more complex for Bandura than it is for Skinner, for whom 'the mind' had no part to play in a scientific psychology (see Gross *et al.*, 2000). In Bandura's (1974) view:

> 'Contrary to mechanistic metaphors, outcomes change behaviour in humans through the intervening influence of thought'.

Box 31.5 Five cognitive/mediating variables influencing the likelihood of learning and/or performance

- The learner must pay *attention* to the relevant clues and ignore those aspects of the model and the environment that are incidental and irrelevant (see Chapter 19). Attention can be influenced by the model's distinctiveness, attractiveness or power (whether or not the model's behaviour has *functional value* for the learner), the learner's level of arousal, and expectations about the model.

- A *visual image* or *semantic code* for the modelled behaviour is recorded in memory. Without an adequate coding system, the learner will fail to store what has been seen or heard (see Gross *et al.*, 2000). Whereas infants are largely confined to immediate imitation, older children can defer imitation because of their superior use of symbols (see Chapter 28).

- *Memory permanence* refers to devices such as rehearsal and organisation, and use of multiple codes to help retain the stored information over long periods (again see Gross *et al.*, 2000).

- *Reproducing the observed motor activities* accurately usually requires several trials to get the muscular 'feel' of the behaviour. Older children enjoy greater muscular strength and control.

- *Motivation* refers to the role of reinforcement, which can be *direct* (as when the child is praised by an adult), *vicarious* (as when a child sees another child being praised: see Box 31.4, pages 338–339) or *self-reinforcement* (as when the child praises itself/feels pleased with itself).

Is SLT a developmental theory?

As noted in Box 31.5, *changes* take place in cognitive or mediating processes as children get older. However, Durkin (1995) believes that these processes essentially apply at *any* age, which means that the theory is not a true theory of development. Bandura resists the notion of a general structural reorganisation of the kind proposed by Piaget (see Chapter 28), and so he fails to take account of cognitive *development* (Grusec, 1992). As Bee (2000) points out, SLT can say how a child might acquire a particular behaviour pattern, but it does not take into account the underlying developmental changes that are occurring. For example, do three-year-olds and ten-year-olds typically learn the same amount or in the same way from modelling? As Bee (2000) notes:

> 'Given Bandura's emphasis on cognitive aspects of the modelling process, a genuinely developmental social learning theory could be proposed, although no such theory now exists'.

Indeed, the importance of cognitive factors is reflected in Bandura's (1986, 1989) re-naming of SLT as *social cognitive theory*. Other important cognitive processes are those relating to the *self*.

Box 31.6 Self-concept, self-monitoring, and self-efficacy

According to Bandura, children learn both overt behaviour/concrete skills and information, and also abstract skills and information through modelling. Indeed, *abstract modelling* is part of his 'social cognitive theory' (1986, 1989). For example, the 'rule' underlying a model's behaviour can be extracted from observing the behaviour, without the rule being made explicit or articulated. In this way, the child can acquire attitudes, values, expectancies, ways of solving problems, and standards of self-evaluation.

By incorporating (or *internalising*) societal standards into its self, the child can monitor its own behaviours in terms of these standards. This *self-monitoring* ensures that behaviour is regulated even in the absence of reinforcement. Indeed, according to Bandura (1971), 'There is no more devastating punishment than self-contempt'; that is, we are our own harshest critics. This mirrors Freud's view of the young child's superego, which is often more punitive than the parents it has replaced (see page 333).

Another internalised standard or expectancy is *self-efficacy*. This refers to our belief that we can act effectively and exercise some control over events that influence our lives (Bandura, 1977a, 1986). This is crucially important for motivation, since how we judge our own capabilities is likely to affect our expectations about future behaviour. For example, if we feel that a model's actions are within our capabilities, then we may attempt to imitate them, but a low sense of self-efficacy regarding the modelled skill is likely to inhibit us (Durkin, 1995).

An evaluation of Bandura's SLT

One of the strengths of Bandura's SLT (and other versions, such as that of Mischel, 1973) is that behaviour can only be understood by taking the actor's self-concept, self-monitoring, self-efficacy and other mediating variables into account. However, these internal processes do not constitute 'personality', a concept which most SL theorists tend to dismiss (Durkin, 1995). Nevertheless, they make the theory far less mechanistic than Skinner's, for example, which focuses entirely on external events. For Bandura (1973):

> 'The environment is only a potentiality, not a fixed property that inevitably impinges upon individuals and to which their behaviour eventually adapts. Behaviour partly creates the environment and the resultant environment, in turn, influences the behaviour'.

This view is called *reciprocal determinism* (Bandura, 1977a, 1986). People are both products *and* producers of their environment (see Chapter 59).

Strictly, none of the theories discussed in this chapter is concerned with personality, since this is usually defined in terms of individual differences. Most research into individual differences in infancy and childhood has focused on temperament, rather than personality.

Freud's psychoanalytic theory laid the foundations for the psychodynamic approach as a whole. Whilst Erikson shared many of Freud's basic ideas, there are also some fundamental differences between them. This is reflected in Erikson's description of *psychosocial* stages of development, which incorporate but go well beyond Freud's *psychosexual* stages. Similarly, Bandura's SLT has its roots in conditioning theories, such as Skinner's, but his emphasis on *observational learning* and *cognitive* factors that mediate between observed behaviour and imitation represent a radically different view of learning.

Summary

- **Personality** refers to **enduring individual differences**. Theories of personality development are either not strictly developmental theories at all (such as SLT), or are more concerned with common developmental patterns (stages) than individual differences (such as psychodynamic theories).

- Most research into individual differences in infants and children has looked at **temperament** rather than personality. Temperament is genetically determined, but personality is the product of an **interaction** between inborn temperament and environmental influences. Theories of temperament fail to consider interactions between inborn differences and **common developmental patterns**.

- All **psychodynamic** theories stem from Freud's **psychoanalytic theory**. According to Freud, the **psychic apparatus** consists of the **id**, **ego** and **superego**. The id and the ego are governed by the **pleasure principle** and **reality principle** respectively. The superego comprises the **conscience** and **ego-ideal**, representing the **punishing** and **rewarding parent** respectively.

- According to Freud's theory of **infantile sexuality**, sexuality is evident from birth. A different **erogenous zone** is the focus during each stage of **psychosexual development**. Too much or too little gratification at any particular stage can cause **fixation** at that stage, resulting in associated **adult personality traits**.

- The **oral stage** (0–1) is sub-divided into the **incorporative** and **biting/aggressive** sub-stages, and the **anal stage** (1–3) comprises the **expulsion** and **retention** sub-stages. The **phallic stage** (3–5/6) is when the **Oedipus complex** occurs, followed by the **latency period** (5/6–puberty) and the **genital stage** (puberty to maturity).

- A boy's Oedipus complex **ends** when he identifies with his father (**identification with the aggressor**), motivated by his **fear of castration/castration anxiety**. Since a girl's Oedipus complex **begins** with her belief that she has already been castrated, Freud found it difficult to explain her identification with her mother. One suggestion was **anaclitic identification**.

- Freud argued that the girl's less complete identification with her mother will result in a weaker superego and sense of separate identity compared with boys. However, there is no supporting evidence for this claim, and **penis envy** has been reinterpreted as envy of men's superior social status.

- Malinowski's study of Trobriand Islanders suggests that the Oedipus complex is **not** universal, contrary to Freud's claim. Freud's own main evidence was the case of Little Hans, which was seriously flawed and has been reinterpreted by others, such as Bowlby.

- Whilst Erikson shared many of Freud's basic ideas, he felt that the psychosexual stages could not explain how development continues beyond physical/sexual maturity. His eight **psychosocial stages** are based on his **epigenetic principle**, but they also take into account the influence of the sociocultural environment.

- Each psychosocial stage centres around a developmental crisis, involving a struggle between an **adaptive** and a **maladaptive** personality characteristic. Whilst every personality represents a blend of both, healthy development involves **more** of the adaptive than the maladaptive characteristic.

- The stages spanning childhood are **basic trust versus basic mistrust** (0–1), **autonomy versus shame and doubt** (1–3), **initiative versus guilt** (3–6) and **industry versus inferiority** (6–12). Other stages span early, middle and late adulthood.

- SLT attempts to reinterpret certain aspects of Freud's theory in terms of **conditioning theory/classical learning theory**. Bandura investigated Freud's concept of identification, largely through laboratory experiments of **imitative aggression**.

- Whilst accepting many of the basic principles of conditioning, Bandura emphasised **observational learning/modelling**, distinguished between **learning** and **performance**, and identified several **cognitive variables** which mediate between observation of a model's behaviour and its imitation. These include **attention**, **memory**, and **motor reproduction**.

- For Bandura, **reinforcement** is both a source of **information** and **motivation**. Reinforcement is **not** needed for learning to take place, but it may be for performance of that learning, whether **direct**, **vicarious** or **self-reinforcement**.

- Self-reinforcement is related to **self-monitoring**, the SLT equivalent of Freud's superego. This represents an **internalised** societal standard or expectancy, another example being **self-efficacy**.

- A limitation of Bandura's SLT is that it is not a true **developmental** theory. However, one of its strengths is that it sees people as shapers of their environment, as well as being shaped by it (**reciprocal determinism**).

Essay Questions

1 Describe and evaluate **one** psychodynamic theory of personality development. (*24 marks*)

2 a Describe **one** social learning account of personality development. (*12 marks*)

   b Evaluate this theory by reference to alternative theories **and/or** research studies. (*12 marks*)

WEB ADDRESSES

http://www.stg.brown.edu/projects/hypertext/landow/HTatBrown/Freud/Psychosexual_Development.html
http://www.uia.org/uiademo/hum/h1543.htm
http://www.uia.org/uiademo/hum/h0285.htm
http://www.wynja.com/personality/theorists.html

32 *Gender Development*

Every known culture distinguishes between male and female, a distinction which is accompanied by widely held beliefs (*stereotypes*: see Chapter 2) about their psychological make-up and behaviours. The study of psychological sex differences is really an attempt to see how accurate these stereotypes are.

Feminist interpretations of sex differences share the belief that social, political, economic and cultural factors determine *gender*, our awareness and understanding of the differences that distinguish males from females. This view is directly opposed to those of sociobiologists and evolutionary psychologists, who argue that sex differences are 'natural', having evolved as a part of the more general adaptation of the human species to its environment (see Chapter 43).

Several other theoretical accounts of gender and gender differences have been advanced, including *biological approaches, biosocial theory, psychoanalytic theory, social learning theory, cognitive–developmental theory* and *gender schema theory*. This chapter considers these various accounts, but begins by defining some of the basic terms needed to evaluate the different theories.

THE 'VOCABULARY' OF SEX AND GENDER

Feminist psychologists (e.g. Unger, 1979) distinguish between *sex* and *gender*. Sex refers to some biological fact about us, such as a particular genetic make-up, reproductive anatomy and functioning, and is usually referred to by the terms 'male' and 'female'. Gender, by contrast, is what culture makes out of the 'raw material' of biological sex. It is, therefore, the social equivalent or social interpretation of sex.

Sexual identity is an alternative way of referring to our biological status as male or female. Corresponding to gender is *gender identity*, our classification of ourselves (and others) as male or female, boy or girl, and so on. Sexual and gender identities correspond for most of us, but not in *transsexualism*. Whilst being anatomically male or female, transexuals firmly believe that they belong to the opposite sex. As a result, their biological sexual identities are fundamentally inconsistent with their gender identities.

Gender role (or *sex role*) refers to the behaviours, attitudes, values, beliefs and so on which a particular society either expects from, or considers appropriate to, males and females on the basis of their biological sex. To be *masculine* (or *feminine*), then, requires males (or females) to conform to their respective gender roles.

All societies have carefully defined gender roles, although their precise details differ between societies. *Gender* (or sex) *stereotypes* are widely held beliefs about psychological differences between males and females which often reflect gender roles (see pages 345–346).

Figure 32.1 *Renee Richards, formerly known as Richard Raskin, one of the world's best-known transsexuals. Born male, Richard had his sex reassigned through surgery and continued her tennis career as a woman*

Sex typing refers to our acquisition of a sex or gender identity and learning the appropriate behaviours (adopting an appropriate *sex role*). Sex typing begins early in Western culture, with parents often dressing their new-born baby boy or girl in blue or pink. Even in infancy's earliest days, our gender influences how people react to us (Condry & Ross, 1985). Indeed, usually the first question asked by friends and relatives of parents with a new-born baby is 'Boy or girl?' By age three or four, most children have some knowledge about their gender. They know, for example, that boys become men and girls become women, and that some games are played by boys and others by girls. A permanent gender identity is usually acquired by age five, and children know that a girl is a girl even if she can climb a tree (Zimbardo & Weber, 1994: see pages 349–350).

BIOLOGY AND SEXUAL IDENTITY

Biologically, sex is not a unidimensional variable, and attempts to identify the biological factors influencing gender identity have produced at least five categories.

Box 32.1 Five categories of biological sex

Chromosomal sex: Normal females inherit two X chromosomes, one from each parent (XX). Normal males inherit one X chromosome from the mother and one Y chromosome from the father (XY). Two chromosomes are needed for the complete development of both internal and external female structures, and the Y chromosome must be present for the complete development of male internal and external structures (Page *et al.*, 1987). For many years it was believed that if the Y chromosome is absent, female external genitals develop. However, a female-determining gene has been located on the X chromosome (Unger & Crawford, 1996). Female embryos begin synthesising large quantities of estrogen, which are thought to play a key role in the development of the female reproductive system. A gene on the Y chromosome called TDF (*testis-determining factor)* appears to be responsible for testis formation and male development (Hodgkin, 1988).

Gonadal sex: This refers to the sexual or reproductive organs (ovaries in females and testes in males). *H-Y antigen*, controlled by genes on the Y chromosome, causes embryonic gonads to be transformed to testes. If H-Y antigen is not present, gonadal tissue develops into ovaries (Amice *et al.*, 1989).

Hormonal sex: When the gonads are transformed to testes or ovaries, genetic influences cease and biological

sex determination is controlled by *sex hormones*. The male sex hormones are called *androgens*, the most important being *testosterone* (secreted by the testes). The ovaries secrete two distinct types of female hormone, *estrogen* and *progesterone.* Although males usually produce more androgens, and females more estrogens, both males and females produce androgens *and* estrogens. So, strictly, there are no 'male' or 'female' hormones (Muldoon & Reilly, 1998).

Sex of the internal reproductive structures: The Wolffian ducts in males and the Mullerian ducts in females are the embryonic forerunners of the internal reproductive structures. In males, these are the prostate gland, sperm ducts, seminal vesicles and testes. In females, they are the Fallopian tubes, womb and ovaries.

Sex of the external genitals: In males, the external genitalia are the penis and scrotum. In females, they are the outer lips of the vagina (*labia majora*). In the absence of testosterone (which influences both the internal and external structures of chromosomal males), female structures develop (see text).

The categories identified in Box 32.1 are usually highly correlated, such that a person tends to be male (or female) in all respects. The categories also tend to be correlated with non-biological aspects of sex, including the sex the baby is assigned to at birth, how it is brought up, gender identity, gender-role identity and so on. Either pre- or post-natally, however, disorders can occur leading to an inconsistency or low correlation between the categories. These disorders can tell us a great deal about the development of gender identity, gender role and gender-role identity.

People with such disorders are called hermaphrodites. *True hermaphrodites* have either simultaneously or sequentially functioning organs of both sexes. They are very rare and their external organs are often a mixture of male and female structures. *Pseudohermaphrodites* are more common. Although they too possess ambiguous internal and external reproductive structures, they are born with *gonads* that match their chromosomal sex (unlike true hermaphrodites).

Box 32.2 Three major types of pseudohermaphroditism

- In *androgen insensitivity syndrome* (AIS) (or *testicular feminising syndrome*), pre-natal development in a chromosomally normal (XY) male is *feminised*. The internal reproductive structures of either sex fail to develop, and the external genitals fail to differentiate into a penis and scrotum. Normal-looking female external genitals and a shallow vagina are present at birth. At puberty, breast development occurs but the individual fails to menstruate. Because of the presence of a very shallow (or 'blind') vagina, little or no surgery is needed for the adoption of a female appearance.

- In *adrenogenital syndrome* (AGS), a chromosomally normal (XX) female is exposed to an excessive amount of androgens during the critical period of pre-natal sexual differentiation. Whilst the internal reproductive structures are unaffected, the external structures resemble those of a male infant. For example, an enlarged clitoris appears to be a penis (see Figure 32.2). These individuals are usually raised as females.

- In *DHT-deficient males* (or 5-alpha-reductase deficiency), a genetic disorder prevents the normal pre-natal conversion of testosterone into *dihydrotestosterone* (DHT). This hormone is necessary for the normal development of male external genitals. These males are usually incorrectly identified as females and raised as girls.

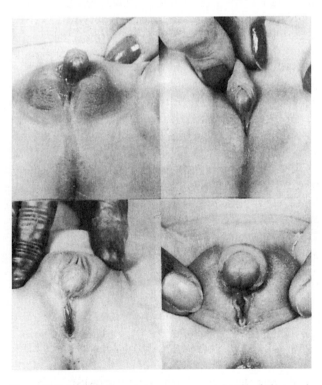

Figure 32.2 *Ambiguous appearance at birth of the genitalia of individuals with the adrenogenital syndrome (XX, but with excessive androgen during pre-natal differentiation) (From Money & Ehrhardt, 1972)*

Supporters of a biological approach argue that males and females are *biologically programmed* for certain kinds of activities compatible with male and female roles. For example, of 18 DHT-deficient males, all but two responded to the dramatic biological changes at puberty (the clitoris-like organ enlarges and becomes a penis and the testes descend) by adopting a male gender-role, despite being raised as females (Imperato-McGinley *et al.*, 1979). Of the two that did not, one acknowledged that he was a male but continued to dress as a female, whilst the other maintained a female gender-identity, married and underwent a sex-change operation. This suggests that their testosterone had pre-programmed masculinity into their brains.

Several researchers have argued that male and female brains are structually different. For example, destruction of small parts of rats' hypothalami resulted in new-born males behaving as though they were female (Dorner, 1976). However, evidence from human studies tends not to support this claim. For example, Daphne Went, although chromosomally male, has a female external appearance, is married, and leads an active and successful life as a woman (Goldwyn, 1979).

However, there is some evidence of sex differences in *hemispheric specialisation*. For example, when males perform spatial tasks, there is greater electrical activity in the right hemisphere (Bryden & Saxby, 1985). In women, both hemispheres are activated. According to McGlone (1980), the right hemisphere is generally the dominant one in men, whilst the left is generally dominant in women (see Box 32.3, page 346).

Despite evidence that the corpus callosum is larger overall in women and longer towards the back of the brain (an example of a 'dimorphic' characteristic), Kimura (1993) has cautioned against accepting this evidence uncritically. It has not been clearly established that the number of fibres is the crucial male-female difference (as has been assumed), and sex differences in cognitive functioning have yet to be related to the size of the corpus callosum (see Chapter 11).

GENDER STEREOTYPES AND GENDER DIFFERENCES

There appears to be a high degree of agreement across 30 countries regarding the characteristics associated with each gender group (Williams & Best, 1994). For example, male-associated terms included 'aggressive', 'determined' and 'sharp-witted', whilst female-associated terms included 'cautious', 'emotional' and 'warm'. However, as far as *actual* differences are concerned, many stereotypes about males and females have little empirical support.

Box 32.3 Some findings relating to gender differences

Aggression: According to Maccoby & Jacklin (1974) and Weisfeld (1994), boys are more verbally and physically aggressive than girls, a difference which appears as soon as social play begins (around two and a half years). Whilst both sexes become less aggressive with age, boys and men remain more aggressive throughout development. However, some studies have shown that women score higher for certain kinds of indirect non-physical aggression (Durkin, 1995), whilst others have found no sex differences at all (e.g. Campbell & Muncer, 1994).

Verbal ability: From pre-school to adolescence, the sexes are very similar with respect to verbal ability. At age 11, however, females become superior, and this increases during adolescence and possibly beyond (Maccoby & Jacklin, 1974). Again, though, evidence suggests that any such differences are so small as to be negligible (Hyde & Linn, 1988).

Spatial ability: Males' ability to perceive figures or objects in space and their relationship to each other is consistently better than that of females in adolescence and adulthood (Maccoby & Jacklin, 1974). However, whilst there is male superiority on some spatial tasks, *within-sex* variability is large. Moreover, when between-sex differences are found, they are usually small (Durkin, 1995).

Mathematical ability: Mathematical skills increase faster in boys, beginning around age 12 or 13 (Maccoby & Jacklin, 1974). However, whilst there are significant sex differences, these are in the *reverse* direction to the stereotype (Hyde *et al.*, 1990).

(Adapted from Durkin, 1995)

Durkin (1995) suggests that:

'The overwhelming conclusion to be drawn from the literature on sex differences is that it is highly controversial'.

A statistically significant difference does not imply a large behavioural difference. Rather, what determines a significant result is the *consistency* of the differences between groups, such that if, for example, all the girls in a school scored 0.5 per cent higher than all the boys on the same test, a small but highly significant result would be produced (Edley & Wetherell, 1995).

Eagly (1983), however, has argued that in at least some cases a significant difference does reflect a substantial sex difference. By combining the results of different but comparable studies (*meta-analysis*: see Chapter 54, page 580), substantial sex differences emerge on some measures. According to Eagly, research has actually tended to *conceal* rather than *reveal* sex differences. However, the differences *within* each gender are, as noted earlier, at least as great as the differences between them (Maccoby, 1980).

BIOSOCIAL THEORY

According to Edley & Wetherell (1995), to ask 'What is the biological basis of masculinity (or femininity)?' is to pose a false question. In their view:

'It requires us to separate what cannot be separated: men [and women] are the product of a complex system of factors and forces which combine in a variety of ways to produce a whole range of different masculinities [and femininities]'.

Biosocial theory takes social factors into account in relation to biological ones. It sees the *interaction* between biological and social factors as important, rather than biology's direct influence. Adults prefer to spend time with babies who respond to them in 'rewarding' ways, and 'demanding' babies tend to receive more attention than 'passive' babies.

As far as other people are concerned, the baby's sex is just as important as its temperament. For example, the 'baby X' experiments (Smith & Lloyd, 1978) involved dressing babies in unisex snowsuits and giving them names which were sometimes in line with their true gender and sometimes not. When adults played with them, they treated the babies according to the gender they believed them to be. This indicates that a person's (perceived) biological make-up becomes part of his or her social environment through others' reactions to it. According to Money & Ehrhardt (1972), 'anatomy is destiny': how an infant is labelled sexually determines how it is raised or socialised. In turn, this determines the child's gender identity, and from this follow its gender role, gender-role identity and sexual orientation.

Key STUDY

Box 32.4 Pseudohermaphrodites and gender identity

Money & Ehrhardt (1972) studied girls with AGS (see Box 32.2, page 345) who were raised as boys and, before age three, had their genitals surgically corrected and were raised as girls. Money and Ehrhardt claim that it is possible to change the sex of rearing without any undue psychological harm being done, provided this occurs within a 'critical' or 'sensitive' period' of about two and a half to three years. However, after this, reassignment to the opposite sex can cause extreme psychological disturbance. Money and Ehrhardt's study of ten people with testicular feminising syndrome showed there was a strong preference for the female role, which also supports the view that sex of rearing is more important than biological sex.

Just because some people appear to be flexible in their psychosexual identities does not in itself disprove that 'built-in biases' still have to be overcome (Diamond, 1978). Money and Ehrhardt's participants are clearly an atypical sample, and there is no evidence that people *in general* are as flexible in their psychosexual orientation and identity.

Key S T U D Y

Box 32.5 The case of the penectomised twin

Money (1974) has reported a case in which, as a result of an accident during a circumcision, one of a pair of twins lost his penis. This penectomised boy was raised as a girl and, at 17 months, 'he' was castrated, estrogen was given, and a vaginal canal constructed. At age four, the child preferred dresses to trousers, took pride in 'his' long hair, and was cleaner than 'his' brother. At age nine, although 'he' had been the dominant twin since birth, 'he' expressed this by being a 'fussy little mother' to 'his' brother. This finding seems to support the view that gender identity (and gender role) is *learned*.

The reversal of original sexual assignment is possible if it takes place early enough and is consistent in all respects, which includes the external genitalia conforming well enough to the new sex. However, castration and the use of estrogen clearly contributed to the ease of reassignment, and probably also account for the unaffected twin being taller. Significantly, when the 'girl' had reached her teens 'she' was an unhappy adolescent, with few friends, uncertain about 'her' gender, and maintaining that boys 'had a better life'. 'She' also looked rather masculine. For Diamond (1982), these findings indicated that biology had ultimately proven irrepressible.

Diamond & Sigmundson (1997) describe another case of a penectomised boy, raised as a girl from eight months of age. Despite all the sex-change surgery and hormone therapy, 'Joan' always felt male, and at age 14 the original surgery was reversed. At 25, 'John' married a woman who already had children. Agreeing with Diamond, Reiner (cited in Fletcher, 1997) argues that:

'The organ that appears to be critical to psychosexual development and adaptation is not the genitalia but the brain'.

SOCIOBIOLOGICAL THEORY

Sociobiologists (evolutionary theorists: see Chapter 43) argue that gender has gradually evolved over the course of human development as part of our broader adaptation to the environment (Lumsden & Wilson, 1983). Males and females have developed different roles as a function of their respective contributions to reproduction and domestic labour (Wilson, 1978; Hoyenga & Hoyenga, 1979). The relatively greater physical strength, lung capacity and so on of males make them better suited to hunting and defending territory and family. The childbearing and milk-producing capacities of females, however, make them ideally suited to childcare and other nurturant roles.

According to *parental investment theory* (Kenrick, 1994), females invest considerably more in reproduction than do males. Society came to be organised in sexually exclusive domestic partnerships as a way of meeting the female's needs for protection and the male's need for preventing his mate from mating with other males. The consequence of this was the evolution of different courtship displays and roles (such as 'playing hard to get') which are still evident in many Western and other cultures. According to Buss (1994), what females universally find attractive in males are the characteristics associated with the provision of resources. Men, by contrast, see physical beauty as being of most importance (see Chapter 4).

The sociobiological approach has been criticised on several grounds. For example, dominance patterns are not, as sociobiological approaches assume, equated with greater aggression. In humans, at least, dominance often relates to status seeking, which implies the role of culturally determined values (Sayers, 1982). Sociobiological approaches to sex differences are also difficult to test: we have only incomplete knowledge about the ways in which our ancestors adapted to their environments. So, our hunches about which characteristics were adaptive and why differences between the sexes evolved are 'educated guesses' at best.

FREUD'S PSYCHOANALYTIC THEORY

Freud's theory is related to his explanation of moral development (see Chapter 30) which, in turn, is part of his theory of psychosexual development (see Chapter 31). Up until the resolution of the Oedipus complex, gender identity is assumed to be flexible. Resolution of the Oedipus complex occurs through *identification* with the same-sex parent, and results in the acquisition of both a superego and gender identity. As well as a weaker conscience, Freud also saw the development of gender identity as being weaker in girls than boys.

There are at least three reasons for doubting a Freudian interpretation of gender identity's development. First, children of a particular age do *not* appear to acquire gender identity in 'one fell swoop' (Krebs & Blackman, 1988). Second, children who grow up in 'atypical' families (e.g. single-parent or lesbian couples) are not necessarily adversely affected in terms of their gender identity (Golombok *et al.*, 1983). Indeed, there is evidence of *more* secure attachments amongst children reared in fatherless families (whether lesbian or heterosexual: Golombok *et al.*, 1997). Third, whilst identification might promote gender identity, children are aware of gender roles well before the age at which Freud believed their complexes are resolved. For example, boys prefer stereotypically masculine toys (such as trucks) and girls stereotypically feminine toys (such as dolls) *in infancy* (O'Brien *et al.*, 1983).

SOCIAL LEARNING THEORY

According to social learning theory (SLT), one reason girls and boys learn to behave differently is that they are *treated differently* by their parents and others. As was seen in the 'baby X' study (see page 346), when informed of a child's biological sex, parents and others often react to it according to their *gender-role expectations*. Thus, girls and boys are often given different toys, have their rooms decorated differently, and are even spoken about in different terms (Rubin *et al.*, 1974). However, Karraker *et al.* (1995) found that this strong sex-typing of infants at birth has declined, and that there were no differences between mothers and fathers in this respect. A consistent and persistent finding is that fathers treat their children in a more gendered way than mothers (Maccoby, 1990). Typically, fathers interact in a more instrumental and achievement-oriented way, and give more attention to their sons, whilst mothers attend equally to sons and daughters (Quiery, 1998).

SLT also emphasises the roles of *observational learning* and *reinforcement*. By observing others behaving in particular ways and then imitating that behaviour, children receive reinforcement from 'significant others' for behaviours considered to be sex-appropriate (Bandura, 1977a: see Chapter 31). Parents tend to positively reinforce boys more for behaviours reflecting independence, self-reliance and emotional control. Girls, however, tend to be reinforced for compliance, dependence, nurturance, empathy and emotional expression (Block, 1979). Fathers tend to reinforce these sex-typed behaviours more than mothers do (Kerig *et al.*, 1993).

Figure 32.3 *Playing with dolls and displaying nurturant behaviour, and playing with guns and displaying assertive, even aggressive, behaviour, conform to female and male gender role expectations/stereotypes respectively. According to social learning theory, children receive parental reinforcement for displaying such gender-appropriate behaviours*

Box 32.6 Findings supporting SLT

- Sears *et al.* (1957) found that parents allowed sons to be more aggressive in their relationships with other children, and towards their parents, than daughters. For some mothers, 'being a boy' meant being aggressive, and boys were often encouraged to fight back. Although parents believe they respond in the same way to aggressive acts committed by boys and girls, they actually intervene much more frequently and quickly when girls behave aggressively (Huston, 1983).

- Boys were more likely to imitate aggressive male models than were girls (Bandura *et al.*, 1961, 1963:

see Box 31.4, pages 338–339) Children are also more likely to imitate a same-sex model than an opposite-sex model, even if the behaviour is 'sex-inappropriate'.

- Although parents are important models, SL theorists are also interested in media portrayals of males and females. A large body of evidence suggests that *gender-role stereotypes* are portrayed by the media, as well as by parents and teachers (Wober *et al.*, 1987). Moreover, children categorised as 'heavy' viewers of television hold stronger stereotyped beliefs than 'lighter' viewers (Gunter, 1986: see also Chapter 9).

SL theorists see the reinforcement of sex-typed behaviours as continuing throughout life rather than being confined to childhood. For example, parents of adolescents endorsed different statements concerning the ways their sons and daughters are treated. 'I encourage my child always to do his/her best' tended to be endorsed for boys, whereas 'I encourage my child to keep control of his/her feelings at all times' tended to be endorsed for girls (Block, 1978).

Although social reinforcement plays a role in young children's sex typing, the evidence concerning modelling is less impressive. Thus, whilst modelling plays an important role in children's socialisation, there is no consistent preference for the same-sex parent's behaviour (Hetherington, 1967). Instead, children prefer to model the behaviour of those with whom they have most contact (usually the mother). Also, there is no significant correlation between the extent to which parents engage in sex-typed behaviours and the strength of sex-typing in their children (Smith & Daglish, 1977). However, fathers' adoption of either traditional (sex-typed) or egalitarian attitudes has been found to correlate with four-year-olds' perceptions of sex roles (Quiery, 1998).

Box 32.7 Findings not supporting SLT

- According to Maccoby & Jacklin (1974), there are no consistent differences in the extent to which boys and girls are reinforced for aggressiveness or autonomy. Rather, there appears to be remarkable uniformity in the sexes' socialisation. This is supported by Lytton & Romney (1991), who found very few sex differences in terms of parental warmth, overall amount of interaction, encouragement of achievement or dependency, restrictiveness and discipline, or clarity of communication.

- Although Bandura *et al.*'s research is often cited, the evidence concerning imitation and modelling is actually inconclusive, and some studies have failed to find that children are more likely to imitate same-sex models than opposite-sex models. Indeed, children have been shown to prefer imitating behaviour that is 'appropriate' to their own sex *regardless* of the model's (Maccoby & Jacklin, 1974).

- The view that *television* can impact upon a passively receptive child audience with messages about sex-role stereotyping, and mould young children's conceptions of gender is oversimplistic (see Chapter 9). For Gunter & McAleer (1997), children respond selectively to particular characters and events, and their perceptions, memories and understanding of what they have seen may often be mediated by the dispositions they bring with them to the viewing situation. Whilst 'heavy' viewers of television might hold stronger stereotyped beliefs than other children, no precise measures were taken of the programmes they actually watched.

COGNITIVE–DEVELOPMENTAL AND GENDER-SCHEMATIC PROCESSING THEORIES

Cognitive–developmental theory

The cognitive–developmental approach (Kohlberg, 1969; Kohlberg & Ullian, 1974) emphasises the child's participation in developing both an understanding of gender and gender-appropriate behaviour (see Chapter 30). Children's discovery that they are male or female *causes* them to identify with members of their own sex (not the other way round, as psychoanalytic and SL theories suggest). Whilst rewards and punishments influence children's choices of toys and activities, these do not mechanically strengthen stimulus–response connections, but provide children with *information* about when they are behaving in ways that other people deem appropriate (see Chapters 30 and 38).

According to cognitive–developmental theorists, young children acquire an understanding of the concepts *male* and *female* in three stages.

Box 32.8 Stages in the development of gender identity

Stage 1 (Gender labelling or basic gender identity): This occurs somewhere around age three (Ruble, 1984) and refers to the child's recognition that it is male or female. According to Kohlberg, knowing one's gender is an achievement that allows us to understand and categorise the world. However, this knowledge is fragile, and children do not yet realise that boys invariably become men and girls always become women.

Stage 2 (Gender stability): By age four or five, most children recognise that people retain their gender for a lifetime. However, there are still limitations, in that children rely on superficial signs (such as the length of a person's hair) to determine their gender (Marcus & Overton, 1978).

Stage 3 (Gender constancy or consistency): At around age six or seven, children realise that gender is *immutable*. So, even if a woman has her hair cut very short, her gender remains constant. Gender constancy represents a kind of *conservation* (see Chapter 28) and, significantly, appears shortly after the child has mastered the conservation of quantity (Marcus & Overton, 1978).

Once children acquire gender constancy, they come to value the behaviours and attitudes associated with their sex. Only at this point do they identify with the adult figures who possess the qualities they see as being most central to their concepts of themselves as male or female (Perry & Bussey, 1979).

Evidence suggests that the concepts of gender identity, stability and constancy do occur in that order across many cultures (Munroe *et al.*, 1984). Slaby & Frey (1975) divided two- to five-year-olds into 'high' and 'low' gender constancy. The children were then shown a silent film of adults simultaneously performing a series of simple activities. The screen was 'split', with males performing activities on one side and females performing activities on the other. Children rated as 'high' in gender constancy showed a marked same-sex bias, as measured by the amount of visual attention they gave to each side of the screen. This supports Kohlberg's belief that gender constancy is a *cause* of the imitation of same-sex models rather than an effect. Children actively construct their gender-role knowledge through purposeful monitoring of the social environment. They engage in *self-socialisation*, rather than passively receiving information (Whyte, 1998).

A major problem for cognitive–developmental theory is that it predicts there should be little or no gender-

appropriate behaviour *before* gender constancy is achieved. However, even in infancy, both sexes show a marked preference for stereotypical male and female toys (Huston, 1983: see page 348). Whilst such children might have developed a sense of gender identity, they are, as far as cognitive–developmental theory is concerned, some years away from achieving gender stability and constancy (Fagot, 1985).

Gender-schematic processing theory

This addresses the possibility that gender identity *alone* can provide children with sufficient motivation to assume sex-typed behaviour patterns (e.g. Bem, 1985; Martin, 1991). Like SLT, this approach suggests that children learn 'appropriate' patterns of behaviour by observation. However, consistent with cognitive–developmental theory, children's active cognitive processing of information also contributes to their sex-typing.

Children learn that strength is linked to the male sex-role stereotype and weakness to the female stereotype, and that some dimensions (including strength–weakness) are more relevant to one gender (males) than the other (Rathus, 1990). So, a boy learns that the strength he displays in wrestling (say) affects others' perceptions of him. Unless competing in some sporting activity, most girls do not see this dimension as being important. However, whilst boys are expected to compete in sports, girls are not, and so a girl is likely to find that her gentleness and neatness are more important in the eyes of others than her strength (Rathus, 1990).

Figure 32.4 *Jane Couch (the 'Fleetwood Assassin'), women's world welter-weight boxing champion, after winning her sex discrimination case in 1998 against the British Boxing Board of Control over its refusal to grant her a license to box professionally*

According to gender-schematic processing theory, then, children learn to judge themselves according to the traits considered to be relevant to their genders. Consequently, the self-concept becomes mixed with the gender schemas of a particular culture which provides standards for comparison. The theory sees gender identity as being sufficient to produce 'sex-appropriate'

behaviour. The labels 'boy' and 'girl', once understood, give children the basis for mixing their self-concepts with their society's gender schemas. Children with gender identity will actively seek information about gender schemas, and their self-esteem will soon become influenced by how they 'measure up' to their gender schema (Rathus, 1990).

CONCLUSIONS

This chapter has considered various theories of gender development and psychological sex differences. Whilst every known culture distinguishes between male and female (reflected in stereotypes regarding typical male/female characteristics and behaviour), the evi-

dence for the truth of such stereotypes is not conclusive. No single theory adequately explains the complex process by which a person acquires his or her gender role. All the perspectives discussed in this chapter have contributed to our understanding of that process, and they should be seen as complementary explanations (Whyte, 1998).

Summary

- Every known society distinguishes between male and female. The study of psychological sex differences attempts to test the accuracy of sex **stereotypes**.

- Feminist psychologists distinguish between **sex** or **sexual identity** (some aspect of our biological make-up as 'male' or 'female') and **gender**. **Gender identity** is how we classify ourselves and others as male or female.

- There is little empirical support for **actual** gender differences in terms of either **aggression**, **verbal**, **spatial** or **mathematical ability**.

- A statistically significant difference does not imply a large behavioural difference, although **meta-analysis** sometimes produces large differences on some measures. However, **within**-gender differences are at least as great as **between**-gender differences.

- **Biologically**, sex refers to five main categories: **chromosomal sex**, **gonadal sex**, **hormonal sex**, **sex of the internal reproductive structures** and **sex of the external genitalia**. These are usually highly correlated with each other, as well as with non-biological factors such as sexual assignment at birth, sex of rearing and gender identity. In **hermaphroditism** and **pseudohermaphroditism**, pre- and post-natal disorders produce an inconsistency between these categories.

- Major types of pseudohermaphroditism are **androgen insensitivity syndrome** (AIS)/**testicular feminising syndrome**, **adrenogenital syndrome** (AGS) and **dihydrotestosterone (DHT)-deficiency/ 5-alpha-reductase decifiency**.

- According to the **biological** approach, males and females are biologically programmed for certain activities compatible with gender roles. The 18 DHT-deficient males studied by Imperato-McGinley *et al.* appear to have masculinity pre-programmed into their brains by testosterone.

- Claims that male and female brains are structurally different are largely based on studies of rats, and are unsupported by human evidence. Whilst studies of **hemispheric specialisation** are consistent with some of the claimed male–female differences in cognitive abilities, evidence that the corpus callosum is sexually dimorphic is far from conclusive.

- **Biosocial theory** stresses the **interaction** of social and biological factors. A person's (perceived) biological make-up (such as sex) becomes part of his or her social environment through others' reactions to it.

- Money and Ehrhardt claim that there is a 'critical' or 'sensitive' period for the development of gender identity. However, their participants were clearly atypical. Cases of penectomised boys raised as girls tend to support the claim that gender identity and gender role are **biologically determined**.

- According to **sociobiologists**, gender has evolved as part of human beings' broader adaptation to the environment. **Parental investment theory** claims that sexually exclusive domestic partnerships meet the female's need for protection and the male's need for preventing his mate from mating with other males.

- **Psychoanalytic theory** sees gender identity as being related to moral and overall psychosexual development. Gender identity is acquired through

identification with the same-sex parent which ends the Oedipus complex. Girls do not resolve their Oedipus complex as effectively as boys, resulting in a weaker conscience and gender identity.

■ However, gender identity develops much more gradually than Freud claimed. Also, studies of children who grow up in 'atypical' families show that their gender identity is not adversely affected.

■ According to **social learning theory** (SLT), girls and boys learn to behave differently through being **treated differently** by parents and others. SLT also stresses the role of **observational learning** and **reinforcement** for imitating sex-appropriate behaviours.

■ Whilst there is some evidence that boys and girls are treated differently by their parents, some researchers claim that socialisation of the sexes is highly uniform.

■ Evidence is inconclusive regarding the importance for imitation of the **sex-appropriateness** of a model's behaviour and the model's sex. There is no consistent preference for the same-sex parent's behaviour, but rather for the parent the child spends most time with.

■ According to the **cognitive–developmental approach**, children's discovery that they are male or female **causes** them to identify with and imitate same-sex models. Rewards and punishments provide children with **information** about when they are behaving in appropriate ways.

■ Three stages in the development of gender identity are **gender labelling** (**basic gender identity**), **gender stability** and **gender constancy** (or **consistency**). Cross-cultural evidence supports this sequence. The claim that children actively construct their gender role knowledge through monitoring their social environment has received experimental support.

■ **Gender-schematic processing theory** maintains that gender identity alone can provide a child with sufficient motivation to assume sex-typed behaviour. Children learn to judge themselves according to the traits seen as relevant to their gender, resulting in a self-concept that is mixed with the gender schemas of a particular culture.

Essay Questions

1 Discuss psychological insights into the development of gender identity and gender roles. (*24 marks*)

2 **a** Describe **one** theory of the development of gender. (*12 marks*)

   b Assess the extent to which this theory is supported by research evidence. (*12 marks*)

WEB ADDRESSES

http://www.upm.edu.my/llsgend.html
http://www.hfni.gsehd.gwu.edu/~tip/theories.html
http://www.apa.org/journals/cntlcntl44131.html
http://www.garysturt.free-online.co.uk/gender.htm

33 *Adolescence*

INTRODUCTION AND OVERVIEW

The word 'adolescence' comes from the Latin *adolescere* meaning 'to grow into maturity'. As well as being a time of enormous physiological change, adolescence is also marked by changes in behaviour, expectations and relationships, with both parents and peers. In Western, industrialised societies, there is generally no single initiation rite signalling the passage into adulthood.

The lack of such initiations into adulthood make this a more difficult transition than it appears to be in more traditional, non-industrialised societies. Relationships with parents in particular, and adults in general, must be renegotiated in a way that allows the adolescent to achieve greater independence. This process is aided by changing relationships with peers.

This chapter examines three major aspects of adolescent development (collectively known as the *classical theory*). These are *'storm and stress'*, which relates to the emotional changes which are triggered by puberty, *identity formation*, which has both individual and social dimensions, and *generation gap*, which refers to the changes in relationships already mentioned. These are discussed in relation to some major theories of adolescence, such as those of Hall, Erikson, Marcia and Coleman. The chapter also considers cultural differences in adolescent behaviour.

THE CHANGING FACE OF ADOLESCENCE

Historically, adolescence has been seen as a period of transition between childhood and adulthood. However, writers today are more likely to describe it as one of *multiple transitions*, involving education, training, employment and unemployment, as well as transitions from one set of living circumstances to another (Coleman & Roker, 1998).

In many ways this change in perspective reflects changes in the adolescent experience compared with that of previous generations. It starts five years earlier, marriage takes place six or seven years later than it did, and co-habitation, perhaps as a prelude to marriage, is rapidly increasing (Coleman & Hendry, 1999). At the same time, there has been an extension in compulsory education, and pressures on the workforce to become more highly skilled place a premium on continuing education. Any delay in acquiring an income may defer passage into adulthood (Hendry, 1999).

Coupled with these 'adulthood-postponing' changes, in recent years adolescents have enjoyed greater self-determination at steadily younger ages. Yet this greater freedom carries with it more risks and greater costs when errors of judgement are made:

'Dropping out' of school, being out of work, teenage pregnancy, sexually transmitted diseases, being homeless, drug addiction and suicide, are powerful examples of the price that some young people pay for their extended freedom'. (Hendry, 1999)

Figure 33.1 *1950s films such as* Rebel Without A Cause, *starring James Dean, have been seen as helping to create the concept of the 'rebellious teenager'.*

Normative and non-normative shifts

One way of categorising the various transitions involved in adolescence is in terms of *normative* and *non-normative* shifts (Hendry & Kloep, 1999; Kloep & Hendry, 1999). These are:

- **normative, maturational shifts:** growth spurt (both sexes), menarche (first menstruation), first nocturnal emissions ('wet dreams'), voice breaking (boys), changes in sexual organs, beginning of sexual arousal, changed romantic relationships, gender role identity, changed relationships with adults, increasing autonomy and responsibility;

- **normative, society-dependent shifts:** change from primary to secondary school, leaving school, getting started in an occupation, acquiring legal rights for voting, purchasing alcohol, sex, driving licence, military service, and co-habitation;

- **non-normative shifts:** examples include parental divorce, family bereavement, illness, natural disasters, war, incest, emigration, disruption of peer network, risk-taking behaviours, 'disadvantage' (because of gender, class, regional or ethnic discrimination), physical and/or mental handicap.

According to Kloep & Hendry (1999):

'Although all adolescents have to cope with the psychosocial challenges associated with their maturing body, new relationships with parents and peers, with school and the transitions toward employment, a growing number encounter additional problems like family disruption, economic deprivation or social or cultural changes'.

A normative shift may become non-normative, if, say, there are other circumstances that cause a normal developmental 'task' to become more difficult, such as the onset of puberty occuring unusually early or late.

PUBERTY: THE SOCIAL AND PSYCHOLOGICAL MEANING OF BIOLOGICAL CHANGES

Puberty and body image

Puberty is one of the most important adjustments that adolescents have to make (Coleman & Hendry, 1999). Even as a purely *biological* phenomenon, puberty is far from being a simple, straightforward process. Whilst all adolescents experience the same bodily changes (see Box 33.1 and Figure 33.2), the sequence of changes may vary within individuals (*intraindividual asynchronies*: Alsaker, 1996). For example, for some girls menstruation may occur very early on in their puberty, whilst for others it

may occur after most other changes (e.g. growth spurt, breast development) have taken place.

Box 33.1 Major changes in puberty

Physiologically, puberty begins when the seminal vesicles and prostate gland enlarge in the male, and the ovaries enlarge in the female. Both males and females experience the *adolescent growth spurt*. Male *secondary sex characteristics* include growth of pubic and then chest and facial hair, and sperm production. In females, breast size increases, pubic hair grows, and menstruation begins.

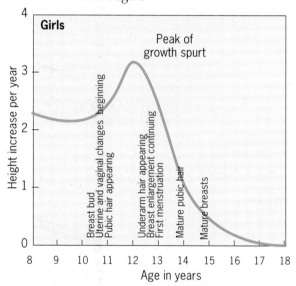

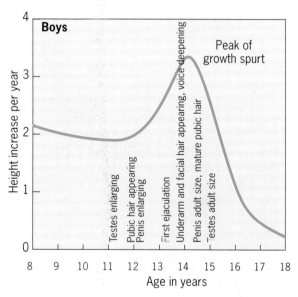

Figure 33.2 *The development of secondary sex characteristics. The curved lines represent the average increase in height from eight to 18 years of age. The characteristics shown may occur earlier or later in a person's development, but usually occur in the order shown (Based on Tanner, 1978, and Tanner & Whitehouse, 1976)*

According to Davies & Furnham (1986), the average adolescent is not only sensitive to, but also critical of, his or her changing physical self. Because of gender and sexual development, young people are inevitably confronted, perhaps for the first time, by cultural standards of beauty in evaluating their own body image (via the media and the reactions of others). This may produce a non-normative shift in the form of dieting practices, leading to eating disorders (see Gross *et al.*, 2000). Young people may be especially vulnerable to teasing and exclusion if they are perceived by their peers as over- or underweight (Kloep & Hendry, 1999).

Gender differences

Whilst puberty may be a normative, maturational shift, it may be a more difficult transition for girls than boys. This is because of the *subjective meaning* of bodily change (what it means for the individual), which mirrors the *socio-cultural significance* of puberty (its significance for society). According to the *cultural ideal hypothesis* (Simmons & Blyth, 1987), puberty will bring boys *closer* to their physical ideal (an increase in muscle distribution and lung capacity produces greater stamina, strength and athletic capacities), whilst girls move *further away* from theirs.

For girls, who begin puberty on average two years ahead of boys, it is normal to experience an increase in body fat and rapid weight gain, thus making their bodies less like the Western cultural ideal of the thin, sylph-like supermodel. In addition, they have to deal with menstruation, which is negatively associated with blood and physical discomfort (Crawford & Unger, 1995).

The importance of timing

Not only are the sexes affected differently by puberty, but if the cultural ideal hypothesis is valid, it follows that *early-maturing boys* will be at an *advantage* relative to their 'on-time' and late-maturing peers (they will be moving faster towards the male ideal), whilst *early-maturing girls* will be at a *disadvantage* (they will be moving faster away from the female ideal). Indeed, according to Alsaker (1996);

> 'Pubertal timing is generally regarded as a more crucial aspect of pubertal development than pubertal maturation itself'.

In other words, it is not the *fact* of puberty that matters as much as *when* it occurs, and it matters mainly in relation to body image and self-esteem. A common finding is that early-maturing girls and late-maturing boys suffer lower self-esteem.

Box 33.2 Why do early-maturing girls and late-maturing boys feel less good about themselves?

One popular explanation is the *deviancy hypothesis*, according to which those who are 'off-time' in physical maturation are socially deviant compared with peers of the same age and sex (Wichstrom, 1998). Since girls begin puberty on average two years before boys, early-maturing girls are the first to enter this deviant position, followed by late-maturing boys.

An alternative explanation is the *developmental readiness hypothesis* (Simmons & Blyth, 1987). In the case of early/sudden puberty, too little time will have been spent on ego development during latency, with early-maturing girls once more being most affected. (This explanation is similar to Coleman's *focal theory*, which is discussed on pages 361–362).

As far as the *cultural ideal hypothesis* is concerned, Wichstrom (1998) maintains that the suggestion that the pubertal girl moves further away from the Western stereotyped female ideal may *not* be true. *Both* boys and girls move closer to their ideals, provided they do not put on excessive weight (Wichstrom, 1998).

According to Wichstrom, the cultural ideal hypothesis is sensitive to changes in time and context. For example, in Norway there may be less emphasis on sterotypical male stature compared with the USA and UK. Perhaps also, the embarrassment and negative affect experienced by American girls when starting their periods and becoming sexually responsive occur less among Norwegian girls, due to relatively greater openness about adolescent sexuality (Wichstrom, 1998).

HALL'S THEORY: ADOLESCENCE AS 'STORM AND STRESS'

This is probably the earliest formal theory of adolescence. Influenced by Darwin's evolutionary theory (see Chapter 37), Hall (1904) argued that each person's psychological development *recapitulates* (or recaptures) both the biological and cultural evolution of the human species. He saw adolescence as a time of 'storm and stress' (or *Sturm und Drang*), which mirrors the volatile history of the human race over the last 2000 years.

Some evidence suggests that emotional reactions are more *intense* and *volatile* during adolescence compared with other periods of life, such as the study by Csikszentmihalyi & Larson (1984: see Box 33.3, page 356). However, more important indicators of storm and stress are (a) mental disorder, and (b) delinquent behaviour.

Key STUDY

Box 33.3 Csikszentmihalyi & Larson's (1984) study of adolescent reactions

Seventy-five Chicago-area high-school students from diverse social and racial backgrounds were asked to wear electronic pagers for a week. Every two hours, the pager signalled to the students who were instructed to write a description of what they were doing and how they felt about it. After a week, they filled out questionnaires about both their general moods and their specific moods during particular activities. About 33 per cent of waking time was spent pursuing leisure activities, the other 60 per cent being more-or-less equally divided between 'maintenence activities' (such as commuting and eating) and 'productive activities' (such as studying and working).

Particularly revealing were the adolescents' extreme mood swings, from extreme happiness to deep sadness (and vice versa) in less than an hour. Adults usually require several hours to reach the same emotional peaks and troughs.

Studies of mental disorder

Several studies have found that *early-maturing girls* score higher on measures of depressive feelings and sadness (e.g. Alsaker, 1992; Stattin & Magnusson, 1990), although this is only true when the measures are taken before or simultaneously with changing schools (Petersen *et al.*, 1991). They have also been reported to have more psychosomatic (psychophysiological) symptoms (e.g. Stattin & Magnusson, 1990), to display greater concerns about eating (e.g. Brooks-Gunn *et al.*, 1989), and to score higher on Offer's psychopathology scale (e.g. Brooks-Gunn & Warren, 1985).

Figure 33.3 *Pre-teens are growing up faster than ever before, and early-maturing girls are most at risk of mental disorder and delinquency*

As far as *early-maturing boys* are concerned, the evidence is much more mixed (Alsaker, 1996). Whilst early maturation is usually found to be advantageous, it has also been found to be associated with *more* psychopathology (e.g. Petersen & Crockett, 1985), depressive tendencies and anxiety (e.g. Alsaker, 1992).

Key STUDY

Box 33.4 The 'Isle of Wight' study (Rutter *et al.*, 1976)

This involved a large (more than 2000), representative sample of 14–15-year-olds, whose parents and teachers completed behaviour questionnaires about them. More detailed data were obtained from two sub-samples: (i) 200 randomly selected from the total population; (ii) 304 with extreme scores on the teacher/parent questionnaires (suggesting 'deviant' behaviour).

Those in both sub-samples were given questionnaires and tests and interviewed by psychiatrists. The major findings regarding rates of psychiatric disorder among the adolescents, compared with a sample of ten-year-olds and the adolescents' parents, are shown in Table 33.1.

Table 33.1 *Percentage of ten-year-olds, 14-15-year-olds, and the latter's parents, displaying psychiatric disorder*

	10-year-olds	14–15-year-olds	Adults (parents)
Males	12.7	13.2	7.6
Females	10.9	12.5	11.9

According to Rutter *et al.* (1976):

- There is a rather modest peak in psychiatric disorders in adolescence.

- Although severe clinical depression is rare, some degree of inner turmoil may characterise a sizeable minority of adolescents. Whilst it is not a myth, it should not be exaggerated.

- A substantial proportion of those adolescents with psychiatric problems had had them since childhood. Also, when problems did first appear during adolescence, they were mainly associated with stressful situations (such as parents' marital discord). According to Rutter *et al.* (1976):

'Adolescent turmoil is fact, not fiction, but its psychiatric importance has probably been overestimated in the past.'

Whilst some adolescents in Western societies may display affective disturbances or disorders, it is a relatively small minority who will show clinical depression or report 'inner turmoil' (Compas *et al.*, 1995). Instead, the majority worry about everyday issues, such as school and examination performance, finding work, family and social relationships, self-image, conflicts with authority, and the future generally (Gallagher *et al.*, 1992).

Studies of delinquent behaviour

Caspi *et al.* (1993) studied all the children born in Dunedin, New Zealand between April 1972 and March 1973, following them up every two years from ages 3-15. Compared with on-time (menarche 12.5-13.5 years) and late maturers (menarche after 13.5), early-maturing girls were more at risk for:

- *early delinquency* (breaking windows, getting drunk, making prank phone calls, stealing from other pupils at school);
- *familiarity with delinquent peers* (having friends or knowing others who engaged in these activities);
- *delinquency* (shoplifting, car theft, smoking marijuana, using weapons).

However, the risk for early delinquency was greater only in mixed-sex schools, and (as with a sample of Swedish girls studied by Magnusson *et al.*, 1985) early maturers were likely to mix with older peers. As for boys, *off-time* (early and late) maturation has been shown to be related to alcohol consumption, with late maturers also being at risk for *later* alcohol problems (Anderson & Magnusson, 1990).

ERIKSON'S THEORY: IDENTITY CRISIS

As noted in Chapter 31, Erikson (1963) believed that it is human nature to pass through a genetically determined sequence of *psychosocial stages*, spanning the whole lifetime. Each stage involves a struggle between two conflicting personality outcomes, one of which is positive (or *adaptive*), and the other negative (or *maladaptive*). Healthy development involves the adaptive outweighing the maladaptive.

The major challenge of adolescence is to establish a strong sense of personal identity. The dramatic onset of puberty, combined with more sophisticated intellectual abilities (see Chapter 28), makes adolescents particularly concerned with finding their own personal place in adult society.

In Western societies, adolescence is a *moratorium*, an authorised delay of adulthood, which frees adolescents from most responsibilities and helps them make the difficult transition from childhood to adulthood. Although this is meant to make the transition easier, it can also have the opposite effect. Most of the societies studied by cultural anthropologists have important public ceremonies to mark the transition from childhood to adulthood. This is in stark contrast to Western, industrialised nations, which leave children to their own devices in finding their identity. Without a clearly defined procedure to follow, this process can be difficult – both for adolescents and their parents (see the 'generation gap' on pages 360–361).

Does society create identity crisis?

As well as the perceived absence of 'rites of passage' in Western society, a problem for both adolescents and their parents at the end of the twentieth century is the related lack of consensus as to where adolescence begins and ends, and precisely what adolescent rights, privileges and responsibilities are. For example, the question 'When do I become an adult?' elicits a response from a teacher which is different from a doctor's, parent's or police officer's (Coleman, 1995).

The 'maturity gap' refers to the incongruity of achieving biological maturity at adolescence without simultaneously being awarded adult status (Curry, 1998). According to Hendry & Kloep (1999):

> 'Young people, as they grow up, find themselves in the trap of having to respond more and more to society's demands in a 'responsible' adult way while being treated as immature and not capable of holding sound opinions on a wide range of social matters'.

One possible escape route from this trap is *risk-taking behaviour* (see page 358).

As well as having to deal with the question 'Who am I?', the adolescent must also ask 'Who will I be?'. Erikson saw the creation of an adult personality as achieved mainly through choosing and developing a commitment to an occupation or role in life. The development of *ego identity* (a firm sense of who one is and what one stands for) is positive, and can carry people through difficult times.

When working with psychiatrically disturbed soldiers in World War II, Erikson coined the term *identity crisis* to describe the loss of personal identity which the stress of combat seemed to have caused. Some years later, he extended the use of the term to include:

> '... severely conflicted young people whose sense of confusion is due ... to a war within themselves'.

Failure to integrate perceptions of the self into a coherent whole results in *role confusion*, which, according to Erikson, can take several forms (see Box 33.5, page 358).

Box 33.5 Four major forms of role confusion

Intimacy: Fear of commitment to, or involvement in, close relationships, arising from a fear of losing one's own identity. This may result in stereotyped and formalised relationships, or isolation.

Time perspective: Inability to plan for the future or retain any sense of time. It is associated with anxieties about change and becoming an adult.

Industry: Difficulty in channelling resources in a realistic way into work or study, both of which require commitment. As a defence, the adolescent may find it impossible to concentrate, or become frentically engaged in a single activity to the exclusion of all others.

Negative identity: Engaging in abnormal or delinquent behaviour (such as drug taking, or even suicide) in an attempt to resolve the identity crisis. This extreme position, which sets such adolescents aside from the crowd, is preferable to the loneliness and isolation that come with failing to achieve distinct and more functional roles in life ('a negative identity is better than no identity').

Related to Erikson's claims about negative identity is *risk-taking behaviour*. Hendry (1999) asks if risk-taking is:

'... part of the psychological make-up of youth – a thrill-seeking stage in a developmental transition – a necessary rite of passage *en route* to the acquisition of adult skills and self-esteem?'

Many teenagers seek out excitement, thrills and risks as earnestly as in their childhood, perhaps to escape a drab existence or to exert some control over their own lives and to achieve *something*. For some, delinquency may be the solution: it could actually be adaptive as a way of facilitating self-definition and expressing autonomy (Compas et al., 1995).

Such conflict seems to be largely absent in societies where the complete transition to adulthood is officially approved and celebrated at a specific age, often through a particular ceremony. These enable both the individual and society to adjust to change and enjoy a sense of continuity (Price & Crapo, 1999).

Box 33.6 Initiation into adulthood in non-Western cultures

Cohen (1964) looked at 45 non-industrialised societies which held adulthood ceremonies. In societies where adult skills were hard and dangerous, or

where father–son relationships were weak but men had to co-operate in hard work, male initiation rituals were dramatic and painful. They allowed the boy to prove his manhood to the community – and to himself.

Sometimes they are designed to *give boys strength*, often by associating them with animals or plants. For example, in the Merina of Madagascar, the boy is associated with the banana tree, which bears much fruit resembling the erect penis (an ideal symbol of virility and fertility). The to-be-initiated boy is removed from his mother's home (a symbol of his attachment to her), before being circumcised in the company of men.

Brown (1963) described 'rites of passage' for girls in 43 societies from all major regions of the world. They most commonly occur where young girls continue to live and work in their mothers' homes after marriage, but they also sometimes occur even when young women permanently leave home. Here, they involve genital operations or extensive tattooing. These dramatically help a girl understand that she must make the transition from dependent child to a woman, who will have to fend for herself in a male-dominated environment (Price & Crapo, 1999).

In recent years, *infibulation*, the most extreme form of female circumcision, has become a global human rights issue. Its purpose is to preserve the virginity of young girls before marriage, and to tame the disturbing power of women. In many traditional Islamic countries, especially Sudan, Ethiopia, and Somalia, millions of young girls continue to undergo painful and risky genital operations.

Although the act of infibulation may, from a Western perspective, deindividualise and depersonalise women:

'It acts as a transition or a rite of passage to a greater female adult collective; one where women hold relatively few advantages in a male-dominated world. It may in fact be one of the few positive status markers for women in traditional Islamic societies'. (Price & Crapo, 1999)

According to Coleman & Roker (1998), an important trend in adolescence research is an increasing focus on identity development among ethnically diverse populations, such as young black women (e.g. Robinson, 1997) and mixed-race young people (Tizard & Phoenix, 1993). Coleman and Roker believe that notions of identity and identity formation are likely to become more central to the study of adolescence as this life stage becomes longer and more fragmented, and entry into adulthood becomes more problematic.

Studies of self-esteem

Tests of Erikson's theory have typically used measures of self-concept (especially *self-esteem*) as indicators of crisis. Girls' dissatisfaction with their appearance begins during puberty, along with a decline in self-esteem (Crawford & Unger, 1995). Comparisons between *early-* and *late-maturing girls* indicate that dissatisfaction with looks is associated with the rapid and normal weight gain that is part of growing up (Attie & Brooks-Gunn, 1989; Blyth *et al.*, 1981).

Early maturers have less positive body images, despite the fact that they date more and earlier. Also, sexual activity is more problematic for adolescent girls (as it is for females in general): there are persisting double standards regarding sex (as reflected in 'slag' and 'stud' for sexually active females and males respectively), together with differential responsibility for contraception and pregnancy.

However, Offer *et al.* (1988) deny that there is any increase in disturbance of the self-image during early adolescence. For Coleman & Hendry (1999), although such disturbance is more likely in early than late adolescence, only a very small proportion of the total adolescent population is likely to have a negative self-image or very low self-esteem.

By contrast, *early-maturing boys* feel more attractive (Tobin-Richards *et al.*, 1983) and tend to be more satisfied with their bodies, looks and muscle development (Blyth *et al.*, 1981; Simmons & Blyth, 1987). However, Alsaker (1996) refers to two recent studies, which have found a correlation between pubertal boys' *dissatisfaction* with their bodies and the development of pubic and body hair. She asks if this reflects some new image of men in advertisements, and a new trend for men to shave their bodies and be less hairy.

Most of these (and other similar) studies have been conducted in the USA, UK and other English-speaking countries. However, a recent study of a very large, nationally representative Norwegian sample found that the global self-esteem of both late-maturing boys and girls suffered, whilst early and on-time maturers (of both sexes) enjoy equally high self-esteem (Wichstrom, 1998).

MARCIA'S THEORY: IDENTITY STATUSES

In an extension of Erikson's work, Marcia (1980) proposed four *statuses* of adolescent identity formation, which characterise the search for identity. A mature identity can only be achieved if an individual experiences several *crises* in exploring and choosing between life's alternatives, finally arriving at a *commitment* or investment of the self in those choices.

Box 33.7 The four identity statuses proposed by Marcia (1980)

Table 33.2 *Four identity statuses as defined by high/low commitment and high/low crisis*

		Degree of crisis	
		High	Low
Degree of commitment to particular role/values	High	Identity achievement	Foreclosure
	Low	Moratorium	Diffusion (or confusion)

Diffusion/confusion: the individual has not really started thinking about the issues seriously, let alone formulated any goals or made any commitment. (This represents the *least mature* status).

Foreclosure: the individual has avoided the uncertainties and anxieties of crisis by quickly and prematurely committing to safe and conventional (parental) goals and beliefs. Alternatives have not been seriously considered.

Moratorium: this is the height of the crisis as described by Erikson (see page 358). Decisions about identity are postponed whilst the individual tries out alternative identities, without committing to any particular one.

Identity achievement: the individual has experienced a crisis but has emerged successfully with firm commitments, goals and ideology. (This represents the *most mature* status.)

Although identity moratorium is a prerequisite for identity achievement, Marcia does *not* see the four statuses as Erikson-type stages. However, evidence suggests that, amongst 12- to 24-year-old men, they are broadly age-related. For example, Meilman (1979) reported that younger men (12-18) were more likely to experience diffusion or foreclosure, whereas older men were increasingly likely to be identity achievers. Irrespective of age, relatively few men were achieving moratorium, which casts doubt on the validity of the theory.

Several *longitudinal* studies have indicated clear patterns of movement from foreclosure and diffusion to moratorium and achievement (Kroger, 1996). However, when applied to females, even Marcia (1980) accepts that his statuses work 'only more or less'. This is an example of *androcentrism*, that is, taking the male experience as the standard, and applying it to both men and women. Erikson's theory has been criticised in a similar way (Gilligan, 1982: see Chapters 34 and 35).

SOCIOLOGICAL APPROACHES: GENERATION GAP

Sociologists see *role change* as an integral aspect of adolescent development (Coleman, 1995). Changing school or college, leaving home and beginning a job, all involve a new set of relationships, producing different and often greater expectations. These expectations themselves demand a substantial reassessment of the self-concept, and *speed up* the socialisation process. Some adolescents find this problematic because of the wide variety of competing socialising agencies (such as the family, mass media and peer group), which often present *conflicting* values and demands.

Sociologists also see socialisation as being more dependent on the adolescent's *own generation* than on the family or other social institutions (*auto-socialisation*: Marsland, 1987). As Marsland says:

'The crucial meaning of youth is withdrawal from adult control and influence compared with childhood'.

Young people withdraw into their peer groups, and this withdrawal is (within limits) accepted by adults. What Marsland is describing here is the *generation gap*.

Parent–adolescent relationships

According to Hendry (1999):

'Adolescence as a transition from childhood to adulthood requires changes from child–parent relationships to young-adult–parent relationships'.

Failure to negotiate new relationships with parents, or having highly critical or rejecting parents, is likely to make adolescents adopt a negative identity (Curry, 1998). Also, parents who rated their own adolescence as stormy and stressful reported more conflict in their relationships with adolescent children, and were less satisfied with their family (Scheer & Unger, 1995). Parents in general are going through a time of transition themselves, reappraising their life goals, career and family ambitions, and assessing whether they have fulfilled their expectations as parents (see discussion of the 'mid-life crisis' in Chapter 34).

However, for most adolescents relationships with parents become more equal and reciprocal and parental authority comes to be seen as open to discussion and negotiation (e.g. Coleman & Hendry, 1999; Hendry *et al.*, 1993). Hendry *et al.*'s (1993) study also suggests that relationships with mothers and fathers do not necessarily change in the same ways and to the same extent.

Key STUDY

Box 33.8 Hendry *et al.*'s (1993) study of adolescent–parent relationships

In a longitudinal Scottish study, Hendry *et al.* (1993) found that parents were chosen in preference to friends when discussing progress and problems at school, and careers, but not necessarily more personal matters. Mothers were preferred over fathers as confidantes in all areas except careers and sex (boys) and problems with mothers (both sexes). Most girls and nearly half the boys chose to confide in their mothers over problems with friends, and nearly half the girls and a third of the boys conveyed doubts about their own abilities to her.

These figures suggest a *disengagement* by fathers. Girls tend to be very uncomfortable discussing pubertal issues with their fathers, and learn almost nothing from them about puberty. A mother's role in enforcing family rules brings her into conflict with the children more readily, but she is still seen as being supportive and caring, not 'distanced' like the father.

Studies conducted in several countries have found that young people get along well with their parents (e.g. Hendry *et al.*, 1993; Kloep & Tarifa, 1993), adopt their views and values, and perceive family members as the most important 'significant others' in their lives (McGlone *et al.*, 1996). Furthermore, most adolescents who had conflicts with their parents already had poor relationships with them before puberty (Stattin & Klackenberg, 1992).

Disagreements between young people and their parents are similar everywhere in Europe, including: Greece (Besevegis & Giannitsas, 1996), Italy (Jackson *et al.*, 1996), Scotland (Hendry *et al.*, 1993), Germany (Fischer *et al.*, 1985), and Albania and Sweden (Kloep & Tarifa, 1993). Teenagers have daily quarrels about how long or often they may stay out, how much they should help at home, the tidiness of their bedrooms, volume of music and school achievement.

According to Jackson *et al.* (1996), disagreements can arise because:

* parents expect greater independence of action from their teenagers;
* parents do not wish to grant as much autonomy as the adolescent demands (with young women having more conflict than young men over independence);
* parents and adolescents have different personal tastes and preferences.

Despite this potential for conflict, evidence suggests that competence as an independent adult can best be achieved within the context of a secure family environment, where exploration of alternative ideas, identities and behaviour is allowed and actively encouraged (Barber & Buehler, 1996). So, whilst detachment and separation from the family are necessary and desirable, young people do *not* have to reject their parents in order to become adults in their own right.

Peer relationships

Adolescent friendship groups (established around mutual interests) are normally embedded within the wider network of peer groups (which set 'norms', and provide comparisons and pressures to conform to 'expected' behaviours). Friendship groups reaffirm self-image, and enable the young person to experience a new form of intimacy and learn social skills (such as discussing and solving conflicts, sharing and self-assertion). They also offer the opportunity to expand knowledge, develop a new identity, and experiment away from the watchful eyes of adults and family (Coleman & Hendry, 1999).

Figure 33.4 *As important as peer relationships are, adolescents – and pre-adolescents – need adults they can look up to and trust*

Generally, peers become more important as providers of advice, support, feedback and companionship, as models for behaviour, and as sources of comparison with respect to personal qualities and skills. However, whilst peer groups and friendship groups become important points of reference in social development, and provide social contexts for shaping day-to-day values, they often support traditional parental attitudes and beliefs. Hence, peer and friendship groups can work in concert with, rather than in opposition to, adult goals and achievements (Hendry, 1999).

COLEMAN'S FOCAL THEORY: MANAGING ONE CHANGE AT A TIME

According to Coleman & Hendry (1990), most theories of adolescence help us to understand young people with serious problems and those belonging to minority or deviant groups. However, what is needed is a theory of *normality*. The picture that emerges from the research as a whole is that, whilst adolescence is a difficult time for some, for the majority it appears to be a period of relative stability. Coleman's (1980) *focal theory* is an attempt to explain how this is achieved.

The theory is based on a study of 800 six-, 11-, 13-, 15- and 17-year-old boys and girls. Attitudes towards self-image, being alone, heterosexual and parental relationships, friendships and large-group situations all changed as a function of age. More importantly, concerns about different issues reached a peak at different ages for both sexes.

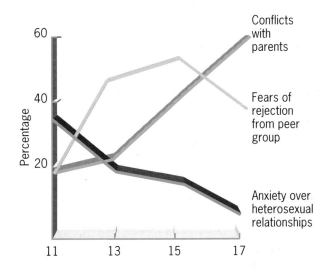

Figure 33.5 *Peak ages of the expression of different themes. These data are for boys only (From Coleman & Hendry, 1990)*

Particular sorts of relationship patterns come into *focus* (are most prominent) at different ages, although no pattern is specific to one age. The patterns overlap and there are wide individual differences.

Coleman believes that adolescents are able to cope with the potentially stressful changes as well as they do by dealing with one issue at a time. They spread the process of adaptation over a span of years, attempting to resolve one issue first before addressing the next. Because different problems and relationships come into focus and are dealt with at different points during the adolescent years, the stresses resulting from the need to adapt do not all have to be dealt with together.

According to Coleman & Hendry (1999), it is those adolescents who, for whatever reason, must deal with *more than one* issue (or normative shift) at a time, that are most likely to experience difficulties. If normative shifts coincide with non-normative ones, the situation is even more problematic (Hendry & Kloep, 1999).

Coleman's original findings have been successfully replicated by Kroger (1985) with large North American and New Zealand samples. Others have successfully tested hypotheses derived from the theory. For example, Simmons & Blyth (1987) predicted that if change (such as puberty):

- occurred at too young an age (causing the individual to be developmentally 'off-time');
- was marked by sharp discontinuity (i.e. sudden change); or
- involved accumulation of significant and temporally close issues (important shifts occurred together),

then adjustment would be more difficult. Their results strongly supported these predictions.

CONCLUSIONS

This chapter has portayed adolescence as involving a number of important transitions from childhood to adulthood, including puberty. The potential for *storm and stress* in Western societies is increased by the lack of clear definitions regarding when adulthood is reached. This makes the task of attaining an adult identity, as well as relationships with parents, more difficult compared with non-industrialised societies.

The chapter discussed storm and stress, *identity crisis* and the *generation gap* in the context of major psychological theories of adolescence, such as those of Hall, Erikson, and Marcia, together with sociological approaches. Whilst these theories all paint a picture of adolescence as an *inherently* difficult developmental stage, the evidence suggests that this is not necessarily so. Certain groups (such as early-maturing girls) may be more vulnerable than others, but the majority seem to cope well. According to Coleman's theory, it is *not* adolescence itself that is stressful, but the timing and combination of the transitions faced by young people.

Summary

- Adolescence means 'to grow into maturity' and involves **multiple transitions**. Compared with previous generations, it begins sooner and ends later. Various 'adulthood-postponing' changes have coincided with increased freedom at earlier ages.

- These transitions or **shifts** can be categorised as **normative maturational**, **normative society-dependent**, and **non-normative**. Normative shifts can become non-normative, as when puberty begins unusually early or late.

- **Puberty**, which marks the start of adolescence, involves the **adolescent growth spurt** and the development of **secondary sex characteristics** (both sexes). Whilst girls typically enter puberty two years before boys, there are important individual differences within each sex (such as **intraindividual asynchronies**).

- Adolescents evaluate their changing body image in terms of cultural standards of beauty, especially as these relate to weight. According to the **cultural ideal hypothesis**, girls move further away from their physical ideal, and **early-maturing girls** face a double disadvantage. By contrast, **early-maturing boys** will move fastest towards their physical ideal.

- Hall's **recapitulation theory** sees adolescence as a time of **storm and stress**. Whilst mood swings are more common during adolescence, rates of mental disorder (and delinquency rates) are only higher in early-maturing girls and adolescents with problems prior to puberty. The evidence for **off-time** maturation in boys is more mixed.

- According to Erikson, adolescence involves a conflict between **ego identity** and **role confusion**. In Western societies, adolescence is a **moratorium**, intended to help ease the transition to adulthood. However, the lack of clear definitions of adulthood, together with the maturity gap, may contribute to the adolescent **identity crisis**.

■ Role confusion can centre around **intimacy**, **time perspective** and **industry**. It can also take the form of **negative identity**, related to which is **risk-taking behaviour**. These problems are largely absent in societies which mark the transition to adulthood by **initiation ceremonies**, although **infibulation** (female circumcision) in Islamic countries is a highly controversial example.

■ Erikson's theory has been tested mainly by measuring **self-esteem**. Whilst self-esteem may decline in early adolescence, especially in girls, this affects only a very small proportion of all adolescents. However, research findings from English-speaking countries may not generalise to other cultures.

■ Marcia's four identity statuses (**diffusion/confusion**, **foreclosure**, **moratorium** and **identity achievement**) are defined by high/low **commitment** and **crisis**. Although these are not meant to be Erikson-type stages, the evidence suggests otherwise, but only for men. This has led to a charge of **androcentrism**.

■ Sociological approaches stress **role change**, the **conflicting** values and demands of different socialising agencies, and **auto-socialisation**, which produces the **generation gap**.

■ Renegotiating relationships with parents is necessary and usually successful. Although relationships usually become more equal and reciprocal, fathers may become **disengaged**, especially from their daughters, whilst mothers remain supportive and caring.

■ Research in various European countries suggests that adolescent–parent relationships are generally good. Whilst there are inevitable disagreements, which may sometimes concern independence, adult status is probably best achieved within the context of a secure family environment.

■ **Friendship groups** (as 'sub-groups' of the wider **peer group**) assume much greater significance during adolescence, such as helping to shape basic values. However, these values are often consistent with parents' values, goals and achievements.

■ According to Coleman's **focal theory**, most adolescents cope as well as they do by spreading the process of adaptation over several years, dealing with one issue at a time. Having to deal with more than one issue at a time is stressful, especially if changes occur too early or suddenly. There is considerable research evidence in support of focal theory.

Essay Questions

1 Discuss psychological insights into the development of identity in adolescence. *(24 marks)*

2 Describe and evaluate research into social relationships in adolescence. *(24 marks)*

WEB ADDRESSES

http://education.indiana.edu/cas/adol/adol.html
http://www.stanford.edu/group/adolescent.ctr/
http://www.hec.ohio-state.edu/famlife/adolescence/adolmain.html
http://csbsnt.csbs.unit.edu/dept/csa

34 *Early and Middle Adulthood*

Assuming we enjoy a normal life-span, the longest phase of the life-cycle will be spent in adulthood. Until recently, however, personality changes in adulthood attracted little psychological research interest. Indeed, as Levinson *et al.* (1978) have observed, adulthood is:

'... one of the best-kept secrets in our society and probably in human history generally'.

This chapter attempts to reveal some of these secrets by examining what theory and research have told us about personality change in adulthood, including the occurrence of crisies and transitions. Many theorists believe that adult concerns and involvements are patterned in such a way that we can speak about *stages* of adult development. *Early* (or young) *adulthood* covers the two decades from 20 to 40, and *middle adulthood* spans the years from 40 to 60 or 65. These are both discussed in this chapter. Later adulthood (or 'old age') is discussed in Chapter 36.

ERIKSON'S THEORY

Chapter 33 described Erikson's views on adolescence and his theory that human development occurs through a sequence of psychosocial stages. As far as early and middle adulthood are concerned, Erikson described two primary developmental crises (the sixth and seventh of his psychosocial stages: see Table 31.1, page 336).

The first is the establishment of *intimacy*, which is a criterion of having attained the psychosocial state of adulthood. By intimacy, Erikson means the ability to form close, meaningful relationships with others without 'the fear of losing oneself in the process' (Elkind, 1970). Erikson believed that a prerequisite for intimacy was the attainment of *identity* (the reconciliation of all our various roles into one enduring and stable personality: see Chapter 33, page 357). Identity is necessary, because we cannot know what it means to love someone and seek to share our life with them until we know who we are, and what we want to do with our lives. Thus, genuine intimacy requires us to give up some of our sense of separateness, and we must each have a firm identity to do this.

Intimacy need not involve sexuality. Since intimacy refers to the essential ability to relate our deepest hopes and fears to another person, and in turn to accept another's need for intimacy, it describes the relationship between friends just as much as that between sexual partners (Dacey, 1982). By sharing ourselves with others, our personal identities become fully realised and consolidated. Erikson believed that if a sense of identity were not established with friends or a partner, then *isolation* (a sense of being alone without anyone to share with or care for) would result. We normally achieve intimacy in *young adulthood* (our 20s and 30s), after which we enter *middle age* (our 40s and 50s). This involves the attainment of *generativity*, the second developmental crisis.

Box 34.1 Generativity

The central task of the middle years of adulthood is to determine life's purpose or goal, and to focus on achieving aims and contributing to the well-being of others (particularly children). Generativity means being concerned with others beyond the immediate family, such as future generations and the nature of the society and world in which those future generations will live. As well as being displayed by parents, generativity is shown by anyone actively concerned with the welfare of young people and in making the world a better place for them to live and work. People who successfully resolve this developmental crisis establish clear guidelines for their lives and are generally productive and happy within this *directive framework*. Failure to attain generativity leads to *stagnation*, in which people become preoccupied with their personal needs and comforts.

Evaluation of Erikson's theory

The sequence from identity to intimacy may not accurately reflect present-day realities. In recent years, the trend has been for adults to live together before marrying, so they tend to marry later in life than people did in the past (see Chapter 35). Many people struggle with identity issues (such as career choice) *at the same time* as dealing with intimacy issues.

Additionally, some evidence suggests that females achieve intimacy *before* 'occupational identity'. The typical life course of women involves passing directly into a stage of intimacy without having achieved personal identity. Sangiuliano (1978) argues that most women submerge their identities into those of their partners, and only in mid-life do they emerge from this and search for separate identities and full independence. There is also a possible interaction between gender and *social class*. For example, amongst working class men, early marriage is seen as a 'good' life pattern. They see early adulthood as a time for 'settling down', having a family and maintaining a steady job. Middle class men and women, by contrast, see early adulthood as a time for exploration, in which different occupations are tried. Marriage tends to occur after this, and 'settling down' does not usually take place before 30 (Neugarten, 1975). There is also evidence of an interaction between gender, *race* and *culture*.

Key STUDY
Box 34.2 Intimacy and identity

Ochse & Plug (1986) studied over 1800 South African black and white men and women. Their findings raise questions about both the *timing* of particular stages and the exact *sequence* of the developmental tasks involved. For example, amongst whites, 25–39-year-old women appear to develop a sense of identity *before men*. This may be because developing a true sense of intimacy must *precede* a sense of identity (*not* vice versa, as Erikson claimed). According to Price and Crapo (1999):

'It is quite feasible that by sharing and risking themselves in close relationships, people may learn to know themselves, to reconcile their conception of themselves with the community recognition of them, and to develop a sense of mutuality with their community'.

Not until this process is complete can a sense of identity be achieved. Due to prevailing social conditions in South Africa (including minority status, high poverty rates, and fragmented living conditions), black women had a difficult time achieving a sense of intimacy and hence of identity. Black men also did not achieve a sense of identity until late in life. In turn, this adversely affected black women, who still experienced a lack of self-definition, intimacy and well-being far into middle age:

'It appears that the experience of the "adult years" was one thing for whites and something quite different for blacks. As social conditions change in South Africa, whole groups of blacks may expect to experience a completely different psychological development than they would have under apartheid.' (Price & Crapo, 1999)

Erikson's psychosocial stages were meant to be *universal*, applying to both sexes in all cultures. However, he acknowledged that the sequence of stages is different for a woman, who suspends her identity as she prepares to attract the man who will marry her. Men achieve identity before achieving intimacy with a sexual partner, whereas for women, Erikson's developmental crises appear to be fused (see Chapter 55). As Gilligan (1982) has observed:

'The female comes to know herself as she is known, through relationships with others'.

All the above evidence suggests that it is almost certainly impossible to describe *universal* stages for adults. Moreover, as seen in Chapter 33, there is evidence of a growing prolongation of adolescence.

Box 34.3 Perpetual adolescence

According to Sheehy (1996), whilst childhood is ending earlier, adults are prolonging adolescence into their 30s. Indeed, many people are not acknowledging maturity until they reach 40. Sheehy suggests that:

'Adolescence is now prolonged for the middle classes until the end of their 20s, and for blue-collar men and women until their mid-20s, as more young adults live at home longer. True adulthood does not begin until 30. Most Baby Boomers, born after World War II, do not feel fully 'grown up' until they are in their 40s, and even then they resist'.

Beaumont (1996) argues that we have evolved into a generation of 'Peter Pans', stuck in adolescence:

'You see them in Hyde Park – 30- and 40-somethings on rollerblades and skateboards, hanging out at Glastonbury or discussing the merits of Oasis versus Blur at dinner parties'.

The fictional models of this 'new generation' are Gary and Tony from the BBC television programme *Men Behaving Badly*, and Patsie and Eddy from *Absolutely Fabulous*. Real-life examples of 'Peter Pans' include Mick Jagger, Cliff Richard and Richard Branson.

Figure 34.1 *Gary and Tony, the 'perpetual adolescents' in BBC TV's* Men Behaving Badly

According to Orbach (cited in Beaumont, 1996), one problem created by adults who refuse to grow up is their own parenting. Unable to look up to figures of authority themselves, they feel a sense of loss and look to their own children for emotional sustenance in a curious role reversal.

LEVINSON *ET AL.*'S 'SEASONS OF A MAN'S LIFE'

Perhaps the most systematic study of personality and life changes in adulthood began in 1969, when Levinson *et al.* interviewed 40 men aged 35 to 45 from a variety of occupational backgrounds. Transcripts were made of the five to ten tape-recorded interviews that each participant gave over several months. Levinson *et al.* looked at how adulthood is actually *experienced*.

In *The Seasons of a Man's Life*, Levinson *et al.* (1978) advanced a *life structure theory*, defining life structure as the underlying pattern or design of a person's life at any given time. Life structure allows us to 'see how the self is in the world and how the world is in the self', and evolves through a series of *phases* or *periods* which give overall shape to the course of adult development. Adult development comprises a sequence of *eras* which overlap in the form of *cross-era transitions*. These last about five years, terminating the outgoing era and initiating the incoming one. The four eras are pre-adulthood (age 0–22), early adulthood (17–45), middle adulthood (40–65) and late adulthood (60 onwards).

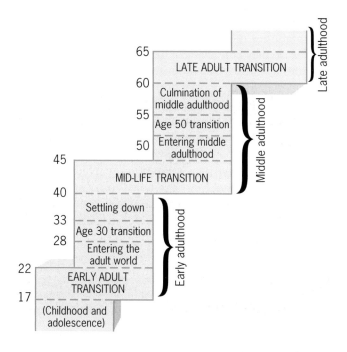

Figure 34.2 *Levinson* et al.'s *theory of adult development. The life-cycle is divided into four major eras that overlap in the form of cross-era transitions (From Gross, 1996)*

The phases or periods alternate between those that are *stable* (or *structure-building*) and *transitional* (or *structure-changing*). Although each phase involves biological, psychological and social adjustments, family and work roles are seen as central to the life structure at any time, and individual development is interwoven with changes in these roles.

The era of early adulthood

Early adult transition (17–22) is a developmental 'bridge' between adolescence and adulthood.

Box 34.4 Separation and attachment

Two key themes of the early adult transition are *separation* and the formation of *attachments* to the adult world. *External* separation involves moving out of the family home, increasing financial independence, and entering more independent and responsible roles and living arrangements. *Internal* separation involves greater psychological distance from the family, less emotional dependence on the parents, and greater differentiation between the self and family. Although we separate from our parents, Levinson *et al.* argue that we never complete the process, which continues throughout life. Attachment involves exploring the world's possibilities, imagining ourselves as part of it, and identifying and establishing changes for living in the world before we become 'full members' of it.

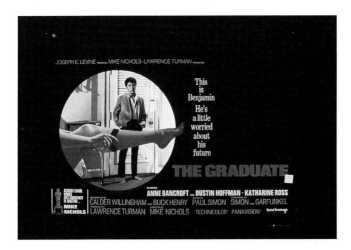

Figure 34.3 *A newly graduated Dustin Hoffman, whilst trying to separate from his parents, is seduced by Anne Bancroft, who is old enough to be his mother!*

Between ages 22 and 28, we *enter the adult world*. This is the first *structure-building* (rather than *structure-changing*) phase and hence is referred to as the *entry life structure for early adulthood*. In it, we try to fashion:

'a provisional structure that provides a workable link between the valued self and adult society'.

In the *novice phase*, we try to define ourselves as adults and live with the initial choices we make concerning jobs, relationships, lifestyles and values. However, we need to create a balance between 'keeping our options open' (which allows us to explore possibilities without being committed to a given course) and 'putting down roots' (or creating stable life structures).

Our decisions are made in the context of our *dreams* (the 'vague sense' we have of ourselves in the adult world and what we want to do with our lives). We must overcome disappointments and setbacks, and learn to accept and profit from successes, so that the dream's 'thread' does not get lost in the course of 'moving up the ladder' and revising the life structure. To help us in our efforts at self-definition, we look to *mentors*, older and more experienced others, for guidance and direction. Mentors can take a *formal* role in guiding, teaching and helping novices to define their dreams. Alternatively, a mentor's role may be *informal*, providing an advisory and emotionally supportive function (as a parent does).

The *age-30 transition* (28–33) provides an opportunity to work on the flaws and limitations of the first life structure, and to create the basis for a more satisfactory structure that will complete the era of young adulthood. Most of Levinson *et al.*'s participants experienced *age-30 crises* which involved stress, self-doubt, feelings that life was losing its 'provisional quality' and becoming more serious, and time pressure. Thus, the participants saw this as being the time for change, if change was needed. However, for a minority the age-30 transition was crisis-free.

Box 34.5 Settling down

The *settling down* (or *culminating life structure for early adulthood*: 33–40) phase represents consolidation of the second life structure. This involves a shift away from tentative choices regarding family and career towards a strong sense of commitment to a personal, familial and occupational future. Paths for success in work and husband and father roles are mapped out and, instead of just beginning to find out what is important and what our opinions are, we see ourselves as responsible adults.

The settling down phase comprises two substages: *early settling down* (33–36) and *becoming one's own man* or *BOOM* (36–40). In the latter, we strive to advance and succeed in building better lives, improve and use our skills, be creative, and in general contribute to society. We want recognition and affirmation from society, but we also want to be self-sufficient and free of social pressure and control. Although a 'boy-man' conflict may be produced, this can represent a step forward. This sub-stage may also see us assume a *mentor role* for someone younger (see above).

The era of middle adulthood

The *mid-life transition* (40–45) involves terminating one life structure, initiating another, and continuing the process of individuation started during the *BOOM* sub-stage. This is a time of soul-searching, questioning and assessing the real meaning of the life structure's achievement. It is sometimes referred to as the *mid-life crisis*, although Levinson *et al.* did not actually use this term. For some people, the change is gradual and fairly painless. For others, however, it is full of uncertainties.

The age-50 mid-life crisis stems from unconscious tensions between attachment and separation, the resurfacing of the need to be creative (which is often repressed in order to achieve a career), and retrospective comparisons between 'dreams' and life's reality.

Most participants in Levinson *et al.*'s study had not reached age 45. Following interviews two years after the study was concluded, some were chosen for more extensive study. However, the evidence for the remaining phases is much less detailed than for the earlier ones.

In entering *middle adulthood* (or *early life structure for middle adulthood*: 45–50), we have resolved (more-or-less satisfactorily) whether what we have committed ourselves to really is worthwhile, and it is again necessary to make choices regarding a new life structure. Sometimes, these choices are defined by *marker events* such as divorce, illness, occupational change, or the death of a loved one. However, the choices may also be influenced by less obvious but significant changes, such as shifts in the enthusiasm for work or in the quality of marriage. As before, the resulting life structure varies in how satisfying it is and how connected it is to the self. It may not be intrinsically happy and fulfilling. The restructuring consists of many steps, and there may be setbacks in which options have to be abandoned ('back to the drawing board').

The validity of the 'mid–life crisis'

Just as the 'identity crisis' is part of the popular stereotype of adolescence (see Chapter 33, page 357), Levinson *et al.* have helped to make the 'mid-life crisis' part of the common-sense understanding of adult development. Like Erikson, Levinson *et al.* see crisis as *inevitable*. As they note:

> 'It is not possible to get through middle adulthood without having at least a moderate crisis in either the mid-life transition or the age-50 transition'.

They also see crisis as *necessary*. If we do not engage in soul searching, we will:

> '... pay the price in a later developmental crisis or in a progressive withering of the self and a life structure minimally connected to the self'.

The view that crisis is both inevitable and necessary (or *normative*, to use Erikson's term) is controversial. People of all ages suffer occasional depression, self-doubt, sexual uncertainty and concerns about the future. Indeed, there appears to be an increasingly wide age range (and a growing number) of people who decide to make radical changes in their life-style, both earlier and later than predicted by Levinson *et al.*'s theory.

'Downshifting'

According to Tredre (1996), the concept of a mid-life crisis is too narrow in that traditionally, or stereotypically, it refers to someone in his or her late 40s, with grown-up children, who gives up a secure and well-paid 'respectable' career, and moves to a small market town or village in order to enjoy a less stressful, more peaceful and generally better quality of life. We need to spread the net wider nowadays and think in terms of early-, mid- and late-life crises: people of all age groups and walks of life are 'feeling the itch'.

Downshifting refers to voluntarily opting out of a pressurised career and interminably long hours in the office, and often involves giving up an exceptionally well-paid job in a high-profile industry in the pursuit of a more fulfilling way of life. Tredre identifies a number of possible reasons for downshifting, including anti-urbanism (fuelled by concerns over urban pollution), crime, violence, and increasing job insecurity.

Box 34.6 Identity crisis and the life cycle

Marcia (1998) also believes that the concept of a mid-life crisis is misleading and too narrow. He argues that 'adolescing' (making decisions about one's identity) occurs throughout the lifespan, whenever we review or reorganise our lives. At the very least, we might expect identity crises to accompany (in Erikson's terms) intimacy–isolation, generativity–stagnation, and integrity–despair (see Chapter 36).

Just as puberty and other changes in early adolescence disrupt the partial identities of childhood, so the demands of intimacy require a reformulation of the initial identity achieved at late adolescence. Similarly, the generative, care-giving requirements of middle age differ from those of being with an intimate partner. The virtues of fidelity, love and care (see Table 31.1, page 336), which derive from positive resolution of young and middle adulthood, do not emerge without a struggle. According to Marcia (1998):

'Periods of adolescing are normal, expectable components of life cycle growth'.

However, whilst crises are not limited to specific times in our lives, those associated with middle (and old) age are especially difficult.

Figure 34.4 *The image of an older man's attraction to younger women is part of the popular concept of the 'mid-life crisis'. It is portrayed here by Woody Allen and Juliette Lewis in* Husbands and Wives

Durkin (1995) notes that a large proportion of middle-aged people actually feel *more* positive about this phase of life than earlier ones, with only ten per cent reporting feeling as though they had experienced a crisis. For Durkin, the mid-life crisis is not as universal as Levinson *et al.* suggest, and the time and extent to which we experience uncomfortable self-assessments vary as a function of several factors (such as personality). Although the evidence is sparse, going through middle age in a relatively peaceful and untroubled way is actually a *favourable* indicator of future development, that is, a *lack* of emotional disturbance predicts *better* rather than poorer functioning in later life (Rutter & Rutter, 1992).

Crisis can stem from several sources, including ineffective adjustment to the normal stresses of growth and transition in middle-age, and the reaction of a particularly vulnerable person to these stresses (Hopson & Scally, 1980). This suggests that the mid-life crisis is not a *stage* through which everyone *must* pass. The diversity of adult experience makes terms like 'stages' and 'seasons' inappropriate. *Themes*, perhaps, is a better term.

Many stressful biological, social and psychological life changes are likely to occur together in any particular society (Bee & Mitchell, 1980). As a result, most people will experience transitions or crises at roughly the same time in their life-cycles. People will differ regarding how much stress they can tolerate before a 'crisis' is experienced, and in how they respond to it when it does occur. Personal growth may be one response, and changing the major 'external' aspects of our lives (by, for example, changing jobs or, getting divorced) another.

Two other components of the mid-life crisis are much less contentious. The first is a wide range of *adaptations* in the life pattern. Some of these stem from role changes that produce fairly drastic consequences, such as divorce, remarriage, a major occupational change, redundancy or serious illness. Others are more subtle, and include the ageing and likely death of parents, the new role of grandparent, and the sense of loss which sometimes occurs when children have all moved away from the family home (*empty-nest distress*). The impact of some of these life or marker events is discussed in Chapter 35.

The second non-controversial component is the significant change in the *internal* aspects of life structures, which occurs regardless of external events. This involves reappraising achievements and remaining ambitions, especially those to do with work and the relationship with our sexual partner. A fundamental development at this time is the realisation that the final authority for life rests with us. (This relates to Gould's, 1978, 1980, theory: see page 371.) Sheehy (1976) has suggested that men in their 40s begin to explore and develop their more 'feminine' selves (by becoming more nurturant, affiliative and intimate). Women, by contrast, discover their more 'masculine' selves (by becoming more action-oriented, assertive, and ambitious). The passing-by in *opposite directions* produces the pain and distress which is the 'mid-life crisis'.

The seasons of a woman's life

Levinson *et al.*'s research was carried out on men, and no women were included in the sample. Similar research investigating women has found similarities with Levinson *et al.*'s findings. However, men and women have been shown to differ in terms of their *dreams*.

Box 34.7 Women's dreams and 'gender splitting'

Levinson (1986) argues that a 'gender-splitting' phenomenon occurs in adult development. Men have fairly unified visions of their futures, which tend to be focused on their careers. Women, however, have 'dreams' which are more likely to be split between a career and marriage. This was certainly true of academics and business women, although the former were less ambitious and more likely to forego a career, whereas the latter wanted to maintain their careers but at a reduced level. Only the *homemakers* had unified dreams (to be full-time wives and mothers, as their own mothers had been).

Roberts & Newton (1987) saw the family as playing a 'supportive' role for men. Women's dreams were constructed around their relationship with the husband and family, which subordinated their personal needs. So, part of *her* dream is *his* success. For Durkin (1995), this difference in women's and men's priorities may put women at greater risk:

'... of disappointment and developmental tension as their investment in others' goals conflict with their personal needs'.

Women who give marriage and motherhood top priority in their 20s tend to develop more individualistic goals for their 30s. However, those who are career-oriented early on in adulthood tend to focus on marriage and family concerns later. Generally, the transitory instability of the early 30s lasts *longer* for women than for men, and 'settling down' is much less clear cut. Trying to integrate career and marriage/family responsibilities is very difficult for most women, who experience greater conflicts than their husbands are likely to.

Gender splitting is relevant to discussion of marriage/partnering and parenthood. The changing roles of women in paid employment and of men in the home are discussed in Chapter 35.

THE VALIDITY OF STAGE THEORIES OF ADULT DEVELOPMENT

Erikson's and Levinson's theories of adult development emphasise a 'ladder-like' progression through an inevitable and universal series of stages/phases. The view that adult development is 'stage-like' has, however,

been criticised (Rutter & Rutter, 1992) on the grounds that it underestimates the degree of *individual variability*. Many members of the mainstream working class population do *not* grow or change in systematic ways. Instead, they show many rapid fluctuations, depending on things like relationships, work demands and other life stresses that are taking place (Craig, 1992).

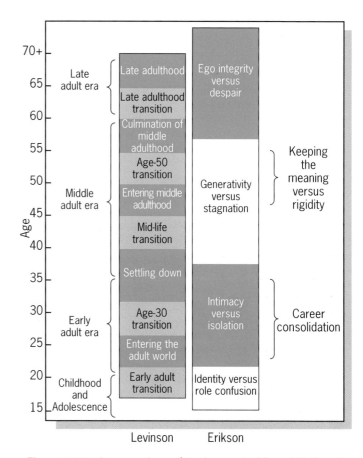

Figure 34.5 *A comparison of Levinson et al.'s and Erikson's adult stages. Note how the former's are defined primarily by age and the latter's by crisis (From Santrock, 1986)*

Stage theories also imply a *discontinuity* of development. However, many psychologists maintain there is also considerable *continuity* of personality during adult life. The popular stereotype sees middle adulthood as the time when a person is responsible, settled, contented and at the peak of achievement. Because of all these criticisms of stage theories, current views of adult development stress the *transitions* and milestones that mark adult life, rather than a rigid developmental sequence (Baltes, 1983, 1987; Schlossberg, 1984). This is commonly referred to as the *life events approach*. Yet, despite the growing unpredictability of changes in adult life, most people still unconsciously evaluate their transitions according to a *social clock*, which determines whether we are 'on time' with respect to particular life events (such as getting married: Schlossberg *et al.*, 1978). If we are 'off time', either early or late, we are *age deviant*. Like other types of deviancy, this can result in social penalties, such as amusement, pity or rejection.

Whilst all cultures have social clocks that define the 'right' time to marry, begin work, have children and so on, these clocks vary greatly between cultures (Wade & Tavris, 1999).

Craig (1992) sees changes in adult thought, behaviour and personality as being less a result of chronological age or specific biological changes, and more a result of personal, social and cultural events or forces. Because of the sheer diversity of experiences in an adult's life, Craig does not believe it is possible to describe major 'milestones' that will apply to nearly everyone. The life events approach is discussed further in Chapter 35.

GOULD'S THEORY OF THE EVOLUTION OF ADULT CONSCIOUSNESS

Whereas Levinson *et al.* discussed adult development in terms of evolving life structures, Gould (1978, 1980) prefers to talk about the evolution of *adult consciousness* which occurs when:

'... we release ourselves from the constraints and ties of childhood consciousness'.

Gould sees the thrust of adult development as being towards the realisation and acceptance of ourselves as creators of our own lives, and away from the assumption that the rules and standards of childhood determine our destiny. His theory is an extension of the Freudian idea of *separation anxiety*. According to Gould, we have to free ourselves of the *illusion of absolute safety*, an illusion which dominated childhood. This involves *transformations*, giving up the security of the past to form our own ideas. We have to replace the concept of parental dependency with a sense of *autonomy*, or owning ourselves. This, however, is difficult because dependency on parents is a normal fea-

ture of childhood. Indeed, without it, childhood would be very difficult. As well as shedding childhood consciousness, Gould believes that our *sense of time* also changes.

Box 34.8 Our changing sense of time

Up until age 18 or so, we feel both protected and constrained by our parents, and never quite believe that we will escape the 'family world'. This is like being in a timeless capsule in which 'the future is a fantasy space that may possibly not exist'. However, we begin to glimpse an endless future and see an infinite amount of time ahead of us.

In our 20s, we become confident about being separated from the family. However, we have not yet formed early-adult life structures. Gould (1980) puts it like this:

'Because of all the new decisions and novel experiences that come with setting up new adult enterprises, our time sense, when we're being successful, is one of movement along a chosen path that leads linearly to some obscure prize decades in the future. There is plenty of time, but we're still in a hurry once we've developed a clearer, often stereotyped, picture of where we want to be by then'.

At the end of our 20s, our sense of time incorporates our adult past as well as future. The future is neither infinite nor linear, and we must choose between different options because there isn't time to take them all. From our mid-30s to mid-40s, we develop a sense of urgency that time is running out. We also become aware of our own mortality which, once attained, is never far from our consciousness. How we spend our time becomes a matter of great importance. Additionally, we begin to question whether our 'prize' (freedom from restrictions by those who have formed us – our parents) either exists or, if it does, whether it has been worth it (cf. Levinson *et al.*'s 'dream').

CONCLUSIONS

This chapter has considered several theories of personality change in early and middle adulthood. The stage theory approach has been popular, although critics

argue that development does not occur in predictable and ordered ways. Whether personality development in adulthood is characterised by stability or change has yet to be resolved.

Summary

- In Erikson's psychosocial theory, young adulthood involves the establishment of **intimacy**. This can be achieved through friendship as well as through a sexual relationship. Failure to achieve intimacy results in a sense of **isolation**. The central task of middle adulthood is the attainment of **generativity**. Failure to achieve generativity results in **stagnation**.

- Many people struggle with issues of identity and intimacy **at the same time**, and women tend to achieve intimacy **before** 'occupational identity', submerging their identities into those of their partners. There are also important social class, racial and cultural differences in the timing of marriage and 'settling down'.

- Levinson *et al.* were concerned with how adulthood is actually **experienced**. Their **life structure theory** identifies **phases** or **periods** which give overall shape to the course of adult development. These are either **stable** (structure-building) or **transitional** (structure-changing). A sequence of **eras** overlaps in the form of **cross-era transitions**.

- **Early adult transition** (17–22) is a developmental bridge between adolescence and adulthood. It involves both internal and external **separation** from parents and **attachment** to the adult world.

- **Entry life structure for early adulthood** (22–28) is the first **structure-building** phase. In the novice phase, we make choices in the context of our **dreams**. We look to **mentors** to help us in the task of self-definition and defining our dreams.

- The **age-30 transition** (28–33) provides an opportunity to create the basis for a more satisfactory life structure that will complete the era of young adulthood. An **age-30 crisis** is commonly experienced.

- The **culminating life structure for early adulthood/settling down** phase (33–40) involves two sub-stages, **early settling down** (33–36) and **becoming one's own man** (BOOM) (36–40). The latter may involve the assumption of a **mentor role** for some younger adult.

- The **mid-life transition** (40–45) is a time of soul-searching and assessing the meaning of the life-structure achievement (**mid-life crisis**).

- In **early life structure for middle adulthood/entering middle adulthood** (45–50), we must again make choices regarding new life structures. These choices are sometimes defined by **marker events**.

- Levinson *et al.* have helped to make the 'mid-life crisis' part of our common-sense understanding of adult development. They see crisis as both inevitable and necessary (**normative**).

- People of all ages suffer crises ('**adolescing**'), and a growing number of people are deciding to make radical changes in their life-style (**downshifting**), both earlier and later than predicted by Levinson *et al.*

- A large proportion of middle-aged people actually feel **more** positive about their lives than earlier, and the mid-life crisis is not as universal as Levinson *et al.* suggest.

- Research involving women has found similarities with Levinson *et al.*'s findings based on their all-male sample. However, there is a '**gender splitting**' that occurs in relation to men's and women's **dreams**. Whilst men have fairly unified, career-focused visions of the future, women's dreams are split between career and marriage/family responsibilities.

- The age-30 transition generally lasts longer for women than for men, and 'settling down' is much less clear cut. Trying to integrate career and marriage and family responsibilities is very difficult for most women.

- The view that adult development is 'stage-like' has been criticised on the grounds that it underestimates **individual variability**. Stage theories also imply a **discontinuity** of development, whilst many psychologists stress the **continuity** of adult personality.

- According to Gould, the thrust of adult development is towards the realisation and acceptance of ourselves as creators of our own lives (adult consciousness) and freeing ourselves of the **illusion of absolute safety**.

- Gould also believes that adult development involves a change in the **sense of time**. By the end of our twenties, the future is seen as neither infinite nor linear, and we must make choices. From our mid-thirties to mid-forties, we sense that time is running out and are aware of our mortality.

Essay Questions

1 Critically consider the evidence for the existence of crises and transitions in early and middle adulthood.

(24 marks)

2 Describe and critically evaluate any **one** theory of development in early and middle adulthood.

(24 marks)

WEB ADDRESSES

http://midmac.med.harvard.edu/research.html
http://www.hope.edu/academic/psychology/335/webrep2/crisis.html
http://www.mhhe.com/socscience/devel/common/middleadulthood.htm

35 *Family and Relationships in Adulthood*

As Chapter 34 showed, evidence concerning the predictability of changes in adult life (or what Levinson, 1986, calls *psychobiosocial transitions*) is conflicting. Three kinds of influence can affect the way we develop in adulthood (Hetherington & Baltes, 1988). *Normative age-graded influences* are biological (such as the menopause) and social (such as marriage and parenting) changes that normally occur at fairly predictable ages. *Normative history-graded influences* are historical events that affect whole generations or cohorts at about the same time (examples include wars, recessions and epidemics). Finally, *non-normative influences* are idiosyncratic transitions, such as divorce, unemployment and illness.

Levinson's (1986) term *marker events* refers to age-graded and non-normative influences. Others prefer the term critical life events to describe such influences, although it is probably more accurate to describe them as *processes*. Some critical life events, such as divorce, unemployment and bereavement, can occur at any time during adulthood (bereavement is discussed in Chapter 36). Others occur late in adulthood, such as retirement (which is also discussed in Chapter 36). Yet others tend to happen early in adulthood, such as marriage (or partnering) and parenting. This chapter examines research findings concerning the impact of marriage, parenting and divorce.

MARRIAGE

Since over 90 per cent of adults marry at least once, marriage is an example of a normative age-graded influence. Marriage is an important transition for young adults, because it involves a lasting personal commitment to another person (and, so, is a means of achieving Erikson's *intimacy*: see Chapter 34), financial responsibilities and, perhaps, family responsibilities. However, it cannot be the *same* type of transition for everyone. In some cultures, for example, people have little choice as to who their partners will be (as is the case in *arranged marriages*: see Chapter 6).

Marriage and preparation for marriage can be very stressful. Davies (1956) identified mental disorders occurring for the first time in those who were engaged to be married. Typically, these were anxiety and depression, which usually began in connection with an event that hinged on the wedding date (such as booking the reception). Since the disorders improved when the engagement was broken off or the wedding took place, Davies concluded that it was the *decision* to make the commitment that was important, rather than the act of getting married itself.

Box 35.1 Cohabitation

Apparently, couples who live together (or *cohabit*) before marriage are *more* likely to divorce later, and be less satisfied with their marriages, than those who marry without having cohabited. Also, about 40 per cent of couples who cohabit do not marry. Whilst this suggests that cohabitation may prevent some divorces, cohabitees who do marry are more likely to divorce. According to Bee (1994), this is because people who choose to cohabit are *different* from those who choose not to. As a group, cohabitees seem to be more willing to flout tradition in many ways (such as being less religious and disgreeing that one should stay with a marriage partner no matter what). Those who do not cohabit include a large proportion of 'more traditional' people.

It has long been recognised that mortality is affected by marital status. Married people tend to live longer than unmarried people, are happier, healthier and have lower rates of various mental disorders than the single, widowed or divorced (see Box 5.6, page 49). The excessive mortality of the unmarried relative to the married has generally been increasing over the past two to three decades, and it seems that divorced (and widowed) people in their twenties and thirties have particularly high risks of dying compared with other people of the same age (Cramer, 1995: see Chapter 36).

Measures of marital adjustment indicate that agreement between partners on various issues (a measure of marital compatability) is positively correlated with other components of relationship adjustment, such as satisfaction, affection and doing various activities together (Eysenck & Wakefield, 1981: and see Box 5.4, page 46 for a discussion of factors that contribute to marital unhappiness and divorce).

Box 35.2 Do men get more from marriage than women?

Bee (1994) argues that the greatest beneficiaries of marriage are men, partly because they are less likely than women to have close confidants outside marriage, and partly because wives provide more emotional warmth and support for husbands than husbands do for wives. Marriage is less obviously psychologically protective for women, not because a confiding and harmonious relationship is any less important for them (indeed, if anything it is *more* important), but because:

- many marriages do not provide such a relationship; and

- other consequences of marriage differ between the sexes.

(The 'advantage' of marriage for men is reflected in the higher rates of men's re-marriage following divorce: see text below.)

Although our attitudes towards education and women's careers have changed, Rutter & Rutter (1992), echoing Levinson's concept of 'gender-splitting' (see Chapter 34), have proposed that:

'The potential benefits of a harmonious relationship may, for a woman, be counterbalanced by the stresses involved in giving up a job or in being handicapped in a career progression or promotion through having to combine a career and parenthood'.

This is discussed further on pages 377–379.

DIVORCE

Although divorce rates in the US have shown a modest decline since 1979, over 45 per cent of marriages still end in divorce (Simons, 1996). In 1996, there were about 1,150,000 divorces in the US, involving over one million children. Following divorce, 84 per cent of children reside with their mothers in single-parent homes, but this is usually only temporary, since 65 per cent of women, and over 75 per cent of men remarry. Rates of cohabitation are high in those who do not remarry. Divorce rates are even higher in remarriages than first marriages; therefore, children who are exposed to multiple marital transitions experience the most adverse consequences in adjustment (Hetherington & Stanley-Hagan, 1999).

So, in recent decades, the structure and stability of families in Western societies have undergone considerable changes. An increasing number of adults live in subsequent cohabiting or remarried relationships and, in turn, these changes have led to a marked rise in the number of children living in step-family situations (Nicholson *et al.*, 1999: see pages 380–381).

Box 35.3 Who is most likely to divorce?

National statistics conceal important racial and ethnic differences. For example, compared with non-Hispanic Whites, African-Americans wait longer before marrying and are less likely to marry, but are also more likely to separate and divorce and to remain separated without a legal divorce. They are also less likely to remarry (Hetherington & Stanley-Hagan, 1999).

According to Turnbull (1995), divorce rates are highest during the first five years of marriage and then peak again after couples have been married for 15–25 years.

Divorce is a stressor for both men and women, since it involves the loss of one's major attachment figure and source of emotional support. However, men appear to experience *more* stress than women, which is perhaps not altogether surprising given the greater benefits to men of marriage (see above). Also, divorce can have serious effects on the psychological adjustment of children whose parents are separating (see pages 380–381).

According to Woollett & Fuller (cited in Cooper, 1996), mothers who have been through a divorce often report experiencing a sense of achievement in their day-to-day activities and a feeling of 'a job well done'. This is because they use their experiences of divorce in a positive way to 'galvanise' them into taking charge of their lives. According to Woollett:

> 'When the marriage breaks down, the mother is thrown into all sorts of things that are unfamiliar. There are new areas, new decisions, and she is forced to cope'.

However, Lewis (cited in Cooper, 1996) warns that:

> 'We must be careful about thinking about the positive changes [divorced women report] because we are always comparing a positive change against the negative feeling that went before. The positive is only relative'.

PARENTHOOD

For most people, parenthood and child-rearing represent key transitions. According to Bee (1994), 90 per cent of adults will become parents, mostly in their twenties and thirties. Parenthood, however, varies in meaning and impact more than any other life transition. It may occur at any time from adolescence to middle age, and for some men, may even occur in late adulthood! Parenthood may also be planned or unplanned, wanted or unwanted, and there are many motives for having children.

Traditionally, parenthood is the domain of the married couple. However, it may involve a single woman, a homosexual couple (see page 381), a cohabiting couple or couples who adopt or foster children. Since the 1950s, there has been a greater acceptability of sexuality among young people, and this has been accompanied by a marked rise in the number of teenage pregnancies.

Equally, though, the increasing importance of work careers for women has also led to more and more couples *postponing* starting a family so that the woman can become better established in her career (see page 378). As a result of this, there is a new class of middle-aged parents with young children (Turnbull, 1995).

Parenthood brings with it several psychological adaptations. For example, many women worry that that their babies may be abnormal, and about the changes in their bodies and how well they will cope with motherhood. Another concern is how the relationship with their husband or partner will be affected. Whilst pregnancy brings many couples closer together, most men take longer than women to become emotionally involved in it – and some feel left out. This feeling of exclusion may continue after the baby is born, as the mother becomes preoccupied with it.

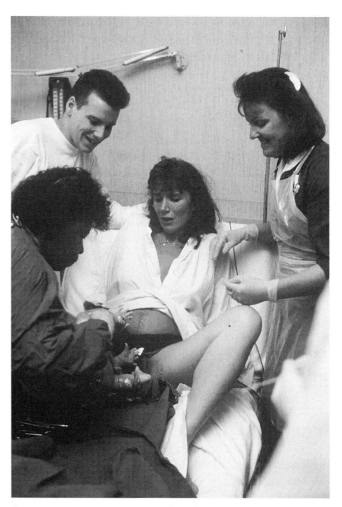

Figure 35.1 *Being at the birth of his child can help to counteract a father's feelings of being excluded during the pregnancy – and afterwards. It can also help him to form an emotional bond with the baby*

Marital satisfaction tends to be highest before children arrive. It then drops and remains relatively low as long as there are dependent children in the home. Finally, it rises again during the 'post-parental' and retirement stages (see Chapter 5, page 47). For new parents, the roles of parent and spouse are at least partially incompatible. New parents report having less time for each other, whether it be conversing, having sex, being affectionate or carrying out routine chores that used to be done together (Bee, 1994).

Parents are, of course, attachment figures for their dependent children. Unlike the relationship with a partner, the relationship with a child is *asymmetrical* (the child is *not* an attachment figure for its parents). This new form of responsibility can be very stressful, and has implications for how parents adapt to these new role demands, and the quality of their interactions with the child (Durkin, 1995). An unhappy couple may stay together not just 'for the kids' sake', but because the parental role has sufficient meaning and value for each partner to outweigh the dissatisfaction with their marriage (Levinson *et al.*, 1978).

Box 35.4 Empty nest or crowded nest: which is more distressing?

Regarding *empty-nest* distress (see Chapter 34, page 369), most parents do not find their children's departure from home to be a distressing time (Durkin, 1995). Indeed, many report that the end of child-rearing responsibilities is a 'liberating experience', and they welcome new opportunities for closer relationships with their partners, personal fulfilment through work, a return to education and so on. The extent to which women report empty-nest distress may be *cohort-related*, that is, it may be more typical of women who reached maturity during historical periods when traditional roles were stressed (Durkin, 1995).

The *crowded nest* (Datan *et al.*, 1987) can, however, be a source of stress. This occurs when grown-up children opt *not* to leave home, which defies the demands of the 'social clock' established by preceding generations. Parents find it difficult to adjust to 'adult children' living at home, especially if the parents themselves are still doing much of the material providing (see Chapter 34, pages 356–366).

Womanhood and motherhood

According to Kremer (1998), in the post-industrial/post-modern world of the 1990s we are still influenced by beliefs and attitudes regarding work and the sexes (or 'gendered employment profiles') inherited from an earlier time. For example, the *motherhood mystique/mandate* refers to the belief that women are born and reared to be, first and foremost, mothers (whilst the 'fatherhood mandate' is hardly, if ever, mentioned). Another example is the stereotype of men as inherently more committed to work than women, whose attitudes towards it are less positive than men's.

The motherhood mandate has at least three important implications. The first is that motherhood is 'natural'. Berryman (in Lacey, 1998) maintains that motherhood is still seen as synonymous with womanhood:

> 'Parenthood is seen as a central, key role in women's lives in a way that it isn't for men. Women who don't become mothers are seen as psychologically inadequate – wanting in some way. But there is plenty of evidence that motherhood doesn't come naturally to all women; it is a skill that many women have to learn'.

For example, Berryman maintains that, because smaller families and fewer siblings are now the norm, many women today have little experience of children when they start their own families – and the reality can come as a shock. This belief that mothering comes 'naturally' is so deep-rooted that women who do not bond immediately with their babies feel inadequate or guilty, or perhaps both: see Bowlby's theory of attachment in Gross *et al.* (2000). However, there are indications that attitudes towards having children are changing.

Box 35.5 Do people still want to become parents?

According to Jones (1995), 20 per cent of women in the UK born between 1960 and 1990 are unlikely to ever become mothers. They are likely to be well-educated, middle-class women, not necessarily pursuing a career, but realising that 'it's OK to go through life without having children' (Root Cartwright, in charge of the British Organisation of Non-Parents (BON)).

Norton (1999) cites a market research survey conducted by Mintel (the *Pre-Family Lifestyles Report*, 1999), involving almost 700 20-34-year-olds without children. It found that more women than men thought it important to be financially secure and established in their careers before starting a family. More significantly, a quarter of women, compared with less than one-fifth of men, saw their work as a career rather than a job.

Married men and women were more likely than co-habiting couples to say they did not want children, with those living alone being keenest on starting a family (85 per cent). Overall, one in ten women said she was undecided about children. One-quarter of the sample did not want to assume the responsibility of parenthood, and only three per cent thought that having children early in adulthood outweighed the financial and career advantages.

A second implication of the motherhood mandate is that most people would probably consider it to be 'unnatural' (or 'wicked') for a mother to leave her children, even if they are left in the care of their father whom she believes will look after them better than she could herself. However, the number of absent mothers targeted by the Child Support Agency trebled between 1995 and 1998, with over 37,000 being approached to pay child maintenance. One in 20 absent parents is a woman (Lacey, 1998). Either there are a lot more 'unnatural' or 'wicked' women out there than was previously thought, or the motherhood mandate needs serious revision!

A third implication is that it is 'unnatural' or simply 'wrong' for a mother of young children to go out to work (see Gross *et al.*, 2000). Related to this is the stereotype concerning women's attitudes towards paid employment. Is there any foundation for this stereotype?

The changing role of women in the work force

Traditionally, men have been seen as dominating the primary employment sector, with their employment histories remaining unbroken from school to retirement. In contrast, women predominate in the secondary employment sector, which is typically unstable, offering poor career prospects and working conditions. There is also a dip or gap in paid employment associated with child-rearing during the mid-twenties to early thirties (Kremer, 1998).

However, at the end of the 1990s employment profiles for both genders are changing rapidly. Women comprise about half the workforce (although a far higher proportion are part-time than men) and mothers are less likely to leave work to care for young children. Yet women are still more likely than men to interrupt their careers, at least temporarily, to take care of children, whilst men rarely do (Craig, 1992; Nicholson, 1993). (This relates to the 'gender-splitting' phenomenon identified by Levinson (1986) and will be discussed further below.)

Women's attitudes to paid employment

Kremer (1998) cites several surveys (conducted in the 1980s and 90s) showing that, despite poorer working conditions, the overwhelming majority of working women prefer to be in paid employment. Additionally, most of those not in work (especially those under 50) would prefer to be. When asked to rate the importance of various factors at work, the differences between men and women are few, and usually only involve clashes between work commitments and domestic responsibilities. Men and women also tend to agree about the *motivation* for working, such as money, stimulation and feeling useful, and, ironically (given their poorer working conditions), women consistently express *higher* job satisfaction (especially part-time workers and those working from home).

Box 35.6 Women, work and evolution

According to Hrdy (1999), these findings should come as no surprise. Arguing from an evolutionary perspective, Hrdy claims that being ambitious is just as natural for a mother as breastfeeding. It is a fallacy to believe that mothers who go out to work are in conflict with their natural instincts. She argues that there is nothing new about working mothers: for most of human existence, and for millions of years before that, primate mothers have combined productive lives with reproduction. This combination of work and motherhood has always entailed trade-offs.

What is new for modern mothers is the *compartmentalisation* of their productive and reproductive lives. The factories, laboratories and offices where women in post-industrial societies go to 'forage' are even less compatible with childcare than jaguar-infested forests and distant groves of mongongo nuts. Hrdy is especially interested in the Pleistocene period, which extends from about 1.6 million years ago (when humans emerged from apes) to the invention of agriculture (about 10,000 years ago). It was during this period that many human instincts – including mothering – evolved through natural selection. Pleistocene woman would have striven for status and 'local clout' among her female peers. Ambition was just as much the driving force for women as for men, serving the Darwinian purpose of producing offspring who survived to adulthood (see Chapter 43).

Figure 35.2 *Nicola Horrlick, City high-flyer and 'superwoman'*

However, a recent survey in the UK (conducted by *Top Sante* magazine and *BUPA*) paints a rather different picture (Brown, 1999). Involving 5000 women, average age 36, the majority in managerial and professional jobs, the survey found that 77 per cent would give up work tomorrow if they could. At an age when most would have expected to be at the pinnacle of their professions, nearly half dream of a life of leisure and almost a third want to be homemakers. 'Superwoman' may exist, but it seems that she feels overworked and disillusioned from juggling the demands of career and family. Contrary to the equation of womanhood with motherhood, many feel under pressure to go out to work and raise families, as they feel that society does not value mothers who stay at home (Brown, 1999). If they are having to juggle career and family, what does this tell us about the contribution of their husbands or partners?

Does 'New Man' exist?

The phenomenon of 'dual-earner couples/marriages' (where the husband works full-time and the wife works at least 20 hours per week) has become quite common, both in the US (Craig, 1992) and the UK (Nicholson, 1993). Compared with more 'traditional' couples, these husbands report more marital dissatisfaction and conflicts over family and work responsibilities, and the wives similarly report higher levels of conflict, as well as a very realistic work overload.

Figure 35.3 *If 'New Man' does exist, it is definitely not Homer Simpson*

Despite some evidence that domestic tasks (especially childcare) are more evenly shared in some dual-earner families, it is nearly always the woman who is still primarily responsible for both housework and childcare, regardless of the age of the children and whether she is

working full- or part-time. Based on studies in eastern and western Europe, and North and South America, it seems that when there are *no* children, working wives do the bulk of the shopping and so on. However, when there are children, the husband's contribution to running the home actually *declines* (in relative terms) with each child: the wife's *increases* by five to ten per cent with each child (Nicholson, 1993). Whilst there are no apparent social class differences in men's contributions to the domestic division of labour, there are cultural ones, with Swedish men doing much more than their North American counterparts (Durkin, 1995).

A survey in the UK (Montgomery, 1993) found that 82 per cent of husbands had never ironed, 73 per cent had never washed clothes, and 24 per cent had never cooked. Kremer (1998) concludes that:

> 'There is little evidence to suggest that domestic responsibilities have been lifted from the shoulders of women. Instead, women's dual roles (home carer and worker) persist. Indeed, even in situations where both partners are not in paid employment, or where the woman is the primary wage earner, then this pattern often still endures'.

Similarly, Quiery (1998) maintains that whilst there have been some changes in fathers' behaviour over the last 15–20 years, they are hardly dramatic and the burden of child-rearing and home-making still falls on mothers. However, evidence from America suggests a rather more significant change might be taking place.

Key **STUDY**

Box 35.7 Are American men participating more in their children's activities?

Pleck (1999) compared 11 studies dating from the mid 1960s to the early 1980s with 13 studies conducted between the mid 1980s and early 1990s. As shown in Figure 35.4 (page 380), fathers' *engagement* with their children (as a percentage of the mothers' engagement) *increased* over that period from 34.3 per cent to 43.5 per cent. Engagement refers to interaction with ones children, such as playing with them, reading to them, and helping them with their homework.

In that same period, fathers' *availability* also increased (again, as a percentage of the mothers') from 51.8 per cent to 65.6 per cent (see Figure 35.5, page 380). Availability is a measure of how much time fathers spend near their children, either interacting with them or not (such as working on the computer whilst the children play video games).

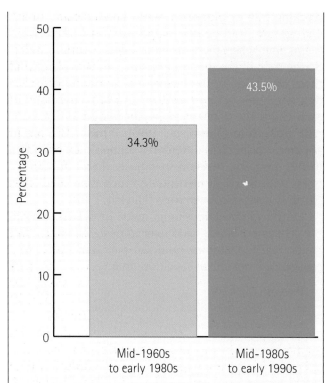

Figure 35.4 *Amount of time fathers interact with their children as percentage of mothers' engagement (From Pleck, 1999)*

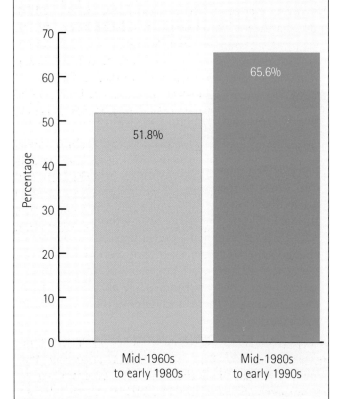

Figure 35.5 *Amount of time fathers are near their children, either interacting or not, as percentage of mothers' availability (From Pleck, 1999)*

Pleck (1999) concludes that although men still perform less childcare than women, men's participation in family activities *is* increasing. However, he points out that most of the relevant data come from studies of *married* fathers, which excludes a substantial proportion of the adult male population. When these other groups are taken into account, the *opposite* picture emerges. For example, the increase in divorce rates since the 1950s has weakened many men's family ties. Most divorced fathers' contact with their children drops off rapidly after divorce. Almost half of all divorced fathers have not seen their children in the past year, and high proportions of them do not pay child maintenance. In addition, the recent increase in the proportion of men who never marry also indicates decreasing family involvement. Most unmarried fathers – teen and adult – refuse to accept any responsibility for their children.

Thus, it seems that American family life (and probably in the UK and other Western countries also) is changing in *two contradictory directions*. In two-parent families, fathers' involvement with children and overall gender equality are increasing. However, two-parent families have become a smaller proportion of all families, and families headed by single mothers have become more common. The overall effect of this is that more children do not have resident fathers (Pleck, 1999).

Pleck also challenges the popular view among social scientists (including psychologists, such as Levinson) that family is more central than work for women's identities, whilst the reverse is true for men. He cites evidence (from both his own and others' research) which shows that family is *far more psychologically central* to men than work, just as it is for women. For example, fathers and mothers experience similar levels of anxiety over separation from their children during the first two years of parenthood. This suggests that 'gender-splitting' may not be such a clearly defined phenomenon as Levinson proposed. However, men are more likely to take workplace emotions home with them than are mothers, who keep these separate from their family experience.

Step-parenthood

In the early 1960s, almost 90 per cent of children spent their childhood and adolescence in homes with two biological, married parents. Now that is true of about 40 per cent of children in the US and about 50 per cent in the UK (Hetherington & Stanley-Hagan, 1999). This is attributed to increases in the divorce, out-of-wedlock childbearing, and dramatically escalating rates of cohabitation.

Although 38 per cent of white American children experience parental divorce before their sixteenth birthday, the figure for African-American children is almost 74 per cent. Thus, compared with white children, more

African-American children experience their parents' marital dissolutions and spend longer in single-parent households, which often include cohabiting partners and relatives.

Key **S T U D Y**

Box 35.8 The effects of living in a step-family

Nicholson *et al.* (1999) examined the effects of living in a step-family during childhood and adolescence on a range of psychosocial outcomes. Data were collected for over 900 children in New Zealand as part of the Christchurch Health and Development Study. They had all lived in step-families (for the first time) from ages six to 16, and were assessed at age 18 in terms of mental health, antisocial behaviour, substance use, restricted life opportunities, and sexual risk-taking.

Compared with a control group (children who had *not* been exposed to step-families for the first time between six and 16), they were more likely to become juvenile offenders, nicotine dependent, to abuse or become dependent on illegal substances, leave school without qualifications, engage in early sexual activity, and have multiple sexual partners. However, when factors such as family socioeconomic status, family history of instability, adversity and conflict, gender and pre-existing child behaviour and attentional problems were controlled for, the differences became non-significant:

'Although young people exposed to living in a stepfamily had increased risks of poor psychosocial outcomes, much of this association appeared to be spurious and arose from confounding social, contextual and individual factors that were present prior to the formation of the stepfamily'. (Nicholson *et al.*, 1999)

Lesbian and gay parenting

In the context of advocating that psychologists should study homosexual relationships in their own terms (and not by comparison with heterosexual ones), Kitzinger & Coyle (1995) suggest that we might want to ask how the children of lesbian/gay couples understand and talk about their parents' relationships and how they can develop positive views about homosexuality in a heterosexual culture. Homosexual couples have always been involved in parenting through partners' previous heterosexual relationships. The recent increase in fostering/adoption of children by gay men, and the ongoing 'lesbian baby boom', mean that many more homosexual couples are parents than used to be the case (see Chapter 6, pages 60–62).

According to Kitzinger *et al.* (1998), research into lesbian/gay parenting was initially concerned with whether or how far the children of lesbians and (to a lesser extent) gay men could be distinguished psychologically from those of heterosexuals. On balance, this research suggested that these children were no more 'at risk' than children raised in heterosexual families.

For example, Taylor (1993) found no evidence that children reared in gay/lesbian families were more disturbed or had greater gender identity confusion than those reared in heterosexual families. Barrett & Robinson (1994) reviewed the impact of gay fathering on children. They stress the need to take into account that these children are likely to have experienced parental divorce and to show the psychological distress that often accompanies it (see Gross *et al.*, 2000). Although these children may be isolated, angry and in need of help sorting out their feelings about homosexuality in general, they are in little danger of being sexually abused, and adjust well to their family situations. Whilst the relationships with their fathers may be stormy at first, they also have the potential for considerable honesty and openness.

Increasingly, psychologists are researching areas directly rooted in the concerns of lesbian/gay parents themselves, including coming out to one's children, and managing different co-parenting arrangements (such as a lesbian mother with her female lover, her ex-husband, a gay male sperm donor, or a gay male co-parent: Kitzinger *et al.*, 1998).

CONCLUSIONS

This chapter has examined research findings concerning the impact of two major normative age-graded influences, marriage/partnering and parenthood, and one non-normative influence, divorce. In the case of parenthood, the changing roles of men and women have been shown to be crucial, especially women's participation in the labour market. This means that to appreciate the impact of various life events, they must be examined in the broader context of social norms, which, at least in Western countries, are constantly shifting. The chapter has also illustrated the mutual influence of different life events involving family and relationships.

Summary

- Marriage and parenting, which tend to happen early in adulthood, are examples of **normative**, **age-graded influences**, whilst divorce is a **non-normative influence**, which can occur at any time during adulthood. These are also called **marker events** or **critical life events**.

- Couples who **cohabit** before marriage are more likely to divorce later, or be less satisfied with their marriages, than those who do not cohabit. Cohabitees appear to be less traditional and religious than non-cohabitees, making them more prepared to flout tradition.

- **Married people** tend to live longer, and are happier, healthier and have lower rates of mental disorder than unmarried people. Men benefit most from marriage, partly because they are less likely than women to have close confidants outside marriage, and partly because wives provide more emotional warmth and support for their husbands than vice versa. The potential benefits of marriage for women may be counterbalanced by **gender-splitting**.

- Sixty-five per cent of women, and over 75 per cent of men remarry following **divorce**, and cohabitation rates are high in those who do not remarry. Divorce rates are even higher in remarriages than first marriages. These changes have led to a marked rise in the number of children living in **step-family situations**.

- Whilst young people living in step-families may be at greater risk of poor psychosocial outcomes, such as juvenile delinquency and drug abuse, much of this can be attributed to problems that existed **prior to** the formation of the step-families.

- Compared with the American population as a whole, African-Americans are more likely to separate and divorce, but are also less likely to remarry. Divorce rates are also highest during the first five years of marriage, and then peak again after 15-25 years.

- **Parenthood** has greater variability in meaning and impact than any other life transition. Whilst pregnancy can bring couples closer together, men can feel excluded, especially after their babies are born.

- Marital satisfaction is highest before children arrive, then it drops whilst there are dependent children at home. There is little evidence for **empty-nest distress**, and marital satisfaction usually increases once children have left home. The **crowded nest** is more likely to be distressing.

- The **motherhood mystique/mandate** can make women who do not bond immediately with their babies feel inadequate. However, women are increasingly **postponing** having children or deciding not to have children at all, giving financial security and career higher priority. This is producing a new class of middle-aged parents with young children.

- The motherhood mandate also implies that it is unnatural for mothers to leave their children, yet the number of absent parents who are women is increasing. Another implication is that it is wrong for a mother of young children to go out to work.

- Women now comprise about half the workforce, and are less likely than they used to be to leave work to care for young children. However, they are still more likely than men are to interrupt their careers.

- Evidence exists that working mothers feel pressurised into going out to work, because society does not value mothers who stay at home. They consequently feel overworked by having to juggle two 'careers'.

- Despite evidence that domestic duties are more evenly shared in some **dual-earner families**, it is invariably the woman who is still primarily responsible for both housework and childcare. However, in relative terms, **married fathers** are **engaging** more with their children and are more **available** to them then they used to be.

- At the same time, most divorced fathers have little contact with their children, an increasing number of men remain unmarried, and most unmarried fathers deny responsibility for their children. The overall effect of this is that more and more children are living without resident fathers.

- Many more **lesbian/gay** couples are parents than used to be the case. Early research examined whether the children of such parents were more 'at risk' than those raised in heterosexual families, but more recently the emphasis has shifted to issues such as co-parenting arrangements.

Essay Questions

1 Discuss psychological research into the effects of marriage (or partnering) **and** parenthood. (*24 marks*)

2 Critically consider the role of gender **and/or** cultural differences in marriage (or partnering) **and/or** divorce. (*24 marks*)

WEB ADDRESSES

http://www.personal.psu.edu/faculty/n/x/nxd10/family3.htm
http://www.ben2ucla.edu/~jeffwood/
http://www.hec.ohio-state.edu/famlife/family/famlinks.htm
http://www.cleveland.cc.nc.us/staff/bolich/psyche/oage4g5.html

36 Cognitive Changes in Late Adulthood

INTRODUCTION AND OVERVIEW

Whilst 'growing up' is normally seen as desirable, 'growing old' usually has much more negative connotations. The negative view of ageing is based on the *decrement* model, which sees ageing as a process of decay or decline in physical and mental health, intellectual abilities and social relationships.

An alternative to the decrement model is the *personal growth model*, which stresses the potential advantages of late adulthood (or 'old age'), such as increased leisure time, reduced responsibilities, and the ability to concentrate only on matters of high priority (Kalish, 1982). This much more positive view is how ageing has been studied within the *lifespan approach*.

This chapter considers some of the theories and research concerned with *adjustment to late adulthood*. It begins by looking at what is meant by the term 'old' and at some of the cognitive and social changes that occur in late adulthood. It then discusses the impact of two major life events, *retirement* (a *normative, age-graded influence*, often taken to mark the 'official' start of old age) and *bereavement* (a *non-normative influence*, although death of one's spouse becomes increasingly likely as we attain late adulthood).

THE MEANING OF 'OLD'

People today are living longer and retaining their health better than any previous generation (Baltes & Baltes, 1993). The proportion of older people in the British population has increased dramatically in recent years. In 1961, two per cent of the population (one million people) were aged 80 or over. By 1991, this figure had risen to four per cent (two million people). The number of centenarians has risen from 271 (in 1951), to 1185 (1971), to 4400 (1991). In 1997, the number stood at 8000 with projections of 12,000 (2001) and 30,000 (2030) (McCrystal, 1997).

Because of this *demographic imperative* (Swensen, 1983), developmental psychologists have become increasingly interested in our later years. But what do we mean by 'old'? Kastenbaum's (1979) *'The ages of me'* questionnaire assesses how people see themselves at the present moment in relation to their age.

Few people, irrespective of their chronological age, describe themselves *consistently* (that is, they tend to give *different* responses to the different questionnaire items). For example, people over 20 (including those in their seventies and eighties) usually describe themselves as feeling younger than their chronological age. We also generally consider ourselves to be *too* old.

Box 36.1 Kastenbaum's 'The ages of me' questionnaire

Figure 36.1 *Whilst (c) might depict someone's chronological age, (a) might correspond to his biological age and (b) might represent his subjective age*

- My **chronological age** is my actual or official age, dated from my time of birth. My chronological age is …

- My **biological age** refers to the state of my face and body. In other people's eyes, I look as though I am about ... years of age. In my own eyes, I look like someone of about ... years of age.

- My **subjective age** is indicated by how I feel. Deep down inside, I really feel like a person of about ... years of age.

- My **functional age,** which is closely related to my **social age,** refers to the kind of life I lead, what I am able to do, the status I believe I have, whether I work, have dependent children and live in my own home. My thoughts and interests are like those of a person of about ... years of age, and my position in society is like that of a person of about .... years of age.

(Adapted from Kastenbaum, 1979)

Ageism

It seems, then, that knowing a person's chronological age tells us little about the sort of life that person leads or what they are like. However, one of the dangerous aspects of *ageism* is that chronological age is assumed to be an accurate indicator of all the other ages. According to Comfort (1977), ageism is:

> '... the notion that people cease to be people, cease to be the same people or become people of a distinct and inferior kind by virtue of having lived a specified number of years ... Like racism, which it resembles, it is based on fear'.

Similarly, Bromley (1977) argues that most people react negatively to the elderly because they seem to deviate from our concept of 'normal' human beings. As part of the 'welfarist approach' to understanding the problems of an ageing society (Fennell *et al.*, 1988), 'they' (i.e. the elderly) are designated as different, occupying another world from 'us' – a process that for all perceived minorities tends to be dehumanising and sets lower or different standards of social value or individual worth (Manthorpe, 1994: see Chapter 3).

Stereotypes of the elderly are more deeply entrenched than (mis)conceptions of gender differences. It is therefore not surprising that people are overwhelmingly unenthusiastic about becoming 'old' (Stuart-Hamilton, 1997). According to Jones (1993), everyone over retirement age is seen as a strange homogeneous mass, with limited abilities, few needs and few rights:

> 'What other section of the population that spans more than 30 years in biological time is grouped together in such an illogical manner? ... As a consequence, older people suffer a great deal ... As for experience and wisdom,

these qualities are no longer valued in this fast-moving high-technology world. They are devalued by the community, as well as by their owners'. (Jones, 1993)

Figure 36.2 *The popularity of Harry Enfield's* Old Gits *can be seen as confirming the existence of an ageist society*

Box 36.2 A decade-by-decade description of 'the elderly'

The young-old (60–69): This period marks a major transition. Most adults must adapt to new role structures in an effort to cope with the losses and gains of the decade. Income is reduced due to retirement. Friends and colleagues start to disappear. Although physical strength wanes somewhat, a great many young-old have surplus energy and seek out new and different activities.

The middle-aged old (70–79): This is often marked by loss or illness. Friends and family may die. The middle-aged old must also cope with reduced participation in formal organisations, which can produce restlessness and irritability. Their own health problems become more severe. The major developmental task is to maintain the personality reintegration achieved in the previous decade.

The old old (80–89): The old old show increased difficulty in adapting to and interacting with their surroundings. They need help in maintaining social and cultural contacts.

The very old old (90–99): Although health problems become more acute, the very old old can successfully alter their activities to make the most of what they have. The major advantage of old age is freedom from responsibilities. If previous crises have been resolved satisfactorily, this decade may be joyful, serene and fulfilling.

(Based on Burnside *et al.*, 1979, and Craig, 1992)

As Box 36.2. suggests, the aged are *not* one cohesive group (Craig, 1992). Rather, they are a collection of sub-groups, each with its unique problems and capabilities, but all sharing to some degree the age-related difficulties of reduced income, failing health and the loss of loved ones. For Craig, however:

'Having a problem is not the same as being a problem, and the all-too-popular view of those over age 65 as needy, non-productive, and unhappy needs revision'.

Similarly, Dietch (1995) has commented that:

'Life's final stage is surrounded by more myths, stereotypes and misinformation than any other developmental phase'.

COGNITIVE CHANGES IN OLD AGE

Consistent with the *decrement model* (see *Introduction and overview*), it is commonly believed that old age is associated with a decrease in cognitive abilities. Until recently, it was thought that intellectual capacity peaked in the late teens or early twenties, levelled off, and then began to decline fairly steadily during middle age and more rapidly in old age.

The evidence on which this claim was based came from *cross-sectional studies* (studying *different* age groups at the *same* time). However, we cannot draw firm conclusions from such studies, because the age groups compared represent different generations with different *experiences* (the *cohort effect*). Unless we know how 60-year-olds, say, performed when they were 40 and 20, it is impossible to say whether or not intelligence declines with age.

An alternative methodology is the *longitudinal study*, in which the *same* people are tested and re-tested at *various* times during their lives. Several such studies have produced data contradicting the results of cross-sectional studies, indicating that at least some people retain their intellect well into middle age and beyond (Holahan & Sears, 1995). However, the evidence suggests that there

are some age-related changes in different *kinds* of intelligence and *aspects* of memory.

Changes in intelligence

Although psychologists have always disagreed about the definition of intelligence, there is general acceptance that it is *multi-dimensional* (composed of several different abilities). *Crystallised intelligence* results from accumulated knowledge, including a knowledge of how to reason, language skills and an understanding of technology. This type of intelligence is linked to education, experience and cultural background, and is measured by tests of general information.

By contrast, *fluid intelligence* refers to the ability to solve novel and unusual problems (those not experienced before). It allows us to perceive and draw inferences about relationships among patterns of stimuli and to conceptualise abstract information, which aids problem-solving. Fluid intelligence is measured by tests using novel and unusual problems not based on specific knowledge or particular previous learning.

Crystallised intelligence *increases* with age, and people tend to continue improving their performance until near the end of their lives (Horn, 1982). Using the *cross-longitudinal* method (in which *different* age groups are *re-tested* over a long period of time), Schaie & Hertzog (1983) reported that fluid intelligence declines for all age groups over time, peaking between 20 and 30. The tendency to continue adding to our knowledge as we grow older could account for the constancy of crystallised intelligence. Alternatively, regular use of our crystallised abilities may help to maintain them (Denney & Palmer, 1981). The decline in fluid intelligence may be an inevitable part of the ageing process related to the reduced efficiency of neurological functioning. However, we may also be less often challenged to use our fluid abilities in old age (Cavanaugh, 1995).

Changes in memory

Some aspects of memory appear to decline with age, possibly because we become less effective at processing information (which may underlie cognitive changes in general: Stuart-Hamilton, 1994). On recall tests, older adults *generally* perform more poorly than younger adults. However, the *reverse* is sometimes true, as shown by Maylor's (1994) study of the performance of older contestants on *Mastermind*. On recognition tests, the differences between younger and older people are less apparent and may even disappear. As far as *everyday memory* is concerned, the evidence indicates that the elderly do have trouble recalling events from their youth and early lives (Miller & Morris, 1993).

WOMEN BECOME FORGETFUL WHILE MEN GET GRUMPIER (REPORT ON AGEING)

Figure 36.3 *Former Conservative Prime Ministers, Margaret Thatcher and Edward Heath, are well known for their political disagreements. If recent reports on ageing are to be believed, Thatcher will have difficulty remembering them, whilst Heath will remember them with irritation*

Significant memory deficits are one feature of *dementia*, the most common form of which is *Alzheimer's disease*. However, over 90 per cent of people over 65 show *little* deterioration (Diamond, 1978), and even very late in life cortical neurons seem capable of responding to enriched conditions by forming new functional connections with other neurons. This is supported by the finding that those who keep mentally active are those who maintain their cognitive abilities (Rogers *et al.*, 1990).

However, there are those who claim that Alzheimer's disease is an accelerated form of normal changes in the ageing brain, so that we would all get the disease if we lived long enough. The opposing view is that cognitive decline is not an inevitable part of ageing, but rather it reflects a disease process which is more likely to affect us as we get older (Smith, 1998). Work by the Oxford Project to Investigate Memory and Ageing (OPTIMA) has used *X-ray computerised tomography* (CT: see Chapter 10) to examine the medial temporal lobe (see Chapter 11). Whilst this tiny area comprises only two per cent of the volume of the whole cerebral cortex, it includes the *hippocampus*, a structure known to be crucial for memory. Also, the neurons of the medial temporal lobe connect with almost all other parts of the cortex, thus any damage to this part of the brain is likely to have consequences for the functioning of the rest of the cortex.

X-ray CT images show that the medial temporal lobe is markedly smaller in people with dementia who eventually die of Alzheimer's disease than in age-matched controls without cognitive deficit. Repeated CT scans over periods of several years have found that shrinkage is slow in control participants (about 1-1.5 per cent per year), compared with an alarming rate of some 15 per cent per year in Alzheimer's patients (Smith, 1998).

These, and other supportive data, led the OPTIMA researchers to conclude that Alzheimer's disease is *dis-*

tinct from normal ageing and that it cannot simply be an acceleration of normal ageing. Although cognitive decline does appear to increase with age for the population as a whole, if we rigorously exclude those with pathological changes (such as early Alzheimer's), then a majority may not show any significant decline. According to Smith (1998):

> 'We must abandon the fatalistic view that mental decline is an inevitable accompaniment of ageing'.

Consistent with this conclusion is the belief that *negative cultural sterotypes* of ageing actually *cause* memory decline in the elderly.

Key S T U D Y

Box 36.3 The influence of stereotypes on memory

Levy & Langer (1994) investigated the memory capabilities of hearing Americans, members of the American deaf community and people from mainland China. It was assumed that members of the deaf community were less likely to have been exposed to negative cultural stereotypes. People from mainland China were chosen because of the high esteem in which Chinese society holds its aged members. The older American deaf participants and the Chinese participants performed much better on memory tasks than the older American hearing participants.

Also, younger hearing Americans held less positive views of ageing than any of the other groups. Amongst the older participants, attitudes towards ageing and memory performance were positively correlated. Levy and Langer believe that negative stereotypes about ageing may become *self-fulfilling prophecies*, in which low expectations mean that people are less likely to engage in activities that will help them maintain their memory abilities.

The subliminal (below conscious awareness) presentation of *negative self-stereotypes* (e.g. 'Because of my age I am forgetful') tended to *worsen* memory performance, whilst *positive self-stereotypes* (e.g. 'Because of my age I have acquired wisdom') tended to *improve* it (Levy, 1996). Levy found no such effect with young participants, for whom stereotypes of ageing are less salient.

SOCIAL CHANGES IN OLD AGE

Social disengagement theory

According to Manthorpe (1994), Cumming & Henry's (1961) *social disengagement theory* represented the first major attempt to produce a theory about individuals' relationships with society. Based on a five-year study of 275 50-90-year-olds in Kansas City, USA, Cumming and Henry claimed that:

> 'Many of the relationships between a person and other members of society are severed and those remaining are altered in quality'.

This social disengagement involves the *mutual withdrawal* of society from the individual (through compulsory retirement, children growing up and leaving home, the death of a spouse and so on) and of the individual from society (Cumming, 1975). As people grow older, they become more solitary, retreat into the inner world of their memories, become emotionally quiescent, and engage in pensive self-reflection.

Cumming sees disengagement as having three components: (a) *shrinkage of life space* refers to the tendency to interact with fewer other people as we grow older, and to occupy fewer roles; (b) *increased individuality* means that in the roles that remain, older people are much less governed by strict rules and expectations; (c) the *acceptance* (even embrace) *of these changes*, so that withdrawal is a voluntary, natural and inevitable process and represents the most appropriate and successful way of growing old.

As far as society is concerned, the individual's withdrawal is part of an inevitable move towards death – the ultimate disengagement (Manthorpe, 1994). By replacing older individuals with younger people, society renews itself and the elderly are free to die (Bromley, 1988).

An evaluation of social disengagement theory

Bee (1994) sees the first two components as difficult to dispute. However, the third is more controversial because of its view of disengagement as a natural, voluntary and inevitable process rather than an imposed one. Bromley (1988) argues that such a view of ageing has detrimental *practical* consequences for the elderly, such as encouraging a policy of segregation, even indifference, and the very destructive belief that old age has no value (see page 385). For Bromley, an even more serious criticism concerns whether *everyone* actually does disengage.

Key STUDY

Box 36.4 Do the elderly disengage?

Havighurst *et al.* (1968) followed up about half the sample originally studied by Cumming & Henry (1961). Although increasing age was accompanied by increasing disengagement, at least some of those studied remained active and engaged, and they

tended to be the happiest. The fact that those who disengage the least are the happiest, have the highest morale and live the longest, contradicts social disengagement's view that withdrawal from mainstream society is a natural and inherent part of the ageing process (Bee, 1994). Whilst some people may choose to lead socially isolated lives and find contentment in them, such disengagement does not appear to be necessary for overall mental health in old age.

Havighurst *et al.* (1968) also identified several different personality types. These included *reorganisers*, who were involved in a wide range of activities and reorganised their lives to compensate for lost activities, and the *disengaged*, who voluntarily moved away from role commitments. Consistent with social disengagement theory, the latter reported low levels of activity but high 'life satisfaction'. However, the disposition to disengage is a *personality dimension* as well as a characteristic of ageing (Bromley, 1988).

Social disengagement theory focuses on the *quantitative changes*, such as the reduced number of relationships and roles in old age. However, according to Carstensen (1996) it is the *qualitative changes* that are crucial:

> 'Although age is associated with many losses, including loss of power, social partners, physical health, cognitive efficiency, and, eventually, life itself – and although this list of losses encompasses the very things that younger people typically equate with happiness – research suggests that older people are at least as satisfied with their lives as their younger counterparts'

Although many of these losses are beyond the older person's control (Rosnow, 1985), such as retirement (see pages 391–392), *friendships* are voluntary, non-institutionalised and relatively enduring relationships which offer comfort and stability. *Informal* support from friends (and other primary relationships) also reduces dependency on social security agencies, the helping professions and other formal organisations (Duck, 1991; Rainey, 1998). It is the *choice* element that differentiates friendships from other types of relationships (Baltes & Baltes, 1986), providing older people control over at least one life domain (Rainey, 1998).

Maintaining close relationships with others is often a significant factor in determining whether older people feel a sense of belonging to the social system. This may become *more* important with age, because society withdraws from older adults both *behaviourally* (compulsory retirement) and *attitudinally* (attributing diminishing powers, abilities and qualities to the elderly). Both relatives and friends are crucial in how life is experienced by the elderly. Overall, individual adaptation to old age on all levels has been shown to be highly dependent on personal tolerance of stress and life events, and on the availability of informal social support networks (Duck, 1991). These findings regarding the role of friendships and other relationships are consistent with *socioemotional selectivity theory* (see pages 390–391).

Activity (or re-engagement) theory

The major alternative to disengagement theory is *activity (or re-engagement) theory* (Havighurst, 1964; Maddox, 1964). Except for inevitable biological and health changes, older people are the same as middle-aged people, with essentially the same psychological and social needs. Decreased social interaction in old age is the result of the withdrawal of an inherently ageist society from the ageing person, and happens against the wishes of most elderly people. The withdrawal is not mutual.

Optimal ageing involves staying active and managing to resist the 'shrinkage' of the social world. This can be achieved by maintaining the activities of middle age for as long as possible, and then finding substitutes for work or retirement (such as leisure or hobbies) and for spouses and friends upon their death (such as grandchildren). It is important for older adults to maintain their *role counts*, to ensure they always have several different roles to play.

An evaluation of activity theory

According to Bond *et al.* (1993), activity theory can be criticised for being:

'... unrealistic because the economic, political and social structure of society prevents the older worker from maintaining a major activity of middle age, namely, "productive" employment'.

The implication seems to be that there really is *no* substitute for paid employment (at least for men: see Chapter 35). According to Dex & Phillipson (1986), society appears to measure people's worth by their ability to undertake paid labour, and the more autonomous people are in their working practice, the more respect they seem to deserve. When someone retires, they not only lose their autonomy and right to work for money, but they also lose their identity: they cease to be a participant in society and their status is reduced to 'pensioner/senior citizen' or simply 'old person'.

As noted in Box 36.4, some elderly people seem satisfied with disengagement, suggesting that activity theory alone *cannot* explain successful ageing. Nevertheless, activity or re-engagement prevents the consequences of disengagement from going too far in the direction of isolation, apathy and inaction.

Figure 36.4 *The elderly couple above seem to fit the stereotype of the withdrawn, isolated, 'disengaged' person, whilst the couple below illustrate an alternative, but less common, stereotype, of the person who remains as active in old age as when s/he was middle-aged*

Just as disengagement may be involuntary (as in the case of poor health), so we may face involuntarily high levels of activity (as in looking after grandchildren). Both disengagement and activity may, therefore, be equally maladaptive. Quite possibly, disengagement theory actually *under*estimates, and activity theory *over*estimates, the degree of control people have over the 'reconstruction' of their lives.

Additionally, both theories see ageing as essentially the same for everyone. They both refer to a legitimate process through which some people come to terms with the many changes that accompany ageing (they represent *options*: Hayslip & Panek, 1989). However, people will select a style of ageing best suited to their personality and past experience or lifestyle, and there is no single 'best way' to age (Neugarten & Neugarten, 1987). For Turner & Helms (1989), personality is the key factor and neither theory can adequately explain successful ageing.

Increasingly, theorists are emphasising the *continuity* between earlier and later phases of life. Satisfaction, morale and adaptations in later life seem to be closely related to a person's life-long personality style and response to stress and change. According to Reedy (1983):

'In this sense, the past is the prologue to the future. While the personality changes somewhat in response to various life events and changes, it generally remains stable throughout all of adult life'.

Social exchange theory

According to Dyson (1980), both disengagement and activity theories fail to take sufficient account of the physical, social and economic factors which might limit people's choices about how they age. Age robs people of the capacity to engage in the reciprocal give-and-take that is the hallmark of social relationships, and thus weakens their attachment to others. In addition, Dowd (1975) argues that:

'Unlike the aged in traditional societies, older people in industrialised societies have precious few power resources to exchange in daily social interaction'.

This inequality of power results in dependence on others and compliance with others' wishes. However, for both Dyson and Dowd there is a more positive aspect to this loss of power. Adjusting to old age in general, and retirement in particular, involves a sort of *contract* between the individual and society. The elderly give up their roles as economically active members of society, but in *exchange* they receive increased leisure time, take on fewer responsibilties and so on. Although the contract is largely unwritten and not enforceable, most people will probably conform to the expectations about being old which are built into social institutions and stereotypes (see Box 36.3, page 387).

Socioemotional selectivity theory

According to *socioemotional selectivity theory* (SST: Carstensen, 1992, 1993; Carstensen & Turk-Charles, 1994), social contact is motivated by various goals, including basic survival, information seeking, development of self-concept and the regulation of emotion. Whilst they all operate throughout life, the importance of specific goals varies, depending on one's place in the life cycle. For example, when *emotional regulation* is the major goal, people are *highly selective* in their choice of social partners, preferring familiar others. This selectivity is at its peak in infancy and old age: the elderly turn increasingly to friends and adult children for emotional support (see pages 388–389).

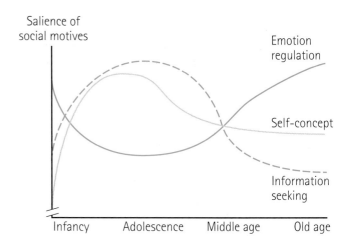

Figure 36.5 *Idealised illustration of the lifespan trajectory (From Carstensen, 1996)*

According to SST, a major factor contributing to these changes in social motives is *construal of the future*, which is indicated by chronological age. When the future is perceived as largely open-ended, long-term goals assume great significance. However, when the future is perceived as limited (see Gould's theory, page 371), attention shifts to the present. Immediate needs, such as emotional states, become more salient. So, contrary to disengagement theory (which sees reduced social contact as being caused by emotional states becoming diluted and dampened down), SST predicts that emotional concerns will become *more* important in old age.

It follows that when younger people hold expectations about the future which are similar to those of the elderly, they should make the same kinds of social choices as those typically made by older people.

Key STUDY

Box 36.5 How a limited future can influence current concerns

Carstensen (1996) describes a study involving a group of healthy gay men, a group of HIV-positive, asymptomatic gay men, and a group of HIV-positive, symptomatic gay men. A group of young, middle-aged and old men representing the general population served as a control group.

The social preferences of the healthy gay men were similar to those of the young men from the control group. Those of the asymptomatic group mimicked those of the middle-aged controls, whilst those of the symptomatic group were strikingly similar to those of the oldest control participants. In other words:

'The closer the men were to the end of their lives, the greater weight they placed on affective qualities of prospective social partners ... changes in social preferences appear to be altered in much the same way when futures are limited by age as when futures are limited by disease'. (Carstensen, 1996)

According to Carstensen (1996), the findings relevant to SST taken together paint quite an optimistic picture. Age-related reduction in social contact appears to be highly selective (rather than reflecting a reduced capacity), such that interaction is limited to those people who are most familiar and can provide the most emotional security and comfort. This is an excellent strategy when time and social energy need to be invested wisely.

Psychosocial theory

Another alternative to disengagement and activity theories is Erikson's *psychosocial theory* (see Chapters 31 and 34). A more valid and useful way of looking at what all elderly people have in common might be to examine the importance of old age as a stage of development, albeit the last (which is where its importance lies).

In old age, there is a conflict between *ego-integrity* (the positive force) and *despair* (the negative force). As with the other psychosocial stages, we cannot avoid the conflict altogether, which occurs as a result of biological, psychological and social forces. The task is to end this stage, and hence life, with *greater* ego-integrity than despair, and this requires us to take stock of our life, reflect on it, and assess how worthwhile and fulfilling it has been.

Box 36.6 The characteristics of ego-integrity

- The belief that life does have a purpose and makes sense.

- Accepting that, within the context of our lives as a whole, what happened was somehow inevitable and could only have happened when and how it did.

- Believing that all life's experiences offer something of value, and that we can learn from everything that happens to us. Looking back, we can see how we have grown psychologically as a result of life's ups and downs, triumphs and failures, calms and crises.

- Seeing our parents in a new light and being able to understand them better, because we have lived through our own adulthood and have probably raised children of our own.

- Realising that we share with all other human beings, past, present and future, the inevitable cycle

of birth and death. Whatever the historical, cultural and other differences, we all have this much in common. In the light of this, death 'loses its sting'.

Fear of death is the most conspicuous symptom of despair. In despair, we express the belief that it is too late to undo the past and turn the clock back in order to right wrongs or do what has not been done. Life is not a 'rehearsal', and this is the only chance we get.

RETIREMENT

Retirement has figured prominently in the discussion above of theories of social adjustment in old age. As a normative, age-graded influence, it is an inevitable and anticipated loss of work, which many people experience without undue psychological upheaval (Raphael, 1984). However, it may be unacceptable to those who, for example, see themselves as 'too young' to stop work.

One consequence of retirement is the loss of everyday, ritualised patterns of activity, which contribute to the very fabric of our lives. Whilst the early weeks of not working may be celebrated, emptiness may be experienced for a time following retirement. As the months pass, frustration and a sense of 'uselessness' can set in, and this may produce an angry and irritable response to the world.

Figure 36.6 *Victor Meldrew (star of BBC TV's* One Foot in the Grave) *seems to personify the sense of frustration and uselessness that often sets in, especially for men, after the 'honeymoon period' of retirement*

Retirement is a *process* and *social role* which unfolds through a series of six phases, each of which requires an adjustment to be made (Atchley, 1982, 1985). The phases do not correspond with any particular chronological ages, occur in no fixed order, and not all of them are necessarily experienced by everyone.

Box 36.7 The six phases in the process of retirement

1 **Pre-retirement phase:** (i) in the *remote* sub-phase, retirement is seen as being in a reasonably distant future; (ii) the *near* sub-phase may be initiated by the retirement of older friends and colleagues and there may be much anxiety about lifestyle changes, especially financial ones.

2 **Honeymoon phase (immediate post-retirement):** This phase typically involves euphoria, partly due to newfound freedom, and is often a busy period (which may be long or short).

3 **Disenchantment phase:** This involves a slowing down after the honeymoon phase, with feelings of being let down and even depression. The degree of disenchantment is related to declining health and finances. Eagerly anticipated post-retirement activities (e.g. travel) may lose their original appeal. Disenchantment may be produced by unrealistic pre-retirement fantasies or inadequate preparation for retirement.

4 **Reorientation phase:** This is a time to develop a more realistic view of life alternatives, and may involve exploring new avenues of involvement, sometimes with the help of community groups (e.g. special voluntary or paid jobs for the retired). This helps to decrease feelings of role loss and is a means of achieving self-actualisation (see Chapter 17).

5 **Stability phase:** This involves the establishment of criteria for making choices, allowing people to deal with life in a fairly comfortable and orderly way. They know what is expected of them, what their strengths and weaknesses are, allowing mastery of the retirement role.

6 **Termination phase:** Illness and disability usually make housework and self-care difficult or impossible, leading to the assumption of a sick or disabled (as opposed to retirement) role.

(From Gross, 1996, and based on Atchley, 1982, and Atchley & Robinson, 1982)

People who retire *voluntarily* seem to have very little or no difficulty in adjusting. However, those who retire because they have reached a compulsory age tend to be dissatisfied at first, although they eventually adapt. The least satisfied are those whose health is poor when they retire (which may have caused their retirement), although health often improves following retirement.

Bromley (1988) believes that it is the *transition* between employment and retirement that causes adjustment problems. Those who are most satisfied in retirement tend to be scientists, writers and other academics, who simply carry on working with little loss of continuity from very satisfying jobs. Those who discover satisfying leisure activities with at least some of the characteristics of work, also adjust well. Conversely, some people decide to take early retirement (for reasons other than ill-health). This means that retirement is not necessarily a sudden and enforced dislocation of a working life, inevitably causing feelings of rejection and producing psychological problems.

Retirement and gender

As noted in Chapter 35, women are increasingly entering the labour market and remaining in it, and so more and more women are having to adjust to their own retirement. At the same time, 'gender-splitting' will mean that home and family still occupy a major part of a working woman's time, and retirement will involve less of a lifestyle change than it will for her husband.

According to Rainey (1998), the increase in working women aged 45–64 is particularly significant. They are the very group who, traditionally, contribute the most time to voluntary organisations and provide informal support for the elderly. There is no evidence that these women are abandoning their caring roles. In fact, these 'women in the middle' appear to be assuming multiple roles: caring for their own families (which includes helping their husbands adjust to retirement), for aged parents, possibly parents-in-law, as well as working. They are caught in the 'caring trap' (Rainey, 1998).

Retirement and unemployment

As noted above, retirement is an anticipated loss of work, whilst unemployment is sudden and generally unanticipated. According to Campbell (1981), retirement is also an accepted and 'honourable' social status (it is 'achieved'), whereas unemployment is not. Moreover, retirement is seen as a proper reward for a lifetime of hard work, whilst unemployment implies failure, being unwanted (or incompetent), and a 'scrounger' who is 'living off the state'. There is a stigma attached to unemployment which can make it a disturbing and degrading experience, whilst most men see retirement as a rather benign condition of life.

BEREAVEMENT

Although the loss, through death, of loved ones can occur at any stage of the life-cycle, it becomes more likely as we get older that we will suffer *bereavement*. The psychological and bodily reactions that occur in people who suffer bereavement are called *grief*. The 'observable expression of grief' (Parkes & Weiss, 1983) is called *mourning*, although this term is often used to refer to the social conventions surrounding death (such as funerals and wearing black clothes).

Approaches to the understanding of grief

According to Archer (1999), grief has been variously depicted as (a) a natural human reaction; (b) a psychiatric disorder; and (c) a disease process. All three approaches contain an element of truth. As far as (a) is concerned, grief is a univeral feature of human existence, found in all cultures. However, its form and the intensity of its expression varies considerably (see pages 395–396). As far as (b) is concerned, although grief itself has never been classified as a mental disorder (see Chapter 46):

> 'The psychiatric framework emphasises the human suffering grief involves, and therefore provides a useful balance to viewing it simply as a natural reaction'. (Archer, 1999)

Regarding (c), although there may be increased rates of morbidity (health deterioration) or mortality (death) amongst bereaved people, these are not necessarily *directly* caused by the grief process. For example, the effects of change in lifestyle (such as altered nutrition or drug intake), or increased attention to physical illness which pre-dated the bereavement, might be mistaken for the effects of grief itself. However, there is substantial evidence that bereaved spouses are more at risk of dying themselves compared with matched non-bereaved controls. This is true mainly for widowers (Stroebe & Stroebe, 1993), and especially for younger widowers experiencing an unexpected bereavement (Smith & Zick, 1996: see Chapter 36).

Stage or phase accounts of grief

According to Archer (1999), a widely held assumption is that grief proceeds through an orderly series of stages or phases, with distinct features. Whilst different accounts vary in the details of particular stages, the two most commonly cited are those of Bowlby (1980) and Kübler-Ross (1969).

Box 36.8 Bowlby's phase theory of grief

According to Bowlby (1980), adult grief is an extension of a general distress response to separation commonly observed in young children (see Gross *et al.*, 2000). Adult grief is a form of *separation anxiety* in response to the disruption of an attachment bond.

1 **Phase of numbing:** Numbness and disbelief, which can last from a few hours up to a week, may be punctuated by outbursts of extremely intense distress and/or anger.

2 **Yearning and searching:** These are accompanied by anxiety and intermittent periods of anger, and can last for months or even years.

3 **Disorganisation and despair:** Feelings of depression and apathy occur when old patterns have been discarded.

4 **Reorganisation:** There is a greater/lesser degree of recovery from bereavement and acceptance of what has occurred.

Kübler-Ross's stage theory: anticipatory grief

Kübler-Ross's (1969) stage view was based on her pioneering work with over 200 terminally ill patients. She was interested in how they prepare for their *own* imminent death (*anticipatory* grief), and so her stages describe the process of dying. However, she was inspired by an earlier version of Bowlby's theory (Parkes, 1995) and her stages were later applied (by other researchers) to grief for others. Her theory remains very influential in nursing and counselling, both with dying patients and the bereaved (Archer, 1999).

Box 36.9 Kübler-Ross's stages of dying

1 **Denial ('No, not me'):** This prevents the patient from being overwhelmed by the initial shock. It may take the form of seeking a second opinion, or holding contradictory beliefs.

2 **Anger ('It's not fair – why me?'):** This may be directed at medical staff and other healthy people who will go on living.

3 **Bargaining ('Please God let me ...'):** This is an attempt to postpone death by 'doing a deal' with God (or fate, or the hospital), much as a child might bargain with its parents in order to get its own way.

4 **Depression ('How can I leave all this behind?'):** This is likely to arise when the patient realises that no bargain can be struck and that death is inevitable. S/he grieves for all the losses that death represents.

5 **Acceptance ('Leave me be, I am ready to die'):** Almost devoid of feelings, the patient seems to have given up the struggle for life, sleeps more and withdraws from other people, as if preparing for 'the long journey'.

Almost all the patients she interviewed initially denied they had life-threatening illnesses, although only three remained in a constant state of denial (the rest drifted in and out). Denial was more common if they had been given the diagnosis in an abrupt or insensitive way, or if they were surrounded by family and/or staff who were also in denial. *Searching* for a second opinion was a very common initial reaction, representing a desperate attempt to change the unpredictable world they had just been catapulted into, back into the world they knew and understood (March & Doherty, 1999).

Depression is a common reaction in the dying. For example, Hinton (1975) reported that 18 per cent of suicides suffered from serious physical illnesses, with four per cent having illnesses that probably would have killed them within six months (see Chapter 50). Terminally ill patients suffer from what Kübler-Ross called *preparatory depression* (as opposed to *reactive*).

Elderly people who have lived a full life have relatively little to grieve for – they have gained much and lost few opportunities. However, people who perceive a life full of mistakes and missed opportunities may, paradoxically, have *more* to grieve for as they begin to realise that these opportunities are now lost forever. This resembles Erikson's *despair* (see page 391), as does *resignation*, which Kübler-Ross distinguished from acceptance. The detachment and stillness of those who have achieved acceptance comes from calmness, whilst in those who have become resigned it comes from despair. The latter cannot accept death, nor can they deny its existence any longer (March & Doherty, 1999).

An evaluation of stage theories of grief

Generally, stage models have not been well supported by subsequent research. Both Bowlby's and Kübler-Ross's accounts were proposed before any prolonged, detailed follow-up studies of bereaved people had been undertaken (Archer, 1999). According to March & Doherty (1999), they represent generalisations from the experience of some individuals and lack the flexibility necessary to describe the range of individual reactions.

Grief is *not* a simple, universal process through which we all go (Stroebe *et al.*, 1993).

Some researchers prefer to talk about the *components* of grief. Ramsay & de Groot (1977), for example, have identified nine such components, some of which occur early and others late in the grieving process.

Box 36.10 Ramsay and de Groot's nine components of grief

1 **Shock:** Usually the first response, most often described as a feeling of 'numbness', which can also include pain, calm, apathy, depersonalisation and derealisation. It is as if the feelings are so strong that they are 'turned off'. This can last from a few seconds to several weeks.

2 **Disorganisation:** The inability to do the simplest thing, or, alternatively, organising the entire funeral and then collapsing.

3 **Denial:** Behaving as if the deceased were still alive is a defence against feeling too much pain. It is usually an early feature of grief, but one that can recur at any time. A common form of denial is searching behaviour (e.g. waiting for the deceased to come home, or having hallucinations of them).

4 **Depression:** This emerges as the denial breaks down but can occur, usually less frequently and intensely, at any point during the grieving process. It can consist of either 'desolate pining' (a yearning and longing, an emptiness interspersed with waves of intense psychic pain') or 'despair' (feelings of helplessness, the blackness of the realisation of powerlessness to bring back the dead).

5 **Guilt:** This can be both real and imagined, for actual neglect of the deceased when they were alive, or for angry thoughts and feelings.

6 **Anxiety:** This can involve fear of losing control of one's feelings, of going mad, or more general apprehension about the future (changed roles, increased responsibilities, financial worries, and so on).

7 **Aggression:** This can take the form of irritability towards family and friends, outbursts of anger towards God or fate, doctors and nurses, the clergy or even the person who has died.

8 **Resolution:** This is an emerging acceptance of the death, a 'taking leave of the dead and acceptance that life must go on'.

9 **Reintegration:** This involves putting acceptance into practice by reorganising one's life in which the deceased has no place. However, pining and

despair may reappear on anniversaries, birthdays, and so on.

(Based on Gross, 1996)

However, many stage theorists have explicitly *denied* that the stages are meant to apply equally and rigidly to everyone. For example, Bowlby (1980) himself said that:

'These phases are not clear cut, and any one individual may oscillate for a time back and forth between any two of them'.

Yet stages provide us with a framework or guidelines for understanding the experiences of bereaved and dying individuals, whilst at the same recognising that that there is a huge variability in the ways individuals react. Stages do not prescribe where an individual 'ought' to be in the grieving process (March & Doherty, 1999).

Cultural influences on reactions to bereavement

Because of this huge individual variability, trying to distinguish 'normal' from 'abnormal' grief seems quite arbitrary (Schuchter & Zisook, 1993). According to Middleton *et al.* (1993), the validity of the concept of pathological grief must be considered in terms of cultural norms. Although grief is a universal response to major loss, its meaning, duration and how it is expressed are all culturally prescribed.

Figure 36.7 *The depth of feeling and public grief caused by the death of Diana, Princess of Wales, was unprecedented*

Inter- and intra-cultural differences

Cultures differ in how they define death and what is an appropriate expression of grief. According to Rosenblatt (1993):

'Culture is such a crucial part of the context of bereavement that it is often impossible to separate an individual's grief from culturally required mourning'

For example, in cultures that believe 'do not grieve because grief will cause the ghost of the deceased to take you away' or 'do not grieve because the deceased has gone to a better life', it is difficult to assess accurately what appears to be muted or restrained grief. Similarly, when the 'rules' say 'cry', and people cry, how do we know the grief is genuine, deeply felt and likely to occur in the absence of the cultural demands for crying (what kind of *attribution* should we make?: see Chapter 1)?

The Jewish rites of mourning are believed to be of therapeutic benefit, enabling the expression, rather than the repression, of grief. For the first few days following the burial, mourners are expected to be distressed and their despair is recognised and supported by relatives and friends who come to pay their respects.

By contrast, the Hindu, Sikh, Muslim and Buddhist religions all discourage too much weeping (Firth, 1993). The Hindus believe that weeping makes a river which the soul of the deceased has to cross, and Sikhs believe the deceased has gone to God. However, the expression of grief is less inhibited in villages on the Indian subcontinent compared with Sikhs and Hindus living in Britain. Similarly, wailing is still very common among Muslims in Muslim countries (Firth, 1993).

Compared with Western women, Japanese women accept their husbands' death with composure and resignation. They believe strongly in an afterlife and that their ancestors are always with them. Their beliefs mitigate feelings of complete loss and, to this extent, they have less to grieve about. The long-lasting grief and depression observed among the bereaved in the UK is partly a result of the *lack* of rituals and beliefs, as well as the lack of an externally-based *end* to the grieving process (March & Doherty, 1999).

Box 36.11 Culture and the length of the grieving process

- In traditional Navajo Indian culture, the expression of grief lasts for four days following the death (March & Doherty, 1999).

- For Hindus in India, the mourning period lasts 10-16 days.

- For orthodox Jews, there are five graduated periods of mourning: (i) between death and the burial (which occurs as soon as can be arranged); (ii) immediate post-burial; (iii) seven days following the burial (the *shiva* week); (iv) thirty days from the burial (marking the official end of mourning, unless it is a parent who has died, in which case it continues for a whole year); finally (v) between 30 days and one year, when the memorial stone is erected (Katz, 1993).

According to Firth (1993), all the major religions of the world teach that there is some sort of continuity or survival after death. They also comfort and reassure the bereaved by helping to make sense of death and personal loss, providing shape and meaning to the grieving process. As Box 36.11 shows, mourning lasts for a clearly defined period in different cultures, providing 'milestones'. These allow the bereaved a gradual time to let go of the deceased and adjust to the psychological and social changes in their lives.

As well as differences between cultures, there are also important differences *within* culturally diverse countries, such as the USA and the UK. For example, WASP (White Anglo-Saxon Protestant) Americans tend to 'psychologise' their emotional pain (e.g. depression), whilst people in many ethnic minority groups tend to 'somatise' theirs (e.g. bodily symptoms: Kleinman & Kleinman, 1985).

CONCLUSIONS

The different meanings of 'old' suggest that chronological age is a poor indicator of what a particular elderly individual is like, both psychologically and socially. However, major theories of social adjustment to old age, such as social disengagement and activity theories, tend to regard the elderly as basically all the same. This implies that there is a particular way of ageing successfully, a view that is not shared by other theories and not supported by research evidence.

Similarly, the view that ageing inevitably involves rapid and generalised cognitive decline is also not supported by research evidence. Both intelligence and memory have many facets, which tend to decline at very different rates.

The impact of retirement and bereavement has also been discussed. Retirement is a socially imposed loss of work, which has both social and psychological effects, as does bereavement. Attempts to identify stages of grief that apply equally to everyone have proved largely unsuccessful, partly because of individual variability and partly because of both inter- and intra-cultural differences in how death and grief are understood and managed.

Summary

- Whilst 'growing up' has positive connotations, 'growing old' has negative ones, reflecting the **decrement model**. An alternative, more positive view, is the **personal growth model**.

- Age can be defined in different ways, specifically **chronological**, **biological**, **subjective** and **functional** (closely related to **social**). Few people, regardless of chronological age, describe themselves consistently.

- One feature of **ageism** is the assumption that chronological age is an accurate indicator of all the other ages. Stereotypes of the elderly are deeply rooted in rapidly changing Western societies, where their experience and wisdom are no longer valued.

- Burnside *et al.*,'s decade-by-decade description is a way of seeing the aged as a collection of sub-groups, each with its own problems and capabilities. We need to change our stereotypes of the elderly as being needy, non-productive and unhappy.

- The claim that intelligence declines fairly rapidly in old age is based on **cross-sectional studies**, which face the problem of the **cohort effect**. **Longitudinal studies** indicate that whilst **crystallised intelligence** increases with age, **fluid intelligence** declines for all age groups over time. This may reflect the inevitable reduction in the efficiency of **neurological** functioning, although we may be less often challenged to use these abilities in old age.

- Some aspects of memory decline with age, perhaps due to less effective **information processing**. Older adults generally perform more poorly than younger adults on recall tests, but the differences are reduced or may even disappear when recognition tests are used.

- Evidence from the **OPTIMA project** suggests that **dementia** (the most common form of which is Alzheimer's disease) is not an accelerated form of normal ageing. Rather, it appears to reflect a disease process which is more likely to affect us as we get older. This means that cognitive decline is not an inevitable accompaniment of ageing.

- **Negative cultural stereotypes** of ageing actually cause memory decline in the elderly, and may become **self-fulfilling prophecies**.

- **Social disengagement theory** refers to the mutual withdrawal of society and the individual. Its most controversial feature is its claim that the elderly accept and even welcome disengagement, and that this is a natural and inevitable process.

- Although old age is undeniably associated with many types of loss, social disengagement theory emphasises the **quantitative** changes to the exclusion of the **qualitative** changes, which may become more important with age. The latter include **friendships**, which are under the older person's control and provide essential informal support.

- **Activity** or **re-engagement theory** claims that older people are psychologically and socially essentially the same as middle-aged people. The withdrawal of society and the individual is not mutual, and optimal ageing involves maintaining the activities of middle age for as long as possible.

- According to **social exchange theory**, older people in **industrialised societies** have **few power resources** to exchange in everyday social interaction, making them dependent on others. However, there is also a largely unwritten contract, whereby the elderly relinquish their roles as economically active members of society in exchange for increased leisure time and fewer responsibilities.

- **Socioemotional selectivity theory** maintains that the importance of different social motives changes at different points in the life cycle. For the elderly, **emotional regulation** assumes major importance, making them highly selective as regards social partners. This change in social motives is largely determined by **construal of the future**.

- According to Erikson's **psychosocial theory**, old age involves a conflict between **ego-integrity** and **despair**. The task of ageing is to assess and evaluate life's value and meaning. Despair is characterised by a fear of death.

- **Retirement** is an inevitable, anticipated loss of work. It is a process and social role which proceeds through six phases, each requiring a different adjustment.

- People who retire **voluntarily** have little or no difficulty in adjusting, compared with those who retire because they have reached retirement age or whose health is poor. It is the **transition** between employment and retirement that causes adjustment problems.

- Compared with unemployment, retirement is an accepted and **honourable social status**, a proper reward for a hard life's work. Whilst unemployment has negative connotations, most men see retirement as a benign condition of life.

- **Grief** has been portrayed as a **natural, universal human reaction** to bereavement, a **psychiatric disorder** and a **disease process**.

- A widely held assumption is that grief proceeds through an orderly **series of stages** or **phases**. The two most commonly cited stage/phase accounts are those of Bowlby and Kübler-Ross.

- Kübler-Ross's account was based on interviews with terminally ill patients, so her stages describe the process of dying (**anticipatory grief**). The stages she identified are **denial**, **anger**, **bargaining**, (**preparatory**) **depression** and **acceptance**. She also distinguished between **acceptance** and **resignation**.

- Stage theories of grief have been criticised for their failure to describe the range of individual reactions. Grief is not a simple, universal process which is the same for everyone. Ramsay and de Groot prefer to talk about **components of grief**, which do not occur in a fixed order and which are not necessarily experienced by everyone.

- However, many stage theorists have themselves denied that the stages are meant to apply equally and rigidly to everyone. Stages provide a framework for understanding bereaved people's experiences, which display a huge variability.

- Although grief is a universal response to major loss, its meaning, duration and how it is expressed are all **culturally prescribed.** Cultures differ in how they define death, and it is often impossible to separate an individual's grief from cuturally required mourning.

- All the world's major religions teach that there is some kind of **after-life**. They also comfort the bereaved by helping to make sense of death and by providing 'milestones', which allow a gradual time to let go of the deceased and adjust to life without them.

Essay Questions

1 Discuss psychological research into the effects of retirement **and/or** bereavement in late adulthood.

(24 marks)

2 **a** Describe **one** theory of how people adjust to old age. *(12 marks)*

b Evaluate this theory by reference to alternative theories **and/or** research studies. *(12 marks)*

WEB ADDRESSES

http://www.aoa.dhhs.gov/
http://www.iog.wayne.edu.apadiv20/newslet.htm
http://www.iog.wayne.edu/APADIV20/lowdiv20.htm
http://www.psy.flinders.edu.au/labs/cogsci3.htm

Comparative Psychology

PART 1: DETERMINANTS OF ANIMAL BEHAVIOUR

37 Evolutionary Explanations of Animal Behaviour

INTRODUCTION AND OVERVIEW

Comparative psychology may be defined as the study of the behaviour of animals with a view to drawing comparisons (similarities and differences) between them. It also involves studying non-human animal behaviour in order to gain a better understanding of human behaviour. The basis of comparative psychology is the evolutionary relationship between all living organisms. According to Charles Darwin and Alfred Russel Wallace (Darwin, 1859), all species are biologically related, and so behaviour patterns are also likely to be related.

Comparative psychologists believe that most of the differences between animals are *quantitative* rather than *qualitative*. It is important to note, however, that the degree to which investigations of non-human animal behaviour are applicable to humans is questionable, and that there may be critical qualitative differences to be considered. This chapter looks at *evolutionary explanations of the behaviour of non-human animals*, including *biological explanations of apparent altruism*.

EVOLUTION

Evolution is the process by which new species arise as the result of gradual changes to the genetic make-up of existing species over long periods of time. The father of evolutionary theory was Charles Darwin (see Figure 37.1, page 400), and an understanding of his *theory of evolution by natural selection* is fundamental to the study of comparative psychology. Although far reaching in its effects, Darwin's theory is actually quite simple.

Box 37.1 A summary of Darwin's theory

- All species tend to produce very many more offspring than can ever survive. For example, Darwin calculated that after 750 years, the descendants of one pair of elephants could number more than 19 million. However, the size of population tends to remain more or less constant, meaning that most of these offspring must die. It also follows that there must be competition for resources, such as mates, food and territories. Therefore, there is a 'struggle for existence' among individuals.

- Individuals within a species differ from one another (*variation*). Much of this variability is inherited (*genetic variation*).

- Competition for resources, together with variation between individuals, means that certain members of the population are more likely to survive and reproduce than others. These individuals will inherit the characteristics of their parents, and evolutionary change takes place through natural selection. Over a long period of time, this process may lead to the considerable differences now observed between living organisms.

- It is important to remember that for natural selection to drive evolutionary change, the environment must select certain individuals, and the differences between individuals must be (to some extent) inherited. Without these two factors, evolution is not likely to occur.

Figure 37.1 *Charles Darwin. His theory of evolution by natural selection forms the basis of comparative psychology*

NATURE VERSUS NURTURE

How much of the variability within a species is due to genetic factors, and how much depends upon the influence of the environment? This *nature* (inherited characteristics) versus *nurture* (acquired characteristics) debate has been hotly contested in biology and psychology (see Chapter 59). However, although certain features may fall neatly into one of these two categories, the question of whether learning *or* evolution underlie any given behaviour is largely meaningless. Any behaviour, however simple or complex, has an element both of inheritance *and* learning about it (the interaction of which is known as *penetrance*). The only point of debate is over the relative importance of the contributions

made to a behaviour by *phylogeny* (inherited, species-specific behaviour patterns) and *ontogeny* (behaviour patterns acquired during the lifetime of the individual, which are not shared with every member of the species). The importance of this, as far as the present chapter is concerned, is that most animal behaviour appears to have some genetic component, and is therefore capable of being influenced by the processes of evolution.

THE EVIDENCE FOR EVOLUTION

Darwin's theory of evolution by natural selection is supported by evidence from four main areas.

Box 37.2 The evidence supporting Darwin's theory

- **Palaeontology**: Fossil records indicate clear evidence for evolution, particularly for the vertebrates (animals with backbones). The most convincing evidence is found in cases where, in successive rock layers from the same locality, a series of fossils exhibit gradual change.

- **Comparative anatomy**: When the anatomy of one group of animals is compared with that of another, resemblances are generally more obvious than differences. One example of this is the pentadactyl ('five-digit') limb, which is found in various forms in all mammals. Comparing the physiology or embryology (development of the embryo) of species also provides evidence for evolution by natural selection.

- **Geographical distribution**: Places with the same climatic conditions in different regions of the world do not always possess the same animal forms. Elephants, for example, live in India and Africa, but not in South America. This phenomenon is best explained by assuming that existing animals are the descendants of extinct populations which were of a more generalised type. These ancestors were dispersed from their place of origin, became geographically isolated (for example by sea or mountains), and evolved along different paths, becoming adapted to their new environments.

- **Artificial selection**: Modern varieties of domesticated animals are very different from their ancestors. They have evolved as a result of humans choosing examples with the most desirable qualities, through selective breeding. Artificial selection is essentially the same as natural selection, except that it is very much quicker, and the features selected may not be of survival value in natural populations.

In addition to the evidence cited above, it is also possible to observe evolution in action over relatively short time periods. Classic examples of this include the development of antibiotic resistance in populations of bacteria, and the evolution of industrial melanism in the peppered moth (*Biston betularia*).

Key STUDY

Box 37.3 The evolution of industrial melanism in the peppered moth?

The peppered moth exists in two genetically determined forms: a light-coloured peppered form (*Biston betularia typica*) and a dark form (*Biston betularia carbonaria*). The first melanic moth (dark type) was reported in Manchester in 1849. By 1900, it had almost replaced the typical mottled form. Clearly, evolution (a change in gene frequency) had occurred.

The most significant selection pressure for peppered moths is visual predation by birds, which remove them from trees when they rest during the day. Kettlewell's (1955) experiments involved releasing moths in various locations and investigating what happened to them. He found that more moths were eaten by birds if they were conspicuous against their backgrounds than if they were camouflaged. In polluted industrial areas (e.g. Manchester), the melanic form was better camouflaged, and predation was largely restricted to the mottled form. In areas not polluted by soot, the reverse was true and the mottled form predominated.

Industrial melanism appears to be a classic example of evolution in action. However, Hailman (1992) has argued that the evidence is far from conclusive. It is not clear whether anyone has actually observed the ratio of peppered to melanic forms change over time. Data from the mid-nineteenth century come from amateur moth collections, not scientific samples. Hailman also claims that it is unlikely that birds eat sufficient numbers of moths to shift the ratio. Furthermore, the correlation between melanic moths in industrial areas and peppered moths elsewhere is far from clear. Without further experiments, industrial melanism may be considered a *myth* of evolutionary biology.

Fitness

Darwin's theory of evolution by natural selection has often been summed up by the phrase 'survival of the fittest'. However, this is an oversimplification. *Fitness* is not a quality that individuals possess, such as size or

speed, but is closely linked with evolutionary success. It may be defined as a measure of the ability of an individual to leave behind offspring. The relative fitness of the offspring is also important. It is likely that at least some of this fitness is genetic in nature and, therefore, determined by natural and sexual selection.

BASIC EVOLUTION THEORY

Figure 37.2 *Is this fish likely to be fitter than one which has not developed legs?*

More recent examinations of Darwin's work have tended to replace the term 'fitness' with '*inclusive fitness*' (Dawkins, 1989). Inclusive fitness may be defined as the total number of an animal's genes present in subsequent generations. These genes will be present in direct offspring and in the offspring of close relatives, such as brothers and sisters. The use of the term inclusive fitness may solve one of the problems of Darwin's theory, that being the existence of *altruistic behaviour* in certain species (see pages 404–406).

Behaviour

As noted in the *Introduction and overview*, this chapter aims to consider evolutionary concepts as explanations of the behaviour of animals. With this in mind, evolution may be more specifically defined as the processes by which animal *behaviour* is altered by means of adaptation through natural selection. It is important to remember that natural selection works by *differential reproduction*. When examining animal behaviour, therefore, we should usually ask 'How does that behaviour enable that animal to produce more offspring?', or 'Why would an animal that performed a different behaviour pattern leave fewer offspring?'

According to Darwin, all species are biologically related to each other through evolution, and so behaviour patterns are also likely to be related. Grier & Burk (1992) suggest that nearly all animal behaviour is influenced by genetic factors to some degree, and that behaviour makes important contributions to an animal's survival and reproductive success. The behaviour of animals must, therefore, be subject to the forces of evolution in the same way as their anatomy and physiology.

One important question which needs to be addressed is how *new* behaviours arise. It is important to realise that most behaviour patterns do not suddenly appear as a whole, especially if they are complex. They probably originate as very small modifications of ancestral behaviour, which conferred a slight but significant advantage (perhaps due to a *mutation*). This behaviour pattern would then spread by natural selection. New behaviour patterns can also arise by combining pre-existing behavioural units (single observable acts) in novel forms.

Instinctive and learned behaviour

The 'nature' versus 'nurture' debate mentioned earlier (see page 400) may also be applied to animal behaviour. In this case, nature traditionally represents *instinctive* behaviours, and nurture represents *learned* behaviours. As will be seen, though, this is an oversimplification because instincts are *not* purely genetic and learning is *not* purely environmental.

Instinctive behaviour evolves gradually, and is modified by natural selection in order to adapt animals to fit a fixed and unchanging environment. Such behaviours are advantageous for animals that have short lifespans, and little or no parental care. These animals have little opportunity or need for learning. Learned behaviour enables animals to discover which responses give the best results in certain circumstances, and to modify their actions accordingly. The ability to learn gives animals an adaptive advantage in that it gives them a greater potential for changing their behaviour to meet changing circumstances within their own lifetime. However, few behaviours can be said to be entirely dominated by either inheritance or learning, and an *interaction* between the two is the norm.

Seligman (1970) suggested that animals are *biologically prepared* to learn some things more readily than others. Some associations, such as taste avoidance, may be more biologically useful (or have greater survival value) than others, and are therefore learned more quickly and are more resistant to *extinction* (see Chapter 38). Research on birdsong has demonstrated the importance of both instinct and learning.

Key STUDY

Box 37.4 The role of genetic and environmental factors in the development of bird song

In the normal course of development, young male white-crowned sparrows (*Zonotrichia leucophrys*) do not start to sing until about two months of age. At this point, the sounds the birds produce are called *subsong*. At around four months, the variable sounds of subsong 'crystallise' into the final adult song characteristics of this species.

If a young male is isolated from other white-crowned sparrows during the *sensitive period* (days 1–50), he produces subsong but it does not crystallise into the proper adult version. This appears to suggest that the ability to produce subsong is instinctive, but that learning is required to develop the correct adult song. Further evidence for the interaction of genetic and environmental factors comes from white-crowned sparrows exposed only to the song of the song sparrow (*Melospiza melodra*) during the sensitive period. These birds learn neither the related species' song nor their own (Ridley, 1995).

As Box 37.4 shows, although most male birds inherit the basics of their song, they need to experience singing and listening to the songs of other birds before they can produce the final form. Similar genetic and environmental factors appear to play a role in the opening of milk bottle tops by blue tits. In this case, the physical ability to remove strips of material is instinctive, but its application to the foil tops of milk bottles is learned (Sherry & Galef, 1984: see page 407).

Evidence for the evolution of behaviour

Explanations of the evolution of behaviour are essentially the same as those of the evolution of anatomy and physiology. However, evidence for the evolution of behaviour is not as easily obtained. For example, behaviour is not easily fossilised. However, fossil records may provide evidence of particular anatomical features which *imply* certain behaviours. The role of head ornaments in dinosaurs, such as the horns of *Triceratops*, has been inferred from the behaviour of animals, such as deer and certain beetles, that have head ornaments today and use them to attract mates or threaten potential rivals (Molnar, 1977).

By far the best evidence for the evolution of animal behaviour comes from *interspecies comparisons* (which is what comparative psychology is all about). To make these comparisons we need a *phylogenetic tree*, which shows the ancestral relations of modern forms based on anatomical and physiological evidence. If we know the evolutionary relationship between a group of species, we can infer whether common behaviour patterns are *homologous* (species share a common ancestor) or *analogous* (similar behaviour patterns evolved in unrelated organisms due to similar environmental pressures).

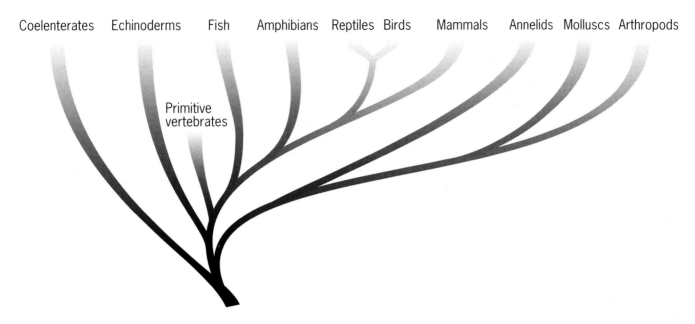

Coelenterates Echinoderms Fish Amphibians Reptiles Birds Mammals Annelids Molluscs Arthropods

Primitive vertebrates

Figure 37.3 *A phylogenetic tree of some large groups of animals*

Convergent evolution is when similar behaviours evolve independently in a number of unrelated species. The social insects represent a good example of convergent evolution, with termites (*Amitermes hastatus*) and the social hymenopterans (ants, bees and wasps) developing this distinctive behaviour independently. *Divergent evolution* is when different behaviours are observed among related species. An example of this is courtship behaviour in ducks, which is typically a distinctive pattern of vocalisations and head and tail movements (Lorenz, 1958). In this case, the behaviour is probably advantageous in ensuring that individuals do not waste time and effort courting members of a different species.

Convergent and divergent evolution form the basis of two approaches to studying comparative psychology. The first considers the function of analogous behaviours among unrelated species, and attempts to explain what caused these behaviours by searching for similar environmental factors. The second looks at differences among closely related species to investigate the evolutionary changes undergone by a particular behavioural unit based on phylogenetic relationships. A comparison of closely related species, living in different habitats, can often reveal those aspects of behaviour which are particularly important in adapting the animal to its environment. It is also possible to combine these two approaches for a detailed study of the evolution of a particular behaviour.

Phylogenetic trees based on behavioural similarities can be constructed and compared to those based on anatomical and physiological evidence. Lorenz (1958) did this with ducks and geese, and found that the grouping of species according to their behaviour is sim-

ilar to, but not exactly identical with, groupings based on anatomical similarity.

Several experimental studies have shown that differences in behaviour can result from differences in genes. For example Benzer (1973) induced genetic mutations that changed behaviour in the fruit fly *Drosophila*. One example of this is the 'amnesiac fly', which learns normally but forgets very rapidly. The physiological basis of these altered behaviour patterns have been investigated, and shown to be due to a mutation in a specific gene (Dudai, 1989). Artificial selection experiments (Cade, 1981) have also demonstrated that genetic factors are important in calling behaviour in crickets (*Gryllus integer*). In humans, however, the situation is more complex, and there are probably very few examples of behaviour being influenced by a *single* gene.

Key **STUDY**

Box 37.5 The genetic basis of 'women's intuition'

Cartwright (2000), however, has suggested the existence of a single gene (or a small cluster of genes on the X chromosome) that plays a major role in normal social skills, such as awareness of other people's feelings, and the ability to chat and make friends. Normal human females have two X chromosomes, one from each parent. Males, on the other hand, have only one X chromosome (inherited from their mother) and a Y chromosome (inherited from their father).

Cartwright (2000) found that girls with Turner's syndrome (who only have one X chromosome) differed in their behaviour depending on whether they inherited this chromosome from their mother or father. Girls who inherit their mother's X chromosome lack social skills, whereas girls who inherit their father's do not.

This may explain why normal girls tend to have rather better social skills than their male counterparts. Cartwright suggests that girls are genetically pre-programmed to learn to interpret social cues. Boys, however, do not have this advantage and have to work harder to achieve the same level of social competence (see also Chapter 32).

When examining the evolution of behaviour, it is important to consider two main points. First, when we talk about genes for a particular behaviour it does not mean that one gene alone codes for that behaviour. It is much more likely that several genes are involved. However, a difference in behaviour between two individuals may be due to a *difference* in a single gene. Second, the fact that genes can be shown to influence behaviour does not imply that genes alone produce the behaviour, or even that the behaviour can be divided up into genetic and environmental components. The way in which behaviour develops is the result of a complex *interaction* between genes and the environment (see Chapter 59).

We should not expect all behaviours to be currently adaptive. Some behaviours may be adaptively 'neutral', in the sense that they no longer serve an essential function in promoting survival. It is also possible for certain behaviours to become *maladaptive*, particularly following a rapid change in ecological conditions. The analysis of any behaviour pattern should include some consideration of the function for which it was originally adapted. In times of rapid ecological change, the behaviour repertoire of many animals will consist of a conglomerate of adaptive, neutral and maladaptive patterns (Davies, 1995).

APPARENT ALTRUISM

Altruism can be defined as the performance of a behaviour which enhances the fitness of the recipient, whilst lowering the fitness of the performer (the *altruist*). For example, a blackbird (*Xanthocephalus xanthocephalus*) will give an alarm call if it detects a potential predator. This benefits individuals nearby, as they are alerted to the risk and so can hide or flee. The altruistic caller suffers not only the very small energetic cost of sounding the alarm but, potentially, a very large cost, having made its whereabouts known to the predator.

If animals really were to perform behaviours that were selfless, surely they would rapidly lose the evolutionary 'race' against those that were not? Selfish

recipients would gain without cost, altruists would encounter costs without gains, and the selfish individuals would win hands down. At least that is what natural selection would predict in a competitive world. The question of how altruism could arise perplexed Darwin, and now presents a central problem for evolutionary biologists. Several attempts have been made to explain how altruistic behaviours are preserved in populations. These theories suggest that there *is* an inherent gain for the altruist, that is, the altruism is only *apparent*. Two different explanations for apparent altruism are *kin selection theory* and *reciprocal altruism theory*.

Kin selection theory

This suggests that traits which directed an individual's altruism towards its relatives, but not to non-relatives, would evolve (Hamilton, 1964). Only those sharing genes would benefit, thus promoting the survival of related individuals which are also likely to be genetically predisposed to be altruistic. The altruist thus gains via *inclusive fitness* (see page 401).

As kin selection relies on altruists helping related individuals, greater altruistic sacrifices would be expected for closer relatives. The relatedness of two individuals can be expressed as the *coefficient of relationship* (r). This is the proportion of genes they share. An offspring shares 50 per cent of its genes with each parent ($r = 0.5$). Full siblings will, on average, share 50 per cent of their genes with each other, as each has inherited some in common from each parent (but not necessarily the same genes).

Table 37.1   *Degree of kinship (relatedness) between different individuals*

Relationship	Expected proportion of shared genes (coefficient of relationship, r)
Identical twins	1.0
Parent/offspring	0.5
Full sibling [brother or sister]	0.5
Grandparent/grandchild	0.25
Aunt, uncle/niece, nephew	0.25
Cousin	0.125
Non-relative	0

Box 37.6 When will altruism evolve?

We would expect altruism to occur if the cost (**c**) of the behaviour to the altruist is low (c is small) and the benefit (**b**) to the recipient is great (b is large). The ratio of benefits to costs (**K**) can be expressed as **b/c** and we would expect this figure to be large where altruism occurs, that is, for the benefits to exceed the costs. If **K = b/c**, then the higher the value of **K**, the greater the probability of altruism occurring. If the costs are too high, altruists are unlikely to survive to be altruistic, and if the gains are too small, the behaviour may not have a significant effect on the recipient.

Of course, the degree of kinship (**r**) matters too. Altruism should only occur when **K > 1/r**. This will only be fulfilled when either the cost/benefit ratio is very favourable, or when the degree of relatedness is very high (so **1/r** is very small). This makes sense: individuals will risk more for close kin as they stand to gain more in terms of inclusive fitness.

(Based on Hamilton, 1964)

Bertram (1976) used his own studies of lions, and those of Schaller (1972), to generate data about a 'typical pride', consisting of four 'resident' females and two 'pride' males. The females may have different mothers and fathers, but tend to remain with the same pride. The males are typically brothers who have taken over a new pride together. Bertram used evidence from observations of copulations, and the movements of animals between prides, to establish the relationships between individuals.

From many examples of different prides, he calculated average coefficients of relationship for each of the adults in a pride. He found that males, related on average by *r* = 0.22, were *more likely* to show altruism than females, whose coefficient of relationship was lower (*r* = 0.15). However, females do demonstrate altruism. For example, when nursing, females will allow cubs of other lionesses in the pride to suckle from them. This is altruistic for the female, as it bears the cost of making milk, which is then unavailable to her own offspring.

Figure 37.4 *A lioness* (Panthera leo*) will altruistically suckle all the cubs in a pride*

The females' behaviour is surprising, because they are not as closely related to one another as are males (nor so closely related to all the cubs in the pride), so they stand to gain less via increased inclusive fitness. A process which is *not* dependent on kinship must be responsible for the females' altruistic behaviour.

Possibly, the communal suckling described above is not truly altruistic after all, and it might be in a female's *own* interests to assist the development of *all* cubs. Her offspring will have a greater chance of survival if the pride is maintained, thus her own reproductive success depends on the survival of other cubs, which may be smaller or more needy than her own. The costs are small, but the potential benefits may be great. Similarly, she is more likely to survive in a larger pride which could sustain her if, for example, she was injured. The lionesses are simply acting in their own interests.

Reciprocal altruism theory

Kin selection can only explain altruism when the helper and recipient are *related*. However, in many cases they are not. For example Packer & Pusey (1982) found that Tanzanian lions forming co-operative groups for hunting included large numbers of non-relatives. Trivers (1971) proposed that in these circumstances, *reciprocal altruism* may be operating. This is where one individual (the altruist) helps another, and is later 'repaid' by assistance from that unrelated recipient. The initial altruist suffers a short-term reduction in individual fitness, but both individuals eventually achieve a gain in fitness.

Key (S T U D Y)

Box 37.7 Reciprocal altruism in vampire bats

One of the most impressive examples of reciprocal altruism is illustrated by vampire bats (*Desmodus rotundus*). Wilkinson (1984) studied kinship relationships between bats at a roost site. He found that bats were only altruistic to one another if they were either close relatives, or unrelated individuals who were regular roost mates. A vampire bat without food will only survive for about two days. If it has been unsuccessful in finding a host from which to suck blood, it returns to the roost and solicits food from a neighbour who regurgitates blood for it. When the altruist and recipient are related, this can be explained by kin selection. Reciprocal altruism can explain regurgitation between unrelated individuals. The bats are aware of which individuals they help and receive help from, and assistance is restricted to those who reciprocate. This would not be the case if the only force at work were kin selection.

For reciprocal altruism to evolve, the benefit from reciprocation must outweigh the cost of donation, that is, the altruist must end up better off in the long run (after the good turn has been repaid). For vampire bats, a small amount of blood given by a well-fed individual represents a very small cost, but is of significant benefit to a starving roost mate. The altruist's donated meal may enable the recipient to survive, enabling it to forage again the next night (and possibly return the favour). The necessity for reciprocity is clear: an individual that failed to reciprocate would not be helped again. *Cheating* would only be an effective strategy in a population of altruists with poor memories. So, reciprocal altruism will only be maintained if the majority of individuals reciprocate.

Box 37.8 The prisoner's dilemma: a model for reciprocal altruism

The prisoner's dilemma is a game which allows us to model the behaviour of two individuals who could *co-operate* or *defect* (Axelrod & Hamilton, 1981). The pay-off from each strategy, co-operation or defection, depends on the strategy employed by the opponent, as illustrated below from the point of view of player X.

		Player Y	
		Co-operate	Defect
Player X	Co-operate	Mutual co-operation (investment pays off)	Sucker (exploited)
	Defect	Cheat (best net result)	Mutual defection (no pains, no gains)

Because the biggest pay-off results from defection when the opponent co-operates, *cheating* can pay. Always defecting avoids being exploited, and might lead to a big net gain, but if both players defect they profit less than if they had both co-operated. Encountering cheats is costly, so individuals should operate strategies which avoid exploitation and maximise mutual co-operation.

Axelrod (1984) investigated many different strategies, of varying complexity, pitting them against one another in computerised games. The winning strategy was the simplest one, '*tit for tat*', which co-operated on the first move and from then on copied the opponent's previous move. By using the strategy of retaliation in response to defection, the opponent is discouraged from cheating. By forgiving as soon as co-operation is resumed, mutual co-operation is encouraged, and this is the most rewarding option for both players.

SOCIOBIOLOGY

Sociobiology can be defined as the systematic study of the biological basis of all social behaviour, including altruism, aggression and sexual behaviour (Hamilton, 1964; Wilson, 1975). Sociobiology differs from classical studies of animal behaviour (known as *ethology*) in that it generally considers the *set of genes*, rather than the individual, as the basic unit of evolution. In other words, it is not as important for individuals to survive as it is for their genes to do so. Sociobiologists have suggested that this may explain the existence of altruism (Dawkins, 1989). What appears as an altruistic act is actually selfish at the gene level (see pages 404–406). This approach has been called the *selfish gene theory*. It proposes that any behaviour of an organism is specifically 'designed' to maximise the survival of its genes. From the 'gene's point of view', a body is a sort of survival machine created to enhance the gene's chances of continued replication.

Sociobiology has been criticised for oversimplifying explanations of behaviour, and overemphasising the role of genetic factors. It has also been suggested that the extension from animal to human behaviour is doubtful, because genetic evolution has been overtaken by *cultural evolution*. Sociobiology is now considered to be outdated. *Behavioural ecology* is the preferred perspective, as it takes into account environmental influences and individual differences, and does not suggest that behaviour is a predetermined inevitability of species and sex.

EVOLUTIONARILY STABLE STRATEGIES (ESSs)

An *evolutionarily stable strategy* (ESS) is a behaviour pattern (or set of behaviour patterns) which, if most of the population adopt it, cannot be bettered by any other strategy and will, therefore, tend to become established by natural selection. Individuals must weigh up the fitness costs and benefits of a particular behaviour, and identify the optimal strategy to enhance their own fitness at that point in time. An ESS is, therefore, an optimum strategy dependent on the circumstances in which it is used. This means that an individual cannot successfully behave differently from the others in a population, even if it appears that there would be a short-term gain by doing so.

Box 37.9 An evolutionarily stable strategy (ESS)

Consider a species in which *both* parents are required to raise the young. If a male of this species had a mutant gene which made it take no part in parenting, it would be able to mate with a great number of females. The short-term gain, in evolutionary terms, is that this male would produce many offspring and, therefore, many copies of his own genes. However, the success of his strategy depends on the behaviour of the female. In this case, she is incapable of raising the young alone and so none of them would survive. The male would not benefit from breaking away from the ESS, and his mutant gene would not survive to change the behaviour of later generations. Although this is an oversimplified example, it serves to illustrate the idea that the evolutionary success of one behaviour pattern depends on the behaviour of others

It should be noted that this ESS is also dependent on *environmental* conditions. If conditions improve, either sex can change its previous stable strategy to further increase its fitness. For example, the male dunnock (a small sparrow-like bird) will desert his mate and their fledglings if he estimates that this particular season provides an abundance of food. In this case, his mate should be able successfully to complete the task of raising their joint offspring on her own. The male is then free to mate with another female, raise another brood and thus increase his fitness. Similarly, female dunnocks are known to mate with more than one male during the breeding season, and to indulge in covert behaviour to accomplish extra-pair matings. In reality, the fledglings in the nest are often *not* the joint offspring of one male and one female.

Cultural evolution

Cultural evolution may be seen as analogous to genetic evolution. *Cultural behaviour* is that which is passed on from one generation to the next, leading to a process of evolutionary change. Those behaviours which are successful or adaptive will be imitated (*selected*), and passed on to future generations (*inherited*). Cultural transmission is more powerful and flexible than its genetic equivalent, mainly because it is considerably faster (Brown, 1986).

Although examples of cultural evolution are most readily available for humans, examples of animal culture also occur. Kawamura (1952) undertook studies of Japanese macaques (*Macaca fuscata*). He left sweet potatoes on the beach for the monkeys, one of whom 'invented' the idea of washing the sand off the potatoes

Figure 37.5 *A blue tit opening milk bottle tops and drinking the milk. This behaviour appears to be influenced by both environmental and genetic factors, and represents an example of cultural evolution*

in the sea. Soon, other monkeys imitated her (Ridley, 1986: see Chapter 39, page 424). Another example of animal culture involves the removal of foil tops off milk bottles, and drinking of the milk, by blue tits (Sherry & Galef, 1984: see Chapter 39, pages 425–426).

Examples of cultural transmission have been observed in animals. However, it is still genetic factors which play by far the largest role in determining behaviour. In humans, however, much of behaviour is due to cultural rather than genetic determinants (see Chapters 43–45). It is for this reason that many psychologists are hesitant to apply the same insights to humans as to non-human animals.

Box 37.10 Some limitations of the evolutionary approach

The evolutionary approach to studying animal behaviour has a number of potential problems. These include:

- Behaviour is always an interaction between genes and the environment, never purely genetic. The further an animal is up the phylogenetic scale, the more its behaviour is determined by experience. Therefore, evolution can only provide a limited understanding of behaviour.

- Behaviour is also culturally transmitted, even in non-human animals.

- Sociobiology has been accused of being extremely selective in the examples of behaviour which it considers, ignoring numerous examples of both non-human and human behaviour which do not fit the theory (Hayes, 1994).

- There is currently little scientific evidence to support the theoretical arguments. However, this assumes a simple relationship between genes and behaviour, which is probably not the case. Furthermore, a lack of scientific evidence in favour of an approach is *not* the same as evidence against this approach.

CONCLUSIONS

In general, comparative psychologists use an evolutionary approach to explain animal behaviour. They ask questions about how particular behaviour patterns contribute to an animal's chances of survival and its reproductive success. The appeal of the evolutionary approach is that it is based on a logical concept (Darwinian natural selection) and produces plausible hypotheses, many of which can be tested. There is a wide range of evidence for the evolution of behaviour, based on both comparative and experimental studies. However, there are also limitations to the evolutionary approach and alternative ways of explaining animal behaviour may be required.

Summary

- **Comparative psychology** may be defined as the study of the behaviour of animals, with a view to drawing comparisons between them. It also involves studying animal behaviour in order to gain a better understanding of human behaviour. The basis of comparative psychology is the evolutionary relationship between all living organisms.

- **Evolution** is the process by which new species arise as the result of gradual changes to existing species over long periods of time. Evolution results from **superior genetic variants** having an advantage in the struggle for existence. These individuals are more likely to **survive** and **reproduce**, resulting in a change in a population's **gene frequency**. This process may gradually lead to the considerable differences now observed between living organisms.

- There is considerable debate as to how much of the variability within a species is due to genetic factors (**nature**), and how much depends on the influence of the environment (**nurture**). However, all behaviour has both an element of inheritance and learning about it, the interaction of which is known as **penetrance**.

- Darwin's theory of evolution by natural selection is supported by evidence from **palaeontology**, **comparative anatomy**, **geographical distribution** and **artificial selection**. It is also possible to observe evolution in action over relatively short time periods. An example of this is the evolution of **industrial melanism** in the peppered moth.

- **Fitness** is a measure of the ability of an individual to leave behind offspring. This term has been replaced by **inclusive fitness**, which refers to the total number of an animal's genes present in subsequent generations. These genes will be present in direct offspring and in the offspring of close relatives. The concept of inclusive fitness may solve one of the problems of Darwin's theory, namely the existence of **altruistic behaviour** in certain species.

- It appears that nearly all animal behaviour is influenced by genetic factors to some degree, and that behaviour makes important contributions to an animal's survival and reproductive success. Behaviour must, therefore, be subject to the forces of evolution in the same way as anatomy and physiology.

- Behaviour may be divided into **instinctive** (predominantly genetic) and **learned** (predominantly environmental). Few behaviours are entirely dominated by either inheritance or learning, and an **interaction** between them is the norm.

- Research suggests that animals are **biologically prepared** to learn some things more readily than others. These associations may have survival value, and are therefore learned more quickly and are more resistant to extinction.

- The best evidence for the evolution of animal behaviour comes from **interspecies comparisons**. **Phylogenetic trees** based on behavioural similarities are generally similar to those based on anatomical and physiological evidence. Also, several experimental studies have shown that differences in behaviour can result from differences in genes.

■ **Altruism** is behaviour performed by an individual at **cost** to itself that **benefits** another individual. For example, the alarm calls of birds are apparently altruistic.

■ It is difficult to explain how truly altruistic behaviours could evolve, since they would disadvantage their performers. Since altruism is preserved in populations, there must be a hidden advantage to the performer.

■ **Kin selection theory** proposes that altruists perform helpful behaviours for **close relatives** in order to reap benefits from the additional shared genes, which are consequently passed into the next generation. This increases the **inclusive fitness** of the altruist. Altruism would be expected between close relatives when the costs were low and the gains high.

■ The vicarious genetic success explained by kin selection only accounts for altruism between **kin** (relatives), not between unrelated individuals. Kin selection cannot explain why, for example, lionesses (which are not closely related to all the cubs in a pride) let cubs suckle communally.

■ Helping behaviours between **non-related individuals** can be explained by **reciprocal altruism**, as seen in vampire bats. Reciprocal altruism relies on animals being able to **recognise** and **remember** one another. They are then able to selectively assist those individuals that have been helpful in the past.

■ **Sociobiology** is the systematic study of the biological basis of all social behaviour. It differs from classical **ethology** in that it considers the **set of genes**, rather than the individual, as the basic unit of evolution. Sociobiology has been criticised for oversimplifying explanations of behaviour and overemphasising the role of genetic factors.

■ **Cultural evolution** may be seen as analogous to genetic evolution. Although examples of cultural transmission have been observed in animals, it is still genetic factors which play by far the largest role in determining their behaviour.

■ In humans, however, much of behaviour is due to cultural rather than genetic determinants. It is for this reason that many psychologists are hesitant to apply the same insights to humans as to animals.

■ The evolutionary approach to studying animal behaviour has a number of potential problems. These include the influence of the environment and cultural transmission upon behaviour, the apparent existence of behaviours which cannot be explained by sociobiology, and the lack of empirical evidence supporting the theoretical arguments.

Essay Questions

1 Critically consider evolutionary explanations of the behaviour of non-human animals. (*24 marks*)

2 Describe and evaluate biological explanations of apparent altruism. (*24 marks*)

WEB ADDRESSES

http://mendel.mbb.sfu.ca
http://www.coedu.usf.edu/behavior/behavior.html
http://www.hbes.com
http://www.world-of-dawkins.com

38 Classical and Operant Conditioning

INTRODUCTION AND OVERVIEW

The *behaviourist* approach has been a major influence in psychology (see Gross *et al.*, 2000). In view of its emphasis on learning, it is not surprising that learning should itself be one of psychology's most researched and discussed topics. There are several different theories of what learning involves. Watson (1913) based his explanation of human learning on *classical conditioning*. Another theory was proposed by Thorndike, and extended by Skinner, for whom *operant conditioning* is the crucial form of all human and non-human learning.

This chapter considers some of the important similarities and differences between these two forms of conditioning, together with their limitations as explanations of *non-human animal learning*. It also considers how conditioning has been interpreted in *cognitive* terms, in particular Tolman's *cognitive behaviourism*.

HOW DO PSYCHOLOGISTS DEFINE LEARNING?

Learning is a *hypothetical construct* (it cannot be directly observed but only *inferred* from observable behaviour), and it normally implies a fairly *permanent* change in a person's behavioural performance. Because temporary fluctuations in behaviour can occur as a result of fatigue, drugs, temperature changes, and so on, this is another reason for taking *permanence* as a minimum requirement for saying that learning has occurred. However, permanent behaviour changes can also result from things that have nothing to do with learning, as when brain damage and changes associated with puberty and other maturational processes alter behaviour. So, if behaviour change is to be counted as learning, the change must be linked to some kind of *past experience*. A fairly representative definition of learning is:

'... the process by which relatively permanent changes occur in behavioural potential as a result of experience' (Anderson, 1995b).

This definition implies a fundamental distinction between *learning* (behavioural potential) and *performance* (actual behaviour) (see Box 38.10, pages 419–420).

Box 38.1 Learning and other abilities

According to Howe (1980), learning is:

'... a biological device that functions to protect the human individual and to extend his capacities'.

In this context, learning is neither independent of, nor entirely separate from, several other abilities, including memory and perception. Indeed, learning and memory may be regarded as two sides of the same coin (see Gross *et al.*, 2000).

Also, most instances of learning take the form of adaptive changes whereby we increase our effectiveness in dealing with the environment, which has undoubted survival value (Howe, 1980). Similarly, Anderson (1995b) describes learning as:

'... the mechanism by which organisms can adapt to a changing and nonpredictable environment'.

Some basic questions about learning

Whilst psychologists generally agree that learning is relatively permanent and due to past experience, there is much less agreement about exactly *what* changes when learning occurs, and what *kinds* of past experience are involved. Psychologists differ as to how much they focus on the *overt, behavioural changes* as opposed to the *covert, cognitive changes*. Whilst Watson and Skinner emphasise the former to the exclusion of the latter, cognitive psychologists are more interested in the latter as they are reflected in the former.

BEHAVIOURIST APPROACHES: LEARNING THEORY (CLASSICAL AND OPERANT CONDITIONING)

The major figures in the behaviourist (learning theory) tradition are shown in Figure 38.1. Skinner appears at the top because of his distinction between *respondents* (or respondent behaviour), which are triggered automatically by particular environmental stimuli, and *operants* (or operant behaviour), which are essentially voluntary.

Related to Skinner's distinction is that between *classical* (Pavlovian) *conditioning* and *operant* (instrumental or Skinnerian) *conditioning*. Although both represent the behaviourist approach to learning, there are important differences between them, hence Skinner's distinction (see Box 38.6, pages 417–418). Neither Hull nor Tolman fits easily into either type of conditioning, which is why they are placed between the others (Hull's drive reduction theory was discussed in Chapter 17).

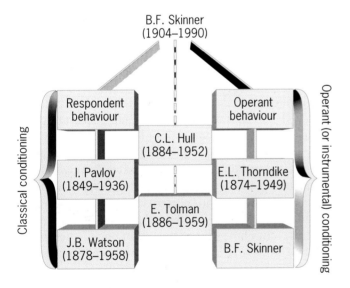

Figure 38.1 *Major figures in the behaviourist (learning theory) tradition*

Classical conditioning

Pavlov was a physiologist interested in the process of digestion in dogs. He developed a surgical technique for collecting a dog's salivary secretions, which incorporated a tube attached to the outside of its cheek so the drops of saliva could be easily measured.

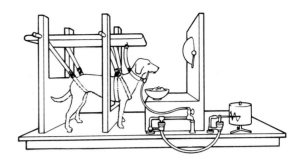

Figure 38.2 *The apparatus used by Pavlov in his experiments on conditioned reflexes*

Pavlov (1927) noticed that the dogs would often start salivating *before* any food was given to them, such as when they looked at the food, saw the feeding bucket or even heard the footsteps of the laboratory assistant about to feed them. These observations led to the study of what is now called *classical* (or Pavlovian) *conditioning*, whereby a stimulus (such as a bell) which would not normally produce a particular response (such as salivation) will eventually do so by being paired repeatedly with another stimulus (such as food) which *does* normally produce the response.

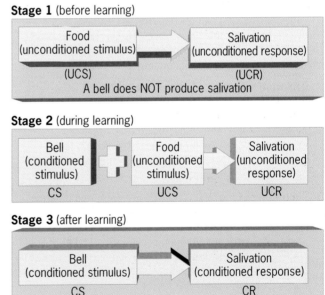

Figure 38.3 *The basic procedure involved in classical conditioning*

Before conditioning, the taste of food will naturally, and automatically, make the dog salivate, but the sound of a bell will not. The food is an *unconditioned stimulus* (UCS) and salivation an *unconditioned response* (UCR), which is automatic, reflexive and biologically built-in. During conditioning, the bell is paired with the food. Because the bell does not naturally produce salivation it is called a *conditioned stimulus* (CS), because its production of salivation is *conditional* upon it being paired with the UCS. The terms used by Pavlov were, in fact, 'conditional' and 'unconditional' but these were mistranslated from the Russian as 'conditioned'/'unconditioned' and have 'stuck'. The CS is also *neutral* with regard to salivation prior to conditioning.

If the bell and food are paired a sufficient number of times, salivation will occur whenever the dog hears the bell and before the food is presented. When this occurs, conditioning has taken place and the salivation is now a *conditioned response* (CR) because it is produced by a conditioned stimulus (CS) – the bell.

This basic procedure can be used with a variety of conditioned stimuli, such as buzzers, metronomes, lights, geometric figures and so on. The exact relationship between the CS and the UCS can also be varied to give different kinds of conditioning.

Table 38.1 *Four types of classical conditioning based on different CS–UCS relationships*

1	Delayed or forward	The CS is presented before the UCS, and remains 'on' whilst the UCS is presented and until the UCR appears. Conditioning has occurred when the CR appears before the UCS is presented. A half-second interval produces the strongest learning. As the interval increases, learning becomes poorer. This type of conditioning is typically used in the laboratory, especially with non-humans.
2	Backward	The CS is presented after the UCS. Generally this produces very little, if any, learning in laboratory animals. However, much advertising uses backward conditioning (e.g. the idyllic tropical scene is set and then the coconut bar is introduced).
3	Simultaneous	The CS and UCS are presented together. Conditioning has occurred when the CS on its own produces the CR. This type of conditioning occurs often in real-life situations (e.g. the sound of the dentist's drill accompanies the contact of the drill with your tooth).
4	Trace	The CS is presented and removed before the UCS is presented, so that only a 'memory trace' of the CS remains to be conditioned. The CR is usually weaker than in delayed or simultaneous conditioning.

Generalisation and discrimination

In *generalisation*, the CR transfers spontaneously to stimuli similar to, but different from, the original CS. For example, if a dog is conditioned using a bell of a particular pitch, and is then presented with a bell a little higher or lower in pitch, it will still salivate. However, if the dog is presented with bells that are increasingly different from the original, the CR will gradually weaken and eventually stop altogether – the dog is showing *discrimination*.

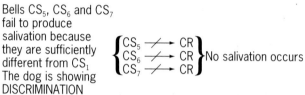

Figure 38.4 *An example of discrimination occurring spontaneously as a result of generalisation stopping*

Key **STUDY**

Box 38.2 Discrimination training and experimental neurosis

Pavlov (1927) *trained* dogs to discriminate in the original conditioning procedure. For example, if a high-pitched bell is paired with food but a low-pitched bell is not, the dog will start salivating in response to the former but not to the latter (*discrimination training*).

Related to discrimination is what Pavlov called *experimental neurosis*. He trained dogs to salivate to a circle but not to an ellipse, and then gradually changed the shape of the ellipse until it became almost circular. When this happened, the dogs started behaving in 'neurotic' ways, whining, trembling, urinating and defecating, refusing to eat and so on. It was as if they did not know how to respond: was the stimulus a circle (in which case, through generalisation, they 'should' salivate) or was it an ellipse (in which case, through discrimination, they 'should' not salivate)?

Extinction and spontaneous recovery

If dogs have been conditioned to salivate to a bell, and the bell is then repeatedly presented *without* food, the CR of salivation gradually becomes weaker and eventually stops altogether (*extinction*). However, if a dog that has undergone extinction is removed from the experimental situation, and then put back a couple of hours or so later, and the bell re-presented, it will start salivating again. Although no further pairing of the bell and food has occurred, the CR of salivation reappears in response to the bell (*spontaneous recovery*). This shows that extinction does not involve an 'erasing' of the original learning, but rather a learning to *inhibit* or *suppress* the CR when the CS is continually presented without a UCS.

Classical conditioning and human behaviour

There have been many laboratory demonstrations of classical conditioning in humans, and the basic procedure is a useful way of thinking about how certain fairly automatic responses may be acquired in real life. The impact of conditioning principles (both classical and operant) within *clinical psychology* has been considerable (see Chapter 53).

Box 38.3 Some general issues relating to conditioning and human behaviour

It is relatively easy to classically condition and extinguish CRs, such as the eye-blink and galvanic skin response (GSR). But what relevance does this have for understanding human learning and memory, let alone thinking, reasoning or problem-solving? In normal adults, the conditioning process can apparently be over-ridden by instructions: simply *telling* participants that the UCS will not occur again causes instant loss of a CR which would otherwise extinguish only slowly (Davey, 1983). Most participants in a conditioning experiment are aware of the experimenter's contingencies (the relationship between stimuli and responses), and in the absence of such awareness often fail to show evidence of conditioning (Brewer, 1974).

There are also important differences between very young children or those with severe learning difficulties, and older children and adults, regarding their behaviour in a variety of *operant* conditioning and discrimination learning experiments. These seem largely attributable to language development (Dugdale & Lowe, 1990).

All this suggests that people have rather more efficient, language- (or rule-) based forms of learning at their disposal than the laborious formation of associations between a CS and UCS. Even behaviour therapy, one of the apparently more successful applications of conditioning principles to human behaviour (see Chapter 53) has given way to *cognitive-behaviour therapies* (see Chapter 54).

(Based on Mackintosh, 1995)

Operant conditioning

Whilst not rejecting Pavlov's and Watson's discoveries, Skinner (1938) argued that most behaviour (human and non-human) is not elicited by specific stimuli. He saw learning as a much more *active* process, in which animals *operate* on their environment. This is *instrumental* in bringing about certain *consequences*, which then determine the probability of that behaviour being repeated.

Thorndike's law of effect

Skinner's study of operant conditioning derived from Thorndike's (1898) *law of effect*. Thorndike built puzzle-boxes, in which cats had to learn to operate a latch that automatically caused the door to spring open. When they managed to escape, they were rewarded with a piece of fish visible from inside the puzzle-box. The cats were deprived of food for a considerable time before the experiments began, and so were highly motivated. Each time, after eating the fish, they were put straight back in and the whole procedure repeated.

At first the cats behaved in a purely random fashion, and it was only by chance that they escaped. However, each time they were returned to the puzzle-box, it took them *less* time to escape. For example, with one of the boxes, the average time for the first escape was five minutes, but after 10–20 trials it was about five seconds.

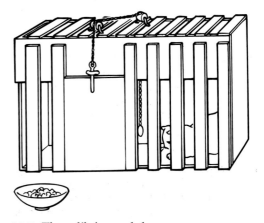

Figure 38.5 *Thorndike's puzzle box*

Thorndike explained this by claiming that the learning was essentially random or *trial-and-error*. There was no sudden flash of insight into how the releasing mechanism worked, but rather a gradual reduction in the number of errors made and hence escape time (see Chapter 27). What was being learned was a connection between the stimulus (the manipulative components of the box) and the response (the behaviour which allowed the cat to escape). Further, the stimulus–response connection is 'stamped in when pleasure results from the act, and stamped out when it doesn't' (the *law of effect*).

Skinner's 'analysis of behaviour'

Skinner used a form of puzzle-box known as a *Skinner box*, intended to automate Thorndike's research and designed for a rat or pigeon to do things in rather than escape from. The box has a lever (in the case of rats) or illuminated discs (in the case of pigeons), under which is a food tray. The experimenter decides exactly what the relationship will be between pressing the lever/pecking the disc and the delivery of a food pellet, giving total *control* of the animal's environment.

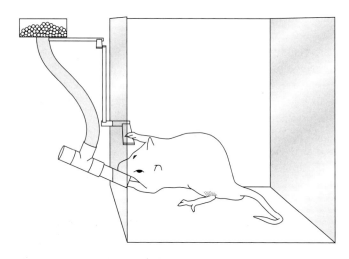

Figure 38.6 *A rat in a Skinner box*

Skinner used the term *strengthen* in place of Thorndike's 'stamping in', and *weaken* in place of 'stamping out', because he regarded Thorndike's terms as too mentalistic and his own as more objective and descriptive.

Box 38.4 Skinner's analysis of behaviour (or the ABC of operant conditioning)

The *analysis of behaviour* requires an accurate but neutral representation of the relationship (or *contingencies*) between:

- *Antecedents* (the stimulus conditions, such as the lever, the click of the food dispenser, a light that may go on when the lever is pressed);

- *Behaviours* (or *operants*, such as pressing the lever);

- *Consequences* (what happens as a result of the operant behaviour, that is, reinforcement or punishment).

This is the ABC of operant conditioning.

According to Skinner's version of the law of effect, 'behaviour is shaped and maintained by its consequences'. The consequences of operants can be *positive reinforcement*, *negative reinforcement*, or *punishment*.

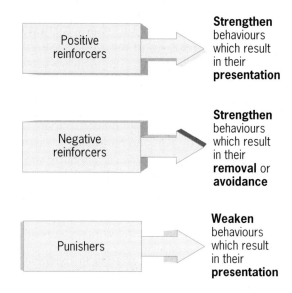

Figure 38.7 *The consequences of behaviour and their effects*

Whilst positive and negative reinforcement both *strengthen* behaviour (making it more probable), each works in a different way. *Positive reinforcement* involves presenting something pleasurable (such as food), whilst *negative reinforcement* involves the removal or avoidance of some 'aversive' (literally 'painful') state of affairs (such as electric shock). *Punishment* has the effect of *weakening* behaviour (making it less probable), through the presentation of an aversive stimulus).

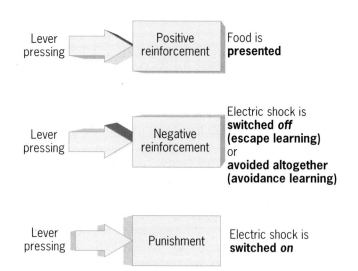

Figure 38.8 *Three possible consequences of lever pressing in a Skinner box*

Reinforcement and reinforcers

Whilst food itself is a *reinforcer*, the presentation of food as a result of lever-pressing is (positive) *reinforcement*. Similarly, an electric shock is a *punisher*, and the presentation of electric shock is called *punishment*.

According to Skinner, whether something is a reinforcer or punisher is decided *retrospectively*, that is, after food or shock has been made contingent on, say, lever-pressing on several occasions. So, if a behaviour is strengthened when followed by food, the food is a reinforcer. However, if shock weakens a behaviour, the shock is a punisher. Reinforcers and punishers cannot be defined independently of the effects they have on behaviour.

Skinner believes that this is a more scientific approach, since the intended and actual effect may not always coincide. For example, if children who feel deprived of their parents' attention find that their parents respond when they are naughty, they are more likely to continue being naughty, even if the parents' response is to shout or smack (at least they get some attention this way!). Similarly, a positive reinforcement can only loosely be called a reward, as 'reward' implies that the rewarder *expects* to strengthen behaviour, whereas 'positive reinforcement' refers to what has been *shown* to strengthen behaviour.

Primary and secondary reinforcers

Primary reinforcers such as food, water, and sex are natural reinforcers (reinforcing in themselves). *Secondary* (or *conditioned*) *reinforcers* acquire their reinforcing properties through association with primary reinforcers, that is, we have to *learn* (through classical conditioning) to find them reinforcing. Examples of human secondary reinforcers are money, cheques and tokens (see Chapter 53, pages 571–572). In a Skinner box, if a click accompanies the presentation of each food pellet, rats will eventually find the click reinforcing on its own, such that the click can be used as a reinforcer for getting rats to learn some new response. Secondary reinforcers often 'bridge the gap' between a response and a primary reinforcer which may not be immediately forthcoming.

Schedules of reinforcement

Another important aspect of Skinner's work is the effects on behaviour of how frequently and regularly (or predictably) reinforcements are presented. Ferster & Skinner (1957) identified five major schedules of reinforcement, each of which produces a characteristic pattern of responding.

Rats and pigeons (and probably most mammals and birds) typically 'work harder' (press the lever/peck the disc at a faster rate) for scant reward. When reinforcements are relatively infrequent and irregular or

unpredictable, they will go on working long after the reinforcement has actually been withdrawn. So, each schedule can be analysed in terms of *pattern and rate of response* and *resistance to extinction* (see Table 38.2, page 416).

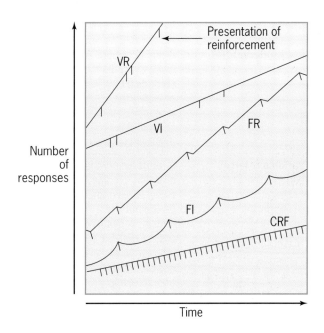

Figure 38.9 *Typical cumulative records for a response (such as lever pressing) reinforced using five schedules of reinforcement. VR = variable ratio; VI = variable interval; FR = fixed ratio; FI = fixed interval; CRF = continuous reinforcement*

A *continuous* schedule is usually used only when some new response is being learned. Once emitted regularly and reliably, it can be maintained by using one of the four *partial* or *intermittent* schedules. However, this change must be gradual. Skinner (1938) originally used an interval schedule because a reinforcer is guaranteed, sooner or later, so long as one response is made during the interval.

Shaping: the reinforcement of successive approximations

Reinforcement can be used to build up relatively complex behaviour (not part of an animal's natural repertoire) by reinforcing closer and closer approximations to the desired behaviour. First, the behaviour must be broken down into a number of small steps, each of which is reinforced in sequence, so that gradually what the learner can do is much more like what the experimenter is trying to teach it. This is the method used by animal trainers, and by Skinner to teach pigeons to play ping-pong. Most human skills are learned in this step-by-step manner.

Table 38.2 *Common reinforcement schedules and associated patterns of response and resistance to extinction*

Reinforcement schedule	Example	Pattern and rate of responding	Resistance to extinction	Example of human behaviour
1 Continuous reinforcement (CRF)	Every single response is reinforced	Response rate is low but steady	Very low – the quickest way to bring about extinction	1 Receiving a high grade for every assignment 2 Receiving a tip for every customer served
2 Fixed interval (FI)	A reinforcement is given every 30 seconds (FI 30), provided the response occurs at least once during that time	Response rate speeds up as the next reinforcement becomes available; a pause after each reinforcement. Overall response rate fairly low	Fairly low – extinction occurs quite quickly	1 Being paid regularly (every week or month) 2 Giving yourself a 15-minute break for every hour's studying done
3 Variable interval (VI)	A reinforcement is given on average every 30 seconds (VI 30), but the interval varies from trial to trial. So, the interval on any one occasion is unpredictable	Response rate is very stable over long periods of time. Still some tendency to increase response rate as time elapses since the last reinforcement	Very high – extinction occurs very slowly and gradually	Many self-employed people receive payment irregularly (depending on when the customer pays for the product or service)
4 Fixed ratio (FR)	A reinforcement is given for a fixed number of responses, however long this may take, e.g. one reinforcement every 10 responses (FR 10)	There is a pronounced pause after each reinforcement, and then a very high rate of responding leading up to the next reinforcement	As in FI	1 Piece work (the more work done, the more money earned) 2 Commission (extra money for so many goods made or sales completed)
5 Variable ratio (VR)	A reinforcement is given on average every 10 responses (VR 10), but the number varies from trial to trial. So, the number of responses required on any one occasion is unpredictable	Very high response rate – and very steady	Very high – the most resistant of all the schedules	Gambling

Figure 38.10 *Elephants behaving in a very un-elephant-like way. They must be* shaped *into displaying this 'unnatural behaviour'*

Shaping also provides an important foundation for *behaviour modification*, which is used to teach children and adults with learning difficulties to use the toilet, feed and dress themselves and other social skills. It has also been used to develop speech in autistic children and adult schizophrenics (see Chapter 53).

Negative reinforcement: escape and avoidance learning

Escape and avoidance learning are the two major ways in which negative reinforcement has been studied in the laboratory. *Escape learning* is relatively simple. For example, rats can learn to press a lever to turn off electric shock.

Avoidance learning is more complex and more relevant to certain aspects of human behaviour, especially the persistence of phobias (see Chapter 53).

Box 38.5 Avoidance learning through negative reinforcement

Most laboratory studies use a *shuttle box*, divided into two compartments, sometimes with a barrier or door between them. Electric shocks can be delivered through the floor of either compartment independently of the other. Only one side is electrified at a time, and the task is to find which is the safe side on any one occasion.

A *warning signal* is given whenever the electrified side is to be changed, so the animal can always avoid being shocked if it switches sides when it hears (or sees) the signal. According to the *two-factor theory* (Mowrer, 1960) or the *two-process theory* (Gray, 1975), the animal first learns to be afraid (the warning signal elicits an anticipatory emotional response of fear or anxiety through *classical conditioning*), and then learns a response to reduce the fear (jumping the barrier is *negatively reinforced* through avoiding the shock before it is switched on).

Punishment

Skinner maintained that with both non-humans and humans, positive (and, to a lesser extent, negative) reinforcement is a much more potent influence on behaviour than punishment, largely because punishment can only make certain responses less likely. Nothing *new* can be taught by punishment alone.

However, Campbell & Church (1969) argue that punishments are, if anything, a *stronger* influence on behaviour than the incentive effects of reinforcements (at least with laboratory animals). The problem, however, is the unpleasant side-effects of stress, anxiety, withdrawal, aggression and so on.

Estes (1970) concluded that punishment merely *suppressed* rats' lever pressing in the short term, but did not weaken it. Others have shown that the strength and duration of the suppression effect depend on the *intensity* of the punishment and the degree of deprivation. However, the response is still suppressed rather than unlearned.

When alternative ways of obtaining reinforcers are available, punishment has a more powerful suppressive effect on the punished behaviour (Howe, 1980). For example, Azrin & Holz (1966) combined punishment and reinforcement so that response A was punished whilst response B, incompatible with A, was positively reinforced. This is something that Skinner advocates with humans.

The antecedents of behaviour: stimulus control

In operant conditioning, the stimulus indicates the likely consequence of emitting a particular response: the operant behaviour is more likely to occur in the presence of some stimuli than others. If a rat has been reinforced for lever pressing, it is more likely to go on doing so as the lever becomes associated both with reinforcement and the action of pressing. Technically, lever pressing is now under the *stimulus control* of the lever, but there is still no inevitability about pressing it, only an *increased probability* (see Box 38.6).

Similarly, drivers' behaviour is brought under the stimulus control of traffic signals, road signs, other vehicles, pedestrians and so on. Much of our everyday behaviour can be seen in this way. Sitting on chairs, answering the telephone, turning on the television and so on, are all operants which are more likely to occur in the presence of those stimuli because of the past consequences of doing so.

A special case of stimulus control is a *discriminative stimulus*. If a rat in a Skinner box is reinforced for lever pressing *only* when a light is on, the light soon becomes a discriminative stimulus (the rat only presses the lever when the light is on).

Box 38.6 Major similarities and differences between classical and operant conditioning

- They are both types of *associative learning*.
- *Generalisation, discrimination, extinction* and *spontaneous recovery* occur in both.
- In classical conditioning, the UCR or CR is *elicited* (triggered automatically) by the UCS or CS (it is essentially a reflex, involuntary response). In operant conditioning, behaviour is *emitted* by the organism and is essentially voluntary.
- In classical conditioning, the stimulus is guaranteed to produce the response, whilst the likelihood of a particular operant response being emitted is a function of the past consequences of such behaviour (it is more or less *probable* but never certain).
- In classical conditioning, the UCS works in essentially the same way *regardless* of whether it is pleasurable (such as food) or aversive (such as electric shock). In operant conditioning, responses that result in pleasurable outcomes are likely to be repeated, whilst those that result in aversive outcomes are not.
- In classical conditioning, completely new stimulus–response connections are formed, whilst operant conditioning involves the strengthening

or weakening of response tendencies already present in the animal's behavioural repertoire.

- In classical conditioning, the reinforcer (the UCS) is presented *regardless* of what the animal does and is presented *before* the response. In operant conditioning, the reinforcer is only presented if the animal emits some specified, pre-selected behaviour, and is presented *after* the behaviour.

- In classical conditioning, the *strength* of conditioning is typically measured in terms of response magnitude (e.g. how many drops of saliva) and/or latency (how quickly a response is produced by a stimulus). In operant, conditioning strength is measured mainly as *response rate* (see Table 38.2, page 416).

Does conditioning work in the same way for all species?

The fact that many experiments involving a variety of species can all be described as classical conditioning, does *not* in itself mean that there is only one mechanism involved, or only one explanation which applies, equally, to all species and all cases (Walker, 1984). Although *conditionability* seems to be an almost universal property of nervous systems, many psychologists have argued that there can be no general laws of learning (Seligman, 1970).

If such laws do exist, one of them is likely to be the *law of contiguity*: events (or stimuli) which occur close together in time and space are likely to become associated with each other. Most of the examples of conditioning considered so far appear to 'obey' the law of contiguity.

Key **STUDY**

Box 38.7 Taste aversion studies

These represent an important exception to the 'law' of contiguity (e.g. Garcia & Koelling, 1966; Garcia *et al.*, 1966). In Garcia *et al.*'s study, rats were given a novel-tasting solution, such as saccharine-flavoured water (the CS), prior to a drug, *apomorphine* (the UCS), which has a *delayed* action, inducing severe intestinal illness (the UCR).

In two separate experiments, the precise time-lapse between tasting the solution and the onset of the drug-induced nausea was either (a) 5, 6, 7, 8, 9, 10, 11, 12, 15, 16, 17, 18, 19, 20, 21 and 22 minutes, or (b) 30, 45, 75, 120 and 180 minutes. In (a), the rats received just four treatments (one every third day),

and in (b) five were given (one every third day). In all cases, a conditioned aversive response to the solution was acquired, that is, intestinal illness became a CR (a response to the solution alone). In some replications, just a single treatment has been needed.

Whilst rats can also be conditioned to novel smells, auditory, visual and tactile stimuli are not so readily associated with internal illness. It is impossible to deter pigeons from water, and for other species taste aversions are very difficult to establish even if the animal is made very ill. Thus, there seem to be definite biological limitations on the likelihood of animals developing conditioned aversions.

Similarly, rats typically learn very quickly to avoid shock in a shuttlebox and to press a lever for food. However, they do not learn very readily to press a lever to avoid shock. Pigeons can be trained quickly to fly from one perch to another in order to avoid shock, but it is almost impossible to train them to peck a disc to avoid shock.

This has led Bolles (1980) and others to conclude that we cannot regard the basic principles of learning as applying equally to all species in all situations. We must take into account the evolutionary history of the species, as well as the individual organism's learning history.

Box 38.8 Seligman's concept of preparedness

According to Seligman (1970), animals are biologically prepared to learn actions that are closely related to the survival of their species (such as learned water or food aversions), and these *prepared* behaviours are learned with very little training. Equally, *contra-prepared* behaviours are contrary to an animal's natural tendencies and so are learned with great difficulty, if at all. Most of the behaviour studied in the laboratory falls somewhere in between these two extremes.

Oakley (1983) believes that *preparedness* in classical and operant conditioning is an inherited characteristic. If in a species' history, individuals have often been exposed to certain biologically significant kinds of association, then the ability to learn rapidly about such associations becomes genetically transmitted.

Much of the relevant human data relates to how easily certain conditioned fear responses can be induced in the laboratory, or how common certain phobias are compared with others (see Chapter 53, page 566). Most human phobias tend to be of non-humans or dangerous places. Most common of all are the fears of snakes, spiders, the dark, high and closed-in places, and often there is no previous evidence for the fear actually having been conditioned (Seligman, 1972).

The role of cognition

According to Mackintosh (1978, 1995), conditioning is *not* reducible to the strengthening of stimulus–response connections through an automatic process called reinforcement. It is more appropriate to think of it as involving the detection and learning of *relations between events* in the environment, whereby animals typically discover what signals food, water, danger or safety.

"Stimulus, response! Stimulus, response! Don't you
ever *think*?"

Figure 38.11 *Even conditioning involves more than just stimulus and response*

Instead of treating salivation or lever-pressing as what is learned, we could regard it simply as a convenient *index* of what has been learned, namely that certain relationships exist in the environment. Indeed, Pavlov himself described the CS as a 'signal' for the UCS, the relationship between CS and the UCS as one of '*stimulus substitution*', and the CR as an '*anticipatory*' response (or '*psychic secretions*'), suggesting that his dogs were *expecting* the food to follow the bell.

To support this interpretation, Rescorla (1968) presented two groups of rats with the same number of CS–UCS pairings, but the second group also received additional presentations of the UCS on its own without the CS. The first group showed much stronger conditioning than the second, indicating that the most important factor (in classical conditioning anyway) is how *predictably* the UCS follows the CS, *not* how often they are paired.

Pavlov's discovery of *higher-order conditioning* also suggests a more complex process than the basic procedure described earlier (see pages 411–413).

Box 38.9 Higher order conditioning

Pavlov (1927) demonstrated that a strong CS could be used in place of food to produce salivation in response to a new stimulus which had never been paired with food. For example, if the CS is a buzzer, it can be paired with, say, a black square in such a way that after ten pairings (using delayed conditioning), the dog will salivate a small but significant amount at the sight of the black square *before* the buzzer is sounded. It is as if the CS were functioning as a UCS.

The buzzer and food pairing is referred to as *first order conditioning*, and the black square and buzzer pairing as *second order conditioning*. Pavlov found that learning could not go beyond third or fourth order conditioning.

COGNITIVE APPROACHES

Cognitive alternatives to conditioning sometimes come in the form of *extensions* of conditioning theory, such as *social learning theory* (see Chapter 31), and sometimes in the form of accounts of learning stemming from a theoretical approach which is diametrically opposed to the S–R approach. A good example of the latter is *insight learning* (see Chapter 27) as proposed by the *Gestalt psychologists* (see Chapter 23).

Tolman's cognitive behaviourism: latent learning and cognitive maps

One of the earliest challenges to Skinner's view that learning cannot take place in the absence of reinforcement came from Tolman (1948). Although studying rats within the behaviourist tradition in the 1920s, 1930s and 1940s, Tolman would today be regarded as a cognitive psychologist, because he explained rats' learning in terms of inferred cognitive processes, in particular *cognitive or mental maps*.

Key STUDY

Box 38.10 Tolman & Honzik's (1930) demonstration of latent learning

Group 1 rats were reinforced every time they found their way through a maze to the food box. *Group 2* rats were never reinforced, and *Group 3* rats received no reinforcement for the first ten days of the experiment but did so from day 11.

Not surprisingly, Group 1 learned the maze quickly and made fewer and fewer mistakes, whilst Group 2 never reduced the time it took to find the food, and moved around aimlessly much of the time. Group 3, however, having apparently made no progress during the first ten days, showed a sudden decrease in the time it took to reach the goal-box on day 11, when they received their first reinforcement, and caught up almost immediately with Group 1.

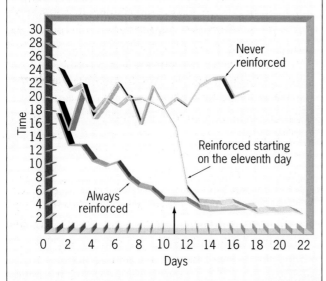

Figure 38.12 *The results of Tolman and Honzik's study of latent learning in rats*

Clearly, Group 3 rats had been learning their way through the maze during the first ten days but the learning was *latent* ('behaviourally silent'), that is, it did not show up in their actual behaviour (performance) until they received the incentive of the reinforcement on day 11.

Tolman and Honzik concluded that reinforcement may be important in relation to *performance* of learned behaviour, but it is not *necessary* for the learning itself.

Tolman's (1948) *place-learning* (or *sign-learning*) theory maintains that rats learn *expectations* as to which part of the maze will be followed by which other part. Tolman called these expectations *cognitive maps*, and they represent a primitive kind of perceptual map of the maze or understanding of its spatial relationships.

Although a cognitive map can only be *inferred* from behaviour, it is difficult to know how else to explain the finding that rats will take short-cuts to the food box if the old path is blocked, or how, if the maze were rotated, they can find the usual food location from several different starting points (Tolman *et al.*, 1946). Similarly, Restle (1957) flooded a maze immediately after a group of rats had learnt to run it, and they were able to swim to the goal-box with no more errors than when they had walked. This clearly supports Tolman's interpretation.

CONCLUSIONS

This chapter has considered some of the major similarities and differences between classical and operant conditioning. Whilst behaviourist psychologists have explained conditioning in stimulus–response terms, it can also be interpreted in terms of cognitive factors. Tolman's cognitive behaviourism is an important alternative to conditioning. Tolman saw cognitive factors as playing a crucial part in the learning process, and distinguished between learning and performance.

Summary

■ Learning is one of psychology's central areas of research, and has played a major part in its development as a scientific discipline.

■ **Theories of learning** differ regarding the nature of the processes involved, especially the role of cognitive factors. However, all agree that learning involves a relatively permanent behaviour change due to past experience. An important distinction is that between **learning** and **performance**, referring to **potential** and **actual** behaviour respectively. Also, learning is

adaptive and closely related to other abilities, particularly memory.

■ Skinner distinguished between **respondent** and **operant behaviours**, which correspond to **classical** (or Pavlovian) and **operant** (or instrumental) **conditioning** respectively.

■ In **classical** conditioning, the pairing of a conditioned (CS) and an unconditioned stimulus (UCS) results in the former eliciting a response that previously was only produced by the latter. **Delayed** (or **forward**), **backward**, **simultaneous**, and **trace** conditioning differ according to the relationship between the conditioned and unconditioned stimuli.

- **Generalisation**, **discrimination**, **extinction** and **spontaneous recovery** apply to both classical and operant conditioning. Spontaneous recovery demonstrates that extinction involves learning to inhibit or suppress the CR, not an erasing of it.

- Compared with classical conditioning, **operant** conditioning sees learning as much more **active**. Skinner was interested in how animals **operate** on their environment, and how their activity is **instrumental** in producing certain **consequences**.

- In classical conditioning, a response is **elicited** by a stimulus and is involuntary, whilst operant responses are **emitted** by the learner and are voluntary. Also, in classical conditioning, the reinforcer is presented regardless of what the learner does **before** the response, whilst in operant conditioning, the reinforcement is contingent upon a specified response being emitted and is presented **after** the response.

- Skinner's work was based on Thorndike's **law of effect**. Skinner designed a form of puzzle-box (a **Skinner box**) and called the consequences of behaviour **positive reinforcement**, **negative reinforcement** and **punishment**. Reinforcement (both positive and negative) **strengthens** behaviour, whilst punishment **weakens** it.

- **Primary reinforcers** are naturally reinforcing, whilst **secondary** (or conditioned) **reinforcers** come to be reinforcing through association with primary reinforcers. **Shaping** involves the reinforcement of **successive approximations** to the desired behaviour.

- Different **schedules of reinforcement** can be analysed in terms of **pattern/rate of response** and **resistance to extinction**. **Variable** schedules involve high, steady rates of response and high resistance to extinction compared with **fixed** and **continuous** schedules.

- **Escape** and **avoidance learning** have been explained by the **two-factor theory**, according to which both classical and operant conditioning are involved. The persistence of human phobias can be understood in terms of avoidance learning.

- **Punishment** seems to involve a **suppression** of behaviour, and is most effective when combined with the reinforcement of an incompatible response.

- In operant conditioning, the stimulus makes certain behaviour **more likely** to occur, but this is not inevitable as it is in classical conditioning. This is called **stimulus control**.

- **Taste aversion** experiments contribute to the view that the basic principles of conditioning do not apply equally to all species in all situations. **Preparedness** helps to explain experimental findings, showing that different species acquire certain conditioned responses more or less easily, and why certain human phobias are more common than others.

- Rather than a simple strengthening of stimulus–response associations, conditioning can be thought of as learning about **relations between events**.

- Tolman's theory of **latent learning** explains how learning can take place in the absence of reinforcement. Rats learn a **cognitive map** of the maze, not the individual movements of walking or running that take them to the food box.

Essay Questions

1 Describe and evaluate **either** classical **or** operant conditioning as an explanation of the behaviour of non-human animals. (*24 marks*)

2 **a** Outline the basic principles of operant conditioning. (*6 marks*)

   b Critically consider the role of operant conditioning in the behaviour of non-human animals.

   (*18 marks*)

WEB ADDRESSES

http://www.indiana.edu/~iuepsyc/Ch_8/C8E1.html
http://www.coedu.usf.edu/behavior/behavior.html
http://spsp.clarion.edu/topps/tptn5031.htm
http://www.coedu.usf.edu/behavior/listserv.html

39 *Social Learning in Non-human Animals*

INTRODUCTION AND OVERVIEW

This chapter examines research into *social learning in non-human animals*. The first part describes how social learning can occur in non-humans through *imitation* and *tutoring*. It considers the factors affecting imitation, including stimulus enhancement and the qualities of a model, and discusses the role of imitation in the acquisition of *antipredator* and *foraging* behaviours.

The second part of the chapter considers evidence for *intelligence* in non-human animals. Included here are *insightfulness* and *mathematical ability*, forms of reasoning not generally associated with non-human animals. Another characteristic which humans might share with non-humans is the ability to identify oneself as an individual and make judgements about others. Research in this area is considered, as is research into *self-recognition* and *awareness of the mental states of others*.

SOCIAL LEARNING IN NON-HUMAN ANIMALS

Several kinds of learning might be classed as 'social', because they occur in the presence of others. However, the surrounding individuals should in some way be *responsible* for that learning, and so improvements in performance that are caused by the presence of an audience or competitors would not satisfy this criterion. Thus, a single barking dog setting off the entire neighbourhood is an example of *contagion*. One animal simply triggers the same, pre-existing response in another, and no learning has occurred. Contagion is also demonstrated by human yawning. To be defined as *social learning*, the acquisition of some new skill must result from the direct effect of other individuals. This can occur in two ways, namely *imitation* and *tutoring*.

To allow social learning to occur, animals must be capable of memorising complex behaviours. They may not necessarily rehearse their new skills immediately, so their memories must be stable over time. In order that opportunities to learn socially can exist, *conspecifics* (members of the same species) must be available for observation. Hence, we would expect to find social learning in gregarious species with good memories.

Imitation and tutoring

In *imitation*, the 'learner' observes a '*model*' that demonstrates a behaviour, which the recipient may or may not imitate. This is a *passive* process, and is interesting as the learning may take place in the absence of immediate reinforcers. Furthermore, there may be a delay in the production of the behaviour by the recipient following the original observation.

Herbert & Harsh (1944) found that cats escaped faster from a puzzle-box if they had previously watched another cat escaping, particularly when they saw the trial-and-error process leading up to the escape of the demonstrator, rather than simply observing a skilled individual. The naïve cats seemed to gain from the experience of watching, but another factor (such as reduced fear or curiosity) must also have been at work to explain why the skilled demonstrator was less effective.

An alternative to imitation is *tutoring*, which involves direct instruction. Here, one animal takes the 'tutor' role and the other the 'learner' role. This is an *active* process, in which the tutor encounters some costs in order to provide an improved learning experience for the recipient. Boesch (1991) describes how chimpanzee mothers influence their infants' ability to crack nuts using tools (see Box 39.1, page 423). Apart from food sharing, the mothers may stimulate interest, facilitate nut-cracking or directly tutor the infant. Some carnivores, such as domestic cats, cheetahs, tigers and meerkats may learn predatory strategies through tutoring by adults (Russell, 1990). The adults capture and maim or restrain prey, so that the juveniles can gain first-hand experience of tackling prey as well as observing hunting behaviour.

Box 39.1 Tutoring in chimpanzees (Boesch, 1991)

Chimpanzees (*Pan trogolodytes*) in the Tai National Park, Ivory Coast, use a hard rock as an anvil upon which to open nuts with a small stone used as a hammer. Mother chimpanzees can improve the way their infants employ these tools by stimulating their interest, facilitating nut-cracking, or directly tutoring them.

Adult chimpanzees usually carry their hammers as they forage. Mothers, however, may leave the stone they are using as a hammer on top of the anvil to attract their young. Whilst the infants show an interest in these tools, so do other potentially thieving chimpanzees. To facilitate infants' attempts to crack nuts open, the mothers may position unopened nuts on the anvil, and place a hammer alongside it before departing.

Adults are better than infants at finding and selecting good tools, and so can facilitate learning by providing effective hammers. One mother produced four good tools for her son (each of which he eventually lost). These were used to open 36 nuts in 40 minutes. The mother, however, spent much of her time searching for new tools, and consumed only eight nuts in the same period. Clearly, such facilitation carries costs for the mother.

Finally, mothers may observe their infants' performance and demonstrate how to overcome difficulties, such as those experienced with panda nuts. These nuts are particularly hard, and have three separate kernels making them difficult to open. One mother, observing her son about to attempt to open the second kernel of a nut with it incorrectly positioned on the anvil, stopped him, cleared the anvil, repositioned the nut and allowed him to continue.

Another mother, observing her daughter unsuccessfully using an irregularly shaped hammer, was given the tool as she approached. The mother took the tool, and very slowly rotated in her hand, taking a full minute to complete this single movement. She then cracked open ten nuts with the hammer in this position, of which her daughter ate more than six. When the infant resumed, she quickly opened four nuts. Previously, she had been varying all aspects of her behaviour and, although she continued to change her posture, she maintained an identical hammer grip to that demonstrated by her mother.

Such instances of social learning carry considerable benefits for the recipients in terms of the speed with which they can acquire new, complex behaviours, and the consequent reduction in risk associated with making fewer errors. Advantages might include avoiding poisonous foods, and gaining access to otherwise inaccessible resources by using new techniques and copying the responses of others to predators. The learner thus profits from the experiences of others. For the tutors, however, there are obvious costs. They relinquish food and other resources (such as tools), thereby increasing their own time and energy expenditure.

Imitation and mimicry

Mimicry can be considered a special case of *imitation*, in which there is no obvious reward. True imitation, by contrast, leads to a reward although it may be indirect or delayed. Pearce (1997) suggests that copying of human behaviours by captive primates such as orang-utans (*Pongo pygmaeus*) provides examples of mimicry. He cites behaviours such as pouring drinks, touching glasses and using a paint brush.

Whilst there may be no tangible rewards, the orang-utans may be reinforced by the human attention such behaviours attract, perhaps in the same way as a naughty child persists even in the face of adult anger. However, Moore (1992) reports an experimental procedure with an African grey parrot (*Psittacus erithacus*), in which no audience was present when the mimicry occurred (the parrot's performance was recorded on video tape following the demonstration by the experimenter).

Compared with operant conditioning (see Chapter 38), imitation is an efficient way to acquire a new behaviour because it removes the need for a lengthy period of trial-and-error. Whilst learners may not imitate perfectly on the first occasion, their initial attempts will more closely resemble the appropriate behaviour than would be the case without a model to guide them. This also reduces risk to the animal. By making fewer errors, it is exposed to less danger from predators, the environment, competitors or poisonous food items. Imitation is therefore a highly effective way to learn complex behaviours like foraging and predator avoidance.

Stimulus enhancement

For an animal learning about the real world, what behaviours are deemed to be sufficiently important to be worth watching and copying? McQuoid & Galef (1992) showed that jungle fowl (*Gallus gallus*) would imitate the food bowl choice of a conspecific. Rather than copying their behaviour, the birds merely seemed to be *attracted* to a particular food bowl as a consequence of seeing the demonstrator feeding from it, and their exploratory responses fortuitously led them to food. The increased attractiveness of an object which is the subject of another individual's attention is called *stimulus enhancement*. The attention of the birds was drawn towards the bowls from which the demonstrators were feeding. They were not imitating actions, but responding to a raised interest in one aspect of their environment. Stimulus enhancement might explain why children only want to have the toy their sibling is playing with!

Unlike McQuoid and Galef, Burt & Guilford (1999) found that pigeons (*Columbia livia*) did *not* show social learning of food location. In their experiment, demonstrator pigeons were trained to find covered boxes of food in a grid on the floor. Experimental birds then watched a demonstrator locating food successfully, whilst other (control) birds were exposed to the grid alone. Burt and Guilford's results showed that those birds which tackled the food-finding task alone were *more* successful at finding the food. A knowledgeable individual did not seem to act as an effective model.

Mammals, by contrast, may be able to learn from conspecifics, at least about what *not* to eat. Galef (1988) allowed a rat to eat food with a distinctive flavour (cinnamon or cocoa). Rats without experience of either flavour were more likely to taste tainted food if they had smelled the flavour on another individual, providing that the smell emanated from the *front*, rather than the *back*, of the animal. The rats were also less likely to taste the food if it was only familiar because they had smelled it soaked onto a wad of cotton wool. The experience of another healthy animal, therefore, seems to be crucial. Through social learning, a rat knows which foods conspecifics have successfully encountered.

What makes a good demonstrator?

Chapter 31 discussed the importance of status or familiarity on the effectiveness of a model for children. What factors affect the probability that a non-human model will be imitated? Nicol & Pope (1999) used chickens (*Gallus gallus domesticus*) to investigate the effect of demonstrator status on the performance of an observer.

Key STUDY

Box 39.2 The effect of demonstrator status

Nicol & Pope's (1999) demonstrator animals were operantly conditioned to find food in a chamber. An observer was then allowed to watch a demonstrator perform the task for five minutes on each of four consecutive days. On the fifth day, the observers were placed in the chamber. Their responses were more likely to be appropriately directed if they had observed a dominant hen than a submissive one or a cockerel.

This suggests that status may affect salience as a demonstrator, perhaps because dominant hens have, in general, a superior foraging ability and so are preferable models. However, in another part of the experiment, Nicol and Pope tested the effect of foraging success on the likelihood of being imitated, and found *no* significant effect. The actual success of the model does not appear to affect its perceived value as a demonstrator.

Foraging

One of the most frequently cited examples of social learning is the acquisition of sweet potato washing by a troop of Japanese macaque monkeys (*Macaca fuscata*) described by Kawai (1965: see also Chapter 37, page 407). In 1953, a single 18-month-old female, Imo, was observed to take sand-covered pieces of sweet potato to the sea and wash the sand off before eating them. The patterned way in which this behaviour appeared in other members of the troop at Koshima led to the claim that it was acquired by social learning. Semushi, Imo's playmate, was the next to exhibit potato washing a month later, followed by another playmate and Imo's mother three months after this. Within five years, 14 of the troop's 15 juveniles and two of the 11 adults were washing potatoes. Since young macaques spend time with their mothers and peers, this pattern implies social learning – other youngsters, and then their mothers, would have been exposed to demonstrations of potato washing.

Figure 39.1 *Sweet potato washing by Japanese macaques*

The claim that social learning explains the spread of potato washing at Koshima has been challenged by Galef (1996). If social learning is a 'fast track', why did sweet potato washing take so long to appear in others? Even after five years, less than two thirds of the troop had acquired the behaviour. A lack of exposure to models might account for the lag in adult or dominant animals, but even some juveniles took several years to learn. This slow appearance compares poorly to other modes of learning. Imo is generally accepted as having been unusually creative, implying that the behaviour could not have arisen spontaneously in other members of the troop. However, in four different locations where macaques received sweet potatoes, washing was observed (Kawai 1965). It is not, therefore, impossible that given the time available, each monkey in the Koshima troop discovered potato washing for itself.

Human intervention may have been an additional factor in the spread of potato washing. Not only did caretakers provide sweet potatoes for the monkeys, but they were selective towards those monkeys that washed them (Green 1975). By such differentiation, the caretakers would have *reinforced* washing behaviour. Finally, this particular troop displayed other feeding behaviours, such as eating caramel, which were unrelated to their natural food sources. So, potato washing by the Koshima troop may not, in fact, be an example of social learning. Instead, the majority of the troop may have washed their potatoes because each independently discovered the behaviour, and was operantly conditioned to continue to do so by humans.

Opening milk bottles

When most British milk was full fat, there was a significant reward for a bird that could peck through the foil cap on the bottle. Blue tits (*Parus caeruleus*) and great tits (*Parus major*) are now sufficiently good at this behaviour that there is a market in bird proof bottle covers (see Figure 37.5, page 407). The behaviour was first described in Southern England, near Southampton, in 1921. The habit spread rapidly across Britain (see Figure 39.2), and certainly faster than could have been accounted for if it were a genetically controlled characteristic. So, social learning may explain its rapid appearance. Fisher & Hinde (1949) reported the behaviour, and suggested that it could be transmitted by imitation. One bird might observe the activities of another with a milk bottle and see it feeding. If the observer then copied the behaviour, it would be rewarded in the form of the cream from the top of the milk, and would continue performing the learned behaviour.

However, it is possible that what is actually occurring is not imitation. For a bird that finds an open bottle, drinking the remainder of the cream might provide an incentive to tamper with future milk bottles it encoun-

ters. The role of other birds in the wild would simply be to abandon open bottles. A study conducted by Sherry & Galef (1984) with the black-capped chickadee offers evidence to support this view (see Box 39.3). Indeed, it seems unlikely that imitation alone could explain the spread of bottle opening in blue-tits, since it apparently arose simultaneously in several different geographical areas.

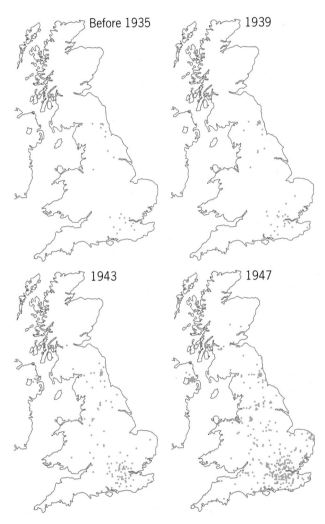

Figure 39.2 *Map showing the spread of milk bottle opening in tits across Britain, 1921–1947*

Key **S T U D Y**

Box 39.3 Imitation or incentive: bottle–opening birds

Sherry & Galef (1984) tested the ability of black-capped chickadees (*Parus atricapillus*) to acquire foil-top opening behaviour. Naïve birds were divided into three groups, which were given different exposure to foil-topped milk containers. The naïve birds observed a trained bird opening a container, received containers already opened by the experimenters, or were given unopened containers (the control group). Following these pre-treatments, each bird was later left alone with three unopened containers.

Those animals given the opportunity to learn by imitation, *and* those with the incentive of exposure to an opened container, learned to peck through the foil top whereas the control birds did not.

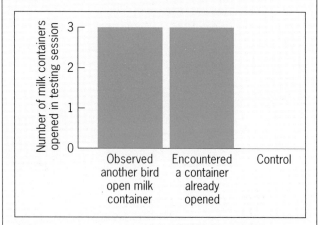

Figure 39.3 *The incentive of exposure to containers providing food is as effective as an opportunity for imitation*

In a further study, Sherry & Galef (1990) investigated whether bottle opening could be acquired by mechanisms other than observation. In that experiment, two naïve birds were housed in adjacent cages. The one that could access a covered cream container was more likely to peck at, and open, the container in the presence of the other than when it was alone. *Social facilitation*, rather than social learning, may be sufficient to account for this observation. The presence of the second bird may reduce fear or motivate competitive foraging behaviour, thus raising the likelihood that a container will be explored and opened by chance.

There seems to be several processes at work, although the relative importance of each is still unclear. Undoubtedly, some animals must acquire the ability to open bottles spontaneously, and this chance discovery has probably happened several, if not many, times. Social factors (imitation and social facilitation) appear to be responsible for some of the spread of this behaviour. Finally, many birds will encounter bottles which have already been opened, and by being reinforced for exploring in that particular context, may learn to peck through the foil tops themselves.

Learning foraging strategies

Fritz & Kotrschal (1999) investigated the social learning of *foraging* in ravens (*Corvus corax*). Prior to the experi-

ment, ravens were fed meat in boxes without lids. When exposed to boxes with lids, naïve ravens jumped onto the box and pecked until they forced the sliding lids apart (see Figure 39.4). Two 'models' were trained to employ a different technique, namely pulling coloured tabs to slide the lids apart. Then, naïve animals were placed in a pair, either with another naïve animal or with a model. Their initial responses to the box, time taken to approach it, and opening technique were recorded.

When first exposed to the boxes, control animals often responded with 'jumping jack' behaviour: approaching the object, pecking at it quickly with the tip of the beak and hopping backwards. In the wild, such a response would serve to test whether a carcass was dead. Despite their 'jumping jacks' sometimes being directed towards the coloured tabs, no control animals opened the lids in this way. By contrast, ravens which had observed the models, approached the boxes faster, often scrounged food from the model's box, and used both levering and tab-pulling. It would appear that the presence of a model did affect the observers' behaviour.

Fritz and Kotrschal concluded that it is not possible to distinguish between the effects of stimulus enhancement and imitation. The ravens may have observed the model's interaction with the tabs, and thus been attracted to them (the tabs became enhanced stimuli). Alternatively, the ravens may have observed and imitated the model's technique. Either explanation can account for the presence of the 'pulling' behaviour in observers and its absence from the repertoire of the control animals.

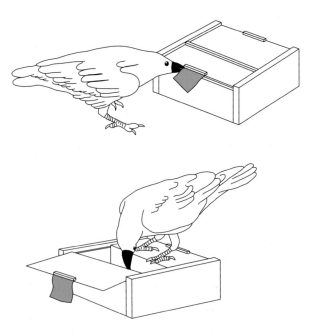

Figure 39.4 *Naïve ravens* (Corvus corax) *obtain food from a closed box by jumping on it and levering the lids apart. Following exposure to a trained model, they will open the lids by pulling the coloured tabs*

Predator avoidance

Blackbirds

An error with food may result in hunger or sickness, but failure to take evasive action in the face of a hunter carries a greater risk. Survival depends on the rapid acquisition of *antipredator behaviour*. By observing and copying the responses of adults to predators, juveniles can learn appropriate responses to specific situations. A bird's experience of the mobbing behaviour of a conspecific may result in social learning.

Curio *et al.* (1978) conducted an experiment in which two blackbirds (*Turdus merula*) could be exposed simultaneously to different stimuli, such that neither could see what object was in the other's field of view. Thus, a mobbing demonstrator might give an appropriate antipredator alarm at the sight of a stuffed owl, whilst the learner was looking at an innocuous stuffed honeyeater. Curio *et al.* found that the naïve birds would begin to respond with an alarm call to the inappropriate, socially learned, stimulus if they had heard mobbing on their initial exposure.

Vervet monkeys

Vervet monkeys (*Cercopithecus aethiops*) learn their alarm calls from adults, who employ different calls for different classes of predator (see Chapter 41). Juveniles are less reliable both in terms of their calling and their responses. They may fine tune their behaviours by observing the calls and responses of adults to particular predator types.

Cheney & Seyfarth (1990) found that whilst infant vervets' calls were not indiscriminate, they were less reliable than those of adults. Although infants gave inappropriate calls to innocent warthogs, mice, tortoises, pigeons and non-predatory birds, there was a 'logic' to their mistakes. They tended to generate snake alarms to things low to the ground (mice and tortoises), leopard alarms to larger, walking animals and eagle alarms to aerial objects such as falling leaves!

This suggests that there may be a genetic predisposition to respond to different categories of objects, which is honed by social experience. Feedback from the responses of adults may reinforce appropriate calls. For example, if a juvenile emits an eagle call to a pigeon, the adults will look up but then ignore the call. However, if the bird is a predator, they too will respond with eagle calls. Discrimination learning (see Chapter 38) would enable the juveniles to perfect their calls by reinforcing appropriate calling, and allowing misdirected calling to be extinguished.

Like their own calling, the responses of young vervets to the calls of others is inconsistent. In an experiment using recorded calls, Seyfarth & Cheney (1986) observed the behaviour of infants on hearing an eagle alarm (see Figure 39.5). Initially, infants appeared startled or con-fused, and looked for their mothers. Subsequently, they watched their mother's response and eventually responded in the same way to the call, by looking upwards into the sky. The infants behaved as if they had modelled their behaviour on that of their mothers.

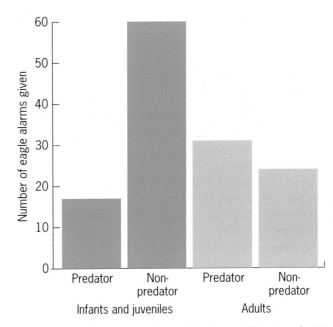

Figure 39.5 *The error rate for eagle alarm calling is only 44 per cent for adult vervet monkeys, but 78 per cent for juveniles (Seyfarth & Cheney, 1986)*

Further evidence for the involvement of both nature and nurture in vervet calls is reported by Bright (1984). Bright found that the calls given by vervets in Senegal and Kenya are very alike, despite the populations having been separated for thousands of generations. The degree of similarity suggests an underlying genetic component, whereas experimental isolation studies suggest that cultural transmission is also involved. Young vervets raised apart from adults, or in the company of other species, produce very different sounds from socially reared individuals.

LEARNING AND INTELLIGENCE

Clearly, there is more to intelligence than the learned conditioned responses acquired by animals via the processes described in Chapter 38. *Latent-learning* (see pages 419–420) and *social learning* (see Chapter 31, pages 337–338) both illustrate the propensity of animals to learn by means other than conditioning. In all of these respects, animal intelligence resembles that of humans, but is there any evidence that animals can demonstrate higher cognitive abilities?

A possible indicator of intelligence might be *language*. Non-humans are apparently less well prepared to acquire new information or skills than humans (see Chapter 41). Few species exhibit any capacity to acquire language, and those that do cannot match the achievement of a human child in speed or complexity. The following sections describe some other areas where non-human animals have demonstrated intelligent behaviour.

Insight learning

Sometimes, we can struggle over a question for hours or weeks, only to find that as soon as we stop trying the answer pops into our head. This experience of suddenly solving a problem, in the apparent absence of any trial-and-error process, is called *insight learning*. Its role in human problem solving is discussed in Chapter 37. Similar behaviour apparently occurs in animals, but is it really insight learning?

Köhler (1925) observed the behaviour of his chimpanzees (*Pan troglodytes*), particularly a male named Sultan, in situations such as those described in Chapter 27 (see Box 27.1, page 285). The tasks used appeared to require the animals to absorb information about the situation, and reapply their knowledge in order to solve a problem. This often involved the retrieval of fruit that was inaccessible except by means of detours or tool use.

In one study, Sultan was given two bamboo rods of about equal length with which to retrieve fruit from outside his cage (see Figure 39.6). Each stick alone was too short to reach the fruit and, having failed, Sultan abandoned his efforts and simply played with the sticks. Whilst playing, he held the sticks in a line such that one could be fitted inside the other. He immediately joined the sticks and ran to the edge of the cage to retrieve the fruit.

Although the sticks fell apart whilst Sultan was raking the fruit in, he immediately reconnected them. Köhler believed this was because Sultan recognised that fitting the sticks together was essential to solving the problem of retrieval. His success appeared to be the product of time spent with the elements of the problem in mind, and the solution arose as a result of insight rather than manipulation.

Box 39.4 Sultan: a reappraisal

Rarely reported are (in Köhler's words) Sultan's 'bad errors', that is, when he engaged in behaviours irrelevant to the situation. Before solving the double stick problem, Sultan had dragged a box up to the bars

then abandoned it, and had lost one of the sticks. He pushed one stick so far out of the cage with the other that he could not retrieve it himself.

Furthermore, when Sultan failed to recognise that one stick could be joined to the other, he was assisted by the observer putting a finger into the end of the wider stick. These events, often omitted from descriptions of Köhler's studies, reduce the credibility of the insightful solutions assumed in such situations.

If Sultan was able to conceptualise the problem, and work through an internal trial-and-error series to determine which approaches might offer effective solutions, a sudden correct response would appear to be 'insightful'. Alternatively, though, his successful retrieval of the fruit could be viewed as the consequence of combining previously learned responses in new ways.

In general, Köhler's descriptions of the chimpanzees' behaviour suggest that they were far from instant, insightful solutions. In fact, the chimpanzees are often described as 'angry' or 'fatigued', and they frequently engaged in varied efforts with a range of potential tools (including their keepers and Köhler himself) to solve a problem. Nevertheless, Köhler observed that Sultan did not attempt to make a double stick from two pieces of the same diameter. He appeared to comprehend the necessity for one stick to have a smaller diameter than the other, without having to engage in trial-and-error.

Figure 39.6 *Evidence for insight learning in animals? Sultan making a double stick*

Evidence against insight learning

Epstein *et al.* (1984) suggested that the behaviour of Köhler's chimpanzees could simply be built up from conditioned responses. Epstein *et al.* used naïve pigeons (*Columba livia*) that were unaccustomed either to moving objects about or standing on them. They were then taught to move a box, to stand on it, or to perform both of these tasks.

When given a problem identical to that shown in Box 27.1 (see page 285), the pigeons failed to reach the food unless they had been taught both component behaviours. They had been reinforced for pushing a box to a spot on the floor (they were not rewarded for pushing it if there was no spot). They had also been taught to stand on a box positioned beneath a banana to reach a food reward. The behaviour of these birds in the test situation closely resembled the chimpanzees' behaviour. They initially stretched up underneath the banana, then suddenly pushed the box, hopped onto it and pecked the food. Birds that had been trained in only *one* of the component tasks failed to generate the necessary sequence.

The study of insightful behaviour is problematic, and the methodology used has been criticised. As the moment of insight is brief and unpredictable, it is hard to record accurately. It is also difficult to determine which characteristics of the preceding behaviour are relevant. Since all the observer sees is the moment of enlightenment, the mechanism of insight learning is open to interpretation.

If insight is believed to result from 'thinking about' the problem, then the animal has a conscious experience and must be forming mental representations of objects and actions. This explanation of insight requires that animals are *aware*. Whilst the notion of awareness in a chimpanzee may be acceptable to some, few psychologists would accept the idea that pigeons are aware. Since both species were able to solve the task described earlier, this would imply that both were 'thinking'.

The argument for the occurrence of insight is also *circular*. If the animal solves a problem, it is deemed to have demonstrated insight because the situation demanded it. However, this cannot be independently verified. The animal *might* have solved the problem by some other means, but it is not possible within the framework of the experiment to differentiate between alternative interpretations.

Like Epstein *et al.*, Schiller (1952) doubted that insight learning occurred *independently* of trial-and-error. He gave 48 chimpanzees sticks that fitted together. Of these, 32 connected them correctly within an hour. There were 20 adults, of which 19 completed the task within five minutes. This might suggest that experience with sticks increases the possibility of a solution being found independently of any insightful behaviour. However,

Schiller concluded that maturational, rather than experiential factors, were responsible for the difference.

By disregarding early experience, we risk 'throwing the baby out with the bath water'. Just because an animal has practised some of the task elements which will assist in its solution does not preclude the possibility that the final steps in reaching the answer could arise as a sudden realisation. A non-physicist is unlikely to be able to resolve the problem of cold fusion, because s/he does not understand the relevant sub-processes. For a physicist who does, the final stages of the problem may arise in a flash.

Animal numeracy

Pfungst (1907, cited in Reber, 1985) investigated Clever Hans, a horse that appeared to be able to count. Horses, in common with most non-human animals, do not generally demonstrate an understanding of the concept of number. Hans was only 'clever' because he learned to respond to very subtle cues from his master, not because he had any capacity for calculation. However, in contrast to the majority of non-human animals, some primates have been shown to display the rudiments of mathematical understanding.

Key **S T U D Y**

Box 39.5 Mathematical understanding in non-humans

By the time human babies begin to speak, they already have some concept of number. Chapter 28 described experiments in which an infant is exposed to an object that subsequently 'disappears' because it is covered up or plunged into darkness. The baby is startled if a different number of objects are present when it can next view the scene. Hauser *et al.* (1996) wanted to find out whether non-human primates would also be surprised in such a situation, so they contrived a mathematical magic show for wild rhesus monkeys (*Macaca mulatta*).

If a monkey sat still for long enough, it was shown a box with no front or top in which there was a platform. The box was then hidden by a screen and the monkey saw the experimenter place two aubergines, one by .one, behind the screen. On some occasions, one of the aubergines was not placed on view in the box, but was hidden. As the screen was removed to reveal the box's contents, the monkey's reaction was observed. The 13 animals exposed to a single aubergine gazed for more than twice as long as the 48 that saw both aubergines. Those confronted with the wrong number of aubergines also appeared 'surprised', suggesting that they 'expected' a particular number of aubergines to be present.

Brannon & Terrace (1998) studied a pair of captive rhesus monkeys (*Macaca mulatta*). The monkeys were trained over a period of six weeks, using a touch sensitive video screen, to respond to the appearance of sets of four images displayed simultaneously. Each image consisted of between one and four items, such as 'three flowers' or 'two circles' (see Figure 39.7). The items varied in terms of colour, shape and size, in order to control for variables such as attractiveness or area which could have obscured the effects of quantity.

The monkeys were rewarded with banana-flavoured treats for touching the boxes in order. If they responded incorrectly, the screen went blank and they had to start again. After 150 trials over five days, it was clear that they could differentiate between 1, 2, 3 and 4 items. After this, the monkeys were presented with new images, displaying between five and nine items. Each was seen only once, and no rewards were given. Even without any additional training, they performed with 75 per cent accuracy, suggesting that they had understood the original relationship and could reapply their understanding of number.

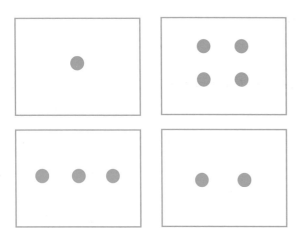

Figure 39.7 *Brannon and Terrace presented chimpanzees with four images on a video monitor. The chimpanzees were able to learn the task of touching the images in numerical order. When the number of items was increased to nine, they were still able to perform the task*

Self-recognition

When faced with a mirror, primates such as chimpanzees and gorillas respond in the same way as naïve humans. Babies, and adults who have gained sight later in life, first respond to the reflection as if it were another individual. This initial reaction disappears as they have the opportunity to observe themselves. Gradually, the acceptance that the reflection is their own image emerges. This is called *self-recognition*.

Evidence for primate self-recognition

Convincing evidence for self-recognition has been provided by Gallup (1970) who gave chimpanzees the opportunity to learn to recognise themselves in a mirror. Initially, they responded with threat gestures and vocalisations, as if they believed their reflection was another chimpanzee. Subsequently, they used the mirror to explore parts of their bodies they could not usually see. The chimpanzees were later anaesthetised and a coloured, non-irritating dye was applied to one eyebrow ridge and the opposite ear. After recovering from the anaesthetic, none of the chimpanzees indicated any interest in the marked areas of their heads until they were given access to a mirror.

Once they could see the marks, the frequency of touching the coloured areas increased. This could be interpreted as a response to novelty rather than a recognition of any change in themselves. However, the chimpanzees would have to be able to recall their *previous appearance* to detect the difference and to direct their hand towards the correct facial area using only their reflection. This implies the occurrence of some self-recognition.

Figure 39.8 *Chimpanzees learn to use mirrors to explore parts of their bodies they cannot usually see*

Evidence against primate self-recognition

Pearce (1997) reports a range of studies similar to Gallup's using species including the orang-utan (*Pongo pygmaeus*) which, like the chimpanzee, displays a capacity to learn to recognise itself. In monkeys and various vertebrates (such as dogs, cats and elephants), self-recognition does not seem to develop with exposure to mirrors. These species react as if the image were another animal, rather like territorial wild birds do in response to their reflection in a window pane.

Doubt has also been cast on the reliability of Gallup's evidence. Swartz & Evans (1991) used Gallup's mark test and found that not all chimpanzees showed evidence of mirror self-recognition (MSR). Bard (1994) suggests a number of reasons for difficulties experienced with mirror self-recognition tasks which could account for the contradictory findings.

Different researchers working with the same species have found varying levels of reliability with MSR, and consequently believe that self-recognition arises at different ages. This variability may result from the detrimental effect of distress and distractions on cognitive ability, and of competing interests on concentration. For example, a human observer may be more interesting than a mirror image. Recovery from anaesthesia, essential to the Gallup mark test, also impairs cognitive functioning. Finally, it is difficult to judge when an animal is focused on a mark or is visually guiding self-directed movements. Thus, observing and assessing the function of eye gaze can be deceptive.

Is self-recognition essential for learning by imitation?

Learning by imitation is a means by which some animals can acquire new behaviours. As this is not apparent in all species, it might be dependent upon self-recognition. If a baby responds in kind to an adult poking its tongue out, does this necessarily mean that it is making a connection beteen the tongue it can see (the adult's) and the one it can feel (its own)?

Some animals are exposed to similar opportunities for imitation, such as the home-raised chimpanzee Viki (see Chapter 41). In this situation, an animal might copy the actions of another individual because it is aware of its own behaviour. This is not, however, the only possible interpretation. Hayes & Hayes (1952) reported that Viki did imitate a range of human actions, such as washing dishes, sometimes on the first occasion they were demonstrated. However, Viki was accustomed to receiving rewards in response to such modelling, and so her reaction could have been 'first-time-lucky' operant behaviour (Heyes, 1994).

Is self-recognition just a conditioned response?

It seems unlikely that a sophisticated response such as an animal's awareness of its own behaviour could be the consequence of operant conditioning. Beninger *et al.* (1974), however, conducted a study in which rats were operantly conditioned to a noise. They received reinforcement for pushing one of four levers, the correct choice being dependent on the behaviour they had been performing when a buzzer sounded. There is no suggestion that the rats were 'aware' of their behaviour at the time of the sound, merely that the posture or activity could become the subject of a conditioned response. So, animals may not have to be self-aware. Their behaviour may simply be manipulated by the reinforcers which are contingent on the situation.

Box 39.6 Why be self-aware?

A behaviour is not likely to arise through a complex and potentially expensive process (in terms of time, energy or investment), if it could be the product of one that is more simple and direct. However, there is evidence that some animals are conscious of themselves and of others. If an animal's awareness of its own behaviour or motives provided sufficient insight to allow it to predict the consequences of its actions, or the responses of others, these would be significant advantages. The self-aware animal might be able to out-wit competitors, avoid danger, or co-operate more effectively. This may be particularly so for primates living in complex social groups.

Theory of mind

From early childhood onwards, humans are described as having a *theory of mind*, that is, a conception of the knowledge, intentions, desires or beliefs held by another individual (see also Chapter 45). Adult humans are very proficient in their use of the theory of mind. When someone reaches out for the TV remote control, we assume s/he wants to change the channel as this is what we would do. There are two stages to this assumption: (1) the self-knowledge which allows us to determine why we behave in a particular way, and (2) the extrapolation of those motives to others. Having grasped the concept of 'theory of mind', we can then exploit it. For example, we may ask to watch a specific programme, thus manipulating the behaviour of the person holding the remote control.

Can animals utilise a theory of mind in the same way? This question presupposes that animals have a 'state of mind' about which others could make inferences. If they do, and we must assume this in order to continue the debate, then are they able to assess the mental states of others? We can approach this question from two perspectives. First, can animals correctly attribute knowledge to others? Second, can animals employ the tactic of *deception,* and if so, can we conclude that they are knowingly altering the beliefs of another individual?

Attribution of knowledge to others

Woodruff & Premack (1979) demonstrated that chimpanzees could learn discriminations which might be explained in terms of theory of mind, but could also have been the consequence of conditioning. Povinelli *et al.* (1990) conducted an experiment in which chimpanzees had to make judgements based on the knowledge they believed human participants to have.

Each chimpanzee was faced with an array of four up-turned cups, one of which contained a piece of food which it would be allowed to eat if it chose correctly. The only clues were from two of the trainers who pointed at different cups. One of these (the knowledgeable trainer) had hidden the food whilst the cups (but not the trainer) were screened from the chimpanzee. The other trainer had been out of the room whilst the chimpanzee watched this procedure.

Over a period of several hundred trials during which, on every occasion, the knowledgeable trainer pointed to the correct cup, the four chimpanzees produced a significant preference for this choice. This could be interpreted as evidence for the development of an understanding of what the trainers knew, that is, their state of mind. Alternatively, the results could be explained more simply in terms of *operant conditioning*: the chimpanzees were effectively reinforced for choosing the cup indicated by the person who had been in the room the longest.

To test for the possibility of operant conditioning, Povinelli *et al.* conducted a further test with the same animals. They were exposed to an identical experimental situation, except that there was a third trainer who actually baited the cups whilst one trainer could watch and the other wore a rather obvious bucket over his head (see Figure 39.9).

In this situation, the chimpanzees' responses were ambiguous. Over 30 trials, three of the four chimpanzees showed a significant preference for the cup indicated by the new-style knowledgeable trainer (the one without a bucket). However, it is still possible that they were learning a more simple association, such as 'choose the one selected by *Trainer-No-Bucket*', rather than actually attributing knowledgeable status to them. An experiment which attempts to overcome this possibility is described in Box 39.7.

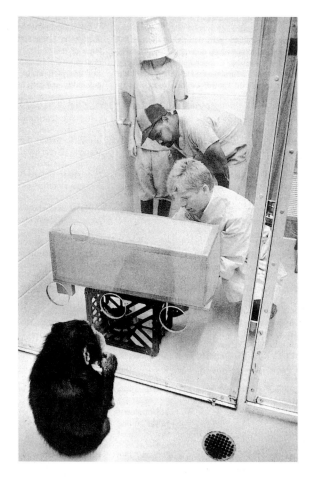

Figure 39.9 *Chimpanzees can learn to select a cup indicated by the trainer who has not had a bucket over his head, and so knows where the food is hidden*

Key (S T U D Y)

Box 39.7 Chimpanzees teaching people

Povinelli *et al.* (1992) investigated the ability of chimpanzees to consider the perspective of others. Their work supports the idea that chimpanzees can convey information to another, previously ignorant individual. The ability of chimpanzees to comprehend the social role of their partner was measured by the speed at which they acquired a new behaviour that they had watched, and had helped another individual to acquire, but had never themselves performed.

The experiment used four pairs (each comprising a chimpanzee and a human), and divided into two conditions. In each pair, one participant was an 'informant', the other an 'operator'. In two pairs, the chimpanzee was the informant. In the others, the chimpanzee played the role of the operator. The pair sat opposite one another, either side of a piece of apparatus with handles at the operator's end. These handles caused pairs of food trays to move within reach of the participants.

In the first stage of the experiment, the operator learned to pull the correct handle to draw a tray visibly baited with food to the edge of the apparatus. This caused the other food tray to reach the informant. This behaviour was acquired rapidly. During the second stage, the operator was unaware of which trays contained food. Human operators covered their ears with their hands and turned away, and the chimpanzees were screened from the apparatus, as the food trays were being baited.

The informants were required to gesture to the operator to indicate which handle to pull, and they generally did this by pointing. The 'informant' chimpanzees readily learned to indicate the correct location, and the 'operators' similarly learned to respond to signalling. Both informants and operators received a food reward for correct signalling and response.

The chimpanzees' comprehension of the role of their partner was tested in the third stage, in which the informant and operator swapped roles. This reversal was achieved by spinning the apparatus round, so that the handles faced the ex-informant (the new operator). Three of the four chimpanzees showed immediate transfer of skills between the two phases of the experiment. Ex-operators spontaneously pointed, and ex-informants responded accurately to pointing by using the correct handle.

Povinelli *et al.* concluded that the chimpanzees had learned the requirements of both roles during the training phase. They could both comprehend the social role of another individual, *and* attribute intention to their behaviour.

Deception

Some animals have demonstrated an awareness of what other individuals know and can profit from this (as in Povinelli *et al.'s* experiments). In Savage-Rumbaugh's experiments with language-trained pygmy chimpanzees (see Chapter 41), there is evidence that they comprehend the deception of others and that this is 'bad'. Might it be possible for chimpanzees to influence the behaviour of others to their own advantage by engaging in deception?

In Woodruff & Premack's (1979) experiment, chimpanzees were exposed to two trainers operating different but consistent strategies. One trainer was always *competitive*, the other *co-operative*. At the start of each trial, a laboratory assistant hid food under one of two containers, whilst the chimpanzee watched but could not access the food. When a trainer appeared, the chimpanzee could obtain the food either by directing him towards the correct container (if he was 'co-operative'), or towards the incorrect container (if he was 'competitive').

The chimpanzees indicated their choice to the trainers by pointing or staring. Some of them were able to achieve the correct response even in the presence of both trainers, suggesting that they were capable of deception – deliberately misinforming the competitive trainer. The chimpanzees took many trials to learn the discrimination, so it is possible that, like the subjects in Povinelli *et al.'s* experiments, they were being operantly conditioned to some subtle cue in the experimental procedure.

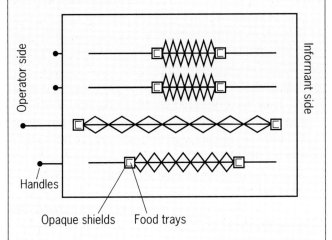

Handles

Opaque shields   Food trays

Figure 39.10 *Apparatus used to test spontaneous communication in chimpanzees (*Pan troglodytes*) (Povinelli et al., 1992)*

CONCLUSIONS

This chapter has looked at social learning in non-human animals. Social learning claims to offer a rapid means to develop new and complex behaviours by imitating conspecifics. This could provide animals in their natural habitats with safe routes to the acquisition of foraging and antipredator behaviours, both essential to survival.

Whilst some behaviours may be learned in this way, through incidental observation or direct tutoring, many experimental examples of apparent social learning can be explained by more simple processes. Independent discovery, stimulus enhancement, facilitation and reinforcement may account for many instances of supposed social learning.

Beyond the acquisition of behaviours by operant conditioning, the evidence for intelligence in non-human animals is largely restricted to chimpanzees. This species demonstrates a range of behaviours, including insight learning, an understanding of number, self-recognition and deception. The studies illustrating these abilities have, however, been criticised and many of the findings can be interpreted in more simplistic ways.

Summary

- **Social learning** is the acquisition of a new skill resulting from the direct effect of other individuals through **imitation** or **tutoring**. It is most likely to occur in gregarious species with good memories.

- Social learning may have benefits for the recipient, such as reduced time to acquire new behaviours, avoiding danger, and access to otherwise inaccessible resources. For the model, however, the costs may include expenditure of time, energy and loss of resources.

- **Mimicry** describes instances of **imitation** in which there is no obvious reward, such as the copying of human behaviours shown by captive chimpanzees.

- **Stimulus enhancement** can explain why an observer may appear to imitate a demonstrator's behaviour. Having seen a model interacting with a particular object, the observer may perceive this as a preferential stimulus and thus be more likely to respond and interact with that item.

- Sweet potato washing by Japanese macaques is often described as an example of social learning. However, this is only one possible explanation for the distribution of a new **foraging** behaviour. Independent discovery and conditioning by humans may also be explanations.

- Young blackbirds can learn an **antipredatory response** to a particular stimulus by imitating the calls they hear their parents utter at the time of their observation. Juvenile vervet monkeys also learn their antipredator calls, although they appear to have a predisposition to respond to certain categories of objects.

- **Insight learning** is the sudden solution of a problem in the absence of any apparent trial and error process. Chimpanzees were thought to be unusual in demonstrating insight learning. However, it is hard to observe the moment of insight, or to decide which preceding elements of the situation are relevant. Much of the process of insight cannot be observed, and so it is open to different interpretations.

- It is unclear whether an animal needs to have a conscious experience in order to form the necessary mental representations to 'think about' a problem. Studies of insight set a problem which, if solved, is taken to signify insight learning. However, this fails to acknowledge that an animal may be able to reach a solution by some other means.

- **Self-recognition** is the understanding that the reflection seen in a mirror is of oneself not another individual. Primates seem to demonstrate self-recognition by their fascination for watching their own mirror images.

- Gallup showed that chimpanzees responded to having their faces painted in the same way as human infants. They were unreactive until they saw themselves in a mirror, and showed self-recognition by attempting to touch the coloured region.

- Apart from chimpanzees and the orang-utan, no other species consistently displays self-recognition. However, the reliability of evidence for **mirror self-recognition** (MSR) has been questioned. Variability in MSR findings could be attributed to the effects of distress, distraction, anaesthesia or difficulties associated with judging where an animal's focus is directed and why.

■ Self-recognition may be a necessary prerequisite for imitation, a learning process associated with intelligence. Whilst animals, particularly primates, can readily learn by imitation, it is unclear whether this is independent of operant behaviour.

■ Being self-aware has advantages. It enables the individual to predict the consequences of its own actions and those of others. This could be used to out-wit competitors, avoid danger, or co-operate effectively. Understanding of the knowledge, intention, desires or beliefs held by another individual is our **theory of mind**.

■ The ability of chimpanzees to utilise a theory of mind can be examined by considering their **attribution of knowledge** to others, and their employment of **deception**. They are able to learn to make a choice based on the knowledge they attribute to a trainer who has seen where food has been hidden. This appears to indicate that the chimpanzees can judge the human's state of mind.

■ **Deception** requires an understanding of the state of mind of other individuals, and the ability to knowingly and falsely alter their beliefs. Whilst research suggests that chimpanzees can use deception, the training of deceptive behaviours takes many trials. Chimpanzees might simply be operantly conditioned to subtle cues in the experimental procedure, rather than being responsive to mental states.

Essay Questions

1 Describe and evaluate explanations relating to the role of social learning in the behaviour of non-human animals. *(24 marks)*

2 Critically consider evidence for intelligence in non-human animals. *(24 marks)*

WEB ADDRESSES

http://www.panix.com/~paleodiet/foraging/
http://pigeon.psy.tufts.edu/psych26/Kohler.htm
http://www.idealibrary.com.links/artid/anbe.1996.0318
http://www.idealibrary.com/links/artid/anbe.1996.0366

40 Animal Navigation

Why does an animal need to know where it is going? Perhaps to return to a familiar location, such as a food cache, or to reach a winter breeding site. Such behaviours are examples of *homing*, that is, navigating back to a known location. *Migrating* animals may travel vast distances to such new environments in order to raise their chances of survival. To home or migrate successfully, animals need to know how to find their goal, that is, to *navigate*. This chapter examines explanations and research studies into homing and migration as examples of animal navigation.

NAVIGATION

According to Greek myth, when Theseus entered the labyrinth to slay the minotaur, he began to unravel a ball of silken thread. The deed done, he was able to use the thread to retrace his footsteps. The simplest technique of navigation used by animals is a *trail*. Foraging ants, for example, use a pheromone trail to guide others to a food source. Some species of loris, a type of tree-dwelling lemur, employ 'urine washing'. The males urinate on one hand, rub this against the other, then rub them on their feet. Consequently, they deposit scent trails through the branches as they travel. By marking their journey, they can then retrace their steps. This technique also allows them to find their way at night (Shorey, 1976).

Navigation requires two aspects of knowledge, knowing *where to go to* and knowing *how to get there*. These are required for both homing and migration, although in the latter the destination may not have been visited before. It could be argued that animals only needed to know the direction, and once on course stopped when a suitable or familiar area was detected. However, is this really navigation? Some animals can cope with being deflected off course and adopt alternative routes. This suggests that they are capable of *true navigation*, that is, they can employ both a 'map' to know where to go (the location of the goal) *and* a 'compass' to know how to get there (the direction without reference to landmarks).

Box 40.1 Navigation: the knowledge

- *Landmarks* are visual characteristics, which might assist birds to both get their bearings at the start of a journey and fine tune their descent.

- *Smell* may be used for both local and long distance detection of home. It might provide either map or compass information.

- *The sun* travels in an arc across the sky, which varies with the season and latitude. In tandem with an internal clock, its position in the sky and pattern of polarised light can provide information about direction.

- *Geomagnetism* is generated as the earth spins and its outer core swirls. Nerve cells which respond to changes in *magnetite* in the brain (see page 441) can detect information about direction and position.

- *Poles*: Although described as north and south, the earth's geomagnetic poles don't align with the geographic poles, and can even swap over.

- *Field lines*: The earth's magnetic field emerges from the poles at right angles to the surface, curving round until they are horizontal at the equator. This dip or inclination provides information to distinguish 'poleward' from 'equatorward' directions and distance from the pole.

- *The stars* appear to rotate around a single point in the night sky. This occurs as the earth spins, and this point represents geographical north or south, depending on which hemisphere an animal is in.

LOCATION BASED NAVIGATION

Chapter 42 discusses *spatial memory* (the ability to remember specific locations within an environment). One important cue for this is the position of fixed objects. However, object position is not just used in familiar locations. Some species use their memory to track their own movements further afield.

Navigation using familiar landmarks is termed *piloting*. Some animals find their way by committing the features of the locality to memory. This enables them to create a mental 'set of directions' that lead to specific sites, such as a nest, and to determine directions relative to their surroundings. Different animals rely predominantly on different senses to provide this information. For gannets, these cues are visual, whereas salmon rely on their sense of *smell*. Such cues cannot, however, provide information for a fledgling migrant on its first outward journey.

Piloting by sight

Cartwright & Collett (1983) and Collett *et al.* (1986) trained bees to find a sucrose solution, and gerbils to find sunflower seeds. The food was always located at a fixed distance and compass bearing from a 40-centimetre-high cylinder. Once trained, the animals persistently searched in the correct location relative to the cylinder, even when no food was present. On some trials, the location of the cylinder and the animals' entry point was varied, to ensure that they were not simply repeating a learned motor sequence from their starting point.

Searching in the correct relative location indicated that they were using a landmark (the cylinder) to orientate, and they subsequently employed other strategies to determine the appropriate direction and distance. For bees, but not gerbils, there is good evidence for the use of a magnetic sense (see Box 40.1, page 436), enabling them to determine the direction to travel away from the cylinder. In the absence of this information about compass bearings, the gerbils might have been orienting with respect to more distant fixed points, such as the doorway.

The strategies used by bees and gerbils to determine distance seemed to differ. When the height of the cylinder was halved, bees searched closer to it, and when it was doubled, they searched farther away. This suggests that the bees were using the size of the retinal image to guide their position. When the retinal image is enlarged (by increasing the height of the cylinder), it reaches threshold size before the bees are close enough, and so they begin their search too far away.

By contrast, the height of the cylinder had little effect on navigation for gerbils. Their distance judgements seemed to rely on 'dead reckoning' (see below). In an experimental test without food (to ensure that they could not use olfactory cues), gerbils were put into the test area and allowed to orientate to the landmark before the lights were extinguished. Tracking under infra-red illumination showed that the gerbils continued on course and stopped to search at the right location, even after travelling as much as 2.5 metres. They seemed to judge how far they had to go once on course, and knew when the appropriate distance was covered. It is not clear from these results, however, whether this decision was based on travelling time or actual distance covered.

Piloting by smell

Salmon are long-distance migrants. After hatching, they swim downstream to the sea. In early spring, several years and many thousands of miles later, they must make the return journey to the river where they hatched to spawn. How do they choose, in an expanse of water apparently devoid of constant features, which way to swim?

Hasler & Larsen (1955) suggested that one possible stable environmental cue might be *smell*, and that the salmon's home-stream may have a specific odour that can be detected and followed along a gradient of increasing concentration. Salmon can apparently make such judgements easily, having the necessary olfactory discrimination to detect subtle variations in the smell of the water (see Figure 40.1, page 438). When Wisby & Hasler (1954) blocked the nostrils of migrating salmon, they failed to return successfully, and similar disorientation has been demonstrated in experiments where the olfactory nerve has been severed.

It is not clear what exactly has such an attractive smell. Salmon may be *imprinting* on the rocks, soil or plants in the stream, or on a combination of these and the pheromonal characteristics of their own population. This is supported by the observation that salmon can discriminate both their own population and their kin (Quinn & Tolson, 1986; Quinn & Hara, 1986).

Dead reckoning

This system of navigation operates by measuring current position with reference to the distance travelled and direction(s) taken. It is about 'knowing the location of the target with respect to yourself', rather than knowing where you, or the target, lies in geographical space. It is more than 'knowing the way there', because an animal

their outward journey they could see, but for the remainder they were covered. On release, the geese headed off in the wrong direction, behaving as if they had only been moved for the portion of the outward journey which they had seen.

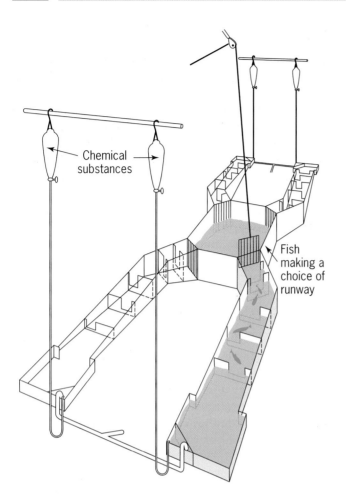

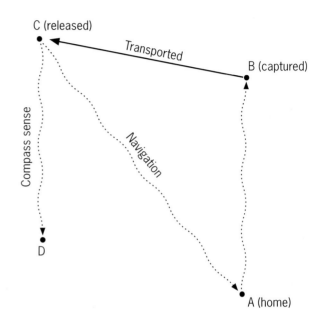

Figure 40.2 *A compass is necessary, but not sufficient, for navigation. An animal capable of returning to its home (A) from C has the ability to navigate. If the animal moves to D it has a compass sense, but is not capable of navigation*

Figure 40.1 *Salmon seem to have sufficient discriminatory power to choose pathways in an experimental setting on the basis of olfaction alone. This would enable them to navigate back to the stream where they hatched on the basis of the smell of each branch in the returning river*

may search haphazardly, but return via the most direct route.

In ants, this knowledge seems to derive from the outward journey (Gallistel, 1990). Wehner & Srinivansan (1981) took foraging desert ants (*Cataglyphis bicolor*) 600 metres away from their nests, and found that they behaved as if they had not been moved at all. From their displaced point, they set off in a compass direction appropriate for their previous location and, more importantly, travelled approximately the same distance as between their previous foraging location and the nest. This would have been entirely correct for an undisplaced individual, but they were unable to take account of their imposed relocation, probably because they had no immediate cues to position and were using dead reckoning (see Figure 40.2).

The ability to measure displacement may depend upon being able to *see* on the outward journey. Saint Paul (1982) displaced geese from their home. For part of

DIRECTION-BASED NAVIGATION

The navigational techniques described so far rely on memory, but there is evidence that some animals can also use navigational systems similar to human orienteering skills. These additional sources of information can account, for example, for the ability of pigeons to home to the loft when they have been transported in enclosed or rotating cages, or even under anaesthetic.

Sun compass

Kramer (1951) demonstrated that birds can use the *sun* as a cue to orientation. He trained caged starlings to search for food located at a particular compass direction, with only the sun and sky to guide them. They maintained accurate bearings, enabling them to forage successfully regardless of the time of day. This suggests that they could compensate for the movement of the sun across the sky.

To test this, Schmidt-Koenig (1961) housed pigeons under artificial lighting schedules to alter their internal clocks. When returned to natural daylight, they misinterpreted the sun's location based on the 'new' time of day, so their foraging behaviour was re-oriented (see Figure 40.3). Similar effects of clock shifting on orientation have been demonstrated in other species, such as monarch butterflies (Perez *et al.*, 1997).

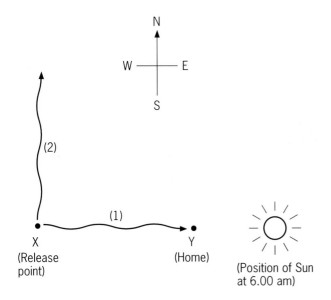

Figure 40.3 *Clock-shifting and altered navigation in homing pigeons. (1) indicates the (correct) path taken by a bird kept in natural light. (2) is the path taken by a bird that has been shifted forward by six hours. The birds must fly east to return home. Pigeon 1 'knows' it is 6.00 am, and therefore the sun is in the east, so it flies towards the sun. Pigeon 2 'thinks' it is noon and therefore the sun is in the south, so it flies at 90° anticlockwise to the sun (believing this to be east, when it is actually north)*

Box 40.2 Multiple navigation mechanisms

Evidence also suggests that pigeons can use more than one mechanism. For example, Ganzhorn *et al.* (1989) released four hour delay clock-shifted pigeons near the equator as noon approached. They would be expected to fly in the opposite direction from home (as they should interpret the position of the sun as being just past its zenith, when it would actually still be rising). In fact, they tended to fly in the correct direction, ignoring the mis-information from the sun compass. This implies that, at least whilst the sun is high in the sky, birds use other systems to navigate accurately. Sandhoppers display *chronometrically compensated lunar orientation*, that is, they can judge direction based on the *moon's* position, adjusting for the time of night. They can do this independently of moon shape and experience of the moon in nature (Ugolini *et al.*, 1999).

Polarised light

Light is made up of waves that travel in all possible directions. *Polarised light* is light which has passed through material acting as a filter. Rather as a turnstile allows people out of but not into an area, a polarising material reflects all waves that are not of a particular orientation. This leaves a set of regular rays of light. An example of such a filter would be the atmosphere. Polarisation through the atmosphere is greatest at an angle of 90 degrees to the rays of the sun. So, when the sun is overhead, less polarised light falls on the surface of the earth compared to sunrise or sunset.

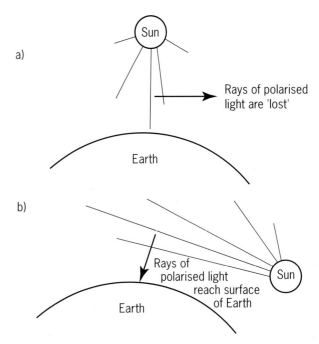

Figure 40.4 *The diagram above shows the sun at (a) the zenith and (b) the azimuth of its path through the sky. Polarisation of sunlight is greatest at 90° to the ambient rays. When the sun is overhead, the polarised rays are 'lost' as they are tangential to the earth. When the sun is lower in the sky, the polarised rays are directed towards the earth's surface. The angle of polarised light can therefore be used as a cue to the whereabouts of the sun, and so as an indicator of direction*

Provided some blue sky is visible, an animal that is capable of detecting polarised light could use this as a cue to the position of the sun, and hence direction, even when the sun was obscured. Pigeons might be able to use this cue as they can be conditioned to respond to polarised light (Kreithen, 1978). It has yet to be demonstrated, however, whether they *actually* use this ability to assist in navigation.

Bees seem to be able utilise information from polarised light. Von Frisch (1956, 1967) showed that honey bees could accurately indicate direction on their return to the hive (see Chapter 41, pages 455–456), even when it was cloudy. It was only necessary for the bees to be able to see a small area of sky to perform their 'dance' in the correct orientation. Von Frisch showed that the orientation of the bees' dance could be altered by exposing them to ultraviolet light from the sun which had been passed through a polarising filter (see Figure 40.4, page 439).

Magnetic sense

When sleeping away from home or after re-arranging your bedroom furniture, you might have had the feeling that you were lying in the 'wrong direction'. This could be because of an innate *magnetic sense*. Some humans seem to be particularly attuned to compass direction, in the absence of any other cues (see Box 40.4, page 441).

The earth is a giant magnet. It has two magnetic poles, approximately at the geographic poles, with lines of magnetic force (field lines) between them. These patterns of magnetic force leave the surface of the earth at the South pole and return at the North pole, describing varying angles of inclination or slope (see Figure 40.5). An animal capable of detecting these field lines could use geomagnetic information as a cue to direction.

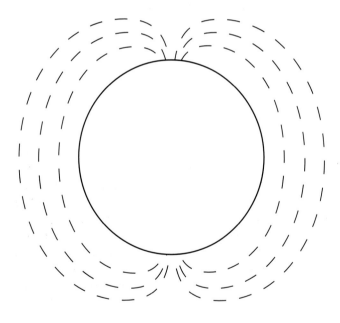

Figure 40.5 *Between the North and South pole run field lines or patterns of magnetism. They are steeply inclined towards the surface of the earth at the poles and horizontal at the equator. This variation could be used by animals as a cue to direction*

The use of an internal compass by animals, especially humans, has been doubted for decades. However, there is strong evidence from a variety of sources that such abilities exist.

Behavioural evidence

Homing pigeons are excellent navigators. The importance of magnetic information to pigeons is suggested by their loss of homing ability during magnetic storms (Gould, 1982), and when their journey passes through an anomalous area in the earth's magnetic field. Experimental demonstrations confirm these observations. For example, pigeons lose their navigational ability (on overcast days) when a magnet is attached to their heads (Larkin & Keeton, 1976).

Key **STUDY**

Box 40.3 The importance of magnetic information to pigeons

Walcott & Brown (1989) studied the ability of pigeons to orientate towards home (indicated by the dashed line in Figure 40.6) when released from Jersey Hill, New York. They recorded the *vanishing bearings* of released pigeons, each one appearing as a dot in Figure 40.6. Although most pigeons were able to home successfully, their initial directions were random. Jersey Hill is known to be an area of magnetic anomaly.

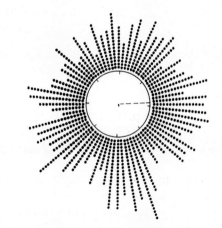

Figure 40.6 *The vanishing bearings of pigeons in Walcott & Brown's (1989) study*

Beason (1989) reported a series of experiments that aimed to discover the source of navigational abilities in the bobolink (*Dolichonyx oryzivorus*), a transequatorial North American migrant. This bird's migratory path extends so far north *and* south of the equator, that it is unable to use the same visual pattern of stars throughout its journey. It is therefore likely that it uses some other cue in addition to a star map.

In Beason's first experiment, bobolinks were caught and housed individually without a view of the natural sky. The birds' movements were recorded on consecutive nights under a planetarium sky. In the control condition, the stellar north coincided with the natural magnetic north (north as indicated by the star patterns was the same as geographical north). In the experimental condition, the star patterns were reversed, so that the apparent stellar south coincided with the natural geomagnetic north. After an average of 2.5 nights, the orientation of the experimental birds had been reversed. They appeared to be using geomagnetic information in preference to stellar information, although their response to the change was not immediate.

To verify the importance of magnetic information, Beason conducted a second experiment, in which the stellar information was unaltered, but the inclination of the local magnetic field was reversed (using a pair of 4 metre electromagnets). So, although magnetic north remained in the same geographical direction, the vertical component of the magnetic field was changed. Again, the bobolinks favoured magnetic over visual (stellar) cues.

Within an average of 2.1 nights, they had reversed their orientation towards the direction indicated by the (altered) magnetic field. Similar effects were described by Wiltschko & Wiltschko (1988) in garden warblers (*Sylvia borin*) and robins (*Erithacus rubecula*). As with bobolinks, robins were found to be using field lines rather than polarity. Birds, it seems, use magnetic information to fly 'poleward' or 'equatorward', rather than 'north' or 'south'.

Physiological evidence

If bobolinks are preferentially following magnetic cues, they must be able to detect them. Beason conducted biochemical and anatomical studies to investigate this, and found evidence for the presence of *magnetite* in the birds' heads. Magnetite is a naturally occurring iron compound, and is magnetic.

In bobolinks, the magnetite was concentrated in the ethmoidal region of the brain (behind the nose). Microelectrodes were used to record activity from neurons in this area in anaesthetised birds. The neurones responded to alterations in the magnetic field around the bird when it was manipulated using electromagnets.

Although this does not indicate exactly where the receptor cells demonstrating a sensitivity to geomagnetic information are, or how they work, it does provide good evidence for the existence of a neural basis to geomagnetic navigation. A similar internal compass may exist in humans.

Box 40.4 Magnetic sense in humans

Murphy (1989) tested participants aged 4–18 for their ability to judge direction. They were invited into a quiet room in their school, and shown four objects around the room which were to be used in place of compass directions. They were asked to sit on a spinning chair and rotated clockwise, then anticlockwise, before stopping at each compass point in a random order. Participants made one estimate in each direction.

Comparison of male and female ability showed that females performed significantly better than chance at all ages from 9–18 years. Boys were much less accurate, performing better than chance only in the 13–14 year old group. To establish that this was the result of *magnetoreception*, Murphy tested 11–18 year old girls in two conditions, with either a brass bar or a magnet attached to the side of their head, following their initial orientation to the room. She found that the girls maintained their ability to reliably pinpoint compass directions in the 'brass bar' condition, but lost this ability with a magnet attached to their head. The magnets would have disrupted their interpretation of natural magnetic fields, thus limiting their magnetoreception.

Stellar map

The use of a stellar map to guide migration was first demonstrated in the garden warbler (*Sylvia borin*) by Sauer & Sauer (1955). These birds breed during the summer in Northern and central Europe, but *over-winter* in Africa, south of the Sahara. In common with other migrant songbirds, a caged warbler will be restless when it would otherwise be migrating. At night, when either a natural starry sky or planetarium is visible, this activity is directional and can be recorded using the apparatus described in Box 40.5. However, research suggests that the stars provide only compass information, rather than a true map. Stars can tell birds where to go, but not when to stop (Emlen 1967).

Key S T U D Y

Box 40.5 Observing *Zugunruhe*, or 'migratory restlessness'

A caged warbler can see the natural starry sky, a planetarium sky, or can receive other cues to direction. Standing on the bottom of the apparatus, the bird gets inky feet. As it becomes restless during the migratory season, it will tend to jump up onto the sides of the cone, leaving footprints. The density of colour in a particular region indicates its preferred direction of travel. The planetarium stars provide directional information, and regardless of whether this corresponds with the night sky, the birds' movements are oriented in line with the star pattern they have seen. When no sky is visible, the birds are still active, but their movements are random. Devoid of this night-time cue, they show migratory restlessness without direction.

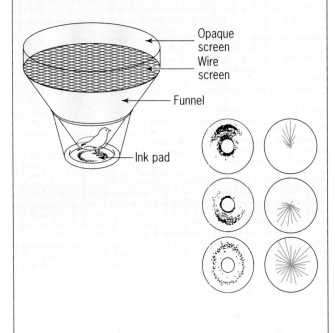

Figure 40.7 *Apparatus used to study migratory restlessness in warblers*

Star positions are not constant, although the positions of stars relative to one another is a stable cue to direction. This is because the pattern of stars on the celestial sphere appears to rotate around a fixed point. In the northern hemisphere this is Polaris, the north star. Even humans can reliably use the constellation the 'Great Bear' (Ursa major) to locate north, regardless of its position in the sky.

Are stellar maps learned or innate?

The ability to use stellar maps as a guide may be learned. Emlen (1972) observed indigo buntings (*Passerina cyanea*), reared in a planetarium where the nightly movement of the stars rotated around Betelgeuse (a star in the constellation of Orion), instead of Polaris. This gave the buntings false reference information. The young birds headed off in the opposite direction from the one they should have done if purely innate migratory mechanisms

were at work. They seemed to be using visual information about celestial rotation to calibrate a star compass.

MIGRATION

Migration refers to cyclical, long-distance travel between two specific locations. It enables animals to have the 'best of both worlds'. Their two homes provide, at different times of year, optimal environments for feeding or breeding. These alternatives must offer considerable advantages over staying in one place. Such journeys have costs, but it is assumed that for the behaviour to have evolved, the benefits must have outweighed the costs for past generations.

Figure 40.8 *Geese, like many migrants, fly from a summer breeding ground to a winter feeding ground each year*

What are the costs and benefits of migration?

Clearly, the costs in terms of energy and time spent travelling are considerable, as the distances are often vast. Inevitably, since the migrant is out of its normal range, it is exposed to greater risks (such as predation), geographical barriers (such as water, mountain ranges or deserts) and man-made obstacles. During a single night in Illinois, seven towers killed 3200 migrating birds (Fisher 1979). Unpredictable weather can also be hazardous, especially as most migrations happen when the seasons change in autumn and spring. Having left their established territory, migrants must return to compete with any conspecifics who have over-wintered, and are thus still resident.

Box 40.6 The costs of migration for the monarch butterfly

The monarch butterfly (*Danaus plexippus*) flies from Canada and North America to over-wintering sites high in the mountains of Mexico. Those that return in the spring may have made a round trip of up to 6700 km! Following a severe rain or snow storm, thousands of monarchs may die around Canada's Great Lakes, and a single freezing winter's night may kill millions of butterflies (Calvert & Brower, 1986). Surprisingly, monarchs are sufficiently robust to be tagged with sticky labels, so that the return of individuals can be recorded.

In contrast to most species, which head somewhere warmer for the winter, the monarchs, by increasing altitude, spend winter in near freezing temperatures. It has been suggested that this helps them to survive the winter by reducing their metabolic rate, so conserving their energy stores for their return flight (Cocker 1998).

Figure 40.9 *A tagged monarch butterfly*

In its favour, migration may offer a habitat that is safer in terms of temperature, weather or absence of predators, which thus promotes survival. Alternatively, the new location may offer readily available water, food, space or mates, or fewer competitors. These would increase the likelihood of raising offspring. In general, animals migrate between a safe place to spend winter and an area of plenty (albeit short lived) to mate during the summer (Urquart, 1987).

Knowing when and where to go

Birds and insects are common migratory animals. Being able to fly, they are better equipped to cover long distances without interruption from geographical features such as water or mountains. Migration in mammals is consequently largely restricted to the bigger, hoofed mammals. Wildebeest (*Connochaetes taurinus*), for example, migrate across the African plains, following the rains and retreating watering holes to find new vegetation to graze.

Figure 40.10 *Wildebeest on their annual migration across Africa in search of rains and fresh grazing*

What triggers migration?

The migration of wildebeest is primarily controlled by the availability of food and water. The impetus to move comes from the absence of resources, and there is immediate information to guide the herd to new pastures because they can see or hear the rains which herald new growth. The migration of loggerhead turtles shows a similarly immediate response to the environment.

Box 40.7 Migration of loggerhead turtles

Female loggerhead turtles lay their eggs in nests on the Atlantic coastline of Florida. The young turtles hatch, cross the beach and swim up to 50 miles to the safety and plenty of the Gulf Stream. This then leads them to the Sargasso Sea, where they spend several years, before returning to a Florida beach. Their migration to the sea is guided by moon and star light reflecting from the water's surface. Captive hatchlings will swim towards a source of light. They are unlikely to use any more sophisticated visual cues, as they are very short-sighted out of water.

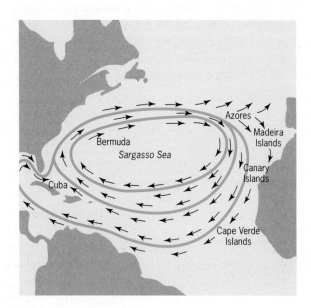

Figure 40.11 *Migratory paths of sea turtles once they have left their nesting beaches in Florida. The arrows indicate the flow of ocean currents*

The triggers for migration may not, however, be so direct. It is clearly better to be able to predict changes in climate, especially when the target location is considerably out of sensory range, than to simply respond to detectable variations. To do this, animals must know when and where to go. They need both an indicator of time, and information about the location of their goal.

Anticipating change allows animals to move before bad weather sets in, and to prepare for the journey, such as eating more if they will be unable to feed in transit. Since changing weather patterns are generally cyclical, animals can use seasonal indicators to initiate movement. In the northern hemisphere, the onset of winter is preceded by shortening day length during autumn. Animals can detect this change and use it as a signal to forewarn them to begin migration. Hence, as daylight hours decrease, animals become restless and move southward to warmer climes. The reverse occurs in spring to return the animals to their northern breeding grounds.

Day length, the key seasonal indicator, is also responsible for setting the biological clock which affects a range of biological functions (see Chapter 13). As autumn approaches and day length shortens, birds respond with an increase in pituitary gland hormones, which stimulate eating and the laying down of fat in preparation for the journey. Additionally, animals become restless, a characteristic exploited by researchers studying migration (see Box 40.5, pages 441–442). Not all species, however, migrate on an annual basis. Eel and hagfish may take several years to travel between their breeding grounds, and so other environmental or internal factors must control such cycles (Siiter, 1999).

Migratory routes

For species that are long lived and migrate in groups, knowing where to go is not an issue. The younger ones just follow the older ones. However, many more find their way without being led. Perdeck (1958) provided evidence to suggest that directional information in migrant birds may be *innate*.

Prior to their migration, Perdeck took adult starlings and hatchlings from Holland to a release site in Switzerland. From there, the adults took account of their displacement and flew on to their normal wintering grounds. The migratory orientation of the young birds, who lacked experience of the migratory route, was correct with respect to their hatching location rather than their new position.

It would appear that visual cues to location will override innate information about destination in instances of conflict. The adults were likely to have been using additional, acquired cues, such as those described earlier on.

Helbig (1991) studied two populations of the black cap (*Sylvia atricapilla*), which exhibited different migratory routes. One orientated to the south-east, the other to the south-west. When individuals from these populations were crossbred, the orientation of their offspring was intermediate between the two parental directions. This suggests that there is a genetic component in migratory route. The urge to migrate may also be genetically controlled (see Box 40.8).

As well as directional information, migrants need to know either the precise location of their goal, or how far away it is. Gwinner (1972) provided evidence for the latter in the garden warbler (*Sylvia borin*). He compared the time spent in flight by migrating juvenile birds unaccompanied by adults, and the period of migratory restlessness in captive juveniles. Calculations showed that the distance the captive birds could have flown during the time they were active closely matched that of their migratory passage. This suggests that their internal clock initiates flight for the journey time required to reach an appropriate destination. Combined with directional information, this ensures that birds will find conspecifics at the new location.

Key **STUDY**

Box 40.8 Is there an innate tendency to migrate?

The tendency to migrate seems to be innate in some species. Biebach (1983) used hand-reared robins (*Erithacus rubecula*) from a population in which some, but not all, of the adults tended to migrate. Of these hand-reared birds, 80 per cent were migrants (as indicated by their migratory restlessness), and 20 per cent were not. The birds were then allowed to mate in migrant/migrant, migrant/non-migrant and non-migrant/non-migrant pairs (five, four, and one pair respectively). In their offspring, almost 90 per cent from the migrant/migrant pairs were also migrants, but only 53 per cent of the other pairings. This suggests that there is a genetic component which predisposes robins to migrate, but that this is neither a simple genetic effect nor the only factor involved.

Studying migration

Where animals go, and how quickly they get there, are two key migration questions. Labelling animals with rings or tags enables researchers to identify where animals have come from, and this method has been used with species from butterflies to baleen whales. Individuals finding the migrants, dead or alive, can return them, or the information, to the researcher who tagged them. The probability of obtaining such information is increased by observing or trapping incoming migrants, some of which may be tagged. This, of course, requires that the animals' destination is known. For some species, this information has been elusive. For example, the over-wintering site of the monarch butterfly (see Box 40.6, page 443) was unknown to Western scientists until 1976.

Oceanic migrants, such as turtles and whales, pose a significant challenge to researchers. To increase the chance of locating the animals, they are fitted with radio transmitters. Using radio receivers, seasonal movements and the migratory routes followed can be readily studied. A baleen whale may travel 12,500 miles per year on its round-trip, a journey untraceable without the aid of electronic tracking equipment.

HOMING

The term *homing* may be used to refer to either the return of animals to their hatching/birth place after natural displacement, or following artificial transportation and release by a captor. Animals may move in search of food, to seek mates, or to find a better habitat. People, be they pigeon fanciers or psychologists, may deliberately relocate animals. In either case, the return of the animal to its nest, loft or birth place is described as homing.

Clearly, it might be possible for animals to use their memories and rely only on piloting to home successfully, since they have 'been that way before'. However, animals may home via a different route than their departure, or travel across featureless expanses, and still successfully return to their home. They must, therefore, be exploiting navigational techniques discussed earlier.

Some bird species show a remarkable ability to home. A Manx shearwater (*Puffinus puffinus*) released from Boston, Massachusetts took only 12 days to fly more than 3000 miles home to its nest in South Wales (Matthews, 1955). The albatross is able to home successfully over even greater distances. Kenyon & Rice (1958) report the Laysan albatross (*Diomedea immutabilis*) homing over distances in excess of 4100 miles!

Homing pigeons are, perhaps, the most impressive. They are able to find their way over hundreds of miles, using a range of navigational mechanisms, such that they are almost impossible to send off course. Their skills include using landmarks, piloting, dead reckoning, sun compass and internal clock, polarised light and a magnetic compass. They may even be able to use two sources of information to provide a co-ordinate based location system (Pearce, 1997: see Box 40.2, page 439).

Other cues which have been investigated include:

* tactile cues, such as the feeling of swimming upstream against the current (Hasler, 1960);

* flying into the prevailing wind (Bellrose, 1967);

* auditory cues, such as those used by whales to navigate through the oceans using echolocation to map the contours of the ocean floor to provide a map (Norris, 1967).

CONCLUSIONS

This chapter has examined navigation in non-human animals. Migration is a behaviour which enhances an animal's fitness. Whilst such journeys have costs, these must be outweighed for migrant species by the benefits to survival and reproduction offered by ensuring safer, warmer or more food-rich habitats throughout the year. Similarly, homing ensures that animals return to the security of a known area and, for some species, the advantages of their own nest or social group.

To home or migrate, animals must to be able to navigate. To find their way, they need the equivalent of a map and in some cases a compass. Such information is available to animals through their memories and their ability to detect and utilise information from landmarks, the sun, polarised light, the stars and the earth's magnetic field.

Summary

- Some animals, such as ants and the loris, find their way by leaving **olfactory trails** to follow. However, using this technique alone they could neither find their way if displaced nor take an alternative, shorter route.

- **True navigation** refers to way-finding without reference to landmarks. It requires both a 'map' to locate the goal and a 'compass' to determine direction.

- **Piloting** is a simple form of navigation relying on memory of **landmarks**. These may be olfactory, visual or auditory. Bees and gerbils use **visual** landmarks to judge direction and distance. To estimate the distance to the goal, bees use the size of the image of the landmark, whereas gerbils use **dead reckoning**.

- The **position of the sun** in its daily arc provides information about direction of travel. Clock-shifted pigeons relying solely on the sun to navigate mis-orient, although the addition of other navigational information can allow such pigeons to home accurately.

- **Polarised light** can be used to indicate direction, even when the sun is obscured. **Geomagnetism** may provide birds, bees and possibly humans with information about direction (toward or away from the pole) and location (from the dip of field lines). Some birds navigate with magnetic information, and can use it to update information from other sources such as the stars.

- **Magnetite** is an iron compound found in the heads of some birds. It is magnetic, and probably involved in their ability to detect geomagnetism. The ability of birds to navigate is disrupted when they fly through magnetically anomalous areas, during magnetic storms, and when they have magnets attached to their heads.

- Birds such as warblers use a **stellar compass** rather than a star map. This stellar information is learned, and can be artificially manipulated in a planetarium.

- **Migration** is long distance travel between two specific locations. It is costly in terms of travelling time and energy spent. Migrants may also risk exposure to predation, poor weather and dangerous obstacles, and face competition from non-migrant residents when they return.

- The benefits of migration may include an environment which offers more space, food or mates, is safer, with better weather and fewer predators or competitors. By optimising their summer and winter habitats, animals maximise their fitness.

- The immediate trigger for migration may be direct, such as availability of food or water, or indirect, such as day length. Animals benefit from being able to anticipate changes, and moving in the right direction before they occur.

- Evidence from starlings and warblers suggests that information about direction and distance of migration are innate. Crossbreeding experiments with robins suggest there is a **genetic** tendency for the birds to show a predisposition to migrate.

- **Homing** is the return of an animal to its place of origin, following natural or artificial displacement. An albatross can home from distances over 4100 miles.

Essay Questions

1 Discuss explanations of homing in non-humans.
(24 marks)

2 Describe and evaluate research studies into homing
   and migration in non-human animals. *(24 marks)*

WEBSITE ADDRESSES

http://www.tbone.biol.sc.edu/
http://www.rin.org.uk/rin_sigs.html
http://www.biologists.com/JEB/01/jeb0110.html
http://www.biologists.com/JEB/182/01/jeb8902.html

41 *Animal Communication and Language*

INTRODUCTION AND OVERVIEW

This chapter explores *animal communication*, both in the natural environment and in the laboratory. Some of the behaviours described in Chapters 39 and 40 require interaction between individuals. Successful exchange of information relies upon individuals being able to signal their knowledge or intentions to one another. Animal communication, like any behaviour, is subject to selection pressures; signals which enhance fitness should evolve. It is reasonable to expect, therefore, that communication should play an essential role in animals' survival and reproduction.

Signals about food, finding a mate, or danger have clear implications for the fitness of both the sender and the receiver. The first part of this chapter considers three different *signalling systems* using *vision*, *sound* and *smell*, and discusses their relative merits for different species. Some of the signalling systems used in the wild are complex, and might even constitute '*language*'. The second part of this chapter discusses research studies of *natural animal language*, and *laboratory attempts to teach language to non-human animals*.

SIGNALLING SYSTEMS IN NON-HUMAN ANIMALS

The function of communication is to serve senders and recipients, but it can only do so if it is effective and reliable. To avoid errors, signals are consistent and situation specific. Species differ in their capacity to communicate, and in the media available within their habitat. Therefore, they use different *signalling systems*. *Visual* (sight), *auditory* (sound), *olfactory* (smell), *tactile* (touch) and *gustatory* (taste) senses are used. Many animals exploit combinations of signals, or use different systems for different functions. This chapter concentrates on discussing the first three sensory systems, but first it will be useful to consider what is meant by the term 'signal'.

What is a signal?

What is a message, and how do we know when one has been communicated? We all know that sending messages is not the same as communicating. We can talk without being listened to, and send e-mails that 'bounce'. *Communication* is a two-way process, in which a message is conveyed from a sender to one or more recipients. Its reception is denoted by a change in the recipient. For example, Tinbergen & Perdeck (1950) studied the begging behaviour of herring gull chicks (*Larus argentatus*). The chicks beg for food using a signal, namely pecking a red spot on the parent bird's bill. The reception of this

signal is indicated by the parent's response of feeding the chick. Note the difference between this *active* communication by the chick, and the *passive* sign (a sign stimulus) of the red spot on the parent's bill.

Figure 41.1 *A chick communicates its need for food with a pecking signal*

Signals provide information of benefit to the recipient. In the herring gull, the parent is informed about when to feed its young to maximise growth and minimise wasted effort. The sender also benefits because the chick gets fed. Other benefits could include gaining a mate through courtship signals (increasing individual fitness), or assisting kin by giving an alarm call (raising inclusive fitness).

For communication to be effective, the sender and recipient must attach the same *meaning* to the signal. Without this correspondence, the mutual benefits are lost. So, a *signal* is a deliberate message, sent to one or more recipients. Decoding the message results in behavioural or other changes in the recipient, and consequent benefits to both parties.

Communication can only evolve if it is of benefit to both signaller and recipient. If it is not, the tendency to expend effort in sending messages or responding to them, will be eliminated by natural selection. Once established, however, communication signals can be exploited, as shown in Table 41.1.

Table 41.1 *Signal legitimacy and effects on fitness*

Effect on fitness		Term used	Description
Signaller	Receiver		
+	+	Communication	Legitimate signaller and receiver
–	+	Eavesdropping	Legitimate signaller, illegitimate receiver
+	–	Deceitful signalling	Illegitimate signaller, legitimate receiver

+ represents an increase in fitness; – represents a decrease in fitness.

Box 41.1 Eavesdropping and deceitful signalling

Unintended recipients may benefit from the content of a message or simply by deducing the location of the sender. For example, the scent released by a female bark beetle to attract a mate also attracts competing females to the signaller's egg-laying site. These *eavesdropping* females gain, because they avoid spending time and energy searching for a suitable tree. The signalling female loses, because her offspring must compete with those of the cheats (Raffa & Berryman, 1983). Predators may be the unintended recipients of calls or displays that provide them with a meal, whilst the signaller suffers the ultimate cost of its life.

Hoverflies (*Helophilus pendulus*) send a *deceitful* message to potential predators by mimicing wasps. This signals that they are dangerous, without incurring the costs associated with generating a sting and venom, and the duped predator loses the chance of a palatable meal. Male cricket frogs (*Acris crepitans blanchardi*) use auditory signals to display their

strength to their competitors, with lower tones indicating a stronger male. Males may be deceitful by lowering the tone of their call during a signalling session, suggesting that they are stronger than they really are (Wagner, 1992). To counter this, other males can judge whether or not to fight as the initial tone produced is usually a reliable indicator of strength.

Visual signalling systems

Visual signalling systems are one of the easiest to study. As illegitimate receivers (eavesdroppers), psychologists can readily observe both the signals sent and the response of target individuals. The visual signalling system is a flexible one, as the nature of the message can be varied according to *position, movement* and *colour*.

Animals can adopt static positions or postures which convey particular meaning to others. These may be exaggerated by physical structures. For example, the threatening stance of a robin (*Erithacus rubecula*) is enhanced by fluffing up the breast feathers. It is better able to defend its territory by looking larger and more aggressive to potential competitors. Postures may form part of a sequence of movements (or *gestures*), such as the courtship dances performed by great crested grebes (*Podiceps cristatus*).

Figure 41.2 *Courtship of the great crested grebe* (Podiceps cristatus) *(Huxley, 1914). On inland waters, from midwinter onwards, the great crested grebe can be seen performing its elaborate courtship dance. The male and female may play different roles, as in assuming the 'cat' position (where their partner stands upright in the 'ghost' position), or during invitations to mate. Sometimes the male and female mirror each other's behaviour, such as during the head-shaking ceremony and in the 'weed' or 'penguin' dance. This is where the birds, each with a beakful of weed, rise up in the water to perform an exaggerated version of the head-shaking ceremony. (a) Cat position, (b), invitation, (c) approach, (d) clicking calls accompany swaying of the heads. (c) and (d) are stages in the head-shaking ceremony*

The use of colour in signalling is clearly seen in the display of peacocks (*Pavo cristatus*: see Box 43.1, page 473). Colour is also fundamental to the responses of robins. A robin will attack just a few red feathers nailed to a stake in its territory, but will ignore a whole stuffed robin that has been painted brown (Lack, 1943). The coloured feathers of a dominant male ruff (*Philomachus pugnax*, a wading bird) indicate his status to females during courtship. Subordinate males have white ruffs and get fewer mates.

When we see a visual signal and the corresponding response of a receiver, we can infer the meaning of the signal. On some occasions, the mechanism by which the signal has arisen is obvious, often because there is some functional significance to the signalling behaviour itself. In the courtship of the common tern (*Sterna hirundo*, a sea bird), the male provides the female with fish to eat. This is a signal for mating to proceed, and implies that the male is a good forager and will provide well for his mate and their young (Nisbet, 1977).

Box 41.2 The evolution of a worthless visual courtship signal

The wedding gift of the male balloon fly (*Hilara sartor*) is difficult to explain, since it consists of a hollow silken ball (Kessel, 1955). Why does he offer it, and why must the female receive this apparently bizarre signal as a prerequisite to mating? The comparative method in animal behaviour offers a way to answer questions about how behaviours may have evolved. It provides a means to deduce hypothetical evolutionary sequences, by identifying a plausible series of changes based on the behaviour of present-day species.

The suggestion is not that these are ancestral forms, but that they represent possible behaviours of earlier forms. There are several thousand species of empid fly (from the same family as *Hilara sartor*), which show diverse courtship patterns. The flow-chart below offers a possible evolutionary pathway, which could have led to the balloon fly's courtship signal. The starting point is a simple, understandable, behaviour. Through the course of evolution, this transforms to one which is apparently worthless and consequently incomprehensible in isolation.

Carnivorous flies hunt for smaller insects, such as midges. The females are courted in isolation.

↓

The male carnivorous flies capture prey, then seek a female. She takes the prey prior to copulation and consumes it to provide herself with energy.

↓

Prey capture and courtship as above, but males with prey form groups to attract females.

↓

As above, but the male restrains the prey with strands of silk.

↓

As above, but the prey is entirely wrapped in silk

↓

As above, but before wrapping, the male removes juices from the prey, so the female receives a non-nutritious husk.

↓

Nectar-feeding species find an insect fragment around which to construct a silk balloon. This is presented to the female before copulation.

↓

Hilara sartor omits the insect fragment, constructing only a silken ball to present to the female.

Behaviours such as those of the balloon fly and grebe are described as being *ritualised*, that is, evolution has operated to make the signal more effective. Ritualisation makes signals *conspicuous* (improving detection by the receiver), and *stereotyped* (reducing the likelihood of a misunderstanding).

When considering the evolution of behaviour, we must remember the explanations given in Chapter 37. Signals, like any other actions, evolve because they are *adaptive*, and enhance the fitness of the signaller. The evolution of communication seems complex, because it appears to require a simultaneous change in the behaviour of both signaller and recipient. There can be no value in a signal, no matter how elaborate, unless it is understood and acted upon by the intended recipient.

This problem is not, however, as complex as it first appears. Novel signals are simply new behaviours to which others respond in advantageous ways. The key element is the *effect* of the action on other individuals, rather than the nature of the signal. It can be similar to existing behaviours, such as variations of aggression, preening or parental care, but does not have to be. Signals may be unrelated to the message conveyed, but still be effective. If, however, new behaviours were to arise which were effective signals, but carried large costs (for example, attracted predators), they would probably be eliminated by natural selection.

Advantages and disadvantages of visual signalling systems

The variables of colour, position and movement offer an enormous variety of messages, and their complexity is one way to ensure that they are understood. If a signal differs greatly from another, it is less likely to be misinterpreted. Some visual signals, such as colours, are enduring and have few costs (they use little energy to maintain). Their permanence ensures that when a potential recipient is encountered, it is unable to avoid the message. Hence, signalling and reception are guaranteed.

One disadvantage of visual signalling is that the certainty of reception relies on encountering conspecifics (members of the same species), and this cannot be assured. Furthermore, postures and gestures are transient (lasting only a short time) and energetic, and are more costly than colour signals. A vigorously moving animal uses energy, and runs the risk of attracting predators. Because the recipient has to be nearby and within a line of sight, visual signalling is not as effective over a long range as other media. Finally, visual signals are useless in the dark unless, of course, the organism is *bioluminescent* (generates its own light), such as fire flies (*Photinus consimilus*).

Auditory signalling systems

Auditory communication, like visual signalling, is highly flexible. Messages can vary in terms of *pitch, volume* or *sequence*. In toads, the pitch of the male's croak indicates his size to females, who prefer deep croaks as these imply bigger, fitter males. The sequence of notes produced by crickets (*Gryllus integer*), using their legs, informs potential mates of the sender's species. In many forms of auditory communication, all three variables are changed, producing a huge array of potential signals. Human language provides an example of communication which exploits this variability to the full (see Chapter 26).

One advantage of living in a social group is a reduction in risk from predators. In animals such as ground squirrels (*Spermophilus beldingi*), this is achieved by the communication of impending threats between group members. For vervet monkeys (*Cercopithecus aethiops*), the nature of the hazard dictates the most appropriate response – there is no point in going up a tree to avoid a martial eagle! For signals to be helpful to the recipients, the message must indicate the appropriate response.

Seyfarth *et al.* (1980) studied vervet alarm calls through observations and field experiments. By using recordings of different calls, they could be sure that it was the auditory message, not some other feature of the situation, that was informing the vervets about appropriate evasive behaviour. They described three distinct alarms for different predators, which produce different responses.

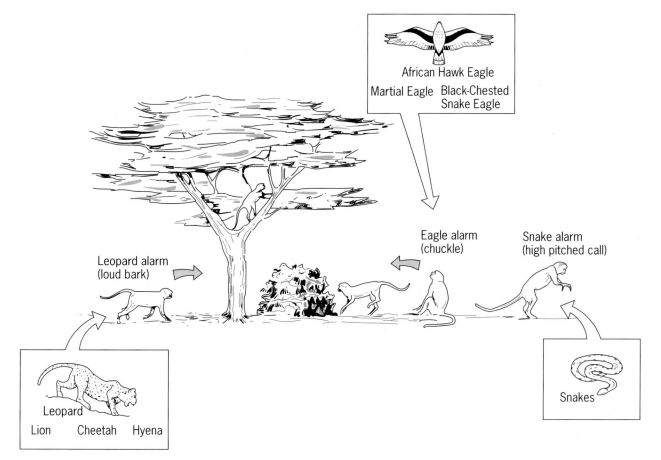

Figure 41.3 *Vervet monkey* (Cercopithecus aethiops) *alarm calls. Different signals elicit appropriate predator-avoidance behaviours*

Advantages and disadvantages of auditory signalling systems

Sound is a highly effective medium for communication. It is both penetrating and flexible. Van Bushkirk (1997) discovered that similar species of bird living in different habitats exploit the auditory medium to their best advantage. Birds living in deciduous forests need penetrating calls to travel long distances. They use lower frequency calls than their 'open country' cousins.

Complex and variable messages can be created with sound, as illustrated by the diversity of bird song. Even when similar species of bird inhabit the same area, they can be distinguished by their song, which is essential for their potential mates. To ensure that a young bird acquires a song that others will recognise, it learns the fine details by listening to adults singing. It knows which adults to copy, because it has an innate 'blue print' on to which to map the correct 'full song' (see Box 37.4, page 402).

If you happen to be looking the wrong way, it is possible to 'miss' a visual signal. It is much more difficult to avoid receiving an auditory message if you are within earshot. On land, sound will permeate some structures and bounce off others, thus travelling 'around corners' which visual signals cannot do.

The features that make sound such a good medium for sending and receiving legitimate messages also make errors more likely and cheating easier. Vervet alarm calls, for example, are learned. During infancy, vervets make errors in their calls and responses with potentially fatal consequences (see Chapter 39, page 427). The sounds intended for conspecifics could be abused by others. Predators, for example, can use messages intended for legitimate receivers to locate prey. It is interesting to note that alarm calls are similar across many species. This is an attempt to counter their illegitimate reception, as the frequencies used make the source hard to locate.

Box 41.3 Deceitful signal senders

Male great tits (*Parus major*) pronounce ownership of their territory using between two and seven different songs. They tend to change song each time they change perch (Krebs, 1977). This behaviour could deceitfully indicate to prospecting males that there were more occupied territories in the area than really existed. However, this may not be the reason that intruders are deterred. They may be aware that all the calls emanate from the same male, but his scope for song may be (correctly) interpreted as an indicator of age or strength. Therefore, the appropriate judgement would be to depart (Yasukawa, 1981).

Olfactory signalling systems

Olfaction is the process of detecting and identifying smells. *Pheromones* are volatile chemicals released by animals, which have an effect on the physiology or behaviour of conspecifics. *Releaser pheromones* have a short-term effect, initiating the performance of a behaviour in the recipient. *Primer pheromones* have longer term effects, often operating by changing the recipient's physiology, such as altering hormone activity.

The territories of many animals are marked by scent. This can be an enduring message that does not require the signaller's continual activity. Pheromones left in urine, or anal scent deposits, clearly indicate the presence of a resident. For example, house mice (*Mus domesticus*) use odours in urine to mark out their territories (Hurst, 1990). Many other species, including badgers (*Meles meles*), otters (*Lutra lutra*), dogs (*Canis familiaris*) and domestic and wild cats mark out their territories using scent.

In some species, the status of an individual can be deduced from its scent marking. Rozenfeld & Rasmont (1991) investigated odour recognition in bank voles (*Clethrionomys glareolus*). Dominant voles deposited their own urine and faeces over that of other rodents, 'over marking' it. Voles can also deduce the sex and status of individuals from their olfactory signals.

Sexual behaviour is highly sensitive to olfactory cues. For example, male moths are attracted to sexually active females by their scent (see Figure 41.4). This is an example of a *releaser pheromone*.

Figure 41.4 *The antennae of a male moth. Some are so sensitive that they can detect a female moth over a mile away*

In order to detect females effectively, males have large fluffy antennae, and are capable of detecting just a few molecules of the pheromone the females release. Each antenna of a male silk worm moth (*Bombix mori*) is covered with about 10,000 sensory hairs. A single molecule of the female's pheromone, *bombykol*, is sufficient to activate a sensory hair cell (Schneider, 1969).

Box 41.4 Pheromones and incest-avoidance

Pheromones can serve another function in sexual behaviour, namely the avoidance of *inbreeding* (being able to select an unrelated mate increases fitness). Simmons (1990) demonstrated that female crickets (*Gryllus bimaculatus*) were sensitive to scent cues as well as auditory ones. The females were able to differentiate between olfactory signals from individuals with various degrees of kinship. They preferred the odour of males who were not related to them.

After the birth of offspring, pheromones are important in the formation of attachments between the mother and offspring. The maintenance of paternal care may also be under pheromonal control. Male California mice (*Peromyscus californicus*) respond with parental behaviour to odours present in their mate's excreta, licking the pups and huddling over them (Gubernick, 1990).

Table 41.2 *Signalling systems compared*

Criterion	System and its effectiveness		
	Vision	Audition	Olfaction
Operates in darkness	✓	✓	✓
Difficult to obstruct	✗	✓	✓
Can reach moving target	✗ & ✓	✓	✓
Operates in windy weather	✓	✓	✗
Unaffected by pollution	✓	✓	✗
Variable messages possible	✓	✓	✗
Lasting message	✗ & ✓	✗	✓
Little risk of attracting predators	✗	✗	✓
Effective without attention of recipient	✗	✓	✓

✓ – signalling system fulfils criterion;
✗ – signalling system does not fulfil criterion.

Advantages and disadvantages of olfactory signalling systems

Communicating by smell combines some of the advantages of both vision and audition. Like auditory signals, smells can cover long distances, and are relatively uninterrupted by obstacles. They can reach recipients who are moving or not paying attention. Olfactory signals can also travel in darkness. Like colours, pheromones are lasting, and require little 'maintenance' to perpetuate. However, olfaction has some disadvantages. Pheromonal signals can be interrupted by poor weather, obliterated by rain, or blown in the wind (which would send an intended recipient off course).

ANIMAL LANGUAGE

Opinion about the existence of language in non-humans is divided (Lewin, 1991). The *discontinuity school* sees language as being uniquely human, and regards communication in non-humans as being fundamentally different from human language (Chomsky, cited in Wyman, 1983). The *continuity school*, by contrast, sees language as part of a cognitive continuum, the roots of which lie in our ape-like ancestors.

According to Darwin's theory of the evolutionary origin of species, humans are only *quantitatively*, rather than *qualitatively*, different from non-humans. If Darwin's assertion about the evolutionary origin of species is correct, then it should be possible to show that non-human communication systems constitute 'language', or that non-humans at least possess the capacity to *learn* language (see Chapter 26, pages 277–279).

Box 41.5 Ten criteria for language

Ten generalised features of language which have sometimes been used to evaluate the existence of language in non-human animals are:

- *Symbolic/semantic:* The communication system uses arbitrary symbols, which have shared meaning for the communicators.
- *Specialisation:* The symbols used are employed only for communication, and are not the by-product of another behavioural system.
- *Displacement:* The system can be used to describe things which are absent in time or space (e.g. past events or hidden objects).
- *Generativity:* The system allows for the production of an infinite variety of novel utterances.

- *Phonological and lexical syntax:* Language is dependent on a rule-based structure. This has rules for the combination of basic units (e.g. sounds: phonological syntax) and the combination of higher level units (e.g. words: lexical syntax).

- *Spontaneous acquisition:* Users acquire basic language spontaneously, without formal instruction or reinforcement. Only then can subsequent languages, or language elements, be learned.

- *Critical period:* The acquisition of fluency in a first language is limited to an early phase in life.

- *Cultural transmission:* Language, with changes accumulated by one generation, is passed to the next by its use.

- *Interchangeable roles:* Language users can be both transmitters and recipients of language.

- *Conversation:* By alternating roles, language users can exchange information about a shared understanding.

One way of resolving the 'animal language' issue is to identify the characteristics that all human languages share, and see if they are also found in non-human communication in the natural world. Another way is to see if non-humans who are given *training* can satisfy particular criteria sufficiently well enough to be considered 'language users'. Evidence for either of these approaches would support the continuity school.

Vervet monkeys

As noted previously (see page 451 and Chapter 39), vervet monkeys use a 'vocabulary' of calls to indicate the presence of specific predators, and each call elicits a different response in others. To what extent does this communication system satisfy the criteria for language identified in Box 41.5?

Symbolic/semantic

Each call is meaningful. Whether it means 'I can see a particular predator' or 'make a particular escape response' is difficult to determine, but the semantic value of each call is indicated by the consistent response from the receivers. The calls themselves are arbitrary (the sounds are not related to their meaning), and so can be described as symbolic.

Specialisation

The extent to which vervet calls are used exclusively for communication is unclear. They may have evolved from

fear responses, but because they are predator specific, this explanation alone is insufficient. An animal that was merely vocalising in response to fear would be unlikely to demonstrate such reliable distinctions in its sounds, or to broadcast its fear so widely.

Displacement and generativity

The criterion of displacement is partially satisfied because the receiver, on hearing the alarm call, makes an appropriate escape response without seeing the predator (it is not simply being alerted to look for a predator). However, the same displacement does not apply to the sender. There is simply no need to send warnings about predators who are not there in time or space. Indeed, to do so would be maladaptive. Vervet calls are not, however, 'generative', because they serve only to communicate about a limited range of events in a restricted way.

Phonological and lexical syntax

Alarm calls cannot be usefully combined. Unlike human language, a sequence of calls does not convey more information, or different meanings, than each call would do individually.

Spontaneous acquisition, critical period and cultural transmission

Cheney & Seyfarth's (1990) observations of young vervets suggests that their calling ability develops as a result of both genetic and cultural factors (see Chapter 39, page 427). Young vervets give alarm calls to a wider category of objects (both animate and inanimate) than adults. However, there is a certain 'logic' in their calling. The existence of a predisposition to respond to particular categories of objects as different predators suggests an innate element to the calls.

Juvenile vervets imitate adult behaviour, and adults refine juvenile behaviour by reiterating their calls only when they are appropriate. This is a cultural element in the transmission of the calls, and essentially resembles the acquisition of human language. As noted in Chapter 26, Chomsky (1965) believes that humans have an innate processing capacity (the *language acquisition device*). This governs the *way* language is learned, but *what* is learnt (the specific language) is determined by the environment.

Interchangeable roles and conversation

The roles of sender and receiver are often interchangeable, although particular individuals may call more often. There is no evidence of conversation between vervets using alarm calls, which are only employed in response to the stimulus of a predator. Juvenile vervets do not produce false alarm calls just to see others respond.

Honey bees

Honey bees (*Apis mellifera*) perform *dances* to communicate complex information about the direction and distance of food sources (see also Chapter 40, pages 439–440).

Key S T U D Y

Box 41.6 The dance of the honey bees (von Frisch, 1956, 1967)

The round dance
This is used by worker bees to communicate that food has been found near to the hive (up to 50 metres away). As shown in Figure 41.5, a bee moves in a circular path, indicated by the arrows, on the vertical face of the comb inside the hive. The dance is attended by other workers, who then leave the hive to search for the food.

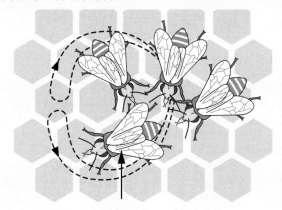

Figure 41.5 *The round dance (see text)*

The waggle dance
Worker bees uses this to communicate that food has been found at a more distant source. The dance indicates both the distance and direction of the food. Like the round dance, it is performed in darkness on the vertical face of the comb. The bee dances in a figure-of-8 pattern, followed by other workers. The angle of the waggle communicates information about the direction in which to fly. The direction of the food source relative to the sun is translated by the dancer into an angle relative to gravity. If the food can be found by flying directly towards the sun, the waggle is performed in a vertical run which points upwards. If the food is directly away from the sun, the worker waggles on a downward-pointing run (see Figure 41.6, a and b).

If the other workers must fly at an angle, say 40° clockwise from the sun, then the dancers tilt the waggle run at 40° clockwise from the vertical (see Figure 41.6, c and d).

Any direction can thus be encoded by the dance. Surprisingly, the distance the bees must fly is indi-

cated by the vigour of the dance (we might expect a bee who had flown a long way to be less active). The number of complete cycles of the dance, and the number and duration of waggles all increase with distance from the hive. A bee that has travelled a long way must ensure her followers know exactly where to go as they have more scope for getting lost.

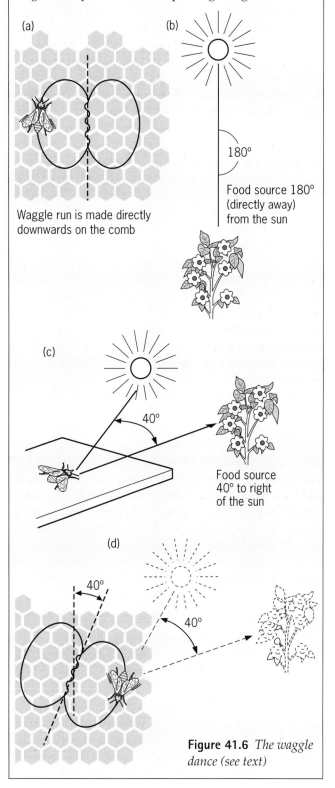

(a) Waggle run is made directly downwards on the comb

(b) 180° Food source 180° (directly away) from the sun

(c) 40° Food source 40° to right of the sun

(d) 40° 40°

Figure 41.6 *The waggle dance (see text)*

The waggle dance is *symbolic*, because it uses angles and vigour to convey meaning about direction and distance respectively. The signals are *specialised*, and by communicating about something which is absent, they also show *displacement*. Moreover, the roles of the transmitter and recipient are *interchangeable*. So, the honey bee dance satisfies at least some of the criteria identified in Box 41.5, pages 453–454.

The symbols used by bees may *not* be truly *arbitrary*. Although the direction of the dance does not point to the food, there is a one-to-one correspondence between the two dimensions. This is like representing numbers with longer and longer words. The bees' signals are restricted to two fixed 'linguistic dimensions', rather than being representative in the way that we can signify *tall* with a small word, *short* with a longer word, and *average* with a longer word still. The size of the concept and the size of the word are unrelated. Similarly, the waggle dance could be described as *generative*, as the bees can communicate about novel locations. However, this is hardly creative on the same scale as human language.

Griffin & Taft (1992) investigated the *sounds* made by honey bees during the waggle dance, and found that they convey the same message as the waggles. The sound's duration correlates closely with the waggle's duration, so the two are equivalent indicators of distance. However, the auditory component may be displaced in time, and is sometimes as long as one second behind the movements. This delay does not appear to communicate any additional information about the food source.

Humans can convey the same message *simultaneously*, using two signalling skills (e.g. saying no and shaking the head). Such reinforcement of a message ensures that it is not misunderstood. Although the waggle dance exhibits displacement by informing other bees about a distant food source, it could be argued that the bees are not 'talking about' that distance, but giving instructions. Certainly, there is no element of *conversation*, and there is little evidence to suggest that the waggle dance satisfies the criteria of *phonological/lexical syntax*, *spontaneous acquisition*, *critical period* or *cultural transmission*. It is therefore unlikely that honey bees have language.

Birds

Box 41.7 Is birdsong true language?

Chapter 37 (see Box 37.4, page 402) discussed the development of birdsong. Such songs are *symbolic* in that the meanings of territoriality or courtship are shared, but they are really only elaborate signals.

Birdsong is, though, a highly *specialised* form of communication. However, it conforms to Chomsky's (1965) idea of a system with a fixed number of signals which are produced in response to a specific range of triggers. Thus, although varied, birdsong cannot be described as *generative*. Similarly, birdsong lacks *syntax*, as there are too few elements to recombine meaningfully. Furthermore, birds do not demonstrate varied, alternating exchanges, which could qualify as *conversations*.

Birds do, however, illustrate clear *spontaneous acquisition* that is restricted to a *critical period* in early life. Changes in song are, as a consequence, passed on to subsequent generations as they absorb the learned element of their song, illustrating *cultural transmission* (see Chapter 37, page 407). As with the bees' waggle dance, birdsong only satisfies a few of the criteria for true language.

Chimpanzees

Chimpanzees (*Pan troglodytes*) use various facial expressions, sounds and gestures to communicate, although none seems complex or varied enough to constitute language. However, there is evidence to suggest that wild primates can learn complex skills and imagine a situation from another individual's perspective (Boesch, 1991). These abilities could imply a *capacity* to learn language.

Boesch observed adult chimpanzees demonstrating techniques for cracking nuts using a stone hammer to their offspring (see Box 39.1, page 423). The observations suggested that adult chimpanzees are able to compare their offspring's performance to an internal concept of the way a behaviour *should* appear. From this, they could anticipate the effects of these actions and the consequences of modifications in performance, both of which are essential to language.

Being able to understand that there can be a viewpoint different from one's own, and predicting the likely outcome of a change in behaviour, is indicative of complex cognitive processes. These perspective and turn-taking skills are fundamental to aspects of language, such as *cultural transmission*, *displacement* and *conversation*.

Further evidence of the chimpanzee's ability to consider the perspective of others has been provided by Povinelli *et al.* (1992: see Box 39.7, pages 432–433). So, although chimpanzees demonstrate little by way of language in the wild, other aspects of their comprehension and behaviour suggest that they may have some skills which underlie language acquisition.

TEACHING LANGUAGE TO NON-HUMAN ANIMALS

As the previous section has shown, studies of non-humans in their natural habitats indicate that *some* aspects of their communication resembles language. Other research has attempted to *teach* language to non-humans. Birds, cetaceans and primates have all been the focus of research interest. Birds are good potential candidates for learning language because:

- they use a complex form of communication in their natural habitat;

- birdsong is, at least in part, *acquired* (indicating that birds are able to learn to communicate);

- they use the auditory channel for communication, making it easy to measure the success of teaching and learning.

Some bird species, such as parrots, are remarkably good mimics. This further enhances their suitability for research into language acquisition. Pepperberg (1983) taught Alex, an African grey parrot (*Psittacus erithacus*), a vocabulary of about 150 spoken words. Alex uses these words to request objects and categorise them (such as *same* or *different*) in response to questions about colour and shape. Although he does not respond with absolute accuracy, the language Alex uses clearly satisfies the criteria of *symbolic/semantic*, *specialised*, and *interchangeable roles*.

Cetaceans

Cetaceans communicate in the wild with a complex array of auditory signals. Their capacity to learn language has been investigated by Herman *et al.* (1984) using two bottlenosed dolphins (*Tursiops truncatus*). Akeakamai was taught with a language based on visual signs, whereas Phoenix was taught an acoustic language.

Using the visual signs, Akeakamai responded accurately to novel four-word sentences whose meaning was dependent upon word order. This indicated that she could comprehend the grammar of the sentences. Phoenix could respond to five-word sentences, where the instruction involved a verb relating two objects, both with related modifiers such as 'surface hoop fetch bottom basket' ('go to the hoop at the surface and take it to the basket at the bottom').

The technique of teaching dolphins to understand, rather than produce, language has the advantage of readily demonstrating their linguistic comprehension. It is easier to set a task and see if an animal performs it (indicating understanding) than to wait for the spontaneous generation of utterances in a language which may or may not have been acquired. The technique also offers greater precision, as the instructions can be rigorously controlled and the responses readily classified as correct or incorrect. However, the technique does not allow for *conversation*. Although the dolphins may comprehend and respond correctly, they cannot reply.

Key **STUDY**

Box 41.8 Syntax in the dolphin

Herman *et al.* (1993) investigated Akeakamai's ability to respond to complex visual language by testing her understanding of syntax. The findings suggested that she could use a rule-based language, as she was able to identify instances of the experimenters breaking the rules. For example, when an anomalous sequence of gestures was presented to her, Akeakamai sometimes rejected them. This indicated an awareness of an error, because she never refused normal sequences. In this sense, Akeakamai's language skills not only satisfy the rules of *symbolic/semantic* and the *specialised criteria*, but also of using *syntax*.

Primates

Early research into the possibility of non-humans acquiring language involved attempts to teach chimpanzees to *speak*. Kellogg & Kellogg (1933) raised Gua alongside their own son, Donald. Although Gua displayed some of the same abilities as Donald, such as moving around and grasping objects, she did not display any evidence of vocalising in the way Donald did. Although she could understand a few words, she failed to utter a single one.

Hayes & Hayes (1951) raised Viki from infancy in their own home. Viki wore nappies, and was generally treated as though she was a human infant. However, despite the intensive training she was given over three years, Viki managed to utter only a few simple words, namely 'mam', 'pap', 'cup' and 'up', and even these were difficult for her trainers to understand.

As Vygotsky (1962) noted, early researchers confused human *language* with human *speech*. Kellogg (1968) pointed out that chimpanzees' vocal apparatus is unsuitable for making English speech sounds, and subsequent research has shown that the brain mechanisms by which humans are able to control their vocal apparatus are not present in chimpanzees. As a result, other studies have attempted to teach language to chimpanzees using *non-vocal techniques*.

Vygotsky (1962) argued that using *sign language* would be a more sensible approach, because the actions involved are within a chimpanzee's competence.

Moreover, because human and chimpanzee hand dexterity are more or less the same, any limitations in acquiring language would be purely cognitive. Research which has used *Ameslan* (American Sign Language: ASL) to teach chimpanzees includes that of Gardner & Gardner (1969, 1977), Patterson & Linden (1981) and Terrace (1979). Alternatives to sign language have used plastic symbols of varying shapes and colours (Premack & Premack, 1972), and a computer keyboard (*lexigram*) consisting of keys which display a geometric pattern (Rumbaugh & Savage-Rumbaugh, 1978).

Box 41.9 Aitchison's criteria for language

Rather than using the ten criteria for language identified in Box 41.5 (see pages 453–454), Aitchison (1983) has proposed that there are *four* features which distinguish between true language (that is, language used by humans) and the communication systems of non-humans:

Semanticity: The use of symbols to mean or refer to objects, actions, relational concepts (such as 'over' and 'in'), and so on.

Displacement: The ability to make reference to events and objects in another time or place.

Creativity: The capacity to combine symbols so as to produce (and understand when the symbols are combined by someone else) 'original' language.

Structure dependence: An understanding of the 'patterned' nature of language and the use of 'structured chunks', such as word order.

A detailed discussion of the findings relating to the various primates that have been studied can be found in Gross & McIlveen (1997). However, Table 41.3 summarises the findings from studies of four primates in terms of Aitchison's criteria for true language.

The findings are at least *supportive* of the view that the ability to acquire language is not unique to humans. However, one of the fiercest critics of such research has been Terrace (1979). He studied a male chimpanzee ('Nim'), who was taught ASL. Nim eventually learned 125 basic signs, and Terrace and his colleagues attempted to record every statement that Nim made.

Table 41.3 *Summary of the findings of studies of four primates in relation to Aitchison's criteria for true language*

	Washoe	Sarah	Lana	Koko
	Female chimpanzee studied by Gardner & Gardner (1969, 1977) and taught ASL	Female chimpanzee studied by Premack (1971), Premack & Premack (1972), and taught with plastic symbols	Female chimpanzee studied by Savage-Rumbaugh *et al.* (1980) and taught using a computer keyboard	Female gorilla studied by Patterson (1980) using ASL
Semanticity criterion	After 5 years could use 160 signs, and generalised these from one situation to another	Learned the meaning of over 100 words, including complex ideas such as 'colour of'	Learned over 100 symbols and could generalise these	After 7 years training had acquired over 400 signs, and understands many English words for those signs
Displacement criterion	Could ask for or refer to absent objects/people	No evidence of this was found	Some evidence that she could refer to things not physically present	Supposedly apologised for a biting incident 3 days before
Structure dependence criterion	Was just as likely to sign 'sweet go' as 'go sweet', although her use of word order eventually became consistent	Could follow instructions and answer simple questions	Could distinguish between 'Tim groom Lana' and 'Lana groom Tim'	No evidence of this displayed
Creativity criterion	Once 8–10 signs were learned, Washoe spontaneously began to combine them (e.g. 'hurry gimme toothbrush')	Did not spontaneously produce new sentences	Was able to combine words in her vocabulary for objects she had no word for (e.g a cucumber was referred to as 'banana which is green')	Was able to combine words in her vocabulary for objects she had no word for (e.g. a Pinocchio doll was referred to as 'elephant baby')

Within two years, they had recorded over 20,000 statements consisting of two or more signs. However, after studying videotapes of Nim, Terrace concluded that whilst Nim could produce a large number of combinations of his 125 signs, he was essentially just imitating his trainers rather than creatively communicating new information.

In Terrace's (1985) view, no research, his own included, has shown spontaneous utterances from non-humans which are 'not whole or partial imitations of the teacher's most recently signed utterances'. According to Rumbaugh & Savage-Rumbaugh (1994), researchers have mistakenly concentrated on the *production* of language rather than its *comprehension*. As they have noted, children understand speech before they can produce it, yet the studies so far described expected primates to generate speech before they had a basis from which to comprehend it. If so, it is not surprising that critics see the studies as demonstrating little more than sophisticated signalling. Without the underlying comprehension, it would be impossible for primates to be productive.

Rumbaugh & Savage-Rumbaugh have conducted several language-learning projects. In these, chimpanzees were reared in *language-structured* environments, in which language was used around them to announce and co-ordinate social activities. For example, in an attempt to overcome the lack of investment in comprehension, two chimpanzees, Sherman and Austin, were initially taught to listen to each other. Eventually, they learned to use language to co-operate for mutual benefit (Anderson *et al.*, 1996).

Figure 41.7 *Panbanisha and Panzee using the lexigram keyboard*

Language acquisition in pygmy chimpanzees

The first attempt to teach a pygmy chimpanzee was with Matata, a wild-born animal, introduced to the laboratory when she was five years old. She was spoken to in English, and used a lexigram keyboard with a matrix of 256 geometrical, coloured shapes. The shapes deliberately bore no resemblance to the items (nouns) or activities (verbs) they represented. Matata learned just eight lexigrams, which functioned only as requests. There was no indication that the shapes had acquired any symbolic representation.

Throughout her training, Matata had Kanzi with her, a new-born infant she had kidnapped six months earlier. No efforts were made to teach Kanzi, but at age two-and-a-half, when he was introduced to the language programme, it became apparent that he had learned the symbols during his mother's lessons! Kanzi spontaneously made requests, named things, and announced what he was going to do. Even at this early stage, it was clear that Kanzi used language differently. He was illustrating reflexiveness without training.

Training was continued with Kanzi, but unlike the formal instruction other animals had received, he was simply exposed to people communicating with each other, and with him, about real events via the keyboard. Kanzi was encouraged to use the keyboard, but was never denied objects or participation in activities for failing to do so. He quickly learned to communicate requests to travel around the research centre, to visit food sites, other chimpanzees, to play games and watch television!

As well as being able to follow simple commands, such as 'give the cereal to Karen', Kanzi can also understand complex sentences. For example, whilst the instruction 'go to the colony room and get the orange' produced hesitation, 'get the orange that is in the colony room' did not. The latter is more complex, and since it produced better

---

Key **S T U D Y**

Box 41.10 Immersing chimpanzees in language

Rumbaugh & Savage-Rumbaugh (1994) were interested in discovering whether the success of teaching by immersion in language could benefit other species which had shown lesser language skills using formal teaching methods. They reared Panzee (a *Pan troglodytes* chimpanzee) and Panbanisha (a bonobo or pygmy chimpanzee: *Pan paniscus*), two chimpanzees of very similar age, in the same language-rich environment. Within two years, both species could learn without formal instruction, but Panbanisha was much more competent.

Because they received no explicit training in language, their learning satisfies the criterion of *spontaneous acquisition* (see Box 41.5, pages 453–454), in a manner analogous to a child's language learning. Early exposure to a language-structured environment lays the foundations for comprehension.

comprehension, Kanzi has apparently grasped *lexical syntax* (Lewin, 1991). This is also demonstrated by Kanzi's acquisition of the rule 'action precedes object', a rule naturally applied by human children.

Key STUDY

Box 41.11 Comparing the comprehension abilities of pygmy chimpanzees with human infants

Savage-Rumbaugh *et al.* (1993) conducted an experiment to compare Kanzi's comprehension of human speech with that of a child, Alia, who had also learned to use the keyboard. Both were tested on over 400 novel sentences, which were specific about actions, places and objects. The required actions were not necessarily obvious, either because they were unusual (putting elastic bands on balls), or referred to unpredictable places or situations (such as being asked to 'get the telephone that is outdoors' when a telephone is in sight).

At age nine, Kanzi was correct 74 per cent of the time. At age two-and-a-half, Alia was correct 65 per cent of the time. Clearly, Kanzi has acquired the ability to comprehend and produce language without formal training. He simply responds to communication around him. As with a child, Kanzi's responses are not pure imitation to acquire meanings for symbols, but reflect an understanding of their use. Chimps raised *without* exposure to a lexigram keyboard never developed an understanding of speech (regardless of their later exposure), because it was not made accessible to them through a narrative in which they could participate. This, like the findings with Matata, suggests that chimpanzees have a *critical period* for language acquisition.

Savage-Rumbaugh's research also suggests that chimpanzees have grasped something akin to *lying* or, at least, an awareness of people tricking one another. In one study, Panbanisha watched a person secretly substitute an insect for some sweets in a box. A second person then tried to open the box, and the first asked Panabanisha 'What is she looking for?' Panbanisha replied that she was looking for some sweets. Apart from indicating *displacement*, this finding also implies that the chimpanzee was aware that other people's thinking was different from her own. Panbanisha knew there were no sweets in the box, and was aware that the second person did not. She added that the first person was being 'bad', which is recognition of her understanding that the second person had been tricked (see Chapter 39, page 433).

Is language unique to humans?

Our ability to determine whether non-humans are capable of language is hampered by our own inability to imagine what they are communicating *about*. We do not know if their thoughts are complex enough to *generate* an infinite variety of messages to transmit, or whether their cognitive processing demands a communication system which can convey information about displaced events, untruths or themselves.

There is evidence to suggest that chimpanzees and cetaceans, and perhaps the parrot, can grasp some complex concepts. Primates also seem to be able to refer to displaced events and objects. Finally, Gallup's (1970) research (see Chapter 39, page 430) suggests that chimpanzees can acquire *self-recognition*. Perhaps chimpanzees at least possess the cognitive requirements for language, which would explain why it is only in that species that communication which closely resembles human language has been observed.

CONCLUSIONS

Signalling systems operating through the senses offer animals different ways of communicating. This chapter has discussed the features of effective signalling, the functions of signalling, and the advantages and disadvantages relating to different types of signalling sytem.

Some signalling systems used by non-humans in their natural habitats enable communication that is sufficiently complex to resemble language. However, this 'natural language' fails to fulfil the criteria for a true language.

Attempts have been made to teach language to a variety of non-humans, including birds, cetaceans and primates. Several species are apparently capable of showing some elements of language acquisition, but it is only in chimpanzees that the more sophisticated aspects of language are exhibited.

Summary

- A **signal** is a deliberate message, sent to one or more recipients. Decoding the message results in behavioural or other changes in the recipient, and consequent benefits to both parties. However, **cheats** might affect the fitness of communicators by **eavesdropping** or **deceitful signalling**.

- Signals may be sent through any sensory system. The **visual**, **auditory** and **olfactory** systems are the ones most commonly used by animals.

- Visual signals include **colours**, **postures** (static signals) and **gestures** (movements). The visual signalling system is capable of generating highly variable messages. However, visual signals can only be detected by receivers who are looking.

- Auditory signals can be varied in terms of **pitch**, **volume** or **sequence**. The auditory signalling system is flexible and penetrating. Many auditory signals are **learned**.

- Olfactory signalling systems use **smells**. **Pheromones** are airborne chemicals which affect a receiver's physiology and behaviour. **Releaser pheromones** have short-term effects on behaviour. **Primer pheromones** can produce long-term effects by, for example, altering hormonal activity.

- If **language** is not a special human characteristic, non-humans should either possess it or be capable of learning it. There are ten **generalised features of language**, which can be used to assess its existence in non-humans.

- **Vervet monkeys** produce alarm calls which are predator-specific and cause adaptive responses in the recipients. These calls satisfy some, but not all, of the ten criteria for language.

- **Honey bees** communicate information about the direction and distance of food sources via the **waggle dance**. This uses angles and vigour of movement to communicate meaning. Although the waggle dance satisfies some criteria for language, it does not satisfy them all.

- **Birds** use songs to communicate about territory and courtship. Although the songs are **specialised**, they are better classified as signals than **symbolic communication**. Birdsong does not satisfy the criteria for language.

- **Chimpanzees** use various facial expressions, sounds and gestures to communicate, but none seem complex or varied enough to constitute language. However, certain chimpanzee attributes, such as the ability to learn complex skills, could imply a capacity to learn language.

- There have been many attempts to **teach language** to non-humans. Because birds use an auditory medium, it is easy to observe their ability to acquire language. The **parrot**, however, satisfies few of the criteria for language.

- **Cetaceans** can learn visual or acoustic languages. **Dolphins** have been taught to comprehend symbols for objects and actions, which can be combined into simple instructions. Their responses to meaningful and nonsensical messages suggest they use a simple form of **syntax**.

- Early attempts to teach **chimpanzees** to talk were unsuccessful. Later attempts used non-vocal techniques, such as **sign language**, **plastic symbols** and **computer keyboards** (**lexigrams**).

- Using Aitchison's four criteria for language, attempts to teach language to chimpanzees can be considered successful. However, critics believe that there are alternative ways of explaining the data that have been obtained.

- Most research has concentrated on language *production* rather than *comprehension*. More recent research uses a **language-structured environment**, in which language is used around non-humans to announce and co-ordinate social activities.

- Using this method, **pygmy chimpanzees** have spontaneously learned to communicate with humans. They are capable of understanding complex sentences, indicating an understanding of **lexical syntax**.

- It appears that chimpanzees have the **cognitive requirements** for language, and that only chimpanzees can communicate in a way which closely resembles human language.

Essay Questions

1 Discuss the use of any two different signalling systems in non-human animals. *(24 marks)*

2 Critically consider research studies into animal language. *(24 marks)*

WEB ADDRESSES

http://www.ozemail.com.au/~ilanit/koko.htm
http://www.primate.wisc.edu/pin
http://www.le.ac.uk/education/resources/SocSci/animlang.html
http://citd.scar.utoronto.ca/LINB27/Introduction/animallanguage.html
http://www.gsu.edu/~wwwlrc/biographies/Kanzi.html

42 *Memory in Non-humans*

INTRODUCTION AND OVERVIEW

Chapter 40 discussed animal navigation, particularly those abilities that resemble human orienteering, namely finding one's way in unfamiliar territory with just a map and a compass. For much of the time, however, animals face a simpler task, since they are moving around a familiar territory or home range where landmarks are known. Familiarity therefore allows individuals to learn both locations and routes. This chapter examines explanations and research studies of *memory in non-human animals*, and considers *the importance of memory in navigation and food caching*.

WHAT CAN ANIMALS REMEMBER?

Much research has investigated the range of *human* memory, its longevity and capacity, as well as the diversity of information which people can store. Do animals need such an ability? Animals certainly seem to be able to learn procedural actions and 'declarative facts', such as routes and locations. They might also have something similar to *'episodic memory'* (see Gross *et al.*, 2000), since they can recall pertinent experiences such as pain or stressful situations. Additionally, their memories are affected by interference and fade over time. However, in contrast to humans, non-humans seem to be programmed to remember some pieces of information more readily than others. For example, a rat will learn an association between noise and pain or taste and illness, but not between noise and illness (Garcia & Koelling, 1966: see Box 38.7, page 418). This suggests that animals' memories are more selective or less flexible than our own.

SPATIAL MEMORY

Spatial memory refers to the learning of an environmental layout, in order to recall the objects or activities associated with particular places. Being able to remember a location might be crucial to an animal's survival. It may need to return there for resources, or to avoid it in case of danger. To investigate the capacity of non-humans to remember spatial information, both observational and experimental studies have been conducted on a range of species.

Regolin & Rose (1999) have demonstrated that long-term memory for a spatial task appears early in an animal's life. They tested two-day-old chicks (*Gallus gallus domesticus*) in a detour experiment. Each chick was expected to find its way round a barrier that separated it from a group of chicks. Whilst the chicks showed some preference for a particular direction, they could learn a specific route that was dictated by introducing a barrier. Regolin and Rose found that the chicks retained this spatial memory for at least 24 hours.

The female digger wasp (*Philanthus triangulum*) excavates a burrow in which she lays eggs. To provide for the larvae, she leaves the burrow to hunt for insects. So that she can return to her own burrow, she conducts an orientation flight before departure, committing the features of the landscape to memory. On her return, it is the spatial arrangement of objects that she remembers, rather than the objects themselves.

Another species of digger wasp remembers the sequence of events performed at a burrow, as well as its location. Being able to remember what happened at a particular place for an animal is rather like playing 'pairs', the game in which face-down playing cards are randomly turned face-up in an attempt to locate a match. Would you be able to remember the location of a particular card a month after playing the game?

Key STUDY

Box 42.1 Memory in digger wasps

As the digger wasp *Philanthus triangulum* flies out from her burrow, she memorises landmarks to guide her return flight. Tinbergen (1951) surrounded a wasp's burrow with a ring of pinecones, then moved them 30 cm away when she was hunting (see Figure 42.1, a and b, page 464). The wasp failed to find her burrow, even though it was just outside the ring, and appeared to be relying solely on her memory of the *spatial arrangement* of the cones.

To test this, Tinbergen replaced the decoy pinecones with a ring of stones, and surrounded the actual burrow with a triangle of pinecones (see Figure 42.1, c and d). The wasp searched for her burrow in the ring of stones, ignoring the pinecones. Her memory *was* for the spatial arrangement, rather than for the cones themselves or for the precise geographical location of the burrow.

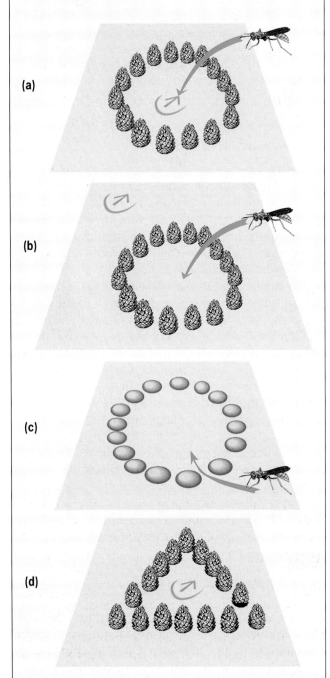

(a)

(b)

(c)

(d)

Figure 42.1 *The confused digger wasp (see text for details)*

Female digger wasps of the species *Ammophilia campestris* may have several burrows at different

stages (being dug, awaiting an egg, needing provisions or being closed). They must therefore remember the behaviours in the correct sequence at many different locations. The process of digging, laying an egg, collecting caterpillars, and opening then re-closing the nest before finally sealing it over, may take several days. On each visit, she must remember which operation is required. It must be like trying to read ten murder-mystery novels by the same author all at once, without confusing the characters or plots.

Holtzman *et al.* (1999) investigated spatial-escape learning in juvenile corn snakes (*Elaphe guttata guttata*). The snakes were required to find an open shelter from a choice of eight possibilities. After 16 trials, the snakes showed several indicators of having learned. For example, they were faster to get to the goal (the one open shelter), travelled a shorter distance to reach it, and spent more time in the adjacent area (less time 'lost'). So, snakes too can rapidly learn a spatial task. Such changes in behaviour are clearly adaptive. Having an effective spatial memory allows animals to spend less time and energy travelling, so they use their resources more efficiently and expose themselves to fewer dangers.

Models of spatial memory

Two models of spatial memory are *spatial adaptation* and *pliancy*.

Spatial adaptation model

Some animals have a greater need than others to remember particular places. If food is clumped, rather than evenly scattered, or if potential mates tend to cluster at regular venues, then an animal will benefit from being able to recall such locations. Species that lay eggs in distributed nest sites, or search widely for mates, tend to have enhanced spatial memories (Sherry *et al.* 1992; 1993).

Such an ecological niche requires a high level of recall for successful habitation. This would put the occupants under selection pressures to adapt, and so improved navigational skills would evolve. The *spatial-adaptation model* (Sherry *et al.*, 1992) suggests a correlation between ecology (living in a spatially demanding niche) and spatial ability.

Key **STUDY**

Box 42.2 Spatial ability in voles

Evidence supporting the spatial adaptation model has been provided by a comparison of spatial ability in male and female rodents. Male meadow voles

(*Microtus pennsylvanicus*) must find their way around a home range which is four times the size of the females'. In the prairie vole (*M. Ochrogaster*), however, each pair shares a territory, and so males and females have equal demands placed on their spatial ability. Gaulin & FitzGerald (1989) compared the maze-learning ability of these animals, and found differences as predicted by spatial-adaptation theory. Male meadow voles, but not prairie voles, showed better spatial skills.

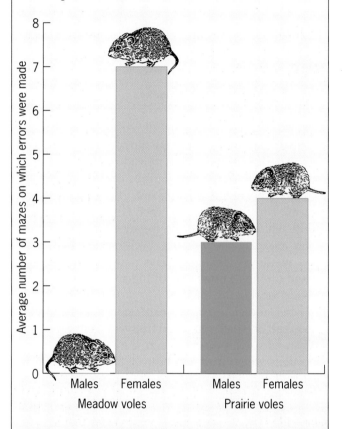

Figure 42.2 *Sex differences in maze learning. Gaulin & FitzGerald (1989) compared errors made in a maze by rodent species where males and females either differ in the size of their home range (meadow vole) or share the same home range (prairie vole)*

Pliancy model

Some evidence contradicts the spatial-adaptation model, and instead suggests that the improved performance observed is the product of selection favouring a more general enhancement in the flexibility of memory. Day *et al.* (1999) studied two related species of lizard, which occupy different ecological niches, one foraging for clumped sedentary prey (*Acanthodactylus boskianus*) and the other for distributed mobile prey (*A. scutellatus*).

When compared on a spatial task, these species performed similarly, suggesting that differences in foraging

strategy alone do not account for variation in such abilities. Both species could use cues in a Barnes maze (see Figure 42.3) to find a hot rock to escape from cold water.

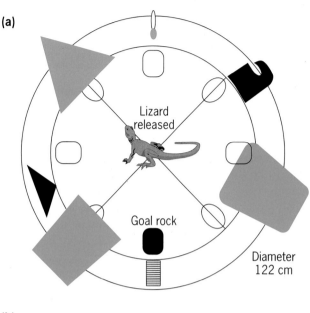

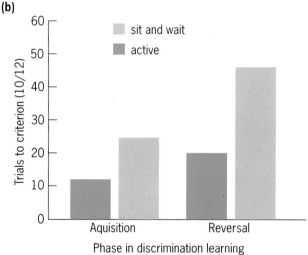

Figure 42.3 *In a Barnes maze test of spatial ability (a), 'active' predatory lizards performed no better than a 'sit-and-wait' species. When compared on a non-spatial task in which the lizards had to learn to choose a palatable rather than unpalatable meal worm according to whether it was against a blue or yellow background, the active predators were faster. They took fewer trials to acquire (and reverse) the visual discrimination (b)*

When Day *et al.* tested the lizards on a non-spatial visual discrimination task, *A. boskianus* performed the reversal task significantly better, and were better at unlearning a previously reinforced response. From this, Day *et al.* concluded that the active foragers have a better memory for complex associations in general, rather than being specifically selected for a predisposition to solve spatial tasks. Their alternative explanation, the *pliancy model*, suggests that such species show a behavioural flexibility. This enables them to learn complex relationships between stimuli and reinforcers, especially in unpredictable situations. In practice, spatial tasks tend to require such adaptability.

FORAGING AND FOOD CACHING

Many studies which demonstrate exceptional spatial ability in animals focus on foraging and food caching behaviour. When an animal forages successfully, it may need to find its way back to the same location on another occasion when the food source has replenished itself. To do this, it must be able to commit the location to memory.

The foraging animal may also be able to find more than it can eat at one time, and so may store some for times when it is less successful, or food is scarce. Caching food is useful, since it keeps for longer and is protected from the roving eyes or noses of competitors, for whom cheating is a cheaper strategy than foraging (see Figure 42.4). However, this strategy demands that the animal hiding the cache can find it later.

Figure 42.4 *A cheetah drags its dead prey high into trees to protect it from theft by stronger but less agile predators*

Learning forage locations

Honeybees, like digger wasps, learn locations in their environment. Chapter 41 showed that successful forager bees communicate distance and direction to other workers in the hive, but how do they acquire their mental map of the nectar's location? Srinivasan *et al.*'s (1997) experiment suggests that they literally 'watch the world whizz by' as they fly.

The bees were trained to find a sugar solution in the middle of a 3.2 metre tunnel, with a transparent top and black-and-white two-centimetre stripes around its walls. In an identical tunnel *without* food, the bees flew

back and forth in diminishing loops until they centred on the point where the food should have been.

When the number of stripes in the tunnel was changed, the bees continued to home in accurately on experimental trials without food, suggesting that they were not using the stripes as landmarks to guide them. However, when the stripes were altered to run horizontally, the bees failed to stop at the appropriate location or at the end of the tunnel. Changing the orientation of the stripes deprived the bees of visual indicators of motion, suggesting that their spatial memory for the distance to their target was based on how much of the world they had passed.

> *Key* **STUDY**
>
> ### Box 42.3 Foraging in chimpanzees
>
> Menzel (1971) studied chimpanzees living under naturalistic conditions in a large outdoor enclosure. For the experiment, they were moved indoors and each was taken on a circuitous journey during which they saw food being hidden in 18 outside locations. When released to find the food, each chimpanzee took a route which minimised the distance travelled, rather than retracing the twisting, backtracking path they had previously followed. This pattern of searching, based on their knowledge of the area, allowed them to find most of the food.
>
> Later, the chimpanzees experienced 18 new food sites, half of which contained fruit and half vegetables. When released to search again, they went first to the locations where fruit had been hidden (preferring to eat fruit over vegetables). Thus, their spatial memory stores information about places *and* facts associated with them, in much the same way as the wasps described in Box 42.1 (see pages 463–464).

Locating food caches

How can squirrels find nuts, hidden weeks or months previously, under a featureless snow-covered lawn? Certainly, their acute sense of smell plays a part, but so too does their memory. Jacobs & Liman (1991) studied handreared grey squirrels (*Sciurus carolinensis*).

Each squirrel was released into a 45 square metre area to bury ten hazelnuts. The exact location of each cache was recorded, and the nuts were then removed. Up to 12 days later, each squirrel was returned to the test area into which new hazelnuts had been placed. These were located at both the individual's own cache sites and at an equal number of randomly chosen sites which had been selected by other squirrels (see Figure 42.5, page 467).

The young squirrels were more likely to recover nuts from their own cache locations, even when they had to travel past the sites chosen by other squirrels to find them, despite the fact that they cannot have smelled or looked different. Clearly, the squirrels had memorised the locations of the food *they* had hidden, and were not relying solely on smell.

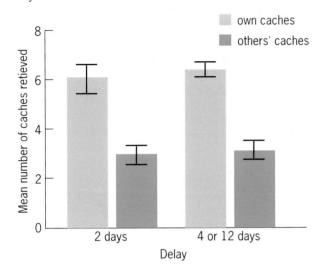

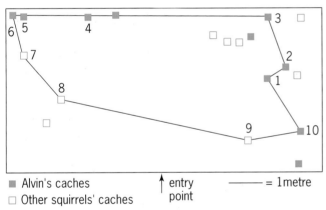

Figure 42.5 *Graph to show number of caches retrieved by squirrels after 2, 4 or 12 days (top), and a schematic representation of the order in which one particular squirrel (Alvin) retrieved caches (bottom)*

Birds, too, may depend on stored food to survive the winter. In Britain, wild marsh tits (*Parus palustris*) will store several hundred seeds a day in crevices in the bark of trees or under stones. In captivity, this species demonstrates an ability to accurately recall the location of cached food for a few days (Cowie *et al.*, 1981; Shettleworth, 1983).

An American species, the black capped chickadee (*Parus atricapillus*), will hide hundreds of seeds and insects in patches of moss or tree bark. These birds can remember the precise location of food items up to 28 days later (Hitchcock & Sherry, 1990). For many ani-

mals, remembering in such detail for long periods of time is probably not useful, as another individual may well have found the food and eaten it.

Key **S T U D Y**

Box 42.4 Spatial memory in black-capped chickadees

Sherry (1984) tested chickadees in an aviary containing small trees with 72 specially-drilled holes, which could be used as cache sites. Each bird was allowed to hide four or five sunflower seeds, and was then taken into a holding cage for 24 hours. The cached seeds were removed and Velcro covers were placed over the holes. This removed any visual or olfactory clues to the storage sites previously chosen by that individual. When returned to the aviary, the chickadees spent more time pecking at the covers and inspecting the sites where they had stored seeds than those where they had not. This suggests that they were relying on their memory of the location, rather than any other cue.

Figure 42.6 *A black-capped chickadee*

Another bird, the Clark's nutcracker (*Nucifraga columbiana*), is even more spectacular in its memory. Single individuals will dig thousands of holes in which to hide small caches of pine seeds during the autumn. Over the winter months, they must recall the location of these carefully covered hoard sites. Experiments similar to those described in Box 42.4 have demonstrated that nutcrackers, like chickadees, recall the precise location of a cache, rather than using cues such as smell or returning to the general location and searching randomly.

In Balda's (1980) study, individual nutcrackers were allowed to dig holes in the aviary floor where they could bury seeds. The bird was then removed, as were its seeds, and the floor of the aviary was swept. Each bird was returned a week later and, on average, 80 per cent of their searching was directed towards their own previous cache sites.

Balda & Kamil (1992) found that Clark's nutcrackers could find their caches up to 40 weeks later! Evidence suggests that species such as the nutcracker may differ from similar but non-hoarding species in their brain development. Specifically, food-hoarders' brains seem to have more neurones in the *hippocampus*, an area implicated in both the formation of long-term memories (see Chapter 11) and spatial memories. These observations support both the spatial-adaptation and pliancy models (Kamil *et al.*, 1999).

COGNITIVE MAPS

The chimpanzees and squirrels described previously were able to memorise specific locations where food was to be found. The routes they took to find the food were not the same as those they had travelled previously. They seemed to be employing an internal representation of the geography of the area. Is this more than just a conditioned response to their environment?

Radial arm maze studies

In a radial arm maze (see Figure 42.7), an animal such as a rat is expected to make a directional choice based on previous experience. Because their performance improves with experience of the maze, their learning might be explained through operant conditioning. However, the responses learned are not readily interpreted within this framework, and have been more effectively explained by the acquisition of a *cognitive map*.

Tolman (1948) first used this term to describe the internal representation an animal builds of the spatial relationships within its environment. Such learning differs from conditioning, because it does not rely on the modification of pre-existing behaviours, and can occur in the absence of obvious reinforcers (see also Chapter 38, pages 419–420).

Key **STUDY**

Box 42.5 How do rats behave in a radial arm maze?

When placed in a radial arm maze, rats explore each arm but apparently not in any systematic way. They do not, as humans might, go round trying each arm in turn, although they do avoid re-entering a previously encountered arm (Olton & Samuelson, 1976).

When a rat is given time to orient in a radial arm maze using external cues, it will readily learn which arm to enter for food. Visual cues placed in the environment around the maze will provide the necessary information for spatial memory to develop.

When radial mazes are extended to make the spatial task more difficult, rats demonstrate a stereotyped response pattern not seen in simpler tasks. Roberts (1979) devised a 24-arm radial maze by branching each part of a standard eight-arm maze into three.

Although rats in this apparatus learned to find food effectively, they appeared to do so by employing a fixed search pattern, such as always turning right when they had returned to the central area. This strategy may be more efficient, but it could also indicate that the rats' memories had reached capacity as they were no longer able to employ the same strategies as before.

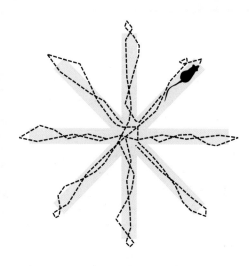

Figure 42.7 *Radial arm maze used for studying cognitive maps*

Detour studies

If an animal builds up a cognitive map of an area or maze through exploration, this could be used to minimise journey time. So, experienced animals should be quicker (Holtzman *et al.*, 1999), able to take a detour around an obstacle (Regolin & Rose, 1999) or take a new, shorter route, if an obstacle is removed. Maier & Schneirla (1935) describe a simple, but elegant study, which demonstrates how a rat can use its cognitive map to shorten its journey (see Figure 42.8, page 469).

The neurobiological basis of cognitive maps

Milner *et al.* (1968) describe the case of H.M., who underwent brain surgery to try and cure his devastating epileptic fits. The surgery, which involved removal of the hippocampus on both sides of the brain, was successful in treating the epilepsy, but left H.M. with severe *amnesia* (see also Gross *et al.*, 2000).

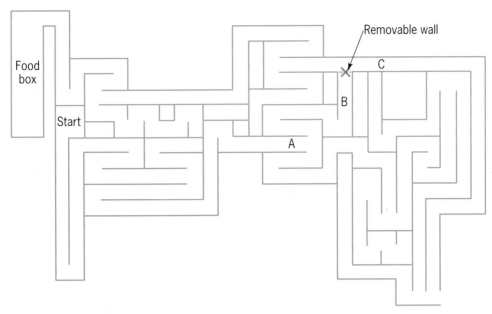

Figure 42.8 *Maier & Schneirla (1935) used a complex maze with several blind alleys. Rats were initially allowed to explore the maze and learned to find the food box. The wall labelled X was then removed, revealing a short-cut between the passages marked B and C. Some rats noticed the change whilst in passage C and explored passage B. On subsequent trials they ran straight from A to B, then took advantage of the short-cut*

Although he had a near-normal memory for things he had learned prior to the operation, his ability to store memories of events after the surgery was very poor. For example, when his parents moved house after his operation, H.M. was unable to learn the new route home.

Hippocampal lesions

Like H.M., rats with hippocampal lesions are poor at tasks which require spatial ability. Morris *et al.* (1982) compared the performance of three groups of rats in a large circular tank filled with water and powdered milk. The murky water conceals a platform to which the rat must swim.

All rats initially find the platform by chance. A control rat rapidly learns where the platform is, so that it can return there quickly when placed in the water. Rats with hippocampal lesions, however, swim in apparently random directions on every trial, failing to benefit from opportunities to learn the platform's location. For both H.M. and the experimental rats, then, hippocampal lesions resulted in the failure to acquire spatial memories.

Lesion studies (see Chapter 10) also suggest that the hippocampus plays a specific role in spatial learning, as opposed to navigation. Bingman & Mench (1990) found that homing pigeons were relatively unaffected by hippocampal lesions in the early stages of a homeward bound flight, because their initial bearings were correct. However, when they were close enough to use landmarks they were less accurate.

Rehkamper *et al.* (1988) found that racing pigeons had larger hippocampal regions than other breeds of pigeon. In the black-capped chickadee (see page 467), the hippocampus increases in size during late autumn when the birds are caching food for winter, so exercising their spatial skills to the full (Smulders *et al.* 1995). Voles also show predictable differences in hippocampal size. Male meadow voles, which must learn their way around a large territory (see Box 42.2, pages 464–465), have a significantly larger hippocampus than the females.

Hippocampal place cells

O'Keefe & Dostrovsky (1971) recorded the activity of individual nerve cells in the hippocampus of rats running in a maze. Some of these cells, called *place cells*, had specific *spatial receptive fields*, that is, they responded strongly only when the rat was in a particular place in the maze. The cells responded to geographical location with respect to environmental cues, such as furniture in the room. If the maze itself was rotated, the hippocampal cells were activated by external cues in the same way. Surprisingly, the receptive fields of deafened and blindfolded rats also remained constant.

Hill & Best (1981) suggested that rats without visual or auditory cues may be using *proprioceptive* (body position) cues to find their way. If the rats remembered how to reach the goal as a sequence of left and right turns, they should be disoriented by being spun, much as being turned around and around in 'pin the tail on the donkey' leaves you very lost. If the deafened, blindfolded rats were placed in a towel and whirled round, and then required to run the maze, their receptive fields were disrupted. This shows that hippocampal cells can use internal or external cues to location.

Hippocampal cells can also integrate different sources of information. Young *et al.* (1994) tested rats in a four-arm radial maze, in which each branch was textured differently (sandpaper, plastic mesh, and so on). Some hippocampal cells responded when a rat was in a particular geographically placed arm, whilst others responded when it was in an arm with a specific texture. Most place cells, however, responded to both cues simultaneously, such as to the 'sandpapered-arm-when-it-pointed-north'.

Neurotransmitters in the hippocampus

The involvement of particular *neurotransmitters* is also being researched. The hippocampus generates theta waves, which can be detected on an EEG (see Chapter 10). If these waves are disrupted by injecting the drug *scopolamine*, spatial learning is impaired (Givens & Olton, 1995). This drug blocks receptor sites for the neurotransmitter *acetylcholine*, and prevents rats from recalling which arm of a T-maze they have most recently entered.

When acetylcholine-producing cells of the hippocampus are damaged, rats perform less well on spatial learning tasks. If healthy cells are transplanted, deficits in performance are reduced (Nilsson *et al.*, 1987). Even in rats with spatial memory impairments due to old age, such transplants can improve maze-learning performance (Gage *et al.*, 1984).

Tang *et al.* (1999) have compared the ability of genetically engineered and normal mice to navigate through a maze. The modified mice had additional sections of an NMDA receptor, a neurotransmitter receptor site which usually only responds when two neurones stimulate it simultaneously. These mice retained their memories for longer, performing better than normal mice on identical mazes.

CONCLUSIONS

Being able to remember locations can enhance an animal's survival by allowing it to find resources or avoid danger. Living in a large territory, foraging for clumped food, or storing and retrieving food caches demands good spatial memory. Non-human animals are able to form cognitive maps to learn spatial relationships in their

DO NON-HUMANS FORGET?

A non-human's memory for an event or location fades with time, and is less likely to be recalled accurately as time passes.

Decay

Decay of memory is illustrated by the black-capped chickadee whose ability to locate a food cache declines after about 28 days (see Box 42.4, page 467). Such forgetting may not be as detrimental as it seems. The longer an animal waits before returning to a hoard site, the greater the chance that any stored food will have rotted or been discovered and eaten by a competitor. To offset this risk, birds retrieve food from their most recent cache sites (Shettleworth, 1984).

Interference

An alternative to decay theory suggests that increased forgetting over time is not simply the result of memories fading, but of *interference* between competing information. An earlier memory may disrupt the learning of new information, or incoming items may displace previous memories or make them harder to retrieve (see Gross *et al.*, 2000). If an animal learns a particular behaviour at a certain time of day, this memory will persist, and can act as a source of interference to the acquisition of other behaviours.

Dallenbach (1924, cited in Hardy & Heyes, 1979) used cockroaches to demonstrate the effects of interference on memory. Two groups of cockroaches were trained to run a maze. Afterwards, one group was allowed to move around freely whilst the others were restrained by placing them in cotton wool. After a delay, the cockroaches were returned to the maze.

Those animals that were able to move had forgotten more than those that were not. By preventing the cockroaches from engaging in other activities, Dallenbach had ensured that reducing interference from memories of more recent spatial experiences would preserve their memory of the maze (see also Gross *et al.*, 2000).

environment. The hippocampus plays a vital role in these memories. Such memories can be forgotten through the processes of decay and interference, although this, too, may be functional, saving animals effort in looking for stolen or rotten food.

Summary

- When memorising its territory or home range, an animal can learn familiar routes or locations to remember the whereabouts of nests or food. Animal memory, including procedural and declarative, resembles that of humans. However, their recall is more limited than our own.

- **Spatial memory** is the learning of an environmental layout, including the objects or activities associated with particular locations. This helps animals to survive by enabling them to return to resources and avoid danger. Animals may acquire spatial memory early in life, since even two-day-old chicks can learn a **detour task**.

- The **spatial adaptation model** suggests that species inhabiting spatially demanding niches have evolved better spatial memories. Evidence from voles suggests that those which need to have good spatial memories, because they have large territories, have better spatial skills. They also have a larger **hippocampus**, the region of the brain where spatial memories are stored.

- According to the **pliancy model**, this enhancement in memory may be a more general increase in the flexibility of learning, rather than being specific to spatial information.

- **Foraging** strategies may depend on spatial memory when food is clumped. For example, bees can learn a particular foraging location by judging the amount of ground they have covered as they fly.

- **Food caching**, the storing of plentiful food for later consumption, places demands on spatial memory. Squirrels can find sites where they buried nuts days previously without the aid of visual or olfactory cues, even when this means passing cache sites chosen by other individuals.

- Evidence from rats in mazes suggests that animals are able to store information about spatial relationships in the environment, rather than just routes. These frameworks are called **cognitive maps**.

- In a **radial arm maze**, rats will learn spatial choices based on visual information, although in complex situations they rely on stereotyped responses rather than cognitive maps. In **detour studies**, animals demonstrate their use of cognitive maps to take short-cuts.

- Lesion studies suggest that the **hippocampus** is essential in the formation of spatial memories. **Hippocampal place cells** have receptive fields that relate directly to specific locations in the environment. They can respond to information about geographical position based on vision, body movements along the route, or tactile cues from the texture of the apparatus.

- Drugs such as **scopolamine**, which block the action of neurotransmitters in the hippocampus, impair **spatial learning**. When cells producing acetylcholine are damaged, spatial memory declines. If healthy cells are transplanted, performance improves.

- Forgetting in animals may occur through **decay** or **interference**. For example, black-capped chickadees are less likely to recall the location of a cache site over time. This is functional, as earlier caches are more likely to have been found by competitors and eaten.

- When cockroaches learn a maze and are either prevented from moving or free to move around, the restrained cockroaches are better at finding their way than those experiencing interference by moving around between learning and recall.

Essay Questions

1. Discuss research studies of memory in non-human animals *(24 marks)*

2. Describe and evaluate research into the importance of memory in **either** navigation **or** foraging behaviour *(24 marks)*

WEB ADDRESSES

http://www.sci.monash.edu.au/psych/research/memory/
http://www.pigeon.psy.tufts.edu/peoplef.htm
http://www.vuw.ac.nz/psych/garry/wham/hall_nyt.html
http://www.biologists.com/JEB/199/01/jeb0131.html

PART 3: EVOLUTIONARY EXPLANATIONS OF HUMAN BEHAVIOUR

43 *Human Reproductive Behaviour*

INTRODUCTION AND OVERVIEW

Evolutionary psychology may be defined as the application of Darwinian principles to human behaviour (see Chapter 37, page 399). This approach assumes that human nature has been shaped by natural selection, and is a recent development of *sociobiology*, which attempts to explain all social behaviour in terms of evolutionary and other biological principles. However, evolutionary psychology is more flexible than sociobiology as it takes into account the role of the mind in mediating the links between genes and human behaviour. This chapter examines *the relationship between sexual selection and human reproductive behaviour*, including evolutionary explanations of *sex differences in parental investment*.

EVOLUTIONARY PSYCHOLOGY: AN INTRODUCTION

Dennett (1996) describes evolutionary psychology as 'a marriage of sociobiology and cognitive psychology'. According to evolutionary psychologists, the human mind has been designed by natural selection to solve problems faced by our ancestors. The evolution of human social behaviour has been adapted for the prehistoric environment in which we lived as hunter-gatherers, known as the *Environment of Evolutionary Adaptedness* (EAA: Davies, 1995). Despite enormous changes in our lifestyle over the last 100,000 years, we may still possess a stone age mind inside a modern skull.

Evolutionary psychology uses Darwinian concepts to generate testable hypotheses about human behaviour, based on the assumption that individuals will act in a way that tends to propagate their genes. However, not all human behaviour represents an adaptation for survival or reproduction. Furthermore, just because a certain behaviour is considered adaptive, it does not

mean that it is developmentally unchangeable or socially desirable.

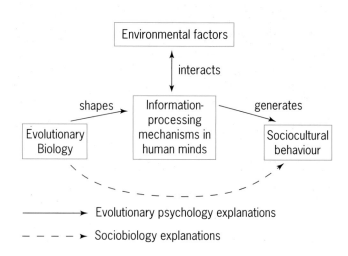

Figure 43.1 *Evolutionary psychology: the marriage of sociobiology and cognitive psychology*

According to Miller (1998), the application of *sexual selection* theory to human behaviour has been the greatest success story in evolutionary psychology. Humans possess specific mental adaptations for choosing mates, selecting their sexual partners on the basis of viability and fertility (indicated by such factors as age, health, social status and disease-resistance). In sexually-reproducing species, it pays to be choosy as the genetic quality of one's mate will determine half the genetic quality of the offspring. However, adaptations for mate choice are probably different for males and females, as what defines a 'good mate' from an evolutionary point of view will be different for the two sexes (see also Chapter 4).

Males and females

Males and females need not be physically or behaviourally different, as *is* the case in *sexually dimorphic* humans (see page 475). Rather, they are simply required to produce different sized gametes (*anisogamy*). 'Males' produce small mobile gametes called *sperm*, and that is what makes them male. 'Females' produce large immobile gametes called *eggs* that have a store of energy which serves to assist the embryo in its development. Sperm are produced in very large numbers. Although each individual sperm has the capacity to fertilise an egg, very few will do so. Eggs are more costly to produce, so females make fewer in a lifetime and release them in significantly smaller numbers than males produce sperm. Overall, males and females put the same amount of energy into making gametes, but spread that energy out differently.

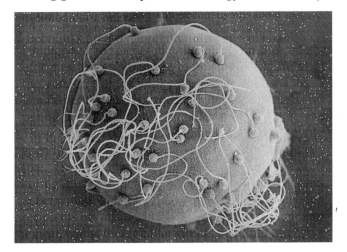

Figure 43.2 *For any species, each gamete (sperm or egg) contains the same amount of genetic information. Eggs, however, are very much bigger, so require greater investment; hence females can afford to produce fewer gametes than males*

A human female is able to produce fertile gametes for only a short proportion of her lifespan, and during this time she is only *fertile* (carrying an egg that can be fertilised) for about two days per month. Once an egg is fertilised, the woman will be pregnant for nine months, during which time she will release no further eggs. A woman who became pregnant at every opportunity would only be fertile for about 900 days in total. Men, by contrast, are fertile for decades. So, whilst females bearing fertile eggs are a scarce resource, fertile males are common. It is this key biological difference that underpins human reproductive behaviour and subsequent parental investment (see pages 477–479).

Sexual selection

Chapter 37 described the extent to which animal behaviour can be explained by evolutionary concepts. The general assumption of this approach is that evolution works almost exclusively through natural selection. However, Darwin himself was aware that natural selection could not explain *all* evolutionary processes. One major problem was to explain the evolution of certain behaviours or anatomical structures which appeared to *reduce* the probability of survival, such as the peacock's tail.

Box 43.1 The peacock's tail

The tail of the peacock (*Pavo cristatus*) appears to have the dual disadvantage of attracting predators and impeding efficient flight, making escape difficult. If it was the case that such tails really increased fitness in some non-obvious way, one would expect them to be present in females also. As natural selection seemed to be unable to explain the existence of such a structure, Darwin proposed the theory of *sexual selection*.

According to Darwin, sexual selection depends on the advantage which certain individuals have over others of the same sex and species solely in respect of reproduction (Darwin, 1871). In the case of the peacock, females appear to prefer males who possess the longest and most brightly-coloured tails. The effects of sexual selection therefore outweigh the disadvantage of owning such a cumbersome appendage (Clamp & Russell, 1998).

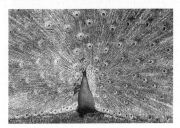

Figure 43.3 *A peacock displaying his extravagant and cumbersome tail. The existence of such a structure is more readily explained by sexual selection than by natural selection*

Evidence suggests that humans are a *mutually* sexually-selected species. In other words, both males and females have evolved preferences for certain behavioural and/or anatomical features in the opposite sex. According to Ridley (1993):

'People are attracted to people of high reproductive and genetic potential – the healthy, the fit and the powerful'. This brings us to the question of exactly how we choose our mates'.

Mate choice: what is attractive?

One way to evaluate the role of sexual selection in human evolution is to compare our species with other primates (the *comparative* approach). We differ from other anthropoid apes in several respects, such as the nature of our facial features, and in having enlarged breasts and buttocks (females) and long penises (males). Much research has looked at the influence of selective mate choice on human facial features. Findings suggest that *average faces* are attractive, but that females with more child-like features (large eyes, small noses and full lips) are preferred, as are males with testosterone-enlarged features, such as strong jaws and large noses (Thornhill & Gangestad, 1993). We also seem to consider bilateral symmetry as an important feature of facial beauty (see Chapter 4, page 38). Furthermore, human faces are extremely well developed for displaying a variety of emotions, many of which are used in courtship (Darwin, 1872).

Box 43.2 The beauty of symmetry

Facial features may be a clue to genetic or nurtured quality, or to character and personality. Studies have shown that men prefer photographs of women with *symmetrical faces*, and vice versa (Cartwright, 2000). It seems likely that *symmetry* (which shows a tendency to be inherited) equates with fitness.

Development may be disturbed by parasites or other infectious agents, and only individuals with the best genes and food supplies will develop perfectly symmetrical faces. For example, the jawlines of males lengthen and broaden during puberty in response to increases in testosterone levels. However, testosterone also suppresses the immune system. Perhaps only the 'fittest' males can develop perfectly sculpted jaws when confronted by immunity-damaging surges of testosterone. Facial symmetry is also the best predictor of body symmetry (see below). Therefore, the human face is probably the main guide to attractiveness and overall genetic fitness (see also Chapter 4).

In addition to facial symmetry, we also appear to find *bodily symmetry* attractive. As suggested in Box 43.2, symmetry advertises biological quality, such as good genes, reproductive vigour and an effective immune system. Research indicates that women with symmetrical male partners have the most orgasms, and women with symmetrical breasts are more fertile than those less evenly endowed (Cartwright, 2000).

Males and females with near-perfect body symmetry also report two or three times as many sexual partners as those with the most asymmetrical bodies. However, this does not necessarily mean that symmetry itself is directly attractive. For example, symmetrical males may be more dominant, or have higher self-esteem, and so be considered more attractive as a result. Furthermore, we may prefer symmetrical bodies because symmetry is what our visual systems happen to respond to most strongly (Cartwright, 2000).

The penis of the human male is the longest, thickest and most flexible of any living primate. It appears that the main influence on the evolution of the human penis was female choice, probably due to factors involved in sexual satisfaction and (indirectly) reproductive success (Eberhard, 1991). Likewise, female human breasts and buttocks have undergone sexual elaboration through mate choice by males. These organs store substantial amounts of fat, so could function as indicators of female nutritional status and hence fertility. Singh (1993) demonstrated that men prefer women who display a low waist-to-hip ratio (WHR), ideally about 0.7. This is concordant with enlarged buttocks, indicating sufficient fat reserves, and a narrow waist, indicating the absence of pregnancy.

Box 43.3 Vital statistics

Despite significant changes over time in the average weight of female centrefolds and beauty queens, one vital statistic has remained constant: the ratio of waist to hip size. Singh (1993) argues that, within reason, a man will find almost any weight of woman attractive so long as her waist is much thinner than her hips, with an ideal ratio of about 0.7. Furthermore, the ratio appears to be consistent across a wide range of cultures.

Ridley (1993) suggests that this preference is due to sexual selection. Larger hips (or hips which *look* larger, compared to a slender waist) may indicate good childbearing capabilities. Alternatively, a thin waist would indicate the absence of pregnancy, something much less common in Pleistocene times than it is today. Thin waists are also associated with high levels of oestrogen and low levels of testosterone, a hormonal balance normally linked to high fertility.

Sexual dimorphism (the differences between the male and female sexes of the same species) is more marked among apes and humans than among monkeys (Crook, 1972). For example, male sexual strategy in humans involves rivalry in acquiring females and a certain amount of aggressiveness in protecting them from other men (McFarland, 1996). This may account for the man's greater size and strength, although it is more likely that this has to do with division of labour within the family (Passingham, 1982).

Many of the differences between the sexes in humans can be attributed to natural selection and to the differing roles of males and females, rather than sexual selection. When considering sexually-selected traits, we must examine those different male and female features that appear to have no direct role in survival or reproduction. Examples of such features include the beard and other male body hair, the change in the male voice that occurs at puberty, and the protruding and rounded breasts of the woman (Wickler, 1967).

Natural selection will favour males who prefer to mate with reproductively capable females. Unfortunately for males seeking to solve this problem, viability and fertility are not attributes that can be observed directly. Instead, males must be able to estimate the *age* of females (which is highly correlated with their reproductive capability), using physical attractiveness as a guide.

Box 43.4 Physical attractiveness is more important in females than males

The physical attractiveness of females occupies a central place in male mate preferences. Males would be expected to use physical features (e.g. clear skin, white teeth), behavioural features (e.g. high energy levels) and reputation (e.g. information regarding the health and prior sexual conduct of a female) as reliable guides to age and reproductive capability. There are several reasons as to why the preference for physical attractiveness should be stronger for males than for females:

• Female reproductive success is not as limited by the problem of obtaining fertile mates.

• Male fertility is less dependent upon age.

• Male fertility cannot be assessed as accurately from physical appearance (due to the above).

(Based on Buss, 1995)

The same arguments apply to female mate preferences, except that physical attractiveness will be less important,

for reasons outlined in Box 43.4. Females should seek to mate with males who show the ability and willingness to invest resources connected with parenting, such as food and protection. For example, American men who marry in a given year earn about 50 per cent more money than unmarried men of the same age, a fact probably due in part to female choice for male resources (Trivers, 1985). However, humans often mate at ages before a man's potential resources are fully known. Therefore, females have to rely on cues that predict the accumulation of resources, such as ambition, industriousness and intelligence (Willerman, 1979).

It has also been speculated that expressions of love and kindness may provide reliable cues to a man's willingness to devote resources to a female and her offspring (Buss, 1987), and to the likelihood of females remaining faithful. The majority of these predictions have been supported by studies across a wide range of cultures. Finally, this account of evolutionary selection pressures yields specific predictions about the nature of male and female deception. Females would be expected to lie about their age, alter their appearance, and conceal prior sexual encounters. Males would be expected to exaggerate their resources, inflate perceptions of their willingness to commit, and feign love to induce a female to mate with them (Buss, 1995: see Box 43.5).

Key **S T U D Y**

Box 43.5 Human mate choice

Figure 43.4 *Males are expected to exaggerate their resources in order to attract females*

Dunbar (1995) studied the 'lonely hearts' columns of magazines and newspapers, and found that men predominantly offer resources and seek attractiveness.

The reverse is usually true in females:

'Professional male (37) looking for attractive female (25–30) to share weekends in his country cottage and life in the city'

'Attractive female (27) seeks professional male for friendship and possibly romance'

Note that in these examples, the male may be exaggerating his resources (indicated by 'professional', 'country cottage' and 'city'). Likewise, the female may lie about her attractiveness, reduce her real age, and try to imply coyness (by indicating that romance is only a possibility).

HUMAN SEXUALITY

Homosexuality

Homosexuality represents a major puzzle for evolutionary psychology. Evidence suggests that genetic factors are involved in the development of male homosexuality (Stevens & Price, 1996). The genes in question probably reduce the sensitivity of the male foetus to the hormone *testosterone*. For example, dizygotic (DZ) twins have a 25 per cent chance of sharing a gay habit, but this becomes 50 per cent for monozygotic (MZ) twins. There is also evidence that the genes are inherited from the mother, either on the X chromosome or in the mitochondria of the egg (Ridley, 1993).

It is not clear whether female homosexuality is influenced by genetic factors to the same degree. However, it is difficult to account for the inclusive fitness of genes which predispose *either* sex to homosexual behaviour. Nevertheless, such genes must have an adaptive advantage, otherwise they would have been eliminated by natural selection.

One theory suggests that homosexuality is influenced by a number of genes, which are predominantly *recessive* (not expressed in the presence of other, *dominant*, genes). These genes would be recessive in heterosexuals, but could provide reproductive advantages when combined with other genes in these individuals (and so transmitted to future generations). Alternatively, the recessive genes could be passed on through the genetic relatives of an exclusive homosexual. These relatives would share genes with the homosexual, who would increase his/her fitness by helping them to raise more children.

The *dominance failure theory* suggests that subordinate males are unable to find female partners, and consequently develop a homosexual orientation. This could have an evolutionary basis if social dominance is determined, at least in part, by genetic factors. The dominance failure theory would also help to account for the fact that

there are more male homosexuals than lesbians. Another solution to the problem of failure in inter-male competition is to assume a female role (*transvestism*) or identity (*transsexualism*).

Key S T U D Y

Box 43.6 Promiscuity and infidelity in homosexual relationships

Before the advent of AIDS, practising male homosexuals were far more *promiscuous* than heterosexual men. For example, a Kinsey Institute study of gay men in San Francisco found that 75 per cent had more than 100 partners whilst 25 per cent had more than 1000 partners (Symons, 1979). In addition, *infidelity* is acknowledged to be a greater factor in male homosexual partnerships than in heterosexual ones. By contrast, lesbians rarely engage in sex with strangers, and usually form long-term partnerships with little risk of infidelity. Most lesbians have fewer than ten partners in their lifetimes (Symons, 1979: but see Chapter 6, page 61).

The reasons for these differences may be found in the evolved adaptations of the male and female psyche. Homosexual men have tended to be promiscuous because their partners are male, and males tend to seek sexual variety. This is also characteristic of heterosexual men, as shown by the existence of relatively large numbers of female prostitutes. According to Symons (1979), homosexual men behave like men, only more so; homosexual women behave like women, only more so.

It should be noted that one objection to evolutionary explanations of homosexuality is that they are *reductionist* (see Chapter 57). There are many different explanations of gender role and gender identity, and some psychologists argue that the evolutionary approach ignores the influence of social, developmental and cultural factors. As it happens, the main aim of evolutionary psychology is to *integrate* an understanding of genetic and environmental influences (see Chapter 32).

Adultery

Studies have shown that, in the UK, more than 20 per cent of children are the offspring of males other than their ostensible father (Ridley, 1993). *Adultery* can be advantageous to both sexes within a monogamous marriage. In short, the male may increase the *quantity* of his mates (resulting in *more* offspring), and the female may increase the *quality* of her mates (resulting in *better* young).

In evolutionary terms, the risk of adultery for women is that they will lose their male partner to another female, and therefore lose the protection and resources he supplies. Males, on the other hand, risk losing their partner to another male, and the consequent investment of a great deal of time and effort bringing up children that are not their own. Both sexes have, therefore, evolved tactics to ensure fidelity by their partner.

Human females exhibit long periods of sexual receptivity, which encourages continued attentiveness from their male partner. They also conceal ovulation, meaning that males must copulate regularly with the same female to ensure fertilisation (see page 479), and guard the woman against advances from other men if he is to be confident of paternity (Lovejoy, 1981).

It has been suggested that human infants have been selected *not* to resemble their fathers (Pagel, 1997). Concealing paternal identity in this way is advantageous as a strategy to avoid paternal neglect, abuse or infanticide when there is a risk that the domestic father is not the biological father. Other research suggests that people are more likely to say of a baby, 'he (or she) looks just like his father' than to say 'he (or she) looks just like his mother', and that it is the mother's relatives who are most likely to say this (Wilson & Daly, 1992). Finally, an evolutionary perspective would also predict that males will place greater importance than females upon *chastity*.

Box 43.7 The importance of chastity

Males who preferred chaste females in the environment of evolutionary adaptedness probably enjoyed greater reproductive success than males who were indifferent to this quality. This is because, prior to the use of modern contraception, female chastity would provide a cue to paternity certainty. As maternity is never in doubt, it is likely that females will place a lower value on chastity than males. However, chastity may also provide a cue to the *future* fidelity of a selected mate, in which case it could be favoured by both sexes. ,

There is great cultural variability in the absolute value placed on chastity (defined as 'no prior experience in sexual intercourse'). For example, it is nearly three times as important in China as in the USA (Buss, 1989). In a sample of 37 different cultures, 23 (62 per cent) showed sex differences in the expected direction, with males valuing chastity more than females. In the other 14 cultures, no significant differences were found. There were no samples in which females preferred chastity in potential mates more than males. It appears that this preference mechanism is more sensitive to cultural conditions than the relatively invariant sex differences found for youth and beauty (see Chapter 4).

Parental investment and sexual selection

Having examined the evolutionary basis of sexual behaviour, we now turn our attention to the consequence of sex – becoming a parent. Trivers (1972) introduced the idea of *parental investment*, defining it as

'... any investment by the parent in an individual offspring that increases the offspring's chance of surviving (and hence reproductive success) at the cost of the parent's ability to invest in other offspring'.

According to Trivers, this investment should include the metabolic investment in gametes (see page 473), and behaviours which assist the survival of the young (such as feeding or guarding from predators).

As noted on page 473, the difference in size of sperm and eggs results in different reproductive strategies for males and females. Receptive females, by their scarcity, are able to 'choose' between males. What do the males offer that the females can use as a basis for choice? One reason a female may choose a particular male is for the genes that have made him healthy and successful.

However, 'good' genes are not the only advantage one male may have over another. A male who is prepared to invest more (assisting the female by providing food or protection, or helping to teach the young) might be preferred by females, because he would increase the chances of her children surviving. To maximise her fitness, therefore, a female should select a mate on the basis of 'good' genes *and* parental investment.

The female strategy should be to court males to ascertain their parenting skills and try to prevent them deserting to mate with other females. Males, by contrast, would benefit from seeking females who are prepared to raise their children alone, enabling the males to mate again. The sexes are in *conflict* because their optimal strategies are opposed to one another. Females want males who will stay, whereas males want females who will let them stray. Nevertheless, there are factors other than sex which influence parental investment.

Box 43.8 Other factors influencing parental investment

Sex of the parent is not the only factor which affects the degree of investment in the young. Following birth, parents can invest in their offspring in a variety of ways: providing warmth, nutrition, teaching or protection. Other factors may come into play to create the evolutionary pressures which determine the extent to which parents offer such assistance to their progeny.

These factors may include the ability of the offspring to fend for themselves, or of the adults to care for them, the complexity of the social group, and the nature and distribution of its food source. Thus, a consideration of investment in gametes, even in conjunction with costs incurred prior to birth, is insufficient to explain the variability of subsequent effort expended by parents on their offspring.

The burden of motherhood

At the time of conception, the female has already made a greater investment in each gamete than has the male (because eggs are bigger). As a result, she has more to lose by the failure of any particular breeding attempt. It is therefore in her interests to continue to invest once she has begun. This results in two evolutionary consequences: she should be more reluctant to begin any investment (that is, be more selective in her choice of mate) and, once committed, should be less likely to abandon her goal.

Box 43.9 Parental investment and mate choice

There are major differences between men and women in terms of the fitness costs of making a poor mate choice (Buss, 1999). A male in the ancestral environment who made a poor choice when selecting a mate could have walked away without incurring much loss. A woman making the same mistake might risk becoming pregnant, and perhaps having to raise the child alone.

The benefits to a woman of making a wise mate choice would have been significant. She could have chosen a man on the basis of his intelligence and reliability, and whether he showed signs that he would be likely to assist with child rearing. A man would also benefit from choosing a mate carefully, such as selecting a woman who was likely to be fertile and who would make a good mother.

However, this only applies to long-term relationships. If a man were seeking a casual sex partner, then the benefits to him of being highly selective would be fewer. In fact, being extremely choosy under these conditions might lower his chances of succeeding in getting a short-term mate. These differences between the sexes in the costs and benefits of being selective have created selection pressure for sex differences in mate choice.

Human females have internal fertilisation and gestation (*pregnancy*). One act of sexual intercourse, which requires minimal male investment, can produce an obligatory and energy-consuming nine-month investment by the woman that prevents other mating opportunities. In addition, only women can engage in the activity of breastfeeding, which lasts as long as four years in some societies (Shostak, 1981). There seems little doubt that 'early' parental investment in humans is an almost exclusively female burden.

The role of the father

Until recent generations, the contribution made to children by the father was simple, but highly significant. As the 'breadwinner', his efforts to provide food and protection enabled his wife to care for their exceedingly *altricial* children (born relatively undeveloped and requiring a great deal of care). The importance of this role is discussed in Box 43.10. Whilst not endorsing the use of evolutionary theory to justify inequalities, it can be used to see how differences in behaviour may have arisen.

Box 43.10 The male as a bread winner

If some males were able to offer material benefits, females would prefer them as partners, as this investment would increase the survival chances of the young. In our society, courting males are required to demonstrate their ability to provide for the family. Females want males who will stay, and ensure provision for them and their young.

Why do girls want to be taken out to restaurants? Perhaps because, although many present-day primates live in food-rich areas, we may not have evolved in such areas. Early humans, probably living on the savannah, would have struggled to find sufficient food, as do baboons (*Papio anubis*) in the same environment.

It is, therefore, unsurprising to observe that male baboons are involved in the care of their young. Here again, they can make an important contribution to survival, and do so. Unlike baby baboons, a human infant cannot cling to its mother. Females with newborn babies would have been restricted in their ability to forage, thus further increasing the male's importance in providing food to ensure the survival of both the lactating female and, therefore, his child.

In humans, males contribute more to parenting than in most other higher primates. Why should this be the case? Human babies are utterly dependent on adult care for several years, so males who invested in helping their mates would reap significant benefits in terms of offspring survival. This would also be true before the birth of the offspring, as human females require relatively more care during the long gestation period than other primates.

Alcock (1993) suggests that, in the course of human evolution, women may have received food from consort males who guarded them during oestrus (the fertile period). If so, then by hiding the exact time of ovulation from the man, the woman could gain greater assistance in terms of food. If the guarding period were extended in this manner, the male might gain the relatively permanent status of 'husband'. The best strategy from the male's point of view would then be to expend further resources on the offspring (which he could relatively safely assume were his own). The male, therefore, ends up making greater parental investment than would have been the case in a 'receptive stage only' guarding strategy.

In the only other pair-bonded higher primate, the gibbon, the pair defend a territory in which the family remain together. Like humans, the babies are altricial, requiring constant care initially, and only dispersing after five to six years. The female looks after the young while they are suckling, and once they are weaned the male takes over. He instructs the juvenile in foraging techniques, whilst the female is preoccupied with the next, newborn, sibling. As the reproductive success of the male is increased by 'freeing' the female to care for the younger offspring, he can fulfil a useful role. His investment in the older sibling raises the survival chances of both that individual in its own right, and of the younger sibling by ensuring it has the full attention of the mother, the only parent who at that time can care for it. Care by the male in this instance makes a significant contribution to increasing his individual fitness.

In humans, therefore, *both* parents contribute to parental care. The male contribution can take many forms, including caring for the pregnant or suckling woman, feeding and protecting defenceless young and caring for juveniles in the difficult time between total parental protection and independence.

CONCLUSIONS

Evolutionary psychologists suggest that humans possess specific mental adaptations for choosing mates, selecting their sexual partners on the basis of viability and fertility. Both males and females have evolved preferences for certain behavioural and/or anatomical features in the opposite sex. Evolutionary psychology also provides plausible explanations of homosexuality and adultery.

Parental investment theory predicts that the sex which invests more in the offspring (females) is more choosy in mate selection. The sex investing less in the offspring (males) will be less choosy in mate selection, and more competitive with its own sex for access to the high-investing sex. Nevertheless, in long-term relationships, both men and women invest heavily in children. Therefore, parental investment theory predicts that both sexes should be discriminating.

Summary

- **Evolutionary psychology** may be defined as the application of Darwinian ideas on evolution to human behaviour, based on the assumption that individuals will act in a way that tends to propagate their genes. This approach takes the view that human nature has been shaped by natural selection, and is a recent development of **sociobiology**.

- The application of **sexual selection** theory to human behaviour has been the greatest success story in evolutionary psychology. Humans possess specific mental adaptations for choosing mates, selecting their sexual partners on the basis of **viability** and **fertility**.

- Adaptations for mate choice are, however, probably different for males and females, as what defines a 'good mate' from an evolutionary point of view will be different for the two sexes.

- Evidence suggests that humans are a **mutually sexually-selected species**. Both males and females have evolved preferences for certain behavioural and/or anatomical features in the opposite sex. In general, people are attracted to others of high reproductive and genetic potential – the healthy, the fit and the powerful.

- When selecting a mate, we find average faces attractive. Females are preferred with more child-like features, as are males with strong jaws and large noses. **Bilateral symmetry** is also an important feature of facial and bodily beauty.

- **Sexual dimorphism** in humans may be partly explained by sexual selection. For example, it appears that the main influence on the evolution of the long human penis was female choice, probably due to factors involved in sexual satisfaction and reproductive success.

- Likewise, males prefer women who display a low waist-to-hip ratio. This is concordant with enlarged buttocks, indicating sufficient fat reserves, and a narrow waist, indicating the absence of pregnancy.

- Males must be able to estimate the age of females (which is highly correlated with their reproductive capability), using **physical attractiveness** as a guide. Females are less concerned with looks, and prefer males who show the ability and willingness to invest resources connected with parenting.

- On this basis, females might be expected to lie about their age, alter their appearance, and conceal prior sexual encounters. Males would be predicted to exaggerate their resources, inflate perceptions of their willingness to commit, and feign love to induce a female to mate with them.

- Evidence suggests that genetic factors are involved in the development of **homosexuality**. This may be in the form of recessive genes, which provide heterosexual 'carriers' with a reproductive advantage, or such genes may be passed on through the relatives of an exclusive homosexual because s/he helps his/her relatives to raise more children.

- The **dominance failure theory** of homosexuality suggests that subordinate males are unable to find female partners, and consequently develop a homosexual orientation. This would account for the fact that there are more male homosexuals than lesbians.

- **Adultery** can be advantageous to both sexes within a monogamous marriage. The male may increase the quantity of his mates, and the female may increase the quality of her mates.

- The risk of adultery for women is that they will lose their male partner to another female, and therefore lose the protection and resources he supplies. Males, on the other hand, risk being **cuckolded** and investing a great deal of time and effort bringing up children that are not their own.

- **Parental investment** is any investment by the parent in an individual offspring that increases the offspring's chance of surviving, at the cost of the parent's ability to invest in other offspring. This investment will include the metabolic cost of gametes and behaviours which assist the survival of the young.

- One reason a female may choose a particular male is the genes that have made him healthy and successful. However, 'good' genes are not the only advantage one male may have over another. A male who is prepared to invest more might be preferred by females, because he would raise the chances of her children surviving.

- Human females make a greater investment in each gamete than do males, and have more to lose by the failure of any particular breeding attempt. This results in two evolutionary consequences: females will be more selective in their choice of a mate, and females will be less likely to abandon any breeding attempt.

- Human males contribute more to parenting than most other higher primates. This is because males who invested in helping their mates would reap significant benefits in terms of offspring survival. In humans, therefore, **both** parents contribute to parental care, and we are a **mutually sexually selected species**.

Essay Questions

1 Discuss psychological insights into the relationship between sexual selection and human reproductive behaviour. *(24 marks)*

2 Critically consider evolutionary explanations of sex differences in parental investment. *(24 marks)*

WEBSITE ADDRESSES

http://evolution.humb.univie.ac.at/jump.html
http://www.indiana.educ/~kinsey
http://www.liv.ac.uk/www/evolpsych/main.htm
http://www.bga.org
http://www.cogsci.soton.ac.uk

44 Evolutionary Explanations of Mental Disorders

INTRODUCTION AND OVERVIEW

Darwinian medicine represents an evolutionary approach to understanding disease. The approach attempts to explain why humans are generally susceptible to certain diseases and not others. As such, it does not replace conventional medicine (which tends to ask 'what' and 'how' questions about disease), but complements it (by also asking 'why' questions). Darwinian medicine suggests that, far from being part of the illness, many symptoms such as fever, vomiting, coughing and fussiness over food may form a vital part of the body's adaptive response towards infection (Davies, 1996). However, natural selection has not had time to change our bodies to cope with modern environmental phenomena, such as fatty diets, pollution or drugs. This mis-match between our design and our environment may be the basis of many preventable modern illnesses, such as heart disease (Nesse & Williams, 1996).

When examined in an evolutionary framework, *mental disorders* (such as anxiety and depression) are essentially the same as the physical diseases mentioned above. In certain cases, there may even be a direct link between physical and mental condition. For example, Sydenham's chorea is an auto-immune disease (characterised by uncontrollable muscle twitches) caused by antibody attack on nerve cells in the basal ganglia of the brain. Many people who suffer from Sydenham's chorea in childhood develop *obsessive–compulsive disorder* later in life (see pages 483–484 and Chapter 51). The brain areas apparently involved in obsessive–compulsive disorder are very close to those damaged by Sydenham's chorea, and some cases of this mental disturbance may result from a malfunctioning of the immune system.

Many psychiatric symptoms are not diseases in themselves, but defences akin to fever and sneezing. According to Nesse & Williams (1996), many of the genes that predispose to mental disorders are likely to have fitness benefits, many of the environmental factors that cause mental disorders are likely to be novel aspects of modern life, and many of the more unfortunate aspects of human psychology are not flaws, but design compromises. This chapter considers evolutionary explanations of mental disorders, focusing on *anxiety* and *affective disorders*.

ANXIETY

Anxiety is a general feeling of dread or apprehensiveness, which is typically accompanied by various physiological reactions. These include increased heart rate, rapid and shallow breathing, sweating and muscle tension (see Chapter 51). The capacity to experience anxiety is vital to survival, and 'an animal incapable of fear is a dead animal' (Nesse, 1987).

Anxiety may be thought of as a form of *vigilance*, which enables an animal to be alert and prepared to act. In many ways, anxiety may be considered as synonymous with *arousal*. Both states prepare the body for appropriate action, such as fighting, fleeing, freezing or submitting. There are also many parallels between anxiety and the immune system.

Box 44.1 Parallels between anxiety and the immune system

The immune system has a *general response* (such as fever and inflammation), and a *specific response* (including the production of antibodies and natural killer cells). So it is with anxiety. General threats release general anxiety, promoting physiological arousal in preparation for fight or flight, and specific objects or situations can cause phobic anxiety.

On some occasions, anxiety promotes *avoidance* or *escape*. This results in removal of the individual from a source of threat, just as disgust, vomiting and sneezing are designed to separate us from agents that cause disease (*pathogens*). On other occasions, anxiety promotes *aggressive defence*, motivating the individual to attack the source of danger. This may be considered synonymous with the attacking of pathogens by the immune system.

Both systems are designed to protect an animal from harm, but both can have harmful effects in certain circumstances. The immune system can over-react (*anaphylaxis*), under-react (*immune deficiency*), or respond to the wrong cue (*allergy* or *auto-immune disease*). Similarly, anxiety can be excessive (*panic*), deficient (*hypophobia*), or a response to a harmless situation. Only in these cases should anxiety truly be considered a mental disorder.

Anxiety evidently works on the 'smoke-detector' principle. The cost of getting killed once is clearly higher than the cost of responding to a hundred false alarms. This was demonstrated by an experiment in which guppies were separated into timid, ordinary, and bold groups on the basis of their reactions (hiding, swimming away or confronting) when approached by a larger predatory fish. Each group was then left in a tank with a predatory fish. After 60 hours, 40 per cent of the timid guppies and 15 per cent of the ordinary guppies were still alive, but none of the bold guppies had survived (Pinker, 1997).

Marks (1987) describes the evolutionary function of fear as follows:

'Fear is a vital evolutionary legacy that leads an organism to avoid threat, and has obvious survival value. It is an emotion produced by the perception of present or impending danger and is normal in appropriate situations. Without fear few would survive long under natural conditions.'

However, whilst anxiety can be useful, it usually seems excessive and unnecessary. Fifteen per cent of the US population has experienced a clinical anxiety disorder (Nesse & Williams, 1996). To explain this apparent excess of anxiety, we need to ask how the mechanisms that regulate anxiety were shaped by the forces of natural selection.

The concept of an *optimal level of anxiety* is presented in Figure 44.1. It is also important to note here that mild anxiety is often associated with increased sexual drive (Hamer & Copeland, 1999). Therefore, if mildly anxious people have more children, this observation alone could account for an optimal level of anxiety.

In order to assess whether anxiety relating to a particular stimulus is appropriate in a given situation, four things need to be known:

- the relative likelihood that a given stimulus signals a danger (as opposed to something harmless);
- the relative frequency of dangerous and non-dangerous stimuli in this location;
- the cost of responding to a false alarm;
- the cost of not responding to a true emergency.

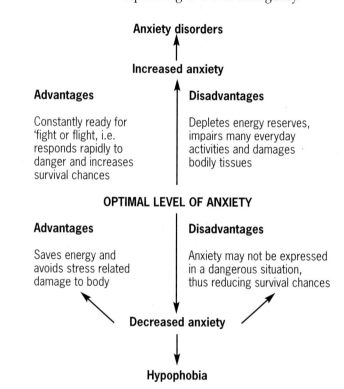

Figure 44.1 *Is there an optimum level of anxiety?*

It is likely that those individuals whose anxiety level is adjusted by rapid and accurate analysis of these things will have a survival advantage. However, in general it pays to err on the side of caution, even if it sometimes results in mistakenly avoiding objects or situations that are harmless.

Phobias

A *phobia* is a type of anxiety disorder, in which there is a persistent and unreasonable fear of an object or situation. The three main types of phobia are *agoraphobia* (commonly defined as a 'fear of open spaces'), *social phobia* (fear of social situations) and *specific phobias* (fear of a specific object or situation).

As noted in Chapter 53 (see page 566), Watson & Rayner (1920) showed that phobias can be acquired through classical conditioning. This behavioural approach to the acquisition of phobias is supported by the effectiveness of behaviour therapies in the treatment of phobic disorders (see Chapter 53, pages 566–568). It is also possible that genetic factors play a role in the development of phobias (Torgersen, 1983). However, many of the studies implicating genetic factors have been criticised, and the extent to which such factors are involved is unclear.

Box 44.2 Preparedness

One interesting observation about the development of phobic disorders is that people are evidently more likely to become phobic towards some stimuli rather than others. Many more people have phobias about spiders and snakes than about cars, in spite of their greater exposure to cars (making an association with that stimulus more likely).

According to Seligman (1971), the objects or situations forming the basis of most phobias were real sources of danger hundreds of thousands of years ago, and those individuals who were sensitive to these stimuli were favoured by natural selection. Indeed, according to Darwin (1877):

> 'May we not suspect that the ... fears of children, which are quite independent of experience, are the inherited effects of real dangers ... during ancient savage time?'

Seligman argued that some associations are more biologically useful than others, such as taste aversion or predator avoidance. These associations are therefore learned more quickly, and are more resistant to extinction. Thus, we have a psychological predisposition or *'preparedness'* to be sensitive to, and become phobic about, some (potentially dangerous) stimuli rather than others. Certain phobias, such as a fear of heights or the dark, are consistent with Seligman's theory (see Box 38.8, page 418).

The preparedness theory has been the subject of much debate in evolutionary psychology. McNally & Steketee (1985) studied snake and spider phobias, and found that in 91 per cent of cases the cause for concern was not a fear of being harmed, but rather a fear of having a panic attack. It has also been suggested that these phobias may be explained by social learning theory (Bandura, 1977a: see Chapter 31, pages 338–341).

Other studies have supported the preparedness theory. For example, monkeys raised in the laboratory have no fear of snakes, and will reach over a snake to get a banana. However, after watching a single video that shows another monkey reacting with alarm to a snake, the monkeys develop a lasting phobia of snakes (Hunt, 1995).

This observation could be explained by a preparedness argument (snakes are dangerous animals) or social learning theory (monkeys learn the fear by copying the behaviour of others). However, if the video shows another monkey demonstrating a fear reaction to a flower, no phobia of flowers is created. Monkeys readily learn a fear of snakes, but not a fear of flowers. Similar findings have been reported for humans (Tomarken *et al.*, 1989).

It has been suggested that phobias may result from novel stimuli not found in the Pleistocene era (see Chapter 43, page 472). However, new dangers such as guns, drugs, radioactivity, and high-fat meals cause too little fear, not too much. In any case, these evolutionarily novel hazards are far too recent for selection to have established specific fears. It should be noted that some novel situations, such as flying, *do* often cause phobias. However, a fear of flying has probably been prepared by the dangers associated with heights and being trapped in a small, enclosed space.

Figure 44.2 *Air disaster films may contribute to a fear of flying*

Seligman's preparedness theory provides a plausible account of the development of some phobias. There is much evidence that the patterning of fears appears to correspond fairly well to specific adaptive problems of ancestral environments, and displays some evidence of cross-cultural generality (Buss, 1999). Nevertheless, the status of fears and phobias as evolved adaptations remains controversial. It is difficult to see, for example, how this approach could explain certain simple phobias and most social phobias, such as public speaking.

Obsessive–compulsive disorder

As noted in Chapter 51, it has been estimated that 1.5 million people in Britain suffer from *obsessive–compulsive disorder* (OCD). Obsessions are involuntary thoughts or images that are recurrent and generally unpleasant (see Box 51.1, page 548). Compulsions are irresistible urges to engage in repetitive behaviours. These behaviours are aimed at reducing or preventing the discomfort associated with some future undesirable event. Compulsives usually recognise that their behaviours are senseless. However, if prevented from engaging in them, they experience intense anxiety which is only reduced when the compulsive ritual is performed (see Chapter 51).

Box 44.3 The functions of checking and cleaning behaviours

An evolutionary consideration of OCD has led to much conjecture as to the functions of ritualistic checking and cleaning behaviours. It appears that checking may have arisen in relation to the defence of resources, such as food supplies, territories and mates. When human communities began to store valuable possessions, these had to be protected against thieves. Security arrangements had to be frequently and thoroughly checked to ensure they were effective.

Genes responsible for *excessive* checking (obsessive–compulsive behaviour) may have negative fitness benefits in terms of reproductive success. In other words, obsessive–compulsives may have fewer children, resulting in selection *against* the genes responsible for excessive checking. Likewise, those genes responsible for inadequate checking would be lost from the gene pool, due to an inability to protect resources. It seems likely that there is an optimal level of checking, and those at the upper end of the continuum are diagnosed as suffering from OCD.

Washing and cleaning behaviour may have evolved as a defence against microorganisms. Since pathogens cannot easily be seen or conceptualised, the notion of `contamination' is common among sufferers of OCD. Those who clean excessively are diagnosed as obsessional, but those who clean too little may suffer increased mortality from infection (Stevens & Price, 1996). OCD, then, may simply represent an *exaggerated* form of behaviours which, at a more moderate level, have (or had) significant fitness benefits.

AFFECTIVE DISORDERS

Affective disorders are the most common type of psychological problem, with a lifetime risk of around 12 per cent for men and 20 per cent for women. Essentially, affective disorders are exaggerations of the universal human capacity to experience sadness and euphoria. However, they are classified as mental disorders when these moods are judged to be extreme (*depression* or *mania*), incapacitating, chronic, or unresponsive to outside influences.

Figure 44.3 *'The mad woman' by Giacome Balla (1871–1958). Affective disorders affect one in five women*

Depression and mania

The characteristic features of depression are low mood, reduced energy, pessimistic thinking, and disturbances of sleep and appetite (see Box 50.1, page 539). The depressed mood is more intense and sustained than ordinary sadness, and is associated with gloomy thoughts of worthlessness, guilt and hopelessness. Depressed people exhibit a general inhibition of activity, and feel unable to cope with the future. Other biological correlates include constipation, amenorrhoea, and the loss of libido.

Mania may be thought of as a mirror image of depression. Mood is elated, self-esteem inflated, and energy levels are high. The future is viewed with extreme optimism, and people suffering from mania often maintain a constant flow of confident speech. Sleep patterns are disturbed by hyperactivity (but this is not seen as a problem), and appetite and libido are increased. Eventually, physical exhaustion intervenes and the euphoric mood may be interrupted by bursts of irritability, and sometimes by moments of depression.

Table 44.1 *Contrasting features of depression and mania*

	Depression	Mania
Mood	Depressed	Elated
Self-esteem	Low	High
Energy	Low	High
Social manner	Submissive	Domineering
Speech	Slow	Rapid
Appetite	Reduced	Increased
Sexual libido	Reduced	Increased
View of the future	Pessimistic	Optimistic

Genetic factors appear to be important determinants of bipolar disorder (mania and depression), which occurs in one out of every 100 people. These genes presumably offer some advantage, either in certain circumstances or in combination with certain other genes. Consistent with this idea is Jamison's (1989) study, which reported a disproportionately higher incidence of bipolar disorder among creative people (see Chapter 50, page 540).

Interestingly, the genetic co-variance between depression and anxiety is very close to 100 per cent (Kendler *et al.*, 1992). This means that the genes that cause anxiety are almost certainly also responsible for depression. The genes differ in their effects according to environmental factors, such as life events. In general, it seems that anxiety results from the the *anticipation* of loss, whereas depression comes from the *experience* of loss (Hamer & Copeland, 1999). The role of genetic and environmental factors in the development of affective disorders is summarised in Figure 44.4.

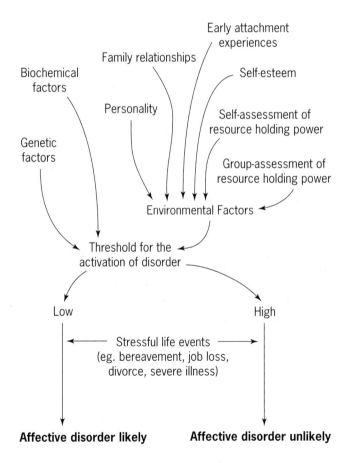

Figure 44.4 *The role of genetic and environmental factors in the development of affective disorders*

The neurotransmitter *serotonin* appears to play a significant role in affective disorders (see Chapter 50, pages 543–544). Studies of vervet monkeys have found that the highest-ranking (*alpha*) male in each group had serotonin

levels that were twice as high as those of other males (Raleigh & McGuire, 1991). When alpha males lose their position, their serotonin levels fall and they begin to show signs of 'depression', such as isolation and lack of appetite.

These behaviours can be prevented by administering antidepressant drugs, such as *fluoxetine* (*Prozac*), that raise serotonin levels (see Chapter 52, pages 558–559). Furthermore, if the alpha male is removed from a group, and Prozac given to another randomly chosen male, that individual always becomes the new alpha-male. These findings suggest that the serotonin system may function, at least in part, to mediate status hierarchies, and that some low mood may be a normal part of status competition (Nesse & Williams, 1996). Nevertheless, it is unclear as to *how* serotonin achieves its effects in this context, and whether elevated serotonin levels lead to high status, or *vice versa*.

Key **STUDY**

Box 44.4 Depression: a response to modern life ?

Some evidence suggests that we may actually be in an epidemic of depression. Nesse & Williams (1996) examined data from 39,000 people in five different parts of the world, and found that young people are far more likely than their elders to have experienced an episode of major depression. Furthermore, the rates were higher in societies with greater degrees of economic development. One particular aspect of modern life that may be implicated in the aetiology of depression is *mass communication*.

Mass communication, especially via television and films, effectively makes us one enormous competitive group. In the ancestral environment, a person would have a good chance of being the best at an activity within his/her small group, such as hunting or tool-making. Even if someone were not the best, the group would probably value their skills. Today, everyone competes with the best in the world. None of us can achieve the fantasy lives we see on television, and our friends and relations may seem inadequate by comparison. Consequently, we are dissatisfied with them, and even more dissatisfied with ourselves. Thus, after being exposed to photographs or stories about desirable potential mates, people decrease their ratings of commitment to their current partners.

There are several reasons to think that the capacity for sadness is an adaptive trait. Sadness is universal, has relatively consistent characteristics across diverse cultures, and is reliably elicited by certain cues, notably those that indicate a *loss*. The losses in question are often of reproductive resources, such as money, a mate, health, or relatives. It could be that a loss signals maladaptive behaviour. The adaptive nature of sadness may be that it changes our behaviour, such that future losses are prevented.

Two features of sadness might increase fitness. First, it may motivate us to stop activities that may be causing losses. Second, it may prevent the usual human tendency of optimism, and enable us to assess our lives more objectively. Studies have found that most of us tend consistently to overestimate our abilities and effectiveness. This is normally adaptive, in that it helps us to succeed in social competition and keeps us pursuing important strategies and relationships even at times when they are not paying off.

Similarly, a manic reaction may be triggered by the perception of a *gain* in reproductive resources (or *resource holding power*: RHP). Gilbert (1990) describes this as a gain in *social attention-holding potential* (SAHP).

Box 44.5 Social attention-holding potential (SAHP)

SAHP refers to the quality and quantity of attention others pay to a particular person. According to Gilbert, humans compete with each other to be attended to, and valued by, those in the group. When group members bestow a lot of quality attention on an individual, that individual rises in status. Ignored individuals are banished to low status. Extreme rises or falls in status may lead to mania or depression respectively.

SAHP may also help to explain the *social phobia* described on page 483. Certain social situations, such as public speaking, may have significant consequences for status (SAHP). The greater the potential consequences, the greater we would expect the accompanying social anxiety to be. Social anxiety presumably functions to motivate efforts to avoid status loss (Buss, 1999).

Overall, we can say that the human capacity to experience sadness and joy probably functions as a punishment and reward system, to discourage or encourage behaviour that will decrease or increase the chances of reproductive success. Depression and mania represent the extremes of this system, promoting adjustment to the altered circumstances. Only if these new circumstances are totally accepted will the affective disorder be resolved.

Attachment theory and affective disorders

Attachment theory (see Gross *et al.*, 2000) represents one possible explanation of affective disorders. According to Stevens & Price (1996):

'The formation of a warm, intimate, and lasting relationship with a dependable attachment figure is the basis of human happiness and security'.

Threats to this relationship can cause anxiety. The loss of an attachment figure may result in depression, whereas joy comes from the restoration of an attachment thought to have been lost.

Depression as a pathological state is particularly likely to occur in individuals who, because of ineffective attachment in childhood, have failed to develop a mature capacity to deal with loss. Evidence supporting this view comes from studies showing that patients prone to depression commonly recall lack of parental affection (Parker, 1984).

However, a problem with attachment theory is that it underestimates the role of individual differences in overcoming childhood trauma. Furthermore, many cases of depression are not readily attributable to the loss of an attachment figure. If there is any loss at all, it may commonly be some other valuable asset, such as a job, status, or financial security (see Chapter 50, pages 540–541).

Rank theory and affective disorders

Whereas attachment theory argues that depression is an adaptive response to losing an attachment figure, *rank theory* proposes that depression is an adaptive response to a loss of status. The function of depression is, therefore, to promote the acceptance of a subordinate role and the reduction in resources that accompanies this role. This has the dual advantage of preventing further losses, and maintaining the *status quo* of a social group. Gaining rank (and thus increasing RHP) is associated with elevated mood, and losing rank (and reducing RHP) with depressed mood.

According to rank theory, depression originally arose as a *submitting* component of ritual conflict. Likewise, mania evolved as the *winning* component of such conflict. An important part of this conflict is *self-assessment*. Both depression and mania reinforce the result of ritual conflict, and establish the respective ranks of the competitors. This idea may also help to explain why the incidence of depression is greater than that of mania: in most human societies there are potentially more losers than winners.

Box 44.6 Self-assessment of resource holding power (RHP)

Assessment is an *algorithmic capacity* (a set of rules) that enables an individual to weigh up whether a rival is stronger or weaker, and to produce the appropriate response (fight, submission or flight). It is on the basis of this *algorithm* (see Chapter 27, page 285) that humans form their internal working models of self in relation to others.

Mental well-being depends on forming estimates of one's own power and attractiveness, which are accurate and stable. Good social adjustment results from accurate self-appraisal, which indicates that we appear strong and attractive to ourselves and others. An inflated self-perception can lead to mania, and a devalued self-perception to depression. Mania or depression is more common in people who are relatively insensitive to external social cues. However, people suffering from alternating mania and depression often have no firm concept of their RHP, and are heavily dependent on outside events, such as the comments of others, and internal physiological factors, such as fluctuations in serotonin and noradrenaline levels.

Despite the above arguments, it is important to point out that both depression and mania are considered *maladaptive* in modern society. An evolutionary explanation of these disorders is that they are pathological conditions based on the (inappropriate) activation of an evolved means of adaptation (Stevens & Price, 1996). However, non-evolutionary explanations of affective disorders may be just as valid.

The incidence of affective disorders

Depression occurs when self-assessment of RHP falls to a critically low level. At this point, the individual in question sees his/herself as a liability to the social group, and is in danger of being rejected. In the ancestral environment this would have very serious consequences, with only a slim chance of survival or reproductive success. However, the act of becoming depressed may elicit nurturance by the rest of the group. This would be expected to enhance perceived RHP, leading to recovery and cohesion of the social group.

In modern societies, people can become isolated without risk to their chances of survival. In these circumstances, the isolated depressive cannot gain RHP in the same manner as our ancestors in the *environment of evolutionary adaptedness* (EAA: see Chapter 43, page 472). This idea might explain the apparent increase in the incidence of depression over the past century (Seligman, 1975).

Sex differences in the incidence of affective disorders

Given that rank is more important to the reproductive success of males than females (see Chapter 43, pages 474–477), we might expect affective disorders to be more common in men. However, these disorders are twice as common in *females* (during the reproductive years) than in males (see Chapter 50, pages 545–546). This could be explained relatively simply if depression *reduced* reproductive success in males more than it did in females. This would result in genes predisposing to depression being selected against more strongly in men, leading to a lower incidence of the disorder.

An alternative explanation of sex differences in affective disorders is that ritual conflicts between men and women (as opposed to inter-male territorial disputes) often result in *winning* for the male, and *submitting* for the female (leading to depression). This may have been particularly true for the polygynous societies common in the EAA.

There is some evidence that when women are given equal opportunities, the incidence of depression among them ceases to be greater than that for men (Wilhelm & Parker, 1989). However, these findings may reflect a trend towards an increasing incidence of depression for males aged 20–40 years. This could be related to the greater competition men are experiencing from women in the employment market.

A final problem for females is the burden of motherhood, including *post-natal depression*. The basis of this condition is unclear, but it is associated with fears of being a bad mother and feeling dominated by the child. This may then invoke a maladaptive submissive routine, which is diagnosed as post-natal depression.

Evolutionary explanations for these gender differences would be strengthened if the differences were universal. However, cross-cultural comparisons of the incidence of affective disorders are inconclusive in this respect, and Cochrane (1995) has suggested a number of *non-biological* explanations for women's greater susceptibility to depression. These include the effects of sexual abuse in childhood (much more common for females), the use of depression as a coping strategy, and the acceptance of a traditional female gender role leading to learned helplessness (see Chapter 50, page 546). It seems clear that the evolutionary approach to psychopathology may be useful, but it is only one of many approaches, and an eclectic approach may be the best way forward.

CONCLUSIONS

This chapter has considered evolutionary explanations of mental disorders, focusing on anxiety and affective disorders. Most phobias appear to be associated with objects or situations which were real sources of danger in the Environment of Evolutionary Adaptedness. Similarly, the checking and cleaning behaviours characteristic of OCD may have been useful for guarding resources or protecting individuals against disease.

The main factors governing mood are the gain or loss of attachment figures and social rank, measured as *resource holding power* (RHP). A loss will lower an individual's relative RHP, resulting in negative self-perception and unhappiness, whereas a gain will raise RHP and invoke happiness. Overall, it seems that the human capacity to experience sadness and joy functions as a punishment and reward system to discourage or encourage behaviour that will decrease or increase the chances of reproductive success. Depression and mania represent the extremes of this system.

Summary

- Many mental disorders are not diseases in themselves, but defences akin to fever or the immune response. Many of the genes that predispose to mental disorders are likely to have fitness benefits, many of the environmental factors that cause mental disorders are likely to be novel aspects of modern life, and many of the more unfortunate aspects of human psychology are not flaws but design compromises.

- **Anxiety** is a general feeling of dread or apprehensiveness, which is typically accompanied by various physiological reactions. The capacity to experience anxiety is vital to survival, and it may be thought of as a form of vigilance which enables an animal to be alert and prepared to act.

- Whilst anxiety can be useful, it usually seems excessive and unnecessary. In general, it seems likely that there is an **optimal level of anxiety**, which has been shaped by natural selection. This enables an individual to react rapidly to a dangerous situation, without depleting energy reserves or damaging bodily tissues by constantly being ready for action.

- A **phobia** is an anxiety disorder in which there is a persistent and unreasonable fear of an object or situation. The objects or situations forming the basis of most phobias were real sources of danger thousands of years ago, and those individuals who were sensitive to these stimuli were favoured by evolution.

- We have a psychological predisposition or **preparedness** to become phobic about certain (potentially dangerous) stimuli. The preparedness theory provides a plausible account of the development of some phobias, but cannot explain certain simple phobias and most social phobias.

- **Obsessive–compulsive disorder** (OCD) is characterised by behaviours such as checking and cleaning. Checking may have arisen in relation to resource defence. Security arrangements for resource defence had to be frequently and thoroughly checked to ensure they were effective. It is likely that there is an **optimal level of checking**, and those at the upper end of the continuum suffer from OCD.

- Washing and cleaning behaviour may have evolved as a defence against microorganisms. Since pathogens cannot easily be seen or conceptualised, the notion of contamination is common among suffers of OCD. Those who clean excessively are diagnosed as obsessional.

- **Genetic factors** appear to be important determinants of alternating **mania** and **depression**. These genes presumably offer some advantage, either in certain circumstances or in combination with certain other genes. The **serotonin system** may function, at least in part, to mediate **status hierarchies**, and some low mood may be a normal part of status competition.

- There are many reasons to think that the capacity for sadness is an adaptive trait. Sadness is universal, has relatively consistent characteristics across diverse cultures, and is reliably elicited by certain cues, notably those that indicate a **loss**. The losses in question are often of **reproductive resources**. The adaptive nature of sadness may be that it changes our behaviour such that future losses are prevented.

- Depression is particularly likely to occur in individuals who, because of **ineffective attachment** in childhood, have failed to develop a mature capacity to deal with loss. However, **attachment theory** underestimates the role of individual differences in overcoming childhood trauma, and many cases of the depression are not readily attributable to the loss of an attachment figure.

- **Rank theory** proposes that depression is an adaptive response to a loss of status. Gaining rank (increasing resource holding power: RHP) is associated with elevated mood, and losing rank (reducing RHP) with depressed mood. However, affective disorders are still maladaptive in modern society.

Essay Questions

1 Discuss evolutionary explanations of depression.
(24 marks)

2 Critically consider the view that anxiety disorders can be explained in evolutionary terms. *(24 marks)*

WEBSITE ADDRESSES

http://www.huxley.net/rankmood
http://www.cogs.susx.ac.uk
http://issid.grc.nia.nih.gov
http://psych.lmu.edu/hbes.htm

45 The Evolution of Intelligence

INTRODUCTION AND OVERVIEW

Intelligence has long been considered a feature unique to human beings, giving us the capacity to devise elaborate strategies for solving problems. However, like all our other features, intelligence is the product of evolutionary change, and can be observed in varying degrees in a range of species. This chapter examines *evolutionary factors in the development of human intelligence*, including the *relationship between brain size and intelligence*. It begins, however, by attempting to define intelligence.

WHAT IS INTELLIGENCE?

Many attempts have been made to define intelligence, with varying degrees of success. Binet & Simon (1915) defined intelligence as 'the faculty of adapting oneself to circumstances'. Wechsler (1944) thought that intelligence was 'the capacity to understand the world and the resourcefulness to cope with its challenges'. A key point in both of these definitions is that intelligence contributes to the *adaptability* of a species, a concept introduced in Chapter 37 (see page 402). With this idea in mind, a useful definition of intelligence is *the ability to devise flexible solutions to problems*.

It seems unlikely that intelligence is a single entity. It is best considered as a collection of aptitudes, including:

- learning a wide range of information;
- applying learned information in new situations;
- thinking, reasoning and original planning.

Together, these abilities produce behaviour we see as 'intelligent'. Byrne (1995) suggested that human intelligence encompasses both special-purpose, hard-wired abilities serving particular needs (such as mate choice, see Chapter 43), and flexible, general-purpose cognitive functions which can be applied widely. To date, psychologists have tended to emphasise the latter abilities. However, evolutionary psychologists believe that we possess many more special-purpose abilities than previously thought.

Box 45.1 The interaction between genetic and environmental influences

For most psychologists, intelligence can be attributed to an *interaction* between genes and the environment (see Chapters 29 and 59). Genes do not fix behaviour, but establish a range of possible reactions to environmental experiences. In turn, environments can affect whether the full range of genetic variability is expressed. Assessments of the extent to which the variation in IQ scores can be attributed to genetic factors suggested a *heritability estimate* of 50 to 60 per cent (Bouchard & Segal, 1988: see page 317). Nevertheless, as pointed out in Chapters 29 and 59, genetic and environmental factors can never be isolated from one another. What is important for evolutionary psychologists is that genes *do* play a role in the development of intelligence, and so this ability can evolve.

Why intelligence?

The human brain is uniquely large among primates. This evolutionary increase in brain size must have been driven by strong selective advantages, because there are significant costs involved. Our large brain is energetically expensive. It makes birth a prolonged, painful and sometimes dangerous process, and continuing growth and maturation of the brain post-birth results in the requirement for extended parental care. Intelligence must be worth all these costs!

According to Plotkin (1995), *unpredictability* is the core concept for an understanding of why intelligence evolved. *Instincts* (adaptive behaviours that are constructed by complex developmental processes from genetic instructions) can deal with some environmental variation, such as physiological and behavioural adaptations for maintaining body temperature in mammals. However, instincts are somewhat inflexible, and intelligence will be selected for in a world of unpredictable change. The faster or more significant the changes, the greater the selection pressure will be for the adaptability provided by intelligence.

In effect, intelligence is best viewed as an *adaptation* which is based on instincts, but which provides much greater flexibility in an unpredictable world. Advanced intellectual abilities are, therefore, spin-offs of the more fundamental forms of knowledge essential to survival. As Byrne (1995) has put it, 'instinct is the mother of intelligence'.

THE EVOLUTION OF HUMAN INTELLIGENCE

There are three main theories that attempt to account for the evolution of human intelligence. These are *ecological* theory, *social* theory and *sexual selection* theory. All three theories rely to a certain extent on the *comparative approach*. This was outlined in Chapter 37, but warrants further examination here.

Box 45.2 The comparative approach

With the comparative approach, the history of intelligence can be inferred from its pattern of occurrence in surviving species. According to Byrne (1995), there are three components to the comparative approach:

- Find reliable differences in the intelligence of living animal species, and ascertain how these differences affect the species' ability to survive under different circumstances.

- Deduce from the above the likely intelligence of the species' extinct ancestors.

- Look for plausible selection pressures that could have favoured the evolutionary changes uncovered, that is, problems to which they seem to be the solutions.

The comparative approach is most useful when restricted to relatively closely related species. In the case of humans, this means monkeys and apes (see Figure 45.1). For example, monkeys and apes have brains that are twice as large as average mammals of their size, and humans have brains three times as large as a monkey or ape of human size (Passingham, 1982). This brain inflation is accomplished by prolonging foetal brain growth for a year after birth. In fact, if our bodies grew proportionally during that period, we would be ten feet tall and weigh half a ton!

Learning and memory (the storage of an internal representation of learned knowledge: see Gross *et al.*, 2000) are forms of intelligence common to humans and a range of other animals. The ability to *manipulate* stored knowledge (reasoning and thought) is a form of intelligence that is probably restricted to a small number of species. *Homo sapiens* is particularly good at this skill, and at sharing learned knowledge (*culture*), for which language is essential (see Chapters 25–27).

Table 45.1 *A summary of human evolution*

Species	Date	Brain size
Chimp–hominid ancestor	6–8 million years ago	450 mm^3
Australopithecus afarensis	2.5–4 million years ago	400–500 mm^3
Homo habilis	1.6–2.3 million years ago	500–800 mm^3
Homo erectus	300,000-1.9 million years ago	750–1250 mm^3
Homo sapiens	Present–45,000 years ago	1350 mm^3

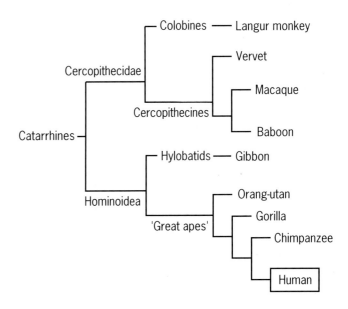

Figure 45.1 *The evolutionary relationship between monkeys, apes and humans*

Ecological theory

One of the main selection pressures that promoted the development of intelligence may have been efficiency in *foraging*. Many simian (monkey-like) primates have to balance their diets via wide-ranging and selective eating. To do this efficiently requires adaptations for finding and obtaining food. *Finding* particular foods over a wide area may require a *cognitive map* (memorised spatial knowledge: see Chapter 38, page 420). Although many species probably have some spatial knowledge, the idea that the advantages of a better cognitive map selected for greater intelligence was first introduced to explain primate intelligence (Byrne, 1995).

This idea is supported by the remarkable navigational skills possessed by many monkeys and apes. For example, chimpanzees in West Africa use round stones as hammers, and larger flat stones as anvils, to break open tough *Panda* and *Coula* nuts. Boesch & Boesch (1984) showed that these stones are often in short supply, and locating them quickly is important when a chimpanzee happens upon a new source of nuts. Rather than random searching, the chimpanzees go straight to the nearest stone of the right type, often using short cuts. This implies that they *remember* where they last saw a useful stone lying, and that they possess a cognitive map of the forest, annotated with rock locations.

Box 45.3 Tool use in humans

Obtaining food involves several skills, such as hunting, tool use and complex food processing. These skills presumably also require intelligence, although objections have been raised to this view. The first stone tools of *Homo habilis* appeared about 2.5 million years ago in Ethiopia. These were very simple indeed (roughly chipped rocks which were no more sophisticated than those made by chimpanzees), and barely improved over the next million years.

They were then replaced by the hand axes and teardrop shaped stone devices of *Homo erectus*. Again, little happened for over a million years until about 200,000 years ago, when there was a sudden and dramatic expansion in the variety and sophistication of tools at about the time that *Homo sapiens* appeared. After that, tools became ever more varied and accomplished until the discovery of metal.

However, all of this development came too late to explain intelligence, which had been increasing over the previous three million years. According to Byrne (1995), tool-making represents a possible candidate for selecting intelligence in the common ancestors of humans and apes, but seems unlikely to have been the source of the subsequent massive brain-size changes leading to modern humans.

Hunting explanations of intelligence suggest that this ability requires the skills of *forethought*, *cunning* and *co-ordination*. However, this suggestion applies equally well to lions, who seem to cope with much smaller brains than ourselves. Similar arguments have been advanced for *gathering* food, but this also applies to many other

species. Baboons must know where to forage at what time, and whether to eat certain insects. Chimpanzees seek out a special plant whose leaves can cure them of worm infections, and they exchange cultural information about how to crack nuts. Most ecological explanations fail the test of applying only to humans (although they could conceivably apply *more strongly* to humans).

There is one final problem with the ecological theory of the development of intelligence. The increase in brain size in the primates, over that of other mammal groups, is chiefly due to *neocortical enlargement* in the brain. This implies a strong selection pressure for neocortical enlargement in primates, and an intellectual function is the only serious candidate for this selection pressure. Therefore, if the ecological theory is correct, and intelligence evolved to cope with large range areas and highly selective diets, we would expect *neocortex ratio* (ratio of neocortex size to that of the rest of the brain) to correlate positively with the complexity of the environment. However, neocortex ratio appears to be unrelated to environmental complexity (Byrne, 1995). Therefore alternatives to the ecological theory must be considered.

Social theory

The environment of a social animal includes not only other species of animals and plants (potentially predators, competitors, parasites or food) and aspects of the physical world, but also members of its own species. An individual's social companions are serious potential competitors for mates and food. Given that they have similar intelligence, this may be the basis for an 'arms race' to be a winner in the social world.

According to *social theory*, interactions with other members of a social group present an intellectual challenge, and primate intelligence has evolved in response to this challenge. Humphrey (1976) argued that the need to compromise between maximising individual gains (by manipulating others) and retaining the benefits of group living, selects for those individuals with the greatest intelligence. According to this view, intelligence is an evolutionary adaptation for solving social problems.

Box 45.4 Group living and the evolution of intelligence

With the exception of the orang utan, which is intelligent but solitary, the most intelligent species are social: bees, parrots, dolphins, elephants, wolves, and, of course, monkeys, gorillas and chimpanzees. Group living could have set the stage for the evolution of intelligence in two ways. First, sociality increases the value of having better information, because information is the one commodity that can be given away and kept at the same time. A more intelligent animal living in a group possesses both the benefit of the knowledge and the benefit of whatever it can get in exchange for that knowledge. Second, group living itself poses new cognitive challenges. Social animals send and receive signals to co-ordinate predation, defence, foraging, and sexual behaviour. They exchange favours, repay and enforce debts, punish cheaters, and join coalitions (Pinker, 1997).

Cosmides & Tooby (1997) have suggested that our ancestors should have evolved to detect violations of social conventions, when those violations could be interpreted as cheating on social contracts (as when B refused to scratch A's back after A had scratched B's back). In other words, human reasoning in social situations should involve a 'search for cheats' strategy. Experimental psychologists have long known that our reasoning powers are affected by the content, and not merely by the logical structure, of arguments (Cronin, 1991). This shows up in people's responses to Wason's (1983) selection task.

Key STUDY

Box 45.5 Wason's selection task

Wason's selection task is a test of logical reasoning in which people are asked to determine whether a conditional rule has been violated (Wason, 1983). What is interesting about this task is that our ability to solve it depends a great deal on the way the problem is presented.

For example, consider the following problem. The four cards below have a letter on one side and a number on the other. *If a card has the letter D on one side then it must have the number 3 on the other side*. Indicate only those card(s) that you definitely need to turn over to see if this rule is violated.

D	F	3	7

The logically correct answer is to turn over only two cards: D (to check that it has a number 3 on the reverse) and 7 (to check that it does *not* have a D on the back). However, people generally perform poorly on a test like this, with only 4–10 per cent being successful.

Now consider another problem involving a conditional rule. The four cards below have information about four people sitting in a bar. One side of the card states what a person is drinking, and the other side tells that person's age. *If a person is drinking beer, then s/he must be over 18 years old*. Indicate only those card(s)

that you definitely need to turn over to see if any of these people are breaking this law.

drinking beer	drinking coke	25 years old	16 years old

The logic of enforcing the rule is, of course, exactly the same. The cards you need to turn over are 'drinking beer' (to check they are over 18 years old) and '16 years old' (to check they are not drinking beer). In this case, an example of detecting a 'cheater' in an example of social exchange, people are much more successful (typically around 75 per cent selecting the correct reply). This suggests that humans may possess cognitive adaptations for social exchange (Cosmides & Tooby, 1997).

According to Cosmides (1989), humans are particularly adept at solving puzzles to do with social exchanges. These have the structure of a social contract: 'if you take the benefit, then you pay the cost'. The reason why we are so much better at applying a conditional rule when it involves a social contract is that we are operating a *search-for-cheats procedure*. We look for people who take the benefit (to ensure they have paid the cost) and for those who do not pay the cost (to check that they have not received the benefit). This is why we do so much better in the second example of the Wason selection task described in Box 45.5 – beer is a 'benefit' that one earns through maturity, and cheaters are underage drinkers. These basic findings have been replicated among the Shiwiar, a foraging people in Ecuador, suggesting that socially-biased problem solving is universal (Cosmides, 1989).

Apes and humans are particularly adept at *tactical deception* (deliberately deceiving others in order to secure a goal). Byrne & Whiten (1988) report an incident in which Paul, a young baboon, saw an adult female, Mel, find a large edible root. He looked around and then gave a sharp cry. The call summoned Paul's mother, who 'assumed' that Mel had just stolen the food from her offspring or threatened him in some way, and chased Mel away. Paul ate the root.

This piece of social manipulation by the young baboon required some intelligence: a knowledge that its call would bring its mother, a guess at what the mother would 'assume' had happened, and a prediction that it would lead to Paul getting the edible root. This type of reasoning is known as *Machiavellian intelligence*, and suggests that deceiving and detecting deception are the primary reason for the evolution of intelligence. This is supported by the finding that there is a strong positive correlation between neocortex ratio and the prevalence of tactical deception in various primates.

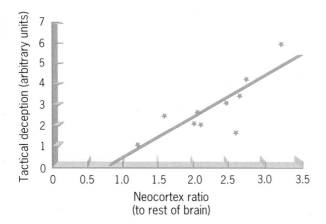

Figure 45.2 *The relationship between the neocortical ratio and the prevalence of tactical deception for various primates (Adapted from Byrne, 1995)*

In order to use tactical deception effectively, a species must have some sort of *'theory of mind'*. Research suggests that certain primates have a limited theory of mind, but that this is mainly confined to apes and humans. This idea fits in with observational studies suggesting that the habit of calculated deception is common in humans, occasional in chimpanzees, rare in baboons and virtually unknown in other animals (Ridley, 1993: see pages 431–433).

Box 45.6 Theory of mind

Research suggests that humans and apes possess an evolved ability to assign beliefs or desires to the actions of others. This ability appears to be generated by a specific cognitive system that is sometimes called a 'theory of mind' module (Leslie, 1987). This module allows us to represent the idea that another individual can have thoughts about certain objects or situations, that is, we can attribute minds to others. For example, we may explain why Peter is looking in the fridge by assuming that he has a *desire* for food and that he *believes* that food can be found in the fridge. This ability is not present at birth, but develops between the ages of 3 and 5 in a characteristic pattern that appears to be universal (see also Chapter 39).

A theory of mind may initially have evolved to allow individuals to predict the behaviour of other members of their social group better. Once it had evolved for that reason, it could be elaborated because it allowed effective tactical deception. Occasionally, the neurological basis of the theory of mind module can be electively damaged. Such damage is thought to be the basis of *autism* in many children, who do not appear to distinguish between living and non-living entities. In other words, autistic children are 'mind-blind' (Pinker, 1997).

Several psychologists have proposed that the human brain is the outcome of a cognitive arms race set in motion by the Machiavellian intelligence of our primate forebears. As Pinker (1997) puts it:

> 'You had better think about what your opponent is thinking about what you are thinking he is thinking'.

What this means is that only humans themselves could provide the necessary challenge to explain their own evolution (Alexander, 1975).

However, the Machiavellian theory applies to *every* social species, so how did humans break away from the pack? The answer to this question is not clear, but may relate to the changes in lifestyle required to cope with the costs of intelligence, such as large brain size, extended childhood, and so on. Alternatively, it could be the result of the development of language. Most animals use communication to manipulate each other, so perhaps our advanced communication system selected for greater deceptive abilities (and better deception-detecting skills), leading to increased intelligence.

As noted on page 492, measures of environmental complexity are unrelated to neocortex ratio. However, group size (a measure of social complexity) *does* correlate positively with neocortical enlargement (see Figure 45.3). This provides strong support for a social origin of human intelligence. However, all apes and monkeys show complex behaviour replete with communication, manipulation, deception and long-term relationships.

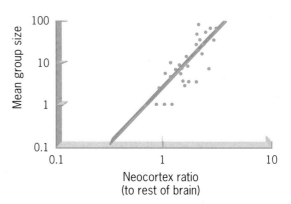

Figure 45.3 *The relationship between group size (social complexity) and neocortex ratio for various primates (adapted from Byrne, 1995)*

Selection for Machiavellian intelligence based on such social complexities should predict much larger brains in other apes and monkeys than we observe. Furthermore, the *insight* special to great apes (see Chapter 39) is not obviously related to brain volume. It is possible that insight requires a 'critical' cortical size, or that great-ape specialities may result from a change in the type of information-processing or neural organisation within the brain. These issues mean we may still have a problem explaining *human* intelligence. Nevertheless, the current consensus in evolutionary psychology is that the social theory is by far the most plausible explanation for the evolution of intelligence.

Sexual selection theory

According to Ridley (1993), the evolution of human intelligence was the result of *sexual competition* between individuals of the same sex. Males compete with males (and females with females) to attract and seduce attractive members of the opposite sex. In many ways, this may simply be seen as a version of the Machiavellian intelligence theory outlined above. But what could have made clever people more likely to win the intra-sex competition, and to have more children than their less intelligent counterparts?

Answers to this question tend to focus on the idea of the brain as a courtship device to attract and retain sexual mates. Its specific evolutionary function is to stimulate and entertain potential partners, and to assess the stimulation attempts of others. Intelligent people are more attractive, and are able to outwit their sexual competitors. The only way that sufficient evolutionary pressure could be sustained in one species to produce our extra-large brains is sexual selection. In a sense, the brain is the human equivalent of a peacock's tail (see Box 43.1, page 473), and 'clever people are sexy people'.

Surveys consistently place intelligence high in lists of desirable characteristics in both sexes, even above such things as beauty and wealth (Miller, 1992). Yet intelligence provides no indication of youth, status, fertility or parental ability, so evolutionists tend to ignore it. However, if intelligence is viewed as being a measure of courtship ability, then mutual sexual selection could account for some of our impressive intellectual abilities.

Box 45.7 Food provision as courtship activity

One important type of courtship activity is the provision of food, predominantly by males (which may suggest a link between the ecological and sexual selection theories for the evolution of intelligence). It has been suggested that, during the Pleistocene era, hunting was overwhelmingly a male activity. Women tended to be busy with child-rearing duties, and men were psychologically and physically prepared for hunting because of their evolutionary history of killing each other. This enabled successful hunters to trade meat with females for sex, a behaviour observed in baboons, chimpanzees and most foraging societies (Pinker, 1997). Indeed, the exchange of resources for sexual access is still an important part of the interactions between men and women all over the world.

Selecting for big brains (intelligence) may also have influenced our mating systems. The large heads of human infants require that they are born helpless and premature at nine months (if they were as advanced at birth as apes, they would be 21 months in the womb), requiring the formation of long-term pair bonds to ensure that parental investment is adequate for survival.

Montagu (1961) argued that humans are born more immature, and remain more immature for a longer period, than any other species. This feature, the retention of juvenile features into adult life, is known as *neotony*. However, although we look like baby apes, we breed at a relatively advanced age. The combination of a slow change in the shape of our head and a long period of youthfulness means that as adults we have astonishingly large brains for an ape. Ridley (1993) proposes that the mechanism by which apemen turned into humans was simply a genetic switch that slowed the developmental clock.

Box 45.8 The importance of neotony in the development of human intelligence

The neotony theory may be closely linked with human mating strategies. If men began selecting mates that appeared youthful (for arbitrary reasons, or because youthfulness implied health and/or fertility), then any gene that slowed the rate of development of adult characteristics in a woman would make her more attractive at a given age than a rival. As a result, she would have more offspring, who would inherit the same neotony gene. Neotony could therefore be a consequence of sexual selection. Since neotony may be a major factor in the development of human intelligence (by enlarging the brain size at adulthood), it is to sexual selection that we should attribute our great intelligence.

A neotony gene would probably make males (and females, since there is no reason why it should be specific to the female sex in its effects) appear more youthful. Therefore, it is possible that neotonous traits were favoured by *female* choice, rather than male choice. Younger males may have made more co-operative hunters and females that wanted meat picked younger-looking men. The conclusion is the same: increased intelligence is favoured by neotony, and neotony is a consequence of sexual selection.

A comparison of the three theories

There are advantages and disadvantages in each of the theories presented in this chapter. It seems likely that ecological factors, sociality and sexual selection have all played a role in the evolution of human intelligence. To what extent they were equally important, or acted over a similar time period during our evolution, is an issue that requires further examination. Nevertheless, at this point in time, the social function of the intellect is supported by the greatest body of evidence, and may be regarded as the generally accepted theory.

Social theory

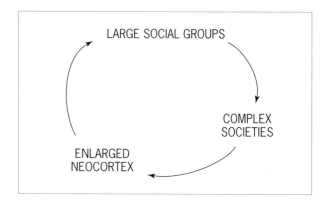

Ecological theory

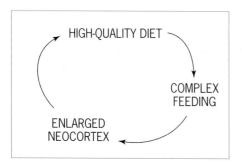

Sexual selection theory

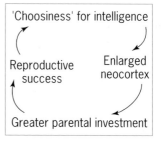

Figure 45.4 *A comparison of the theories explaining the evolution of intelligence. The size of each diagram indicates the likely contribution of the factors focused on by the theory to the development of human intelligence*

CONCLUSIONS

Intelligence is a key component of the adaptability of a species in that it provides the ability to devise flexible solutions to problems. Genetic factors play a significant role in the development of intelligence, and so this ability is subject to the forces of evolution. The three main theories that have been proposed to account for the evolution of human intelligence are ecological theory, social theory and sexual selection theory. All of these are plausible, although the exact nature of the selective forces that shaped our intelligence remains unclear.

Summary

■ **Intelligence** has long been considered to be a feature unique to humans, giving us the capacity to devise elaborate strategies for solving problems. However, intelligence is a product of evolutionary change, and can be observed in varying degrees in a range of species.

■ Definitions of intelligence tend to emphasise its contribution to the **adaptability** of a species. A useful way to view intelligence is as the ability to devise flexible solutions to problems. Byrne suggests that human intelligence encompasses both special-purpose, hardwired abilities serving particular needs, and flexible, general-purpose cognitive functions which can be applied widely.

■ **Unpredictability** is the core concept for an understanding of why intelligence evolved. The more unpredictable the environment, the greater the selection pressure will be for the adaptability provided by intelligence. Intelligence is best viewed as an adaptation based on **instincts**.

■ The **ecological theory** proposes that one of the main selection pressures that promoted the development of intelligence was efficiency in foraging. Intelligence is an adaptation that increases the efficiency of **finding** food (requiring a **cognitive map**) and **obtaining** food (which involves several skills).

■ There are several problems with ecological theory. Advances in tool technology were probably the **result** of increasing intelligence, not the **cause**. Also, foraging explanations fail the test of applying only to humans, and the **neocortex ratio** is apparently unrelated to environmental complexity.

■ According to **social theory**, the need to compromise between maximising individual gains (by manipulating others) and retaining the benefits of group living, selects for those individuals with the greatest intelligence. This theory sees intelligence as an evolutionary adaptation for solving social problems.

■ Our ancestors should have evolved to detect violations of social conventions, when those violations could be interpreted as cheating on social contracts. Thus, human reasoning in social situations should involve a 'search for cheats' strategy. Cross-cultural studies suggest that socially-biased problem solving is universal.

■ Apes and humans are particularly adept at **tactical deception**. This suggests that deceiving and detecting deception are the primary reasons for the evolution of intelligence. In support of this, there is a strong correlation between neocortex ratio and the prevalence of tactical deception in various primates.

■ **Sexual selection theory** proposes that the evolution of human intelligence was the result of sexual competition between individuals of the same sex. The brain functions as a **courtship device** to attract and retain sexual mates. Intelligent people are more attractive, and are able to outwit their sexual competitors.

■ It is likely that ecological factors, sociality and sexual selection have all played a role in the evolution of human intelligence. However, social factors have probably been dominant, although the exact nature of the selective forces that shaped human intelligence remains unclear.

Essay Questions

1 Describe and evaluate theories of the evolution of human intelligence. *(24 marks)*

2 Critically consider research into the relationship between brain size and intelligence. *(24 marks)*

WEB ADDRESSES

http://psych.st-and.ac.uk:8080/people/lect/rwb.html
http://cognweb.english.ucsb.edu/index.html
http://www.psych.ucsb.edu/research/cep
http://www.psy.utexas.edu/psy/idep-homepage/AIDEPonline.html

UNIT 5

Individual Differences and Perspectives

Individual Differences

46 Classificatory Systems

INTRODUCTION AND OVERVIEW

Of all the biological and psychological models of abnormality, the most influential has been the biological (medical) model. An integral part of this model is the *diagnosis* of mental disorders through the use of *classificatory systems*. Two currently used classificatory systems both derive from the work of Kraepelin (1913). In Britain and most other parts of the world, the classificatory system used is ICD-10. The system currently used in North America is DSM-IV. This chapter describes these approaches to the classification of psychological abnormality and examines research into the reliability and validity of classification and diagnosis. It begins, however, by briefly looking at the history of attempts to classify abnormal behaviour.

A BRIEF HISTORY OF CLASSIFICATORY SYSTEMS

Sorting people into categories in order to predict their behaviour is not new. The first attempt at a unified classification of psychological abnormality was made by the Ancient Greek physician Hippocrates. He identified three categories of abnormal behaviour: *mania* (abnormal excitement), *melancholia* (abnormal dejection) and *phrenitis* (brain fever). Later, another Greek physician, Asclepiades, described differences between hallucinations, delusions and illusions, and explained how each could be used as a diagnostic sign. Attempts at beginning a classificatory system were made by Pinel, who grouped disorders he believed were psychological or mental in

nature into a category called *neurosis* (functional diseases of the nervous system), which was divided into several types.

The first comprehensive attempt to classify abnormal behaviours was developed by Kraepelin (1913), who published a classificatory system that brought together earlier systems, and simultaneously elaborated on them in important ways. After carefully observing hospitalised patients and examining their records, Kraepelin proposed 18 distinct types of mental disorder, each with a characteristic pattern of *symptoms* (a *syndrome*), a distinct developmental course, particular underlying physical causes and a characteristic outcome. Kraepelin's work was important in the development of two classificatory systems introduced after the Second World War.

Box 46.1 The ICD and DSM classificatory systems

In 1948, the World Health Organisation (WHO) was created and, shortly afterwards, published the *International Standard Classification of Diseases, Injuries and Causes of Death* (ICD). The sixth revision of the ICD manual (ICD-6) provided a classification of all diseases and disorders, including those the WHO considered to be *psychological* in nature. Independently, the American Psychiatric Association (1952) published the first edition of its *Diagnostic and Statistical Manual of Mental Disorders* (DSM), which contained a classification of mental disorders based on a scheme developed by the US Army in World War II.

Both ICD and DSM have undergone several revisions since their introduction. The most recent revision of the

ICD is the tenth (ICD-10). The *Clinical Descriptions and Diagnostic Guidelines of the ICD-10 Classification of Mental and Behavioural Disorders* (CDDG) was published in 1992, and the *Diagnostic Criteria for Research* (DCR) in 1993. The version of DSM currently in use is *DSM-IV*, published in 1994 by the American Psychiatric Association.

Kraepelin's system is also embodied in the 1983 *Mental Health Act (England and Wales)*, which identifies three categories of *mental disturbance* or *mental disorder*. These are *mental illness* (neurosis, organic psychosis and functional psychosis), *personality disorder* and *mental impairment*.

ICD-10 AND DSM-IV

ICD-10 identifies 11 major categories of mental disorder. These are detailed in Box 46.2, together with examples of *some* of the disorders included in these categories.

Box 46.2 Major categories in ICD-10 and some specific examples of disorders included in those categories

1 **Organic, including symptomatic, mental disorders:** dementia in Alzheimer's disease; personality and behavioural disorders due to brain disease, damage and dysfunction

2 **Mental and behavioural disorders due to psychoactive substance use:** substances include alcohol, cannabinoids, cocaine and hallucinogens

3 **Schizophrenia, schizotypal and delusional disorders:** schizophrenia (paranoid, hebephrenic, catatonic, undifferentiated, residual, simple, other and unspecified types); schizotypal disorder

4 **Mood (affective) disorders:** manic episode (including hypomania); bipolar affective disorder; depressive episode; recurrent depressive disorder; persistent mood (affective) disorders (including cyclothymia and dysthymia)

5 **Neurotic, stress-related and somatoform disorders:** phobic anxiety disorders (including agoraphobia, social phobias and specific (isolated) phobias); anxiety disorders (including panic disorder, generalised anxiety disorder); obsessive–compulsive disorder; reaction to severe stress and adjustment disorders (including post-traumatic stress disorder); dissociative (conversion) disorders (including dissociative amnesia, fugue and multiple personality disorder); somatoform disorders (including hypochondriacal disorders)

6 **Behavioural syndromes associated with physiological disturbances and physical factors:** eating disorders (including anorexia nervosa and bulimia

nervosa); non-organic sleep disorders (including sleep-walking, night terrors); sexual dysfunction not caused by organic disorder or disease

7 **Disorders of adult personality and behaviour:** specific personality disorders (including paranoid, schizoid, dissocial, emotionally unstable, anxious or avoidant, and dependent); habit and impulse disorders (including pathological gambling, fire-setting and stealing); gender and identity disorders (including transsexualism); disorders of sexual preference (including fetishism, voyeurism and paedophilia)

8 **Mental retardation:** mental retardation which is mild, moderate, severe or profound

9 **Disorders of psychological development:** specific disorders of speech and language (including expressive, specific speech articulation and receptive language disorders); specific developmental disorders of scholastic skills (including disorders of reading, spelling, arithmetic); pervasive developmental disorder (including childhood autism, atypical autism, Rett's syndrome, Asperger's syndrome)

10 **Behavioural and emotional disorders with onset usually occurring in childhood and adolescence:** hyperkinetic disorder (including disorders of activity and attention, hyperkinetic conduct disorder); conduct disorders; mixed disorders of conduct and emotion

11 **Unspecified mental disorder:** mental disorder not otherwise specified.

Box 46.3 identifies the major categories and *some* specific examples of disorders recognised in DSM-IV.

Box 46.3 Major categories in DSM-IV and some specific examples of disorders included in those categories

1   **Delirium, dementia, amnestic and other cognitive disorders:** dementias (e.g. of Alzheimer's type); amnestic disorders

2   **Schizophrenic and other psychotic disorders:** schizophrenia (paranoid, disorganised, catatonic, undifferentiated and residual types); schizophreniform disorder; schizoaffective disorder

3   **Substance-related disorders:** alcohol-use disorders; hallucinogen-use disorders; opioid-use disorders; sedative, hypnotic or anxiolytic substance-use disorders

4   **Mood disorders:** depressive disorders (e.g. major depressive disorder); bipolar disorders (e.g. bipolar I disorder, such as single manic episode, and bipolar II disorder, i.e. recurrent major depressive episodes with hypomania); cyclothymic disorder

5   **Anxiety disorders:** panic disorder (with or without agoraphobia); agoraphobia; specific or simple phobia; social phobia; obsessive–compulsive disorder; post-traumatic stress disorder

6   **Somatoform disorders:** somatisation disorder; conversion disorder; hypochondriasis

7   **Dissociative disorders:** dissociative disorder; dissociative fugue; dissociative identity disorder or multiple personality disorder; depersonalisation disorder

8   **Adjustment disorders:** adjustment disorder (with anxiety, depressed mood, disturbance of conduct, mixed disturbance of emotions and conduct, or mixed anxiety and depressed mood)

9   **Disorders first diagnosed in infancy, childhood or adolescence:** mental retardation (mild, moderate, severe, profound); learning disorders (reading disorder, mathematic disorder, disorder of written expression); disruption-behaviour and attention deficit disorders (attention deficit/hyperactivity disorder)

10 **Personality disorders:** paranoid; schizoid; schizotypal; antisocial; borderline; histrionic; narcissistic; avoidant; dependent; obsessive–compulsive

11 **Sexual and gender identity disorders:** sexual desire disorders; sexual arousal disorders; paraphilias (e.g. exhibitionism, fetishism, voyeurism); gender identity disorders (in children or in adolescents and adults)

12 **Impulse control disorders not elsewhere classified:** intermittent explosive disorder; kleptomania; pyromania; pathological gambling

13 **Factitious disorders:** factitious disorder with predominantly psychological or physical signs and symptoms

14 **Sleep disorders:** dyssomnias (e.g. primary insomnia, narcolepsy); parasomnias (e.g. sleep terror disorder, sleepwalking disorder)

15 **Eating disorders:** anorexia nervosa; bulimia nervosa

16 **Mental disorders due to a general medical condition not elsewehere classified:** catatonic disorder due to a general medical condition; personality change due to a general medical condition

17 **Other conditions that may be a focus of clinical attention:** relational problems (e.g. partner or sibling relational problem); problems related to abuse or neglect (e.g. physical and/or sexual abuse of child); additional conditions that may be a focus of clinical attention (e.g. bereavement, occupational problem, phase of life problem).

Comparing ICD-10 and DSM-IV

ICD-10 and DSM-IV overlap extensively and, for many categories, are virtually identical (Cooper, 1995). For example, what ICD-10 calls *mental and behavioural disorders due to psychoactive substance use* are referred to as *substance-related disorders* in DSM-IV.

From Boxes 46.2 and 46.3 it is also clear, however, that each system uses a different *number* of major categories, and that differences arise because of the larger number of discrete categories used in DSM-IV to classify disorders that appear under a smaller number of more general categories in ICD. For example, *neurotic, stress-related* and *somatoform* disorders appear as a single category in ICD-10, and include those appearing under four headings in DSM-IV (*anxiety disorders, somatoform disorders, dissociative disorders* and *adjustment disorders*). Similarly, what ICD-10 calls *disorders of adult personality and behaviour* appears under four headings in DSM (*personality disorders, sexual and gender identity disorders, impulse control disorders not elsewhere classified* and *factitious disorders*).

Additionally, a general DSM-IV category can incorporate more than one ICD-10 category. For example, what DSM-IV calls *disorders usually first diagnosed in infancy, childhood or adolescence*, is categorised by ICD-10 as *behavioural and emotional disorders with onset usually occurring in childhood or adolescence, disorders of psychological development* and *mental retardation*.

Box 46.4 The Chinese classification of mental disorders

China, which makes up 20 per cent of the world's population, has its own classificatory sysem, the *Chinese Classification of Mental Disorders* (CCMD). The revised second edition (CCMD-2-R) was published in 1995. It classifies mental disorders into ten broad groups, and contains operationalised diagnostic criteria for its listed categories. Some Chinese psychiatrists feel that CCMD-2-R is redundant, because ICD-10, with which it is very similar, helps international exchange. However, other Chinese psychiatrists see it as having distinct advantages. One of these is its inclusion of *culture-distinctive categories* (*culture-bound syndromes*: see Chapter 48), and the exclusion of diagnostic categories felt not to be suitable for use in China (e.g. pathological gambling).

Psychosis and neurosis

One of abnormal psychology's oldest distinctions has been between *psychosis* and *neurosis*. As a psychiatrist's joke has it, the psychotic believes that 2 + 2 = 5, whilst the neurotic knows that 2 + 2 = 4, but is really bothered by the fact. Of course, the distinction is much more complex than the joke would suggest.

Box 46.5 The traditional distinctions made between psychosis and neurosis

Effects on personality: Only a part of personality is affected in neurosis. In psychosis, the whole of personality is affected.
Contact with reality: The neurotic maintains contact with reality, whereas the psychotic loses contact. *Hallucinations* and *delusions*, for example, represent the inability to distinguish between subjective experience and external reality.
Insight: The neurotic has insight, and recognises a problem exists. The psychotic lacks this insight.
Relationship of disorder with 'normal' behaviour: Neurotic behaviours are an exaggeration of normal behaviour. Psychotic behaviours are discontinuous with normal behaviour.
Relationship of disorder with pre-morbid personality: Neurotic disturbances are related to the individual's personality prior to the disorder (the pre-morbid personality). Psychotic disorders are not related to the pre-morbid personality.

Although the traditional distinction between psychosis and neurosis has been dropped in present classificatory systems, ICD-10 still uses the term *neurotic*, and DSM-IV the term *psychotic*. Gelder *et al.* (1989) identify four reasons for abolishing the distinction:

- Disorders that were included under the broad categories of neurosis and psychosis actually had little in common. So, diverse conditions were grouped together under these broad headings.
- It is less informative to classify a disorder as neurotic or psychotic than to classify it as a disorder *within* those very broad categories. For example, the label *schizophrenic* is much more informative than the label *psychotic*.
- The criteria used to distinguish neurosis and psychosis are all liable to exceptions.
- The neuroses were grouped because of the view that they shared common origins (a view strongly influenced by the psychodynamic model: see Gross *et al.*, 2000), rather than on the basis of observable commonalities between them.

Despite moves to abolish the distinction between psychosis and neurosis, the terms are still used in everyday psychiatric practice, as they are convenient terms for disorders that cannot be given more precise diagnoses. They are also still in general use as, for example, is the case with the term *antipsychotic drugs* to describe drugs used to treat schizophrenia (see Box 52.1, pages 557–558).

CLASSIFICATORY SYSTEMS AND THE CONCEPT OF MENTAL ILLNESS

Although neither DSM-IV nor ICD-10 uses the term *mental illness* (see page 504), much of the vocabulary used in the area of psychological abnormality comes from medicine. For example, abnormal behaviour is referred to as *psychopathology*, and is classified on the basis of its *symptoms*, the classification being called a *diagnosis*. *Therapy* refers to methods used to change behaviour, and therapies are often conducted in *mental hospitals*. Indeed, the individual is usually referred to as a *patient*, and considered *cured* when the abnormal behaviour is no longer displayed.

The tendency to think about abnormal behaviour as indicative of some *underlying illness* has been defended because it is more *humane* to regard a disturbed individual as *ill* or *mad* rather than simply *bad* (Blaney, 1975). Critics argue that the label *mentally ill* removes *responsibility* for behaviour, and a person so described is seen as being a 'victim' to whom something has happened and who needs 'care'. However, the label *mentally ill* may be more stigmatising than the label *bad* or *morally defective*, since illness is something a person has no control over, whilst 'being bad' implies an element of choice.

Box 46.6 Labelling

Szasz (1974, 1994) argues that stigmatising labels are used for political purposes by those in power to exclude people who have upset the social order. Of course, behaviours that society does not approve of can result in imprisonment. The imprisoned person is, however, still seen as being responsible for his or her behaviour. Yet in the former Soviet Union, for example, political dissidents were diagnosed as schizophrenic for expressing views that only people whom the authorities saw as 'not being in their right minds' would express. Since those views *were* expressed, dissidents were obviously 'not in their right minds'.

Labelling has many other negative consequences (MacLeod, 1998). For example, people react to 'former mental patients' more negatively than to people with the same symptoms who are not so labelled (Farina, 1992). Labelling also denies people's uniqueness if they are pigeon-holed and stereotyped in terms of a diagnostic category. A label may even become *self-fulfilling*: a person might respond to being labelled by behaving in a way that is consistent with the label, thus *confirming* the label that was originally applied (Comer, 1998).

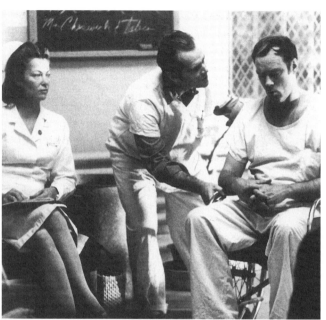

Figure 46.1 *A still from* One Flew Over the Cuckoo's Nest *(1975). McMurphy (Jack Nicholson) is trying to persuade an unresponsive member of the ward therapy group to vote for a change in the ward routine at the state mental hospital where both are patients. McMurphy is an anti-conformist, a charming, but manipulative rebel, who gets involved in a power struggle with 'Big Nurse' Ratched (Louise Fletcher); she succeeds in preventing the desired change. Eventually, McMurphy is crushed by the system, which labels his rebellious behaviour 'mental illness', and 'treats' it, initially by ECT and finally by lobotomy (see Chapter 52). In this way, not only is his rebelliousness stopped, but his entire personality is destroyed*

Szasz (1962) argued that psychiatry assumes that mental illness is caused by diseases or disorders of the nervous system, particularly the brain, and that these manifest themselves in terms of abnormal thinking and behaviour. If this is so, then they should be called *diseases of the brain* or *neurophysiological disorders*. This would remove the confusion between disorders with a physical or organic basis, and the 'problems in living' the person might have. The former, of course, must be seen in an anatomical and physiological context, whereas the latter must be seen in an ethical and social one.

For Szasz, the vast majority of 'mental illnesses' are actually 'problems in living', and it is the exception rather than the rule to come across an individual suffering from some organic brain disorder, who would be considered 'mentally ill'. This fact is recognised by those psychiatrists who distinguish between *organic psychoses*, which have an underlying physical cause, and *functional psychoses*, which either do not or have yet to be shown to have an underlying physical cause (Bailey, 1979: see below). Indeed, even if the functional psychoses could be shown to be organic, there would still be many disorders

which even organic psychiatrists would accept cannot be conceived of as bodily diseases (Heather, 1976).

Furthermore, if an illness does not affect the brain, then how can something like the mind (a non-spatial, non-physical entity) be conceived of as suffering from a disorder of a physico-chemical nature? (see Chapter 57). Like Szasz, Bailey (1979) has argued that organic mental illnesses are not actually mental illnesses at all. Rather, they are *physical illnesses* in which mental symptoms are manifested, and these aid diagnosis and treatment. Additionally, functional mental illnesses are also not illnesses. Rather, they are disorders of *psychosocial or interpersonal functioning* (Szasz's 'problems in living'), in which mental symptoms are important in determining an appropriate form of therapy.

As a result of this debate, neither DSM-IV nor ICD-10 uses the term *mental illness*. Instead, *mental disorder* is used, which DSM-IV defines as:

'... a clinically significant behaviour or psychological syndrome or pattern that occurs in a person and that is associated with present distress (a painful symptom), disability (impairment of one or more important areas of functioning), a significant increased risk of suffering death, pain, disability or an important loss of freedom. In addition, this syndrome or pattern must not be merely an expectable response to a particular event such as, for example, the death of a loved one'.

ICD-10 uses the term *mental disorder* to imply the existence of a clinically recognisable set of symptoms or behaviours, associated in most cases with distress and interference with personal functions.

Box 46.7 The end of 'organic'?

DSM-IV has removed the category *organic mental disorders* and replaced it with *delirium, dementia, amnestic and other cognitive disorders*, because it implies that other disorders in the manual do not have an organic component. According to Henderson *et al.* (1994), because research has shown that biological factors influence a whole range of disorders, it is misleading to use the term *organic*. Consequently, the concept of psychological abnormality has become even more 'medicalised' than ever. Whilst ICD-10 retains a separate category for *organic disorders*, the use of the word organic has been challenged as 'a neuropsychiatrist's nightmare' (Lewis, 1994), although DSM-IV's preference for *cognitive* instead of *organic* may be seen as undervaluing the frequent behavioural component in many cognitive (or organic) disorders (Henderson *et al.*, 1994).

THE GOALS OF CLASSIFICATION

Whatever their differences and similarities, both DSM-IV and ICD-10 have certain *goals*. The first is *to provide a common shorthand language*, that is, a common set of terms with agreed-on meanings. Diagnostic categories summarise large amounts of information about characteristic symptoms and a disorder's typical cause, along with its typical age of onset, predisposing factors, course, prevalence, sex ratio and associated problems. This allows effective communication between professionals, research on different aspects of disorders, and an evaluation of appropriate treatment (see below).

The second goal concerns *understanding the origins of disorders*. If disorders have different origins, these might be uncovered by grouping people according to behavioural similarities and then looking for other similarities. For example, a group of people displaying a particular behaviour might show, say, a certain structural brain abnormality, or have had similar early experiences. Accurate diagnosis is necessary to enable research to be carried out into their origins. Any conclusions are likely to be biased if people have been assigned to the wrong

grouping. Additionally, misdiagnoses produce inaccurate estimates about the *incidence* and *prevalence* of mental disorders, as well as misleading information about their causes and correlates. Fewer mistakes would be made if more was known about the causes and natural history of disorders.

The third goal concerns *treatment plans*. Since a wide variety of therapies exist (see Chapters 52 to 54), accurate diagnosis is necessary to match a disorder to a treatment and ensure maximum benefit for the individual. By treating everybody as new and unique, it is difficult to predict how to treat any one person. Therefore, knowing that a person's symptoms are similar to those of another person whose progress followed a particular course, or who benefitted from a certain kind of treatment, can also be helpful.

Some problems with the classification of mental disorders

The goals of classification can only be achieved if the classification of abnormal behaviour is both *reliable* and *valid* (Comer, 1998). In one of psychology's most famous investigations, Rosenhan (1973) reported what happened when eight psychiatrically normal people from various backgrounds presented themselves at the admissions offices of different American psychiatric hospitals, complaining of hearing bizarre and disembodied voices saying 'empty', 'hollow' and 'thud'.

Key STUDY

Box 46.8 On being sane in insane places

All of Rosenhan's (1973) *pseudopatients* were admitted to the hospitals, most being diagnosed as schizophrenic. Once admitted, they behaved normally. However, their diagnoses seemed to bias the staff's interpretation of their behaviours. For example, pacing a corridor out of boredom was interpreted as 'anxiety' by the staff. When one pseudopatient began to make notes, it was recorded as 'patient engages in writing behaviour'.

Shortly after admission, the pseudopatients stopped claiming to hear voices, and all were eventually discharged with diagnoses of 'schizophrenia in remission' (a lessening in the degree of schizophrenic symptoms). The only people who were apparently suspicious of them were their 'fellow' patients, one of whom commented, 'You're not crazy, you're a journalist or a professor. You're checking up on the hospital'. It took between seven and 52 days (the average being 19) for staff to be convinced that the pseudopatients were 'well enough' to be discharged.

(Based on Gross, 1999)

In a second study, members of a teaching hospital were told about Rosenhan's findings, and informed that more pseudopatients would try to gain admission to the hospital during a particular three-month period. Each staff member was asked to rate every new patient as an impostor or not. During the period, 193 patients were admitted, of whom 41 were confidently alleged to be impostors by at least one member of staff. Twenty three were suspected by one psychiatrist, and a further 19 were suspected by one psychiatrist *and* one other staff member. However, Rosenhan did not send *any* pseudopatients. All of those who presented themselves for admission were *genuine*.

The reliability of classificatory systems

In this context, *reliability* refers to the consistency of a diagnosis across repeated measurements. Clearly, no classificatory system is of value unless users can agree with one another when trying to reach a diagnosis. Kreitman (1961) suggested five main groups of variables that affect the reliability of diagnosis, relating to:

- psychiatrists;
- the psychiatric examination;
- the patients;
- the method of analysis;
- nomenclature (names) and reporting.

Using these variables, Kreitman *et al.* (1961) found an overall diagnostic agreement of 63 per cent, whilst Zigler & Phillips (1961) reported a range of 54–84 per cent agreement in studies assessing reliability for broad categories of disorder. However, Kendell (1975) showed that when more differentiated categories were used (such as specific types of anxiety), reliability ranged from only 32 to 57 per cent.

Davison & Neale (1994) have reported that the highest agreement rate is for *psychosexual disorders*, and the lowest for *somatoform disorders*. Although agreement for some disorders is low, they are as good as those in some medical diagnoses. For example, an agreement rate of only 66 per cent has been reported for cause of death when death certificates were compared with post-mortem reports, and agreement between doctors regarding angina, emphysema and tonsillitis (diagnosed without a definitive laboratory test) was no better, and sometimes worse, than that for schizophrenia (Falek & Moser, 1975).

There have been several attempts to improve the reliability of diagnosis. The *US–UK Diagnostic Project* (Cooper *et al.*, 1972) arose from the observation that schizophrenia was much more likely to be diagnosed by American than British psychiatrists, whereas for manic depression the reverse was true. Cooper *et al.* found that when specific criteria for the two disorders were established and the clinicians trained in these, the agreement level rose significantly. Agreement can also be improved

if psychiatrists use standardised interview schedules or special instruments such as Wing *et al.*'s (1974) *Present State Examination* (Okasha *et al.*, 1993).

In DSM-III (1980), a system of *multiaxial classification* was introduced. DSM-II (1968) required only a 'diagnostic label' (such as schizophrenia) to be used. However, DSM-III and DSM-IV make use of five different axes, which represent different areas of functioning.

Box 46.9 The five axes used in DSM–IV

Axis I: Clinical syndromes and other conditions that may be a focus of clinical attention: This lists all the mental disorders (except personality disorders and mental retardation). A person with more than one disorder has all listed, with the principal disorder listed first. 'Other conditions' may include problems related to abuse or neglect, academic problems and 'phase of life' problems.

Axis II: Personality disorders: These are life-long, deeply ingrained, inflexible and maladaptive traits and behaviours, which may occur quite independently of Axis I clinical disorders. They are likely to affect an individual's ability to be treated.

Axis III: General medical conditions: This lists any medical conditions that could potentially affect a person's mental state, and hence would be relevant to understanding and treating a disorder.

Axis IV: Psychosocial and environmental problems: These are problems that might affect the diagnosis, treatment and prognosis of a diagnosed disorder. For example, a person may have experienced a stressful event such as divorce or the death of a loved one. Ratings are made from one to seven, with seven indicating a *catastrophic* event or events.

Axis V: Global assessment of functioning: On this, the clinician provides a rating of the person's psychological, social and occupational functioning. Using the *global assessment of functioning scale*, 1 denotes *persistent danger* and 100 *superior functioning* with no symptoms.

Rather than being assigned to a single category, people are assessed more broadly, giving a more global and in-depth picture. Axes I, II and III are compulsory in terms of diagnosis, but Axes IV and V are optional. Although ICD-10 does not have the same separate axes, broad types of *aetiology* or causes (such as organic causes, substance use and stress) are built into its groupings of disorders.

During ICD-10's construction, it was agreed that the incomplete and controversial state of knowledge about the causes of mental disorders meant that classification should be worked out on a *descriptive* basis. This implied that disorders should be grouped according to similarities and differences of symptoms and signs, so that a particular disorder should appear only in one diagnostic category. Unfortunately, this did not appeal to clinicians, who like to give prominence to causes (aetiology) wherever possible. Consequently, ICD-10 includes broad types of aetiology within its various categories. Whilst ICD-10 is 'impure' from a classificatory view, it is much more likely to be used by clinicians (Cooper, 1995). DSM-IV, by contrast, makes no assumptions about causation when a diagnosis is made, and is *atheoretical*.

Both DSM-IV and ICD-10 appear to be much more reliable than their predecessors, and ICD-10's clinical guidelines are suitable for widespread international use because of their high reliability (Sartorius *et al.*, 1993). Holmes (1994) reports that the use of *decision trees* (as shown in Figure 46.2), and *computer programs* to aid diagnosis, has also increased reliability. Even so, there is still room for subjective interpretation in the diagnostic process. For example, in *mania* (see Chapter 52, page 539), the elevated mood must be 'abnormally and persistently elevated', and the assessment on Axis V requires comparison between the individual 'and an average person', which begs the question of what an average person actually is (Davison & Neale, 1994).

The validity of classificatory systems

Validity refers to an estimation of a particular measure's accuracy. In this context, validity is the extent to which a diagnosis reflects an actual disorder. Clearly, reliability and validity are closely related. If a disorder cannot be agreed upon, the different views expressed cannot all be correct. Because there is no absolute standard against which a diagnosis can be compared for most disorders, validity is much more difficult to assess, and there is no guarantee that a person has received the 'correct' diagnosis (Holmes, 1994).

One purpose of making a diagnosis is to enable a suitable program of *treatment* to be chosen (the third goal of classification identified on page 505). However, there is only a 50 per cent chance of correctly predicting what treatment people will receive on the basis of the diagnosis they are given (Heather, 1976). Indeed, in a 1000 cases studied by Bannister *et al.* (1964), there was *no* clear-cut relationship between diagnosis and treatment, one reason being that factors other than diagnosis may be equally important in deciding on a particular treatment.

Critics of classificatory systems argue that the diagnostic process cannot be valid if the label a person is given does not allow a clinician to make a judgement about the

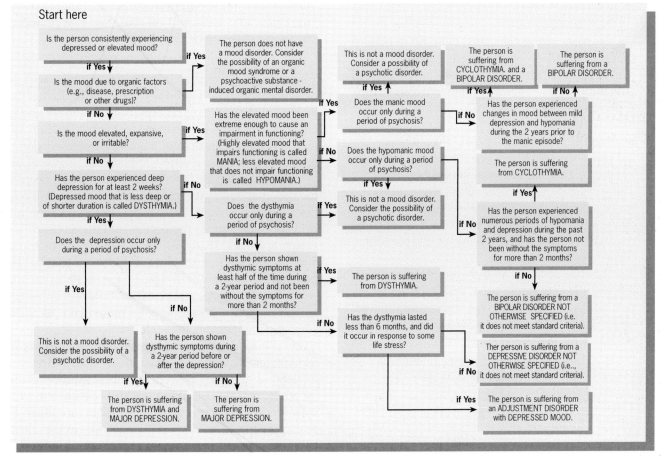

Figure 46.2 *Decision tree for mood disorder. Note that cyclothymia (or cyclothymic disorder) is defined as numerous periods of hypomania and depression during the past two years but absent for more than two months. Dysthymia (or dysthymic disorder) refers to a depressed mood that is less severe or shorter lasting than major depression (From Holmes, 1994)*

disorder's cause or a prediction about prognosis and likely response to treatment. As Mackay (1975) has observed:

> 'The notion of illness implies a relatively discrete disease entity with associated signs and symptoms, which has a specific cause, a certain probability of recovery and its own treatments. The various states of unhappiness, anxiety and confusion which we term "mental illness" fall far short of these criteria in most cases'.

Defenders of classificatory systems have countered their critics by comparing psychiatric diagnosis with medical diagnosis. As noted previously, medical diagnosis is not problem-free. Moreover, whilst Rosenhan's (1973) study is widely interpreted as a damning indictment of psychiatric diagnosis, his claims can be disputed.

Box 46.10 Some challenges to Rosenhan's (1973) study

As the clinicians in Rosenhan's study were *not* required to distinguish between normal and abnormal, the study tells us nothing about the accuracy of diagnosis *per se*. Rather, the study was really assessing whether people pretending to have mental disorders could be detected. Spitzer (1975) has made the following observations:

- On the basis of the clinicians' data, no diagnoses other than those given were justified. Each pseudopatient insisted on admission, which itself is an important symptom of emotional disturbance. A person who swallowed a litre of blood, and then went to hospital vomiting blood, would probably be diagnosed as having a peptic ulcer. Just because the physician failed to notice the deception would not imply that diagnosis was impossible.
- The pseudopatients' behaviour after admission was *not* normal. Normal people would say, 'I'm not crazy, I just pretended to be. Now I want to be released'. At least, initially, however, the pseudopatients remained impassive.
- The label *in remission* (which the pseudopatients left with) is very rarely used, and implies that the psychiatrists knew there was something different about them. All the non-psychotic pseudopatients observed by the psychiatrists were, by virtue of being given the label *in remission*, diagnosed as non-psychotic. This, of course, is a 100 per cent record of accuracy.
- The use of the word 'insane', whilst catchy, is inaccurate. 'Insane' is not a psychiatric diagnostic category, but a legal term decided in a court of law. As such, Rosenhan used the term *incorrectly*.

(Based on Gross, 1999)

Some other issues surrounding classificatory systems

When Kraepelin visited south-east Asia at the turn of the century, he noted that there were *cultural variations* in mental disorders. Despite this, he considered mental disorder to be universal. As he noted:

> 'Mental illness in Java showed broadly the same clinical picture as we see in our country ... The overall similarity far outweighed the deviant features'. (cited in Dein, 1994)

Box 46.11 Transcultural psychiatry

Until quite recently, Western diagnostic categories were viewed as universal, and non-Western patterns of unusual or undesirable behaviour were seen as variants of these Western categories. According to Dein (1994), *transcultural psychiatry* was preoccupied with the pursuit of *culture-bound syndromes* and the systematic attempt to fit them into Western psychiatric categories. The view was taken that, whilst the expression of a disorder might be culturally variable, there was a core hidden within the disorder which is common to all cultures (Littlewood, 1992). Unfortunately, the difficulty with this is that the *biological core* remained elusive (see Chapter 48).

Transcultural psychiatry is 'now synonymous with the psychiatry of ethnic minorities' (Dein, 1994). Rather than looking at the pathological aspects of immigrant groups' cultures, emphasis has changed to a preoccupation with race and racism. In Britain, markedly increased rates of schizophrenia among Afro-Caribbean immigrants, and overdoses among British Asian women, have been the themes that have attracted most attention. Although black people account for only five per cent of the total British population, 25 per cent of patients on psychiatric wards are black (Banyard, 1996: see Figure 46.3, page 509). According to Littlewood & Lipsedge (1989), black patients in psychiatric hospitals are more likely than white patients to see a junior doctor, rather than a consultant or senior doctor, and are more likely to receive some types of therapy than others.

Several explanations have been advanced to explain the higher incidence of diagnosed schizophrenia in immigrant groups. One concerns the misinterpretation by white, middle class psychiatrists of behaviour which is perfectly ordinary within Afro-Caribbean culture. For white people, dominoes is a quiet affair, the silence being broken only when a player 'knocks' to indicate a domino cannot be played. The way Caribbean men play dominoes, however, could be seen as 'aggressive' and 'threatening' by a white observer, who might consider such behaviour to be indicative of a psychological problem (Banyard, 1996).

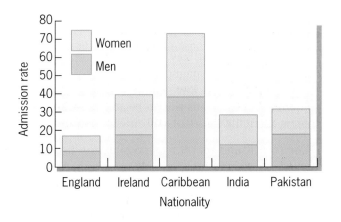

Figure 46.3 *Country of birth and hospital admission for schizophrenia (From Banyard, 1996)*

Another explanation derives from the observation that of those people from Caribbean backgrounds diagnosed as schizophrenic, only 15 per cent showed the classic diagnostic indicators. The other 85 per cent had a distinctive pattern of symptoms which some psychiatrists refer to as *West Indian psychosis* (Littlewood & Lipsedge, 1989). Littlewood and Lipsedge have argued that mental illness in ethnic minorities is often an intelligible response to disadvantage and racism.

Box 46.12 The adaptive paranoid response

One of the major 'symptoms' displayed by members of ethnic minorities is the feeling of being persecuted (a *delusion of persecution*: see Chapter 49, page 529).

CONCLUSIONS

This chapter has looked at classificatory systems currently used in the diagnosis of abnormal behaviour. Two important classificatory systems are ICD-10 and

Delusions are false beliefs. If a person believes that someone is 'out to get me', when this is not the case, s/he is deluded. But if someone really *is* being persecuted, the belief is an accurate perception of the world, rather than a delusion. The term *adaptive paranoid response* describes a mental disorder brought about by a hostile environment. In a society which is intolerant of minority groups, survival depends at least partly on a 'healthy' cultural paranoia, which is a demanding requirement.

Several other issues have also interested transcultural psychiatrists. Littlewood (1992), for example, has challenged the international validity of DSM-IV on the grounds that the assumptions Axis V (global assessment of functioning) makes about nuclear family life, occupation and education are *ethnocentric* (see Chapter 55). Scheper-Hughes (1991) discusses the political implications of psychiatric diagnosis and the way that psychiatric diagnoses may function as ideologies, which mystify reality, obscure relations of power and domination, and prevent people from grasping their situations in the world. In Brazil, for example, hunger is medicalised into a diagnosis of *nervos* and treated by medication, an example of psychosocial stress being misidentified in biological terms.

Do we need both ICD and DSM?

Since ICD-10 and DSM-IV are so similar, the need for both of them has been questioned. From the perspective of the WHO, there is a statutory obligation to the member states of the United Nations Organisation to update the ICD at regular intervals (which, until recently, has been every ten years). The American Psychiatric Association has no such obligation, but would probably argue that national classifications are able to reflect national traditions and usage (Cooper, 1995).

DSM-IV. Although generally accepted as being useful, the reliability and validity of both systems have been brought into question.

Summary

- The medical model is the most influential model of abnormality. Central to it is the **classification** and **diagnosis** of mental disorders. Kraepelin's original system proposed 18 distinct disorders, each with its own characteristic pattern of **symptoms** (a **syn-**

drome), distinct developmental course, underlying physical causes, and outcome.

- The **ICD** and **DSM** classificatory systems derive from Kraepelin's work. Their latest versions are **ICD-10** and **DSM-IV**. The former is used in Britain and most other parts of the world. The latter is used extensively in North America.

- The two systems overlap considerably. However, DSM-IV uses a larger number of categories to classify disorders that appear under a smaller number of more general ICD-10 categories. Conversely, a general DSM-IV category sometimes incorporates more than one ICD-10 category.

- Neither ICD-10 nor DSM-IV makes the traditional distinction between **neurosis** and **psychosis**, one reason being that there are exceptions to all the criteria used to make it. However, ICD-10 still uses the term 'neurotic' and DSM-IV the term 'psychotic'. Psychiatrists find it convenient to use them in everyday practice.

- Because of the debate about the meaning of 'mental illness', both DSM-IV and ICD-10 use the term **mental disorder** instead. DSM-IV has dropped the category 'organic mental disorders', because it misleadingly implies that other disorders are not influenced by biological factors. This makes the concept of abnormality more medical than it has ever been.

- Three main **goals** of classificatory systems are providing a common shorthand language concerning a disorder's relevant aspects, understanding a disorder's origins, and setting up treatment plans. These goals can only be achieved if classificatory systems are both **reliable** and **valid**.

- **Reliability** refers to the **consistency** with which different users reach the same diagnosis. The degree of agreement varies depending on how broad or specific the category is, and between different disorders. Overall, reliability is as good as in some medical diagnoses.

- DSM-IV uses **multi-axial classification**. This provides a more global and in-depth assessment than just applying a single diagnostic label. Whilst ICD-10 does not have separate axes, broader types of cause (such as organic, substance use and stress) are built into its groupings of disorders. This makes it less 'pure' than DSM-IV from a classificatory perspective, but more attractive to clinicians who prefer highlighting aetiology.

- **Validity** is the extent to which a diagnosis reflects an actual disorder. Whilst reliability and validity are related, there is no absolute standard against which a diagnosis can be matched, making validity difficult to assess.

- Studies showing the low predictability of treatment based on patients' diagnoses suggest that classificatory systems have low validity. Similarly, validity requires that clinicians should be able to make judgements about the causes of a disorder and its prognosis.

- Rosenhan found that it was possible for 'pseudopatients' to gain admission into various American psychiatric hospitals, suggesting that clinicians cannot distinguish between the 'sane' and 'insane'. This, and the finding that the genuinely disturbed were sometimes suspected of being pseudopatients, have been taken to indicate that psychiatric diagnosis is neither reliable nor valid. Rosenhan's research has, however, been extensively criticised.

- Until recently, Western diagnostic categories were seen as universal, with a biological 'core' of disorders sometimes hidden by cultural variations. **Transcultural psychiatry** is concerned with these variations or **culture-bound syndromes**. It looks at the incidence of different disorders among different cultural/ethnic groups, different hospitalisation rates, and issues of race and racism within psychiatry.

- Axis V **on DSM-IV** (global assessment of functioning) has been accused of being **ethnocentric**. Psychiatric diagnoses may function as ideologies, preventing people from appreciating the power relationships in their societies.

Essay Questions

1 Describe and evaluate ICD **and** DSM as ways of classifying psychological abnormality. *(30 marks)*

2 Discuss research into the reliability **and** validity of any one approach to the classification of psychological abnormality. *(30 marks)*

WEB ADDRESSES

http://www.who.ch
http://www.psych.org/main.html
http://www.apa.org/science/lib.html
http://mentalhelp.net/prof.htm
http://www.sterling.holycross.edu/departments/psychology/

47 Multiple Personality Disorder (Dissociative Identity Disorder)

INTRODUCTION AND OVERVIEW

In the ICD-10 classificatory system (see Chapter 46), *multiple personality disorder* (MPD) is classified under the category heading *neurotic, stress-related and somatoform disorder*. In DSM-IV, it is classified as a *dissociative disorder*, and has recently been re-named *dissociative identity disorder* (DID). This chapter identifies the clinical characteristics of MPD, and describes some case studies of the disorder. Whether MPD is a spontaneous and genuine mental disorder, or one which is manufactured either by people themselves or their therapists (an *iatrogenic* phenomenon), has been hotly debated. This chapter examines this debate.

CHARACTERISTICS AND CASE STUDIES OF MPD

Of all the mental disorders recognised by the ICD-10 and DSM-IV classificatory systems, perhaps the most bizarre and least well-understood is MPD. Broadly, MPD takes the form of a separation or *dissociation* of one part of the self from its other parts. This has led to the common confusion between MPD and *schizophrenia*, in which splitting also occurs. However, the splitting in schizophrenia is of a different kind from that involved in MPD (see Chapter 49).

MPD is defined as the existence within a person of two or more distinct, integrated and well-developed personalities or personality states. At least two of these personalities recurrently take full control of the person's behaviour. In its most basic form, MPD is termed 'alternating personality': two personalities alternate, each unaware of the thoughts and behaviour of the other (they are *mutually amnesic*). Typically, one personality (the primary or host) appears more often than the other(s).

In classic cases, the personalities and personality states each have unique memories, behaviour patterns and social relationships. In more complex forms of the disorder, personalities 'eavesdrop' on their rivals when one personality is *'dominant'* and controlling behaviour. The *'subordinate'* personalities are thus fully aware of the thoughts and behaviours of the dominant personality, and are *co-conscious* (or *mutually cognisant*) with it. However, whilst the subordinate personalities are aware of the dominant personality, the latter is often unaware of the former (a *one-way amnesic relationship*). Co-conscious personalities can express their awareness through automatic writing (in which a person writes a message without awareness or conscious control), or some other indirect way (such as auditory hallucinations).

The sub-personalities have been reported to differ in several ways, including eyeglass prescriptions, handedness, allergies, susceptibility to alcohol and IQ (Lilienfeld, 1995). Sometimes, they are so different from the core personality that they can be described as 'polar opposites'. Thus, if one personality is 'conformist' and 'nice', the other might be 'rebellious' and 'nasty'. Lipton's (1943) study of 'Maud K.', and her alternate personality 'Sara', is a good example of this.

Key STUDY

Box 47.1 'Maud K.' and 'Sara'

In general demeanour, Maud was quite different from Sara. She walked with a swinging, bouncing gait contrasted to Sara's sedate one. [Whereas] Sara was depressed, Maud was ebullient and happy … Maud used a lot of rouge and lipstick, painted her fingernails and toenails deep red, and put a red ribbon in her hair. She liked red and was quickly attracted by anything of that colour. Sara's favourite colour was blue. She was a mature intelligent individual. Her IQ [was] 128 [Maud's IQ was 43] … Sara did not smoke and was very awkward when she attempted it. Maud had a compulsion to smoke ... Maud had no conscience, no sense of right and wrong. She saw no reason for not always doing as she pleased. She felt no guilt over her incestuous and promiscuous sexual relationships. Sara, on the other hand, had marked guilt feelings over her previous immoral behaviour.

(Adapted from Lipton, 1943)

MPD is often accompanied by a *fugue* ('flight'), a kind of extension of *amnesia* (memory loss), in which the individual flees from home and self by wandering off on a journey, not knowing how s/he got there, and unable to recall his/her true identity. The MPD sufferer assumes a new identity but, unlike many amnesics, does not experience confusion or disorientation. It is usually a brief episode, lasting hours or days rather than weeks. In MPD, the fugue is usually a period of time during which one of the alternate personalities is in control, leaving the 'original' personality unable to account for his/her actions (see Box 47.3, page 513).

The transition from one personality to another is called *switching*. It is usually sudden, and often triggered by traumatic or stressful events. Periods of severe headache, followed by unexplained amnesia, are typically taken as being suggestive of MPD. Personality alternation can last from minutes to years, although the former is more common. Sometimes, personality alternation is marked by changes in body posture and tone of voice. Changes in physiological and neurological activity can also accompany personality alternation.

Physiological and neurological changes were documented by Ludwig *et al.* (1972) in their study of 'Jonah', a 27-year-old man. Jonah was admitted to hospital complaining of severe headaches and memory lapses. During his stay, hospital attendants noticed personality changes whenever these episodes occurred. As well as the primary personality of Jonah, who was a shy, polite and highly conventional individual, three other distinct personalities were identified.

The first, 'Sammy', remembered emerging at age six when Jonah's mother stabbed his stepfather, and Sammy persuaded the parents never to fight again in front of the children. Sammy was aware of the other personalities, and could co-exist in consciousness with Jonah, or set Jonah aside and take over. Sammy emerged every time Jonah was in trouble or needed legal advice. Sammy, the intellectual and rational personality, was designated 'the lawyer' (in contrast to Jonah's designation as 'the square').

The second personality, 'King Young', emerged when Jonah was six or seven, and was only indirectly aware of the other personalities. Jonah's mother had occasionally dressed him in girl's clothes, and Jonah had become confused about his sexual identity. Glib, and very much 'a ladies man', King Young emerged whenever Jonah encountered difficulties with women. He was designated 'the lover'. 'Usoffa Abdulla', designated 'the warrior', was the third personality. He emerged when Jonah was ten and a gang of boys beat him up without provocation. When Jonah lost consciousness, Usoffa took over and was so violent that he nearly killed several of Jonah's attackers. Aware of Jonah, but only indirectly aware of the others, Usoffa's role was to protect and watch over Jonah. Capable of ignoring pain, Usoffa appeared at the first sign of physical danger to Jonah, and left after the problem had been (usually violently) resolved.

Key **S T U D Y**

Box 47.2 Assessing Jonah's personalities

Ludwig *et al.* asked each of the four personalities to supply words of personal emotional significance. For each personality, two of these words were selected and interspersed with twelve neutral words, giving a total of twenty words. Each personality was then presented with the twenty words, and his *galvanic skin response* (a measure of the electrical response of the skin, and taken to be indicative of physiological arousal) was measured. Whilst Jonah responded to the emotional words of *all* the other personalities, they responded to their own words but not to those supplied by the other personalities.

Each personality was also assessed using an *electroencephalogram* (EEG: see Chapter 10). Table 47.1 shows some of the measures and differences between the personalities.

Table 47.1 *EEG measures of Jonah and his alternate personalities (From Schreiber, 1973)*

Measure	Jonah	Sammy	King Young	Usoffa
Alpha wave frequency (Hz)	10.5	9.5	9.5	10.5
Alpha wave amplitude (mV)	20.0	20.0	30.0	15.0
% time alpha wave	53.0	20.0	52.0	41.0
% time delta wave	31.0	75.0	18.0	45.0

Case studies of MPD have been reported for over 400 years, and the disorder explained in ways reflecting prevailing cultural beliefs. So, MPD has at times been thought to indicate possession by spirits, reincarnation and clairvoyance (Mair, 1999). More recently, various biological and psychological explanations have been proposed.

Box 47.3 Some explanations of MPD

- **The psychodynamic model:** Psychodynamic theorists see MPD as extreme *repression* (see Gross *et al.*, 2000) in which memories of a traumatic event are repressed excessively and dysfunctionally. The reaction has its roots in childhood experiences, particularly *abusive parenting* (see page 518). A child exposed to trauma and abuse takes flight from the world by regularly pretending to be another person looking on from afar.

- **The biological (medical) model:** According to double brain theory (DBT: see also Chapter 12, page 127), 'multiple personality' is the alternate functioning of the left and right cerebral hemispheres. According to the theory, we are all *two* persons. However, it is only under extreme conditions (e.g. following a *commissurotomy*, in which the two cerebral hemispheres are separated, or severe stress or trauma) that the existence of these two selves becomes apparent, both subjectively and behaviourally. A commissurotomy results in a *'split-brain' patient* (see Chapter 12), whilst severe stress or trauma causes MPD.

- **State-dependent learning:** If we learn something in one state or context, it is better remembered when that state or context is re-created (see Gross *et al.*, 2000). This could be because arousal states are part of the memory process, and different arousal states are associated with different memories. In MPD, particular arousal states may be tied exclusively to certain memories, thoughts and abilities (that is, the different sub-personalities).

- **Self-hypnosis:** In self-hypnosis, people actively induce themselves to forget unpleasant events (cf. repression above). Some researchers believe that MPD originates in early childhood (see page 518), when children are generally very suggestible and excellent hypnotic subjects. Abused and traumatised children (see page 518) may escape their threatening world by self-hypnosis, mentally separating themselves from their bodies and their surroundings, and fulfilling a wish to become some other person(s).

(From Comer, 1998, and Gross, 1999)

MPD: A GENUINE OR 'MANUFACTURED' DISORDER?

The first case of MPD recorded in detail is that of Mary Reynolds of Pennsylvania (Mitchell, 1816). In Plumer's (1860) account of the case, two independent states of consciousness were described. The number of reported cases of MPD peaked in the late nineteenth century, when there was much fascination with *hypnosis* as a pathway to the unconscious mind and the paranormal (Mair, 1999).

Figure 47.1 *Stills from the film* The Three Faces of Eve. *It was this film that brought multiple personality disorder to public attention*

Prince (1900) described 24 reported cases, and argued that in more fully developed forms the secondary or 'disintegrated' personality would 'approximate to that of normal life and might pass before the world as mentally healthy'. The publication of Prince's (1905) book saw another increase in the number of reported cases. Taylor & Martin (1944) identified 76 cases occurring over 128 years, and suggested there might be as many more (Merskey, 1992). One of the most famous cases was reported by Thigpen & Cleckley (1954). A book of the case was published (*The Three Faces of Eve*: Thigpen & Cleckley, 1957), and shortly afterwards, a film of it made. From that point the number of cases, *and* personalities, increased almost exponentially!

About half of the documented cases have ten or more personalities (the average being fifteen for women and eight for men: Comer, 1998), and can have over 100. Before 1980, there were only 200 documented cases in the entire world. By 1984, more than 1000 cases had been reported in the United States alone. So, whilst MPD used to be considered both puzzling *and* rare, it is estimated that one per cent of the population may have multiple personalities and require treatment for the disorder (Mair, 1999).

Table 47.2 *An illustrative history of documented MPD cases from 1954*

- **Horton & Miller (1972):** 'Gloria' was a very disturbed 16-year-old, who ultimately manifested *four* different personalities.

- **Schreiber (1973):** 'Sybil' had *17* alternative personalities, including adults, a teenager, two males ('Mike' and 'Sid') and a baby ('Ruthie')

- **Hawksworth & Schwarz (1977):** Henry Hawksworth had *five* personalities, and claimed that another version of himself, 'Johnny', lived inside a ventriloquist's doll.

- **Sizemore & Pittillo (1977):** The original 'Eve White' (see text) revealed herself as Christine Sizemore, and claimed *nine* personalities *before* Eve Black, and a total of *22* in all.

- **Keyes (1981):** W S Milligan evidently possessed *ten*, and possibly as many as *23* different personalities, including 'Adalana', a girl who would enjoy washing dishes when it was required, and 'Tommy', a 16-year-old escape artist.

- **Chase (1988):** Chase describes her own experiences with 'the Troops', *92* personalities who evidently resided within her.

- **Williamson (1999):** Williamson's mother was diagnosed with MPD, and apparently has *95* separate personalities. Perhaps cynically, Williamson notes that: 'her diagnosis may explain why she has been married nine times – only 86 more husbands and she'll have paired off all the folks in her head'.

As noted previously, one of the most famous cases of MPD is that of Thigpen & Cleckley (1954). They studied a 25-year-old woman who was referred to them because of 'severe and blinding headaches'. It became clear that 'Eve White' was experiencing marital problems and personal frustrations. Several days after Eve had visited their office, Thigpen and Cleckley received a letter, in which the handwriting of the last paragraph was very different from the previous paragraphs (see Figure 47.2):

'What was the meaning of such a letter? Though unsigned, the postmark, the content, and the familiar penship in most of the message revealed that this had been written by Eve White. However, it raised puzzling

questions. Had some child found the uncompleted page, scribbled those words, and perhaps as a whim mailed it in an already addressed envelope? Perhaps. The handwriting of the last paragraph certainly suggested the work of a child. Could Eve White herself, as a puerile prank, have decided to disguise her characteristic handwriting and added this inconsequential note? And if so, why? She seemed to be a circumspect, matter-of-fact person, meticulously truthful and consistently sober and serious about her grave troubles'. (Thigpen & Cleckley, 1954)

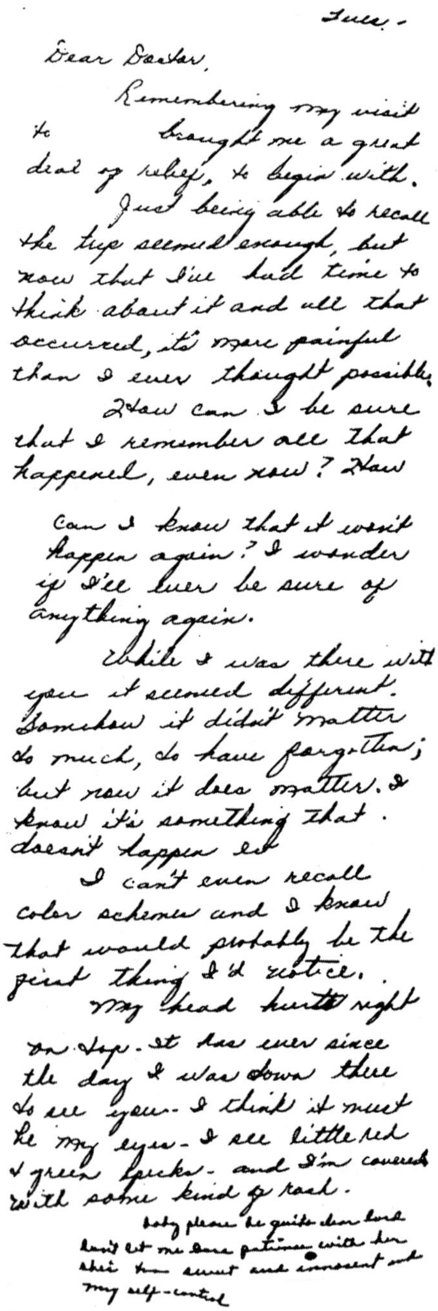

Figure 47.2 *The letter sent to Thigpen and Cleckley by Eve White. Note the change in handwriting in the last four lines*

Box 47.4 'Eve Black' and 'Jane'

Thigpen and Cleckley 'contacted' a second personality, 'Eve Black'. Initially, this was achieved through hypnosis, but later she emerged spontaneously. Eve White was the dominant personality, and had no knowledge of Eve Black's existence, although Eve Black had been alternating with Eve White for some years. Whenever Eve Black surfaced, all that Eve White could report was that she had 'blackouts'. Eve Black, however, was co-conscious with Eve White. She knew everything that she did, and would talk about her with flippancy and contempt.

Whilst Eve White was serious, quiet and bland, Eve Black was carefree, mischievous and uninhibited. She would 'come out' at the most inappropriate times, leaving Eve White with hangovers, bills and a reputation in locals bars that she could not explain. After eight months of treatment, Eve White suffered a major setback. Her original symptoms returned, but were more intense and frequent. This was the prelude to the appearance of a third and more mature personality, 'Jane'. Jane was co-conscious with both Eve White and Eve Black, although she had no memory of their activities up to the time of her appearance.

Simulation and MPD

Several attempts have been made to validate MPD's existence, but many researchers are sceptical about it. For Aldridge-Morris (1989), it is unhelpful to regard MPD as a discrete clinical entity, and the view of many psychiatrists and clinical psychologists is that at least some cases of MPD are *simulations*. Indeed, in at least one case, a patient *admitted* that she had reported her multiple personalities to please the doctors who first told her that that was her condition (Merskey, 1992).

Certainly, MPD can be induced experimentally using hypnosis, and some researchers argue that this supports the view that many apparent cases of MPD are faked (Spanos *et al.*, 1985). However, Spanos *et al.* also point out that individuals predisposed to MPD may have a tendency towards suggestibility and fantasy, making them especially susceptible to cues from others (including therapists: see pages 517–518). This same tendency may also confer a talent for adopting or enacting *roles*. From this perspective, the role-taking explanation does not necessarily mean that MPD does not exist. Rather, MPD cases:

'... can perhaps be conceptualised as uniquely capable of creating and entering a fantasy world inhabited by their own imaginary identities' (Lilienfeld, 1995).

Thigpen & Cleckley (1954), however, were concerned that they might have been 'hoodwinked' by a skilful actress. At the suggestion of the editor of the journal in which their article was published, they gave Eve the Semantic Differential attitude scale, a technique for evaluating the connative meanings of words. The test scores were analysed 'blind' by two other researchers.

Eve White, Eve Black and Jane were each tested twice, at two-monthly intervals. Eve White emerged as socialised, perceiving the world 'normally', but showing an unsatisfactory attitude towards herself. Eve Black displayed a 'violent kind of adjustment', saw herself as perfect, and perceived the world 'abnormally'. Jane had the most 'healthy' perception of the world and the most satisfactory self-evaluation. Because each personality's ratings were more similar to themselves on the second testing than to those of the other personalities, this was taken as indicating that the three personalities were distinct.

This was apparently confirmed by London *et al.* (1969, cited in Gross, 1999), who analysed frame-by-frame a 30-minute film of Eve made by Thigpen and Cleckley. London *et al.* looked for facial regularities and other transformations of expressive behaviour. All three personalities 'appeared' in the film, and all showed *'transient microstrabismus'* (the deviation of one eye from the axis of the other, such as one moving to the left, the other to the right, or one moving and the other not moving). Significantly, each personality showed a *different* microstrabismus pattern.

Box 47.5 The role of the media in MPD

According to Thigpen & Cleckley (1984), some features of MPD can be role-played through *observational learning*. The portrayal of MPD in films (e.g. *The Three Faces of Eve*) and in books (e.g. *When Rabbit Howls*: Chase, 1988) has made the disorder well-known, and provided 'detailed examples of the symptoms and course of multiple personality' (Spanos *et al.*, 1985). In support of this, Fahy *et al.* (1989) reported a patient who had seen *The Three Faces of Eve* and read the book *Sybil* (Schreiber, 1973: see also page 518). Directing her attention away from the 'alternate personalities' led to their decline. This would make MPD a *doxogenic* disorder (from 'doxe' meaning opinion, and 'geon', to produce), that is, a disorder due to a person's opinions, these being largely formed through *media influences*.

But why would people be motivated to simulate MPD? According to Wessely (1993), one review of MPD:

'... noted that it was common among cases to attribute antisocial acts that they had performed to their other selves as a way of avoiding blame. In America, MPD has been used as a successful defence in rape and other serious crimes'.

Altrocchi (1980), for example, describes the case of Arthur D. Wayne Bicknall, who was acquitted of drink-driving in 1976 by a Californian judge. His psychiatrist testified that one of Bicknall's other personalities ('Johnnie') was the true criminal. Similarly, in 1978, a Californian jury acquitted Ester Minor of forgery after three psychiatrists (including the one that testified on Bicknall's behalf) and two psychologists had testified that it was 'Raynell Potts' who had actually carried out the crime without Minor's knowledge.

Box 47.6 The 'Hillside Strangler'

Using MPD as a defence is not, however, always successful. One example of this was Kenneth Bianchi, known as the 'Hillside Strangler'. He was shown to be simulating MPD to escape the death penalty for the sadistic murders of ten young women in Los Angeles. Bianchi was discovered by prosecution lawyers to have imitated a psychologist, and had sufficient knowledge of psychological methods and jargon to simulate MPD. He was caught out when, after being casually told by a psychiatrist that most cases of MPD have *three* personalities, Bianchi, who claimed to have *two* personalities, promptly produced a third!

Bianchi was later diagnosed as suffering from *dissocial personality disorder*. Some of the characteristics of this include 'superficial charm and good "intelligence"', 'absence of nervousness', 'untruthfulness and insincerity' and 'lack of remorse or shame'. All of these are conducive to criminal behaviour, and useful to simulate another mental disorder to avoid detection for a crime.

In a variation of the above cases, Wessely (1993) described a court case in Wisconsin, USA, in which a man was tried for the rape of a 27-year-old Korean-born woman, identified in court as 'Sarah'. The trial attracted much publicity, because Sarah was alleged to have 46 different personalities, including 'Sam', a creature that 'evolved from a small animal which lives beneath tables and growls when frightened'. Six of the personalities were sworn in, and gave testimony in court. The defendant was found guilty of rape, because whilst one of the personalities had consented to sex, at least some of the other 45 had not (see McIlveen *et al.* 1994, for a full description of the case).

Box 47.7 What rights do alternate personalities have?

Some psychologists believe that alternate personalities satisfy the basic criteria for *personhood* – they are conscious, with thoughts, beliefs and (perhaps) their own body-schema (Apter, 1991).

- If there is someone *who* the secondary selves are, is it the original person, or someone else?
- Does the secondary person(s) have a right to life?
- Is the fusion of personalities into one 'self' (as happens in therapy) the death of them?
- Are the secondary personalities entitled to vote, just as the primary personality is?

(From Gross, 1999)

Further support for the view that MPD cases are simulated comes from Rathus (1984). Rathus claims to have seen:

'... mini-epidemics of claimed multiple personality on psychiatric wards, when patients had been confronted with socially unacceptable behaviour and found out that others were attributing such behaviour to other personalities dwelling within them'.

Of course, this does not mean that there is no such thing as MPD, but it does suggest that some people attempt to escape responsibility by attributing behaviour to 'forces beyond their control'.

It is also worth noting that MPD is diagnosed in women at least three times as often as it is in men (Comer, 1998), and that the majority of females are young whereas the majority of therapists are older men. Prince (1905), for example, was 44 when he studied Miss Beauchamp, a 23-year-old. Miss Beauchamp is actually on record as pleading to be hypnotised by Prince: 'And I do want you, please, please, to hypnotise me again. You know it is the only thing that has ever helped me' (Prince, 1905). The possibility that Miss Beauchamp generated alternate personalities to retain Prince's interest cannot be ruled out!

The diagnosis of all dissociative disorders is not straightforward, since it relies on an individual's self-report. Moreover, because some psychiatrists might not even contemplate the possibility that an individual is lying, distinguishing between the fraudulent and genuine can be difficult (Wessely, 1993). With amnesia, for example, even expert psychiatrists find it difficult to distinguish between simulators and the genuinely affected (Schacter, 1986).

Box 47.8 Detecting simulation

As noted earlier, alternate personalities differ in various ways, including body posture and tone of voice. However, these behaviours are relatively easy to simulate, as is performance on personality questionnaires and intelligence tests. The EEG (as used by Ludwig *et al.*, 1972: see Box 47.2, page 512) has been used to detect simulators. *Evoked potentials* (regular patterns of electrical activity in the brain in response to some controlled stimulus, such as a flashing light) *may* accompany personality alteration (Goleman, 1985). Additionally, in one study in which actors *pretended* to have MPD, changes in EEG activity were *not* exhibited (Putnam, 1992).

Coons *et al.* (1982) are more sceptical. They believe that EEG differences between alternating personalities reflect differences in mood, concentration and muscle tension, rather than some important difference between the brains of non-MPD and MPD individuals. As Sue *et al.* (1994) have remarked:

'Although the claimed evidence supports the existence of [MPD], reliable methods to determine [its] validity do not currently exist'.

Iatrogenesis and MPD

According to Carson *et al.* (1988), because MPD can be induced experimentally, it might be that it is 'an artificial creation produced inadvertently by suggestions of the therapist'. An *iatrogenic disorder* is a condition or disorder produced by a physician or therapist through mechanisms such as selective attention, reinforcement, and expectations placed on the patient or individual. It has been proposed that MPD occurs when a potential 'sufferer' encounters a therapist who believes and/or is interested in the disorder (Frick, 1995).

Thigpen & Cleckley (1984) discussed the 'epidemic' of MPD cases that had swept the United States since the publication of *The Three Faces of Eve*. They revealed that thousands of people who *sought* to be diagnosed as suffering from MPD had been referred to them. To see Thigpen and Cleckley, people often used various voices on the telephone or wrote letters in different handwriting. Thigpen and Cleckley, however, diagnosed only *one* further case of MPD, and suggested that 'a competition [seems] to have developed among some doctors to see who could diagnose the most cases', to which Wessely (1993) suggests they might have added, 'and whose cases could have the most personalities'.

Wessely's view is supported by the observation that most MPD cases have been reported in the United States, where public interest in the disorder seems greatest, and by a general acceptance that some cases may have been wittingly or unwittingly encouraged by therapists eager for publicity. For Wessely:

'[By finding] a therapist who will collude in this new, dramatic piece of theatre ... the therapist [acts] as the midwife for the new personalities'.

MPD is virtually unknown in other parts of the world (Takahashi, 1990). Indeed, it was omitted from early drafts of ICD-10, since some advisers pointed out that its diagnosis is never made in those countries where ICD is used (which might make it a *culture-bound syndrome*: see Chapter 48). When Aldridge-Morris (1989) wrote to the British Psychological Society (BPS) and the Royal College of Psychiatrists asking whether British professionals had experience of MPD, he received few replies. Four were from professionals who believed they might have seen a total of six cases between them, but even these were tentative. For Aldridge-Morris:

It is clear that some therapists have an astronomically higher probability of meeting such patients than their colleagues, and the vast majority (dare one say 'all'?) are in the United States'.

If MPD is an artificial creation produced either deliberately or accidentally by a therapist's suggestions, it ought to be possible to detect this. Berman (1975), for example, suggests that genuine cases can be detected by:

* discovering whether the split appeared *before* the therapy began, and/or

* examining whether or not the reported personalities lead 'separate lives' beyond the confines of the therapeutic setting.

Box 47.9 MPD: Consciously contrived or absorption in the 'role'?

According to Carson *et al.* (1988), MPD cases may involve 'elements of "performance" whose deliberateness is less consciously contrived than it is an absorption in the "role"'. With respect to 'elements of performance', Berman (1975) says:

'There are good reasons for doubting the tales of split personalities: the therapist's intense involvement with their patients; their own belief in the reality of the splitting; the use of hypnosis and other methods of suggestion. [However], whilst some cases might be fictitious, and whilst in others a therapist's expectations may have unconsciously encouraged the birth of the personalities detected, I believe that true cases of multiple personality do occur'.

Berman believes that the use of hypnosis in getting MPD sufferers to switch from one personality to another indicates that the power of suggestion, along with the individual's desire to please the therapist, plays some role in transforming what Rycroft (1978) describes as 'severe, but less exotic, emotional responses' into 'much more interesting cases of MPD'. However, Carson *et al.* (1988) believe that the distinction between 'true and genuine' and 'false and fraudulent' is actually a false dichotomy, and that MPD may reflect unconscious efforts by the person involved to play various roles.

Childhood abuse and MPD

MPD is typically first diagnosed in late adolescence or early adulthood. However, the initial signs of dissociation usually develop in early childhood, before the age of eight (Mair, 1999). As noted previously (see page 516), the vast majority of cases are female, and most have been physically, often sexually, abused as children. For example, Coons *et al.* (1982) describe the case of 'Lucy', a 23-year-old woman who was sexually abused by an alcoholic father when she was five.

Key **STUDY**

Box 47.10 'Lucy'

Lucy was raped at the age of 21, and began having frequent periods of amnesia and headaches (Lucy had in fact experienced amnesia from the age of five). Lucy had at least three other personalities:

'Linda', the personality who originated at age five was confident, aggressive, and normally good-humoured, but would fly into a rage at the slightest provocation. 'Sally', a personality formed to cope with the rape experience, was reclusive, distrustful and nearly mute. 'Sam', a male secondary personality, served as a rescuer personality when Sally made one of her many suicide attempts.

(From Coons *et al.*, 1982)

Although various explanations of MPD have been proposed (see Box 47.3, page 513), the link between childhood *abuse* and MPD is a dominant perspective, and adults diagnosed with MPD are now believed to have started dissociating in early childhood as a response to trauma usually involving *sexual* abuse (Mair, 1999). Indeed, some regard MPD as being *caused* by abuse. For example, Ross (1997) says that '[MPD] is a little girl imagining the abuse is happening to someone else'.

Mair believes that the publication of *Sybil* (Schreiber, 1973: see Table 47.2, page 514) strongly influenced the development of this MPD–severe early trauma link, *even though the author offered little factual evidence of Sybil's childhood*. Many MPD cases claim to have been abused in childhood, in many unpleasant ways. However, memories reported by people suffering from dissociative disorders may be unreliable (Kluft, 1996), and corroboration of an adult's report of childhood abuse is difficult. For Mair (1999), the general pattern is of *some* abuse in *some* individuals. Moreover, whilst abuse might *contribute* to a present problem, it does not mean that a present problem can *only* be explained as a response to the abuse, or that the mechanism of the response is understood. The link between MPD and severe childhood trauma may not be as clear-cut as some psychologists believe.

CONCLUSIONS

This chapter has identified the clinical characteristics of MPD and described some case studies of it. It has also examined the issue of whether MPD is a genuine mental disorder or one which is manufactured either by people themselves or their therapists. The status of MPD is unclear. A view shared by many researchers is that MPD never occurs as a spontaneous natural event in adults. For Merskey (1992):

'Many of these [people] have had terrible experiences and awful problems in their lives. The [issue] is not whether or not [they] need treatment – they do – but rather under what label and with which ideas'.

Summary

- **Multiple personality disorder** (MPD) is one of the most bizarre and least well-understood mental disorders. Broadly, it takes the form of a **separation** or **dissociation** of one part of the self from its other parts. In DSM-IV, MPD is called **dissociative identity disorder**.

- MPD is defined as the existence within a person of two or more distinct, integrated and well-developed personalities or personality states. In its most basic form, MPD is termed '**alternating personality**'.

- Sometimes, the sub-personality or personalities are so different from the core personality that they can be described as '**polar opposites**'. The transition from one personality to another is called **switching**. It is usually sudden, and often triggered by traumatic or stressful events.

- Changes in physiological and neurological activity sometimes accompany personality alternation, and the disorder has been explained in terms of **repression**, **double brain theory**, **state-dependent learning** and **self-hypnosis**.

- Recently, the number of reported cases of MPD and the number of alternate personalities identified have increased dramatically. In one case, 95 apparently separate personalities have been claimed.

- Several attempts have been made to validate MPD's existence, but many researchers are sceptical. It has been claimed that at least some cases of MPD are **simulations**.

- Because some features of MPD can be role-played through **observational learning**, the disorder may be **doxogenic**. The media portrayal of MPD may play a role in its 'development'.

- MPD has been used as a defence by criminals. Sometimes this has been successful, and sometimes the defendant's simulation has been exposed.

- It has also been argued that MPD is an artificial creation produced intentionally or unintentionally by therapists eager for publicity. This would make MPD an **iatrogenic disorder**. Most MPD cases have been reported in the United States, where interest in the disorder seems greatest.

- MPD is typically first diagnosed in late adolescence or early adulthood. However, the first signs of dissociation usually develop before the age of eight.

- Some researchers believe that MPD is a response to childhood **physical abuse**. However, the link between MPD and severe childhood trauma is not clear-cut.

- MPD's status is unclear. However, an important issue is not whether MPD sufferers need treatment, but rather under what label they are treated and with which ideas.

Essay Questions

1 Using case studies, discuss pychological insights into multiple personality disorder. *(30 marks)*

2 Discuss the view that multiple personality disorder is an iatrogenic phenomenon. *(30 marks)*

WEB ADDRESSES

http://www.dissociation.com/
http://www.nami-org/helpline/multpers.htm
http://york.39.ncl.ac.uk/www/MPDlink.html
http://www.tezcat.com/~tina/dissoc.shtml

48 Culture-bound Syndromes

INTRODUCTION AND OVERVIEW

In DSM-IV, a *culture-bound syndrome* (CBS) is defined as:

'... recurrent, locality-specific patterns of aberrant behaviour and troubling experience that may or may not be linked to a particular DSM-IV category. Many of these patterns are indigenously [within the culture in which they occur] considered to be 'illnesses' or at least afflictions, and most have local names'.

This chapter describes case studies of some of the syndromes which are apparently bound by culture, and examines the arguments for and against their status as true culture-bound syndromes.

SOME EXAMPLES OF CBSs

Despite DSM-IV's use of non-operationalised words like 'aberrant' and 'troubling', there is, as Berry *et al.* (1992) have observed:

'... nothing more intriguing [for researchers] than discovering another unique way of "being mad"! The rich reports of "culture-bound syndromes" have ... led to the claim that there are unique, local forms [of mental disorder] not known beyond a particular culture. These 'exotic' disorders are usually described and interpreted in terms which relate to the particular culture in which they are reported. Gradually these CBSs enter the [Western] psychiatric literature'.

At least 36 apparent CBSs have been identified (Humphreys, 1999). For example, *pibloqtoq* is found in Greenland, Alaska and the Canadian arctic. It is characterised by an uncontrollable urge to leave one's shelter, tear off one's clothes, and expose oneself to the Arctic weather. Another CBS related to climate is *pa-feng*, which occurs in China. Sufferers fear an excess of *yin* (or 'negative energy': see Box 48.6, page 523) from exposure to the wind. The behavioural response to this is to wrap up in warm clothes and eat hot food.

Some CBSs involve 'spiritual possession'. One of these is *windigo*, once common among the Algonquin Indians of Canada. It is characterised by depression, appetite loss, nausea and a dream about possession by a supernatural monster (the windigo) that eats humans. The windigo has the power to turn those possessed by it into cannibals. If a cure cannot be found, the sufferer often pleads for death to avoid the cannibalistic desires. Other CBSs involving spiritual possession include *zar* (North Africa) and *hsieh-ping* (Taiwan).

A disorder which appears widely in African students, often just prior to school and university examinations, is called *brain fag*. It owes its name to the individual's explanation of the illness as being due to 'tiredness of the brain' (it is 'fagged out').

Key STUDY

Box 48.1 A case of brain fag in Tanzania

As a result of his symptoms, a 22-year-old African male had to refrain from studying for the equivalent of English A level examinations in biology, chemistry and physics. He complained of being unable to study because of the feeling of pressure around his head. He was convinced that the effect of print was to constrict his pupils, and this made him experience a feeling of tiredness in the brain, somehow related to the amount of light getting into his eyes. Additionally, he was unable to understand or remember what he had read.

The onset of the disturbance was sudden. Initially, he beat his chest with his fists, and was not able to keep still. He sang hymns to which he put his own words, expressing his troubles to the world. In his agitated state, he complained that all objects around him were brightly coloured, and from time to time they changed colour from yellow to black and white.

Because he had made a disturbance in the street, he was, in the usual Tanzanian fashion, arrested, handcuffed and taken to hospital. According to his schoolfriends, he had experienced difficulty in getting off to sleep, nightmares, an inability to concentrate on his studies, and a marked loss of appetite.

(Adapted from Harris, 1981)

ARE CBSs TRULY 'CULTURE-BOUND'?

There has been much controversy over whether CBSs are truly culture-bound or merely 'local expressions of some universal disorders already known and classified' (Berry *et al.*, 1992; see Box 46.11, page 508). Some CBSs can clearly be subsumed by a disorder identified in Western classificatory systems. For example, *kuru* is a progressive psychosis and dementia found in cannibalistic groups in New Guinea. It results from an aberrant protein which is capable of replicating itself by deforming other proteins in the brain. Because kuru has been identified with a form of *Creutzfeldt–Jakob disease*, it would be classified as an *organic mental disorder*.

Susto and latah

Susto and *latah* are also regarded as being examples of apparent, rather than real, CBSs. Susto is a disorder that occurs in the Andean highlands of Peru, Bolivia and Columbia. It is characterised by insomnia, apathy, depression and anxiety, and is believed to result from contact with supernatural beings (e.g. witches) which cause the soul to leave the body. Latah (which means 'ticklish') occurs in Malaysia and Indonesia, usually amongst uneducated, middle-aged or elderly women. It is characterised by evidently uncontrollable imitative behaviour. Movements and speech are imitated, and the individual complies to the demands of others and behaves in ways they normally would not (e.g. uttering obscenities).

Despite their behavioural differences, susto and latah share an important similarity. Susto is typically brought on by *fright*, and latah's onset is often the result of a sudden or startling (*frightening*) stimulus, such as being tickled. In Yap's (1974) view, this is sufficient for both to be regarded as local expressions of '*primary fear reaction*', a condition recognised and classified in Western classificatory systems (Berry *et al.*, 1992).

Box 48.2 Matiruku: A Fijian 'madness'?

Matiruku comes from 'mati' meaning low water or tide, and 'ruku', in the morning. Figuratively, matiruku means 'a person periodically "cranky"'. Two Fijian words for 'cranky' are 'yavavala', meaning to be frequently in motion and intensely industrious, and 'bulabula', meaning healthy, full of life, fertile (of land), strong, and fresh (of the wind). In Fijian language, matiruku describes a *condition* of 'periodic insanity', rather than a person suffering from it. So,

Fijians talk about people *having* matiruku, rather than *being* a matiruku.

Rather than being a CBS, Price & Karim (1978) argued that it is a form of *hypomania*, a mood disorder (see Chapter 50). Their view is supported by the finding that matiruku does not occur in children, apparently has no precipitating factors, involves an elevated mood, an increase in talkativeness, sleep disturbances, and total reversibility of the condition. The intensification of hypomanic symptoms in the morning has also been reported in at least some Western cases of hypomania (Winokur *et al.*, 1969).

Dhat

Dhat has been described as a 'true culture-bound sex neurosis', commonly found in India. It is a syndrome characterised by severe anxiety and hypochondriacal concerns with the discharge of semen, whitish discolouration of urine, and feelings of weakness and exhaustion. It seems unlikely, though, that dhat is a true CBS.

The origins of dhat lie in the early Hindu belief that semen is derived from the blood, and that its loss produces mental and physical impairments. Many cultures share this belief. For example, the loss of semen has been considered a waste of the 'vital male sexual essence' in China (Tannahill, 1980), and in our own culture in Victorian times, semen was described as:

'The purest, essential and spirituous portion of the blood ... derived from every part of the system, particularly the brain and spinal cord' (Haller & Haller, 1974).

Box 48.3 Spermatorrhea

In 1840, the *Lancet* medical journal carried an editorial on the mental impairment, moral degradation and physical debility caused by loss of semen, mainly by masturbation. Dangerfield (1843) described *spermatorrhea* as a disorder whose primary symptoms were bodily complaints, anxiety, depression and sexual difficulties as a result of semen loss.

Various treatment measures for spermatorrhea were devised, including the insertion of wooden blocks, the size of pigeon eggs, into the rectum. These were kept there day and night to compress the prostate and force semen back into the bladder. Another treatment, the attachment to the penis of an electric alarm, triggered by a nocturnal erection, sounds mild by comparison!

Pre- and Victorian doctors believed that virtuous young men absorbed spermatic fluid, which enriched the blood and vitalised the brain and, in Victorian times, many men agreed. According to Singh (1992), the shared doctor–patient view of Victorian England is like the one that *currently* exists between traditional village healers and some native Indians.

In Western culture now, the idea that semen is a precious body fluid whose loss is detrimental to health is widely acknowledged to be untrue, and increased medical knowledge has been accompanied by an increased permissiveness. India is still largely a non-permissive society, and discussing sexuality openly is a taboo. Because a large majority of the Indian population receives no sex education, ignorance about sexual matters is widely prevalent. For Singh (1992):

> 'Ignorance thus breeds ignorance, with "quacks" and self-appointed "sexologists" perpetrating erroneous views, just as happened in the West earlier. Dhat syndrome thus appears to be a variation of the centuries-old false beliefs and ignorance. It is "culture-bound" only in the sense that it represents the immense "cultural" difference between the scientifically aware medical population and the myth-oriented native population'.

Amok

Although kuru, susto, latah, matiruku and dhat are probably *not* CBSs, there are several disorders whose status as genuine CBSs is stronger. One of these is *amok* (Witthower, 1969). Amok means 'to engage furiously in battle', and probably originated in the cultural training for warfare which the early Javanese and Malays adopted from the Hindu states of India (Westermeyer, 1973). In battle, Malay warriors would typically charge forward brandishing their daggers shouting 'Amok! Amok!' (a practice similar to the Viking behaviour called *berserker*, from which the word 'berserk' derives: Leff, 1981). As well as reinforcing their own courage, the intention was to terrify their opponents into believing they could expect no mercy, and that the only way to preserve their lives was to run away.

Epic poems praised legendary warriors who behaved in this way, and those in battle were encouraged to emulate them through self-sacrificial, fanatical charges, indiscriminate slaughter and refusal to surrender. With the introduction of Islam into Malaysia in the fourteenth century, amok occasionally became an act of religious fanaticism, and the faithful were induced to slay indiscriminately all 'infidels' with no concern for their own lives.

Box 48.4 An Amok attack

Amok outside the context of battle was first described by European travellers to Malaysia in the mid-sixteenth century. In the classic case, an assailant (a *pengamok*) attacks, without warning, anyone within reach. The attack, conducted with a *keris* (dagger), would last until the assailant was overwhelmed or killed. If alive, he (there are few reported cases of amok committed by females: Schmidt *et al.*, 1977) would fall asleep or into a stupor for several days, and apparently have no recollection of his actions. Usually, the pengamok would have been quiet or withdrawn for days before the episode occurred.

According to Carr (1978), Malays are taught from childhood that one never confronts another person, let alone expresses aggression. However, such diffidence *could* be interpreted by another person as a sign of weakness and inferiority. In a society with stringent rules and sanctions against confrontation and aggression, amok would act as a 'loophole': if a person's self-esteem were insulted, amok would enable him to restore his integrity. Because the perceived insults could have come from a number of individuals, it is not surprising that a pengamok should vent his anger against society (Kon, 1994).

Such violence would be incomprehensible in a culture which did not sanction confrontation and aggression, and as a result likely to be attributed to something like spirit possession. The Malay concept of courage could also contribute to amok. According to Kon (1994), Malays have a more fatalistic concept of courage than is found in most Western cultures. Theirs is a willingness to face up to a hopeless situation, and take on an adversary when it is beyond one's capacity (cf. the Muslim belief that one's fate is in the hands of Allah).

Whether amok is a genuine CBS or not depends on whether the cultural element is primary, or if culture 'overlays' a primary mental disorder. Carr & Tan (1976) found that whilst those pengamoks who survived were typically deemed 'insane' by the local police, and detained indefinitely in psychiatric institutions, there was very little evidence of mental disturbances *before or after* the episode of amok. However, Schmidt *et al.* (1977) diagnosed nearly all the 14 cases they interviewed as having mental disorders, schizophrenia being the most common diagnosis.

The status of amok as a genuine CBS would also be challenged if episodes of it were to occur in non-Malaysians outside Malaysia.

Box 48.5 Amok in other cultures?

- **Papua New Guinea:** Burton-Bradley (1968) reported seven cases in young adult males, collected over eight years. There was *no* evidence of mental disorder in any of the cases.

- **Laos:** Westermeyer (1973) reported 18 cases of amok with grenades, perpetrated by young males. Most episodes were preceded by interpersonal discord, insults or personal loss. Most occurred in the context of social drinking, but there was no history of alcohol abuse. Of the eight who survived, four escaped the police. Of the four who were detained, only one was diagnosed as mentally disordered.

- **North America:** Arboleda-Florez (1979) described the cases of the '*Calgary Mall Sniper*', '*The Madman in the Tower*' and the '*Memorial Day Man*'. The first of these was suffering from schizoid personality disorder with paranoid features. There was no evidence of mental disorder in the other two. All three were male.

- **United Kingdom:** In August 1987, Michael Ryan, a 27-year-old dressed in a combat jacket, stalked Hungerford killing 15 people, including his mother. He finally shot himself. Although a loner with a passion for guns, there was no history of mental disorder (Burton-Bradley, 1987).

- Other cases have been reported in **Trinidad, India, Liberia, Africa, Siberia** and **Polynesia.**

(Based on Kon, 1994)

At least some of the cases identified in Box 48.5 are very similar to those occurring in south-east Asia and, all other things being equal, would suggest that amok is *not* a genuine CBS. According to Arboleda-Florez (1979), the ingredients necessary for amok to occur *can* come from *any* culture at *any* time. These ingredients are:

- a society in transition;
- a feeling of alienation;
- a need for assertiveness.

The incidence of amok in the rest of the world is, however, *rare* compared with Malaysia and its neighbouring countries, such as Indonesia. This argues for a strong cultural element to amok but, possibly, culture might merely amplify a universal pattern of violent behaviour (Kon, 1994). Additionally, Kline (1963) found that the incidence of amok in Chinese immigrants to Indonesia was as high as the local Indonesians (who are culturally similar to the Malays). Although there are Chinese immigrants in countries all over the world, there are no reports of amok amongst the Chinese except where they live in close proximity to the Malays. A society with a tradition of amok evidently facilitates the further expression of such behaviour (Kon, 1994).

Koro

Another disorder which might be a true CBS is *koro*. Koro means 'head of the turtle', and the disorder is also known as *suk-yeong* ('shrinking penis'). Amongst men, it is characterised by the following beliefs:

- the penis is shrinking;
- it will disappear into the abdomen, and if this happens;
- its disappearance will cause death.

Koro is much less common amongst women, who believe that the breasts and labia are shrinking (Yap, 1951). The belief that death will occur arises from the further belief that ghosts do not possess genitals, and because the individual's genitals are shrinking, s/he will turn into a ghost. These beliefs are typically accompanied by an intense anxiety state and associated physiological reactions, such as palpitations, sweating, breathlessness and bodily spasms. Preventative manoeuvres, such as tying, clamping or grasping the genitals, are also conducted, although these can sometimes produce medical complications.

Box 48.6 The origins of koro

Koro was originally described as a culture-bound psychogenic syndrome occurring amongst the Chinese of southern coastal China and among overseas Chinese in south-east Asia (Yap, 1965). It is considered to be a CBS as it is strongly influenced by the cultural beliefs of the Chinese concerning activity of the Yang (male) and Yin (female) humours in human beings. These were first described by Chu Chen Hang over 700 years ago. The disease was first described in the *Yellow Emperor's Book of Medicine* in 3000 BC. The cases presented had a *chronic course*, although by the time of the Chin Dynasty, koro was described as having an *acute onset* and was associated with sexual activity. The *New Collection of Remedies*, published in 1834, indicated that koro could be precipitated after sexual excess or misdemeanours (real or fantasised), or following exposure to raw or ('cold') food, such as bananas (Devan & Hong, 1987).

Although primarily a disorder of the young, koro can occur in the elderly. For example, the oldest sufferer reported by the Koro Study Team (1969) was 70. Koro tends to be short-lived, and can be recurrent. It may affect single individuals, but can affect groups. Indeed, 'epidemics' can occur if enough fear is generated by the spreading of rumours. 'Epidemics' have been reported in Singapore, Indonesia (Gwen, 1968), China (Rin, 1965), Hong Kong (Yap, 1965), north-east Thailand (Harrington, 1982) and, interestingly (see Box 48.10, page 526), Assam, in North Eastern India (Dutta, 1983).

The Koro Study Team (1969) reported an 'epidemic' of the disorder in Singapore. Cases appeared after rumours had spread about some men having koro after eating pork from pigs inoculated against swine fever. The number of cases rapidly increased, and it became a common sight to see men appearing at admission rooms, with chop-sticks and other mechanical aids tied to their sex organs. The Koro Study Team reported on 450 cases, 95 per cent being young Chinese males. Most were of acute onset and brief duration, but 17 per cent had recurrent attacks. Simple treatment measures, such as reassurance and suggestion, were all that was required.

Koro has been explained in terms of a variety of mental disorders, including:

- obsessional disorder;
- acute castration fear;
- anxiety reaction;
- schizophrenia;
- depersonalisation syndrome;
- psychophysiological dysfunctions.

As noted, one major characteristic in koro is the belief or conviction that (in males) the penis is shrinking. If the grounds on which the belief is held are shown to be false, then it would amount to a *delusion* (see Chapter 49, page 529).

Key STUDY

Box 48.7 Are the beliefs in koro delusional?

An attempt to validate the authenticity of a sufferer's experience of penile shrinkage was undertaken by Oyebode *et al.* (1986). They used a penile plethysmograph, which measures changes in penile circumference, and found that the conviction of penile shrinkage *does* correspond with a true physiological change in penile circumference below a baseline measure of it. So, the conviction that the penis is shrinking would appear *not* to be a delusion. According to

Oyebode *et al.*, there are two explanations for this finding:

- the person they studied had dysfunctional autonomic control of his penile size, leading to more frequent or marked diminution of his penile size than would be normal, or
- the changes in his penile size were normal, but awareness of them was heightened by personal factors, such as obsessional self-scrutiny or sexual conflicts.

However, because there are no data on changes in penile size in men not displaying the symptoms of koro, it is difficult to reach firm conclusions about how this particular case can be explained.

There have, however, been questions raised about koro as a genuine CBS. Although the confined geographical origin of cases initially reported suggested that it only affected people from particular cultures, it has also been reported in people of various cultural backgrounds. These include the United Kingdom (Adeniran & Jones, 1994), Canada (Ede, 1976), France (Bourgeois, 1968) and the United States (Bychowski, 1952).

Such cases might suggest that koro is not as culture-bound as Yap (1965) asserted, because mechanisms involving cultural beliefs are not apparently related to any of them. However, a careful analysis of the non-Chinese cases indicates that *most* are *secondary* to a major mental disorder. For example, in several cases the koro symptoms were secondary to schizophrenia and depression, and the symptoms disappeared once the mental disorder had been successfully treated. As a result, the term *atypical koro* has been applied to such cases.

It is also possible to distinguish between *complete* and *incomplete* forms of koro. The non-Chinese cases typically display the incomplete form because they lack important elements of koro's psychopathology, namely an absence of the belief that the penis will disappear into the abdomen and/or a lack of the fear of death as a result of this.

Key STUDY

Box 48.8 A case of 'incomplete' koro

The case was that of a 44-year-old man, born and bred in England. There was no family history of psychiatric illness. He was referred by his general practitioner on account of a 20-year-old belief that his penis recurrently shrank and disappeared into his abdomen. He believed that the origins of these symptoms could be traced to his childhood, when his penis was pulled during a game with other boys.

His fears started gradually after he had completed his military service. Two years before referral he had been unable to find his penis while attempting to urinate, and wet his trousers. Since then he had to sit on the toilet to urinate, and refused to carry out his job as a plumber on building sites that did not have lavatories. On further questioning, it transpired that apart from his routine trip to work, he was afraid of going out on his own, and that social situations and gatherings made him very anxious.

The case report confirmed his social phobias, agoraphobic symptoms, panic attacks and the specific fear that his penis shrank episodically and went into his abdomen. He did not believe, however, that this symptom endangered his life. When pressed about the irrationality of his fear, he would look embarrassed and change the topic. He was not suicidal. He was physically healthy. His agoraphobia and social phobia were successfully treated using psychotherapeutic drugs (see Chapter 52) and behavioural therapy, and he no longer feared that his penis would shrink. One year after referral he had maintained all his gains and had developed a full social life.

(Adapted from Berrios & Morley, 1984)

In the *majority* of non-Chinese cases, then, the use of the label 'koro' is inappropriate. A number of alternatives have been proposed, including *genital retraction syndrome* (Anderson, 1990), although this implies an organic rather than psychological disturbance (Heyman & Fahy, 1992). A more appropriate term would be *koro-like states* (Berrios & Morley, 1984). At least some Chinese cases display the *complete* form of koro, and so 'complete koro' refers to the CBS type whereas 'incomplete koro' is not culture-bound. Thus, koro would appear not to be a unitary phenomenon (Sachdev, 1985).

Box 48.9 Koro and koro–like states

- **'True' or 'classical' koro:** Common in the Chinese, and not related to an underlying mental disorder. Short-lived, but can be recurrent. Treatable by simple measures, such as reassurance. *Indisputably cultural in origin.*

- **Koro-like state (a) – koro 'grafted' upon an underlying mental disorder:** Koro is typically *associated* with anxiety states, but is also sometimes evident in depression, schizophrenia and brief psychotic states. *Probably cultural in origin.*

- **Koro-like state (b) – koro as a symptom of a mental disorder:** Koro is based on a *delusion* or the result of depersonalisation and possibly accompanying schizophrenia. Requires treatment other than reassurance. Disappears when the underlying disorder is treated. More likely in non-Chinese individuals. *Not culturally determined.*

(Modified from Devan & Hong, 1987)

Durst & Rosca-Rebaudengo (1988) suggested that a fourth category could be added to those in Box 48.9, namely *koro as a symptom of organic disorders*. They studied a patient with a tumour of the corpus callosum (see Box 12.7, pages 121–122) who displayed true koro symptoms:

'[At the time the tumour was diagnosed], his sexual appetite and performance decreased. His behaviour became bizarre, in that he was obsessed with his penis. He was petrified that it would shrink and disappear into his abdomen, after which, he was convinced, he would die. In order to prevent the dissolution of his penis, he felt compelled to perform manoeuvres aimed at pulling it outward. He started to exhibit his penis to his family, and even strangers, in an attempt at reassurance. His delusional conviction worsened, and he claimed that his penis had shrunk to 1 cm in length. At the same time, he became aggressive towards his wife and children, and expressed suicidal intentions'.

Because of his suicidal tendencies and failure to respond to psychotherapeutic drugs, he was given electroconvulsive therapy (ECT: see Chapter 52). As well as his depression and anxiety subsiding, the symptoms of koro also disappeared. Given that the tumour was exerting pressure on his thalami and hypothalamus, and given the latter's well-established involvement in sexual behaviour, Durst and Rosca-Rebaudengo concluded that the koro symptoms were a result of this.

However, the case report indicates that the individual had apparently had a fear of sexual inadequacy since he was seventeen, whereas his tumour did not become apparent until he was 24. Moreover, the tumour enlarged one year after he was discharged from hospital, but the koro symptoms did not recur. This suggests that the symptoms and the tumour were *coincidentally* rather than *causally* related. Because ECT was effective in treating depression, it could be that the koro symptoms were *part* of the depression, which would classify the individual as koro-like state (b) in Box 48.9.

The overall picture, then, appears to be that whilst koro-like states might be seen beyond the cultures in which 'true' koro occurs, 'true' koro is not seen outside those cultures. However, a report of a koro epidemic outside China and south-east Asia challenges this.

Box 48.10 A koro epidemic in Assam

In 1982, Assam, in North Eastern India, experienced an epidemic of koro, which lasted from June until the middle of September. The locals called the epidemic *Jinjinia Bemar*, indicating a disease characterised by a tingling sensation of the body. However, those affected were also convinced that their genitals were shrinking. The epidemic started with a rumour that a lethal disease had struck the people, bringing instant death or making them impotent. Initially, those affected did not seek medical help, but tried to combat it using various preventative measures. These included drinking gallons of lemon water, smearing chalk paste or lime paste over the ear lobes and genitals, and avoiding all outdoor activities.

At the end of July, people began to consult medical and psychiatric experts. Both sexes were affected. Often, a male would come for help either grasping his penis or with it tied securely with broad ribbons or elastic bands. Once psychiatrists recognised that what they were dealing with was koro, the benign nature of the disorder was communicated to people through the mass media, and the intensity of the panic faded away. Only a few sporadic fresh cases were recorded after the epidemic subsided in the middle of September 1982.

(Based on Dutta, 1983)

CBSs, CULTURAL RELATIVITY AND ETHNOCENTRISM

As noted on page 520, CBSs are regarded as being 'outside' the mainstream of psychological abnormality, as defined by, and enshrined in, the DSM-IV and ICD-10 classificatory systems of Western psychiatry. These systems *define* what is and what is not a mental disorder.

The fact that CBSs may be quite common within a particular culture makes no difference. If they are limited (or apparently limited) to other cultures, they are *excluded* from the mainstream classification of mental disorders. Since the disorders occur in groups that are seen as 'alien' in primarily racial terms, the concept of a CBS is therefore one that has been generated by the ideology of Western psychiatry: mental disorder in the West is seen as being culturally neutral, whereas disorders that are distinctively different from those seen in the West are regarded as 'culture-bound' (Fernando, 1991).

Researchers distinguish between modern, scientific psychiatry and traditional *ethnopsychiatry* (the study of culture-relative or culture-specific disorders), seeing the former as telling us about authentic illness, whilst the latter tells us about illness that is contaminated/distorted by culture. Fernando (1991) believes that anthropology and psychiatry have colluded in regarding psychiatric disorders seen in Western (white) societies as being on a different plane from those in non-Western (black, 'primitive' societies):

> 'When culture "distorts" a syndrome beyond a certain point, a CBS is identified. Practitioners go along with this approach, seeing symptom constellations in the West as the standard, and those in other cultures as anomalies'. (Fernando, 1991)

This represents a form of *ethnocentrism* within Western psychiatry, and in keeping with this view, Fernando believes that the concept of a CBS has a distinctly *racist* connotation.

Similarly, Littlewood & Lipsedge (1989) argue that it is wrong to look at beliefs about 'madness' in other cultures as if they are only more or less accurate approximations to a 'scientific' (accurate, objective) description. A cultural understanding of mental disorder is as important in Western as in any other culture. Indeed, some general features of those 'ritual patterns' usually classed as CBSs are applicable to Western neurosis (Littlewood & Lipsedge, 1989), and disorders such as *anorexia nervosa* and *premenstrual syndrome* (see Chapter 13) may be examples of *Western* CBSs (Fernando, 1991). It is somewhat ironic that the name of one CBS described in the present chapter has become part of the vocabulary of English-speaking Western societies ('running *amok*').

CONCLUSIONS

This chapter has described case studies of some of the syndromes which are believed to be unique to particular cultures. Of these, some can easily be subsumed by disorders identified in Western classificatory systems. For others, however, it is much more difficult to do this, and there are strong arguments both for and against their status as true CBSs.

Summary

- In DSM-IV, culture-bound syndromes (CBSs) are defined as 'recurrent, locality-specific patterns of aberrant behaviour and troubling experience that may or may not be linked to a particular DSM-IV category'. At least 36 CBSs have been identified, including **pibloqtoq**, **pa-feng**, **windigo**, **zar**, **hsieh-ping** and **brain fag**.

- There has been much controversy over whether CBSs are truly culture-bound, or merely local expressions of some universal disorders already known and classified.

- Some CBSs can be easily subsumed by a disorder identified in Western classificatory systems. Examples include **kuru**, **susto**, **latah** and **matiruku**.

- **Dhat** has been described as a 'true culture-bound sex neurosis'. It is commonly found in India, but is culture-bound only in the sense that a represents a cultural difference between the scientifically aware and myth-oriented native populations of India.

- **Amok** is a disorder found in Malaysia, whose status as a genuine CBS is stronger. Although amok-type behaviour has been found outside Malaysia, its incidence is rare, which argues for a strong cultural element to the disorder.

- **Koro** is characterised by a belief that the penis is shrinking, it will disappear into the abdomen, and that if this happens it will cause death. It was originally described as a CBS occurring amongst native Chinese and overseas Chinese in south-east Asia.

- Koro's status as a CBS has been challenged by its observation in people of various cultural backgrounds, including the United Kingdom, Canada, France and the United States. In most non-Chinese cases, though, koro is secondary to a major mental disorder (**atypical koro**), and the symptoms disappear when the major disorder has been successfully treated.

- Non-Chinese cases are usually **incomplete** forms of koro, because they lack important elements of its psychopathology. Whilst **koro-like states** might be seen beyond the cultures in which true koro occurs, true koro is not seen outside those cultures.

- Some researchers believe that the concept of a CBS is one which has been generated by the ideology of Western psychiatry, which may be **ethnocentric**. Indeed, the concept of a CBS has a distinctly racist connotation.

Essay Questions

1 Using case studies, discuss psychological insights into culture-bound syndromes. (*30 marks*)

2 Discuss arguments for and against the view that some mental disorders are cultural in origin.

(*30 marks*)

WEB ADDRESSES

http://nursingworld.org/tan/98janfeb/mental.htm
http://weber.ucsd.edu/~thall/cbs_links.html
http://www.cmeinc.com/pt/p980145.html
http://www.stlcc.cc.mo.us/mc/users/vritts/psypath.htm
http://www.mc-mlmhs/cultures/issuessay/dissues.htm

49 *Schizophrenia*

INTRODUCTION AND OVERVIEW

Of all the disorders identified in ICD-10 and DSM-IV, schizophrenia is the most serious. Kraepelin (1913) called the disorder *dementia praecox* (*senility of youth*), believing that it occurred early in adult life and was characterised by a progressive deterioration or dementia. However, Bleuler (1911) observed that it also began in later life and was not always characterised by dementia. Bleuler coined the word *schizophrenia* to refer to a *splitting* of the mind's various functions in which the personality loses its unity.

This chapter describes the clinical characteristics of schizophrenia. It also examines the psychological and biological explanations of the disorder, including evidence on which these explanations are based.

THE CLINICAL CHARACTERISTICS OF SCHIZOPHRENIA

As noted, schizophrenia is a disorder in which personality loses its unity. It should not be confused with *multiple personality disorder*, in which personality splits into two or more separate *identities* (see Chapter 47). The confusion probably arises because the word *schizophrenia* derives from the Greek words *schizein* (to split) and *phren* (the mind). As will be seen, schizophrenia is a 'splitting' between thoughts and feelings, the consequences being bizarre and maladaptive behaviour.

In Britain, schizophrenia's diagnosis relies on *first-rank symptoms* (Schneider, 1959). The presence of one or more of these, in the absence of brain disease, is likely to result in a diagnosis of schizophrenia. The three first rank symptoms are *passivity experiences and thought disturbances*, *hallucinations* and *primary delusions*.

Passivity experiences and thought disturbances

These include *thought insertion* (the belief that thoughts are being inserted into the mind from outside, under the control of external forces), *thought withdrawal* (the belief that thoughts are being removed from the mind under the control of external forces), and *thought broadcasting* (the belief that thoughts are being broadcast or otherwise made known to others). External forces may include 'the Martians', 'the Communists' and 'the Government', and the mechanism by which thoughts are affected is often a 'special ray' or a radio transmitter. Thought broadcasting is also an example of a *delusion* (see page 529).

Hallucinations

Hallucinations are perceptions of stimuli not actually present. They may occur in any sense modality, but the most common are *auditory*. Typically, voices come from outside the individual's head and offer a 'running commentary' on behaviour in the third person (such as 'He is washing his hands. Now he'll go and dry them.'). Sometimes, they will comment on the individual's character, usually insultingly, or give commands. However, they may also be perceived as amusing and reassuring (Chadwick & Birchwood, 1994).

Somatosensory hallucinations involve changes in how the body feels. It may, for example, be described as 'burning' or 'numb'. *Depersonalisation*, in which the person reports feeling separated from the body, may also occur. Hallucinations are often distortions of real environmental perceptual cues, so that noises from (say) a heating system are heard as voices whispering (Frude, 1998).

Box 49.1 What causes auditory hallucinations?

At least some auditory hallucinations may be projections of the individual's *own* thoughts. According to Silbersweig *et al.* (1995), a breakdown occurs in 'dialogue' between the frontal lobes (which deal with intentions) and the temporal lobes (which process language and register the consequences of actions). This results in a failure to integrate behaviour with the perception of its consequences. In auditory hallucinations, normal thoughts may progress via internal language into a form in which they can be articulated and, if desired, spoken. This involves a *feedback loop* which warns the next stage of the process what is happening, and tells us that the inner speech is our own. Auditory hallucinations may occur because the feedback loop is broken. So, schizophrenics talk to themselves without realising it. This is supported by the observation of increased activity in Broca's area (see Chapter 12) during auditory hallucinations (McGuire *et al.*, 1995).

Primary delusions

Delusions are false beliefs which persist even in the presence of disconfirming evidence.

- A *delusion of grandeur* is the belief that one is somebody who is or was important or powerful (such as Jesus Christ or Napoleon).

- A *delusion of persecution* is the belief that one is being plotted or conspired against, or being interfered with by certain people or organised groups.

- A *delusion of reference* is the belief that objects, events and so on have a (typically negative) personal significance. For example, a person may believe that the words of a song specifically refer to him/her.

- A *delusion of nihilism* is the belief that nothing really exists and that all things are simply shadows. The belief that one has been dead for years and is observing the world from afar is also common.

All delusions are held with extraordinary conviction, and the person may be so convinced of their truth that they are acted on, even if this involves murder.

"No, Mr Hennessey, you just THINK you're delusional!"

Figure 49.1 *Delusions are strongly held false beliefs which persist even in the presence of disconfirming evidence*

Key STUDY
Box 49.2 Capgras syndrome

Capgras syndrome is a delusion in which sufferers believe that family members and others are *imposters*. Ramachandran & Hirstein (cited in Johnston, 1997) report the case of D.S., who suffered damage to his brain's right hemisphere following a traffic accident. D.S. shows no physiological response to people's faces or pictures of himself, and is convinced that his parents are 'doubles'. Ramachandran and Hirstein believe that when we meet people, the brain creates memory 'files' about them. When we next meet them, our emotional responses cause their files to be retrieved rather than new ones opened. This does not happen in Capgras syndrome, because the links between pattern recognition and emotion have been severed (de Bruxelles, 1999: see also Chapter 21, page 217).

First rank symptoms are subjective experiences, and can only be inferred on the basis of the individual's verbal reports. Hallucinations are the least important first rank symptom, because they are not exclusive to schizophrenia (which is also true of delusions: see Chapter 50). Slater & Roth (1969) identify four different characteristics of schizophrenia directly observable from behaviour. These are *thought process disorder*, *disturbances of affect*, *psychomotor disorders* and *lack of volition*.

Figure 49.2 *There is considerable similarity between the paintings produced by psychotic patients and this section of a picture of Hell, painted by the sixteenth-century Dutch painter Hieronymus Bosch*

Thought process disorder

Although constantly bombarded by sensory information, we are usually able to attend selectively to some and exclude the rest (see Chapter 19). This ability is impaired in schizophrenia, and leads to overwhelming and unintegrated ideas and sensations which affect concentration. Thus, schizophrenics are easily distracted. Their failure to maintain an *attentional focus* is reflected in the inability to maintain a focus of thought. In turn, this is reflected in the inability to maintain a focus in language.

The classic disturbance in the *form* of schizophrenic thought (as opposed to its *content*) involves *loose associations* (or *derailment*). The individual shifts from topic to topic as new associations arise, and fails to form coherent and logical thoughts. As a result, language is often rambling and disjointed. Often, one idea triggers an association with another. When associations become too loose, incoherence results (a *word salad*).

Box 49.3 Loose associations and word salad

'I am the nun. If that's enough, you are still his. That is a brave cavalier, take him as your husband, Karoline, you well know, though you are my Lord, you were just a dream. If you are the dove-cote, Mrs K. is still beset by fear. Otherwise I am not so exact in eating. Handle the gravy carefully. Where is the paint brush? Where are you, Herman?'

(From Bleuler, 1911)

A word's sound may also trigger an association with a similar sounding word (*clang association*) as in:

'The King of Spain feels no pain in the drain of the crane. I'm lame, you're tame: with fame, I'll be the same'.

Schizophrenic thought is also reflected in *neologisms*, the invention of new words (such as *putenance* and *amoriation*: Vetter, 1969), or the combination of existing words in a unique fashion (such as 'belly bad luck and brutal and outrageous' to describe stomach ache). Other characteristics include *thought blocking*, *literal interpretation*, *poverty of content* and *perseveration*.

Disturbances of affect

In some cases, thought process disorder is brief and intermittent. However, disturbances of affect (*emotional disturbances*), and other characteristic disturbances, tend to be fairly stable. The three main types of emotional disturbance are *blunted*, *flattened* and *inappropriate affect*.

Blunted affect

This is an apparent lack of emotional sensitivity, in which the person responds impassively to events that would ordinarily evoke a strong emotional reaction. For example, when told that a close relative had died, a schizophrenic might respond in a monotonic voice: 'Really? Is that so?'.

Flattened affect

This is a more pervasive and general absence of emotional expression, in which the person appears devoid of any sort of emotional tone. Flattened affect may reflect the schizophrenic's 'turning off' from stimuli they are incapable of dealing with, for self-protection.

Inappropriate affect

This is the display of an emotion which is incongruous with its context. For example, when asked if a meal was enjoyable or when offered a gift, the person may become agitated and violent. However, the receipt of bad news may be followed by uncontrolled giggling.

Psychomotor disorders

In some schizophrenics, motor behaviour is affected. In *catatonia*, the individual assumes an unusual posture which is maintained for hours or even days (*catatonic stupor*). Attempts to alter the posture can be met with resistance and sometimes violence. In *stereotypy*, the person engages in purposeless, repetitive movements, such as rocking back and forth or knitting an imaginary sweater. Instead of being mute and unmoving, the individual may be wild and excited, showing frenetically high levels of motor activity (*catatonic excitement*).

Lack of volition

This is a withdrawal from interactions with other people. It sometimes involves living an asocial and secluded life, through loss of drive, interest in the environment, and so on. More disturbed individuals appear to be oblivious to others' presence, and completely unresponsive when people like friends and relatives attempt contact.

TYPES OF SCHIZOPHRENIA

Both ICD-10 and DSM-IV distinguish between different types of schizophrenia. This is because the disorder's characteristics are so variable.

Hebephrenic schizophrenia

The most severe type of schizophrenia is *hebephrenic* (or *disorganised*) *schizophrenia* (*hebephrenic* means 'silly mind'). It is most often diagnosed in adolescence and young adulthood, and is usually progressive and irreversible. Its main characteristics are incoherent language, disorganised behaviour, delusions, vivid hallucinations (often sexual or religious) and loose associations. It is also characterised by flattened or inappropriate affect, and extreme social withdrawal and impairment.

Simple schizophrenia

This usually appears during late adolescence and has a slow, gradual onset. Principally, the individual withdraws from reality, has difficulty in making or keeping friends, is aimless and lacks drive, and shows a decline in academic or occupational performance. Males often become drifters or tramps, whilst females may become prostitutes. Simple schizophrenia is only recognised by ICD-10 which, whilst acknowledging that it is controversial, retains it because some countries still use it.

Catatonic schizophrenia

The major characteristic of catatonic schizophrenia is a striking impairment of motor activity. Individuals may hold unusual and difficult positions until their limbs grow swollen, stiff and blue from lack of movement. An interesting feature is *waxy flexibility*, in which the individual maintains a position into which he or she has been manipulated by others.

Catatonic schizophrenics may engage in *agitated catatonia*, bouts of wild, excited movement, and may become dangerous and unpredictable. In *mutism*, the person is apparently totally unresponsive to external stimuli. However, catatonic schizophrenics often *are* aware of what others were saying or doing during the catatonic episode, as evidenced by their reports after the

episode has subsided. Another characteristic is *negativism*, in which the individual sits either motionless and resistant to instructions, or does the opposite of what has been requested.

Paranoid schizophrenia

This has the presence of well-organised, delusional thoughts as its dominant characteristic. Paranoid schizophrenics show the highest level of awareness, and least impairment, in the ability to carry out daily functions. Thus, language and behaviour appear relatively normal. However, the delusions are usually accompanied by hallucinations which are typically consistent with them. It tends to have a later onset than the other schizophrenias, and is the most *homogenous* type (paranoid schizophrenics are more alike than simple, catatonic and hebephrenic schizophrenics).

Undifferentiated (or atypical) schizophrenia

This is a 'catch-all' category for people who either fit the criteria for more than one type, or do not appear to be of any clear type. For example, disorders of thought, perception and emotion, without the features particular to the types described above, would result in the label undifferentiated being applied.

Other disorders

These include *schizophreniform psychosis* (similar to schizophrenia, but lasting for less than 6 months), *schizotypal disorder* (eccentric behaviour and unusual thoughts and emotions resembling those of schizophrenia, but without characteristic schizophrenic abnormalities), and *schizoaffective disorder* (episodes in which both schizophrenic and affective characteristics are prominent, but which do not justify a diagnosis of either schizophrenia or an affective disorder).

Key STUDY

Box 49.4 **Markers for schizophrenia**

Davidson *et al.* (1999) measured intelligence, social functioning, organisational ability, interest in physical activity, and autonomy in 9000 healthy male adolescents. Those who were later hospitalised for schizophrenia had significantly *lower* test scores than those who were not hospitalised. The simple assessment tools used by Davidson *et al.* thus appear to allow early identification of either the presence of, or vulnerability to, schizophrenia.

THE COURSE OF SCHIZOPHRENIA

The characteristics of schizophrenia rarely appear in 'full-blown' form. Typically, there are three phases in schizophrenia's development. The *prodromal phase* usually occurs in early adolescence (*process schizophrenia*), or in relatively well-adjusted people in early adulthood (*reactive schizophrenia*). The individual becomes less interested in work, school, leisure activities and so on. Typically, s/he becomes increasingly withdrawn, eccentric and emotionally flat, cares little for health and appearance, and shows lowered productivity at either work or school. This phase may last from a few weeks to years.

In the *active phase*, schizophrenia's major characteristics appear. In some people, this phase lasts only a few months, whereas in others it lasts a lifetime. If and when it subsides (usually after therapy), the person enters the *residual phase*. This is characterised by a lessening of the major characteristics and a more-or-less return to the prodromal phase. Around 25 per cent of schizophrenics regain the capacity to function normally, ten per cent remain permanently in the active phase, and 50–65 per cent alternate between the residual and active phases (Bleuler, 1978).

Box 49.5 The concept of schizophrenia

Whether schizophrenia is a single disorder with several types, or whether each type is a distinct disorder, has been hotly debated. Gelder *et al.* (1989) believe that, with the possible exception of paranoid schizophrenia, the other types are actually of doubtful validity and difficult to distinguish between in clinical practice. Because of this lack of reliability, it has been argued that the concept of schizophrenia is 'almost hopelessly in tatters' and that there is no such entity as schizophrenia (Sarbin, 1992).

PSYCHOLOGICAL EXPLANATIONS OF SCHIZOPHRENIA

Behavioural explanations

According to the behavioural model, schizophrenia can be explained in terms of conditioning and observational learning. Ullman & Krasner (1969) argue that people show schizophrenic behaviour when it is more likely than normal behaviour to be reinforced. In psychiatric institutions, staff may unintentionally reinforce schizo-phrenic behaviour by paying more attention to those displaying it. Patients can 'acquire' the characteristics by observing others being reinforced for behaving bizarrely. Alternatively, schizophrenia may be acquired through the *absence* of reinforcement for attending to appropriate objects.

Certainly, schizophrenic behaviour can be modified through conditioning (see Chapter 53), although little evidence suggests that such techniques can affect the expression of thought disorders. Moreover, it is difficult to see how schizophrenic behaviour patterns can be acquired when people have had no opportunity to observe them. For these reasons at least, it is generally accepted that the behavioural model contributes little to understanding schizophrenia's *causes* (Frude, 1998).

Psychodynamic explanations

One psychodynamic explanation proposes that schizophrenia results from an ego which has difficulty in distinguishing between the self and the external world. Another account attributes it to a *regression* to an infantile stage of functioning. Freud believed that schizophrenia occurred when a person's ego either became overwhelmed by the demands of the id, or was besieged by unbearable guilt from the superego (see Chapter 31).

Rather than resolving the intense *intrapsychic conflict*, the individual retreats to the pre-ego state of *primary narcissism*, in which only its own needs are felt. Initially, *regressive symptoms* occur, and the individual may experience delusions of self-importance. Fantasies become confused with reality, which gives rise to hallucinations and delusions (Freud called these *restitutional symptoms*), as the individual attempts to regain contact with reality.

The incoherent delusions and bizarre speech patterns displayed in schizophrenia *may* make sense when preceded by the phrase 'I dreamed …'. However, schizophrenic behaviour is *not* that similar to pre-ego infantile behaviour, and the psychodynamic model cannot predict schizophrenic outcome on the basis of theoretically predisposing early experiences. This has resulted in it being given little credibility.

The role of social and family relationships

According to Bateson *et al.* (1956), parents predispose children to schizophrenia by communicating in ways that place them in 'no-win' situations. A father might, for example, complain about his daughter's lack of affection (the *primary communication*), whilst simultaneously telling her that she is too old to hug him when she tries to be affectionate (the *metacommunication*). Bateson *et al.* used the term *double bind* to describe such contradictory multiple verbal and non-verbal messages. Children who experience double binds may lose their grip on reality and see their own feelings, perceptions, knowledge and so on as being unreliable indicators of it.

Similarly, *deviant communication* within families may lead to children doubting their own feelings and perceptions. Wynne *et al.* (1977) propose that some parents often refuse to recognise the meaning of words used by their children, and instead substitute words of their own. This can be confusing if the children are young, and may play a role in schizophrenia's development.

Box 49.6 Marital schism and marital skew

Schizophrenics' families are sometimes marked by *marital schism* or *marital skew* (Lidz, 1973). When both parents are preoccupied with their own problems, they threaten the household's continuity, and marital schism occurs. Marital skew occurs when one disturbed parent dominates the household. According to Fromm-Reichman (1948), the *schizophrenogenic* mother is one who generates schizophrenic children. Such mothers are domineering, cold, rejecting and guilt-producing. Fromm-Reichman argued that, in conjunction with passive and ineffectual fathers, such mothers 'drive' their children to schizophrenia.

The view that social and family interactions play a causal role in schizophrenia's development lacks empirical support, and has difficulty in explaining why abnormal patterns develop in some rather than all the children in a family. Klebanoff (1959) has suggested that the family patterns correlated with schizophrenia actually constitute a *reasonable* response to an unusual child. Thus, children who were brain-damaged and retarded tended to have mothers that were more possessive and controlling than mothers of non-disturbed children. Although family factors probably do not play a causal role in schizophrenia's development, how the family reacts to offspring when the symptoms have appeared may play a role in influencing an individual's functioning. Families high in *expressed emotion* (EE) frequently express criticism, disapproval and hostility, and are highly intrusive. When EE is reduced, the recurrence of schizophrenic characteristics is reduced (Linszen *et al.*, 1997).

Cognitive explanations

As noted previously, schizophrenia is characterised by disturbances in thought, perception, attention and language. The cognitive model views these as *causes* rather than *consequences* of the disorder. Maher (1968) sees the

bizarre use of language as the result of faulty information processing. When words with multiple meanings to an individual (*vulnerable words*) are used, a person may respond in a personally relevant but semantically irrelevant or inappropriate way.

The cognitive model proposes that catatonic schizophrenia may be the result of a breakdown in *auditory selective attention* (see Chapter 19). Because our information-processing abilities are limited, we need to purposefully select information to process. Impairment of the selective attention mechanism would result in the senses being bombarded with information. The catatonic schizophrenic's lack of interaction with the outside world may occur because it is the only way that sensory stimulation can be kept to a manageable level (Finkelstein *et al.*, 1997: see Box 49.8, page 534).

BIOLOGICAL EXPLANATIONS OF SCHIZOPHRENIA

Genetic influences

Schizophrenia tends to run in families. The likelihood of a person developing it is about one in 100. However, with one schizophrenic parent, the likelihood increases to one in five. If both parents are schizophrenic, it increases to about one in two or one in three (Rees *et al.*, 1999). These observations have led some researchers to propose that schizophrenia can be explained in *genetic* terms.

Gottesman & Shields (1972) examined the history of 45,000 individuals treated at two London hospitals between 1948 and 1964. They identified 57 schizophrenics with twins who agreed to participate in their study. Using diagnosis and hospitalisation as the criteria for schizophrenia, the researchers reported a *concordance rate* (see Gross *et al.*, 2000) of 42 per cent for identical (monozygotic or MZ) twins and nine per cent for non-identical (dizygotic or DZ) twins.

Other studies have consistently reported concordance rates which are higher for MZs than DZs (see Table 49.1, page 534). In *all* of them, though, the concordance rate is less than the theoretically expected 100 per cent. However, Heston (1970) found that if a MZ had a schizophrenic disorder, there was a 90 per cent chance that the other twin had *some sort* of mental disorder.

Of course, the *environment* may play an influential role, and given that twins tend to be raised in the same environment, it would be reckless to attribute Heston's (and others') findings exclusively to genetic factors. However, when MZs are separated at birth (and presumably raised in different environments), the concordance rate is as high as that obtained for MZs raised in the same environment (Gottesman, 1991).

Table 49.1 *Concordance rates for schizophrenia for identical (MZ) and non-identical (DZ) twins (Based on Rose et al., 1984)*

Study	'Narrow' concordance *		'Broad' concordance *	
	% MZs	% DZs	% MZs	% DZs
Rosanoff *et al.* (1934) USA (41 MZs, 53 DZs)	44	9	61	13
Kallmann (1946) USA (174 MZs, 296 DZs)	59	11	69	11–14
Slater (1953) England (37 MZs, 58 DZs)	65	14	65	14
Gottesman & Shields (1966) England (24 MZs, 33 DZs)	42	15	54	18
Kringlen (1968) Norway (55 MZs, 90 DZs)	25	7	38	10
Allen *et al.* (1972) USA (95 MZs, 125 DZs)	14	4	27	5
Fischer (1973) Denmark (21 MZs, 41 DZs)	24	10	48	20

(* 'Narrow' based on attempt to apply a relatively strict set of criteria when diagnosing schizophrenia. 'Broad' includes 'borderline schizophrenia', 'schizoaffective psychosis' and 'paranoid with schizophrenia-like features'.)

Key **S T U D Y**

Box 49.7 The adopted children of schizophrenic mothers

Looking at MZs reared apart is one way round the problem of controlling environmental factors. Another is to study children of schizophrenic parents brought up in foster or adoptive homes. The usual method is to compare the incidence of schizophrenia in the biological and adoptive parents of adopted children with the disorder.

Heston (1966) compared 47 children of schizophrenic mothers adopted before the age of one month with 50 children raised in the homes of their biological and non-schizophrenic mothers. Psychiatrists' 'blind' testing of the children revealed that ten per cent with schizophrenic mothers were diagnosed as schizophrenic, whereas no children of non-schizophrenic mothers were so diagnosed. Also, children of schizo-

phrenic mothers were more likely than children of non-schizophrenic mothers to be:

'... morally defective, sociopathic, neurotic, criminal and to have been discharged from the armed forces on psychiatric grounds' (Heston, 1966).

Kety *et al.* (1968) examined Denmark's *Folkregister*, a life-long record of Danish citizens. The researchers compiled lists of adopted children who either developed or did not develop schizophrenia. Its incidence in the adoptive families of those who developed the disorder (five per cent) was as low as in the adoptive families of those who did not develop it. However, in those who did develop schizophrenia, its incidence in the biological families was far higher than expected (21 per cent).

If the disposition towards schizophrenia is environmental, the incidence would be higher among adoptive relatives with whom the adopted child shared an environment. However, if hereditary factors are important, the incidence would be higher in biological than in adoptive relatives (which is what the researchers found).

Klaning *et al.* (1996) have looked at the incidence of schizophrenia in twins *as a population* and found that it is higher than in the general population. This might be due to twins' greater exposure to perinatal complications (such as low birth weight) which could lower the 'threshold' for developing schizophrenia. Alternatively, the psychological environment might be different for twins and provide a greater risk of developing the disorder.

From what has been said, genetic factors appear to play some (and perhaps a major) role in schizophrenia (Milunsky *et al.*, 1999). However, attempts to identify the gene or genes *responsible* have not been successful. Claims have been made about genetic markers on chromosomes 5 and 22, and then quickly retracted in the light of subsequent research. As noted, even if genes are involved, genetic factors alone cannot be responsible.

Box 49.8 Chromosome 15 and the alpha–7 nicotinic receptor

Many schizophrenics are chain-smokers. This may not be coincidental. An area on chromosome 15 is apparently responsible for a site in the brain (the alpha-7 nicotinic receptor) that plays a role in filtering information. A genetic defect in this area of chromosome 15 is thought to be implicated in schizophrenia. However, this site in the brain can be stimulated by nicotine (Court *et al.*, 1999). Malfunctioning neurons might therefore be implicated in schizophrenia, and chain-smoking may be an unwitting form of 'self-medication' (Dalack *et al.*, 1999).

Biochemical influences

One way in which genes may influence behaviour is through biochemical agents in the brain (see Gross *et al.*, 2000). According to the *inborn-error of metabolism hypothesis*, some people inherit a metabolic error which causes the body to break down naturally occurring chemicals into toxic ones which are responsible for schizophrenia's characteristics. Osmond & Smythies (1953) noted that there were similarities between the experiences of people who had taken hallucinogenic drugs, and those diagnosed as schizophrenic.

Some evidence supports the view that the brain produces its own *internal hallucinogens*. For example, Smythies (1976) found small amounts of hallucinogen-like chemicals in schizophrenics' cerebrospinal fluid, whilst Murray *et al.* (1979) reported that the hallucinogen *dimethyltryptamine* (DMT) was present in schizophrenics' urine. Moreover, when DMT levels decreased, schizophrenic symptoms also decreased. However, later research indicated that schizophrenia's characteristics were *different* from those produced by hallucinogenic drugs, and researchers turned to other biochemicals.

Perhaps because hallucinogenic drugs are chemically similar to the neurotransmitters *noradrenaline* and *dopamine* (which occur naturally in the brain), they became the focus of research, with dopamine receiving most attention. The earliest theory implicating dopamine proposed that schizophrenia was caused by its *excess* production, and post-mortem studies of diagnosed schizophrenics showed higher than normal concentrations of dopamine, especially in the limbic system (Iversen, 1979). However, rather than producing more dopamine *per se*, it is widely accepted that more dopamine is *utilised* as a result of overly sensitive postsynaptic receptors for it, or because of above normal reactivity to dopamine due to an increased number of receptor sites. For example, the density of one site (the D4 receptor) is six times greater in schizophrenic than non-schizophrenic brain tissue (Davis *et al.*, 1991).

Dopamine's role is supported by several lines of evidence. For example, in non-schizophrenics, cocaine and amphetamine produce delusions of persecution and hallucinations similar to those observed in some types of schizophrenia. Both drugs are known to cause the stimulation of dopamine receptors. Additionally, cocaine and amphetamine *exacerbate* schizophrenic symptoms (Davis, 1974). Research also indicates that drugs which treat schizophrenia (see Chapter 52) reduce the concentration of brain-dopamine by blocking dopamine receptors and preventing them from becoming stimulated (Kimble, 1988).

Box 49.9 The diathesis–stress and vulnerability–stress models

Genetic factors might create a predisposition to schizophrenia, which interacts with other factors to produce the disorder. Whilst most environments are conducive to normal development, some may trigger mental disorders. The *diathesis–stress model* is one explanation of an *interaction* between genetic and biochemical factors, and accounts for the finding that not everybody who might be genetically predisposed to schizophrenia (by virtue of, say, having a schizophrenic parent) develops it.

The model proposes that schizophrenia occurs as a result of a biological vulnerability (*diathesis*) to a disorder interacting with personally significant environmental stressors. Genetic vulnerability puts a person at risk, but environmental stressors (like leaving home or losing a job) must be present for the gene to be 'switched on'. The *vulnerability–stress model* (Nuechterlein & Dawson, 1984) is an extension of the diathesis–stress model, and specifies the genetically determined traits that can make a person vulnerable. These include hyperactivity and information-processing deficits.

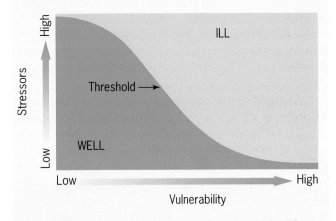

Figure 49.2 *The relationship between vulnerability and stressors as influences on schizophrenia (From Norman & Malla, 1993)*

Although the evidence linking dopamine to schizophrenia is impressive, its causal role has been questioned. For example, dopamine's availability could be just *one* factor in the sequence of schizophrenia's development rather than the *only* factor. More importantly, drugs used to treat schizophrenia are not always effective, and some drugs affect *serotonin* (see Chapter 52).

Drugs are evidently only helpful in treating what Kraepelin called the *positive* (or *Type 1*) *symptoms* of schizophrenia (Crow, 1995). These include the classic symptoms of delusions, hallucinations and thought dis-order. The *negative* (or *Type 2*) *symptoms* of decreased speech, lack of drive, diminished social interaction and loss of emotional response, are little affected by drug treatment. This has led to the proposal that the positive symptoms have one cause (possibly related to dopamine), whereas the negative symptoms have some other cause.

Neurodevelopmental influences

One possible cause of the negative symptoms is *brain damage*, and 'a considerable body of evidence points to the existence of structural abnormalities in the brains of schizophrenics' (McNeill *et al.*, 1993). Many schizophrenics display symptoms clearly indicating neurological disease, especially with regard to eye movements. These include decreased rate of eye blink, staring, lack of blink reflex in response to a tap on the forehead, poor visual pursuit movements, and poor pupillary reactions to light (Arango *et al.*, 1999). Post-mortems suggest a disease that had occurred earlier in life and had partially healed, or one that was slowly progressing at the time of death.

Some schizophrenics underwent difficult births, and their brains might have suffered a lack of oxygen (Nicolson *et al.*, 1999). The apparent decline in the number of cases of schizophrenia might be related to improvements in maternity care. Research using imaging devices to compare schizophrenic and non-schizophrenic brains has been reviewed by Jeannerod (1999) and Staal *et al.* (1999).

Several kinds of structural abnormality have been discovered in schizophrenics' brains, including an unusually small corpus collosum, high densities of white matter in the right frontal and parietal lobes, a smaller volume of temporal lobe grey matter, unusually large ventricles (the hollow spaces in the brain filled with cerebrospinal fluid), indicating the loss of brain tissue elsewhere, and changes in regional cerebral blood flow (Ambrus *et al.*, 1999).

Chua & McKenna (1995) have argued that the only well-established structural abnormality in schizophrenia is lateral ventricular enlargement, and even this is modest and shows considerable overlap with the non-schizophrenic population. However, Min *et al.* (1999) claim that there are substantial shape differences in the *thalami* of schizophrenics, whilst Jonsson *et al.* (1999) argue strongly for a greater disorientation of neurons in the *hippocampi*.

Box 49.10 The viral theory of schizophrenia

If schizophrenia is a result of the brain's failure to develop normally for some reason (which would make it a *neurodevelopmental disorder*), it is important to know when this damage occurs. One theory suggests that the damage may be due to a *viral infection*. Seasonal variations in chickenpox and measles (both caused by viruses) are well known. According to Torrey *et al.* (1977), the finding that significantly more people who develop schizophrenia are born in late winter and early spring than at other times of the year is not a statistical quirk.

Torrey *et al.* (1993) believe that schizophrenia may be the result of a virus affecting pre-natal development, especially during the second trimester of pregnancy, when the developing brain is forming crucial interconnections. For example, in normal development, *pre-alpha cells* are formed in the middle of the brain and migrate towards the cortex. In schizophrenic brains, however, the cells get only 85 per cent of the way to their final destination. Support for a viral theory comes from longitudinal studies conducted by O'Callaghan *et al.* (1991, 1993) who reported an increased risk for schizophrenia for those in the fifth month of foetal development during the 1957 *influenza pandemic*. The virus may remain latent until puberty or adulthood, and could be re-activated by hormonal changes or another viral infection.

Bracha *et al.* (1991) have shown that one MZ twin who develops schizophrenia is more likely to have various hand deformities compared with the other twin. Since the hands are formed during the second trimester of pregnancy, the same pre-natal trauma or virus which affects the brain may also affect the hands. To explain schizophrenia's tendency to run in families, Stevens (1982) has proposed that whatever causes the damage affects only people with an *inherited susceptibility* to schizophrenia, and does not affect those with non-schizophrenic heredity.

At present, there is little agreement over the plausibility of viral theories (Parker *et al.*, 2000). Some researchers, for example, have failed to find an association between births during the 1957 influenza epidemic and the later development of schizophrenia. It is ridiculous to suggest that the alleged schizophrenogenic effects of the epidemic were genuine and present in Finland, England, Wales and Edinburgh (as some studies have reported), but absent in the rest of Scotland and the United States (which other studies have found), since the virus that caused the epidemic could not have changed (Crow & Done, 1992).

Others have failed to find evidence of *any* significant associations between later schizophrenia and maternal exposure to a variety of infectious diseases other than influenza (O'Callaghan *et al.*, 1994). As Claridge (1987) has remarked, the season of birth effect has many equally plausible explanations, one being that it might reflect the cycles of sexual activity among the parents of future psychotics, a hypothesis which does not seem to have attracted much attention, despite its credibility as an explanation for the data.

CONCLUSIONS

This chapter has described schizophrenia's clinical characteristics and examined psychological and biological explanations for the disorder. Some of these are more plausible than others and have received considerable empirical support. However, an explanation which is accepted by all of those working in the area so far remains elusive.

Summary

- Schizophrenia is the most serious of all the disorders identified in ICD-10 and DSM-IV. In Britain, its diagnosis is based on Schneider's **first rank symptoms** (**passivity experiences and thought disorder**, **hallucinations**, and **primary delusions**).

- First rank symptoms can only be inferred from the individual's verbal reports. Four characteristics directly observable from behaviour are **thought process disorder, disturbances of affect/emotional disturbances, psychomotor disturbances** and **lack of volition**.

- Both ICD-10 and DSM-IV distinguish between different types of schizophrenia. **Hebephrenic** (**disorganised**), **catatonic**, **paranoid**, and **undifferentiated** (**or atypical**) schizophrenias are recognised by both systems. ICD-10 also recognises **simple** schizophrenia.

- The course of schizophrenia is characterised by **prodromal**, **active**, and **residual phases**. The term **process schizophrenia** is used when the prodromal phase occurs in early adolescence. **Reactive schizophrenia** refers to the prodromal phase occurring in early adulthood.

- The **behavioural model** can account for schizophrenia's maintenance, but has difficulty explaining its origins. The **psychodynamic model**'s explanation is a poor predictor of a schizophrenic outcome. Neither model contributes much to understanding schizophrenia's causes.

- Social and family relationships (**double bind, deviant communication**, and **marital schism/skew**) have also been implicated in schizophrenia. However, it is difficult to explain why only **some** children in a family develop schizophrenia, and family patterns may be a response to an unusual child rather than a cause of abnormality.

- **Cognitive** explanations see schizophrenia as a consequence of **faulty information processing**. Catatonic schizophrenia may be the result of the inability to **attend selectively** to information.

- The observation that schizophrenia tends to run in families, and that schizophrenic parents have a greater chance of producing schizophrenic offspring, suggests that **genetic** factors may be involved in the disorder.

- There are higher **concordance rates** for schizophrenia in MZ than DZ twins, and a higher incidence of schizophrenia in **adopted** children of schizophrenic parents. Whilst genetic factors appear to play at least some role in schizophrenia, attempts to identify the gene or genes responsible have been equivocal.

■ One way in which genes can influence behaviour is by altering **brain biochemistry**. The **inborn-error of metabolism hypothesis** claims that some people inherit metabolic errors. Another hypothesis proposes that the brain produces its own 'internal hallucinogens'. However, it is generally accepted that this hypothesis is unlikely to be true.

■ Explanations implicating **dopamine** have received more support. Schizophrenia is not caused by an excess of dopamine, but by the manner of its utilisation. Schizophrenics apparently have more numerous or densely packed dopamine **receptor sites**.

■ Cocaine and amphetamine stimulate dopamine receptors, producing schizophrenia-like symptoms in non-schizophrenics, and exacerbating the symptoms of diagnosed schizophrenics. Drugs which block dopamine receptors reduce schizophrenic symptoms.

■ The **diathesis–stress model** proposes that schizophrenia is the result of an **interaction** between biological vulnerability and personally significant environmental stressors. The **vulnerability–stress model** specifies the genetically determined traits that can make a person vulnerable.

■ Schizophrenia's **positive (Type 1) symptoms** might have one cause (related to dopamine), whilst its **negative (Type 2)** symptoms might have some other cause (related to brain damage).

■ Damage may be caused by oxygen deficits at birth. However, although there are several structural differences between schizophrenic and non-schizophrenic brains, these are modest and overlap considerably in the two populations.

■ Schizophrenia might be a **neurodevelopmental disorder,** in which the brain fails to develop normally. One cause might be a **viral infection**. However, the evidence concerning viral theories is inconclusive and sometimes contradictory.

Essay Questions

1 a Outline the clinical characteristics of schizophrenia.
(5 marks)

b Discuss biological explanations of schizophrenia.
(25 marks)

2 Critically consider biological **and** psychological explanations of schizophrenia. *(30 marks)*

WEB ADDRESSES

http://www.mentalhealth.com
http://www.rcpsych.ac.uk
http://www.schizophrenia.com/research/research.html
http://www.nimh.nih.gov.publicat/schizoph.htm

50 *Depression*

INTRODUCTION AND OVERVIEW

Mood (or *affective*) *disorders* involve a prolonged and fundamental disturbance of mood and emotions. Mood is a pervasive and sustained emotional state that colours perceptions, thoughts and behaviours. At one extreme is *manic disorder* (or *mania*), characterised by wild, exuberant and unrealistic activity, and a flight of ideas or distracting thoughts. At the other is *depressive disorder*. Mania usually occurs in conjunction with depression, and in such cases is called *bipolar disorder*. However, when mania occurs alone, the term bipolar is also used, the term *unipolar* being reserved for the experience of depression only. The term *manic–depressive* refers to both the unipolar and bipolar forms of affective disorder.

This chapter describes the clinical characteristics of depression. It also examines the psychological and biological explanations of the disorder, including evidence on which these explanations are based.

THE CLINICAL CHARACTERISTICS OF DEPRESSION

Depression has been called the 'common cold' of psychological problems (Seligman, 1973). It is the most common psychological problem people face. During the coming year, most of us will experience some symptoms of depression (Beck & Young, 1978). When a loved one dies or a relationship ends, depression is a normal reaction. Indeed, most psychologically healthy people occasionally 'get the blues' or 'feel down'. However, this usually passes fairly quickly. For a diagnosis of *clinical depression*, several characteristics need to have co-occurred for a period of time.

Box 50.1 The characteristics of clinical depression

Clinical depression is defined by persistent low mood for at least two weeks, plus at least five of the following:

* decreased appetite or weight loss or increased appetite or weight gain (a change of 0.5 kg per week over several weeks or 4.5 kg in a year when not dieting);

* difficulty in sleeping (*insomnia*) or sleeping longer than usual (*hypersomnia*);

* loss of energy or tiredness to the point of being unable to make even the simplest everyday decisions;

* an observable slowing down or agitation. To discharge feelings of restlessness, people will often wring their hands, pace about or complain (*agitated depression*);

* a markedly diminished loss of interest or pleasure in activities previously enjoyed;

* feelings of self-reproach or excessive or inappropriate guilt over real or imagined misdeeds. These may develop into *delusions* (see Chapter 49, page 529);

* complaints or evidence of diminished ability to think or concentrate;

* recurrent thoughts of death (not just a fear of dying), suicide, suicidal thoughts without a specific plan, or a suicide attempt or a specific plan for committing suicide.

(Adapted from Nemeroff, 1998)

Unipolar depression can occur at any age, and may appear gradually or suddenly. In Britain, around five per cent of adults aged between 18 and 74 will experience serious depression. However, the number of people seeking help from their GPs for depression was *nine million* in 1998 (BPS, 1999).

Key STUDY

Box 50.2 A case of depression

A 55-year-old man has suffered from decreased appetite and a 23 kg weight loss over the past six months. His appetite.loss has been accompanied by a burning pain in his chest, back and abdomen, which he is convinced indicates a fatal abdominal cancer. He is withdrawn and isolated, unable to work, uninterested in friends and family, and unresponsive to their attempts to make him feel better. He awakes at 4 a.m. and is unable to fall back asleep. He claims to feel worse in the mornings and to improve slightly as the day wears on. He is markedly agitated and speaks of feelings of extreme unworthiness. He says that he would be better off dead and that he welcomes his impending demise from cancer.

(Adapted from Spitzer *et al.*, 1981)

Figure 50.1 *Sir Winston Churchill was a sufferer of alternating periods of mania and depression. He called the depressive episodes his 'black dog'*

Key STUDY

Box 50.3 A case of bipolar disorder

For four months, Mrs S. has spent most of her time lying in bed. She appears sad and deep in thought and often states, 'I'm no good to anyone; I'm going to be dead soon'. She expresses feelings of hopelessness and listlessness and has difficulty concentrating. Suddenly, one day, her mood seems to be remarkably better. She is pleasant, verbalises more and appears somewhat cheerful. The following day, however, her speech rate is increased, she moves rapidly, shows a flight of ideas, and intrudes into everyone's activities. Over a couple of days, this activity increases to the point where she is unable to control her actions and attempts to break the furniture.

(Adapted from Spitzer *et al.*, 1981)

Deeply embedded within psychiatric thinking is the distinction between *endogenous* and *exogenous* (or *reactive*) depression. Endogenous ('coming from within') was used to describe depression arising from biochemical disturbances in the brain. Exogenous ('coming from the outside') was used to describe depression occurring as a reaction (hence *reactive*) to stressful life experiences. However, this distinction is controversial, and endogenous is now used to describe a cluster of symptoms, rather than the origins of the depression (Williams & Hargreaves, 1995).

As noted previously, bipolar disorder is characterised by alternating periods of mania and depression, apparently unrelated to external events. Their duration and frequency vary from person to person. Sometimes, manic and depressive episodes may be separated by long periods of normal functioning. For others, the episodes quickly follow one another. These unending cycles can be destructive for the people affected, their families and friends.

Bipolar disorder generally appears in the early 20s. Unlike depression (which is more prevalent in women: see pages 545–546), bipolar disorder is equally prevalent in men and women, although the disorder itself is much less common than depression. Interestingly, there is a disproportionately higher incidence of bipolar disorder among creative people (Jamison, 1989). For example, of 47 award-winning British writers and artists, 38 per cent were treated for the disorder (see also Post, 1994). In the general population, the figure is about one per cent.

PSYCHOLOGICAL EXPLANATIONS OF DEPRESSION

Behavioural explanations

The behavioural model focuses on the role played by *reinforcement* (see Chapter 38). Ferster (1965) proposed that depression is a result of a *reduction* in reinforcement. Lewinsohn (1974) expanded Ferster's theory, and proposed that certain events, such as the death of a loved one, induce depression because they reduce positive reinforcement.

Depressed people may be less socially active. Initially, this leads to concern and attention from their friends. Lewinsohn argues that this *reinforces* the depressed behaviour. However, after a while concern and attention wane. Thus, reinforcement is reduced and this exacerbates the depression. The depressed individual is therefore caught in a cycle from which escape is difficult.

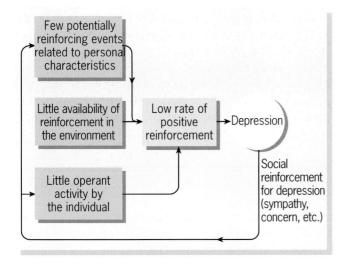

Figure 50.2 *Lewinsohn's model of depression*

Lewinsohn sees people lacking social skills as prime candidates for depression, because social ineptness is unlikely to bring reinforcement from others. Consequently, the socially unskilled individual may exhibit the form of passive behaviour characterising depression. Depressed people report having fewer pleasant experiences than non-depressed people, and greater depression is correlated with fewer pleasant experiences (Peterson, 1993). However, whilst depression might *follow* a reduction in pleasant experiences, it could *precede* a reduction in those experiences, implying that people who become depressed might lower their participation in reinforcing events.

Cognitive–behavioural and cognitive explanations

Seligman's (1975, 1992) research represents a link between behavioural and cognitive perspectives. Seligman & Maier (1967) conducted an experiment in which dogs were restrained, so that they could not avoid electric shocks. The dogs appeared to become passively resigned to the receipt of the shocks. Later, when they were placed in a situation in which they *could* escape the shocks, they made no attempt to do so. Seligman called this phenomenon *learned helplessness*.

Box 50.4 Learned helplessness

Seligman argued that the dogs' behaviours (which included lethargy, sluggishness, and appetite loss) were similar to those exhibited by depressed humans. Depressed people (like dogs) learn from experience to develop an expectancy that their behaviours will be fruitless in bringing about an environmental change. When people feel helpless to influence their encounters with pleasurable and unpleasurable stimuli, they become depressed.

Seligman's account was criticised because it failed to address the issue of why some depressed people blame themselves for their depression, whilst others blame the external world, and the observation that depressed people tend to attribute their successes to luck rather than ability. Abramson *et al.*'s (1978) revised version of learned helplessness theory is based on the attributions or interpretations people make of their experiences (see Chapter 1).

According to Abramson *et al.*, people who attribute failure to *internal* ('It's my fault'), *stable* ('It's going to last forever') and *global* ('It's going to affect everything I do') causes, and attribute successes to luck, are more likely to become depressed. This is because these factors lead to the perception that they are helpless to change things for the better. This *attributional style* (see Chapter 1) derives from learning histories, especially in the family and at school.

Questionnaires assessing how people interpret adversities in life predict (to some degree) their future susceptibility to depression (Kinderman & Bentall, 1997). However, although cognitions of helplessness often accompany depressive episodes, the cognitive pattern changes once the depressive episode ends. According to Gotlib & Colby (1995), people who were formerly depressed are actually no different from people who have never been depressed in terms of their tendencies to view negative events with an attitude of helpless resignation. This suggests that an attitude of helplessness could be a *symptom* rather than a *cause* of depression.

Box 50.5 Beck's cognitive triad model

A similar account to Seligman's is Beck's (1974, 1997) cognitive model which states that:

'An individual's emotional response to an event or experience is determined by the conscious meaning placed on it'.

Beck believes that depression is based in self-defeating *negative beliefs* and *negative cognitive sets* (tendencies to think in certain ways) that develop as a result of experience. Certain childhood and adolescent experiences (such as the loss of a parent or criticism from teachers) lead to the development of a cognitive triad consisting of three interlocking negative beliefs. These concern the *self*, the *world* and the *future*, and cause people to have a distorted and constricted outlook on life. The beliefs lead people to magnify bad, and minimise good, experiences. The cognitive triad is maintained by several kinds of distorted and illogical interpretations of real events that contribute to depression (see also Chapter 54).

Some depressed people do describe their world in the ways outlined by Beck (Whisman & McGarvey, 1995). However, correlations do not imply causality, and it could be that depressed feelings and logical errors of thought are both caused by a third factor (perhaps a biochemical imbalance: see pages 543–545). Additionally, the perception and recall of information in more negative terms might be the *result* of depression rather than the *cause* of it.

Other research has looked at the role of *depressogenic schemata* (cognitions which may precipitate depression, and remain latent until activated by *stress*). Several types of stressor may activate dysfunctional beliefs in people. For example, *sociotropic* individuals may be stressed by negative interactions with, or rejections by, others, whereas *autonomous* individuals may be stressed by a failure to reach personal goals (Haaga & Beck, 1992). According to Teasdale's (1988) *differential activation hypothesis*, the increased accessibility of negative thoughts after an initial shift in mood may explain why some people suffer persistent rather than transient depression (Scott, 1994).

Psychodynamic explanations

Psychodynamic approaches to mood disorders were first addressed by Abraham (1911). However, it was Freud (1917) who attempted to apply psychodynamic principles. He noted a similarity between the grieving that occurs when a loved one dies and depressive symptoms. For Freud, depression was an excessive and irrational grief response to loss that evokes feelings associated with real or imagined loss of affection from the person on whom the individual was most dependent as a child. Thus, depressed people become dependent

and clinging or, in extreme cases, regress to a childlike state. The greater the experience of loss in childhood, the greater the regression that occurred during adulthood. The evidence for Freud's account is, however, mixed. Some studies report that children who have lost a parent are particularly susceptible to depression later on (Palosaari & Aro, 1995). Others, however, have failed to find such a susceptibility (Parker, 1992).

Freud also argued that unresolved and repressed hostility towards one's parents was important. When loss is experienced, anger is evoked and turned *inward* on the self, because the outward expression of anger is unacceptable to the superego. This self-directed hostility creates feelings of guilt, unworthiness and despair, which may be so intense as to motivate *suicide* (the ultimate form of inward-directed aggression). Freud further believed that grief was complicated by inevitable mixed feelings. As well as affection, mourners are likely to have had at least occasionally angry feelings towards the deceased. However, these unacceptable feelings are also redirected towards the self, leading to lowered self-esteem and guilty feelings.

Psychodynamic theorists see bipolar disorder as the result of the alternating dominance of personality by the superego (in the depressive phase of the disorder). This floods the individual with exaggerated ideas of wrongdoing and associated feelings of guilt and worthlessness. The ego (in the manic phase) then attempts to defend itself by rebounding and asserting supremacy. As a response to the ego's excessive display, the superego dominates, resulting in guilty feelings which plunge the individual again into depression.

Box 50.6 Weaknesses of the psychodynamic model's account of depression

At least four reasons suggest that the psychodynamic model is inadequate in explaining mood disorders in general, and depression in particular:

- There is no direct evidence that depressed people interpret the death of a loved one as desertion or rejection of themselves (Davison & Neale, 1990).

- If anger is turned inward, we would not expect depressed people to direct excessive amounts of hostility towards those close to them. This does, however, occur (Weissman & Paykel, 1974).

- There is little evidence for a direct connection between early loss and the risk of depression in adult life (Crook & Eliot, 1980).

- Since symbolic loss cannot be observed, this aspect of the theory cannot be experimentally assessed.

BIOLOGICAL EXPLANATIONS OF DEPRESSION

Genetic influences

Based on the observation that mood disorders tend to run in families, a *genetic* basis for them has been proposed. People with first-degree relatives (relatives with whom an individual shares 50 per cent of his/her genes – parents and siblings) who have a mood disorder are much more likely to develop one than people with unaffected first-degree relatives (Oruc *et al.*, 1998). Allen (1976) has reported a higher average concordance rate for bipolar disorder in MZs (72 per cent: the highest for *any* mental disorder) than in DZs (14 per cent).

For major depression, the average concordance rate for MZs is 46 per cent and only 20 per cent for DZs (McGuffin *et al.*, 1996). The fact that concordance rates for bipolar disorder and major depression differ suggests that, if genetic factors *are* involved, they are different for the two disorders. As noted in Chapter 49, however, data from families and twins are limited by the fact that they usually share the same environment. However, as with schizophrenia, this problem has been at least partially overcome by adoption studies. Adopted children who later develop a mood disorder appear to be much more likely to have a biological parent who has a mood disorder, becomes alcoholic or commits suicide, even though the adopted children are raised in very different environments (Wender *et al.*, 1986).

Key **S T U D Y**

Box 50.7 DNA markers and mood disorders

DNA markers have been used to identify the gene or genes involved in mood disorders. This approach looks at the inheritance of mood disorders within high-risk families, and then searches for a DNA segment that is inherited along with a predisposition to develop the disorder. Egeland *et al.* (1987) studied 81 people from four high-risk families, all of whom were members of the Old Order Amish community in Pennsylvania. Fourteen were diagnosed as having a bipolar disorder, and all had specific genetic markers at the tip of chromosome 11. However, subsequent research has failed to replicate this finding in other populations in which bipolar disorder appears to be inherited.

Whilst these data do not invalidate those of Egeland *et al.*, other researchers have failed to support their findings when the analysis was extended to other Amish relatives (Kelsoe *et al.*, 1989). This suggests at least two possibilities: the gene for bipolar disorder may not actually be on chromosome 11, or several genes play a role, only one of which is on chromosome 11. The latter is supported by the observation that a gene on the X chromosome has also been implicated in bipolar disorder. (Nemeroff, 1998).

Cells use a gene called SERT to make a serotonin transporter protein, which plays an important role in the transmission of information between neurons (Ogilvie *et al.*, 1996). In most people, part of this gene (the *second intron*) contains ten or 12 repeating sections of DNA. However, in a significant number of people with depression, this part of the gene has only nine repeating sequences. The fact that serotonin is strongly implicated in depression (see below) and that newer anti-depressant drugs (see Chapter 52) interact with the serotonin transporter protein, offers one of the strongest hints yet that genes may be involved in depression (Frisch *et al.*, 1999), although other research disputes SERT's role (Seretti *et al.*, 1999).

Biochemical influences

As mentioned in Chapter 49 (see page 535), genes act by directing biochemical events. *Biochemical processes* which may play a causal role in affective disorders involve imbalances in the neurotransmitters *serotonin* and *noradrenaline*. Schildkraut (1965) proposed that too much noradrenaline at certain sites causes mania, whereas too little causes depression. Later research suggested that serotonin plays a similar role.

Some evidence supports Schildkraut's proposals. For example, non-humans given drugs that diminish noradrenaline production become sluggish and inactive, two symptoms of depression (Wender & Klein, 1981). Similar effects occur when humans are given *reserpine*, used to treat high blood pressure. Additionally, drugs which are effective in reducing depression (see Chapter 52, pages 558–559) increase brain levels of noradrenaline and/or serotonin (Lemonick, 1997). *Iproniazid* (used to treat tuberculosis) produces elation and euphoria, and increases noradrenaline and serotonin levels. Lithium carbonate (a treatment for mania: see Chapter 52, page 559) decreases noradrenaline and serotonin levels.

Research also indicates that depressed people's urine contains lower than normal levels of compounds produced when noradrenaline and serotonin are broken down by enzymes (Teuting *et al.*, 1981), suggesting lower than normal activity of noradrenaline and serotonin-secreting neurones in the brain. Abnormally high levels of noradrenaline compounds have been found in the urine of manic people (Kety, 1975), and the level of these compounds fluctuates in people with bipolar disorder (Bunney *et al.*, 1972).

Box 50.8 The permissive amine theory of mood disorder

Schildkraut's theory was weakened by the finding that whilst noradrenaline *and* serotonin are lower in depression, lower levels of serotonin are also found in mania. Thus, it cannot be a simple case of an excess or deficiency of these neurotransmitters that causes mania or depression. An attempt to reconcile these observations is Kety's *permissive amine theory of mood disorder* (noradrenaline and serotonin are examples of *biogenic amines*, hence the theory's name).

According to Kety, serotonin plays a role in limiting noradrenaline levels. When serotonin levels are normal, so are noradrenaline levels, and only normal highs and lows are experienced. However, when serotonin is deficient it cannot play its limiting role, and so noradrenaline levels fluctuate beyond normal high and low levels, leading to mania and depression.

Whilst drugs that alleviate depression increase noradrenaline and serotonin levels, they do so only in the period immediately after taking the drug. Within a few days, the levels return to baseline. The problem for Kety's theory is that antidepressant effects do *not* occur during the period when transmitter levels are elevated. All anti-depressants take some time before they alleviate depression (see Chapter 52, page 558). This suggests that depression cannot be explained simply in terms of a change in neurotransmitter levels. It is more likely that the drugs act to reduce depression by increasing the *sensitivity* of receiving neurons, thereby allowing them to utilise limited neurotransmitter supplies in a more effective way (Kennett, 1999).

Additionally, antidepressant drugs are not always effective in reducing depression, not everyone suffering from depression shows reduced neurotransmitter levels, and not everyone displaying mania shows increased noradrenaline levels. Whilst it is likely that neurotransmitters play a role in mood disorders, these findings demonstrate that their exact role remains to be determined (Wolpert, 1999).

Box 50.9 Structural differences in the brains of depressives

Part of the brain called the subgenual prefrontal cortex, which is located about 2.5 inches (6 cm) behind the bridge of the nose, is known to play an important role in the control of emotion. In depressed people, it is eight per cent less active than in non-depressed people, and there is 40–50 per cent less tissue in the

depressed. This deficit may result from a catastrophic loss of an as yet unknown subset of neurons by an also unknown cause. (Nemeroff, 1998)

External factors and biochemical influences

Whilst the evidence suggests that affective disorders are heritable and that biochemical factors are involved, the exact cause-and-effect relationships remain to be established. If a gene is involved, its exact mode of transmission must be complex, given the variation in the severity and manner of the expression of mood disorders. Serotonin might act as the regulator, or serotonin and noradrenaline might play different roles in different types of mood disorders. Also, the possibility that neurotransmitter levels change *as a result* of the mood disorder, rather than being its cause, cannot be excluded. For example, environmental stimuli may cause depression which causes biochemical changes in the brain. Noradrenaline levels are lower in dogs in whom learned helplessness has been induced (Miller *et al.*, 1977). The dogs did not inherit such levels, but acquired them as a result of their experiences.

Two sub-types of *seasonal affective disorder* (SAD) of particular interest are *winter depression* (associated with appetite, weight and sleep gain) and *summer depression* (associated with weight, sleep and appetite loss).

Box 50.10 The pineal gland, melatonin and the treatment of winter depression

Winter depression might be regulated by the *pineal gland*, a tiny structure located close to the brain's centre. As noted in Chapter 13, the pineal gland is believed to have evolved by convergence and fusion of a second pair of *photoreceptors* (Morgan, 1995). It secretes the hormone *melatonin*, which influences serotonin's production. Melatonin production is controlled by the presence or absence of direct light stimulation to the eyes. It is produced when it is dark, but its production is suppressed when it is light. In winter depression, melatonin production may be desynchronised as a result of decreasing natural light exposure during the winter months (see Chapter 14).

One way of treating winter depression is to re-phase the rhythm of melatonin production, and this is the principle underlying *phototherapy*. Sufferers of winter depression are seated in front of extremely bright lights (the equivalent to the illumination of 2500 candles on a surface one metre away being the most effective: Wehr & Rosenthal, 1989). Exposure to this light for just over one hour each evening reverses the symptoms within three to four days.

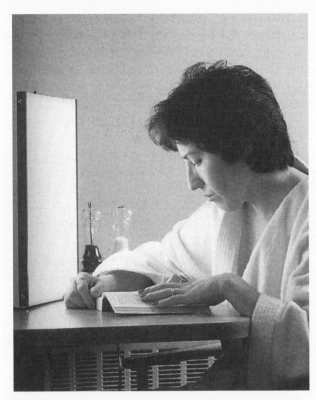

Figure 50.3 *Exposure to bright lights has been shown to be effective for some people in treating winter depression.*

In summer depression, a mechanism other than decreasing light exposure must play a role (Partonen & Lonnqvist, 1998). Laboratory studies of non-humans have shown that changes in magnetic field exposure, which alter the direction of the magnetic field, are correlated with decreased melatonin synthesis and serotonin production (Rudolph *et al.*, 1993). Kay (1994) hypothesises that *geomagnetic storms* might partly account for the bimodal annual distribution of depression (that is, summer *and* winter depression). Kay found a 36 per cent increase in male hospital admissions for depression in the second week following such storms, and believes that the effects of geomagnetic storms on melatonin synthesis and serotonin production are the same in humans and non-humans.

Bush (cited in Whittell, 1995) has investigated the high suicide rate in the remote Alaskan hinterland, where suicide levels among the state's 15–24 year olds are six times the USA average. Bush argues for a link between the *aurora borealis* (or Northern lights), a source of changes in geomagnetism, and electrical activity in the brain. Additionally, the British finding that new mothers and pregnant women are 60 per cent more likely to suffer depression if they live near high-voltage electricity cables than those who do not, coupled with

clusters of suicides in people living close to such cables, suggests that electromagnetic fields *might* be involved this disorder (Westhead, 1996).

Whatever seasonal depression's causes, the anti-depressant drug *sertraline* is effective, at least in winter depression, and produces even better effects than *phototherapy* (see Box 50.10), which is inconvenient, costly and associated with headaches and eye strain (Syal, 1997).

Box 50.11   Pets and depression

Borna disease virus (BDV) was first identified in horses in Germany over 100 years ago. As well as causing behavioural problems in horses, the virus also affects sheep, rabbits and cats. Humans with some behavioural problems are six times more likely to have contracted BDV. If BDV causes emotional problems in humans (it is believed to attack neurons which control mood), it could explain the unusually high suicide and depression rates in rural areas.

(Based on Wilson, 1999)

SEX DIFFERENCES IN DEPRESSION

According to Cochrane (1995), when all relevant factors are controlled for, depression contributes most highly to the overall rate of treatment for mental disorders in women, who are two to three times more likely than men to become clinically depressed (Williams & Hargreaves, 1995).

Several factors may account for the sex difference. These include hormonal fluctuations associated with the menstrual cycle, childbirth, the menopause, taking oral contraceptives, brain chemistry and diet (Leutwyler, 1997).

Key S T U D Y

Box 50.12 Brain biochemistry and diet

According to Diksic *et al.* (cited in Highfield, 1997b), serotonin is made by men's brain stems at a rate 52 per cent higher than in women. This could be due to the way men and women develop. One possibility is that dieting during the teenage years might alter brain biochemistry. Smith *et al.* (1997) found that women experienced symptoms of depression when *tryptophan*, a protein component, was removed from their diets. Tryptophan is an amino-acid precursor of serotonin, and even a standard 1000-calorie carbohydrate-restricted diet can lower blood plasma levels of it enough to alter serotonin function.

The evidence concerning hormonal and other factors is, however, weak. For example, although one in ten women who have just given birth are sufficiently depressed to need medical or psychological help, no specific causal hormonal abnormality has been identified. It is just as plausible to suggest that social factors (such as the adjustment to a new role) are as important as any proposed physical factors (Murray, 1995).

Cochrane (1995) has summarised non-biological explanations of women's greater susceptibility to depression. For example, girls are very much more likely to be sexually abused than boys, and victims of abuse are at least twice as likely to experience clinical depression in adulthood, compared with non-abused individuals. Abuse alone, then, might explain the sex difference. An alternative account is based on the fact that the sex difference is greatest between the ages of 20 and 50, the years when marriage, child-bearing, motherhood and the *empty nest syndrome* (see Chapter 35) will be experienced by a majority of women.

Although women are increasingly becoming part of the labour force (see Chapter 35), being a full-time mother and wife, having no employment outside of the home, and lacking an intimate and confiding relationship, are increasingly being seen as risk factors for depression (Wu & DeMaris, 1996). The acceptance of a traditional female gender role may contribute to *learned helplessness* (see page 541), because the woman sees herself as having little control over her life.

Depression may be seen as a *coping strategy* that is available to women (Cochrane, 1983). Not only is it more acceptable for women to admit to psychological problems, but such problems may represent a means of changing an intolerable situation. As Callaghan & O'Carroll (1993) have observed:

'Unhappiness about their domestic, social, and political circumstances lies at the root of many women's concerns. This unhappiness must not be medicalised and regarded as a "female malady".'

CONCLUSIONS

Like schizophrenia, depression is a serious mental disorder with distinct clinical characteristics. Psychological and biological explanations have been advanced to explain depression. All have received support, although we are still some way from a single accepted explanation.

Summary

- At one extreme of **mood/affective disorder** is **manic disorder/mania**. At the other is **depressive disorder**. Mania on its own or, more usually, in conjunction with depression, is called **bipolar disorder**. **Unipolar disorder** refers to depression only. **Manic–depression** refers to both unipolar and bipolar disorders.

- Depression is the most common mental disorder, and can be a response to certain life events or just part of 'everyday life'. To be diagnosed as **clinically depressed**, a person must display persistent low mood for at least two weeks, plus at least five other symptoms identified in diagnostic criteria.

- The traditional distinction between **endogenous** and **exogenous/reactive** depression is controversial. Endogenous no longer denotes depression's origins, but refers to a cluster of symptoms. Depression can occur at any age and is more common in women.

- **Behavioural** explanations of depression focus on the role played by a reduction in **positive reinforcement**. **Cognitive–behavioural** accounts use the concept of **learned helplessness** to explain depression. However, learned helplessness on its own cannot account for depressed peoples' **attributional styles**.

- According to Beck's **cognitive model**, depression is based in self-defeating **negative beliefs** and **cognitive sets**. The **cognitive triad** leads people to exaggerate their bad experiences and minimise their good experiences.

■ **Depressogenic schemata** may be activated by rejections from others (in **sociotropic** individuals), or a failure to reach personal goals (in **autonomous** individuals). The **differential activation hypothesis** is an attempt to explain persistent and transient depression.

■ The **psychodynamic model** proposes that both **actual** and **symbolic losses** cause us to re-experience parts of childhood, and depression may involve a regression to a childlike dependency. However, the psychodynamic model is inadequate in explaining mood disorders in general and depression in particular.

■ Because mood disorders run in families, they might have a **genetic** basis. This is supported by the higher concordance rate in MZs than DZs. DNA markers have been used to identify the gene(s) involved, although the data are equivocal in this respect. The SERT gene offers the strongest evidence yet for a genetic basis to mood disorders.

■ Lower than normal levels of activity in **serotonin**- and **noradrenaline**-secreting neurons may be a causal factor in depression. Kety's **permissive amine theory** describes their interaction, but is inconsistent with some evidence. Whilst neurotransmitters probably play a role in mood disorders, exactly what it is remains to be discovered.

■ Seasonal variations in the incidence of depression are well-established. **Winter depression** is almost certainly caused by the desynchronisation of **melatonin,** as a result of decreasing natural light exposure in winter.

■ **Summer depression** is more difficult to explain. Geomagnetic factors may be involved in summer and winter depression, by influencing melatonin synthesis and serotonin production.

■ Biological explanations of sex differences in depression implicate the menstrual cycle, childbirth, the menopause, oral contraceptives, and the influence of dieting on brain biochemistry.

■ Psychological explanations of sex differences in depression implicate sexual abuse, the stress associated with marriage, childbearing, motherhood, and the 'empty nest syndrome'. Depression may even be a **coping strategy** for women.

Essay Questions

1 **a** Outline the clinical characteristics of depression.
    (*5 marks*)

   b Discuss biological explanations of depression.
    (*25 marks*)

2 Discuss the view that depression can be better explained in psychological than biological terms.
    (*30 marks*)

WEB ADDRESSES

http://www.mentalhealth.com
http://www.psych.helsinki.fi/~janne/asdfaq/
http://www.psycom.net/depression.central
http://www.gene.ucl.ac.uk/users/dcurtis/lectures/pgenfunc.html

51 *Anxiety Disorders*

INTRODUCTION AND OVERVIEW

Researchers generally agree that some anxiety is *biologically adaptive*, because it produces enhanced vigilance and a more realistic appraisal of a situation, allowing us to develop appropriate *coping responses* (see Gross *et al.*, 2000). Some people, however, experience anxiety which is so overwhelming that it interferes with normal everyday functioning. Such anxiety is experienced as a general feeling of dread or apprehensiveness, typically accompanied by various physiological reactions, including increased heart rate, rapid and shallow breathing, sweating, muscle tension and a dryness of the mouth.

Anxiety disorders form a category in DSM-IV that is subsumed by the category *neurotic, stress-related* and *somatoform disorders* in ICD-10. DSM-IV recognises four types of anxiety disorder: *panic disorder* and *generalised anxiety disorder*, *phobic disorders* (called *phobic anxiety disorders* in ICD-10), *obsessive–compulsive disorder*, and *post-traumatic stress disorder* (which ICD-10 includes under the heading *stress and adjustment disorders*). This chapter describes the clinical characteristics of obsessive–compulsive disorder and post-traumatic stress disorder. It also examines the psychological and biological explanations of these disorders, including evidence on which these explanations are based.

THE CLINICAL CHARACTERISTICS OF OBSESSIVE–COMPULSIVE DISORDER (OCD)

As its name suggests, in *obsessive–compulsive disorder* (OCD) the profound anxiety is reflected in obsessions and compulsions. *Obsessions* are recurrent thoughts or images that do not feel voluntarily controlled, and are experienced as senseless or repugnant. It is for this reason that they are anxiety-provoking. *Compulsions* are irresistible urges to engage in repetitive behaviours. These are performed according to rules or *rituals*, as a way of reducing or preventing the anxiety associated with some future undesirable event (Shafran, 1999).

All of us have thoughts and behaviour patterns that are repeated, but these are only problematic if they cause personal distress or interfere with daily life. OCD sufferers experience significant personal and social problems, and may have difficulty in maintaining a job, finishing school, and developing relationships (Goodman, 1999). OCD has recently undergone a dramatic change in status (Tallis, 1995). Once regarded as a rare disorder, it now occupies a central position in clinical psychology and contemporary psychiatry. OCD is the fourth most common psychological problem in the USA, and in Britain it is estimated that one to one-and-a-half million people suffer from it. Females are slightly more likely to be OCD sufferers, and the disorder usually begins in young adulthood, and sometimes in childhood (Rothenberg, 1998).

Box 51.1 Characteristics of obsessional thought

Frequently, obsessional thoughts take the form of violent *images*, such as killing oneself or others. However, they can take other forms. The four most common obsessional characteristics are:

- *impaired control over mental processes* (such as repetitive thoughts over a loved one's death);
- *concerns of losing control over motor behaviours* (such as killing someone);
- *fear of contamination* (by, for example, germs);
- *checking behaviours* (such as concern over whether a door has been locked).

Whatever form the thoughts take, they cannot be resisted and are extremely unpleasant for the sufferer.

(From Sanavio, 1988)

Often, compulsions arise from obsessions. For example, a person persistently thinking about contamination by germs may develop complex rituals for avoiding contamination. These are repeated until the person is satisfied that this is the case, even if the hands become raw as a result of being washed hundred of times a day. The most common compulsive behaviours are checking and washing (Shafran, 1999).

Shakespeare's character Lady Macbeth, who acquired a hand-washing compulsion after helping her husband murder the King of Scotland is, perhaps, the most famous fictional OCD sufferer. The late billionaire Howard Hughes, who constantly wore gloves, walked on clean paper, bathed repeatedly and refused to see people for fear of being contaminated by them, is, perhaps, the most well-known non-fictional sufferer, along with Charles Darwin, Martin Luther and John Bunyan (Bennett, 1997). Compulsives recognise that their behaviours are senseless, yet they experience intense anxiety if they are prevented from engaging in them. This anxiety is only reduced when the ritualistic behaviour is performed.

Key STUDY

Box 51.2 A case of obsessive thoughts leading to compulsive behaviour

Shirley K., a 23-year-old housewife, complained of frequent attacks of headaches and dizziness. During the preceding three months, she had been disturbed by recurring thoughts that she might harm her two-year-old son either by stabbing or choking him (the obsessional thought). She constantly had to go to his room, touch the boy and feel him breathe in order to reassure herself that he was still alive (the compulsive act), otherwise she became unbearably anxious. If she read a report in the daily paper of the murder of a child, she would become agitated, since this reinforced her fear that she, too, might act on her impulse.

(From Goldstein & Palmer, 1975)

PSYCHOLOGICAL EXPLANATIONS OF OCD

Psychodynamic explanations

According to the psychodynamic model, obsessions are *defence mechanisms* (see Gross *et al.*, 2000) that serve to occupy the mind and *displace* more threatening thoughts. Laughlin (1967), for example, sees the intrusion of obsessional thoughts as preventing the arousal of anxiety 'by

serving as a more tolerable substitute for a subjectively less welcome thought or impulse'. Certainly, something like this might be practised by athletes who 'psych themselves up' before a competitive event. From a psychodynamic perspective (and also from a cognitive perspective: see page 550), the 'tolerable substitute' might function to exclude self-defeating doubts and thoughts. However, it is difficult to see what thoughts of killing someone (which, as noted in Box 51.1, is one of the more common obsessional thoughts) are a more tolerable substitute *for*.

Box 51.3 Other psychodynamic approaches to OCD

According to *object relations theorists*, disturbed relationships in early life leave some people with a 'split' view of the world. Believing that thoughts, emotions, actions and persons are either *all* good or *all* bad, they must resort to 'ego-alien' obsessions to tolerate the negative aspects of their thinking or feelings. Some *ego psychologists* interpret the aggressive impulses experienced by people with OCD as an unfulfilled need for self-expression, to try to overcome feelings of vulnerability or insecurity.

(Adapted from Comer, 1998)

Behavioural explanations

The behavioural model sees OCD as a way of reducing anxiety. If a particular thought or behaviour reduces anxiety, then it should (because it is *reinforcing*: see Chapter 38, pages 414–415) become more likely to occur. This *anxiety-reduction hypothesis* explains why OCD is maintained, but it does not explain the disorder's development. However, the *superstition hypothesis* does. Skinner (1948a) argued that what we call 'superstition' develops as a result of a chance association between a behaviour and a reinforcer. In Skinner's experiments, pigeons were given food at regular intervals irrespective of their behaviour. After a while, they displayed idiosyncratic movements, presumably because these were the movements they were making when the food was given.

The superstition hypothesis can account for many compulsive rituals (O'Leary & Wilson, 1975). Amongst soccer players, for example, many superstitious behaviours exist. These include always being last on to the pitch, and always putting the left sock on before the right. Such behaviours may occur because they were, in the past, associated with success. If such rituals are not permitted, anxiety is aroused. However, whilst chance associations between behaviours and reinforcers might explain the persistence of some *behaviours*, the development of obsessional *thoughts* is much more difficult for the behavioural model to explain.

Cognitive explanations

As noted earlier (see page 548), all of us have thoughts and behaviours that are repeated. However, most of us do not develop OCD. This is because we can selectively ignore and dismiss thoughts, even if they are unwanted, unpleasant and intrusive (Clayton *et al.*, 1999). Cognitively-based research indicates that OCD sufferers differ from non-sufferers in several important ways (Ehntholt *et al.*, 1999):

- they believe that their thoughts are capable of harming themselves or others, and feel they must eliminate them;

- they have higher standards of conduct and morality, and perceive their thoughts as being more unacceptable;

- they feel they can and should have perfect control over their thoughts, otherwise they will be unable to control their behaviour;

- they are more depressed and have lower self-esteem.

Because OCD sufferers find their intrusive thoughts extremely repulsive, they attempt to *neutralise* them. This involves thinking or behaving in ways designed to 'correct' their thoughts, such as deliberately thinking 'good thoughts', checking for possible danger sources, or repeatedly washing their hands (Salkovskis *et al.*, 1997). When such tactics reduce anxiety, they are reinforced, and become more likely to be used in the future. Eventually, though, the tactics are employed so often that they become, by definition, obsessional or compulsive. As Comer (1998) notes:

> 'At the same time, because the neutralising strategy was effective, the individual becomes convinced that the initial intrusive thought must indeed have been dangerous and in need of elimination. That thought now feels even more reprehensible and worrisome; as a result, it begins to occur so frequently that it too becomes an obsession'.

Key STUDY

Box 51.4 Is there a memory bias in OCD?

Radomsky & Rachman (1999) compared non-OCD sufferers, anxious participants, and OCD sufferers with a fear of contamination, on their recall for 'contaminated' (touched by the experimenter) and 'non-contaminated' objects. OCD sufferers had a better recall of 'contaminated' than 'non-contaminated' objects, whereas the other two groups showed no difference in their recall of the two types of objects.

Because there were no differences between the three groups in terms of their general memory ability,

a *memory bias* clearly operates in OCD. Presumably, memory deficits are a result of the way in which OCD sufferers process information. This is another promising cognitive approach to understanding OCD's causes.

BIOLOGICAL EXPLANATIONS OF OCD

Genetic influences

Comings & Comings' (1987) finding that people with OCD often have first-degree relatives with some sort of anxiety disorder suggests a genetic basis to OCD. Other research with MZ twins also points to a genetic component (Pauls & Alsobrook, 1999). However, the finding that in over half of the families of OCD sufferers members become actively *involved* in the rituals, indicates the potential influence of *learning* (which supports the behavioural model: Tallis, 1995). This might be particularly applicable to OCD's development in childhood: children with a parent who engages in ritualistic behaviour may see such behaviour as the norm (see Chapter 31).

Biochemical influences

One biochemical account of OCD is based on the finding that the only psychotherapeutic drugs which are effective in treating the disorder are those that increase the activity of the neurotransmitter *serotonin*. These include selective serotonin reuptake inhibitors (SSRIs) and monoamine oxidase inhibitors (MAOIs), both of which have the effect of increasing serotonin activity, and are more commonly associated with the treatment of depression (see Chapter 52). This has led to the proposal that OCD is a result of low serotonin activity. However, it can take up to eight to 12 weeks of drug treatment before a measurable clinical improvement is observed, and most sufferers who take SSRIs or MAOIs do not fully improve. Moreover, up to a half do not show *any* clinically meaningful improvement (McDougle *et al.*, 1999).

Box 51.5 Hallucinogens and OCD

Most hallucinogenic drugs enhance the activity of two types of serotonin receptor site (5-HT2A and 5-HT2C). The more strongly a hallucinogenic drug binds to a receptor site, the more potent its hallucinogenic effects are. Delgado & Moreno (1998) suggest that activation of the 5-HT2A and 5-HT2C receptor sites may be important for the improvement of OCD symptoms. So, activation of those receptor sites by hallucinogens *might* lead to an acute reduction of, as well as longer-lasting beneficial effects on, OCD's symptoms. Clearly, though, there are important issues relating to the use of hallucinogens as a treatment for OCD.

Another neurotransmitter that has been implicated in OCD is *dopamine* (see also Chapter 49). One drug that acts to enhance dopamine's effects is *quinpirole*. Szechtman *et al.* (1999) treated rats with quinpirole, and found that their behaviour met the ethological criteria of *compulsive checking* in OCD (see Box 51.1, page 548). Moreover, when rats that had been given quinpirole were given *clorgyline* (a MAOI: see above), their checking behaviour stopped. According to Szetchtman *et al.*, dopamine systems may play a role in OCD, and MAOIs may exert their effects by acting at MAOI-displaceable quinpirole binding sites.

It has also been suggested that *neuropeptides* play a role in OCD. Some of the influences these have (e.g. on fixed-action patterns and stereotyped behaviour) may relate to some of the characteristics of OCD (McDougle *et al.*, 1999). Additionally, neuropeptidergic and monoaminergic (including *serotonin*) systems interact, and are co-localised among specific populations of neurons. It is possible that serotonin, dopamine and neuropeptides (along with other as yet unknown substances) are all implicated in OCD (Fitzgerald *et al.*, 1999).

Brain structures

Another biological approach to OCD proposes that the disorder is a result of faulty functioning of the *caudate nuclei* and the *orbital frontal cortex*. The latter, which is part of the cortex just above the eyes, generates impulses about primitive activities, such as violence and sexuality. These are sent to the caudate nuclei, which filters some of them and passes the most powerful ones to the *thalami* (the brain's sensory relay station). Impulses that reach the thalami are subjected to higher cognitive analysis (they are thought about) and, possibly, behavioural initiation (they are acted on). According to Salloway & Cummings (1996), it is overactivity in the orbital frontal cortex and/or the caudate nuclei that leads to the constant and repetitive thoughts and actions that characterise OCD.

Studies using scanning and imaging devices (see Chapter 10) indicate that the orbital frontal cortex is more active in OCD sufferers than control participants (Crespo-Facorro *et al.*, 1999), whilst clinical studies suggest that OCD's symptoms arise or subside following damage to either the orbital frontal cortex or the caudate nuclei (Max *et al.*, 1995). It could even be that low serotonin activity and heightened brain activity are *both* involved in OCD.

As Comer (1998) notes:

> 'Serotonin plays a very active role in the operation of the orbital region and the caudate nuclei, so low serotonin activity might well be expected to disrupt the proper functioning of these areas ... Such abnormalities [may] set up some kind of biological predisposition for the development of this disorder ... The precise roles of these factors, however, are not yet fully understood'.

THE CLINICAL CHARACTERISTICS OF POST-TRAUMATIC STRESS DISORDER (PTSD)

During the First World War, many soldiers experienced *shell shock*, a shock-like state which followed the traumatic experiences of prolonged combat. Prior to being described as a clinical condition, it had been taken as evidence of cowardice, and sometimes resulted in summary trial and execution. In World War II, *combat exhaustion* was used to describe a similar reaction, characterised by terror, agitation or apathy, and insomnia.

Today, the term *post-traumatic stress disorder* (PTSD) is used to describe an anxiety disorder occurring in response to an extreme psychological or physical trauma, which is outside the range of 'normal' human experience (Thompson, 1997). PTSD affects both men and women, across all age groups (Weintraub & Ruskin, 1999). As well as war, such traumas include a physical threat to one's self or family, witnessing other peoples' deaths, and being involved in a natural or human-made disaster. In Britain, several disasters associated with PTSD have been extensively researched. These include the deaths of over 90 spectators at the Hillsborough football ground in 1989, and the bombing of the PanAm airliner that crashed at Lockerbie in 1992.

One civilian disaster causing PTSD in those who survived it was the collision between two jumbo jets that killed 582 passengers in Tenerife in 1977. A combination of environmental and human factors led to a Dutch airliner colliding with an American one. Many passengers were killed instantly, but some survived.

Key **STUDY**

Box 51.6 A case of PTSD

Martin lost his wife and blames himself for her death, because he sat stunned and motionless for some 25 seconds after the Dutch jumbo jet hit. He saw nothing but fire and smoke in the aisles, but roused himself and led his wife to a jagged hole above and behind his seat. Martin climbed out onto the wing and reached down and took hold of his wife's hand, but 'an explosion from within literally blew her out of my hands and pushed me back and down onto the wing'. He reached the runway, turned to go back after her, but the plane blew up seconds later.

Five months later, Martin was depressed and bored, had 'wild dreams', a short temper and became easily confused and irritated. 'What I saw there will terrify me forever', he says. He told the psychologist who interviewed him that he avoided television and movies, because he couldn't know when a frightening scene would appear.

(Adapted from Perlberg, 1979)

Figure 51.1 *Despite being trained to deal with emergency situations, members of the emergency services cannot be prepared for major disasters, such as the Lockerbie, Hillsborough and* Herald of Free Enterprise *disasters. Police involved in the 1989 Hillsborough disaster were awarded (in 1996) substantial financial compensation for the 'mental injury' they suffered (post-traumatic stress disorder), and can be considered 'peripheral' victims of the disaster (see page 553)*

Hunt (1997) has studied apparent PTSD amongst people in their sixties and seventies, evidently disturbed by their experiences in World War II. This is hardly surprising if it is assumed that they have been bothered *continuously* since the war. However, this assumption is apparently false, as most got on with their lives, raised families, and so on (Bender, 1995). For some reason, the memories seem to be coming back to disturb them now that they have retired (see page 554).

PTSD following the capsize of the cross-channel ferry *Herald of Free Enterprise* in Zeebrugge in 1993 has also been extensively researched (Joseph *et al.*, 1993). Studies of those who survived the disaster have shown that even *very young children* can be emotionally disturbed by a trauma. Yule (1993), for example, reports that child survivors of recent disasters show PTSD's clinical characteristics, including distressing recollections of the event, avoidance of reminders, and signs of increased physiological arousal, manifested as sleep disturbances and poor concentration.

Often, these children do not confide their distress to parents or teachers for fear of upsetting them. Consequently, their school work is affected, and they can be thrown off their educational career course. However, when asked sympathetically and straightforwardly, they usually share their reactions. Pynoos *et al.*'s (1993) research also indicates that PTSD is not limited to adults. They found a strong correlation between children's proximity to the epicentre of the 1988 Armenian earthquake and the overall severity of PTSD's core components, with girls reporting more persistent anxiety than boys.

Key S T U D Y

Box 51.7 Children and the *Challenger* disaster

In January 1986, the *Challenger* space shuttle exploded shortly after lift-off, killing all on board. Terr *et al.* (1999) compared East Coast children, who *saw* the event on television, with West Coast children, who *heard* about it first. More than 60 per cent of all children feared at least one stimulus related to *Challenger* within the first five to seven weeks of the explosion. However, the East Coast children were significantly more symptomatic than the West Coast children. Three of the East Coast children met DSM criteria for PTSD, although no children met these criteria one year later. According to Terr *et al.*, distant traumas appear to be one of a newly defined spectrum of trauma-related conditions that include relatively fleeting characteristics and a few longer-lasting ones. These may affect large numbers of normal children.

PTSD may occur immediately following a traumatic experience, or weeks, months, and even years later. In the Vietnam war, there were relatively few cases of shell shock or combat fatigue, probably because of the rapid turnover of soldiers in and out of the combat zone. However, on their return home, soldiers found it more difficult to *adjust* to civilian life than did those in the two World Wars.

As well as tiredness, apathy, nightmares, depression, social withdrawal, and a general lack of responsiveness ('*emotional anaesthesia*'), veterans reported *flashbacks* of events they had witnessed or participated in, and avoidance of thoughts associated with them. They also showed *hyperalertness*, exaggerated startle reactions, and felt guilty that they had survived but others had not. At least some reported using alcohol or drugs to try and curb disturbing symptoms, as have victims of sexual abuse (Davis & Wood, 1999). Many veterans also cut themselves off from society, to escape the sense of not being able to fit in as a result of their experiences.

Box 51.8 DSM-IV and ICD-10 criteria for PTSD

In DSM-IV, a diagnosis of PTSD is made if the clinical characteristics continue for longer than a month and produce clinically significant distress. When the characteristics are observed within four weeks of the traumatic event and last for less than a month, a diagnosis of *acute stress disorder* is more likely. In all other respects, though, the characteristics of acute and post-traumatic stress disorders are virtually identical (Comer, 1998).

Peters *et al.* (1999) tested the assumption that participants receiving an ICD-10 diagnosis of PTSD would receive the same diagnosis using DSM-IV. Agreement between the two systems was only moderately high, and Peters *et al.* concluded that ICD-10 and DSM-IV PTSD cannot be assumed to be identical. Nearly half of the discrepancies could be accounted for by DSM-IV's requirement of 'clinically significant distress' (see above). Around twenty per cent of discrepancies were a result of DSM-IV's requirement for there to be a 'general numbing of responsiveness'.

PSYCHOLOGICAL EXPLANATIONS OF PTSD

Behavioural explanations

Whilst OCD sufferers tend not to have common background factors, all PTSD sufferers share the experience of a profoundly traumatising event or events, even though these may be different from one another in various ways. However, the event(s) alone cannot explain the onset and maintenance of PTSD. According to the behavioural model, *classical conditioning* (see Chapter 38) plays a role in PTSD. Pavlov (1927), for example, conducted experiments that produced what he called *traumatic mental imprinting*. In these experiments, dogs were presented with stimuli that elicited fear responses.

The dogs associated these stimuli with particular environmental cues, which then became capable of eliciting the fear response themselves in the absence of any other stimulus (see also Chapter 53).

Humans often show fear reactions to stimuli that were present at the time a trauma occurred. Hunt (1997), for example, interviewed veterans of the Normandy landings in World War II around the time of the fiftieth anniversary events in 1994. Many reported still being troubled by their memories of the war in general, but in particular were adversely affected by specific memories which had been revived by the anniversary commemorations.

Key STUDY
Box 51.9 Stimulus generalisation and PTSD

Stimulus generalisation is the tendency for stimuli similar to an original stimulus in a learning situation to produce the response originally acquired (see Chapter 37). Grillon & Morgan (1999) studied the 'startle' response in a group of PTSD and non-PTSD Gulf War veterans. Unlike the non-PTSD group, the PTSD group showed a lack of differential startle response in the presence of a conditioned stimulus with or without an unconditioned stimulus, and an increase in 'baseline' startle during a second conditioning experiment. These findings suggest that people with PTSD tend to generalise fear across stimuli and are sensitised by stress.

Cognitive explanations

Classical conditioning cannot be the only mechanism involved in PTSD, since not everyone who is exposed to a traumatic event develops the disorder. Green (1994) reports that PTSD develops in about 25 per cent of those who experience traumatic events, although the range is quite large, being about 12 per cent for accidents and 80 per cent for rape. A *dose-effect* relationship between a stressor's severity and the degree of consequent psychological distress also operates (Puttnam, 1996). Presumably, individual differences in how people perceive events, as well as the *recovery environment* (such as support groups), also play influential roles.

Paton (1992), for example, found that relief workers at Lockerbie reported differences between what they expected to find and what they actually encountered, and this was a source of stress. This was also reported by Dixon *et al.* (1993) in their study of PTSD amongst 'peripheral' victims of the *Herald of Free Enterprise* disaster. For relief workers, then, some way of increasing *predictability* (and hence *control*: see Gross *et al.*, 2000), which would minimise the differences between what is expected and what is observed, would be useful. Amongst the Normandy veterans, Hunt (1997) found that support systems, in the form of comradeship, were *still* important, and used by veterans as a means of coping with the traumatic memories (and often the physical consequences) of their war experiences.

The return of memories many years after a traumatic event suggests that keeping busy with socially valued life roles enables a person to *avoid* processing the traumatic memories. The unfortunate consequence of this, however, is that memories do not get integrated into a person's views about the world. To resolve the discrepancy, Bender (1995) suggests that people must process their traumatic experiences and integrate them into their world views. In behavioural terms, thinking about the traumatic event would lead to *extinction* of the responses associated with it.

Key **STUDY**

Box 51.10 Cognitive factors affecting the development and maintenance of PTSD

Dunmore *et al.* (1999) have identified some of the cognitive factors that influence the development and maintenance of PTSD, at least in assault victims. They investigated factors relating to PTSD's onset by comparing people with and without PTSD. Factors related to the maintenance of PTSD were investigated by comparing people who had recovered from PTSD with those whose PTSD was persistent. Cognitive factors associated with PTSD's onset included *detachment during assault* and *failure to perceive positive responses from others*.

Factors associated with the onset *and* maintenance of PTSD included appraisal of aspects of the assault itself (such as *mental confusion* and *appraisal of emotions*), appraisal of what came after the assault (such as *negative responses of others*), dysfunctional strategies (such as *avoidance/safety seeking*) and global beliefs impacted by the assault. According to Dunmore *et al.*, these factors may contribute to PTSD directly, by generating a sense of ongoing threat, or in two *indirect* ways:

- by motivating cognitive and behavioural strategies that prevent recovery;
- by affecting the nature of the traumatic memory.

Psychodynamic explanations

Psychodynamic theorists have tended to concentrate on *childhood abuse* as a precipitator for later vulnerability to PTSD following a traumatic experience. Abused children might psychologically *dissociate* themselves from the experience and memory of abuse (see Chapter 47, page 518). This may then become a habitual way of dealing with other traumatic events as well, 'thus setting the stage for the development of an acute or post-traumatic stress disorder' (Comer, 1998). There is, however, little, if any, support for a psychodynamic account of PTSD, and it seems equally plausible to propose that a history of abuse might actually *protect* an individual, because of the stronger defence mechanisms that individual would have developed.

BIOLOGICAL EXPLANATIONS OF PTSD

Biochemical influences

Some researchers have focused on the autonomic, hypothalamic-pituitary-adrenal axis and sympatho-adreno-medullary axis systems (see Gross *et al.*, 2000). It has been proposed that a traumatic event has an extreme effect on the normal stress response. In one study of neuroendocrine and psychophysiological responses in PTSD, Liberzon *et al.* (1999a) found that PTSD-diagnosed combat veterans showed higher baseline responses in measures of skin conductance, heart rate, plasma cortisol and catecholamines (epinephrine, norepinephrine and dopamine) than a group of combat veterans without PTSD and a group who had not been in combat. They also showed exaggerated responses on those measures in response to combat sounds, whereas the other two groups did not differ on any measure.

Genetic influences

It could be that some people display an elevated biological response to trauma, because they inherit a genetic predisposition to do so (Comer, 1998). Twin studies are suggestive of this (True *et al.*, 1993), as is research which indicates that there is an increased prevalence of PTSD in the adult children of Holocaust survivors, even though these children do not report a greater exposure to those events identified in DSM or ICD criteria for PTSD (Yehuda, 1999). However, it is difficult to know to what extent the similar vulnerabilities in twins and family members of trauma survivors is related to biological or genetic influences, as opposed to experiential influences, because of the large degree of shared environment. As Yehuda notes, in connection with family members:

'At-risk family members, such as children, may be more vulnerable to PTSD as a result of witnessing the extreme suffering of a parent with chronic PTSD rather than because of inherited genes. But even if the [predisposition] for PTSD were somehow "biologically transmitted" to children of trauma survivors, [it] is still a consequence of the traumatic stress in the parent. Thus, even the most biological explanations for vulnerability must at some point deal with the fact that a traumatic event has occurred'.

Neurological factors

Some researchers have investigated brain structures which might be *damaged* by extreme stress states. For example, Bremner (1999) found that PTSD-diagnosed people who were Vietnam combat veterans, or had been abused as children, showed a reduction in volume of the *hippocampus*, and had deficits on measures of hippocampal function. This might indicate that traumatic stressors can have long-term effects on the function of some brain structures. Other researchers have used non-invasive scanning techniques (see Chapter 10) to investigate brain activation in people diagnosed with PTSD when trauma-related stimuli are presented to them.

Key STUDY

Box 51.11 Brain activity in Vietnam veterans

Liberzon *et al.* (1999b) compared the brain activity of Vietnam combat veterans with PTSD with that of combat veterans without PTSD, and a group who had not been in combat, to combat sounds. Whilst all three groups showed increased activity in several limbic regions of the brain (see Chapter 18), only the combat veterans with PTSD shown increased activity in the region of the *nucleus accumbens/left amygdala* (which has been implicated in fear: Nemeroff, 1998). So, the limbic brain regions may mediate the response to aversive stimuli in both 'healthy' people and PTSD sufferers. Similar research has been conducted by Zubieta . (1999). They have shown that the *medial prefrontal cortex* is more active when PTSD-diagnosed combat veterans are exposed to combat sounds. Interestingly, this increase in activity was *not* found in combat-exposed veterans without PTSD, or people who had not been in combat.

CONCLUSIONS

This chapter has described the clinical characteristics of obsessive–compulsive disorder (OCD) and post-traumatic stress disorder (PTSD), and psychological and biological explanations for them. A variety of psychological and biological explanations have been proposed for both disorders. Although there is some support for all of the explanations, researchers do not yet agree about how the two disorders can best be explained.

Summary

- **Obsessive–compulsive disorder** (OCD) is characterised by recurrent thoughts or images that do not feel voluntarily controlled (**obsessions**), and irresistible urges to engage in repetitive behaviours (**compulsions**).

- OCD affects around one to one-and-a-half million people in Great Britain, and is the fourth most common psychological problem in the United States. It usually begins in young adulthood, and sometimes in childhood.

- The four most common obsessional characteristics are **impaired control over mental processes**, **concerns of losing control over motor behaviours**, **fears of contamination**, and **checking behaviours**.

- Compulsions may arise from obsessions, and compulsives recognise that their behaviours are senseless, but experience intense anxiety if prevented from engaging in them.

- **Psychodynamic** theorists regard obsessions as **defence mechanisms** that serve to occupy the mind and **displace** threatening thoughts with more tolerable substitutes. However, it is difficult to see what some obsessional thoughts are a more tolerable substitute for.

- The **anxiety-reduction hypothesis**, a **behavioural** explanation, accounts for OCD's maintenance but not its origins. The **superstition hypothesis** proposes that compulsions arise through chance associations between behaviours and reinforcers. However, this does not explain the development of intrusive thoughts.

- **Cognitive** explanations of OCD suggest that sufferers attempt to neutralise their intrusive thoughts by thinking or behaving in ways designed to 'correct' them. When these thoughts or behaviours reduce anxiety, they are reinforced. However, they are then used so often that they become, by definition, obsessional or compulsive.

- Both **genetics** and **biochemistry** may be causal factors in OCD. Low **serotonin** activity has been linked to OCD. **Dopamine** and **neuropeptides** may also be involved in the disorder.

- Brain structures that have been implicated in OCD include the **caudate nuclei** and the **orbital frontal cortex**, although the precise roles of these structures is not yet fully understood.

- **Post-traumatic stress disorder** (PTSD) is a response to an extreme psychological/physical trauma beyond the range of normal human experience. It has been observed in both children and adults, and may occur immediately after a trauma or years later.

- PTSD is characterised by **tiredness, nightmares, apathy, social withdrawal**, and **'emotional anaesthesia'**. Other characteristics include **'flashbacks', hyperalertness** and **guilt**. ICD-10 and DSM-IV PTSD are not identical. This is because of DSM-IV's requirement of 'clinically significant distress', and ICD-10's requirement for a 'general numbing of responsiveness'.

- **Classical conditioning** is involved in PTSD to the extent that sufferers often show reactions to stimuli present at the time of the trauma. However, not everyone exposed to a traumatic event develops PTSD. This depends on the stressor's nature and severity, individual differences, and the **recovery environment**.

- Certain **cognitive factors** influence PTSD's development, at least in assault victims. These include **detachment during assault** and **failure to perceive positive responses from others**. Other factors (such as **mental confusion, appraisal of emotions**, and **avoidance/safety seeking**) are associated with PTSD's onset **and** maintenance.

- **Psychodynamic** explanations of PTSD concentrate on **childhood abuse** as a precipitator for later vulnerability to PTSD. However, there is little, if any, support for such an account.

- PTSD may have an extreme effect on the normal **stress response**, and people may display an elevated biological response to trauma because they inherit a **genetic predisposition** to do so. Various brain structures may actually be damaged by extreme stress states. One of these is the **hippocampus**.

- Combat veterans with PTSD show increased activity in the **nucleus accumbens/left amygdala**, which have been implicated in the fear response. The **medial prefrontal cortex** is also more active in PTSD-diagnosed combat veterans, although the reason for this is not yet understood.

Essay Questions

1 Describe and evaluate psychological **and** biological explanations of obsessive–compulsive disorder.
(30 marks)

2 **a** Outline the clinical characteristics of post-traumatic stress disorder (PTSD). *(5 marks)*

   b Describe **one** explanation of PTSD. *(10 marks)*

   c Evaluate this explanation in terms of research studies **and/or** alternative explanations. *(15 marks)*

WEB ADDRESSES

http://www.mentalhealth.com
http://www.nimh.hih.gov/publicat/ocd.htm
http://www.long-beach.va.gov.ptsd/stress.html
http://www.trauma-pages.com

52 Biological (Somatic) Therapies

INTRODUCTION AND OVERVIEW

The biological (medical) model sees mental disorders as being caused largely, if not exclusively, by physical factors. As a result, the biological model's favoured therapeutic approaches are physical, and collectively known as *somatic therapies*. The early and middle parts of the twentieth century saw the introduction of a variety of extraordinary treatments for mental disorders, whose names conjure up disturbing images of what they involved (David, 1994). These include *carbon dioxide inhalation therapy*, *nitrogen shock therapy*, *narcosis therapy*, *insulin coma therapy* and *malaria therapy*.

Although many somatic therapies have been abandoned, three are still used (and their names, too, may conjure up disturbing images). These are *chemotherapy*, *electroconvulsive therapy* and *psychosurgery*. This chapter describes the use and mode of action of these therapies, and considers some of the issues surrounding them.

CHEMOTHERAPY

The use of *drugs* to treat mental disorders has been the most influential of the currently used somatic therapies, and around a quarter of all medications prescribed in Britain through the National Health Service are *psychotherapeutic* drugs. The three main types of drug are *neuroleptics*, *antidepressants* and *antimanics*, and *anxiolytics*.

Neuroleptics

Neuroleptics were the forerunners of the 'drug revolution' in the treatment of mental disorders. They were introduced in the 1950s following the accidental discovery that they calmed psychotic individuals. Since they lessened the need for the physical restraint (such as straitjackets) of seriously disturbed individuals, they were seen as a great advance in treatment. Neuroleptics are also known as *major tranquillisers*, although this term is misleading, because they generally tranquillise without impairing consciousness (BNF, 1999). The term

antipsychotics is also used to describe them, because they are mainly used to treat schizophrenia and other severe disorders, such as mania and amphetamine abuse.

Box 52.1 The neuroleptic drugs

Examples: The most widely used group is that of the *phenothiazines* and include *chlorpromazine hydrochloride* (marketed under the trade names *Thorazine* and *Largactil*). The butyrophenone group includes *haloperidol* (e.g. *Haldol*) and *droperidol* (e.g. *Droleptan*). One of the more recent neuroleptics is *clozapine* (*Clozaril*), a member of the *dibezazepines* group, which was developed to avoid the side-effects (see below) of the phenothiazines. It is used with people unresponsive to, or intolerant of, 'conventional' neuroleptics.

Mode of action: Most neuroleptics block D2 and D3 *dopamine* receptors in the brain (Joyce & Gurevich, 1999). The result of this is that dopamine cannot excite post-synaptic receptors (see Chapter 49, page 535). Neuroleptics also inhibit the functioning of the hypothalamus (which contains dopamine secreting neurons). The hypothalamus plays a role in arousal, and neuroleptic drugs prevent arousal signals from reaching higher brain regions. Rather than blocking D2 or D3 receptors, clozapine blocks D4 receptors, and for that reason is known as an *atypical* neuroleptic. Neuroleptics may also affect other receptors, including those for serotonin.

Side-effects: Of many that have been reported, the more extreme include blurred vision, *neuroleptic malignant syndrome* (which produces delirium, coma and, sometimes, death) and *extrapyramidal symptoms*. These consist of *akathisia* (restlessness), *dystonia* (abnormal body movements, one of which is known as the 'Thorazine shuffle'), and *tardive dyskinesia*. Tardive (late onset) dyskinesia (movement disorder) is an irreversible condition resembling Parkinson's disease. Some side-effects can be controlled by the use of other drugs, such as *procyclidine* (*Kemadrin*).

Attempts to limit side-effects include *targeted strategies* or *drug holidays*, in which the drugs are discontinued during periods of remission, and reinstituted when early signs of relapse occur. *Agranulocytosis* (a decrease in the number of infection-fighting white blood cells) is a side-effect of clozapine and some other neuroleptics. It occurs in about two per cent of users, and is potentially fatal. Blood tests must be given on a regular basis. When the cell count drops too low, the drug's use must be permanently discontinued. Newer atypical neuroleptics such as *risperidone* (*Risperdal*) may avoid many of the side-effects described above. Risperidone is also more effective than 'conventional' neuroleptics (Wirshing *et al.*, 1999). *Olanzapine* (*Zyprexa*) has a similar action to clozapine, and has also been linked to haematological complications (Naumann *et al.*, 1999). Other atypical neuroleptics include *quetiapine* (*Seroquel*) and *zotepine* (*Zoleptil*).

Long-acting *depot injections* are used when compliance with oral treatment is unreliable. However, they may give rise to a higher incidence of extrapyramidal reactions than oral preparations (BNF, 1999).

Typical neuroleptics are effective in reducing schizophrenia's *positive* symptoms (see Chapter 49, pages 535–536), and allow other therapies to be used when the symptoms are in remission. However, some people fail to respond to the drugs, especially those displaying schizophrenia's *negative* symptoms, such as apathy and withdrawal. *Atypical* neuroleptics can reduce negative symptoms (Pallanti *et al.*, 1999). However, antipsychotic

drugs do not *cure* schizophrenia, but *reduce* its prominent symptoms (Hutton, 1998). Relapse occurs after several weeks if the drugs are stopped. Additionally, neuroleptics are of little value in treating social incapacity and other difficulties in adjusting to life outside the therapeutic setting. As a result, relapse is common (Green, 1996).

Antidepressants and antimanics

Antidepressants are classified as *stimulants*, and were also introduced in the 1950s. As well as treating depression, they have been used in the treatment of panic disorder, specific phobias, obsessive–compulsive disorder and eating disorders (Balon, 1999; Sheehan, 1999).

Box 52.2 Antidepressants

Examples: The *monoamine oxidase inhibitor* (MAOI) group includes *phenelzine* (marketed under the trade name *Nardil*) and *moclobemide* (*Manerix*). The tricyclic group includes *imipramine hydrochloride* (*Tofranil*) and *doxepin* (*Sinequan*). The tetracyclic group includes *fluoxetine* (*Prozac*) and *sertraline* (*Lustral*). Because of their mode of action (see below), the tetracyclics are also known as *selective serotonin re-uptake inhibitors* (SSRIs).

Mode of action: MAOIs are so called because they inhibit (or block) the uptake of the enzyme that deactivates *noradrenaline* and *serotonin*. Thus, they are believed to act directly on these neurotransmitters. The tricyclic group prevents the re-uptake of noradrenaline and serotonin by the cells that released them, making these neurotransmitters more likely to reach receptor sites. The tetracyclics block the action of an enzyme that removes serotonin from the synapses between neurons (hence serotonin levels are elevated).

Side-effects: MAOIs require adherence to a special diet. Amine-rich food (such as some cheeses, pickled herrings and yeast extracts) must be avoided. Failure to do so results in the accumulation of an amine called *tyramine*, which causes cerebral haemorrhage. However, 'reversible' selective MAOIs reduce the dietary dangers of traditional MAOIs. Both MAOIs and the tricyclics are associated with cardiac arrhythmias and heart block, dry mouth, blurred vision and urinary retention. Tetracyclic drugs like Prozac are also not free from serious side-effects, including impairment of sexual function and abnormal aggression (Breggin, 1996). The most recent antidepressants include *reboxetine* (*Edronax*), which exerts its effects exclusively on noradrenaline (Lemonick, 1997).

None of the antidepressants identified in Box 52.2 exerts an *immediate* change in mood (Stevenson & Baker, 1996). For example, *tricyclics* can take up to four weeks before a noticeable improvement is observed (and with individuals who are so depressed that they are contemplating suicide, this is clearly a drawback). However, when mood improves, psychological therapies can be used to try and get at the root of the depression. MAOIs are generally less effective than tricyclics, and because of dietary requirements and the fact that they have more side-effects than tricyclics, MAOIs are the least preferred antidepressant drug.

Blind Lemon's career had been going steadily downhill since he started taking the Prozac.

Figure 52.1 *For some people, anti-depressants can bring about a significant improvement in their mood*

Prozac, an SSRI antidepressant, was introduced in 1987. It has been termed the 'happy pill' and its users 'the happy, shiny people' (Kramer, 1993). Because Prozac was believed to have fewer side-effects than the tricyclics, it has been widely prescribed as a treatment for depression. The claim that Prozac can increase happiness and create a 'more interesting personality' has produced astonishing sales. More than 37 million people worldwide take the drug (O'Neill, 1999). In 1996, American *children* aged between six and 18 received 735,000 prescriptions for Prozac and other SSRIs (Laurence, 1997).

Although antidepressants are effective when used in the short term with severe depression, they are not useful on a long-term basis. Indeed, they do not alleviate depression in all people, and controlled studies suggest their effectiveness is no greater than psychotherapy and cognitive therapy (see Chapters 53 and 54). As Box 52.2 illustrates (see page 558), one side-effect (especially of the tricyclics) is *urinary retention*. Controversially, this has been used to treat *nocturnal enuresis* (bedwetting) in children, even when other simple measures have not been tried.

Lithium carbonate was approved as an antimanic drug in 1970, but was actually first used in the mid-nineteenth century for *gouty mania* (Garrod, 1859). It is used to treat both bipolar and unipolar disorder. Lithium salts (such as *lithium carbonate* and *lithium citrate*) flatten out cycles of manic behaviour. Once the manic phase in bipolar disorder has been eliminated, the depressed phase does not return. Lithium salts appear to be 'miracle drugs', in that within two weeks of taking them, 70–80 per cent of manic individuals show an improvement in mood.

Box 52.3 Antimanics

Examples: The inorganic salts lithium carbonate and lithium citrate are marketed under a variety of trade names including *Camcolit* and *Liskonum* (both lithium carbonate) and *Litarex* and *Priadel* (both lithium citrate).

Mode of action: By increasing the re-uptake of *noradrenaline* and *serotonin*, it is believed that lithium salts decrease their availability at various synaptic sites. The precise mode of action is not, however, known.

Side-effects: These include depressed reactions, hand tremors, dry mouth, weight gain, impaired memory and kidney poisoning. If lithium becomes too concentrated in the bloodstream, side effects include nausea, diarrhoea and, at very high levels, coma and death. As a result, users' blood and urine is regularly checked (Schou, 1997).

Anxiolytics

These are classified as *depressants,* and are also known as *anti-anxiety drugs* or *minor tranquillisers*. Anxiety was first treated with synthetic *barbiturates* (such as *phenobarbitol*). However, because of their side-effects and the introduction of other anxiolytic drugs, their use gradually declined. Anxiolytics are used to reduce anxiety and tension in people whose disturbances are not severe enough to warrant hospitalisation (Ballenger, 1995). The drugs are effective in reducing the symptoms of *generalised anxiety disorder*, especially when used in the short term and in combination with psychological therapies. They are also used to combat withdrawal symptoms associated with opiate and alcohol addiction. However, anxiolytics are of little use in treating the anxiety that occurs in sudden, spontaneous *panic attacks*.

Box 52.4 Anxiolytics

Examples: The propanediol group includes *meprobamate* (marketed under the trade name *Equasegic*). The *benzodiazepine* group includes *chlordiazepoxide* (*Librium*), *diazepam* (*Valium*) and *alprazolam* (*Xanax*).

Mode of action: Their general effect is to depress CNS activity, which causes a decrease in activity of the sympathetic branch of the ANS. This produces decreased heart and respiration rate, and reduces feelings of nervousness and tension without inducing tiredness. Since benzodiazepine receptor sites exist in the limbic system, that group might exert their effect by mimicking or blocking a naturally occurring substance yet to be discovered.

Side-effects: These include drowsiness, lethargy, tolerance, dependence, withdrawal (manifested as tremors and convulsions) and toxicity. *Rebound anxiety* (anxiety which is even more intense than that originally experienced) can occur when their use is stopped. Rebound anxiety may be physiological or psychological in origin. Newer anxiolytics, such as *buspirone hydrochloride* (*Buspar*), seem to be as effective as established anxiolytics, although unpleasant side-effects (including hallucinations and amnesia) have also been reported (BNF, 1999).

The term *minor tranquillisers* might suggest that anxiolytic drugs are 'safe'. However, one of their dangers is that overdose can lead to death, especially when taken with alcohol. As Box 52.4 shows, anxiolytics also produce addiction. Although it is generally agreed that anxiolytic use should be limited to people whose anxiety is clearly handicapping their work, leisure and family relationships, they are all too commonly prescribed. Indeed, Valium is the most prescribed of all drugs. An astonishing 8000 tons of *benzodiazepines* were consumed in the United States alone in 1977, and 21 million prescriptions issued in Britain alone in 1989 (Rassool & Winnington, 1993). As with other drugs, their use with children (to relieve acute anxiety and related insomnia caused by fear) is controversial, and the use of benzodiazepines during pregnancy has been linked with vascular and limb malformations in the offspring (MacDonald, 1996).

Box 52.5 Assessing the effectiveness of chemotherapy

Sometimes, the mere belief or expectation that a treatment will be effective can be sufficient to convince a person that s/he has been helped, and to thus show signs of improvement. This is called the *placebo effect*. To try to assess a drug's effectiveness and overcome the placebo effect, researchers used *double blind control*. In this, the person administering the treatment and the person receiving it are kept ignorant as to the exact nature of the treatment being studied. Since neither knows what has actually been given, the expectations of both are minimised.

In studies assessing the effectiveness of chemotherapy, the placebo treatment is an inert pill or injection. Achieving satisfactory double blind control is not always straightforward. For example, people can sometimes tell if they are receiving a placebo because of the *absence* of side-effects. However, this can be overcome by using *active placebos*, which mimic a drug's side-effects but exert no other effect (Fisher & Greenberg, 1980).

For example, Heimberg *et al.* (1999) compared the effectiveness of a MAOI anti-depressant (*phenelzine sulphate*) with cognitive–behavioural therapy (CBT: see Chapter 54) in the treatment of social phobia. Some participants received twelve weeks treatment of either the anti-depressant or a placebo. Others received twelve weeks of CBT or 'educational–supportive group therapy' (a placebo equivalent of CBT). At the end of the twelve weeks, the MAOI and CBT treatments were more effective, in terms of response rates and other measures, than their placebo counterparts. Whilst MAOI therapy was more effective than CBT on some measures, the fact that both were superior to the respective placebos indicates that they are useful in the treatment of social phobia.

ELECTROCONVULSIVE THERAPY

Sakel (1933, cited in Fink, 1984) found that inducing a hypoglycaemic coma by means of insulin seemed to be effective in treating certain psychoses. Later, von Meduna claimed that schizophrenia and epilepsy were *biologically incompatible*, that is, schizophrenia rarely occurred in epilepsy and vice versa. Drawing on his observation that psychotic individuals prone to epilepsy showed less severe symptoms following an epileptic fit, von Meduna advocated inducing major epileptiform fits in psychotics, in order to 'drive out', and hence 'cure', their schizophrenia.

Von Meduna used *Cardiazol*, a cerebral stimulant, to induce the epileptic fit. However, this method was unsatisfactory, not least because it induced feelings of impending death during the conscious phase of its action! Various alternatives were tried until, after visiting an abattoir and seeing animals rendered unconscious by means of electric shocks, Cerletti and Bini (Bini, 1938) advocated passing an electric current across the temples to induce an epileptic fit. Although there have been refinements to Cerletti and Bini's original procedures, *electroconvulsive therapy* (ECT) is still administered in essentially the same way.

Box 52.6 The procedures used in ECT

Following a full physical examination (necessary because heart conditions, chest diseases and peptic ulcers can be accentuated by ECT), the person is required to fast for three to four hours prior to treatment, and empty the bladder immediately before treatment. Whilst being psychologically prepared, dentures, rings and other metallic objects are removed and a loose-fitting gown worn.

Forty-five to sixty minutes before treatment, an *atropine sulphate* injection is given. This prevents the heart's normal rhythm from being disturbed and inhibits the secretion of mucus and saliva. An anxiolytic drug may also be given if a person is particularly apprehensive. With the person lying supine, head supported by a pillow, a short-acting barbiturate anaesthetic followed by a muscle relaxant is given, the latter ensuring that a reduced convulsion will occur. Oxygen is given before and after treatment, and a mouth gag is applied to prevent the tongue or lips being bitten.

In *bilateral* ECT, saline-soaked lint-covered electrodes are attached to each temple, and electricity passes through the frontal lobes. In *unilateral* ECT, two electrodes are attached to the temple and mastoid region of the non-dominant cerebral hemisphere, through which the electricity passes. With the chin held still, a current of around 200 milliamps, flowing at 110 volts, is passed from one electrode to another for a brief period (around 0.5–4 seconds).

Because of the use of muscle relaxants, the only observable sign of the fit is a slight twitching of the eyelids, facial muscles, and toes. When the convulsion, which lasts from half a minute to two minutes, is complete and the jaw relaxed, an airway is inserted into the mouth and oxygen given until breathing resumes unaided. The person is turned into the left lateral position, head on the side, and carefully observed until the effects of the muscle relaxant and anaesthetic have worn off and recovery is complete.

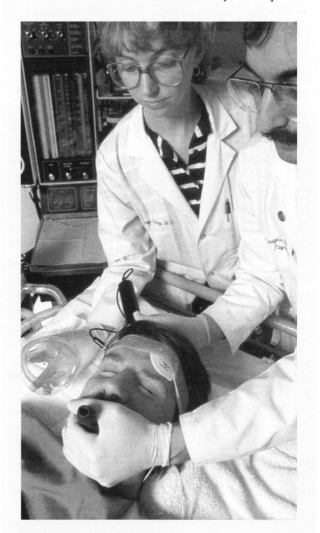

Figure 52.2 *ECT as it is carried out today. Despite the technical improvements, ECT is a highly controversial treatment*

Typically, six to nine ECT treatments, occurring over two to four weeks, will be administered, the amount being gauged by the individual's response (Freeman, 1995). Although originally used to treat schizophrenia, ECT's usefulness with that disorder has been seriously questioned, and today it is primarily used to treat severe depression, bipolar disorder and certain obsessive–compulsive disorders. In Britain, around 20,000 people a year undergo ECT (Johnston, 1996). According to Comer (1998), ECT is 'highly effective' in 60–70 per cent of people with severe depression, and particularly useful with those who harbour suicidal feelings because its effects are immediate (unlike the antidepressant drugs: see page 559).

Box 52.7 Explaining ECT's effectiveness

Whilst ECT's effectiveness in certain disorders is beyond dispute, its use has been questioned on the grounds that it is not known why the beneficial effects occur. It might be due to the *anterograde* and *retrograde amnesia* that occur as a side-effect. However, *unilateral ECT* (see Box 52.5, page 560), which minimises memory disruption, is also effective in reducing depression. As a result, a 'memory loss' theory is unlikely to be true.

Given ECT's nature and the negative publicity it has received, a person might deny his/her symptoms to avoid the 'punishment' the therapy is perceived as being, which *extinguishes* the abnormal behaviour. This possibility has been tested by applying *sub-convulsive shocks*. However, these do not seem to be beneficial and, since they are as unpleasant as convulsive shocks, a 'punishment' theory account is also unlikely to be true.

The most plausible account of ECT's effectiveness is that it produces various biochemical changes in the brain, which are greater than those produced by anti-depressant drugs. However, many physiological changes occur when ECT is administered, and it is difficult to establish which of these are important. Since ECT appears to be most effective in the treatment of depression, and since both noradrenaline and serotonin have been strongly implicated in that disorder (see Chapter 50), it is most likely that these neurotransmitters are affected.

ECT has also been criticised on *ethical* grounds. Indeed, in 1982, it was outlawed in Berkeley, California, by voter referendum, and its use was punishable by a fine of up to $500 and six months in jail. As noted earlier, ECT has a negative public image deriving from horrific descriptions in books and films. Some of its opponents have described the therapy as being 'about as scientific as kicking a television set because it is not working' (Heather, 1976). Certainly, the primitive methods once used were associated with bruises and bone fractures (a consequence of the restraint used by nursing staff during the convulsion), and with pain when an individual failed to lose consciousness during the treatment. However, the use of muscle relaxants minimises the possibility of fractures, and anaesthetics rule out the possibility of the individual being conscious during treatment (see Box 52.6, page 561).

Yet whilst ECT is now considered to be a 'low-risk' therapeutic procedure, Breggin (1996) has argued that brain damage can occur following its administration (at least in non-humans 'sacrificed' immediately after

receiving ECT). Breggin has also pointed out that whilst ECT is typically seen as a treatment of 'last resort', which should be preceded by a careful assessment of the costs and benefits for a particular individual, such assessments are not always routine. Although this may be true in the United States, under Section 58 of the Mental Health Act (1983), ECT's use in Britain requires an individual's consent or a second medical opinion before it can be administered.

PSYCHOSURGERY

Psychosurgery refers to surgical procedures that are performed on the brain to treat mental disorders. The term is properly used when the intention is to *purposely* alter psychological functioning. Thus, whilst removing a brain tumour might affect a person's behaviour, it would not constitute a psychosurgical procedure.

Psychosurgical techniques, albeit primitive ones, have been carried out for a long time (see Gross *et al.*, 2000). In medieval times, psychosurgery involved 'cutting the stone of folly' from the brains of those considered to be 'mad'. Modern psychosurgical techniques can be traced to the Second International Neurological Conference held in London in 1935, when Jacobsen reported the effects of removing the pre-frontal areas (the forward-most portion) of the frontal lobes in chimpanzees. The procedure apparently abolished the violent outbursts some of the chimpanzees had been prone to.

In the audience was Moniz, a Portugese neuropsychiatrist. Moniz was sufficiently impressed by Jacobsen's findings to persuade a colleague, Lima, to carry out surgical procedures on the frontal lobes of schizophrenics and other disturbed individuals, in an attempt to reduce their aggressive behaviour. The procedure involved severing the neural connections between the pre-frontal areas and the hypothalamus and thalami, the rationale being that thought (mediated by the cortex) would be disconnected from emotion (mediated by lower brain centres).

The *leucotomy* or *pre-frontal lobotomy* seemed to be successful in reducing aggressive behaviour in unmanageable patients. The original 'apple corer' technique involved drilling a hole through the skull covering on each side of the head, and then inserting a blunt instrument which was rotated in a vertical arc (see Figure 52.3, page 563). This procedure followed the unsuccessful technique of injecting alcohol to destroy areas of frontal lobe brain tissue. Moniz originally used the technique on schizophrenics and people who were compulsive and anxiety-ridden. After a year, a 70 per cent 'cure' rate was claimed by Moniz and Lima.

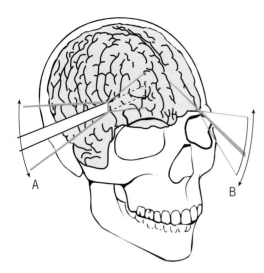

Figure 52.3 *The 'apple corer' technique originally used by Moniz and Lima. A leucotome is inserted into the brain and rotated in a vertical arc*

Also at the 1935 conference was Freeman, a neurologist who was not trained as a surgeon. Freeman & Watts (1942) developed and popularised the 'standard' prefrontal lobotomy. In the absence of alternative therapeutic techniques, and with the seemingly high success rate claimed by Moniz and others, the operation became extremely common. Estimates vary as to the number of operations performed in the United States following Freeman and Watts' pioneering work. Kalinowsky (1975) puts it at around 40,000, whilst Valenstein's (1980) estimate is 25,000. Although not surgically trained, Freeman developed his own psychosurgical technique called the *transorbital lobotomy*.

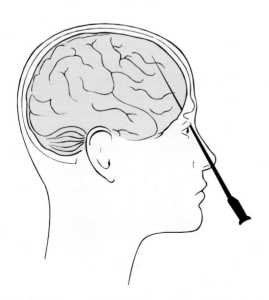

Figure 52.4 *The transorbital lobotomy. A needle-like instrument is inserted into the brain through the eye socket using a hammer. The instrument is then rotated in a horizontal arc*

Psychosurgery was largely abandoned in the late 1950s following the introduction of the psychotherapeutic drugs, and various other reasons.

Box 52.8 Some reasons for the abandonment of psychosurgery

Lack of scientific basis: The theoretical rationale for Moniz's operation was vague and misguided, with researchers *not entirely clear* why beneficial effects should occur. Indeed, David (1994) has questioned whether even now knowledge of the frontal lobes (what David calls '*frontal lobology*') is anything more than 'psychiatry's new pseudoscience'. Moniz's reports of success were also exaggerated, and whilst he was awarded the Nobel prize for medicine in 1949 'for his discovery of the therapeutic value of leucotomy in the treatment of some psychoses', it is ironic that he was shot and paralysed by a patient on whom he had performed a lobotomy! (Valenstein, 1990).

Consistency and irreversibility: Psychosurgery produces inconsistent outcomes. Behaviour change occurs in some individuals but not others, although who will be affected, and how, is difficult to predict. Psychosurgical procedures cannot be reversed.

Side-effects: Some of the severe and permanent side-effects associated with psychosurgery are (in no particular order):

apathy; impaired judgement; reduced creativity; epileptic-type seizures; severe blunting of emotions; intellectual impairments; hyperactivity; distractability; impaired learning ability; overeating; partial paralysis; memory loss; personal slovenliness; childlike behaviour; indifference to others; death.

Lack of evaluation: One surgeon noted that the *cingulotomy* (see page 564) produces 'little or no changes in intellectual and discriminative ability', using the ability to *knit* after the operation as the criterion for change (Winter, 1972).

Consent: Psychosurgical techniques were routinely used with people who could not give their consent to the operation. However, Section 58 of the revised Mental Health Act in Britain introduced stringent provisions regarding information to those referred for psychosurgery and their consent to treatment (Rappaport, 1992).

Given the reasons identified above, it is perhaps surprising to learn that, although controversial, psychosurgery is still performed today. However, it is very much a treatment of last resort, used only when other treatment methods have failed. It is also occasionally used for pain control in the terminally ill. According to Snaith (1994), over 20 operations a year are conducted in Britain.

Modern lobotomies (*capsulotomies*) involve cutting two tiny holes in the forehead which allow radioactive electrodes to be inserted into the frontal lobe to destroy tissue by means of beta rays. Other psychosurgical techniques involve the destruction of small amounts of tissue in precisely located areas of the brain, using a computer controlled electrode which is heated to 68°C. One application of the *thermocapsulatomy* is to interrupt the neural pathways between the limbic system and hypothalamus in the hope of alleviating depression.

Psychosurgical techniques reduce the risk of suicide in severe depression from 15 per cent to one per cent (Verkaik, 1995). The *cingulotomy* cuts the cingulum bundle (a small bundle of nerve fibres connecting the prefrontal cortex with parts of the limbic system). This is used to treat obsessive–compulsive disorder, and evidently does so effectively (Lippitz *et al.*, 1999).

Even more controversial than ECT, psychosurgery continues to have a negative image amongst both professionals and the public (Mindus *et al.*, 1999). However, according to Valenstein (1973):

'There are certainly no grounds for either the position that all psychosurgery necessarily reduces all people to a 'vegetable status' or that it has a high probability of producing miraculous cures. The truth, even if somewhat wishy-washy, lies in between these extreme positions'.

CONCLUSIONS

Biological (somatic) therapies derive from the medical model, and have long been used to treat abnormal behaviour. This chapter has described the use and mode of action of three somatic approaches to therapy. Although controversial, they continue to be used today in the treatment of certain mental disorders.

Summary

- **Biological (somatic) approaches** are favoured by the medical model, and include **chemotherapy, electroconvulsive therapy** (ECT) and **psychosurgery**.

- The most influential somatic approach is chemotherapy (drugs). Three main types of psychotherapeutic drug are the **neuroleptics, antidepressants** and **antimanics,** and **anxiolytics**.

- The neuroleptics (**major tranquillisers** or **antipsychotics**) are mainly used to treat schizophrenia, mania and amphetamine abuse. Most exert their effects by blocking D2 or D3 dopamine receptors, whilst **atypical neuroleptics** act on D4 receptors.

- Although effective, neuroleptics have many unpleasant and sometimes permanent side-effects. These include **neuroleptic malignant syndrome** and **extrapyramidal symptoms**.

- Neuroleptics reduce schizophrenia's **positive** symptoms, but are less effective with its **negative** symptoms. They do not cure schizophrenia, and are of little value in treating social incapacity and other difficulties in adjusting to life in the outside world. As a result, relapse is common.

- **Antidepressants** are also used to treat disorders other than depression. **Selective serotonin reuptake inhibitors** (SSRIs) are widely accepted as being more beneficial than **monoamine oxidase inhibitors** (MAOIs) and **tricyclics**. SSRIs affect serotonin levels, whilst MAOIs and tricyclics influence both serotonin and noradrenaline. Newer antidepressants (e.g. **reboxetine**) only influence noradrenaline.

- Antidepressants take time to exert their effects, which limits their use with people who are suicidally depressed. Whilst they may be useful in the short term, they are not useful on a long-term basis. All are associated with unpleasant side-effects, and some are controversially used to treat other problems (such as bedwetting).

- Salts of the metal lithium (**lithium carbonate** and **lithium citrate**) are used to treat both bipolar and unipolar depression, as well as mania. Within two weeks of taking them, 70–80 per cent of manic individuals show an improvement in mood. They increase the re-uptake of noradrenaline and serotonin. However, unpleasant side-effects are also associated with their use.

- **Anxiolytic drugs (anti-anxiety drugs** or **minor tranquillisers)** depress CNS activity, producing a decrease in activity in the sympathetic branch of the ANS. Some may mimic or block naturally occurring brain substances. Side-effects include **rebound anxiety**. They also produce **addiction**. Despite this, their use is still widespread.

■ **ECT** is used to treat depression, bipolar disorder, and certain obsessive–compulsive disorders. Typically, six to nine treatments will be administered over two to four weeks.

■ Although it is not known exactly why ECT is effective, the most plausible theory attributes its effectiveness to **biochemical changes** in the brain. Because it is not known exactly how it works, ECT continues to be controversial.

■ **Psychosurgery** involves performing surgical procedures on the brain to purposely alter psychological functioning. Originally, the **leucotomy/pre-frontal lobotomy** was used with aggressive schizophrenics as was the **transorbital lobotomy**. At least 25,000 psychosurgical operations were performed in the United States alone.

■ Psychosurgery was largely abandoned in the 1950s following the introduction of psychotherapeutic drugs. Operations often lacked a sound theoretical rationale, did not produce consistent benefits, and were associated with many side-effects. However, some surgical procedures are still performed, although only as a last resort.

Essay Questions

1　Discuss the use of any **two** biological (somatic) therapies in the treatment of mental disorders. *(30 marks)*

2　Describe and evaluate issues surrounding the use of biological (somatic) therapies in the treatment of mental disorders. *(30 marks)*

WEB ADDRESSES

http://www.breggin.com
http://www.mentalhealth.com
http://www.noah.cuny.edu/illness/mentalhealth/cornell/tests/ect.html
http://neurosurgery.mgh.harvard.edu.psysurg.htm
http://lcweb.gov/lexico/liv/p/Psychosurgery.html

Behavioural Therapies

Behavioural therapies use the principles of classical and operant conditioning to treat mental disorders. The term *behaviour therapies* is reserved for those approaches which are based on *classical conditioning*. Those that use *operant conditioning* are called *behaviour modification techniques* (Walker, 1984). This chapter describes the use and mode of action of behavioural therapies, and considers some of the issues surrounding them.

THERAPIES BASED ON CLASSICAL CONDITIONING: BEHAVIOUR THERAPIES

Phobias: a suitable case for behaviour therapy

Being afraid of something that might *objectively* cause us harm is a normal reaction. However, some people show an intense, persistent and *irrational* fear of, and desire to avoid, particular objects, activities or situations. When such behaviour interferes with normal, everyday functioning, a person has a *phobia*. Encountering the phobic stimulus results in intense anxiety. Although a phobic usually acknowledges that the anxiety is out of proportion to the actual danger the phobic stimulus poses, this does little to reduce the fear, and s/he is highly motivated to avoid it.

Watson & Rayner (1920) showed that by repeatedly pairing a neutral stimulus with an unpleasant one, a *fear* response to the neutral stimulus could be classically conditioned. According to Wolpe (1969), classical conditioning explains the development of *all* phobias. Certainly, the pairing of a neutral stimulus with a frightening experience is acknowledged by *some* phobics as marking their phobias' onset. Moreover, the *resilient* nature of some phobias (their *resistance to extinction*) can also be explained in conditioning terms.

Box 53.1 The two-process or two-factor theory of phobias

According to Mowrer's (1947) *two-process* or *two-factor theory*, phobias are acquired through *classical conditioning* (factor 1) and maintained through *operant conditioning* (factor 2), because the avoidance of the phobic stimulus and the associated reduction in anxiety is *negatively reinforcing*. An alternative explanation, Rachman's (1984) *safety-signal hypothesis*, sees avoidance as being motivated by the *positive* feelings of safety.

If maladaptive behaviours can be learned, they can presumably be *unlearned* since the same principles governing the learning of adaptive behaviours apply to maladaptive ones. Therapies based on classical conditioning concentrate on stimuli that elicit new responses which are contrary to the old, maladaptive ones. Three therapeutic approaches designed to treat phobic behaviour are *implosion therapy*, *flooding* and *systematic desensitisation*. Two therapies designed to treat other disorders (*aversion therapy* and *covert sensitisation*) exert their effects by *creating* phobias.

Implosion therapy and flooding

Implosion therapy and flooding both work on the principle that if the stimulus evoking a fear response is repeatedly presented without the unpleasant experience that accompanies it, its power to elicit the fear response will be lost.

Implosion therapy

In implosion therapy, the therapist repeatedly exposes the person to vivid *mental images* of the feared stimulus

in the safety of the therapeutic setting. This is achieved by the therapist getting the person to imagine the most terrifying form of contact with the feared object using *stimulus augmentation* (vivid verbal descriptions of the feared stimulus, to supplement the person's imagery). After repeated trials, the stimulus eventually loses its anxiety-producing power, and the anxiety extinguishes (or *implodes*) because no harm comes to the individual in the safe setting of the therapist's room.

Flooding

In flooding, the individual is forced to *confront* the object or situation eliciting the fear response. For example, an *acrophobic* (a person with a fear of heights) might be taken to the top of a tall building and physically prevented from leaving. By preventing avoidance of, or escape from, the feared object or situation, the fear response is eventually *extinguished*. Wolpe (1973) describes a case in which an adolescent girl afraid of cars was forced into the back of one. She was then driven around continuously for four hours. Initially, her fear reached hysterical heights. Eventually, it receded, and by the end of the journey had disappeared completely.

Implosion therapy and flooding are effective with certain types of phobia (Wolpe, 1997). However, for some people, both lead to increased anxiety, and the procedures are too traumatic. As a result, they are used with considerable caution.

Key **STUDY**

Box 53.2 Using virtual reality to treat phobias

Computer-generated virtual environments have been tested on people suffering from various phobias (Rose & Foreman, 1999). The hardware consists of a head-mounted display and a sensor that tracks head and right hand movements, so that the user can interact with objects in the virtual environment. The equipment is integrated with a square platform surrounded by a railing. This aids exposure by giving the user something to hold on to and an edge to feel.

Software creates a number of virtual environments to confront different phobias. Those for *acrophobia* include:

* three footbridges hovering 7, 50 and 80 metres above water;

* four outdoor balconies with railings at various heights in a building ranging up to 20 floors high;

* a glass elevator simulating the one at Atlanta's Marriott Hotel which rises 49 floors.

People using virtual reality:

'... had the same sensations and anxiety as they did *in vivo* [in the actual presence of the phobic stimulus]. They were sweating, weak at the knees and had butterflies in the stomach. When the elevator went up and down, they really felt it. We are trying to help people confront what they are scared of' (Rothbaum, cited in Dobson, 1996).

Rothbaum sees virtual reality as holding the key to the treatment of phobia, because it is easier to arrange and less traumatic than real exposure to phobia-causing situations. Compared with a control group of acrophobics, Rothbaum and her team reported a 100 per cent improvement in 12 participants after two months of 'treatment'.

Figure 53.1 *Head-mounted display, similar to that used in the treatment of people with phobias*

Systematic desensitisation

Implosion therapy and flooding both use extinction to alter behaviour. However, neither trains people to substitute the maladaptive behaviour (fear) with an adaptive and *desirable* response. Jones (1924) showed that fear responses could be eliminated if children were given candy and other incentives in the presence of the feared stimulus. Her method involved *gradually* introducing the feared stimulus, bringing it closer and closer to the children, whilst at the same time giving them candy, until no anxiety was elicited in its presence. For many years, Jones's work went unrecognised. Wolpe (1958) popularised and refined it under the name *systematic desensitisation* (SD).

In one version of SD, the individual initially constructs an *anxiety hierarchy* (a series of scenes or events rated from lowest to highest in terms of the amount of anxiety they elicit).

Box 53.3 An anxiety hierarchy generated by a person with thanatophobia (fear of death), where 1 = no anxiety and 100 = extreme anxiety

Ratings	Items
5	Seeing an ambulance
10	Seeing a hospital
20	Being inside a hospital
25	Reading an obituary notice of an old person
30–40	Passing a funeral home
40–55	Seeing a funeral
55–65	Driving past a cemetery
70	Reading the obituary of a young person who died of a heart attack
80	Seeing a burial assemblage from a distance
90	Being at a funeral
100	Seeing a dead man in a coffin

(Based on Wolpe & Wolpe, 1981)

Once the hierarchy has been constructed, *relaxation training* is given. This will be the adaptive substitute response, and is the response most therapists use. Training aims to achieve complete relaxation, the essential task being to respond quickly to suggestions to feel relaxed and peaceful. After relaxation training, the person is asked to imagine, as vividly as possible, the scene at the bottom of the hierarchy, and is simultaneously told to remain calm and relaxed (called *graded pairing*).

Box 53.4 Reciprocal inhibition and SD

Wolpe was influenced by the concept of *reciprocal inhibition* which, as applied to phobias, maintains that it is impossible to experience two incompatible emotional states (such as anxiety and relaxation) simultaneously. If the individual finds that anxiety is increasing, the image is terminated, and the therapist attempts to help him/her regain the sense of relaxation. When thinking about the scene at the bottom of the hierarchy no longer elicits anxiety, the next scene in the hierarchy is presented. *Systematically*, the hierarchy is worked through until the individual can imagine any of the scenes without experiencing discomfort. When this happens, s/he is *desensitised*. Once the hierarchy has been worked through, the person is required to confront the anxiety-producing stimulus in the real world.

One problem with SD is its dependence on a person's ability to conjure up vivid images of encounters with a phobic stimulus. A way of overcoming this is to use photographs or slides displaying the feared stimulus. Another approach involves *in vivo* encounters. For example, an arachnophobic may be desensitised by gradually approaching spiders, the method used by Jones (1924: see page 567). This *in vivo* desensitisation is almost always more effective and longer lasting than other desensitisation techniques (Wilson & O'Leary, 1978).

SD, implosion therapy and flooding are all effective in dealing with specific fears and anxieties. Compared with one another, flooding is more effective than SD (Marks, 1987) and implosion therapy (Emmelkamp *et al.*, 1992), whilst implosion therapy and SD do not differ in their effectiveness (Gelder *et al.*, 1989).

The fact that flooding is apparently the superior therapy suggests that *in vivo* exposure to the anxiety's source is crucial (Hellström & Öst, 1996). Because implosion therapy and SD do *not* differ in their effectiveness, systematically working through a hierarchy might not be necessary. Indeed, presenting the hierarchy in *reverse* order (from most to least frightening), randomly, or in the standard way (from least to most frightening) does not influence SD's effectiveness (Marks, 1987).

Aversion therapy

The therapies just considered are all appropriate in the treatment of phobias occurring in specific situations. *Aversion therapy* (AT), by contrast, is used with people who want to *extinguish* the *pleasant* feelings associated with socially undesirable behaviours, like excessive drinking or smoking. SD tries to substitute a pleasurable response for an aversive one. AT *reverses* this, and pairs an unpleasant event with a desired but socially undesirable behaviour. If this unpleasant event and desired behaviour are repeatedly paired, the desired behaviour should eventually elicit negative responses.

Box 53.5 AT and alcohol abuse

Perhaps AT's best known application has been in the treatment of *alcohol abuse*. In one method, the problem drinker is given a drug that induces nausea and vomiting, but *only* when combined with alcohol. When a drink is taken, the alcohol interacts with the drug to produce nausea and vomiting. It does not take many pairings before alcohol begins to elicit an aversive fear response (becoming nauseous).

In another method, the problem drinker is given a warm saline solution containing a drug which induces nausea and vomiting without alcohol (Elkins, 1991). Immediately before vomiting begins, an alcoholic beverage is given, and the person is required to smell, taste and swill it around the mouth before swallowing it. The aversive fear response may generalise to other alcohol-related stimuli, such as pictures of bottles containing alcohol. However, to avoid *generalisation* to all drinks, the individual may be required to take a soft drink in between the aversive conditioning trials.

AT has been used with some success in the treatment of alcohol abuse and other behaviours (most notably cigarette smoking, overeating and children's self-injurious behaviour). It has also found its way into popular culture. In Burgess's (1962) novel *A Clockwork Orange*, the anti-social 'hero', Alex, gains great enjoyment from rape and violent behaviour. When caught, he can choose between prison and therapy, and opts for the latter. He is given a nausea-inducing drug and required to watch films of violence and rape. After his release, he feels nauseous whenever he contemplates violence and rape. However, because the therapy took place with Beethoven's music playing, Alex acquires an aversion towards Beethoven as well!

Box 53.6 AT and homosexuality

One of the most controversial (and non-fictional) applications of AT was with sexual 'aberrations' such as homosexuality (Beresford, 1997). Male homosexuals, for example, were shown slides of nude males followed by painful but safe electric shocks. The conditioned response to the slides was intended to generalise to homosexual fantasies and activities beyond the therapeutic setting. Later, the individual might have been shown slides of nude women, and an electric shock terminated when a sexual response occurred (Adams *et al.*, 1981).

Whatever its use, AT is unpleasant, and not appropriate without an individual's *consent*, or unless all other approaches to treatment have failed. As noted, evidence suggests that the therapy is effective. However, those undergoing it often find ways to continue with their problem behaviours. People have the cognitive abilities to discriminate between the situation in which aversive conditions occur and situations in the real world. In some cases, then, cognitive factors will 'swamp' the conditioning process, and this is one reason why AT is not always effective.

AT does not involve classical conditioning alone, and actually combines it with operant conditioning. Once the classically conditioned fear has been established, the person is inclined to avoid future contact with the problem stimulus (an *operant* response) in order to alleviate fear of it (which is *negatively reinforcing*). Critics see AT as being inappropriate unless the individual learns an *adaptive* response. For this reason, most behaviour therapists try to *shape* (see page 571) new adaptive behaviours *at the same time* as extinguishing existing maladaptive ones.

Covert sensitisation

Silverstein (1972) has argued that AT is unethical and has the potential for misuse and abuse. As a response to this, some therapists use *covert sensitisation* (CS) as an alternative and 'milder' form of aversion therapy. CS is a mixture of AT and SD. Essentially, people are trained to punish themselves using their *imaginations* (hence the term *covert*). *Sensitisation* is achieved by associating the undesirable behaviour with an exceedingly disagreeable consequence.

Box 53.7 CS and alcohol abuse

A heavy drinker might be asked to imagine being violently sick all over him/herself on entering a bar, and feeling better only after leaving and breathing fresh air. The individual is also instructed to rehearse an alternative 'relief' scene, in which the decision not to drink is accompanied by pleasurable sensations. CS can be helpful in controlling overeating and cigarette smoking, as well as excessive drinking (Emmelkamp, 1994).

THERAPIES BASED ON OPERANT CONDITIONING: BEHAVIOUR MODIFICATION TECHNIQUES

Behaviours under voluntary control are strongly influenced by their consequences. As noted in Chapter 38, actions producing positive outcomes tend to be repeated, whereas those producing negative outcomes tend to be suppressed. Therapies based on classical conditioning usually involve *emotional responses* (such as anxiety), although *observable behaviours* (such as gradually approaching an object that elicits anxiety) are also influenced. Therapies based on operant conditioning are aimed *directly* at observable behaviours.

There are several therapies based on operant conditioning, all involving three main steps. The first is to identify the undesirable or maladaptive behaviour. The next is to identify the reinforcers that maintain such behaviour. The final step is to restructure the environment, so that the maladaptive behaviour is no longer reinforced. One way to eliminate undesirable behaviours is to *remove* the reinforcers that maintain them, the idea being that their removal will *extinguish* the behaviour they reinforce. Another way is to use aversive stimuli to *punish* voluntary maladaptive behaviours.

As well as eliminating undesirable behaviours, operant conditioning can be used to increase desirable behaviours. This can be achieved by providing *positive reinforcement* when a behaviour is performed, and making the reinforcement *contingent* on the behaviour being manifested *voluntarily*.

Therapies based on extinction

The behavioural model proposes that people learn to behave in abnormal ways when they are unintentionally reinforced by others for doing so (see Chapter 49, page 532). For example, a child who receives parental attention when s/he shouts is likely to engage in this behaviour in the future, because attention is reinforcing. If abnormal behaviours can be *acquired* through operant conditioning, they can be *eliminated* through it. With a disruptive child, parents might be instructed to *ignore* the behaviour, so that it is *extinguished* from the child's behavioural repertoire.

If this is to be effective, however, the therapist must be able to identify and eliminate the reinforcer that is maintaining the adaptive behaviour, and this is not always easy.

Key STUDY
Box 53.8 Behaviour modification using extinction

A 20-year-old woman reluctantly sought help for 'compulsive face-picking'. Whenever the woman found some little blemish or pimple, she would pick and scratch at it until it became a bleeding sore. As a result, her face was unsightly. Everyone was distressed except the individual herself, who seemed remarkably unconcerned. Her family and fiancé had tried several tactics to stop the face-picking, including appealing to her vanity, pleading and making threats.

The therapist felt that the face-picking was being maintained by the attention her family and fiancé were giving it. As long as she continued, the pattern of inadvertent reinforcement was maintained, and she would remain the centre of attention. Once the therapist had identified the behaviours that were reinforcing the face-picking, the parents and fiancé were instructed not to engage in these and to ignore the face-picking entirely. They were also told that it would probably get worse before it improved.

After a temporary increase in face-picking, it was quickly extinguished when attention was no longer given. To prevent the behaviour from reappearing, the parents and fiancé were encouraged to provide plenty of loving attention and to support the woman contingent upon a variety of healthy, adaptive behaviours.

(Based on Crooks & Stein, 1991)

Therapies based on punishment

In AT, an aversive stimulus, such as an electric shock, is used to classically condition a negative response to a desired but undesirable stimulus. Aversive stimuli can also be used to *punish* voluntary maladaptive behaviours.

Key STUDY
Box 53.9 Behaviour modification using punishment

Cowart & Whaley (1971) studied an emotionally disturbed infant who was hospitalised because he persistently engaged in self-mutilating behaviour to such an extent that he had to be restrained in his crib. Electrodes were attached to the infant's leg, and he was placed in a room with a padded floor (the self-mutilation involved violently banging his head against the floor). When the infant began the self-mutilating behaviour, he was given an electric shock. Initially, he was startled, but continued self-mutilating, at which point another shock was given. There were very few repetitions before self-mutilation stopped, and the infant could be safely let out of his crib.

It is generally agreed that therapies using punishment are not as effective as those employing positive reinforcement (see below) in bringing about behaviour change. At least one reason for not using punishment is the tendency for people to *overgeneralise* behaviour. Thus, behaviours which are *related* to the punished behaviour are also not performed. Moreover, punishment tends to produce only a temporary suppression of undesirable behaviour, and unless another reinforcement-inducing behaviour pattern is substituted for the punished behaviour, it will resurface (see Chapter 38, page 417).

There are also ethical issues surrounding the use of punishment, particularly with very young children. In Cowart and Whaley's study, however, the infant was engaging in a behaviour which was clearly very harmful, and with these sorts of behaviour, punishment is actually extremely effective. Presumably, the physical well-being that occurred from not self-mutilating was sufficiently reinforcing to maintain the new behaviour pattern.

Therapies based on positive reinforcement

Behaviour shaping

Isaacs *et al.* (1960) describe the case of a 40-year-old male schizophrenic who had not spoken to anyone for 19 years. Quite accidentally, a therapist discovered that the man loved chewing gum, and decided to use this as a way of getting him to speak.

Initially, the therapist held up a piece of gum. When the patient looked at it, it was given to him. The patient began to pay attention to the therapist, and would look at the gum as soon as the therapist removed it from his pocket. Later, the therapist held up the gum and waited until the patient moved his lips. When this occurred, he was immediately given the gum. However, the therapist then began to give the gum *only* when the patient made a sound.

At the point when the patient reliably made a sound when the gum was shown, the therapist held the gum and instructed him to 'Say gum'. After 19 years of silence, the patient said the word. After six weeks, he spontaneously said 'Gum, please', and shortly afterwards began talking to the therapist. This approach is known as *behaviour shaping*, and has been most notably used with the chronically disturbed and people with learning difficulties, who are extremely difficult to communicate with.

Key STUDY

Box 53.10 Using positive reinforcement to treat anorexia nervosa

A young anorectic woman was in danger of dying, because she had drastically curtailed her eating behaviour and weighed only 47 lbs. In the first stage of therapy, the therapist established an appropriate reinforcer that could be made contingent upon eating. The reinforcer chosen was social, and whenever the anorectic swallowed a bite of food, she was rewarded by the therapist talking to her and paying her attention. If she refused to eat, the therapist left the room and she remained alone until the next meal was served (which is 'time out' from positive reinforcement rather than punishment).

After a while, her eating behaviour gradually increased, and the therapist introduced other rewards contingent upon her continuing to eat and gain weight. These included having other people join her at meal times or being allowed to have her hair done. Eventually, the woman gained sufficient weight to be discharged from the hospital. Because people are likely to regress if returned to a non-supportive institutional setting, the woman's parents were instructed how to continue reinforcing her for appropriate eating behaviours. At follow-up nearly three years later, the woman was still maintaining an adequate weight.

(Based on Bachrach *et al.*, 1965)

Token economies

Ayllon & Haughton (1962) reported that staff at one hospital found it particularly difficult to get withdrawn schizophrenics to eat regularly. Ayllon and Haughton noticed that the staff were actually exacerbating the problem by coaxing the patients into the dining room and, in some cases, even feeding them. The researchers reasoned that the increased attention was reinforcing the patients' uncooperativeness and decided that the hospital rules should be changed. For example, if patients did not arrive at the dining hall within 30 minutes of being called, they were locked out. Additionally, staff were no longer permitted to interact with patients at meal times. Because their uncooperative behaviours were no longer being reinforced, the patients quickly changed their eating habits. Then, the patients were made to pay one penny in order to enter the dining hall. The pennies could be earned by showing socially appropriate *target behaviours*, and their frequency also began to increase.

Ayllon and Haughton's approach was refined by Ayllon & Azrin (1968) in the form of a *token economy system*. In this, patients are given tokens in exchange for desirable behaviour. The therapist first identifies what a patient likes (such as watching television or smoking cigarettes). When a productive activity occurs (such as making a bed or socialising with other patients), the patient is given tokens that can be exchanged for 'privileges'. The tokens therefore become conditioned reinforcers for desirable and appropriate behaviours.

Ayllon and Azrin showed that tokens were effective in eliciting and maintaining desired behaviours. The amount of time spent performing desired behaviours was highest when the reinforcement contingencies were imposed, and lowest when they were not. Ayllon and Azrin also discovered that token economies had an effect on patient and staff morale, in that the patients were less apathetic and irresponsible, whilst the staff became more enthusiastic about their patients and the therapeutic techniques.

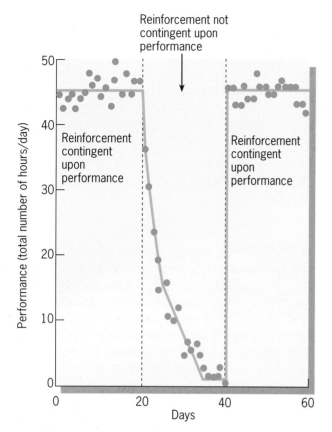

Figure 53.2 *The effects of a token economy on hospitalised patients' performance of target behaviours*

As well as being used with the chronically disturbed, token economies have also been used in programmes designed to modify the behaviour of children with *conduct disorders*. Schneider & Byrne (1987) awarded tokens to children who engaged in helpful behaviours, and removed the tokens for inappropriate behaviours such as arguing or not paying attention.

Box 53.11 Token economies: some issues

Despite their effectiveness in producing behaviour change with various disorders, issues have been raised about token economies. Eventually, tokens will have to be replaced by other social reinforcers, both within and outside the therapeutic setting. The individual is gradually 'weaned off' the tokens in the therapeutic setting, and can be transferred to a 'half-way house' or some other community live-in arrangement where more social reinforcers can be used. Unfortunately, this is not always successful, and there tends to be a high re-hospitalisation rate for discharged individuals.

Token economies can lead to 'token learning' (people might only indulge in a behaviour if they are

directly rewarded for it: Baddeley, 1997). Whilst this might be effective within the confines of the therapeutic setting, Baddeley sees it as quite unproductive in other settings, where it is necessary to learn on a subtler and less immediate reward system.

SOME GENERAL COMMENTS ABOUT BEHAVIOURAL THERAPIES

One criticism of behavioural therapies is that they focus only on the observable aspects of a disorder. The behavioural model considers the maladaptive behaviour to be the disorder, and the disorder is 'cured' when the behaviour is changed. Although critics accept that behavioural therapies can alter behaviour, they argue that such therapies fail to identify a disorder's *underlying* causes. One consequence of this is *symptom substitution*, in which removing one symptom simply results in another, and perhaps more serious, problem behaviour replacing it.

As noted earlier, behaviours learnt under one set of conditions may not generalise to other conditions. The behavioural model sees behaviours as being controlled by the environment, so it is not surprising that behaviours altered in one context do not endure in a very different one (Ost *et al.*, 1997). Indeed, Rimm (1976) sees this as behaviour therapy's major limitation. To avoid it, therapists attempt to extend the generality of changed behaviours by working (as far as possible) in environments which are representative of real life. They also encourage people to avoid environments that elicit maladaptive behaviours, to return for follow-up treatment, and teach them how to modify their behaviour on a continuing basis.

The most serious criticism of behavioural therapies is *ethical* (see Chapter 56). Techniques involving punishment, in particular, have been criticised for exercising authoritarian control and for dehumanising and 'brainwashing' people. Another criticism is that behavioural therapists manipulate people and deprive them of their freedom (see Chapter 57). As has been seen, it is the therapist, rather than the person, who controls the reinforcers, and therapists do not encourage people to seek insight concerning their disorders.

However, supporters of the behavioural model argue that they do not treat disorders without consent and that, in a sense, we are all 'naïve behaviour therapists'. For example, when we praise people or tell them off for a particular behaviour, we are using behaviour modification techniques: all therapists are doing is using such approaches in a systematic and consistent way. Therapists who use behavioural methods are *not* attempting to control behaviour, but helping people to control their *own* behaviour (see Chapter 56, pages 608–609).

CONCLUSIONS

Various behaviour therapies and behaviour modification techniques have been used to treat mental disorders. Behaviour therapies used to treat phobias include implosion therapy, flooding and systematic desensitisation. Aversion therapy and covert sensitisation create a phobia towards a pleasurable but undesirable behaviour. Behaviour modification techniques include behaviour shaping and token economies. These have been used to treat various disorders, including schizophrenia. Although supporters of the behavioural model see all of these therapies as being highly effective, opponents believe that important criticisms can be made of them which limit their application.

Summary

- Behavioural therapies try to change behaviour based on whatever means are most effective. **Behaviour therapies** use classical conditioning principles whilst **behaviour modification techniques** use operant conditioning.

- If maladaptive behaviours can be acquired through classical conditioning, they can presumably be unlearned through it. **Implosion therapy**, **flooding**, and **systematic desensitisation** (SD) are used to treat **phobias**, and attempt to produce new responses that are contrary to the old, maladaptive ones.

- Neither implosion therapy nor flooding trains people to substitute maladaptive behaviour with adaptive/desirable behaviour. SD does, with **relaxation** being the adaptive substitute response used by most therapists.

- Flooding is more effective than SD and implosion therapy. Implosion therapy and SD are equally effective. This suggests that *in vivo* exposure to the phobic stimulus is important, and that systematic progression through a hierarchy is unnecessary.

- **Aversion therapy** (AT) is used to extinguish the pleasant feelings associated with an undesirable behaviour. This is achieved by repeatedly pairing an unpleasant stimulus with the undesirable behaviour until it eventually elicits an unpleasant response. AT uses both classical and operant conditioning

- Although useful in the treatment of some problem behaviours, there are important ethical issues associated with AT's use. For that reason, **covert sensitisation** is sometimes employed. This method has been used to control excessive drinking, overeating and smoking.

- Behaviour therapies usually involve emotional responses as well as observable behaviours. Therapies based on operant conditioning are aimed **directly** at observable behaviours. When the reinforcers that maintain an undesirable/maladaptive behaviour have been identified, the environment is restructured so that they are no longer reinforced.

- Undesirable behaviours can be **extinguished** by removing the reinforcers that maintain them. Alternatively, aversive stimuli can be used to **punish** the behaviours. Desirable behaviours can be increased by making **positive reinforcement** contingent on voluntary behaviours being performed.

- **Punishment** by electric shock has been used to treat self-mutilating behaviour. However, punishment only **suppresses** an undesirable behaviour, which will resurface unless substituted by a behaviour that is reinforced. Punishment also raises ethical issues, particularly when used to treat children.

- **Behaviour shaping** and the **token economy** system both use **positive reinforcement** to change behaviour. These methods are effective in eliciting and maintaining desired behaviours. However, they are limited by a **lack of generalisation** beyond the therapeutic setting. Token economies, for example, can lead to 'token learning'. To avoid lack of generalisation, therapists try to work in environments that are as representative of real life as possible.

- By focusing on a disorder's observable aspects, behavioural therapies fail to identify its underlying causes. One consequence of this is **symptom substitution**.

- Although critics accept that behavioural therapies can be effective, they see therapists as manipulating, dehumanising, and controlling people and depriving them of their freedom. Therapists sees themselves as helping people to control their own behaviour.

Essay Questions

1 Discuss the use of therapies based on classical conditioning in the treatment of mental disorders.

(30 marks)

2 Critically consider issues surrounding the use of therapies based on operant conditioning. *(30 marks)*

WEB ADDRESSES

http://mentalhealth.com
http://psychcentral.com
http://fox.klte/~Kerosfi/psychotherapy
http://www.discoveryhealth.com

54 *Alternatives to Biological and Behavioural Therapies*

INTRODUCTION AND OVERVIEW

Biological (somatic) and behavioural therapies are effective ways of treating some mental disorders. However, therapies based on the *psychodynamic* and *cognitive* models are also used to treat certain mental disorders, and might even do so *more* effectively than biological and behavioural therapies. This chapter describes the use and mode of action of some therapies based on the psychodynamic model (namely *psychoanalysis* and *psychoanalytically oriented psychotherapies*) and the cognitive model (so-called *cognitive–behavioural therapies*, which include *modelling, rational–emotive therapy* and *cognitive restructuring therapy*). It also examines some of the issues surrounding therapies derived from these two models.

PSYCHOANALYSIS

The psychodynamic model sees mental disorders as stemming from the demands of the *id* and/or the *super-ego*. If the *ego* is too weak to cope with these, it defends itself by *repressing* them into the unconscious. However, the conflicts do not disappear, but find expression through behaviour (and this is the disorder a person experiences).

For Freud (1894), it is not enough to change a person's present behaviours. To bring about a permanent 'cure', the problems giving rise to the behaviours must also be changed. According to Freud, psychological problems have their origins in events that occurred earlier in life. He did not see present problems as the *psychoanalyst's* domain, because people will already have received sympathy and advice from family and friends. If such support was going to help, it would have done so already, and there would be no need for a psychoanalyst to be consulted.

Box 54.1 Psychoanalysis: the only game in town?

According to Eisenberg (1995), there was a time 'when psychoanalysis was the only game in town'. However, whilst there are more than 400 psychotherapies (Holmes, 1996), the popularity of psychodynamic approaches (those based on psychoanalysis) has declined over the years. For example, between 1961 and 1982, the proportion of therapists identifying themselves as psychoanalysts dropped from 41 to 14 per cent (Smith, 1982). Nonetheless, therapies based on the psychodynamic model are, 'one of Britain's most recession-proof industries' (Laurance, 1993), and more than 100,000 people are currently receiving some form of psychodynamically-based therapy.

The purpose of *psychoanalysis* is to uncover the unconscious conflicts responsible for an individual's mental disorder. In Freud's words, psychoanalysis aims to 'drain the psychic abscess' and 'make the unconscious conscious'. The first step is therefore to bring the conflicts into consciousness. Ultimately, this helps the *analysand* (the person undergoing psychoanalysis) to gain *insight*, or conscious awareness, of the repressed conflicts. The rationale is that once a person understands the reason for a behaviour, the ego can deal more effectively with it and resolve the conflict (Schwartz, 1999).

Techniques used in psychoanalysis

Freud and his followers used, or developed, several techniques to bring conflicts into consciousness, including *hypnosis*, and the interpretation of *dreams* (see Chapter 15), *faulty actions* ('*Freudian slips*') and *physiological cues* (Gross & McIlveen, 1998). However, the most widely used technique is *free association*.

Free association

In this, the analysand lies on a comfortable couch so that the analyst cannot be seen (which prevents the latter from distracting the former, and interfering with concentration). The analysand is encouraged to say whatever comes to mind, no matter how trivial or frivolous it might seem. Freud called this the *basic rule* of psychoanalysis. He believed that the ego ordinarily acts as a censor, preventing threatening unconscious impulses from entering consciousness. By free-associating, the censor could be 'by-passed'. Although free association is the most widely used technique, it takes several sessions before analysands 'open up'.

Box 54.2 Introducing an analysand to free association

In ordinary conversation, you usually try to keep a connecting thread running through your remarks, excluding any intrusive ideas or side issues so as not to wander too far from the point, and rightly so. But in this case, you must talk differently. As you talk, various thoughts will occur to you which you would like to ignore because of certain criticisms and objections. You will be tempted to think, 'that is irrelevant or unimportant or nonsensical,' and to avoid saying it. Do not give in to such criticism. Report such thoughts in spite of your wish not to do so. Later, the reason for this injunction, the only one you have to follow, will become clear. Report whatever goes through your mind. Pretend that you are a traveller, describing to someone beside you the changing views which you see outside the train window.

(From Ford & Urban, 1963)

During analysis, the analyst remains '*anonymous*' and does not express emotion or evaluate the analysand's attitudes. The analyst does not reveal information about him/herself, since whilst the analyst needs to learn a great deal about the analysand, the reverse is not true (although Freud himself evidently broke this rule in all 43 cases he studied: Sapsted, 1998). This form of interaction ensures that the analysand does not form a close, personal relationship with the analyst, but views him or her purely as an 'anonymous and ambiguous stimulus'. Whilst the analysand free-associates, the analyst acts as a sort of *sounding board*, often repeating and clarifying what the analysand has said. Thus, the analysand tells a story and the analyst helps interpret it in terms of repressed conflicts and feelings.

The main form of communication between the analyst and analysand is the analyst's *interpretive comments*. Sometimes, the analyst may need to draw attention to the

analysand's *resistances*. Freud believed that what analysands do *not* say is as important as what they do say. During free association, analysands may express an unwillingness to discuss openly some aspects of their lives. For example, they may disrupt the session, change the subject whenever a particular topic comes up, joke about something as though it was unimportant, arrive late for a session, or perhaps miss it altogether.

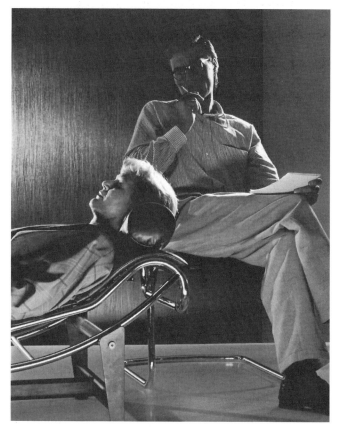

Figure 54.1 *During psychoanalysis, the analysand usually reclines on a couch, while the analyst sits behind to avoid distracting the analysand. Although the analyst traditionally plays a passive role, occasionally he or she will offer an interpretation to help the analysand reach an insight*

Box 54.3 Freud's description of resistance

The analysand endeavours in every sort of way to extricate himself from [the rule of free association]. At one moment he declares that nothing occurs to him, at the next that so many things are crowding in on him that he cannot get hold of anything. Presently we observe with pained astonishment that he has given way first to one and then to another critical objection; he betrays this to us by the long pauses that he introduces into his remarks. He then admits that there is something he really cannot say – he would be ashamed to; and he allows this reason to prevail against his promise. Or he says that something has occurred to him, but it concerns another person and not himself and is therefore exempt from being reported. Or, what has now occurred to him is really too unimportant, too silly and senseless; I cannot possibly have meant him to enter into thoughts like that. So it goes on in innumerable variations.

(From Freud, 1894)

Freud saw resistance as natural, because it is painful to bring unconscious conflicts into conscious awareness. It also indicates that the analyst is getting close to the source of the problem, and that the unconscious is struggling to avoid 'giving up its secrets'. Although resistance hinders therapy, it provides useful information for both analysand and analyst in the form of clues about the repressed conflict's nature.

As therapy progresses, analysts may *privately deduce* the nature of what is behind the analysand's statements, and attempt to generate further associations. For example, the analysand may apologise for saying something believed to be trivial. The analyst tells the analysand that what appears trivial might relate to something important. By appropriately timing this intervention, significant new associations may result. The analyst does not suggest what is important in what the analysand has said. The goal is to help the analysand discover this him/herself.

Box 54.4 Confrontation and reconstruction

As therapy continues, the analyst may try to explain the analysand's behaviour in a way which is new to him/her. For example, analysands may be informed that their anger does not come from where they think it does, but rather that they are angry because the analyst reminds them of someone. In *confrontation*, the analyst tells the analysand exactly what is being revealed in the free associations. In *reconstruction*, the analyst provides hypothetical historical statements of hitherto buried fragments of the analysand's past. For example, the analysand may be told that the anger is a repetition of feelings experienced as a child, and that the analyst stands for the objects of that anger.

Transference

Once interpretation is complete and the unconscious conflict has been brought into consciousness, the analyst and the analysand repeat and 'live out' the conflict. The associated feelings which have been repressed for so long then become available for 'manipulation' by the analyst. Freud called this process *transference* or *transference neurosis*. In it, the original source of the conflict is *displaced* onto the analyst who now becomes the object of the analysand's emotional responses (see Box 54.4). Depending on the nature of the conflict, the feelings may be positive and loving or negative and hostile. By exploring the transference relationship, psychoanalysis assumes that unconscious conflicts can be brought out into the open, understood and resolved. According to Thomas (1990):

'Over the years, it has become increasingly clear to practising analysts that the process of transference ... is one of the most important tools they have. It has become so central to theory and practice that many, though not all, analysts believe that making interpretations about transference is what distinguishes psychoanalysis from other forms of psychotherapy. When attention is focused on the transference and what is happening in the here and now, the historical reconstruction of childhood events and the search for the childhood origins of conflicts may take second place'.

Box 54.5 Countertransference and training analysis

Freud discovered that transference operated in both directions, and that he could transfer his own feelings onto his analysands. A male analysand, for example, could be viewed as a 'rebellious son'. Freud called the placing of clients into his own life *countertransference*. To avoid displacing their own repressed childhood feelings and wishes onto their patients, analysts undergo a *training analysis*. This permits them to understand their own conflicts and motivations, so they become opaque concerning their own behaviours and feelings to avoid countertransference with their analysands.

Whether the avoidance of countertransference is absolutely necessary is, however, debatable. As Thomas (1990) has observed:

'In Freud's time, countertransference feelings were considered to be a failing on the part of the analyst. These feelings were to be controlled absolutely. Now, countertransference is considered an unavoidable outcome of the analytic process, irrespective of how well prepared the analyst is by analytic training and its years of required personal analysis ... most modern analysts are trained to observe their own countertransference feelings and to use these to increase their understanding of the analysand's transference and defences'.

The feelings associated with transference are the same for men and women. They include:

- attachment to the analyst;
- overestimation of the analyst's qualities;
- jealousy of those connected with the analyst.

Sometimes, transference takes on an exaggerated form known as acting out, in which the analysand engages in the impulses stirred up by therapy. However, the analysand must be convinced that 'acting out' the conflict through transference does *not* constitute a true resolution of the problem. By itself, then, transference does not bring about the required change.

Quite clearly, transference is crucial, because without it the analyst's interpretations would not even be considered by the analysand. Freud believed that psychoanalysis was ineffective with disorders like schizophrenia and depression because people with these disorders could not produce transference. Whilst he believed that schizophrenia's and depression's origins could be explained in psychodynamic terms, they reduce the capacity for transference for some reason, and since people experiencing those disorders are completely indifferent to the analyst, the analyst cannot influence them (Boyer & Giovachini, 1980).

Achieving insight and working through

Once an analysand consciously understands the roots of the conflict, *insight* has been achieved, and the analysand must be helped to deal with the conflict maturely and rationally. Whilst insight sometimes comes from the recovery of the memory of a repressed experience, the notion of a psychoanalytic 'cure' resulting from the sudden recall of a single traumatic incident cannot be true, since psychodynamic therapists feel that troubles seldom stem from a single source. Instead, they are *over-determined* (see Chapter 57, page 616). For Freud, analysands gained insight through a gradual increase in self-knowledge (a process of *re-education*). This increase often involves repetitive consideration of all aspects of the conflict, allowing the individual to face reality and deal with it effectively, rather than deny and distort it. This is called *working through*.

To break down the complex ego defences which have been developed to cope with the conflict, and to bring about a lasting personality change, the analysand and analyst need to work through every implication of the

problem with complete understanding by the analysand. This is necessary to prevent the conflict from being repressed into the unconscious again. As a result, the individual is strengthened and therefore becomes capable of handling different aspects of the conflict without having to resort to *defence mechanisms* (see Gross *et al.*, 2000). The ultimate goal of psychoanalysis, then, is a deep-seated modification of personality, so as to allow people to deal with problems on a realistic basis.

Box 54.6 Contemporary perspectives on classical psychoanalysis

Classical psychoanalysis is both intense, time-consuming and expensive (£30 to £40 per 50-minute session), involving perhaps three to six sessions per week over several years. Moreover, during its course, an analysand may be vulnerable and helpless for long periods. This occurs when the analysand's old defences and resistances are broken down, but the ego is still not strong enough to cope adequately with the conflict. Although some psychoanalysts still rigidly adhere to Freud's protracted techniques, there has been a shift in the theoretical basis of psychoanalysis and:

'The Aunt Sally of classical Freudianism is simply not relevant to present-day psychoanalysis' (Holmes, 1996).

For Garfield & Bergin (1994):

'The cornerstones of early Freudian metapsychology were repression, the unconscious, and infantile sexuality. Contemporary psychoanalysis views all three in a different light'.

PSYCHOANALYTICALLY ORIENTED PSYCHOTHERAPIES

Analysts who are more flexible in fitting the therapeutic sessions to a person's needs are known as *psychoanalytically oriented psychotherapists*. Most psychoanalytically oriented psychotherapies involve briefer treatment and use face-to-face interaction (*focal psychotherapies*). Although they also emphasise restructuring the entire personality, more attention is paid to the analysand's current life and relationships than to early childhood conflicts. Freudian principles are followed (the aim of therapy is still to gain insight, and free expression is emphasised), but these therapies enable those who cannot afford protracted therapy, or whose time is limited by other commitments, to be treated (Cohn, 1994).

Perhaps the most influential of those who have revised Freudian therapeutic approaches are the *ego psychologists* or *ego analysts*. Rather than emphasising the id's role, these therapists focus on the ego and the way in which it acts as the *executive* of personality (see Chapter 29). As well as personality being shaped by inner conflicts, contemporary analysts believe that it may be shaped by the external environment.

Box 54.7 Contemporary therapeutic approaches derived from psychoanalysis

Ego analysts are sometimes referred to as the *second generation* of psychoanalysts. They believe that Freud over-emphasised the influence of sexual and aggressive impulses and underestimated the ego's importance. Erikson (1965), for example, spoke to clients directly about their values and concerns, and encouraged them to consciously fashion particular behaviours and characteristics. For Erikson, the ego's cognitive processes are constructive, creative and productive. This is different from Freud's therapeutic approach of establishing conditions in which patients could 'shore up' the ego's position.

Unlike Freud, who saw analysands as perpetual victims of their past who could not completely overcome their childhood conflicts, Horney (1924) saw them as capable of overcoming abuse and deprivation through self-understanding and productive adult relationships. Freud's emphasis on unconscious forces and conflicts was disputed by Freud's daughter, Anna Freud (1966). She believed a better approach was to concentrate on the ways in which the ego perceives the world.

Klein (1950) and Mahler (1975) have stressed the child's separation from the mother and interpersonal relationships as being important in psychological growth. *Object relations theorists* believe that some people have difficulty in telling where the influences of significant others end and their 'real selves' begin. Mahler's approach to therapy is to help people separate their own ideas and feelings from those of others so they can develop as true individuals.

As noted earlier, one of the major differences between classical psychoanalysis and psychoanalytically oriented psychotherapies is the *time* spent in therapy. Roth & Fonagy (1996) argue that there is a high 'relapse rate' in all types of brief therapies when those who have undergone treatment are not followed up for long periods of time. Therapy's ultimate goal must be good outcome sustained at follow-up, but as Holmes (1996) has remarked:

'Modern health services seem always to be in a hurry; time is money; but the cost of major cardiac surgery is still far greater than, say, the 100–200 hours of psychotherapy that are needed to make a significant impact on borderline personality disorder. An emphasis on sufficient time is a central psychoanalytic dimension that should be preserved at all costs'.

THERAPIES BASED ON THE PSYCHODYNAMIC MODEL: SOME ISSUES

At least some people who have undergone psychoanalysis claim that it has helped them achieve insight into their problems, and has provided long-term relief from the repressed feelings that were interfering with healthy functioning. However, although Freud's theories and his therapeutic approach have been influential, they have also been subject to much criticism, and there have been numerous explanations of 'why Freud was wrong' (Webster, 1995) and several calls to 'bury Freud' (Tallis, 1996). One problem with Freud's work is that it is difficult to study scientifically, since concepts like transference, insight, unconscious conflicts and repression are either vague or difficult to measure.

Much of the evidence favouring psychoanalysis derives from carefully selected case studies, which may be biased. In cases where psychoanalysis fails to produce significant changes, analysts can blame the analysand. If an analysand accepts an insight into a behaviour but does not change that behaviour, the insight is said to be merely *intellectual* (Carlson, 1987).

Box 54.8 Psychoanalysis as a closed system

The 'escape clause' of intellectual insight makes the argument for insight's importance completely circular, and therefore illogical: if the analysand improves, the improvement is due to insight, but if the analysand's behaviour remains unchanged, then real insight did not occur. Carlson (1987) likens this to the logic of wearing a charm in the belief that it will cure an illness. If the illness is cured, then the charm works. If it is not cured, then the individual does not believe sufficiently in its power. Psychoanalysis is a *closed system*. A critic who raises questions about the validity of psychoanalysis is described as suffering from *resistance*, since the critic cannot recognise the therapy's 'obvious' value.

Assessing the effectiveness of psychoanalysis

Eysenck (1952) made the first systematic attempt to evaluate psychoanalysis's effectiveness. He examined psychoanalysis and *eclectic psychotherapy* (psychotherapy incorporating various approaches rather than the single approach used in psychoanalysis). Prior to Eysenck's study, psychotherapy's value and effectiveness had not been seriously questioned.

Key **STUDY**

Box 54.9 Eysenck's assessment of psychoanalysis's effectiveness

According to Eysenck, psychoanalysis was 'unsupported by any scientifically acceptable evidence'. Looking at studies conducted between 1920 and 1944, Eysenck discovered that in only 44 per cent of cases using psychoanalysis could the person be considered 'cured', 'much improved' or 'improved'. Using the same criteria to assess eclectic psychotherapy, the figure was 64 per cent.

Eysenck argued that many people with psychological problems improve *without* any professional treatment (*spontaneous remission*). Eysenck compared the two therapies with a *control group* of people with similar problems, but who did not receive any form of professional treatment (e.g. they were treated only custodially in an institution). Using data reported by Landis (1938) and Denker (1946), Eysenck found that 66 per cent satisfied the 'cured', 'much improved' or 'improved' criteria. He concluded that:

'There thus appears to be an inverse correlation between recovery and psychotherapy: the more psychotherapy, the smaller the recovery rate'.

Eysenck's claim that no treatment is at least as effective, if not more effective, than professional treatment was not greeted enthusiastically by psychoanalysts and eclectic psychotherapists. Nor was his additional claim that it was unethical for therapists to *charge* people for their services, when the evidence suggested they were paying for nothing (Eysenck, 1992).

Eysenck's research did not, however, escape criticism. For example, researchers questioned his inclusion as 'failures' those people who 'dropped out' of therapy, on the grounds that somebody who leaves therapy cannot necessarily be counted as 'not cured'. When Eysenck's figures were reanalysed taking this into account, the figure of 44 per cent for psychoanalysis rose to a considerably higher 66 per cent (Oatley, 1984).

Bergin (1971) argued that psychoanalysis's success rate increased to 83 per cent if 'improvement' was measured differently, whilst Malan *et al.* (1975) suggested that Eysenck's control group differed in important ways from those who received therapy (a point Eysenck acknowledged). 'Untreated' individuals actually had one assessment interview, which some of them perceived as a powerful impetus for *self-induced change*. Since the interview clearly influenced some people, they could hardly be considered to have 'spontaneously recovered'. Even Landis (1938), whose article was one from which Eysenck derived his spontaneous remission figure, noted differences between those who did and did not receive therapy.

Key **STUDY**

Box 54.10 Psychotherapy versus behaviour therapy

Sloane *et al.* (1975) compared psychotherapy with behaviour therapy and no therapy at all. Participants were matched according to age, sex and disorder, and randomly assigned to a course of psychotherapy or behaviour therapy, or were placed on a waiting list for therapy without actually receiving any treatment. Highly experienced experts in either psychotherapy or behaviour therapy interviewed participants before the study began and, without knowing to which group they had been assigned, at various times later on. After four months, 80 per cent of those who received psychotherapy *or* behaviour therapy had either improved or recovered. For those who received no therapy, the figure was 48 per cent, suggesting that contrary to Eysenck's (1952) claim, psychotherapy *did* have a significant effect.

When participants were assessed one year later, those who received psychotherapy or behaviour therapy had maintained their improvement, whereas those who had not received therapy had made small but significant gains towards the levels of the two treatment groups. So, whilst spontaneous remission may occur (as Eysenck had claimed), both therapies were still better than no therapy at all.

Meta–analytic studies of psychotherapy's effectiveness

Smith *et al.* (1980) used *meta-analysis* to assess psychotherapy's effectiveness. This allows researchers to *combine* the results of all the studies concerned with a particular phenomenon, and produce an 'average estimate' of the effect size of whatever has been investigated. Smith *et al.* combined the results from 475 studies concerned with therapy effectiveness, some of which had used very different ways of measuring how effective a therapy was. Those receiving psychodynamic therapies scored significantly *higher* than those who received no therapy on many of the measures. However, there was considerable overlap in the outcomes for treated and untreated individuals, and psychodynamic therapies were more effective with some disorders (e.g. anxiety disorders) than others (e.g. schizophrenia).

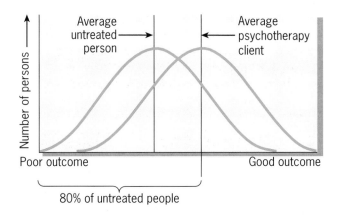

Figure 54.2 *Normal distribution curves showing improvement by those treated with psychotherapy as compared with untreated people (Based on Smith* et al., *1980)*

Smith *et al.* concluded that psychodynamic therapies:

'... benefit people of all ages ... The average person who receives therapy is better off at the end of it than 80 per cent of persons who do not. [However], this does not mean that everyone who receives psychotherapy improves ... Some people do not improve, and a small number gets worse [Smith *et al.* report a figure of nine per cent]'.

Unfortunately, over half the people receiving treatment in the 475 studies were *students*, who are not representative of the general population. Also in some of the studies, the psychological problems treated were not particularly serious (Shapiro & Shapiro, 1982). More important was the inclusion of methodologically *flawed* studies. Prioleau *et al.* (1983) reanalysed Smith *et al.*'s data, and found only 32 studies free from methodological defects. After examining these, Prioleau *et al.* reached a different conclusion from Smith *et al.*:

'Thirty years after Eysenck first raised the issue of [psychotherapy's effectiveness], ... we are still not aware of a single convincing demonstration [of its benefit]'.

The issue of psychotherapy's effectiveness has yet to be resolved. Some evidence suggests that psychotherapy can be at least as effective as chemotherapy in treating certain disorders (Garfield, 1992). For Andrews (1993), however, dynamic psychotherapy is no better than routine clinical care, and:

'The lack of evidence for efficacy despite considerable research, the real possibility of harm and the high cost all make dynamic psychotherapy unlikely to be a preferred option of the health service'.

Box 54.11 Does the type of person receiving therapy influence its effectiveness?

Some people choose particular therapies over others, that is, they *self-select* a therapy. This makes it difficult to assess therapies, because some people will either change therapists or leave therapy completely. It also makes comparisons between therapies difficult, since in both cases *only* those people who remain can be evaluated. Despite this, it appears that psychodynamic therapies are most effective with well-educated, articulate, strongly motivated and confident people experiencing light to moderate depression, anxiety disorders or interpersonal problems. This is called the *YAVIS effect*, since such people tend to be **y**oung, **a**rticulate, **v**erbal, **i**ntelligent and **s**uccessful.

COGNITIVE–BEHAVIOURAL THERAPIES

According to the cognitive model, mental disorders result from distortions in people's cognitions. The aim of cognitively-based therapies is to show people that their distorted or irrational thoughts are the main contributors to their difficulties. If faulty modes of thinking can be *modified* or *changed*, then disorders can be alleviated.

Therapies based on the cognitive model, then, aim to change maladaptive behaviour by changing the way people *think*. Cognitive–behavioural therapies have been viewed as techniques really belonging to the domain of the behavioural model. In some cases, the dividing line between a therapy based on the behavioural model and one based on the cognitive model is very fine and arbitrary. Indeed, therapists identifying their orientation as primarily behavioural or cognitive may actually be doing the same thing.

Supporters of the cognitive model, however, believe that behaviour change results from changes in cognitive processes, and hence cognitive–behavioural therapies can be separated from purely behavioural ones. Like psychodynamic therapies, cognitive–behavioural therapies aim to produce *insight*. However, rather than focusing on the past, they try to produce insight into *current cognitions*.

MODELLING

As noted in Chapter 31, certain kinds of learning cannot be *solely* explained in terms of classical or operant conditioning. According to Bandura (1969, 1984) and other *social learning theorists*, humans and some non-humans can learn directly *without* experiencing an event, and can acquire new behaviours from others simply by observing them (*observational learning*). Moreover, whether we see people being rewarded or punished can strengthen or reduce our own inhibitions against behaving in similar ways. If we see a positive outcome for a behaviour, our restraint against performing it is lowered (*response disinhibition*). However, if we see a negative outcome, our restraint is heightened (*response inhibition*).

Bandura argues that maladaptive behaviours can be altered by exposing those demonstrating them to appropriate *models* (others performing actions the person is afraid to perform). As well as changing behaviour, this approach aims to change *thoughts* and *perceptions*.

Box 54.12 illustrates *participant modelling* (or *guided participation)*, which involves observing the therapist's behaviour and then imitating it. This is more effective than having people watch filmed or video-taped models (*symbolic modelling*: Menzies & Clarke, 1993). Modelling has been successfully used with various phobias and, as well as eliminating undesirable behaviours, has also been used to establish new and more appropriate behaviours.

Key STUDY

Box 54.12 An application of modelling to ophidiophobia (fear of snakes)

After constructing an anxiety hierarchy with participants, the therapist performed the behaviour fearlessly at each step. Gradually, participants were led into touching, stroking and then holding the snake's body with gloved and bare hands whilst the therapist held the snake securely by the head and tail. If a participant was unable to touch the snake following ample demonstration, she was asked to place her hands on the therapist's and to move her hand down gradually until it touched the snake's body. After participants no longer felt apprehension about touching the snake under these conditions, anxieties about contact with the snake's head area and entwining tail were extinguished.

The therapist again performed the tasks fearlessly, and then the therapist and participant performed the responses jointly. As participants became less fearful, the therapist gradually reduced his participation and control over the snake, until eventually participants

were able to hold the snake in their laps without assistance, to let the snake loose in the room and retrieve it, and to let it crawl freely over their bodies. Progress through the graded approach tasks was paced according to the participants' apprehensiveness. When they reported being able to perform one activity with little or no fear, they were eased into a more difficult interaction.

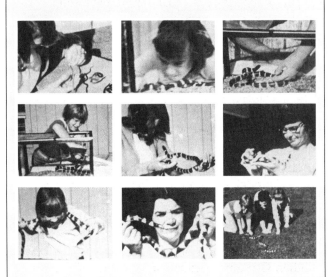

Figure 54.3 *As this sequence of photographs shows, modelling can be an effective way of treating phobias*

(From Bandura, 1971)

In *assertiveness training*, people with difficulty in asserting themselves in interpersonal situations are required to perform in the presence of a group who provide feedback about the adequacy of performance. Then, the therapist assumes the individual's role and models the appropriate assertive behaviour. The individual is asked to try again, this time imitating the therapist. The alternation between *behavioural rehearsal* and modelling continues until the assertive role has been mastered. When this occurs, the skills are tried out in real-life situations. This approach has also been widely used in *social skills training*, in which people who lack the ability to function effectively in certain situations observe others performing the desired behaviours and then attempt to imitate them.

One reason for modelling's effectiveness is the development of *self-efficacy* (Bandura, 1977b: see Box 31.6, page 340). Being able to perform a behaviour that was previously impossible raises a person's evaluation of the degree to which s/he can cope with difficult situations. According to Bandura, when people encounter new situations in which they have difficulty, they are much more willing to engage in behaviours that were previously avoided.

ELLIS' RATIONAL–EMOTIVE THERAPY (RET)

Rational–emotive therapy (RET) was developed in the 1950s by Ellis. After becoming dissatisfied with what he called the 'passivity of psychoanalysis', Ellis, a trained psychoanalyst, developed his own therapeutic approach. For several years, this therapy was regarded as being on the periphery. However, RET is now practised by many therapists, particularly in the USA.

Box 54.13 The A–B–C model of RET

Ellis (1958, 1962) argued that many emotional difficulties are due to the *irrational beliefs* people bring to bear on their experiences, and the reinforcement these receive through being repeated. For Ellis (1997), irrational beliefs can be understood as part of the A–B–C model. According to this, a significant *activating* event or *adversity* (A) triggers a highly charged emotional *consequence* (C). However, to say that A is the cause of C is not *always* correct, even though it may appear to be as far as the person is concerned. Rather, C occurs because of a person's *belief system* (B). Inappropriate emotions, such as depression and guilt, can only be abolished if a change occurs in beliefs and perceptions.

To illustrate this, suppose someone telephones several friends to invite them out for a drink, but finds that none is able to accept the invitation. This activating event (A) might produce the emotional consequence (C) that the person feels depressed, isolated and worthless. For Ellis, C occurs because of the person's belief system (B) which holds that because no one has accepted the invitation, it must mean that no one likes him/her (which Ellis calls an *'awfulising'* statement).

RET aims to help people find flaws in their thinking and 'to make mincemeat' of these maladaptive cognitions by creating D, a *dispute belief system* which has no severe emotional consequences. In the example used in Box 54.13, D might run along the lines of 'people have already made plans to go out, and just because they can't accept my invitation doesn't mean they don't like me'.

Ellis proposes that two of the most common maladaptive cognitions people hold are:

* they are worthless unless they are perfectly competent at everything they try, and,
* they must be approved of and loved by everyone they meet.

Because such beliefs make impossible demands on people who hold them, they lead to anxiety, failure and, frequently, mental disorder.

Box 54.14 Some common irrational beliefs encountered in RET

* Certain people I must deal with are thoroughly bad and should be severely blamed and punished for it.
* It is awful and upsetting when things are not the way I would like them to be.
* My unhappiness is always caused by external events; I cannot control my emotional reactions.
* If something unpleasant might happen, I should keep dwelling on it.
* It is easier to avoid difficulties and responsibilities than to face them.
* I should depend on others who are stronger than I am.
* Because something once strongly affected my life, it will do so indefinitely.
* There is always a perfect solution to human problems, and it is awful if this solution is not found.

(Based on Ellis, 1984)

Once the irrational beliefs have been identified, therapy continues by guiding the person to substitute more logical or realistic thoughts for the maladaptive ones, a task which Ellis believes can be accomplished 'by any therapist worth his or her salt'. Ellis sees the rational–emotive therapist as an *exposing and nonsense-annihilating scientist*. Therapists claim that the universe is logical and rational, and the appropriate means of understanding it is the scientific method of controlled observation. People have the *capacity* for rational understanding and the *resources* for personal growth. However, they also have the capacity to delude themselves and accept irrational beliefs.

As noted earlier, the first stage in therapy is for people to recognise and question their irrational beliefs. Rather than remaining 'anonymous', as a classical psychoanalyst would do, and occasionally offering some form of interpretation, the rational–emotive therapist will show the person how to ask questions like '*Where* is the evidence that I am a worthless person if I am not universally approved?', '*Who* says I must be perfect?' and '*Why* must things go exactly the way I would like them to go?'

Once people have recognised and analysed their beliefs, they are taught to substitute more realistic alternatives to engender *full acceptance*. Rather than measuring themselves against impossible standards, a rational–emotive therapist emphasises that failures should not be seen as 'disastrous', confirming a lack of self-worth, but merely as 'unfortunate' events.

Box 54.15 Some rational alternatives to irrational beliefs

Irrational belief: I *must* prove myself to be thoroughly competent, adequate and achieving, or I *must* at least have real competence or talent at something important.
Rational alternative belief: What I do doesn't have to be perfect to be good. I will be happier if I achieve at a *realistic* level rather than strive for perfection.

Irrational belief: I *have* to view life as awful, terrible, horrible, or catastrophic when things do not go the way I would like them to go.
Rational alternative belief: If I can't change the situation, it may be unfortunate but not catastrophic. I *can* make plans for my life to be as enjoyable as possible.

Irrational belief: I *must* have sincere love and approval almost all the time from all the people who are significant to me.
Rational alternative belief: I would *like* to be approved, but I do not *need* such approval.

(Based on Lange & Jakubowksi, 1976)

Rational–emotive therapists use various approaches to minimise self-defeating beliefs. Rather than focusing on people's histories, they focus on the 'here and now'. As Ellis (1984) puts it:

'Therapists do not spend a great deal of time ... encouraging long tales of woe, sympathetically getting in tune with emotionalising or carefully and incisively reflecting feelings.'

Ellis is not interested in what he calls 'long-winded dialogues', which he sees as 'indulgent'. Rather, RET aims to help people *get* better rather than *feel* better during therapy, and to accept reality 'even when it is pretty grim'.

Indeed, by providing people with warmth, support, attention and caring, their need for love (which is usually the central core of their circumstances: Elkins, 1980) is *reinforced*. There is also the possibility that people become dependent on the therapy and the therapist. The direct approach used in RET is illustrated in Box 54.16, in which Ellis discusses the problems experienced by a 25-year-old female.

Box 54.16 RET in action

Therapist: The same crap! It's always the same crap. Now, if you would look at the crap – instead of 'Oh, how stupid I am! He hates me! I think I'll kill myself!' – then you'd get better right away.
Person: You've been listening! (*laughs*)
Therapist: Listening to what?
Person: (*laughs*) Those wild statements in my mind, like that, that I make.
Therapist: That's right! Because I know that you have to make those statements – because I have a good theory. And according to my theory, people couldn't get upset unless they made those nutty statements to themselves ... Even if I loved you madly, the next person you talk to is likely to hate you. So I like brown eyes and he likes blue eyes, or something. So then you're dead! Because you really think: 'I've got to be accepted! I've got to act intelligently!' Well, why?
Person: (*very soberly and reflectively*) True.
Therapist: You see?
Person: Yes.
Therapist: Now, if you will learn that lesson, then you've had a very valuable session. Because you don't have to upset yourself. As I said before: if I thought you were the worst [*expletive deleted*] who ever existed, well that's my opinion. And I'm entitled to it. But does that make you a turd?
Person: (*reflective silence*)
Therapist: Does it?
Person: No.
Therapist: What makes you a turd?
Person: *Thinking* that you are.
Therapist: That's right! Your *belief* that you are. That's the only thing that could ever do it. And you never have to believe that. See? You control your thinking. I control my thinking – *my* belief about you. But you don't have to be affected by that. You *always* control what you think.

(From Ellis, 1984)

RET is apparently effective for some disorders, such as social phobia, especially when used in conjunction with behavioural therapies (Woody *et al.*, 1997). However, for other disorders (such as agoraphobia), RET is less effective than other therapies (Haaga & Davison, 1993). Clearly, RET is an active and directive therapeutic approach, and one in which the therapist's personal beliefs and values are an inevitable part of what goes on during therapy. However, Ellis' (1984) views that 'no one and nothing is supreme', that 'self-gratification' should be encouraged, and that 'unequivocal love, commitment, service and … fidelity to any interpersonal commitment, especially marriage, leads to harmful consequences' have been disputed (Bergin, 1980).

The argumentative approach to therapy, in which the therapist attacks those beliefs regarded as foolish and illogical, has also been questioned, particularly by those who stress the importance of *empathy* in therapy. For example, Fancher (1996) believes that all cognitive therapies rely on a commonsense view of cognition, and falsely assume that therapists are capable of identifying 'faulty thinking': what is foolish and irrational to the therapist may not be foolish and irrational in terms of the individual's own experiences.

RET is effective in producing behaviour change amongst those who are self-demanding and feel guilty for not living up to their own standards of perfection (Brandsma *et al.*, 1978). For people with severe thought disorders (as in schizophrenia), however, the therapy is ineffective, since people with such disorders do not respond to an Ellis-type analysis of their problems (Ellis, 1993).

BECK'S COGNITIVE RESTRUCTURING THERAPY

Like Ellis, Beck was originally trained as a psychoanalyst. As with RET, Beck's (1967) therapy assumes that disorders stem primarily from irrational beliefs that cause people to behave in maladaptive ways. Beck's approach is specifically designed to treat *depressed* people. Depressed people suffer from a *cognitive triad* of negative beliefs about *themselves*, their *futures* and their *experiences* (Beck *et al.*, 1979). Such beliefs are seen as arising from faulty information-processing and faulty logic.

Beck's therapy aims to identify the implicit and self-defeating assumptions depressed people make about themselves, change their validity and substitute more adaptive assumptions. Box 54.17 illustrates an exchange between a therapist using Beck's approach and a student, who believed that she would not get into the college to which she had applied.

Box 54.17 Beck's therapeutic approach to therapy in action

Therapist: Why do you think you won't be able to get into the university of your choice?
Student: Because my grades were not really so hot.
Therapist: Well, what was your grade average?
Student: Well, pretty good up until the last semester in high school.
Therapist: What was your grade average in general?
Student: As and Bs.
Therapist: Well, how many of each?
Student: Well, I guess, almost all of my grades were As but I got terrible grades my last semester.
Therapist: What were your grades then?
Student: I got two As and two Bs.
Therapist: Since your grade average would seem to come out to almost all As, why do you think you won't be able to get into the university?
Student: Because of competition being so tough.
Therapist: Have you found out what the average grades are for admissions to the college?
Student: Well, somebody told me that a B+ average would suffice.
Therapist: Isn't your average better than that?
Student: I guess so.

(From Beck *et al.*, 1979)

Note how the therapist attempts to reverse the 'catastrophising beliefs' held by the student concerning herself, her situation and her future. Note also how the therapist takes a gentler, less confrontational and more experiential approach to the student than a rational–emotive therapist would.

Box 54.17 illustrates the strategy of identifying a person's self-impressions which, although not recognised as such, are misguided. Once the self-impressions have been identified, the therapist's role is to attempt to disprove rather than confirm the negative self-image (Williams, 1992). By sharing knowledge of the cognitive model, the person undergoing therapy may then understand the origins of the disorder, and ultimately develop skills to apply effective interventions independently.

Given its original purpose, it is not surprising that Beck's approach to therapy is most successful in treating depression (Beck, 1997). However, the therapy has also been adapted and used successfully with eating disorders (Walsh *et al.*, 1997). Whether Beck's approach can be applied to schizophrenia and personality disorders has been hotly debated (Beck & Freeman, 1990; Tarrier *et al.*, 1993).

SOME OTHER APPLICATIONS OF COGNITIVE–BEHAVIOURAL THERAPIES

Like other therapies, cognitive–behavioural therapies have received considerable scrutiny as to their worth (De Rubeis *et al.*, 1999). These therapies are particularly helpful in the treatment of *panic disorder* (Barlow, 1997). The physiological reactions that occur in this disorder are similar to those of a heart attack. They include increased heart rate, rapid and shallow breathing, sweating, muscle tension and a dryness of the mouth. Other reactions are chest pain and a tingling in the hands or feet.

Clark (1993) has argued that the core disturbance in this disorder is an abnormality in thinking. When external or internal stressors cause increased physiological activity, this is noticed but interpreted in '*catastrophic*' ways (e.g., 'I am having a heart attack'). This leads to even more physiological activity, and so a *positive feedback loop* between cognitions and bodily reactions occurs.

Because of their fears, people become *hypervigilant* and repeatedly scan their bodies for signs of danger, which results in their noticing sensations which other people would not be aware of. Additionally, subtle *avoidance behaviours* prevent them from disconfirming their negative beliefs. For example, people convinced that they are suffering from cardiac disease may avoid exer-

cise, and rest whenever a palpitation occurs in the belief that this will prevent a fatal heart attack.

Clark *et al.* (1999) have shown that six to seven one-hour sessions of cognitive–behavioural therapy is highly effective in changing the cognitions and behaviour of 90 per cent of panic disorder sufferers. However, whether therapies derived from the cognitive model can and should be used with other disorders is less clear-cut. For example, James & Blackburn (1995) found that of the few well-controlled studies examining cognitively based therapies' effectiveness, there was little evidence to suggest that improvement occurred in obsessive–compulsive disorder. Moreover, whilst anxiety is reduced in social phobia, therapy does not necessarily lead to improved social functioning (Stravynski & Greenberg, 1998). Against this, however, are findings indicating that cognitively based therapies can have a significant impact on conditions such as:

- schizophrenia (Kingdon & Turkington, 1994);
- chronic fatigue syndrome (Sharpe *et al.*, 1996);
- the psychological effects of unemployment (Proudfoot *et al.*, 1997);
- bulimia nervosa (Spangler, 1999);
- adolescent depression (Clarke *et al.*, 1999);
- adult depression (Jarrett *et al.*, 1999).

CONCLUSIONS

This chapter has described the use and mode of action of therapies based on the psychodynamic and cognitive models of abnormality. Although less popular than they once were, psychoanalysis and psychoanalytically oriented psychotherapies are still used today. However, several important issues surround their use, and at least

some professionals believe them to be of little help in the treatment of mental disorders.

Cognitive–behavioural therapies have been used to treat several types of disorder, especially panic disorder and depression. Their effectiveness with these disorders is well established, and some types of cognitive–behavioural therapy have a significant impact on other types of mental disorder.

Summary

- **Psychoanalysis** initially aims to uncover the unconscious conflicts responsible for a person's mental disorder, and make them conscious. By providing **insight** into these, the ego can deal more effectively with them.

- The most widely used technique to make the unconscious conscious is **free association**. The **basic rule** of psychoanalysis is that the analysand says whatever comes to mind. The analyst acts as a **sounding board**,

offering **interpretive comments** and drawing attention to the analysand's **resistances**.

- The analyst may **privately deduce** what lies behind the analysand's free associations, or use **confrontation** and **reconstruction**. The now conscious conflict can be manipulated by the analyst through **transference/transference neurosis**. Transference may take the form of **acting out**.

- Psychoanalysis ultimately aims to produce a deep-seated modification of personality. This allows people to deal with problems without having to resort to

defence mechanisms. However, **insight** does not constitute a cure. It is achieved through a process of 're-education' and an increase in self-knowledge involving **working through**.

■ **Psychoanalytically oriented psychotherapies** are briefer and more flexible approaches. Freudian principles are still followed, although more attention is paid to the analysand's current life and relationships.

■ Important revisions of psychoanalysis have been made by **ego psychologists/ego analysts**. Personality is seen as being shaped as much by the external environment as inner conflicts.

■ Freud's theories and his therapeutic approach have been extensively criticised. Some critics contend that psychoanalysis is a **closed** system. Others believe that psychoanalysis is ineffective in treating mental disorders.

■ One **meta-analytic** study of the effectiveness of psychoanalysis indicated that psychodynamic therapies are effective, although some people show no improvement and a small percentage actually gets worse. However, when this study was re-analysed, the claim that psychoanalysis is ineffective is supported.

■ **Cognitive–behavioural therapies** attempt to show people that their distorted/irrational thoughts are the main contributors to their disorders. By changing faulty thinking, disorders can be treated effectively.

■ **Modelling** is useful in the treatment of phobia, and also effective in **assertiveness training** and **social skills training**. One reason for this is the development of **self-efficacy**.

■ **Rational–emotive therapy** (RET) aims to help people find flaws in their irrational thinking by creating a **dispute belief system**. RET is an active, direct and argumentative approach, which has been questioned by those who stress **empathy's** importance in therapy. However, it is effective for certain disorders.

■ Beck's **cognitive restructuring therapy** also sees disorders as stemming from irrational beliefs. The therapy is specifically designed to treat **depression**, and is effective in doing this. Beck's therapy identifies depressed people's implicit and self-defeating assumptions, but is less confrontational than RET.

■ Cognitive–behavioural therapies have been particularly useful in treating **panic disorder**. They have also been shown to have an impact on schizophrenia, chronic fatigue syndrome, bulimia nervosa, adolescent and adult depression, and the psychological effects of unemployment.

Essay Questions

1 Discuss issues surrounding the use of therapies derived from the psychodynamic model of abnormality. *(30 marks)*

2 Describe and evaluate **one** cognitive–behavioural approach to the treatment of mental disorders. *(30 marks)*

WEB ADDRESSES

http://www.apsa.org
http://www.aapsa.org
http://www.divpsa.org
http://mindstreet.com.cbt.html
http://www.beckinstitute.org

Perspectives

55 Bias in Psychological Theory and Research

INTRODUCTION AND OVERVIEW

Mainstream academic psychology, modelling itself on classical, orthodox, natural science (such as physics and chemistry), claims to be *objective*, *unbiased*, and *value-free*. Collectively this is referred to as the *positivist* view of science, or *positivism* (see Chapter 58). As applied to the study of humans, this implies that it is possible to study people as they 'really are', without the psychologist's characteristics influencing the outcome of the investigation in any way.

This chapter shows that a view of psychology as unbiased and value-free is mistaken. It discusses two major forms of bias (namely, *sexism* and *ethnocentrism*, relating to gender and culture respectively), which permeate much psychological theory and research.

Much of the chapter's content is relevant to the topic of prejudice and discrimination. As Chapter 3 showed, prejudice and discrimination can be understood as characteristics of *individuals* or of *social groups*, *institutions* and even *whole societies*. With bias in psychological theory and research, it is sometimes individual psychologists, and sometimes 'psychology as a whole' that are being accused of bias.

GENDER BIAS: FEMINIST PSYCHOLOGY, SEXISM AND ANDROCENTRISM

Not surprisingly, most of the criticism of mainstream psychology regarding its gender bias has come from *feminist psychology*, which Wilkinson (1997) defines as:

> '... psychological theory and practice which is explicitly informed by the political goals of the feminist movement'.

Whilst feminism and feminist psychology can take a variety of forms, two common themes are the valuation of women as worthy of study in their own right (not just in comparison with men), and recognition of the need for social change on behalf of women (Unger & Crawford, 1996).

Feminist psychology is openly political and sets out to challenge the discipline of psychology for its inadequate and damaging theories about women, and for its failure to see power relations as central to social life (Unger & Crawford, 1992). More specifically, it insists on exposing and challenging the operation of male power in psychology:

> 'Psychology's theories often exclude women, or distort our experience by assimilating it to male norms or man-made stereotypes, or by regarding "women" as a unitary category, to be understood only in comparison with the unitary category "men" ... Similarly, psychology [screens out] ... the existence and operation of social and structural inequalities between and within social groups' (Wilkinson, 1991).

Psychology obscures the social and structural operation of male power by concentrating its analysis on people as individuals (*individualism*). Responsibility (and pathology) are located within the individual, to the total neglect of social and political oppression. By ignoring or minimising the *social context*, psychology obscures the mechanisms of oppression. For example, the unhappiness of some women after childbirth is treated as a problem in individual functioning (with possible hormonal causes), thus distracting attention away from the difficult material situation in which many new mothers find themselves (Wilkinson, 1997: see Chapter 50, pages 545–546).

Box 55.1 Some major feminist criticisms of psychology

- Much psychological research is conducted on all-male samples, but then either fails to make this clear or reports the findings as if they applied equally to women and men.

- Some of the most influential theories within psychology as a whole are based on studies of males only, but are meant to apply equally to women and men.

- If women's behaviour differs from men's, the former is often judged to be pathological, abnormal or deficient in some way (*sexism*). This is because the behaviour of men is, implicitly or explicitly, taken as the 'standard' or norm against which women's behaviour is compared (*androcentrism* – male-centredness, or the *masculinist* bias).

- Psychological explanations of behaviour tend to emphasise biological (and other internal) causes, as opposed to social (and other external) causes (*individualism*). This gives (and reinforces) the impression that psychological sex differences are inevitable and unchangeable. This reinforces widely held stereotypes about men and women, contributing to the oppression of women (another form of *sexism*).

- Heterosexuality (both male and female) is taken, implicitly or explicitly, as the norm, so that homosexuality is seen as abnormal (*heterosexism*).

Exercise 1

Try to think of (at least) one example for each of the five major criticisms of psychological theory and research made in Box 55.1. Regarding the fourth point, how does this relate to attribution theory as discussed in Chapter 1?

The feminist critique of science

In many ways, a more fundamental criticism of psychology than those listed in Box 55.1 is feminists' belief that scientific enquiry itself (whether this be within psychology or not) is biased.

Psychology's claims to be a science are based on its methods (especially the experiment), and the belief that it is a value-free discipline (see Chapter 58). However, as far as the latter is concerned, can scientific enquiry be neutral, wholly independent of the value system of the human scientists involved? According to Prince & Hartnett (1993):

> 'Decisions about what is, and what is not, to be measured, how this is done, and most importantly, what constitutes legitimate research are made by individual scientists within a socio-political context, and thus science is ideological.'

As far as scientific method is concerned, many feminist psychologists argue that it is gender-biased. For example, Nicolson (1995) identifies two major problems associated with adherence to the 'objective' investigation of behaviour for the way knowledge claims are made about women and gender differences.

First, the experimental environment takes the individual 'subject's *behaviour*' as distinct from the 'subject' herself as the unit of study. Therefore, it becomes deliberately blind to the behaviour's *meaning*, including the social, personal and cultural contexts in which it is enacted. As a result, claims about gender differences in competence and behaviour are attributed to *intrinsic* (either the product of 'gender role socialisation' or biology) as opposed to contextual qualities. This is another reference to *individualism* (see above).

Second, experimental psychology, far from being context-free, takes place in a very specific context which typically disadvantages women (Eagly, 1987). In an experiment, a woman becomes anonymous, stripped of her social roles and accompanying power and knowledge she might have achieved in the outside world. She is placed in this 'strange', environment, and expected to respond to the needs of (almost inevitably) a male experimenter who is in charge of the situation, with all the social meaning ascribed to gender power relations.

The belief that it is possible to study people 'as they really are', removed from their usual socio-cultural context (in a 'de-contextualised' way), is completely invalid:

> 'Psychology relies for its data on the practices of socialised and culture-bound individuals, so that to explore 'natural' or 'culture-free' behaviour (namely that behaviour unfettered by cultural, social structures and power relations) is by definition impossible' (Nicolson, 1995).

Feminist psychologists offer a critical challenge to psychological knowledge on gender issues by drawing on other disciplines, such as sociology. According to Giddens (1979), for example:

'There is no static knowledge about people to be 'discovered' or 'proved' through reductionist experimentation, and thus the researcher takes account of context, meaning and change over time'.

Exercise 2

Do you agree with Nicolson's claim that all human behaviour is 'culture-bound? What about 'instinctive' behaviours, such as eating, drinking and sex: does culture play a part here too? If so, in what ways? (These questions are equally relevant to the section on culture bias.)

Some practical consequences of gender bias

According to Kitzinger (1998), questions about sex differences (and similarities) are not just *scientific* questions, they are also highly *political*. Some answers to these questions have been used to keep women out of universities, or to put them in mental hospitals. Other answers have been used to say that women should be encouraged to go on assertiveness training courses, or to argue that women should have all the same rights and opportunities as men. In other words, the *science* of sex differences research is always used for *political* reasons:

'However much psychologists may think or hope or believe that they are doing objective rsearch and discovering truths about the world they are always influenced ... by the social and political context in which they are doing their research'. (Kitzinger, 1998)

For Prince & Hartnett (1993), scientific psychology has *reified* concepts such as personality and intelligence (treating abstract or metaphorical terms as if they were 'things' or entities):

'... and the scientific psychology which 'objectively' and 'rationally' produced means of measuring these reifications has been responsible for physical assaults on women such as forced abortions and sterilisations'.

Between 1924 and 1972, more than 7500 women in the state of Virginia alone were forcibly sterilised, in particular, 'unwed mothers, prisoners, the feeble-minded, children with discipline problems'. The criterion used in all cases was mental age as measured by the Stanford–Binet intelligence test (Gould, 1981).

Having convinced society that intelligence 'exists' in some objective way, and having produced a means of measuring it, psychologists could then promote and justify discrimination against particular social groups. Another example of the use of intelligence tests to justify blatant discrimination (although not specifically against women) involved the army alpha and beta tests, which influenced the passing of the 1924 Immigration Restriction Act in the USA (see Gross, 1999).

Box 55.2 Psychology's influence on immigration policy in the USA

Debates in Congress leading to passage of the Immigration Restriction Act of 1924 continually made reference to data from the army alpha and beta tests. *Eugenicists* (who advocate 'selective breeding' in humans in order to 'improve' genetic stock) lobbied for immigration limits and for imposing harsh quotas against nations of inferior stock. In short, Southern and Eastern Europeans, who scored lowest on the army tests, should be kept out. The eugenicists battled and won one of the greatest victories of scientific racism in American history. 'America must be kept American', proclaimed President Coolidge as he signed the bill.

Throughout the 1930s, Jewish refugees, anticipating the Holocaust, sought to emigrate, but were refused admission. Estimates suggest that the quotas barred up to six million Southern, Central and Eastern Europeans between 1924 and 1939:

'We know what happened to many who wished to leave, but had nowhere to go. The paths to destruction are often indirect, but ideas can be agents as sure as guns and bombs' (Gould, 1981).

(From Gould, 1981)

In the 1993 preface to *In a Different Voice* (1982), Gilligan says that at the core of her work on moral development in women and girls (see Chapter 30, page 328) was the realisation that within psychology, and in society at large, 'values were taken as facts'. She continues:

'In the aftermath of the Holocaust ... it is not tenable for psychologists or social scientists to adopt a position of ethical neutrality or cultural relativism ... Such a hands-off stance in the face of atrocity amounts to a kind of complicity'.

Whilst the example she gives is clearly extreme, it helps to illustrate the argument that not only do psychologists (and other scientists) have a responsibility to make their values explicit about important social and political issues, but failure to do so may (unwittingly) contribute to prejudice, discrimination and oppression. These considerations are as relevant to a discussion of the ethics of psychological research as they are to gender (and culture) bias, and are discussed in more detail in Chapter 56.

The masculinist bias and sexism: a closer look

Box 55.1 (see page 589) identified the masculinist bias (*androcentrism*) and sexism as two major criticisms of mainstream psychology made by feminist psychologists. Whilst each of these can take different forms, emphasis here will be given to (a) the argument that men are taken as some sort of standard or norm, against which women are compared and judged, and (b) gender bias in psychological research.

The male norm as the standard

According to Tavris (1993):

> 'In any domain of life in which men set the standard of normalcy, women will be considered abnormal, and society will debate woman's 'place' and her 'nature'. Many women experience tremendous conflict in trying to decide whether to be 'like' men or 'opposite' from them, and this conflict is itself evidence of the implicit male standard against which they are measuring themselves. This is why it is normal for women to feel abnormal'.

Tavris gives two examples of why it is normal for women to feel abnormal. First, in 1985, the American Psychiatric Association proposed two new categories of mental disorder for inclusion in the revised (third) edition of the *Diagnostic and Statistical Manual of Mental Disorders* (DSM-III-R: see Chapter 46). One was *masochistic personality*. In DSM-II, this was described as one of the psychosexual disorders, in which sexual gratification requires being hurt or humiliated. The proposal was to extend the term so that it became a more pervasive personality disorder, in which one seeks failure at work, at home, and in relationships, rejects opportunities for pleasure, puts others first (thereby sacrificing one's own needs) plays the martyr, and so on.

Whilst not intended to apply to women exclusively, these characteristics are associated predominantly with the female role. Indeed, according to Caplan (1991), it represented a way of calling *psychopathological* the behaviour of women who conform to social norms for a 'feminine woman' (the 'good wife syndrome').

In short, such a diagnostic label was biased against women, and perpetuated the myth of women's masochism. The label was eventually changed to *self-defeating personality disorder,* and was put in the appendix of DSM-III-R.

Exercise 3

If you were proposing a parallel diagnosis for men who conform to social norms for a 'masculine man', what characteristics would this have to include, and what would you call it? Could you justify extending sadism to conformist men?

Tavris's second example of why it is normal for women to feel abnormal concerns *causal attributions* made about men's and women's behaviours. When men have problems, such as drug abuse, and behave in socially unacceptable ways, as in rape and other forms of violence, the causes are looked for in their upbringing. Women's problems, however, are seen as the result of their psyche or hormones. This is another form of *individualism*, with the further implication that it could have been different for men (they are the victims of their childhood, for example), but not for women ('that's what women are like').

The 'mismeasure of woman'

According to Tavris, the view that man is the norm and woman is the opposite, lesser or deficient (the problem) constitutes one of three currently competing views regarding the 'mismeasure of woman' (meant to parallel Gould's, 1981, *The Mismeasure of Man*, a renowned critique of intelligence testing: see Gross, 1999). It is the view that underpins so much psychological research designed to discover why women aren't 'as something' (moral, intelligent, rational) as men (what Hare-Mustin & Maracek, 1988 call *alpha-bias*). It also underlies the enormous self-help industry, whereby women consume millions of books and magazines advising them how to become more beautiful, independent and so on. Men, being normal, feel no need to 'fix' themselves in corresponding ways (Tavris, 1993).

Box 55.3 A demonstration of the 'mismeasure of woman'

Wilson (1994) states that the reason 95 per cent of bank managers, company directors, judges and university professors in Britain are men is that men are 'more competitive', and because 'dominance is a personality characteristic determined by male hormones'.

Wilson also argues that women in academic jobs are less productive than men: 'objectively speaking, women may already be over-promoted'. Women who do achieve promotion to top management positions 'may have brains that are masculinised'.

The research cited by Wilson to support these claims comes partly from the psychometric testing industries which provide 'scientific' evidence of women's inadequacies, such as (compared with men) their lack of mathematical and spatial abilities. Even if women are considered to have the abilities to perform well in professional jobs, they have personality defects (in particular, low self-esteem and lack of assertiveness) which impede performance.

According to Wilson (1994):

'These differences [in mental abilities, motivation, personality and values] are deep-rooted, based in biology, and not easily dismantled by social engineering. Because of them we are unlikely to see the day when the occupational profiles of men and women are the same'.

(From Wilson, 1994, and Wilkinson, 1997)

Exercise 4

Try to identify examples of *individualism* in Box 55.3. Can you formulate some arguments against Wilson's claims?

Sexism in research

The American Psychological Association's Board of Social and Ethical Responsibility set up a Committee on Nonsexist Research, which reported its findings as *Guidelines for Avoiding Sexism in Psychological Research* (Denmark *et al.*, 1988). This maintains that gender bias is found at all stages of the research process:

- question formulation;
- research methods and design;
- data analysis and interpretation, and
- conclusion formulation.

The principles set out in the *Guidelines* are meant to apply to other forms of bias too: race, ethnicity, disability, sexual orientation and socio-economic status.

Box 55.4 Examples of gender bias at each stage of the research process

- **Question formulation:** It is assumed that topics relevant to white males are more important and 'basic' (e.g. the effects of TV violence on aggression in boys: see Chapter 9), whilst those relevant to white females, or ethnic minority females or males, are more marginal, specialised, or applied (e.g. the psychological correlates of pregnancy or the menopause).

- **Research methods and design:** Surprisingly often, the sex and race of the participants, researchers, and

any confederates who may be involved, are not specified. As a consequence, potential interactions between these variables are not accounted for. For example, men tend to display more helping behaviour than women in studies involving a young, female confederate 'victim' (see Chapter 8). This could be a function of either the sex of the confederate or an interaction between the confederate and the participant, rather than sex differences between the participants (which is the conclusion usually drawn).

- **Data analysis and interpretation:** Significant *sex differences* may be reported in very misleading ways, because the wrong sorts of comparisons are made. For example:

  'The spatial ability scores of women in our sample is significantly lower than those of men, at the 0.01 level'. You might conclude from this that women cannot or should not become architects or engineers. However, 'Successful architects score above 32 on our spatial ability test ... engineers score above 31 ... 12 per cent of women and 16 per cent of men in our sample score above 31; 11 per cent of women and 15 per cent of men score above 32'. What conclusions would you draw now? (Denmark *et al.*, 1988)

- **Conclusion formulation:** Results based on one sex only are then applied to both. This can be seen in some of the major theories within developmental psychology, notably Erikson's psychosocial theory of development (1950: see Chapters 33 and 34), Levinson *et al.*'s (1978) *Seasons of a Man's Life* (see Chapter 34), and Kohlberg's theory of moral development (1969: see Chapter 30). These all demonstrate *beta-bias* (Hare-Mustin & Maracek, 1988), and are discussed further below.

(Based on Denmark *et al.*, 1988)

Sexism in theory

Gilligan (1982) gives Erikson's theory of lifespan development (based on the study of males only) as one example of a sexist theory, which portrays women as 'deviants'. In one version of his theory, Erikson (1950) describes a series of eight *universal* stages, so that, for both sexes, in all cultures, the conflict between *identity* and *role confusion* (adolescence) precedes that between *intimacy* and *isolation* (young adulthood). In another version, he acknowledges that the sequence is *different* for the female, who postpones her identity as she prepares to attract the man whose name she will adopt, and by whose status she will be defined (Erikson, 1968). For women, intimacy seems to go along with identity: they come to know themselves through their relationships with others (Gilligan, 1982).

Despite his observation of sex differences, the sequence of stages in Erikson's psychosocial theory remains unchanged (see Chapter 31, page 336). As Gilligan points out:

> 'Identity continues to precede intimacy as male experience continues to define his [Erikson's] life-cycle concept'.

Similarly, Kohlberg's (1969) six-stage theory of moral development was based on a 20-year longitudinal study of 84 boys, but he claims that these stages are universal (see Chapter 30). Females rarely attain a level of moral reasoning above stage three ('Good boy–nice girl' orientation), which is supposed to be achieved by most adolescents and adults. This leaves females looking decidedly morally deficient.

Like other feminist psychologists, Gilligan argues that psychology speaks with a 'male voice', describing the world from a male perspective and confusing this with absolute truth (*beta-bias*). The task of feminist psychology is to listen to women and girls who speak in a 'different voice' (Gilligan, 1982; Brown & Gilligan, 1992). Gilligan's work with females has led her to argue that men and women have qualitatively different conceptions of morality, with moral dilemmas being 'solved' in terms of care, responsibility and relationships. Men are more likely to stress rights and rules. By stressing the *differences* between men and women (an *alpha-biased* approach), Gilligan is attempting to redress the balance, created by Kohlberg's beta-biased theory.

Exercise 5

In what ways is Freud's psychoanalytic theory (especially the psychosexual stages of development) sexist (or what Grosz, 1987, calls 'phallocentric')? Repeat this exercise for Levinson *et al.*'s theory of adult development, and any other theory you are familiar with.

CULTURE BIAS

In discussing gender bias, several references have been made to cultural bias. Denmark *et al.*'s (1988) report on sexism is meant to apply equally to all other major forms of bias, including cultural (see Box 55.4 page 592). Ironically, many feminist critics of Gilligan's ideas have argued that women are not a cohesive group who speak in a single voice, a view which imposes a false sameness upon the diversity of women's voices across differences of age, ethnicity, (dis)ability, class and other social divisions (Wilkinson, 1997).

Exercise 6

Before reading on, ask yourself what is meant by the term 'culture'. How is it related to 'race', 'ethnicity' and 'sub-cultures'?

Cross-cultural psychology and ethnocentrism

According to Smith & Bond (1998), cross-cultural psychology studies *variability* in behaviour among the various societies and cultural groups around the world. For Jahoda (1978), its additional goal is to identify what is *similar* across different cultures, and thus likely to be our common human heritage (the *universals* of human behaviour).

Cross-cultural psychology is important because it helps to correct *ethnocentrism*, the strong human tendency to use our own ethnic or cultural groups' norms and values to define what is 'natural' and 'correct' for everyone ('reality': Triandis, 1990). Historically, psychology has been dominated by white, middle class males in the USA. Over the last century, they have enjoyed a monopoly as both the researchers and the 'subjects' of the discipline (Moghaddam & Studer, 1997). They constitute the core of psychology's *First World* (Moghaddam, 1987).

Box 55.5 Psychology's First, Second and Third Worlds

- The USA, the *First World* of psychology, dominates the international arena and monopolises the manufacture of psychological knowledge, which it exports to other countries around the globe, through control over books and journals, test manufacture and distribution, training centres and so on.

- The *Second World* countries comprise Western European nations and Russia. They have far less influence in shaping psychology around the world, although, ironically, it is in these countries that modern psychology has its philosophical roots (see Chapte 58). Just as the countries of the Second World find themselves overpowered by American popular culture, they also find themselves overwhelmed by US-manufactured psychological knowledge.

- *Third World* countries are mostly importers of psychological knowledge, first from the USA but also from the Second World countries with which they historically had colonial ties (such as Pakistan and England). India is the most important Third World 'producer' of psychological knowledge, but even there most research follows the lines established by the US and, to a lesser extent, Western Europe.

(From Moghaddam & Studer, 1997)

According to Moghaddam *et al.* (1993), American researchers and participants:

' ... have shared a lifestyle and value system that differs not only from that of most other people in North America, such as ethnic minorities and women, but also the vast majority of people in the rest of the world'.

Yet the findings from this research, and the theories based upon it, have been applied to *people in general*, as if culture makes no difference. An implicit equation is made between 'human being' and 'human being from Western culture' (the *Anglocentric* or *Eurocentric bias)*.

When members of other cultural groups have been studied, it has usually been to *compare* them with Western samples, using the behaviour and experience of the latter as the 'standard'. As with androcentrism, it is the failure to acknowledge this bias which creates the misleading and false impression that what is being said about behaviour can be generalised without qualification.

Cross-cultural psychologists do *not* equate 'human being' with 'member of Western culture', because for them, cultural background is the crucial *independent variable*. In view of the domination of First World psychology, this distinction becomes crucial. At the same time, the search for universal principles of human behaviour is quite valid (and is consistent with the 'classical' view of science: see page 589 and Chapter 58).

What is culture?

Herskovits (1955) defines culture as 'the human-made part of the environment'. For Triandis (1994):

'Culture is to society what memory is to individuals. In other words, culture includes the traditions that tell 'what has worked' in the past. It also encompasses the way people have learned to look at their environment and themselves, and their unstated assumptions about the way the world is and the way people should act'.

The 'human-made' part of the environment can be broken down into *objective* aspects (such as tools, roads and radio stations) and *subjective* aspects (such as categorisations, associations, norms, roles and values). This allows us to examine how subjective culture influences behaviour (Triandis, 1994). Whilst culture is made by humans, it also helps to 'make' them: humans have an interactive relationship with culture (Moghaddam *et al.*, 1993).

Much cross-cultural research is actually based on 'national cultures', often comprising a number of subcultures, which may be demarcated by religion (as in Northern Ireland), language (Belgium), or race (Malaysia and Singapore). However, such research often fails to provide any more details about the participants than the name of the country (national culture) in which the study was done. When this happens, we pay two 'penalties'.

First, when we compare national cultures, we can lose track of the enormous diversity found within many of the major nations of the world, and differences found *between* any two countries might well also be found between carefully selected subcultures *within* those countries. Second, there is the danger of implying that national cultures are unitary systems, free of conflict, confusion and dissent. This is rarely the case (Smith & Bond, 1998).

How do cultures differ?

Definitions of culture such as those above stress what *different cultures* have in common. To evaluate research findings and theory that are culturally biased, it is even more important to consider the ways in which *cultures are different* from each other. Triandis (1990) identifies several *cultural syndromes*, which he defines as:

' ... a pattern of values, attitudes, beliefs, norms and behaviours that can be used to contrast a group of cultures to another group of cultures'.

Box 55.6 Three major cultural syndromes used to contrast different cultures

Three major cultural syndromes are *cultural complexity*, *individualism–collectivism*, and *tight vs loose cultures*.

- **Cultural complexity** refers to how much attention people must pay to time. This is related to the number and diversity of the roles that members of the culture typically play. More industrialised and technologically advanced cultures, such as Japan, Sweden and the USA, are more complex in this way. (The concept of time also differs between cultures: see Chapter 25, page 260).

- **Individualism–collectivism** refers to whether one's identity is defined by personal choices and achievements (the autonomous individual: individualism) or by characteristics of the collective group to which one is more or less permanently attached, such as the family, tribal or religious group, or country (collectivism). Whilst people in every culture display both, the relative emphasis in the West is towards individualism, and in the East towards collectivism. Broadly, capitalist politico-economic systems are associated with individualism, whilst socialist societies are associated with collectivism.

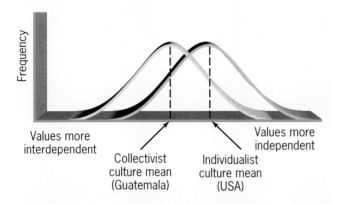

Figure 55.1 *Hypothetical distributions of interdependent/independent value scores in a collectivist and an individualist national culture (From Smith & Bond, 1998)*

- **Tight cultures** expect their members to behave according to clearly defined norms, and there is very little tolerance of deviation from those norms (see the criteria of normality/abnormality in Gross *et al.*, 2000). Japan is a good example of a tight culture, and Thailand an example of a **loose culture**.

(Based on Smith & Bond, 1998, and Triandis, 1990, 1994)

The emic–etic distinction

Research has to begin somewhere and, inevitably, this usually involves an instrument or observational technique rooted in the researcher's own culture (Berry, 1969). These can be used for studying *both* cross-cultural differences *and* universal aspects of human behaviour (or the 'psychic unity of mankind').

Exercise 7

Try to identify some behaviours (both normal and abnormal) which can be considered to have both universal (common to all cultures) and culture-specific features.

The distinction between culture-specific and universal behaviour is related to what cross-cultural psychologists call the *emic–etic distinction*, first made by Pike (1954) to refer to two different approaches to the study of behaviour. The *etic* looks at behaviour from outside a

particular cultural system, the *emic* from the inside. This derives from the distinction made in linguistics between phon*etics* (the study of universal sounds, independently of their meaning) and phon*emics* (the study of universal sounds as they contribute to meaning: see Chapter 26, page 270).

'Etics' refers to culturally general concepts, which are easier to understand (because they are common to all cultures), whilst 'emics' refers to culturally specific concepts, which include all the ways that particular cultures deal with etics. It is the emics of another culture that are often so difficult to understand (Brislin, 1993).

The research tools that the 'visiting' psychologist brings from 'home' are an emic for the home culture, but when they are assumed to be valid in the 'alien' culture and are used to compare them, they are said to be an *imposed etic* (Berry, 1969). Many attempts to replicate American studies in other parts of the world involve an imposed etic: they all assume that the situation being studied has the same meaning for members of the alien culture as it does for members of the researcher's own culture (Smith & Bond, 1998).

The danger of imposed etics is that they are likely to involve imposition of the researcher's own cultural biases and theoretical framework. These simply may not 'fit' the phenomena being studied, resulting in their distortion. A related danger is *ethnocentrism* (see page 593).

Box 55.7 Intelligence as an imposed etic

Brislin (1993) gives the example of the concept of intelligence. The etic is 'solving problems, the exact form of which hasn't been seen before', a definition which at least recognises that what constitutes a 'problem' differs between cultures. However, is the emic of 'mental quickness' (as measured by IQ tests, for example) universally valid? Among the Baganda people of Uganda, for example, intelligence is associated with slow, careful, deliberate thought (Wober, 1974). Nor is quick thinking necessarily a valid emic for all schoolchildren within a culturally diverse country like the USA (Brislin, 1993).

Psychologists need to adapt their methods, so that they are studying the same processes in different cultures (Moghaddam *et al.*, 1993). But how do we know that we are studying the same processes? What does 'same' mean in this context? For Brislin (1993), this is the problem of *equivalence*. The very experience of participating in psychological testing will be strange and unfamiliar to members of non-Western cultures (Lonner, 1990).

Even if measures are adapted for use in other cultures, psychologists should be aware that simply being asked to do a test may be odd for some people (Howat, 1999). For a detailed discussion of different kinds of equivalence, see Gross (1995).

Advantages of cross–cultural research

It may now seem obvious (almost 'common sense') to state that psychological theories must be based on the study of people's behaviours from all parts of the world. However, it is important to give specific reasons and examples in support of this argument.

Box 55.8 Major advantages of cross-cultural research

- **Highlighting implicit assumptions:** Cross-cultural research allows investigators to examine the influence of their own beliefs and assumptions, revealing how human behaviour cannot be separated from its cultural context.

- **Separating behaviour from context:** Being able to stand back from their own cultural experiences allows researchers to appreciate the impact of situational factors on behaviour. They are thus less likely to make the *fundamental attribution error* (see Chapter 1), or to use a 'deficit model' to explain the performances of minority group members.

- **Extending the range of variables:** Cross-cultural research expands the range of variables and concepts that can be explored. For example, people in individualist and collectivist cultures tend to explain behaviour in different ways, with the latter less likely to make *dispositional attributions* (see Chapter 1).

- **Separating variables:** Cross-cultural research allows the separation of the effects of variables that may be confounded within a particular culture. For example, studying the effects of television on school achievement is very difficult using just British or American samples, since the vast majority of these families own (at least) one TV set!

- **Testing theories:** Only by conducting cross-cultural research can Western psychologists be sure whether their theories and research findings are relevant outside of their own cultural contexts. For example, Thibaut and Kelley's exchange theory of relationships (see Chapter 5, page 45), and Sherif *et al.*'s 'Robber's Cave' field experiment on intergroup conflict (see Box 3.6, page 25) have all failed the replication test outside of North American settings.

(Based on Rogoff & Morelli, 1989; Brislin, 1993; Moghaddam *et al.*, 1993, and Smith & Bond, 1998)

Cross–cultural versus cultural psychology

Several criticisms have been made of cross-cultural psychology, mainly from *cultural psychologists*, for whom mind is embedded in a sociohistorical process that shapes and creates 'multiple realities' (Shweder, 1990). Instead of trying to identify universal 'laws' of psychological functioning (a major goal of cross-cultural psychology), cultural psychologists adopt a *relativistic* approach and stress the *uniqueness* of different cultures (as in *indigenous* psychology). Whilst cross-cultural psychology is an outgrowth of 'mainstream' psychology (see Chapter 58), with an emphasis on natural scientific methods, cultural psychology can be seen as a rejection of mainstream psychology, favouring the use of qualitative and ethnographic approaches (Martin, 1998: see Gross *et al.*, 2000).

CONCLUSIONS

This chapter considered many different examples of how mainstream psychology is biased and, therefore, much less objective and value-free than is required by the positivist view of science it has traditionally modelled itself on. Whilst gender and culture bias are often discussed separately, this chapter showed that they are actually quite closely related. Despite its shortcomings,

Moghaddam & Studer (1997) believe that cross-cultural psychology is one of the avenues through which minorities have begun to have their voices heard in psychology and that:

' ... there has been a demand that psychology make good its claim to being the science of *humankind* by including women and non-whites as research participants.'

Summary

- A **positivist** study of people implies an objective, value-free psychology, in which the psychologist's characteristics have no influence on the investigation's outcome. However, **sexism** and **ethnocentrism** pervade much psychological theory and research.

- **Feminist psychologists** challenge mainstream psychology's theories about women, who are either excluded from research studies or whose experiences are assimilated to/matched against male norms (**androcentrism/the masculinist bias**).

- Male power and social and political oppression are screened out through **individualism,** thus playing down the **social context**. This reinforces popular gender stereotypes, contributing to women's oppression.

- Feminist psychologists also challenge psychology's claim to be an objective, value-free science. Decisions about what constitutes legitimate research are made by individual scientists within a socio-political context, making science ideological.

- Scientific method itself is gender-biased, concentrating on the 'subject's' behaviour, rather than its meaning, and ignoring contextual influences. These typically include a male experimenter who controls the situation.

- Using psychometric test results, Wilson argues that men and women differ in terms of mental abilities, motivation, personality, and values, which are based in biology. This demonstrates **alpha-bias**.

- According to Denmark *et al.*, gender bias is found at all stages of the **research process**. The last stage (conclusion formulation) is related to **theory construction**. Levinson *et al.*'s, Erikson's, and Kohlberg's theories all claim to present **universal** accounts of development. In fact, they are based on all-male samples and describe the world from male perspectives (**beta-bias**).

- **Cross-cultural psychology** is concerned with both behavioural **variability** between cultural groups and behavioural **universals**. It also helps to correct **ethnocentrism**.

- American researchers and participants share a lifestyle and value system which differ from those of both most other North Americans and the rest of the world's population. Yet the research findings are applied to **people in general**, disregarding culture's relevance (the **Anglocentric/Eurocentric bias**).

- **Culture** is the human-made part of the environment, comprising both **objective** and **subjective** aspects. When cross-cultural researchers compare national cultures, they fail to recognise the great diversity often found **within** them, implying that national cultures are free of conflict and dissent.

- Cultural differences can be assessed in terms of three major **cultural syndromes**, namely, **cultural complexity**, **individualism–collectivism**, and **tight vs. loose cultures**. Whilst members of every culture display both individualism and collectivism, the relative emphasis in the West is towards the former, and in the East towards the latter.

- The distinction between culture-specific and universal behaviour corresponds to the **emic–etic distinction**. When Western psychologists study non-Western cultures, they often use research tools which are emic for them but an **imposed etic** for the culture being studied. This involves imposition of the researcher's own cultural biases and theoretical framework, producing distortion of the phenomenon under investigation.

- Cross-cultural research allows researchers to examine the influence of their own beliefs and assumptions, and to appreciate the impact of situational factors on behaviour. It also allows separation of the effects of variables that may usually be confounded within the researchers' own cultures.

- Only by doing cross-cultural research can Western psychologists be sure that their theories and research findings are relevant outside their own cultural contexts.

- Cross-cultural psychology is an outgrowth of mainstream psychology, adopting a natural scientific approach. **Cultural psychologists** reject this approach in favour of qualitative and ethnographic methods, stressing the **uniqueness** of different cultures.

Essay Questions

1 'Whilst psychologists claim to study "human beings", their theories and research studies in fact apply only to a very limited sample of the world's population.'

Critically consider the view that psychological theory **and/or** research studies are culturally biased.

(30 marks)

2 Critically consider the view that psychological theory **and/or** research studies are gender-biased.

(30 marks)

WEB ADDRESSES

http://www.vix.com/men/articles/genderbiastest/html
http://www.millisecond.com/seandr/psych/BuchResp.html
http://www.iupui.edu/~anthkb/ethnocen.htm
http://www.nova.edu/ssss/FemMed/fmp.html

56 *Ethical Issues in Psychology*

One of psychology's unique features is that people are both the investigators and the subject matter (see Chapter 58, page 633). This means that the 'things' studied in a psychological investigation are capable of thoughts and feelings. Biologists and medical researchers share this problem of subjecting living, sentient things to sometimes painful, stressful or strange and unusual experiences.

Just as Orne (1962) regards the psychological experiment as primarily a *social situation* (which raises questions of objectivity: see Chapter 58, page 633), so every psychological investigation is an *ethical situation* (raising questions of propriety and responsibility). Similarly, just as *methodological* issues permeate psychological research, so do *ethical* issues. For example, the *aims* of psychology as a science (see Chapter 58) concern what is *appropriate* as much as what is *possible*. Social psychology's use of stooges to deceive naïve participants (see Gross *et al.*, 2000), and the surgical manipulation of animals' brains in physiological psychology (Chapters 10, 16 and 17) are further examples of the essential difference between the study of the physical world and that of humans and non-humans. What psychologists can and cannot do is determined by the effects of the research on those being studied, as much as by what they want to find out.

Gross *et al.* (2000) discuss several ethical issues arising from the study of social influence , including *protection from harm*, *deception* and *informed consent*, and *debriefing*. Gross *et al.* show how *codes of conduct* and *ethical guidelines* have been produced to protect human participants, regardless of the particular research being conducted.

However, psychologists are *practitioners* as well as scientists and investigators. They work in practical and clinical settings, where people with psychological problems require help (see Chapters 52–54). Whenever the possibility of *changing* people arises, ethical issues also arise, just as they do in medicine and psychiatry. This chapter looks at the ethical issues faced by psychologists as *scientists/investigators*, both of humans and non-humans, and as *practitioners*.

CODES OF CONDUCT AND ETHICAL GUIDELINES

Whilst there are responsibilities and obligations common to both the scientist and practitioner roles, there are also some important differences. These are reflected in the *codes of conduct and ethical guidelines* published by the major professional bodies for psychologists – the British Psychological Society (BPS) and the American Psychological Association (APA).

The *Code of Conduct for Psychologists* (BPS, 1985: see Figure 56.1, page 600) applies to the major areas of both research and practice, and there are additional documents designed for the two areas separately. The *Ethical Principles for Conducting Research with Human Participants* (BPS, 1990, 1993) and the *Guidelines for the Use of Animals in Research* (BPS and the Committee of the Experimental Psychological Society, 1985) obviously apply to the former, whilst, for example, the *Guidelines for the Professional Practice of Clinical Psychology* (BPS, 1983) apply to the latter.

Exercise 1

Do you think it is necessary for psychologists to have written codes of conduct and ethical guidelines? What do you consider to be their major functions?

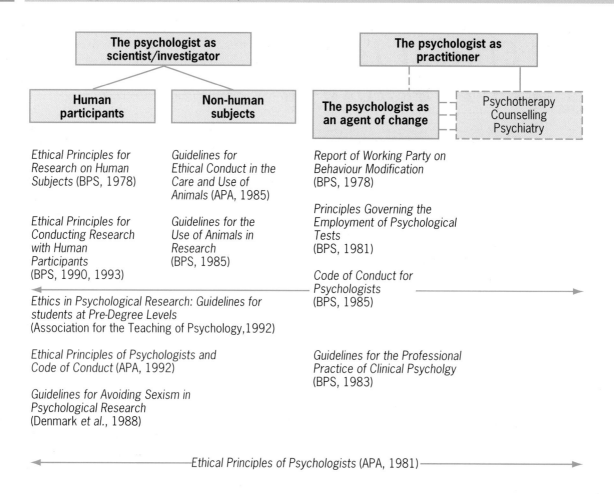

Figure 56.1 *Major codes of conduct/ethical guidelines published by the British Psychological Society (BPS) and the American Psychological Association (APA)*

PSYCHOLOGISTS AS SCIENTISTS/INVESTIGATORS: HUMAN PARTICIPANTS

Widening the ethical debate: protecting the individual versus harming the group

Gross *et al.*'s (2000) discussion of the ethics of psychological research focuses on the vulnerability of individual participants, and psychologists' responsibilities to ensure that they do not suffer in any way from their experience of participating. Whilst 'protection of participants' is one of the specific principles included in the *Ethical Principles for Conducting Research with Human Participants* (BPS, 1990, 1993), *all* the principles (informed consent, avoidance of deception, and so on) are designed to prevent any harm coming to the participant, or the avoidance of overt 'sins' (Brown, 1997).

As important as this is, little attention is paid to errors of omission or covert expressions of damaging assumptions, attitudes and values which are, often unconsciously, helping to shape the research questions (see Chapters 55 and 58). Whilst individual participants may be protected from overt harm, the *social groups* to which they belong (and which they represent in the research context) may be harmed as a consequence of the research findings.

Exercise 2

Re-read Chapter 55. Try to identify some fundamental values and biases that are potentially damaging to particular social groups. In what ways are these values/biases harmful to these groups?

Box 56.1 The ethics of ethical codes: underlying assumptions

According to Brown (1997), one core assumption underlying ethical codes is that what psychologists do as researchers, clinicians, teachers and so on is basically harmless and inherently valuable because it is based on 'science' (defined as *positivism*: see Chapter 58). Consequently, it is possible for a psychologist to conduct technically ethical research but still do great harm. For example, a researcher can adhere strictly to 'scientific' research methodologies, get technically adequate informed consent from participants (and not breach any of the other major prescribed principles), but still conduct research which claims to show the inferiority of a particular group. Because it is conducted according to 'the rules' (both methodological and ethical), the question of whether it is ethical in the broader sense to pursue such matters is ignored.

For example, neither Jensen (1969) nor Herrnstein (1971) was ever considered by mainstream psychology to have violated psychology's ethics by the questions they asked regarding the intellectual inferiority of African Americans (see Chapter 29). Individual black participants were not harmed by being given IQ tests, and might even have found them interesting and challenging. However, the way the findings were interpreted and used:

' ... weakened the available social supports for people of colour by stigmatising them as genetically inferior, thus strengthening the larger culture's racist attitudes. Research ethics as currently construed by mainstream ethics codes do not require researchers to put the potential for this sort of risk into their informed consent documents' (Brown, 1997).

Jensen's and Herrnstein's research (highlighted by Herrnstein and Murray in '*The Bell Curve*', 1994) has profoundly harmed black Americans. Ironically, the book has received much *methodological* criticism, but only black psychologists (such as Hilliard, 1995, and Sue, 1995) have raised the more fundamental question of whether simply conducting such studies might be ethically dubious. As Brown observes:

'To ask this question about the risks of certain types of inquiry challenges science's hegemony as the source of all good in psychology'.

Herrnstein and Murray, Rushton (1995), Brand (cited in Richards, 1996a) and others, like the Nazi scientists of the 1930s, claim that the study of race differences is a purely 'objective' and 'scientific' enterprise (Howe, 1997).

If it is thought unethical to deceive individual black or female participants about the purposes of some particular study, but ethically acceptable to use the results to support the claim that blacks or women are genetically inferior, then this narrow definition of ethics makes it an ineffective way of guiding research into socially sensitive issues (Howitt, 1991). Formal codes continue to focus narrowly on risks to the individual participant, in the specific context of the investigation, but neglect questions about the risks to the group to which the participant belongs.

'As long as research ethics avoid the matter of whether certain questions ethically cannot be asked, psychologists will conduct technically ethical research that violates a more general ethic of avoiding harm to vulnerable populations' (Brown, 1997).

Protecting the individual versus benefiting society

If the questions psychologists ask are limited and shaped by the values of individual researchers, they are also limited and shaped by considerations of *methodology* (what it is *possible* to do, practically, when investigating human behaviour and experience). For example, in the context of intimate relationships (see Chapters 4–6), Brehm (1992) claims that, by its nature, the laboratory experiment is extremely limited in the kinds of questions it allows psychologists to investigate.

Conversely, and just as importantly, there are certain aspects of behaviour and experience which *could* be studied experimentally, although it would be unethical to do so, such as 'jealousy between partners participating in laboratory research' (Brehm, 1992). Indeed:

'All types of research in this area involve important ethical dilemmas. Even if all we do is to ask subjects to fill out questionnaires describing their relationships, we need to think carefully about how this research experience might affect them and their partner' (Brehm, 1992).

So, what it may be *possible* to do may be *unacceptable*, but equally, what may be *acceptable* may not be *possible*. However, just as focusing on protection of individual participants can work to the detriment of whole groups (see above), so it can discourage psychologists from carrying out *socially meaningful* research (what Brehm, 1992, calls the *ethical imperative*) which, potentially, may improve the quality of people's lives. Social psychologists in particular have a *two-fold* ethical obligation, to individual participants *and* to society at large (Myers, 1994). This relates to discussion of psychology's *aims* as a science (see Chapter 58). Similarly, Aronson (1992) argues that social psychologists are:

'... obligated to use their research skills to advance our knowledge and understanding of human behaviour for the ultimate aim of human betterment. In short, social psychologists have an ethical responsibility to the society as a whole'.

Talking about the aim of 'human betterment' raises important questions about basic *values*. It opens out the ethical debate in such a way that values must be addressed and recognised as part of the research process (something advocated very strongly by feminist psychologists: see above and Chapter 55).

Exercise 3

Before reading on, try to think of some examples of how research findings that you are familiar with might be used to *benefit people in general*. You may find it useful to focus on social psychology.

Box 56.2 An example of the benefits of social psychological research

In many bystander intervention studies (e.g. Latané & Darley, 1968: see Chapter 8), people are deceived into believing that an 'emergency' is taking place. Many of Latané and Darley's participants were very distressed by their experiences, especially those in the experiment in which they believed another participant was having an epileptic fit. Yet when asked to complete a post-experimental questionnaire (which followed a very careful debriefing), *all* said they believed the deception was justified and would be willing to participate in similar experiments again. None reported any feelings of anger towards the experimenter.

Beaman *et al.* (1978) built on these earlier experiments. They used a lecture to inform students about how bystanders' refusals to help can influence both one's interpretation of an emergency and feelings of responsibility. Two other groups of students heard either a different lecture or no lecture at all. Two weeks later, as part of a different experiment in a different location, the participants found themselves (accompanied by an unresponsive stooge) walking past someone who was slumped over or sprawled under a bike. Of those who had heard the lecture about helping behaviour, 50 per cent stopped to offer help compared with 25 per cent who had not.

This suggests that the results of psychological research can be used to make us more aware of influences on behaviour, making it more likely that we will act differently armed with that knowledge from how we might otherwise have done. In the case of bystander intervention, this 'consciousness-raising' is

beneficial in a tangible way to the person who is helped. Being more sensitive to the needs of others, and feeling satisfied by having helped another person, may also be seen as beneficial to the helper.

The 'double obligation dilemma'

The dilemma faced by social psychologists (regarding their obligations to society and individual participants) is greatest when investigating important areas such as conformity, obedience and bystander intervention (Aronson, 1992). In general, the more important the issue, (i) the greater the potential benefit for society, and (ii) the more likely an individual participant is to experience distress and discomfort. This is because the more important the issue, the more essential the use of *deception* becomes (see Gross *et al.*, 2000).

Psychologists want to know how people are likely to behave if they found themselves in that situation *outside the laboratory*. This raises several crucial *methodological* questions (such as experimental realism, external validity or mundane realism: see Chapter 58 and Gross *et al.*, 2000). However, the key *ethical* issue hinges on the fact that the use of deception *both* contributes enormously (and perhaps irreplaceably) to our understanding of human behaviour (helping to satisfy the obligation to society), and at the same time significantly increases individual participants' distress (detracting from the responsibility to protect individuals).

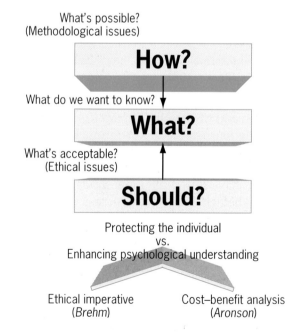

Figure 56.2 *Ethical and methodological constraints on the questions that psychologists can try to answer through the research process*

Box 56.3 Some proposed solutions to the 'double obligation dilemma

- Having accepted that, under certain circumstances, deception is permissible, most psychologists still advocate that it should not be used unless it is considered *essential* (Milgram, 1992; Aronson, 1992). This is consistent with the BPS *Ethical Principles*.

- Aronson (1992) advocates a *cost–benefit analysis*: weighing how much 'good' (benefits to society) will derive from doing the research against how much 'bad' will happen to the participants.

- Milgram (1992) believes that if the experimental creation of stress or conflict were excluded on principle, and only studies which produced positive emotions were allowed, this would produce

  '... a very lopsided psychology, one that caricatured rather than accurately reflected human experience'.

  Traditionally, the most deeply informative experiments in social psychology include those examining how participants resolve *conflicts*, such as Asch's studies of conformity (truth versus conformity: see Gross *et al.*, 2000), Latané and Darley's bystander intervention studies (getting involved in another's troubles versus not getting involved: see Chapter 8), and Milgram's own obedience experiments (internal conscience versus external authority: see Gross *et al.*, 2000).

- Two compromise solutions to the problem of not being able to obtain informed consent are *presumptive consent* (of 'reasonable people') and *prior general consent*. In the former, the views of many people are obtained about an experimental procedure's acceptability. These people would not participate in the actual experiment (if it went ahead), but their views could be taken as evidence of how people in general would react to participation.

  Prior general consent could be obtained from people who might, subsequently, serve as experimental participants. Before volunteering to join a pool of research volunteers, people would be explicitly told that sometimes participants are misinformed about a study's true purpose and sometimes experience emotional stress. Only those agreeing would be chosen (Milgram, 1992). This is a compromise solution, because people would be giving their 'informed consent' (a) well in advance of the actual study, (b) only in a very general way, and (c) without knowing what specific manipulations/deceptions will be used in the particular experiment in which they participate. It seems to fall somewhere between 'mere' consent and full 'informed consent' (and could be called *semi- or partially informed consent*).

PSYCHOLOGISTS AS SCIENTISTS/INVESTIGATORS: NON-HUMAN SUBJECTS

The BPS Scientific Affairs Board published its *Guidelines for the Use of Animals in Research* (1985), in conjunction with the Committee of the Experimental Psychological Society. It offers a checklist of points which investigators should carefully consider when planning experiments with living non-humans. Researchers have a general obligation to:

'... avoid, or at least to minimise, discomfort to living animals ... discuss any future research with their local Home Office Inspector and colleagues who are experts in the topic ... seek ... Widespread advice as to whether the likely scientific contribution of the work ... justifies the use of living animals, and whether the scientific point they wish to make may not be made without the use of living animals' [BPS, 1985].

This raises two fundamental questions: (a) how do we know non-humans suffer?, and (b) what goals can ever justify subjecting them to pain and suffering?

How do we know that non-humans suffer?

Exercise 4

Identify examples of experiments involving non-humans in which they suffered pain and distress. Try to specify *in what ways* suffering occurred.

Box 56.4 Some criteria for judging non–human suffering

- Disease and injury are generally recognised as major causes of suffering. Consequently, research such as Brady's (1958) 'executive monkey' experiments would probably not even be debated in the current climate (Mapstone, 1991). Brady attached pairs of monkeys to an apparatus which gave electric shocks, such that one monkey (the 'executive': see Figure 56.3, page 604) could prevent the shock by pressing a lever, but the other could not. The former developed ulcers and eventually died.

- Even if we are sure that non-humans are not suffering physically, their confinement might cause mental suffering not affecting their external condition (Dawkins, 1980). For example, apparently healthy zoo and farm animals often show bizarre behaviours.

Figure 56.3 *An 'executive monkey'*

- We must *find out* about non-human suffering by careful observation and experimentation. Because different species have different requirements, lifestyles, and, perhaps, emotions, we cannot *assume* that we know about their suffering or well-being without studying them species by species (Dawkins, 1980).

Drawing on the Institute of Medical Ethics (IME) Working Party's report (Haworth, 1992), Bateson (1986, 1992) has proposed criteria for assessing animal suffering, including:

- possessing receptors sensitive to noxious or painful stimulation, and

- having brain structures comparable to the human cerebral cortex.

Bateson (1992) tentatively concludes that insects probably do not experience pain, whereas fish and octopi probably do. However, the boundaries between the presence and absence of pain are 'fuzzy'.

Exercise 5

Try to formulate arguments for and against the use of non-humans in research. This should not be confined to *psychological* research, since much of the debate takes place in relation to medicine, pharmacology and so on.

How can we justify experiments with non-humans?

The question of suffering wouldn't arise if non-humans were not being used in experiments in the first place. According to Gray (1987), the main justifications for non-human experimentation are the *pursuit of scientific knowledge* and the *advancement of medicine*.

To justify the use of non-humans, especially when very stressful procedures are used, the research must be rigorously designed and the potential results must represent a significant contribution to our knowledge of medicine, pharmacology, biopsychology or psychology as a whole. This is a safeguard against distressing research being carried out for its own sake, or at the researcher's whim.

The *Guidelines* state that if the non-humans are confined, constrained, harmed or stressed in any way, the experimenter must consider whether the knowledge to be gained justifies the procedure. Some knowledge is trivial, and experiments must not be done simply because it is possible to do them. To take the executive monkeys experiments again (see Box 56.4), the medical justification (to discover why business executives develop ulcers) was insufficient to justify their continuation. The monkeys' obvious suffering superseded even the combination of scientific and medical justification. However, there are other cases where, whilst the scientific justification may be apparent, the medical justification is much less so, such as Olds & Milner's (1954) experiments where non-humans' brains are stimulated via implantation of a permanent electrode (electrical self-stimulation of the brain/ES-SB: see Box 17.5, page 170).

Figure 56.4 *Animal Liberation Front activists with beagles after a raid on a laboratory owned by 'Boots the Chemist'*

Safeguards for non-human subjects

Whatever practical application Olds and Milner's ES-SB experiments may have subsequently had (such as pain/anxiety relief in psychotics, epileptics and cancer patients), they don't seem to have been conducted with such human applications in mind. Can the scientific knowledge gained about ES-SB as a very powerful positive reinforcer *on its own* justify the rats' eventual 'sacrifice'? The very least required of researchers is that the minimum of suffering is caused, both during and following any surgical procedure and by any electric shock or food deprivation, the most objected-to treatments (Gray, 1987).

Box 56.5 Some safeguards for non-human subjects

- Gray (1987) claims that food deprivation is *not* a source of suffering, and that rats (the most commonly used experimental subjects in psychology) are either fed once a day when experimentation is over, or maintained at 85 per cent of their free-feeding (*ad lib.*) body weight. Both are actually *healthier* than allowing them to eat *ad lib.* Electric shock may cause *some* but not *extreme* pain (based on observations of the animals' behaviour). The level permitted is controlled by the Home Office (HO) inspectors, who monitor implementation of The Animals (Scientific Procedures) Act (1986). The average level used in the UK is 0.68 milli-amperes, for an average of 0.57 seconds. This produces an unpleasant tickling sensation in humans.

- Procedures causing pain or distress are illegal, unless the experimenter holds an HO licence and relevant certificates. Even then, there should be no alternative ways of conducting the experiment without the use of aversive stimulation. Similarly, it is illegal in the UK to perform any surgical or pharmacological procedure on vertebrates (or one invertebrate – the octopus) without an HO licence and relevant certification. Such procedures must be performed by experienced staff.

- The *Guidelines* stress the importance of understanding *species differences* in relation to (i) caging and social environment, (ii) the stress involved in marking wild animals for identification or attaching them with radio transmitters, and (iii) the duration of food/drink deprivation. Field workers should disturb non-humans as little as possible. Even simple observation of non-humans in the wild can have marked effects on their breeding and survival.

- The number of non-humans used in laboratory experiments is declining. For example, in the UK, the Netherlands, Germany and several other European countries, the numbers have fallen by half since the 1970s (Mukerjee, 1997). However, the UK still uses approximately three million non-humans a year in experiments (85 per cent of which are mice, rats and other rodents). By comparison, over 700 million non-humans are killed for food every year (Nursing Times, 1996).

- The UK, Australia, Germany and several other countries require a utilitarian *cost–benefit analysis* (non-human pain, distress and death *versus* acquisition of new knowledge and the development of new medical therapies for humans) to be performed before any non-human experiment can proceed (Mukerjee, 1997; Rowan, 1997). Interestingly, this is what most non-scientists also seem to do (Aldhous *et al.*, 1999: see Box 56.7, pages 606–607).

Despite these safeguards, the very existence of the 1986 Act condones the use of non-humans. Legally, the Act aims to spare animals 'unnecessary' pain and distress; implicitly, the law accepts that some research will involve suffering for the non-human subjects. In this way, we signal our unease but accept that there is no alternative. Under the Act, applications for project licences have to say whether they have considered alternatives to using non-humans, and in granting the licence the Home Secretary must weigh up the likely benefit of the research against the adverse effects on the animal subjects. However, there is no remit to consider whether the proposed research is truly necessary (Seymour, 1996). Also, the Medicines Act (1968) requires that all new medicines have undergone a range of tests on non-humans before they can be tested on humans (Lyall, 1993: see Box 56.6, page 606).

The medical justification argument

The strongest argument for non-human experiments is undoubtedly the advancement of medical knowledge and treatments. However, it is easy for *scientific* and *ethical* issues to become confused. Demonstrations of what has been achieved in a practical sense from non-human experiments represents only a *minimum* requirement for their justification. So, only if it can be convincingly shown, for example, that many drugs used in the treatment of human diseases (including anti-cancer drugs, AIDS treatments, anti-epileptic and anti-depressant drugs: Green, 1994) have been developed using non-humans, and could not have been developed otherwise, can the ethical debate begin.

Box 56.6 Are non-human experiments scientifically useful?

The case for

- Non-human experiments have played a crucial role in the development of modern medical treatments, and will continue to be necessary as researchers seek to alleviate existing ailments and respond to the emergence of new diseases.

- The causes of and vaccines for dozens of infectious diseases, including diphtheria, tetanus, rabies, whooping cough, tuberculosis, poliomyelitis, measles, mumps, and rubella, have been determined largely through non-human experimentation. It has also led to the development of antibacterial and antibiotic drugs.

- Non-human research has also been vital to areas of medicine, such as open-heart surgery, kidney failure and organ transplantation, diabetes, malignant hypertension, and gastric ulcers.

- There are no basic differences between the physiologies of laboratory animals and humans. Both control their internal biochemistries by releasing the same basic endocrine hormones, both send out similar chemical transmitters from neurons in the CNS and PNS, and both react in the same way to infection or tissue injury. Non-human models of disease (see below) are intended to provide a means of studying a particular procedure (such as gene therapy for cystic fibrosis).

The case against

- Through genetic manipulation, surgical intervention, or injection of foreign substances, researchers produce diseases in laboratory animals that 'model' human diseases. However, evolutionary pressures have produced innumerable subtle differences between species, and the knock-on effect of applying a stimulus to one particular organ system on the non-human's overall physiological functioning is often unpredictable and not fully understood.

- Important medical advances have been delayed because of misleading results from non-human experiments. Cancer research is especially sensitive to physiological differences between species. Rats and mice, for example, synthesise about 100 times the recommended daily allowance of vitamin C believed to help the (human) body ward off cancer. Penicillin is toxic to guinea-pigs, whilst morphine stimulates cats (the opposite effect to that in humans).

- The stress of handling, confinement, and isolation alters a non-human's physiology, introducing a variable that makes extrapolating results to humans even more difficult. Laboratory stress can increase non-humans' susceptibility to infectious disease and certain tumours, as well as influencing hormone and antibody levels.

- Non-human experiments to test the safety of drugs are confounded by the fact that tests on different species often produce conflicting results.

(Based on Barnard & Kaufman, 1997, Botting & Morrison, 1997, Mukerjee, 1997, and Sawyer, 1996)

Green (1994), Carlson (1992) and many other biopsychologists believe that the potential benefits of non-human experiments is sufficient to justify their use.

Exercise 6

Critically consider the claim that particular non-human species, namely those that are closest to us in an evolutionary sense, should be given 'special consideration' in the context of animal experiments.

Box 56.7 Chimpanzees, AIDS and moral responsibility

What will become of several hundred research 'veterans' that are now considered to be of no further value to medical science? Their plight is a direct consequence of their genetic similarity to human beings, which makes them ideal models for the study of several diseases afflicting people worldwide, and the quest to find vaccines against them. During the 1970s, chimpanzees started to be used in large numbers in biomedical research in the USA. This came with the development of vaccines against hepatitis B, and later in a still unrealised search for a hepatitis C vaccine.

Some scientists lobbied for retirement facilities for the chimpanzees, but many began to seriously consider euthanasia as the only practical way to alleviate the crisis. Ironically, it was the AIDS epidemic in the mid-1980s which 'saved' the very chimpanzees that were 'used up'. Once again, they became 'surrogate human beings', this time in the development of HIV vaccines.

Yet by the mid-1990s, scientists began to turn to human volunteers for the initial testing of HIV vaccines, leaving large numbers of 'redundant' chimpanzees, which have a lifespan of up to 40 years. A report by the US National Research Council (1997) concluded that chimpanzees should be afforded special consideration, on ethical grounds, over other non-humans, and that euthanasia is *not* an acceptable means of population control. This is consistent with one of the findings of a recent MORI poll conducted in the UK, namely that people are more likely to oppose experiments on monkeys than those on mice. Only those experiments designed to test or develop drugs to treat childhood leukemia were seen as justifying monkeys' suffering (Aldhous *et al.*, 1999).

(Based on Mahoney, 1998)

Speciesism: extending the medical justification argument

According to Gray (1991), whilst most people (both experimenters and animal rights activists) would accept the ethical principle that inflicting pain is wrong, we are sometimes faced with having to choose between different ethical principles, which may mean having to choose between human and non-human suffering. Gray believes that *speciesism* (discriminating against and exploiting animals because they belong to a particular [non-human] species: Ryder, 1990) *is* justified, and argues that:

> 'Not only is it not wrong to give preference to the interests of one's own species, one has a duty to do so'.

Such a moral choice involves establishing a calculus (Dawkins, 1990), which pits the suffering of non-humans against the human suffering which the former's use will alleviate. For Gray (1991):

> 'In many cases the decision not to carry out certain experiments with animals (even if they would inflict pain or suffering) is likely to have the consequence that more people will undergo pain or suffering that might otherwise be avoided'.

One of the problems associated with the pro-speciesism argument is that medical advance may only become possible after extensive development of knowledge and scientific understanding in a particular field (Gray, 1991). In the meantime, scientific understanding may be the only specific objective that the experiment can readily attain. It is at this interim stage that the suffering imposed on experimental animals will far outweigh any (lesser) suffering eventually avoided by people, and this is at the core of the decisions that must be made by scientists and ethical committees.

PSYCHOLOGISTS AS PRACTITIONERS

Clinical psychologists (as well as educational psychologists, psychotherapists, psychiatrists, social workers, nurses, counsellors and other professionals) are concerned with bringing about *psychological change*. It is in their capacities as *agents of change* that clinical psychologists face their greatest ethical challenges.

Exercise 7

Consider some of the ethical issues faced by psychologists attempting to change other people's behaviour. Some are of a general nature, such as freedom versus determinism (see Chapter 57), others will overlap with ethical principles governing research (such as confidentiality and informed consent), and yet others may be specific to particular therapeutic approaches (see Chapters 52–54).

According to Fairbairn & Fairbairn (1987), clinical psychologists:

> '... must decide how they will interact with those who seek their help; for example, whether in general they will regard them as autonomous beings with rights and responsibilities, or rather as helpless individuals, incapable of rational choice'.

Fairbairn and Fairbairn argue that two quite common beliefs likely to detract from an explicit consideration of professional ethics and values in psychological practice are (a) that psychology is a value-free science, and (b) that therapists should be value-neutral or 'non-directive'.

Psychology as value-free science

Central to clinical (and counselling) psychology is the *scientist–practitioner model* of helping (Dallos & Cullen, 1990). This sees clinical psychology as being guided by, and operating within, the framework of the general scientific method (see Chapters 55 and 58). If clinical psychologists view clinical psychology as having firm foundations in positivist science, they may disregard ethics because these are not amenable to objective consideration. However, even if the psychological knowledge used in clinical practice was always the result of the application of an objective scientific method, moral questions of an interpersonal kind are bound to arise *at the point at which it is applied* (Fairbairn & Fairbairn, 1987).

This distinction between possession of knowledge and its application ('science' versus 'technology') is fundamental to any discussion of ethics, because it is related to the notion of *responsibility*. Presumably, clinical psychologists *choose* which techniques to use with clients and how to use them. The mere existence (and even the demonstrated effectiveness) of certain techniques does not *in itself* mean that they must be used. Similarly, the kind of research which clinical psychologists consider worth doing (and which then provides the scientific basis for the use of particular techniques) is a matter of choice, and reflects views regarding the nature of people and how they can be changed (see Gross *et al.*, 2000).

Box 56.8 Criticisms of scientific behaviour therapy and modification

- Because of (rather than despite) its espoused status as a value-free, applied science, behaviour therapy and modification tend to devalue and thereby dehumanise their clients by treating people, for 'scientific' purposes as if they were 'organisms' as opposed to 'agents', helpless victims of forces outside their control. This criticism also applies to medical psychiatry and classical psychoanalysis, except that both see the controlling forces as being internal (organic abnormalities or intra-psychic forces, respectively) as opposed to environmental contingencies (see Gross *et al.*, 2000).

- Clients soon come to believe that they are abnormal, helpless and also worthless, because this is part of the culture-wide stereotype of 'mental illness' and related terms. Negative self-evaluation and passivity characterise many, if not most, mental health clients, who think and behave like passive organisms. The solution lies in helping people recover, or discover, their agency.

(Based on Trower, 1987)

Therapists as value-neutral and non-directive

If psychology as a value-free science involves not regarding or treating clients fully as human beings, this second major issue is about the therapist or psychologist functioning as something less than a complete person within the therapeutic situation. Providing help and support in a non-directive, value-free way is a tradition for psychotherapists and counsellors (Fairbairn & Fairbairn, 1987). However, such an approach may seem to require remaining aloof and distant from the client which, in turn, may entail not treating the client with respect as a person, since this requires the therapist to recognise that the client is a person like him- or herself.

Exercise 8

Evaluate the claim that it is possible for therapists not to have any influence over their clients/patients.

The influence of the therapist

Adopting what is thought to be a value-free position in therapy may lead therapists to deny the importance or influence of their own moral values, which are often hidden in therapy. This kind of influence is much more subtle and covert than the coercion that can operate on hospitalised psychiatric patients, even voluntary ones. The in-patient is subjected to strong persuasion to accept the treatment recommendations of professional staff. As Davison & Neale (1994) observe:

> 'Even a 'voluntary' and informed decision to take psychotropic medication or to participate in any other therapy regimen is often (maybe usually) less than free'.

Box 56.9 Therapist influence in psychodynamic and behaviour therapy

The issue of the therapist's influence on the patient/client has been central to a long-standing debate between traditional (psychodynamic) psychotherapists and behaviour therapists (who are usually clinical psychologists by training: see Chapters 53 and 54). Psychotherapists regard behaviour therapy as unacceptable (even if it works), because it is manipulative and demeaning of human dignity. By contrast, they see their own methods as fostering the autonomous development of the patient's inherent potential, helping the patient to express his or her true self, and so on. Instead of influencers, they see themselves as 'psychological midwives', present during the birth, possessing useful skills, but there primarily to make sure that a natural process goes smoothly.

However, this is an exaggeration and misrepresentation of both approaches. For many patients, the 'birth' would probably not happen at all without the therapist's intervention, and s/he undoubtedly influences the patient's behaviour. Conversely, behaviour therapists are at least partly successful because they establish active, cooperative relationships with the patients, who play much more active roles in the therapy than psychotherapists believe.

All therapists, of whatever persuasion, if they are at all effective, influence their patients. Both approaches comprise a situation in which one human being (the therapist) tries to act in a way that enables another human being to act and feel differently, and this is as true of psychoanalysis as it is of behaviour therapy.

(From Wachtel, 1977)

The crucial issue is the *nature* of the therapist's influence, rather than whether or not influence occurs. One ethical issue is whether the influence is exerted in a direction that is in the patient's interest, or in the service of the therapist's needs. Another is whether the patient is fully informed about the kind of influence the therapist wishes to exert, and the kind of ends being sought (the issue of *informed consent*). Therapist *neutrality* is a myth. Therapists influence their clients in subtle yet powerful ways. According to Davison & Neale (1994):

'Unlike a technician, a psychiatrist cannot avoid communicating and at times imposing his own values upon his patients. The patient usually has considerable difficulty in finding the way in which he would wish to change his behaviour, but as he talks to the psychiatrist his wants and needs become clearer. In the very process of defining his needs in the presence of a figure who is viewed as wise and authoritarian, the patient is profoundly influenced. He ends up wanting some of the things the psychiatrist thinks he should want'.

In the above quotation, we can add 'psychologist' and 'psychotherapist' to 'psychiatrist'.

Freedom and behavioural control

Whilst a behavioural technique such as *systematic desensitisation* is mainly limited to anxiety reduction, this can at least be seen as enhancing the patient's freedom, since anxiety is one of the greatest restrictions on freedom. By contrast, methods based on *operant conditioning* can be applied to almost any aspect of a person's behaviour. Those who use operant methods (such as the *token economy*) often describe their work rather exclusively in terms of *behavioural control*, subscribing to Skinner's (1971) view of freedom as an illusion (see Chapter 57, pages 617–618).

Wachtel (1977) believes that, when used in institutional settings (such as with long-term schizophrenic patients in psychiatric hospitals), the token economy is so subject to abuse that its use is highly questionable. It may be justifiable if it works, and if there is clearly no alternative way of rescuing the patient from an empty and destructive existence. However, as a routine part of how society deals with deviant behaviour, this approach raises very serious ethical questions. One of these relates to the question of *power*. Like the experimental 'subject' relative to the experimenter, the patient is powerless relative to the institutional staff responsible for operating the token economy programme:

'Reinforcement is viewed by many – proponents and opponents alike – as somehow having an inexorable controlling effect upon the person's behaviour and rendering him incapable of choice, reducing him to an automaton or duly wound mechanism' (Wachtel, 1977).

It is the reinforcing agent's power to physically deprive uncooperative patients of 'privileges' that is the alarming feature of the token economy (see Chapter 54, pages 571–572).

The abuse of patients by therapists

In recent years, there has been considerable criticism of psychotherapy (especially Freudian psychoanalysis), including its ethical shortcomings. Masson (1988) believes that there is an imbalance of power involved in the therapeutic relationship, and individuals who seek therapy need protection from the therapist's constant temptation to abuse, misuse, profit from and bully the client. The therapist has almost absolute emotional power over the patient, and Masson catalogues many examples of patients' emotional, sexual and financial abuse at their therapists' hands.

Not surprisingly, Masson's attack has stirred up an enormous controversy. Holmes (1992) agrees with the core of Masson's (1992) argument, namely that:

'No therapist, however experienced or distinguished, is above the laws of the unconscious, and all should have access to supervision and work within a framework of proper professional practice'.

However, in psychotherapy's defence, Holmes points out that exploitation and abuse are by no means confined to psychotherapy. Lawyers, university teachers, priests and doctors are also sometimes guilty (the case of Harold Shipman, the serial-killer doctor, being one, albeit rather extreme, example). All these professional groups have ethical standards and codes of practice (often far more stringent than the law of the land), with disciplinary bodies which impose severe punishments (usually expulsion from the profession). We should not condemn an entire profession because of the transgressions of a small minority.

CONCLUSIONS

This chapter considered the ethics of psychological research, with both human participants and non-human subjects, as well as ethical issues arising from the psychologist's role as a professional involved in behaviour change. Discussion of ethical issues has, in various ways, struck at the heart of psychology itself, requiring us to ask what psychology is *for*. According to Hawks (1981), prevention rather than cure should be a primary aim of psychology, enabling people to cope by themselves, without professional help, thus 'giving psychology away' to people/clients. For Bakan (1967), the significant place in society of the psychologist is more that of the teacher than expert or technician.

Summary

- Psychology's subject matter consists of sentient things with thoughts and feelings. This makes every psychological investigation an ethical situation, with research determined as much by its effects on those being studied, as by what psychologists want to find out. Clinical psychologists also face ethical issues in their roles as agents of behavioural change.

- Various **codes of conduct** and **ethical guidelines** exist to regulate psychological research with humans and non-humans, as well as the practice of clinical and other applied branches of psychology.

- The BPS's *Ethical Principles* identifies several guiding principles for research with human participants, including consent/informed consent and withdrawal from the investigation, deception, protection of participants, debriefing, and confidentiality.

- Whilst ethical codes serve to protect individual participants, underlying assumptions may harm the **social groups** they represent. For example, technically ethical research (which protects individuals) may reinforce racist attitudes (thereby harming social groups). Formal codes neglect wider issues regarding the ethical acceptability of **socially sensitive research**.

- Psychological research must be **socially meaningful** (the **ethical imperative**). This applies particularly to social psychologists, such as those engaged in bystander intervention studies. Using results from earlier studies to make participants more aware of situational influences on behaviour, can increase the likelihood that they will subsequently offer help.

- The dual obligation to individual participants and to society produces a dilemma regarding the use of deception. Three possible solutions are conducting a **cost–benefit analysis**, and obtaining **presumptive** or **prior general consent**.

- Two fundamental issues relating to the use of **non-humans** in research are how we assess their suffering, and the goals used to justify any suffering that is caused. Whilst physical suffering is obvious, mental suffering is less overt. Species need to be studied individually, but more general criteria (such as possessing pain receptors) can also be applied.

- The main justifications for non-human experimentation are the **pursuit of scientific knowledge** and the **advancement of medicine**. Safeguards exist to minimise pain and distress in experiments, including the BPS Guidelines and the Animals (Scientific Procedures) Act monitored by Home Office inspectors.

- The medical justification argument presupposes that medical benefits have actually resulted from non-human experiments. Scientific opinion is divided about this, with some researchers stressing the biological similarities between species, and others stressing subtle differences which can result in misleading and conflicting results.

- Gray advocates **speciesism,** by arguing that we are morally obliged to inflict pain on non-humans in order to reduce potential human suffering. This is often a long-term goal, and ethical decisions centre around justifying non-human suffering in the short-term when only scientific knowledge is achievable.

- Clinical psychologists and other **agents of change** are likely to neglect professional ethics, because of the twin beliefs that psychology is a value-free science (as embodied in the **scientist–practitioner model** of helping) and that therapists should be value-neutral/'non-directive'.

- However effective a particular technique may be, clinical psychologists still **choose** which techniques to use and what research is worth doing.

- Behaviour therapy and modification treat people as helpless organisms, reinforcing stereotypes of the 'mentally ill' which clients then internalise, resulting in low self-esteem and passivity.

■ Psychiatric in-patients are subjected to subtle coercion to accept particular treatments, and therapists may exert an even more covert influence over their clients.

■ Whilst psychodynamic therapists have traditionally accused behaviour therapists of manipulating and dehumanising their clients/patients, **all** therapists influence their clients/patients. The crucial issue is the **nature** of that influence.

■ The **token economy** is often described in terms of **behavioural control** (based on Skinner's rejection of free will). Within institutions, staff have the **power** to deprive patients of 'privileges'. There is also a power imbalance between therapists and their clients. In both situations, abuse of power may occur.

Essay Questions

1 Describe and evaluate arguments for and against the use of non-human animals in psychological research.
(*30 marks*)

2 'Researchers' only responsibility is the protection of their participants.'

Discuss this view of the role of psychologists as investigators of human behaviour and experience, using examples from different areas of psychology.
(*30 marks*)

WEB ADDRESSES

http://www.bps/org.uk.charter/codofcon.htm
http://www.psy.herts.ac.uk/Docs/EthicalGuidelines.html
http://www.informin.co.uk/LM/LM119/LM119_AnimalExp. html
http://altweb.jhsph.edu/
http://lwww.aalas.org

PART 2: DEBATES

57 Free Will and Determinism, and Reductionism

INTRODUCTION AND OVERVIEW

As Chapter 58 shows, any discussion of psychology's scientific status raises fundamental questions about the nature of the person or, at least, the image of the person that underlies major psychological theories, and which is implicit in much of the study of human behaviour. This chapter discusses two of these fundamental questions. One, debated by Western philosophers for centuries, is whether we choose to act as we do, or whether behaviours are caused by influences beyond our control (*free will versus determinism*). The other, which has a shorter history and is debated by philosophers of science, concerns the validity of attempts to explain complex wholes in terms of their constituent parts (*reductionism*). One example of this is the relationship between the mind (or consciousness) and the brain (the '*mind–body problem*').

FREE WILL AND DETERMINISM

What is free will?

One way of approaching this question is to consider examples of behaviour where 'free will' (however defined) is clearly *absent*.

Box 57.1 A case of Tourette's disorder

Tim is 14 and displays a variety of twitches and tics. His head sometimes jerks and he often blinks and grimaces. Occasionally, he blurts out words, usually vulgarities. He does not mean to do it and is embarrassed by it, but he cannot control it. Because of his strange behaviour, most other children avoid him. His isolation and embarrassment are interfering with his social development. Tim suffers from a rare condition called Tourette's disorder.

(From Holmes, 1994)

Exercise 1

What specific aspects of Tim's disorder are relevant to understanding the concept of 'free will'? If you think Tim lacks it, what led you to this conclusion? Think of other behaviours (normal or abnormal) that demonstrate a lack of free will.

Intuition tells us that people have the ability to choose their own courses of action, determine their behaviours and, to this extent, have *free will*. Simultaneously, though, this freedom is exercised only within certain physical, political, sociological and other environmental constraints. However, the positivistic, mechanistic nature of scientific psychology (see Chapter 58) implies that behaviour is *determined* by external (or internal) events or stimuli, and that people are passive responders. To this extent, people are *not* free. *Determinism* also implies that behaviour occurs in a regular, orderly manner which (in principle) is totally predictable. For Taylor (1963), determinism maintains that:

'In the case of everything that exists, there are antecedent conditions, known or unknown, given which that thing could not be other than it is ... More loosely, it says that everything, including every cause, is the effect of some cause or causes; or that everything is not only determinate but causally determined'.

'Everything that exists' includes people and their thoughts and behaviours, so a 'strict determinist' believes that thought and behaviours are no different from (other) 'things' or events in the world. However, this begs the question of whether thoughts and behaviours are the same *kind of thing or event* as, say, chemical reactions in a test tube, or neurons firing in the brain. We don't usually ask if the chemicals 'agreed' to combine in a certain way, or if the neurons 'decided' to fire. Unless we were trying to be witty, we would be guilty of *anthropomorphism* (attributing human abilities and characteristics to non-humans).

Figure 57.1 *This painting by Gustave Dore of the Old Testament story of Lot's wife being turned to stone ('The Rescue of Lot') illustrates the human capacity for free will*

It is only *people* who can agree and make decisions. These abilities and capacities are part of our concept of a person, which, in turn, forms an essential part of 'everyday' or commonsense psychology (see Gross *et al.*, 2000). Agreeing and deciding are precisely the kinds of things we do *with our minds* (they are mental processes or events), and to be able to agree and make decisions, it is necessary to 'have a mind'. So, free will implies having a mind. However, having a mind does not imply free will: it is possible that decisions and so on are themselves *caused* (determined), even though they seem to be freely chosen.

Exercise 2

Try to explain what someone means when he or she says: 'I had no choice but to ...' or 'You leave me no choice ...'. Can you interpret this in a way that is consistent with a belief in free will?

Different meanings of 'free will'

One of the difficulties with the free will versus determinism debate is the ambiguity of the concepts involved.

Having a choice

The 'actor' could have behaved differently, given the same circumstances. This contrasts sharply with a common definition of determinism, namely that things could only have happened as they did, given everything that happened previously.

Not being coerced or constrained

If someone puts a loaded gun to your head and tells you to do something, your behaviour is clearly not free: you have been *forced* to act this way. This is usually where the philosophical debate about 'free' will *begins*. It is also related to what James (1890) called *soft determinism* (see page 616).

Voluntary

If 'involuntary' conveys reflex behaviour (such as the eye-blink response to a puff of air directed at the eye), then 'voluntary' implies 'free' (the behaviour is not automatic). By definition, most behaviour (human and non-human) is *not* reflex, nor is it usually the result of coercion. So is most behaviour free?

Box 57.2 Evidence for the distinction between voluntary and involuntary behaviour

Penfield's (1947) classic experiments involved stimulating the cortex of patients about to undergo brain surgery (see Chapter 10, page 100). Even though the cortical area being stimulated was the same as that which is involved when we normally ('voluntarily') move our limbs, patients reported feeling that their arms and legs were being moved passively, quite a different experience from initiating the movement themselves. This demonstrates that the *subjective experience* (*phenomenology*) of the voluntary movement of one's limbs cannot be *reduced* to the stimulation of the appropriate brain region (otherwise Penfield's patients should not have reported a difference). Doing things voluntarily simply *feels* different from the 'same' things 'just happening'. Similarly, see Delgado's (1969) study (page 108).

If this is true for bodily movements, then it adds weight to the claim that having free will is an undeniable part of our subjective experience of ourselves as people. The sense of self is most acute (and important and real for us) where moral decisions and feelings of responsibility for past actions are involved (Koestler,

1967). See text and Box 57.3, page 615, for further discussion of free will and moral responsibility.

One demonstration of people's belief in their free will is *psychological reactance* (Brehm, 1966; Brehm & Brehm, 1981: see Chapter 17). A common response to the feeling that our freedom is being threatened is the attempt to regain or reassert it, which is related to the need to be free from others' controls and restrictions, to determine our own actions, and not be dictated to. A good deal of contrary (resistant) behaviour, otherwise known as 'bloody-mindedness' ('Don't tell me what to do!') seems to reflect this process (Carver & Scheier, 1992).

Similar to this need to feel free from others' control is *intrinsic motivation or self-determination* (Deci, 1980; Deci & Ryan, 1987). This refers to people's intrinsic interest in things, such that they do not need to be offered extrinsic incentives for doing them. Engaging in such activities is motivated by the desire for competence and self-determination.

So what happens if someone is offered an extrinsic reward for doing something which is already interesting and enjoyable in itself? Lepper *et al.* (1973) found that the activity loses its intrinsic appeal, and motivation is reduced (the *paradox of reward*: see Box 17.7, page 171). This has implications for accounts of moral development based on learning theory principles, especially operant conditioning (see Chapters 31 and 38).

Exercise 3

How could you account for the 'paradox of reward' in terms of attributional principles, specifically, internal and external causes? (See Chapter 1.)

Deliberate control

Norman & Shallice (1986) define divided attention as an upper limit to the amount of processing that can be performed on incoming information at any one time. They propose three levels of functioning, namely *fully automatic processing*, *partially automatic processing*, and *deliberate control* (see Chapter 20, page 204). Deliberate control corresponds to free will.

Driving a car is a sensory–motor skill, performed by experienced drivers more-or-less automatically. It does not require deliberate, conscious control, unless some unexpected event disrupts the performance (such as putting your foot on the brake when there is an obstacle ahead: this is a 'rule of the game'). However, on an icy road this can be risky, since the steering wheel has a different 'feel' and the whole driving strategy must be changed. After doing it several times, this too may become a semi-automatic routine:

'But let a little dog amble across the icy road in front of the driver, and he will have to make a 'top-level decision' whether to slam down the brake, risking the safety of his passengers, or run over the dog. And if, instead of a dog, the jaywalker is a child, he will probably resort to the brake, whatever the outcome. It is at this level, when the pros and cons are equally balanced, that the subjective experience of freedom and moral responsibility arises' (Koestler, 1967).

As we move downwards from conscious control, the subjective experience of freedom diminishes. According to Koestler:

'Habit is the enemy of freedom ... Machines cannot become like men, but men can become like machines'.

Koestler also maintains that the second enemy of freedom is very powerful (especially negative) emotion:

'When [emotions] are aroused, the control of decisions is taken over by those primitive levels of the hierarchy which the Victorians called 'the Beast in us' and which are in fact correlated to phylogenetically older structures in the nervous system'.

The arousal of these structures results in 'diminished responsibility' and 'I couldn't help it' (Koestler, 1967).

Exercise 4

In Koestler's quote above, (a) what does 'phylogenetically older structures' mean? and (b) what are the major 'primitive levels of the hierarchy' correlated with these structures? (See Chapter 18, pages 175–178.)

Why should psychologists be interested in the concept of free will?

As noted in the *Introduction and overview*, the philosophical debate about free will and determinism is centuries old. It can be traced back at least to the French philosopher Descartes (1596–1650), whose ideas had a great influence on both science in general and psychology in particular (see Chapter 58, page 625). For much of its history as a separate, scientific discipline, psychology has operated as if there were no difference between natural, physical phenomena and human thought and behaviour (see pages 618–619).

During the period 1913–1956, psychology (at least in the USA) was dominated by behaviourism, Skinner being particularly influential. Skinner's beliefs about the influence of mental phenomena on behaviour, and those concerning free will, are discussed on pages 617–618.

Exercise 5

Try to identify some (other) ways in which the issue of free will is relevant to psychological theory and practice. For example, how does the notion of free will relate to criteria for defining and diagnosing mental disorders?

Free will and psychological abnormality

Definitions of abnormality, and the diagnosis and treatment of mental disorders, often involve implicit or explicit judgements about free will and determinism. In a general sense, mental disorders can be seen as the partial or complete breakdown of the control people normally have over their thoughts, emotions and behaviours. For example, *compulsive* behaviour, by definition, is behaviour which a person cannot help but do: s/he is 'compelled' to do it. People are *attacked* by panic, *obsessed* by thoughts of germs, or become the *victims* of thoughts which are *inserted* into their mind from outside and are under external influence (see Chapter 49, page 528). In all these examples, things are happening to, or being done to, the individual (instead of the individual *doing them*), both from the individual's perspective and that of a psychologist or psychiatrist.

Being judged to have lost control (possession of which is usually thought of as a major feature of normality), either temporarily or permanently, is a legally acceptable defence in cases of criminal offences.

Box 57.3 Forensic psychiatry, diminished responsibility and the law

Forensic psychiatry deals with assessment and treatment of mentally disturbed offenders. The 1983 Mental Health Act has several clauses providing for the compulsory detention of prisoners (either whilst awaiting trial or as part of their sentences) in hospital. Psychiatrists, as expert witnesses, can play important roles in advising the Court about:

* fitness to plead;
* mental state at the time of the offence;
* diminished responsibility.

The defence of *diminished responsibility* (for murder) was introduced in England and Wales in the 1957 Homicide Act, largely replacing the plea of 'not guilty by reason of insanity', which was based on the 'McNaughton Rules' of 1843.

If accepted, there is no trial and a sentence of manslaughter is passed. If not accepted, a trial is held and the jury must decide whether the accused (at the time the crime was committed) was suffering from an abnormality of mind, and if so, whether it was such as to substantially impair his/her responsibility.

Peter Sutcliffe, the 'Yorkshire Ripper', was found guilty of the murder of 13 women and the attempted murder of seven others, despite his defence that he heard God's voice telling him to 'get rid' of prostitutes. In finding him guilty of murder, the jury did not necessarily reject the defence's argument that he was suffering from paranoid schizophrenia, only that it did not constitute a mental abnormality of sufficient degree to substantially impair responsibility for his acts. Sutcliffe was sentenced to 20 concurrent terms of life imprisonment, which he served initially in an ordinary prison before being sent to Broadmoor Special Hospital.

(Based on Gelder *et al.*, 1989, and Prins, 1995)

Free will and moral accountability

Underlying the whole question of legal (and moral) responsibility is the presupposition that people are, at least some of the time, able to control their behaviours and choose between different courses of action. How else could we ever be held responsible for *any* of our actions? In most everyday situations and interactions, we attribute responsibility, both to ourselves and others, unless we have reason to doubt it. According to Flanagan (1984):

'It seems silly to have any expectations about how people ought to act, if everything we do is the result of some inexorable causal chain which began millennia ago. 'Ought', after all, seems to imply 'can', therefore, by employing a moral vocabulary filled with words like 'ought' and 'should', we assume that humans are capable of rising above the causal pressures presented by the material world, and, in assuming this we appear to be operating with some conception of freedom, some notion of free will'.

Free will as an issue in major psychological theories

Most major theorists in psychology have addressed the issue of free will and determinism, including James, Freud, Skinner, and Rogers.

James and soft determinism

James pioneered psychology as a separate, scientific discipline. In *The Principles of Psychology* (1890), he devoted a whole chapter to the 'will', which he related to attention:

'The most essential achievement of the will ... when it is most 'voluntary' is to *attend* to a different object and hold it fast before the mind ... Effort of attention is thus the essential phenomenon of will'.

For James, there was a conflict. Belief in determinism seemed to fit best with the scientific view of the world, whilst belief in free will seemed to be required by our social, moral, political, and legal practices, as well as by our personal, subjective experience (see above). His solution to this conflict was two-fold.

First, he distinguished between the scientific and non-scientific worlds. Psychology as a science could only progress by assuming determinism, but this does not mean that belief in free will must be abandoned in other contexts. So, scientific explanation is not the only useful kind of explanation.

Second, he drew a further distinction between *soft* and *hard* determinism. According to *soft determinism*, the question of free will depends on the type(s) of cause(s) our behaviour has, not whether it is caused or not caused (the opposite of 'not caused' is 'random', not 'free'). If our actions have, as their immediate (proximate) cause, processing by a system such as *conscious mental life* (or CML, which includes consciousness, purposefulness, personality and personal continuity), then they count as free, rational, voluntary, purposive actions.

According to *hard determinism*, CML is itself caused, so that the immediate causes are only part of the total causal chain which results in the behaviour we are trying to explain. Therefore, as long as our behaviour is caused at all, there is no sense in which we can be described as acting freely.

Freud and psychic determinism

Although in most respects their ideas about human behaviour are diametrically opposed, Freud and Skinner shared the fundamental belief that free will is an illusion. However, in keeping with their theories as a whole, their reasons are radically different.

Exercise 6

Based on what you already know about Freud's psychoanalytic theory, try to identify those parts which are most relevant to his rejection of free will.

According to Strachey (1962):

'Behind all of Freud's work ... we should posit his belief in the universal validity of the law of determinism ... Freud extended the belief (derived from physical phenomena) uncompromisingly to the field of mental phenomena'.

Similarly, Sulloway (1979) maintains that all of Freud's work in science (and Freud saw himself very much as a scientist) was characterised by an abiding faith in the notion that all vital phenomena, including psychical (psychological) ones, are rigidly and lawfully determined by the principle of cause and effect. One major example of this was the extreme importance he attached to the technique of *free association*.

Box 57.4 How 'free' is Freud's 'free association'?

'Free association' is a misleading translation of the German *'freier Einfall'*, which conveys much more accurately the intended impression of an uncontrollable 'intrusion' (*'Einfall'*) by pre-conscious ideas into conscious thinking. In turn, this pre-conscious material reflects *unconscious* ideas, wishes and memories (what Freud was really interested in), since here lie the principal cause(s) of neurotic problems.

It is a great irony that 'free' association should refer to a technique used in psychoanalysis meant to reveal the *unconscious causes* of behaviour (see Chapter 54, page 576). It is because the causes of our thoughts, actions and supposed choices are unconscious (mostly *actively repressed*), that we *think* we are free. Freud's application of this general philosophical belief in causation to mental phenomena is called *psychic determinism*.

(Based on Sulloway, 1979)

For Freud, part of what 'psychic determinism' conveyed was that in the universe of the mind, there are no 'accidents'. No matter how apparently random or irrational behaviour may be (such as 'parapraxes' or 'Freudian slips'), unconscious causes can always account for them, and this also applies to hysterical symptoms and dreams. As Gay (1988) states, 'Freud's theory of the mind is ... strictly and frankly deterministic'. However:

- Freud accepted that true accidents, in the sense of forces beyond the victim's control (e.g. being struck by lightning), can and do occur, and are not unconsciously caused by the victim.

- One of the aims of psychoanalysis is to 'give the patient's ego *freedom* to decide one way or another' (Freud, quoted in Gay, 1988), so therapy rests on the belief that people *can* change. However, Freud saw the extent of possible change as being very limited.

- One aspect of psychic determinism is *overdetermination*, that is, much of our behaviour has *multiple* causes, both conscious and unconscious. So, although our conscious choices, decisions and intentions may genuinely influence behaviour, they never tell the whole story.

- Despite never having predicted in advance what choice or decision a patient would make, Freud maintained that these are not arbitrary, and can be understood as revealing personality characteristics (Rycroft, 1966). What Freud often did was to explain his patients' choices, neurotic symptoms, and so on *not* in terms of causes (the *scientific* argument), but by trying to make sense of them and give them meaning (the *semantic* argument). Indeed, the latter is supported by the title of, arguably, his greatest book, *The Interpretation of Dreams* (1900) (as opposed to *The 'Cause' of Dreams*).

Skinner and the illusion of free will

Like Freud, Skinner sees free will as an illusion. However, whilst Freud focused on 'the mind', especially unconscious thoughts, wishes, and memories, Skinner's *radical behaviourism* eliminates all reference to mental or private states as part of the explanation of behaviour (including theories like Freud's!).

Although Skinner does not deny that pain and other internal states exist, they have no 'causal teeth' and hence no part to play in scientific explanations of (human) behaviour (Garrett, 1996). Free will (and other '*explanatory fictions*') cannot be defined or measured objectively, nor are they needed for successful prediction and control of behaviour (for Skinner, the primary aims of a science of behaviour). It is only because the causes of human behaviour are often hidden from us in the environment, that the myth or illusion of free will survives.

Exercise 7

Given what you know about Skinner's theory of operant conditioning and his 'analysis of behaviour', try to identify the causes of human behaviour which he believes are often hidden from us in the environment (see Chapter 38).

Skinner argues that when what we do is dictated by force or punishment, or by their threat (negative reinforcement), it is obvious to everyone that we are not acting freely. For example, when the possibility of prison stops us committing crimes, there is clearly no choice involved, because we know what the environmental causes of our behaviour are. Similarly, it may sometimes be very obvious which positive reinforcers are shaping behaviour (a bonus for working over-time, for example). However, most of the time we are unaware of environmental causes, and it looks (and feels) as if we are behaving freely. Yet all this means is that we are free of punishments or negative reinforcement, and behaviour is still determined by the pursuit of things that have been positively reinforced in the past. When we perceive others as behaving freely, we are simply unaware of their reinforcement histories (Fancher, 1996).

Box 57.5 The freedom myth and the rejection of punishment

In *Beyond Freedom and Dignity*, Skinner (1971) argued that the notion of 'autonomous man', upon which so many of Western society's assumptions are based, is both false and has many harmful consequences. In particular, the assumption that people are free *requires* that they are constantly exposed to punishment and its threat as a negative reinforcer (Fancher, 1996).

Based on experiments with rats and pigeons, Skinner argued that positive reinforcement is more effective than negative reinforcement or punishment in producing lasting conditioning effects. In Skinner's version of Utopia (described in his novel *Walden Two*, 1948b), negative reinforcement is completely abandoned as a means of social control. Children are reared only to seek positive reinforcement contingent upon their showing socialised, civilised behaviour. Inevitably, they grow up to be cooperative, intelligent, sociable and happy.

Exercise 8

What *ethical* issues are raised by Skinner's advocacy of a utopian society like *Walden Two*? In what ways does this Utopia reflect Skinner's beliefs about the aims of a scientific psychology?

Skinner and moral responsibility

Clearly, Skinner's belief that free will is an illusion conflicts with the need to attribute people with free will if we are to hold them (and ourselves) morally (and legally) responsible for their behaviour. Skinner (1971) himself acknowledges that freedom and dignity are:

' ... essential to practices in which a person is held responsible for his conduct and given credit for his achievements'.

However, Skinner equates 'good' and 'bad' with 'beneficial to others' (what is rewarded) and 'harmful to others' (what is punished) respectively, thus removing morality from human behaviour. For Skinner, 'oughts' are not 'moral imperatives': they reflect *practical*, rather than moral, guidelines and rules (Morea, 1990).

According to Garrett (1996), if we are rational, thinking creatures, capable of assessing ethical rules and principles, and evaluating the goodness of our lives, then we have all the freedom needed to reasonably prefer democratic to non- (or anti-) democratic forms of government (as expressed in *Walden Two* and *Beyond Freedom and Dignity*).

A further consequence of Skinner's rejection of the notion of 'autonomous man' is what Ringen (1996) calls *the behaviour therapist's dilemma*, which is closely related to some of the most fundamental *ethical* issues faced by psychologists as *agents of change* (see Chapter 56, pages 607–609).

Box 57.6 The behaviour therapist's dilemma

Ringen (1996) claims that there is a deep tension between two features of modern clinical psychology. On the one hand, Skinner (1971) argues that scientific considerations support *radical behaviourism* as the most appropriate framework for understanding and facilitating the development of effective behaviour therapy (including methods based on both classical and operant conditioning). On the other hand, an increasingly significant ethical and legal constraint on therapeutic practice, the doctrine of *informed consent*, obliges behaviour therapists (and other practitioners in the helping professions, including psychiatry) to acknowledge the autonomy of those who come to them for help.

The behaviour therapist's dilemma describes a widely accepted assessment of why these two aspects of modern clinical psychology are in tension, namely, that *either* radical behaviourism is false *or* human beings never act autonomously. This involves having to choose between alternatives that many contemporary behaviour therapists would find it difficult to defend.

(From Ringen, 1996)

Rogers, freedom and the fully functioning person

According to Gross *et al.* (2000), Rogers was perhaps the most influential *humanistic, phenomenological* psychologist. As such, he stressed the process of self-actualisation and the necessity of adopting the other person's perspective if we are to understand that person, and in particular, his/her self-concept.

Understanding the self-concept is also central to Rogers' *client-centred therapy* (see Gross & McIlveen, 1999). His experience as a therapist convinced him that real change does occur in therapy: people choose to see themselves and their life situations differently. Therapy and life are about free human beings struggling to become more free. Personal experience is important, but it does not imprison us. How we react to our experience is something we ourselves choose and decide (Morea, 1990).

Exercise 9

According to Rogers, in what ways are individuals prevented from recognising their *true* feelings and behaviour? In what respects is Rogers' view of human beings a more optimistic one than, say, Freud's?

Rogers' deep and lasting trust in human nature did not, however, blind him to the reality of evil *behaviour*:

'In my experience, every person has the capacity for evil behaviour. I, and others, have had murderous and cruel impulses ... feelings of anger and rage, desires to impose our wills on others ... Whether I ... will translate these impulses into behaviour depends ... on two elements: social conditioning and voluntary choice' (Rogers, 1982, cited in Thorne, 1992).

By making the distinction between 'human nature' and behaviour, Rogers retains his optimistic view of human beings. However, this did not exclude altogether a deterministic element in his later writings. In *Freedom to Learn for the '80s* (1983), he states that it is becoming clear from science that human beings are complex machines and not free. So how can this be reconciled with self-actualisation, psychological growth, and the freedom to choose?

One proposed solution is in the form of a version of soft determinism. Unlike neurotic and incongruent people whose defensiveness forces them to act in ways they would prefer not to, the healthy, fully functioning person:

' ... not only experiences, but utilises, the most absolute freedom when he spontaneously, freely and voluntarily chooses and wills that which is absolutely determined'.

The fully functioning person chooses to act and be the way s/he has to. It is the most satisfying way to behave (Morea, 1990).

REDUCTIONISM

What is reductionism?

Together with positivism, mechanism, determinism, and empiricism, reductionism represents part of 'classical' science (see Chapter 58). Luria (1987) traces the origins of reductionism to the mid-nineteenth-century view within biology that the organism is a complex of organs, and the organs are complexes of cells. To explain the basic laws of the living organism, we have to study as carefully as possible the features of separate cells.

From its biological origins, reductionism was extended to science in general. For example, the properties of a protein molecule could be uniquely determined or predicted in terms of properties of the electrons or protons making up its atoms. Consistent with this view is Garnham's (1991) definition of reductionism as:

' ... the idea that psychological explanations can be replaced by explanations in terms of brain functioning or even in terms of physics and chemistry'.

Although reductionism's ultimate aim (according to its supporters) is to account for all phenomena in terms of microphysics, *any* attempt to explain something in terms of its components or constituent parts may be thought of as reductionist. A useful definition, which is consistent with this broader view, is that of Rose *et al.* (1984), for whom reductionism is:

' ... the name given to a set of general methods and modes of explanation both of the world of physical objects and of human societies. Broadly, reductionists try to explain the properties of complex wholes – molecules, say, or societies – in terms of the units of which those molecules or societies are composed'.

Rose (1997) identifies four major types of reductionism (or different meanings of the term).

Box 57.7 Different meanings of reductionism

- **Reductionism as methodology:** This refers to the attempt to isolate variables in the laboratory in order to simplify the living world's enormous complexity, flux and multitude of interacting processes. This is the basis of the experiment, which reflects natural science's attempt to identify cause-and-effect relationships (see Chapter 58).

- **Theory reduction:** This refers to science's aim to capture as much of the world in as few laws or principles as possible. It is related to:

- **Philosophical reductionism:** This refers to the belief that because science is unitary, and because physics is the most fundamental of the sciences, ultimately all currently separate disciplines (including psychology) will be 'reduced' to physics (see the quotes from Garnham (1991), above, and Crick (1994), page 621).

- **Reductionism as ideology:** This refers to the very marked tendency in recent years to identify genes responsible for a whole range of complex human behaviours, including stress, anxiety, depression, personality, homosexuality, intelligence, alcoholism, criminality and violence.

(Based on Rose, 1997)

Rose calls the claim that there is a direct causal link between genes and behaviour *neurogenetic determinism.* It involves a sequence of (false) assumptions and arguments, one of which is the dichotomy between genetic and environmental causes (or nature and nurture: see Chapter 59).

Exercise 10

There are many examples of psychological theories and concepts which fit either or both of Garnham's and Rose *et al.'s* definitions. These can be found in all areas of psychology, but below are a few of the more 'obvious' examples. For each one, try to explain (a) why the theory or concept is reductionist, and (b) what the strengths and/or weaknesses of such an approach are.

i   According to *structuralism* (e.g. Wundt), perception is simply a series of sensations (see Chapter 58).
ii   According to Watson's *peripheralism*, thought consists of tiny movements of the vocal chords (see Chapter 25).
iii   Intelligence is a person's performance on a standardised intelligence test (his/her IQ score: see Chapter 29).
iv   Psychological sex differences are caused by biological factors (such as hormones: see Chapter 32).
v   According to Freud, personality development involves progress through a series of *psychosexual* stages (see Chapter 31).
vi   Schizophrenia is caused by an excess of the neurotransmitter, dopamine (see Chapter 49).
vii   According to Adorno *et al.*, anti-semitism (and other forms of racism) are symptomatic of the *authoritarian personality* (see Chapter 3).

The mind–body problem: what is the relationship between mind and brain?

Perhaps the oldest and most frequently debated example of reductionism is the *mind–body problem* (or the *problem of mind and brain*). Originally a philosophical issue, it continues to be discussed, often passionately, by neurophysiologists, biologists, neuropsychologists and psychologists in general.

Whilst it is generally agreed that the mind (or consciousness) is a property of human beings (as is walking upright on two legs), and that without the human brain there would be no consciousness, a 'problem' remains.

Box 57.8 The problem of the mind–brain relationship

- How can two 'things' be related when one of them is physical (the brain has size, weight, shape, density, and exists in space and time) and the other apparently lacks all these characteristics?

- How can something that is non-physical/non-material (the mind) influence or produce changes in something that is physical (the brain/body)?

The 'classic' example given by philosophers to illustrate the problem is the act of deciding to lift one's arm. (This example also illustrates the exercise of [free] will: see text.) From a strictly scientific perspective, this kind of causation should be impossible, and science (including psychology and neurophysiology) has traditionally rejected any brand of *philosophical dualism*, that is, the belief in the existence of two essentially different kinds of 'substance', the physical body and the non-physical mind (see Box 57.9).

From an evolutionary perspective, could consciousness have equipped human beings with survival value *unless* it had causal properties (Gregory, 1981), that is, unless it could actually bring about changes in behaviour? Our subjective experiences tell us that our minds *do* affect behaviour, and that consciousness *does* have causal properties (just try lifting your arm). However, many philosophers and scientists from various disciplines have not always shared the layperson's common sense understanding.

Figure 57.2 *The capacity of alcohol and other, illegal, drugs to change mood and behaviour clearly demonstrates the interaction between mind and brain*

Whilst there are many theories of the mind–brain relationship, most are not strictly relevant to the debate about reductionism. Box 57.9 and Figure 57.3 (see page 621) summarise most of the major theories, but emphasis will be given to reductionist approaches, especially as they impinge on *psychological* theories.

Box 57.9 Some major theories of the mind–brain relationship

- Theories fall into two main categories: *dualism* (which distinguishes between mind and brain), and *monism* (which claims that only mind *or* matter is real).

- According to Descartes' seventeenth-century dualist theory (which first introduced the mind–body problem into philosophy), the mind can influence the brain, but not vice versa. Whilst *epiphenomenology* sees the mind as a kind of by-product of the brain (the mind has no influence on the brain), *interactionism* sees the influence as two-way.

- *Psychophysical parallelists* are dualists who believe that there is no mind–brain interaction at all: mental and neural events are merely perfectly synchronised or correlated.

- According to *mentalism/idealism*, only mental phenomena are real. *Phenomenological* theories, such as that of Rogers, and *constructionist* explanations of behaviour, have a mentalist 'flavour'.

- Most monist theories take one or other form of *materialism*.

- The *peripheralist* version of materialism is illustrated by Skinner's *radical behaviourism* (see Gross *et al.*, 2000). During the 1930s, Skinner denied the existence of mental phenomena (as had Watson, the founder of behaviourism). However, from 1945 he began to adopt a less extreme view, recognising their existence, but defining them as *covert/internal actions*, subject to the same laws as overt behavioural events (those of conditioning). This *is* a form of reductionism.

- *Centralist materialism* (or *mind–brain identity theory*) identifies mental processes with purely physical processes in the central nervous system. Whilst it is logically possible that there might be separate, mental, non-physical phenomena, it just turns out that, as a matter of fact, mental states are identical with physical states of the brain. We are, simply, very complicated physico-chemical mechanisms.

- *Eliminative materialism* represents an extreme reductionist form of (centralist) materialism: see page 621.

(Based on Flanagan, 1984; Gross, 1995, and Teichman, 1988)

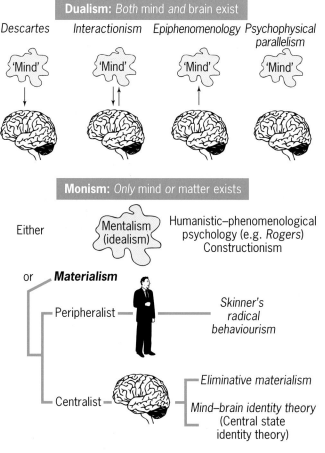

Dualism: *Both* mind *and* brain exist

Descartes   *Interactionism*   *Epiphenomenology*   *Psychophysical parallelism*

'Mind'   'Mind'   'Mind'   'Mind'

Monism: *Only* mind *or* matter exists

Either   Mentalism (idealism)   Humanistic–phenomenological psychology (e.g. *Rogers*) Constructionism

or   **Materialism**

Peripheralist — *Skinner's radical behaviourism*

Centralist — *Eliminative materialism*

Mind–brain identity theory (Central state identity theory)

Figure 57.3 *An outline of the major theories of the mind–brain relationship*

Exercise 11

Using your knowledge of physiological psychology, try to relate the examples below to the theories outlined in Box 57.9 (see page 620) and Figure 57.3. Specifically, do these examples involve *interactions* between mind and brain, and, if so, in what direction is the influence taking place?

a The effects of psychoactive drugs (see Chapter 52).
b Electrical stimulation of the brain (see Chapter 10).
c Sperry's study of split-brain patients (see Chapter 12).
d Stress (see Gross *et al.*, 2000).

Reductionist theories of the mind–brain relationship

As Box 57.9 (see page 620) shows, *eliminative materialism* is an extreme form of reductionist materialism. What makes it reductionist is the attempt to *replace* a psychological account of behaviour with an account in terms of neurophysiology. An example of this approach is Crick's (1994) *The Astonishing Hypothesis: The Scientific Search for the Soul*.

According to Crick:

> 'You, your joys and your sorrows, your memories and your ambitions, your sense of personality and free will, are in fact no more than the behaviour of a vast assembly of nerve cells and their associated molecules'.

But is this a valid equation to make? According to Smith (1994), the mind and brain problem is radically different from other cases of *contingent identity* (identical as a matter of fact) with which it is usually compared, such as 'a gene is a section of the DNA molecule'. What is different is reductionism, and the related issue of exactly what is meant by *identity*.

Box 57.10 Different meanings of 'identity' relevant to the mind–brain relationship

Whilst it is generally agreed that we cannot have a mind without a brain, mind states and brain states are not systematically correlated, and the neurophysiological and neurological evidence points towards *token identity*. For example, we cannot just assume that the same neurophysiological mechanisms will be used by two different people both engaged in the 'same' activity of reading (Broadbent, 1981). There are many ways that 'the brain' can perform the same task.

But it is precisely this kind of systematic correlation that mind–brain identity has been taken to imply, whereby whenever a mind state of a certain type occurs, a brain state of a certain type occurs (*type identity*). Token identity means that there must always be a place for an autonomous psychological account of human thought and action.

(Based on Harré *et al.*, 1985)

According to Penrose (1990), there is a built-in *indeterminacy* in the way that individual neurons and their synaptic connections work (their responses are inherently unpredictable). Yet, despite this unpredictability at the level of the individual units or components, the system as a whole is predictable. The 'nervous system' (or sub-systems within it) does not operate randomly, but in a highly organised, structured way.

Consciousness, intelligence, and memory are properties of the brain as a system, *not* properties of the individual units, and they could not possibly be predicted from analysing the units. Instead, they 'emerge' from interactions between the units that compose the system (and so are called *emergent properties*). The whole is greater than the sum of its parts (Rose, 1997: see Chapter 23, page 232).

Can you be a materialist without being a reductionist?

According to Rose (1992):

> 'The mind is never replaced by the brain. Instead we have two distinct and legitimate languages, each describing the same unitary phenomena of the material world'.

Rose speaks as a materialist and an *anti-reductionist*, who believes that we should learn how to translate between mind language and brain language (although this may be impossibly difficult: see Box 57.7, page 619). Whilst most materialists are also reductionists, and vice versa, this is not necessarily so. Freud, for example, was a materialist who believed that no single scientific vocabulary (such as anatomy) could adequately describe (let alone explain) all facets of the material world. He believed in the *autonomy of psychological explanation*.

The fact that there are different 'languages' for describing minds and brains (or different *levels of description* or *universes of discourse*) relates to the question of the relevance of knowing, say, what is going on inside our brains when we think or are aware. For Eiser (1994):

> 'The firing of neurons stands to thought in the same relation as my walking across the room (etc.) stands to my getting some coffee. It is absolutely essential in a causal or physical sense, and absolutely superfluous ... to the logic of the higher-order description. In short, I can accept that it happens, and then happily ignore it'.

This explains how it is possible to be simultaneously a materialist (the brain is necessarily implicated in everything we do and the mind does not represent a different kind of reality) *and* an anti-reductionist (we can describe and explain our thinking without having to 'bring my brain into it'). Two separate levels of description are involved.

CONCLUSIONS

Given psychology's intellectual and historical roots in philosophy and natural science, it is hardly surprising that psychological theories have contributed to the debate about free will versus determinism, and reductionism. The possession of free will is a fundamental aspect of our common sense concept of a person. Therefore, any theory calling itself psychological must have something to say about this issue. Equally, belief (or not) in the independence of psychological from neurophysiological explanations of behaviour, is crucial to the survival of psychology itself as a separate discipline. This chapter has tried to capture some of the essential features of both these issues.

Summary

- Our intuitive belief in **free will** conflicts with the scientific belief in **determinism**. Determinism also implies behaviour's complete predictability and that everything (including thoughts and behaviour) has a cause. Whilst free will implies having a mind, the things we do with our minds may themselves be determined.

- Free will is an ambiguous concept and can denote having a choice, not being coerced or constrained, voluntary (as opposed to reflex), and deliberate control (as opposed to automatic information processing). The more automatic our behaviours, the weaker our subjective experience of freedom becomes.

- Penfield demonstrated that voluntarily moving one's limbs involves a different **subjective experience** compared with brain stimulation causing one's limbs to move. This supports the view that free will is part of our experience of being a person, which is demonstrated by **psychological reactance**. Similar to this need to feel free from others' control is **intrinsic motivation/self-determination**.

- Definitions of abnormality, and the diagnosis/treatment of mental disorders, often involve judgements about free will. Temporary or permanent loss of control is a legally acceptable defence in criminal cases, as in the **diminished responsibility** defence (for murder).

■ For James, a conflict exists between science's belief in determinism and belief in free will as required by other social institutions. He proposed that psychology as a science could only progress by assuming determinism, but belief in free will could be maintained in other contexts. James also distinguished between **soft** and **hard determinism**, the former allowing **conscious mental life** to be the immediate cause of behaviour.

■ Freud extended the law of determinism to mental phenomena (**psychic determinism**). Ironically, 'free' association was used in psychoanalysis to reveal the **unconscious causes** of behaviour, our ignorance of which creates an **illusion** of freedom.

■ However, Freud's concept of **overdetermination** allows the **conscious** mind a role in influencing behaviour, and he often tried to interpret the **meaning** of patients' thoughts and behaviours (rather than look for causes).

■ Skinner's radical behaviourism involves a rejection of **explanatory fictions**, such as free will and other mentalistic terms. The illusion of free will survives because the environmental causes of behaviour are often hidden from us. He advocated that only positive reinforcement should be used as a means of social control.

■ Skinner rejects the notion of 'autonomous man' and removes morality from human behaviour, by equating 'good' and bad' with what is rewarded and punished respectively. One consequence of this is the **behaviour therapist's dilemma**.

■ Rogers stressed self-actualisation, psychological growth and the freedom to choose. The need to understand a person's self-concept is central to his **client-centred therapy**, which enables people to change and become more free.

■ However, whilst remaining optimistic about 'human nature', Rogers argued that science shows people to be complex machines and not free. The fully functioning person chooses to act the way s/he must.

■ Originating in biology, **reductionism** became part of science in general. Although its supporters see reductionism's ultimate aim as accounting for all phenomena (including psychological) in terms of microphysics, **any** attempt to explain something in terms of its components is reductionist. Rose identifies **reductionism as methodology**, **theory reduction**, **philosophical reductionism** and **reductionism as ideology** (**neurogenetic determinism**).

■ Whilst it is generally agreed that a brain is necessary for consciousness, the problem remains of how the non-physical mind can influence the physical brain. From a strictly scientific perspective, such influence should be impossible. However, from an evolutionary perspective, consciousness should be able to produce behaviour change.

■ Theories of the **mind–brain relationship** are either **dualist** or **monist**. Dualist theories include Descartes' original dualism, epiphenomenology, interactionism, and psychophysical parallelism. Monist theories include mentalism/idealism, **peripheralist materialism** (such as Skinner's radical behaviourism) and **centralist materialism/mind–brain identity theory**.

■ Skinner's definition of mental phenomena as **covert/internal actions** is reductionist, as is **eliminative materialism**, which attempts to **replace** psychological accounts of behaviour with neurophysiological ones. The latter confuses **type identity** with **token identity**.

■ Whilst individual neurons and their synaptic connections are unpredictable, the nervous system overall is highly organised. **Emergent properties** (such as intelligence and consciousness) reflect the activity of the brain as a system, and could not possibly be predicted from analysis of its components.

■ Whilst most materialists are also reductionists, some argue that psychology and neurophysiology constitute distinct **levels of description/universes of discourse**, which cannot replace each other. Freud, for example, believed in the **autonomy of psychological explanation**.

Essay Questions

1 Discuss the free will and determinism debate in relation to **two** theoretical approaches (e.g. Freud, Skinner). (*30 marks*)

2 Describe and evaluate arguments for and against reductionism as a form of explanation, using examples from psychological theory and research studies.

(*30 marks*)

WEB ADDRESSES

http://www.determinism.net
http://www.siu.edu/~philos/faculty/Manfedi/intro/freedom.html
http://www.ptproject.ilstu.edu/pt/fwdl.htm
http://cswww.essex.ac.uk/Research/FSS/MISC/reduction.html

58 *Psychology as a Science*

INTRODUCTION AND OVERVIEW

Psychology is commonly defined as the *scientific* study of behaviour and cognitive processes (or mind or experience). In effect, this book as a whole has been looking at how different psychologists have put this definition into practice, through their use of various investigative methods to study a wide variety of behaviours and cognitive processes.

The present chapter turns the spotlight once more on that definition of psychology. It does this by examining the nature of science (including the major features of scientific method), and by tracing some of the major developments in psychology's history as a scientific discipline. This enables the question of how appropriate it is to use scientific method to study human behaviour and cognitive processes to be addressed, and the validity of this widely accepted definition to be assessed.

SOME PHILOSOPHICAL ROOTS OF SCIENCE AND PSYCHOLOGY

As noted in Chapter 57, Descartes was the first to distinguish formally between mind and matter (*philosophical dualism*), which had an enormous impact on the development of both psychology as a science and science in general. Dualism allowed scientists to treat matter as inert and completely distinct from themselves, which meant that the world could be described *objectively*, without reference to the human observer. Objectivity became the ideal of science, and was extended to the study of human behaviour and social institutions by Comte in the mid-1800s, who called it *positivism*.

Descartes also promoted *mechanism*, the view that the material world comprises objects which are assembled like a huge machine and operated by mechanical laws. He extended this view to living organisms, including, eventually, the human body. Because the mind is non-material, Descartes believed that, unlike the physical world, it can be investigated only through *introspection* (observing one's own thoughts and feelings). He was also one of the first advocates of *reductionism* (see Chapter 57).

Empirism refers to the ideas of the seventeenth- and eighteenth-century British philosophers, Locke, Hume and Berkeley. They believed that the only source of true knowledge about the world is sensory experience (what comes to us through our senses or what can be inferred about the relationship between such sensory facts). Empirism is usually contrasted with *nativism* (or *ratio-*

nalism), according to which knowledge of the world is largely innate or inborn (see, for example, Chapter 24).

Figure 58.1 *René Descartes (1596–1650)*

Exercise 1

Try to identify examples of psychological theory and research which reflect empirist or nativist views. (Another way of doing this is to ask where in psychology the *nature–nurture* or *heredity and environment* debate takes place: see Chapter 59.)

The word *'empirical'* ('through the senses') is often used to mean 'scientific', implying that what scientists do, and what distinguishes them from non-scientists, is carry out experiments and observations as ways of collecting data or 'facts' about the world (hence, 'empirical methods' for 'scientific methods'). *Empiricism* (as distinct from empirism) proved to be one of the central influences on the development of physics and chemistry.

Empiricism and psychology

Prior to the 1870s, there were no laboratories specifically devoted to psychological research, and the early scientific psychologists had trained mainly as physiologists, doctors, philosophers, or some combination of these. The two professors who set up the first two psychological laboratories deserve much of the credit for the development of academic psychology. They were Wundt (1832–1920) in Germany, and James (1842–1910) in the USA (Fancher, 1979).

Wundt's contribution

A physiologist by training, Wundt is generally regarded as the 'founder' of the new science of experimental psychology, or what he called 'a new domain of science' (1874). Having worked as Helmholtz's assistant (see Chapter 23, page 239), Wundt eventually became professor of 'scientific philosophy' at Leipzig University in 1875, illustrating the lack of distinct boundaries between the various disciplines which combined to bring about psychology's development (Fancher, 1979).

Figure 58.2 *Wilhelm Wundt (1832–1920)*

In 1879, Wundt converted his 'laboratory' at Leipzig into a 'private institute' of experimental psychology. For the first time, a place had been set aside for the explicit purpose of conducting psychological research, and hence 1879 is widely accepted as the 'birthdate' of psychology as a discipline in its own right. From its modest beginnings, the institute began to attract people from all over the world, who returned to their own countries to establish laboratories modelled on Wundt's.

Box 58.1 Wundt's study of the conscious mind: introspective psychology and structuralism

Wundt believed that conscious mental states could be scientifically studied through the systematic manipulation of antecedent variables (those that occur before some other event), and analysed by carefully controlled techniques of *introspection*. Introspection was a rigorous and highly disciplined technique for analysing conscious experience into its most basic elements (*sensations* and *feelings*). Participants were always advanced psychology students, who had been carefully trained to introspect properly.

Sensations are the raw sensory content of consciousness, devoid of all 'meaning' or interpretation, and all conscious thoughts, ideas, perceptions and so on were assumed to be combinations of sensations. Based on his experiment in which he listened to a metronome beating at varying rates, Wundt concluded that *feelings* could be analysed in terms of *pleasantness–unpleasantness, tension–relaxation,* and *activity–passivity*.

Wundt believed that introspection made it possible to cut through the learned categories and concepts that define our everyday experience of the world, and so expose the 'building blocks' of experience. Because of introspection's central role, Wundt's early brand of psychology was called *introspective psychology* (or *introspectionism*), and his attempt to analyse consciousness into its elementary sensations and feelings is known as *structuralism*.

(Based on Fancher, 1979)

Exercise 2

1 Consider the difficulties that might be involved in relying on introspection to formulate an account of the nature of conscious experience (i.e. an account that applies to *people in general*).
2 In what ways is structuralism *reductionist*? (see Chapter 57).
3 Which major theory of perception rejects this structuralist approach? Outline its principal features (see Chapter 23).

James' contribution

James taught anatomy and physiology at Harvard University in 1872, and by 1875 was calling his course *The Relations Between Physiology and Psychology*. In the same year, he established a small laboratory, used mainly for teaching purposes. In 1878, he dropped anatomy and physiology, and for several years taught 'pure psychology'.

His view of psychology is summarised in *The Principles of Psychology* (1890), which includes discussion of instinct, brain function, habit, the stream of consciousness, the self, attention (Chapters 19 and 20), perception (Chapter 24), free will (Chapter 57), emotion (Chapter 18), and memory.

Figure 58.3 *William James (1842–1910)*

The Principles of Psychology provided the famous definition of psychology as 'the Science of Mental Life'. Ironically, however, James was very critical both of his book and of what psychology could offer as a science. He became increasingly interested in philosophy and disinterested in psychology, although in 1894 he became the first American to call favourable attention to the recent work of the then little known Viennese neurologist, Sigmund Freud (Fancher, 1979).

James proposed a point of view (rather than a theory) that directly inspired *functionalism*, which emphasises the purpose and utility of behaviour (Fancher, 1979). Functionalism, in turn, helped to stimulate interest in *individual differences*, since they determine how well or poorly individuals adapt to their environments. These attitudes made Americans especially receptive to Darwin's (1859) ideas about individual variation, evolution by natural selection, and the 'survival of the fittest' (see Chapters 43–45).

Watson's behaviourist revolution: a new subject matter for psychology

Watson took over the psychology department at Johns Hopkins University in 1909, and immediately began cutting psychology's ties with philosophy and strengthening those with biology. At that time, Wundt's and James's studies of consciousness were still the 'real' psychology, but Watson was doing research on non-humans and became increasingly critical of the use of introspection.

Figure 58.4 *John Broadus Watson (1878–1958)*

In particular, Watson argued that introspective reports were unreliable and difficult to verify. It is impossible to check the accuracy of such reports, because they are based on purely private experience, to which the investigator has no possible means of access. As a result, Watson redefined psychology in his famous 'behaviourist manifesto' of 1913.

Box 58.2 Watson's (1913) 'behaviourist manifesto'

'Watson's article 'Psychology as the behaviourist views it' is often referred to as the 'behaviourist manifesto', a charter for a truly scientific psychology. It was *behaviourism* which was to represent a rigorous empirist approach within psychology for the first time. According to Watson:

'Psychology as the behaviourist views it is a purely objective natural science. Its theoretical goal is the prediction and control of behaviour. Introspection forms no essential part of its methods, nor is the scientific value of its data dependent upon the readiness with which they lend themselves to interpretation in terms of consciousness. The behaviourist … recognises no dividing line between man and brute. The behaviour of a man … forms only a part of the behaviourist's total scheme of investigation.'

Three features of this 'manifesto' deserve special mention:

- Psychology must be purely objective, excluding all subjective data or interpretations in terms of conscious experience. This redefines psychology as the 'science of behaviour' (rather than the 'science of mental life').

- The goals of psychology should be to predict and control behaviour (as opposed to describing and explaining conscious mental states), a goal later endorsed by Skinner's *radical behaviourism* (see Gross *et al.*, 2000).

- There is no fundamental (*qualitative*) distinction between human and non-human behaviour. If, as Darwin had shown, humans evolved from more simple species, then it follows that human behaviour is simply a more complex form of the behaviour of other species (the difference is merely *quantitative*, one of degree). Consequently, rats, cats, dogs and pigeons became the major source of psychological data. Since 'psychological' now meant 'behaviour' rather than 'consciousness', non-humans that were convenient to study, and whose environments could easily be controlled, could replace people as experimental subjects.

(Based on Fancher, 1979, and Watson, 1913)

Exercise 3

Try to formulate arguments for *and* against Watson's claim that there is only a *quantitative* difference between the behaviour of humans and non-humans.

In his 1915 Presidential address to the American Psychological Association, Watson talked about his recent 'discovery' of Pavlov's work on conditioned reflexes in dogs. He proposed that the conditioned reflex could become the foundation for a full-scale human psychology.

The extreme environmentalism of Locke's empirism (see page 625) lent itself well to the behaviourist emphasis on learning (through the process of Pavlovian or classical conditioning). Whilst Locke had described the mind at birth as a *tabula rasa* ('blank slate') on which experience writes, Watson, in rejecting the mind as suitable for a scientific psychology, simply swapped mind for behaviour: it is now behaviour that is shaped by the environment.

According to Miller (1962), empirism provided psychology with both a *methodology* (stressing the role of observation and measurement) and a *theory*, including analysis into elements (such as stimulus–response units) and *associationism* (which explains how simple elements can be combined to form more complex ones).

Behaviourism also embodied positivism, in particular the emphasis on the need for scientific rigour and objectivity. Humans were now conceptualised and studied as 'natural phenomena', with subjective experience, consciousness and other characteristics (traditionally regarded as distinctive human qualities) no longer having a place in the behaviourist world.

The cognitive revolution

Academic psychology in the USA and the UK was dominated by behaviourism for the next 40 years. However, criticism and dissatisfaction with it culminated in a number of 'events', all taking place in 1956, which, collectively, are referred to as the 'cognitive revolution'.

This new way of thinking about and investigating people was called the *information-processing approach*. At its centre is the *computer analogy*, the view that human cognition can be understood by comparing it with the functioning of a digital computer. It was now acceptable to study the mind again, although its conceptualisation was very different from that of Wundt, James and the other pioneers of the 'new psychology' prior to Watson's 'behaviourist revolution'.

Box 58.3 The 1956 'cognitive revolution'

- At a meeting at the Massachusetts Institute of Technology (MIT), Chomsky introduced his theory of language (see Chapter 26), Miller presented a paper on the 'magical number seven' in short-term memory (see Gross *et al.*, 2000), and Newell and Simon presented a paper on the logical theory machine (or logic theorist), with a further paper by Newell *et al.* (1958), which Newell & Simon (1972) extended into the general problem solver (GPS: see Chapter 27).

- The first systematic attempt to investigate concept formation (in adults) from a cognitive psychological perspective was reported (Bruner *et al.*, 1956).

- At Dartmouth College, New Hampshire (the 'Dartmouth Conference'), ten academics met to discuss the possibilities of producing computer programs that could 'behave' or 'think' intelligently. These academics included McCarthy (generally attributed with having coined the term 'artificial intelligence'), Minsky, Simon, Newell, Chomsky and Miller.

(Based on Eysenck & Keane, 1995)

Science, scientism and mainstream psychology

Despite this major change in psychology after 1956, certain central assumptions and practices within the discipline have remained essentially the same, and these are referred to as *mainstream psychology*. Harré (1989) refers to the mainstream as the 'old paradigm', which he believes continues to be haunted by certain 'unexamined presuppositions', one of which is *scientism*, defined by Van Langenhove (1995) as:

'... the borrowing of methods and a characteristic vocabulary from the natural sciences in order to discover causal mechanisms that explain psychological phenomena'.

Scientism maintains that all aspects of human behaviour can and should be studied using the methods of natural science, which claims to be the sole means of establishing 'objective truth'. This can be achieved by studying phenomena removed from any particular context ('context-stripping' exposes them in their 'pure' form), and in a *value-free* way (there is no bias on the investigator's part). The most reliable way of doing this is through the laboratory experiment, the method providing the greatest degree of control over relevant variables (see Gross *et al.*, 2000, and Box 58.8, pages 635–636). As noted on page 625, these beliefs and assumptions add up to the traditional view of science known as positivism.

Exercise 4

Try to find examples of experimental studies of human behaviour that fit the definition of 'context-stripping' given above. Probably the 'best' examples will come from social psychology, which in itself should suggest criticisms of this approach to studying behaviour. (See also Chapter 55, page 589.)

Although much research has moved beyond the confines of the laboratory experiment, the same positivist logic is still central to how psychological inquiry is conceived and conducted. Method and measurement still have a privileged status:

'Whether concerned with mind or behaviour (and whether conducted inside or outside the laboratory), research tends to be constructed in terms of the separation (or reduction) of entities into independent and dependent variables and the measurement of hypothesised relationships between them' (Smith *et al.*, 1995).

Despite the fact that since the mid-1970s the natural sciences model has become the subject of vigorous attacks, psychology is still to a large extent dominated by it. The most prominent effect of this is the dominance of experiments (Van Langenhove, 1995). This has far-reaching effects on the way psychology *pictures* people as more or less passive and mechanical information-processing devices, whose behaviour can be split up into variables. It also affects the way psychology *deals* with people. In experiments, people are not treated as single individuals, but as interchangeable 'subjects'. There is no room for individualised observations.

WHAT DO WE MEAN BY 'SCIENCE'?

The major features of science

Most psychologists and philosophers of science would probably agree that for a discipline to be called a science, it must possess certain characteristics. These are summarised in Box 58.4 and Figure 58.5 (see page 630).

Box 58.4 The major features of science

- **A definable subject matter:** This changed from conscious human thought to human and non-human behaviour, then to cognitive processes within psychology's first 80 years as a separate discipline.

- **Theory construction:** This represents an attempt to explain observed phenomena, such as Watson's attempt to account for (almost all) human and non-human behaviour in terms of classical conditioning, and Skinner's subsequent attempt to do the same with operant conditioning.

- **Hypothesis testing:** This involves making specific predictions about behaviour under certain specified conditions (for example, predicting that by combining the sight of a rat with the sound of a hammer crashing down on a steel bar just behind his head, a small child will learn to fear the rat, as in the case of Little Albert: see page 556).

- **The use of empirical methods:** These are used to collect data (evidence) relevant to the hypothesis being tested.

What is 'scientific method'?

The account given in Box 58.4 and Figure 58.5 of what constitutes a science is non-controversial. However, it fails to tell us how the *scientific process* takes place, the sequence of 'events' involved (such as where the theory comes from in the first place, and how it is related to observation of the subject matter), or the exact relationship between theory construction, hypothesis testing and data collection.

Collectively, these 'events' and relationships are referred to as (the) *scientific method*. Table 58.1 (see page 630) summarises some common beliefs about both science and scientific method together with some alternative views.

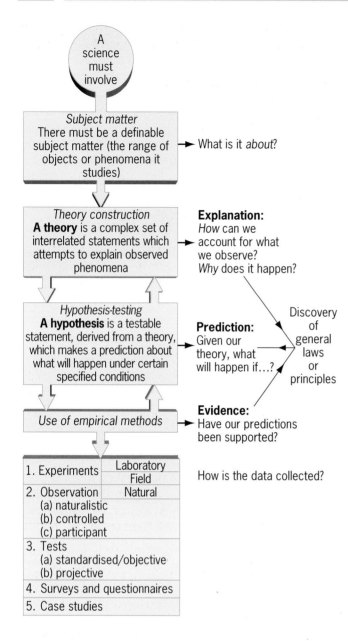

Figure 58.5 *A summary of the major features of a science*

Table 58.1 *Some common beliefs, and alternative views about, 'science' and 'scientific method'*

Common beliefs

▲ Scientific discovery begins with simple, unbiased, unprejudiced observation (i.e. the scientist simply 'samples' the world without any preconceptions, expectations or predetermined theories).

■ From the resulting sensory evidence ('data'/sense-data), generalised statements of fact will take shape (i.e. we gradually build up a picture of what the world is like based on a number of separate 'samples').

✳ The essential feature of scientific activity is the use of empirical methods, through which the sensory evidence is gathered (i.e. what distinguishes science from non-science is performing experiments and so on).

◆ The truth about the world (the objective nature of things, what the world is 'really like') can be established through properly controlled experiments and other ways of collecting 'facts' (i.e. science can tell us about reality as it is *independently* of the scientist or the activity of observing it).

▼ Science involves the steady accumulation of knowledge, so that each generation of scientists adds to the discoveries of previous generations.

Alternative views

▲ There is no such thing as 'unbiased' or 'unprejudiced' observation. Our observation is always selective, interpretative, pre-structured and directed (i.e. we must have at least some idea of what we are looking for, otherwise we cannot know when we have found it).

■ 'Data' do not constitute 'facts': evidence usually implies measurement, numbers, recordings and so on which need to be interpreted in the light of a theory. Facts do not exist objectively and cannot be discovered through 'pure observation'. 'Fact' = Data + Theory (Deese, 1972).

✳ Despite the central role of data collection, data alone do not make a science. Theory is just as crucial, because without it, data have no meaning (see second bullet above).

◆ Scientific theory and research reflect the biases, prejudices, values and assumptions of the individual scientist, as well as of the scientific community to which he or she belongs. Science is *not* value-free (see Chapter 55).

▼ Science involves an endless succession of long, peaceful periods ('normal science') and 'scientific revolutions' (Kuhn, 1962: see Table 58.3, page 632).

▲ Science has a warm, human, exciting, argumentative, creative 'face' (Collins, 1994: see Box 58.5, page 631).

(Based on Medawar, 1963, and Popper, 1972)

Box 58.5 The inner world of scientists

According to Richards & Wolpert (1997), scientists, outside their own habitat, are a poorly understood species. If they feature in popular awareness at all, it is through a limited set of media stereotypes. With a few exceptions, if scientists are not mad or bad, they are perceived as personality-free, their measured tones and formal reports implying ways of thinking and working far removed from the intellectual and emotional messiness of other human activities.

Richards and Wolpert engaged in a series of conversations with several eminent scientists (including chemists, immunologists, biologists, biochemists, neuro- and evolutionary biologists) in an attempt to redress the balance, and give a rare glimpse of the human reality of scientific life.

Scientists think and feel about their work using the same psychological apparatus as the rest of us. The human qualities of science come over very strongly: its energy and imaginative richness, the frustration, love and despair which enslaves its practitioners.

For example, Mitchison (an immunologist) says that experiments start with 'the act of creation':

'Not all experiments you think of are good experiments, but thinking of one is just wonderful, eureka! It's fantastic'.

According to Edelman (an immunologist and neurobiologist), stumbling upon the solution to a problem when you least expect to find it is a '... remarkable pleasure'. Some scientists are like voyeurs, with '... almost a lustful feeling of excitement when a secret of nature is revealed'.

(Adapted from Richards & Wolpert, 1997)

As a result of the first two beliefs identified in Table 58.1 (see page 630), Popper (1972) has revised the stages of the scientific process as proposed by the classical view (the *inductive method*). This, together with Popper's revised version, is shown in Table 58.2.

Can psychology be a science if psychologists cannot agree what psychology is?

As previously noted, definitions of psychology have changed during its lifetime, largely reflecting the influence and contributions of its major theoretical *approaches* or orientations. In this chapter, it has been seen that each approach rests upon a different image of what people are like, which in turn determines what is important to study, as well as the methods of study that can and should be used. Consequently, different approaches can

be seen as self-contained disciplines, as well as different facets of the same discipline (Kuhn, 1962; Kline, 1988).

Table 58.2 *Comparison between the classical, inductive view of science and Popper's revised version*

Inductive method	Popper's version
Observation and method	Problem (usually a refutation of an existing theory or prediction)
Inductive generalisation	Proposed solution or new theory
Hypothesis	Deduction of testable statements (hypotheses) from the new theory. This relates to the *hypothetico-deductive method*, which is usually contrasted with/opposed to the inductive method. In practice, *both* approaches are involved in the scientific process and are complementary.
Attempted verification of hypothesis	Tests or attempts to refute by methods including observation and experiment
Proof or disproof	Establishing a preference between competing theories
Knowledge	

(Based on Popper, 1972)

Exercise 5

What is the underlying image of the person associated with each of the major theoretical approaches within psychology? Which of these do you consider captures your own experience, and your experience of others, most accurately, and why?

Kuhn argues that a field of study can only legitimately be considered a science if a majority of its workers subscribe to a common, global perspective or *paradigm*. According to Kuhn, this means that psychology is *pre-paradigmatic*: it lacks a paradigm, without which it is still in a state (or stage) of *pre-science*. Whether psychology has, or has ever had, a paradigm, is hotly debated (see Table 58.3, page 632).

Is a theoretical approach the same as a paradigm?

As Table 58.3 (page 632) shows, Kuhn (a philosopher of science), along with some psychologists, maintains that psychology is still a pre-science. Others believe that psychology has already undergone at least two revolutions, and is in a stage of normal science, with cognitive psychology the current paradigm. A third view, which represents a blend of the first two, is that psychology currently, and simultaneously, has a number of paradigms.

Table 58.3 *Kuhn's three stages in the development of a science, and some views about how they apply to psychology*

Stages in the development of a science (▲) and their application to psychology (■)

▲ *Pre-science:* No paradigm has evolved, and there are several schools of thought or theoretical orientations.

■ Like Kuhn, Joynson (1980) and Boden (1980) argue that psychology is pre-paradigmatic. Kline (1988) sees its various approaches as involving different paradigms.

▲ *Normal science:* A paradigm has emerged, dictating the kind of research that is carried out and providing a framework for interpreting results. The details of the theory are filled in and workers explore its limits. Disagreements can usually be resolved within the limits allowed by the paradigm.

■ According to Valentine (1982), behaviourism comes as close as anything could to a paradigm. It provides: (i) a clear definition of the subject matter (behaviour, as opposed to 'the mind'); (ii) fundamental assumptions, in the form of the central role of learning (especially conditioning), and the analysis of behaviour into stimulus–response units, which allow prediction and control; (iii) a methodology, with the controlled experiment at its core.

▲ *Revolution:* A point is reached in almost all established sciences where the conflicting evidence becomes so overwhelming that the old paradigm has to be abandoned and is replaced by a new one (*paradigm shift*). For example, Newtonian physics was replaced by Einstein's theory of relativity. When this paradigm shift occurs, there is a return to normal science.

■ Palermo (1971) and LeFrancois (1983) argue that psychology has already undergone several paradigm shifts. The first paradigm was *structuralism*, represented by Wundt's introspectionism. This was replaced by Watson's *behaviourism*. Finally, *cognitive psychology* largely replaced behaviourism, based on the computer analogy and the concept of information processing. Glassman (1995) disagrees, claiming that there never has been a complete reorganisation of the discipline as has happened in physics.

(Based on Gross, 1996)

For example, Smith & Cowie (1991) identify psychoanalysis, behaviourism, sociobiology, the information-processing, and cognitive–developmental approaches as paradigms, with the last being the most important as far as child development is concerned (see Chapter 28). For Davison & Neale (1994) there are 'four major paradigms of contemporary abnormal psychology', namely, the biological, psychoanalytic, learning (behaviourist) and cognitive (see Gross *et al.*, 2000).

Lambie (1991) believes that it is a mistake to equate 'paradigm' with 'approach'. As noted in Table 58.2, whilst theory is an essential part of a paradigm, there is much more involved than this. For example, different

theories can coexist within the same overall approach, such as classical and operant conditioning within 'learning theory' (the behaviourist approach), and Freud's and Erikson's theories within the psychodynamic approach.

One of the 'ingredients' that makes a paradigm different from an approach is its *social psychological* dimension. Paradigms refer to assumptions and beliefs held in common by most, if not all, the members of a given scientific community. This issue is discussed further in the following section.

IS IT APPROPRIATE TO STUDY HUMAN BEHAVIOUR USING SCIENTIFIC METHODS?

The social nature of science: the problem of objectivity

'Doing science' is part of human behaviour. When psychologists study what people do, they are engaging in some of the very same behaviours they are trying to understand (such as thinking, perceiving, problem-solving and explaining). This is what is meant by the statement that psychologists are part of their own subject matter, which makes it even more difficult for them to be objective than other scientists.

According to Richards (1996b):

'Whereas in orthodox sciences there is always some external object of enquiry – rocks, electrons, DNA, chemicals – existing essentially unchanging in the non-human world (even if never finally knowable 'as it really is' beyond human conceptions), this is not so for Psychology. 'Doing Psychology' is the human activity of studying human activity; it is human psychology examining itself – and what it produces by way of new theories, ideas and beliefs about itself is also part of our psychology!'.

Knowable 'as it really is' refers to objectivity, and Richards is claiming that it may be impossible for *any* scientist to achieve complete objectivity. One reason for this relates to the *social nature of scientific activity*. As Rose (1997) says:

'How biologists – or any scientists, perceive the world is not the result of simply holding a true reflecting mirror up to nature: it is shaped by the history of our subject, by dominant social expectations and by the patterns of research funding'.

Does this mean that 'the truth' only exists 'by agreement'? Does science tell us not about what things are 'really' like, but only what scientists happen to believe is the truth at any particular time?

Exercise 6

Given what was said earlier about the sometimes very intense feelings aroused in individual scientists during the course of their work (see Box 58.5), in what ways do you think science can be described as a social activity? (It might be useful to think about why you do practical work – other than because you have to!)

According to Richardson (1991), whatever the *logical* aspects of scientific method may be (deriving hypotheses from theories, the importance of refutability and so on), science is a very *social* business. Research must be qualified and quantified to enable others to replicate it, and in this way the procedures, instruments and measures become standardised, so that scientists anywhere in the world can check the truth of reported observations and findings. This implies the need for universally agreed conventions for reporting these observations and findings (Richardson, 1991).

Collins (1994) takes a more extreme view, arguing that the results of experiments are more ambiguous than they are usually taken to be, whilst theory is more flexible than most people imagine:

'This means that science can progress only within communities that can reach consensus about what counts as plausible. Plausibility is a matter of social context so science is a "social construct"' (Collins, 1994).

Kuhn's concept of a paradigm also stresses the role of agreement or consensus among fellow scientists working within a particular discipline. Accordingly, 'truth' has more to do with the popularity and widespread acceptance of a particular framework within the scientific community than with its 'truth value'. The fact that revolutions do occur (paradigm shifts: see Table 58.3) demonstrates that 'the truth' can and does change.

For example, the change from Newtonian to Einsteinian physics reflected the changing popularity of these two accounts. For Planck, who helped to shape the 'Einsteinian revolution':

'A new scientific theory does not triumph by convincing its opponents and making them see the light, but rather because its opponents eventually die, and a new generation grows up that is familiar with it' (cited in Kuhn, 1970).

The popularity or acceptability of a theory, however, must be at least partly determined by how well it explains and predicts the phenomena in question. In other words, *both* social and 'purely' scientific or rational criteria are relevant.

However, even if there are widely accepted ways of 'doing science', 'good science' does not necessarily mean 'good psychology'. Is it valid to study human behaviour and experience as part of the natural world, or is a different kind of approach needed altogether? After all, it is not just psychologists who observe, experiment and theorise (Heather, 1976).

The psychology experiment as a social situation

To regard empirical research in general, and the experiment in particular, as objective involves two related assumptions. The first is that researchers only influence the *participant's* behaviour (the outcome of the experiment) to the extent that they decide what hypothesis to test, how the variables are to be operationalised, what design to use, and so on. The second assumption is that the only factors influencing the participants' performance are the objectively defined variables manipulated by the experimenter.

Exercise 7

Try to formulate some arguments *against* these two assumptions. What do the experimenter and participant bring with them into the experimental situation that is not directly related to the experiment, and how may this (and other factors) influence what goes on in the experimental situation? (See Chapter 55.)

Experimenters are people too: the problem of experimenter bias

According to Rosenthal (1966), what the experimenter is *like* is correlated with what s/he *does*, as well as influencing the participant's perception of, and response to, the experimenter. This is related to *experimenter bias*.

Box 58.6 Some examples of experimenter bias

According to Valentine (1992), experimenter bias has been demonstrated in a variety of experiments, including reaction time, psychophysics, non-human learning, verbal conditioning, personality assessment, person perception, learning and ability, as well as in everyday life situations.

What these experiments consistently show is that if one group of experimenters has one hypothesis about what it expects to find and another group has the opposite hypothesis, both groups will obtain results that support their respective hypotheses. The results are *not* due to the mishandling of data by biased experimenters, but the experimenter's bias somehow creates a changed environment, in which participants actually behave differently.

Experimenters who had been informed that rats learning mazes had been specially bred for this ability ('maze-bright'), obtained better learning from their rats than did experimenters who believed that their rats were 'maze-dull' (Rosenthal & Fode, 1963; Rosenthal & Lawson, 1961). In fact, both groups of rats were drawn from the *same* population and were *randomly* allocated to the 'bright' or 'dull' condition. The crucial point is that the 'bright' rats did actually learn faster. The experimenters' expectations in some way concretely changed the situation, although *how* this happened is far less clear.

In a natural classroom situation, children whose teachers were told that they would show academic 'promise' during the next academic year, showed significantly greater IQ gains than children for whom such predictions were not made (although this group also made substantial improvements). The children were, in fact, *randomly* allocated to the two conditions, but the teachers' expectations actually produced the predicted improvements in the 'academic promise' group, that is, there was a *self-fulfilling prophecy* (Rosenthal & Jacobson, 1968).

(Based on Valentine, 1992, and Weisstein, 1993)

Exercise 8

How could you explain the findings from the studies described in Box 58.6? How could experimenter expectations actually bring about the different performances of the two groups of rats and children?

Participants are psychologists too: demand characteristics

Instead of seeing the person being studied as a passive responder to whom things are done ('subject'), Orne (1962) stresses what the person *does*, implying a far more active role. Participants' performance in an experiment could be thought of as a form of problem-solving behaviour. At some level, they see the task as working out the true purpose of the experiment and responding in a way which will support (or not support, in the case of the unhelpful participant) the hypothesis being tested.

In this context, the cues which convey the experimental hypothesis to participants represent important influences on their behaviour, and the sum total of those cues are called the *demand characteristics* of the experimental situation. These cues include:

'... the rumours or campus scuttlebut [gossip] about the research, the information conveyed during the original situation, the person of the experimenter, and the setting of the laboratory, as well as all explicit and implicit communications during the experiment proper' (Orne, 1962).

This tendency to identify the demand characteristics is related to the tendency to play the role of a 'good' (or 'bad') experimental participant.

Box 58.7 The lengths that some people will go to to please the experimenter

Orne (1962) points out that if people are asked to do five push-ups as a favour, they will ask 'Why?', but if the request comes from an experimenter, they will ask 'Where?' Similarly, he reports an experiment in which people were asked to add sheets of random numbers, then tear them up into at least 32 pieces. Five-and-a-half hours later, they were still at it and the experimenter had to stop them!

This demonstrates very clearly the strong tendency to want to please the experimenter, and not to 'upset the experiment'. It is mainly in this sense that Orne sees the experiment as a social situation, in which the people involved play different but complementary roles. In order for this interaction to proceed fairly smoothly, each must have some idea of what the other expects of him or her.

The expectations referred to in Box 58.7 are part of the culturally shared understandings of what science in general, and psychology in particular, involves and without which the experiment could not 'happen' (Moghaddam *et al.*, 1993). So, not only is the experiment a social situation, but science itself is a *culture-related phenomenon*. This represents another respect in which science cannot claim complete objectivity.

The problem of representativeness

Traditional, mainstream experimental psychology adopts a *nomothetic* ('law-like') approach. This involves generalisation from limited samples of participants to 'people in general', as part of the attempt to establish general 'laws' or principles of behaviour (see Figure 58.5, page 630).

Exercise 9

Figure 58.6 (see page 635) captures a fairly typical scene as far as participant characteristics in mainstream psychological research are concerned.

Figure 58.6

In this photograph of one of Asch's famous conformity experiments (see Gross *et al.*, 2000), what are the most apparent characteristics of the experimental participants, and how are they similar to/different from those of Asch (who is pictured furthest right)?

Despite the fact that Asch's experiments were carried out in the early 1950s, very little has changed as far as participant samples are concerned. In American psychology, at least, the typical participant is a psychology undergraduate, who is obliged to take part in a certain number of studies as a course requirement, and who receives 'course credit' for so doing (Krupat & Garonzik, 1994).

Mainstream British and American psychology has implicitly equated 'human being' with 'member of Western culture'. Despite the fact that the vast majority of research participants are members of Western societies, the resulting findings and theories have been applied to 'human beings', as if culture made no difference (they are culture-bound and culture-blind: Sinha, 1997). This Anglocentric or Eurocentric bias (a form of *ethnocentrism*) is matched by the androcentric or masculinist bias (a form of *sexism*), according to which the behaviours and experiences of men are taken as the standard against which women are judged (see Chapter 55).

In both cases, whilst the bias remains implicit and goes unrecognised (and is reinforced by psychology's claim to be objective and value-free), research findings are taken as providing us with an objective, scientifically valid, account of what 'women/people in general are like'. Once we realise that scientists, like all human beings, have prejudices, biases and values, their research and theory begin to look less objective, reliable and valid than they did before (see Chapter 55).

The problem of artificiality

Criticisms of traditional empirical methods (especially the laboratory experiment) have focused on their *artificiality*, including the often unusual and bizarre tasks that people are asked to perform in the name of science (see Box 58.7, page 634). Yet we cannot be sure that the way people behave in the laboratory is an accurate indication of how they are likely to behave outside it (Heather, 1976).

What makes the laboratory experiment such an unnatural and artificial situation is the fact that it is almost totally structured by one 'participant' – the experimenter. This relates to *power differences* between experimenters and their 'subjects', which is as much an *ethical* as a practical issue (see Chapter 56).

Traditionally, participants have been referred to as 'subjects', implying something less than a person, a dehumanised and depersonalised 'object'. According to Heather (1976), it is a small step from reducing the person to a mere thing or object (or experimental 'subject'), to seeing people as machines or machine-like ('mechanism' = 'machine-ism' = mechanistic view of people). This way of thinking about people is reflected in the popular definition of psychology as the study of 'what makes people tick' (see page 625).

The problem of internal versus external validity

If the experimental setting (and task) is seen as similar or relevant enough to everyday situations to allow us to generalise the results, we say that the study has high *external* or *ecological validity*. But what about *internal validity*? Modelling itself on natural science, psychology attempts to overcome the problem of the complexity of human behaviour by using *experimental control* (what Rose, 1997, calls *reductionism* as *methodology*: see Box 57.7, page 619). This involves isolating an independent variable (IV) and ensuring that extraneous variables (variables other than the IV likely to affect the dependent variable) do not affect the outcome (see Gross *et al.*, 2000). But this begs the crucial question: *how do we know when all the relevant extraneous variables have been controlled?*

Box 58.8 Some difficulties with the notion of experimental control

- Whilst it is relatively easy to control the more obvious *situational variables*, this is more difficult with *participant variables* (such as age, gender and culture), either for practical reasons (such as the availability of these groups), or because it is not always obvious exactly what the relevant variables are. Ultimately, it is down to the experimenter's judgement and intuition: what s/he believes is important (and possible) to control (Deese, 1972).

- If judgement and intuition are involved, then control and objectivity are matters of degree, whether it is in psychology or physics (see Table 58.1, page 630).

- It is the *variability/heterogeneity* of human beings that makes them so much more difficult to study than, say, chemicals. Chemists don't usually have to worry about how two samples of a particular chemical might be different from each other, but psychologists definitely do have to allow for individual differences between participants.

- We cannot just assume that the IV (or 'stimulus' or 'input') is identical for every participant, definable in some objective way, independently of the participant, and exerting a standard effect on everyone. The attempt to define IVs (and DVs) in this way can be regarded as a form of *reductionism* (see Chapter 57).

- Complete control would mean that the IV alone was responsible for the DV, so that experimenter bias and the effect of demand characteristics were irrelevant. But even if complete control were possible (even if we could guarantee the *internal validity*

of the experiment), a fundamental dilemma would remain. The greater the degree of control over the experimental situation, the more different it becomes from real-life situations (the more artificial it gets and the lower its *external validity*).

As Box 58.8 indicates, in order to discover the relationships between variables (necessary for understanding human behaviour in natural, real-life situations), psychologists must 'bring' the behaviour into a specially created environment (the laboratory), where the relevant variables can be controlled in a way that is impossible in naturally-occurring settings. However, in doing so, psychologists have constructed an artificial environment and the resulting behaviour is similarly artificial. It is no longer the behaviour they were trying to understand!

CONCLUSIONS

Psychology as a separate field of study grew out of several other disciplines, both scientific (such as physiology), and non-scientific (in particular philosophy). For much of its life as an independent discipline, and through what some call revolutions and paradigm shifts, it has taken the natural sciences as its model (scientism). This chapter highlighted some of the major implications of adopting

methods of investigating the natural world and applying them to the study of human behaviour and experience. In doing this, the chapter has also examined what are fast becoming out-dated and inaccurate views about the nature of science. Ultimately, whatever a particular science may claim to have discovered about the phenomena it studies, scientific activity remains just one more aspect of human behaviour.

Summary

- **Philosophical dualism** enabled scientists to describe the world **objectively**, which became the ideal of science. Its extension by Comte to the study of human behaviour and social institutions is called **positivism**. Descartes extended **mechanism** to the human body, but the mind remained accessible only through **introspection**.

- **Empirism** emphasises the importance of sensory experience, as opposed to **nativism's** claim that knowledge is innate. 'Empirical' implies that the essence of science is collecting data/'facts' through experiments and observations. Empirism influenced psychology through its influence on physiology, physics and chemistry.

- Wundt is generally regarded as the founder of the new science of experimental psychology, establishing its first laboratory in 1879. He used **introspection** to

study conscious experience, analysing it into its basic elements (**sensations** and **feelings**). This is called **structuralism**.

- James is the other pioneer of scientific psychology. He influenced several important research areas, and helped make Freud's ideas popular in America. His views influenced **functionalism** which, in turn, stimulated interest in **individual differences**.

- Watson's criticisms of introspection culminated in his 1913 'behaviourist manifesto'. He argued that for psychology to be objective, it must study behaviour rather than mental life, its goals should be the prediction and control of **behaviour**, and there are only **quantitative** differences between human and non-human behaviour.

- Instead of the mind being influenced by experience (as Locke believed), Watson saw **behaviour** as shaped by the environment. Empirism provided both a **methodology** and a **theory** (including analysis into elements and **associationism**). Consciousness and subjective experience had no place in the behaviourist world, and people were studied as 'natural phenomena'.

- Dissatisfaction with behaviourism culminated in the 1956 'cognitive revolution'. At the centre of this new **information-processing approach** lay the **computer analogy**.

- Despite this major change, **mainstream** psychology (the 'old paradigm') has survived. **Scientism** maintains that all aspects of human behaviour can and should be studied using the methods of natural science. It involves 'context-stripping' and the **value-free**, objective use of laboratory experiments in particular. People are seen as passive and mechanical information-processing devices and treated as interchangeable 'subjects'.

- A science must possess a definable **subject matter**, involve **theory construction** and **hypothesis testing**, and use **empirical methods** for data collection. However, these characteristics fail to describe the **scientific process** or **scientific method**.

- Whilst the classical view of science is built around the **inductive method**, Popper's revised view stresses the **hypothetico-deductive method**. The two methods are complementary.

- Different theoretical **approaches** can be seen as self-contained disciplines, making psychology **pre-paradigmatic** and so still in a stage of **pre-science**. According to Kuhn, only when a discipline possesses a paradigm has it reached the stage of **normal science**, after which **paradigm shifts** result in **revolution** (and a return to normal science).

- Even where there are external objects of scientific enquiry (as in chemistry), complete **objectivity** may be impossible. Whatever the **logical** aspects of scientific method may be, science is a very **social** activity. Consensus among colleagues is paramount, as shown by the fact that revolutions involve re-defining 'the truth'.

- **Experimenter bias** and **demand characteristics** make psychological research (especially experiments) even less objective than the natural sciences. Environmental changes are somehow produced by experimenters' expectations, and demand characteristics influence participants' behaviours by helping to convey the experimental hypothesis.

- Participants' performance is a form of problem-solving behaviour and reflects their playing the roles of 'good' (or 'bad') experimental participants. The experiment is a social situation and science itself is **culture-related**.

- The **artificiality** of laboratory experiments is largely due to their being totally structured by experimenters. Also, the higher an experiment's **internal validity**, the lower its **external validity** becomes. Whilst certain **situational variables** can be controlled quite easily, this is more difficult with **participant variables**.

Essay Questions

1 a Define the term 'science'. (*5 marks*)
   b Outline the development of psychology as a separate discipline. (*10 marks*)
   c With reference to **two** areas/branches of psychology (e.g. physiological, developmental), assess the extent to which psychology can be regarded as a science. (*15 marks*)

2 Describe and evaluate arguments for and against the claim that psychology is a science. (*30 marks*)

WEB ADDRESSES

http://elvers.stjoe.udayton.edu/history/people/Wundt.html
http://mfp.es.emory.edu/james.html
http://www.users.csbsju.edu/~tcredd/pb/pbnames.html
http://www.lucknow.com/horus/guide/cm106.html

59 Nature and Nurture

The debate concerning the influence of nature and nurture (or heredity and environment) is one of the longest-running, and most controversial, both inside and outside psychology. It deals with some of the most fundamental questions that human beings (at least those from Western cultures) ask about themselves, such as 'How do we come to be the way we are?' and 'What makes us develop in the way we do?'.

These and similar questions have been posed (sometimes explicitly, sometimes implicitly) throughout this book in relation to a wide range of topics. These include aggression (Chapter 7), perceptual abilities (Chapter 24), language acquisition (Chapter 26), intelligence (Chapter 29), personality development (Chapter 31), gender development (Chapter 32), schizophrenia (Chapter 49), and depression (Chapter 50). In some of these examples, the focus of the debate is on an ability *shared by all human beings* (such as language and perception), whilst in others the focus is on *individual differences* (such as intelligence and schizophrenia). In both cases, however, certain assumptions are made about the exact meaning of 'nature' and 'nurture', as well as about how they are related.

The first part of this chapter looks at the history of the nature–nurture debate within psychology, including the viewpoints of some of the major theorists. It then considers the meaning of 'nature' and 'nurture'. By distinguishing different types of environment, such as *shared* and *non-shared*, it is easier to understand the *relationship* between nature and nurture, including *gene–environment correlation* and *gene–environment interaction*. The final part of the chapter discusses *behaviour genetics* and the concept of *heritability*.

THE HISTORY OF THE NATURE–NURTURE DEBATE: NATIVISM, EMPIRISM AND INTERACTIONISM

Nativism is the philosophical theory according to which knowledge of the world is largely innate or inborn: nature (heredity) is seen as determining certain abilities and capacities. The French philosopher Descartes was a seventeenth-century nativist theorist who, as noted in Chapter 58, had an enormous impact on science in general, including psychology. At the opposite philosophical extreme is *empirism*, associated mainly with seventeenth-century British philosophers, and even more influential on the development of psychology. A key empirist was Locke, who believed that at birth the human mind is a *tabula rasa* (or 'blank slate'). This is gradually 'filled in' by learning and experience.

Exercise 1

Try to identify psychological (and other) theories which adopt an *extreme* position regarding the nature–nurture issue. Which particular features of the theories made you classify them in this way?

Nativism and empirism are extreme theories in that they were trying to answer the question 'Is it nature or nurture?', as if *only* one or the other could be true. Early psychological theories tended to reflect these extremes, as in Gesell's concept of *maturation* and Watson's *behaviourism*.

Box 59.1 Gesell and Watson: two extreme viewpoints

According to Gesell (1925), one of the American pioneers of developmental psychology, *maturation* refers to genetically programmed patterns of change. The instructions for these patterns are part of the specific hereditary information passed on at the moment of conception (Bee, 2000). All individuals will pass through the same series of changes, in the same order, making maturational patterns *universal* and *sequential*. They are also *relatively impervious to environmental influence*.

Gesell was mainly concerned with infants' psychomotor development (such as grasping and other manipulative skills, and locomotion, such as crawling and walking). These abilities are usually seen as 'developing by themselves', according to a genetically determined timetable. Provided the baby is physically normal, practice or training are not needed – the abilities just 'unfold'.

For Watson (1925), environmental influence is all-important (see Chapter 58), and human beings are completely malleable:

'Give me a dozen healthy infants, well-formed, and my own specialised world to bring them up in and I'll guarantee to take any one at random and train him to become any type of specialist I might select – a doctor, lawyer, artist, merchant-chief and, yes, even beggar-man and thief, regardless of his talents, penchants, abilities, vocations and race of his ancestors'.

Watson (1928) also claimed that there is no such thing as an inheritance of capacity, talent, temperament, mental constitution and character:

'The behaviourists believe that there is nothing from within to develop. If you start with the right number of fingers and toes, eyes, and a few elementary movements that are present at birth, you do not need anything else in the way of raw material to make a man, be that man genius, a cultured gentleman, a rowdy or a thug'.

Exercise 2

Try to identify psychological theories and areas of research in which the process of maturation plays an important role. Examples are most likely to be found in developmental psychology.

The concept of maturation continues to be influential within psychology. Not only does maturation explain major biological changes, such as puberty (see Chapter 33) and physical aspects of ageing (see Chapter 36), but all stage theories of development assume that maturation underpins the universal sequence of stages. Examples include Freud's psychosexual theory (see Chapter 31), Erikson's psychosocial theory (see Chapters 31, 33, 34 and 36), and Piaget's theory of cognitive development (see Chapter 28). Watson's extreme empirism (or *environmentalism*) was adopted in Skinner's *radical behaviourism*, which represents a major model of both normal and abnormal behaviour (see Chapters 38 and 53).

Are nativism and empirism mutually exclusive?

As noted in Box 59.1 (see page 638), maturationally determined developmental sequences occur regardless of practice or training. However, as Bee (2000) points out:

'These powerful, apparently automatic maturational patterns require at least some minimal environmental support, such as adequate diet and opportunity for movement and experimentation'.

At the very least, the environment must be *benign*, that is, it must not be harmful in any way, preventing the ability or characteristic from developing. More importantly, the ability or characteristic cannot develop without environmental 'input'. For example, the possession of a language acquisition device (LAD) as proposed by Chomsky (1965: see Chapter 26) must be applied to the particular linguistic data provided by the child's linguistic community, so that the child will only acquire *that* language (although it could just as easily have acquired *any* language). This is an undeniable fact about language acquisition, which Chomsky himself recognised.

Another example of the role of the environment involves vision. One of the proteins required for development of the visual system is controlled by a gene whose action is triggered only by visual experience (Greenough, 1991). So, *some* visual experience is needed for the genetic programme to operate. Although every (sighted) child will have some such experience under normal circumstances, examples like these tell us that maturational sequences do not simply 'unfold'. The system appears to be 'ready' to develop along particular pathways, but it requires experience to trigger the movement (Bee, 2000).

Another way of considering the interplay between nature and nurture is to look at Freud's and Piaget's developmental theories. Although maturation underlies the sequence of stages in both theories, the role of experience is at least as important.

Box 59.2 Nature and nurture in Freud's and Piaget's developmental theories

For Freud it is not the sexual instinct itself that matters, but rather the reactions of significant others (especially parents) to the child's attempts to satisfy its sexual needs. Both excessive frustration *and* satisfaction can produce long-term effects on the child's personality, such as fixation at particular stages of development (see Box 31.1, page 334).

Although Freud is commonly referred to as an instinct theorist (suggesting that he was a nativist), his concept of an instinct was very different from the earlier view of unlearned, largely automatic (pre-programmed) responses to specific stimuli (based on non-human species: see Chapter 37). Instead of using the German word '*Instinkt*', he used '*Trieb*' ('drive'), which denotes a relatively undifferentiated form of energy capable of almost infinite variation through experience (see Gross *et al*., 2000).

As a biologist, Piaget stressed the role of *adaptation* to the environment. This involves the twin processes of *assimilation* and *accommodation*, which in turn are related to (*dis-*)*equilibration* (see Chapter 28). These mechanisms are part of the biological 'equipment' of human beings, without which intelligence would not change (the individual would not progress through increasingly complex stages of development). However, the infant actively explores its environment and *constructs* its own knowledge and understanding of the world (the child as scientist: Rogoff, 1990). According to Piaget (1970), intelligence consists:

' ... neither of a simple copy of external objects nor of a mere unfolding of structures preformed inside the subject, but rather ... a set of structures constructed by continuous interaction between the subject and the external world'.

Both Freud's and Piaget's theories demonstrate that:

' There is a trade-off in nature between pre-specification, on the one hand, and plasticity, on the other, leading ultimately to the kind of flexibility one finds in the human mind' (Karmiloff-Smith, 1996).

Maturation is an example of what Karmiloff-Smith means by 'pre-specification', and *inborn biases* represent another example. For example, very young babies already seem to understand that unsupported objects will fall (move downward), and that a moving object will continue to move in the same direction unless it encounters an obstacle (Spelke, 1991: see Chapter 24). However, these 'pre-existing conceptions' are merely the *beginning* of the story. What then develops is the result of experience filtered through these initial biases, which *constrain* the number of developmental pathways that are possible (Bee, 2000).

According to Bee (2000), no developmental psychologists today would take seriously the 'Is it nature or nurture?' form of the debate. Essentially, every facet of a child's development is a product of some pattern of interaction between the two. Until fairly recently, however, the theoretical pendulum was well over towards the nurture/environmental end of the continuum. In the last decade or so, there has been a marked swing back towards the nature/biological end, partly because of the

impact of *sociobiology* and its more recent off-shoot *evolutionary psychology* (see Chapters 43–45).

Exercise 3

Draw a diagram, representing a continuum, with 'extreme nativism' (nature) at one end and 'extreme empirism' (nurture) at the other. Then place theories along the continuum to indicate the emphasis they give to either nature or nurture – or both. The theories can be drawn from any area of psychology. They are likely to include those identified in Exercise 1, but should also reflect the approaches discussed in Chapter 55. Some examples are given in Figure 59.3 on page 642.

What do we mean by 'nature'?

In the *Introduction and overview*, it was noted that some examples of the nature–nurture debate involve abilities or capacities common to all human beings (such as language and perception), whilst others involve individual differences (such as intelligence and schizophrenia). According to Plomin (1994), it is in the latter sense that the debate 'properly' takes place, and much of the rest of this chapter will reflect this individual differences approach.

Within *genetics* (the science of heredity), 'nature' refers to what is typically thought of as inheritance, that is, differences in genetic material (chromosomes and genes) which are transmitted from generation to generation (from parents to offspring). The 'father' of genetics, Gregor Mendel (1866), explained the difference between smooth and wrinkled seeds in garden peas in terms of different genes. Similarly, modern human genetics focuses on genetic differences between individuals, reflecting the use of the word 'nature' by Galton, who coined the phrase *nature–nurture* in 1883 as it is used in the scientific arena (Plomin, 1994).

So, what are genes? Genes are the basic unit of hereditary transmission, consisting of large molecules of deoxyribonucleic acid (DNA). These are extremely complex chemical chains, comprising a ladder-like, double helix structure (discovered by Watson & Crick in 1953: see Figure 59.1, page 641).

The genes, which occur in pairs, are situated on the *chromosomes*, which are found within the nuclei of living cells. The normal human being inherits 23 pairs of chromosomes, one member of each pair from each parent. The twenty-third pair comprises the sex chromosomes, which are two Xs in females, and an X and a Y in males (see Chapter 32 and Figure 59.2, page 641).

The steps of the gene's double helix (or 'spiral staircase': Plomin, 1994) consist of four nucleotide bases (adenine, thymine, cytosine and guanine). These can occur in any order on one side of the double helix, but the order on the other side is always fixed, such that adenine always pairs with thymine, and cytosine always pairs with guanine. Taking just one member of each of the 23 pairs of chromosomes, the human *genome* comprises more than three billion nucleotide base pairs (Plomin, 1994). Two major functions of genes are *self-duplication* and *protein synthesis*.

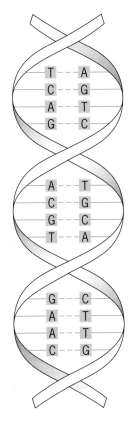

thymine is bound to adenine

cytosine is bound to guanine

Figure 59.1 *The structure of a DNA molecule represented schematically. This shows its double-stranded coiled structure and the complementary binding of nucleotide bases, guanine (G) to cytosine (C) and adenine (A) to thymine (T)*

Self-duplication

DNA copies itself by unzipping in the middle of the spiral staircase, with each half forming its complement: when a cell divides, all the genetic information (chromosomes and genes) contained within the cell nucleus is reproduced. This means that the 'offspring' cells are identical to the 'parent' cells (*mitosis*), but this process applies only to *non-gonadal* (non-reproductive) cells (such as skin, blood and muscle cells).

The reproductive (or germ) cells (ova in females, sperm in males) duplicate through *meiosis*, whereby each cell only contains half the individual's chromosomes and genes. Which member of a chromosome pair goes to any particular cell seems to be determined randomly. The resulting germ cells (*gametes*), therefore, contain 23 chromosomes, one of which will be either an X (female) or a Y (male). When a sperm fertilises an ovum, the two sets of chromosomes combine to form a new individual with a full set of 46 chromosomes.

Protein synthesis

The 'genetic code' was 'cracked' in the 1960s. Essentially, DNA controls the production of *ribonucleic acid* (RNA) within the cell nucleus. This 'messenger' RNA moves outside the nucleus and into the surrounding cytoplasm, where it is converted by ribosomes into sequences of amino acids, the building blocks of proteins and enzymes.

Genes that code for proteins and enzymes are called *structural genes*, and they represent the foundation of classical genetics (Plomin, 1994). The first single-gene disorders discovered in the human species involved metabolic disorders caused by mutations (spontaneous changes) in structural genes. A much-cited example is *phenylketonuria*, which is discussed in relation to gene–environment interaction (see pages 645–646).

Most genes are *regulator* genes, which code for products that bind with DNA itself and serve to regulate other genes. Unlike the structural genes which are 'deaf'

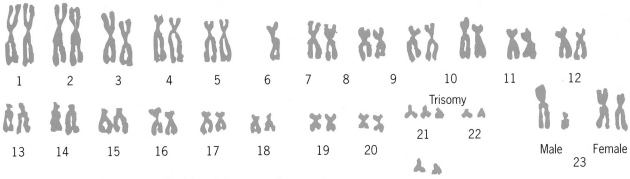

Figure 59.2 *A sample karyotype. The 21st chromosome has one too many chromosomes, a common problem. This is called a 'trisomy'. The 23rd chromosome pair is shown with both male and female versions. In a normal karyotype, only one such pair would be found*

to the environment, the regulator genes communicate closely with the environment and change in response to it (Plomin, 1994).

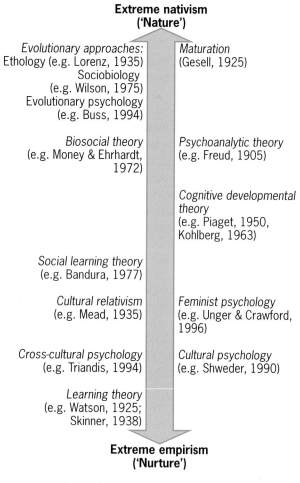

Extreme nativism ('Nature')

Evolutionary approaches:
Ethology (e.g. Lorenz, 1935)
Sociobiology
(e.g. Wilson, 1975)
Evolutionary psychology
(e.g. Buss, 1994)

Maturation
(Gesell, 1925)

Biosocial theory
(e.g. Money & Ehrhardt, 1972)

Psychoanalytic theory
(e.g. Freud, 1905)

Cognitive developmental theory
(e.g. Piaget, 1950, Kohlberg, 1963)

Social learning theory
(e.g. Bandura, 1977)

Cultural relativism
(e.g. Mead, 1935)

Feminist psychology
(e.g. Unger & Crawford, 1996)

Cross-cultural psychology
(e.g. Triandis, 1994)

Cultural psychology
(e.g. Shweder, 1990)

Learning theory
(e.g. Watson, 1925; Skinner, 1938)

Extreme empirism ('Nurture')

Figure 59.3 *A continuum representing the position of various psychological (and other) theories on the nature–nurture debate*

Neurogenetic determinism: are there genes 'for' anything?

As noted in Chapter 57 (see Box 57.7, page 619), several claims have been made in recent years about the discovery of genes 'for' a wide range of complex human behaviours (*reductionism as ideology*: Rose, 1997). Related to this is what Rose calls *neurogenetic determinism*, the claim that there is a direct causal link between genes and behaviour. This involves the false assumption that causes can be classified as *either* genetic or environmental, and there are additional reasons for doubting the validity of neurogenetic determinism.

The phrase 'genes for' is a convenient, but misleading, shorthand used by geneticists. In the case of eye colour, for example (which, from a genetic point of view, is one of the more simple characteristics – or *phenotypes*), there is a difference in the biochemical pathways that

lead to brown and to blue eyes. In blue-eyed people, the gene for a particular enzyme (which catalyses a chemical transformation *en route* to the synthesis of the pigment) is either missing or non-functional for some reason. A gene 'for' blue eyes now has to be reinterpreted as meaning 'one or more genes *in whose absence* the metabolic pathway that leads to pigmented eyes terminates at the blue-eye stage' (Rose, 1997).

As more is learned about the human genome, geneticists come to realise that many supposedly 'single-gene disorders' result from different gene mutations in different people. They may show a similar clinical picture, such as high blood cholesterol levels with an enhanced risk of coronary heart disease. However, the gene mutation, and hence the enzyme malfunction, that results in the disorder may be very different in each case. This also means that a drug which effectively treats the condition in one person may simply not work in another, whose cholesterol accumulation is caused by *different* biochemical factors (Rose, 1997).

Box 59.3 Is there more to heredity than DNA?

Cells not only inherit genes, they also inherit a set of instructions that tell the genes when to become active, in which tissue and to what extent. Without this 'epigenetic' instruction manual, multicellular organisms would be impossible. Every cell, whether a liver or skin cell, inherits exactly the same set of genes. However, the manual has different instructions for different cell types, allowing the cell to develop its distinctive identity. It seems that the instruction manual is wiped clean during the formation of germ cells, ensuring that all genes are equally available, until the embryo begins to develop specific tissues. However, there is evidence to suggest that changes in the epigenetic instruction manual can sometimes be passed from parent to offspring.

For example, pregnant women facing the brunt of the Nazi siege of the Netherlands at the end of World War II were reduced to near starvation. Some miscarried, but if they successfully gave birth, their babies appeared quite normal after a period of catch-up growth, and seemed no different from their better-nourished peers when tested at age 18. Many of these war babies now have children of their own (the grandchildren of the war-time pregnant mothers). Even girls who had themselves been of normal weight at birth produced babies who were either underweight or grew into small adults, despite the post-war generation being well fed. Thus, there is a sort of 'sleeper effect', whereby the effects of starvation skipped a generation.

Such 'awkward' findings are very difficult for geneticists to explain. However, one possible explanantion is in the form of an epigenetic phenomenon called 'imprinting' (Reik, cited in Vines, 1998). Genes exist in pairs and they behave in exactly the same way regardless of which parent they come from. However, in some cases an imprinted gene is activated only if it comes from the father, and in other cases only if it comes from the mother. Some sort of 'mark' must persist through the generations to tell the offspring's cells which genes to re-imprint. Whatever the precise mechanism by which they operate, the existence of imprinted genes demonstrates that not all genes are wiped totally clean of their epigenetic marks.

(Based on Ceci & Williams, 1999; Vines, 1998)

What do we mean by 'nurture'?

Exercise 4

What do you understand by the term 'environment'? Try to identify different uses of the term and different 'levels' at which the environment exists.

When the term 'environment' is used in a psychological context, it usually refers to all those *post-natal* influences (or potential sources of influence) lying *outside/external to* the individual's body. These include other people, both members of the immediate family and other members of society, opportunities for intellectual stimulation, and the physical circumstances of the individual's life ('environs' = 'surroundings'). These influences are implicitly seen as impinging on a passive individual, who is *shaped by* them (as shown in Figure 59.4).

On all three counts, this view of the environment seems inadequate. It is not just the individual person who is 'immersed in'/influenced by his/her environment, but during mitosis the specific location of any particular cell is constantly changing as the cluster of cells of which it is a part is constantly growing. At an even more micro-level, the cell nucleus (which contains the DNA) has as its environment the cytoplasm of the cell (see Figure 59.5).

As noted in Box 29.3 (see page 313), pre-natal non-genetic factors (such as the mother's excessive alcohol consumption during pregnancy) account for the largest proportion of biologically caused learning difficulties and lowered IQ. Finally, and most significantly, not only is 'nature' and 'nurture' a false dichotomy (see *Conclusions*, page 648), but it is invalid to regard the environment as existing independently of the individual (that is, objectively). Not only do people's environments influence them, but people make their own environ-

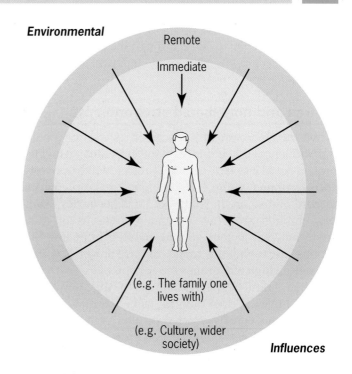

Figure 59.4 *Traditional, extreme behaviourist/environmentalist view of the environment as a set of external, post-natal influences acting upon a purely passive individual*

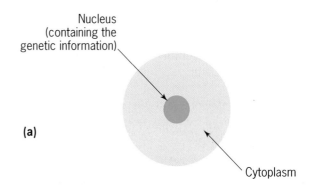

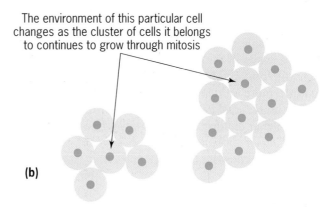

Figure 59.5 *For the nucleus of an individual cell, the environment is the surrounding cytoplasm (a). The specific location of any particular cell is constantly changing during mitosis (b)*

ments (Scarr, 1992: see Box 59.4). A way of thinking about how people do this is through the concept of *non-shared environments*, which is, in turn, related to *gene–environment correlation*.

Shared and non-shared environments

When the environment is discussed as a set of (potential) influences that impinge on the individual, it is often broken down into factors such as overcrowding, poverty, socioeconomic status (SES), family break-up, marital discord and so on. In studies of intelligence, for example, children are often compared in terms of these environmental factors, so that children from low SES groups are commonly found to have lower IQs than those from high SES groups (see Chapter 29).

When families are compared in this way, it is assumed that children from the same family will all be similarly and equally affected by those environmental factors (*shared environment*). For most characteristics, however, most children within the same family are not very similar. In fact, they are often extremely varied in personality, abilities and psychological disorders. This observation is most striking when two adopted children are brought up in the same family: they are usually no more alike than any two people chosen at random from the general population (Plomin, 1996; Rutter & Rutter, 1992).

This substantial within-family variation does *not* mean that family environment is unimportant. Rather, as Plomin (1996) puts it:

> 'Environmental influences in development are doled out on an individual-by-individual basis rather than on a family-by-family basis'.

In other words, differences between children growing up together is exactly what we would expect to find, because it is the *non-shared environment* which has greater influence on development than the shared environment. Different children in the same family have different experiences. For example, Dunn & Plomin (1990) found that the ways in which parents respond differently to their different children (*relative differences*) are likely to be much more influential than the overall characteristics of the family (*absolute differences*). So, it may matter very little whether children are brought up in a home that is less loving or more punitive than average, whereas it may matter considerably that one child receives less affection or more punishment than his/her sibling. These findings imply:

> '... that the unit of environmental transmission is not the family, but rather micro-environments within families' (Plomin & Thompson, 1987).

Gene–environment correlations

The concept of non-shared environments helps explain *how* the environment influences development, which is far more sophisticated and useful than the original 'Is it nature or nurture?' question (see page 639). However, we need to understand the processes by which non-shared environments arise: *why* do parents treat their different children differently, and *how* do children in the same family come to have different experiences? In trying to answer this question, psychologists and behaviour geneticists (see page 647) have, paradoxically, stressed the role of *genetic differences*. A major example of this approach is the concept of *gene–environment correlation*.

Box 59.4 Gene–environment correlations

Plomin *et al*. (1977) identified three types of gene–environment correlations:

- **Passive gene–environment correlations:** Children passively inherit from their parents environments that are correlated with their genetic tendencies. For example, parents who are of above average IQ are likely to provide a more intellectually stimulating environment than lower IQ parents.

- **Reactive gene–environment correlations:** Children's experiences derive from the reactions of other people to the children's genetic tendencies. For example, babies with a sunny, easy-going and cheerful disposition/temperament are more likely to elicit friendly reactions from others than miserable or 'difficult' babies (see Box 59.5, page 646 and Chapter 31). It is widely accepted that some children are easier to love (Rutter & Rutter, 1992). Similarly, aggressive children tend to experience aggressive environments, because they tend to evoke aggressive responses in others (see Chapter 7).

- **Active gene–environment correlations:** Children construct and reconstruct experiences consistent with their genetic tendencies. Trying to define the environment *independently* of the person is futile, since every person's experience is different. According to Plomin (1994):

'Socially, as well as cognitively, children select, modify and even create their experiences. Children select environments that are rewarding or at least comfortable, *niche-picking*. Children modify their environments by setting the background tone for interactions, by initiating behaviour, and by altering the impact of environments ... they can create environments with their own propensities, *niche-building*'.

Gene–environment interactions

As seen above, the concept of gene–environment correlations is related to that of non-shared environments, which helps to explain how the environment exerts its influence. Another way of considering the environment's impact is to identify examples of *gene–environment interactions*.

Genetically speaking, *phenylketonuria* (PKU) is a simple characteristic. It is a bodily disorder caused by the inheritance of a single recessive gene from each parent. Normally, the body produces the amino acid *phenylalanine hydroxylase* which converts *phenylalanine* (a substance found in many foods, particularly dairy products) into *tyrosine*. In the presence of the two recessive PKU genes, however, this process fails and phenylalanine builds up in the blood, depressing the levels of other amino acids. Consequently, the developing nervous system is deprived of essential nutrients, leading to severe mental retardation and, without intervention, eventually, death.

The relationship between what the child inherits (the two PKU genes – the *genotype*) and the actual signs and symptoms of the disease (high levels of phenylalanine in the blood, and mental retardation – the *phenotype*) appears to be straightforward, direct and inevitable: given the genotype, the phenotype will occur. However, a routine blood test soon after birth can detect the presence of the PKU genes, and an affected baby will be put on a low-phenylalanine diet. This prevents the disease from developing. In other words, an environmental intervention will *prevent* the phenotype from occurring.

According to Jones (1993):

> '[The] nature [of children born with PKU genes] has been determined by careful nurturing and there is no simple answer to the question of whether their genes or their environment is more important to their well-being'.

Exercise 5

Try to identify some examples of gene–environment interactions that involve *behaviour*, as distinct from bodily diseases such as PKU. Two relevant areas are intelligence (Chapter 29) and schizophrenia (Chapter 49).

If there is no one-to-one relationship between genotype and phenotype in the case of PKU, it is highly likely that there will be an even more complex interaction in the case of intelligence, certain mental disorders, personality and so on. One such example is *cumulative deficit*, which was discussed in Chapter 29 (see page 318). Another is the concept of *facilitativeness*.

According to Horowitz (1987, 1990), a highly *facilitative* environment is one in which the child has loving and responsive parents, and is provided with a rich array of stimulation. When different levels of facilitativeness are combined with a child's initial *vulnerabilities/susceptibilities*, there is an interaction effect. For example, a *resilient* child (one with many protective factors and a few vulnerabilities) may do quite well in a poor environment. Equally, a vulnerable child may do quite well in a highly facilitative environment. Only the vulnerable child in a poor environment will do really poorly.

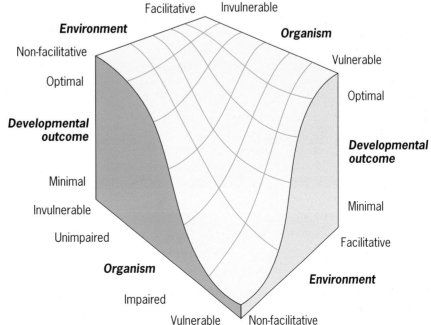

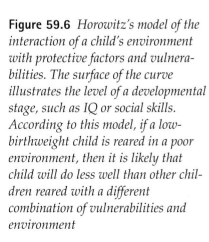

Figure 59.6 *Horowitz's model of the interaction of a child's environment with protective factors and vulnerabilities. The surface of the curve illustrates the level of a developmental stage, such as IQ or social skills. According to this model, if a low-birthweight child is reared in a poor environment, then it is likely that that child will do less well than other children reared with a different combination of vulnerabilities and environment*

This interactionist view is well supported by a 30-year longitudinal study which took place on the Hawaiian island of Kanuai.

Key **STUDY**

Box 59.5 Werner's 'Children of the Garden Island'

Starting in 1955, Werner and her colleagues studied all of the nearly 700 children born on Kanuai in a given period and followed them up when they were two, ten, 18 and 31–32-years old. Werner became interested in a number of 'high risk'/'vulnerable' children, who, despite exposure before the age of two to four or more risk factors, went on to develop healthy personalities, stable careers and strong interpersonal relationships. These risk factors were: reproductive stress (either difficulties during pregnancy and/or during labour and delivery), and discordant and impoverished home lives, including divorce, uneducated, alcoholic or mentally disturbed parents.

As infants, these resilient children were typically described as 'active' 'affectionate', 'cuddly', 'easy-going', and 'even-tempered', with no eating or sleeping habits causing distress to their carers. These are all temperamental characteristics, which elicit positive responses from both family members and strangers. There were also environmental differences between the resilient and non-resilient children, such as smaller family size, at least two years between themselves and the next child, and a close attachment to at least one carer (relative or regular baby-sitter). They also received considerable emotional support from outside the family, were popular with their peers, and had at least one close friend. School became a refuge from a disordered household.

Of the 72 children classified as resilient, 62 were studied after reaching their thirties. As a group, they seemed to be coping well with the demands of adult life. Three-quarters had received some college education, nearly all had full-time jobs and were satisfied with their work. According to Werner (1989):

'As long as the balance between stressful life events and protective factors is favourable, successful adaptation is possible. When stressful events outweigh the protective factors, however, even the most resilient child can have problems'.

Exercise 6

In what ways can culture be thought of as an environmental influence on an individual's behaviour? Try to identify examples from different areas of psychology, but Chapter 55 might be a good place to begin.

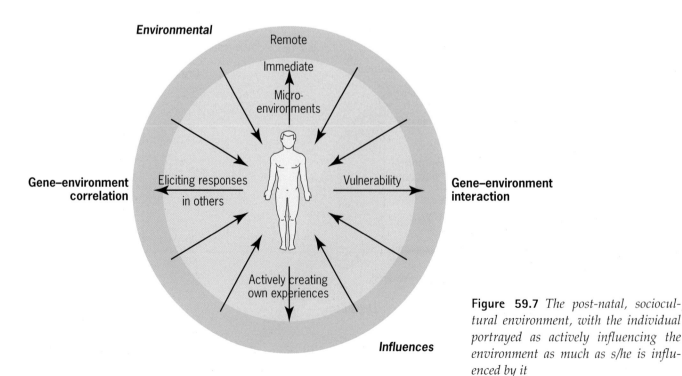

Figure 59.7 *The post-natal, sociocultural environment, with the individual portrayed as actively influencing the environment as much as s/he is influenced by it*

Behaviour genetics and heritability: How much nature and how much nurture?

Behaviour genetics

According to Pike & Plomin (1999), 'Behaviour geneticists explore the origins of individual differences ... in complex behaviours'. More specifically, they attempt to quantify how much of the *variability* for any given trait (such as intelligence, aggressiveness or schizophrenia) can be attributed to (a) genetic differences between people (*heritability*), (b) *shared environments*, and (c) *non-shared environments* (see pages 643–644). The heritability of intelligence was discussed in Chapter 29, as were the two major methods used by behaviour genetics, namely *twin studies* and *adoption studies* (also see Chapter 49).

If genetic factors are important for a trait, identical twins (MZs) will be more similar than non-identical twins (DZs). To the extent that twin similarity cannot be attributed to genetic factors, the *shared environment* is implicated. To the extent that MZs differ *within* pairs, *non-shared environmental* factors are implicated. Because adopted siblings are genetically unrelated to their adoptive family members, the degree of similarity between them is a direct measure of *shared environmental influence* (Pike & Plomin, 1999).

One interesting finding from behaviour genetic research is that the effects of a shared environment seem to *decrease* over time. In a ten-year longitudinal study of over 200 pairs of adoptive siblings, Loehlin *et al.* (1988) found that at an average age of eight, the correlation for IQ was 0.26. This is similar to other studies of young adoptive siblings, and suggests that shared environment makes an important contribution at this age. However, by age 18 the correlation was close to zero. According to Pike & Plomin (1999):

> 'These results represent a dramatic example of the importance of genetic research for understanding the environment. Shared environment is important for *g* [general intelligence] during childhood when children are living at home. However, its importance fades in adolescence as influences outside the family become more salient'.

This conclusion might at first appear paradoxical, yet behaviour genetics provides the best available evidence for the importance of *non-genetic* factors in behavioural development (Plomin, 1995). For example, the concordance rate of MZs for schizophrenia is 40 per cent, which means that most such pairs are *discordant* for diagnosed schizophrenia (see Chapter 49). Whilst there can be no genetic explanation for this, 20 years ago the message from behaviour genetics research was that genetic factors play the major role. Today, the message is

that these same data provide strong evidence for the importance of environmental factors as well as genetic factors (Plomin, 1995). Additionally, the data from twin studies are open to interpretation because not all MZs are equally identical. This is due to certain critical *environmental* factors.

Box 59.6 One placenta or two: are some identical twins more identical than others?

During the first weeks following conception, the embryo is surrounded by an *amnion*, a thin but durable membrane which holds fluid serving as a shock absorber. Surrounding the amnion is another membrane (the *chorion*), which later becomes the placenta. Splitting of the fertilised ovum to produce MZs can occur at different points during early development.

In about 40 per cent of cases, this happens almost immediately after fertilisation, producing entirely separate chorions. So, each twin will have its own placenta (*dichorionic placentation*), but will have identical fingerprints, hairswirls and facial asymmetries. In the other 60 per cent or so of cases, the splitting occurs somewhat later, resulting in the twins sharing a chorion (and later a placenta: *monochorionic placentation*). When this happens, both twins are exposed to similar environmental toxins and diseases.

If MZs that have shared a placenta are no more *concordant* for schizophrenia (no more alike in the degree to which they are diagnosed as schizophrenic) than are DZs or ordinary siblings, then this throws doubt on the claim that genetic factors are the major influence in determining schizophrenia (Davis *et al.*, cited in Ceci & Williams, 1999). What makes MZs so similar might be due to a *shared uterine environment*, rather than shared genes.

Adverse outcomes (such as schizophrenia and retardation) are more dependent on characteristics of the uterine environment than are positive outcomes (Bronfenbrenner & Ceci, 1994). This implies that the role of genetic factors in *pathological* conditions might have been *overestimated*, whilst their role in *normal* functioning is probably unaffected by whether the MZs had separate or shared placentas.

(Based on Ceci & Williams, 1999)

Heritability

According to Ceci & Williams (1999), *heritability* is one of the most controversial concepts in psychology. As noted earlier, it is a statistical measure of the genetic contribution to differences between individuals, that is, it tells us what proportion of individual differences within a population (*variance*) can be attributed to genes. However, this does *not* mean that 'biology is destiny' Indeed, as also noted above, behaviour genetics has helped confirm the importance of environmental factors, which generally account for as much variance in human behaviour as genes do (Plomin & DeFries, 1998). Even when genetic factors do have an especially powerful effect, as in PKU, environmental interventions can often fully or partly overcome the genetic 'determinants'.

Box 59.7 Some 'facts' about heritability

- The degree of heritability (or *heritability estimate*/h²) is *not set in stone*: the relative influence of genes and environment can change. For example, if environmental factors were made almost identical for all members of a hypothetical population, any differences in a particular characteristic (say, intelligence) in that population would then have to be attributed to genetics. Heritability would be closer to 100 per cent than 50 per cent.

- At the same time, however, equating the environment would probably reduce the size of differences observed among individuals. If all children enjoyed the best environment possible, they would probably differ much *less* than if some had been given the worst possible environment.

- Within the *same* population, h² will differ depending on which trait is being measured (for example, it is higher for IQ than for most aspects of personality).

- h² will also differ for the *same* trait when assessed in *different* populations.

- h² will tend to be higher in a good environment than a poor one; the former provides the necessary resources for the biological potential to be realised.

- h² is a way of explaining what makes people different, *not* the relative contribution of genes and environment to any *individual's* make-up.

- The explanation of individual differences *within* groups bears *no* relation to the explanation of differences *between* groups (see Chapter 29).

(Based on Ceci & Williams, 1999; Plomin & DeFries, 1998)

According to Ceci & Williams (1999):

'Heritability estimates are highly situational: they are descriptions of the relative contributions of genes and environments to the expression of a trait in a specific group, place and time. Such estimates tell us nothing about the relative contributions if the group, place or time is changed.'

Exercise 7

Based on your reading of this chapter, what conclusions would you draw about the influence of nature and nurture?

CONCLUSIONS

According to Ceci & Williams (1999):

'Nearly all responsible researchers agree that human traits are jointly determined by both nature and nurture, although they may disagree about the relative contributions of each'.

They also point out that not all biological influences on development are genetic: some are critical features of the intrauterine environment that are sometimes mistaken for genetic influences (see page 647 and Box 29.4, page 344). So, 'biological' does *not* mean 'genetic', and just as importantly, 'environment' can refer to biological, psychological, social, and cultural influences.

In the 1950s, the extreme environmentalism of behaviourism dominated thinking about nature–nurture, but the 1960s saw the adoption of a more balanced view. The 1980s and 1990s saw psychology becoming much more accepting of genetic influence (Plomin, 1996). Plomin (1995) maintains that:

'Research and theory in genetics (nature) and in environment (nurture) are beginning to converge ... the common ground is a model of active organism–environment interaction in which nature and nurture play a duet rather than one directing the performance of the other ... It is time to put the nature–nurture controversy behind us and to bring nature and nurture together in the study of development in order to understand the processes by which genotypes become phenotypes'.

Similarly, Ceci & Williams (1999) conclude like this:

'The battle today seems more over the specific genetic and environmental mechanisms than over whether genes or environments matter'.

Summary

- The **nature–nurture debate** concerns fundamental questions about the causes of human development, sometimes focusing on behaviours and abilities **shared by all human beings**, and sometimes on **individual differences**.

- **Nativists** see knowledge of the world as largely innate, whilst **empirists** stress the role of learning and experience. These extreme viewpoints are reflected in early psychological theories, such as Gesell's **maturation** and Watson's **behaviourism**, respectively.

- Maturation refers to genetically programmed patterns of change, which are **universal**, **sequential** and **relatively impervious to environmental influence**.

- Watson saw human beings as completely malleable, such that the environment could be designed to make any infant become any specified type of adult. He rejected the idea of inheritance of capacity, talent, or temperament.

- The concept of maturation continues to be influential in psychology, as in biological processes such as puberty and ageing, and stage theories of development. Watson's **environmentalism** was adopted in Skinner's **radical behaviourism**.

- Nativism and empirism are not mutually exclusive. Not only must the environment be **benign**, but particular environmental input is often necessary, as in the application of Chomsky's LAD to particular linguistic data.

- In both Freud's and Piaget's theories, experience is just as important as the underlying maturation. For Freud, it is others' reactions to the child's sexual needs that matter more than the sexual instinct itself. For Piaget, intelligence involves the **construction** of mental structures through the child's interaction with its environment.

- **Genetics** is the science of heredity. **Genes** are the basic units of hereditary transmission, and consist of large molecules of **deoxyribonucleic acid (DNA)**. Genes occur in pairs on the **chromosomes** found within the cell nucleus.

- Two major functions of genes are **self-duplication** and **protein synthesis**. Self-duplication occurs through **mitosis** (in the case of non-reproductive cells) and **meiosis** (in the case of reproductive cells). Genes that code for proteins and enzymes are called **structural genes**. Most genes are *regulator* genes.

- **Neurogenetic determinism** makes the false assumption that causes can be classified as **either** genetic **or** environmental. Also, the phrase 'genes for' is a convenient but misleading shorthand for complex biochemical processes.

- Cells inherit genes along with an 'epigenetic' instruction manual, without which multicellular organisms would be impossible. Changes in the instruction manual may be passed from parent to offspring. Heredity may thus involve more than DNA.

- The term 'environment' is commonly used to refer to **post-natal** influences lying **outside** the body of a passive individual who is **shaped by them**. However, environments exist for individual cells as well as the cell nucleus, and **pre-natal** non-genetic factors play a major part in learning difficulties and lowered IQ.

- **People make their own environments**, as well as being influenced **by them**. For most characteristics, the **shared environment** seems to have little impact on development compared with the **non-shared environment**.

- The concept of non-shared environments helps explain **how** the environment influences development. Two ways in which non-shared environments arise are **gene–environment correlations** and **gene–environment interactions**.

- Three types of gene–environment correlations are **passive**, **reactive** and **active**. The last of these illustrates the futility of trying to define the environment **independently** of the person, since every individual's experience is different. Two aspects of active gene–environment correlations are **niche-picking** and **niche-building**.

- PKU is an example of gene–environment interaction, demonstrating the lack of a one-to-one relationship between **genotype** and **phenotype**. Other examples include **cumulative deficit** and Horowitz's concept of **facilitativeness**.

- **Behaviour genetics** attempts to quantify how much of the **variability** for any particular trait is due to **heritability**, **shared environnments**, and **non-shared environments**. Most relevant data show the importance of **both** genetic and environmental factors.

- **Heritability estimates** describe the relative contributions of genes and environment for particular traits, in a specific population, at a particular place and time. If the environment changes for the whole population, so will the heritability estimates for specific traits.

■ Heritability estimates are measures of individual differences **within** groups, and can tell us nothing about **between**-group differences or particular individuals within a group.

■ It is generally agreed that human traits are determined by **both** nature **and** nurture. Where researchers may still disagree is over the relative contributions of each, and the specific genetic and environmental mechanisms involved.

Essay Questions

1 a Examine the assumptions made by **two** theories/theoretical approaches regarding the relationship between nature and nurture. (*15 marks*)

   b Assess the extent to which research evidence supports the view that nature and nurture interact. (*15 marks*)

2 'Instead of asking '*how much* does each contribute'. we should be investigating *how* each contributes'.

   Discuss this view of the relationship between nature and nurture. (*30 marks*)

WEB ADDRESSES

http://objana.com/frog/natnurt.html
http://genetics.nature.com
http://www.apa.org/releases/mother.html
http://www.learner.org/exhibits/personality/genes.html

Appendices

Appendix 1
Data Analysis

INTRODUCTION AND OVERVIEW

As noted in Gross *et al*. (2000), if a theory predicts a *difference* between conditions of an experimental study, it is not enough simply to demonstrate that such a difference does indeed occur. The difference would need to be *large enough* to rule out mere chance effects. This would also apply to a predicted *correlation*, or an *association* between data gathered in an observational study, and so on. In all cases we would need to show that the difference or association was not one which we would expect to get just by chance.

The phrase 'just by chance' refers to the variation we would expect just through sampling errors, and the small deviations in performance resulting from people and conditions varying slightly over time. What we expect, then, is a *convincing* difference, and this is known in statistical terms as a *significant difference*.

This appendix recognises that readers will need to conduct practical work as part of their A level course and that they will be asked to analyse their gathered data for significance as a part of that process, reporting this in a scientific fashion as part of a coursework assignment.

The appendix takes you through the logic and rationale of significance tests and introduces those relevant to the current AQA (A) A level specification. Calculated examples are given, in which you are directed to the statistical tables on pages 663–670 in order to make a final significance decision.

SIGNIFICANCE TESTING

Significance testing is concerned with the interpretation of patterns among data, especially those which *appear* to support theoretical predictions. Suppose we hypothesise that, because of the existence of male and female stereotypes, males estimate their own IQs at a higher level than do females. This is a hypothesis about the *population* of male and female IQ estimates. To test the hypothesis, we would take two *samples* of men and women and ask them to estimate their own IQ. We would then calculate the mean IQs for both groups. Were we to find that the men did, on average, rate their IQ higher than did the women, this would *support* the hypothesis, but not necessarily in a convincing way. Why not? Because *whenever* we take two samples from the *same* population, we will always find some, usually small, difference between them. The differences found might not convince us that males really do differ from females.

The proposal that two samples come from the same population is called the *null hypothesis*. If the male and female populations in the above example are the same, then each time we take two samples at random, there is a fifty-fifty chance that the male mean will be higher than the female mean. The other 50 per cent of the time the female mean will be higher than the male mean. The support for a difference between males and females, then, is so far not very impressive. There is a 50 per cent chance of the male mean being the higher, even if the male and female populations are the same. We therefore don't just want the male sample mean to be higher than the female sample mean: we want the difference to be a *large* one, and an *unlikely* one, if the null hypothesis were true.

Significance testing helps us to make a tentative claim about the populations that samples are drawn from. If we obtain a large enough difference, we are able to say that it is unlikely that the two samples came from identical populations. What we can say, with some caution, is that it is *likely* that the male and female populations are different.

The convention among statisticians for many years has been to reason as follows:

- assume that the two samples were drawn at random from the *same population*;

- determine the probability of obtaining the difference found if the two samples were drawn from the same population;

- if this probability is very small, conclude that the samples were *not* drawn from the same population.

THE NULL AND ALTERNATIVE HYPOTHESES

The assumption that two samples come from the same population is the *null hypothesis* (or H_0). It is an assumption based on the notion that any difference between two samples drawn from the same population is due to random variation between the samples selected. The null hypothesis assumes that two samples are drawn from the *same* population, or from populations that are *identical*. (Note that if you are conducting a correlation (see pages 656–657), the H_0 is usually that the correlation in the underlying population is zero.)

The *alternative hypothesis* is the assumption that the two samples come from *different* populations. It is usually this hypothesis that we would like to support in a research investigation.

The probability of results occurring under the null hypothesis

Hopefully, you will be familiar enough with simple mathematics to recall that probability is measured as a value somewhere between 0 and 1. For example, the probability of obtaining a head from a toss of a coin is ½ or 0.5. This is *exactly* half since there are only two equally likely things that can happen – we have a 1-in-2 chance of getting a head. With a pack of cards, the probability of drawing a heart at random is ¼, since one in four of the cards is a heart. If a magician finds the very card you thought of earlier, we tend to be surprised since the probability of him or her doing this 'by chance' is ¹⁄₅₂, or around 0.02. More formally, the phrase 'by chance' means 'if the null hypothesis is true'. The null hypothesis here is based on the notion that the magician is only guessing, and drawing cards at random from a shuffled pack. The H_0 holds that the frequency of the magician's correct guesses *should be* 1 in 52. Against these odds, the magician's feat appears outstanding.

Statisticians accept as significant *those results which have a probability of occurrence of less than 0.05 under H_0*. That is:

If the probability of a result occurring, if the null hypothesis is true, is found to be less than 0.05, the result is said to be 'significant'.

Yet another way of putting this is that we accept (provisionally) that two populations are *different* when the difference found between two samples would occur less than five times in 100 (0.05) if we drew many pairs of samples from the same population.

Imagine that really annoying breakfast incident where you drop a piece of toast butter side down onto the carpet. 'Not again!', you despair, 'That happens *every* time. Why couldn't it drop the other way?' Your younger sister pipes up, 'You can't really imagine the toast has a will to fall butter side down, surely? Have you actually noticed the times it *didn't* fall that way? You know, really it's just like tossing a coin. Fate hasn't got it in for you. It's just that you don't compare the events properly. Here, I know, let's test that idea.'

Your sister then sets up an investigation for you. Rather than butter a piece of toast and run the risk of ruining the carpet, she puts a cross on one side. You and she then throw the toast in the air 1000 times and record the results – cross up or down. The results are 511 down, 489 up. Is this evidence for a bias toward toast falling with the cross down? Your sister holds the *null hypothesis*, that the 'population' of tosses (which is infinite – you could go on all day and night) contains 50 per cent up and 50 per cent down results. You hold the *alternative hypothesis* that the toast tends to fall butter side (i.e. cross) down, that is, the population contains far more down than up results. To test for significance, you have to calculate the probability of getting 511 crosses down, *if the null hypothesis is true*. You should find that the probability of getting 511 crosses down in 1000 throws is quite high, if the *true* cross-down rate is 50 per cent. In other words, it is not at all unusual to get 511 butter sides down if the 'true' down rate is 50 per cent. Here, you would have to retain the null hypothesis, even if it would mean losing face with your sister.

Adapted from 'Murphy's Law' (1991), a QED programme available from BBC Education and Training.

Calculating the probability of results occurring under the null hypothesis

A significance test tells us the probability of our results occurring *if the null hypothesis is true*. If that probability is small (less than 0.05), we can reject the null hypothesis and claim support for the alternative hypothesis. We can say that the null hypothesis is *probably* not true. However, remember that we have not calculated the probability that the null hypothesis is true or not; we have calculated the probability of our results occurring *if it is true*. Also, we have neither *proved* that the alternative hypothesis is true nor *shown* that the null hypothesis is false. Scientific researchers are always aware that there are several possible interpretations of a result.

They talk of *gaining support* for their research hypothesis, rather than providing conclusive proof that it is true.

TESTS OF DIFFERENCE FOR DATA OBTAINED FROM RESEARCH STUDIES WITH A RELATED DESIGN*

Two fairly simple statistical tests which can be used when conducting a study with a *related design* (see Gross *et al.*, 2000) are the *sign test* and the *Wilcoxon matched pairs signed ranks test*.

Table A1.1 shows some results from a fictitious study in which participants who had volunteered not to eat for 12 hours were asked to recall words from a list containing 20 food-related words and 20 non-food related words. The numbers of food-related words correctly recalled appear in column 2. The numbers in column 3 are the numbers of food-related words recalled from another list given when the *same* participants were tested at a later date when they had just been given a good meal (they were 'satiated'). Assuming that hunger affects memory recall, we might expect participants to recall more food-related words when hungry than when satiated. The fact that participants might have differing memory abilities is accounted for by using the same people in both conditions.

Table A1.1 *Numbers of food-related words correctly recalled by participants when hungry and satiated*

1 Participant letter	2 Food words recalled when hungry	3 Food words recalled when satiated	4 Diff	5 Sign of diff	6 Rank of diff
A	13	5	+8	+	7.5
B	8	9	−1	−	1.5
C	16	9	+7	+	6
D	12	6	+6	+	5
E	12	12	0	n/a	n/a
F	8	9	−1	−	1.5
G	12	4	+8	+	7.5
H	14	12	+2	+	3
I	18	14	+4	+	4
J	15	6	+9	+	9

* A 'related' research design produces 'pairs' of data values, as in a repeated measures or matched pairs design (see Gross *et al.*, 2000).

The (binomial) sign test

Use the sign test when:

- you are expecting a *difference* between conditions;
- the data are in *related pairs* (e.g. each person has a score in both conditions of an experiment);
- you want to use only a *sign* for each pair of values (e.g. whether they improved or worsened).

Calculation of the sign test

Procedure	Calculation on our data
1 Calculate the difference between each pair of scores, always subtracting in the same direction.	See Table A1.1 column 4.
2 Note the sign of each difference (+ or −). Ignore differences of zero.	See Table A1.1 column 5.
3 Find *S* – the number of the less frequent signs.	*S* = 2. There are fewer negative signs.
4 Consult Table 1 (Appendix 3, page 663) and the line for *N* (the number of pairs of scores excluding differences of zero).	Relevant line is *N* = 9 (participant E had a zero difference).
5 For significance, *S* must be *less than or equal to* the appropriate table value.	For a two-tailed test* and $p < 0.05$, *S* must be *less than or equal to* 1, which it is not.
6 Make statement of significance.	The difference is not significant, and the null hypothesis must be *retained*.

*A crude rule is that one-tailed tests are used where a *directional* prediction has been made, and two-tailed tests where the prediction is *non-directional*. If you *do* make a directional prediction, then, if the results go in the opposite direction, *even if they reach the critical value at $p < 0.05$*, you may not claim the result to be significant. It is easier to reach significance for a one-tailed test, but the cost is that you have to put all your eggs in one basket. You cannot use the advantage of one-tailed tests, then switch sides if your results come out the wrong way. In fact, statisticians hotly debate the issue of whether to use one- or two-tailed tests in psychology. Some say only two-tailed tests should ever be used, irrespective of whether the hypothesis is directional or non-directional. For the sake of simplicity, all tests in this section are conducted as two-tailed. For further explanation, see Coolican (1999).

The result in step 6 indicates that the probability of two out of nine signs being negative, assuming that each sign is equally likely to be negative or positive, is greater than 0.05. In other words, two negative signs is a relatively *likely* outcome *if the null hypothesis is true*. The null hypothesis is that there are equal numbers of negative and positive signs in the underlying population, and our result has more than a 5-in-100 chance of occurring if the null hypothesis is true. Therefore, our result does not discredit the null hypothesis. In other words, on the evidence of the test, we are unable to say that 'these results are very unlikely if hunger has no affect on memory'.

Limitations of the sign test

The sign test is really only meant for *nominal* or *categorical* level data. A good example might be where a researcher *only* knew that patients had improved or worsened under therapy and did not have a measured result for each individual (i.e. a score or at least a rank position). The sign test did not use all the information available for each person, but reduced each pair of score values to a *difference sign*. A more powerful test, which uses more of the available information, is the Wilcoxon signed ranks matched pairs test.

The Wilcoxon signed ranks matched pairs test

Use the Wilcoxon test when:

- you are expecting a *difference* between conditions;
- the data are in *related* pairs (e.g. each person has a score in both conditions of an experiment);
- you have a *measured variable* and are using the *ranks* of the values (*ordinal data*).

The Wilcoxon test takes account of the *sizes* of the differences between scores, by looking at the *rank* for each difference relative to the others. Using the sign test, we said that we wanted only a few negative signs, if any. In the Wilcoxon, if we look at column 4 of Table A1.1 (see page 654), we want any negative differences, if there are any at all, *to be as small as possible*.

Calculation of the Wilcoxon signed ranks matched pairs test

Procedure	Calculation on our data
1 Calculate the difference between each pair of scores, always subtracting in the same direction.	See Table A1.1 column 4.
2 Note the sign of each difference. *Ignore differences of zero.*	See Table A1.1 column 5.
3 Rank the differences from the smallest to the largest, ignoring the + and – signs.	See Table A1.1 column 6.
4 Find the *sum of the ranks* of positive differences, and the sum of ranks of negative differences. The *smaller* of these is *T*.	Sum of ranks of *negative* differences (participants B and F with 1.5 each) is the smaller, so *T* = 3.

5 Find line for *N* (excluding differences of zero) in Table 2 (Appendix 3, page 664).	Relevant line is *N* = 9 (participant E had a zero difference).
6 For significance, *T* must be *less than or equal to* the appropriate table value.	For a two-tailed test at $p < 0.05$, *T* must be *less than or equal to* 5, which it is.
7 Make statement of significance.	The difference *is* significant ($p < 0.05$), and the null hypothesis can be *rejected*.

This result indicates that our test of the motivational memory effect was 'successful'. The weaker sign test did not give this result, but the conclusion from the Wilcoxon test, using *ranks* of score differences (more information), is that the total of the ranks for the 'wrong' differences (those that discredit our research hypothesis) is trivial. It had a probability of occurrence of less than 0.05 if the null hypothesis (that the two scores in each pair came from identical populations) was true.

We therefore reject the null hypothesis and accept *provisionally* the alternative hypothesis, that higher numbers of food-related words are recalled when participants are hungry. Remember, this is not a statement about our particular results (more food-related words *were* recalled when participants were hungry than when they were satiated), but a tentative claim about what *would* happen if larger numbers of people (the 'population') could be tested.

A stronger test

An even stronger test of difference for paired data is the *related* t *test*, which uses the actual values obtained rather than just their ranks (see Coolican, 1999).

TESTS OF DIFFERENCE FOR UNRELATED SETS OF DATA

The Mann–Whitney test

Use the Mann–Whitney test when:

- you are expecting a *difference* between conditions;
- the data are *unrelated* (each person has a score in only one of the groups of data);
- you have a *measured variable* and are using the *ranks* of the values (*ordinal data*).

Suppose that the data in Table A1.1 (see page 654) had not been obtained from a repeated measures experiment (the same people in both conditions), but from an *independent groups* experimental design. In this new study, a group of ten people are tested after 12 hours food deprivation, and a *separate* sample of ten people (the control group) are tested when 'satiated'. This has the advantage that we can use an identical word list in both conditions. The table of data obtained might appear as in Table A1.2.

Table A1.2 *Numbers of food-related words correctly recalled by hungry and satiated participants*

1 Food words recalled by hungry participants (condition A)	2 Rank of column 1 values	3 Food words recalled by satiated participants (condition B)	4 Rank of column 3 values
13	15	5	2
8	5.5	9	8
16	19	9	8
12	12	6	3.5
12	12	12	12
8	5.5	9	8
12	12	4	1
14	16.5	12	12
18	20	14	16.5
15	18	6	3.5
Sum of ranks: R_A = 135.5		R_B = 74.5	

Calculation of the Mann–Whitney U test

Procedure	Calculation on our data
1 Rank all the values in the two groups as one set.	See columns 2 and 4, Table A1.2.
2 Find the total of the *ranks* in each group. Call one group total R_A (the smaller one if numbers are unequal) and the other group total R_B.	Call the 'hungry' condition A and the 'satiated' condition B. R_A = 135.5 R_B = 74.5
3 Use the following formula to calculate U_A: $U_A = N_A N_B + \dfrac{N_A(N_A + 1)}{2} - R_A$ where N_A is the number of participants in group A, and N_B is the number in group B.	$U_A = 10 \times 10 + \dfrac{10(10 + 1)}{2} - 135.5$ $= 100 + \dfrac{110}{2} - 135.5$ $= 100 + 55 - 135.5$ $= 19.5$

4 Then calculate U_B from:

$$U_B = N_A N_B + \frac{N_B(N_B + 1)}{2} - R_B \qquad U_B = 10 \times 10 + \frac{10(10 + 1)}{2} - 74.5$$

$$= 100 + \frac{110}{2} - 74.5$$

$$= 100 + 55 - 74.5$$

$$= 80.5$$

[note: to check you have calculated correctly, $U_A + U_B$ should = $N_A N_B$]

5 Select the smaller of U_A and U_B and call it U.	Since 19.5 < 80.5, U = 19.5.
6 Check the value of U against critical values in Table 3, Appendix 3, pages 665–666, taking into account N in each group (where N_A is the number of participants in group R_A and N_B is the number of participants in group R_B) and whether the test is one- or two-tailed.	The two sample sizes are 10 and 10. For $p < 0.05$, U must be *less than or equal to* 23 (two-tailed), which it is.
7 Make statement of significance.	The difference *is* significant ($p < 0.05$) and the null hypothesis can be *rejected*.

The result of the Mann–Whitney test indicates that the same values as obtained in Table A1.1 (see page 654) produce a significant difference, even when they come from two separate groups of people.

A stronger test

A stronger test for independent data is the *unrelated t test* (see Coolican, 1999).

CALCULATING A CORRELATION COEFFICIENT

Suppose that the number of cigarettes smoked per day by eight people and their attitude towards smoking were measured. As Table A1.3 shows (see page 657), if these data are rank ordered for each variable, people tend to get much the same rank on one variable as they do on the other. The *Spearman correlation coefficient (rho)* is derived from a calculation based on the *lack of difference* between each pair of ranks. The lower the differences, the better is the match (*correlation*) between one variable and the other.

Table A1.3 *Paired scores on smoking attitude and average number of cigarettes smoked per day*

1 Participant	2 Average number of cigarettes smoked per day (variable 1)	3 Rank of column 2 values	4 Smoking attitude score (variable 2)	5 Rank of column 4 values	6 Difference, d (column 3 – column 5)	7 d^2
A	5	3	27	5	−2	4
B	8	4	16	3	1	1
C	0	1	5	1	0	0
D	25	8	35	8	0	0
E	20	7	28	6	1	1
F	1	2	14	2	0	0
G	10	5	23	4	1	1
H	15	6	32	7	−1	1
						$\Sigma d^2 = 8$

Spearman's correlation coefficient (rho)

Use Spearman's rho when:

- you are investigating the *correlation* between two variables;

- the data are *related* (each person has a score on both variables);

- you have a *measured variable* and are using the *ranks* of the values (*ordinal data*).

Spearman's rho (or r_s) is calculated using the formula:

$$r_s = 1 - \frac{6 \times \Sigma d^2}{N(N^2 - 1)}$$

and the table below describes the procedure for calculating it.

Calculation of Spearman's rho

Procedure	Calculation on our data
1 Rank order the values of the first variable, from lowest (rank 1) to highest.	See column 3 of Table A1.3.
2 Repeat this procedure for the second variable.	See column 5 of Table 1.3.
3 Subtract the rank for each participant's variable 2 score from the rank of their variable 1 score (column 3–column 5), and call the difference d.	See column 6 of Table A1.3.
4 Square each of the d values (d^2).	See column 7 of Table A1.3.
5 Add up all the d^2 values (Σd^2)	Total of column 7 = 8.
6 Insert the result of step 5 into the formula for r_s above, where N is the number of pairs of scores.	$r_s = 1 - \dfrac{6 \times 8}{10(10^2 - 1)}$ $= 1 - \dfrac{48}{990} = 1 - 0.048.$

Our calculated value for the correlation between the pairs of scores, $r_s = 0.952$.

Checking for significance

We can check to see whether this is a *significant* correlation by testing it against the null hypothesis that the population correlation is actually zero. Table 5, Appendix 3 (see page 668) indicates that for $N = 8$, and significance at $p < 0.05$ (two-tailed), the calculated correlation coefficient needs to be *greater* than 0.738. Since the calculated value is greater than the table value, the correlation is significant.

Significance and strength

Note that *significant* does not necessarily mean *strong*. With a high value for N, a fairly low correlation coefficient can be significant, but for low N we need a relatively high correlation value for significance.

The use of chi-square (χ^2) on frequency tables

Use chi-square when:

- you have *categorical variables* and are comparing frequencies (you cannot compare percentages or ratios, for example);

- you are expecting a *difference* between frequency distributions (or an association between two categorical variables);

- the data are *unrelated* (i.e. people or cases cannot appear in more than one cell of the frequency table – see below).

Suppose, for the sake of time and convenience, we had asked much simpler questions about smoking behaviour and attitude. Suppose we had simply asked people whether they smoked or not, and whether they agreed with banning smoking in all public places. Instead of *measuring* people's attitude to smoking and asking how many they smoked per day, each person might have just been *categorised* as either a smoker or a non-smoker, and as either for or against the ban. The data that we might have gathered from the participants are shown in Table A1.4.

Table A1.4 *Observed frequencies of smokers and non-smokers for and against a ban on smoking*

	Smokers	Non-smokers	Total (R)
Against ban	34 (a)	12 (b)	46
For ban	16 (c)	38 (d)	54
Total (C)	50	50	100 (T)

As we might expect, more smokers have voted against the ban, and more non-smokers have voted for it. So, the distribution of smokers across the 'for' and 'against' categories is different from the distribution of non-smokers. We now need to know if the difference between the distributions is large enough to count as significant.

The null hypothesis would be that the two distributions are the same. That is, being a smoker (or non-smoker) is *not* associated with being for or against the ban. In that case, we would expect both smokers *and* non-smokers to be split in the same way across the 'for' and 'against' categories. 54 per cent of people were for the ban and 46 per cent against. Hence, 54 per cent of the smokers should be for the ban and 46 per cent against it. This gives 27 for and 23 against. The same frequencies should be observed in the non-smokers. This is how we calculate what are called the *expected frequencies* in a chi-square test. 'Expected' here does *not* mean what we actually expect, but *what would be expected under the null hypothesis*. The formula for calculating the expected frequencies in any table is:

$$\text{Expected frequency } (E) = \frac{R \times C}{T}$$

for each 'cell' of the table, where R = the relevant row total (a + b or c + d), C = the relevant column total (a + c or b + d) and T = the total number of observations (a + b + c + d).

For Table A1.4 this gives:

Cell a: $\dfrac{50 \times 46}{100} = 23$ Cell b: $\dfrac{50 \times 46}{100} = 23$

Cell c: $\dfrac{50 \times 54}{100} = 27$ Cell d: $\dfrac{50 \times 54}{100} = 27$

Table A1.5 gives the expected frequencies derived from the observed frequencies in Table A1.4.

Table A1.5 *Expected frequencies of smokers and non-smokers for and against a ban on smoking*

	Smokers	Non-smokers	Total (R)
Against ban	23 (a)	23 (b)	46
For ban	27 (c)	27 (d)	54
Total (C)	50	50	100 (T)

The formula to use when calculating chi-square is:

$$\chi^2 = \sum \frac{(O - E)^2}{E}$$

where O = the observed frequency for a cell and E = the expected frequency for that cell.

In the procedure described below, the data in Table A1.4 are labelled O (for observed), and the corresponding data in Table A1.5 are labelled E (for expected). Each cell is dealt with in turn and identified by its letter. Hence the first row deals with the observed and expected values in Cell a (34 and 23 respectively).

Procedure for calculating chi–square on our data

Step: 1	2 $O-E$	3 $(O-E)^2$	4 $(O-E)^2/E$	5 Total of column 4 results
Cell a:	34 − 23 = 11	11^2 = 121	121/23 = 5.26	5.26
Cell b:	12 − 23 = −11	-11^2 = 121	121/23 = 5.26	5.26
Cell c:	16 − 27 = −11	-11^2 = 121	121/27 = 4.48	4.48
Cell d:	38 − 27 = 11	11^2 = 121	121/27 = 4.48	4.48
			χ^2 =	19.48

This procedure gives a chi-square value of 19.48. In order to be significant, the calculated χ^2 value must be *greater* than the value that appears in Table 4 in Appendix 3 (see page 667). Note that this kind of chi-square test is *always* two-tailed, whatever the predictions were. However, before consulting Table 4 we must calculate *degrees of freedom* (df). These are used instead of N when determining significance.

To calculate df use:

$$df = (R - 1) \times (C - 1)$$

where *R* and *C* are the numbers of rows and columns respectively.

In the above example, df $= (2 - 1) \times (2 - 1) = 1$.

According to Table 4, for 1 df and $p < 0.05$ we need a chi-square value of at least 3.84. Our calculated value of 19.48 easily exceeds this, and so we have a significant result. This supports the hypothesis that being against a smoking ban is associated with being a smoker.

CHOOSING THE APPROPRIATE TEST

A statistical test must be *appropriate* for the data you are testing. To decide which test is appropriate you must answer the following questions:

Step 1: Are you looking for a *difference* between sets of data or a *correlation* between two variables?

Experiments usually test the difference between results in two conditions. Treat data in frequency tables like Table A1.4 as a *difference* between distributions.

Step 2: At what *level* of measurement are the data being treated (categorical or measured)?

Either you have *categorical/nominal* data for each person (such as did/ didn't improve, or smoker/ non-smoker) or you have an individual *score* or *position* for each person (such as time to read words or rank in group on attractiveness). When using this book, *treat interval data as ordinal*.

Step 3: If you are looking for a *difference*, is the design *related* or *unrelated*?

Are there two scores for each person or for two *related* people such as a matched pair? If not, and each person has only one score or appears in only one cell of a frequency table, the design is *unrelated*.

Table A1.6 *Table for choosing an appropriate significance test on your data*

Nature of hypothesis test	Type of research design: Unrelated	Related
Difference:		
categorical variable (nominal level data)	chi-square	sign test
measured variable[1] (ordinal level data)	Mann–Whitney	Wilcoxon matched pairs
Correlation[2] (ordinal level data)		Spearman's rho

[1] Treat interval level scores as ordinal by ranking them.
[2] Correlational data *must* be related.

Appendix 2
Report Writing

INTRODUCTION AND OVERVIEW

A research report tells the reader everything they need to know about the research study, and it does this in a logical order. Reports usually run as follows:

- Title and abstract
- Introduction, hypotheses and/or aims
- Method
- Results
- Discussion
- References.

Include appendices at the end where necessary, to provide useful but not essential information. The sections above tell the reader:

- *why* you carried out the research (the rationale for your hypotheses);
- *how* you did the research (method);
- *what* you found (results);
- a discussion of the findings in the light of what you set out to show or test.

The following notes on writing a research report are important and, if followed carefully, will improve your marks for practical reports.

Title

Simply state the IV–DV effect (or correlation) you are looking for, e.g. 'The effect of hot and cold weather on the likelihood of giving money to a street beggar'.

Abstract

In fewer than 150–200 words, perhaps only six sentences, give the main features of the study, including the hypotheses tested, overall design, *main findings* and conclusions for theory. It is essential to give the nature and direction of results. Hence, you should *not* just say 'The results showed that long-term memory decays over time'. The reader needs to know more specifically what happened, e.g: 'Fewer words were recalled with a six-hour delay after presentation compared with a delay of only three hours'.

Introduction

Write no more than a couple of sides of A4 about the background theory that leads into the rationale for your study. Don't write, say, three sides on unrelated memory theory simply because your study is about some aspect of memory. Stick closely to your hypothesis and make sure you *do* provide a rationale for, and introduce, your *particular study*. By this stage in your report, the reader should know what you are about to attempt, in broad outline at least.

Hypothesis(es)

State these in specific terms, following the detail provided in your introduction, e.g. 'Participants recall more words after a three-hour delay than after a six-hour delay', *not* in the more general way: 'Participants' memories get worse over time'.

Method

You should usually divide this into the four following sub-sections and there should be no overlap between them, i.e. no repeated content:

- **Design** – the skeleton of the research. Is it experimental? If so, give the type of design (e.g. repeated measures). If not, describe the approach – observational, interview, questionnaire, correlational, case study, etc. Give the independent variable and dependent variable where relevant, in *operational* terms. Don't say the dependent variable is, for example, the 'participants' scores' or 'participants' memory'. Do say it is the 'number of words correctly recalled'. State the conditions of the independent variable. If the design is non-experimental you still need to give operational definitions of your measures. If the study is correlational, state which variables are going to be correlated with which.

- **Participants** – not just how many and the sex breakdown, if relevant, but also: where were they from exactly? How were they recruited? What selection procedures were used?

- **Materials** – don't simply provide a list. Describe in sentences what was used to obtain data from the participants (but not the computer software used in the analysis of results). State how observations were coded or questionnaires scored (though these can be included in the early part of the results section instead).

- **Procedure** – record the exact steps taken with each (group of) participant(s) and in the piloting of any materials (e.g. questionnaire). Do *not* state the obvious fact that 'results were collected and analysed'.

Results

Start with a *description* in words (text) of your main findings (means of groups, standard deviations, etc., whichever is most appropriate). Support this with a numbered table (e.g. 'Table 1') which has a clear heading and labels for columns and rows. It must *stand alone* so the reader can understand it without having to refer to the text. A chart (known as a 'figure', e.g. 'Figure 1') can also be provided to support the data. This too must have a clear heading. Do not litter your report with charts. You will not gain any extra marks – one chart is usually enough. Do not draw a bar chart with a column representing each participant's individual score. This is not a useful *summary* of data. Do not include tables of raw scores (one or two for each participant). All data presented must be a *summary only* of the values found. If raw data are to be included, then put these into an appendix.

Do not define for the reader what a mean or standard deviation is (or how a Mann–Whitney test works). Assume they are familiar with basic statistical tools.

Follow the description of the results with an *analysis*. This is very often a significance test of two groups' scores (e.g. their means). Or, instead, it might be a correlation. Always state *exactly* what is being tested. Never say 'the results were tested'; say instead, e.g., 'the means

of errors made in the alone and audience conditions were tested for significant difference ...'. State *which* test you are using and *why*, e.g. level of data measurement (ordinal), type of test (differences), type of design (related/unrelated). State the test result (e.g. the value of Mann-Whitney U). Then immediately state the level of probability for this statistic to occur under the null hypothesis (e.g. 'This is significant with $p < 0.05$). State whether the test is one- or two-tailed, and df or N (where appropriate). Finally state whether the null hypothesis is to be rejected or retained (not 'accepted' or 'proven' etc.).

Discussion

Start by discussing the implications of your results – the *theory from your introduction* which is supported or challenged and in *what* ways and *why*. Discuss any special, unusual or marked findings. Discuss reasons why the findings may be invalid or have failed to show the expected effect. This is a critique of your design, a search for possible confounding variables, sampling errors, etc. Discuss how far the finding might safely be generalised, given that you will usually have tested only a tiny sample of any population. Give recommendations for improving the research next time. Discuss ways in which the research could be *extended* to test more theory, but avoid the knee-jerk reactions of 'we should test more participants' or 'we should test for sex differences' unless you can provide a *good reason for doing so*. Finally give an overall conclusion which summarises the results and implications.

References

Each named researcher you have mentioned in your text should appear in your reference list. Exceptions to this are secondary references in your text. You might have said, for instance, 'Craik & Lockhart, 1972, in Gross, 1996'. In this case you can provide just the 'Gross, 1996' details in your reference list. Background texts you have consulted but not mentioned should *not* appear in your references but may go in some other list entitled 'background reading' or 'bibliography' (although this is usually not required). References should include *all* details of the publication, not just a repeat of the name and date. The format in which you should present your references is as follows:

For books: The author's (or authors') name, initials, (year of publication) *Title*. Place of publication: publisher.

For journal articles: Name(s), initials, (year of publication) Title. *Journal, volume,* [part], page numbers.

REPORTS OF QUALITATIVE DATA

In preparing a report on the analysis of qualitative data, several major principles need to be borne in mind:

Data fit – all data must be included

The report must recognise *all* aspects of the data gathered. For instance, one cannot conveniently 'ignore' the one statement by a school student which is contrary to your expectations about the degree of independence experienced by college students. If there is too great a mismatch between the raw data and developed categories, the data need to be looked at again thoroughly until the 'fit' becomes closer.

Journalism must be avoided

Magazine articles might well avoid such 'awkward' items of information like the one described above; a qualitative research report may not. As examination boards begin to include more emphasis on qualitative reports, markers will be on the lookout for quality reports and will not give much credit to those which amount to no more than a vivid description of 'A day with my baby brother' or 'Watching chimps play at the zoo'.

The researcher must remain objective

Although the researcher may have strong views concerning the topic of investigation, at the level of mere description and tentative interpretation, all possible views must be taken into account. For instance, a tentative conclusion that 'colleges provide students with a greater sense of independence than do schools' must be tempered with recognition that the researcher is also a college student and may well have, unwittingly perhaps, prompted information that confirmed his or her own initial feelings on the matter.

Use actual data, not paraphrase

The report should include (anonymously, of course) some of the actual statements made by participants, in particular those which typify the developed categories or themes.

The report must be psychological

The report must relate your findings to relevant psychological theory or research. It cannot just be a description of your baby brother's behaviour or of school/college interviews. In the latter case, for example, the work might well have been inspired by reading about psychological theories of adolescence and the possibility of identity crisis. This should be made clear in the introduction, and the discussion should relate your findings to established theory, research and debate.

Further reading and support

For more detail on qualitative data analysis in general, including more information on how to proceed and examples of qualitative reports, see Coolican (1999). For whole books on the subject, see Hayes (1997), which has accessible chapters including a very clear account of grounded theory, by Pidgeon and Henwood. Other edited texts include Richardson (1996) and Banister *et al.* (1994).

Appendix 3
Statistical Tables

Table 1 CRITICAL VALUES IN THE BINOMIAL SIGN TEST

	Level of significance for one–tailed test				
	0.05	0.025	0.01	0.005	0.0005
N	Level of significance for two–tailed test				
	0.10	0.05	0.02	0.01	0.001
5	0	–	–	–	–
6	0	0	–	–	–
7	0	0	0	–	–
8	1	0	0	0	–
9	1	1	0	0	–
10	1	1	0	0	–
11	2	1	1	0	0
12	2	2	1	1	0
13	3	2	1	1	0
14	3	2	2	1	0
15	3	3	2	2	1
16	4	3	2	2	1
17	4	4	3	2	1
18	5	4	3	3	1
19	5	4	4	3	2
20	5	5	4	3	2
25	7	7	6	5	4
30	10	9	8	7	5
35	12	11	10	9	7

Calculated S must be *equal to* or *less than* the table (critical) value for significance at the level shown.

SOURCE: F. Clegg, *Simple Statistics*, Cambridge University Press, 1982. With the kind permission of the author and publishers.

Table 2 CRITICAL VALUES OF *T* IN THE WILCOXON SIGNED RANKS TEST

	Level of significance for a one-tailed test			
	0.05	0.025	0.01	0.001
	Level of significance for a two-tailed test			
N	0.1	0.05	0.02	0.002
5	*T* ≤ 0			
6	2	0		
7	3	2	0	
8	5	3	1	
9	8	5	3	
10	11	8	5	0
11	13	10	7	1
12	17	13	9	2
13	21	17	12	4
14	25	21	15	6
15	30	25	19	8
16	35	29	23	11
17	41	34	27	14
18	47	40	32	18
19	53	46	37	21
20	60	52	43	26
21	67	58	49	30
22	75	65	55	35
23	83	73	62	40
24	91	81	69	45
25	100	89	76	51
26	110	98	84	58
27	119	107	92	64
28	130	116	101	71
29	141	125	111	78
30	151	137	120	86
31	163	147	130	94
32	175	159	140	103
33	187	170	151	112

Calculated *T* must be *equal to* or *less than* the table (critical) value for significance at the level shown.

SOURCE: Adapted from R. Meddis, *Statistical Handbook for Non-Statisticians*, McGraw-Hill, London (1975), with the kind permission of the author and publishers.

Table 3a CRITICAL VALUES OF U FOR A ONE-TAILED TEST AT 0.025; TWO-TAILED TEST AT 0.05* (MANN–WHITNEY)

n_2 \ n_1	20	19	18	17	16	15	14	13	12	11	10	9	8	7	6	5	4	3	2	1
1	—	—	—	—	—	—	—	—	—	—	—	—	—	—	—	—	—	—	—	—
2	2	2	2	2	1	1	1	1	1	0	0	0	0	—	—	—	—	—	—	—
3	8	7	7	6	6	5	5	4	4	3	3	2	2	1	1	0	—	—	—	—
4	13	13	12	11	11	10	9	8	7	6	5	4	4	3	2	1	0	—	—	—
5	20	19	18	17	15	14	13	12	11	9	8	7	6	5	3	2	1	0	—	—
6	27	25	24	22	21	19	17	16	14	13	11	10	8	6	5	3	2	1	—	—
7	34	32	30	28	26	24	22	20	18	16	14	12	10	8	6	5	3	1	—	—
8	41	38	36	34	31	29	26	24	22	19	17	15	13	10	8	6	4	2	0	—
9	48	45	42	39	37	34	31	28	26	23	20	17	15	12	10	7	4	2	0	—
10	55	52	48	45	42	39	36	33	29	26	23	20	17	14	11	8	5	3	0	—
11	62	58	55	51	47	44	40	37	33	30	26	23	19	16	13	9	6	3	0	—
12	69	65	61	57	53	49	45	41	37	33	29	26	22	18	14	11	7	4	1	—
13	76	72	67	63	59	54	50	45	41	37	33	28	24	20	16	12	8	4	1	—
14	83	78	74	67	64	59	55	50	45	40	36	31	26	22	17	13	9	5	1	—
15	90	85	80	75	70	64	59	54	49	44	39	34	29	24	19	14	10	5	1	—
16	98	92	86	81	75	70	64	59	53	47	42	37	31	26	21	15	11	6	1	—
17	105	99	93	87	81	75	67	63	57	51	45	39	34	28	22	17	11	6	2	—
18	112	106	99	93	86	80	74	67	61	55	48	42	36	30	24	18	12	7	2	—
19	119	113	106	99	92	85	78	72	65	58	52	45	38	32	25	19	13	7	2	—
20	127	119	112	105	98	90	83	76	69	62	55	48	41	34	27	20	13	8	2	—

* Dashes in the body of the table indicate that no decision is possible at the stated level of significance.

For any n_1 and n_2 the observed value of U is significant at a given level of significance if it is *equal* to or *less* than the critical values shown.

SOURCE: R. Runyon and A. Haber (1976) *Fundamentals of Behavioural Statistics* (3rd ed.) Reading, Mass.: McGraw-Hill, Inc., with kind permission of the publisher.

Table 3b CRITICAL VALUES OF *U* FOR A ONE-TAILED TEST AT 0.05; TWO-TAILED TEST AT 0.10* (MANN-WHITNEY)

n_1

n_2	1	2	3	4	5	6	7	8	9	10	11	12	13	14	15	16	17	18	19	20
1	—	—	—	—	—	—	—	—	—	—	—	—	—	—	—	—	—	—	0	0
2	—	—	—	—	0	0	0	1	1	1	1	2	2	2	3	3	3	4	4	4
3	—	—	0	0	1	2	2	3	3	4	5	5	6	7	7	8	9	9	10	11
4	—	—	0	1	2	3	4	5	6	7	8	9	10	11	12	14	15	16	17	18
5	—	0	1	2	4	5	6	8	9	11	12	13	15	16	18	19	20	22	23	25
6	—	0	2	3	5	7	8	10	12	14	16	17	19	21	23	25	26	28	30	32
7	—	0	2	4	6	8	11	13	15	17	19	21	24	26	28	30	33	35	37	39
8	—	1	3	5	8	10	13	15	18	20	23	26	28	31	33	36	39	41	44	47
9	—	1	3	6	9	12	15	18	21	24	27	30	33	36	39	42	45	48	51	54
10	—	1	4	7	11	14	17	20	24	27	31	34	37	41	44	48	51	55	58	62
11	—	1	5	8	12	16	19	23	27	31	34	38	42	46	50	54	57	61	65	69
12	—	2	5	9	13	17	21	26	30	34	38	42	47	51	55	60	64	68	72	77
13	—	2	6	10	15	19	24	28	33	37	42	47	51	56	61	65	70	75	80	84
14	—	2	7	11	16	21	26	31	36	41	46	51	56	61	66	71	77	82	87	92
15	—	3	7	12	18	23	28	33	39	44	50	55	61	66	72	77	83	88	94	100
16	—	3	8	14	19	25	30	36	42	48	54	60	65	71	77	83	89	95	101	107
17	—	3	9	15	20	26	33	39	45	51	57	64	70	77	83	89	96	102	109	115
18	—	4	9	16	22	28	35	41	48	55	61	68	75	82	88	95	102	109	116	123
19	0	4	10	17	23	30	37	44	51	58	65	72	80	87	94	101	109	116	123	130
20	0	4	11	18	25	32	39	47	54	62	69	77	84	92	100	107	115	123	130	138

* Dashes in the body of the table indicate that no decision is possible at the stated level of significance.

For any n_1 and n_2 the observed value of *U* is significant at a given level of significance if it is *equal* to or *less* than the critical values shown.

SOURCE: R. Runyon and A. Haber (1976) *Fundamentals of Behavioural Statistics* (3rd ed.) Reading, Mass.: McGraw-Hill, Inc., with kind permission of the publisher.

Table 4 CRITICAL VALUES OF χ^2

	Level of significance for a one tailed–test					
	0.10	0.05	0.025	0.01	0.005	0.0005
	Level of significance for a two-tailed test					
df	0.20	0.10	0.05	0.02	0.01	0.001
1	1.64	2.71	3.84	5.41	6.64	10.83
2	3.22	4.60	5.99	7.82	9.21	13.82
3	4.64	6.25	7.82	9.84	11.34	16.27
4	5.99	7.78	9.49	11.67	13.28	18.46
5	7.29	9.24	11.07	13.39	15.09	20.52
6	8.56	10.64	12.59	15.03	16.81	22.46
7	9.80	12.02	14.07	16.62	18.48	24.32
8	11.03	13.36	15.51	18.17	20.09	26.12
9	12.24	14.68	16.92	19.68	21.67	27.88
10	13.44	15.99	18.31	21.16	23.21	29.59
11	14.63	17.28	19.68	22.62	24.72	31.26
12	15.81	18.55	21.03	24.05	26.22	32.91
13	16.98	19.81	22..36	25.47	27.69	34.53
14	18.15	21.06	23.68	26.87	29.14	36.12
15	19.31	22.31	25.00	28.26	30.58	37.70
16	20.46	23.54	26.30	29.63	32.00	39.29
17	21.62	24.77	27.59	31.00	33.41	40.75
18	22.76	25.99	28.87	32.35	34.80	42.31
19	23.90	27.20	30.14	33.69	36.19	43.82
20	25.04	28.41	31.41	35.02	37.57	45.32
21	26.17	29.62	32.67	36.34	38.93	46.80
22	27.30	30.81	33.92	37.66	40.29	48.27
23	28.43	32.01	35.17	38.97	41.64	49.73
24	29.55	33.20	36.42	40.27	42.98	51.18
25	30.68	34.38	37.65	41.57	44.31	52.62
26	31.80	35.56	38.88	42.86	45.64	54.05
27	32.91	36.74	40.11	44.14	46.96	55.48
28	34.03	37.92	41.34	45.42	48.28	56.89
29	35.14	39.09	42.69	49.69	49.59	58.30
30	36.25	40.26	43.77	47.96	50.89	59.70
32	38.47	42.59	46.19	50.49	53.49	62.49
34	40.68	44.90	48.60	53.00	56.06	65.25
36	42.88	47.21	51.00	55.49	58.62	67.99
38	45.08	49.51	53.38	57.97	61.16	70.70
40	47.27	51.81	55.76	60.44	63.69	73.40
44	51.64	56.37	60.48	65.34	68.71	78.75
48	55.99	60.91	65.17	70.20	73.68	84.04
52	60.33	65.42	69.83	75.02	78.62	89.27
56	64.66	69.92	74.47	79.82	83.51	94.46
60	68.97	74.40	79.08	84.58	88.38	99.61

Calculated value of χ^2 must *equal* or *exceed* the table (critical) values for significance at the level shown.
Abridged from R. A. Fisher and F. Yates, *Statistical Tables for Biological, Agricultural and Medical Research* (6th ed.) Longman Group UK Ltd (1974).

Table 5 CRITICAL VALUES OF SPEARMAN'S RHO (r_s)

	Level of significance for a one-tailed test			
	0.05	0.025	0.01	0.005
	Level of significance for a two-tailed test			
N	0.10	0.05	0.02	0.01
4	1.000			
5	0.900	1.000	1.000	
6	0.829	0.886	0.943	1.000
7	0.714	0.786	0.893	0.929
8	0.643	0.738	0.833	0.881
9	0.600	0.700	0.783	0.833
10	0.564	0.648	0.745	0.794
11	0.536	0.618	0.709	0.755
12	0.503	0.587	0.671	0.727
13	0.484	0.560	0.648	0.703
14	0.464	0.538	0.622	0.675
15	0.443	0.521	0.604	0.654
16	0.429	0.503	0.582	0.635
17	0.414	0.485	0.566	0.615
18	0.401	0.472	0.550	0.600
19	0.391	0.460	0.535	0.584
20	0.380	0.447	0.520	0.570
21	0.370	0.435	0.508	0.556
22	0.361	0.425	0.496	0.544
23	0.353	0.415	0.486	0.532
24	0.344	0.406	0.476	0.521
25	0.337	0.398	0.466	0.511
26	0.331	0.390	0.457	0.501
27	0.324	0.382	0.448	0.491
28	0.317	0.375	0.440	0.483
29	0.312	0.368	0.433	0.475
30	0.306	0.362	0.425	0.467

For *n* > 30, the significance of r_s can be tested by using the formula:

$$t = r_s \sqrt{\left(\frac{n-2}{1-r_s^2}\right)} \qquad df = n - 2$$

and checking the value of *t* in table 6.

Calculated r_s must *equal* or *exceed* the table (critical) value for significance at the level shown.

SOURCE: J.H. Zhar, Significance testing of the Spearman Rank Correlation Coefficient, *Journal of the American Statistical Association*, 67, 578–80. With the kind permission of the publishers.

Table 6 CRITICAL VALUES OF *t*

	Level of significance for a one-tailed test			
	0.05	0.025	0.01	0.005
	Level of significance for a two-tailed test			
df	0.10	0.05	0.02	0.01
1	6.314	12.706	31.821	63.657
2	2.920	4.303	6.965	9.925
3	2.353	3.182	4.541	5.841
4	2.132	2.776	3.747	4.604
5	2.015	2.571	3.365	4.032
6	1.943	2.447	3.143	3.707
7	1.895	2.365	2.998	3.499
8	1.860	2.306	2.896	3.355
9	1.833	2.262	2.821	3.250
10	1.812	2.228	2.764	3.169
11	1.796	2.201	2.718	3.106
12	1.782	2.179	2.681	3.055
13	1.771	2.160	2.650	3.012
14	1.761	2.145	2.624	2.977
15	1.753	2.131	2.602	2.947
16	1.746	2.120	2.583	2.921
17	1.740	2.110	2.567	2.898
18	1.734	2.101	2.552	2.878
19	1.729	2.093	2.539	2.861
20	1.725	2.086	2.528	2.845
21	1.721	2.080	2.518	2.831
22	1.717	2.074	2.508	2.819
23	1.714	2.069	2.500	2.807
24	1.711	2.064	2.492	2.797
25	1.708	2.060	2.485	2.787
26	1.706	2.056	2.479	2.779
27	1.703	2.052	2.473	2.771
28	1.701	2.048	2.467	2.763
29	1.699	2.045	2.462	2.756
30	1.697	2.042	2.457	2.750
40	1.684	2.021	2.423	2.704
60	1.671	2.000	2.390	2.660
120	1.658	1.980	2.358	2.617
∞	1.645	1.960	2.326	2.576

Calculated *t* must *equal* or *exceed* the table (critical) value for significance at the level shown.

SOURCE: Abridged from R.A. Fisher and F. Yates, *Statistical Tables for Biological Agricultural and Medical Research* (6th ed.) Longman Group UK Ltd (1974)

Table 7 RANDOM NUMBERS

03 47 43 73 86	39 96 47 36 61	46 98 63 71 62	33 26 16 80 45	60 11 14 10 95
97 74 24 67 62	42 81 14 57 20	42 53 32 37 32	27 07 36 07 51	24 51 79 89 73
16 76 62 27 66	56 50 26 71 07	32 90 79 78 53	13 55 38 58 59	88 97 54 14 10
12 56 85 99 26	96 96 68 27 31	05 03 72 93 15	57 12 10 14 21	88 26 49 81 76
55 59 56 35 64	38 54 82 46 22	31 62 43 09 90	06 18 44 32 53	23 83 01 30 30
16 22 77 94 39	49 54 43 54 82	17 37 93 23 78	87 35 20 96 43	84 26 34 91 64
84 42 17 53 31	57 24 55 06 88	77 04 74 47 67	21 76 33 50 25	83 92 12 06 76
63 01 63 78 59	16 95 55 67 19	98 10 50 71 75	12 86 73 58 07	44 39 52 38 79
33 21 12 34 29	78 64 56 07 82	52 42 07 44 38	15 51 00 13 42	99 66 02 79 54
57 60 86 32 44	09 47 27 96 54	49 17 46 09 62	90 52 84 77 27	08 02 73 43 28
18 18 07 92 46	44 17 16 58 09	79 83 86 16 62	06 76 50 03 10	55 23 64 05 05
26 62 38 97 75	84 16 07 44 99	83 11 46 32 24	20 14 85 88 45	10 93 72 88 71
23 42 40 64 74	82 97 77 77 81	07 45 32 14 08	32 98 94 07 72	93 85 79 10 75
52 36 28 19 95	50 92 26 11 97	00 56 76 31 38	80 22 02 53 53	86 60 42 04 53
37 85 94 35 12	83 39 50 08 30	42 34 07 96 88	54 42 06 87 98	35 85 29 48 38
70 29 17 12 13	40 33 20 38 26	13 89 51 03 74	17 76 37 13 04	07 74 21 19 30
56 62 18 37 35	96 83 50 87 75	97 12 25 93 47	70 33 24 03 54	97 77 46 44 80
99 49 57 22 77	88 42 95 45 72	16 64 36 16 00	04 43 18 66 79	94 77 24 21 90
16 08 15 04 72	33 27 14 34 90	45 59 34 68 49	12 72 07 34 45	99 27 72 95 14
31 16 93 32 43	50 27 89 87 19	20 15 37 00 49	52 85 66 60 44	38 68 88 11 80
68 34 30 13 70	55 74 30 77 40	44 22 78 84 26	04 33 46 09 52	68 07 97 06 57
74 57 25 65 76	59 29 97 68 60	71 91 38 67 54	13 58 18 24 76	15 54 55 95 52
27 42 37 86 53	48 55 90 65 72	96 57 69 36 10	96 46 92 42 45	97 60 49 04 91
00 39 68 29 61	66 37 32 20 30	77 84 57 03 29	10 45 65 04 26	11 04 96 67 24
29 94 98 94 24	68 49 69 10 82	53 75 91 93 30	34 25 20 57 27	40 48 73 51 92
16 90 82 66 59	83 62 64 11 12	67 19 00 71 74	60 47 21 29 68	02 02 37 03 31
11 27 94 75 06	06 09 19 74 66	02 94 37 34 02	76 70 90 30 86	38 45 94 30 38
35 24 10 16 20	33 32 51 26 38	79 78 45 04 91	16 92 53 56 16	02 75 50 95 98
38 23 16 86 38	42 38 97 01 50	87 75 66 81 41	40 01 74 91 62	48 51 84 08 32
31 96 25 91 47	96 44 33 49 13	34 86 82 53 91	00 52 43 48 85	27 55 26 89 62
66 67 40 67 14	64 05 71 95 86	11 05 65 09 68	76 83 20 37 90	57 16 00 11 66
14 90 84 45 11	75 73 88 05 90	52 27 41 14 86	22 98 12 22 08	07 52 74 95 80
68 05 51 18 00	33 96 02 75 19	07 60 62 93 55	59 33 82 43 90	49 37 38 44 59
20 46 78 73 90	97 51 40 14 02	04 02 33 31 08	39 54 16 49 36	47 95 93 13 30
64 19 58 97 79	15 06 15 93 20	01 90 10 75 06	40 78 78 89 62	02 67 74 17 33
05 26 93 70 60	22 35 85 15 13	92 03 51 59 77	59 56 78 06 83	52 91 05 70 74
07 97 10 88 23	09 98 42 99 64	61 71 62 99 15	06 51 29 16 93	58 05 77 09 51
68 71 86 85 85	54 87 66 47 54	73 32 08 11 12	44 95 92 63 16	29 56 24 29 48
26 99 61 65 53	58 37 78 80 70	42 10 50 67 42	32 17 55 85 74	94 44 67 16 94
14 65 52 68 75	87 59 36 22 41	26 78 63 06 55	13 08 27 01 50	15 29 39 39 43

References

ABEL, E.L. (1977) The relationship between cannabis and violence: A review. *Psychological Bulletin*, 84, 193–211.

ABRAHAM, K. (1911) Notes on the psychoanalytical investigation and treatment of manic-depressive insanity and allied conditions. Originally written in 1911 and later published in E. Jones (Ed.) *Selected Papers of Karl Abraham, MD*. London: The Hogarth Press.

ABRAHAMS, C. & SHANLEY, E. (1992) *Social Psychology for Nurses*. London: Edward Arnold.

ABRAMS, D. & MANSTEAD, A.S.R. (1981) A test of theories of social facilitation using a musical task. *British Journal of Social Psychology*, 20, 271–278.

ABRAMSON, L.Y. & MARTIN, D.J. (1981) Depression and the causal inference process. In J.M. Harvey, W. Ickes & R.F. Kidd (Eds) *New Directions in Attribution Research*, Volume 3. Hillsdale, NJ: Erlbaum.

ABRAMSON, L.Y., SELIGMAN, M.E.P. & TEASDALE, J.D. (1978) Learned helplessness in humans: Critique and reformulation. *Journal of Abnormal Psychology*, 87, 49–74.

ADAM, K. & OSWALD, I. (1977) Sleep is for tissue restoration. *Journal of the Royal College of Physicians*, 11, 376–388.

ADAM, K. & OSWALD, I. (1983) Protein synthesis, bodily renewal and the sleep-wake cycle. *Clinical Science*, 65, 561–567.

ADAMS, H.E., TOLLISON, C.S. & CARSON, T.P. (1981) Behaviour therapy with sexual preventative medicine. In S.M. Turner, K.S. Calhoun & H.E. Adams (Eds) *Handbook of Clinical Behaviour Therapy*. New York: Wiley.

ADAMS, J.A. (1976) Issues for a closed-loop theory of motor learning. In G.E. Stelmach (Ed.) *Motor Control: Issues and Trends*. London: Academic Press.

ADAMS, R.J. & MAURER, D. (1984) Detection of contrast by the new-born and two-month-old infant. *Infant Behaviour and Development*, 7, 415–422.

ADENIRON, R.A. & JONES, J.R. (1994) Koro: culture-bound disorder or universal symptom? *British Journal of Psychiatry*, 164, 559–561.

ADORNO, T.W., FRENKEL-BRUNSWICK, E., LEVINSON, J.D. & SANFORD, R.N. (1950) *The Authoritarian Personality*. New York: Harper & Row.

AHMED, K. (1998) Island's youth pass TV test. *The Guardian*, 29 April, 6.

AHUHJA, A. (1998) Body clocks could be the death of us. *The Times*, 13 April, 16.

AITCHISON, J. (1983) *The Articulate Mammal*. London: Hutchinson.

AITCHISON, J. (1996) Wugs, woggles and whatsits. *The Independent* (Section Two), 28 February, 8.

ALCOCK, J. (1993) *Animal Behaviour* (5th edition). Sunderland, MA: Sinauer.

ALDHOUS, P., COGHLAN, A. & COPLEY, J. (1999) Let the People Speak. *New Scientist*, 162 (2187), 26–31.

ALDRIDGE-MORRIS, R. (1989) *Multiple Personality. An Exercise in Deception*. London: Lawrence Erlbaum Associates.

ALEXANDER, R.D. (1975) The search for a general theory of behaviour. *Behavioural Science*, 20, 77–100.

ALLEN, M. (1976) Twin studies of affective illness. *Archives of General Psychiatry*, 33, 1476–1478.

ALLPORT, D.A. (1980) Attention and performance. In G. Claxton (Ed.) *Cognitive Psychology: New Directions*. London: Routledge & Kegan Paul.

ALLPORT, D.A. (1989) Visual attention. In M. Posner (Ed.) *Foundations of Cognitive Science*. Cambridge, MA: MIT Press.

ALLPORT, D.A. (1993) Attention and control. Have we been asking the wrong questions? A critical review of twenty-five years. In D.E. Meyer & S.M. Kornblum (Eds) *Attention and Performance*, Volume XIV. London: MIT Press.

ALLPORT, D.A., ANTONIS, B. & REYNOLDS, P. (1972) On the division of attention: A disproof of the single-channel hypothesis. *Quarterly Journal of Experimental Psychology*, 24, 225–235.

ALLPORT, G.W. (1954) *The Nature of Prejudice*. Reading, MA: Addison-Wesley.

ALLPORT, G.W. (1955) *Theories of Perception and the Concept of Structure*. New York: Wiley.

ALLPORT, G.W. & PETTIGREW, T.F. (1957) Cultural influences on the perception of movement: The trapezoidal illusion among Zulus. *Journal of Abnormal and Social Psychology*, 55, 104–113.

ALSAKER, F.D. (1992) Pubertal timing, overweight, and psychological adjustment. *Journal of Early Adolescence*, 12, 396–419.

ALSAKER, F.D. (1996) The impact of puberty. *Journal of Child Psychology & Psychiatry*, 37 (3), 249–258.

ALTROCCHI, J. (1980) *Abnormal Behaviour*. New York: Harcourt Brace Jovanovich.

AMATO, P.R. (1983) Helping behaviour in urban and rural environments: Field studies based on a taxonomic organisation of helping episodes. *Journal of Personality and Social Psychology*, 45, 571–586.

AMBRUS, E., SZEKERES, G., KERI, S., CSERNAY, L., JANKA, Z. & PAVICS, L. (1999) Regional cerebral blood flow changes in schizophrenic patients detected by SPECT studies under resting and active conditions. *Orv. Hetil.*, 140, 1783–1786.

AMERICAN PSYCHIATRIC ASSOCIATION (1952) *Diagnostic and Statistical Manual of Mental Disorders*. Washington, DC: American Psychiatric Association.

AMERICAN PSYCHIATRIC ASSOCIATION (1968) *Diagnostic and Statistical Manual of Mental Disorders* (2nd edition). Washington, DC: American Psychiatric Association.

AMERICAN PSYCHIATRIC ASSOCIATION (1980) *Diagnostic and Statistical Manual of Mental Disorders* (3rd edition). Washington, DC: American Psychiatric Association.

AMERICAN PSYCHIATRIC ASSOCIATION (1987) *Diagnostic and Statistical Manual of Mental Disorders* (3rd edition, revised). Washington, DC: American Psychiatric Association.

AMERICAN PSYCHIATRIC ASSOCIATION (1994) *Diagnostic and Statistical Manual of Mental Disorders* (4th edition). Washington DC: American Psychiatric Association.

AMERICAN PSYCHOLOGICAL ASSOCIATION (1981) Ethical principles of psychologists. *American Psychologist*, 36, 633–638.

AMERICAN PSYCHOLOGICAL ASSOCIATION (1985) *Guidelines for Ethical Conduct in the Care and Use of Animals*. Washington, DC: American Psychological Association.

AMERICAN PSYCHOLOGICAL ASSOCIATION (1992) Ethical principles of psychologists and code of conduct. *American Psychologist*, 47, 1597–1612.

AMICE, V., BERCOVI, J., NAHOUL, K., HATAHET, M. & AMICE, J. (1989) Increase in H-Y antigen positive lymphocytes in hirsute women: Effects of cyproterone acetate and estradiol treatment. *Journal of Clinical Endocrinology and Metabolism*, 68, 58–62.

AMIR, Y. (1969) Contact hypothesis in ethnic relations. *Psychological Bulletin*, 71, 319–342.

AMIR, Y. (1994) The contact hypothesis in intergroup relations. In W.J. Lonner & R.S. Malpass (Eds) *Psychology and Culture*. Boston: Allyn & Bacon.

ANAND, B.K. & BROBECK, J.R. (1951) Hypothalamic control of food intake in rats and cats. *Yale Journal of Biological Medicine*, 24, 123–140.

ANDERSON, A., HOLMES, B. & ELSE, L. (1996) Zombies, dolphins & blindsight. *New Scientist*, 4 May, 20–27.

ANDERSON, C.A. & FORD, C.M. (1986) Affect of the game player: Short-term effects of highly and mildly aggressive video games. *Personality & Social Psychology Bulletin*, 12, 390–402.

ANDERSON, D.N. (1990) Koro: the genital retraction symptoms after stroke. *British Journal of Psychiatry*, 157, 142–144.

ANDERSON, D.R., LORCH, E.P., FIELD, D.E., COLLINS, P.A. & NATHAN, J.G. (1986) Television viewing at home: Age trends in visual attention and time with TV. *Child Development*, 57, 1024–1033.

ANDERSON, J. (1974) Bystander intervention in an assault. Paper presented at the meeting of the Southeastern Psychological Association, Hollywood, FL.

ANDERSON, J.R. (1995a) *Cognitive Psychology and its Implications*. New York: W.H. Freeman & Company.

ANDERSON, J.R. (1995b) *Learning and Memory: An Integrated Approach*. Chichester: Wiley.

ANDERSON, T. & MAGNUSSON, D. (1990) Biological maturation and the development of drinking habits and alcohol abuse among young males. A prospective longitudinal study. *Journal of Youth & Adolescence*, 19, 33–41.

ANDREWS, G. (1993) The essential psychotherapies. *British Journal of Psychiatry*, 162, 447–451.

ANNIS, R.C. & FROST, B. (1973) Human visual ecology and orientation anisotropies in acuity. *Science*, 182, 729–731.

APTER, A. (1991) The problem of Who: Multiple personality, personal identity and the double brain. *Philosophical Psychology*, 4, 219–248.

ARANGO, C., BARTKO, J.J., GOLD, J.M. & BUCHANAN, R.W. (1999) Prediction of neuropsychological performance by neurological signs in schizophrenia. *American Journal of Psychiatry*, 156, 1349–1357.

ARBOLEDA-FLOREZ, J. (1979) Amok. In R.C. Simons & C. Hughes (Eds), *The Culture-Bound Syndromes: Folk Illness of Psychiatric and Anthropological Interest*. Doredecht: Reidel.

ARCHER, J. (1999) *The Nature of Grief: The Evolution and Psychology of Reactions to Loss*. London: Routledge.

ARGYLE, M. (1983) *The Psychology of Interpersonal Behaviour* (4th edition). Harmondsworth: Penguin.

ARGYLE, M. (1988) *Bodily Communication* (2nd edition). London: Methuen.

ARGYLE, M. & HENDERSON, M. (1984) The rules of friendship. *Journal of Social and Personal Relationships*, 1, 211–237.

ARKES, H.R. & BLUMER, C. (1985) The psychology of sunk cost. *Organisational Behaviour & Human Decision Processes*, 35, 124–140.

ARKIN, R., COOPER, H. & KOLDITZ, T. (1980) A statistical review of the literature concerning the self-serving bias in interpersonal influence situations. *Journal of Personality and Social Psychology*, 48, 435–448.

ARMSBY, R.E. (1971) A re-examination of the development of moral judgement in children. *Child Development*, 42, 1241–1248.

ARONSON, E. (1980) *The Social Animal* (3rd edition). San Francisco: W.H. Freeman.

ARONSON, E. (1992) *The Social Animal* (6th edition). New York: Freeman.

ARONSON, E. & LINDER, D. (1965) Gain and loss of esteem as determinants of interpersonal attraction. *Journal of Experimental Social Psychology*, 1, 156–171.

ARONSON, E., BRIDGEMAN, D.L. & GEFFNER, R. (1978) The effects of a co-operative classroom structure on student behaviour and attitudes. In D. Bar-Tal & L. Saxe (Eds) *Social Psychology of Education*. New York: Wiley.

ARONSON, E., WILLERMAN, B. & FLOYD, J. (1966) The effect of a pratfall on increasing attractiveness. *Psychonomic Science*, 4, 227–228.

ASCH, S.E. (1946) Forming impressions of personality. *Journal of Abnormal and Social Psychology*, 41, 258–290.

ASCHOFF, J. & WEVER, R. (1981) The circadian system in man. In J. Aschoff (Ed.) *Handbook of Behavioural Neurology* (Volume 4). New York: Plenum Press.

ASERINSKY, E. & KLEITMAN, N. (1953) Regularly occurring periods of eye motility and concomitant phenomena during sleep. *Science*, 118, 273–274.

ASHMORE, R. & DEL BOCA, F. (1976) Psychological approaches to understanding intergroup conflicts. In P. Katz (Ed.) *Towards the Elimination of Racism*. New York: Pergamon.

ASLIN, R.N., PISONI, D.B. & JUSCZYK, P.W. (1983) Auditory development and speech perception in infancy. In P.H. Mussen (Ed.) *Handbook of Child Psychology* (4th edition). New York: Wiley.

ASSOCIATION FOR THE TEACHING OF PSYCHOLOGY (1992) Ethics in psychological research: Guidelines for students at pre-degree levels. *Psychology Teaching*, 4–10, New Series, No. 1.

ATCHLEY, R.C. (1982) Retirement: Leaving the world of work. *Annals of the American Academy of Political and Social Science*, 464, 120–131.

ATCHLEY, R.C. (1985) *Social Forces and Ageing: An Introduction to Social Gerontology*. Belmont, California: Wadsworth.

ATCHLEY, R.C. & ROBINSON, J.L. (1982) Attitudes towards retirement and distance from the event. *Research on Ageing*, 4, 288–313.

ATTIE, I. & BROOKS-GUNN, J. (1989) Development of eating problems in adolescent girls: A longitudinal study. *Developmental Psychology*, 25, 70–79.

ATTNEAVE, F. (1954) Some informational aspects of visual perception. *Psychological Review*, 61, 183–193.

ATWOOD, M.E. & POLSON, P.G. (1976) A process model for water-jug problems. *Cognitive Psychology*, 8, 191–216.

AX, A.F. (1953) The physiological differentiation of fear and anger in humans. *Psychosomatic Medicine*, 15, 422–433.

AXELROD, R. (1984) *The Evolution of Co-operation*. New York: Basic Books.

AXELROD, R. & HAMILTON, W.D. (1981) The evolution of co-operation. *Science*, 211, 1390–1396.

AYLLON, T. & AZRIN, N.H. (1968) *The Token Economy: A Motivational System for Therapy and Rehabilitation*. New York: Appleton Century Crofts.

AYLLON, T. & HAUGHTON, E. (1962) Control of the behaviour of schizophrenic patients by food. *Journal of the Experimental Analysis of Behaviour*, 5, 343–352.

AZRIN, N.H. & HOLZ, W.C. (1966) Punishment. In W.K. Honig (Ed.) *Operant Behaviour: Areas of Research and Application*. New York: Appleton-Century-Crofts.

BACHRACH, A., ERWIN, W. & MOHN, J. (1965) The control of eating behaviour in an anorexic by operant conditioning. In L. Ullman & L. Krasner (Eds) *Case Studies in Behaviour Modification*. New York: Holt, Rinehart & Winston.

BADDELEY, A.D. (1986) *Working Memory*. Oxford: Oxford University Press.

BADDELEY, A.D. (1997) *Human Memory: Theory and Practice* (revised edition). East Sussex: Psychology Press.

BADDELEY, A.D. & HITCH, G. (1974) Working memory. In G.H. Bower (Ed.) *Recent Advances in Learning and Motivation*, Volume 8. New York: Academic Press.

BAHRICK, L.E., WALKER, A.S. & NEISSER, U. (1981) Selective looking by infants. *Cognitive Psychology*, 13, 377–390.

BAILEY, C.L. (1979) Mental illness – a logical misrepresentation? *Nursing Times*, May, 761–762.

BAILEY, S. (1993) Fast forward to violence. *Criminal Justice Matters*, 3, 6–7

BAILLARGEON, R. (1987) Object permanence in three-and-a-half and four-and-a-half-month-old infants. *Developmental Psychology*, 33, 655–664.

BAKAN, D. (1967) *On Method*. San Francisco: Jossey-Bass Inc.

BALASUBRAMAMIAM, V., KANATA, T.S. & RAMAMURTHI, B. (1970) Surgical treatment of hyperkinetic and behaviour disorders. *International Surgery*, 54, 18–23.

BALDA, R.P. (1980) Recovery of cached seeds by a captive *Nucifraga caryocatactes*. *Zeitschrift für Tierpsychologie*, 52, 331–346.

BALDA, R.P & KAMIL, A.C. (1992) Long-term spatial memory in Clark's nutcracker, *Nucifraga columbiana*. *Animal Behaviour*, 44, 761–769.

BALL, S. & NUKI, P. (1996) Most under-11s watch violent videos. *The Sunday Times*, 23 July, 1.

BALLENGER, J.C. (1995) Benzodiazepines. In A.F. Schatzber & C.B. Nemeroff (Eds) *The American Psychiatric Press Textbook of Psychopharmacology*. Washington, D.C.: American Psychiatric Press.

BALON, R. (1999) Fluvoxamine for phobia of storms. *Acta Psychiatria Scandinavia*, 100, 244–245.

BALTES, M.M. & BALTES, P.B. (1986) *The Psychology of Control and Ageing*. Hillsdale, NJ: Erlbaum.

BALTES, P.B. (1983) Life-span developmental psychology: Observations on history and theory revisited. In R.M. Lerner (Ed.) *Developmental Psychology: Historical and Philosophical Perspectives*. Hillsdale, NJ: Erlbaum.

BALTES, P.B. (1987) Theoretical propositions of life-span developmental psychology: On the dynamics of growth and decline. *Developmental Psychology*, 23, 611–626.

BALTES, P.B. & BALTES, M.M. (1993) *Successful Ageing: Perspectives from the Behavioural Sciences*. Cambridge: Cambridge University Press.

BANDURA, A. (1965) Influence of model's reinforcement contingencies on the acquisition of imitative responses. *Journal of Personality & Social Psychology*, 1, 589–595.

BANDURA, A. (1969) *Principles of Behaviour Modification*. New York: Holt, Rinehart & Winston.

BANDURA, A. (1971) *Social Learning Theory*. Englewood Cliffs, NJ: Prentice-Hall.

BANDURA, A. (1973) *Aggression: A Social Learning Analysis*. London: Prentice Hall.

BANDURA, A. (1974) Behaviour theory and models of man. *American Psychologist*, 29, 859–869.

BANDURA, A. (1977a) *Social Learning Theory* (2nd edition). Englewood Cliffs, NJ: Prentice-Hall.

BANDURA, A. (1977b) Self-efficacy: Toward a unifying theory of behaviour change. *Psychological Review*, 84, 191–215.

BANDURA, A. (1984) Recycling misconceptions of perceived self-efficacy. *Cognitive Therapy and Research*, 8, 231–235.

BANDURA, A. (1986) *Social Foundations of Thought and Action*. Englewood Cliffs, NJ: Prentice-Hall.

BANDURA, A. (1989) Social cognitive theory. In R. Vasta (Ed.) *Six Theories of Child Development*. Greenwich: JAI Press.

BANDURA, A. (1994) Social cognitive theory of mass communication. In J. Bryant & D. Zillman (Eds) *Media Effects: Advances in Theory and Research*. Hove: Erlbaum.

BANDURA, A., ROSS, D. & ROSS, S.A. (1961) Transmission of aggression through imitation of aggressive models. *Journal of Abnormal and Social Psychology*, 63, 575–582.

BANDURA, A., ROSS, D. & ROSS, S.A. (1963) Imitation of film-mediated aggressive models. *Journal of Abnormal and Social Psychology*, 66, 3–11.

BANICH, M.T. (1997) *Neuropsychology: The Neural Bases of Mental Function*. Boston: Houghton Miflin.

BANISTER, P., BURMAN, E., PARKER, I., TAYLOR, M. & TINDALL, C. (1994) *Qualitative Methods in Psychology*. Buckingham: Open University.

BANNISTER, D., SALMON, P. & LIEBERMAN, D.M. (1964) Diagnosis–treatment relationships in psychiatry: A statistical analysis. *British Journal of Psychiatry*, 110, 726–732.

BANYARD, P. (1996) *Applying Psychology to Health*. London: Hodder & Stoughton.

BARBER, B.K. & BUEHLER, C. (1996) Family cohesion and enmeshment: Different constructs, different effects. *Journal of Marriage & the Family*, 58 (2), 433–441.

BARD, K.A. (1994) Developmental issues in the evolution of mind. *American Psychologist*, 49, 760.

BARD, P. (1928) A diencephalic mechanism for the expression of rage with special reference to the sympathetic nervous system. *American Journal of Physiology*, 84, 490–515.

BARKER, R., DEMBO, T. & LEWIN, K. (1941) Frustration and regression: An experiment with young children. *University of Iowa Studies in Child Welfare*, 18, 1–314.

BARLOW, D.H. (1997) Cognitive–behavioural therapy for panic disorder: Current status. *Journal of Clinical Psychiatry*, 58 (Suppl. 2), 32–36.

BARNARD, N.D. & KAUFMAN, S.R. (1997) Animal research is wasteful and misleading. *Scientific American*, February, 64–66.

BARON, R.A. (1972) Aggression as a function of ambient temperature and prior anger arousal. *Journal of Personality & Social Psychology*, 21, 183–189.

BARON, R.A. (1977) *Human Aggression*. New York: Plenum.

BARON, R.A. (1989) *Psychology: The Essential Science*. London: Allyn & Bacon.

BARON, R.A. & BELL, P.A. (1975) Aggression and heat: Mediating effects of prior provocation and exposure to an aggressive model. *Journal of Personality & Social Psychology*, 31, 825–832.

BARON, R.A. & BELL, P.A. (1976) Aggression and heat: The influence of ambient temperature, negative affect, and a cooling drink on physical aggression. *Journal of Personality & Social Psychology*, 33, 245–255.

BARON, R.A. & BYRNE, D. (1997) *Social Psychology* (8th edition). London: Allyn & Bacon.

BARON, R.A. & RICHARDSON, D.R. (1994) *Human Aggression* (2nd edition). New York: Plenum.

BARRETT, M.D. (1989) Early language development. In A. Slater & G. Bremner (Eds) *Infant Development*. Hove: Erlbaum.

BARRETT, R. & ROBINSON, B. (1994) Gay dads. In A.E. Gottfried & A.W. Gottfried (Eds) *Redefining Families*. New York: Plenum Press.

BARROWCLOUGH, A. (1999) The Ku Klux Klan is here. *The Times* (Part 3), July 21, 37, 40.

BARTLETT, F.C. (1932) *Remembering*. Cambridge: Cambridge University Press.

BARTLETT, J.C. & SEARCY, J. (1993) Inversion and configuration of faces. *Cognitive Psychology*, 25, 281–316.

BATES, E., O'CONNELL, B. & SHORE, C. (1987) Language and communication in infancy. In J.D. Osofsky (Ed.) *Handbook of Infant Development* (2nd edition). New York: Wiley.

BATESON, G., JACKSON, D., HALEY, J. & WEAKLAND, J. (1956) Toward a theory of schizophrenia. *Behavioural Science*, 1, 251–264.

BATESON, P. (1986) When to experiment on animals. *New Scientist*, 109 (1496), 30–32.

BATESON, P. (1992) Do animals feel pain? *New Scientist*, 134 (1818), 30–33.

BATSON, C.D. & OLESON, K.C. (1991) Current status of the empathy–altruism hypothesis. In M.S. Clark (Ed.) *Prosocial Behaviour. Review of Personality and Social Psychology*, 12. Newbury Park, CA.: Sage.

BAUMEISTER, R.F. & LEARY, M.R. (1995) The need to belong: Desire for interpersonal attachments as a fundamental human motivation. *Psychological Bulletin*, 117, 497–529.

BAUMGART, P., WALGER, P., FUCHS, G., DORST, K.G., VETTER, H. & RAHN, K.H. (1989) Twenty-four-hour blood pressure is not dependent on endogenous circadian rhythm. *Journal of Hypertension*, 7, 331–334.

BAYLEY, N. (1969) *Bayley Scales of Infant Development*. New York: Psychological Corporation.

BEAMAN, A.L., BARNES, P.J., KLENTZ, B., & MCQUIRK, B. (1978) Increasing helping rates through information dissemination: Teaching pays. *Personality & Social Psychology Bulletin*, 4, 406–411.

BEASON, R.C. (1989) *Magnetic sensitivity and orientation in the bobolink*. Paper presented at the Royal Institute of Navigation Conference, 1989.

BEAUMONT, J.G. (1988) *Understanding Neuropsychology*. Oxford: Blackwell.

BEAUMONT, P. (1996) Thirtysomethings who won't grow up. *The Observer*, 19 May, 11.

BECK, A.T. (1967) *Depression: Causes and Treatment*. Philadelphia: University of Philadelphia Press.

BECK, A.T. (1974) The development of depression: A cognitive model. In R.J. Friedman & M.M. Katz (Eds) *The Psychology of Depression: Contemporary Theory and Research*. New York: Wiley.

BECK, A.T. (1997) Cognitive therapy: Reflections. In J.K. Zeig (Ed.), *The Evolution of Psychotherapy: The Third Conference*. New York: Brunner/Mazel.

BECK, A.T. & FREEMAN, A. (1990) *Cognitive Therapy of Personality Disorders*. New York: Guilford Press.BECK, A.T. & YOUNG, J.E. (1978) College blues. *Psychology Today*, September, 80–92.

BECK, A.T., RUSH, A.J., SHAW, B.F. & EMORY, G. (1979) *Cognitive Therapy of Depression*. New York: Guilford Press.

BEE, H. (1992) *The Developing Child* (7th edition). New York: HarperCollins.

BEE, H. (1994) *Lifespan Development*. New York: HarperCollins.

BEE, H. (2000) *The Developing Child* (9th edition). Boston: Allyn & Bacon.

BEE, H. & MITCHELL, S.K. (1980) *The Developing Person: A Lifespan Approach*. New York: Harper & Row.

BELLROSE, F.C. (1967) Orientation in waterfowl migration. In R.M. Storm (Ed.) *Animal Orientation and Navigation*. Corvallis: Oregon State University Press, pp.73–99.

BELLUR, R. (1995) Interpersonal attraction revisited: Cross-cultural conceptions of love. *Psychology Review*, 1, 24–26.

BEM, D.J. (1967) Self-perception: An alternative interpretation of cognitive dissonance phenomena. *Psychological Review*, 74, 183–200.

BEM, D.J. (1972) Self-perception theory. In L. Berkowitz (Ed.) *Advances in Experimental Social Psychology*, Volume 6. New York: Academic Press.

BEM, S.L. (1985) Androgyny and gender schema theory: A conceptual and empirical integration. In T.B. Sonderegger (Ed.) *Nebraska Symposium on Motivation*. Nebraska, NE: University of Nebraska Press.

BENDER, M. (1995) The war goes on. *The Psychologist*, 8, 78–79.

BENINGER, R.J., KENDALL, S.B. & VANDERWOF, C.H. (1974) The ability of rats to discriminate their own behaviours. *Canadian Journal of Psychology*, 28, 79–91.

BENNETT, M. (1993) Introduction. In M. Bennett (Ed.) *The Child as Psychologist: An Introduction to the Development of Social Cognition*. Hemel Hempstead: Harvester Wheatsheaf.

BENNETT, W. (1997) Daughter dead after living like a monk in a room for 14 years. *The Daily Telegraph*, 5 September, 3.

BENTLEY, E. (2000) *Awareness: Biorhythms, Sleep and Dreaming*. London: Routledge.

BENZER, S. (1973) Genetic dissection of behaviour. *Scientific American*, 229, 24–37.

BEREITER, C. & ENGELMAN, S. (1966) *Teaching Disadvantaged Children in The Pre-School*. Englewood Cliffs, NJ: Prentice-Hall.

BERESFORD, D. (1997) Army gave gays shock treatment. *The Guardian*, 17 June, 13.

BERGER, H. (1929) Über das Elektrenkephalogramm des Menschen. *Archiv für Psychiatrie und Nevenkrankheiten*, 87, 527–570.

BERGIN, A.E. (1971) The evaluation of therapeutic outcomes. In A.E. Bergin & S.L. Garfield (Eds) *Handbook of Psychotherapy and Behaviour Change: An Empirical Analysis*. New York: Wiley.

BERGIN, A.E. (1980) Psychotherapy and religious values. *Journal of Consulting and Clinical Psychology*, 48, 642–645.

BERKO, J. (1958) The child's learning of English morphology. *Word*, 14, 150–177.

BERKOWITZ, L. (1966) On not being able to aggress. *British Journal of Clinical and Social Psychology*, 5, 130–139.

BERKOWITZ, L. (1968) Impulse, aggression and the gun. *Psychology Today*, September, 18–22.

BERKOWITZ, L. (1978) Whatever happened to the frustration–aggression hypothesis? *American Behavioural Scientist*, 21, 691–708.

BERKOWITZ, L. (1989) The frustration–aggression hypothesis: an examination and reformation. *Psychological Bulletin*, 106, 59–73.

BERKOWITZ, L. (1990) On the formation and regulation of anger and aggression – a cognitive neoassociationistic analysis. *American Psychologist*, 45, 494–503.

BERKOWITZ, L. (1993) *Aggression: Its Causes, Consequences and Control*. New York: McGraw-Hill.

BERKOWITZ, L. (1995) A career on aggression. In G.G. Brannigan & M.R. Merrens (Eds) *The Social Psychologists: Research Adventures*. New York: McGraw-Hill.

BERKOWITZ, L. & GEEN, R.G. (1966) Film violence and the cue properties of available targets. *Journal of Personality and Social Psychology*, 3, 525–530.

BERKOWITZ, L. & LE PAGE, A. (1967) Weapons as aggression-eliciting stimuli. *Journal of Personality and Social Psychology*, 7, 202–207.

BERLIN, B. & KAY, P. (1969) *Basic Colour Terms: Their Universality and Evolution*. Berkeley, CA: University of California Press.

BERMAN, E. (1975) Tested and documented split personality. *Psychology Today*, August, 78-81.

BERNSTEIN, B. (1961) Social class and linguistic development: A theory of Social Learning. In A.H. Halsey, J. Floyd & C.A. Anderson (Eds) *Education, Economy and Society*. London: Collier-Macmillan Ltd.

BERRIOS, G.E. & MORLEY, S.J. (1984) Koro-like symptom in a non-Chinese subject. *British Journal of Psychiatry*, 145, 331–334.

BERRY, D.S. & WILLINGHAM, J.K. (1997) Affective traits, responses to conflict and satisfaction in romantic relationships. *Journal of Research in Personality*, 31, 564–576.

BERRY, D.T.R. & WEBB, W.B. (1983) State measures and sleep stages. *Psychological Reports*, 52, 807–812.

BERRY, J.W. (1969) On cross-cultural compatability. *International Journal of Psychology*, 4, 119–128.

BERRY, J.W., POORTINGA, Y.H., SEGALL, M.H. & DASEN, P.R. (1992) *Cross-Cultural Psychology*. Cambridge: Cambridge University Press.

BERSCHEID, E. & WALSTER, E.M. (1974) Physical attractiveness. In L. Berkowitz (Ed.) *Advances in Experimental Social Psychology*, Volume 7. New York: Academic Press.

BERSCHEID, E. & WALSTER, E.M. (1978) *Interpersonal Attraction* (2nd edition). Reading, MA: Addison-Wesley.

BERSCHEID, E., DION, K., HATFIELD, E. & WALSTER, G.W. (1971) Physical attractiveness and dating choice: A test of the matching hypothesis. *Journal of Experimental and Social Psychology*, 7, 173–189.

BERTENTHAL, B.I. & FISCHER, K.W. (1978) Development of self-recognition in the infant. *Developmental Psychology*, 14, 44–50.

BERTRAM, B.C.R. (1976) Kin selection in lions and in evolution. In P.P.G. Bateson & R.A. Hinde (Eds) *Growing Points in Ethology*. Cambridge: Cambridge University Press.

BESEVEGIS, E. & GIANNITSAS, N. (1996) Parent–adult relations and conflicts as perceived by adolescents. In L. Verhofstadt-Deneve, I. Kienhorst & C. Braet (Eds) *Conflict and Development in Adolescence*. Leiden: DSWO Press.

BIANCHI, A. (1992) Dream chemistry. *Harvard Magazine*, September–October, 21–22.

BICKMAN, L. (1971) The effects of another bystander's ability to help on bystander intervention in an emergency. *Journal of Experimental Social Psychology*, 7, 367–379.

BIEBACH, H. (1983) Genetic determination of partial migration in the European robin (*Erithacus rubecula*). *Auk*, 100, 601–606.

BIEDERMAN, I. (1987) Recognition-by-components: A theory of human image understanding. *Psychological Review*, 94, 115–147.

BIERHOFF, H.W. & KLEIN, R. (1988) Prosocial behaviour. In M. Hewstone, W. Stroebe, J.P. Codol & G.M. Stephenson (Eds) *Introduction to Social Psychology*. Oxford: Blackwell.

BINET, A. & SIMON, T.H. (1915) *Method of Measuring the Development of the Intelligence of Young Children*. Chicago: Chicago Medical Book Company.

BINGMAN, V.P. & MENCH, J.A. (1990) Homing behaviour of hippocampus and parahippocampus lesioned pigeons following short-distance releases. *Behavioural Brain Research*, 40, 227–238.

BINI, L. (1938) Experimental researches on epileptic attacks induced by electric current. *American Journal of Psychiatry*, Supplement 94, 172–183.

BLAIR, R.J.R., JONES, L., CLARK, F. & SMITH, M (1997) The psychopathic individual: A Lack of responsiveness to distress cues? *Psychophysiology*, 34, 192–198.

BLAKEMORE, C. (1988) *The Mind Machine*. London: BBC Productions.

BLANEY, P. (1975) Implications of the medical model and its alternatives. *American Journal of Psychiatry*, 132, 911–914.

BLASI, A, (1980) Bridging moral cognition and moral action: A critical review of the literature. *Psychological Bulletin*, 88, 1–44.

BLAU, P.M. (1964) *Exchange and Power in Social Life*. New York: Wiley.

BLEULER, E. (1911) *Dementia Praecox or the Group of Schizophrenias*. New York: International University Press.

BLEULER, M.E. (1978) The long-term course of schizophrenic psychoses. In L.C. Wynne, R.L. Cromwell & S. Mathyse (Eds) *The Nature of Schizophrenia: New Approaches to Research and Treatment*. New York: Wiley.

BLOCH, V. (1976) Brain activation and memory consolidation. In Rosenzweig, M.A. & Bennett, E.L. (Eds) *Neural Mechanisms of Learning and Memory*. Cambridge, MA: MIT Press.

BLOCK, J. (1978) Review of H.J. Eysenck and S.B.G. Eysenck, The Eysenck Personality Questionnaire. In O. Buros (Ed.) *The Eighth Mental Measurement Yearbook*. Highland Park, NJ: Gryphon.

BLOCK, J. (1979) Another look at sex differentiation in the socialisation behaviours of mothers and fathers. In F. Denmark & J. Sherman (Eds) *Psychology of Women: Future Directions of Research*. New York: Psychological Dimensions.

BLOOD, R.O. & WOLFE, D.M. (1969) *Husbands and Wives: The Dynamics of Married Lives*. New York: Free Press.

BLOOM, B.S. (1964) *Stability and Change in Human Characteristics*. New York: Harcourt Brace Jovanovich.

BLUNDELL, J.E. & HILL, A.J. (1995) Hunger and appetite. In B. Parkinson & A.M. Colman (Eds) *Emotion and Motivation*. London: Longman.

BLYTH, D.A., SIMMONS, R.G., BULCROFT, R., FELT, D., VANCLEAVE, E.F. & BUSH, D.M. (1981) The effects of physical development on self-image and satisfaction with body-image for early adolescent males. *Research in Community & Mental Health*, 2, 43–73.

BNF (1999) *British National Formulary*. Number 38. London: British Medical Association/Royal Pharmaceutical Society of Great Britain.

BODEN, M. (1980) Artificial intelligence and intellectual imperialism. In A.J. Chapman & D.M. Jones (Eds) *Models of Man*. Leicester: British Psychological Society.

BODEN, M. (1987) *Artificial Language and Natural Man* (2nd edition). Cambridge, MA: Harvard University Press.

BOESCH, C. (1991) Teaching among wild chimpanzees. *Animal Behaviour*, 41, 530–532.

BOESCH, C. & BOESCH, H. (1984) Mental map in wild chimpanzees: An analysis of hammer transports for nut cracking. *Primates*, 25, 160–170.

BOGEN, J.E. (1969) The other side of the brain. *Bulletin of the Los Angeles Neurological Societies*, 34, 3.

BOKERT, E. (1970) The effects of thirst and related auditory stimulation on dream reports. Paper presented to the Association for the Physiological Study of Sleep, Washington DC.

BOLLES, R.C. (1967) *Theory of Motivation*. New York: Harper & Row.

BOLLES, R.C. (1980) Ethological learning theory. In G.M. Gazda & R.J. Corsini (Eds) *Theories of Learning: A Comparative Approach*. Itaska, ILL.: Free Press.

BOND, J., COLEMAN, P. & PEACE, S. (Eds) (1993) *Ageing in Society: An Introduction to Social Gerontology*. London: Sage.

BORBELY, A. (1986) *Secrets of Sleep*. Harmondsworth: Penguin.

BORKE, H. (1975) Piaget's mountains revisited: Changes in the egocentric landscape. *Developmental Psychology*, 11, 240–243.

BORNSTEIN, M.H. (1976) Infants are trichromats. *Journal of Experimental Child Psychology*, 19, 401–419.

BORNSTEIN, M.H. (1988) Perceptual development across the life-cycle. In M.H. Bornstein & M.E. Lamb (Eds) *Perceptual, Cognitive and Linguistic Development*. Hove: Erlbaum.

BOTTING, J.H. & MORRISON, A.R. (1997) Animal research is vital to medicine. *Scientific American*, 67–79, February.

BOUCHARD, T.J. & McGUE, M. (1981) Familial studies of intelligence: A review. *Science*, 212, 1055–1059.

BOUCHARD, T.J. & SEGAL, N.L. (1988) Heredity, environment and IQ. In *Instructor's Resource Manual* to accompany G. Lindzay, R. Thompson & B. Spring *Psychology* (3rd edition). New York: Worth Publishers.

BOUCHARD, T.J., LYKKEN, D.T., McGUE, M., SEGAL, N.L. & TELLEGEN, A. (1990) Sources of human psychological differences: The Minnesota study of twins reared apart. *Science*, 250, 223–228.

BOURGEOIS, M. (1968) Un koro charentais (transposition, ethnopsychiatrique). *Annales-Medicales-Psychologiques*, 126, 749.

BOURNE, L.E., DOMINOWSKI, R.L. & LOFTUS, E.F. (1979) *Cognitive Processes*. Englewood Cliffs, NJ: Prentice-Hall.

BOWER, T.G.R. (1966) The visual world of infants. *Scientific American*, 215, 80–92.

BOWER, T.G.R. (1971) The object in the world of the infant. *Scientific American*, 225, 38–47.

BOWER, T.G.R. (1979) *Human Development*. San Francisco: W.H. Freeman.

BOWER, T.G.R. & WISHART, J.G. (1972) The effects of motor skill on object permanence. *Cognition*, 1, 28–35.

BOWER, T.G.R., BROUGHTON, J.M. & MOORE, M.K. (1970) Infant responses to approaching objects: An indicator of response to distal variables. *Perception and Psychophysics*, 9, 193–196.

BOWIE, I. (1991) Eye structure: A functional view. *Nursing Standard*, 5 (50), 54–55.

BOWLBY, J. (1973) *Attachment and Loss*. Volume 2: *Separation*. Harmondsworth: Penguin.

BOWLBY, J. (1980) *Attachment and Loss*. Volume 3: *Loss, Sadness and Depression*. London: Hogarth Press.

BOYER, B. & GIOVACHINI, P. (1980) *Psychoanalytic Treatment of Schizophrenia, Borderline and Characterological Disorders* (2nd edition). New York: Jason Aronson.

BRACHA, H.S., TORREY, E.F., BIGELOW, L.B., LOHR, J.B. & LININGTON, B.B. (1991) Subtle signs of prenatal maldevelopment of the head ectoderm in schizophrenia: A preliminary monozygotic twin study. *Biological Psychiatry*, 30, 719–725.

BRADBURY, J. (1984) *Violent offending and drinking patterns*. Institute of Criminology Monograph. Victoria University of Wellington: Wellington.

BRADBURY, T.N. & FINCHAM, F.D. (1990) Attributions in marriage: Review and critique. *Psychological Bulletin*, 107, 3–33.

BRADDICK, O.J. (1974) A short range process in apparent motion. *Vision Research*, 14, 519–527.

BRADSHAW, J.L. & WALLACE, G. (1971) Models for the processing and identification of faces. *Perception & Psychophysics*, 9, 443–448.

BRADY, J.V. (1958) Ulcers in executive monkeys. *Scientific American*, 199, 95–100.

BRADY, J.V. & NAUTA, W.J.H. (1953) Subcortical mechanisms in emotional behaviour: Affective changes following septal forebrain lesions in the albino rat. *Journal of Comparative and Physiological Psychology*, 46, 339–346.

BRAINERD, C.J. (1978) Neo-Piagetian training experiments revisited: Is there any support for the cognitive-developmental stage hypothesis? *Cognition*, 2, 349–370.

BRAINERD, C.J. (1983) Modifiability of cognitive development. In S. Meadows (Ed.) *Development of Thinking*. London: Methuen.

BRANDSMA, J.M., MAULTSBY, M.C. & WELSH, R. (1978) 'Self-help techniques in the treatment of alcoholism.' Unpublished manuscript cited in G.T. Wilson & K.D. O'Leary *Principles of Behaviour Therapy*. Englewood Cliffs, NJ: Prentice-Hall.

BRANNON, E.M. & TERRACE, H.S. (1998) Ordering of the numerosities 1 to 9 by monkeys. *Science*, 282, 746–749.

BREGGIN, P. (1996) *Toxic Psychiatry*. London: Fontana.

BREHM, J.W. (1966) *A Theory of Psychological Reactance*. New York: Academic Press.

BREHM, S.S. (1992) *Intimate Relationships* (2nd edition). New York: McGraw-Hill.

BREHM, S.S. & BREHM, J.W. (1981) *Psychological Reactance: A Theory of Freedom and Control*. New York: Academic Press.

BREHM, S.S. & KASSIN, S.M. (1996) *Social Psychology* (3rd edition). New York: Houghton Mifflin.

BREMNER, J.D. (1999) Does stress damage the brain? *Biological Psychiatry*, 45, 797–805.

BRENNEN, T., BAGULEY, T., BRIGHT, J. & BRUCE, V. (1990) Resolving semantically induced tip-of-the-tongue states for proper nouns. *Memory & Cognition*, 18, 339–347.

BREWER, M.B. & KRAMER, R.M. (1985) The psychology of intergroup attitudes and behaviour. *Annual Review of Psychology*, 36, 219–243.

BREWER, W.F. (1974) There is no convincing evidence for operant or classical conditioning in adult humans. In W.B. Weimar & D.S. Palermo (Eds) *Cognition and the Symbolic Processes*. Hillsdale, NJ: Lawrence Erlbaum.

BRIGHT, M. (1984) *Animal Language*. London: British Broadcasting Corporation.

BRINER, R. (1999) Feeling and smiling. *The Psychologist*, 12, 16–19.

BRISLIN, R. (1993) *Understanding Culture's Influence on Behaviour*. Orlando, FL: Harcourt Brace Jovanovich.

BRITISH PSYCHOLOGICAL SOCIETY & THE COMMITTEE OF THE EXPERIMENTAL PSYCHOLOGICAL SOCIETY (1985) . Leicester: BPS (*Guidelines for the use of animals in research.*)

BRITISH PSYCHOLOGICAL SOCIETY (1978) Ethical principles for research on human subjects. *Bulletin of the British Psychological Society*, 31, 48–49.

BRITISH PSYCHOLOGICAL SOCIETY (1981) Principles governing the employment of psychological tests. *Bulletin of the British Psychological Society*, 34, 317–318.

BRITISH PSYCHOLOGICAL SOCIETY (1983) *Guidelines for the professional practice of clinical psychology*. Leicester: British Psychological Society.

BRITISH PSYCHOLOGICAL SOCIETY (1985) A code of conduct for psychologists. *Bulletin of the British Psychological Society*, 38, 41–43.

BRITISH PSYCHOLOGICAL SOCIETY (1990) Ethical principles for conducting research with human participants. *The Psychologist*, 3 (6), 269–272.

BRITISH PSYCHOLOGICAL SOCIETY (1993) Ethical principles for conducting research with human participants (revised). *The Psychologist*, 6 (1), 33–35.

BRITISH PSYCHOLOGICAL SOCIETY (1999) Increase in depression. *The Psychologist*, 12, 277.

BROADBENT, D.E. (1954) The role of auditory localisation and attention in memory span. *Journal of Experimental Psychology*, 47, 191–196.

BROADBENT, D.E. (1958) *Perception and Communication*. Oxford: Pergamon.

BROADBENT, D.E. (1981) Non-corporeal explanations in psychology. In A.F. Heath (Ed.) *Scientific Explanation*. Oxford: Clarendon Press.

BROADBENT, D.E. (1982) Task combination and selective intake of information. *Acta Psychologica*, 50, 253–290.

BROCKNER, J. & RUBIN, Z. (1985) *Entrapment in Escalating Conflict*. New York: Springer-Verlag.

BRODBECK, A. & IRWIN, O. (1946) The speech behaviour of infants without families. *Child Development*, 17, 145–146.

BROMLEY, D.B. (1977) Speculations in social and environmental gerontology. *Nursing Times* (Occasional Papers), 53–56, 21 April.

BROMLEY, D.B. (1988) *Human Ageing: An Introduction to Gerontology* (3rd edition). Harmondsworth: Penguin.

BRONFENBRENNER, U. (1960) Freudian theories of identification and their derivatives. *Child Development*, 31, 15–40.

BRONFENBRENNER, U. & CECI, S.J. (1994) Nature–nurture in developmental perspective: A bioecological theory. *Psychological Review*, 101, 568–586.

BROOKS, J. & WATKINS, M. (1989) Recognition memory and the mere exposure effect. *Journal of Experimental Psychology: Learning, Memory and Cognition*, 15, 968–976.

BROOKS, L. (1999) Quality time spurs early rise. *The Guardian*, 3 March, 5.

BROOKS-GUNN, J. & WARREN, M.P. (1985) The effects of delayed menarche in different contexts. Dance and non-dance students. *Journal of Youth & Adolescence*, 14, 285–300.

BROOKS-GUNN, J., ATTIE, H., BURROW, C., ROSSO, J.T. & WARREN, M.P. (1989) The impact of puberty on body and eating concerns in athletic and nonathletic contexts. *Journal of Early Adolescence*, 9, 269–290.

BROWN, B. & GROTBERG, J.J. (1981) *Headstart: A Successful Experiment*. Courrier (Paris International Children's Centre).

BROWN, H. (1985) *People, Groups and Society*. Milton Keynes: Open University Press.

BROWN, J. (1999) Superwoman is feeling overworked and fed up. *Oxford Times* (Business Supplement), July/August, 11.

BROWN, J.D. & SMART, S. (1991) The self and social conduct: Linking self-representations to prosocial behaviour. *Journal of Personality and Social Psychology*, 60, 368–375.

BROWN, J.K. (1963) A cross-cultural study of female initiation rites. *American Anthropologist*, 65, 837–853.

BROWN, L.M. & GILLIGAN, C. (1992) *Meeting at the Crossroads: Women's Psychology and Girls' Development*. Cambridge, MA.: Harvard University Press.

BROWN, L.S. (1997) Ethics in psychology: Cui bono? In D. Fox & I. Prilleltensky (Eds) *Critical Psychology: An Introduction*. London: Sage.

BROWN, R. (1965) *Social Psychology*. New York: The Free Press.

BROWN, R. (1970) The first sentences of child and chimpanzee. In R. Brown (Ed.) *Psycholinguistics*. New York: Free Press.

BROWN, R. (1973) *A First Language: The Early Stages*. Cambridge, MA: Harvard University Press.

BROWN, R. (1986) *Social Psychology: The Second Edition*. New York: Free Press.

BROWN, R. & LENNEBERG, E.H. (1954) A study in language and cognition. *Journal of Abnormal and Clinical Psychology*, 49, 454–462.

BROWN, R., CAZDEN, C.B. & BELLUGI, U. (1969) The child's grammar from one to three. In J.P. Hill (Ed.) *Minnesota Symposium on Child Psychology*, Volume 2. Minneapolis: University of Minnesota Press.

BROWN, R.J. (1988) Intergroup relations. In M. Hewstone, W. Stroebe, J.P. Codol & G.M. Stephenson (Eds) *Introduction to Social Psychology*. Oxford: Blackwell.

BROWN, R.J. (1996) Intergroup relations. In M. Hewstone, W. Stroebe & G.M. Stephenson (Eds) *Introduction to Social Psychology* (2nd edition). Oxford: Blackwell.

BROWN, R.J. & TURNER, J.C. (1981) Interpersonal and intergroup behaviour. In J.C. Turner & H. Giles (Eds) *Intergroup Behaviour*. Oxford: Blackwell.

BRUCE, V. (1995) Perceiving and Recognising Faces. In I. Roth & V. Bruce *Perception and Representation: Current Issues* (2nd edition). Buckingham: Open University Press.

BRUCE, V. & GREEN, P.R. (1990) *Visual Perception* (2nd edition). Hove: Erlbaum.

BRUCE, V. & YOUNG, A.W. (1986) Understanding face recognition. *British Journal of Psychology*, 77, 305–327.

BRUCE, V., BURTON, A.M. & DENCH, N. (1994) What's distinctive about a distinctive face? *Quarterly Journal of Experimental Psychology*, 47A, 119–141.

BRUNER, J.S. & POSTMAN, L. (1949) On the perception of incongruity. *Journal of Personality*, 18, 206–223.

BRUNER, J.S. & TAGIURI, R. (1954) The perception of people. In G. Lindzey (Ed.) *Handbook of Social Psychology*, Volume 2. London: Addison Wesley.

BRUNER, J.S. (1957) On perceptual readiness. *Psychological Review*, 64, 123–152.

BRUNER, J.S. (1975) The ontogenesis of speech acts. *Journal of Child Language*, 2, 1–21.

BRUNER, J.S. (1978) Acquiring the uses of language. *Canadian Journal of Psychology*, 32, 204–218.

BRUNER, J.S. (1983) *Child's Talk: Learning to Use Language*. Oxford: Oxford University Press.

BRUNER, J.S., BUSIEK, R.D. & MINTURN, A.L. (1952) Assimilation in the immediate reproduction of visually perceived figures. *Journal of Experimental Psychology*, 44, 151–155.

BRUNER, J.S., GOODNOW, J.J., & AUSTIN, G.A. (1956) *A Study of Thinking*. New York: Wiley.

BRYANT, J. & ZILLMAN, D. (Eds) (1994) *Media Effects: Advances in Theory and Research*. Hove: Erlbaum.

BRYDEN, M. & SAXBY, L. (1985) Developmental aspects of cerebral lateralisation. In J. Obrzat & G. Hynd (Eds) *Child Neuropsychology, Volume 1: Theory and Research*. Orlando, FLA: Academic Press.

BUEHLER, C. & LEGGE, B.H. (1993) Mothers' receipt of social support and their psychological well being following marital separation. *Journal of Social and Personal Relationships*, 10, 21–38.

BUNNEY, W., GOODWIN, F. & MURPHY, D. (1972) The 'switch process' in manic-depressive illness. *Archives of General Psychiatry*, 27, 312–317.

BURGER, F. (1982) The 46-hour-a-week habit. *The Boston Globe*, 2 May

BURGESS, A. (1962) *A Clockwork Orange*. Harmandsworth: Penguin.

BURNE, J. (1998) Dream a little dream. *The Guardian*, 18 August, 15.

BURNE, J. (1999) Don't worry, be happy. *The Guardian* (Supplement), 24 August, 8–9.

BURNSIDE, I.M., EBERSOLE, P. & MONEA, H.E. (1979) *Psychological Caring Throughout the Lifespan*. New York: McGraw-Hill.

BURR, W.R. (1970) Satisfaction with various aspects of marriage over the life cycle: A random middle class sample. *Journal of Marriage and the Family*, 32, 29–37.

BURT, C. (1966) The genetic determination of differences in intelligence: A study of monozygotic twins reared together and apart. *British Journal of Psychology*, 57, 137–153.

BURT DE PERERA, T. & GUILFORD, T. (1999) The social transmission of spatial information in homing pigeons. *Animal Behaviour*, 57, 715–719.

BURTON, A.M., BRUCE, V. & JOHNSTON, R.A. (1990) Understanding face recognition with an interactive activation model. *British Journal of Psychology*, 81, 361–380.

BURTON-BRADLEY, B.G. (1968) The amok syndrome in Papua New Guinea. *Medical Journal of Australia*, 1, 252–256.

BURTON-BRADLEY, B.G. (1987) The Hungerford Massacre and its aftermath. *British Journal of Psychiatry*, 151, 866.

BUSS, A.H. & PLOMIN, R. (1984) *Temperament: Early Developing Personality Traits*. Hillsdale, NJ: Erlbaum.

BUSS, D.M. (1987) Sex differences in human mate selection criteria: An evolutionary perspective. In C. Crawford, D. Krebs & M. Smith (Eds). *Sociobiology and Psychology: Ideas, Issues and Applications*. Hillside, NJ: Erlbaum.

BUSS, D.M. (1988) The evolutionary biology of love. In R.J. Sternberg & M.L. Barnes (Eds) *The Psychology of Love*. New Haven, CT: Yale University Press.

BUSS, D.M. (1989) Sex differences in human mate preferences: Evolutionary hypotheses tested in 37 cultures. *Behavioural & Brain Sciences*, 12, 1–49.

BUSS, D.M. (1994) Mate preference in 37 cultures. In W.J. Lonner & R.S. Malpass (Eds) *Psychology and Culture*. Boston: Allyn & Bacon.

BUSS, D.M. (1995) Evolutionary psychology: A new paradigm for psychological science. *Psychological Inquiry*, 6, 1–49.

BUSS, D.M. (1999) *Evolutionary Psychology*. Boston, MA: Allyn & Bacon.

BUSS, M. & SHACKELFORD, T.K. (1997) Susceptibility to infidelity in the first year of marriage. *Journal of Research in Personality*, 31, 193–221.

BUUNK, B.P. (1996) Affiliation, attraction and close relationships. In M. Hewstone, W. Stroebe & G.M. Stephenson (Eds) *Introduction to Social Psychology* (2nd edition). Oxford: Blackwell.

BUUNK, B. & HUPKA, R.B. (1987) Cross-cultural differences in the elicitation of sexual jealousy. *Journal of Sexual Research*, 23, 12–22.

BYCHOWSKI, G. (1952) *Psychotherapy of Psychosis*. New York: Grunne & Stratton.

BYRNE, R.W. (1995) *The Thinking Ape*. Oxford: Oxford University Press.

BYRNE, R.W. & WHITEN, A. (1988) *Machiavellian Intelligence: Social Expertise and the Evolution of Intellect in Monkeys, Apes and Humans*. Oxford: Clarendon Press.

CADE, W.H. (1981) Alternative mating strategies: Genetic differences in crickets. *Science*, 212, 563–564.

CALLAGHAN, P. & O'CARROLL, M. (1993) Making women mad. *Nursing Times*, 89, 26–29.

CALVERT, W.H. & BROWER, L.P. (1986) The location of the monarch butterfly (*Danaus plexipuss*) overwintering colonies in Mexico in relation to topography and climate. *Journal of the Lepidoperists' Society*, 40, 164–187.

CALVIN, W.H. (1994) The emergence of language. *Scientific American*, October, 79–85.

CAMPBELL, A. (1981) *The Sense of Well-Being in America*. New York: McGraw-Hill.

CAMPBELL, A. & MUNCER, S. (1994) Men and the meaning of violence. In J. Archer (Ed.) *Male Violence*. London: Routledge.

CAMPBELL, B.A. & CHURCH, R.M. (1969) (Eds) *Punishment and Aversive Behaviour*. New York: Appleton-Century-Crofts.

CAMPBELL, D.T. (1967) Stereotypes and the perception of group differences. *American Psychologist*, 22, 817–829.

CAMPFIELD, L.A., BRANDON, P. & SMITH, F.J. (1985) On-line continuous measurement of blood-glucose and meal pattern in free-feeding rats: The role of glucose in meal initiation. *Brain Research Bulletin*, 14, 605–616.

CAMPOS, J.J., LANGER, A. & KROWITZ, A. (1970) Cardiac responses on the visual cliff in pre-locomotor human infants. *Science*, 170, 196–197.

CANNON, W.B. (1927) The James-Lange theory of emotions: A critical reexamination and an alternative theory. *American Journal of Psychology*, 39, 106–124.

CANNON, W.B. (1929) *Bodily Changes in Pain, Hunger, Fear, and Rage*. New York: Appleton.

CANNON, W.B. & WASHBURN, A.L. (1912) An explanation of hunger. *American Journal of Physiology*, 29, 441–454.

CAPLAN, P.J. (1991) Delusional dominating personality disorder (DDPD). *Feminism & Psychology*, 1 (1), 171–174.

CAPRON, C. & DUYME, M. (1989) Assessment of effects of socio-economic status on IQ in full cross-fostering study. *Nature*, 340, 552–554.

CARLSON, N.R. (1977) *Physiology of Behaviour*. Boston: Allyn & Bacon.

CARLSON, N.R. (1987) *Discovering Psychology*. London: Allyn & Bacon.

CARLSON, N.R. (1988) *Foundations of Physiological Psychology*. Boston: Allyn & Bacon.

CARLSON, N.R. (1992) *Foundations of Physiological Psychology* (2nd edition). Boston: Allyn & Bacon.

CARNEGIE, D. (1937) *How To Win Friends and Influence People*. New York: Simon & Schuster.

CARR, J.E. (1978) Ethnobehaviourism and the culture-bound syndromes: The case of amok. *Culture, Medicine and Psychiatry*, 2, 269–293.

CARR, J.E. & TAN, E.K. (1976) In search of true amok: Amok as viewed within the Malay culture. *American Journal of Psychiatry*, 133, 1295–1299.

CARROLL, D.W. (1986) *Psychology of Language*. Monterey, CA: Brooks/Cole Publishing Co.

CARROLL, J.B. & CASAGRANDE, J.B. (1958) The function of language classifications in behaviour. In E.E. Maccoby, T.M. Newcombe & E.L. Hartley (Eds) *Readings in Social Psychology* (3rd edition). New York: Holt, Rinehart & Winston.

CARSON, R.C., BUTCHER, J.N. & COLEMAN, J.C. (1988) *Abnormal Psychology and Everyday Life* (8th edition). London: Scott, Foresman & Co.

CARSTENSEN, L.L. (1992) Social and emotional patterns in adulthood: Support for socioemotional selectivity theory. *Psychology and Ageing*, 7, 331–338.

CARSTENSEN, L.L. (1993) Motivation for social contact across the life span: A theory of socioemotional selectivity. In J. Jacobs (Ed.) *Nebraska Symposium on Motivation 1992, Developmental Perspectives on Motivation*, Volume 40. Lincoln: University of Nebraska Press.

CARSTENSEN, L.L. (1996) Socioemotional selectivity: A life span developmental account of social behaviour. In M.R. Merrens & G.C. Brannigan (Eds) *The Developmental Psychologists: Research Adventures across the Life Span*. New York: McGraw-Hill.

CARSTENSEN, L.L. & TURK-CHARLES, S. (1994) The salience of emotion across the adult life course. *Psychology and Ageing*, 9, 259–264.

CARTER, R. (1998) *Mapping the Mind*. London: Weidenfeld & Nicolson.

CARTWRIGHT, B.A. & COLLETT, T.S. (1983) Landmark learning in bees: Experiments and models. *Journal of Comparative Physiology*, 151, 521–43.

CARTWRIGHT, J. (2000) *Evolution and Human Behaviour*. Basingstoke: Macmillan.

CARTWRIGHT, R.D., LLOYD, S., KNIGHT, S. & TRENHOLME, I. (1984) Broken dreams: A study of the effects of divorce and depression on dreams. *Psychiatry*, 47, 251–259.

CARVER, C.S. & SCHEIER, M.F. (1992) *Perspectives on Personality* (2nd edition). Boston: Allyn & Bacon.

CASE, R. (1985) *Intellectual Development*. London: Methuen.

CASPI, A., LYNAM, T.E., MOFFITT, T.E. & SILVA, P.A. (1993) Unravelling girls' delinquency: Biological, dispositional and contextual contributions to adolescent misbehaviour. *Developmental Psychology*, 29, 19–30.

CAVANAUGH, J.C. (1995) Ageing. In P.E. Bryant & A.M. Colman (Eds) *Developmental Psychology*. London: Longman.

CAVE, S. (1998) *Applying Psychology to the Environment*. London: Hodder & Stoughton.

CECI, S.J. & WILLIAMS, W.M. (Eds) (1999) *The Nature–Nurture Debate: The Essential Readings*. Oxford: Blackwell.

CHADWICK, P. & BIRCHWOOD, M. (1994) The omnipotence of voices. *British Journal of Psychiatry*, 164, 190–201.

CHAIKIN, A.L. & DARLEY, J.M. (1973) Victim or perpetrator? Defensive attribution of responsibility and the need for order and justice. *Journal of Personality and Social Psychology*, 25, 268–275.

CHAPMAN, L.J. & CHAPMAN, J.P. (1969) Illusory correlation as an obstacle to the use of valid psychodiagnostic signs. *Journal of Abnormal Psychology*, 74, 271–280.

CHARLTON, B. (1996) How to get inside the thinking brain. *The Times*, 5 February, 12.

CHASE, M. & MORALES, F. (1990) The atonia and myoclonia of active (REM) sleep. *Annual Review of Psychology*, 41, 557–584.

CHASE, T. (1988) *When Rabbit Howls*. London: Sidgwick & Jackson.

CHENEY, D.L. & SEYFARTH, R.M. (1990) *How Monkeys See the World*. Chicago: University of Chicago Press.

CHERRY, E.C. (1953) Some experiments on the recognition of speech with one and two ears. *Journal of the Acoustical Society of America*, 25, 975–979.

CHERRY, E.C. & TAYLOR, W.K. (1954) Some further experiments on the recognition of speech with one and two ears. *Journal of the Acoustical Society of America*, 26, 554–559.

CHERRY, F. & BYRNE, D.S. (1976) Authoritarianism. In T. Blass (Ed.) *Personality Variables in Social Behaviour*. Hillsdale, NJ: Erlbaum.

CHOI, P. (1999) Why I study … the menstrual cycle. *The Psychologist*, 12, 8–9.

CHOI, P. & McKEOWN, S. (1997) What are young undergraduate women's qualitative experiences of the menstrual cycle? *Journal of Psychosomatic Obstetrics & Gynecology*, 18, 259–265.

CHOMSKY, N. (1957) *Syntactic Structures*. The Hague: Mouton.

CHOMSKY, N. (1965) *Aspects of the Theory of Syntax*. Cambridge, MA: MIT Press.

CHOMSKY, N. (1968) *Language and Mind*. New York: Harcourt Brace Jovanovich.

CHOMSKY, N. (1979) *Language and Responsibility*. Sussex: Harvester Press.

CHUA, S.E. & McKENNA, P.J. (1995) Schizophrenia – a brain disease? A critical review of structural and functional cerebral abnormality in the disorder. *British Journal of Psychiatry*, 166, 563–582.

CLAMP, A.G. & RUSSELL, J. (1998) *Comparative Psychology*. London: Hodder & Stoughton.

CLARIDGE, G. (1987) The continuum of psychosis and the gene. *British Journal of Psychiatry*, 150, 129–133 (correspondence).

CLARK, D.M. (1993) Treating panic attacks. *The Psychologist*, 6, 73–74.

CLARK, D.M., SALKOVSKIS, P.M., HACKMANN, A., WELLS, A., LUDGATE, J. & GELDER, M. (1999) Brief cognitive therapy for panic disorder: A randomized controlled trial. *Journal of Consulting & Clinical Psychology*, 67, 583–589.

CLARK, K.B. & CLARK, M. (1947) Racial identification and preference in negro children. In T.M. Newcomb & E.L. Hartley (Eds) *Readings in Social Psychology*. New York: Holt.

CLARK, R.D. & WORD, L.E. (1974) Where is the apathetic bystander? Situational characteristics of the emergency. *Journal of Personality and Social Psychology*, 29, 279–287.

CLARKE, G.N., ROHDE, P., LEWINSOHN, P.M., HOPS, H. & SEELEY, J.R. (1999) Cognitive–behavioural treatment of adolescent depression: efficacy of acute group treatment and booster sessions. *Journal of the American Academy of Child & Adolescent Psychiatry*, 38, 272–279.

CLAYTON, I.C., RICHARDS, J.C. & EDWARDS, C.J. (1999) Selective attention in obsessive–compulsive disorder. *Journal of Abnormal Psychology*, 108, 171–175.

CLORE, G.L. & BYRNE, D.S. (1974) A reinforcement-affect model of attraction. In T.L. Huston (Ed.) *Foundations of Interpersonal Attraction*. New York: Academic Press.

CLORE, G.L., BRAY, R.M., ITKIN, S.M. & MURPHY, P. (1978) Interracial attitudes and behaviour at a summer camp. *Journal of Personality and Social Psychology*, 36, 706–712.

COCHRANE, R. (1983) *The Social Creation of Mental Illness*. London: Longman.

COCHRANE, R. (1995) Women and depression. *Psychology Review*, 2, 20–24.

COCHRANE, R. (1996) Marriage and madness. *Psychology Review*, 3, 2–5.

COCKER, J. (1998) Where Monarchs spend the winter. *Journal of the Association for the Teaching of Psychology*, 7, 2–20.

COHEN, D.B. (1973) Sex role orientation and dream recall. *Journal of Abnormal Psychology*, 82, 246–252.

COHEN, Y.A. (1964) *The Transition from Childhood to Adolescence: Cross-cultural Studies in Initiation Ceremonies, Legal Systems, and Incest Taboos*. Chicago: Aldine.

COHN, E.G. (1993) The prediction of police calls for service: The influence of weather and temporal variables on rape and domestic violence. *Journal of Environmental Psychology*, 13, 71–83.

COHN, H.W. (1994) What is existential psychotherapy? *British Journal of Psychiatry*, 165, 699–701.

COLBY, A. & KOHLBERG, L. (Eds) (1987) *The Measurement of Moral Judgement*. New York: Cambridge University Press.

COLBY, A., KOHLBERG, L., GIBBS, J. & LIEBERMAN, M. (1983) A longitudinal study of moral development. *Monographs of the Society for Research in Child Development*, 48, (1–2, Serial No. 200).

COLEMAN, J.C. (1980) *The Nature of Adolescence*. London: Methuen.

COLEMAN, J.C. (1995) Adolescence. In P.E. Bryant & A.M. Colman (Eds) *Developmental Psychology*. London: Longman.

COLEMAN, J.C. & HENDRY, L. (1990) *The Nature of Adolescence* (2nd edition). London: Routledge.

COLEMAN, J.C. & HENDRY, L. (1999) *The Nature of Adolescence* (3rd edition). London: Routledge.

COLEMAN, J.C. & ROKER, D. (1998) Adolescence. *The Psychologist*, 11(12), 593–596.

COLLEE, J. (1993) Symbol minds. *The Observer Life Magazine*, 26 September, 14.

COLLETT, T.S., CARTWRIGHT, B.A. & SMITH, B.A. (1986) Landmark learning and visuo-spatial memories in gerbils. *Journal of Comparative Physiology*, 158, 835–51.

COLLINS, H. (1994) *Times Higher Education Supplement*, 18, 30 September.

COLLINS, R.C. (1983) Headstart: An update on program effects. *Newsletter of the Society for Research in Child Development*. Summer, 1–2.

COLLIS, G.M. & SCHAFFER, H.R. (1975) Synchronization of visual attention in mother-infant pairs. *Journal of Child Psychology and Psychiatry*, 16, 315–320.

COMER, R. (1998) *Abnormal Psychology* (3rd edition). New York: W.H. Freeman & Co.

COMFORT, A. (1977) *A Good Age*. London: Mitchell Beazley.

COMINGS, D.E. & COMINGS, B.G. (1987) Hereditary agoraphobia and obsessive-compulsive behaviour in relatives of patients with Gilles de la Tourette's syndrome. *British Journal of Psychiatry*, 151, 195–199.

COMPAS, B.E., HINDEN, B.R. & GERHARDT, C.A. (1995) Adolescent development: Pathways and processes of risk and resilience. *Annual Review of Psychology*, 46, 265–293.

COMSTOCK, G. & PAIK, H. (1991) *Television and the American Child*. New York: Academic Press.

CONDRY, J.C. & ROSS, D.F. (1985) Sex and aggression: The influence of gender label on the perception of aggression in children. *Child Development*, 56, 225–233.

CONNOR, S. (1997) Mute boy speaks after brain is halved. *The Sunday Times*, 4 May, 10.

CONNOR, S. (1998) Science finds a way of treating fear. *The Sunday Times*, 22 February, 11.

COOK, E. (1997) Is marriage driving women mad? Real Life. *Independent on Sunday*, 10 August, 1–2.

COOLICAN, H. (1997) Thinking about prejudice. *Psychology Review*, 4, 26–29.

COOLICAN, H. (1999) *Research Methods and Statistics in Psychology* (3rd edition). London: Hodder & Stoughton.

COONS, P.M., MILSTEIN, V. & MARLEY, C. (1982) EEG studies of two multiple personalities and a control. *Archives of General Psychiatry*, 39, 823-825.

COOPER, G. (1994) Napoleon island to end TV exile. *Independent on Sunday*, 12 June, 7.

COOPER, G. (1996) How nursery breeds bad behaviour. *Independent*, 13 September, 3.

COOPER, J.E., KENDELL, R.E., GURLAND, B.J., SHARPE, L., COPELAND, J.R.M. & SIMON, R. (1972) *Psychiatric Diagnosis in New York and London*. Oxford: Oxford University Press.

COOPER, P.J. (1995) Eating disorders. In A.A. Lazarus & A.M. Colman (Eds) *Abnormal Psychology*. London: Longman.

COOPER, R.S., ROTIMI, C.N. & WARD, R. (1999) The puzzle of hypertension in African-Americans. *Scientific American*, 253, 36–43.

COREN, S. & GIRGUS, J.S. (1978) *Seeing is Deceiving: The Psychology of Visual Illusions*. Hillsdale, NJ: Erlbaum.

CORNWELL, T. (1997) Board tones down Ebonics policy. *Times Educational Supplement*, 31 January, 14.

CORRIGAN, R. (1978) Language development as related to stage-6 object permanence development. *Journal of Child Language*, 5, 173–189.

CORSARO, W.A. (1993) Interpretive reproduction in the 'sculoa materna'. *European Journal of Psychology of Education*, 8, 357–374.

CORTEEN, R.S. & WOOD, B. (1972) Autonomic responses to shock-associated words in an unattended channel. *Journal of Experimental Psychology*, 94, 308–313.

COSMIDES, L. (1989) The logic of social exchange: Has natural selection shaped how humans reason? Studies with the Wason selection task. *Cognition*, 31, 187–276.

COSMIDES, L. & TOOBY, J. (1995) Cognitive adaptations for social exchange. In J. Barkow, L. Cosmides & J. Tooby (Eds.) *The Adapted Mind*. New York: Oxford University Press.

COTMAN, C.W. & McGAUGH, J.L. (1980) *Behavioural Neuroscience*. New York: Academic Press.

COURT, J., SPURDEN, D., LLOYD, S., McKEITH, I., BALLARD, C., CAIRNS, N., KERWIN, R., PERRY, R. & PERRY, E. (1999) Neuronal nicotinic receptors in dementia with Lewy bodies and schizophrenia: Alpha-bungarotoxin and nicotine binding in the thalamus. *Journal of Neurochemistry*, 73, 1590–1597.

COWART, J. & WHALEY, D.L. (1971) Punishment of self-mutilation behaviour. Cited in D.L. Whaley & R.W. Malott *Elementary Principles of Behaviour*. New York: Appleton Century Crofts.

COWIE, R.J., KREBS, J.R. & SHERRY, D.F. (1981) Food storage by marsh tits. *Animal Behaviour*, 29, 1252–1259.

COX, V.C., PAULUS, P.B. & MCCAIN, G. (1984) Prison crowding research: The relevance for prison housing standards and a general approach regarding crowding phenomena. *American Psychologist*, 39, 1148–1160.

CRAIG, G.J. (1992) *Human Development* (6th edition). Englewood Cliffs, NJ: Prentice-Hall.

CRAMER, D. (1995) Special issue on personal relationships. *The Psychologist*, 8, 58–59.

CRAMER, D. (1998) *Close Relationships*. London: Arnold.

CRANDELL, L.E. & HOBSON, R.P. (1999) Individual differences in young children's IQ: A social–developmental perspective. *Journal of Child Psychology & Psychiatry*, 40(3), 455–464.

CRATTY, B.J. (1970) *Perceptual and Motor Development in Children*. New York: MacMillan.

CRAWFORD, M. & UNGER, R.K. (1995) Gender issues in psychology. In A.M. Colman (Ed.) *Controversies in Psychology*. London: Longman.

CRESPO-FACORRO, B., CABRANES, J., LOPEZ-IBOR ALCOCER, M., PAYA, B., FERNANDEZ PEREZ, C., ENCINAS, M., AYUSO MATEOS, J. & LOPEZ-IBOR, J. (1999) Regional cerebral blood flow in obsessive–compulsive patients with and without a chronic tic disorder: A SPECT study. *European Archives of Psychiatry and Clinical Neuroscience*, 249, 156–161.

CRICK, F. (1994) *The Astonishing Hypothesis: The Scientific Search for the Soul*. London: Simon & Schuster.

CRICK, F. & MITCHISON, G. (1983) The function of dream sleep. *Nature*, 304, 111–114.

CROCKER, J., THOMPSON, L., McGRAW, K. & INGERMAN, C. (1987) Downward comparison, prejudice, and evaluation of others: Effects of self-esteem and threat. *Journal of Personality and Social Psychology*, 52, 907–916.

CROMER, R.F. (1974) The development of language and cognition: The cognition hypothesis. In B.M. Foss (Ed.) *New Perspectives in Child Development*. Harmondsworth: Penguin.

CRONIN, H. (1991) *The Ant and the Peacock*. Cambridge: Cambridge University Press.

CROOK, J.H. (1972) Sexual selection, dimorphism and social organisation in the primates. In B. Campbell (Ed.) *Sexual Selection and the Descent of Man*, 1871–1971. Chicago: Aldine.

CROOK, T. & ELIOT, J. (1980) Parental death during childhood and adult depression: A critical review of the literature. *Psychological Bulletin*, 87, 252–259.

CROOKS, R.L. & STEIN, J. (1991) *Psychology: Science, Behaviour and Life* (2nd edition). London: Holt, Rinehart & Winston Inc.

CROW, T.J. (1995) Brain changes and negative symptoms in schizophrenia. 9th World Congress of Psychiatry (1993, Rio de Janeiro, Brazil). *Psychopathology*, 28, 18–21.

CROW, T.J. & DONE, D.J. (1992) Prenatal exposure to influenza does not cause schizophrenia. *British Journal of Psychiatry*, 161, 390–393.

CROWNE, D.P. & MARLOWE, D. (1964) *The Approval Motive*. New York: Wiley.

CSIKSZENTMIHALYI, M. & LARSON, R. (1984) *Being Adolescent: Conflict and Growth in the Teenage Years*. New York: Basic Books.

CUMBERBATCH, G. (1987) *The Portrayal of Violence on British Television*. London: BBC Publications.

CUMBERBATCH, G. (1997) Media violence: Science and common sense. *Psychology Review*, 3, 2–7.

CUMMING, E. (1975) Engagement with an old theory. *International Journal of Ageing and Human Development*, 6, 187–191.

CUMMING, E. & HENRY, W.E. (1961) *Growing Old: The Process of Disengagement*. New York: Basic Books.

CURIO, E., ERNST, V. & VIETH, W. (1978) Cultural transmission of enemy recognition. *Science*, 202, 899–901.

CURRY, C. (1998) Adolescence. In K. Trew & J. Kremer (Eds) *Gender & Psychology*. London: Arnold.

CURTISS, S. (1977) *Genie: A Psycholinguistic Study of a Modern-Day 'Wild Child'*. London: Academic Press.

CZEISLER, C.A., MOORE-EDE, M.C. & COLEMAN, R.M. (1982) Rotating shift work schedules that disrupt sleep are improved by applying circadian principles. *Science*, 217, 460–463.

DACEY, J.S. (1982) *Adolescents Today* (2nd edition). Glenview, Illinois: Scott, Foresman & Company.

DALACK, G.W., BECKS, L., HILL, E., POMERLEAU, O.F. & MEADOR-WOODRUFF, J.H. (1999) Nicotine withdrawal and psychiatric symptoms in cigarette smokers with schizophrenia. *Neuropsychopharmacology*, 21, 195–202.

DALE, P.S. (1976) *Language Development: Structure and Function* (2nd edition). New York: Holt, Rinehart and Winston.

DALGLEISH, T. (1998) Emotion. In M. Eysenck (Ed.) *Psychology: An Integrated Approach*. Harlow: Addison Wesley/Longman Ltd.

DALLOS, R. & CULLEN, C. (1990) Clinical psychology. In I. Roth (Ed.) *Introduction to Psychology*, Volume 2. Hove/E.Sussex/Milton Keynes: Open University Press/Lawrence Erlbaum Associates Ltd.

DALTON, K. (1964) *The Premenstrual Syndrome*. Springfield, ILL: Charles C. Thomas.

DANGERFIELD, G.N. (1843) The symptoms, pathology, causes and treatment of spermatorrhea. *Lancet*, i, 211–216.

DARLEY, J.M. (1991) Altruism and prosocial behaviour research: Reflections and prospects. In M.S. Clark (Ed.) *Prosocial Behaviour, Review of Personality and Social Psychology*, 12. Newbury Park: CA: Sage.

DARLEY, J.M. & HUFF, C.W. (1990) Heightened damage assessment as a result of the intentionality of the damage causing act. *British Journal of Social Psychology*, 29, 181–188.

DARLEY, J.M. & LATANÉ, B. (1968) Bystander intervention in emergencies: Diffusion of responsibility. *Journal of Personality and Social Psychology*, 8, 377–383.

DARLINGTON, R.B. (1991) The long-term effects of model preschool programs. In L. Okagaki & R.J. Sternberg (Eds) *Directors of Development*. Hillsdale, NJ: Erlbaum.

DARWIN, C. (1859) *The Origin of Species by Means of Natural Selection*. London: John Murray.

DARWIN, C. (1871) *The Descent of Man and Selection in Relation to Sex*. London: John Murray.

DARWIN, C. (1872) *The Expression of Emotion in Man and Animals*. London: John Murray.

DARWIN, C. (1877) A biographical sketch of an infant. *Mind*, 2, 285–294.

DASEN, P.R. (1994) Culture and cognitive development from a Piagetian perspective. In W.J. Lonner & R.S. Malpass (Eds) *Psychology and Culture*. Boston: Allyn & Bacon.

DATAN, N., RODEHEAVER, D. & HUGHES, F. (1987) Adult development and ageing. *Annual Review of Psychology*, 38, 153–180.

DAVEY, G.C.L. (1983) An associative view of human classical conditioning. In G.C.L. Davey (Ed.) *Animal Models of Human Behaviour: Conceptual, Evolutionary, and Neurobiological Perspectives*. Chichester: Wiley.

DAVID, A., BLAMIRE, A. & BREITER, H. (1994) Functional Magnetic Resonance Imaging: A new technique with implications for psychology and psychiatry. *British Journal of Psychiatry*, 164, 2–7.

DAVID, A.S. (1994) Frontal lobology: Psychiatry's new pseudoscience. *British Journal of Psychiatry*, 161, 244–248.

DAVIDSON, M., REICHENBERG, A., RABINOWITZ, J., WEISER, M., KAPLAN, Z. & MARK, M. (1999) Behavioural and intellectual markers for schizophrenia in apparently healthy male adolescents. *American Journal of Psychiatry*, 156, 1328–1335.

DAVIDSON, R.J. (1992) Anterior cerebral asymmetry and the nature of emotion. *Brain and Cognition*, 20, 280–299.

DAVIES, D.L. (1956) Psychiatric illness in those enagaged to be married. *British Journal of Preventive and Social Medicine*, 10, 123–127.

DAVIES, E. & FURNHAM, A. (1986) Body satisfaction in adolescent girls. *British Journal of Medical Psychology*, 59, 279–288.

DAVIES, J.C. (1969) The J-curve of rising and declining satisfactions as a cause of some great revolutions and a contained rebellion. In H.D. Graham & T.R. Gurr (Eds) *The History of Violence in America: Historical and Comparative Perspectives*. New York: Praeger.

DAVIES, R. (1995) Selfish altruism. *Psychology Review*, 1, 2–9

DAVIES, R. (1996) Evolutionary determinants of behaviour. In M. Cardwell, L. Clark & C. Meldrum (Eds) *Psychology for A Level*. London: HarperCollins.

DAVIS, D., CAHAN, S. & BASHI, J. (1977) Birth order and intellectual development: The confluence model in the light of cross-cultural evidence. *Science*, 196, 1470–1472.

DAVIS, J.A. (1959) A formal interpretation of the theory of relative deprivation. *Sociometry*, 22, 280–296.

DAVIS, J.M. (1974) A two-factor theory of schizophrenia. *Journal of Psychiatric Research*, 11, 25–30.

DAVIS, K.L., KAHN, R.S., KO, G. & DAVIDSON, M. (1991). Dopamine in schizophrenia; a review and reconceptualization. *American Journal of Psychiatry*, 148, 1474–1486.

DAVIS, T.M. & WOOD, P.S. (1999) Substance abuse and sexual trauma in a female veteran population. *Journal of Substance Abuse & Treatment*, 16, 123–127.

DAVISON, G. & NEALE, J. (1990) *Abnormal Psychology* (5th edition). New York: Wiley.

DAVISON, G. & NEALE, J. (1994) *Abnormal Psychology* (6th edition). New York: Wiley.

DAWKINS, M.S. (1980) The many faces of animal suffering. *New Scientist*, November 20.

DAWKINS, M.S. (1990) From an animal's point of view: Motivation, fitness and animal welfare. *Behavioural and Brain Sciences*, 13, 1–9.

DAWKINS, R. (1976) *The Selfish Gene*. Oxford: Oxford University Press.

DAWKINS, R. (1989) *The Selfish Gene* (2nd edition). Oxford: Oxford University Press.

DAY, L.B., CREWS, D. & WILCZYNSKI, W. (1999) Spatial and reversal learning in congeneric lizards with different foraging strategies. *Animal Behaviour*, 57, 393–407.

DAY, R & WONG, S. (1996) Anomalous perceptual asymmetries for negative emotional stimuli in the psychopath. *Journal of Abnormal Psychology*, 105, 648–652.

DE BRUXELLES, S. (1999) Crash victim thinks wife is an imposter. *The Times*, 5 March, 7.

DE LA RONDE, C. & SWANN, W. (1998) Partner verification: Restoring shattered images of our intimates. *Journal of Personality & Social Psychology*, 75, 374–382.

DE PAULO, B.M. & FISHER, J.D. (1981) Too tuned-out to take: The role of non-verbal sensitivity in help-seeking. *Personality and Social Psychology Bulletin*, 7, 201–205.

DE RUBEIS, R., GELFAND, L., TANG, T. & SIMONS, A. (1999) Medications versus cognitive behaviour therapy for severely depressed outpatients: Meta-analysis of four randomised comparisons. *American Journal of Psychiatry*, 156, 1007–1013.

DE SILVA, P. (1997) Jealousy in couple relationships: Nature, assessment and therapy. *Behaviour Research and Therapy*, 35, 973–985.

DE VILLIERS, P.A. & DE VILLIERS, J.G. (1979) *Early Language*. Cambridge, MA: Harvard University Press.

DEAUX, K. (1972) To err is humanising: But sex makes a difference. *Representative Research in Social Psychology*, 5, 20–28.

DECI, E.L. (1980) *The Psychology of Self-determination*. Lexington, MA.: D.C. Heath.

DECI, E.L. & RYAN, R.M. (1987) The support of autonomy and the control of behaviour. *Journal of Personality & Social Psychology*, 53, 1024–1037.

DEESE, J. (1972) *Psychology as Science and Art*. New York: Harcourt Brace Jovanovich.

DEIN, S. (1994) Cross-cultural psychiatry. *British Journal of Psychiatry*, 165, 561–564.

DELBOEUF, J.L.R. (1892) Sur une nouvelle illusion d'optique. *Bulletin de L'Academie Royale de Belgique*, 24, 545–558.

DELGADO, J.M.R. (1969) *Physical Control of the Mind*. New York: Harper & Row.

DELGADO, P.L. & MORENO, F.A. (1998) Hallucinogens, serotonin and obsessive–compulsive disorder. *Journal of Psychoactive Drugs*, 30, 359–366.

DELK, J.L. & FILLENBAUM, S. (1965) Differences in perceived colour as a function of characteristic colour. *American Journal of Psychology*, 78, 290–293.

DEMENT, W.C. (1960) The effects of dream deprivation. *Science*, 131, 1705–1707.

DEMENT, W.C. (1974) *Some Must Watch While Some Must Sleep*. San Francisco: W.H. Freeman.

DEMENT, W.C. & KLEITMAN, N. (1957) Cyclical variations in EEG during sleep and their relation to eye movements, body motility and dreaming. *Electroencephalography and Clinical Neurophysiology*, 9, 673–690.

DEMENT, W.C. & WOLPERT, E. (1958) The relation of eye movements, body motility and external stimuli to dream content. *Journal of Experimental Psychology*, 55, 543–553.

DENKER, R. (1946) Results of treatment of psychoneuroses by the general practitioner: A follow-up study of 500 cases. *New York State Journal of Medicine*, 46, 356–364.

DENMARK, F., RUSSO, N.F., FRIEZE, I.H. & SECHZER, J.A. (1988) Guidelines for avoiding sexism in psychological research: A report of the *ad hoc* committee on nonsexist research. *American Psychologist*, 43, 582–585.

DENNETT, D.C. (1996) *Darwin's Dangerous Idea: Evolution and the Meanings of Life*. London: Penguin.

DENNEY, N. & PALMER, A. (1981) Adult age differences on traditional problem-solving measures. *Journal of Gerontology*, 36, 323–328.

DEREGOWSKI, J. (1972) Pictorial perception and culture. *Scientific American*, 227, 82–88.

DERMER, M. & THIEL, D.L. (1975) When beauty may fail. *Journal of Personality and Social Psychology*, 31, 1168–1176.

DEUTSCH, F.M. & LAMBERTI, D.M. (1986) Does social approval increase helping? *Personality and Social Psychology Bulletin*, 12, 149–157.

DEUTSCH, J.A. & DEUTSCH, D. (1963) Attention: Some theoretical considerations. *Psychological Review*, 70, 80–90.

DEUTSCH, J.A. & DEUTSCH, D. (1967) Comments on 'Selective attention: Perception or response?' *Quarterly Journal of Experimental Psychology*, 19, 362–363.

DEUTSCH, M. & COLLINS, M.E. (1951) *Interracial Housing: A Psychological Evaluation of a Social Experiment*. Minneapolis, MN: University of Minnesota Press.

DEVALOIS, R.L. & JACOBS, G.H. (1984) Neural mechanisms of colour vision. In I. Darian-Smith (Ed.) *Handbook of Physiology*, Volume 3. Bethesda, MD: American Physiological Society.

DEVAN, G.S. & HONG, O.S. (1987) Koro and schizophrenia in Singapore. *British Journal of Psychiatry*, 150, 106–107.

DEX, S. & PHILLIPSON, C. (1986) Social policy and the older worker. In C. Phillipson & A. Walker (Eds) *Ageing and Social Policy: A critical assessment*. Aldershot: Gower.

DI GIACOMO, J.P. (1980) Intergroup alliances and rejections within a protest movement (analysis of social representations). *European Journal of Social Psychology*, 10, 329–344.

DIAMOND, M. (1978) Sexual identity and sex roles. *The Humanist*, March/April.

DIAMOND, M. (1982) Sexual identity, monozygotic twins reared in discordant roles, and a BBC follow-up. *Archives of Sexual Behaviour*, 11, 181–186.

DIAMOND, M. & SIGMUNDSON, H.K. (1997) Sex reassignment at birth. *Paediatric & Adolescent Medicine*, 151, 298–304.

DIAMOND, R. & CAREY, S. (1986) Why faces are and are not special: An effect of expertise. *Journal of Experimental Psychology: General*, 115, 107–117.

DIENER, E. (1980) Deindividuation: The absence of self-awareness and self-regulation in group members. In P.B. Paulus (Ed.) *Psychology of Group Influence*. Hillsdale, NJ: Erlbaum.

DIENER, E., FRASER, S.C., BEAMAN, A.L. & KELEM, R.T. (1976) Effects of deindividuation variables on stealing among Halloween trick-or-treaters. *Journal of Personality and Social Psychology*, 33, 178–183.

DIETCH, J.T. (1995) Old age. In D. Wedding (Ed.) *Behaviour and Medicine* (2nd edition). St Louis, MO: Mosby-Year Book.

DION, K.K. & BERSCHEID, E. (1974) Physical attractiveness and peer perception among children. *Sociometry*, 37, 1–12.

DION, K.K. & DION, K.L. (1995) On the love of beauty and the beauty of love: Two psychologists study attraction. In G.G. Brannigan & M.R. Merrens (Eds) *The Social Psychologists: Research Adventures*. New York: McGraw-Hill.

DION, K.K., BERSCHEID, E. & WALSTER, E. (1972) What is beautiful is good. *Journal of Personality and Social Psychology*, 24, 285–290.

DION, K.L. & DION, K.K. (1993) Gender and ethnocultural comparisons in styles of love. *Psychology of Women Quarterly*, 17, 463–473.

DIXON, P., REHLING, G. & SHIWACH, R. (1993) Peripheral victims of the Herald of Free Enterprise disaster. *British Journal of Medical Psychology*, 66, 193–202.

DOBSON, R. (1996) Confront your phobias in virtual reality. *The Sunday Times*, 21 January, 14.

DOBSON, R. (1999a) Breakthrough in foetal brain scans. *The Sunday Times* (News Review), 29 August, 10.

DOBSON, R. (1999b) Slaves to the rhythm. *The Sunday Times* (Lifestyle), 25 April, 33–34.

DOCKRAY, G.J., GREGORY, R.A. & HUTCHINSON, J.B. (1978) Isolation, structure and biological activity of two cholecystokinin octapeptides from the sheep brain. *Nature*, 274, 711–713.

DODWELL, P.C. (1995) Fundamental processes in vision. In R.L. Gregory & A.M. Colman (Eds) *Sensation and Perception*. London: Longman.

DOLLARD, J., DOOB, L.W., MOWRER, O.H. & SEARS, R.R. (1939) *Frustration and Aggression*. New Haven, CT: Harvard University Press.

DONALDSON, M. (1978) *Children's Minds*. London: Fontana.

DONCHIN, E. (1975) On evoked potentials, cognition and memory. *Science*, 190, 1004–1005.

DONNERSTEIN, E. & BERKOWITZ, L. (1981) Victim reactions in aggressive erotic films as a factor in violence against women. *Journal of Personality and Social Psychology*, 41, 710–724.

DONNERSTEIN, E. & WILSON, W. (1976) Effects of noise and perceived control on ongoing and subsequent aggressive behaviour. *Journal of Personality and Social Psychology*, 34, 774–781.

DONNERSTEIN, E., LINZ, D. & PENROD, S. (1987) *The Question of Pornography*. London: The Free Press.

DORNER, G. (1976) *Hormones and Brain Differentiation*. Amsterdam: Elsevier.

DOTY, R.M., PETERSON, W.E. & WINTER, D.G. (1991) Threat and authoritarianism in the United States 1978–1987. *Journal of Personality and Social Psychology*, 61, 629–640.

DOVIDIO, J.F. (1995) With a little help from my friends. In G.G. Brannigan & M.R. Merrens (Eds) *The Social Psychologists: Research Adventures*. New York: McGraw-Hill.

DOVIDIO, J.F., ALLEN, J.L. & SCHROEDER, D.A. (1990) Specificity of empathy-induced helping: Evidence for altruistic motivation. *Journal of Personality and Social Psychology*, 59, 249–260.

DOVIDIO, J.F., PILIAVIN, J.A., GAERTNER, S.L., SCHROEDER, D.A. & CLARK, R.D. (1991) The arousal: Cost-reward model and the process of intervention. In M.S. Clark (Ed.) *Prosocial Behaviour: Review of Personality and Social Psychology*, 12. Newbury Park, CA: Sage.

DOWD, J.J. (1975) Ageing as exchange: A preface to theory. *Journal of Gerontology*, 30, 584–594.

DOWD, M. (1984) Twenty years after the murder of Kitty Genovese, the question remains: Why? *The New York Times*, B1, B4.

DRABMAN, R.S. & THOMAS, M.H. (1974) Does media violence increase children's toleration of real-life aggression? *Developmental Psychology*, 10, 418–421.

DRIVER, J. (1996) Attention and segmentation. *The Psychologist*, 9, 119–123.

DRYER, D.C. & HOROWITZ, L.M. (1997) When do opposites attract? Interpersonal complementarity versus similarity. *Journal of Personality & Social Psychology*, 72, 592–603.

DUCK, S. (1988) *Relating to Others*. Milton Keynes: Open University Press.

DUCK, S. (1991) *Friends for Life* (2nd edition). Hemel Hempstead: Harvester Wheatsheaf.

DUCK, S. (1992) *Human Relationships* (2nd edition). London: Sage.

DUCK, S. (1995) Repelling the study of attraction. *The Psychologist*, 8, 60–63.

DUCK, S. (Ed.) (1982) *Personal Relationships 4: Dissolving Personal Relationships*. London: Academic Press.

DUDAI, Y. (1989) *The Neurobiology of Memory*. Oxford: Oxford University Press.

DUGDALE, N. & LOWE, C.F. (1990) Naming and stimulus equivalence. In D.E. Blackman & H. Lejeune (Eds) *Behaviour Analysis in Theory and Practice: Contributions and Controversies*. Hillsdale, NJ: Lawrence Erlbaum.

DUNBAR, G., LEWIS, V. & HILL, R. (1999) Control processes and road-crossing skills. *The Psychologist*, 12(8), 398–399.

DUNBAR, R. (1995) Are you lonesome tonight? *New Scientist*, 145, 26–31.

DUNCAN, G. (1993) *Economic deprivation and childhood development*. Paper presented at the biennial meetings of the Society for Research in Child Development, New Orleans. April.

DUNCAN, H.F., GOURLAY, N. & HUDSON, W. (1973) *A Study of Pictorial Perception among Bantu and White Primary-school Children in South Africa*. Johannesburg: Witwatersrand University Press.

DUNCAN, J. & HUMPHREYS, G.W. (1992) Beyond the search surface: Visual search and attentional engagement. *Journal of Experimental Psychology*: Human Perception and Performance, 18, 578–588.

DUNCKER, K. (1945) On problem-solving. *Psychological Monographs*, 58 (Whole No. 270).

DUNMORE, E., CLARK, D.M. & EHLERS, A. (1999) Cognitive factors involved in the onset and maintenance of posttraumatic stress disorder (PTSD) after physical or sexual assault. *Behaviour Research and Therapy*, 37, 809–829.

DUNN, J. & PLOMIN, R. (1990) *Separate Lives: Why Siblings are so Different*. New York: Basic Books.

DURKIN, K. (1995) *Developmental Social Psychology: From Infancy to Old Age*. Blackwell.

DURST, R. & ROSCO-REBAUDENGO, P. (1988) Koro secondary to a tumour of the corpus callosum. *British Journal of Psychiatry*, 153, 251–254.

DUTTA, D. (1983) Koro epidemic in Assam. *British Journal of Psychiatry*, 143, 309–310.

DUTTON, D.G. & ARON, A.P. (1974) Some evidence for heightened sexual attraction under conditions of high anxiety. *Journal of Personality and Social Psychology*, 30, 510–517.

DWORETZKY, J.P. (1981) *Introduction to Child Development*. St Paul, Minnesota: West Publishing Co.

DYSON, J. (1980) Sociopolitical influences on retirement. *Bulletin of the British Psychological Society*, 33, 128–130.

EAGLY, A.H. (1983) Gender and social influence: A social psychological analysis. *American Psychologist*, September.

EAGLY, A.H. (1987) *Sex Differences in Social Behaviour: A Social Role Interpretation*. Hillsdale, NJ.: Erlbaum.

EAGLY, A.H. & CROWLEY, M. (1986) Gender and helping behaviour: A meta-analytic review of the social psychological literature. *Psychological Bulletin*, 100, 232–308.

EAGLY, A.H. & WOOD, W. (1999) The origins of sex differences in human behaviour. *American Psychologist*, 54, 408–423.

EAGLY, A.H., ASHMORE, R., MAKHIJANI, M. & LONGON, L. (1991) What is beautiful is good but … a meta-analytic review of research on the physical attractiveness stereotype. *Psychological Bulletin*, 110. 107–128.

EBERHARD, W.G. (1991) Copulatory courtship and cryptic female choice in insects. *Biological Reviews*, 66, 1–31.

ECKENSBERGER, L.H. (1994) Moral development and its measurement across cultures. In W.J. Lonner & R.S. Malpass (Eds) *Psychology and Culture*. Boston: Allyn & Bacon.

ECKENSBERGER, L.H. (1999) Socio-moral development. In D. Messer & S. Millar (Eds) *Exploring Developmental Psychology: From Infancy to Adolescence*. London: Arnold.

ECKENSBERGER, L.H. & ZIMBA, R. (1997) The development of moral judgement. In J.W. Berry, P.R. Dasen & T.S. Saraswathi (Eds) *Handbook of Cross-cultural Psychology*, Volume 2: *Basic Processes and Human Development*. Boston: Allyn & Bacon.

EDE, A. (1976) Koro in an Anglo-Saxon Canadian. *Canadian Psychiatric Association Journal*, 21, 389–392.

EDLEY, N. & WETHERELL, M. (1995) *Men in Perspective: Practice, Power and Identity*. Hemel Hempstead: Harvester Wheatsheaf.

EDWARDS, J. (1999) A crime to shame the nation. *The Mirror*, 17 August, 1.

EGELAND, J., GERHARD, D., PAULS, D., SUSSEX, J., KIDD, K., ALLEN, C., HOSTETTER, A. & HOUSEMAN, D. (1987) Bipolar affective disorder linked to DNA markers on chromosome 11. *Nature*, 325, 783–787.

EHNTHOLT, K.A., SALKOVSKIS, P.M. & RIMES, K.A. (1999) Obsessive–compulsive disorder, anxiety disorder and self-esteem: An exploratory study. *Behaviour Research and Therapy*, 37, 771–781.

EHRENFELS, C. Von (1890) Über Gestaltqualitäten. *Vierteljahresschrift für Wissenschaftliche Philosophie und Soziologie*, 14, 249–292.

EIMAS, P.D. (1975) Speech perception in early infancy. In L.B. Cohen and P. Salapatek (Eds) *Infant Perception: From Sensation to Cognition*, Volume 2. New York: Academic Press.

EISENBERG, I. (1995) The social construction of the human brain. *American Journal of Psychiatry*, 152, 1563–1575.

EISENBERG, N. (1982) The Development of Reasoning regarding Prosocial Behaviour. In N. Eisenberg (Ed.) *The development of prosocial behaviour*. New York: Academic Press.

EISENBERG, N. (1986) *Altruistic Emotion, Cognition and Behaviour*. Hillsdale, NJ.: Erlbaum.

EISENBERG, N. (1996) In search of the good heart. In M.R. Merrens & G.C. Brannigan (Eds) *The Developmental Psychologists: Research Adventures across the Life Span*. New York: McGraw-Hill.

EISENBERG, N., MILLER, R.A., SHELL, R., MCNALLEY, S. & SHEA, C. (1991) Prosocial development in adolescence: A longitudinal study. *Developmental Psychology*, 27(5), 849–857.

EISER, J.R. (1983) From attributions to behaviour. In M. Hewstone (Ed.) *Attribution Theory: Social and Functional Extensions*. Oxford: Blackwell.

EISER, J.R. (1994) *Attitudes, Chaos and the Connectionist Mind*. Oxford: Blackwell.

EKMAN, P., FRIESEN, W.V. & SIMONS, R.C. (1985) Is the startle reaction an emotion? *Journal of Personality and Social Psychology*, 49, 1416–1426.

ELKIND, D. (1970) Erik Erikson's eight ages of man. *New York Times Magazine*, 5 April.

ELKIND, D. (1976) *Child Development and Education: A Piagetian Perspective*. Oxford: Oxford University Press.

ELKINS, R. (1991) An appraisal of chemical aversion (emetic therapy) approaches to alcohol treatment. *Behaviour Research and Therapy*, 29, 387–414.

ELKINS, R.L. (1980) Covert sensitisation treatment of alcoholism. *Addictive Behaviours*, 5, 67–89.

ELLENBERG, L. & SPERRY, R.W. (1980) Lateralised division of attention in the commissurotomised and intact brain. *Neuropsychologia*, 18, 411–418.

ELLIOTT, J. (1977) The power and pathology of prejudice. In P. Zimbardo & F.L. Ruch (Eds) *Psychology and Life* (9th edition). Glenview, IL: Scott, Foreseman and Co.

ELLIOTT, J. (1990) In *Discovering Psychology. Program 20 (PBS Video Series)*. Washington, DC: Annenberg/CPB Program.

ELLIS, A. (1958) *Rational Psychotherapy*. California: Institute for Rational Emotive Therapy.

ELLIS, A. (1962) *Reason and Emotion in Psychotherapy*. Secaucus, NJ: Lyle Stuart (Citadel Press).

ELLIS, A. (1984) Rational–emotive therapy. In R. Corsini (Ed.) *Current Psychotherapies* (3rd edition). Itasca, Il: Peacock.

ELLIS, A. (1993) Reflections on rational–emotive therapy. *Journal of Consulting and Clinical Psychology*, 61, 199–201.

ELLIS, A. (1997) The evolution of Albert Ellis and rational emotive behaviour therapy. In J.K. Zeig (Ed.) *The Evolution of Psychotherapy: The Third Conference*. New York: Brunner/Mazel.

ELLIS, H.D. & YOUNG, A.W. (1990) Accounting for delusional misidentifications. *British Journal of Psychiatry*, 157, 239–248.

ELLISON, G.D. & FLYNN, J.P. (1968) Organised aggressive behaviour in cats after surgical isolation of the hypothalamus. *Archives Italiennes de Biologie*, 106, 1–20.

EMLEN, S.T. (1967) Migratory orientation in the Indigo bunting *Passerina cyanea*. Parts I & II. *Auk*, 84, 309–42, 463–89.

EMLEN, S.T. (1972) The ontogenetic development of orientation capabilities. In S.R. Galler, K. Schmidt-Koenig, G.J. Jacobs & R.E. Bellville (Eds), *Animal Orientation & Navigation*. Washington D.C., NASA, pp.191–210.

EMLER, N., OHANA, J. & DICKINSON, J. (1990) Children's representations of social relations. In G. Duveen & B.Lloyd (Eds) *Social Representations and the Development of Knowledge*. Cambridge: Cambridge University Press.

EMMELKAMP, P.M. (1994) Behaviour therapy with adults. In A.E. Bergin & S.L. Garfield (Eds) *Handbook of Psychotherapy and Behaviour Change* (4th edition). New York: Wiley.

EMMELKAMP, P.M.G., BOUMAN, T.K. & SCHOLING, A. (1992) *Anxiety Disorders: A Practitioner's Guide*. New York: Plenum.

EMPSON, J.A.C. (1989) *Sleep and Dreaming*. London: Faber and Faber.

EMPSON, J.A.C. & CLARKE, P.R.F. (1970) Rapid eye movements and remembering. *Nature*, 228, 287–288.

EPSTEIN, R.C.E., KIRSHNIT, R.P. & RUBIN, L.C. (1984) 'Insight' in the pigeon: Antecendents and determinants of an intelligent performance. *Nature*, 308, 61–62.

ERIKSEN, C.W. (1990) Attentional search of the visual field. In D. Brogan (Ed.) *Visual Search*. London: Taylor & Francis.

ERIKSEN, C.W. & YEH, Y.Y. (1987) Allocation of attention in the visual field. *Journal of Experimental Psychology: Human Perception and Performance*, 11, 583–597.

ERIKSON, E.H. (1950) *Childhood and Society*. New York: Norton.

ERIKSON, E.H. (1963) *Childhood and Society* (2nd edition). New York: Norton.

ERIKSON, E.H. (1965) *Childhood and Society*. London: Penguin Books.

ERIKSON, E.H. (1968) *Identity: Youth and Crisis*. New York: Norton.

ERLENMEYER-KIMLING, L. & JARVIK, L.F. (1963) Genetics and intelligence: A review. *Science*, 142, 1477–1479.

ERON, L.D. & HUESMANN, L.R. (1985) The role of television in the development of pro-social and anti-social behaviour. In D. Olweus, M. Radke-Yarrow, & J. Block (Eds) *Development of Anti-Social and Pro-Social Behaviour*. Orlando, FL: Academic Press.

ESTES, W.K. (1970) *Learning Theory and Mental Develoment*. New York: Academic Press.

EVANS, C. (1984) *Landscapes of the Night: How and Why We Dream*. New York: Viking.

EVANS, J. ST. B.T. & OVER, D.E. (1996) *Rationality and Reasoning*. Hove: Psychology Press.

EYSENCK, H.J. (1952) The effects of psychotherapy: An evaluation. *Journal of Consulting Psychology*, 16, 319–324.

EYSENCK, H.J. (1954) *The Psychology of Politics*. London: Routledge & Kegan Paul.

EYSENCK, H.J. (1992) The outcome problem in psychotherapy. In W. Dryden & C. Feltham (Eds) *Psychotherapy and its Discontents*. Buckingham: Open University Press.

EYSENCK, H.J. & WAKEFIELD, J.A. (1981) Psychological factors as predictors of marital satisfaction. *Advances in Behaviour Research and Therapy*, 3, 151–192.

EYSENCK, M.W. (1982) *Attention and Arousal: Cognition and Performance*. Berlin: Springer.

EYSENCK, M.W. (1984) *A Handbook of Cognitive Psychology*. London: Lawrence Erlbaum Associates.

EYSENCK, M.W. (1993) *Principles of Cognitive Psychology*. Hove: Erlbaum.

EYSENCK, M.W. (1994) Attention. In C.C. French & A.M. Colman (Eds) *Cognitive Psychology*. London: Longman.

EYSENCK, M.W. (1997a) Doing two things at once. *Psychology Review*, 4 (1) 10–12.

EYSENCK, M.W. (1997b) Absent-mindedness. *Psychology Review*, 3, 16–18.

EYSENCK, M.W. & KEANE, M.J. (1995) *Cognitive Psychology: A Student's Handbook* (3rd edition). Hove: Erlbaum.

FAGOT, B.L. (1985) Beyond the reinforcement principle: Another step toward understanding sex role development. *Developmental Psychology*, 21, 1097–1104.

FAHY, T., ABAS, M. & BROWN, J.C. (1989) Multiple personality: A symptom of psychiatric disorder. *British Journal of Psychiatry*, 154, 99-101.

FAIRBAIRN, G. & FAIRBAIRN, S. (1987) Introduction. In S. Fairbairn & G. Fairbairn (Eds) *Psychology, ethics and change*. London: Routledge & Kegan Paul.

FALEK, A. & MOSER, H.M. (1975) Classification in schizophrenia. *Archives of General Psychiatry*, 32, 59–67.

FANCHER, R.E. (1979) *Pioneers of Psychology*. New York: Norton.

FANCHER, R.E. (1996) *Pioneers of Psychology* (3rd edition). New York: Norton.

FANTZ, R.L. (1961) The origin of form perception. *Scientific American*, 204, 66–72.

FARBER, S.L. (1981) *Identical Twins Reared Apart*. New York: Basic Books.

FARINA, A. (1992) The stigma of mental disorders. In A.G. Miller (Ed.) *In the Eye of the Beholder*. New York: Praeger.

FARR, R. (1998) From collective to social representations: Aller et retour. *Culture and Psychology*, 4, 275–296.

FARR, R.M. & MOSCOVICI, S. (Eds) (1984) *Social Representations*. Cambridge: Cambridge University Press.

FARRAR, M.J. (1992) Negative evidence and grammatical morpheme acquisition. *Developmental Psychology*, 28, 90–98.

FEATHER, N.T. & SIMON, J.G. (1971) Attribution of responsibility and valence of success and failure in relation to initial confidence and task performance. *Journal of Personality and Social Psychology*, 18, 173–188.

FEIGENBAUM, E.A. & McCORDUCK, P. (1983) *The Fifth Generation*. New York: Addison-Wesley.

FEINGOLD, A. (1992) Good-looking people are not what we think. *Psychological Bulletin*, 111, 304–341.

FELIPE, N.J. & SOMMER, R. (1966) Invasion of personal space. *Social Problems*, 14, 206–214.

FELMLEE, D.H. (1995) Fatal attractions: Affection and disaffection in intimate relationships. *Journal of Social and Personal Relationships*, 12, 295–311.

FENNELL, G., PHILLIPSON, C. & EVERS, H. (1988) *The Sociology of Old Age*. Milton Keynes: Open University Press.

FENSON, L., DALE, P.S., REZNICK, J.S., BATES, E., THAL, D.J. & PETHICK, S.J. (1994) Variability in early communicative development. *Monographs of the Society for Research in Child Development*, 59 (5, Serial No. 242).

FERNANDO, S. (1991) *Mental Health, Race and Culture*. London: Macmillan, in conjunction with MIND.

FERRY, G. (1999) How do we think? *Oxford Today*, 12, 24–26.

FERSTER, C. (1965) Classification of behaviour pathology. In L. Krasner & L. Ullman (Eds) *Research in Behaviour Modification*. New York: Holt, Rinehart & Winston.

FERSTER, C.B. & SKINNER, B.F. (1957) *Schedules of Reinforcement*. New York: Appleton-Century-Crofts.

FESTINGER, L. (1954) A theory of social comparison processes. *Human Relations*, 7, 117–140.

FESTINGER, L., PEPITONE, A. & NEWCOMB, T. (1952) Some consequences of deindividuation in a group. *Journal of Abnormal and Social Psychology*, 47, 382–389.

FESTINGER, L., SCHACHTER, S. & BACK, K. (1950) *Social Pressures in Informal Groups: A Study of Human Factors in Housing*. Stanford, CA: Stanford University Press.

FINCHAM, F. (1997) Understanding marriage. From fish scales to milliseconds. *The Psychologist*, 10, 543–547.

FINK, M. (1984) Meduna and the origins of convulsive therapy in suicidal patients. *American Journal of Psychiatry*, 141, 1034–1041.

FINKELSTEIN, J.R.J., CANNON, T.D., GUR, R.E., GUR, R.C. & MOBERG, P. (1997) Attentional dysfunctions in neuroleptic-naïve and neuroleptic-withdrawn schizophrenic patients and their siblings. *Journal of Abnormal Psychology*, 106, 203–212.

FIRTH, S. (1993) Cross-cultural perspectives on bereavement. In D. Dickenson & M. Johnson (Eds) *Death, Dying and Bereavement.* London: Sage (in association with the Open University).

FISCHER, A., FUCHS, W. & ZINNECKER, J. (1985) Jugenliche und Erwachsene '85. In Jugenwerk der Deutschen Shell (Ed.) *Arbeitsbericht und Dokumentation,* Volume 5. Leverskusen: Leske und Budrich.

FISCHMAN, J. (1985) Mapping the mind. *Psychology Today,* September, 18–19.

FISHER, A.C. (1979) Mysteries of bird migration. *National Geographic,* 152(2), 154–193.

FISHER, J. & HINDE, R.A. (1949) The opening of milk bottles by birds. *British Birds,* 10, 337–403.

FISHER, S. & GREENBERG, R. (1977) *Scientific Credibility of Freud's Theories.* New York: Basic Books.

FISHER, S. & GREENBERG, R. (Eds) (1980) *A Critical Appraisal of Biological Treatments for Psychological Distress: Comparisons with Psychotherapy and Placebo.* Hillsdale, NJ: Erlbaum.

FISKE, S.T. & NEUBERG, S.L. (1990) A continuum of impression formation, from category-based to individuating processes: Influences of information and motivation on attention and interpretation. In L. Berkowitz (Ed.) *Advances in Experimental Social Psychology,* Volume 23. New York: Academic Press.

FISKE, S.T. & TAYLOR, S.E. (1991) *Social Cognition* (2nd edition). New York: McGraw-Hill.

FITZGERALD, K.D., MacMASTER, F.P., PAULSON, L.D. & ROSENBERG, D.R. (1999) Neurobiology of childhood obsessive–compulsive disorder. *Child and Adolescent Psychiatric Clinics of North America,* 8, 533–575.

FLANAGAN, O.J. (1984) *The Science of the Mind.* Cambridge, Mass.: MIT Press.

FLAVELL, J.H. (1982) Structures, stages and sequences in cognitive development. In W.A. Collins (Ed.) *The Concept of Development: The Minnesota Symposia on Child Development,* Volume 15. Hillsdale, NJ: Erlbaum.

FLAVELL, J.H. (1986) The development of children's knowledge about the appearance–reality distinction. *American Psychologist,* 41, 418–425.

FLAVELL, J.H., GREEN, F.L. & FLAVELL, E.R. (1990) Developmental changes in young children's knowledge about the mind. *Cognitive Development,* 5, 1–27.

FLAVELL, J.H., MILLER, P.H. & MILLER, S.A. (1993) *Cognitive Development* (3rd edition). Englewood Cliffs, NJ.: Prentice-Hall.

FLETCHER, D. (1997) Boy raised as girl after surgical accident. *Daily Telegraph,* 15 March, 3.

FLETCHER, G.J. & WARD, C. (1988) Attribution theory and processes: Cross-cultural perspectives. In M.Bond (Ed.) *The Cross-Cultural Challenge to Psychology.* Newbury Park, CA: Sage.

FLOWERS, J.H., WARNER, J.L. & POLANSKY, M.L. (1979) Response and encoding factors in ignoring irrelevant information. *Memory and Cognition,* 7, 86–94.

FODOR, J.A. & PYLYSHYN, Z.W. (1981) How direct is visual perception? Some reflections on Gibson's 'ecological approach'. *Cognition,* 9, 139–196.

FOLKARD, S., HUME, K.I., MINORS, D.S., WATERHOUSE, J.M. & WATSON, F.L. (1985) Independence of the circadian rhythm in alertness from the sleep/wake cycle. *Nature,* 313, 678–679.

FOOT, H.C. (1994) *Group and Interactive Learning.* Computational Mechanics Publications.

FORD, C.S. & BEACH, F.A. (1951) *Patterns of Sexual Behaviour.* New York: Harper & Row.

FORD, D.H. & URBAN, H.B. (1963) *Systems of Psychotherapy: A Comparative Study.* New York: Wiley.

FORD, R. (1998) Study fails to link film violence to crime. *The Times,* 8 January, 9.

FOULKES, D. (1971) Longitudinal studies of dreams in children. In Masserman, J. (Ed.) *Science and Psychoanalysis.* New York: Grune & Stratton.

FOULKES, D. (1985) *Dreaming: A Cognitive-Psychological Analysis.* Hillsdale, NJ: Lawrence Erlbaum Associates.

FOULKES, D., SULLIVAN, B., KERR, N.H. & BROWN, L. (1988) Appropriateness of dream feelings to dreamed situations. *Cognition and Emotion,* 2, 29–39.

FOX, J.L. (1984) The brain's dynamic way of keeping in touch. *Science,* 225, 82–821.

FRANKO, D.L. & OMORI, M. (1999) Subclinical eating disorders in adolescent women: A test of the continuity hypothesis and its psychological correlates. *Journal of Adolescence,* 22, 389–396.

FREAN, A. (1994) Researchers study TV's arrival on media-free island. *The Times,* 6 June, 8.

FREEDMAN, J.L. (1975) *Crowding and Behaviour.* San Francisco: Freeman.

FREEDMAN, J.L., LEVY, A.S., BUCHANAN, R.W. & PRICE, J. (1972) Crowding and human aggressiveness. *Journal of Experimental Social Psychology,* 8, 528–548.

FREEMAN, C. (Ed.) (1995) *The ECT Handbook.* London: Gaskell.

FREEMAN, H. & WATTS, J.W. (1942) *Psychosurgery.* Springfield, Ill.: Thomas.

FREUD, A. (1966) *Normality and Pathology in Childhood.* London: Hogarth Press.

FREUD, S. (1891) *On Aphasia.* Translated by E. Stengel (1950). Image: New York.

FREUD, S. (1894) The defence neuropsychoses. In J. Strachey (Ed.) *The Standard Edition of the Complete Psychological Works of Sigmund Freud,* Volume 1. London: The Hogarth Press, 1953.

FREUD, S. (1900) *The Interpretation of Dreams.* London: Hogarth Press.

FREUD, S. (1905) *Three Essays on the Theory of Sexuality.* Pelican Freud Library, Vol. 7 Harmondsworth: Penguin.

FREUD, S. (1909) *Analysis of a Phobia in a Five-Year-Old Boy.* London: The Hogarth Press.

FREUD, S. (1917) *Mourning and Melancholia.* London: The Hogarth Press.

FREUD, S. (1920/1984) *Beyond the Pleasure Principle.* Pelican Freud Library (11). Harmondsworth: Penguin.

FREUD, S. (1923/1984) *The Ego and the Id.* Pelican Freud Library (11). Harmondsworth: Penguin.

FREUD, S. (1924) The passing of the Oedipus complex. In E. Jones (Ed.) *Collected Papers of Sigmund Freud,* Volume 5. New York: Basic Books.

FREUD, S. (1933) *New Introductory Lectures on Psychoanalysis.* New York: Norton.

FRICK, W.B. (1995) The subpersonalities controversy: A reply to my critics. *Journal of Human Psychology,* 35, 97-101.

FRIEDMAN, M.I. & STRICKER, E.M. (1976) The physiological psychology of hunger: A physiological perspective. *Psychological Review,* 83, 409–431.

FRISCH, A., POSTILNICK, D., ROCKAH, R. *et al.* (1999) Association of unipolar major depressive disorder with genes of the serotonergic and dopaminergic pathways. *Molecular Psychiatry,* 4, 389–392.

FRITZ, J. & KOTRSCHAL, K. (1999) Social learning in common ravens, *Corvus corax. Animal Behaviour,* 57, 785–793.

FRODI, A. (1975) The effect of exposure to weapons on aggressive behaviour from a cross-cultural perspective. *International Journal of Psychology,* 10, 283–292.

FROMM, E. (1941) *Escape From Freedom.* New York: Farrar & Rinehart.

FROMM, E. (1962) *The Art of Loving.* London: Unwin Books.

FROMM-REICHMAN, F. (1948) Notes on the development of treatment of schizophrenics by psychoanalytic psychotherapy. *Psychiatry,* 11, 263–273.

FROST, J.A., BINDER, J.R., SPRINGER, J.A., HEMMEKE, T.A., BELLGOWAN, P.S.F., RAO, S.M. & COX, R.W. (1999) Language processing is strongly lateralised in both sexes: Evidence from functional MRI. *Brain,* 122, 199–208.

FRUDE, N. (1998) *Understanding Abnormal Psychology.* Oxford: Blackwell.

FURNHAM, A. & HEAVEN, P. (1999) *Personality and Social Behaviour.* London: Arnold.

FURTH, H.G. (1966) *Thinking Without Language.* New York: Free Press.

GADOW, J.D. & SPRAFKIN, J. (1989) Field experiments of television violence: Evidence for an environmental hazard? *Paediatrics*, 83, 399–405.

GADOW, J.D. & SPRAFKIN, J. (1993) Television violence and children. *Journal of Emotional and Behavioural Disorders*, 1, 54–63.

GAGE, F.H., BJORKLUND, A., STEVENI, U., DUNNETT, S.B. & KELLY, P.A.T. (1984) Intrahippocampal septal grafts ameliorate learning impairments in aged rats. *Science*, 225, 533–536.

GAHAGAN, J. (1980) Social interaction. In J. Rasford & E. Govier (Eds) *A Textbook of Psychology*. London: Sheldon Books.

GAHAGAN, J. (1991) Understanding other people, understanding self. In J. Radford & E. Govier (Eds) *A Textbook of Psychology* (2nd edition). London: Routledge.

GALEF, B.G. (Jr) (1988) Communication of information concerning the diets in social central-place foraging species: *Rattus norvegicus*. In T.R. Zentall & B.G. Galef Jr. (Eds), *Social Learning Psychological and Biological Perspectives*. Hillsdale, N.J: Lawrence Erlbaum Associates.

GALEF, B.G. (Jr.) (1996) Tradition in animals: Field observations and Laboratory Analyses. In M. Bekoff & D. Jamieson (Eds) *Readings in Animal Cognition*. Cambridge, MA: Massachusetts Institute of Technology Press.

GALLAGHER, M., MILLAR, R., HARGIE, O. & ELLIS, R. (1992) The personal and social worries of adolescents in Northern Ireland: Results of a survey. *British Journal of Guidance & Counselling*, 30(3), 274–290.

GALLISTEL, C.R. (1990) *The Organization of Learning*. Cambridge, MA: MIT Press.

GALLUP, G.G. (Jr) (1970) Chimpanzees: Self-recognition. *Science*, 167, 86–87.

GANZHORN, J.U., KIEPENHEUER, J., RANVAUD, R. & SCHMIDT-KOENIG, K. (1989) How accurate is the sun compass of the homing pigeon? *Proceedings of the Royal Institute of Navigation Conference 1989: Orientation and Navigation – Birds, Humans and other Animals*.

GARBER, H.L. (1988) *The Milwaukee Project: Preventing Mental Retardation in Children at Risk*. Washington, DC: American Association on Mental Retardation.

GARCIA, J. & KOELLING, R.A. (1966) The relation of cue to consequence in avoidance learning. *Psychonomic Science*, 4, 123–124.

GARCIA, J., ERVIN, F.R. & KOELLING, R.A. (1966) Learning with prolonged delay of reinforcement. *Psychonomic Science*, 5 (3), 121–122.

GARDNER, R.A. & GARDNER, B.T. (1969) Teaching sign language to a chimpanzee. *Science*, 165(3894), 664–672.

GARDNER, R.A. & GARDNER, B.T. (1977) Comparative psychology and language acquisition. In K. Salzinger & R. Denmark (Eds) *Psychology: The State of the Art*. New York: Annals of the New York Academy of Science.

GARFIELD, S. (1992) Response to Hans Eysenck. In W. Dryden & C. Feltham (Eds) *Psychotherapy and its Discontents*. Buckingham: Open University Press.

GARFIELD, S. & BERGIN, A. (1994) Introduction and historical overview. In A. Bergin & S. Garfield (Eds) *Handbook of Psychotherapy and Behaviour Change*. Chichester: Wiley.

GARNHAM, A. (1988) *Artificial Intelligence: An Introduction*. London: Routledge, Kegan Paul.

GARNHAM, A. (1991) *The Mind in Action*. London: Routledge.

GARRETT, R. (1996) Skinner's case for radical behaviourism. In W. O'Donohue & R.F. Kitchener (Eds) *The Philosophy of Psychology*. London: Sage.

GARROD, A.B. (1859) *The Nature and Treatment of Gout and Rheumatic Gout*. London: Walton & Maberly.

GAUKER, C. (1990) How to learn language like a chimpanzee. *Philosophical Psychology*, 3, 31–53.

GAULIN, S.J.C. & FITZGERALD, R.W. (1989) Sexual selection for spatial learning ability. *Animal Behaviour*, 37, 322–331.

GAY, P. (1988) *Freud: A Life for our Time*. London: J.M. Dent & Sons.

GAZZANIGA, M.S. (1967) The split-brain in man. *Scientific American*, 221, 24–29.

GAZZANIGA, M.S. (1983) Right hemisphere language following brain bisection: A 2-year perspective. *American Psychologist*, 38, 525–537.

GAZZANIGA, M.S. (1998) The split brain revisited. *Scientific American*, 273, 35–39.

GEEN, R.G. (1995) Social motivation. In Parkinson, B. & Colman, A.M. (Eds) *Emotion and Motivation*. London: Longman.

GEEN, R.G. & BERKOWITZ, L. (1966) Some conditions facilitating the occurrence of aggression after the observation of violence. *Journal of Personality*, 35, 666–676.

GEEN, R.G. & O'NEAL, E.C. (1969) Activation of cue-elicited aggression by general arousal. *Journal of Personality & Social Psychology*, 11, 289–292.

GEISELMAN, P.J. (1983) 'The role of hexoses in hunger motivation.' (Unpublished doctoral dissertation, University of California, Los Angeles.)

GELDER, M., GATH, D. & MAYON, R. (1989) *The Oxford Textbook of Psychiatry* (2nd edition). Oxford: Oxford University Press.

GELMAN, R. (1978) Counting in the pre-schooler: What does and does not develop. In R.S. Siegler (Ed.) *Children's Thinking: What Develops?* Hillsdale, NJ: Erlbaum.

GELMAN, R. (1979) Preschool thought. *American Psychologist*, 34, 900–905.

GELMAN, R. & BAILLARGEON, R. (1983) A review of some Piagetian concepts. In J.H. Flavell & E.M. Markman (Eds) *Cognitive Development*, Volume 3 in P.H. Mussen (Ed.) *Handbook of Child Psychology* (4th edition). New York: Wiley.

GERBNER, G. (1972) Violence in television drama: Trends and symbolic functions. In G.A. Comstock & E.A. Rubenstein (Eds) *Television and Social Behaviour*, Volume 1, *Media Content and Control*. Washington, DC: US Government Printing Office.

GERBNER, G. & GROSS, L. (1976) Living with television: The violence profile. *Journal of Communication*, 26, 173–199.

GERBNER, G., GROSS, L., MORGAN, M. & SIGNORIELLI, N. (1980) The 'mainstreaming' of America: Violence profile No. II. *Journal of Communication*, 30, 10–29.

GERBNER, G., GROSS, L., SIGNORIELLI, N. & MORGAN, M. (1986) *Television's mean world: Violence profile No. 14–15*. Philadelphia: Annenberg School of Communications, University of Pennsylvania.

GERGEN, K.J. (1973) Social psychology as history. *Journal of Personality and Social Psychology*, 26, 309–320.

GERGEN, K.J. & GERGEN, M.M. (1981) *Social Psychology*. New York: Harcourt Brace Jovanovich,

GERGEN, K.J., GERGEN, M.M. & BARTON, W. (1973) Deviance in the dark. *Psychology Today*, 7, 129–130.

GERRARD, N. (1997) Nicaragua's deaf children. *The Observer Review*, 30 March, 1.

GESCHWIND, N. (1972) Language and the brain. *Scientific American*, 226, 76–83.

GESCHWIND, N. (1979) *The Brain*. San Francisco: Freeman.

GESELL, A. (1925) *The Mental Growth of the Preschool Child*. New York: Macmillan.

GIBBS, J.C. & SCHNELL, S.V. (1985) Moral development 'versus' socialisation. *American Psychologist*, 40, 1071–1080.

GIBSON, E.J. & WALK, P.D. (1960) The visual cliff. *Scientific American*, 202, 64–71.

GIBSON, E.J., SHAPIRO, F. & YONAS, A. (1968) 'Confusion matrices of graphic patterns obtained with a latency measure: A program of basic and applied research.' (*Final Report Project No. 5-1213*, Cornell University.)

GIBSON, J.J. (1950) *The Perception of the Visual World*. Boston: Houghton Mifflin.

GIBSON, J.J. (1966) *The Senses Considered as Perceptual Systems*. Boston: Houghton Mifflin.

GIBSON, J.J. (1979) *The Ecological Approach to Visual Perception*. Boston: Houghton Mifflin.

GIDDENS, A. (1979) *Central Problems in Social Theory*. Basingstoke: Macmillan.

GILBERT, D.T. (1995) Attraction and interpersonal perception. In A. Tesser (Ed.) *Advanced Social Psychology*. New York: McGraw-Hill.

GILBERT, G.M. (1951) Stereotype persistence and change among college students. *Journal of Abnormal and Social Psychology*, 46, 245–254.

GILBERT, P. (1990) Changes: Rank, status and mood. In S. Fischer & C.L. Cooper (Eds) *On the Move: The Psychology of Change and Transition*. New York: John Wiley.

GILFORD, R. & BENGSTON, V. (1979) Measuring marital satisfaction in three generations: Positive and negative dimensions. *Journal of Marriage and the Family*, 41, 387–398.

GILLIE, O. (1976) Pioneer of IQ faked his research. *The Sunday Times*, 29 October, H3.

GILLIGAN, C. (1982) *In a Different Voice: Psychological Theory and Women's Development*. Cambridge, MA: Harvard University Press.

GILLIGAN, C. (1993) Letter to Readers (Preface) In *In A Different Voice*. Cambridge, MA.: Harvard University Press.

GILOVICH, T. (1983) Biased evaluation and persistence in gambling. *Journal of Personality and Social Psychology*, 44, 1110–1126.

GINSBERG, H.P. (1981) Piaget and education: The contributions and limits of genetic epistemology. In K. Richardson & S. Sheldon (Eds) *Cognitive Development to Adolescence*. Milton Keynes: Open University Press.

GIVENS, B.S. & OLTON, D.S. (1995) Cholinergic and GABAergic modulation of medial septal area: Effect on working memory. *Behavioural Neuroscience*, 104, 849–855.

GLASSMAN, W.E. (1995) *Approaches to Psychology* (2nd edition). Buckingham: Open University.

GLEASON, J. (1967) Do children imitate? *Proceedings of the International Conference on Oral Education of the Deaf*, 2, 1441–1448.

GLEITMAN, H. & JONIDES, J. (1978) The effect of set on categorisation in visual search. *Perception and Psychophysics*, 24, 361–368.

GLEITMAN, I.R. & WANNER, E. (1988) Current issues in language learning. In H.M. Bornstein & M.E. Lamb (Eds) *Developmental Psychology: An Advanced Textbook* (2nd edition). Hillsdale, NJ: Erlbaum.

GLUCKSBERG, S. & COWAN, N. (1970) Memory for non-attended auditory material. *Cognitive Psychology*, 1, 149–156.

GLUCKSBERG, S. & WEISBERG, R. (1966) Verbal behaviour and problem-solving: Some effects of labelling upon availability of novel functions. *Journal of Experimental Psychology*, 71, 659–664.

GOFFMAN, E. (1968) *Asylums – Essay on the Social Situation of Mental Patients and Other Inmates*. Harmondsworth: Penguin.

GOFFMAN, E. (1971) *The Presentation of Self in Everyday Life*. Harmondsworth: Penguin.

GOLDIN-MEADOW, S. & FELDMAN, H. (1977) The development of a language-like communication without a language model. *Science*, 197, 401–403.

GOLDSTEIN, M. & PALMER, J. (1975) *The Experience of Anxiety: A Casebook* (2nd edition). New York: Oxford University Press.

GOLDSTEIN, M.C. (1979) Pahari and Tibetan polyandry revisited. *Ethnology*, 17, 325–337.

GOLDWYN, E. (1979) The fight to be male. *The Listener*, 24 May, 709–712.

GOLEMAN, D. (1985) New focus on multiple personality. *The New York Times*, May 21, C1 & C6.

GOLOMBOK, S., SPENCER, A. & RUTTER, M. (1983) Children in lesbian and single-parent households: Psychosexual and psychiatric appraisal. *Journal of Child Psychology and Psychiatry*, 24, 551–572.

GOLOMBOK, S., TASKER, F., & MURRAY, C. (1997) Children raised in fatherless families from infancy: family relationships and the socioemotional development of children of lesbian and single heterosexual mothers. *Journal of Child Psychology & Psychiatry*, 38 (7), 783–791.

GOMBRICH, E.H. (1960) *Art and Illusion*. London: Phaidon.

GOODMAN, W.K. (1999) Obsessive–compulsive disorder: Diagnosis and treatment. *Journal of Clinical Psychiatry*, 60, 27–32.

GOODWIN, R. (1991) A re-examination of Rusbult's responses to dissatisfaction typology. *Journal of Social and Personal Relationships*, 8, 569–574.

GOODWIN, R. (1995) Personal relationships across cultures. *The Psychologist*, 8, 73–75.

GOPNIK, A. & ASTINGTON, J.W. (1988) Children's understanding of representational change and its relation to the understanding of false belief and the appearance–reality distinction. *Child Development*, 59, 26–37.

GOPNIK, A. & WELLMAN, H.M. (1994) The theory theory. In L.A. Hirschfeld & S.A. Gelman (Eds) *Mapping the Mind*. Cambridge: Cambridge University Press.

GORANSON, R.E. & KING, D. (1970) *Rioting and daily temperature: Analysis of the U.S. riots in 1967*. Unpublished manuscript, York University.

GORDON, I.E. (1989) *Theories of Visual Perception*. Chichester: Wiley.

GORDON, R.M. (1978) Emotion labelling and cognition. *Journal for the Theory of Social Behaviour*, 8, 125–135.

GOTLIB, I.A. & COLBY, C.A. (1995) *Psychological Aspects of Depression: Towards a Cognitive-Interpersonal Integration*. Chichester: Wiley.

GOTTESMAN, I. (1991) *Schizophrenia Genesis*. New York: W.H. Freeman.

GOTTESMAN, I.I. & SHIELDS, J. (1972) *Schizophrenia and Genetics: A Twin Study Vantage Point*. New York: Academic Press.

GOTTLIEB, G. (1975) Development of species identification in ducklings. III. Maturational rectification of perceptual deficit caused by auditory deprivation. *Journal of Comparative and Physiological Psychology*, 89, 899–912.

GOULD, J.L. (1982) The map sense of pigeons. *Nature*, 296, 205–211.

GOULD, R.L. (1978) *Transformations: Growth and Change in Adult Life*. New York: Simon & Schuster.

GOULD, R.L. (1980) Transformational tasks in adulthood. In S.I. Greenspan & G.H. Pollock (Eds) *The Course of Life: Psychoanalytic Contributions Toward Understanding Personality Development*, Volume 3: *Adulthood and the Ageing Process*. Washington, DC: National Institute for Mental Health.

GOULD, S.J. (1981) *The Mismeasure of Man*. Harmondsworth: Penguin.

GRAY, J.A. (1975) *Elements of a Two-Process Theory of Learning*. London: Academic Press.

GRAY, J.A. (1987) The ethics and politics of animal experimentation. In H. Beloff & A.M. Colman (Eds) *Psychology Survey*, No.6. Leicester: British Psychological Society.

GRAY, J.A. (1991) On the morality of speciesism. *The Psychologist*, 4 (5), 196–198.

GRAY, J.A. & WEDDERBURN, A.A. (1960) Grouping strategies with simultaneous stimuli. *Quarterly Journal of Experimental Psychology*, 12, 180–184.

GREGORY, R.L. (1970) *The Intelligent Eye*. London: Weidenfeld & Nicolson.

GREGORY, R.L. (1981) *Mind in Science*. Harmondsworth: Penguin.

GREEN, B.L. (1994) Psychosocial research in traumatic stress: An update. *Journal of Traumatic Stress*, 7, 341–363.

GREEN, S. (1975) Dialects in Japanese monkeys. *Zeitschrift für Tierpsychologie*, 38, 305–314.

GREEN, S. (1980) Physiological studies I and II. In Radford, J. & Govier, E. (Eds) *A Textbook of Psychology*. London: Sheldon Press.

GREEN, S. (1994) *Principles of Biopsychology*. Sussex: Lawrence Erlbaum Associates.

GREEN, S. (1996) Drugs and psychological disorders. *Psychology Review*, 3, 25–28.

GREEN, S. (1998) Sleeping. *Psychology Review*, 5, 23–26.

GREENBERG, J., PSYZCZYNSKI, T. & SOLOMON, S. (1982) The self-serving attributional bias: Beyond self-presentation. *Journal of Experimental Social Psychology*, 18, 56–67.

GREENBERG, R. & PEARLMAN, C. (1967) Delerium tremens and dreaming. *American Journal of Psychiatry*, 124, 133–142.

GREENBERG, R., PILLARD, R. & PEARLMAN, C. (1972) The effect of dream (stage REM) deprivation on adaptation to stress. *Psychosomatic Medicine*, 34, 257–262.

GREENE, J. (1987) *Memory, Thinking and Language*. London: Methuen.

GREENE, J. (1990) Perception. In I. Roth (Ed.) *Introduction to Psychology*, Volume 2. Milton Keynes: Open University Press.

GREENFIELD, P.M. (1984) *Mind and the Media: The Effects of Television, Video Games and Computers*. Cambridge, MA: Harvard University Press.

GREENFIELD, P.M. & SMITH, J.H. (1976) *The Structure of Communication in Early Language Development*. New York: Academic Press.

GREENOUGH, W.T. (1991) Experience as a component of normal development: Evolutionary considerations. *Developmental Psychology*, 27, 11–27.

GREGORY, R.L. (1966) *Eye and Brain*. London: Weidenfeld & Nicolson.

GREGORY, R.L. (1972) Visual illusions. In B.M. Foss (Ed.) *New Horizons in Psychology 1*. Harmondsworth: Penguin.

GREGORY, R.L. (1973) *Eye and Brain* (2nd edition). New York: World Universities Library.

GREGORY, R.L. (1980) Perceptions as hypotheses. *Philosophical Transactions of the Royal Society of London, Series B*, 290, 181–197.

GREGORY, R.L. (1983) Visual illusions. In J. Miller (Ed.) *States of Mind*. London: BBC Productions.

GREGORY, R.L. (1996) Twenty-five years after 'The Intelligent Eye'. *The Psychologist*, 9, 452–455.

GRIER, J.W. & BURK, T. (1992) *Biology of Animal Behaviour*. Dubuque, IA: WCB Communications.

GRIFFIN, D.R. & TAFT, L.D. (1992) Temporal separation of honeybee dance sounds from waggle movements. *Animal Behaviour*, 44, 583–584.

GRIFFIN, J. (1998) *The Origins of Dreams*. London: ETSI.

GRIFFIT, W. (1970) Environmental effects on interpersonal affective behaviour: Ambient effective temperature and attraction. *Journal of Personality & Social Psychology*, 15, 240–244.

GRIFFITHS, M. (1990) The cognitive psychology of gambling. *Journal of Gambling Studies*, 6, 31–42.

GRIFFITHS, M. (1993) Are computer games bad for children? *The Psychologist*, 6, 401–407.

GRIFFITHS, M. (1997a) Video games and aggression. *The Psychologist*, 10, 397–401.

GRIFFITHS, M. (1997b) Selling hope: The psychology of the National Lottery. *Psychology Review*, 4(1), 26–30.

GRIFFITHS, M. (1998) Violent video games: Are they harmful? *Psychology Review*, 4, 28–29.

GRIFFITHS, M. (1999) Internet addiction: Fact or fiction. *The Psychologist*, 12, 246–250.

GRIFFITT, W. & VEITCH, R. (1971) Hot and crowded: Influence of population density and temperature on interpersonal affective behaviour. *Journal of Personality & Social Psychology*, 17, 92–98.

GRILLON, C. & MORGAN, C. (1999) Fear-potentiated startle conditioning to explicit and contextual cues in Gulf War veterans with posttraumatic stress disorder. *Journal of Abnormal Psychology*, 108, 134–142.

GROOME, D., DEWART, H., ESGATE, A., GURNEY, K., KEMP, R. & TOWELL, N. (1999) *An Introduction to Cognitive Psychology : Processes and Disorders*. London: Psychology Press.

GROSS, R. (1995) *Themes, Issues and Debates in Psychology*. London: Hodder & Stoughton.

GROSS, R. (1996) *Psychology: The Science of Mind and Behaviour* (3rd edition). London: Hodder & Stoughton.

GROSS, R. (1999) *Key Studies in Psychology* (3rd edition). London: Hodder & Stoughton.

GROSS, R. & McILVEEN, R. (1997) *Cognitive Psychology*. London: Hodder & Stoughton.

GROSS, R. & McILVEEN, R. (1998) *Psychology: A New Introduction*. London: Hodder & Stoughton.

GROSS, R. & McILVEEN, R. (1999) *Therapeutic Approaches to Abnormal Behaviour*. London: Hodder & Stoughton.

GROSS, R., McILVEEN, R., COOLICAN, H., CLAMP, A. & RUSSELL, J. (2000) *Psychology: A New Introduction* (2nd edition). London: Hodder & Stoughton.

GROSZ, E.A. (1987) Feminist theory and the challenge of knowledge. *Women's Studies International Forum*, 10, 475–480.

GROTE, N. & FRIEZE, I. (1994) The measurement of friendship-based love in intimate relationships. *Personal Relationships*, 1, 275–300.

GRUENDEL, J.M. (1977) Referential overextension in early language development. *Child Development*, 48, 1567–1576.

GRUSEC, J.E. (1992) Social learning theory and developmental psychology: The legacies of Robert Sears and Albert Bandura. *Developmental Psychology*, 28, 776–786.

GRUSH, J.E. (1976) Attitude formation and mere exposure phenomena: A non-artifactual explanation of empirical findings. *Journal of Personality and Social Psychology*, 33, 281–290.

GUBERNICK, D.J. (1990) A maternal chemosignal maintains paternal behaviour in the biparental California mouse, *Peromyscus californicus*. *Animal Behaviour*, 39, 936–942.

GUERIN, B.J. (1993) *Social Facilitation*. Cambridge: Cambridge University Press.

GUNTER, B. (1986) *Television and Sex-Role Stereotyping*. London: IBA and John Libbey.

GUNTER, B. (1998) Telebuddies: Can watching TV make us more considerate? *Psychology Review*, 4, 6–9.

GUNTER, B. & HARRISON, J. (1998) *Violence on Television: An Analysis of the Amount, Nature, Location and Origin of Violence in British Programmes*. London: Routledge.

GUNTER, B. & McALEER, J.L. (1997) *Children and Television – The One-Eyed Monster?* (2nd edition) London: Routledge.

GUPTA, U. & SINGH, P. (1992) Exploratory study of love and liking and types of marriage. *Indian Journal of Applied Psychology*, 19, 92–97.

GUR, R.C., SKOLNICK, B.E. & GUR, R.E. (1994) Effects of emotional discrimination tasks on cerebral blood flow: Regional activation and its relation to performance. *Brain and Cognition*, 25, 271–286.

GUSTAFSON, G. & HARRIS, K. (1990) Women's responses to young infants' cries. *Developmental Psychology*, 26, 144–152.

GWEN, A.L. (1968) Koro, its origin and nature as a disease entity. *Singapore Medical Journal*, 9, 3–7.

GWIAZDA, J., BRILL, S., MOHINDRA, I. & HELD, R. (1980) Preferential looking acuity in infants from two to 58 weeks of age. *American Journal of Optometry and Physiological Optics*, 57, 428–432.

GWINNER, E. (1972) Endogenous timing factors in bird migration. In S.R. Galler, K. Schmidt-Koenig, G.J. Jacobs & R.E. Bellville (Eds), *Animal Orientation & Navigation*. Washington D.C., NASA.

HAAGA, D.A. & BECK, A.T. (1992) Cognitive therapy. In S. Pakyel (Ed.) *Handbook of Affective Disorders* (2nd edition). Cambridge: Cambridge University Press.

HAAGA, D.A. & DAVISON, G.C. (1993) An appraisal of rational-emotive therapy. *Journal of Consulting and Clinical Psychology*, 61, 215–220.

HABER, R.N. & HERSHENSON, M. (1980) *The Physiology of Visual Perception*. New York: Holt, Rinehart & Winston.

HACK, M., TAYLOR, C.B.H., KLEIN, N., EIBEN, R., SCHATSCHNEIDER, C. & MERCURI-MINICH, N. (1994) School-age outcomes in children with birth weights under 750g. *The New England Journal of Medicine*, 331, 753–759.

HAGELL, A. & NEWBURN, T. (1994) *Young Offenders and the Media*. London: Batsford.

HAIGH, J. (1995) Inferring gamblers' choice of combinations in the National Lottery. *Bulletin – The Institute of Mathematics and Its Applications*, 31, 132–136.

HAILMAN, J. (1992) The necessity of a 'show me' attitude in science. In J.W. Grier & T. Burk, (Eds) *Biology of Animal Behaviour* (2nd edition). Dubuque, IO: W.C. Brown.

HAITH, M.M. (1990) Progress in the understanding of sensory and perceptual processes in early infancy. *Merrill-Palmer Quarterly*, 36, 1–26.

HALL, C.S. (1966) *The Meaning of Dreams*. New York: McGraw-Hill.

HALL, C.S. (1984) 'A ubiquitous sex difference in dreams' revisited. *Journal of Personality & Social Psychology*, 46, 1109–1117.

HALL, C.S. & VAN DE CASTLE, R.L. (1966) *The Content Analysis of Dreams*. E. Norwalk, CT: Appleton-Century-Crofts.

HALL, E.T. (1959) *The Silent Language*. New York: Doubleday.

HALL, G.S. (1904) *Adolescence*. New York: Appleton & Co.

HALLER, J.S. & HALLER, R.M. (1974) *The Physician and Sexuality in Victorian America*. Chicago: University of Illinois Press.

HALLIGAN, P.W. (1995) Drawing attention to neglect: The contribution of line bisection. *The Psychologist*, 8, 257–264.

HALLORAN, J.D. & CROLL, P. (1972) Television programmes in Great Britain. In G.A. Comstock & E.A. Rubenstein (Eds) *Television and Social Behaviour*, Volume 1, *Media Content and Control*. Washington, DC: US Government Printing Office.

HALPERN, D. (1995) *Mental Health and the Built Environment*. London: Taylor & Francis.

HAMER, D. & COPELAND, P. (1999) *Living With Our Genes*. London: Macmillan.

HAMILTON, D.L. & GIFFORD, R.K. (1976) Illusory correlation in interpersonal perception: A cognitive basis of stereotypic judgements. *Journal of Experimental Social Psychology*, 12, 392–407.

HAMILTON, W.D. (1964) The genetical evolution of social behaviour I, II. *Journal of Theoretical Biology*, 7, 1–52.

HAMPSON, P.J. (1989) Aspects of attention and cognitive science. *Irish Journal of Psychology*, 10, 261–275.

HAMPSON, P.J. & MORRIS, P.E. (1996) *Understanding Cognition*. Oxford: Blackwell.

HANLON, M. (1999) Tribe who can't tell the difference between blue, green and purple. *The Express*, 18 March, 38–39.

HARDIE, E.A. (1997) PMS in the workplace: Dispelling the myth of the cyclic dysfunction. *Journal of Occupational and Organisational Psychology*, 70, 97–102.

HARDY, M. & HEYES, S. (1979) *Beginning Psychology*. London: Weidenfeld & Nicolson.

HARE-MUSTIN, R. & MARACEK, J. (1988) The meaning of difference: Gender theory, post-modernism and psychology. *American Psychologist*, 43, 455–464.

HARGREAVES, D., MOLLOY, C. & PRATT, A. (1982) Social factors in conservation. *British Journal of Psychology*, 73, 231–234.

HARLOW, J. (1999a) Love equation gives secret of good marriage. *The Sunday Times*, 25 April, 9.

HARLOW, J. (1999b) Health experts say net nerds are sick people. *The Sunday Times*, 22 August, 11.

HARRÉ, R. (1983) *Personal Being*. Oxford: Blackwell.

HARRÉ, R. (1989) Language games and the texts of identity. In J. Shotter & K.J. Gergen (Eds) *Texts of Identity*. London: Sage.

HARRÉ, R., CLARKE, D., & De CARLO, N. (1985) *Motives and Mechanisms: An Introduction to the Psychology of Action*. London: Methuen.

HARRINGTON, J.A. (1982) Epidemic psychosis. *British Journal of Psychiatry*, 141, 98–99.

HARRIS, B. (1981) A case of brain fag in east Africa. *British Journal of Psychiatry*, 138, 162–163.

HARRIS, M. (1998) Perception. In P. Scott & C. Spencer (Eds) *Psychology: A Contemporary Introduction*. Oxford: Blackwell.

HARROWER, J. (1998) *Applying Psychology to Crime*. London: Hodder & Stoughton.

HARTMANN, E.L. (1973) *The Functions of Sleep*. New Haven, CT: Yale University Press.

HARVEY, J.H. & WEARY, G. (1984) Current issues in attribution theory and research. *Annual Review of Psychology*, 35, 427–459.

HASKINS, R. (1989) Beyond metaphor: The efficacy of early childhood education. *American Psychologist*, 44, 274–282.

HASLER, A.D. (1960) Homing orientation in migratory fishes. *Ergebnisse der Biologie*, 23, 94–115.

HASLER, A.D. & LARSEN, J.A. (1955) The homing salmon. *Scientific American*, 193(2), 72–77.

HASS, A. (1979) *Teenage Sexuality: A Survey of Teenage Sexual Behaviour*. New York: Macmillan.

HASTE, H., MARKOULIS, D. & HELKAMA, K. (1998) Morality, Wisdom and the Life Span. In A. Demetriou, W. Doise & C. van Lieshout (Eds) *Life-Span Developmental Psychology*. Chichester: John Wiley & Sons Ltd.

HASTIE, R. & PARK, B. (1986) The relationship between memory and judgement depends on whether the judgement task is memory based or on-line. *Psychological Bulletin*, 93, 258–268.

HATFIELD, E. & RAPSON, R. (1987) Passionate love/sexual desire: Can the same paradigm explain both? *Archives of Sexual Behaviour*, 16, 259–278.

HAUSER, M.D., MACNEILAGE, P. & WARE, M. (1996) Numerical representations in primates. *Proceedings of the National Academy of Science*, 93, 1514–1517.

HAVIGHURST, R.J. (1964) Stages of vocational development. In H. Borrow (Ed.) *Man in a World of Work*. Boston: Houghton Mifflin.

HAVIGHURST, R.J., NEUGARTEN, B.L. & TOBIN, S.S. (1968) Disengagement and patterns of ageing. In B.L. Neugarten (Ed.) *Middle Age and Ageing*. Chicago: University of Chicago Press.

HAWKES, N. (1998) Tongue-twisters. *The Times*, 23 February, 15.

HAWKINS, S.A. & HASTIE, R. (1990) Hindsight: Biased judgements of past events after the outcomes are known. *Psychological Bulletin*, 107, 311–327.

HAWKS, D. (1981) The dilemma of clinical practice – Surviving as a clinical psychologist. In I. McPherson & M. Sutton (Eds) *Reconstructing Psychological Practice*. London: Croom Helm.

HAWKSWORTH, H. & SCHWARZ, T. (1977) *The Five of Me*. Chicago: Henry Regnery.

HAWORTH, G. (1992) The use of non-human animals in psychological research: the current status of the debate. *Psychology Teaching*, 46–54. New Series, No.1.

HAY, D.C. & YOUNG, A.W. (1982) The human face. In A.W. Ellis (Ed) *Normality and Pathology in Cognitive Functions*. London: Academic Press.

HAYES, K. & HAYES, C. (1951) Intellectual develpment of a house-raised chimpanzee. *Proceedings of the American Philosophical Society*, 95, 105–109.

HAYES, K. & HAYES, C. (1952) Imitation in a home-raised chimpanzee, *Journal of Comparative Physiology & Psychology*. 45, 450–459.

HAYES, N. (1994) *Principles of Comparative Psychology*. Hove: Lawrence Erlbaum Associates.

HAYES, N. (1997) *Doing Qualitative Analysis in Psychology*. Hove: Psychology Press.

HAYES, N. (1998) Spreading the word: How social representations happen. *Psychology Review*, 4, 29–31.

HAYSLIP, B. & PANEK, P.E. (1989) *Adult Development and Ageing*. New York: Harper & Row.

HEARNSHAW, L. (1979) *Cyril Burt: Psychologist*. Ithaca, NY: Cornell University Press.

HEAROLD, S. (1986) A synthesis of 1043 effects of television on social behaviour. In G. Comstock (Ed.) *Public Communication and Behaviour*. New York: Academic Press.

HEATHER, N. (1976) *Radical Perspectives in Psychology*. London: Methuen.

HEBB, D.O. (1949) *The Organisation of Behaviour*. New York: Wiley.

HEBER, R. & GARBER, H. (1975) The Milwaukee Project: A study of the use of familial retardation to prevent cultural retardation. In B.Z. Friedlander, G.M. Sterrit & G.E. Kirk (Eds) *Exceptional Infant*, Volume 3: *Assessment and Intervention*. New York: Brunner/Mazel.

HEIDER, E. (1972) Universals in colour naming and memory. *Journal of Experimental Psychology*, 93, 10–20.

HEIDER, E. & OLIVER, D. (1972) The structure of the colour space in naming and memory for two languages. *Cognitive Psychology*, 3, 337–354.

HEIDER, F. (1946) Attitudes and cognitive organisation. *Journal of Psychology*, 21, 107–112.

HEIDER, F. (1958) *The Psychology of Interpersonal Relations*. New York: Wiley.

HEIMBERG, R., LIEBOWITZ, M., HOPE, D. *et al.* (1999) Cognitive behavioural group therapy vs phenelzine therapy for social phobia: 12-week outcome. *Archives of General Psychiatry*, 55, 1133–1141.

HELBIG, A.J. (1991) Inheritance of migratory direction in a bird species: A cross breeding experiment with SE- and SW-migrating black caps (*Sylvia atricapilla*). *Behav. Ecol. Sociobiol.*, 28, 9–12.

HELLER, R.F., SALTZSTEIN, H.D. & CASPE, W.B. (1992) Heuristics in medical and non-medical decision-making. *Quarterly Journal of Experimental Psychology*, 44A, 211–235.

HELLSTRÖM, K. & ÖST, L.-G. (1996) Prediction of outcome in the treatment of specific phobia. A cross validation study. *Behaviour Research and Therapy*, 34, 403–411.

HENDERSON, A.S., JABLENSKY, A. & SARTORIUS, N. (1994) ICD-10: A neuropsychiatrist's nightmare? *British Journal of Psychiatry*, 165, 273–275.

HENDRICK, S.S., HENDRICK, C. & ADLER N.L. (1986) Romantic relationships. Love, satisfaction and staying together. *Journal of Personality & Social Psychology*, 54, 980–988.

HENDRY, L.B. (1999) Adolescents and society. In D. Messer & F. Jones (Eds) *Psychology and Social Care*. London: Jessica Kingsley.

HENDRY, L.B. & KLOEP, M. (1999) Adolescence in Europe – an important life phase? In D. Messer & S. Millar (Eds) *Exploring Developmental Psychology: From Infancy to Adolescence*. London: Arnold.

HENDRY, L.B., SHUCKSMITH, J., LOVE, J.G. & GLENDINNING, A. (1993) *Young People's Leisure and Lifestyles*. London: Routledge.

HENSLEY, W.E. (1981) The effects of attire, location, and sex on aiding behaviour: A similarity explanation. *Journal of Non-Verbal Behaviour*, 6, 3–11.

HEPWORTH, J.T. & WEST, S.G. (1988) Lynchings and the economy: A time series analysis of Hovland and Sears (1940). *Journal of Personality and Social Psychology*, 55, 239–247.

HERBERT, M.J. & HARSH, C.M. (1944) Observational learning by cats. *Journal of Comparative Psychology*, 37, 81–95.

HERMAN, J. & ROFFWARG, H. (1983) Modifying oculomotor activity in awake subjects increases the amplitude of eye movement during REM sleep. *Science*, 220, 1074–1076.

HERMAN, L.M., KUCZAJ II, S.A. & HOLDER, M.D. (1993) Responses to anomolous gestural sequences by a language-trained dolphin: Evidence for processing of semantic relations and syntactic information. *Journal of Experimental Psychology: General*, 122(2), 184–194.

HERMAN, L.M., RICHARDS, D.G. & WOLF, J.P. (1984) Comprehension of sentences by bottle nosed dolphins. *Cognition*, 16, 129–219.

HERRNSTEIN, R.J. (1971) IQ. *Atlantic Monthly*, September, 43–64.

HERRNSTEIN, R.J. & MURRAY, C. (1994) *The Bell Curve: Intelligence and Class Structure in American Life*. New York: Free Press.

HERSHENSON, M., MUNSINGER, H. & KESSEN, W. (1965) Preference for shapes of intermediate variability in the newborn human. *Science*, 147, 630–631.

HERSKOWITS, M.J. (1955) *Man and His Works: The Science of Cultural Anthropology*. New York: Alfred K. Knopf.

HESS, R.D. & SHIPMAN, V. (1965) Early experience and the socialisation of cognitive modes in children. *Child Development*, 36, 860–886.

HESTON, L.L. (1966) Psychiatric disorders in foster-home-reared children of schizophrenic mothers. *British Journal of Psychiatry*, 122, 819–825.

HESTON, L.L. (1970) The genetics of schizophrenia and schizoid disease. *Science*, 167, 249–256.

HETHERINGTON, A.W. & RANSON, S.W. (1942) The relation of various hypothalamic lesions to adiposity in the rat. *Journal of Comparative Neurology*, 76, 475–499.

HETHERINGTON, E.M. (1967) The effects of familial variables on sex-typing, on parent-child similarity, and on imitation in children. In J.P. Hill (Ed.) *Minnesota Symposium on Child Psychology*, Volume 1. Mineapolis, MN: University of Minnesota Press.

HETHERINGTON, E.M. & BALTES, P.B. (1988) Child psychology and life-span development. In E.M. Hetherington, R. Lerner, & M. Perlmutter (Eds) *Child Development in Life-Span Perspective*. Hillsdale, NJ: Erlbaum.

HETHERINGTON, E.M. & STANLEY-HAGAN, M. (1999) The adjustment of children with divorced parents: A risk and resiliency perspective. *Journal of Child Psychology & Psychiatry*, 40(1), 129–140.

HEWSTONE, M. & BROWN, R.J. (1986) Contact is not enough: An intergroup perspective on the contact hypothesis. In M. Hewstone & R.J. Brown (Eds) *Contact and Conflict in Inter–group Encounters*. Oxford: Blackwell.

HEWSTONE, M. & FINCHAM, F. (1996) Attribution theory and research: Basic issues and applications. In M. Hewstone, W. Stroebe & G.M. Stephenson (Eds) *Introduction to Social Psychology* (2nd edition). Oxford: Blackwell.

HEWSTONE, M. & JASPARS, J.M.F. (1982) Explanations for racial discrimination: The effect of group discussion on intergroup attributions. *European Journal of Social Psychology*, 12, 1–16.

HEWSTONE, M., STROEBE, W. & STEPHENSON, G.M. (1996) *Introduction to Social Psychology* (2nd edition). Oxford: Blackwell.

HEYES, C. M. (1994) Social cognition in primates. In N.J. Mackintosh, (Ed.) *Animal Learning and Cognition*. London: Academic Press.

HEYMAN, I. & FAHY, T.A. (1992) Koro-like symptoms in a man affected with the Human Immunodeficiency Virus. *British Journal of Psychiatry*, 160, 119–121.

HIGHFIELD, R (1996a) Want to know what she's thinking? *The Daily Telegraph*, 28 August, 12.

HIGHFIELD, R. (1996b) Scientists shed light on the origins of our body clock. *The Daily Telegraph*, 5 May, 6.

HIGHFIELD, R. (1997a) Forgetfulness opens windows on the mind. *The Daily Telegraph*, 18 July, 3.

HIGHFIELD, R. (1997b) Depression in women due to 'chemistry'. *The Daily Telegraph*, 13 May, 5.

HIGHFIELD, R. (1999a) Why you need an ice cold beer. *The Daily Telegraph*, 5 May, 22.

HIGHFIELD, R. (1999b) Unique view through eyes of blind man who sees colour. *Daily Telegraph*, 23 November, 17.

HIGHFIELD, R. (2000) Size matters – which is why some men get short shrift. *The Daily Telegraph*, 13 January, 9.

HILGARD, E.R., ATKINSON, R.L. & ATKINSON, R.C. (1979) *Introduction to Psychology* (7th edition). New York: Harcourt Brace Jovanovich.

HILL, A.J. & BEST, P.J. (1981) Effects of deafness and blindness on the spatial correlates of hippocampal unit activity in the rat. *Experimental Neurology*, 74, 204–217.

HILL, C.Y., RUBIN, Z. & PEPLAU, A. (1976) Breakups before marriage: The end of 103 affairs. *Journal of Social Issues*, 32, 147–167.

HILL, E. & WILLIAMSON, J. (1998) Choose six numbers, any numbers. *The Psychologist*, 11(1), 17–21.

HILLIARD, A.G. (1995) The nonscience and nonsense of the bell curve. *Focus: Notes from the Society for the Psychological Study of Ethnic Minority Issues*, 10–12.

HILTON, D.J. & SLUGOSKI, B.R. (1986) Knowledge-based causal attribution: The Abnormal Conditions Focus model. *Psychological Review*, 93, 75–88.

HINTON, J. (1975) *Dying*. Harmondsworth: Penguin.

HIRSCH, H. (1995) *Genocide and the Politics of Memory*. Chapel Hill, NC: The University of North Carolina Press.

HISCOCK, J. (1996) Schools recognise 'Black English'. *The Daily Telegraph*, 21 December, 12.

HITCHCOCK, C.L. & SHERRY, D.F. (1990) Long-term memory for cache sites in the black-capped chickadee. *Animal Behaviour*, 40, 701–712.

HOBBES, T. (1651) *Leviathan*. London: Dent, 1914.

HOBSON, J.A. (1988) *The Dreaming Brain*. New York: Basic Books.

HOBSON, J.A. (1989) Dream theory: A new view of the brain-mind. *The Harvard Medical School Mental Health Letter*, 5, 3–5.

HOBSON, J.A. (1995) Sleeping and dreaming. In D. Kimble & A.M. Colman (Eds.) *Biological Aspects of Behaviour*. London: Longman.

HOBSON, J.A. & McCARLEY, R.W. (1977) The brain as a dream state generator: An activation-synthesis hypothesis of the dream process. *American Journal of Psychiatry*, 134, 1335–1348.

HOCHBERG, J.E. (1970) Attention, organisation and consciousness. In D.I. Mostofsky (Ed.) *Attention: Contemporary Theory and Analysis*. New York: Appleton Century Crofts.

HOCHBERG, J.E. (1971) Perception. In J.W. Kling & L.A. Riggs (Eds) *Experimental Psychology*. New York: Holt.

HOCHBERG, J.E. (1978) Art and perception. In E.C. Carterette & H. Friedman (Eds) *Handbook of Perception*, Volume 10. London: Academic Press.

HODGKIN, J. (1988) Everything you always wanted to know about sex. *Nature*, 331, 300–301.

HODKIN, B. (1981) Language effects in assessment of class-inclusion ability. *Child Development*, 52, 470–478.

HOFFMAN, M.L. (1975) Altruistic behaviour and the parent-child relationship. *Journal of Personality and Social Psychology*, 31, 937–943.

HOGG, M.A. & VAUGHAN, G.M. (1998) *Social Psychology: An Introduction* (2nd edition). Hemel Hempstead: Prentice Hall/Harvester Wheatsheaf.

HOHMANN, G.W. (1966) Some effects of spinal cord lesions on experienced emotional feelings. *Psychophysiology*, 3, 143–156.

HOLAHAN, C.K. & SEARS, R.R. (1995) *The Gifted Group in Later Maturity*. Stanford, CA: Stanford University Press.

HOLLIN, C. & HOWELLS, K. (1997) Controlling violent behaviour. *Psychology Review*, 3, 10–14.

HOLMES, D.S. (1994) *Abnormal Psychology* (2nd edition). New York: HarperCollins.

HOLMES, J. (1992) Response to Jeffrey Masson. In W. Dryden & C. Feltham (Eds) *Psychotherapy and its Discontents*. Buckingham: Open University Press.

HOLMES, J. (1996) Psychoanalysis – An endangered species? *Psychiatric Bulletin*, 20, 321–322.

HOLTGRAVES, T. & SKEEL, J. (1992) Cognitive biases in playing the lottery: Estimating the odds and choosing the numbers. *Journal of Applied Social Psychology*, 22, 934–952.

HOLTZMAN, D.A., HARRIS, T.H., ARANGUREN, G. & BOSTOCKS, E. (1999) Spatial learning of an escape task by young corn snakes, *Elaphe guttata guttata*. *Animal Behaviour*, 57, 51–60.

HOMANS, G.C. (1974) *Social Behaviour: Its Elementary Forms* (2nd edition). New York: Harcourt Brace Jovanovich.

HONZIK, M.P., MacFARLANE, H.W. & ALLEN, L. (1948) The stability of mental test performance between two and eighteen years. *Journal of Experimental Education*, 17, 309–324.

HOPSON, B. & SCALLY, M. (1980) Change and development in adult life: Some implications for helpers. *British Journal of Guidance and Counselling*, 8, 175–187.

HORGAN, J. (1993) Eugenics revisited. *Scientific American*, June, 92–100.

HORN, J.L. (1982) The ageing of human abilities. In B. Wolman (Ed.) *Handbook of Developmental Psychology*. Englewood Cliffs, NJ: Prentice-Hall.

HORNEY, K. (1924) On the genesis of the castration complex in women. *International Journal of Psychoanalysis*, v, 50–65.

HOROWITZ, F.D. (1987) *Exploring Developmental Theories: Toward a Structural/Behavioural Model of Development*. Hillsdale, NJ: Erlbaum.

HOROWITZ, F.D. (1990) Developmental models of individual differences. In J. Colombo & J. Fagan (Eds) *Individual Differences in Infancy: Reliability, Stability, Predictability*. Hillsdale, NJ: Erlbaum.

HORTON, P. & MILLER, D. (1972) The etiology of multiple personality. *Comprehensive Psychiatry*, 13, 151-159.

HOUSTON, J.P., HAMMEN, C., PADILLA, A. & BEE, H. (1991) *Invitation to Psychology* (3rd edition). London: Harcourt Brace Jovanovich.

HOVLAND, C.I. & SEARS, R.R. (1940) Minor studies in aggression, VI: Correlation of lynchings with economic indices. *Journal of Psychology*, 2, 301–310.

HOWARD, J.A., BLUMSTEIN, P. & SCHWARTZ, P. (1987) Social or evolutionary theories? Some observations on preferences in mate selection. *Journal of Personality and Social Psychology*, 53, 194–200.

HOWAT, D. (1999) Social and cultural diversity. *Psychology Review*, 5 (3), 28–31.

HOWE, M. (1980) *The Psychology of Human Learning*. London: Harper & Row.

HOWE, M. (1990) *The Origins of Exceptional Abilities*. Oxford: Blackwell.

HOWE, M. (1995) Hothouse tots: Encouraging and accelerating development in young children. *Psychology Review*, 2, 2–4.

HOWE, M. (1997) *IQ in Question: The Truth about Intelligence*. London: Sage.

HOWE, M. (1998) Can IQ Change? *The Psychologist*, 11(2), 69–71.

HOWE, M. & GRIFFEY, H. (1994) *Give Your Child a Better Start*. London: Michael Joseph.

HOWITT, D. (1991) *Concerning Psychology: Psychology Applied to Social Issues*. Milton Keynes: Open University Press.

HOYENGA, K.B. & HOYENGA, K.T. (1979) *The Question of Sex Differences*. Boston: Little Brown.

HRDY, S.B. (1999) *Mother Nature*. London: Chatto & Windus.

HUBBARD, P. (1991) Evaluating computer games for language learning. *Simulation and Gaming*, 22, 220–223.

HUBEL, D.H. & WIESEL, T.N. (1962) Receptive fields, binocular interaction and functional architecture in the cat's visual cortex. *Journal of Physiology*, 160, 106–154.

HUBEL, D.H. & WIESEL, T.N. (1965) Receptive fields of single neurons in the two non-striate visual areas, 18 and 19 of the cat. *Journal of Neurophysiology*, 28, 229–289.

HUBEL, D.H. & WIESEL, T.N. (1968) Receptive fields and functional architecture of monkey striate cortex. *Journal of Physiology*, 195, 215–243.

HUBEL, D.H. & WIESEL, T.N. (1977) Functional architecture of the macaque monkey visual cortex. *Proceedings of the Royal Society of London, Series B*, 198, 1–59.

HÜBER-WEIDMAN, H. (1976) *Sleep, Sleep Disturbances and Sleep Deprivation*. Cologne: Kiepenheuser & Witsch.

HUDSON, W. (1960) Pictorial depth perception in sub-cultural groups in Africa. *Journal of Social Psychology*, 52, 183–208.

HUESMANN, L.R. & ERON, L.D. (Eds) (1986) *Television and the Aggressive Child: A Cross-National Comparison*. Hove: Erlbaum.

HUESMANN, L.R., ERON, L.D., KLEIN, R., BRICE, P. & FISCHER, P. (1983) Mitigating the imitation of aggressive behaviours by changing children's attitudes about media violence. *Journal of Personality and Social Psychology*, 44, 899–910.

HUGGETT, C. & OLDCROFT, C. (1996) The experience of living in a secluded cave for a month. *Proceedings of the British Psychological Society 27th Annual Student Conference, School of Education, University of Wales*, Cardiff, 27 April.

HUMPHREY, N.K. (1976) The social function of the intellect. In P. Bateson & R. Hinde (Eds) *Growing Points in Ethology*. Cambridge: Cambridge University Press.

HUMPHREYS, G.W. & RIDDOCH, M.J. (1987) *To See But Not to See – A Case Study of Visual Agnosia*. London: Erlbaum.

HUMPHREYS, P.W. (1999) Culture-bound syndromes. *Psychology Review*, 6, 14–18.

HUNT, E. & AGNOLI, A. (1991) The Whorfian hypothesis: A cognitive psychological perspective. *Psychological Review*, 98, 377–389.

HUNT, J. McVicker (1961) *Intelligence and Experience*. New York: Ronald Press.

HUNT, J. McVicker (1969) Has compensatory education failed? Has it been attempted? *Harvard Educational Review*, 39, 278–300.

HUNT, L. (1995) Why a fear of spiders is all in the genes. *The Independent*, 20 December, 17.

HUNT, N. (1997) Trauma of war. *The Psychologist*, 10, 357–360.

HUPKA, R.B. (1981) Cultural determinants of jealousy. *Alternative Lifestyles*, 4, 310–356

HURST, J.L. (1990) Urine marking in populations of wild house mice, *Mus domesticus*, Rutty.I. Communication between males. *Animal Behaviour*. 40, 209–222.

HUSTON, A.C. (1983) Sex-typing. In E.M. Hetherington (Ed.) *Socialisation, personality and social development*, Volume 4 in P.H. Mussen (Ed.) *Handbook of Child Psychology*. New York: Wiley.

HUTTON, A. (1998) Mental health: Drug update. *Nursing Times*, 94, February, 11.

HUXLEY, J.S. (1914) The courtship of the great crested grebe (*Podiceps cristatus*); with an additional theory of sexual selection. *Proceedings of the Zoological Society of London*, 35, 491–562.

HYDE, J.S. & LINN, M.C. (1988) Gender differences in verbal ability: A meta-analysis. *Psychological Bulletin*, 104, 53–69.

HYDE, J.S., FENNEMA, E. & LAMON, S. (1990) Gender differences in mathematics performance: A meta-analysis. *Psychological Bulletin*, 107, 139–155.

IMPERATO-McGINLEY, J., PETERSON, R., GAUTIER, T. & STURLA, E. (1979) Androgens and the evolution of male-gender identity among pseudohermaphrodites with 5–alpha-reductase deficiency. *New England Journal of Medicine*, 300, 1233–1237.

INHELDER, B. & PIAGET, J. (1958) *The Growth of Logical Thinking*. London: Routledge & Kegan Paul.

IRWIN, A. (1996) Diet advice that's hard to follow. *The Daily Telegraph*, 17 September, 5.

IRWIN, A. (1997) People 'not designed for night work'. *The Daily Telegraph*, 22 September, 6.

ISAACS, W., THOMAS, J. & GOLDIAMOND, I. (1960) Application of operant conditioning to reinstate verbal behaviour in psychotics. *Journal of Speech and Hearing Disorders*, 25, 8–12.

ITTELSON, W.H. (1952) *The Ames Demonstrations in Perception*. Princeton, NJ: Princeton University Press.

IVERSEN, L.L. (1979) The chemistry of the brain. *Scientific American*, 241, 134–149.

IWAO, S. (1993) *The Japanese Woman: Traditional Image and Changing Reality*. New York: Free Press.

IWASA, N. (1992) Postconventional reasoning and moral education in Japan. *Journal of Moral Education*, 21(1), 3–16.

JACKENDOFF, R. (1993) *Patterns in the Mind: Language and Human Nature*. Hemel Hempstead: Harvester-Wheatsheaf.

JACKSON, S., CICOGANI, E. & CHARMAN, L. (1996) The measurement of conflict in parent–adolescent relationships. In L. Verhofstadt-Deneve, I. Kienhorst & C. Braet (Eds) *Conflict and Development in Adolescence*. Leiden: DSWO Press.

JACOBS, L. & LIMAN, E. (1991) Grey squirrels remember the locations of buried nuts. *Animal Behaviour*, 41, 103–110.

JAHODA, G. (1978) Cross-cultural perspectives. In H. Tajfel & C. Fraser (Eds) *Introducing Social Psychology*. Harmondsworth: Penguin.

JAHODA, G. (1988) Critical notes and reflections on 'social representations'. *European Journal of Social Psychology*, 18, 195–209.

JAMES, I.A. & BLACKBURN, I.-M. (1995) Cognitive therapy with obsessive-compulsive disorder. *British Journal of Psychiatry*, 166, 144–150.

JAMES, W. (1884) What is an emotion? *Mind*, 9, 188–205.

JAMES, W. (1890) *The Principles of Psychology*. New York: Henry Holt & Company.

JAMISON, K. (1989) Mood disorders and patterns of creativity in British writers and artists. *Psychiatry*, 52, 125–134.

JANKOWIAK, W.R. & FISCHER, E.F. (1992) A cross-cultural perspective on romantic love. *Ethnology*, 31, 149–155.

JANOWITZ, H.D. & GROSSMAN, M.I. (1949) Effects of variations in nutritive density on intake of food in dogs and cats. *American Journal of Physiology*, 158, 184–193.

JARRETT, R.B., SCHAFFER, M., McINTIRE, D. WITT-BROWDER, A., KRAFT, D. & RISSER, R.C. (1999) Treatment of atypical depression with cognitive therapy or phenelzine: a double-blind, placebo-controlled trial. *Archives of General Psychiatry*, 56, 431–437.

JASNOS, T.M. & HAKMILLER, K.L. (1975) Some effects of lesion level and emotional cues on affective expression in spinal cord patients. *Psychological Reports*, 37, 859–870.

JEANNEROD, M. (1999) The contribution of functional neuroimaging to the understanding of schizophrenic psychosis. *Bulletin of the Academy of National Medicine*, 183, 477–484.

JELLISON, J.M. & OLIVER, D.F. (1983) Attitude similarity and attraction: An impression management approach. *Personality and Social Psychology Bulletin*, 9, 111–115.

JENSEN, A. (1969) How much can we boost IQ and scholastic achievement? *Harvard Educational Review*, 39, 1–23.

JENSEN-CAMPBELL, L.A., GRAZIANO, W.G. & WEST, S.G. (1995) Dominance, prosocial orientation and females preferences: Do nice guys really finish last? *Journal of Personality and Social Psychology*, 68, 427–440.

JOHANSSON, G. (1975) Visual motion perception. *Scientific American*, 14, 76–89.

JOHNSON, R.D. & DOWNING, L.E. (1979) Deindividuation and valence of cues: Effects on prosocial and antisocial behaviour. *Journal of Personality and Social Psychology*, 37, 1532–1538.

JOHNSON, R.N. (1972) *Aggression in Man and Animals*. Philadelphia: Saunders.

JOHNSON, T.J., FEIGENBAUM, R. & WEIBY, M. (1964) Some determinants and consequences of the teacher's perception of causation. *Journal of Experimental Psychology*, 55, 237–246.

JOHNSTON, D.K. (1988) Adolescents' solutions to dilemmas in fables: Two moral orientations – two problem-solving strategies. In C. Gilligan, J.V. Ward & J.M. Taylor (Eds) *Mapping the Moral Domain*. Cambridge, MA: Harvard University Press.

JOHNSTON, L. (1996) Move to outlaw electro therapy. *The Observer*, 12 December, 14.

JOHNSTON, R. (1997) This is not my beautiful wife … *New Scientist*, 22 March, 19.

JOHNSTON, W.A. & DARK, V.J. (1986) Selective attention. *Annual Review of Psychology*, 37, 43–75.

JOHNSTON, W.A. & HEINZ, S.P. (1978) Flexibility and capacity demands of attention. *Journal of Experimental Psychology*: General, 107, 420–435.

JOHNSTON, W.A. & HEINZ, S.P. (1979) Depth of non-target processing in an attention task. *Journal of Experimental Psychology*, 5, 168–175.

JOHNSTON, W.A. & WILSON, J. (1980) Perceptual processing of non-targets in an attention task. *Memory and Cognition*, 8, 372–377.

JONES, E.E. & DAVIS, K.E. (1965) From acts to dispositions: The attribution process in person perception. In L. Berkowitz (Ed.) *Advances in Experimental Social Psychology*, Volume 2. New York: Academic Press.

JONES, E.E., DAVIS, K.E. & GERGEN, K. (1961) Role playing variations and their informational value for person perception. *Journal of Abnormal and Social Psychology*, 63, 302–310.

JONES, E.E. & NISBETT, R.E. (1971) *The Actor and the Observer: Divergent Perceptions of the Causes of Behaviour*. Morristown, NJ: General Learning Press.

JONES, F. (1998) Risk taking and everyday tasks. *The Psychologist*, 12(2), 70–71.

JONES, H. (1993) Altered Images. *Nursing Times*, 89(5), 58–60.

JONES, J. (1995) New breed of non-parents turn back on family. *Observer*, 16 April.

JONES, M. C. (1924) The elimination of children's fears. *Journal of Experimental Psychology*, 7, 382–390.

JONES, S. (1993) *The Language of the Genes*. London: Flamingo.

JONSSON, S.A., LUTS, A., GULDBERG-KJAER, N. & OHMAN, R. (1999) Pyramidal neuron size in the hippocampus of schizophrenics correlates with total cell count and degree of cell disarray. *European Archives of Psychiatry and Clinical Neuroscience*, 249, 169–173.

JOSEPH, S., YULE, W., WILLIAMS, R. & HODGKSINSON, P. (1993) Increased substance use in survivors of the Herald of Free Enterprise. *British Journal of Medical Psychology*, 66, 185–192.

JOUVET, M. (1967) Mechanisms of the states of sleep: A neuropharmacological approach. *Research Publications of the Association for the Research in Nervous and Mental Diseases*, 45, 86–126.

JOUVET, M. (1983) Hypnogenic indolamine-dependent factors and paradoxical sleep rebound. In Monnier, E. & Meulders, A. (Eds) *Functions of the Nervous System*, Volume 4: *Psychoneurobiology*. New York: Elsevier.

JOYCE, J. & GUREVICH, E. (1999) D3 receptors and the actions of neuroleptics in the ventral striatopalladial system of schizophrenics. *Annals of the New York Academy of Science*, 877, 595–613.

JOYCE, S. & SCHRADER, A.M. (1999) Twenty years of the Journal of Homosexuality: A bibliometric examination of the first 24 volumes, 1974–1993. *Journal of Homosexuality*, 37, 3–24.

JOYNSON, R.B. (1980) Models of man: 1879–1979. In A.J. Chapman & D.M. Jones (Eds) *Models of Man*. Leicester: British Psychological Society.

JUEL-NIELSEN, N. (1965) Individual and environment: A psychiatric and psychological investigation of monozygous twins raised apart. *Acta Psychiatrica et Neurologica Scandinavia*, (Suppl. 183).

KAGAN, J. (1971) *Change and Continuity in Infancy*. New York: Wiley.

KAGAN, J. (1984) *The Nature of the Child*. New York: Basic Books.

KAGAN, J., REZNICK, J.S. & SNIDMAN, N. (1990) The temperamental qualities of inhibition and lack of inhibition. In M. Lewis & S.M. Miller (Eds) *Handbook of Developmental Psychopathology*. New York: Plenum Press.

KAHNEMAN, D. (1973) *Attention and Effort*. Englewood Cliffs, NJ: Prentice-Hall.

KAHNEMAN, D. & HENIK, A. (1979) Perceptual organisation and attention. In M. Kubovy & J.R. Pomerantz (Eds) *Perceptual Organisation*. Hillsdale, NJ: Erlbaum.

KAHNEMAN, D. & TVERSKY, A. (1984) Changing views of attention and automaticity. In R. Parasuraman, D.R. Davies & J. Beatty (Eds) *Varieties of Attention*. New York: Academic Press.

KALES, A., KALES, J.D. & BIXLER, E.O. (1974) Insomnia: An approach to management and treatment. *Psychiatric Annals*, 4, 28–44.

KALINOWSKY, L. (1975) Psychosurgery. In A. Freedman, H. Kaplan & B. Sadock (Eds) *Comprehensive Textbook of Psychiatry*. Baltimore: Williams & Wilkins.

KALISH, R.A. (1982) *Late Adulthood: Perspectives on Human Development*. Monterey, CA: Brooks-Cole.

KALNINS, I.V. & BRUNER, J.S. (1973) The co-ordination of visual observation and instrumental behaviour in early infancy. *Perception*, 2, 307–314.

KAMIL, A.C., BALDA, R.P. & GOOD, S. (1999) Patterns of movement and orientation during caching and recovery by Clark's nutcrackers, *Nucifraga columbiana*. *Animal Behaviour*, 57(6), 1327–35.

KAMIN, L.J. (1974) *The Science and Politics of IQ*. Harmondsworth: Penguin.

KANIZSA, A. (1976) Subjective Contours. *Scientific American*, 234, 48–52.

KARLINS, M., COFFMAN, T.L. & WALTERS, G. (1969) On the fading of social stereotypes: Studies in three generations of college students. *Journal of Personality and Social Psychology*, 13, 1–16.

KARMILOFF-SMITH, A. (1996) The Connectionist Infant: Would Piaget turn in his Grave? *Society for Research in Child Development Newsletter*, Fall, 1–2 and 10.

KARRAKER, K.H., VOGEL, D.A. & LAKE, M.A. (1995) Parents' gender-stereotyped perceptions of newborns: The eye of the beholder revisited. *Sex Roles*, 33(9/10), 687–701.

KASSER, T. & SHARMA, Y.S. (1999) Reproductive freedom, educational equality and females' preference for resource-acquisition characteristics in mates. *Psychological Sciences*, 10, 374–377.

KASTENBAUM, R. (1979) *Growing Old – Years of Fulfilment*. London: Harper & Row.

KATONA, G. (1940) *Organising and Memorising*. New York: Columbia University Press.

KATZ, D. & BRALY, K. (1933) Racial stereotypes of one hundred college students. *Journal of Abnormal and Social Psychology*, 28, 280–290.

KATZ, J.S. (1993) Jewish Perspectives on Death, Dying and Bereavement. In D. Dickenson & M. Johnson (Eds) *Death, Dying and Bereavement*. London: Sage (in association with the Open University).

KATZEV, A., WARNER, R. & ALCOCK, A. (1994) Girls or boys: Relationship of child gender to marital instability. *Journal of Marriage & the Family*, 56, 89–100.

KAWAI, M. (1965) Newly acquired pre-cultural behavior of the natural troop of Japanese monkeys on Koshima Islet. *Primates*, 6, 1–30.

KAWAMURA, S. (1959) The process of sub-culture propagation among Japanese macaques. *Primates*, 2, 43–55.

KAY, R.W. (1994) Geomagnetic storms: Association with incidence of depression as measured by hospital admission. *British Journal of Psychiatry*, 164, 403–409.

KEEGAN, P. (1999) In the line of fire. *The Guardian* (G2), 1 June, 2–3.

KEENEY, T.J., CANNIZZO, S.R. & FLAVELL, J.H. (1967) Spontaneous and induced verbal rehearsal in a recall task. *Child Development*, 38, 953–966.

KEESEY, R.E. & POWLEY, T.L. (1975) Hypothalamic regulation of body weight. *American Scientist*, 63, 558–565.

KELLEY, H.H. (1967) Attribution theory in social psychology. In D. Levine (Ed.) *Nebraska Symposium on Motivation*, Volume 15. Lincoln, NE: Nebraska University Press.

KELLEY, H.H. (1972) Causal schemata and the attribution process. In E.E. Jones, D.E. Kanouse, H.H. Kelley, S. Valins & B. Weiner (Eds) *Attribution: Perceiving the Causes of Behaviour*. Morristown, NJ: General Learning Press.

KELLEY, H.H. (1983) Perceived causal structures. In J.M.F. Jaspars, F.D. Fincham & M. Hewstone (Eds) *Attribution Theory and Research: Conceptual, Developmental and Social Dimensions*. London: Academic Press.

KELLOGG, W.N. (1968) Communication and language in the home-raised chimpanzee. *Science*, 162, 423–427.

KELLOGG, W.N. & KELLOGG, L.A. (1933) *The Ape and the Child*. New York: McGraw Hill.

KELSOE, J.R., GINNS, E.I., EGELAND, J.A. & GERHARD, D.S. (1989) Re-evaluation of the linkage relationship between chromosome 11 loci and the gene for bipolar disorder in the Old Order Amish. *Nature*, 342, 238–243.

KENDELL, R.E. (1975) *The Role of Diagnosis in Psychiatry*. Oxford: Blackwell.

KENDLER, K.S., NEALE, M.C., KESSLER, R.C., HEATH, A.C. & EAVES, L.J. (1992) Major depression and generalised anxiety disorder: Same genes, (partly) different environments? *Archives of General Psychiatry*, 49, 716–722.

KENNETT, G. (1999) Serotonin – the brain's mood modulator. *Biological Sciences Review*, 12, 28–31.

KENRICK, D.T. (1994) Evolutionary social psychology: From sexual selection to social cognition. *Advances in Experimental Social Psychology*, 26, 75–121.

KENYON, K.W. & RICE, D.W. (1958) Homing of Laysan albatrosses. *Condor*, 60, 3–6.

KEPHART, W.M. (1967) Some correlates of romantic love. *Journal of Marriage & the Family*, 29, 470–474.

KERCKHOFF, A.C. (1974) The social context of interpersonal attraction. In T.L. Huston (Ed.) *Foundations of Interpersonal Attraction*. New York: Academic Press.

KERCKHOFF, A.C. & DAVIS, K.E. (1962) Value consensus and need complementarity in mate selection. *American Sociological Review*, 27, 295–303.

KERIG, P.K., COWAN, P.A. & COWAN, C.P. (1993) Marital quality and gender differences in parent–child interaction. *Developmental Psychology*, 29(6), 931–939.

KERTESZ, A. (1979) Anatomy of jargon. In J. Brown (Ed.) *Jargonapahasia*. New York: Academic Press.

KESSEL, E.L. (1955) Mating activities of balloon flies. *Systematic Zoology*, 4, 97–104.

KESTENBAUM, G.I. & WEINSTEIN, L. (1985) Personality, psychopathology and developmental issues in male adolescent video game use. *Journal of the American Academy of Child Psychiatry*, 24, 325–337.

KETTLEWELL, H.B.D. (1955) Selection experiments on industrial melanism in the Lepidoptera. *Heredity*, 9, 323–342.

KETY, S.S. (1975) Biochemistry of the major psychoses. In A. Freedman, H. Kaplan & B. Sadock (Eds) *Comprehensive Textbook of Psychiatry*. Baltimore: Williams & Wilkins.

KETY, S.S., ROSENTHAL, D., WENDER, P.H. & SCHULSINGER, F. (1968) The types and prevalence of mental illness in the biological and adoptive families of adopted schizophrenics. In D. Rosenthal & S.S. Kety (Eds) *The Transmission of Schizophrenia*. Elmsford, NY: Pergamon Press.

KEYES, D. (1981) *The Minds of Billy Milligan*. New York: Random House.

KIMBLE, D.P. (1988) *Biological Psychology*. New York: Holt, Rinehart & Winston.

KIMURA, D. (1993) Sex differences in the brain. *Scientific American*, 267 (3), September, 80–87 (Special issue).

KINDERMAN, P. & BENTALL, R.P. (1997) Causal attributions in paranoia and depression: Internal, personal, and situational attributions for negative events. *Journal of Abnormal Psychology*, 106, 341–345.

KINGDON, D.G. & TURKINGTON, D. (1994) *Cognitive Behavioural Therapy for Schizophrenia*. East Sussex: Lawrence Erlbaum.

KINGDON, J.W. (1967) Politicians' beliefs about voters. *American Political Science Review*, 61, 137–145.

KITZINGER, C. (1998) Challenging Gender Biases: Feminist psychology at work. *Psychology Review*, 4(3), 18–20.

KITZINGER, C. & COYLE, A. (1995) Lesbian and gay couples: Speaking of difference. *The Psychologist*, 8, 64–69.

KITZINGER, C., COYLE, A., WILKINSON, S. & MILTON, M. (1998) Towards lesbian and gay psychology. *The Psychologist*, 11(11), 529–533.

KLANING, U., MORTENSEN, P.B. & KYVIK, K.D. (1996) Increased occurrence of schizophrenia and other psychiatric illnesses among twins. *British Journal of Psychiatry*, 168, 688–692.

KLEBANOFF, L.D. (1959) A comparison of parental attitudes of mothers of schizophrenics, brain injured and normal children. *American Journal of Psychiatry*, 24, 445–454.

KLEIN, M. (1950) *Contributions to Psycho-analysis*. London: Hogarth Press.

KLEINER, K.A. (1987) Amplitude and phase spectra as indices of infants' pattern preference. *Infant Behaviour and Development*, 10, 49–59.

KLEINMAN, A. & KLEINMAN, J. (1985) Somatization: The interconnections in Chinese society among culture, depressive experiences and the meanings of pain. In A. Kleinman & B. Good (Eds) *Culture and Depression: Studies in the Anthropology and Cross-cultural Psychiatry of Affect and Disorder*. Berkeley: University of California Press.

KLEITMAN, N. (1963) *Sleep and Wakefulness* (2nd edition). Chicago: University of Chicago Press.

KLINE, N.S. (1963) Psychiatry in Indonesia. *American Journal of Psychiatry*, 119, 809–815.

KLINE, P. (1988) *Psychology Exposed*. London: Routledge.

KLOEP, M. & HENDRY, L.B. (1999) Challenges, risks and coping in adolescence. In D. Messer & S. Millar (Eds) *Exploring Developmental Psychology: From Infancy to Adolescence*. London: Arnold.

KLOEP, M. & TARIFA, F. (1993) Albanian children in the wind of change. In L.E. Wolven (Ed.) *Human Resource Development*. Hogskolan: Ostersund.

KLUFT, R.P. (1996) Treating the traumatic memories of patients with dissociative identity disorder. *American Journal of Psychiatry*, 153, 103–110.

KLÜVER, H. & BUCY, P. (1937) 'Psychic blindness' and other symptoms following bilateral temporal lobectomy in Rhesus monkeys. *American Journal of Physiology*, San Diego, CA: Edits.

KOESTLER, A. (1967) *The Ghost in the Machine*. London: Pan.

KOFFKA, K. (1935) *The Principles of Gestalt Psychology*. New York: Harcourt Brace and World.

KOHLBERG, L. (1963) The development of children's orientations toward a moral order: 1. Sequence in the development of moral thought. *Human Development*, 6, 11–33.

KOHLBERG, L. (1969) Stage and sequence: The cognitive developmental approach to socialisation. In D.A. Goslin (Ed.) *Handbook of Socialisation Theory and Research*. Chicago: Rand McNally.

KOHLBERG, L. (1978) Revisions in the theory and practice of moral development. *Directions for Child Development*, 2, 83–88.

KOHLBERG, L. (1984) *Essays on Moral Development: The Psychology of Moral Development*, Volume 2. New York: Harper & Row.

KOHLBERG, L. & NISAN, M. (1987) A longitudinal study of moral judgement in Turkish males. In A. Colby & L. Kohlberg (Eds) *The Measurement of Moral Judgement*. New York: Cambridge University Press.

KOHLBERG, L. & ULLIAN, D.Z. (1974) Stages in the development of psychosexual concepts and attitudes. In R.C. Van Wiele (Ed.) *Sex Differences in Behaviour*. New York: Wiley.

KÖHLER, W. (1925) *The Mentality of Apes*. New York: Harcourt Brace.

KOLTZ, C. (1983) Scapegoating. *Psychology Today*, December, 68–69.

KON, Y. (1994) Amok. *British Journal of Psychiatry*, 165, 658–689.

KORO STUDY TEAM (1969) The Koro epidemic in Singapore. *Singapore Medical Journal*, 10, 234–242.

KOUKKOU, M. & LEHMANN, D. (1983) Dreaming: The functional state-shift hypothesis. *British Journal of Psychology*, 142, 221–231.

KRAEPELIN, E. (1913) *Clinical Psychiatry: A Textbook for Physicians* (translated by A. Diffendorf). New York: Macmillan.

KRAMER, G. (1951) Eine neue Methode zur Eforschung der Zugorientierung und die bisher damit erzielten Ergebnisse. *Proc. X. Ornithol. Congr. Uppsala* 195, 269–80.

KRAMER, P. (1993) *Listening to Prozac – A Psychiatrist Explores Mood-Altering Drugs and the Meaning of the Self*. New York: Viking.

KREBS, D. & BLACKMAN, R. (1988) *Psychology: A First Encounter*. New York: Harcourt Brace Jovanovich.

KREBS, J. (1977) The significance of song repertoires: The Beau Geste hypothesis. *Animal Behaviour*, 25, 475–478.

KREITHEN, M.L. (1978) Sensory mechanisms for animal orientation – Can any new ones be discovered? In K. Schmidt-Kooenig & W.T. Keeton (Eds) *Animal Migration, Navigation and Homing*. Berlin: Springer.

KREITMAN, N. (1961) The reliability of psychiatric diagnosis. *Journal of Mental Science*, 107, 876–886.

KREITMAN, N., SAINSBURY, P. & MORRISSEY, J. (1961) The reliability of psychiatirc assessment: An analysis. *Journal of Mental Science*, 107, 887-908.

KREMER, J. (1998) Work. In K. Trew & J. Kremer (Eds) *Gender & Psychology*. London: Arnold.

KROGER, J. (1985) Separation-individuation and ego identity status in New Zealand university students. *Journal of Youth & Adolescence*, 14, 133–147.

KROGER, J. (1996) *Identity in Adolescence: The Balance between Self and Other* (2nd edition). London: Routledge.

KRUPAT, E. & GARONZIK, R. (1994) Subjects' expectations and the search for alternatives to deception in social psychology. *British Journal of Social Psychology*, 33, 211–222.

KÜBLER-ROSS, E. (1969) *On Death and Dying*. London: Tavistock/Routledge.

KUDRIMOTO, H., SKAGGS, W., BARNES, B., MCNAUGHTON, J., GERRARD, M., SUSTER, M. & WEAVER, K. (1996) REM sleep and the reactivation of recent correlation patterns in hippocampal neuronal ensembles. *Society for Neuroscience Abstracts*, 1871.

KUHN, T.S. (1962) *The Structure of Scientific Revolutions*. Chicago: University of Chicago Press.

KUHN, T.S. (1970) *The Structure of Scientific Revolutions* (2nd edition). Chicago: University of Chicago Press.

KULIK, J.A. & BROWN, R. (1979) Frustration, attribution of blame and aggression. *Journal of Experimental Social Psychology*, 15, 183–194.

KULIK, J.A. & MAHLER, H.I.M. (1989) Stress and affiliation in a hospital setting: Pre-operative roommate preferences. *Personality and Social Psychology Bulletin*, 15, 183–193.

KURDEK, L.A. (1994) The nature and correlates of relationship quality in gay, lesbian and heterosexual cohabiting couples: A test of the individual difference, interdependence, and discrepancy models. In B. Greene & G.M. Herek (Eds.) *Lesbian and Gay Psychology: Theory, Research and Clinical Applications*. London: Sage.

KURUCZ, J. & FELDMAR, G. (1979) Prosopo-affective agnosia as a symptom of cerebral organic disease. *Journal of the American Geriatrics Society*, 27, 225–230.

LaBERGE, D. (1983) Spatial extent of attention to letters and words. *Journal of Experimental Psychology: Human Perception and Performance*, 9, 371–379.

LABOUVIE-VIEF, G. (1980) Beyond formal operations: uses and limits of pure logic in life-span development. *Human Development*, 22, 141–161.

LABOV, W. (1970) The logic of non-standard English. In F. Williams (Ed.) *Language and Poverty*. Chicago: Markham.

LABOV, W. (1973) The boundaries of words and their meanings. In C.J.N. Bailey & R.W. Shuy (Eds) *New Ways of Analysing Variations in English*. Washington, DC: Georgetown University Press.

LACEY, H. (1998) She's leaving home. *Real Life: Independent on Sunday*, 31 May.

LACHMAN, S.J. (1984) Processes in visual misperception: Illusions for highly structured stimulus material. Paper presented at the 92nd annual convention of the American Psychological Association, Toronto, Canada.

LACK, D. (1943) *The Life of the Robin*. London: Witherby.

LAKOFF, G. (1987) *Women, Fire and Dangerous Things: What Categories Reveal About The Mind*. Chicago: University of Chicago Press.

LAMBERT, W.W., SOLOMON, R.L. & WATSON, P.D. (1949) Reinforcement and extinction as factors in size estimation. *Journal of Experimental Psychology*, 39, 637–641.

LAMBIE, J. (1991) The misuse of Kuhn in psychology. *The Psychologist*, 4 (1), 6–11.

LAND, E.H. (1977) The retinex theory of colour vision. *Scientific American*, 237, 108–128.

LANDIS, C. (1938) Statistical evaluation of psychotherapeutic methods. In S.E. Hinde (Ed.) *Concepts and Problems of Psychotherapy*. London: Heineman.

LANGE, A.J. & JAKUBOWSKI, P. (1976) *Responsible Assertive Behaviour: Cognitive/Behavioural Procedures for Trainers*. Champaign, ILL: Research Press.

LANGE, C. (1885) Om Sindsbevaegelser. et psychko. fysiolog. studie. English translation in K. Dunlap (Ed.) *The Emotions*. London: Hafner, 1967.

LANGER, E.J. (1975) The illusion of control. *Journal of Personality & Social Psychology*, 32, 311–328.

LANGLOIS, J. & ROGGMAN, L. (1994) Attractive faces are only average. *Psychological Science*, 1, 115–121.

LANGLOIS, J., ROGGMAN, L. & RISER-DANNER, L. (1990) Infants' differential social responses to attractive and unattractive faces. *Developmental Psychology*, 26, 153–159.

LARKIN, T.S. & KEETON, W.T. (1976) Bar magnets mask the effect of normal magnetic disturbances on pigeon orientation. *Journal of Comparative Physiology*, 110, 227–231.

LASHLEY, K. (1926) Studies of cerebral function in learning: VII The relation between cerebral mass, learning and retention. *Journal of Comparative Neurology*, 41, 1–48.

LATANÉ, B. & DARLEY, J.M. (1968) Group inhibitions of bystander intervention in emergencies. *Journal of Personality and Social Psychology*, 10, 215–221.

LATANÉ, B. & RODIN, J. (1969) A lady in distress: Inhibiting effects of friends and strangers on bystander intervention. *Journal of Experimental Social Psychology*, 5, 189–202.

LATANÉ, B., NIDA, S. & WILLIAMS, D.W. (1981) The effects of group size on helping behaviour. In J.P. Rushton & R.M. Sorrentino (Eds) *Altruism and Helping Behaviour*. Hillsdale, NJ: Erlbaum.

LAU, R.R. & RUSSELL, D. (1980) Attributions in the sports pages. *Journal of Personality and Social Psychology*, 39, 29–38.

LAUGHLIN, H.P. (1967) *The Neuroses*. Washington, DC: Butterworth.

LAURANCE, J. (1993) Is psychotherapy all in the mind? *The Times*, 15 April, 7.

LAURENCE, C. (1997) Cheer up, son – take Prozac. *The Daily Telegraph*, 4 December, 27.

LAVIE, P. (1998) *The Enchanted World of Sleep*. London: Yale University Press.

LAWSON, E.A. (1966) Decisions concerning the rejected channel. *Journal of Experimental Psychology*, 18, 260–265.

LAZARUS, R.S. (1982) Thoughts on the relations between emotion and cognition. *American Psychologist*, 37, 1019–1024.

LAZARUS, R.S. (1999) *Stress and Emotion: A New Synthesis*. London: Free Association Books.

LE BON, G. (1879) *The Crowd: A Study of the Popular Mind*. London: Unwin.

LE DOUX, J. (1996) *The Emotional Brain: The Mysterious Underpinnings of Emotional Life*. New York: Simon & Schuster.

LE FANU, J. (1994) May I examine your dream? *The Times*, 13 January, 15.

LEE, A. (1996) St. Helena study shows benefit of television. *The Times*, 3 August, 7.

LEE, K., CAMERON, C.A., XU, F., FU, G. & BOARD, J. (1997) Chinese and Canadian children's evaluations of lying and truth telling: Similarities and differences in the context of pro- and antisocial behaviours. *Child Development*, 68, 924–934.

LEE, L. (1984) Sequences in separation: A framework for investigating endings of the personal (romantic) relationship. *Journal of Social and Personal Relationships*, 1, 49–74.

LEFF, J. (1981) *Psychiatry Around the Globe: A Transcultural View*. New York: Dekker.

LEFKOWITZ, M.M., ERON, L.D., WALDER, L.O. & HUESMANN, L.R. (1972) Television violence and child aggression: A follow-up study. In G.A. Comstock & E.A. Rubenstein (Eds) *Television and Social Behaviour*, Volume 3. *Television and Adolescent Aggressiveness*. Washington, DC: US Government Printing Office.

LeFRANCOIS, G.R. (1983) *Psychology*. Belmont, CA: Wadsworth Publishing Co.

LeFRANCOIS, G.R. (1986) *Of Children: An Introduction to Child Development*. Belmont, CA: Wadsworth.

LEMONICK, M.D. (1997) The Mood Molecule. *Time*, September 29, 67–73.

LENNEBERG, E.H. (1967) *Biological Foundations of Language*. New York: Wiley.

LEPPER, M.R., GREENE, D., & NISBETT, R.E. (1973) Undermining children's intrinsic interest with extrinsic reward: A test of the overjustification hypothesis. *Journal of Personality & Social Psychology*, 28, 129-137.

LESLIE, A.M. (1987) Pretence and representation: The origins of 'theory of mind'. *Psychological Review*, 94, 412–426.

LEUTWYLER, K. (1997) Depression's double standard. *Scientific American* (special issue), 7, 53–54.

LEVIN, I.P. & GAETH, G.J. (1988) How consumers are affected by the framing of attribution information before and after consuming the product. *Journal of Consumer Research*, 15, 374–378.

LEVINE, N.E. (1988) *The Dynamics of Polyandry: Kinship, Domesticity and Population in the Tibetan Border*. Chicago: University of Chicago Press.

LEVINE, R., SATO, S., HASHIMOTO, T. & VERMA, J. (1995) Love and marriage in 11 cultures. *Journal of Cross-Cultural Psychology*, 26, 554–571.

LEVINGER, G. (1980) Toward the analysis of close relationships. *Journal of Experimental Social Psychology*, 16, 510–554.

LEVINSON, D.J. (1986) A conception of adult development. *American Psychologist*, 41, 3–13.

LEVINSON, D.J., DARROW, D.N., KLEIN, E.B., LEVINSON, M.H. & McKEE, B. (1978) *The Seasons of a Man's Life*. New York: A.A. Knopf.

LEVY, B. & LANGER, E. (1994) Ageing free from negative stereotypes: Successful memory in China and among the American deaf. *Journal of Personality and Social Psychology*, 66, 989–997.

LEVY, J. (1983) Language, cognition and the right hemisphere: A response to Gazzaniga. *American Psychologist*, 38, 538–541.

LEVY, J., TREVARTHEN, C. & SPERRY, R.W. (1972) Perception of bilateral chimeric figures following hemispheric disconnection. *Brain*, 95, 61–78.

LEVY, R. (1996) Improving memory in old age through implicit self-stereotyping. *Journal of Personality & Social Psychology*, 71, 1092–1107.

LEVY, S., STROESSNER, S. & DWECK, C. (1998) Stereotype formation and endorsement: The role of implicit theories. *Journal of Personality & Social Psychology*, 74, 16–34.

LEWIN, R. (1991) Look who's talking now. *New Scientist*, 27 April, 48–52.

LEWINSOHN, P.M. (1974) A behavioural approach to depression. In R. Friedman & M. Katz (Eds) *The Psychology of Depression: Contemporary Theory and Research*. Washington, DC: Winston/Wiley.

LEWINSOHN, P.M., HOPS, H. & ROBERTS, R.E. (1993) Adolescent psychopathology: I. Prevalence and incidence of depression and other DSM-3-R disorders in high school students. *Journal of Abnormal Psychology*, 102, 133–144.

LEWIS, M. & ROWE, D. (1994) Good news. Bad news. *The Psychologist*, 7, 157–160.

LEWIS, S. (1994) ICD-10: A neuropsychiatrist's nightmare? *British Journal of Psychiatry*, 164, 157–158.

LEWONTIN, R. (1976) Race and intelligence. In N.J. Block & G. Dworkin (Eds) *The IQ Controversy: Critical Readings*. New York: Pantheon.

LEY, R.G. & BRYDEN, M.P. (1979) Hemispheric differences in processing emotions and faces. *Brain and Language*, 7, 127–138.

LEYENS, J.P. & CODOL, J.P. (1988) Social cognition. In M. Hewstone, W. Stroebe, J.P. Codol & G.M. Stephenson (Eds) *Introduction to Social Psychology*. Oxford: Blackwell.

LEYENS, J.P. & DARDENNE, B. (1996) Basic concepts and approaches in social cognition. In M. Hewstone, W. Stroebe & G.M. Stephenson (Eds) *Introduction to Social Psychology* (2nd edition). Oxford: Blackwell.

LIBERZON, I., ABELSON, J., FLAGEL, S., RAZ, J. & YOUNG, E. (1999a) Neuroendocrine and psychophysiologic responses in PTSD: A symptom provocation study. *Neuropsychopharmacology*, 21, 40–50.

LIBERZON, I., TAYLOR, S., AMDUR, R., JUNG, T., CHAMBERLAIN, K., MINOSHIMA, S., KOEPPE, R. & FIG, L. (1999b) Brain activation in PTSD in response to trauma-related stimuli. *Biological Psychiatry*, 45, 817–826.

LIDZ, T. (1973) Commentary on 'A critical review of recent adoption, twin and family studies of schizophrenia: Behavioural genetics perspectives'. *Schizophrenia Bulletin*, 2, 402–412.

LIEBERT, R.M. & BARON, R.A. (1972) Some immediate effects of televised violence on children's behaviour. *Developmental Psychology*, 6, 469–475.

LIEBERT, R.M. & SPRAFKIN, J. (1988) *The Early Window: Effects of Television on Children and Youth*. New York: Pergamon Press.

LIGHT, P. (1986) Context, conservation and conversation. In M. Richards & P. Light (Eds) *Children of Social Worlds*. Cambridge: Polity Press.

LIGHT, P. & GILMOUR, A. (1983) Conservation or conversation? Contextual facilitation of inappropriate conservation judgements. *Journal of Experimental Child Psychology*, 36, 356–363.

LIGHT, P., BUCKINGHAM, N. & ROBBINS, A.H. (1979) The conservation task as an interactional setting. *British Journal of Educational Psychology*, 49, 304–310.

LILIENFELD, S.O. (1995) *Seeing Both Sides: Classic Controversies in Abnormal Psychology*. Pacific Grove, CA: Brooks/Cole Publishing Co.

LINSZEN, D.H., DINGERMANS, P.M., NUGTER, M.A. *et al.* (1997) Patient attributes and expressed emotion as risk factors for psychotic relapse. *Schizophrenia Bulletin*, 23, 119–130.

LINVILLE, P.W., FISCHER, G.W. & SALOVEY, P. (1989) Perceived distributions of the characteristics of in-group and out-group members: Empirical evidence and a computer simulation. *Journal of Personality and Social Psychology*, 57, 165–188.

LIPPITZ, B., MINDUS, P., MEYERSON, B., KIHLSTROM, L. & LINDQUIST, C. (1999) Lesion topography and outcome after thermocapsulotomy or gamma knife capsulotomy for obsessive–compulsive disorder: Relevance of the right hemisphere. *Neurosurgery*, 44, 452–458.

LIPPMANN, W. (1922) *Public Opinion*. New York: Harcourt.

LIPTON, S. (1943) Dissociated personality: A case report. *Psychiatric Quarterly*, 17, 35-36.

LISAK, D. & ROTH, S. (1988) Motivational factors in non-incarcerated sexually aggressive men. *Journal of Personality & Social Psychology*, 55, 795–802.

LITTLEWOOD, R. (1992) Psychiatric diagnosis and racial bias: Empirical and interpretive approaches. *Social Science and Medicine*, 34, 141–149.

LITTLEWOOD, R. & LIPSEDGE, M. (1989) *Aliens and Alienists: Ethnic Minorities and Psychiatry*. London: Unwin Hyman.

LLEWELLYN-SMITH, J. (1996) Courses for gifted children are often 'a waste of time'. *The Sunday Telegraph*, 8 September, 5.

LLOYD, P., MAYES, A., MANSTEAD, A.S.R., MEUDELL, P.R. & WAGNER, H.L. (1984) *Introduction to Psychology – An Integrated Approach*. London: Fontana.

LOCKE, J. (1690) *An Essay Concerning Human Understanding*. New York: Mendon (reprinted, 1964).

LOEHLIN, J.C., WILLERMAN, L. & HORN, J.M. (1988) Human behaviour genetics. *Annual Review of Psychology*, 39, 101–133.

LOFTUS, E.F. (1980) *Memory*. Reading, MA: Addison and Wesley.

LOFTUS, G. (1974) Reconstructing memory: The incredible eyewitness. *Psychology Today*, December, 116–119.

LOFTUS, G. & LOFTUS, E.F. (1983) *Mind at Play: The Psychology of Video Games*. New York: Basic Books.

LOGAN, G.D. (1988) Toward an instance theory of automatisation. *Psychological Review*, 95, 492–527.

LONNER, W. (1990) An overview of cross-cultural testing and assessment. In R. Brislin (Ed.) *Applied Cross-Cultural Psychology*. Newbury Park, CA: Sage.

LOO, C.M. (1972) The effects of spatial density on the social behaviour of children. *Journal of Applied Social Psychology*, 2, 372–381.

LOOMIS, A.L., HARVEY, E.N. & HOBART, A. (1937) Cerebral states during sleep as studied by human brain potentials. *Journal of Experimental Psychology*, 21, 127–144.

LORD, C.G., ROSS, L. & LEPPER, M.R. (1979) Biased assimilation and attitude polarisation: The effects of prior theories on subsequently considered evidence. *Journal of Personality and Social Psychology*, 37, 2098–2107.

LORENZ, K. (1935) The companion in the bird's world. *Auk*, 54, 245–273.

LORENZ, K. (1958) The evolution of behaviour. *Scientific American*, 199, 67–78.

LOVAAS, O.I. (1987) Behavioural treatment and normal educational and intellectual functioning in young autistic children. *Journal of Consulting & Clinical Psychology*, 55, 3–9.

LOVEJOY, C.O. (1981) The origin of man. *Science*, 211, 341–350.

LOWE, G. (1994) The mating game. *The Psychologist*, 7, 225.

LUCE, G.G. (1971) *Body Time: The Natural Rhythms of the Body*. St. Albans: Paladin.

LUCE, G.G. & SEGAL, J. (1966) *Sleep*. New York: Coward, McCann & Geoghegan.

LUCHINS, A.S. (1942) Mechanisation in problem-solving: The effect of Einstellung. *Psychological Monographs*, 54 (Whole No. 248).

LUCHINS, A.S. & LUCHINS, E.H. (1959) *Rigidity of Behaviour*. Eugene, OR: University of Oregon Press.

LUDWIG, A.M., BRANDSMA, J.M., WILBUR, C.B., BENFELDT, F. & JAMESON, D.H. (1972) An objective study of multiple personality. *Archives of General Psychiatry*, 26, 298-310.

LUGARESSI, E., MEDORI, R., MONTAGNA, P., BARUZZI, A., CORTELLI, P., LUGARESSI, A., TINUPER, A., ZUCCONI, M. & GAMBETTI, P. (1986) Fatal familial insomnia and dysautonomia in the selective degeneration of thalamic nuclei. *New England Journal of Medicine*, 315, 997–1003.

LUMSDEN, C.J. & WILSON, E.O. (1983) *Promethean Fire*. Cambridge, MA: Harvard University Press.

LURIA, A.R. (1973) *The Working Brain: An Introduction to Neuropsychology* (translated by B. Haigh). New York: Basic Books.

LURIA, A.R. (1980) *Higher Cortical Functions in Man* (2nd edition, revised). New York: Basic Books.

LURIA, A.R. (1987) Reductionism. In R.L. Gregory (Ed.) *The Oxford Companion to the Mind*. Oxford: Oxford University Press.

LURIA, A.R. & YUDOVICH, F.I. (1971) *Speech and the Development of Mental Processes in the Child*. Harmondsworth: Penguin.

LYALL, J. (1993) Animal Rites. *Nursing Times*, 89(10), 18–19.

LYKKEN, D.T. & TELLEGREN, A. (1993) Is human mating adventitious or the result of lawful choice?: A twin study of mate selection. *Journal of Personality and Social Psychology*, 65, 56–68.

LYONS, J. (1970) *Chomsky*. London: Fontana.

LYTTON, H. & ROMNEY, D.M. (1991) Parents' differential socialisation of boys and girls: A meta-analysis. *Psychological Bulletin*, 109, 267–296.

MACCOBY, E.E. (1980) *Social Development – Psychological Growth and the Parent-Child Relationship*. New York: Harcourt Brace Jovanovich.

MACCOBY, E.E. (1990) Gender and relationships: A developmental account. *American Psychologist*, 45, 513–520.

MACCOBY, E.E. & JACKLIN, C.N. (1974) *The Psychology of Sex Differences*. Stanford, CA: Stanford University Press.

MacDONALD, V. (1996) Drug blunder resurfaces in children. *The Sunday Telegraph*, 15 December, 5.

MACKAY, D. (1975) *Clinical Psychology: Theory and Therapy*. London: Methuen.

MACKAY, D.C. & NEWBIGGING, P.L. (1977) The Poggendorf and its variants do arouse the same perceptual processes. *Perception and Psychophysics*, 21, 26–32.

MACKAY, D.G. (1973) Aspects of the theory of comprehension, memory and attention. *Quarterly Journal of Experimental Psychology*, 25, 22–40.

MACKINTOSH, N.J. (1978) Cognitive or associative theories of conditioning: implications of an analysis of blocking. In S.H. Hulse, M. Fowler, & W.K. Honig (Eds) *Cognitive Processes in Animal Behaviour*. Hillsdale, NJ: Lawrence Erlbaum.

MACKINTOSH, N.J. (1995) Classical and operant conditioning. In N.J. Mackintosh & A.M. Colman (Eds) *Learning and Skills*. London: Longman.

MACLEAN, P.D. (1949) Psychosomatic disease and the 'visceral brain': Recent developments bearing on the Papez theory of emotion. *Psychosomatic Medicine*, 11, 338–353.

MACLEOD, A. (1998) Therapeutic interventions. In M. Eysenck (Ed.) *Psychology: An Integrated Approach*. Harlow: Addison Wesley/Longman Ltd.

MADDOX, G.L. (1964) Disengagement theory: A critical evaluation. *The Gerontologist*, 4, 80–83.

MAES, M., DE MEYER, F., THOMPSON, P., PEETERS, D. & COSYNS, P. (1994) Synchronised animal rhythms in violent suicide rate, ambient temperature and the light–dark span. *Acta Psychiatrica Scandinvica*, 90, 391–396.

MAGNUSSON, D., STATTIN, H. & ALLEN, V.L. (1985) Biological maturation and social development: A longitudinal study of some adjustment processes from mid-adolescence to adulthood. *Journal of Youth & Adolescence*, 14, 267–283.

MAGUIRE, E., GADIAN, D., JOHNSRUDE, I., GOOD, C., ASHBURNER, J., FRACKOWIAK, R. & FRITH, D. (2000) Navigation-related structural change in the hippocampi of taxi drivers. *Proceedings of the National Academy of Sciences*, 97(6), 10.1073/pnas 070039597, 14 March.

MAGUIRE, E.A., FRACKOWIAK, S.J. & FRITH, C.D. (1997) Recalling routes around London: Activation of the right hippocampus in taxi drivers. *Journal of Neuroscience*, 17, 7103–7110.

MAHER, B. (1968) The shattered language of schizophrenia. *Psychology Today*, 30ff.

MAHLER, M. (1975) *The Psychological Birth of the Human Infant*. London: Hutchinson.

MAHONEY, J. (1998) Mates past their prime. *Times Higher Educational Supplement*, 25 September, 18.

MAIER, N.R.F. (1931) Reasoning in humans II: The solution of a problem and its appearance in consciousness. *Journal of Comparative Psychology*, 12, 181–194.

MAIER, N.R.F. & SCHNEIRLA, T.C. (1935) *Principles of Animal Psychology*. New York: McGraw-Hill.

MAIN, M., KAPLAN, N. & CASSIDY, J. (1985) Security in infancy, childhood and adulthood: A move to the level of representation. In I. Bretherton & E. Waters (Eds) *Growing Points of Attachment Theory and Research*. (Monographs of the Society for Research in Child Development, Volume 50, Serial No. 209.) Chicago: University of Chicago Press

MAIR, K. (1999) Development of a dogma: Multiple personality and child abuse. *The Psychologist*, 12, 588-591.

MAJOR, B. (1980) Information acquisition and attribution processes. *Journal of Personality and Social Psychology*, 39, 1010–1023.

MALAN, D.H., HEATH, E.S., BACAL, H.A. & BALFOUR, F.H.G. (1975) Psychodynamic changes in untreated neurotic patients. *Archives of General Psychiatry*, 32, 110–126.

MALINOWSKI, B. (1929) *The Sexual Life of Savages*. New York: Harcourt Brace Jovanovich.

MALMSTROM, P. & SILVA, M. (1986) Twin talk: Manifestations of twin status in the speech of toddlers. *Journal of Child Language*, 13, 293–304.

MANDLER, G. (1962) Emotion. In R. Brown (Ed.) *New Directions in Psychology*. New York: Holt, Rinehart & Winston.

MANDLER, G. (1984) *Mind and Body: The Psychology of Emotion and Stress*. New York: Norton.

MANN, L. (1981) The baiting crowd in episodes of threatened suicide. *Journal of Personality and Social Psychology*, 41, 703–709.

MANSTEAD, A.S.R. & SEMIN, G.R. (1980) Social facilitation effects: Mere enhancement of dominant responses? *British Journal of Social and Clinical Psychology*, 19, 19–36.

MANTHORPE, J. (1994) Life Changes. *Nursing Times*, 90 (18), 66–67.

MAPSTONE, E. (1991) Special issue on animal experimentation. *The Psychologist*, 4 (5), 195.

MAQUET, P., PETERS, J-M., ARTS, J., DELFIORE, G., DEGUELDRE, C., LUXEN, A. & FRANCK, G. (1996) Functional neuroanatomy of human rapid-eye-movement sleep and dreaming. *Nature*, 383, 163–166.

MARANON, G. (1924) Contribution à l'etude de l'action emotive de l'adrenaline. *Revue Française d'Endocrinologie*, 2, 301–325.

MARATSOS, M.P. (1983) Some current issues in the study of the acquisition of grammar. In J.H. Flavell & E.M. Markman (Eds) Cognitive Development, Volume 3. In P.H. Mussen (Ed.) *Handbook of Child Psychology* (4th edition). New York: Wiley.

MARCH, P. & DOHERTY, C. (1999) Dying and bereavement. In D. Messer & F. Jones (Eds) *Psychology and Social Care*. London: Jessica Kingsley Publishers.

MARCIA, J.E. (1980) Identity in adolescence. In J. Adelson (Ed.) *Handbook of Adolescent Psychology*. New York: Wiley.

MARCIA, J.E. (1998) Pier Gynt's life cycle. In E. Skoe & A. von der Lippe (Eds) *Personality Development in Adolescence*: A cross national and lifespan perspective. London: Routledge.

MARCUS, D.E. & OVERTON, W.F. (1978) The development of cognitive gender constancy and sex-role preferences. *Child Development*, 49, 434–444.

MARK, V. & ERVIN, F. (1970) *Violence and the Brain*. New York: Harper & Row.

MARKS, I. (1987) *Fears, Phobias and Rituals: Panic, Anxiety and Their Disorders*. New York: Oxford University Press.

MARKS, M. & FOLKARD, S. (1985) Diurnal rhythms in cognitive performance. In J. Nicholson & H. Beloff (Eds) *Psychology Survey 5*. Leicester: British Psychological Society.

MARR, D. (1982) *Vision: A Computational Investigation into the Human Representation and Processing of Visual Information*. San Francisco, CA: W.H. Freeman.

MARRONE, M (1998) *Attachment and Interaction*. London: Jessica Kingsley Publishers.

MARSHALL, G. & ZIMBARDO, P. (1979) Affective consequences of inadequately explaining physiological arousal. *Journal of Personality and Social Psychology*, 37, 970–988.

MARSLAND, D. (1987) *Education and Youth*. London: Falmer.

MARTIN, C.L. (1991) The role of cognition in understanding gender effects. *Advances in Child Development and Behaviour*, 23, 113–149.

MARTIN, G. (1998) Psychology and culture: Two major paradigms. *Psychology Teaching, New Series* (6), 21–23.

MARTIN, P. (1999) Sleep keeps us alert and intelligent. A lack of it can spell disaster. So why aren't we getting enough? *The Sunday Times Magazine*, 17 January, 35–40.

MARVIN, R.S. (1975) Aspects of the pre-school child's changing conception of his mother. Cited in C.G. Morris (1988) *Psychology: An Introduction* (6th edition). Englewood Cliffs, NJ: Prentice-Hall.

MASLACH, C. (1978) Emotional consequences of arousal without reason. In C.E. Izard (Ed.) *Emotions and Psychopathology*. New York: Plenum Publishing Company.

MASLOW, A. (1954) *Motivation and Personality*. New York: Harper & Row.

MASLOW, A. (1968) *Towards a Psychology of Being* (2nd edition). New York: Van Nostrand Reinhold.

MASSARO, D.W. (1989) *Experimental Psychology: An Information Processing Approach*. New York: Harcourt Brace Jovanovich.

MASSON, J. (1988) *Against Therapy: Emotional Tyranny and the Myth of Psychological Healing*. New York: Athaneum.

MASSON, J. (1992) The tyranny of psychotherapy. In W. Dryden & C. Feltham (Eds) *Psychotherapy and its Discontents*. Buckingham: Open University Press.

MATLIN, M. (1989) *Cognition* (2nd edition). Fort Worth, TX: Holt, Rinehart & Winston.

MATTHEWS, G.V.T. (1955) *Bird Navigation*. Cambridge: Cambridge University Press.

MATTHEWS, R. (1997a) Bad news poses health threat to TV audience. *The Sunday Telegraph*, 30 March, 3.

MATTHEWS, R. (1997b) Why being a born loser is all in the mind. *The Sunday Telegraph*, 9 March, 16.

MAUNSELL, J.H.R. & NEWSOME, W.T. (1987) Visual processing in monkey extrastriate cortex. *Annual Review of Neuroscience*, 10, 363–401.

MAURICE, D. (1998) The Von Sallmann Lecture 1996: An opthalmological explanation of REM sleep. *Experimental Eye Research*, 66, 139–145.

MAX, J., SMITH, W., LINDGREN, S., & ROBIN, D. (1995) Case study: Obsessive–compulsive disorder after severe traumatic brain injury in an adolescent. *Journal of the American Academy of Child & Adolescent Psychiatry*, 34, 45–49.

MAYER, J. & MARSHALL, N.B. (1956) Specificity of Gold Thioglucose for ventromedial hypothalamic lesions and obesity. *Nature*, 178, 1399–1400.

MAYKOVICH, M.K. (1975) Correlates of racial prejudice. *Journal of Personality and Social Psychology*, 32, 1014–1020.

MAYLOR, E.A. (1994) Ageing and the retrieval of specialised and general knowledge: Performance of ageing masterminds. *British Journal of Psychology*, 85, 105–114.

McARTHUR, L.A. (1972) The how and why of why: Some determinants and consequences of causal attribution. *Journal of Personality and Social Psychology*, 22, 171–193.

McBURNEY, D.H. & COLLINS, V.B. (1984) *Introduction to Sensation and Perception* (2nd edition). Englewood Cliffs, NJ: Prentice-Hall.

McCALL, R.B., APPLEBAUM, M.I. & HOGARTY, P.S. (1973) Developmental changes in mental test performance. *Monographs for the Society of Research in Child Development*, 38, (3, Whole No. 150).

McCANN, J.J. (1987) Retinex theory and colour constancy. In R.L. Gregory (Ed.) *Oxford Companion to the Mind*. Oxford: Oxford University Press.

McCANNE, T.R. & ANDERSON, J.A. (1987) Emotional responding following manipulation of facial feedback. *Journal of Personality and Social Psychology*, 52, 759–768.

McCAULEY, C. & STITT, C.L. (1978) An individual and quantitative measure of stereotypes. *Journal of Personality and Social Psychology*, 36, 929–940.

McCLELLAND, D.C. (1958) Methods of measuring human motivation. In J.W. Atkinson (Ed.) *Motives in Fantasy, Action and Society*. Princeton, NJ: Van Nostrand.

McCLELLAND, D.C. & ATKINSON, J.W. (1948) The projective expression of need: I. The effect of different intensities of the hunger drive on perception. *Journal of Psychology*, 25, 205–222.

McCRYSTAL, C. (1997) Now you can live forever, or at least for a century. *The Observer*, 15 June, 3.

McDONALD, S. & PEARCE, S. (1996) Clinical insights into pragmatic theory: frontal lobe deficits and sarcasm. *Brain and Language*, 53, 81–104.

McDOUGALL, W. (1908) *An Introduction to Social Psychology*. London: Methuen.

McDOUGLE, C.J., BARR, L.C., GOODMAN, W.K. & PRICE, L.H. (1999) Possible role of neuropeptides in obsessive–compulsive disorder. *Psychoneuroendocrinology*, 24, 1–24.

McFARLAND, D. (1996) *Animal Behaviour* (2nd edition). Harlow: Longman.

McGARRIGLE, J. & DONALSON, M. (1974) Conservation accidents. *Cognition*, 3, 341–350.

McGHEE, P. (1996) Make or break. *Psychology Review*, 2, 27–30.

McGHEE, P.E. (1976) Children's appreciation of humour: A test of the cognitive congruency principle. *Child Development*, 47, 420–426.

McGLONE, F., PARK, A. & ROBERTS, C. (1996) *Relative Values*. Family Policy Studies Centre: BSA.

McGLONE, J. (1980) Sex differences in human brain asymmetry: A critical survey. *Behaviour and Brain Sciences*, 3, 215–227.

McGOVERN, L.P. (1976) Dispositional social anxiety and helping behaviour under three conditions of threat. *Journal of Personality*, 44, 84–97.

McGUFFIN, P., KATZ, R., WATKINS, S. & RUTHERFORD, J. (1996) A hospital-based twin register of heritability of DSM-IV unipolar depression. *Archives of General Psychiatry*, 53, 129–136.

McGUIRE, P.K., SILBERSWEIG, D.A., WRIGHT, L. & MURRAY, R.M. (1995) Abnormal monitoring of inner speech: A physiological basis for auditory hallucinations. *Lancet*, 346, 596–600.

McGUIRE, W.J. (1969) The nature of attitudes and attitude change. In G. Lindzey & E. Aronson (Eds) *Handbook of Social Psychology*, Volume 3 (2nd edition). Reading, MA: Addison-Wesley.

McGURK, H. (1975) *Growing and Changing*. London: Methuen.

McILROY, A.J. (1994) Screen test for children of St. Helena. *The Daily Telegraph*, 19 September, 9.

McILVEEN, R., LONG, M. & CURTIS, A. (1994) *Talking Points in Psychology*. London: Hodder & Stoughton.

McLEOD, P., DRIVER, J., DIENES, Z. & CRISP, J. (1991) Filtering by movement in visual search. *Journal of Experimental Psychology: Human Perception and Performance*, 17, 55–64.

McNALLY, R.J. & STEKETEE, G.S. (1985) The etiology and maintenance of severe animal phobias. *Behaviour Research and Therapy*, 23, 431–435.

McNEIL, T.F., CANTOR-GRAAE, E, NÖRDSTROM, L.G. (1993) Head circumference in 'pre-schizophrenic' and control neonates. *British Journal of Psychiatry*, 162, 517–523.

McNEILL, D. (1970) *The Acquisition of Language*. New York: Harper & Row.

McNEILL, J.E. & WARRINGTON, E.K. (1993) Prosopagnosia: A face-specific disorder. *Quarterly Journal of Experimental Psychology*, 46A, 1–10.

McQUOID, L.M. & GALEF, B.G. (Jr) (1992) Social influences on feeding site selection by Burmese fowl (*Gallus gallus*). *Journal of Comparative Psychology*, 106, 136–141.

MEAD, M. (1935) *Sex and Temperament in Three Primitive Societies*. New York: Dell.

MEADOWS, S. (1993) *The Child as Thinker: The Acquisition and Development of Cognition in Childhood*. London: Routledge.

MEADOWS, S. (1995) Cognitive development. In P.E. Bryant & A.M. Colman (Eds) *Developmental Psychology*. London: Longman.

MEDAWAR, P.B. (1963) *The Art of the Soluble*. Harmondsworth: Penguin.

MEDDIS, R. (1975) *The Sleep Instinct*. London: Routledge, Kegan & Paul.

MEDDIS, R. (1979) The evolution and function of sleep. In D.A. Oakley & H.C. Plotkin (Eds) *Brain, Behaviour and Evolution*. London: Methuen.

MEHLER, J. & DUPOUX, E. (1994) *What Infants Know*. Oxford: Blackwell.

MEILMAN, P.W. (1979) Cross-sectional age changes in ego identity status during adolescence. *Developmental Psychology*, 15, 230–231.

MELHUISH, E.C. (1982) Visual attention to mothers' and strangers' faces and facial contrast in one-month-olds. *Developmental Psychology*, 18, 299–333.

MELTZOFF, A. & MOORE, M. (1983) Newborn infants imitate adult facial gestures. *Child Development*, 54, 702–709.

MELTZOFF, A. & MOORE, M. (1992) Early imitation within a functional framework: The importance of person identity, movement and development. *Infant Behaviour and Development*, 15, 479–505.

MENDEL, G. (1866) Versuche Über Pflanzenhybriden [Experiments in plant hybridisation]. *Verhandlungen des Naturs-forschunden Vereines in Bruenn*, 4, 3–47.

MENZEL, E.W. (1971) Communication about the environment in a group of young chimpanzees. *Folia Primat*, 15, 220–232.

MENZIES, R.G. & CLARKE, J.C. (1993) A comparison of in vivo and vicarious exposure in the treatment of childhood water phobias. *Behaviour Research and Therapy*, 31, 9–15.

MERSKEY, H. (1992) The manufacture of personalities. The production of multiple personality disorder. *British Journal of Psychiatry*, 160, 327–340.

MESSER, D. (1995) Seeing and pulling faces. *The Psychologist*, 8, 77.

MEYER, J.P. & PEPPER, S. (1977) Need compatibility and marital adjustment in young married couples. *Journal of Personality and Social Psychology*, 35, 331–342.

MICHELINI, R.L. & SNODGRASS, S.R. (1980) Defendant characteristics and juridic decisions. *Journal of Research in Personality*, 14, 340–350.

MIDDLETON, W., MOYLAN, A., RAPHAEL, B., BURNETT, P. & MARTINEK, N. (1993) An international perspective on bereavement-related concepts. *Australian & New Zealand Journal of Psychiatry*, 27, 457–463.

MIDGLEY, C. (1998) TV violence has little impact on children, study finds. *The Times*, 12 January, 5.

MIKULA, G. (1994) Perspective-related defferences in interpretations of injustice by victims and victimizers: A test with close relationships. In M.J. Lerner & G. Mikula (Eds) *Injustice in Close Relationships: Entitlement and the Affectional Bond*. New York: Plenum.

MILAVSKY, J.R., KESSLER, R.C., STIPP, H. & RUBENS, W.S. (1982) *Television and Aggression: A Panel Study*. New York: Academic Press.

MILGRAM, S. (1992) *The Individual in a Social World* (2nd edition). New York: McGraw-Hill.

MILLER, D.T. & ROSS, M. (1975) Self-serving biases in the attribution of causality: Fact or fiction? *Psychological Bulletin*, 82, 213–225.

MILLER, E. & MORRIS, R. (1993) *The Psychology of Dementia*. Chichester: Wiley.

MILLER, G.A. (1962) *Psychology: The Science of Mental Life*. Harmondsworth: Penguin.

MILLER, G.A. (1978) The acquisition of word meaning. *Child Development*, 49, 999–1004.

MILLER, G.A. & McNEILL, D. (1969) Psycholinguistics. In G. Lindzey & E. Aronson (Eds) *The Handbook of Social Psychology*, Volume 3. Reading, MA: Addison-Wesley.

MILLER, G.F. (1998) How mate choice shaped human nature: A review of sexual selection and human evolution. In C. Crawford & D. Krebs (Eds) *Handbook of Evolutionary Psychology*. Mahwah, NJ: Erlbaum.

MILLER, J.G. (1984) Culture and the development of everyday social explanation. *Journal of Personality and Social Psychology*, 46, 961–978.

MILLER, L. (1987) The emotional brain. *Psychology Today*, 22, 35–42.

MILLER, N.E. (1941) The frustration–aggression hypothesis. *Psychological Review*, 48, 337–342

MILLER, N.E. (1995) Clinical-experimental interactions in the development of neuroscience: A primer for non-specialists and lessons for young scientists. *American Psychologist*, 50, 901–911.

MILLER, W.R., ROSELLINI, R.A. & SELIGMAN, M.E.P. (1977) Learned helplessness and depression. In J.D. Maser & M.E.P. Seligman (Eds) *Psychopathology: Experimental Models*. San Francisco: W.H. Freeman.

MILLS, J. & CLARK, M.S. (1980) 'Exchange in communal relationships.' (Unpublished manuscript.)

MILNER, B. (1971) Interhemispheric differences in the localisation of psychological processes in man. *British Medical Bulletin*, 27, 272–277.

MILNER, B., CORKIN, S. & TEUBER, H. (1968) Further analysis of the hippocampal amnesic syndrome: 14-year follow-up study of H.M.. *Neuropsychologia*, 6, 215–234.

MILNER, D. (1996) Children and racism: Beyond the value of the dolls. In W.P. Robinson (Ed.) *Social Groups and Identities*. Oxford: Butterworth/Heineman.

MILNER, D. (1997) Racism and childhood identity. *The Psychologist*, 10, 123–125.

MILUNSKY, J., HUANG, X.L., WYANDT, H.E. & MILUNSKY, A. (1999) Schizophrenia susceptibility gene locus at Xp22.3. *Clinical Genetics*, 55, 455–460.

MIN, S.K., AN, S.K., JON, D.I. & LEE, J.D. (1999) Positive and negative symptoms and regional cerebral perfusion in antipsychotic-naïve schizophrenic patients: A high resolution SPECT study. *Psychiatry Research*, 90, 159–168.

MINARD, R.D. (1952) Race relations in the Pocohontas coalfield. *Journal of Social Issues*, 8, 29–44.

MINDUS, P., EDMAN, G. & ANDREEWITCH, S. (1999) A prospective, long-term study of personality traits in patients with intractable obsessional illness treated by capsulotomy. *Acta Psychiatria Scandinavia*, 99, 40–50.

MINORS, D. (1997) Melatonin – hormone of darkness. *Biological Sciences Review*, 10, 39–41.

MISCHEL, W. (1973) Toward a cognitive social learning reconceptualisation of personality. *Psychological Review*, 80, 252–283.

MISCHEL, W. & MISCHEL, H.N. (1976) A cognitive social learning approach to morality and self-regulation. In T. Lickona (Ed.) *Moral Development and Behaviour: Theory, Research and Social Issues*. New York: Holt, Rinehart & Winston.

MITA, T.H., DERMER, M. & KNIGHT, J. (1977) Reversed facial images and the mere exposure hypothesis. *Journal of Personality and Social Psychology*, 35, 597–601.

MITCHELL, J. (1974) *Psychoanalysis and Feminism*. Harmondsworth: Penguin.

MITCHELL, S.L. (1816) A double consciousness, or a duality of person in the same individual. *Medical Repository* (New Series), 3, 185–186.

MITCHELL, T.R. & LARSON, J.B. Jnr. (1987) *People in Organisations: An Introduction to Organisational Behaviour* (3rd edition). New York: McGraw-Hill.

MOERK, E.L. (1989) The LAD was a lady, and the tasks were ill-defined. *Developmental Review*, 9, 21–57.

MOERK, E.L. & MOERK, C. (1979) Quotations, imitations and generalisations: Factual and methodological analyses. *International Journal of Behavioural Development*, 2, 43–72.

MOGHADDAM, F.M. (1987) Psychology in the three worlds: As reflected by the crisis in social psychology and the move towards indigenous third world psychology. *American Psychologist*, 42, 912–920.

MOGHADDAM, F.M. (1998) *Social Psychology: Exploring Universals Across Cultures*. New York: W.H. Freeman & Co.

MOGHADDAM, F.M. & STUDER, C. (1997) Cross-cultural psychology: The frustrated gladfly's promises, potentialities and failures. In D. Fox & D. Prilleltensky (Eds) *Critical Psychology: An Introduction*. London: Sage.

MOGHADDAM, F.M., TAYLOR, D.M. & WRIGHT, S.C. (1993) *Social Psychology in Cross-cultural Perspective*. New York: W.H. Freeman & Co.

MOLNAR, R.E. (1977) Analogies in the evolution of combat and display structures in ornithopods and ungulates. *Evolutionary Theory*, 3, 165–190.

MONEY, J. (1974) Prenatal hormones and postnatal socialisation in gender identity differentiation. In J.K. Cole & R. Dienstbier (Eds) *Nebraska Symposium on Motivation*. Lincoln: University of Nebraska Press.

MONEY, J. & EHRHARDT, A. (1972) *Man and Woman, Boy and Girl*. Baltimore, MD: The Johns Hopkins University Press.

MONK, T. & FOLKARD, S. (1992) *Making Shift-work Tolerable*. Basingstoke: Taylor & Francis.

MONTAGU, A. (1961) Neonatal and infant immaturity in man. *Journal of the American Medical Association*, 178, 56–57.

MONTGOMERY, P. (1993) Paid and unpaid work. In J. Kremer & P. Montgomery *Women's Working Lives*. Belfast: HMSO.

MOORE, B.R. (1992) Avian imitation and a new form of mimicry: Tracing the evolution of complex learning. *Behavior*, 122, 231–263.

MOORE, C. & FRYE, D. (1986) The effect of the experimenter's intention on the child's understanding of conservation. *Cognition*, 22, 283–298.

MOORE-EDE, M.C. (1993) *The 24 Hour Society*. London: Piatkus.

MORAY, N. (1959) Attention in dichotic listening: Affective cues and the influence of instructions. *Quarterly Journal of Experimental Psychology*, 11, 56–60.

MOREA, P. (1990) *Personality: An Introduction to the Theories of Psychology*. Harmondsworth: Penguin.

MORGAN, E. (1995) Measuring time with a biological clock. *Biological Sciences Review*, 7, 2–5.

MORGAN, M.J. (1969) Estimates of length in a modified Müller-Lyer figure. *American Journal of Psychology*, 82, 380–384.

MORLAND, J. (1970) A comparison of race awareness in northern and southern children. In M. Goldschmid (Ed.) *Black Americans and White Racism*. Monterey, CA: Brooks/Cole.

MORRIS, C.G. (1988) *Psychology: An Introduction* (6th edition). London: Prentice-Hall.

MORRIS, R.G.M., GARRUD, P., RAWLINS, J.N.P. & O'KEEFE, J. (1982) Place navigation impaired rats with hippocampal lesions. *Nature*, 297, 681–683.

MORUZZI, G. & MAGOUN, H.W. (1949) Reticular formation and activation of the EEG. *Electroencephalography and Clinical Neurophysiology*, 1, 455–473.

MOSCOVICI, S. (1961) *La Psychoanalyse: Son Image et Son Public*. Paris: Presses Universitaires de France.

MOSCOVICI, S. (1976) *La Psychoanalyse: Son Image et Son Public* (2nd edition). Paris: Presses Universitaires de France.

MOSCOVICI, S. (1981) On social representations. In J.P. Forgas (Ed.) *Social Cognition: Perspectives on Everyday Understanding*. London: Academic Press.

MOSCOVICI, S. (1984) The phenomenon of social representations. In R.M. Farr & S. Moscovici (Eds) *Social Representations*. Cambridge: Cambridge University Press.

MOSCOVICI, S. (1998) Social consciousness and its history. *Culture and Psychology*, 4, 411–429.

MOSCOVICI, S. & HEWSTONE, M. (1983) Social representations and social explanations: From the 'naive' to the 'amateur' scientist. In M. Hewstone (Ed.) *Attribution Theory: Social and Functional Extensions*. Oxford: Blackwell.

MOWRER, O.H. (1947) On the dual nature of learning – a reinterpretation of 'conditioning' and 'problem-solving'. *Harvard Educational Review*, 17, 102–148.

MOWRER, O.H. (1960) *Learning Theory and Behaviour*. New York: John Wiley.

MOYER, K.E. (1976) *The Psychobiology of Aggression*. New York: Harper & Row.

MUKERJEE, M. (1997) Trends in animal research. *Scientific American*, 63, February.

MUKHAMETOV, L.M. (1984) Sleep in marine mammals. In A. Borbely & J. Valatx (Eds) *Sleep Mechanisms*. Springer: Munich.

MULDOON, O. & REILLY, J. (1998) Biology. In K. Trew & J. Kremer (Eds) *Gender & Psychology*. London: Arnold.

MULLEN, B. & JOHNSON, C. (1990) Distinctiveness-based illusory correlations and stereotyping: A meta-analytic integration. *British Journal of Social Psychology*, 29, 11–28.

MULLER, H.J. & MAXWELL, J. (1994) Perceptual integration of motion and form information: Is the movement filter involved in form discrimination? *Journal of Experimental Psychology: Human Perception and Performance*, 20, 397–420.

MUMMENDEY, A. (1996) Aggressive behaviour. In M. Hewstone, W. Stroebe & G.M. Stephenson (Eds) *Introduction to Social Psychology* (2nd edition). Oxford: Blackwell.

MUMMENDEY, A. & OTTEN, S. (1989) Perspective specific differences in the segmentation and evaluation of aggressive interaction sequences. *European Journal of Social Psychology*, 19, 23–40.

MUNDY-CASTLE, A.C. & NELSON, G.K. (1962) A neuropsychological study of the Kuysma forest workers. *Psychologia Africana*, 9, 240–272.

MUNROE, R.H., SHIMMIN, H.S. & MUNROE, R.L. (1984) Gender understanding and sex-role preference in four cultures. *Developmental Psychology*, 20, 673–682.

MUNSINGER, H. (1975) The adopted child's IQ: A critical review. *Psychological Bulletin*, 82, 623–659.

MURPHY, R.G. (1989) *The development of magnetic compass orientation in children*. Paper presented at the Royal Institute of Navigation Conference, 1989.

MURRAY, H.A. (1938) *Explorations in Personality*. New York: Oxford University Press.

MURRAY, I. (1999) Einstein's mind was the shape of a genius. *The Times*, 18 June, 7.

MURRAY, I & WHITWORTH, D. (1999) TV a threat to toddlers, doctors say. *The Times*, 5 August, 1.

MURRAY, J. (1995) *Prevention of Anxiety and Depression in Vulnerable Groups*. London: Gaskell.

MURRAY, R., OON, M., RODNIGHT, R., BIRLEY, J. & SMITH, A. (1979) Increased excretion of dimethyltryptamine and certain features of psychosis. *Archives of General Psychiatry*, 36, 644–649.

MURSTEIN, B.I. (1972) Physical attractiveness and marital choice. *Journal of Personality and Social Psychology*, 22, 8–12.

MURSTEIN, B.I. (1976) The stimulus-value-role theory of marital choice. In H. Grunebaum & J. Christ (Eds) *Contemporary Marriage: Structures, Dynamics and Therapy*. Boston: Little, Brown.

MURSTEIN, B.I. (1987) A clarification and extension of the SVR theory of dyadic parting. *Journal of Marriage and the Family*, 49, 929–933.

MURSTEIN, B.I. & MacDONALD, M.G. (1983) The relation of 'exchange orientation' and 'commitment' scales to marriage adjustment. *International Journal of Psychology*, 18, 297–311.

MURSTEIN, B.I., MacDONALD, M.G. & CERETO, M. (1977) A theory of the effect of exchange orientation on marriage and friendship. *Journal of Marriage and the Family*, 39, 543–548.

MYERS, D.G. (1990) *Exploring Psychology*. New York: Worth.

MYERS, D.G. (1994) *Exploring Social Psychology*. New York: McGraw-Hill.

MYERS, D.G. (1998) *Psychology* (5th edition). New York: Worth.

NAHEMOW, L. & LAWTON, M.P. (1975) Similarity and propinquity in a friendship formation. *Journal of Personality and Social Psychology*, 32, 205–213.

NAPOLITAN, D.A. & GOETHALS, G.R. (1979) The attribution of friendliness. *Journal of Experimental Social Psychology*, 15, 105–113.

NATHANS, J. (1989) The genes for colour vision. *Scientific American*, 226, 42–49.

NATIONAL INSTITUTE OF MENTAL HEALTH (1982) *Television and Behaviour: Ten Years of Scientific Progress and Implications for the Eighties*, Volume 1. Washington, DC: US Government Printing Office.

NAUMANN, R., FELBER, W., HEILEMANN, H. & REUSTER, T. (1999) Olanzapine-induced agranulocytosis. *Lancet*, 354, 566-567.

NAVON, D. & GOPHER, D. (1979) On the economy of the human processing system. *Psychological Review*, 86, 214–255.

NAVON, D. (1977) Forest before trees: The precedence of global features in visual perception. *Cognitive Psychology*, 9, 353–383.

NAVON, D. (1984) Resources – A theoretical soup stone? *Psychological Review*, 91, 216–234.

NEBES, R.D. (1974) Hemispheric specialisation in commissurotomised man. *Psychological Bulletin*, 81, 1–14.

NEISSER, U. & BECKLEN, R. (1975) Selective looking: Attending to visually specified events. *Cognitive Psychology*, 7, 480–494.

NEISSER, U. (1967) *Cognitive Psychology*. New York: Appleton Century Crofts.

NEISSER, U. (1976) *Cognition and Reality*. San Francisco, CA: W.H. Freeman.

NELSON, K. (1973) Structure and strategy in learning to talk. *Monographs of the Society for Research in Child Development*, 38, 149.

NELSON, K. (1977) Facilitating children's syntax acquisition. *Developmental Psychology*, 13, 101–107.

NELSON, S.A. (1980) Factors influencing young children's use of motives and outcomes as moral criteria. *Child Development*, 51, 823–829.

NEMEROFF, C.B. (1998) The neurobiology of depression. *Scientific American*, 278, 28–35.

NESSE, R.M. (1987) An evolutionary perspective on panic disorder and agoraphobia. *Ethology & Sociobiology*, 8, 73–84.

NESSE, R.M. & WILLIAMS, G.C. (1996) *Evolution and Healing*. London: Phoenix.

NEUGARTEN, B.L. (1975) The future of the young-old. *The Gerontologist*, 15, 4–9.

NEUGARTEN, B.L. & NEUGARTEN, D.A. (1987) The changing meanings of age. *Psychology Today*, 21, 29–33.

NEWCOMB, T.M. (1943) *Personality and Social Change*. New York: Holt, Rinehart & Winston.

NEWCOMB, T.M. (1953) An approach to the study of communication. *Psychological Review*, 60, 393–404.

NEWCOMB, T.M. (1961) *The Acquaintanceship Process*. New York: Holt, Rinehart & Winston.

NEWCOMB, T.M. (1978) The acquaintance process: Looking mainly backwards. *Journal of Personality and Social Psychology*, 36, 1075–1083.

NEWELL, A. & SIMON, H.A. (1972) *Human Problem-Solving*. Englewood Cliffs, NJ: Prentice-Hall.

NEWELL, A., SHAW, J.C. & SIMON, H.A. (1958) Elements of a theory of human problem-solving. *Psychological Review*, 65, 151–166.

NEWMAN, H.H., FREMAN, F.N. & HOLZINGER, K.J. (1937) *Twins: A Study of Heredity and the Environment*. Chicago, ILL: University of Chicago Press.

NEWSON, E. (1994) Video violence and the protection of children. *Psychology Review*, 1, 2–6.

NEWSTEAD, S. (1995) Language and thought: The Whorfian hypothesis. *Psychology Review*, 1, 5–7.

NICHOLSON, J. (1977) *Habits*. London: Macmillan

NICHOLSON, J. (1993) *Men and Women: How Different Are They?* (2nd edition). Oxford: Oxford University Press.

NICHOLSON, J.M., FERGUSSON, D.M. & HORWOOD, L.J. (1999) Effects on later adjustment of living in a stepfamily during childhood and adolescence. *Journal of Child Psychology & Psychiatry*, 40 (3), 405–416.

NICOL, C.J. & POPE, S.J. (1999) The effects of demonstrator social status and prior foraging success on social learning in laying hens. *Animal Behaviour*, 57, 163–171.

NICOLSON, P. (1995) Feminism and psychology. In J.A.Smith, R. Harre, & L. Van Langenhove (Eds) *Rethinking Psychology*. London: Sage.

NICOLSON, R., MALASPINA, D., GIEDD, J.N., HAMBURGER, S., LENANE, M., BEDWELL, J., FERNANDEZ, T., BERMAN, A., SUSSER, E. & RAPOPORT, J.L. (1999) Obstetrical complications and childhood-onset schizophrenia. *American Journal of Psychiatry*, 156, 1650–1652.

NILSSON, O.G., SHAPIRO, M.L. GAGE, F.H., OLTON, D.S. & BJORKLUND, A. (1987) Spatial learning and memory following fimbria–fornix transection and grafting of fetal septal neurons to the hippocampus. *Experimental Brain Research*, 67, 195–215.

NISBET, I.C.T. (1977) Courtship feeding and clutch size in common terns, *Sterna hirundo*. In B. Stonehouse & C.M. Perrins (Eds), *Evolutionary Ecology*. London: Macmillan.

NISBETT, R.E. (1972) Hunger, obesity and the ventromedial hypothalamus. *Psychological Review*, 79, 433–453.

NORMAN, D.A. (1968) Toward a theory of memory and attention. *Psychological Review*, 75, 522–536.

NORMAN, D.A. (1969) Memory while shadowing. *Quarterly Journal of Experimental Psychology*, 21, 85–93.

NORMAN, D.A. (1976) *Memory and Attention* (2nd edition). Chichester: Wiley.

NORMAN, D.A. (1981) Categorisation of action slips. *Psychological Review*, 88, 1–15.

NORMAN, D.A. & BOBROW, D.G. (1975) On data-limited and resource-limited processes. *Cognitive Psychology*, 7, 44–64.

NORMAN, D.A. & SHALLICE, T. (1986) Attention to action: Willed and automatic control of behaviour. In R.J. Davidson, G.E. Schwartz & D. Shapiro (Eds) *The Design of Everyday Things*. New York: Doubleday.

NORMAN, R.M.G. & MALLA, A.K. (1993) Stressful life events and schizophrenia I: A review of the research. *British Journal of Psychiatry*, 162, 161–166.

NORRIS, K.S. (1967) Some observations on the migration and orientation of marine mammals. In R.M. Storm (Ed.) *Animal Orientation and Navigation*. Corvallis: Oregon State University Press, pp.101–125.

NORTON, C. (1999) Maternal instinct 'is extinct for one woman in five'. *The Independent*, 27 October, 7.

NORTON, C. & HERBERT, I. (1998) How a dead man provoked an ethical dilemma that has convulsed the NHS. *The Independent*, 8 July, 3.

NUECHTERLEIN, K.H. & DAWSON, M.E. (1984) A heuristic vulnerability/stress model of schizophrenic episodes. *Schizophrenia Bulletin*, 10, 300–311.

NURSING TIMES (1996) *Nursing Times*, 92 (5), 27.

NUTTALL, N. (1996) Missing ingredient may control gluttons' appetite. *The Times*, 4 January, 3.

O'BRIEN, M., HUSTON, A.C. & RISLEY, T. (1983) Sex-typed play of toddlers in a day-care centre. *Journal of Applied Developmental Psychology*, 4, 1–9.

O'CALLAGHAN, E., SHAM, P.C. & TAKEI, N. (1993) Schizophrenia after prenatal exposure to 1957 A2 influenza epidemic. *The Lancet*, 337, 1248–1250.

O'CALLAGHAN, E., SHAM, P.C., TAKEI, N., MURRAY, G.K., GLOVER, G., HARE, E.H. & MURRAY, R.M. (1994) The relationship of schizophrenic births to sixteen infectious diseases. *British Journal of Psychiatry*, 165, 353–356.

O'CALLAGHAN, E., SHAM, P.C., TAKEI, N., MURRAY, G.K., HARE, E.H. & MURRAY, R.M. (1991) Schizophrenia following prenatal exposure to influenza epidemics between 1939 and 1960. *British Journal of Psychiatry*, 160, 461–466.

O'KEEFE, J. & DOSTROVSKY, T. (1971) The hippocampus as a spatial map: Preliminary evidence from unit activity in the freely moving rat. *Brain Research*, 34, 171–175.

O'LEARY, K.D. & WILSON, G.T. (1975) *Behaviour Therapy: Application and Outcome*. Englewood Cliffs, NJ: Prentice-Hall.

O'NEILL, S. (1996) A little kindness goes a long way. *The Daily Telegraph*, 31 August, 1.

O'NEILL, S. (1999) Coroner calls for warning note on Prozac packets. *The Daily Telegraph*, 3 November, 6.

OAKES, P.J., HASLAM, S.A. & TURNER, J.C. (1994) *Stereotyping and Social Reality*. Oxford: Blackwell.

OAKHILL, J.V. (1984) Why children have difficulty reasoning with three-term series problems. *British Journal of Developmental Psychology*, 2, 223–230.

OAKLEY, D.A. (1983) The varieties of memory: A phylogenetic approach. In A.R. Mayes (Ed.) *Memory in Humans and Animals*. Wokingham: Van Nostrand.

OATLEY, K. (1984) *Selves in Relation: An Introduction to Psychotherapy and Groups*. London: Methuen.

OCHSE, R. & PLUG, C. (1986) Cross-cultural investigation of the validity of Erikson's theory of personality development. *Journal of Personality & Social Psychology*. 50, 1240–1252.

OFFER, D., OSTROV, E., HOWARD, K.I. & ATKINSON, R. (1988) *The Teenage World: Adolescents' Self-Image in Ten Countries*. New York: Plenum Press.

OGILVIE, A.D., BATTERSBY, S., BUBB, V.J., FINK, G., HARMAR, A.J., GOODWIN, G.M. & SMITH, C.A.D. (1996) Polymorphism in the serotonin transporter gene associated with susceptibility to major depression. *The Lancet*, 347, 731–733.

OHTSUKA, T. (1985) Relation of spectral types to oil droplets in cones of turtle retina. *Science*, 229, 874–877.

OKASHA, A., SADEK, A., AL-HADDAD, M.K. & ABDEL,–MAWGOUD, M. (1993) Diagnostic agreement in psychiatry: A comparative study between ICD-9, ICD-10 and DSM-III-R. *British Journal of Psychiatry*, 162, 621–626.

OLDS, J. & MILNER, P. (1954) Positive reinforcement produced by electrical stimulation of the septal area and other regions of the rat brain. *Journal of Comparative & Physiological Psychology*, 47, 419–427.

OLTON, D.S. & SAMUELSON, R.J. (1976) Rememberances of places passed: Spatial memory in rats. *Journal of Experimental Psychology: Animal Processes*, 2, 96–116.

ONO, T., SQUIRE, L.R., RAICHLE, M.E., PERRETT, D.I. & FUKUDA, M. (Eds) *Brain Mechanisms of Perception and Memory. From Neurone to Behaviour.* Oxford: Oxford University Press.ORNE, M.T. (1962) On the social psychology of the psychological experiment: with particular reference to demand characteristics and their implications. *American Psychologist*, 17, 776–783.

ORNSTEIN, R. (1986) *The Psychology of Consciousness* (2nd edition, revised). Harmondsworth: Penguin.

ORUC, L., CERIC, I. & LOGA, S. (1998) Genetics of mood disorders: An overview. Part One. *Medical Archives,* 52, 107–112.

OSMOND, H. & SMYTHIES, J. (1953) Schizophrenia: A new approach. *The Journal of Mental Science*, 98, 309–315.

ÖST, L.-G., BRANDBERG, M. & ALM, T. (1997) One versus five sessions of exposure in the treatment of flying phobia. *Behaviour Research and Therapy*, 35, 987–996.

OSWALD, I. (1966) *Sleep*. Harmondsworth: Penguin.

OSWALD, I. (1974) *Sleep* (2nd edition). Harmondsworth: Penguin.

OSWALD, I. (1980) Sleep as a restorative process: Human clues. *Progress in Brain Research*, 53, 279–288.

OWUSU-BEMPAH, K. & HOWITT, D. (1999) Even their soul is defective. *The Psychologist*, 12, 126–130.

OYEBODE, F., JAMIESON, R., MULLANEY, J. & DAVISON, K. (1986) Koro – a psychophysiological dysfunction? *British Journal of Psychiatry*, 148, 212–214.

PACKER, C. & PUSEY, A.E. (1982) Co-operation and competition within coalitions of lions: Kin selection or game theory? *Nature*, 296, 740–742.

PAGE, D., MOSHER, R., SIMPSON, E., FISHER, E., MARDON, G., POLLOCK, J., McGILLIVRAY, B., CHAPPELLE, A. & BROWN, L. (1987) The sex-determining region of the human Y-chromosome encodes a finger protein. *Cell*, 51, 1091–1104.

PAGEL, M. (1995) Speaking your mind. *Times Higher*, 7 July, 17–18.

PAGEL, M. (1997) Desperately concealing father: A theory of parent–infant resemblance. *Animal Behaviour*, 53, 973–981.

PALERMO, D.S. (1971) Is a scientific revolution taking place in psychology? *Psychological Review*, 76, 241–263.

PALLANTI, S., QUERCIOLI, L. & PAZZAGLI, A. (1999) Effects of clozapine on awareness of illness and cognition in schizophrenia. *Psychiatry Research*, 86, 239–249.

PALOSAARI, U.K. & ARO, H.M. (1995) Parental divorce, self-esteem and depression: An intimate relationship as a protective factor in young adulthood. *Journal of Affective Disorders*, 35, 91–96.

PAPEZ, J.W. (1937) A proposed mechanism of emotion. *Archives of Neurology and Psychiatry*, 38, 725–743.

PARFIT, D. (1987) Divided minds and the nature of persons. In C. Blakemore & S. Greenfield (Eds) *Mindwaves*. Oxford: Blackwell.

PARKE, R.D., BERKOWITZ, L., LEYENS, J.P., WEST, S.G. & SEBASTIAN, R.J. (1977) Some effects of violent and non-violent movies on the behaviour of juvenile delinquents. In L. Berkowitz (Ed.) *Advances in Experimental Social Psychology*, Volume 10. New York: Academic Press.

PARKER, G. (1984) The measurement of pathological parental style and its relevance to psychiatric disorder. *Social Psychiatry*, 19, 75–81.

PARKER, G. (1992) Early environment. In E.S. Paykel (Ed.), *Handbook of Affective Disorders*. New York: Guildford.

PARKER, G., MAHENDRAN, R., KOH, E.S. & MACHIN, D. (2000) Season birth in schizophrenia: No latitude at the equator. *British Journal of Psychiatry*, 176, 68–70.

PARKES, C.M. (1995) Attachment and bereavement. In T. Lundin (Ed.) *Grief and Bereavement: Proceedings from the Fourth International Conference on Grief and Bereavement in Contemporary Society, Stockholm, 1994.* Stockholm: Swedish Association for Mental Health.

PARKES, C.M. & WEISS, R.S. (1983) *Recovery From Bereavement*. New York: Basic Books.

PARKS, M.R. & FLOYD, K. (1996) Making friends in cyberspace. *Journal of Communication*, 46, 80–97.

PARTONEN, T. & LONNQVIST, J. (1998) Seasonal affective disorder. *Lancet*, 352, 1369–1374.

PASCUAL-LEONE, J. (1980) Constructive problems for constructive theories: The current relevance of Piaget's work and a critique of information-processing simulation psychology. In R.H. Kluwe & H. Spads (Eds) *Developmental Models of Thinking*. New York: Academic Press.

PASSINGHAM, R.E. (1982) *The Human Primate*. New York: W.H. Freeman.

PATON, D. (1992) Disaster research: The Scottish dimension. *The Psychologist*, 5, 535–538.

PATRICK, G.T.W. & GILBERT, J.A. (1898) On the effects of loss of sleep. The *Psychological Review*, 3, 469–483.

PATTERSON, F.G. (1980) Innovative uses of language by a gorilla: A case study. In K. Nelson (Ed.) *Children's Language* (Volume 2) New York: Gardner Press.

PATTERSON, F.G. & LINDEN, E. (1981) *The Education of Koko*. New York: Holt, Rinehart & Winston.

PAULS, D.L. & ALSOBROOK, J.P. (1999) The inheritance of obsessive–compulsive disorder. *Child and Adolescent Psychiatric Clinics of North America*, 8, 481–496.

PAVLOV, I.P. (1927) *Conditioned Reflexes*. Oxford: Oxford University Press.

PEARCE, J.M. (1997) *Animal Learning and Cognition: An Introduction.* Hove: Psychology Press.

PENFIELD, W. (1947) Some observations on the cerebral cortex of man. *Proceedings of the Royal Society*, 134, 349.

PENFIELD, W. & ROBERTS, L. (1959) *Speech and Brain Mechanisms*. Princeton: Princeton University Press.

PENNINGTON, D.C., GILLEN, K. & HILL, P. (1999) *Social Psychology*. London: Arnold.

PENROD, S. (1983) *Social Psychology*. Englewood Cliffs, NJ: Prentice-Hall.

PENROSE, R. (1990) *The Emperor's New Mind*. Oxford: Oxford University Press.

PEPLAU, L.A. (1981) What homosexuals want in relationships. *Psychology Today*, 15 (March), 28–38.

PEPLAU, L.A. (1982) Research on homosexual couples: An overview. *Journal of Homosexuality*, 8, 3–8.

PEPLAU, L.A. (1991) Lesbian and gay relationships. In J.C. Gonsiorek & J.D. Weinrich (Eds) *Homosexuality: Research Implications for Public Policy*. London: Sage.

PEPPERBERG, I.M. (1983) Cognition in the African grey parrot: preliminary evidence for auditory/vocal comprehension of class concept. *Animal Learning & Behaviour*, 11, 179–185.

PERDECK, A.C. (1958) Two types of orientation in migratory starlings, *Sturnus vulgaris L.*, and chaffinches, *Fringilla coelebs L.*, as revealed by displacement experiments. *Ardea*, 46, 1–37.

PEREZ, S.M, TAYLOR, O.R. & LANDER, R . (1997) A sun compass in Monarch butterflies. *Nature*, 387(6628), 29.

PERLBERG, M. (1979) Trauma at Tenerife: The psychic aftershocks of a jet disaster. *Human Behaviour*, 49–50.

PERRET, D.J., MAY, K.A. & YOSHIKAWA, S. (1994) Facial shape and judgements of female attractiveness. *Nature*, 368, 239–242.

PERRY, D.G. & BUSSEY, K. (1979) The social learning theory of sex differences: Imitation is alive and well. *Journal of Personality and Social Psychology*, 37, 1699–1712.

PETERS, L., SLADE, T & ANDREWS, G. (1999) A comparison of ICD-10 and DSM-IV criteria for post traumatic stress disorder. *Journal of Traumatic Stress*, 12, 335–343.

PETERSEN, A.C. & CROCKETT, L. (1985) Pubertal timing and grade effects on adjustment. *Journal of Youth & Adolescence*, 14, 191–206.

PETERSEN, A.C., SARIGIANI, P.A. & KENNEDY, R.E. (1991) Adolescent depression: Why more girls? *Journal of Youth & Adolescence*, 20, 247–271.

PETERSON, C. (1993) Helpless behaviour. *Behaviour Research & Therapy*, 31, 289–295.

PETITTO, L.A. (1988) "Language" in the prelinguistic child. In F.S. Kessell (Ed.) *The Development of Language and Language Researchers: Essays in Honour of Roger Brown*. Hillsdale, NJ: Erlbaum.

PETTIGREW, T.F. (1958) Personality and sociocultural factors in intergroup attitudes: A cross-national comparison. *Journal of Conflict Resolution*, 2, 29–42.

PHILLIPS, D.P. (1986) National experiments on the effects of mass media violence on fatal aggression: Strengths and weaknesses of a new approach. In L. Berkowitz (Ed.) *Advances in Experimental Social Psychology*, Volume 19. New York: Academic Press.

PHILLIPS, J.L. (1969) *The Origins of Intellect: Piaget's Theory*. San Francisco: W.H. Freeman.

PIAGET, J. (1932) *The Moral Judgement of the Child*. London: Routledge & Kegan Paul.

PIAGET, J. (1950) *The Psychology of Intelligence*. London: Routledge & Kegan Paul.

PIAGET, J. (1952) *The Child's Conception of Number*. London: Routledge & Kegan Paul.

PIAGET, J. (1970) Piaget's theory. In P.H. Mussen (Ed.) *Carmichael's Manual of Child Psychology* (3rd edition), Volume 1. New York: Wiley.

PIAGET, J. (1973) *The Child's Conception of the World*. London: Paladin.

PIAGET, J. & INHELDER, B. (1956) *The Psychology of the Child*. London: Routledge & Kegan Paul.

PIAGET, J. & INHELDER, B. (1969) *The Psychology of the Child*. London: Routledge & Kegan Paul.

PIAGET, J. & SZEMINSKA, A. (1952) *The Child's Conception of Number*. London: Routledge & Kegan Paul.

PIKE, A. & PLOMIN, R. (1999) Genetics and development. In D. Messer & S. Millar (Eds) *Exploring Developmental Psychology: From Infancy to Adolescence*. London: Arnold.

PIKE, K.L. (1954) Emic and etic standpoints for the description of behaviour. In K.L. Pike (Ed.) *Language in Relation to a Unified Theory of the Structure of Human Behaviour* (Prelim. Edition). Glendale, CA: Summer Institute of Linguistics.

PILIAVIN, I.M., RODIN, J. & PILIAVIN, J.A. (1969) Good Samaritanism: An underground phenomenon? *Journal of Personality and Social Psychology*, 13, 289–299.

PILIAVIN, J.A. & PILIAVIN, I.M. (1972) Effects of blood on reactions to a victim. *Journal of Personality and Social Psychology*, 23, 353–362.

PILIAVIN, J.A., DOVIDIO, J.F., GAERTNER, S.L. & CLARK, R.D. (1981) *Emergency Intervention*. New York: Academic Press.

PINE, K. (1999) Theories of cognitive development. In D. Messer & S. Millar (Eds) *Exploring Developmental Psychology: From Infancy to Adolescence*. London: Arnold.

PINEL, J.P.J. (1993) *Biopsychology* (2nd edition). Boston: Allyn & Bacon.

PINEO, P.C. (1961) Disenchantment in the later years of marriage. *Journal of Marriage and Family Living*, 23, 3–11.

PINKER, S. (1994) *The Language Instinct: How the Mind Creates Language*. New York: Morrow.

PINKER, S. (1997) *How the Mind Works*. New York: Norton.

PLECK, J.H. (1999) Balancing Work and Family. *Scientific American Presents*, 10 (2), 38–43.

PLOMIN, R. (1988) The nature and nurture of cognitive abilities. In R.J. Sternberg (Ed.) *Advances in the Psychology of Human Intelligence*, Volume 4. Hillsdale, NJ: Erlbaum.

PLOMIN, R. (1994) *Genetics and Experience: The Interplay Between Nature and Nurture*. Thousand Oaks, CA: Sage.

PLOMIN, R. (1995) Genetics and children's experiences in the family. *Journal of Child Psychology & Psychiatry*, 36, 33–68.

PLOMIN, R. (1996) Nature and Nurture. In M.R. Merrens & G.C. Brannigan (Eds) *The Developmental Psychologists: Research Adventures Across the Life Span*. New York: McGraw-Hill.

PLOMIN, R. & DeFRIES, J.C. (1980) Genetics and intelligence: Recent data. *Intelligence*, 4, 15–24.

PLOMIN, R. & DeFRIES, J.C. (1998) The genetics of cognitive abilities and disabilities. *Scientific American*, May, 62–69.

PLOMIN, R., DeFRIES, J.C. & LOEHLIN, J.C. (1977) Genotype–environment interaction and correlation in the analysis of human behaviour. *Psychological Bulletin*, 84, 309–322.

PLOMIN, R. & THOMPSON, R. (1987) Life-span developmental behavioural genetics. In P.B. Baltes, D.L. Featherman & R.M. Lerner (Eds) *Life-Span Development and Behaviour*, Volume 8. Hillsdale, NJ: Erlbaum.

PLOTKIN, H. (1995) *The Nature of Knowledge*. London: Penguin.

PLUMER, W.S. (1860) Mary Reynolds: A case of double consciousness. *Harper's Magazine*, 20, 807–812.

POGGIO, T. & KOCH, C. (1987) Synapses that compute motion. *Scientific American*, 255, 46–92.

POLLITT, E. & GORMAN, K.S. (1994) Nutritional deficiencies as developmental risk factors. In C.A. Nelson (Ed.) *The Minnesota Symposia on Child Development*, Volume 27. Hillsdale, NJ: Erlbaum.

POPPER, K. (1972) *Objective Knowledge: An Evolutionary Approach*. Oxford: Oxford University Press.

POSNER, M.I. (1980) Orienting of attention. *Quarterly Journal of Experimental Psychology*, 32, 3–25.

POSNER, M.I. & PETERSEN, S.E. (1990) The attention system of the human brain. *Annual Review of Neuroscience*, 13, 25–42.

POSNER, M.I., NISSEN, M.J. & OGDEN, W.C. (1978) Attended and unattended processing modes: The role of set for spatial location. In H.L. Pick & I.J. Saltzman (Eds) *Modes of Perceiving and Processing Information*. Hillsdale, NJ: Erlbaum.

POSNER, M.I., SNYDER, C.R.R. & DAVIDSON, B.J. (1980) Attention and the detection of signals. *Journal of Experimental Psychology: General*, 109, 160–174.

POST, F. (1994) Creativity and psychopathology. A study of 291 world-famous men. *British Journal of Psychiatry*, 165, 22–34.

POVINELLI, D.J., NELSON, K.E. & BOYSEN, S.T. (1990) Inferences about guessing and knowing by chimpanzees (*Pan troglodytes*). *Journal of Comparative Psychology*, 104, 203–210.

POVINELLI, D.J., NELSON, K.E. & BOYSEN, S.T. (1992) Comprehension of role reversal in chimpanzees: Evidence of empathy? *Animal Behaviour*, 43, 633–640.

PREMACK, A.J. & PREMACK, D. (1972) Teaching language to an ape. Scientific American, 227, 92–99.

PREMACK, D. (1971) Language in chimpanzees? *Science*, 172, 808–822.

PREMACK, D. & WOODRUFF, G. (1978) Does the chimpanzee have a theory of mind? *Behavioural & Brain Sciences*, 4, 515–526.

PRENTICE-DUNN, S. & ROGERS, R.W. (1983) Deindividuation in aggression. In R.G. Geen & E.I. Donnerstein (Eds) *Aggression: Theoretical and Empirical Reviews*, Volume 2. New York: Academic Press.

PRICE, R.A. & VANDENBERG, S.G. (1979) Matching for physical attractiveness in married couples. *Personality and Social Psychology Bulletin*, 5, 398–400.

PRICE, W.F. & CRAPO, R.H. (1999) *Cross-Cultural Perspectives in Introductory Psychology* (3rd edition). Belmont, CA: Wadsworth Publishing Company.

PRINCE, J. & HARTNETT, O. (1993) From 'psychology constructs the female' to 'females construct psychology'. *Feminism & Psychology*, 3 (2), 219–224.

PRINCE, J. & KARIM, I. (1978) Matiruku, a Fijian madness: An initial assessment. *British Journal of Psychiatry*, 133, 228–230.

PRINCE, M. (1900) *The Problem of Multiple Personality*. Paris: International Congress of Psychology.

PRINCE, M. (1905) *The Dissociation of Personality*. New York: Oxford University Press.

PRINS, H. (1995) *Offenders, Deviants or Patients?* (2nd edition) London: Routledge.

PRIOLEAU, L., MURDOCK, M. & BRODY, N. (1983) An analysis of psychotherapy versus placebo studies. *Behaviour and Brain Sciences*, 6, 273–310.

PROUDFOOT, J., GUEST, D., CARSON, J., DUNN, G. & GRAY, J. (1997) Effects of cognitive-behavioural training on job-find among long-term unemployed people. *Lancet*, 250, 96–100.

PUCETTI, R. (1977) Sperry on consciousness: A critical appreciation. *Journal of Medicine and Physiology*, 2, 127–146.

PUSHKIN, I. & VENESS, T. (1973) The development of racial awareness and prejudice in children. In P. Watson (Ed.) *Psychology and Race*. Harmondsworth: Penguin.

PUTNAM, F.W. (1992) Are alter personalities fragments or figments? *Psychoanalytic Inquiry*, 12, 95-111.

PUTTNAM, F.W. (1996) Posttraumatic stress disorder in children and adolescents. In L.J. Dickstein, M.B. Riba & J.M. Oldham (Eds) *Review of Psychiatry* (Volume 15). Washington, DC: American Psychiatric Press.

PYNOOS, R.S., GOENIJIAN, A., TASHJIAN, M., KARAKASHIAN, M., MANJIKAN, R., MANOUKIAN, G., STEINBERG, A.M. & FAIRBANKS, L.A. (1993) Post–traumatic stress reactions in children after the 1988 Armenian earthquake. *British Journal of Psychiatry*, 163, 239–247.

QUATTRONE, G.A. (1982) Overattribution and unit formation: When behaviour engulfs the person. *Journal of Personality and Social Psychology*, 42, 593–607.

QUATTRONE, G.A. (1986) On the perception of a group's variability. In S. Worchel & W. Austin (Eds) *The Psychology of Intergroup Relations*, Volume 2. New York: Nelson-Hall.

QUIERY, N. (1998) Parenting and the family. In K. Trew & J. Kremer (Eds) *Gender & Psychology*. London: Arnold.

QUINN, T.P. & HARA, T.J. (1986) Sibling recognition and olfactory sensitivity in juvenile coho salmon (*Onchorhynchus kisutch*). *Canadian Journal of Zoology*, 64, 921–925.

QUINN, T.P. & TOLSON, G.M. (1986) Evidence of chemically mediated population recognition in coho salmon (*Onchorhynchus kisutch*). *Canadian Journal of Zoology*, 64, 84–87.

RABBITT, P.M.A. (1967) Ignoring irrelevant information. *American Journal of Psychology*, 80, 1–13.

RABIN, A.S., KASLOW, N.J. & REHM, L.P. (1986) Aggregate outcome and follow-up results following self-control therapy for depression. Paper presented at the American Psychological Convention.

RACHMAN, S. (1984) Agoraphobia – a safety signal perspective. *Behaviour Research and Therapy*, 22, 59–70.

RADFORD, T. (1997) Obesity gene found in cousins. *The Guardian*, 24 June, 8.

RADOMSKY, A.S. & RACHMAN, S. (1999) Memory bias in obsessive–compulsive disorder (OCD). *Behaviour Research and Therapy*, 37, 605–618.

RAFAL, R.D. & POSNER, M.I. (1987) Deficits in human visual spatial attention following thalamic lesions. *Proceedings of the National Academy of Science*, 84, 7349–7353.

RAFFA, K.F. & BERRYMAN, A.A. (1983) The role of host resistance in the colonisation behaviour and ecology of bark beetles (*Coleoptera: Scolytidae*). *Ecological Monographs*, 63, 27–49.

RAICHLE, M.E. (1994) Visualising the mind. *Scientific American*, 269, 36–42.

RAINEY, N. (1998) Old age. In K. Trew & J. Kremer (Eds) *Gender and Psychology*. London: Arnold.

RALEIGH, M. & McGUIRE, M. (1991) Serotonin in vervet monkeys. *Brain Research*, 559, 181–190.

RAMACHANDRON, V.S. & ANSTIS, S.M. (1986) The perception of apparent motion. *Scientific American*, 254, 80–87.

RAMSAY, R. & de GROOT, W. (1977) A further look at bereavement. Paper presented at EATI conference, Uppsala. Cited in P.E. Hodgkinson (1980) Treating abnormal grief in the bereaved. *Nursing Times*, 17 January, 126–128.

RAPHAEL, B. (1984) *The Anatomy of Bereavement*. London: Hutchinson.

RAPPAPORT, Z.H. (1992) Psychosurgery in the modern era: Therapeutic and ethical aspects. *Medicine and Law*, 11, 449–453.

RASSOOL, G.H. & WINNINGTON, J. (1993) Using psychoactive drugs. *Nursing Times*, 89, 38–40.

RATHUS, S.A. (1984) *Psychology* (3rd edition). London: Holt, Reinhart & Winston.

RATHUS, S.A. (1990) *Psychology* (4th edition). New York: Holt, Rinehart & Winston.

RAZRAN, G. (1950) Ethnic dislikes and stereotypes: A laboratory study. *Journal of Abnormal and Social Psychology*, 45, 7–27.

REASON, J.T. (1979) Actions not as planned: The price of automatisation. In G. Underwood & R. Stevens (Eds) *Aspects of Consciousness: Volume 1, Psychological Issues*. London: Academic Press.

REASON, J.T (1984) Absent-mindedness. In J. Nicholson & H. Beloff (Eds) *Psychology Survey 5*. Leicester: British Psychological Society.

REASON, J.T. (1992) Cognitive underspecification: Its variety and consequences. In B.J. Baars (Ed.) *Experimental Slips and Human Error: Exploring the Architecture of Volition*. New York: Plenum Press.

REASON, J.T & MYCIELSKA, K. (1982) *Absentmindedness: The Psychology of Mental Lapses and Everyday Errors*. Englewood Cliffs, NJ: Prentice-Hall.

REBER, A.S. (1985) *The Penguin Dictionary of Psychology*. Harmondsworth: Penguin.

REBOK, G. (1987) *Life-Span Cognitive Development*. New York: Holt, Rinehart & Winston.

RECHTSCHAFFEN, A. & KALES, A. (1968) A manual of standardised terminology, techniques, and scoring system for sleep stages of human subjects. *National Institute of Health Publication 204*. Washington, DC: US Government Printing Office.

RECHTSCHAFFEN, A., GILLILAND, M., BERGMANN, B. & WINTER, J. (1983) Physiological correlates of prolonged sleep deprivation in rats. *Science*, 221, 182–184.

REEDY, M.N. (1983) Personality and ageing. In D.S. Woodruff & J.E. Birren (Eds) *Ageing: Scientific Perspectives and Social Issues* (2nd edition). Monterey, CA: Brooks/Cole.

REES, M.I., FENTON, I., WILLIAMS, N.M. *et al.* (1999) Autosome search for schizophrenia susceptibility genes in multiply affected families. *Molecular Psychiatry*, 4, 353–359.

REGAN, D.T. & TOTTEN, J. (1975) Empathy and attribution: Turning observers into actors. *Journal of Personality and Social Psychology*, 32, 850–856.

REGOLIN, L. & ROSE, S.P.R. (1999) Long-term memory for a spatial task in young chicks. *Animal Behaviour*, 57, 1185–1191.

REHKAMPER, G., HAASE, E. & FRAHM, H.D. (1988) Allometric comparison of brain weight and brain structure in different breeds of the domestic pigeon, *Columbia liva f.d.* (fantails, homing pigeons, strassers). *Brain, Behavior and Evolution*, 31, 141–149.

REICH, B. & ADCOCK, C. (1976) *Values, Attitudes and Behaviour Change*. London: Methuen.

REILLY, T., ATKINSON, G. & WATERHOUSE, J. (1997) *Biological Rhythms and Exercise*. Oxford: Oxford University Press.

REINBERG, A. (1967) Eclairement et cycle menstruel de la femme. Rapport au Colloque International du CRNS, la photoregulation de la reproduction chez les oiseaux et les mammifères, Montpelier.

REISENZEIN, R. (1983) The Schachter theory of emotion: Two decades later. *Psychological Bulletin*, 94, 239–264.

REISS, I.R. (1986) *Journey into Sexuality: An Exploratory Voyage*. Englewood Cliffs, NJ: Prentice-Hall.

RENNER, M.J. (1992) Curiosity and exploitation. In L.R. Squire (Ed.) *Encyclopaedia of Learning and Memory*. New York: MacMillan.

RESCORLA, R.A. (1968) Probability of shock in the presence and absence of CS in fear conditioning. *Journal of Comparative and Physiological Psychology*, 66, 1–5.

REST, J.R. (1983) Morality. In J.H. Flavell & E. Markman (Eds) *Handbook of Child Psychology*, Volume 3. New York: Wiley.

RESTLE, F. (1957) Discrimination of cues in mazes: A resolution of the 'place versus response' question. *Psychological Review*, 64, 217–228.

RHEINGOLD, H.L. (1961) The effect of environmental stimulation upon social and exploratory behaviour in the human infant. In B.M. Foss (Ed.) *Determinants of Infant Behaviour*, Volume 1. London: Methuen.

RHEINGOLD, H.L., GERWITZ, J.L. & ROSS, H.W. (1959) Social conditioning of vocalisations in the infant. *Journal of Comparative & Physiological Psychology*, 51, 68–73.

RHODES, T. (1999) Internet lonely heart logs on for a year of solitude. *The Sunday Times*, 19 December, 21.

RICE, M. (1989) Children's language acquisition. *American Psychologist*, 44, 149–156.

RICHARDS, A. & WOPERT, L. (1997) The Insiders' Story. *Independent on Sunday Review*, 27 September, 44–45.

RICHARDS, G. (1996a) Arsenic and old race. *Observer Review*, 5 May, 4.

RICHARDS, G. (1996b) *Putting Psychology in its Place*. London: Routledge.

RICHARDSON, K. (1991) *Understanding Intelligence*. Milton Keynes: Open University Press.

RICHARDSON, J.T.E. (Ed.) (1996) *Handbook of Qualitative Research Methods for Psychology and the Social Sciences*. Leicester: BPS Books.

RIDLEY, M. (1986) *The Problems of Evolution*. New York: Oxford University Press.

RIDLEY, M. (1993) *The Red Queen*. London: Penguin.

RIDLEY, M. (1995) *Animal Behaviour* (2nd edition). Cambridge, MA: Blackwell.

RIEGEL, K.F. (1976) The dialectics of human development. *American Psychologist*, 31, 689–700.

RIMM, D.C. (1976) Behaviour therapy: Some general comments and a review of selected papers. In R.L. Spitzer & D.F. Klein (Eds) *Evaluation of Psychological Therapies*. Baltimore: Johns Hopkins University Press.

RIN, H. (1965) A study of the aetiology of Koro in respect to the Chinese concept of illness. *International Journal of Social Psychiatry*, 11, 7–15.

RINGEN, J. (1996) The behaviour therapist's dilemma: Reflections on autonomy, informed consent, and scientific psychology. In W. O'Donohue & R.F. Kitchener (Eds) *The Philosophy of Psychology*. London: Sage Publications.

RIVERS, W.H.R. (1901) Vision. In A.C. Haddon (Ed.) *Reports of the Cambridge Anthropological Expedition to the Torres Straits*, Volume 2, Part 1. Cambridge: Cambridge University Press.

RIVERS, W.H.R. (1906) *The Todas*. New York: Macmillan.

ROBERTS, R. & NEWTON, P.M. (1987) Levinsonian studies of women's adult development. *Psychology and Ageing*, 39, 165–174.

ROBERTS, W.A. (1979) Spatial memory in the rat on a hierarchical maze. *Learning & Motivation*, 10, 117–140.

ROBERTSON, J. (1995) Recovery of brain function: People and nets. *The Psychologist*, 8, 253.

ROBINSON, J.O. (1972) *The Psychology of Visual Illusions*. London: Hutchinson.

ROBINSON, L. (1997) Black adolescent identity and the inadequacies of western psychology. In J. Roche & S. Tucker (Eds) *Youth in Society*. London: Sage.

ROCHFORD, G. (1974) Are jargon aphasics dysphasic? *British Journal of Disorders of Communication*, 9, 35.

ROCK, I. (1983) *The Logic of Perception*. Cambridge, MA: MIT Press.

ROCK, I. (1984) *Perception*. New York: W.H. Freeman.

RODIN, F. & SLOCHOWER, J. (1976) Externality in the non-obese: Effects of environmental responsiveness on weight. *Journal of Personality and Social Psychology*, 33, 338–344.

ROGERS, C.R. (1983) *Freedom to Learn in the 80s*. Columbus, OH: Charles Merrill.

ROGERS, J., MEYER, J. & MORTEL, K. (1990) After reaching retirement age physical activity sustains cerebral perfusion and cognition. *Journal of the American Geriatric Society*, 38, 123–128.

ROGOFF B. & MORELLI, G. (1989) Perspectives on children's development from cultural psychology. *American Psychologist*, 44, 343–348.

ROGOFF, B. (1990) *Apprenticeship in Thinking: Cognitive Development in Social Context*. New York: Oxford University Press.

ROKEACH, M. (1948) Generalised mental rigidity as a factor in ethnocentrism. *Journal of Abnormal and Social Psychology*, 43, 254–278.

ROKEACH, M. (1960) *The Open and Closed Mind*. New York: Basic Books.

ROKER, D., PLAYER, K. & COLEMAN, J. (1998) Exploring adolescent altruism: British young people's involvement in voluntary work and campaigning. In M. Yates & J. Youniss (Eds) *Community Service and Civil Engagement in Youth: International Perspectives*. Cambridge: Cambridge University Press.

ROSE, D. & FOREMAN, N. (1999) Virtual reality. *The Psychologist*, 12, 550–554.

ROSE, S. (1992) *The Making of Memory: From Molecule to Mind*. London: Bantam Books.

ROSE, S. (1997) *Lifelines: Biology, Freedom, Determinism*. Harmondsworth: Penguin.

ROSE, S., LEWONTIN, R.C., & KAMIN, L.J. (1984) *Not in our Genes: Biology, Ideology and Human Nature*. Harmondsworth: Penguin.

ROSE, S.A. & BLANK, M. (1974) The potency of context in children's cognition: an illustration through conservation. *Child Development*, 45, 499–502.

ROSENBAUM, M.E. (1986) The repulsion hypothesis: On the non-development of relationships. *Journal of Personality and Social Psychology*, 51, 1156–1166.

ROSENBLATT, P.C. (1993) The social context of private feelings. In M.S. Stroebe, W. Stroebe & R.O. Hansson (Eds) *Handbook of Bereavement: Theory, Research and Intervention*. New York: Cambridge University Press.

ROSENHAN, D.L. (1973) On being sane in insane places. *Science*, 179, 365–369.

ROSENKILDE, C.E. & DIVAC, I. (1976) Time-discrimination performance in cats with lesions in prefrontal cortex and caudate nucleus. *Journal of Comparative & Physiological Psychology*, 90, 343–352.

ROSENTHAL, A.M. (1964) *Thirty-Eight Witnesses*. New York: McGraw-Hill.

ROSENTHAL, R. (1966) *Experimenter Effects in Behavioural Research*. New York: Appleton-Century-Crofts.

ROSENTHAL, R. & FODE, K.L. (1963) The effects of experimenter bias on the performance of the albino rat. *Behavioural Science*, 8, 183–189.

ROSENTHAL, R. & JACOBSON. L. (1968) *Pygmalion in the Classroom: Teacher Expectation and Pupils' Intellectual Development*. New York: Holt.

ROSENTHAL, R. & LAWSON, R. (1961) 'A longitudinal study of the effects of experimenter bias on the operant learning of laboratory rats.' (Unpublished manuscript, Harvard University.)

ROSNOW, I. (1985) Status and role change through the life cycle. In R.H. Binstock & E. Shanas (Eds) *Handbook of Ageing and the Social Sciences* (2nd edition). New York: Van Nostrand Reinhold.

ROSS, C.A. (1997) *Dissociative Identity Disorder: Diagnosis, Clinical Features and Treatment of Multiple Personality*. New York: Wiley.

ROSS, E.D. (1981) The aprosodias: Functional-anatomic organisation of the affective components of language in the right hemisphere. *Archives of Neurology*, 38, 561–569.

ROSS, L. (1977) The intuitive psychologist and his shortcomings. In L. Berkowitz (Ed.) *Advances in Experimental Social Psychology*, Volume 10. New York: Academic Pres.

ROSS, M. & FLETCHER, G.J.O. (1985) Attribution and social perception. In G. Lindzey & E. Aronson (Eds) *Handbook of Social Psychology*, Volume 2 (3rd edition). New York: Random House.

ROSSI, E.I. (1973) The dream protein hypothesis. *American Journal of Psychiatry*, 130, 1094–1097.

ROTH, A. & FONAGY, P. (1996) *Research on the efficacy and effectiveness of the psychotherapies: A report to the Department of Health*. London: HMSO.

ROTH, I. (1986) An introduction to object perception. In I. Roth & J.P. Frisby (Eds) *Perception and Representation*. Milton Keynes: Open University Press.

ROTH, I. (1995) Object Recognition. In I. Roth & V. Bruce (Eds) *Perception and Representation: Current Issues* (2nd edition). Buckingham: Open University Press.

ROTHENBERG, A. (1998) Diagnosis of obsessive–compulsive illness. *Psychiatric Clinics of North America*, 21, 791–801.

ROTTER, J.B. (1966) Generalised expectancies for internal versus external control of reinforcement. *Psychological Monographs*, 30(1), 1–26.

ROTTON, J. (1993) Atmospheric and temporal correlates of sex crimes: Endogenous factors do not explain seasonal differences in rape. *Environmental Behaviour*, 25, 625–642.

ROWAN, A.N. (1997) The benefits and ethics of animal research. *Scientific American*, 64–66, February.

ROWAN, J. (1978) *The Structured Crowd*. London: Davis Poynter.

ROZENFELD, F.M. & RASMONT, R. (1991) Odour cue recognition by dominant male bank voles, *Clethrionomys glareolus*. *Animal Behaviour*, 41, 839–850.

RUBIN, E. (1915) *Synsoplevede Figurer*. Kobenhaun: Gyldendalske Boghandel.

RUBIN, F. (Ed.) (1968) *Current Research in Hypnopaedia*. New York: Elsevier.

RUBIN, J.Z., PROVENZANO, F.J. & LURIA, Z. (1974) The eye of the beholder: Parents' views on sex of new-borns. *American Journal of Orthopsychiatry*, 44, 512–519.

RUBIN, Z. (1973) *Liking and Loving*. New York: Holt, Rinehart & Winston.

RUBIN, Z. & McNEIL, E.B. (1983) *The Psychology of Being Human* (3rd edition). London: Harper & Row.

RUBLE, D.N. (1984) Sex-role development. In M.C. Bornstein & M.E. Lamb (Eds) *Developmental Psychology: An Advanced Textbook*. Hillsdale, NJ: Erlbaum.

RUDOLPH, K., WIRZ-JUSTICE, A. & KRAUCHI, K. (1993) Static magnetic fields decrease nocturnal pineal cAMP in the rat. *Brain Research*, 446, 159–160.

RUMBAUGH, D.M. & SAVAGE-RUMBAUGH, E.S. (1978) Chimpanzee language research: Status and potential. *Behaviour Research Methods and Instrumentation*, 10, 119–131.

RUMBAUGH, D. & SAVAGE-RUMBAUGH, S. (1994) *Language and Apes*. APA Psychology Teacher Network.

RUNCIMAN, W.G. (1966) *Relative Deprivation and Social Justice*. London: Routledge & Kegan Paul.

RUSBULT, C. (1987) Responses to dissatisfaction in close relationships: The exit–voice–loyalty–neglect model. In D. Perlman & S. Duck (Eds) *Intimate Relationships: Development, Dynamics and Deterioration*. London: Sage.

RUSHTON, J.P. (1995) *Race, Evolution and Behaviour*. New Brunswick, NJ: Transaction Publishers.

RUSSEK, M. (1971) Hepatic receptors and the neurophysiological mechanisms in controlling feeding behaviour. In S. Ehrenpreis (Ed.) *Neurosciences Research*, Volume 4. New York: Academic Press.

RUSSELL, J. (1990) Is object play in young carnivores practice for predation? Unpublished PhD thesis, University College London.

RUSSELL, M.J., SWITZ, G.M. & THOMPSON, K. (1980) Olfactory influences on the human menstrual cycle. *Pharmacology, Biochemistry and Behaviour*, 13, 737–738.

RUTTER, M. (and the English and Romanian Adopteer (ERA) study team) (1998) Developmental Catch-up, and Deficit Following Adoption after Severe Global Early Privation. *Journal of Child Psychology &Psychiatry*, 39(4), 465–476.

RUTTER, M. & RUTTER, M. (1992) *Developing Minds: Challenge and Continuity Across the Life Span*. Harmondsworth: Penguin.

RUTTER, M., GRAHAM, P., CHADWICK, D.F.D. & YULE, W. (1976) Adolescent turmoil: Fact or fiction? *Journal of Child Psychology & Psychiatry*, 17, 35–56.

RYBACK, R.S. & LEWIS, O.F. (1971) Effects of prolonged bed rest on EEG sleep patterns in young, healthy volunteers. *Electroencephalography and Clinical Neurophysiology*, 31, 395–399.

RYCROFT, C. (1966) Introduction: Causes and Meaning. In C. Rycroft (Ed.) *Psychoanalysis Observed*. London: Constable & Co. Ltd.

RYCROFT, C. (1978) *Introduction to M. Prince, The Dissociation of Personality*. New York: Oxford University Press (1905).

RYDER, R. (1990) Open reply to Jeffrey Gray. *The Psychologist*, 3, 403.

SABBAGH, K. & BARNARD, C. (1984) *The Living Body*. London: Macdonald.

SACHDEV, P.S. (1985) Koro epidemic in India. *Australian & New Zealand Journal of Psychiatry*, 19, 433–438.

SACKHEIM, H.A. (1982) Hemispheric asymmetry in the expression of positive and negative emotions. *Archives of Neurology*, 39, 210–218.

SACKS, O. (1985) *The Man who Mistook his Wife for a Hat and Other Clinical Tales*. New York: Summit Books.

SAINTPAUL, U.V. (1982) Do geese use path integration for walking home? In F. Papi & H.G. Wallraff (Eds) *Avian Navigation*. New York, Springer.

SALAPATEK, P. (1975) Pattern perception in early infancy. In L.B. Cohen & P. Salapatek (Eds) *Infant Perception: From Sensation to Cognition*, Volume 1. *Basic Visual Processes*. London: Academic Press.

SALKOVSKIS, P.M., WESTBROOK, D., DAVIS, J., JEAVONS, A. & GLEDHILL, A. (1997) Effects of neutralising on intrusive thoughts: An experiment investigating the etiology of obsessive–compulsive disorder. *Behaviour Research and Therapy*, 35, 211–219.

SALLOWAY, S. & CUMMINGS, I. (1996) Subcortical structures and neuropsychiatric illness. *Neuroscientist*, 2, 66–75.

SAMEROFF, A.J. & SEIFER, R. (1989) Social Regulation of Developmental Communities. Paper presented at the annual meeting of the American Association for the Advancement of Science, San Francisco.

SAMUEL, J. & BRYANT, P. (1984) Asking only one question in the conservation experiment. *Journal of Child Psychology & Psychiatry*, 25, 315–318.

SANAVIO, E. (1988) Obsessions and compulsions: The Padua Inventory. *Behaviour Research & Therapy*, 26, 169–177.

SANBONMATSU, D.M., SHAVITT, S., SHERMAN, S.J. & ROSKO-EWOLDSEN, D.R. (1987) Illusory correlation in the perception of performance by self or a salient other. *Journal of Experimental Social Psychology*, 23, 518–543.

SANFORD, R.N. (1937) The effects of abstinence from food upon imaginal processes. A further experiment. *Journal of Psychology*, 3, 145–159.

SANGIULIANO, I. (1978) *In Her Time*. New York: Morrow.

SANTROCK, J.W. (1986) *Psychology: The Science of Mind and Behaviour*. Dubuque, IA: William C. Brown.

SAPIR, E. (1929) The study of linguistics as a science. *Language*, 5, 207–214.

SAPSTED, D. (1998) Freud broke own rules on patients. *The Daily Telegraph*, 11 February, 11.

SARBIN, T.R. (1992) The social construction of schizophrenia. In W. Flack, D.R. Miller & M. Wiener (Eds) *What is Schizophrenia?* New York: Springer-Verlag.

SARTORIUS, N., KAELBER, C.T. & COOPER, J.E. (1993) Progress toward achieving a common language in psychiatry. Results from the field trials accompanying the clinical guidelines of mental and behavioural disorders in ICD–10. *Archives of General Psychiatry*, 50, 115–124.

SATZ, P. (1979) A test of some models of hemispheric speech organisation in the left- and right-handed. *Science*, 203, 1131–1133.

SAUER, F. & SAUER, E. (1955) Zur Frage der nachtlichen Zugorientierung von Grasmucken. *Rev. Suisse Zool.* 62, 250–59.

SAVAGE-RUMBAUGH, E.S. (1990) Language as a cause-effect communication system. *Philosophical Psychology*, 3, 55–76.

SAVAGE-RUMBAUGH, E.S., MURPHY, J., SEVEIK, R.A., WILLIAMS, S., BRAKKE, K. & RUMBAUGH, D.M. (1993) Language comprehension in ape and child. *Monographs of the Society for research in Child Development*, 58, 3–4.

SAVAGE-RUMBAUGH, E.S., RUMBAUGH, D.M. & BOYSEN, S.L. (1980) Do apes have langauge? *American Scientist*, 68, 49–61.

SAWYER, L. (1996) … Or An Abomination? *Nursing Times*, 92(5), 28.

SAYERS, J. (1982) *Biological Politics: Feminist and Anti-Feminist Perspectives*. London: Tavistock.

SCARR, S. (1984) *Mother Care/Other Care*. New York: Basic Books.

SCARR, S. (1992) Developmental theories for the 1990s: Development and individual differences. *Child Development*, 63, 1–19.

SCARR, S. & WEINBERG, R. (1976) IQ test performance of black children adopted by white families. *American Psychologist*, 31, 726–739.

SCARR, S. & WEINBERG, R. (1978) Attitudes, interests, and IQ. *Human Nature*, April, 29–36.

SCHACHTER, S. (1959) *The Psychology of Affiliation: Experimental Studies of the Sources of Gregariousness*. Stanford, CA: Stanford University Press.

SCHACHTER, S. (1964) The interaction of cognitive and physiological determinants of emotional state. In L. Berkowitz (Ed.) *Advances in Experimental Social Psychology*, Volume 1. New York: Academic Pres.

SCHACHTER, S. & SINGER, J.E. (1962) Cognitive, social and physiological determinants of emotional state. *Psychological Review*, 69, 379–399.

SCHACTER, D.L. (1986) Amnesia and crime. *American Psychologist*, 41, 186-195.

SCHAFFER, H.R. (1989) Early social development. In A. Slater & G. Bremner (Eds) *Infant Development*. Hove: Erlbaum.

SCHAIE, K.W. & HERTZOG, C. (1983) Fourteen-year cohort-sequential analysis of adult intellectual development. *Developmental Psychology*, 19, 531–543.

SCHALLER, G.B. (1972) *The Serengeti Lion*. Chicago: University of Chicago Press.

SCHEER, S.D. & UNGER, D.G. (1995) Parents' perceptions of their adolescence – implications for parent–youth conflict and family satisfaction. *Psychological Reports*, 76(1), 131–136.

SCHEERER, M. (1963) Problem-solving. *Scientific American*, 208, 118–128.

SCHEPER-HUGHES, N. (1991) *Death Without Weeping: The Violence of Everyday Life in Brazil*. Los Angeles: University of California Press.

SCHERER, K. & BOST, J. (1997) *Internet use patterns: Is there Internet dependency on campus?* Paper presented at the 105th Annual Convention of the American Psychological Association, Chicago, IL, August.

SCHIFF, N., DUYME, M., DUMARET, A., STEWART, J., TOMKIEWICZ, S. & FEINGOLD, J. (1978) Intellectual status of working-class children adopted early into upper-middle-class families. *Science*, 200, 1503–1504.

SCHIFFMAN, R. & WICKLUND, R.A. (1992) The minimal group paradigm and its minimal psychology. *Theory and Psychology*, 2, 29–50.

SCHILDKRAUT, J. (1965) The catecholamine hypothesis of affective disorders: A review of supporting evidence. *American Journal of Psychiatry*, 122, 509–522.

SCHILLER, P. (1952) Innate constituents of complex responses in primates. *Psychology Review*, 59, 177–191.

SCHLOSSBERG, N.K. (1984) Exploring the adult years. In A.M. Rogers &C.J. Scheirer (Eds) *The G. Stanley Hall Lecture Series* (vol.4). Washington, DC: American Psychological Association.

SCHLOSSBERG, N.K., TROLL, L.E. & LEIBOWITZ, Z. (1978) *Perspectives on Counselling Adults: Issues and Skills*. Monterey, CA: Brooks/Cole.

SCHMIDT, K., HILL, L. & GUTHRIE, G. (1977) Running amok. *International Journal of Social Psychiatry*, 23, 264–274.

SCHMIDT-KOENIG K. (1961) Die sonne als Kompass im Heim-Orientierungs-system der Brieftauben. *Zietschrift für Tierpsychologie*, 68, 221–44.

SCHNEIDER, B.H. & BYRNE, B.M. (1987) Individualising social skills training for behaviour-disordered children. *Journal of Consulting & Clinical Psychology*, 55, 444–445.

SCHNEIDER, D. (1969) Insect olfaction: Deciphering system for chemical messages. *Science*, 163, 1031–1037.

SCHNEIDER, K. (1959) *Clinical Psychopathology*. New York: Grune & Stratton.

SCHNEIDER, W. & FISK, A.D. (1982) Degree of consistent training: Improvements in search performance and automatic process development. *Perception and Psychophysics*, 31, 160–168.

SCHNEIDER, W. & SHIFFRIN, R.M. (1977) Controlled and automatic human information processing: I. Detection, search and attention. *Psychological Review*, 84, 1–66.

SCHOU, M. (1997) Forty years of Lithium treatment. *Archives of General Psychiatry*, 54, 9–13.

SCHREIBER, F.R. (1973) *Sybil*. Harmondsworth: Penguin.

SCHROEDER, D.A., PENNER, L.A., DOVIDIO, J.F. & PILIAVIN, J.A. (1995) *The Psychology of Helping and Altruism: Problems and Puzzles*. New York: McGraw-Hill.

SCHUCHTER, S.R. & ZISOOK, S. (1993) The course of normal grief. In M.S. Stroebe, W. Stroebe & R.O. Hansson (Eds) *Handbook of Bereavement: Theory, Research and Intervention*. New York: Cambridge University Press.

SCHULER, S.R. (1987) *The Other Side of Polyandry: Property, Stratification and Nonmarriage in the Nepal Himalayas*. Boulder, CO: Westview Press.

SCHWARTZ, G.E., WEINBERGER, D.A. & SINGER, J.A. (1981) Cardiovascular differentiation of happiness, sadness, anger, and fear following imagery and exercise. *Psychosomatic Medicine*, 43, 343–364.

SCHWARTZ, J. (1999) *Cassandra's Daughter: A History of Psychoanalysis in Europe and America*. London: Allen Lane.

SCOLLON, R. (1976) *Conversations With a One-Year-Old*. Honolulu: University of Hawaii Press.

SCOTT, J. (1994) Cognitive therapy. *British Journal of Psychiatry*, 164, 126–130.

SEARS, R.R., MACCOBY, E.E. & LEVIN, H. (1957) Patterns of Child Rearing. New York: Harper & Row.

SEGAL, M.W. (1974) Alphabet and attraction: An unobtrusive measure of the effect of propinquity in the field setting. *Journal of Personality and Social Psychology*, 30, 654–657.

SEGALL, M.H., CAMPBELL, D.T. & HERSKOVITS, M.J. (1963) Cultural differences in the perception of geometrical illusions. *Science*, 139, 769–771.

SEGALL, M.S., DASEN, P.R., BERRY, J.W. & POORTINGA, Y.P. (1990) *Human Behaviour in Global Perspective: An Introduction to Cross-Cultural Psychology*. Oxford: Pergamon Press.

SELFRIDGE, O.G. (1959) Pandemonium: A paradigm for learning. *Symposium on the Mechanisation of Thought Processes*. London: HMSO.

SELIGMAN, M.E.P. (1970) On the generality of the laws of learning. *Psychological Review*, 77, 406–418.

SELIGMAN, M.E.P. (1971) Phobias and preparedness. *Behaviour Therapy*, 2, 307–320.

SELIGMAN, M.E.P. (1972) *Biological Boundaries of Learning*. New York: Academic Press.

SELIGMAN, M.E.P. (1973) Fall into hopelessness. *Psychology Today*, 7, 43–47.

SELIGMAN, M.E.P. (1975) *Helplessness: On Depression, Development and Death*. San Francisco: W.H. Freeman.

SELIGMAN, M.E.P. (1992) Wednesday's children. *Psychology Today*, 25, 61.

SELIGMAN, M.E.P. & MAIER, S.F. (1967) Failure to escape traumatic shock. *Journal of Experimental Psychology*, 74, 1–9.

SELLEN, A.J. & NORMAN, D.A. (1992) The psychology of slips. In B.J. Baars (Ed) *Experimental Slips and Human Error: Exploring the Architecture of Volition*. New York: Plenum Press.

SEM-JACOBSEN, C.W. (1968) *Depth-Electrographic Stimulation of the Human Brain and Behaviour*. Springfield, ILL: Charles C. Thomas.

SERETTI, A., CUSIN, C., LATTUADA, E., DI BELLA, D., CATALANO, M. & SMERALDI, E. (1999) Serotonin transporter gene (5-HTTLPR) is not associated with depressive symptomatology in mood disorders. *Molecular Psychiatry*, 4, 280–283.

SERGENT, J. (1984) An investigation into component and configurational processes underlying face recognition. *British Journal of Psychology*, 75, 221–242.

SERPELL, R.S. (1976) *Culture's Influence on Perception*. London: Methuen.

SEYFARTH, R.M. & CHENEY, D.L. (1986) Vocal development in vervet monkeys. *Animal Behaviour*, 34, 1640–1658.

SEYFARTH, R.M., CHENEY, D.L. & MARLER, P. (1980) Monkey responses to three different alarm calls: Evidence for predator classification and semantic communication. *Science*, 210, 801–803.

SEYMOUR, J. (1996) Beastly Dilemmas. *Nursing Times*, 92 (5), 24–26.

SHAFFER, L.H. (1975) Multiple attention in continuous verbal tasks. In P.M.A. Rabbitt & S. Dornic (Eds) *Attention and Performance* (Volume V). London: Academic Press.

SHAFRAN, R. (1999) Obsessive–compulsive disorder. *The Psychologist*, 12, 588–591.

SHAPIRO, C.M., BORTZ, R., MITCHELL, D., BARTEL, P. & JOOSTE, P. (1981) Slow-wave sleep: A recovery period after exercise. *Science*, 214, 1253–1254.

SHAPIRO, D.A. & SHAPIRO, D. (1982) Meta-analysis of comparative therapy outcome studies: A replication and refinement. *Psychological Bulletin*, 92, 581–604.

SHARPE, M., HAWTON, K., SIMKIN, S., HACKMANN, A., KLIMES, I., PETO, T., WARRELL, S., & SEAGROAT, V. (1996) Cognitive-behavioural therapy for the chronic fatigue syndrome: A randomised controlled trial. *British Medical Journal*, 312, 22–26.

SHEEHAN, D. (1999) Current concepts in the treatment of panic disorder. *Journal of Clinical Psychiatry*, 60 (Supplement 18), 16–21.

SHEEHY, G. (1976) *Passages – Predictable Crises of Adult Life*. New York: Bantam Books.

SHEEHY, G. (1996) *New Passages*. New York: HarperCollins.

SHEFFIELD, F.D. & ROBY, T.B. (1955) Reward value of a non-nutritive sweet taste. *Journal of Comparative & Physiological Psychology*, 43, 471–481.

SHERIF, M. (1966) *Group Conflict and Co-operation: Their Social Psychology*. London: Routledge & Kegan Paul.

SHERIF, M., HARVEY, O.J., WHITE, B.J., HOOD, W.R. & SHERIF, C.W. (1961) *Intergroup Conflict and Co-operation: The Robber's Cave Experiment*. Norman, OK: University of Oklahoma Press.

SHERRY, D.F. (1984) Food storage by black-capped chickadees: memory for the location and contents of caches. *Animal Behaviour*, 32, 451–464.

SHERRY, D.F. & GALEF, B.G. (1984) Cultural transmission without imitation: Milk bottle opening by birds. *Animal Behaviour*, 32, 937–938.

SHERRY, D.F. & GALEF, B.G. (1990) Social learning without imitation: More about milk bottle opening by birds. *Animal Behaviour*, 40, 987–989.

SHERRY, D.F., FORBES, M.R.L., KHURGEL, M. & IVY, G.O. (1993) Females have a larger hippocampus than males in the brood-parasitic brown-headed cowbird. *Proceedings of the National Academy of Sciences USA*, 90, 7839–7843.

SHERRY, D.F., JACOBS, L.F. & GAULIN, S.J. (1992) Spatial memory and adaptive specialization of the hippocampus. *Trends in Neuroscience*, 15, 298–303.

SHETTLEWORTH, S.J. (1983) Memory in food-hoarding birds. *Scientific American*, 248(3), 102–110.

SHETTLEWORTH, S.J. (1984) Learning and behavioral ecology. In J.R Kreb & N.B. Davies (Eds) *Behavioural Ecology: An Evolutionary Approach*. Sunderland, MA: Sinauer.

SHIELDS, J. (1962) *Monozygotic Twins Brought Up Apart and Brought Up Together*. London: Oxford University Press.

SHIFFRIN, R.M. & SCHNEIDER, W. (1977) Controlled and automatic human information processing: II. Perceptual learning, automatic attending and a general theory. *Psychological Review*, 84, 127–190.

SHIH, M., PITTINSKY, T. & AMBADY, N. (1999) Stereotype susceptibility: Identity salience and shifts in quantitative performance. *Psychological Science*, 10, 80–83.

SHOREY, H.H. (1976) *Animal Communication by Pheromones*. New York: Academic Press.

SHORTLIFFE, E.H. (1976) *Computer-Based Medical Consultations: MYCIN*. New York: American Elsevier.

SHOSTAK, M. (1981) *Nisa: The Life and Words of a Kung woman*. Cambridge, MA: Harvard University Press.

SHOTLAND, R.L. & HEINOLD, W.D. (1985) Bystander response to arterial bleeding: Helping skills, the decision-making process, and differentiating the helping response. *Journal of Personality and Social Psychology*, 49, 347–356.

SHUREN, J.E., BROTT, T.G., SCHEFFT, B.K. & HOUSTON, W. (1996) Preserved colour imagery in an achromatopsic. *Neuropsychologia*, 34, 485–489.

SHWEDER, R.A. (1990) Cultural psychology: What is it? In J.W. Stigler, R.A. Shweder & G. Herdt (Eds) *Cultural Psychology*. Cambridge: Cambridge University Press.

SHWEDER, R.A. (1991) *Thinking Through Cultures: Expeditions in Cultural Psychology*. Cambridge, MA: Harvard University Press.

SHWEDER, R.A., MAHAPATRA, M. & MILLER, J.G. (1987) Culture and moral development. In J. Kagan & S. Lamb (Eds) *The Emergence of Morality in Young Children*. Chicago: University of Chicago Press.

SIEGLER, R.S. (1976) Three aspects of cognitive development. *Cognitive Psychology*, 4, 481–520.

SIEGLER, R.S. (1989) How domain-general and domain-specific knowledge interact to produce strategy choices. *Merrill-Palmer Quarterly*, 35, 1–26.

SIFFRE, M. (1975) Six months alone in a cave. *National Geographic*, March, 426–435.

SIGALL, H. & LANDY, D. (1973) Radiating beauty: Effects of having a physically attractive partner on person perception. *Journal of Personality and Social Psychology*, 28, 218–224.

SIITER, R. (1999) *Introduction to Animal Behavior*. Pacific Grove, California: International Thomson Publishing.

SILBERSWEIG, D.A., STERN, E., FRITH, C. *et al.* (1995) A functional neuroanatomy of hallucinations in schizophrenia. *Nature*, 378, 176–179.

SILVERMAN, I. (1971) Physical attractiveness and courtship. *Sexual Behaviour*, September, 22–25.

SILVERN, S.B. (1986) Classroom use of video games. *Education Research Quarterly*, 10, 10–16.

SILVERSTEIN, C. (1972) Behaviour modification and the gay community. Paper presented at the annual conference of the Association for the Advancement of Behaviour Therapy, New York.

SIMMONS, L.W. (1990) Pheromonal cues for the recognition of kin by female crickets, *Gryllus bimaculatus*. *Animal Behaviour*, 40, 192–195.

SIMMONS, R.G. & BLYTH, D.A. (1987) *Moving into Adolescence: The Impact of Pubertal Change and School Context*. New York: Aldine de Gruyter.

SIMON, H.A. & HAYES, J.R. (1976) The understanding process: Problem isomorphs. *Cognitive Psychology*, 8, 165–190.

SIMONS, R.L. (1996) The effects of divorce on adult and child adjustment. In R.L. Simons (Ed.) *Understanding Differences Between Divorced and Intact Families: Stress, Interaction, and Child Outcomes*. Thousand Oaks, CA: Sage.

SIMPSON, J.A., CAMPBELL, B. & BERSCHEID, E. (1986) The association between romantic love and marriage: Kephart (1967) twice revisited. *Personality & Social Psychology Bulletin*, 12, 363–372.

SIMPSON, J.A., GANGESTAD, S.W., CHRISTENSEN, P.N. & LECK, K. (1999) Fluctuating asymmetry, sociosexuality and intrasexual competitive tactics. *Journal of Personality & Social Psychology*, 76, 159–172.

SIMS, A.C.P. & GRAY, P. (1993) The Media, Violence and Vulnerable Viewers. Document presented to the Broadcasting Group, House of Lords.

SINCLAIR-de-ZWART, H. (1969) Developmental psycholinguistics. In D. Elkind & J. Flavell (Eds) *Handbook of Learning and Cognitive Processes*, Volume 5. Hillsdale, NJ: Erlbaum.

SINGER, D. (1989) Children, adolescents, and television – 1989. *Paediatrics*, 83, 445–446.

SINGER, J.E., BRUSH, C.A. & LIBLIN, J.C. (1965) Some aspects of deindividuation: Identification and conformity. *Journal of Experimental Social Psychology*, 1, 356–378.

SINGH, B.R. (1991) Teaching methods for reducing prejudice and enhancing academic achievement for all children. *Educational Studies*, 17, 157–171.

SINGH, D. (1993) Adaptive significance of female attractiveness: The role of waist to hip ratio. *Journal of Personality & Social Psychology*, 65, 293–307.

SINGH, S.P. (1992) Is dhat culture-bound? *British Journal of Psychiatry*, 160, 280–281.

SINHA, D. (1997) Indigenizing psychology. In J.W. Berry, Y.H. Poortinga & J. Pandey (Eds) *Handbook of Cross-cultural Psychology* (2nd edition), Volume 1. Boston: Allyn & Bacon.

SIZEMORE, C.C. & PITTILLO, E.S. (1977) *I'm Eve*. New York: Doubleday.

SKEELS, H.M. & DYE, H.B. (1939) A study of the effects of differential stimulation on mentally retarded children. *Proceedings of the American Association of Mental Deficiency*, 44, 114–136.

SKEELS, H.M. (1966) Adult status of children with contrasting early life experiences. *Monographs of the Society for Research in Child Development*, 31, (Whole No. 3).

SKINNER, B.F. (1938) *The Behaviour of Organisms*. New York: Appleton-Century-Crofts.

SKINNER, B.F. (1948a) Superstition in the pigeon. *Journal of Experimental Psychology*, 38, 168–172.

SKINNER, B.F. (1948b) *Walden Two*. New York: Macmillan.

SKINNER, B.F. (1957) *Verbal Behaviour*. New York: Appleton-Century-Crofts.

SKINNER, B.F. (1971) *Beyond Freedom and Dignity*. New York: Knopf.

SKINNER, B.F. (1985) 'Cognitive science and behaviourism.' (Unpublished manuscript. Harvard University.)

SKRIVER, J. (1996) Naturalistic decision-making. *The Psychologist*, 9, 321–322.

SLABY, R.G. & FREY, K.S. (1975) Development of gender constancy and selective attention to same-sex models. *Child Development*, 46, 839–856.

SLATER, A. (1989) Visual memory and perception in early infancy. In A. Slater & G. Bremner (Eds) *Infant Development*. Hove: Erlbaum.

SLATER, A. (1994) Perceptual development in infancy. *Psychology Review*, 1, 12–16.

SLATER, A. & MORISON, V. (1985) Shape constancy and slant perception at birth. *Perception*, 14, 337–344.

SLATER, E. & ROTH, M. (1969) *Clinical Psychiatry* (3rd edition). Ballière-Tindall and Cassell.

SLAVIN, R. & MADDEN, N. (1979) School practices that improve race relations. *American Edcuation Research Journal*, 16, 169–180.

SLOANE, R., STAPLES, F., CRISTOL, A., YORKSTON, N. & WHIPPLE, K. (1975) *Psychotherapy Versus Behaviour Therapy*. Cambridge, MA: Harvard University Press.

SLOBIN, D.I. (1975) On the nature of talk to children. In E.H. Lenneberg & E. Lenneberg (Eds) *Foundations of Language Development*, Volume 1. New York: Academic Press.

SLOBIN, D.I. (1979) *Psycholinguistics* (2nd edition). Glenview, ILL: Scott, Foresman and Company.

SLOBIN, D.I. (1986) *The Cross-Linguistic Study of Language Acquisition*. Hillsdale, NJ: Erlbaum.

SLUCKIN, W. (1965) *Imprinting and Early Experiences*. London: Methuen.

SLUGOSKI, B. & HILTON, D. (2000) Conversation. In W.P. Robinson & H. Giles (Eds) *Handbook of Language and Social Psychology* (2nd edition). Chichester: Wiley.

SMITH, A.D. (1998) Ageing of the Brain: Is Mental Decline Inevitable? In S. Rose (Ed.) *From Brains to Consciousness: Essays on the New Sciences of the Mind*. Harmondsworth: Penguin.

SMITH, C. & LLOYD, B.B. (1978) Maternal behaviour and perceived sex of infant. *Child Development*, 49, 1263–1265.

SMITH, C.U.M. (1994) You are a group of neurons. *The Times Higher Educational Supplement*, 27 May, 20–21.

SMITH, D. (1982) Trends in counselling and psychotherapy. *American Psychologist*, 37, 802–809.

SMITH, E.M., BROWN, H.O., TOMAN, J.E.P. & GOODMAN, L.S. (1947) The lack of cerebral effects of D-tubo-curarine. *Anaesthesiology*, 8, 1–14.

SMITH, J.A., HARRÉ, R., & VAN LANGENHOVE, L. (1995) Introduction. In J.A.Smith, R. Harré & L. Van Langenhove (Eds) *Rethinking Psychology*. London: Sage.

SMITH, J.R., BROOKS-GUNN, J. & KLEBANOV, P.K. (1997) Consequences of living in poverty for young children's cognitive and verbal ability and early school achievement. In G.J. Duncan & J. Brooks-Gunn (Eds), *Consequences of Growing Up Poor*. New York: Russell Sage Foundation.

SMITH, K.A., FAIRBURN, C.G. & COWEN, P.J. (1997) Relapse of depression after rapid depletion of tryptophan. *The Lancet*, 349, 915–919.

SMITH, K.R. & ZICK, C.D. (1996) Risk of mortality following widowhood: Age and sex differences by mode of death. *Social Biology*, 43, 59–71.

SMITH, M.L., GLASS, G.V. & MILLER, T.I. (1980) *The Benefits of Psychotherapy*. Baltimore: Johns Hopkins University Press.

SMITH, P.B. (1995) Social influence proceses. In M. Argyle & A.M. Colman (Eds) *Social Psychology*. London: Longman.

SMITH, P.K. & COWIE, H. (1991) *Understanding Children's Development* (2nd edition). Oxford: Basil Blackwell.

SMITH, P.K. & DAGLISH, L. (1977) Sex differences in parent and infant behaviour in the home. *Child Development*, 48, 1250–1254.

SMITH, P.K., COWIE, H. & BLADER, M. (1998) *Understanding Children's Development* (3rd ed.). Oxford: Blackwell.

SMULDERS, T.V., SASSON, A.D. & DEVOOGD, T.J. (1995) Seasonal variation in hippocampal volume in a food storing bird, the black-capped chickadee. *Journal of Neurobiology*, 27, 15–25.

SMYTHIES, J. (1976) Recent progress in schizophrenia research. *The Lancet*, 2, 136–139.

SNAITH, R.P. (1994) Psychosurgery: Controversy and enquiry. *British Journal of Psychiatry*, 161, 582–584.

SNAREY, J.R. (1987) A question of morality. *Psychology Today*, June, 6–8.

SNAREY, J.R., REIMER, R. & KOHLBERG, L. (1985) Development of sociomoral reasoning among kibbutz adolescents: A longitudinal cross-cultural study. *Developmental Psychology*, 21(1), 3–17.

SNOW, C.E. (1977) Mother's speech research: From input to interaction. In C.E. Snow and C.A. Ferguson (Eds) *Talking to Children: Language Input and Acquisition*. New York: Cambridge University Press.

SNOW, C.E. (1983) Saying it again: The role of expanded and deferred imitations in language acquisition. In K.E. Nelson (Ed.) *Children's Language*, Volume 4. New York: Gardner Press.

SNYDER, F. (1970) The phenomenology of dreaming. In H. Madow & C. Snow (Eds.) *The Psychodynamic Implication of the Physiological Studies on Dreams*. Springfield: ILL.: Charles C. Thomas.

SOBER, E. (1992) The evolution of altruism: Correlation, cost and benefit. *Biology and Philosophy*, 7, 177–188.

SOLOMON, R. & CORBIT, J. (1974) An opponent-process theory of motivation. *Psychological Review*, 81, 119–145.

SOLSO, R.L. (1995) *Cognitive Psychology* (4th edition). Boston: Allyn & Bacon.

SOMMER, R. (1969) *Personal Space: The Behavioural Basis of Design*. Englewood Cliffs, NJ: Prentice-Hall.

SPANGLER, D.L. (1999) Cognitive–behavioural therapy for bulimia nervosa: An illustration. *Journal of Clinical Psychology*, 55, 699–713.

SPANIER, G.B. & LEWIS, R.A. (1980) Marital quality: A review of the seventies. *Journal of Marriage and the Family*, 42, 825–840.

SPANOS, N.P., WEEKES, J.R. & BERTRAND, L.D. (1985) Multiple personality: A social psychological perspective. *Journal of Abnormal Psychology*, 94, 362–376.

SPELKE, E.S. (1991) Physical knowledge in infancy: Reflections on Piaget's theory. In S. Carey & R. Gelman (Eds) *The epigenesis of mind: Essays on biology and cognition*. Hillsdale, NJ: Erlbaum.

SPELKE, E.S., HIRST, W.C. & NEISSER, U. (1976) Skills of divided attention. *Cognition*, 4, 215–230.

SPERRY, R.W. (1964) The great cerebral commissure. *Scientific American*, 210, 42–52.

SPERRY, R.W. (1974) Lateral specialisation in the surgically separated hemispheres. In F.O. Schmitt & F.G. Worden (Eds) *The Neurosciences: Third Study Program*. Cambridge, MA: MIT Press.

SPERRY, R.W. (1982) Some effects of disconnecting the cerebral hemispheres. *Science*, 217, 1223–1226.

SPERRY, R.W., GAZZANIGA, M.S. & BOGEN, J.E. (1969) Inter-hemispheric relationships: The neocortical commisures; syndromes of hemisphere disconnection. In P.J. Vinken & G.W. Bruyn (Eds.) *Handbook of Clinical Neurology*, Volume 4. New York: Wiley.

SPINNEY, L. (1997) Brain operation left woman with no sense of fear. *The Daily Telegraph*, 11 January, 7.

SPITZER, R.L. (1975) On pseudoscience in science, logic in remission and psychiatric diagnosis: A critique of Rosenhan's 'On being sane in insane places'. *Journal of Abnormal Psychology*, 84, 442–452.

SPITZER, R.L., SKODAL, A.E., GIBBON, M. & WILLIAMS, J.B.W. (Eds) (1981) *DSM-III Case Book*. Washington, DC: American Psychiatric Association.

SPRECHER, S., ARON, A., HATFIELD, E. & CORTESE, A. (1994) Love: American style, Russian style and Japanese style. *Personal Relationships*, 1, 349–369.

SRINIVASAN, M.V., ZHANG, S.W. & BIDWELL, N.J. (1997) Visually mediated odometry in honeybees. *Journal of Experimental Biology*, 200, 2513–2522.

STAAL, W.G., HULSHOFF POL, H.E. & KAHN, R.S. (1999) Outcome of schizophrenia in relation to brain abnormalities. *Schizophrenia Bulletin*, 25, 337–348.

STATTIN, H. & KLACKENBERG, G. (1992) Family discord in adolescence in the light of family discord in childhood. Paper presented at the Conference Youth – TM. Utrecht.

STATTIN, H. & MAGNUSSON, D. (1990) *Pubertal Maturation in Female Development*. Hillsdale: Erlbaum.

STEELE, C.M. & SOUTHWICK, L. (1985) Alcohol and social behaviour 1: The psychology of drunken excess. *Journal of Personality & Social Psychology*, 48, 18–34.

STEPHAN, C.W. & LANGLOIS, J. (1984) Baby beautiful: Adult attributions of infant competence as a function of infant attractiveness. *Child Development*, 55, 576–585.

STERNBERG, R.J. (1986) A triangular theory of love. *Psychological Review*, 93, 119–135.

STERNBERG, R.J. (1988) Triangulating love. In R.J. Sternberg & M.L. Barnes (Eds) *The Psychology of Love*. New Haven, CT: Yale University Press.

STERNBERG, R.J. & GRIGORENKO, E. (Eds) (1997) *Intelligence, Heredity and Environment*. New York: Cambridge University Press.

STEVENS, A. & PRICE, J. (1996) *Evolutionary Psychiatry*. London: Routledge.

STEVENS, J.R. (1982) Neurology and neuropathology of schizophenia. In F.A. Henn & G.A. Nasrallah (Eds) *Schizophrenia as a Brain Disease*. New York: Oxford University Press.

STEVENSON, G.I. & BAKER, R. (1996) Brain Chemistry. *Education in Chemistry*, 33, 124–128.

STEWART, V.M. (1973) Tests of the 'carpentered world' hypothesis by race and environment in America and Africa. *International Journal of Psychology*, 8, 83–94.

STIRLING, J. (2000) *Cortical Functions*. London: Routledge.

STOKES, P. (1999) Horror film boys convicted of stabbing friend. *The Daily Telegraph*, 7 August, 5.

STORMS, M.D. (1973) Videotape and the attribution process: Reversing actors' and observers' points of view. *Journal of Personality and Social Psychology*, 27, 165–175.

STOUFFER, S.A., SUCHMAN, E.A., DeVINNEY, L.C., STARR, S.A. & WILLIAMS, R.M. (1949) *The American Soldier: Adjustment During Army Life*, Volume 1. Princeton, NJ: Princeton University Press.

STRACHEY, J. (1962–1977) *Sigmund Freud: A sketch of his life and ideas*. This appears in each volume of the Pelican Freud Library: originally written for the *Standard Edition of the Complete Psychological Works of Sigmund Freud, 1953–1974*. London: Hogarth Press.

STRAUCH, I. & MEIER, B. (1996) *In Search of Dreams: Results of Experimental Dream Research*. Albany, N.Y.: SUNY.

STRAUS, M., GELLES, R. & STEINMETZ, S. (1980) *Behind Closed Doors: Violence in the American Family*. Garden City, NY: Anchor Press.

STRAVYNSKI, A. & GREENBERG, D. (1998) The treatment of social phobia: A critical assessment. *Acta Psychiatria Scandinavia*, 98, 171–181.

STROEBE, M.S. & STROEBE, M. (1993) The mortality of bereavement: A review. In M.S. Stroebe, W. Stroebe & R.O. Hansson (Eds) *Handbook of Bereavement: Theory, Research and Intervention*. New York: Cambridge University Press.

STROEBE, M.S., STROEBE, W. & HANSSON, R.O. (1993) Contemporary themes and controversies in bereavement research. In M.S. Stroebe, W. Stroebe & R.O. Hansson (Eds) *Handbook of Bereavement: Theory, Research and Intervention*. New York: Cambridge University Press.

STROOP, J.R. (1935) Studies of interference in serial verbal reactions. *Journal of Experimental Psychology*, 18, 643–662.

STUART-HAMILTON, I. (1994) *The Psychology of Ageing: An Introduction* (2nd edition). London: Jessica Kingsley.

STUART-HAMILTON, I. (1997) Adjusting to Later Life. *Psychology Review*, 4 (2), 20–23, November.

SUE, D., SUE, D. & SUE, S. (1994) *Understanding Abnormal Behaviour* (4th edition). Boston: Houghton Mifflin.

SUE, S. (1995) Implications of the Bell curve: Whites are genetically inferior in intelligence? *Focus: Notes from the Society for the Psychological Study of Ethnic Minority Issues*, 16–17.

SULLOWAY, F.J. (1979) *Freud, Biologist of the Mind: Beyond the Psychoanalytic Legend*. New York: Basic Books.

SUMNER, W.G. (1906) *Folkways*. Boston: Ginn.

SURREY, D. (1982) 'It's like good training for life'. *Natural History*, 91, 71–83.

SUTHERLAND, P. (1992) *Cognitive Development Today: Piaget and his Critics*. London: Paul Chapman Publishing.

SWARTZ, K.B. & EVANS, S. (1991) Not all chimpanzees (Pan troglodytes) show self-recognition. *Primates*, 32, 483–496.

SWEET, W.H., ERVIN, F. & MARK, V.H. (1969) The relationship of violent behaviour to focal cerebral disease. In Garattini, S. & Sigg, E.B. (Eds) *Aggressive Behaviour*. New York: Wiley.

SWENSEN, C.H. (1983) A respectable old age. *American Psychologist*, 46, 1208–1221.

SYAL, R. (1997) Doctors find pick-me-up for SAD people. *The Sunday Times*, 19 January, 4.

SYLVA, K. (1996) Education: Report on the Piaget-Vygotsky centenary conference. *The Psychologist*, 9, 370–372.

SYMONS, D. (1979) *The Evolution of Human Sexuality*. New York: Oxford University Press.

SZASZ, T.S. (1962) *The Myth of Mental Illness*. New York: Harper & Row.

SZASZ, T.S. (1974) *Ideology and Insanity*. Harmondsworth: Penguin.

SZASZ, T.S. (1994) *Cruel Compassion – Psychiatric Control of Society's Unwanted*. New York: Wiley.

SZECHTMAN, H., CULVER, K. & EILAM, D. (1999) Role of dopamine systems in obsessive–compulsive disorder (OCD): Implications from a novel psychostimulant-induced animal model. *Polish Journal of Pharmacology*, 51, 55–61.

TAJFEL, H. (1969) Social and cultural factors in perception. In G. Lindzey & E. Aronson (Eds) *Handbook of Social Psychology*, Volume 3. Reading, MA: Addison-Wesley.

TAJFEL, H. (Ed.) (1978) *Differentiation Between Social Groups: Studies in the Social Psychology of Intergroup Relations*. London: Academic Press.

TAJFEL, H. & BILLIG, M. (1974) Familiarity and categorization in inter-group behaviour. *Journal of Experimental Social Psychology*, 10, 159–170.

TAJFEL, H. & TURNER, J.C. (1986) The social identity theory of intergroup behaviour. In S. Worchel & W. Austin (Eds) *Psychology of Intergoup Relations*. Chicago: Nelson-Hall.

TAJFEL, H., BILLIG, M.G. & BUNDY, R.P. (1971) Social categorization and intergroup behaviour. *European Journal of Social Psychology*, 1, 149–178.

TAKAHASHI, Y. (1990) Is multiple personality disorder really rare in Japan? *Dissociation*, 3, 57–59.

TALLIS, F. (1995) *Obsessive Compulsive Disorder: A Cognitive and Neuropsychological Perspective*. Chichester: Wiley.

TALLIS, R. (1996) Burying Freud. *The Lancet*, 347, 669–671.

TANAKA, J.W. & FARAH, M.J. (1993) Parts and wholes in face recognition. *Quarterly Journal of Experimental Psychology*, 46A, 225–246.

TANG, Y., SHIMIZU, E., DUBE, G.R., RAMPAN, C., KERCHNER, G.A., ZHUO, M., LIU, G. & TSEIN, J. (1999) Genetic enhancement of learning and memory in mice, *Nature*, 401, 63–69.

TANNAHILL, R. (1980) *Sex in History*. London: Hamish Hamilton.

TANNER, J.M. (1978) *Fetus into Man: Physical Growth from Conception to Maturity*. Cambridge, MA: Harvard University Press.

TANNER, J.M. & WHITEHOUSE, R.H. (1976) Clinical longitudinal standards for height, weight, height velocity, weight velocity and stages of puberty. *Archives of Disorders in Childhood*, 51, 170–179.

TARRIER, N., BECKETT, R. & HARWOOD, S. (1993) A trial of two cognitive behavioural methods of treating drug-resistant residual psychotic symptoms in schizophrenic patients. *British Journal of Psychiatry*, 162, 524–532.

TAVRIS, C. (1993) The mismeasure of woman. *Feminism & Psychology*, 3 (2), 149–168.

TAYLOR, D.M. & PORTER, L.E. (1994) A multicultural view of stereotyping. In W.J. Lonner & R.S. Malpass (Eds) *Psychology and Culture*. Boston: Allyn & Bacon.

TAYLOR, G. (1993) Challenges from the margins. In J. Clarke (Ed.) *A Crisis in Care*. London: Sage.

TAYLOR, R. (1963) *Metaphysics*. Englewood Cliffs, NJ: Prentice-Hall.

TAYLOR, S.E., PEPLAU, L.A. & SEARS, D.O. (1994) *Social Psychology* (8th edition). Englewood Cliffs, NJ: Prentice-Hall.

TAYLOR, S.P. & SEARS, J.D. (1988) The effects of alcohol and persuasive social pressure on human physical aggression. *Aggressive Behaviour*, 14, 237–243.

TAYLOR, W.S. & MARTIN, M.F. (1944) Multiple personality. *Journal of Abnormal & Social Psychology*, 39, 281–330.

TEASDALE, J. (1988) Cognitive vulnerability to persistent depression. *Cognition and Emotion*, 2, 247–274.

TEICHMAN, J. (1988) *Philosophy and the Mind*. Oxford: Blackwell.

TEIGEN, K.H. (1994) Variants of subjective problems : Concepts, norms and biases. In G. Wright & P. Ayton (Eds) *Subjective Probability*. Chichester: John Wiley.

TEITELBAUM, P.H. (1955) Sensory control of hypothalamic hyperphagia. *Journal of Comparative & Physiological Psychology*, 48, 156–163.

TEITELBAUM, P.H. & EPSTEIN, A.N. (1962) The lateral hypothalamic syndrome: Recovery of feeding and drinking after hypothalamic lesions. *Psychological Review*, 67, 74–90.

TEIXEIRA, J.M.A. (1999) Association between maternal anxiety in pregnancy and increased uterine artery resistance index: Cohort based study. *British Medical Journal*, 318 (7177), 153–157.

TERR, L., BLOCH, D., MICHEL, B., SHI, H., REINHARDT, J. & METAYER, S. (1999) Children's symptoms in the wake of Challenger: A field study of distant-traumatic effects and an outline of related conditions. *American Journal of Psychiatry*, 156, 1536–1544.

TERRACE, H.S. (1979) *Nim*. New York: Knopf.

TERRACE, H.S. (1985) In the beginning was the 'name'. *American Psychologist*, 40, 1011–1028.

TEUTING, P., ROSEN, S. & HIRSCHFELD, R. (1981) *Special Report on Depression Research*. Washington, DC: NIMH-DHHS Publication No. 81–1085.

THIBAUT, J.W. & KELLEY, H.H. (1959) *The Social Psychology of Groups*. New York: Wiley.

THIGPEN, C.H. & CLECKLEY, H.M. (1954) A case of multiple personality. *Journal of Abnormal & Social Psychology*, 9, 135–151.

THIGPEN, C.H. & CLECKLEY, H.M. (1957) *The Three Faces of Eve*. New York: McGraw-Hill.

THIGPEN, C.H. & CLECKLEY, H.M. (1984) On the incidence of multiple personality disorder. *International Journal of Clinical & Experimental Hypnosis*, 32, 63–66.

THOMAS, A. & CHESS, S. (1977) *Temperament and Development*. New York: Brunner/Mazel.

THOMAS, J.C. (1974) An analysis of behaviour in the 'hobbit-orcs' problem. *Cognitive Psychology*, 28, 167–178.

THOMAS, K. (1990) Psychodynamics: The Freudian approach. In I. Roth (Ed.) *Introduction to Psychology*. Hove: Lawrence Erlbaum Associates Ltd.

THOMAS, R. (1999) Lack of sleep leaves night-owl Britons retarded. *The Observer*, 21 March, 1.

THOMAS, R.M. (1985) *Comparing Theories of Child Development* (2nd edition). Belmont, CA: Wadsworth Publishing Company.

THOMPSON, C. (1943) 'Penis envy' in Women. *Psychiatry*, 6, 123–125.

THOMPSON, L.A., DETTERMAN, D.K. & PLOMIN, R. (1991) Associations between cognitive abilities and scholastic achievement: Genetic overlap but environmental differences. *Psychological Science*, 2, 158–165.

THOMPSON, P. (1980) Margaret Thatcher – a new illusion. *Perception*, 9, 483–484.

THOMPSON, S.B.N. (1997) War experiences and post-traumatic stress disorder. *The Psychologist*, 10, 349–350.

THORNDIKE, E. L. (1898) Animal intelligence: An experimental study of the associative processes in animals. *Psychological Review Monograph Supplement 2* (Whole No. 8).

THORNDIKE, E.L. (1911) *Animal Intelligence*. New York: Macmillan.

THORNE, B. (1992) *Rogers*. London: Sage Publications.

THORNHILL, R. & GANGESTAD, S.W. (1993) Human facial beauty: Averageness, symmetry and parasite resistance. *Human Nature*, 4, 237–269.

TILLEY, A.J. & EMPSON, J.A.C. (1978) REM sleep and memory consolidation. *Biological Psychology*, 6, 293–300.

TIMONEN, S., FRANZAS, B. & WISCHMANN, K. (1964) Photosensibility of the human pituitary. *Annales Chirurgiae et Gynaecologiae Feminae*, 53, 156–172.

TINBERGEN, N. (1951) *The Study of Instinct*. Oxford: Clarendon Press.

TINBERGEN, N. (1966) *Animal Behaviour*. Nederland: Time Life International.

TINBERGEN, N. & PERDECK, A.C. (1950) On the stimulus situation releasing the begging response in the newly hatched herring gull chick (*Larus a. argentatus Pont.*). *Behaviour*, 3, 1–38.

TIPPER, S.P. & DRIVER, J. (1988) Negative priming between pictures and words: Evidence for semantic analysis of ignored stimuli. *Memory and Cognition*, 16, 64–70.

TITCHENER, E.B. (1903) *Lectures on the Elementary Psychology of Feeling and Attention*. New York: Macmillan.

TIZARD, B. & PHOENIX, A. (1993) *Black, White or Mixed Race?* London: Routledge.

TIZARD, B., JOSEPH, A., COOPERMAN, O. & TIZARD, J. (1972) Environmental effects on language development: A study of young children in long-stay residential nurseries. *Child Development*, 43, 337–358.

TOBIN-RICHARDS, M.H., BOXER, A.M. & PETERSEN, A.C. (1983) The psychological significance of pubertal change: Sex differences in perceptions of self during early adolescence. In J. Brooks-Gunn & A.C. Petersen (Eds) *Girls at Puberty: Biological and Psychosocial Perspectives*. New York: Plenum.

TOLMAN, E.C. (1923) The nature of instinct. *Psychological Bulletin*, 20, 200–216.

TOLMAN, E.C. (1948) Cognitive maps in rats and man. *Psychological Review*, 55, 189–208.

TOLMAN, E.C. & HONZIK, C.H. (1930) Introduction and removal of reward and maze-learning in rats. *University of California Publications in Psychology*, 4, 257–275.

TOLMAN, E.C., RITCHIE, B.F., & KALISH, D. (1946) Studies in spatial learning. 1: Orientation and the short-cut. *Journal of Experimental Psychology*, 36, 13–25.

TOMARKEN, A.J. & DAVIDSON, R.J. (1994) Frontal brain activation in repressors and non-repressors. *Journal of Abnormal Psychology*, 103, 334–349.

TOMARKEN, A.J., MINEKA, S. & COOK, M. (1989) Fear-relevant selective associations and covariation bias. *Journal of Abnormal Psychology*, 98, 381–394.

TOMKINS, S.S. (1962) *Affect, Imagery, and Consciousness*, Volume 1: *The Positive Affects*. New York: Springer-Verlag.

TOMLINSON-KEASEY, C. (1985) *Child Development: Psychological, Sociocultural, and Biological Factors*. Chicago: Dorsey Press.

TONG, S. (1998) Declining blood lead levels and changes in cognitive functioning during childhood: The Port Pirie cohort study. *Journal of the American Medical Association*, 280 (22), 1915–1919.

TORGERSEN, S. (1983) Genetic factors in anxiety disorders. *Archives of General Psychiatry*, 40, 1085–1089.

TORREY, E.E., BOWLER, A.E., RAWLINGS, R. & TERRAZAS, A. (1993) Seasonability of schizophrenia and stillbirths. *Schizophrenia Bulletin*, 19, 557–562.

TORREY, E.F., TORREY, B.B. & PETERSON, M.R. (1977) Seasonality of schizophrenic births in the United States. *Archives of General Psychiatry*, 34, 1065–1070.

TOVEE, M.J., REINHART, S., EMERY, J.L. & CORNELISSEN, P.L. (1998) Optimum body-mass index and maximum sexual attractiveness. *The Lancet*, 352, 548.

TRABASSO, T. (1977) The role of memory as a system in making transitive inferences. In R.V. Kail & J.W. Hagen (Eds) *Perspectives on the Development of Memory and Cognition*. Hillsdale, NJ: Erlbaum.

TREDRE, R. (1996) Untitled article. *Observer Life*, 12 May, 16–19.

TREISMAN, A.M. (1960) Contextual cues in selective listening. *Quarterly Journal of Experimental Psychology*, 12, 242–248.

TREISMAN, A.M. (1964) Verbal cues, language and meaning in selective attention. *American Journal of Psychology*, 77, 206–219.

TREISMAN, A.M. (1988) Features and objects: The fourteenth Bartlett memorial lecture. *Quarterly Journal of Experimental Psychology*, 40A, 201–237.

TREISMAN, A.M. & GEFFEN, G. (1967) Selective attention: Perception or response. *Quarterly Journal of Experimental Psychology*, 19, 1–18.

TREISMAN, A.M. & GELADE, G. (1980) A feature-integration theory of attention. *Cognitive Psychology*, 12, 97–136.

TREISMAN, A.M. & RILEY, J.G.A. (1969) Is selective attention selective perception or selective response?: A further test. *Journal of Experimental Psychology*, 79, 27–34.

TREISMAN, A.M. & SATO, S. (1990) Conjunction search revisited. *Journal of Experimental Psychology: Human Perception and Performance*, 16, 459–478.

TREISMAN, A.M. & SCHMIDT, H. (1982) Illusory conjunctions in the perception of objects. *Cognitive Psychology*, 14, 107–141.

TRIANDIS, H. (1990) Theoretical concepts that are applicable to the analysis of ethnocentrism. In R.W. Brislin (Ed.) *Applied Cross-Cultural Psychology*. Newbury Park, CA.: Sage.

TRIANDIS, H. (1994) *Culture and Social Behaviour*. New York: McGraw-Hill.

TRIESCHMANN, R.B. (1980) *Spinal Cord Injuries*. New York: Pergamon Press.

TRIVERS, R.L. (1971) The evolution of reciprocal altruism. *Quarterly Review of Biology*, 46, 35–57.

TRIVERS, R.L. (1972) Parental investment and sexual selection. In B. Campbell (Ed.) *Sexual Selection and the Descent of Man*. Chicago: Aldine.

TRIVERS, R.L. (1985) *Social Evolution*. New York: Benjamin Cummings.

TROWER, P. (1987) On the ethical bases of 'scientific' behaviour therapy. In S. Fairbairn & G. Fairbairn (Eds) *Psychology, Ethics and Change*. London: Routledge & Kegan Paul.

TROWLER, P. (1988) *Investigating the Media*. London: Unwin Hyman Limited.

TRUE, W., RICE, L., EISEN, S.A. *et al.* (1993) A twin study of genetic and environmental contributions to the liability of posttraumatic stress symptoms. *Archives of General Psychiatry*, 50, 257–264.

TURNBULL, C.M. (1961) *The Forest People*. New York: Simon & Schuster.

TURNBULL, S.K. (1995) The middle years. In D. Wedding (Ed.) *Behaviour and Medicine* (2nd edition). St. Louis, MO: Mosby-Year Book.

TURNER, J.C. (1991) *Social Influence*. Milton Keynes: Open University Press.

TURNER, J.S. & HELMS, D.B. (1989) *Contemporary Adulthood* (4th edition). Fort Worth, FL: Holt, Rinehart & Winston.

TVERSKY, A. (1972) Elimination by aspects: A theory of choice. *Psychological Review*, 79, 281–299.

TVERSKY, A. & KAHNEMAN, D. (1971) Belief in the law of small numbers. *Psychological Bulletin*, 76, 105–110.

TVERSKY, A. & KAHNEMAN, D. (1973) Judgement under uncertainty: Heuristics and biases. *Science*, 185, 1124–1131.

TVERSKY, A. & KAHNEMAN, D. (1980) Causal schemas in judgements under uncertainty. In M. Fishbein (ed.) *Progress in Social Psychology*. Hillsdale, NJ: Erlbaum.

TVERSKY, A. & KAHNEMAN, D. (1986) Rational choice and the framing of decisions. *Journal of Business*, 59, 5251–5278.

TYERMAN, A. & SPENCER, C. (1983) A critical test of the Sherifs' Robber's Cave experiment: Intergroup competition and co-operation between groups of well-acquainted individuals. *Small Group Behaviour*, 14, 515–531.

TYLER, T.R. & COOK, F.L. (1984) The mass media and judgement of risk: Distinguishing impact on personal and societal level judgements. *Journal of Personality and Social Psychology*, 47, 693–708.

UGOLINI , A., MELIS, C. & INNOCENTI, R. (1999) Moon orientation in adult and young sandhoppers. *Journal of Comparative Physiology – Sensory Neural and Behavioral Physiology*, 184(1), 9–12.

ULLMAN, L.P. & KRASNER, L. (1969) *A Psychological Approach to Abnormal Behaviour*. Englewood Cliffs, NJ: Prentice-Hall.

UNDERWOOD, G. (1974) Moray vs. the rest: The effects of extended shadowing practice. *Quarterly Journal of Experimental Psychology*, 26, 368–372.

UNGER, R. (1979) *Female and Male*. London: Harper & Row.

UNGER, R. & CRAWFORD, M. (1992) *Women and Gender: A Feminist Psychology*. New York: McGraw-Hill.

UNGER, R.K. & CRAWFORD, M. (1996) Women and gender: A feminist psychology (2nd edition). New York: McGraw-Hill.

US RIOTS COMMISSION (1968) Report of the National Advisory Commission on Civil Disorder. New York: Bantam Books.

VAIDYANATHAN, P, & NAIDOO, J. (1991) Asian Indians in Western countries: Cultural identity and the arranged marriage. In N. Bleichrodt & P. Drenth (Eds) *Contemporary Issues in Cross-Cultural Psychology*. Amsterdam: Swets & Zeitlinger.

VALENSTEIN, E.S. (1973) *Brain Control*. New York: John Wiley and Sons.

VALENSTEIN, E.S. (1977) The brain and behaviour control. In E.S. Valenstein (Ed.) *Master Lectures on Behaviour Control*. Washington, DC: American Psychological Association.

VALENSTEIN, E.S. (1980) Rationale and psychosurgical procedures. In E.S. Valenstein (Ed.) *The Psychosurgery Debate*. San Francisco: W.H. Freeman.

VALENSTEIN, E.S. (1990) The prefrontal area and psychosurgery. *Progress in Brain Research*, 85, 539–554.

VALENTINE, E.R. (1982) *Conceptual Issues in Psychology*. London: Routledge.

VAN BUSHKIRK, J. (1997) in A. Barnett, The sounds that say it all as birds sing their hearts out. *New Scientist*, 2084, 16.

VAN ESSEN, D.C. (1985) Functional organisation of primate visual cortex. In A. Peters. & E.G. Jones (Eds) *Cerebral Cortex*, Volume 2 – *Visual Cortex*. New York: Plenum Press.

VAN LANGENHOVE, L. (1995) The theoretical foundations of experimental psychology and its alternatives. In J.A.Smith, R. Harré, & L. Van Langenhove (Eds) *Rethinking Psychology*. London: Sage.

VAN LEHN, K. (1983) On the representation of procedures in repair theory. In H.P. Ginsburg (Ed.) *The Development of Mathematical Thinking*. London: Academic Press.

VANNEMAN, R.D. & PETTIGREW, T.F. (1972) Race and relative deprivation in the urban United States. *Race*, 13, 461–486.

VERKAIK, R. (1995) The kindest cut of all? *The Sunday Times*, 30 July, 18–19.

VERNON, M.D. (1955) The functions of schemata in perceiving. *Psychological Review*, 62, 180–192.

VETTER, H.J. (1969) *Language Behaviour and Psychopathology*. Chicago: Rand McNally.

VINES, G. (1998) Hidden Inheritance. *New Scientist*, 160 (2162), 26–30.

VIVIAN, J. & BROWN, R. (1995) Prejudice and intergroup conflict. In M. Argyle & A.M. Colman (Eds) *Social Psychology*. London: Longman.

VIVIAN, J., BROWN, R.J. & HEWSTONE, M. (1994) 'Changing attitudes through intergroup contact: The effects of membership salience.' (Unpublished manuscript, Universities of Kent and Wales, Cardiff.)

VON FRISCH, K. (1956) *The Dancing Bees*. New York: Harcourt Brace Jovanovich.

VON FRISCH, K. (1967) *The Dance Language and Orientation of Bees*. Cambridge, MA: Harvard University Press.

VON WRIGHT, J.M., ANDERSON, K. & STENMAN, U. (1975) Generalisation of conditioned GSRs in dichotic listening. In P.M.A. Rabbitt & S. Dornic (Eds) *Attention and Performance* (Volume I). London: Academic Press.

VYGOTSKY, L. (1962) *Thought and Language*. Cambridge, MA: MIT Press (originally published in 1934).

VYGOTSKY, L.S. (1978) *Mind in Society*. Cambridge, MA: Harvard University Press.

VYGOTSKY, L.S. (1981) The genesis of higher mental functions. In J.V. Wertsch (Ed.) *The Concept of Activity in Soviet Psychology*. Armonk, NY: Sharpe.

WACHTEL, P.L. (1977) *Psychoanalysis and Behaviour Therapy: Towards an Integration*. New York: Basic Books.

WADA, J. & RASMUSSEN, T. (1966) Intracarotid injection of sodium amytal for lateralisation of cerebral speech dominance. *Journal of Neurosurgery*, 17, 266–282.

WADE, C. & TAVRIS, C. (1993) *Psychology* (3rd edition). New York: HarperCollins.

WADE, C. & TAVRIS, C. (1999) *Invitation to Psychology*. New York: Longman.

WAGENAAR, W.A. (1988) *Paradoxes of Gambling Behaviour*. Hove: Lawrence Erlbaum.

WAGNER, W.E., JR. (1992) Deceptive or honest signalling of fighting ability? A test of alternative hypotheses for the function of changes in call dominant frequency by male cricket frogs. *Animal Behaviour*, 44, 449–462.

WAHBA, N. & BRIDWELL, L. (1976) Maslow reconsidered: A review of research on the need hierarchy theory. *Organisation Behaviour and Human Performance*, 15, 212–240.

WALCOTT, C. & BROWN, A.I. (1989) *The disorientation of pigeons at Jersey Hill*. Paper presented at the Royal Institute of Navigation Conference, 1989.

WALKER, L.J. (1984) Sex differences in the development of moral reasoning: A critical review. *Child Development*, 55, 677–691.

WALKER, L.J. (1989) A longitudinal study of moral reasoning. *Child Development*, 60, 157–166.

WALKER, L.J. (1995) Sexism in Kohlberg's moral psychology? In W.M. Kurtines & J. Gewirtz (Eds) *Moral Development: An Introduction*. Needham Heights, MA: Allyn & Bacon.

WALKER, L.J. (1996) Is One Sex Morally Superior? In M.R. Merrens & G.C. Brannigan (Eds) *The Developmental Psychologists : Research Adventures Across the Life Span*. New York: McGraw-Hill.

WALKER, L.J., DEVRIES, B. & TREVATHAN, S.D. (1987) Moral stages and moral orientations in real-life and hypothetical dilemmas. *Child Development*, 58, 842–858.

WALKER, M.B. (1992) *The Psychology of Gambling*. Oxford: Butterworth Heinemann.

WALKER, S. (1984) *Learning Theory and Behaviour Modification*. London: Methuen.

WALLACE, P. (1999) *The Psychology of the Internet*. Cambridge: Cambridge University Press.

WALSH, B.T., WILSON, G.R., LOEB, K.L. *et al.* (1997) Medication and psychotherapy in the treatment of bulimia nervosa. *American Journal of Psychiatry*, 154, 523–531.

WALSTER, E. (1966) The assignment of responsibility for an accident. *Journal of Personality & Social Psychology*, 5, 508–516.

WALSTER, E., ARONSON, E. & ABRAHAMS, D. & ROTTMAN, L. (1966) Importance of physical attractiveness in dating behaviour. *Journal of Personality and Social Psychology*, 4, 508–516.

WALTON, G.E., BOWER, N.J.A. & BOWER, T.G.R. (1992) Recognition of familiar faces by newborns. *Infant Behaviour and Development*, 16, 233–253.

WARD, S.H. & BRAUN, J. (1972) Self-esteem and racial preference in Black children. *American Journal of Orthopsychiatry*, 42 (4), 644–647.

WARK, P. & BALL, S. (1996) Death of innocence. *The Sunday Times*, 23 June, 12.

WASON, P.C. (1960) On the failure to eliminate hypotheses in a conceptual task. *Quarterly Journal of Experimental Psychology*, 12, 129–140.

WASON, P.C. (1983) Realism and rationality in the selection task. In J. Evans (Ed.) *Thinking and Reasoning: Psychological Approaches*. London: Routledge & Kegan Paul.

WATSON, J.B. (1913) Psychology as the behaviourist views it. *Psychological Review*, 20, 158–177.

WATSON, J.B. (1925) *Behaviourism*. New York: Norton.

WATSON, J.B. (1928) *Psychological Care of Infant and Child*. New York: Norton.

WATSON, J.B. & RAYNER, R. (1920) Conditioned emotional reactions. *Journal of Experimental Psychology*, 3, 1–14.

WATSON, J.D. & CRICK, F.H.C. (1953) Molecular structure of nucleic acid: A structure for deoxyribose nucleic acid. *Nature*, 171, 737–738.

WATSON, R.J. (1973) Investigation into deindividuation using a cross-cultural survey technique. *Journal of Personality & Social Psychology*, 25, 342–345.

WEARY, G. & ARKIN, R.M. (1981) Attributional self-presentation. In J.H. Harvey, W.J. Ickes & R.F. Kidd (Eds) *New Directions in Attributional Research*, Volume 3. Hillsdale, NJ: Erlbaum.

WEATHERLEY, D. (1961) Anti-semitism and expression of fantasy aggression. *Journal of Abnormal and Social Psychology*, 62, 454–457.

WEBB, W.B. (1975) *Sleep: The Gentle Tyrant*. Englewood Cliffs, NJ: Prentice-Hall.

WEBB, W.B. (1982) Sleep and biological rhythms. In W.B. Webb (Ed.) *Biological Rhythms, Sleep and Performance*. Chichester: John Wiley & Sons.

WEBB, W.B. & CAMPBELL, S. (1983) Relationships in sleep characteristics of identical and fraternal twins. *Archives of General Psychiatry*, 40, 1093–1095.

WEBB, W.B. & CARTWRIGHT, R.D. (1978) Sleep and dreams. *Annual Review of Psychology*, 29, 223–252.

WEBSTER, R. (1995) *Why Freud was Wrong: Sin, Science and Psychoanalysis*. London: HarperCollins.

WECHSLER, D. (1944) *The Measurement of Adult Intelligence*. Baltimore, MD: Williams & Wilkins.

WEGNER, D.M. & VALLACHER, R.R. (1976) *Implicit Psychology: An Introduction to Social Cognition*. Oxford: Oxford University Press.

WEGNER, D.M., BENEL, D.C. & RILEY, E.N. (1976) Changes in perceived inter-trait correlations as a function of experience with persons. Paper presented at the meeting of the SouthWestern Psychological Association, Alberquerque (April).

WEHNER, R. & SRINIVASAN, M.V. (1981) Searching behavior of desert ants, genus *Cataglyphis* (Formicidae. Hymenoptera). *Journal of Comparative Physiology*, 142, 315–338.

WEHR, T. & ROSENTHAL, N. (1989) Seasonability and affective illness. *American Journal of Psychiatry*, 146, 201–204.

WEINBERG, R. (1989) Intelligence and IQ: Landmark issues and great debates. *American Psychologist* 44, 98–104.

WEINER, B. (1986) *An Attributional Theory of Motivation and Emotion*. New York: Springer-Verlag.

WEINER, B. (1995) *Judgements of Responsibility*. New York: Guildford.

WEINER, M.J. & WRIGHT, F.E. (1973) Effects of undergoing arbitrary discrimination upon subsequent attitudes toward a minority group. *Journal of Applied Social Psychology*, 3, 94–102.

WEINTRAUB, D. & RUSKIN, P. (1999) Posttraumatic stress disorder in the elderly: A review. *Harvard Review of Psychiatry*, 7, 144–152.

WEISFELD, G. (1994) Aggression and dominance in the social world of boys. In J. Archer (Ed.) *Male Violence*. London: Routledge.

WEISKRANTZ, L. (1986) *Blindsight: A Case Study and Implications*. Oxford: Oxford University Press.

WEISKRANTZ, L. (1988) *Thought Without Language*. Oxford: Oxford University Press.

WEISSMAN, M. & PAYKEL, E. (1974) *The Depressed Woman*. Chicago: University of Chicago Press.

WEISSTEIN, N. (1993) Psychology constructs the female; or, The fantasy life of the male psychologist (with some attention to the fantasies of his friend, the male biologist and the male anthropologist). *Feminism & Psychology*, 3 (2), 195–210.

WELLS, P.A., WILLMOTH, T. & RUSSELL, R.J.H. (1995) Does fortune favour the bald?: Psychological correlates of hair loss in males. *British Journal of Psychology*, 86, 337–344.

WENDER, P.H. & KLEIN, D.F. (1981) The promise of biological psychiatry. *Psychology Today*, 15, 25–41.

WENDER, P.H., KETY, S.S., ROSENTHAL, D., SCHULSINGER, F., ORTMANN, J. & LUNDE, I. (1986) Psychiatric disorders in the biological and adoptive families of individuals with affective disorders. *Archives of General Psychiatry*, 43, 923–929.

WERNER, E.E. (1989) Children of the Garden Island. *Scientific American*, April, 106–111.

WERTHEIMER, M. (1970) *A Brief History of Psychology*. New York: Holt Rinehart & Winston.

WESSELY, S. (1993) Who is the real me? *The Times*, 12 December, 21.

WESTERMARCK, E.R. (1894) *The History of Human Marriage* (3 Vols.). New York: Macmillan.

WESTERMEYER, J. (1973) Grenade amok in Laos: A psychosocial perspective. *International Journal of Psychosocial Psychiatry*, 19, 1–5.

WESTHEAD, R. (1996) Power line link to the baby blues. *The Sunday Telegraph*, 15 September, 2.

WETHERELL, M. (1982) Cross-cultural studies of minimal groups: Implications for the social identity theory of intergroup relations. In H. Tajfel (Ed.) *Social Psychology and Intergroup Relations*. Cambridge: Cambridge University Press.

WHISMAN, M.A. & McGARVERY, A.L. (1995) Attachment, depressotypic cognitions, and dysphoria. *Cognitive Therapy and Research*, 19, 633–650.

WHITE, B.L. (1971) *Human Infants: Experience and Psychological Development*. Englewood Cliffs, NJ: Prentice-Hall.

WHITE, G.L. (1980) Physical attractiveness and courtship progress. *Journal of Personality and Social Psychology*, 39, 660–668.

WHITTELL, G. (1995) Spectacular northern lights linked to suicidal depression. *The Times*, 15 April, 9.

WHITTELL, G. (1996) Black American slang wins place in classroom. *The Times*, 21 December, 11.

WHORF, B.L. (1956) *Language, Thought and Reality*. Cambridge, MA: MIT Press.

WHYTE, J. (1998) Childhood. In K. Trew & J. Kremer (Eds) *Gender and Psychology*. London: Arnold.

WHYTE, W.W. (1956) *The Organization Man*. New York: Simon and Schuster.

WICHSTROM, L. (1998) Self-concept development during adolescence: Do American truths hold for Norwegians? In E. Skoe & A. von der Lippe (Eds) *Personality Development in Adolescence: A Cross National and Life Span Perspective*. London: Routledge.

WICKENS, C.D. (1992) *Engineering Psychology and Human Performance* (2nd edition). New York: HarperCollins.

WICKLER, W. (1967) Socio-sexual signals and their intraspecific imitation among primates. In D. Morris (Ed.) *Primate Ethology*. London: Weidenfeld & Nicolson.

WILDER, D.A. (1984) Intergroup contact: The typical member and the exception to the rule. *Journal of Experimental Social Psychology*, 20, 177–194.

WILDING, J.M. (1982) *Perception: From Sense to Object*. London: Hutchinson.

WILHELM, K. & PARKER, G. (1989) Is sex necessarily a risk factor to depression? *Psychological Medicine*, 19, 401–413.

WILKINSON, G.S. (1984) Reciprocal food sharing in the vampire bat. *Nature*, 308, 181–184.

WILKINSON, S. (1991) Feminism & psychology: From critique to reconstruction. *Feminism & Psychology*, 1 (1), 5–18.

WILKINSON, S, (1997) Feminist Psychology. In D. Fox & D. Prilleltensky (Eds) *Critical Psychology: An Introduction*. London: Sage.

WILLERMAN, L. (1979) *The Psychology of Individual and Group Differences*. San Francisco: W.H. Freeman.

WILLIAMS, J.E. & BEST, D.L. (1994) Cross-cultural views of women and men. In W.J. Lonner & R.S. Malpass (Eds) *Psychology and Culture*. Boston: Allyn & Bacon.

WILLIAMS, J.M.G. (1992) *The Psychological Treatment of Depression*. London: Routledge.

WILLIAMS, J.M.G. & HARGREAVES, I.R. (1995) Neuroses: Depressive and anxiety disorders. In A.A. Lazarus & A.M. Colman (Eds) *Abnormal Psychology*. London: Longman.

WILLIAMS, K.B. & WILLIAMS, K.D. (1983) Social inhibition and asking for help: The effects of number, strength and immediacy of potential help givers. *Journal of Personality and Social Psychology*, 44, 67–77.

WILLIAMS, M. (1981) *Brain Damage, Behaviour and the Mind*. Chichester: Wiley.

WILLIAMS, T.M. (Ed.) (1986) *The Impact of Television: A National Experiment in Three Communities*. New York: Academic Press.

WILLIAMSON, E.M. (1999) The 95 faces of a mother from Hell. *The Sunday Telegraph* (Review), 8 August, 4.

WILNER, D.M., WALKLEY, R. & COOK, S.W. (1955) *Human Relations in Interracial Housing: A Study of the Contact Hypothesis*. Minneapolis: University of Minnesota Press.

WILSON, E. (1999) Warning: pets may cause depression. *The Guardian* (supplement), 20 July, 14–15.

WILSON, E.O. (1975) *Sociobiology – The New Synthesis*. Cambridge, MA: Harvard University Press.

WILSON, E.O. (1978) *On Human Nature*. Cambridge, MA: Harvard University Press.

WILSON, G. (1994) Biology, sex roles and work. In C. Quest (Ed.) *Liberating Women from Modern Feminism*. London: Institute of Economic Affairs, Health & Welfare Unit.

WILSON, G.T. & O'LEARY, K.D. (1978) *Principles of Behaviour Therapy*. Englewood Cliffs, NJ: Prentice-Hall.

WILSON, M. & DALY, M. (1992) The man who mistook his wife for a chattel. In J. Barkow, L. Cosmides & J. Tooby (Eds) *The Adapted Mind*. New York: Oxford University Press.

WILSON, R.S. (1983) The Louisville Twin Study: Developmental synchronies in behaviour. *Child Development*, 54, 298–316.

WILTSCHKO, W. & WILTSCHKO, R. (1988) Magnetic orientation in birds. *Current Ornithology*, 5, 67–121.

WINCH, R.F. (1958) *Mate Selections: A Study of Complementary Needs*. New York: Harper.

WINEBERG, H. (1994) Marital reconciliation in the United States: Which couples are successful? *Journal of Marriage and the Family*, 56, 80–88.

WINOKUR, G., CLAYTON, P.J. & REICH, T.R. (1969) *Manic–Depressive Illness*. St. Louis: Mosby.

WINTER, A. (1972) Depression and intractible pain treated by modified prefrontal lobotomy. *Journal of Medical Sociology*, 69, 757–759.

WIRSHING, D., MARSHALL, B., GREEN, M., MINTZ, J., MARDER, S. & WIRSHING, W. (1999) Risperidone in treatment-refractory schizophrenia. *American Journal of Psychiatry*, 156, 1374–1379.

WISBY, W.J. & HASLER, A.D. (1954) The effect of olfactory occlusion on migrating silver salmon (*Oncorhynchus kisutch*). *Journal of Fish. Res. Bd. Can.* 11, 472–478.

WITKIN, H.A., DYK, R.B., FATERSON, H.F., GOODENOUGH, D.R. & KARP, S.A. (1962) *Psychological Differentiation*. London: Wiley.

WITTGENSTEIN, L. (1961) *Tractatus Logico-Philosophicus* (translated by D.F. Pears & B.F. McGuinness). London: Routledge & Kegan Paul (originally published in 1921).

WITTHOWER, E.D. (1969) Perspectives of transcultural psychiatry. *International Journal of Psychiatry*, 8, 811–824.

WOBER, J.M., REARDON, G. & FAZAL, S. (1987) *Personality, Character Aspirations and Patterns of Viewing Among Children*. London: IBA Research Papers.

WOBER, M. (1974) Towards an understanding of the Kiganda concept of intelligence. In J.W. Berry & P.R. Dasen (Eds) *Culture and Cognition*. London: Methuen.

WOLF, S. & WOLFF, H.G. (1947) *Human Gastric Function*. New York: Oxford University Press.

WOLPE, J. (1958) *Psychotherapy by Reciprocal Inhibition*. Stanford, CA: Stanford University Press.

WOLPE, J. (1969) For phobia: A hair of the hound. *Psychology Today*, 3, 34–37.

WOLPE, J. (1973) *The Practice of Behaviour Therapy*. New York: Pergamon Press.

WOLPE, J. (1997) From psychoanalytic to behavioural methods in anxiety disorders. In J.K. Zeig (Ed) *The Evolution of Psychotherapy: The Third Conference*. New York: Brunner/Mazel.

WOLPE, J. & WOLPE, D. (1981) *Our Useless Years*. Boston: Houghton-Mifflin.

WOLPERT, L. (1999) *Malignant Sadness: The Anatomy of Depression*. London: Faber.

WOOD, D.J., BRUNER, J.S. & ROSS, G. (1976) The role of tutoring in problem-solving. *Journal of Child Psychology & Psychiatry*, 17, 89–100.

WOOD, J.T. & DUCK, S. (1995) *Understanding Relationship Processes 6: Understudied Relationships: Off the Beaten Track.* Thousand Oaks, CA: Sage.

WOODRUFF, G. & PREMACK, D. (1979) Intentional communication in the chimpanzee: The development of deception. *Cognition,* 7, 333–362.

WOODWORTH, R.S. (1918) *Dynamic Psychology.* New York: Columbia University Press.

WOODY, S.R., CHAMBLESS, D.L. & GLASS, C.R. (1997) Self-focused attention in the treatment of social phobia. *Behaviour Research and Therapy,* 35, 117–129.

WU, X. & DeMARIS, A. (1996) Gender and marital status differences in depression: The effects of chronic strains. *Sex Roles,* 34, 299–319.

WUNDT, W. (1874) *Grundzuge der Physiologischen Psychologie.* Leipzig: Engelmann.

WYMAN, A. (1983) *Animal Talk: Instinct or Intelligence?* Detroit Free Press, 25 October, 1B, 2B.

WYNNE, L.C., SINGER, M.T., BARTKO, J.J. & TOOHEY, M.L. (1977) Schizophrenics and their families: Recent research on parental communication. In J.M. Tanner (Ed.) *Developments in Psychiatric Research.* London: Hodder & Stoughton.

YAP, P.M. (1951) Mental disorders peculiar to certain cultures: a survey of comparative psychiatry. *Journal of Mental Science,* 97, 313–327.

YAP, P.M. (1965) Koro – a culture-bound depersonalisation syndrome. *British Journal of Psychiatry,* 111, 43–49.

YAP, P.M. (1974) *Comparative Psychiatry.* Toronto: University of Toronto Press.

YARBUS, A.L. (1967) *Eye Movements and Vision* (B. Haigh, trans.). New York: Plenum.

YASUKAWA, K. (1981) Song repertoires in the red-winged blackbird (*Agelaius phoniceus*): A test of the Beau Geste hypothesis. *Animal Behaviour,* 29, 114–125.

YEHUDA, R. (1999) Biological factors associated with susceptibility to posttraumatic stress disorder. *Canadian Journal of Psychiatry,* 44, 34–39.

YIN, R.K. (1969) Looking at upside-down faces. *Journal of Experimental Psychology,* 81, 141–145.

YIP, A. (1999) Same-sex couples. *Sociology Review,* 8 (3), 30–33.

YOUNG, A. (1997) Finding the mind's construction in the face. *The Psychologist,* 10, 447–452.

YOUNG, A. & BRUCE, V. (1998) Pictures at an exhibition: The science of the face. *The Psychologist,* 11(3), 120–125.

YOUNG, A.W., HAY, D.C. & ELLIS, A.W. (1985) The faces that launched a thousand ships: Everyday difficulties and errors in recognising people. *British Journal of Psychology,* 76, 495–523.

YOUNG, A.W., HELLAWELL, D.J. & HAY, D.C. (1987) Configurational information in face perception. *Perception,* 16, 747–759.

YOUNG, A.W., NEWCOMBE, F., DE HAAN, E.H.F., SMALL, M. & HAY, D.C. (1993) Face perception after brain injury: Selective impairments affecting identity and expression. *Brain,* 116, 941–959.

YOUNG, B.J., FOX, G.D., & EICHENBAUM, H. (1994) Correlates of hippocampal complex-spike cell activity in rats performing a nonspatial radial arm maze task. *Journal of Neuroscience,* 14, 6553–6563.

YULE, W. (1993) Children's trauma from transport disasters. *The Psychologist,* 7, 318–319.

ZAIDEL, E. (1983) A response to Gazzaniga. *American Psychologist,* 38, 542–546.

ZAJONC, R.B. & MARKUS, G.B. (1975) Birth order and intellectual development. *Psychological Review,* 82, 74–88.

ZAJONC, R.B. (1968) Attitudinal effects of mere exposure. *Journal of Personality and Social Psychology,* Monograph Supplement 9, Part 2, 1–27.

ZAJONC, R.B. (1984) On the primacy of affect. *American Psychologist,* 39, 117–123.

ZEBROWITZ, L.A. (1990) *Social Perception.* Milton Keynes: Open University Press.

ZEKI, S. (1980) The representation of colours in the visual cortex. *Nature,* 284, 412–418.

ZEKI, S. (1992) The visual image in mind and brain. *Scientific American,* 267, 43–50.

ZEKI, S. (1993) *A Vision of the Brain.* Oxford: Blackwell.

ZIGLER, E. & PHILLIPS, L. (1961) Psychiatric diagnosis and symptomatology. *Journal of Abnormal Psychology,* 63, 69–75.

ZIGLER, E. & STYFCO, S.J. (1993) Using research and theory to justify and inform Head Start expansion. Social Policy Report, *Society for Research in Child Development,* 7(2), 1–21.

ZILLMAN, D. (1978) Attribution and misattribution of excitatory reactions. In J.H. Harvey, W. Ickes & R.F. Kidd (Eds) *New Directions in Attribution Research,* Volume 2. New York: Erlbaum.

ZILLMAN, D. (1982) Transfer of excitation in emotional behaviour. In J.T. Cacioppo & R.E. Petty (Eds) *Social Psychophysiology: A Sourcebook.* New York: Guilford Press.

ZILLMAN, D. & BRYANT, J. (1974) Effect of residual excitation on the emotional response to provocation and delayed aggressive behaviour. *Journal of Personality and Social Psychology,* 30, 782–791.

ZILLMAN, D. & BRYANT, J. (1984) Effects of massive exposure to pornography. In M.N. Malamuth & E. Donnerstein (Eds) *Pornography and Sexual Aggression.* New York: Academic Press.

ZIMBARDO, P.G. (1969) The human choice: Individuation, reason, and order versus deindividuation, impluse, and chaos. In W.J. Arnold & D. Levine (Eds) *Nebraska Symposium on Motivation.* Lincoln: University of Nebraska Press.

ZIMBARDO, P.G. & WEBER, A.L. (1994) *Psychology.* New York: HarperCollins.

ZINBERG, D.S. (1997) Ebonics unleashes tongues. *The Times Higher Education Supplement,* 14 February, 14.

ZUBIETA, J., CHINITZ, J., LOMBARDI, U., FIG, L., CAMERON, O. & LIBERZON, I. (1999) Medial frontal cortex involvement in PTSD symptoms: A SPECT study. *Journal of Psychiatric Research,* 33, 259–264.

ZUCKERMAN, M. (1979) *Sensation Seeking: Beyond the Optimum Level of Arousal.* Hillsdale, NJ: Erlbaum.

Index

Page numbers in **bold** indicate definitions of words/concepts.